D1471500

Collins

Collins
English-Japanese Dictionary

Collins

Collins
English-
Japanese
Dictionary

HarperCollins Publishers
Westerhill Road
Bishopbriggs
Glasgow
G64 2QT
Great Britain

First Edition 2005

Previously published as Collins-Shubun
Pocket English-Japanese Dictionary

Latest Reprint 2006

© HarperCollins Publishers & Shubun
International Co., Ltd 1993

ISBN-13 978-0-00-722430-2
ISBN-10 0-00-722430-3

Collins® and Bank of English® are
registered trademarks of HarperCollins
Publishers Limited

www.collins.co.uk

A catalogue record for this book is
available from the British Library

HarperCollins Publishers,
10 East 53rd Street, New York, NY 10022

COLLINS POCKET ENGLISH-JAPANESE
DICTIONARY.
First US Edition 2000

ISBN-13 978-0-06-273758-8
ISBN-10 0-06-273758-9

Library of Congress Cataloging-in-
Publication Data has been applied for

www.harpercollins.com

HarperCollins books may be purchased
for educational, business, or sales
promotional use. For information, please
write to: Special Markets Department,
HarperCollins Publishers, 10 East 53rd
Street, New York, NY 10022

Typeset by Tosho Printing Co., Ltd

Printed in Great Britain by Clays Ltd,
St Ives plc

Acknowledgements
We would like to thank those authors and
publishers who kindly gave permission
for copyright material to be used in the
Collins Word Web. We would also like to
thank Times Newspapers Ltd for
providing valuable data.

ORIGINAL MATERIAL BY
CollinsBilingual

JAPANESE LANGUAGE EDITION
Richard C. Goris
Yukimi Okubo

EDITORIAL ADMINISTRATION
Jill Campbell

CONTENTS

Authors' Foreword

Dictionary compilers have been labeled "harmless drudges", but we have found little drudgery in compiling the Collins-Shubun English-Japanese Dictionary. On the contrary, we have experienced great pleasure in rising to the challenge of producing a book that was not run-of-the-mill.

To begin with, we had several advantages. We had the dictionary framework provided in electronic form by Collins Dictionary Division. Then we had computers running powerful Japanese word processing software. Together these factors saved us from the drudgery (and writer's cramp) caused by writing thousands and thousands of manuscript pages by hand. They also eliminated the drudgery of correcting in proof the innumerable mistakes introduced by typesetters misinterpreting our handwriting.

The challenge of producing "a better mousetrap" also provided motivation that eliminated drudgery.

In order to keep the dictionary truly pocket-sized, we aimed at providing one translation for each word, or for each meaning of a word. Where several possible translations existed, we chose the one with the highest frequency of usage in modern Japanese. We also tried to give translations that were the cultural equivalent of the English. Thus, if the English word conveyed a sense of dignity, we used a dignified Japanese expression; if the English was a slangy word, we provided a slangy Japanese word or phrase. Where this was not possible, we have provided glosses to clarify the difference.

There were some exceptions. When the English word had several Japanese equivalents, each used with equal frequency, and generally interchangeable, we gave the two or three most frequent, separated by commas.

In this category fell words that could be expressed either by a Chinese compound (2 or more Chinese characters used as a single word) or by a purely Japanese word. There were also words that could be expressed by a Japanese translation or a "Japanized" foreign loan word of equal frequency. In this case we gave the Japanese translation first, followed by a comma and the loan word. Where the Japanese translation existed, but was outlandish and seldom used, we gave only the loan word. In such cases the loan word is generally listed as a headword in standard Japanese dictionaries.

Finally, we discussed every entry thoroughly before adopting it. Thus we feel we have met our goal of providing a small, portable, but extremely useful dictionary - useful to the language student and the native speaker alike.

Our efforts would have been futile without the support, aid, and counsel of the editorial staff of Collins Dictionaries and Shubun. Shubun's board of experts and editors included Kazuo Shibuya, Shiruki Furukawa, Ari Matsue, and Kazuko Namiki. On the other side of the ocean we had in particular the aid of Lorna Sinclair-Knight, Jeremy Butterfield, and the hard-working Jill Campbell, in addition to other anonymous advisors.

To all and sundry, a handshake and a deep bow of gratitude.

Richard C. Goris
Yukimi Okubo

著 者 前 書

辞書を書く人というと「ひたすらこつこつ働く，人畜無害な凡人」と見る向きもあるが，当の私達はコリンズ・秀文英和辞典を書くに際し，ことさら単調な仕事を余儀なくされたという感じは全く覚えなかった．平凡でない辞書を作ろうというチャレンジに答えることにむしろ大きな喜びを感じた．

第一に苦労を軽減する要素がいくつかあった．まずコリンズ社の辞書部門よりコービルドのデータベースから頻度によって抽出され，フォーマット化されたた語彙リストのフロッピーディスクが提供された．これを強力な日本語ワープロソフトでコンピュータ操作し，日本語訳等を入力した．こうして何千枚もの原稿を手書きする苦労（と書痙の危険）を避けられ，同時に植字段階で起こるエラーを校正で直す苦労も避けることができた．

第二に，「より優れたもの」を作るというチャレンジも作業の単調さを吹き飛ばす動機にもなった．

当書をポケット版の限度内に抑えるためには，原則として一見出し語に対して，あるいは見出し語の一意味に対して一つだけの訳語をつけることにした．複数の訳語が可能な場合，最も頻度の高いものを選んだ．また，英語の語彙に対して文化的に同じ含みの訳語を選ぶように努力した．例えば，英単語が格調の高い語であれば，格調の高い日本語訳をつけた．一方，俗語のような英語に対してはそれに相当する日本語の俗語をつけた．これが不可能な場合，補足説明をつけた．

いくつか例外がある．複数の日本語訳が可能で，頻度が同じぐらいで置き換えもきく場合，二つか三つを併記してコンマで分けた．こういう語には漢語的表現またはやまとことばに訳せる語が多かった．その他に純粋な日本語もしくは外来語で表せる語もあった．その場合，日本語と外来語を併記してコンマで分けた．しかし日本語訳がおかしかったり頻度が低かったりする場合，外来語だけを記載した．この様な外来語はたいがい国語辞典で見出し語として使われている．

熟考と討論を重ねて最後に訳語を選択した．こうして小型でポケット版であるにもかかわらず，language student，native speaker 双方に大いに役立つ画期的な辞典の作成に成功したと確信する．

コリンズ社辞典編集部門及び秀文インターナショナルの編集スタッフの支援と助言なしには私達の努力だけではこの辞書を作れなかったと思う．秀文側にあっては特に渋谷一夫，古川知己，松江亜里，並木和子，そして海の向こうにあっては Lorna Sinclair-Knight, Jeremy Butterfield, Jill Campbell，その他の皆さん方に深く感謝の意を表する．

R．C．ゴリス

大久保　雪美

PUBLISHER'S FOREWORD

As the 21st century approaches and the countries of the world become more internationalized, the importance of English as a world language is felt ever more keenly by society. This awareness spotlights certain problems concerning the bilingual dictionaries, particularly English-Japanese dictionaries, published in Japan.

To begin with, there is the habit of crowding into each entry, without rhyme or reason, all the possible translations of a headword that can be thought of, a habit that has persisted since the Meiji Era.

Secondly, in a great many cases, scientific data on the use of words and phrases is very scarce, making it extremely difficult to improve on the present situation.

Dictionary users are becoming increasingly dissatisfied with the growing volume of unsorted data that is being thrust at them. Things have reached a point where the dictionary makers appear to have lost touch with the needs of their users.

What the users really want is well-ordered data, that is, clear, uncluttered information on the meaning of the words of a language. They need fundamental information on actual usage of the words of a language, information on situation and context in which a word or phrase is used, information on what normally comes before or after various words and phrases. This in turn requires a wealth of background information about the actual state of a language. Fortunately, we have been able to join forces with HarperCollins Publishers of Britain, who have at their disposal the largest data bank in the world of the English language. This data bank furnished us with, among other things, information on word frequency, which guided the choice of headwords; and information on situation, context, variation in meaning etc, which is shown in parentheses (the "indicators") in each entry. The result has been the revolutionary dictionary that we present here, for use throughout the world, in preparation for the 21st century, a truly original publication.

Instead of being laboriously typeset from a hand-written manuscript, the dictionary was composed entirely on a computer in a form that permitted electronic typesetting machines to transform the data directly into the printed page. Throughout the project the authors maintained constant, real-time contact with the editorial staff of Collins Dictionary Division through electronic mail and other modern means.

All Japanese entries in the main text have their pronunciation indicated in romaji, so that anyone anywhere in the world can use this dictionary to study Japanese through the medium of English.

At the same time Japanese users of the dictionary, even if already proficient in English, can gain confidence in their use of the language by noting the information about usage given in the parenthetical "indicators" in each entry.

Shubun International, Ltd.

出版する立場から

21世紀の幕開けが近づく一方、さらに国際化が一層進展し世界語としての英語の重要性がますます高まっているのが昨今の社会情勢と言えましょう。このような背景を踏まえ、我が国の外国語特に英和辞典の将来を考えてみるといくつかの問題点がはっきりしてくる。

まず第一に明治以来の伝統に従って狭い紙面に未整理のままと言ってよい程の訳語という名称の語義の網羅振りが指摘できよう。

第二に多くの場合、言語使用に付いて科学的データに乏しく、思い切った革新の道を拓くことが極めて困難といった状況が指摘できましょう。

肥大化する情報量に辞典使用者もうんざりの感さえするのである。使用者が何を求めているのか図りかねているのが現状とも言える状況である。

辞典使用者は小気味よく整理された情報の提供、すなわち今や簡潔・明解な言語の意味を求めている。ある言語の意味とは、ある語（句）がどのような場面・文脈・前後関係の中で何を伝達しようとしているのか示すことであり、かつ最も基本的なことである。このためには当該言語使用の実態について豊富なデータが必要となる。幸いなことに今日世界最大規模のdata bank of the English languageを活用する英国ハーパーコリンズ社と提携、使用頻度及び語句の意味の使用範囲「indicators」のデータを駆使した21世紀を指向した世界で使える画期的な英和辞典の完成をここに見る運びと相成った次第である。これこそ独創的知的生産物財産とも言うべきかなである。

原稿執筆も従来のような組み上げられた順序ではなく項目単位と言うべき方式で完全にコンピュータ化完成され、原稿執筆終了即組版完了ともなった点は画期的な技術革新の成果でもあった。電子時代の申し子でもある電子メール等最新の技術によりコリンズ社辞典編集部門と執筆のデスクが結ばれ、リアルタイムに意志伝達が行われたのである。

このように完成された本辞典は、日本語全てにローマ字による発音表記を付し、世界の何処にあっても英語を媒介とし日本語の習得を可能ならしめる効果的な内容とした。

また特に我が国の英語既習者の社会人にとって意味使用範囲「indicators」の明示による活用は英語使用に自信を与える英語習得への開眼となると信ずる。

株式会社　秀文インターナショナル

INTRODUCTION

We are delighted you have decided to buy the Collins Shubun Pocket English-Japanese Dictionary and hope you will enjoy and benefit from using it at school, at home, on holiday or at work.

This introduction gives you a few tips on how to get the most out of your dictionary-not simply from its comprehensive wordlist but also from the information provided in each entry.

The Collins Shubun English-Japanese Dictionary begins by listing the abbreviations used in the text and follows with a guide to Japanese pronunciation and a chart of the two Japanese scripts "hiragana" and "katakana" together with the Roman letter transliteration used in this dictionary.

USING YOUR COLLINS SHUBUN POCKET DICTIONARY

A wealth of information is presented in the dictionary, using various typefaces, sizes of type, symbols, abbreviations and brackets. The conventions and symbols used are explained in the following sections.

Headwords

The words you look up in a dictionary -"headwords"- are listed alphabetically. They are printed in bold type for rapid identification. The headwords appearing at the top of each page indicate the first and last word dealt with on the page in question.

Information about the usage or form of certain headwords is given in brackets after the phonetic spelling. This usually appears in abbreviated form (e. g., *(fam)*, (COMM).

Common expressions in which the headword appears are shown in bold italic type (e. g., **account**... *of no account*).

When such expressions are preceded by a colon, it means that the headword is used mainly in that particular expression (e. g., **aback**... *adv*: *to be taken aback*).

Phonetic spellings

The phonetic spelling of each headword (indicating its pronunciation) is given in square brackets immediately after the headword (e. g., **able** [ei'bəl]). The phonetics show a standardized US English pronunciation in IPA (International Phonetic Alphabet) symbols. A list of these symbols is given on page (13).

Translations

Headword translations are given in ordinary type and, where more than one meaning or usage exists, these are separated by a semicolon. You will often find other words in brackets before the translations. These offer suggested contexts in which the headword might appear (e. g., **absentee** (from school, meeting etc) or provide synonyms (e. g. **able** (capable) or (skilled)). A white lozenge precedes a gloss giving information for the non-English native speaker.

"Keywords"

Special status is given to certain English words which are considered as "key" words in the language. They may, for example, occur very frequently or have several types of usage (e. g., **a**, **be**). A combination of lozenges and numbers helps you to distinguish different parts of speech and different meanings. Further helpful information is provided in brackets.

Grammatical Information

Parts of speech are given in abbreviated form in italics after the phonetic spellings of headwords (e. g., *vt*, *adv*, *conj*) and headwords with several parts of speech have a black lozenge before each new part of speech (e. g., **wash**).

使用上の注意

本辞典は英単語の意味を知りたい日本人だけでなく日本語を勉強している外国人も使えるよう，すべての訳語，補足説明などを日本文字とローマ字で併記した．ローマ字は原則としてヘボン式に従い，ローマ字：仮名対照表を (17)―(18) ページに示した．またローマ字には日本語のアクセントも加えた．右上がりのアクセント記号 (á) は声の上がりを，右下がりの記号 (à) は声の下がりを，記号のない場合は平坦に発音する事を示す．

見出し語は太字の立体活字で示した．つづりは米国の標準に従ったが，英国の標準がそれと異なる場合，アルファベット順にこれも示した．

> 例：**anaemia** [əniːˈmiːə] *etc (BRIT)* = **anemia** *etc*

続いて発音を [ ] の中に国際音標文字で示した．発音記号表は (13) ページにある．アクセントは ['] の記号でアクセントのある音節の後に示した．

> 例：**able** [eiˈbəl]

品詞は斜字の略語で示した．例：**able** [eiˈbəl] *adj*

品詞に続いて訳語を日本語とローマ字で示した．原則として1つの意味に対して1つだけ最も頻度の高い訳語を採用した．

> 例：**blockade**... 封鎖 fúsa

頻度が同じぐらいで複数の訳語がある場合，これを示すと共にコンマ (,) で分けた．

> 例：**blood**... 血 chi, 血液 ketsúèki

訳語の前に丸括弧 ( ) の中でその見出し語についての情報を記した．

立体の大文字はその語が使われる「分野」などを示す．

> 例：**blood**... (BIO) 血 chi, 血液 ketsúèki

すなわち，**blood** は「生物学」という分野の語である．

立体の小文字はその他の情報を示す．

> 例：**bleat**... *vi* (goat, sheep) 鳴く nakú

すなわち，bleat という動詞はヤギやヒツジについて使う語である．

> 例：**aperture**... (hole) 穴 aná; (gap) すき間 sukíma; (PHOT) アパーチャ ápàcha

この例では類語を使って見出し語の意味をはっきりさせている．また，このように1つの見出し語に対して複数の意味がある場合，セミコロン (;) で分ける．

見出し語の成句はその都度改行して太字の斜字で示した．

> 例：**bearing**...
>
>   *to take a bearing*...
>
>   *to find one's bearings*...

成句は主語＋動詞形式のものでも文頭の大文字と文尾のピリオドをつけずにあくまでも成句として扱った。ただし疑問を表す成句には？をつけた。

> 例：**anyone**...
> > *anyone could do it*
> > *can you see anyone?*

表示，標識，立て札などに使う成句は「...」で囲んだ.

> 例：**entry**...
> > 「*no entry*」...

改行なしで品詞などに続くコロン（:）＋ 太斜字の成句は見出し語などがその成句以外には殆ど使われない事を示す．

> 例：**aback** [əbæk'] *adv*: *to be taken aback* 仰天する gyōten suru

丸括弧の中で *also*: に続く立体太字の語句はその意味では同意語である事を示す．

> 例：**go about** *vi* (*also*: **go around**: rumor) 流れる nagárerù.

ここでは「噂が流れる」という意味では go about でも go around でも使える事を示している.

特殊記号：

♦：最初に示した品詞と品詞が異なったものにつけた.

> 例：**abdicate**... *vt* (responsibility, right) 放棄する ...
> > ♦*vi* (monarch) 退位する ...

◇：補足説明を示す.

/：見出し語，成句の中で置き換えられる部分を示す．日本語訳やローマ字の中でこれを〔 〕で示した.

> 例：**abide**... *vt*: *I can't abide it/him* 私はそれ〔彼〕が大嫌いだ watáku-
> > shi wá soré〔karè〕ga dáĭkirai da

KEYWORD：このタイトルは頻度の高い重要な語で特に徹底的に取り扱った見出し語（たとえば **be, can**）を示す.

Phonetic Symbols 発音記号表

[ɑː] father, hot, knowledge

[æ] at, have, cat

[ai] my, buy, like

[au] how, mouth

[e] men, says, friend

[ei] say, take, rain

[eːr] air, care, where

[ə] above, payment, label

[əːr] girl, learn, burn, worm

[i] sit, women, busy

[iː] see, bean, city

[ou] no, know, boat

[ɔi] boy, boil

[ʊ] book, could, put

[uː] tool, soup, blue

[ɔː] law, walk, story

[ʌ] up, cut, above

[p] put, cup

[b] be, tab

[d] down, had

[t] too, hot

[k] come, back

[g] go, tag

[s] see, cups, force

[z] rose, buzz

[ʃ] she, sugar

[ʒ] vision, pleasure

[tʃ] church

[dʒ] jam, gem, judge

[f] farm, half, phone

[v] very, eve

[θ] thin, both

[ð] this, other

[l] little, ball

[r] rat, bread

[m] move, come

[n] no, run

[ŋ] sing, bank

[h] hat, reheat

[j] yes

[w] well, away

Table of Abbreviations 略語表

adj	adjective	形容詞
abbr	abbreviation	略語
adv	adverb	副詞
ADMIN	administration	管理
AGR	agriculture	農業
ANAT	anatomy	解剖学
ARCHIT	architecture	建築
AUT	automobiles	自動車関係
aux vb	auxiliary verb	助動詞
AVIAT	aviation	航空
BIO	biology	生物学
BOT	botany	植物学
BRIT	British English	英国つづり／用法
CHEM	chemistry	化学
COMM	commerce, finance, banking	商業，金融関係
COMPUT	computing	コンピュータ関係
conj	conjunction	接続詞
cpd	compound	形容詞的名詞
CULIN	cookery	料理
def art	definite article	定冠詞
dimin	diminutive	指小辞
ECON	economics	経済学
ELEC	electricity, electronics	電気，電子工学
excl	exclamation, interjection	感嘆詞
fam(!)	colloquial usage (! particularly offensive)	口語（！特に悪質なもの）
fig	figurative use	比喩
fus	(phrasal verb) where the particle cannot be separated from the main verb	vt fusを見よ
gen	in most or all senses; generally	たいがいの意味では，一般に
GEO	geography, geology	地理学，地質学
GEOM	geometry	幾何学
indef art	indefinite article	不定冠詞

inf(!)	colloquial usage (! particularly offensive)	口語（！特に悪質なもの）
infin	infinitive	不定詞
inv	invariable	変化しない
irreg	irregular	不規則な
LING	grammar, linguistics	文法，語学
lit	literal use	文字通りの意味
MATH	mathematics	数学
MED	medical term, medicine	医学
METEOR	the weather, meteorology	気象関係
MIL	military matters	軍事
MUS	music	音楽
n	noun	名詞
NAUT	sailing, navigation	海事
num	numeral adjective or noun	数詞
obj	(grammatical) object	目的語
pej	pejorative	蔑称
PHOT	photography	写真
PHYSIOL	physiology	生理学
pl	plural	複数
POL	politics	政治
pp	past participle	過去分詞形
prep	preposition	前置詞
pron	pronoun	代名詞
PSYCH	psychology, psychiatry	精神医学
pt	past tense	過去形
RAIL	railroad, railway	鉄道
REL	religion	宗教
SCOL	schooling, schools and universities	学校教育
sing	singular	単数
subj	(grammatical) subject	主語
superl	superlative	最上級
TECH	technical term, technology	技術(用語)，テクノロジー
TEL	telecommunications	電信電話
TV	television	テレビ
TYP	typography, printing	印刷

US	American English	米国つづり／用法
vb	verb	動詞
vi	verb or phrasal verb used intransitively	自動詞
vt	verb or phrasal verb used transitively	他動詞
vt fus	phrasal verb where the particle cannot be separated from main verb	パーチクルを動詞から分けられない句動詞
ZOOL	zoology	動物学
®	registered trademark	登録商標

THE ROMANIZATION AND PRONUNCIATION OF JAPANESE

There are several systems for writing Japanese in Roman characters, but the most understandable and least confusing to the speaker of English is the Hepburn ("hebon" in Japanese) system. The following table illustrates this system, with its "hiragana" and "katakana" equivalents, as it has been adopted in this dictionary.

a	i	u	e	o	ā	ī	ū	ē	ō
あ	い	う	え	お	—	—	うう	—	おお/おう
ア	イ	ウ	エ	オ	アー	イー	ウー	エー	オー

ka	ki	ku	ke	ko	kya	—	kyu	—	kyo
か	き	く	け	こ	きゃ	—	きゅ	—	きょ
カ	キ	ク	ケ	コ	キャ	—	キュ	—	キョ

ga	gi	gu	ge	go	gya	—	gyu	—	gyo
が	ぎ	ぐ	げ	ご	ぎゃ	—	ぎゅ	—	ぎょ
ガ	ギ	グ	ゲ	ゴ	ギャ	—	ギュ	—	ギョ

sa	shi	su	se	so	sha	shi	shu	she	sho
さ	し	す	せ	そ	しゃ	し	しゅ	しぇ	しょ
サ	シ	ス	セ	ソ	シャ	シ	シュ	シェ	ショ

za	ji	zu	ze	zo	ja	ji	ju	je	jo
ざ	じ	ず	ぜ	ぞ	じゃ	じ	じゅ	じぇ	じょ
ザ	ジ	ズ	ゼ	ゾ	ジャ	ジ	ジュ	ジェ	ジョ

ta	chi	tsu	te	to	cha	chi	chu	che	cho
た	ち	つ	て	と	ちゃ	ち	ちゅ	ちぇ	ちょ
タ	チ	ツ	テ	ト	チャ	チ	チュ	チェ	チョ

da	ji	zu	de	do	ja	ji	ju	je	jo
だ	ぢ	づ	で	ど	ぢゃ	ぢ	ぢゅ	ぢぇ	ぢょ
ダ	ヂ	ヅ	デ	ド	ヂャ	ヂ	ヂュ	ヂェ	ヂョ

na	ni	nu	ne	no		nya	—	nyu	—	nyo
な	に	ぬ	ね	の		にゃ	—	にゅ	—	にょ
ナ	ニ	ヌ	ネ	ノ		ニャ	—	ニュ	—	ニョ
ha	hi	fu	he	ho		hya	—	hyu	—	hyo
は	ひ	ふ	へ	ほ		ひゃ	—	ひゅ	—	ひょ
ハ	ヒ	フ	ヘ	ホ		ヒャ	—	ヒュ	—	ヒョ
ba	bi	bu	be	bo		bya	—	byu	—	byo
ば	び	ぶ	べ	ぼ		びゃ	—	びゅ	—	びょ
バ	ビ	ブ	ベ	ボ		ビャ	—	ビュ	—	ビョ
pa	pi	pu	pe	po		pya	—	pyu	—	pyo
ぱ	ぴ	ぷ	ぺ	ぽ		ぴゃ	—	ぴゅ	—	ぴょ
パ	ピ	プ	ペ	ポ		ピャ	—	ピュ	—	ピョ
ma	mi	mu	me	mo		mya	—	myu	—	myo
ま	み	む	め	も		みゃ	—	みゅ	—	みょ
マ	ミ	ム	メ	モ		ミャ	—	ミュ	—	ミョ
ya	—	yu	—	yo						
や	—	ゆ	—	よ						
ヤ	—	ユ	—	ヨ						
ra	ri	ru	re	ro		rya	—	ryu	—	ryo
ら	り	る	れ	ろ		りゃ	—	りゅ	—	りょ
ラ	リ	ル	レ	ロ		リャ	—	リュ	—	リョ
wa	—	—	—	wo		n				
わ	—	—	—	を		ん				
ワ	—	—	—	ヲ		ン				

Consonants:

Pronounce the consonants as you would in English. Exceptions are "w" in the objective particle "wo", "r", "g", and "f". In "wo" the "w" is normally not pronounced, but is written to distinguish it easily from other words that are pronounced "o". (Japanese word-processing software also usually requires that you type "wo" to get を or ヲ.)

"R" is pronounced with a very slight trill. Do not pronounce it as in the English word "rich"; you probably will not be understood. If you trill it as in Italian or Spanish, you can be understood, but you will sound foreign. The best strategy is to listen and imitate. Lacking access to native speakers, try pronouncing "r" as you would "d", but with the tongue farther forward, touching the upper teeth instead of the palate.

"G" is perfectly understandable pronounced as in English "get", "go" etc, and many Japanese always pronounce it in this way. Cultured people, however, prefer a softer, slightly nasal pronunciation, which they call a "half-voiced" or "nasal-voiced" "k". It is similar to the "ng" in "sing", but coming at the beginning of a syllable.

"F" also is quite understandable when given its usual English fricative value, with the lower lip touching the upper teeth. The Japanese, however, normally pronounce it by simply narrowing the gap between the lower lip and the teeth, without actually touching the lip to the teeth. Thus some individuals pronounce it much closer to "h" than to the English "f".

"N" at the end of a syllable or word is syllabic, that is, it is a syllable in its own right, with full syllabic length, as in English "butt*on*". In this dictionary when syllabic "n" is followed by a vowel or "y", a hyphen is inserted to indicate the proper pronunciation: e. g., 勧誘 かんゆう kan-yū, as opposed to 加入 かにゅう kanyū.

Before "p", "b", or "m", "n" naturally becomes an "m" sound; but in this dictionary, in keeping with the practice of other romanized dictionaries, the Japanese ん is consistently transliterated as "n", not "m" : e. g., 文法 ぶんぽう bunpō, not bumpō.

Double consonants are pronounced in Japanese, as in US English "cattail". In "katakana" and "hiragana" they are indicated by a lowercase っ or ッ before the consonant to be doubled, and in this dictionary are printed as double consonants: か っぱ "kappa", いった "itta". The one exception is the combination っち, which we express as "tch" : マッチ, "matchi".

A few Japanese exclamations are written with a lowercase っ at the end, indicating an articulated "t" sound at the end. These we have romanized with a quarter-sized "t" : しっ "shiₜ" (equivalent to the English "ssh !").

The sounds [ti:] and [di:] do not exist in Japanese. They are usually expressed as

ティ and ディ, which we romanize as "ti" and "di". Other sounds in loan words without Japanese equivalents are generally corrupted to some similar sound, e. g., "v" to "b".

Vowels:

The 5 Japanese vowels are the fundamental Latin vowels: [ɑː], [iː], [uː], [e], and [o]. "U" is pronounced without rounding the lips, keeping them relaxed. A rounded "u" is understandable, but sounds outlandishly foreign. Again, listen and imitate.

The vowels can be long or short. Long vowels are pronounced the same as short vowels, but for double their length, with no break. Pay strict attention to this, for vowel length is essential to both meaning and comprehension. Using a short vowel for a long one, or vice versa, can produce a word of entirely different meaning from the one intended. In this dictionary, long vowels are marked with a macron: ā, ī, ū, ē, ō.

The syllable "-su" at the end of a word, especially in the verbal ending "-masu" frequently drops the "u", so that only the "s" is heard. This occurs more often in the east than in the west of the country. There are no hard and fast rules, so the student needs to rely on his experience from listening to spoken Japanese.

Japanese accents:

Japanese words do not have a strong tonic accent as in most European languages. Instead they are inflected, with the voice rising or falling gently on certain syllables, and remaining flat on others. Using the correct "accent" or inflection is necessary for intelligibility of speech, and often serves to distinguish between words of similar spelling. For example, depending on the "accent", "momo" can mean either "peach" or "thigh"; "kaki" can be either "persimmon" or "oyster"; "atsui" can be "hot" or "thick".

The Japanese accent is difficult to depict graphically with any accuracy, for there are no standard conventions. Many dictionaries simply ignore the problem, leaving the foreign student to his own devices. Language classes for foreigners both in Japan and abroad frequently do not teach accents explicitly, but rely on imitation of pronunciation by a native Japanese model.

We felt that the foreign student needed something to aid the memory in trying to pronounce words already learned in the past, as well as a guide to pronunciation of words being looked up in the dictionary. We settled on the accute accent (á) to indicate a rising inflection, and the grave accent (à) to indicate a falling inflection. No mark at all means that the voice is held flat on that syllable.

The one exception in this dictionary is when two "i"s occur together, as in the word for "good" いい ii. In most cases like this, the first "i" requires a rising inflection (í), and the second a falling inflection (ì). However, with standard typefaces this produces an unesthetic effect (íì). Therefore, we have omitted the accent mark of the second "i" in such cases: a rising inflection on the first of a "double i" combination indicates also a falling inflection on the second letter: íi = í ì.

Doubtless the foreign student will be somewhat disconcerted to see such inflection marks on "n" in this dictionary. Remember that final "n" is always syllabic and may be pronounced by itself in Japanese. Thus, "n" can also have a rising or falling inflection, or be flat, as the case may be.

Accent differs markedly from region to region in Japan, particularly between the east and the west. The speech patterns of the Kanto region have generally been adopted as the standards for a "common" language, to be taught in the schools and used by television and radio announcers. Although the accents in this dictionary have followed the guidance of an expert in the field, we lay no claim to absolute accuracy. Our aim has been to guide the foreign student to a pronunciation that, if used, will be understandable in any part of the country, even when the listeners themselves follow a different standard of pronunciation.

English Irregular Verb Forms　不規則動詞表

arise 　arising	arose	arisen	·持ち上る mochíagaru
awake 　awaking	awoke	awaked	目が覚める me ga samérù
be 　am, is, are 　being	was, were	been	である de árù
bear	bore	born(e)	支える sasáerù
beat	beat	beaten	殴る nagúrù
become 　becoming	became	become	なる nárù
begin 　beginning	began	begun	始める hajímeru
behold	beheld	beheld	見る mírù
bend	bent	bent	曲げる magérù
beseech	besought	besought	嘆願する tañgan suru
beset 　besetting	beset	beset	襲う osóu
bet 　betting	bet, betted	bet, betted	かける kakérù
bid 　bidding	bid, bade	bid, bidden	競りに加わる serí ni kuwawarù
bind	bound	bound	縛る shibárù
bite 　biting	bit	bitten	かむ kámù
bleed	bled	bled	出血する shukkétsu suru
blow	blew	blown	吹く fúkù
break	broke	broken	割る warú
breed	bred	bred	繁殖させる hañshoku sasérù
bring	brought	brought	持って来る motté kurù
build	built	built	建てる tatérù
burn	burned, burnt	burned, burnt	燃やす moyásu
burst	burst	burst	破裂させる harétsu sasérù
buy	bought	bought	買う kaú
can	could	(been able)	出来る dekírù

cast	cast	cast	投げる nagérù
catch	caught	caught	捕まえる tsukámaeru
choose	chose	chosen	選ぶ erábù
choosing			
cling	clung	clung	しがみつく shigámitsukù
come	came	come	来る kúrù
coming			
cost	cost	cost	の値段である no nedán de arù
creep	crept	crept	忍び足で歩く shinóbiàshi de arúkù
cut	cut	cut	切る kirù
cutting			
deal	dealt	dealt	配る kubárù
dig	dug	dug	掘る hórù
digging			
dive	dived	dived	飛込む tobíkomù
diving	*also US* dove		
do	did	done	する sùrú
does			
draw	drew	drawn	描く kákù
dream	dreamed, dreamt	dreamed, dreamt	夢を見る yumé wo mirù
drink	drank	drunk	飲む nómù
drive	drove	driven	運転する uñten suru
driving			
dwell	dwelt	dwelt	住む súmù
eat	ate	eaten	食べる tabérù
fall	fell	fallen	落ちる ochírù
feed	fed	fed	食べさせる tabésaserù
feel	felt	felt	感じる kañjirù
fight	fought	fought	戦う tatákaù
find	found	found	見付ける mitsúkeru
flee	fled	fled	逃げる nigérù
fling	flung	flung	投げる nagérù
fly	flew	flown	飛ぶ tobú
flies			
forbid	forbade	forbidden	禁ずる kiñzurù
forbidding			

forecast	forecast	forecast	予報する yohṓ suru
forego	forewent	foregone	なしで我慢する náshǐ de gámàn suru
foresee	foresaw	foreseen	予想する yosṓ suru
foretell	foretold	foretold	予言する yogén suru
forget	forgot	forgotten	忘れる wasúrerù
forgetting			
forgive	forgave	forgiven	許す yurúsù
forgiving			
forsake	forsook	forsaken	見捨てる misúterù
forsaking			
freeze	froze	frozen	凍る kṓrù
freezing			
get	got	got	手に入れる tḗ ni irerù
getting		US gotten	
give	gave	given	与える atáerù
giving			
go	went	gone	行く ikú
goes			
grind	ground	ground	ひく hikú
grow	grew	grown	成長する seíchō suru
hang	hung, hanged	hung, hanged	掛ける kakérù
have	had	had	持っている móttè iru
has ; having			
hear	heard	heard	聞く kikú
hide	hid	hidden	隠す kakúsù
hiding			
hit	hit	hit	打つ utsú
hitting			
hold	held	held	持つ mótsù
hurt	hurt	hurt	痛める itámerù
keep	kept	kept	保管する hokán suru
kneel	knelt, kneeled	knelt, kneeled	ひざまずく hizámazukù
know	knew	known	知っている shittḕ irù
lay	laid	laid	置く okú
lead	led	led	先導する seńdō suru
lean	leaned, leant	leaned, leant	傾く katámukù
leap	**leaped, leapt**	leaped, leapt	跳躍する chṓyaku suru

learn	learned, learnt	learned, learnt	学ぶ manábù
leave	left	left	去る sárù
leaving			
lend	lent	lent	貸す kásù
let	let	let	許す yurúsù
letting			
lie	lay	lain	横になる yokó ni narù
lying			
light	lighted, lit	lighted, lit	火を付ける hí wo tsukérù
lose	lost	lost	失う ushínaù
losing			
make	made	made	作る tsukúrù
making			
may	might	—	かも知れない ka mo shirenài
mean	meant	meant	意味する ímì suru
meet	met	met	会う áù
mistake	mistook	mistaken	間違える machígaerù
mistaking			
mow	mowed	mowed, mown	刈る karú
must	(had to)	(had to)	しなければならない shinákereba naranài
pay	paid	paid	払う haráù
put	put	put	置く okú
putting			
quit	quit, quitted	quit, quitted	やめる yamérù
quitting			
read	read	read	読む yómù
rid	rid	rid	取除く torínozokù
ridding			
ride	rode	ridden	乗る nórù
riding			
ring	rang	rung	鳴る narú
rise	rose	risen	上がる agárù
rising			
run	ran	run	走る hashírù
running			
saw	sawed	sawn	のこぎりで切る nokógirì de kírù
say	said	said	言う iú

see	saw	seen	見る mírù
seek	sought	sought	求める motómerù
sell	sold	sold	売る urú
send	sent	sent	送る okúrù
set	set	set	置く ókù
setting			
shake	shook	shaken	振る fúrù
shaking			
shall	should	—	しましょう shimashō
shear	sheared	sheared, shorn	毛を刈る ké wò karú
shed	shed	shed	落す otósù
shedding			
shine	shone	shone	照る térù
shining			
shoot	shot	shot	そ撃する sogéki suru
show	showed	shown	見せる misérù
shrink	shrank	shrunk	縮む chijímù
shut	shut	shut	閉める shimérù
shutting			
sing	sang	sung	歌う utáù
sink	sank	sunk	沈没する chiñbotsu suru
sit	sat	sat	座る suwárù
sitting			
slay	slew	slain	殺す korósù
sleep	slept	slept	眠る nemúrù
slide	slid	slid	滑る subérù
sliding			
sling	slung	slung	投げる nagérù
slit	slit	slit	切り開く kiríhirakù
slitting			
smell	smelled, smelt	smelled, smelt	匂う nióù
sneak	sneaked	sneaked	こっそり行く kossórì ikú
	also US snuck	*also US* snuck	
sow	sowed	sown, sowed	まく mákù
speak	spoke	spoken	話す hanásù
speed	sped, speeded	sped, speeded	スピードを出す supídò wo dásù
spell	spelled, spelt	spelled, spelt	つづりを言う tsuzúri wò iú
spend	spent	spent	過ごす sugósù

spill	spilled, spilt	spilled, spilt	こぼす kobósù
spin	spun	spun	紡ぐ tsumúgù
spinning			
spit	spat	spat	つばを吐く tsúbà wo hákù
spitting			
split	split	split	裂く sákù
splitting			
spoil	spoiled, spoilt	spoiled, spoilt	台無しにする daínashi ni surù
spread	spread	spread	広げる hirógerù
spring	sprang	sprung	跳ぶ tobú
stand	stood	stood	立つ tátsù
steal	stole	stolen	盗む nusúmù
stick	stuck	stuck	くっつく kuttsúkù
sting	stung	stung	刺す sásù
stink	stank	stunk	におう nióù
stride	strode	stridden	大またに歩く ómàta ni arúkù
striding			
strike	struck	struck, stricken	打つ útsù
striking			
strive	strove	striven	努力する dóryòku suru
striving			
swear	swore	sworn	誓う chikáù
sweep	swept	swept	掃く hákù
swell	swelled	swelled, swollen	はれる harérù
swim	swam	swum	泳ぐ oyógù
swimming			
swing	swung	swung	振る furú
take	took	taken	とる tórù
taking			
teach	taught	taught	教える oshíerù
tear	tore	torn	破る yabúrù
tell	told	told	述べる nobérù
think	thought	thought	考える kañgaerù
throw	threw	thrown	投げる nagérù
thrust	thrust	thrust	強く押す tsúyòku osú
tread	trod	trodden	歩く arúkù
wake	waked, woke	waked, woken	起す okósù
waking			

waylay	waylaid	waylaid	待伏せする machíbuse suru
wear	wore	worn	着る kirú
weave weaving	wove, weaved	woven, weaved	織る orú
wed wedding	wedded, wed	wedded, wed	結婚する kekkón suru
weep	wept	wept	泣く naku
win winning	won	won	勝つ katsù
wind	wound	wound	巻く makú
withdraw	withdrew	withdrawn	取出す torídasu
withhold	withheld	withheld	拒む kobámù
withstand	withstood	withstood	耐える taérù
wring	wrung	wrung	絞る shibórù
write writing	wrote	written	書く kakù

A

A [ei] *n* (MUS: note) イ音 í-òn; (: key) イ調 íchò

KEYWORD

a [ei, ə] (*before vowel or silent h:* **an**) *indef art* 1 1つの hitótsu no, ある árù ◊ 通常日本語では表現しない tsūjō nihongo de wa hyōgen shínái

a book/girl/mirror 本〔少女, 鏡〕hòn 〔shōjo, kagámi〕

an apple りんご ríngo

she's a doctor 彼女は医者です kánojo wa ishá desu

2 (instead of the number "one") 1つの hitótsù no

a loaf and 2 pints of milk, please パン1本と ミルク2パイント下さい pan íppoñ-to mírùku nipáiñto kudasái

a year ago 1年前 ichinen máè

a hundred/thousand etc pounds 100〔1000〕ポンド hyaku〔sen〕póñdò

3 (in expressing ratios, prices etc) 1つ当り... hitotsu átàri...

3 a day/week 1日〔1週間〕当り3つ ichi-nichi〔isshūkan〕átàri mittsú

10 km an hour 時速10キロメーター jí-sòku jukkirométà

£5 a person 1人当たり5ポンド hitori átàri gopóñdò

30p a kilo 1キロ30ペンス ichíkìro san-juppénsù

AA [eiei'] *n abbr* (= *Alcoholics Anonymous*) アルコール依存症自主治療協会 a-rúkòru izoñshō jishúchiryō kyōkai; (*BRIT*: = *Automobile Association*) 英国自動車連盟 eíkoku jidōsha reñmei

AAA [trip'əlei] *n abbr* (= *American Automobile Association*) 米国自動車連盟 beíkoku jidōsha reñmei

aback [əbæk'] *adv*: *to be taken aback* 仰天する gyōteñ suru

abandon [əbæn'dən] *vt* (person) 見捨てる misúterù; (car) 乗捨てる norísuterù;

(give up: search, idea, research) やめる yaméru

◆*n* (wild behavior): *with abandon* 羽目を外して hamé wò hazúshite

abashed [əbæʃt'] *adj* (person) 恥ずかしがっている hazúkashigattè irú

abate [əbeit'] *vi* (lessen: storm, terror, anger) 治まる osámarù

abattoir [æbətwɑ:r'] (*BRIT*) *n* と殺場 tosátsujō

abbey [æb'i:] *n* 修道院 shúdòin

abbot [æb'ət] *n* 修道院長 shúdòinchō

abbreviate [əbri:'vi:eit] *vt* (essay, word) 短縮する tañshuku suru

abbreviation [əbri:vi:ei'ʃən] *n* (short form) 短縮形 tañshukukei

abdicate [æb'dikeit] *vt* (responsibility, right) 放棄する hōki suru

◆*vi* (monarch) 退位する taí-i suru

abdication [æbdikei']ʃən] *n* (of responsibility, right) 放棄 hōki; (by monarch) 退位 taí-i

abdomen [æb'dəmən] *n* 腹部 fukúbù

abduct [æbdʌkt'] *vt* ら致する ráchì suru

aberration [æbərei'ʃən] *n* (unusual behavior, event etc) 異状 ijō

abet [əbet'] *vt see* **aid**

abeyance [əbei'əns] *n*: *in abeyance* (law) 無視されて múshì sarete; (matter) 保留されて horyū sarete

abhor [æbhɔ:r'] *vt* (cruelty, violence etc) ひどく嫌う hídòku kiráu

abide [əbaid'] *vt*: *I can't abide it/him* 私はそれ〔彼〕が大嫌いだ watákushi wà soré〔karè〕gà daíkirai da

abide by *vt fus* (law, decision) ...に従う ...ni shitágaù

ability [əbil'iti:] *n* (capacity) 能力 nṓryoku; (talent, skill) 才能 saínō

abject [æb'dʒekt] *adj* (poverty) 極度の kyókùdo no; (apology) 卑屈な hikútsu na

ablaze [əbleiz'] *adj* (building etc) 炎上している eñjō shite iru

able [ei'bəl] *adj* (capable) 出来る dekírù;

(skilled) 有能な yū́nō na
to be able to do something ...をする事が出来る ...wo suru koto gà dékirù

able-bodied [ei'bəlbɑːd'iːd] *adj* (person) がん健な gańken na

ably [ei'bliː] *adv* (skilfully, well) 上手に jốzu ni

abnormal [æbnɔːr'məl] *adj* (behavior, child, situation) 異常な ijố na

aboard [əbɔːrd'] *adv* (NAUT, AVIAT) ...に乗って ...ni nottě
♦*prep* (NAUT, AVIAT) ...に乗って ...ni nottě

abode [əboud'] *n* (LAW): *of no fixed abode* 住所不定の jū́shofutèi no

abolish [əbɑː'liʃ] *vt* 廃止する haíshi suru

abolition [æbəliʃ'ən] *n* 廃止 haíshi

abominable [əbɑːm'inəbəl] *adj* (conditions) ひどい hídoì; (behavior) 忌わしい imáwashiì

aborigine [æbəridʒ'əniː] *n* 原住民 geńjūmìn

abort [əbɔːrt'] *vt* (MED: fetus) 流産する ryū́zan suru; (plan, activity) 中止する chū́shi suru

abortion [əbɔːr'ʃən] *n* (MED) 妊娠中絶 nińshinchūzètsu
to have an abortion 妊娠を中絶する nińshin wò chūzetsu suru

abortive [əbɔːr'tiv] *adj* (attempt, action) 不成功の fuséìkō no

abound [əbaund'] *vi* (exist in large numbers) ...が多い ...ga ối
to abound in/with (possess in large numbers) ...に富む ...ni tómù

KEYWORD

about [əbaut'] *adv* 1 (approximately) 約 yákù, 大よそ őyoso, ...ぐらい ...gúrài
about a hundred/thousand etc dollars 約100(1000)ドル yákù hyakú(sen) dòru
it takes about 10 hours 10時間ぐらいかかります jūjikan gúrài kakarimásù
at about 2 o'clock 2時頃 niji górò
I've just about finished ほぼ終ったところです hóbò owatta tokoro desù
2 (referring to place) あちこちに achíko-

chì ni
to leave things lying about 物をあちこちに散らかしたままにする monò wo achíkochì ni chirakashita mamá ni sùrù
to run/walk etc about あちこち走り回る〔歩き回る〕achíkochì hashirimawárù〔arukimawárù〕
3: *to be about to do something* ...するところである ...suru tokoro dè árù
he was about to cry/leave/wash the dishes/go to bed 彼は泣き出す〔帰る、皿を洗う、寝る〕ところだった kárè wa nakidasu(kaeru, sara wo arau, neru) tokoro dattá
♦*prep* 1 (relating to) ...について ...ni tsúìte, ...に関して ...ni kànshite
a book about London ロンドンについての本 róndòn ni tsúìte no hon
what is it about? それは何についてですか sore wa nán ni tsúìte desu ká
we talked about it 私たちはそれについて話し合った watakushitachì a sore ni tsúìte hanashiáttà
what/how about having some coffee? コーヒーでも飲みましょうか kōhī de mò nomimashố kà
2 (referring to place) ...のあちこちに ...no achíkochì ni
to walk about the town 町をあちこち歩き回る machí wo achíkochì arukimawárù
her clothes were scattered about the room 部屋のあちこちに彼女の服が散らかっていた heya no achíkochì ni kánojò no fukú gà chirakatte itá

about-face [əbaut'feis] *n* (MIL) 回れ右 mawáremigì; (*fig*): *to do an about-face* 一変する ippén suru

about-turn [əbaut'təːrn] *n* = **about-face**

above [əbʌv'] *adv* (higher up, overhead) 上の方に ué no hồ ni; (greater, more) 以上に ijố ni
♦*prep* (higher than) ...より上に ...yốrì ué ni; (greater than, more than: in number, amount etc) ...以上 ...íjố; (: in rank etc) 上である ué de arù

mentioned above 上記の jōki no

above all まず第一に mázù daí-ichi ni

aboveboard [əbʌv'bourd'] *adj* 公明正大 な kōmeiseidai na

abrasive [əbrei'siv] *adj* (substance) 研磨 の kénma no; (person, manner) とげとげ しい togétogeshiì

abreast [əbrest'] *adv* (people, vehicles) 横に並んで yokó ni narande

to keep abreast of (*fig*: news etc) ...に ついていく ...ni tsúite ikú

abridge [əbridʒ'] *vt* (novel, play) 短縮す る tañshuku suru

abroad [əbrɔːd'] *adv* 海外に kaígai ni

abrupt [əbrʌpt'] *adj* (sudden: action, end- ing etc) 突然の totsúzen no; (curt: per- son, behavior) ぶっきらぼうな bukkírabō na

abruptly [əbrʌpt'li:] *adv* (leave, end) 突 然 totsúzen; (speak) ぶっきらぼうに buk- kírabō ni

abscess [æb'ses] *n* のうよう nōyō

abscond [æbskɑːnd'] *vi* (thief): *to abscond with* ...を持ち逃げする ...wo mochínige suru; (prisoner): *to abscond (from)* (...から) 逃亡する (...kara) tōbō suru

absence [æb'səns] *n* (of person: from home etc) 不在 fuzái; (: from school, meeting etc) 欠席 kessékì; (: from work) 欠勤 kekkín; (of thing) 無い事 nái kotó

absent [æb'sənt] *adj* (person: from home etc) 不在の fuzái no; (: from school, meeting etc) 欠席の kessékì no; (: from work) 欠勤の kekkín no; (thing) 無い nái

absentee [æbsənti:'] *n* (from school, meeting etc) 欠席者 kessékishà; (from work) 欠勤者 kekkínsha

absent-minded [æb'səntmain'did] *adj* 忘れっぽい wasúreppoì

absolute [æb'səluːt] *adj* (complete) 全く の mattáku no; (monarch, rule, power) 専制的な señseiteki na; (principle, rule etc) 絶対的な zettáiteki na

absolutely [æbsəluːt'liː] *adv* (totally) 全 く mattáku; (certainly) その通り sonō tōrì

absolution [æbsəluː'ʃən] *n* (REL) 罪の許

し tsúmì no yurúshì

absolve [æbzɑːlv'] *vt*: *to absolve some- one (from blame, responsibility, sin)* ...の (...を) 許す ...no (...wò) yurúsù

absorb [æbsɔːrb'] *vt* 吸収する kyūshū su- ru; (assimilate: group, business) 併合す る heígō suru

to be absorbed in a book 本に夢中にな っている hón ni muchū ni nattě irú

absorbent cotton [æbsɔːr'bənt-] (*US*) *n* 脱脂綿 dasshímèn

absorbing [æbsɔːr'biŋ] *adj* 夢中にさせる muchū ni saseru

absorption [æbsɔːrp'ʃən] *n* 吸収 kyūshū; (assimilation: of group, business etc) 併 合 heígō; (interest) 夢中になる事 muchū ni narū kotó

abstain [æbstein'] *vi*: *to abstain (from)* (eating, drinking) 控える hikáe- rù; (voting) 棄権する kikén suru

abstemious [æbsti:'mi:əs] *adj* (person) 節制する sesséi suru

abstention [æbsten'ʃən] *n* (refusal to vote) 棄権 kikén

abstinence [æb'stənəns] *n* 禁欲 kiń-yo- ku

abstract [æb'strækt] *adj* (idea, quality) 抽象的な chūshōteki na; (ART) 抽象派の chūshōha no; (LING): *abstract noun* 抽 象名詞 chūshōmeishi

abstruse [æbstruːs'] *adj* 分かりにくい wakárinikuì

absurd [æbsəːrd'] *adj* ばかげた bakágetà

abundance [əbʌn'dəns] *n* 豊富さ hōfusa

abundant [əbʌn'dənt] *adj* 豊富な hōfu na

abuse [*n* əbjuːs' *vb* əbjuːz'] *n* (insults) の のしり nonóshiri; (ill-treatment) 虐待 gyakútai; (misuse: of power, drugs etc) 乱用 rañ-yō

♦*vt* (insult) ののしる nonóshirù; (ill- treat) 虐待する gyakútai suru; (misuse) 乱用する rañ-yō suru

abusive [əbjuː'siv] *adj* (person) 口の悪い kuchí no waruì; (language) 侮辱的な bu- jókuteki na

abysmal [əbiz'məl] *adj* (performance, failure) 最低の saítei no; (ignorance etc)

ひどい hidói

abyss [əbis'] *n* 深えん shiñ-en

AC [ei'si:] *abbr* = **alternating current**

academic [ækədem'ik] *adj* (person) インテリの iñteri no; (year, system, books, freedom etc) 教育関係の kyóikukañkei no; (pej: issue) 理論的な riróñteki na
♦*n* 学者 gakúsha

academy [əkæd'əmi:] *n* (learned body) アカデミー akádēmī; (school) 学院 gakúin
   academy of music 音楽学院 oñgaku gakúin

accelerate [æksel'əreit] *vt* (process) 早める hayámerù
♦*vi* (AUT) 加速する kasóku suru

acceleration [ækselərei'ʃən] *n* (AUT) 加速 kasóku

accelerator [æksel'əreitə:r] *n* アクセル ákùseru

accent [æk'sent] *n* (pronunciation) なまり namári; (written mark) アクセント符号 akúsento fugó; (fig: emphasis, stress) 強調 kyóchō, アクセント akúsento

accept [æksept'] *vt* (gift, invitation) 受取る ukétoru; (fact, situation, risk) 認める mitómeru; (responsibility, blame) 負う oú

acceptable [æksep'təbəl] *adj* (offer, gift) 受入れられる uké-irerarerù; (risk etc) 許容できる kyoyó dekirù

acceptance [æksep'təns] *n* (of gift, offer etc) 受取る事 ukétoru koto; (of risk etc) 許容 kyoyó; (of responsibility etc) 負う事 oú koto

access [æk'ses] *n* (to building, room) 入る事 háiru kotó; (to information, papers) 利用する権利 riyó suru keñri
   to have access to (child etc) ...への面会権がある ...e no meñkaikeñ ga árù

accessible [ækses'əbəl] *adj* (place) 行きやすい ikíyasuì; (person) 面会しやすい meñkai shiyasuì; (available: knowledge, art etc) 利用しやすい riyó shiyasuì

accessory [ækses'ə:ri:] *n* (dress, COMM, TECH, AUT) アクセサリー ákùsesarī; (LAW): *accessory to* ...の共犯者 ...no kyóhañsha

accident [æk'sidənt] *n* (chance event) 偶然 gúzen; (mishap, disaster) 事故 jíkò
   by accident (unintentionally) うっかり ukkárì; (by chance) 偶然に gúzen ni

accidental [æksiden'təl] *adj* (death) 事故による jíkò ni yorú; (damage) 偶発的な gúhatsuteki na

accidentally [æksiden'təli:] *adv* (by accident) 偶然に gúzen ni

accident-prone [æk'sidəntproun'] *adj* 事故に会いがちな jíko ni aigachi na

acclaim [əkleim'] *n* 賞賛 shósan
♦*vt*: *to be acclaimed for one's achievements* 功績で有名である kóseki dè yúmei de arù

acclimate [əklai'mit] (*US*) *vt* = **acclimatize**

acclimatize [əklai'mətaiz] *vt*: *to become acclimatized (to)* (...に) 慣れる (...ni) narérù

accolade [ækəleid'] *n* (*fig*) 賞賛 shósan

accommodate [əkɑːm'ədeit] *vt* (subj: person) 泊める toméru; (: car, hotel etc) 収容できる shúyō dekirù; (oblige, help) ...に親切にして上げる ...ni shíñsetsu ni shite agérù

accommodating [əkɑːm'ədeitiŋ] *adj* 親切な shíñsetsu na

accommodation [əkɑːmədei'ʃən] *n* 宿泊設備 shukúhakusetsùbi

accommodations [əkɑːmədei'ʃənz] (*US*) *npl* 宿泊設備 shukúhakusetsùbi

accompaniment [əkʌm'pənimənt] *n* 伴奏 bañsō

accompany [əkʌm'pəni:] *vt* (escort, go along with) ...に付きそう ...ni tsukísoù; (MUS) ...の伴奏をする ...no bañsō wò suru

accomplice [əkɑːm'plis] *n* 共犯者 kyóhañsha

accomplish [əkɑːm'pliʃ] *vt* (finish: task) 成遂げる nashítogerù; (achieve: goal) 達成する tasséi suru

accomplished [əkɑːm'pliʃt] *adj* (person) 熟練の jukúren no; (performance) 優れた sugúretà

accomplishment [əkɑːm'pliʃmənt] *n* (completion, bringing about) 遂行 suíkō;

(skill: *gen pl*) 才能 saínō

accord [əkɔːrd'] *n* (treaty) 協定 kyṓtei
♦*vt* 与える atáeru
of his own accord 自発的に jihátsuteki ni

accordance [əkɔːr'dəns] *n*: *in accordance with* (someone's wishes, the law etc) ...に従って ...ni shitágatte

according [əkɔːr'diŋ]: *according to* *prep* (person, account) ...によると ...ni yorú to

accordingly [əkɔːr'diŋli] *adv* (appropriately) それに応じて soré nǐ ṓjite; (as a result) それで soré de

accordion [əkɔːr'diːən] *n* アコーデオン ákōdeon

accost [əkɔːst'] *vt* ...に近寄って話し掛ける ...ni chikáyottè hanáshikakerù

account [əkaunt'] *n* (COMM: bill) 勘定書 kanjōgaki; (: monthly account) 計算書 keísansho; (in bank) 口座 kṓza; (report) 報告 hṓkoku
of no account 構わない kamáwanài
on account つけで tsukế de
on no account 何があっても... (すべき)でない naní ga atte mo ...(subeki) de naí
on account of ...のために ...no tamé ni
to take into account, take account of ...を考慮に入れる ...wò kṓryo ni iréru

accountable [əkaun'təbəl] *adj*: *accountable (to)* (...に) 申開きする義務がある (...ni) mṓshihiraki suru gimù ga árù

accountancy [əkaun'tənsiː] *n* 会計士の職 kaíkeìshi no shokú

accountant [əkaun'tənt] *n* 会計士 kaíkeìshi

account for *vt fus* (explain) 説明する setsúmei suru; (represent) ...(の割合)を占める ...(no waríai) wò shimérù

account number *n* (at bank etc) 口座番号 kṓzabangō

accounts [əkaunts'] *npl* (COMM) 勘定 kanjō

accredited [əkred'itid] *adj* (agent etc) 資格のある shikáku no arù

accrued interest [əkruːd'-] *n* 累積利息 ruísekirisòku

accumulate [əkjuːm'jəleit] *vt* 貯める tamếru
♦*vi* 貯まる tamáru

accuracy [æk'jərəsiː] *n* 正確さ seíkakusa

accurate [æk'jərit] *adj* 正確な seíkaku na

accurately [æk'jəritliː] *adv* (count, shoot, answer) 正確に seíkaku ni

accusation [ækjuːzei'ʃən] *n* 非難 hínàn

accuse [əkjuːz'] *vt*: *to accuse someone (of something)* (crime, incompetence) (...だと) ...を責める (...dá tò) ...wo semếrù

accused [əkjuːzd'] *n* (LAW): *the accused* 容疑者 yōgishà

accustom [əkʌs'təm] *vt* 慣れさせる narésaserù

accustomed [əkʌs'təmd] *adj* (usual): *accustomed to* ...に慣れている ...ni narétè irú

ace [eis] *n* (CARDS, TENNIS) エース ḕsu

ache [eik] *n* 痛み itámi
♦*vi* (be painful) 痛む itámù, ...が痛い ...ga itáî
my head aches 頭が痛い atáma gà itáî

achieve [ətʃiːv'] *vt* (aim) 成遂げる nashítogerù; (result) 上げる agếru; (victory, success) 獲得する kakútoku suru

achievement [ətʃiːv'mənt] *n* (completion) 完成 kanseí; (success, feat) 業績 gyṓseki

acid [æs'id] *adj* (CHEM: soil etc) 酸性の sanseí no; (taste) 酸っぱい suppáî
♦*n* (CHEM) 酸 sáñ; (*inf*: LSD) LSD erúesudî

acid rain *n* 酸性雨 sanseiù

acknowledge [æknɑːl'idʒ] *vt* (letter, parcel: *also*: **acknowledge receipt of**) 受け取った事を知らせる ukétotta koto wò shiráserù; (fact, situation, person) 認める mitómeru

acknowledgement [æknɑːl'idʒmənt] *n* (of letter, parcel) 受領通知 juryṓtsūchi

acne [æk'niː] *n* にきび níkîbi

acorn [ei'kɔːrn] *n* ドングリ dóñguri

acoustic [əku:s'tik] *adj* (related to hearing) 聴覚の chōkaku no; (guitar etc) アコースティックの akōsùtikku no

acoustics [əku:s'tiks] *n* (science) 音響学 oṅkyōgaku

♦*npl* (of hall, room) 音響効果 oṅkyōkōka

acquaint [əkweint'] *vt*: **to acquaint someone with something** (inform) ...に...を知らせる ...ni ...wò shiráseru

to be acquainted with (person) ...と面識がある ...to meṅshiki ga arù

acquaintance [əkwein'təns] *n* (person) 知合い shiríai; (with person, subject) 知識 chíshìki

acquiesce [ækwi:es'] *vi*: **to acquiesce (to)** (...) を承諾する (...wò) shōdaku suru

acquire [əkwai'əːr] *vt* (obtain, buy) 手に入れる te ni iréru; (learn, develop: interest, skill) 取得する shutóku suru

acquisition [ækwiziʃ'ən] *n* (obtaining etc) 入手 nyūshu; (development etc) 獲得 kakútoku; (thing acquired) 取得物 shutókubùtsu

acquit [əkwit'] *vt* (free) 無罪とする múzài to suru

to acquit oneself well 見事な働きをする migòto na határaki wo suru

acquittal [əkwit'əl] *n* 無罪判決 muzái haṅketsu

acre [ei'kəːr] *n* エーカー ềkā

acrid [æk'rid] *adj* (smell, taste, smoke) 刺激的な shigékiteki na

acrimonious [ækrəmou'ni:əs] *adj* (remark, argument) 辛らつな shiríratsu na

acrobat [æk'rəbæt] *n* アクロバット akúrobattò

acrobatic [ækrəbæt'ik] *adj* (person, movement, display) アクロバット的な akúrobattoteki na

acronym [æk'rənim] *n* 頭字語 tōjigo

across [əkrɔ:s'] *prep* (from one side to the other of) ...を渡って ...wo watátte; (on the other side of) ...の向こう側に ...no mukōgawa ni; (crosswise over) ...と交差して ...to kōsa shite

♦*adv* (direction) 向こう側へ mukōgawa e; (measurement) 直径が...で chokkéi ga

... de

to run/swim across 走って〔泳いで〕渡る hashítte (oyóide)wataru

across from ...の向いに ...no mukái ni

acrylic [əkril'ik] *adj* アクリルの ákùriru no

♦*n* アクリル ákùriru

act [ækt] *n* (action) 行為 kṓi; (of play) 幕 makú; (in a show etc) 出し物 dashímòno; (LAW) 法 hṓ

♦*vi* (do something, take action) 行動する kōdō suru; (behave) 振舞う furúmaù; (have effect: drug, chemical) 作用する sáyō suru; (THEATER) 出演する shutsúen suru; (pretend) ...の振りをする ...no furí wò suru

♦*vt* (part) ...に扮する ...ni fuṅ surù

in the act of ...しているさなかに ...shité iru sanàka ni

to act as ...として勤める ...toshite tsutómerù

acting [æk'tiŋ] *adj* (manager, director etc) 代理の daíri no

♦*n* (activity) 演技 éṅgi; (profession) 演劇 eṅgeki

action [æk'ʃən] *n* (deed) 行為 kṓi; (motion) 動き ugókí; (MIL) 戦闘 seṅtō; (LAW) 訴訟 soshṓ

out of action (person) 活動不能で katsúdōfunō de; (thing) 作動不能で sadṓfunō de

to take action 行動を起す kōdō wo okósù

action replay *n* (TV) 即時ビデオ再生 sokúji bideo saìsei

activate [æk'təveit] *vt* (mechanism) 作動させる sadṓsaserù

active [æk'tiv] *adj* (person, life) 活動的な katsúdōteki na

active volcano 活火山 kakkázàn

actively [æk'tivli:] *adv* (participate) 積極的に sekkyōkuteki ni; (discourage) 強く tsúyòku; (dislike) 非常に hijṓ ni

activist [æk'tivist] *n* 活動家 katsúdōka

activity [æktiv'əti:] *n* (being active) 活動 katsúdō; (action) 動き ugókí; (pastime, pursuit) 娯楽 goráku

actor [æk'təːr] *n* 俳優 haíyū

actress [æk'tris] *n* 女優 joyú

actual [æk'tʃuəl] *adj* 実際の jissái no

actually [æk'tʃuːəliː] *adv* (really) 本当に hoñtō ni; (in fact) 実は jitsú wa

acumen [əkjuː'mən] *n* 判断力 hañdañryoku

acupuncture [æk'jupʌŋktʃəːr] *n* 針 hárí

acute [əkjuːt'] *adj* (illness) 急性の kyúsei no; (anxiety, pain) 激しい hagéshiî; (mind, person) 抜け目の無い nukéme no nai; (MATH): *acute angle* 鋭角 eíkaku; (LING): *acute accent* 鋭アクセント eíakùsento

ad [æd] *n abbr* = **advertisement**

A.D. [eidiː'] *adv abbr* (= *Anno Domini*) 西暦...年 seíreki ...neñ

adamant [æd'əmənt] *adj* (person) 譲らない yuzúranai

Adam's apple [æd'əms-] *n* のど仏 nodóbotòke

adapt [ədæpt'] *vt* (alter, change) 適応させる tekíō saserù
♦*vi*: *to adapt (to)* (に)適応する (...ni) tekíō suru

adaptable [ədæp'təbəl] *adj* (device, person) 適応性のある tekíōsei no arù

adapter [ədæp'təːr] *n* (ELEC) アダプター adáputā

adaptor [ədæp'təːr] *n* = **adapter**

add [æd] *vt* (to a collection etc) 加える kuwáeru; (comment etc) 付加える tsukékuwaerù; (figures: *also*: **add up**) 合計する gőkei suru
♦*vi*: *to add to* (increase) ...を増す ...wo masú

adder [æd'əːr] *n* ヨーロッパクサリヘビ yőroppà kusárihebî

addict [æd'ikt] *n* (to drugs etc) 中毒者 chúdokushà; (enthusiast) マニア mánìa

addicted [ədik'tid] *adj*: *to be addicted to* (drink etc) ...中毒にかかっている ...chúdoku ni kakâttè irú; (*fig*: football etc) ...マニアである ...mánìa de arù

addiction [ədik'ʃən] *n* (to drugs etc) 中毒 chúdoku

addictive [ədik'tiv] *adj* (drug) 習慣性のある shúkansei no arù; (activity) 癖になる kusé ni narù

addition [ədiʃ'ən] *n* (adding up) 足し算 tashízàn; (thing added) 加えられた物 kuwáerareta monó
in addition なお náð
in addition to ...の外に ...no hokâ ni

additional [ədiʃ'ənəl] *adj* 追加の tsuíka no

additive [æd'ətiv] *n* 添加物 teñkabùtsu

address [ədres'] *n* (postal address) 住所 júsho; (speech) 演説 eñzetsu
♦*vt* (letter, parcel) ...に宛名を書く ...ni aténa wð kákù; (speak to: person) ...に話し掛ける ...ni hanáshikakerù; (: audience) ...に演説する ...ni eñzetsu suru; (problem): *to address (oneself to) a problem* 問題に取組む mofidai ni torikumù

adept [ədept'] *adj*: *adept at* ...が上手な ...ga jőzu na

adequate [æd'əkwit] *adj* (enough: amount) 十分な júbuñ na; (satisfactory: performance, response) 満足な máñzoku na

adhere [ædhiːr'] *vi*: *to adhere to* (stick to) ...にくっつく ...ni kuttsúkù; (*fig*: abide by: rule, decision, treaty etc) ...を守る ...wo mamórù; (: hold to: opinion, belief etc) ...を固守する ...wo kőshū suru

adhesive [ædhiː'siv] *n* 粘着材 neñchakuzài

adhesive tape *n* (*US*: MED) ばん創こう bañsőkō; (*BRIT*) 粘着テープ neñchaku tépu

ad hoc [æd hɑːk'] *adj* (decision, committee) 特別な tokúbetsu na

adjacent [ədʒei'sənt] *adj*: *adjacent to* ...の隣の ...no tonári no

adjective [æd'ʒiktiv] *n* 形容詞 keíyòshi

adjoining [ədʒɔi'niŋ] *adj* (room etc) 隣の tonári no

adjourn [ədʒəːrn'] *vt* (trial) 休廷にする kyútei ni suru; (meeting, discussion) 休会にする kyúkai ni suru
♦*vi* (trial) 休廷する kyútei suru; (meeting) 休止する kyúshi suru

adjudicate [ədʒuː'dikeit] *vt* (contest) ...の審査員を勤める ...no shiñsa-ìn wo tsutőmerù

adjust [əʤʌst'] *vt* (change: approach etc) 調整する chōsei suru; (rearrange: clothing, machine etc) 調節する chōsetsu suru

♦*vi: to adjust (to)* 適応する tekíō suru

adjustable [əʤʌst'əbəl] *adj* 調節できる chōsetsu dekirù

adjustment [əʤʌst'mənt] *n* (PSYCH) 適応 tekíō; (to machine) 調節 chōsetsu; (of prices, wages) 調整 chōsei

ad-lib [ædlib'] *vi* アドリブで話す adóribu dè hanásù

ad lib [ædlib'] *adv* (speak) アドリブで a-dóribu de

administer [ædmin'istər] *vt* (country) 統治する tōchi suru; (department) 管理する kánri suru; (MED: drug) 投与する tōyo suru

to administer justice 裁く sabákù

administration [ædministrei'ʃən] *n* (management) 管理 kánri; (government) 政権 seíken

administrative [ædmin'istreitiv] *adj* (work, error etc) 管理的な kánriteki na

administrator [ædmin'istreitər] *n* 管理者 kánrishà

admiral [æd'mərəl] *n* 海軍大将 kaígun taíshō

Admiralty [æd'mərəlti:] (*BRIT*) *n: the Admiralty* (*also*: **Admiralty Board**) 海軍省 kaígunshō

admiration [ædmərei'ʃən] *n* 感心 kańshin

admire [ædmai'ər] *vt* (respect) ...に感心する ...ni kańshin suru; (appreciate) 観賞する kańshō suru

admirer [ædmai'ərər] *n* (suitor) 男友達 otōkotomodachi; (fan) ファン fáñ

admission [ædmiʃ'ən] *n* (admittance) 入場 nyūjō; (entry fee) 入場料 nyūjōryō; (confession) 自白 jiháku

admit [ædmit'] *vt* (confess) 自白する ji-háku suru; (permit to enter) 入場させる nyūjō saserù; (to club, organization) 入会させる nyūkai saserù; (to hospital) 入院させる nyūin saserù; (accept: defeat, responsibility etc) 認める mitómeru

admittance [ædmit'əns] *n* 入場 nyūjō

admittedly [ædmit'idli:] *adv* 確かに...であるが táshìka ni ...de árù ga

admit to *vt fus* (murder etc) ...を自白する ...wo jiháku suru

admonish [ædmɑːn'iʃ] *vt* (rebuke) たしなめる tashínamerù; (LAW) 忠告する chū-koku suru

ad nauseam [æd nɔː'ziːəm] *adv* (repeat, talk) いやという程 iyá to iú hodō

ado [ədu:'] *n: without (any) more ado* さっさと sássà to

adolescence [ædəles'əns] *n* 10代 jūdai

adolescent [ædəles'ənt] *adj* 10代の jūdai no

♦*n* ティーンエージャー tíñèjā

adopt [ədɑːpt'] *vt* (child) 養子にする yōshi ni suru; (policy, attitude) とる torù; (accent) まねる manérù

adopted [ədɑːp'tid] *adj* (child) 養子の yōshi no

adoption [ədɑːp'ʃən] *n* (of child) 養子縁組 yōshieñgumi; (of policy etc) 採択 saítaku

adoptive [ədɑːp'tiv] *adj: adoptive father/mother* 養父(母) yōfu(bo)

adoptive country 第2の祖国 dáì ni no sōkòku

adore [ədɔːr'] *vt* (person) 崇拝する sūhai suru

adorn [ədɔːrn'] *vt* (decorate) 飾る kazáru

adrenalin [ædren'əlin] *n* アドレナリン a-dōrenarín

Adriatic [eidri:æt'ik] *n: the Adriatic (Sea)* アドリア海 adóriakài

adrift [ədrift'] *adv* (NAUT: loose) 漂流して hyōryū shite

adult [ədʌlt'] *n* (person) 大人 otóna; (animal, insect) 成体 seítai

♦*adj* (grown-up: person) 大人の otóna no; (: animal etc) 成体の seítai no; (for adults: literature, education) 成人向きの seíjinmuki no

adultery [ədʌl'təri:] *n* かん通 kańtsū

advance [ædvæns'] *n* (movement, progress) 進歩 shíñpo; (money) 前借り maégari

♦*adj* (booking, notice, warning) 事前の jizén no

♦*vt* (money) 前貸する maégashi suru

♦*vi* (move forward) 前進する zeńshin suru; (make progress) 進歩する shińpo suru

to make advances (to someone) (gen) (...に) 言い寄る (...ni) iíyorù

in advance (book, prepare etc) 前もって maémottè

advanced [æd'vænst'] *adj* (SCOL: studies) 高等の kốtō no; (country) 先進の seńshin no; (child) ませた máseta

advancement [ædvæns'mənt] *n* (improvement) 進歩 shińpo; (in job, rank) 昇進 shôshin

advantage [ædvæn'tidʒ] *n* (supremacy) 有利な立場 yúri na táchìba; (benefit) 利点 rítèn; (TENNIS) アドバンテージ adóbañtēji

to take advantage of (person) ...に付込む ...ni tsukékomù; (opportunity) 利用する riyố suru

advantageous [ædvəntei'dʒəs] *adj*: *advantageous (to)* (...に) 有利な (...ni) yúri na

advent [æd'vent] *n* (appearance: of innovation) 出現 shutsúgen; (REL): *Advent* 待降節 taíkōsetsù

adventure [ædven'tʃəːr] *n* 冒険 bốken

adventurous [ædven'tʃəːrəs] *adj* (bold, outgoing) 大胆な daítañ na

adverb [æd'vəːrb] *n* 副詞 fukúshi

adversary [æd'vəːrseːriː] *n* (opponent, *also* MIL) 敵 tekí

adverse [ædvəːrs'] *adj* (effect, weather, publicity etc) 悪い warúi

adversity [ædvəːr'sitiː] *n* 逆境 gyakkyố

advert [æd'vəːrt] (*BRIT*) *n abbr* = **advertisement**

advertise [æd'vəːrtaiz] *vi* (COMM: in newspaper, on television etc) 広告する kốkoku suru

♦*vt* (product, event, job) ...を広告する ...wo kốkoku suru

to advertise for (staff, accommodation etc) ...を求める広告を出す ...wo motómerù kốkoku wo dasu

advertisement [ædvəːrtaiz'mənt] *n* 広告 kốkoku

advertiser [æd'vəːrtaizəːr] *n* (in newspaper, on television etc) 広告主 kốkokunùshi

advertising [æd'vəːrtaiziŋ] *n* (advertisements) 広告 kốkoku; (industry) 広告業界 kốkokugyồkai

advice [ædvais'] *n* (counsel) 忠告 chúkoku; (notification) 知らせ shiráse

a piece of advice 一つの忠告 hítotsu no chúkoku

to take legal advice 弁護士に相談する beńgoshì ni sốdan suru

advisable [ædvai'zəbəl] *adj* 望ましい nozómashiî

advise [ædvaiz'] *vt* (give advice to: person, company etc) ...に忠告する ...ni chúkoku suru; (inform): *to advise someone of something* ...に...を知らせる ...ni ...wo shiráserù

to advise against something/doing something ...(するの) を避けた方がいいと忠告する ... (surú no) wo sakéta hō gà fi to chúkoku suru

advisedly [ædvai'zidliː] *adv* (deliberately) 意図的に itóteki ni

adviser [ædvai'zəːr] *n* (counsellor, consultant: to private person) 相談相手 sốdan aitè; (: to company person) 顧問 kômòn

advisor [ædvai'zəːr] *n* = **adviser**

advisory [ædvai'zəːriː] *adj* (role, capacity, body) 顧問の kômòn no

advocate [æd'vəkit] *vt* (support, recommend) 主張する shuchô suru

♦*n* (LAW: barrister) 弁護士 beńgoshì; (supporter): *advocate of* ...の主張者 ...no shuchốsha

Aegean [idʒi:'ən] *n*: *the Aegean (Sea)* エーゲ海 ếgekài

aerial [eːr'iːəl] *n* アンテナ añtena

♦*adj* (attack, photograph) 航空の kốkū no

aerobics [eːrou'biks] *n* エアロビクス eárobikùsu

aerodynamic [eːroudainæm'ik] *adj* 空力的な kűrikiteki na

aeroplane [eːr'əplein] (*BRIT*) *n* 飛行機 híkōki

aerosol [eːr'əsɔːl] *n* スプレー缶 supúrē

kan

aerospace industry [eːr'əspeis-] *n* 宇宙開発業界 uchūkaīhatsugyōkai

aesthetic [esθet'ik] *adj* 美的な bitéki na

afar [əfɑːr'] *adv: from afar* 遠くから tôku kara

affable [æf'əbəl] *adj* (person) 愛想の良い aísō no yoî; (behavior) 感じの良い kaṅji no yoî

affair [əfeːr'] *n* (matter, business, question) 問題 moñdai; (romance: *also*: **love affair**) 浮気 uwáki

affect [əfekt'] *vt* (influence, concern: person, object) ...に影響を与える ...ni efkyō wò atáerù; (subj: disease: afflict) 冒す okásù; (move deeply) 感動させる kaň-dō saserù

affected [əfek'tid] *adj* (behavior, person) 気取った kidóttà

affection [əfek'ʃən] *n* (fondness) 愛情 aîjō

affectionate [əfek'ʃənit] *adj* (person, kiss) 愛情深い aîjōbukaî; (animal) 人なつこい hitónatsukoî

affiliated [əfil'iːeitid] *adj* (company, body) 関連の kaáren no

affinity [əfin'əti:] *n* (bond, rapport): *to have an affinity with/for* ...に魅力を感じる ...ni miryôku wò kaṅjiru; (resemblance): *to have an affinity with* ... に似ている ...ni nitê iru

affirmative [əfəːr'mətiv] *adj* (answer, nod etc) 肯定の kôtei no

affix [əfiks'] *vt* (stamp) はる harú

afflict [əflikt'] *vt* (subj: pain, sorrow, misfortune) 苦しめる kurúshimerù

affluence [æf'luːəns] *n* 裕福さ yūfukusà

affluent [æf'luːənt] *adj* (wealthy: family, background, surroundings) 裕福な yûfuku na

  the affluent society 豊かな社会 yútàka na shákaî

afford [əfɔːrd'] *vt* (have enough money for) 買う余裕がある kaú yoyû ga arù; (permit oneself: time, risk etc) する余裕がある surú yoyû ga arù; (provide) 与える atáeru

affront [əfrʌnt'] *n* (insult) 侮辱 bujóku

Afghanistan [æfgæn'istæn] *n* アフガニスタン afúganisùtan

afield [əfiːld'] *adv: far afield* 遠く tôku

afloat [əflout'] *adv* (floating) 浮んで ukánde

afoot [əfut'] *adv: there is something afoot* 何か怪しい事が起っている nánīka ayāshii koto gà okóttè irú

afraid [əfreid'] *adj* (frightened) 怖がっている kowágattè irú

  to be afraid of (person, thing) ...を怖がる ...wo kowágarù

  to be afraid to ...をするのを怖がる ...wo suru no wò kowágarù

  I am afraid that (apology) 申訳ないが ... môshiwakenai ga

  I am afraid so/not 残念ですがその通りです〔違います〕zaǹneñ desu ga sonô tòri desu〔chigáimasù〕

afresh [əfreʃ'] *adv* (begin, start) 新たにárāta ni

Africa [æf'rikə] *n* アフリカ afúrika

African [æf'rikən] *adj* アフリカの afúrika no

  ♦*n* アフリカ人 afúrikajìn

aft [æft] *adv* (to be) 後方に kôhō ni; (to go) 後方へ kôhō e

after [æf'təːr] *prep* (of time) ...の後に ...no átò ni; (of place) ...の後ろに ...no ushíro ni; (of order) ...の次に ...no tsugí ni

  ♦*adv* 後に átò ni

  ♦*conj* ...してから ...shitê kara

  what/who are you after? 何〔だれ〕を捜していますか nánī〔dárè〕wo sagáshitè imásu ka

  after he left 彼が帰ってから kárè ga kaếtte kara

  after having done ...してから ...shitê kara

  to name someone after someone ...に因んで...に名を付ける ...ni chínaǹde ...ni na wo tsukérù

  it's twenty after eight (US) 8時20分だ hachíji nijíppùn da

  to ask after someone ...の事を尋ねる ...no kotô wò tazúnerù

  after all (in spite of everything) どうせ

dóse; (in spite of contrary expectations etc) 予想を裏切って yosó wò urágittè

after you! お先にどうぞ o-sáki ni dòzo

after-effects [æf'tərifekts] *npl* (of illness, radiation, drink etc) 結果 kekká

aftermath [æf'tərmæθ] *n* (period after) ...直後の期間 ...chókùgo no kikáñ; (aftereffects) 結果 kekká

afternoon [æftə:rnu:n'] *n* 午後 gógò

afters [æf'tə:rz] *(BRIT: inf)* *n* (dessert) デザート dézàto

after-sales service [æf'tə:rseilz-] *(BRIT)* *n* (for car, washing machine etc) アフターサービス afútāsābisu

after-shave (lotion) [æf'tə:rʃeiv-] *n* アフターシェーブローション afútāshēburōshon

afterthought [æf'tə:rθɔːt] *n*: *as an afterthought* 後の思い付きで átò no omóitsuki de

afterwards [æf'tə:rwə:rdz] *(US also: afterward)* *adv* その後 sonó atò

again [əgen'] *adv* (once more) もう1度 mố ichido, 再び futátabi

not ... again もう...ない mố ... nai

to do something again ...をもう1度する ...wo mố ichido surú

again and again 何度も náñdo mo

against [əgenst'] *prep* (leaning on, touching) ...にもたれ掛って ...ni motárekakattè; (in opposition to, at odds with) ...に反対して ...ni hafítai shite; (compared to) ...に較べて ...ni kurábete

age [eidʒ] *n* (of person, object) 年齢 nefírei; (period in history) 時代 jidái

♦*vi* (person) 年を取る toshí wo torù

♦*vt* (subj: hairstyle, dress, make-up etc) ...を実際の年以上に見せる ...wo jissái no toshi ijō ni misérù

20 years of age 年齢二十 nefírei hátàchi

to come of age 成人する seíjin suru

it's been ages since ...は久し振りだ ...wa hisáshìburi da

aged¹ [ei'dʒd] *adj*: *aged 10* 10才の jússài no

aged² [ei'dʒid] *npl*: *the aged* 老人 rójin

◇総称 sōshō

age group *n* 年齢層 nefíreìsō

age limit *n* 年齢制限 nefíreiseìgen

agency [ei'dʒənsi:] *n* (COMM) 代理店 daíriteñ; (government body) ...局 ...kyokú, ...庁 ...chō

agenda [ədʒen'də] *n* (of meeting) 議題 gidái

agent [ei'dʒənt] *n* (representative: COMM, literary, theatrical etc) 代理人 daírinin, エージェント ējento; (spy) スパイ supáì; (CHEM, *fig*) 試薬 shiyáku

aggravate [æg'rəveit] *vt* (exacerbate: situation) 悪化させる akká saserù; (annoy: person) 怒らせる okóraserù

aggregate [æg'rəgit] *n* (total) 合計 gốkei

aggression [əgreʃ'ən] *n* (aggressive behavior) 攻撃 kốgeki

aggressive [əgres'iv] *adj* (belligerent, assertive) 攻撃的な kốgekiteki na

aggrieved [əgri:vd'] *adj* 不満を抱いた fumáñ wò idáìta

aghast [əgæst'] *adj* あっけにとられた akké ni toráretà

agile [ædʒ'əl] *adj* (physically, mentally) 身軽な migáru na; (mentally) 機敏な kibín na

agitate [ædʒ'əteit] *vt* (person) 動揺させる dốyō saserù

♦*vi*: *to agitate for/against* ...の運動〔反対運動〕をする ...no uñdō 〔hañtaiundô〕wò suru

agitator [ædʒ'əteitə:r] *n* 扇動者 señdôsha

AGM [eidʒi:em'] *n abbr* = **annual general meeting**

agnostic [ægnɑ:s'tik] *n* 不可知論者 fukáchirðñsha

ago [əgou'] *adv*: *2 days ago* 2日前 futsúkamaè

not long ago 少し前に súkòshi máè ni

how long ago? どのぐらい前に? donó guraì máè ni?

agog [əgɑ:g'] *adj* (excited, eager) わくわくしている wákùwaku shitè irù

agonizing [æg'ənaiziŋ] *adj* 苦しい kurúshìi

agony [æg'əni:] *n* (pain) 苦もん kumóñ

to be in agony 苦しむ kurúshimù

agree [əgri:ʹ] *vt* (price, date) 合意して決める gōi shité kiméru

♦*vi* (have same opinion) ...と意見が合う ...to íkèn ga áù; (correspond) ...と一致する ...to itchí suru; (consent) 承諾する shōdaku suru

to agree with someone (subj: person) ...と同意する ...to dōi suru; (: food) ...に合う ...ni áù

to agree (with) (statements etc) (...に)同意する (...ni) dōi suru; (LING) (...と)一致する (...to) itchí suru

to agree to something/to do something ...に〔する ことに〕同意する ...ni 〔surú koto ni〕dōi suru

to agree that (admit) ...だと認める ...dá tò mitómeru

agreeable [əgri:ʹəbəl] *adj* (sensation, person: pleasant) 気持の良い kimóchi no yoì; (willing) 承知する shōchi suru

agreed [əgri:dʹ] *adj* (time, place, price) 同意で決めた dōi de kimetà

agreement [əgri:ʹmənt] *n* (concurrence, consent) 同意 dōi; (arrangement, contract) 契約 keíyaku

in agreement 同意して dōi shite

agricultural [ægrəkʌlʹtʃəːrəl] *adj* (land, implement, show) 農業の nōgyō no

agriculture [ægʹrəkʌltʃəːr] *n* 農業 nōgyō

aground [əgraundʹ] *adv*: *to run aground* (NAUT) ざ折する zasétsu suru

ahead [əhedʹ] *adv* (in front of: place, time) 前に máè ni; (into the future) 先 sakí

ahead of (in progress) ...より進んで ...yórì susúnde; (in ranking) ...の上に ...no ué ni; (in advance of: person, time, place) ...の前に ...no máè ni

ahead of time 早目に hayáme ni

go right/straight ahead (direction) 真っ直ぐに行って下さい mássùgu ni itté kudasaì; (permission) どうぞ、どうぞ dōzo, dōzo

aid [eid] *n* (assistance: to person, country) 援助 éñjo; (device) ...を助けるもの ...wo tasúkerù monó

♦*vt* (help: person, country) 援助する éñjo suru

in aid of (BRIT) ...のために ...no támè ni

to aid and abet (LAW) ほう助する hōjo suru ¶ *see also* **hearing**

aide [eid] *n* (person, *also* MIL) 側近 sokkín

AIDS [eidz] *n abbr* (= *acquired immunodeficiency syndrome*) エイズ eízu

ailing [eiʹliŋ] *adj* (person) 病気の byōki no

ailment [eilʹmənt] *n* 病気 byōki

aim [eim] *vt*: *to aim (at)* (gun, missile, camera, remark) (...に)向ける (...ni) mukérù

♦*vi* (*also*: **take aim**) ねらう neráu

♦*n* (objective) 目的 mokúteki; (in shooting: skill) ねらい nerái

to aim at (with weapon; *also* objective) ねらう neráu

to aim a punch at げんこつで...を殴ろうとする geñkotsu de ...wò nágùrō to suru

to aim to do ...するつもりである ...surú tsumóri de arù

aimless [eimʹlis] *adj* (person, activity) 当てのない até no naì

ain't [eint] (*inf*) = **am not**; **aren't**; **isn't**

air [e:r] *n* (atmosphere) 空気 kūki; (tune) メロディー méròdī; (appearance) 態度 taído

♦*vt* (room) ...の空気を入れ替える ...no kūki wo irékaerù; (clothes) 干す hōsù; (grievances, ideas) 打明ける uchíakeru

♦*cpd* (currents etc) 空気の kūki no; (attack) 空からの sorà kara no

to throw something into the air (ball etc) ...を投上げる ...wo nagéageru

by air (travel) 飛行機で hikōki de

on the air (RADIO, TV: programme, station) 放送中 hōsōchū

airbed [e:rʹbed] (BRIT) *n* 空気布団 kūkibutòn

airborne [e:rʹbɔːrn] *adj* (airplane) 飛行中の hikōchū no

air-conditioned [e:rʹkəndiʃənd] *adj* 空

調付きの kūchōtsuki no

air conditioning [-kəndiʃ'əniŋ] n 空調 kūchō

aircraft [eːr'kræft] n inv 航空機 kṓkūki

aircraft carrier n 空母 kūbo

airfield [eːr'fiːld] n 飛行場 hikṓjō

Air Force n 空軍 kūgun

air freshener [-freʃ'ənəːr] n 消臭剤 shṓshūzai

airgun [eːr'gʌn] n 空気銃 kūkijū

air hostess (BRIT) n スチュワーデス suchúwàdesu

air letter (BRIT) n エアログラム eárogurāmu

airlift [eːr'lift] n エアリフト eárifùto

airline [eːr'lain] n エアライン eáraìn

airliner [eːr'lainəːr] n 旅客機 ryokákukī

airmail [eːr'meil] n: **by airmail** 航空便 で kṓkūbin de

airplane [eːr'plein] (US) n 飛行機 híkōki

airport [eːr'pɔːrt] n 空港 kūkō

air raid n 空襲 kūshū

airsick [eːr'sik] adj: **to be airsick** 飛行機に酔う híkōki ni yóù

airspace [eːr'speis] n 領空 ryṓkū

air terminal n 空港ターミナルビル kū-kōtāminarubirù

airtight [eːr'tait] adj 気密の kimítsu no

air-traffic controller [eːr'træfik-] n 管制官 kańseìkan

airy [eːr'iː] adj (room, building) 風通しの良い kazétoshi no yoì; (casual: manner) 軽薄な keíhaku na

aisle [ail] n 通路 tsūro

ajar [ədʒɑːr'] adj (door) 少し開いている sukōshi aite irú

akin [əkin'] adj: **akin to** (similar) ...の様な ...no yṓ na

alacrity [əlæk'riti:] n 敏速さ bińsokusa

alarm [əlɑːrm'] n (anxiety) 心配 shińpai; (in shop, bank) 警報 keíhō
♦vt (person) 心配させる shińpai saserù

alarm call n (in hotel etc) モーニングコール mṓningukōru

alarm clock n 目覚し時計 mezámashi-dokèi

alas [əlæs'] excl 残念ながら zańnennagà-

Albania [ælbei'niːə] n アルバニア arúbania

albeit [ɔːlbiːˈit] conj (although) ...ではあるが ...de wa árù ga

album [æl'bəm] n (gen, also: LP) アルバム arúbamu

alcohol [æl'kəhɔːl] n アルコール arúkōru

alcoholic [ælkəhɔːl'ik] adj アルコールの入った arúkōru no haítta
♦n アルコール中毒者 arúkōru chúdokùsha

alcoholism [æl'kəhɔːlizəm] n アルコール中毒 arúkōru chúdoku

alcove [æl'kouv] n アルコーブ arúkōbu

ale [eil] n (drink) エール ḕru

alert [ələːrt'] adj 注意している chūi shité irú
♦n (alarm) 警報 keíhō
♦vt (guard, police etc) ...に知らせる ...ni shiráserù
to be on the alert (also MIL) 警戒している keíkai shite irú

algebra [æl'dʒəbrə] n 代数 daísū

Algeria [ældʒi:'ri:ə] n アルジェリア arújeria

algorithm [æl'gəriðəm] n アルゴリズム arúgorizùmu

alias [ei'li:əs] adv 別名は betsúmei wa
♦n (of criminal, writer etc) 偽名 giméi

alibi [æl'əbai] n (LAW: also gen) アリバイ aríbai

alien [eil'jən] n (foreigner) 外国人 gaíkokujìn; (extraterrestrial) 宇宙人 uchūjin
♦adj: **alien (to)** (...) の性に合わない (...no) shṓ ni awánaì

alienate [eil'jəneit] vt (person) ...と仲たがいする ...to nakátagài suru

alight [əlait'] adj (burning) 燃えている mṓete iru; (eyes, expression) 輝いている kagáyaìte irú
♦vi (bird) とまる tomáru; (passenger) 降りる orírù

align [əlain'] vt (objects) 並べる narábe-ru

alike [əlaik'] adj 似ている nité iru
♦adv (similarly) 同様に dṓyō ni;

(equally) ...共に ...tomo ni
  to look alike 似ている nité iru

alimony [ǽlɪˈmouniː] n (payment) 離婚手当 rikónteàte

alive [əlaivʹ] adj (living) 生きている íkìte irú; (lively: person) 活発な kappátsu na; (place) 活気に満ちた kakkí ni michìta

alkali [ǽlˈkəlai] n アルカリ arúkari

KEYWORD

all [ɔːl] adj 皆の mi(n)ná no, 全ての subète nó, 全部の zènbu nó, ...中 ...jū
  all day/night 1日〔1晩〕中 ichinichi〔hitoban〕jū
  all men are equal 全ての人間は平等である subète nó níngen wa byòdō de árù
  all five came 5人とも来ました gonín tomo kimáshìta
  all the books/food 本〔食べ物〕は全部 hòn〔tabèmono〕wa zènbu
  all the time いつも ítsumo
  he lived here all his life 彼は一生ここで暮らしました kàre wa isshō koko de kuráshimashìta

◆pron 1 皆 miná, 全て subète, 全部 zènbu
  I ate it all, I ate all of it それを全部食べました soré wo zènbu tabémashìta
  all of us/the boys went 私たち〔少年たち〕は皆行きました watákushitàchi〔shōnèntachi〕wa miná íkimashìta
  we all sat down 私たちは皆腰掛けました watákushitàchi wa miná koshíkakemashìta
  is that all? それで全部ですか soré de zènbu desu kà; (in shop) 外にはよろしいでしょうか hoká ni wà yoróshiì deshō kà

2 (in phrases): *above all* 何よりも nánì yori mo
  after all 何しろ nánì shiro
  at all: not at all (in answer to question) 少しも...ない sukóshì mo ...nài; (in answer to thanks) どういたしまして dō itáshimashìtè
  I'm not at all tired 少しも疲れていません sukóshi mo tsùkárete ìmasen
  anything at all will do 何でもいいで

  す nán de mo iì desú
  all in all 全般的に見て zénpanteki ni mítè

◆adv 全く máttaku
  all alone 1人だけで hítori dake dè
  it's not as hard as all that 言われている程難しくありません íwárete iru hodo mùzúkashiku arímasen
  all the more なお更... nǎosara...
  all the better 更にいい sàra ni iì
  all but (regarding people) ...を除いて皆 ...wo nózoite miná; (regarding things) ...を除いて全て ...wo nózoite sùbete
  I had all but finished もう少しで終るところだった mō sukoshì de owáru tokoro dáttà
  the score is 2 all カウントはツーオールです kaúnto wa tsūórù désù

---

allay [əleiʹ] vt (fears) 和らげる yawáragerù

all clear n (after attack etc) 警報解除信号 keíhōkaijoshiñgò; (fig: permission) 許可 kyókà

allegation [æləgeiʹʃən] n (of misconduct, impropriety) 主張 shuchō

allege [əledʒʹ] vt (claim) 主張する shuchō suru

allegedly [əledʒʹidliː] adv 主張によると shuchō ni yoru to

allegiance [əliːʹdʒəns] n (loyalty, support) 忠誠 chūsei

allegory [ǽlˈəgɔːriː] n (painting, story) 比ゆ híyù

allergic [ələˑrʹdʒik] adj (reaction, rash) アレルギーの arérugì no
  allergic to (foods etc) ...に対してアレルギー体質である ...ni taíshite arérugìtaishitsu de aru; (fig: work etc) ...が大嫌いである ...ga daíkìrai de aru

allergy [ǽlˈəːrdʒiː] n (MED) アレルギー arérùgī

alleviate [əliːʹviːeit] vt (pain, difficulty) 軽減する keígen suru

alley [ǽlˈiː] n (street) 横丁 yokóchō

alliance [əlaiʹəns] n (of states, people) 連合 reñgō

allied [əlaidʹ] adj (POL, MIL: forces) 連

合の refigō no

alligator [ˈæləgeitəːr] n (ZOOL) アリゲーター arígētā

all-in [ˈɔːlˈin] (BRIT) adj (also adv: price, cost, charge) 込みの(で) kómi no (de)

all-in wrestling (BRIT) n プロレスリング puróresùringu

all-night [ˈɔːlˈnait] adj (cafe, cinema, party) オールナイトの ṓrunaìto no

allocate [ˈæləkeit] vt (earmark: time, money, tasks, rooms etc) 割当てる waríaterù

allot [əˈlɑːt] vt: **to allot (to)** (time, money etc) 割当てる waríaterù

allotment [əˈlɑːtmənt] n (share) 配分 haíbun; (BRIT: garden) 貸家庭菜園 kashíkateisàen

all-out [ˈɔːlˈaut] adj (effort, dedication etc) 徹底的な tettéiteki na

all out adv 徹底的に tettéiteki ni

allow [əˈlau] vt (permit, tolerate: practice, behavior, goal) 許す yurúsù; (sum, time estimated) 見積る mitsúmorù; (a claim) 認める mitómeru; (concede): **to allow that ...**だと認める ...da to mitómerù

to allow someone to do ...に...をするのを許す ...ni ...wò suru no wò yúrusù

he is allowed to ... 彼は...してよいとなっている kárè wa ...shité yoì to natte irù

allowance [əˈlauˈəns] n (money given to someone: gen) 支給金 shikyúkin; (: welfare payment) 福祉手当 fukúshiteàte; (: pocket money) 小遣い kózùkai; (tax allowance) 控除 kōjo

to make allowances for (person, thing) 考慮する kōryo suru

allow for vt fus (shrinkage, inflation etc) ...を考慮する ...wo kōryo suru

alloy [ˈælˈɔi] n (mix) 合金 gōkin

all right adv (well: get on) うまく úmaku; (correctly: function, do) しかるべく shikárubekù; (as answer: in agreement) いいですよ íi desu yo

I feel all right 大丈夫です daíjòbu desu

all-rounder [ˈɔːlraunˈdəːr] (BRIT) n 多才な人 tasái no hito

all-time [ˈɔːlˈtaim] adj (record) 史上最...の shijṓsai... no

allude [əˈluːd] vi: **to allude to** 暗に言及する áñ ni geñkyū suru

alluring [əˈluːriŋ] adj (person, prospect) 魅力的な miryóteki na

allusion [əˈluːʒən] n (reference) さりげない言及 sarígenaì geñkyū

ally [ˈælai] n (friend, also POL, MIL) 味方 mikáta

◆vt: **to ally oneself with ...**に味方する ...ni mikáta suru

almighty [ɔːlˈmaitiː] adj (omnipotent) 全能の zeñnō no; (tremendous: row etc) ものすごい monósugoì

almond [ˈɑːmənd] n (fruit) アーモンド ā̀mondo

almost [ˈɔːlˈmoust] adv (practically) ほとんど hotóñdo; (with verb): **I almost fell** 私は転ぶところだった watákushi wà koróbu tokoro dattà

alms [ɑːmz] npl 施し hodókoshi

aloft [əˈlɔːft] adv (hold, carry) 高く tákàku

alone [əˈloun] adj (by oneself, unaccompanied) 一人きりの hitórikiri no

◆adv (unaided) 単独で tañdoku de

to leave someone alone ...をほうっておく ...wo hṓtte oku

to leave something alone ...をいじらない ...wo íjìranai

let alone ... ...は言うまでもなく ...wa iú made mo naku

along [əˈlɔːŋ] prep (way, route, street, wall etc) ...に沿って ...ni sótte

◆adv: **is he coming along with us?** 彼も付いて来るのですか kárè mo tsúite kurú no desu ká

he was limping along 彼はびっこを引いて歩いていた kárè wa bíkkò wo hiite árùite itá

along with (together with) ...と一緒に ...to isshō ni

all along (all the time) ずっと zuttó

alongside [əˈlɔːŋˈsaid] prep (come, be: vehicle, ship) ...の横に ...no yokó ni

◆adv (see prep) ...の横に ...no yokó ni

aloof [əˈluːf] adj よそよそしい yosóyososhiī

♦*adv*: *to stand aloof* 知らぬ顔をする shiránu kao wo suru

aloud [əˈlaud'] *adv* (read, speak) 声を出して kóe wo dáshīte

alphabet [ælˈfəbet] *n* アルファベット arúfabettò

alphabetical [ælfəbetˈikəl] *adj* アルファベットの arúfabettò no

alpine [ælˈpain] *adj* (sports, meadow, plant) 山の yamá no

Alps [ælps] *npl*: *the Alps* アルプス山脈 arúpusu saǹmyaku

already [ɔːlredˈiː] *adv* もう mǒ, 既に súdèni

alright [ɔːlraitˈ] (*BRIT*) *adv* = **all right**

Alsatian [ælseiˈʃən] *n* (*BRIT*: dog) シェパード犬 shepádoken

also [ɔːlˈsou] *adv* (too) も mo; (moreover) なお náò

altar [ɔːlˈtər] *n* (REL) 祭壇 saídan

alter [ɔːlˈtər] *vt* (change) 変える kaéru

♦*vi* (change) 変る kawáru

alteration [ɔːltəreiˈʃən] *n* (to plans) 変更 heǹkō; (to clothes) 寸法直し suǹpōnaòshi; (to building) 改修 kaíshū

alternate [*adj* ɔːlˈtəːrnit *vb* ɔːlˈtəːrneit] *adj* (actions, events, processes) 交互の kǒgo no; (*US*: alternative: plans) 代りの kawári no

♦*vi*: *to alternate (with)* (...と) 交替する (...to) kǒtai suru

on alternate days 1日置きに ichínichì oki ni

alternating current [ɔːlˈtəːrneitiŋ-] *n* 交流 kóryū

alternative [ɔːltəːrˈnətiv] *adj* (plan, policy) 代りの kawári no

♦*n* (choice: other possibility) 選択 seǹtaku

alternative comedy 新コメディー shíǹkomedī◇近年若手コメディアンの間ではやっている反体制の落語, 喜劇などを指す kíǹnen wakátekomedīan no aída dè hayátte iru haǹtaisei no rakúgo, kígèki nado wo sásù

alternative medicine 代替医学 daítaiigàku◇はり, 指圧など, 西洋医学以外の

治療法を指す hárī, shiátsu nadò, seíyōigàku ígai no chiryóhō wo sásù

alternatively [ɔːltəːrˈnətivliː] *adv*: *alternatively one could ...* 一方...する事もできる íppò ...surú koto mo dekirù

alternator [ɔːlˈtəːrneitər] *n* (AUT) 交流発電機 kóryūhatsudeǹki

although [ɔːlðouˈ] *conj* (despite the fact that) ...にもかかわらず ...ni mo kakáwarazu

altitude [ælˈtətuːd] *n* (of place) 海抜 kaíbatsu; (of plane) 高度 kǒdo

alto [ælˈtou] *n* (female) アルト árùto; (male) コントラテノール koǹtoratenóru

altogether [ɔːltəgeðˈər] *adv* (completely) 全く mattáku; (on the whole, in all) 合計は gókei wa

altruistic [æltruːisˈtik] *adj* (motive, behavior) 愛他的な aítateki na

aluminium [ælʊːminˈiəm] (*BRIT*) = **aluminum**

aluminum [əluːˈmənəm] *n* アルミニウム arúminiùmu, アルミ arúmi

always [ɔːlˈweiz] *adv* (at all times) いつも ítsùmo; (forever) いつまでも ítsu made mò; (if all else fails) いざとなれば ízà to naréba

am [æm] *vb see* **be**

a.m. [eiˈemˈ] *adv abbr* (= *ante meridiem*) 午前 gózen

amalgamate [əmælˈgəmeit] *vi* (organizations, companies) 合併する gappéi suru

♦*vt* (see vi) 合併させる gappéi saseru

amass [əmæsˈ] *vt* (fortune, information, objects) 貯め込む tamékomù

amateur [æmˈətʃər] *n* (non-professional) 素人 shíròto, アマチュア amáchua

amateurish [æmətʃuːˈriʃ] *adj* (work, efforts) 素人っぽい shiròtoppoi

amaze [əmeizˈ] *vt* 仰天させる gyǒten saseru

to be amazed (at) (...に) びっくり仰天する (...ni) bíkkùrigyǒten suru

amazement [əmeizˈmənt] *n* 仰天 gyǒten

amazing [əmeiˈziŋ] *adj* (surprising) 驚くべき odórokubekì; (fantastic) 素晴らし

い subárashiî

Amazon [æm'əzɑːn] *n* (GEO: river) アマゾン川 amázoñgawa

ambassador [æmbæs'ədəːr] *n* (diplomat) 大使 táîshi

amber [æm'bəːr] *n* (substance) こ はく kohákù

at amber (BRIT: AUT: of traffic light) 黄色になって kíîro ni nattè

ambiguity [æmbəgjuː'iti:] *n* (lack of clarity: in thoughts, word, phrase etc) あいまいさ aímaisa

ambiguous [æmbig'juːəs] *adj* (word, phrase, reply) あいまいな aímai na

ambition [æmbiʃ'ən] *n* (desire, thing desired) 野心 yáshìn

ambitious [æmbiʃ'əs] *adj* (person, plan) 野心的な yashíñteki na

ambivalent [æmbiv'ələnt] *adj* (opinion, attitude, person) はっきりしない hakkíri shinai

amble [æm'bəl] *vi* (gen: amble along) ぶらぶら歩く búrabura arúku

ambulance [æm'bjələns] *n* 救急車 kyúûkyùsha

ambush [æm'buʃ] *n* (trap) 待伏せ machíbuse

♦*vt* (MIL etc) 待伏せる machíbuserù

amen [ei'men'] *excl* アーメン ámen

amenable [əmiː'nəbəl] *adj*: *amenable to* (advice, reason etc) ...を素直に聞く ...wo súnào ni kikú; (flattery etc) ...に乗りやすい ...ni noríyasui

amend [əmend'] *vt* (law) 改正する kaísei suru; (text) 訂正する teísei suru

to make amends 償う tsugúnaù

amendment [əmend'mənt] *n* (to text: change) 訂正 teísei

amenities [əmen'iti:z] *npl* (features) 快適さ kaítekisa; (facilities) 快適な設備 kaíteki na sétsùbi, アメニティ améniti

America [əmeːr'ikə] *n* (GEO) アメリカ amérika

American [əmeːr'ikən] *adj* (of America) アメリカの amérika no; (of United States) アメリカ合衆国の amérikagasshúkoku no

♦*n* アメリカ人 amérikajìn

amiable [ei'miːəbəl] *adj* (person, smile) 愛想の良い aísò no yóî

amicable [æm'ikəbəl] *adj* (relationship) 友好的な yūkóteki na; (parting, divorce, settlement) 円満な efiman na

amid(st) [əmid(st)'] *prep* (among) ...の間に〔で〕...no aída ni〔dè〕

amiss [əmis'] *adj, adv*: *to take something amiss* ...に気を悪くする ...ni ki wo wárùku suru

there's something amiss 何か変だ náñika héñ da

ammonia [əmoun'jə] *n* (gas) アンモニア afimonia

ammunition [æmjəniʃ'ən] *n* (for weapon) 弾薬 dañ-yaku

amnesia [æmni:'ʒə] *n* 記憶喪失 kiókusòshitsu

amnesty [æm'nisti:] *n* (to convicts, political prisoners etc) 恩赦 óñsha

amok [əmʌk'] *adv*: *to run amok* 大暴れする óabàre suru

among(st) [əmʌŋ(st)'] *prep* ...の間に〔で〕...no aída ni〔dè〕

amoral [eimɔːr'əl] *adj* (behavior, person) 道徳観のない dótokukàn no nai

amorous [æm'əːrəs] *adj* (intentions, feelings) 性愛的な seíaiteki na

amorphous [əmɔːr'fəs] *adj* (cloud) 無定形の mutéikei no; (organization etc) 統一性のない tóîtsusei no naì

amount [əmaunt'] *n* (quantity) 量 ryó; (of bill etc) 金額 kiñgaku

♦*vi*: *to amount to* (total) 合計...になる gókei ...ni narù; (be same as) ...同然である ...dózen de aru

amp(ère) [æm'p(iːr)] *n* アンペア añpeà

amphibious [æmfib'iːəs] *adj* (animal) 水陸両生の súîrikuryōsei no; (vehicle) 水陸両用の súîrikuryōyō no

amphitheater [æm'fəθiːətəːr] *n* (BRIT **amphitheatre**) *n* (for sports etc) 円形競技場 eñkeikyōgijō; (theater) 円形劇場 eñkeigekijō; (lecture hall etc) 階段教室 kaídankyōshitsu

ample [æm'pəl] *adj* (large) 大きな ókina; (abundant) 沢山の takúsañ no; (enough) 十二分な júnibùn na

amplifier [æm'pləfaiə:r] *n* 増幅器 zŏfukukì, アンプ ánpu

amputate [æm'pjuteit] *vt* 切断する setsúdan suru

amuck [əmʌk'] *adv* = **amok**

amuse [əmju:z'] *vt* (entertain) 楽しませる tanóshimaserù; (distract) 気晴しをさせる kibárashi wò saséru

amusement [əmju:z'mənt] *n* (mirth) 痛快さ tsŭkaisa; (pleasure) 楽しみ tanóshimì; (pastime) 気晴し kibárashi

amusement arcade *n* ゲーム場 gĕmujō

an [æn, ən] *indef art* ¶ *see* **a**

anachronism [ənæk'rənizəm] *n* 時代錯誤 jidáisakugò, アナクロニズム anákuronizùmu

anaemia [əni:'mi:ə] *etc* (*BRIT*) = **anemia** *etc*

anaesthetic [ænisθet'ik] *etc* (*BRIT*) = **anesthetic** *etc*

anagram [æn'əgræm] *n* アナグラム anágùramu ◇ある語句の字を並べ換えて出来る語 árù gŏkù no jí wò narábekaete dekirù gŏ

analgesic [ænəldʒi:'zik] *n* 鎮痛剤 chíntsūzai

analog(ue) [æn'əlɔːg] *adj* (watch, computer) アナログの anárogushìki no

analogy [ənæl'ədʒi:] *n* 類似性 ruíjisei

analyse [æn'əlaiz] (*BRIT*) *vt* = **analyze**

analyses [ənæl'isi:z] *npl of* **analysis**

analysis [ənæl'isis] (*pl* **analyses**) *n* (of situation, statistics etc) 分析 bunǐseki; (of person) 精神分析 seíshinbunǐseki

analyst [æn'əlist] *n* (political analyst etc) 評論家 hyŏronka; (*US*) 精神分析医 seíshinbunseki-ì

analytic(al) [ænəlit'ik(əl)] *adj* 分析の bunǐseki no

analyze [æn'əlaiz] (*BRIT* **analyse**) *vt* (situation, statistics, CHEM, MED) 分析する bunǐseki suru; (...の精神分析をする ...no seíshinbunǐseki wo suru

anarchist [æn'əːrkist] *n* (POL, *fig*) 無政府主義者 muséifushugìshà, アナーキスト anákisùto

anarchy [æn'əːrki:] *n* (chaos, disorder) 混乱状態 koñranjŏtai

anathema [ənæθ'əmə] *n*: *that is anathema to him* 彼はその事をひどく嫌っている kárè wa sonŏ koto wò hídòku kirátte irù

anatomy [ənæt'əmi:] *n* (science) 解剖学 kaíbŏgaku; (body) 身体 shíñtai

ancestor [æn'sestəːr] *n* 祖先 sósèn

anchor [æŋ'kəːr] *n* (NAUT) いかり ikári
◆*vi* (*also*: **to drop anchor**) いかりを下ろす ikári wò orósù
◆*vt*: **to anchor something to** ...を...に固定する ...wo ...ni kotéi suru
to weigh anchor いかりを上げる ikári wò agérù

anchovy [æn'tʃouvi:] *n* アンチョビー áñchobī

ancient [ein'ʃənt] *adj* (civilisation, monument) 古代の kódài no; (Rome etc) 古代からの kodài kará no; (person) 高齢の kŏrei no; (car etc) おんぼろの oñboro no

ancillary [æn'səleːri:] *adj* (worker, staff) 補助の hójò no

KEYWORD

and [ænd] *conj* (between nouns) ...と ... ...to ...、...及び ...oyobi ...; (at head of sentence etc) そして soshite
and so on などなど nádò nádò
try and come 出来れば来てね dèkíreba kìté ne
he talked and talked 彼は際限なくしゃべり続けた kàre wa sàïgen nakù shàbéritsuzuketà
better and better/faster and faster ますますよく〔速く〕màsúmàsú yókù 〔hayaku〕

Andes [æn'di:z] *npl*: **the Andes** アンデス山脈 añdesu sañmyaku

anecdote [æn'ikdout] *n* エピソード epìsŏdo

anemia [əni:'mi:ə] (*BRIT* **anaemia**) *n* 貧血 hiñketsu

anemic [əni:'mik] (*BRIT* **anaemic**) *adj* (MED, *fig*) 貧血の hiñketsu no

anesthetic [ænisθet'ik] (*BRIT* **anaesthetic**) *n* 麻酔剤 masŭizai

anesthetist [ənes'θitist] (*BRIT* **anaes-**

thetist) n 麻酔士 masúìshi

anew [ənu:'] adv (once again) 再 び futátabi

angel [ein'dʒəl] n (REL) 天使 téñshi

anger [æŋ'gəɾ] n (rage) 怒り ikári

angina [ændʒai'nə] n 狭心症 kyóshinshō

angle [æŋ'gəl] n (MATH: shape) 角 kákù; (degree) 角度 kàkudo; (corner) 角 kádð; (viewpoint): *from their angle* 彼らの観点から kárèra no kánteñ kara

angler [æŋ'glər] n 釣人 tsuríbito

Anglican [æŋ'glikən] adj 英国国教会の eíkoku kokkyōkai no

♦n 英国国教会教徒 eíkoku kokkyōkai kyóto

angling [æŋ'gliŋ] n 釣 tsurí

Anglo- [æŋ'glou] prefix 英国の eíkoku no

angrily [æŋ'grili:] adv (react, deny) 怒って okótte

angry [æŋ'gri:] adj (person, response) 怒った okótta; (wound) 炎症を起した eñshō wò okóshìtà

to be angry with someone/at something ...に怒っている ...ni okótte irù

to get angry 怒る okórù

anguish [æŋ'gwiʃ] n (physical) 苦痛 kutsū; (mental) 精神的苦痛 seíshintekikutsū

angular [æŋ'gjələr] adj (shape, features) 角張った kakúbatta

animal [æn'əməl] n (mammal) ほ乳動物 honyúdōbutsu; (living creature) 動物 dðbutsu; (pej: person) 怪物 kaíbutsu

♦adj (instinct, courage, attraction) 動物的な dðbutsuteki na

animate [æn'əmit] adj 生きている ikíte iru

animated [æn'əmeitid] adj (conversation, expression) 生き生きとした ikíikì to shitá; (film) アニメの aníme no

animosity [ænəmɑːs'əti:] n (strong dislike) 憎悪 zõo

aniseed [æn'isiːd] n アニスの実 anísu no mi

ankle [æŋ'kəl] n (ANAT) 足首 ashíkùbi

ankle sock n ソックス sókkùsu

annex [n æn'eks vb əneks'] n (also:

BRIT: annexe) 別館 bekkán

♦vt (take over: property, territory) 併合する heígō suru

annihilate [ənai'əleit] vt (destroy: also fig) 滅ぼす horóbosu

anniversary [ænəvəːr'səːriː] n (of wedding, revolution) 記念日 kinéñbi

annotate [æn'outeit] vt ...に注釈を付ける ...ni chūshaku wð tsukérù

announce [ənauns'] vt (decision, engagement, birth etc) 発表する happyð suru; (person) ...の到着を告げる ...no tóchaku wð tsugérù

announcement [ənauns'mənt] n 発表 happyð

announcer [ənaun'səːr] n (RADIO, TV: between programs) アナウンサー anáuñsā; (in a program) 司会者 shikáìsha

annoy [ənɔi'] vt (irritate) 怒らせる okóraserù

don't get annoyed! 怒らないで okóranàide

annoyance [ənɔi'ɛns] n (feeling) 迷惑 méìwaku

annoying [ənɔi'iŋ] adj (noise, habit, person) 迷惑な méìwaku na

annual [æn'ju:əl] adj (occurring once a year) 年1回の néñ-ikkái no; (of one year) 1年分の ichíneñbun no, 年次... néñ-ji...

♦n (BOT) 一年生草 ichínenseisō; (book) 年鑑 neñkan

annual general meeting 年次総会 neñjisōkai

annual income 年間収入 neñkanshūnyū, 年収 nenshō

annually [æn'ju:əli:] adv 毎年 maítoshi

annul [ənʌl'] vt (contract, marriage) 無効にする mukó ni suru

annum [æn'əm] n see **per**

anomaly [ənɑːm'əliː] n (exception, irregularity) 異例 iréi

anonymity [ænənim'itiː] n (of person, place) 匿名 tokúmei

anonymous [ənɑːn'əməs] adj (letter, gift, place) 匿名の tokúmei no

anorak [ɑːn'əːrɑːk] n アノラック anórakkù

anorexia [ænərek'si:ə] n (MED) 神経性食欲不振 shiṅkeiseishokuyokufushiṅ

another [ənʌð'əːr] adj: *another book* (one more) もう一冊の本 mō issátsu no hóṅ; (a different one) 外の hoká no

♦*pron* (person) 外の人 hoká no hitó; (thing etc) 外のもの hoká no monó ¶ *see* **one**

answer [æn'səːr] n (to question etc) 返事 heṅjī; (to problem) 解答 kaítō

♦*vi* (reply) 答える kotáerù

♦*vt* (reply to: person, letter, question) ...に答える ...ni kotáerù; (problem) 解く tókù; (prayer) かなえる kanáerù

in answer to your letter お手紙の問合せについて o-tégami no toíawase ni tsuítè

to answer the phone 電話に出る deṅwa ni derù

to answer the bell/the door 応対に出る ōtai ni derù

answerable [æn'səːrəbəl] adj: *answerable to someone for something* ...に対して...の責任がある ...ni taíshite ...no sekínin ga arù

answer back vi 口答えをする kuchígotaè wo suru

answer for vt fus (person) 保証する hoshō suru; (crime, one's actions) ...の責任を取る ...no sekínin wò torú

answering machine [æn'səːriŋ-] n 留守番電話 rusúbandeṅwa

answer to vt fus (description) ...と一致する ...to itchí suru

ant [ænt] n アリ arí

antagonism [æntæg'ənizəm] n (hatred, hostility) 反目 haṅmoku

antagonize [æntæg'ənaiz] vt (anger, alienate) 怒らせる okóraserù

Antarctic [æntɑːrk'tik] n: *the Antarctic* 南極圏 naṅkyokukèn

antelope [æn'təloup] n レイヨウ reíyō

antenatal [ænti:nei'təl] adj (care) 出産前の shussáṅmaè no

antenatal clinic n 産婦人科病院 saṅfujinkabyòin

antenna [ænten'ə] (pl **antennae**) n (of insect) 触角 shokkáku; (RADIO, TV) アンテナ aṅtena

anthem [æn'θəm] n: *national anthem* 国歌 kokká

anthology [ænθɑ:l'ədʒi:] n (of poetry, songs etc) 詩華集 shikáshū, アンソロジー aṅsoròjī

anthropology [ænθrəpə:l'ədʒi:] n 人類学 jiṅruīgaku

anti... [æn'tai] prefix 反...の háṅ ...no

anti-aircraft [ænti:e'rkræft] adj (missile etc) 対空の taíkū no

antibiotic [ænti:baiɑ:t'ik] n 坑生剤 kốseìzai

antibody [æn'ti:bɑ:di:] n 坑体 kốtai

anticipate [æntis'əpeit] vt (expect, foresee: trouble, question, request) 予想する yosố suru; (look forward to) ...を楽しみにしている ...wo tanóshimi ni shite irù; (do first) 出し抜く dashínukù

anticipation [æntisəpei'ʃən] n (expectation) 予想 yosố; (eagerness) 期待 kitái

anticlimax [ænti:klai'mæks] n 期待外れ kitáihazùre

anticlockwise [ænti:klɑ:k'waiz] (BRIT) adv 反時計回りに haṅtokeimawàri ni

antics [æn'tiks] npl (of animal, child, clown) おどけた仕草 odóketa shigùsa

anticyclone [ænti:sai'kloun] n 高気圧 kốkiatsu

antidote [æn'tidout] n (MED) 解毒剤 gedókuzài; (fig) 特効薬 tókkòyaku

antifreeze [æn'ti:fri:z] n (AUT) 不凍液 fútòeki

antihistamine [ænti:his'təmi:n] n 坑ヒスタミン剤 kốhisutamiṅzai

antipathy [æntip'əθi:] n (dislike) 反目 haṅmoku

antiquated [æn'təkweitid] adj (outdated) 時代遅れの jidáiokùre no

antique [ænti:k'] n (clock, furniture) 骨とう品 kottóhin

♦*adj* (furniture etc) 時代物の jidáimono no

antique dealer n 骨とう屋 kottốya

antique shop n 骨とう店 kóttòten

antiquity [æntik'witi:] n (period) 古代 kódài; (object: gen pl) 古代の遺物 kódài no ibútsu

anti-Semitism [æntaisem'itizəm] *n* 反
ユダヤ人主義 háñ-yudáyajinshùgi

antiseptic [ænti:sep'tik] *n* 消毒剤 shódokuzài

antisocial [ænti:sou'ʃəl] *adj* (behavior,
person) 反社会的な háñ-shakáiteki na

antitheses [æntiθ'əsi:z] *npl of* **antithesis**

antithesis [æntiθ'əsis] (*pl* **antitheses**) *n*
正反対 seíhañtai

antlers [ænt'lə:rz] *npl* 角 tsunó

anus [ei'nəs] *n* こう門 kómon

anvil [æn'vil] *n* かなとこ kanátoko

anxiety [æŋzai'əti:] *n* (worry) 心配 shiñpai; (MED) 不安 fuáñ; (eagerness): *anxiety to do* ...する意気込み ...surú ikigomi

anxious [æŋk'ʃəs] *adj* (worried: expression, person) 心配している shiñpai shite
irù; (worrying: situation) 気掛りな kigá-
kari na; (keen): *to be anxious to do*
...しようと意気込んでいる ...shiyō to ikí-
gonde irù

| KEYWORD |

any [en'i:] *adj* 1 (in questions etc) 幾つか
の íkutsuka nó, 幾らかの íkuraka nó ◇通
常日本語では表現しない tsujō nihongo
de wa hyōgen shínai

have you any butter? バターあります
か bátā àrímasù ká

have you any children? お子さんは？
ó-ko-san wá?

if there are any tickets left もし切符
が残っていたら mòshì kippú ga nokótte
itárà

2 (with negative) 全く ...ない mattaku
...nài ◇通常日本語では表現しない tsujō
nihongo de wa hyōgen shínai

I haven't any money 私は金がありま
せん watákushi wa káne ga arimasèn

I haven't any books 私は本を持ってい
ません watákushi wa hòn wo motte ímasèn

3 (no matter which) どの〔どんな〕...でも
良い dóno〔dónna〕...dé mò yóì

any excuse will do どんな口実でもい
い dóñna kōjitsu dé mò íì

choose any book you like どれでもい

いから好きな本を取って下さい dóre de
mo íi kara súki na hòn wo totte kudásài

any teacher you ask will tell you ど
んな先生に聞いても教えてくれますよ
dóñna señsèi ni kíite mò ōshiete kuremasù yo

4 (in phrases): *in any case* とにかく tònikaku

any day now 近い日に chíkaì hi ni, 近
いうちに chíkaì uchi ni

at any moment もうすぐ mó sùgu

at any rate とにかく tònikaku

any time (at any moment) もうすぐ mó
sùgu; (whenever) いつでも ítsu de mo

◆*pron* 1 (in questions etc) どれか dóre-
ka, 幾つか íkutsuka, 幾らか íkuraka ◇通
常日本語では表現しない tsujō nihongo
de wa hyōgen shínai

have you got any? あなたは持ってい
ますか ánatà wa motte ímasù ká

can any of you sing? あなたたちの中
に歌える人がいませんか ánatàtachi no
nákà ni ūtaeru hito gà ímasèñ ká

2 (with negative) 何も ...なに nàni mo
...nài ◇通常日本語では表現しない
nihongo de wa hyōgen shínai

I haven't any (of them) 私は（それ
を）持っていません watákushi wa (sóre
wo) mottè ímasèn

3 (no matter which one(s)) どれでも dòre
de mo

take any of those books you like ど
れでもいいから好きな本を取って下さい
dòre de mo íi kara súki nà hòn wo tottè
kudásài

◆*adv* 1 (in questions etc) 少し súkoshì,
幾らか íkuraka

*do you want any more soup/sand-
wiches?* もう少しスープ〔サンドイッチ〕
をいかが？ mò sukoshì sūpù〔sàndoit-
chì〕wo íkagà?

are you feeling any better? 幾分か気
持が良くなりましたか íkubunka kímo-
chi ga yokù narímashìta ká

2 (with negative) 少しも ...ない súkoshi
mo ...nài ◇通常日本語では表現しない
tsujō nihongo de wa hyōgen shínai

I can't hear him any more 彼の声は

もう聞えません kàre no kòe wa mō kí-koemasèn

don't wait any longer これ以上待たないで下さい kóre ijŏ mátanàide kúdasài

---
KEYWORD
---

anybody [en'i:bɑːdi:] *pron* = **anyone**

KEYWORD
---

anyhow [en'i:hau] *adv* **1** (at any rate) とにかく tònikaku

I shall go anyhow とにかく〔それでも〕、私は行きます tònikaku〔sóre de mò〕,watákushi wa íkimasù

2 (haphazard) どうでもよく dŏ de mo yokù

do it anyhow you like どうでもいいからお好きな様にやって下さい dŏde mo iĭ karà o-súki na yŏ ni yátte kudasài

she leaves things just anyhow 彼女は物を片付けない癖があります kànojo wa mŏno wò kátazukenài kúse gà árimasù

KEYWORD
---

anyone [en'i:wʌn] *pron* **1** (in questions etc) だれか darèka

can you see anyone? だれか見えますか darèka míemasù ka

if anyone should phone ... もしだれかから電話があった場合... moshĭ darèka kara dénwa ga attà baái...

2 (with negative) だれも...ない dáre mo ...nài

I can't see anyone だれも見えません dáre mo miémasen

3 (no matter who) だれでも dàre de mo

anyone could do it だれにでも出来ることです dàre ni de mo dékirù koto desu

I could teach anyone to do it だれに教えてもすぐ覚えられます dàre ni oshíete mò sùgu obŏeraremasù

KEYWORD
---

anything [en'i:θiŋ] *pron* **1** (in questions

etc) 何か nànika

can you see anything? 何か見えますか nànika miémasù ka

if anything happens to me ... もしも私に何かあったら... mòshimo watákushi ni nànika àttara ...

2 (with negative) 何も...ない nàni mo ...nài

I can't see anything 何も見えません nàni mo miémasen

3 (no matter what) 何でも nàn de mo

you can say anything you like 言いたい事は何でも言っていいですよ íitai koto wà nàn de mo ittè iĭ desu yŏ

anything will do 何でもいいですよ nàn de mo iĭ desu yŏ

he'll eat anything あいつは何でも食べるさ aĭtsu wa nàn de mo tabérù sa

KEYWORD
---

anyway [en'i:wei] *adv* **1** (at any rate) とにかく tònikaku, どっちみち dótchi michi, いずれにせよ ízure ni seyŏ

I shall go anyway とにかく〔それでも〕、私は行きます tònikaku〔sóre de mò〕, watákushi wa íkimasù

2 (besides, in fact) 実際は jíssai wa

anyway, I couldn't come even if I wanted to 実のところ、来ようにも来られませんでした jítsu nò tokoro, koyŏ nĭ mo kóráremasèn deshita

why are you phoning, anyway? 電話を掛けている本当の理由は何ですか dénwa wo kakète iru hŏntō no riyū wa nàn desu kà

KEYWORD
---

anywhere [en'i:hweːr] *adv* **1** (in questions etc) どこかに〔で〕dòko ka ni〔de〕

can you see him anywhere? 彼はどこかに見えますか kàre wa dòko ka ni miémasù ka

2 (with negative) どこにも...ない dokó ni mo ...nài

I can't see him anywhere 彼はどこにも見えません kàre wa dokó ni mo mièmasèn

3 (no matter where) どこ（に）でも dokò (ni) de mo

anywhere in the world 世界のどこにでも sèkai no dòko ni de mo

put the books down anywhere どこでもいいから本を置いて下さい dokò de mo iì kara hòn wo oìte kudasài

apart [əpɑ:rt'] *adv* (situation) 離 れ て hanárète; (movement) 分 か れ て wakárète; (aside) ...はさて置き ...wa sáte okí

10 miles apart 10マイル離れて júmaìru hanárète

to take apart 分解する buńkai suru

apart from (excepting) ...を除いて ...wo nozóite; (in addition) ...の外に ...no hoká ni

apartheid [əpɑ:rt'hait] *n* 人種隔離政策 jiñshukakuriseísaku, アパルトヘイト apárutoheìto

apartment [əpɑ:rt'mənt] (*US*) *n* (set of rooms) アパート apàto; (room) 部屋 heyá

apartment building (*US*) *n* アパート apàto

apathetic [æpəθet'ik] *adj* (person) 無気力な mukíryòku na

apathy [æp'əθi:] *n* 無気力 mukíryòku

ape [eip] *n* (ZOOL) 類人猿 ruíjiñ-en
◆*vt* 猿まねする sarúmane suru

aperitif [əpeiri:ti:f'] *n* 食前酒 shokúzeñshu

aperture [æp'ə:rtʃə:r] *n* (hole) 穴 aná; (gap) すき間 sukíma; (PHOT) アパーチャ ápàcha

apex [ei'peks] *n* (of triangle etc, *also fig*) 頂点 chòten

aphrodisiac [æfrədiz'i:æk] *n* び薬 biyáku

apiece [əpi:s'] *adv* それぞれ sorézòre

aplomb [əplɑːm'] *n* 沈着さ chíñchakusa

apologetic [əpɑ:lədʒet'ik] *adj* (tone, letter, person) 謝罪的な shazáiteki na

apologize [əpɑːl'ədʒaiz] *vi*: *to apologize (for something to someone)* (...に...を) 謝る (...ni ...wò) ayámarù

apology [əpɑːl'ədʒi:] *n* 陳謝 chíñsha

apostle [əpɑːs'əl] *n* (disciple) 使徒 shítò

apostrophe [əpɑːs'trəfi:] *n* アポストロフィ apósùtorofi

appall [əpɔ:l'] (*BRIT* **appal**) *vt* (shock) ぞっとさせる zottó saseru

appalling [əpɔ:l'iŋ] *adj* (shocking: destruction etc) 衝撃的な shògekiteki na; (awful: ignorance etc) ひどい hidòi

apparatus [æpəræt'əs] *n* (equipment) 器具 kígù; (in gymnasium) 設備 sétsùbi; (organisation) 組織 sòshìki

apparel [əpær'əl] *n* 衣服 ffúku

apparent [əpær'ənt] *adj* (seeming) 外見上の gaíkenjò no; (obvious) 明白な meíhaku na

apparently [əpær'əntli:] *adv* 外見は gaíken wa

apparition [æpəriʃ'ən] *n* (ghost) 幽霊 yùrei

appeal [əpiːl'] *vi* (LAW) (to superior court) 控訴する kòso suru; (to highest court) 上告する jòkoku suru
◆*n* (LAW) (to superior court) 控訴 kòso; (to highest court) 上告 jòkoku; (request, plea) アピール ápìru; (attraction, charm) 魅力 miryóku, アピール ápìru

to appeal (to someone) for (help, calm, funds) (...に) ...を求める (...ni) ...wò motómerù

to appeal to (be attractive to) ...の気に入る ...no ki ní irù

it doesn't appeal to me それは気に入らない soré wa ki ní iranaì

appealing [əpi:'liŋ] *adj* (attractive) 魅力的な miryókuteki na

appear [əpi:r'] *vi* (come into view, develop) 現れる aráwarerù; (LAW: in court) 出廷する shuttéi suru; (publication) 発行される hakkò sarerù; (seem) ...に見える ...ni miérù

to appear on TV/in "Hamlet" テレビ〔ハムレット〕に出演する térèbi〔hámùretto〕ni shutsúen suru

it would appear that ... ...だと思われる ...da to omówarerù

appearance [əpi:'rəns] *n* (arrival) 到着 tòchaku; (look, aspect) 様子 yòsu; (in public) 姿を見せる事 súgàta wo misérù kotó; (on TV) 出演 shutsúen

appease [əpiːz'] *vt* (pacify, satisfy) な だ める nadámerù

appendices [əpen'dəsiːz] *npl of* **appendix**

appendicitis [əpendisai'tis] *n* 盲腸炎 mōchōen, 虫垂炎 chūsuíen

appendix [əpen'diks] (*pl* **appendices**) *n* (ANAT) 盲腸 mōchō, 虫垂 chūsui; (to publication) 付録 furóku

appetite [æp'itait] *n* (desire to eat) 食欲 shokúyoku; (*fig*: desire) 欲 yokú

appetizer [æp'itaizəːr] *n* (food) 前菜 zeń-sai; (drink) 食前酒 shokúzeñshu

appetizing [æp'itaiziŋ] *adj* (smell) お い しそうな oíshisō na

applaud [əplɔːd'] *vi* (clap) 拍手する hákù-shu suru

♦*vt* (actor etc) ...に拍手を送る ...ni hákù-shu wo okúrù; (praise: action, attitude) ほめる homérù

applause [əplɔːz'] *n* (clapping) 拍手 há-kùshu

apple [æp'əl] *n* リンゴ riñgo

apple tree *n* リンゴの木 riñgo no ki

appliance [əplai'əns] *n* (electrical, domestic) 器具 kigú

applicable [æp'likəbəl] *adj* (relevant): **applicable (to)** (...に) 適応する (...ni) tekíō suru

applicant [æp'likənt] *n* (for job, scholarship) 志願者 shigáñsha

application [æplikei'ʃən] *n* (for a job, a grant etc) 志願 shigáñ; (hard work) 努力 dóryòku; (applying: of cream, medicine etc) 塗布 tófù; (: of paint) 塗る事 nurú koto

application form *n* 申請書 shiñseisho

applied [əplaid'] *adj* (science, art) 実用の jitsúyō no

apply [əplai'] *vt* (paint etc) 塗る nurú; (law etc: put into practice) 適用する te-kíyō suru

♦*vi*: **to apply (to)** (be applicable) (...に) 適用される (...ni) tekíyō sarerù; (ask) (...に) 申込む (...ni) mōshikomù

to apply for (permit, grant) ...を申請する ...wo shiñsei suru; (job) ...に応募する

...ni ōbo suru

to apply oneself to ...に精を出す ...ni séī wo dásù

appoint [əpɔint'] *vt* (to post) 任命する niñ-mei suru

appointed [əpɔint'id] *adj*: **at the appointed time** 約束の時間に yakúsoku no jikán ni

appointment [əpɔint'mənt] *n* (of person) 任命 niñmei; (post) 職 shokú; (arranged meeting: with client, at hairdresser etc) 会う約束 áù yakúsoku

to make an appointment (with someone) (...と) 会う約束をする (...to) áù yakúsoku wò suru

appraisal [əprei'zəl] *n* (evaluation) 評価 hyōka

appreciable [əpriː'ʃiːəbəl] *adj* (difference, effect) 著しい ichíjirushìì

appreciate [əpriː'ʃiːeit] *vt* (like) 評価する hyōka suru; (be grateful for) 有難く思う arígatakù omóù; (understand) 理解する ríkài suru

♦*vi* (COMM: currency, shares) 値上りす る neágari suru

appreciation [əpriːʃiːei'ʃən] *n* (enjoyment) 観賞 kañshō; (understanding) 理解 ríkài; (gratitude) 感謝 káñsha; (COMM: in value) 値上り neágari

appreciative [əpriː'ʃətiv] *adj* (person, audience) よく反応する yokú hañnō su-ru; (comment) 賞賛の shōsan no

apprehend [æprihend'] *vt* (arrest) 捕 ま える tsukámaerù

apprehension [æprihen'ʃən] *n* (fear) 不 安 fuán

apprehensive [æprihen'siv] *adj* (fearful: glance etc) 不安の fuán no

apprentice [əpren'tis] *n* (plumber, carpenter etc) 見習い mínarai

apprenticeship [əpren'tisʃip] *n* (for trade, *also fig*) 見習い期間 mínáraikikàn

approach [əprouʧ'] *vi* 近付く chikázukù

♦*vt* (come to: place, person) ...に近付く ...ni chikázukù; (ask, apply to: person) ...に話を持掛ける ...ni hanáshi wò mochí-kakerù; (situation, problem) ...と取組む ...to toríkumù, ...にアプローチする ...ni apúrōchi suru

◆*n* (advance: of person, typhoon etc: *also fig*) 接近 sekkín; (access, path) 入路 nyúro; (to problem, situation) 取組み方 toríkumikata

approachable [əprou'tʃəbəl] *adj* (person) 近付きやすい chikázukiyasuì; (place) 接近できる sekkín dekirù

appropriate [*adj* əprou'ri:it *vb* əprou'ri:eit] *adj* (apt, relevant) 適当な tekítō na

◆*vt* (property, materials, funds) 横取りする yokódori suru

approval [əpru:'vəl] *n* (approbation) 承認 shōnin; (permission) 許可 kyóka

on approval (COMM) 点検売買で teñkenbaíbai de

approve [əpru:v'] *vt* (authorize: publication, product, action) 認可する nífika suru; (pass: motion, decision) 承認する shṓnin suru

approve of *vt fus* (person, thing) ...を良いと思う ...wo yóì to omóù

approximate [əpra:k'səmit] *adj* (amount, number) 大よその ōyoso no

approximately [əpra:k'səmitli:] *adv* (about, roughly) 大よそ ṓyoso, 約 yákù

apricot [æp'rikɑ:t] *n* (fruit) アンズ añzu

April [eip'rəl] *n* 4月 shigátsu

April Fool's Day *n* エープリルフール ēpurirufúru

apron [ei'prən] *n* (clothing) 前掛け maékake, エプロン epúron

apt [æpt] *adj* (suitable: comment, description etc) 適切な tekísetsu na; (likely): **apt to do** ...しそうである ...shisṓ de arù

aptitude [æp'tətu:d] *n* (capability, talent) 才能 saínō

aqualung [æk'wəlʌŋ] *n* アクアラング akúarañgu

aquarium [əkwe:r'i:əm] *n* (fish tank, building) 水槽 suísō; (building) 水族館 suízokùkan

Aquarius [əkwe:r'i:əs] *n* 水がめ座 mizúgameza

aquatic [əkwæt'ik] *adj* (animal, plant, sport) 水生の suísei no

aqueduct [æk'widʌkt] *n* 導水橋 dṓsuikyō

Arab [ær'əb] *adj* アラビアの arábia no, アラブの árabu no

◆*n* アラビア人 arábiajìn, アラブ (人) árabu(jìn)

Arabian [ərei'bi:ən] *adj* アラビアの arábia no

Arabic [ær'əbik] *adj* (language, numerals, manuscripts) アラビア語の arábiago no

◆*n* (LING) アラビア語 arábiago

arable [ær'əbəl] *adj* (land, farm, crop) 耕作に適した kṓsaku ni tekishíta

arbitrary [ɑ:r'bitre:ri:] *adj* (random: attack, decision) 勝手な katté na

arbitration [ɑ:r'bitrei'ʃən] *n* (of dispute, quarrel) 仲裁 chūsai

arc [ɑ:rk] *n* (sweep, *also* MATH) 弧 kò

arcade [ɑ:rkeid'] *n* (round a square, *also* shopping mall) アーケード ākēdo

arch [ɑ:rtʃ] *n* (ARCHIT) アーチ àchi; (of foot) 土踏まず tsuchífumàzu

◆*vt* (back) 丸める marúmeru

archaeology [ɑ:rki:ɑ:l'ədʒi:] *etc* (*BRIT*) = **archeology** *etc*

archaic [ɑ:rkei'ik] *adj* 時代遅れの jidáiokùre no

archbishop [ɑ:rtʃbiʃ'əp] *n* 大司教 daíshikyō

archenemy [ɑ:rtʃ'en'əmi:] *n* 宿敵 shukúteki

archeologist [ɑ:rki:ɑ:l'ədʒist] *n* 考古学者 kṓkogakùsha

archeology [ɑ:rki:ɑ:l'ədʒi:] *n* 考古学 kṓkogàku

archery [ɑ:r'tʃə:ri:] *n* 弓道 kyúdō

archetype [ɑ:r'kitaip] *n* (person, thing) 典型 teñkei

archipelago [ɑ:rkəpel'əgou] *n* 列島 rettṓ

architect [ɑ:r'kitekt] *n* (of building) 建築技師 keñchikugishì

architectural [ɑ:r'kitektʃə:rəl] *adj* 建築の keñchiku no

architecture [ɑ:r'kitektʃə:r] *n* (design of buildings) 建築 keñchiku; (style of building) 建築様式 keñchikuyōshiki

archives [ɑːr'kaivz] *npl* (collection: of papers, records, films etc) 記録収集 kirókushūshū, アーカイブス ākaibusu

Arctic [ɑːrk'tik] *adj* (cold etc) 北極圏の hokkyókukèn no
♦*n: the Arctic* 北極圏 hokkyókukèn

ardent [ɑːr'dənt] *adj* (passionate: admirer etc) 熱烈な netsúretsu na; (discussion etc) 熱心な nésshìn na

arduous [ɑːr'dʒuːəs] *adj* (task, journey) 困難な kónnan na

are [ɑːr] *vb see* be

area [eːr'iːə] *n* (region, zone) 地域 chíiki; (part of place) 区域 kúiki; (*also in room*: e.g. dining area) エリア éría; (MATH etc) 面積 mēñseki; (of knowledge, experience) 分野 búñ-ya

arena [əriː'nə] *n* (for sports, circus etc) 競技場 kyōgijō

aren't [eːrnt] = **are not**

Argentina [ɑːrdʒəntiː'nə] *n* アルゼンチン arúzeñchin

Argentinian [ɑːrdʒəntiːn'iːən] *adj* アルゼンチンの arúzeñchin no
♦*n* アルゼンチン人 arúzenchiñjin

arguably [ɑːr'gjuːəbliː] *adv* 多分...だろう tábùn ...dárò

argue [ɑːr'gjuː] *vi* (quarrel) けんかする keñka suru; (reason) 論じる roñjiru
to argue that ... ...だと主張する ...da to shuchō suru

argument [ɑːr'gjəmənt] *n* (reasons) 論議 róñgi; (quarrel) けんか keñka

argumentative [ɑːrgjəmen'tətiv] *adj* (person) 議論好きな giróñzuki na; (voice) けんか腰の keñkagoshi no

aria [ɑːr'iːə] *n* (MUS) アリア ária

arid [ær'id] *adj* (land) 乾燥した kañsō shita; (subject, essay) 面白くない omóshirokùnai

Aries [eːr'iːz] *n* 牡羊座 ohítsujiza

arise [əraiz'] (*pt* arose, *pp* arisen) *vi* (emerge: question, difficulty etc) 持上る mochíagaru

arisen [əriz'ən] *pp of* arise

aristocracy [ærista:k'rəsiː] *n* 貴族階級 kizőkukaìkyū

aristocrat [əris'təkræt] *n* 貴族 kizőku

arithmetic [əriθ'mətik] *n* (MATH, *also*: calculation) 算数 sañsū

ark [ɑːrk] *n: Noah's Ark* ノアの箱舟 nóà no hakóbùne

arm [ɑːrm] *n* (ANAT) 腕 udé; (of clothing) 袖 sodé; (of chair etc) ひじ掛け hijíkake; (of organization etc) 支部 shíbù
♦*vt* (person, nation) 武装させる busố saseru
arm in arm 腕を組合って udé wò kumíatte

armaments [ɑːr'məmənts] *npl* 兵器 héìki

armchair [ɑːrm'tʃeːr] *n* ひじ掛けいす hijíkakeìsu

armed [ɑːrmd] *adj* (soldier, conflict, forces etc) 武装した busố shita

armed robbery *n* 武装強盗 busốgồtō

armistice [ɑːr'mistis] *n* 停戦 teísen

armor [ɑːr'mər] (*BRIT* **armour**) *n* (HISTORY: knight's) よろい yorói; (MIL: tanks) 装甲部隊 sốkōbutài

armored car [ɑːr'mərd kɑːr'] *n* 装甲車 sốkōsha

armpit [ɑːrm'pit] *n* わきの下 wakí no shìtá

armrest [ɑːrm'rest] *n* ひじ掛け hijíkake

arms [ɑːrmz] *npl* (weapons) 武器 búkì; (HERALDRY) 紋章 mofishō

army [ɑːr'miː] *n* (MIL) 軍隊 gúntai; (*fig*: host) 大群 taígun

aroma [ərou'mə] *n* (of foods, coffee) 香り kaóri

aromatic [ærəmæt'ik] *adj* (herb, tea) 香りのよい kaóri no yoì

arose [ərouz'] *pt of* arise

around [əraund'] *adv* (about) 回りに mawári ni; (in the area) そこら辺に sokórahen ni
♦*prep* (encircling) ...の回りに ...no mawári ni; (near) ...の近辺に ...no kíñpen ni; (*fig*: about: dimensions) ...およそ óyoso, 約 yákù; (: dates, times) ...ごろ ...górò

arouse [ərauz'] *vt* (from sleep) 起す okósù; (interest, passion, anger) 引起こす hikíokosù

arrange [əreindʒ'] *vt* (organize: meeting, tour etc) 準備する júñbi suru; (put in

order: books etc) 整とんする seíton suru; (: flowers) 生ける ikérù
to arrange to do something ...する手配をする ...surú tehái wo suru

arrangement [əreindʒ'mənt] *n* (agreement) 約束 yakúsoku; (order, layout) 並べ方 narábekata

arrangements [əreindʒ'mənts] *npl* (plans, preparations) 手配 tehái

array [ərei'] *n*: **array of** (things, people) 多数の tásū no

arrears [əri:rz'] *npl* (money owed) 滞納金 taínōkin
to be in arrears with one's rent 家賃が滞納になっている yáchìn ga taínō ni natte irù

arrest [ərest'] *vt* (detain: criminal, suspect) 逮捕する taího suru; (someone's attention) 引く hikú
♦*n* (detention) 逮捕 taího
under arrest 逮捕されて taího saréte

arrival [ərai'vəl] *n* (of person, vehicle, letter etc) 到着 tóchaku
new arrival (person) 新入り shiñ-iri; (baby) 新生児 shiñseîji

arrive [əraiv'] *vi* (traveller, news, letter) 着く tsúkù, 到着する tóchaku suru; (baby) 生れる umáreru

arrogance [ær'əgəns] *n* 尊大さ soñdaisa

arrogant [ær'əgənt] *adj* 尊大な soñdai na

arrow [ær'ou] *n* (weapon) 矢 ya; (sign) 矢印 yajírùshi

arse [ɑ:rs] (*BRIT*: *inf!*) *n* けつ ketsú

arsenal [ɑ:r'sənəl] *n* (for weapons) 兵器庫 heíkikò; (stockpile, supply) 保有兵器 hoyúheìki

arsenic [ɑ:r'sənik] *n* ひ素 hísò

arson [ɑ:r'sən] *n* 放火 hókà

art [ɑ:rt] *n* (creative work, thing produced) 芸術品 geíjutsuhin, 美術品 bijútsuhin; (skill) 芸術 geíjutsu, 美術 bíjùtsu

Arts [ɑ:rts] *npl* (SCOL) 人文科学 jiñbunkagàku

artefact [ɑ:r'təfækt] *n* 工芸品 kógeihin

artery [ɑ:r'tə:ri:] *n* (MED) 動脈 dốmyaku; (*fig*: road) 幹線道路 kañsendòro

artful [ɑ:rt'fəl] *adj* (clever, manipulative) こうかつな kókatsu na

art gallery *n* (large, national) 美術博物館 bijútsuhakubutsukàn; (small, private) 画廊 garố

arthritis [ɑ:rθrai'tis] *n* 関節炎 kañsetsuen

artichoke [ɑ:r'titʃouk] *n* アーティチョーク ātíchōku
Jerusalem artichoke キクイモ kikúimo

article [ɑ:r'tikəl] *n* (object, item) 物品 buppín; (in newspaper) 記事 kíjì; (in document) 条項 jókō
article of clothing 衣料品 iryóhin

articles [ɑ:r'tikəlz] *npl* (*BRIT*) (LAW: training) 見習い契約 mináraikeîyaku

articulate [*adj* ɑ:rtik'jəlit *vb* ɑ:rtik'jəleit] *adj* (speech, writing) 表現力のある hyốgeñryoku no arù
♦*vt* (fears, ideas) 打ち明ける uchíakeru

articulated lorry [ɑ:rtik'jəleitid-] (*BRIT*) *n* トレーラートラック torérātorakkù

artificial [ɑ:rtəfiʃ'əl] *adj* (synthetic: conditions, flowers, arm, leg) 人工の jiñkō no; (affected: manner) 装った yosóotta; (: person) きざな kízà na

artificial respiration *n* 人工呼吸 jiñkōkokyù

artillery [ɑ:rtil'ə:ri:] *n* (MIL: corps) 砲兵隊 hóheitai

artisan [ɑ:r'tizən] *n* (craftsman) 職人 shokúnin

artist [ɑ:r'tist] *n* (painter etc) 芸術家 geíjutsuka; (MUS, THEATER etc) 芸能人 geínōjin; (skilled person) 名人 meíjin

artistic [ɑ:rtis'tik] *adj* 芸術的な geíjutsuteki na

artistry [ɑ:r'tistri:] *n* (creative skill) 芸術 geíjutsu

artless [ɑ:rt'lis] *adj* (innocent) 無邪気な mújàki na

art school *n* 美術学校 bijútsugakkò

KEYWORD

as [æz] *conj* **1** (referring to time) ...していa時 ...shíte iru tokì, ...しながら ...shínagàra

as the years went by 年月が経つにつれて toshítsuki ga tatsù ni tsurétè

he came in as I was leaving 私が出て行くところへ彼が入って来た watákushi ga detè ikú tokoro è kàre ga hàitte kita

as from tomorrow 明日からは ásu kàra wa

2 (in comparisons) ...と同じぐらいに ...to onáji gurài ni

as big as ...と同じぐらい大きい ...to onáji gurài ōkiì

twice as big as ...より2倍も大きい ...yorì nibái mo ōkiì

as much/many as ...と同じ量〔数〕...to onáji ryō〔kazu〕

as much money/many books as ...と同じぐらい沢山の金〔本〕...to onáji gurài takúsan nò kanê〔hon〕

as soon as ...すると直ぐに ...surú to sugù ni

3 (since, because) ...であるから ...de árù kara, ...であるので ...de árù no de, ...なので ...na no de

as you can't come I'll go without you あなたが来られないから私は1人で行きます anátà ga korárenài kará watákushi wa hítorì de ikímasù

he left early as he had to be home by 10 彼は10時までに家に帰らなければならなかったので早めに出て行きました kàre wa jūji made ni iê nì kaéranàkereba naránàkatta no de hayáme ni detè ikímashìta

4 (referring to manner, way) ...様に ...yō nì

do as you wish お好きな様にして下さい o-súki na yō ni shité kudasaì

as she said 彼女が言った様に kánojò ga ittá yō nì

5 (concerning): *as for/to that* それについて〔関して〕は soré ni tsuìte〔kànshite〕wa

6: *as if/though* ...であるかの様に ...de árù ka no yō nì

he looked as if he was ill 彼は病気の様に見えました kárè wa byōki no yō nì miémashìta ¶ *see also* long; such; well

♦*prep* (in the capacity of) ...として ...to-shite

he works as a driver 彼は運転手です kárè wa úntènshu desu

as chairman of the company, he ... 会社の会長として彼は... káisha no káichō toshite kárè wa...

he gave it to me as a present 彼はプレゼントとしてこれをくれました kárè wa purézènto toshite korê wo kuremashìta

a.s.a.p. [eieseipi'] *abbr* (= *as soon as possible*) 出来るだけ早く dekíru dake hayàku

asbestos [æsbes'təs] *n* 石綿 ishíwata, アスベスト asúbesùto

ascend [əsend'] *vt* (hill) 登る nobóru; (ladder, stairs) 上る nobóru, 上がる agáru

ascend the throne 即位する sókùi suru

ascendancy *n* [əsen'dənsi:] 優勢 yūsei

ascent [əsent'] *n* (slope) 上り坂 nobórizaka; (climb: of mountain etc) 登はん tōhan

ascertain [æsə:rtein'] *vt* (details, facts) 確認する kakúnin suru

ascribe [əskraib'] *vt*: *to ascribe something to* (put down: cause) ...を...のせいにする ...wo ...no seî ni suru; (attribute: quality) ...が...にあると見なす ...ga ...ni árù to minásù; (: work of art) ...が...の作品だとする ...ga ...no sakúhin da tò suru

ash [æʃ] *n* (gen) 灰 haì; (tree) トネリコ tonériko

ashamed [əʃeimd'] *adj* (embarrassed, guilty) 恥ずかしい hazúkashiì

to be ashamed of (person, action) ...を恥ずかしく思う ...wo hazúkashikù omoù

ashen [æʃ'ən] *adj* (face) 青ざめた aōzameta

ashore [əʃɔːr'] *adv* (be) 陸に rikú ni; (swim, go etc) 陸へ rikú e

ashtray [æʃ'trei] *n* 灰皿 haízara

Ash Wednesday *n* 灰の水曜日 haî no sufyòbi

Asia [ei'ʒə] *n* アジア ájìa

Asian [ei'ʒən] *adj* アジアの ájìa no
♦*n* アジア人 ajíajìn

aside [əsaid'] *adv* (to one side, apart) わ

きへ〔に〕wakí e(ni)

◆*n* (to audience etc) 傍白 bóhaku

ask [æsk] *vt* (question) 尋ねる tazúnerù, 聞く kikú; (invite) 招待する shōtai suru

to ask someone something ...に...を聞く ...ni ...wo kíkù

to ask someone to do something ...に...をするように頼む ...ni ...wo suru yō ni tanómù

to ask someone about something ...に...について尋ねる ...ni ...ni tsuítè tazúnerù

to ask (someone) a question (...に) 質問をする (...ni) shitsúmoñ wo suru

to ask someone out to dinner ...を外での食事に誘う ...wo sótò de no shokúji ni sasoú

ask after *vt fus* (person) ...の事を尋ねる ...no kotó wò tazúnerù

askance [əskǽns'] *adv*: *to look askance at someone/something* ...を横目で見る ...wo yokóme de mirù

askew [əskjuː'] *adv* (clothes) 乱れて midárète

ask for *vt fus* (request) 願う negáu; (look for: trouble) 招く manéku

asking price [æs'kiŋ-] *n* 言値 iíne

asleep [əsliːp'] *adj* (sleeping) 眠っている nemútte irù

to fall asleep 眠る nemúru

asparagus [əspær'əgəs] *n* アスパラガス asúparagàsu

aspect [æs'pekt] *n* (element: of subject) 面 méñ; (direction in which a building etc faces) 向き múkì; (quality, air) 様子 yōsu

aspersions [əspəːr'ʒənz] *npl*: *to cast aspersions on* ...を中傷する ...wo chūshō suru

asphalt [æs'fɔːlt] *n* アスファルト asúfarùto

asphyxiation [æsfiksiːei'ʃən] *n* 窒息 chissóku

aspirations [æspərei'ʃənz] *npl* (hopes, ambitions) 大望 taíbō

aspire [əspai'əːr] *vi*: *to aspire to* ...を熱望する ...wo netsúbō suru

aspirin [æs'pəːrin] *n* (drug) アスピリン asúpirin; (tablet) アスピリン錠 asúpiriñjō

ass [æs] *n* (ZOOL) ロバ róbà; (*inf*: idiot) ばか bákà; (*US*: *inf!*) けつ ketsú

assailant [əsei'lənt] *n* 攻撃者 kōgekisha

assassin [əsǽs'in] *n* 暗殺者 añsatsushà

assassinate [əsǽs'əneit] *vt* 暗殺する añsatsu suru

assassination [əsæsinei'ʃən] *n* 暗殺 añsatsu

assault [əsɔːlt'] *n* (attack: LAW) 強迫 kyōhaku; (: MIL, *fig*) 攻撃 kōgeki

◆*vt* (attack) 攻撃する kōgeki suru; (sexually) ...を暴行する ...wo bōkō suru

assemble [əsem'bəl] *vt* (gather together: objects, people) 集める atsúmerù; (TECH: furniture, machine) 組立てる kumítaterù

◆*vi* (people, crowd etc) 集まる atsúmarù

assembly [əsem'bliː] *n* (meeting) 集会 shūkai; (institution) 議会 gíkài; (construction: of vehicles etc) 組立て kumítate

assembly line *n* 組立てライン kumítateraìn

assent [əsent'] *n* (approval to plan) 同意 dóì

assert [əsəːrt'] *vt* (opinion, innocence, authority) 主張する shuchō suru

assertion [əsəːr'ʃən] *n* (statement, claim) 主張 shuchō

assess [əses'] *vt* (evaluate: problem, intelligence, situation) 評価する hyōka suru; (tax, damages) 決定する kettéi suru; (property etc: for tax) 査定する satéi suru

assessment [əses'mənt] *n* (evaluation) 評価 hyōka; (of tax) 決定 kettéi; (of property etc) 査定 satéi

asset [æs'et] *n* (useful quality, person etc) 役に立つ物 yakú ni tatsù monó

assets [æs'ets] *npl* (property, funds) 財産 zaísan; (COMM) 資産 shísàn

assiduous [əsidʒ'uːəs] *adj* (care, work) 勤勉な kiñben na

assign [əsain'] *vt*: *to assign (to)* (date) (...の日にちを) 決める (...no hiníchi wò) kiméru; (task, resources) (...に) 割当てる (...ni) waríaterù

assignment [əsain'mənt] *n* (task) 任務 nímmu; (SCOL) 宿題 shukúdai

assimilate [əsim'əleit] *vt* (learn: ideas etc) 身に付ける mi ni tsukérù; (absorb: immigrants) 吸収する kyúshū suru

assist [əsist'] *vt* (person: physically, financially, with information etc) 援助する éñjo suru

assistance [əsis'təns] *n* (help: with advice, money etc) 援助 éñjo

assistant [əsis'tənt] *n* (helper) 助手 joshú, アシスタント ashísùtanto; (BRIT: also: shop assistant) 店員 teñ-in

associate [adj, n əsou'ʃi:it vb əsou'ʃi:eit]
adj: **associate member** 準会員 juñkaìin
♦*n* (at work) 仲間 nakáma
♦*vt* (mentally) 結び付ける musúbitsukerù
♦*vi*: **to associate with someone** ...と交際する ...to kōsai suru

associate professor 助教授 jókyòju

association [əsousi:ei'ʃən] *n* (group) 会 kaì; (involvement, link) 関係 kañkei; (PSYCH) 連想 reñsō

assorted [əsɔ:r'tid] *adj* (various, mixed) 色々な iróiro na

assortment [əsɔ:rt'mənt] *n* (gen) ...の色々 ...no iróiro; (of things in a box etc) 詰合せ tsuméawase

assume [əsu:m'] *vt* (suppose) 仮定する katéi suru; (responsibilities etc) 引受ける hikfukerù; (appearance, attitude) 装う yosóoù

assumed name [əsu:md'-] *n* 偽名 giméi

assumption [əsʌmp'ʃən] *n* (supposition) 仮定 katéi; (of power etc) 引受ける事 hikfukerù kotó

assurance [əʃu:r'əns] *n* (assertion, promise) 約束 yakúsoku; (confidence) 自信 jishín; (insurance) 保険 hokén

assure [əʃu:r'] *vt* (reassure) 安心させる añshin saseru; (guarantee: happiness, success etc) 保証する hoshō suru

asterisk [æs'tərisk] *n* 星印 hoshíjirùshi, アステリスク asúterisùku

asteroid [æs'tərɔid] *n* 小惑星 shōwakùsei

asthma [æz'mə] *n* ぜん息 zeñsoku

astonish [əstɑːn'iʃ] *vt* 仰天させる gyốten saserù

astonishment [əstɑːn'iʃmənt] *n* 仰天 gyōten

astound [əstaund'] *vt* びっくり仰天させる bikkúrì gyốten saserù

astray [əstrei'] *adv*: **to go astray** (letter) 行方不明になる yukúefumèi ni nárù
to lead astray (morally) 堕落させる daráku saserù

astride [əstraid'] *prep* ...をまたいで ...wo matáìde

astrologer [æstrɑ:l'ədʒə:r] *n* 星占い師 hoshíuranaìshi

astrology [əstrɑ:l'ədʒi:] *n* 占星術 señseìjutsu

astronaut [æs'trənɔ:t] *n* 宇宙飛行士 uchúhikòshi

astronomer [əstrɑ:n'əmə:r] *n* 天文学者 teñmongakùsha

astronomical [æstrənɑ:m'ikəl] *adj* (science, telescope) 天文学の teñmoñgaku no; (fig: odds, price) 天文学的な teñmongakuteki na

astronomy [əstrɑ:n'əmi:] *n* 天文学 teñmoñgaku

astute [əstu:t'] *adj* (operator, decision) 抜け目のない nukéme no naì

asylum [əsai'ləm] *n* (refuge) 避難所 hinánjo; (mental hospital) 精神病院 seíshinbyóin

---

KEYWORD

at [æt] *prep* **1** (referring to position, direction) ...に〔で〕... ni(de), ...の方へ ...no hố e

at the top 一番上に〔で〕ichíban ue nì 〔de〕

at home/school 家〔学校〕に〔で〕ié 〔gákkō〕nì〔dè〕

at the baker's パン屋に〔で〕pàn-ya ní 〔de〕

to look at something ...の方に目を向ける ...no hố ni mè wo mukéru, ...を見る ...wo míru

to throw something at someone ...目掛けて...を投げる ...megákète ...wo nagérù

2 (referring to time) ...に ...ni
at 4 o'clock 4時に yójì ni
at night 夜 (に) yórù (ni)
at Christmas クリスマスに kurísumàsu ni
at times 時々 tokídoki
3 (referring to rates, speed etc) ...で〔に〕 ...de(ni)
at £1 a kilo 1キロ1ポンドで ichíkìro ichípòndo de
two at a time 1度に2つ ichído nì futátsu
at 50 km/h 時速50キロメーターで jisóku gòjúkkiromētā de
4 (referring to manner) ...で〔に〕 ...de(ni)
at a stroke 一撃で ichígeki de
at peace 平和に hefwa ni
5 (referring to activity) ...して ...shíte
to be at work 仕事している shígoto shite iru
to play at cowboys カウボーイごっこをして遊ぶ kaúbōigokkò wo shité asobu
to be good at something ...するのがうまい ...surú nò ga umáì
6 (referring to cause) ...に〔で〕 ... ni(de)
shocked/surprised/annoyed at something ...にショックを感じて〔驚いて, 怒って〕 ...ni shókkù wo kánjite(odórolte, okóttè)
I went at his suggestion 彼の勧めで私は行きました kárè no susúme de wàtákushi wa ìkímashìta

ate [eit] *pt of* eat
atheist [ei'θi:ist] *n* 無神論者 mushínronsha
Athens [æθ'ənz] *n* アテネ átène
athlete [æθ'li:t] *n* 運動家 uńdōka, スポーツマン supóʻtsumàn
athletic [æθlet'ik] *adj* (tradition, excellence etc) 運動の uńdō no, スポーツのsúpōtsu no; (sporty: person) スポーツ好きの supótsuzuki no; (muscular: build) たくましい takúmashìī
athletics [æθlet'iks] *n* 運動競技 uńdōkyògi
Atlantic [ætlæn'tik] *adj* (coast, waves etc) 太西洋の taíseìyō no

♦*n*: *the Atlantic (Ocean)* 太西洋 taiseíyō
atlas [æt'ləs] *n* 地図帳 chizúchō, アトラス atòrasu
atmosphere [æt'məsfi:r] *n* (of planet) 大気 taíkì; (of place) 雰囲気 fuń-ikì
atom [æt'əm] *n* (PHYSICS) 原子 géǹshi
atomic [ətɑ:m'ik] *adj* 原子の géǹshi no
atom(ic) bomb *n* 原子爆弾 geńshibakùdan
atomizer [æt'əmaizə:r] *n* 噴霧器 fuńmukì
atone [ətoun'] *vi*: *to atone for* (sin, mistake) 償う tsugúnaù
atrocious [ətrou'ʃəs] *adj* (very bad) ひどい hidóì
atrocity [ətrɑ:s'iti:] *n* (act of cruelty) 残虐行為 zańgyakukòi
attach [ətætʃ'] *vt* (fasten, join) 付ける tsukérù; (document, letter) とじる tojírù; (importance etc) 置く okú
to be attached to someone/something (like) ...に愛着がある ...ni aíchaku ga arù
attaché [ætæʃei'] *n* 大使館員 taíshikaǹ-in
attaché case *n* アタッシェケース atásshekèsu
attachment [ətætʃ'mənt] *n* (tool) 付属品 fuzókuhin; (love): *attachment (to someone)* (...への) 愛着 (...é no) aíchaku
attack [ətæk'] *vt* (MIL) 攻撃する kógeki suru; (subj: criminal: assault) 襲う osóu; (idea: criticize) 非難する hínàn suru; (task etc: tackle) ...に取掛る ...ni toríkakarù
♦*n* (assault: MIL) 攻撃 kógeki; (on someone's action) 襲撃 shúgeki; (fig: criticism) 非難 hínàn; (of illness) 発作 hossá
heart attack 心臓発作 shińzōhossà
attacker [ətæk'ə:r] *n* 攻撃者 kógekìsha
attain [ətein'] *vt* (also: attain to: results, rank) 達する tassúru; (: happiness) 手に入れる te ni irérù; (: knowledge) 得る érù
attainments [ətein'mənts] *npl* (achievements) 業績 gyóseki
attempt [ətempt'] *n* (try) 試み kokóromi
♦*vt* (try) 試みる kokóromirù

to make an attempt on someone's life ...の命をねらう ...no ínóchi wò neráu

attempted [ətemp'tid] *adj* (murder, burglary, suicide) ...未遂 ...mísùi

attend [ətend'] *vt* (school, church) ...に通う ...ni kayóu; (lectures) ...に出席する ...ni shusséki suru; (patient) 看護する kángo suru

attendance [əten'dəns] *n* (presence) 出席 shusséki; (people present) 出席率 shussékirītsu

attendant [əten'dənt] *n* (helper) 付添い tsukísoi; (in garage etc) 係 kákàri
♦*adj* (dangers, risks) 付き物の tsukímòno no

attend to *vt fus* (needs etc) ...の世話をする ...no sewá wò suru; (affairs etc) ...を片付ける ...wo katázukerù; (patient) ...を看護する ...wo kángo suru; (customer) ...の用を聞く ...no yō wo kikú

attention [əten'ʃən] *n* (concentration, care) 注意 chūi
♦*excl* (MIL) 気を付け ki wo tsuké

for the attention of ... (ADMIN) ...気付け ...kitsúke

attentive [əten'tiv] *adj* (intent: audience etc) 熱心に聞く nésshìn ni kikú; (polite: host) 気配り十分の kikúbàrijūbùn no

attest [ətest'] *vi: to attest to* (demonstrate) ...を立証する ...wo risshō suru; (LAW: confirm) ...を確認する ...wo kakúnin suru

attic [æt'ik] *n* 屋根裏部屋 yanéurabeya

attitude [æt'ətu:d] *n* (mental view) 態度 táido; (posture) 姿勢 shiséi

attorney [ətə:r'ni:] *n* (lawyer) 弁護士 bengòshi

Attorney General *n* 法務長官 hōmuchōkan

attract [ətrækt'] *vt* (draw) 引付ける hikítsukerù; (someone's interest, attention) 引く hikú

attraction [ətræk'ʃən] *n* (charm, appeal) 魅力 miryóku; (gen pl: amusements) 呼び物 yobímono, アトラクション atórakùshon; (PHYSICS) 引力 fīnryoku; (fig: towards someone, something) 引かれる事 hikáreru koto

attractive [ətræk'tiv] *adj* (man, woman) 美ぼうの bibō no; (interesting: price, idea, offer) 魅力的な miryókuteki na

attribute [*n* æt'rəbjuːt *vb* ətrib'juːt] *n* 属性 zokúsei
♦*vt: to attribute something to* (cause) ...を...のせいにする ...wo ...no sei ni surù; (poem, painting) ...が...の作とする ...ga ...no sakú to surù; (quality) ...にある と考える ...ni ...ga arú to kangáerù

attrition [ətriʃ'ən] *n: war of attrition* 消耗戦 shōmōsen

aubergine [ou'bəːrʒin] *n* (BRIT) (vegetable) なす násù; (color) なす紺 nasúkon

auburn [ɔː'bəːrn] *adj* (hair) くり色 kurfíro

auction [ɔːk'ʃən] *n* (also: *sale by auction*) 競り serí
♦*vt* 競りに掛ける serí ni kakérù

auctioneer [ɔːkʃəniːr'] *n* 競売人 kyōbainīn

audacity [ɔːdæs'iti:] *n* (boldness, daring) 大胆さ daítansa; (pej: impudence) ずうずうしさ zúzúshisà

audible [ɔːd'əbəl] *adj* 聞える kikóeru

audience [ɔːd'iːəns] *n* (at event) 観客 kankyaku; (RADIO) 聴取者 chōshushà; (TV) 視聴者 shíchōsha; (public) 世間 sekén; (interview: with queen etc) 謁見 ekkén

audio-typist [ɔːd'iːoutai'pist] *n* (BRIT) 書取りタイピスト kakítori taipisùto ◇口述の録音テープを聞いてタイプを打つ人 kōjutsu nò rokúon tēpù wo kiíte taipù wo utsu hitó

audio-visual [ɔːd'iːouviʒ'uːəl] *adj* (materials, equipment) 視聴覚の shíchōkaku no

audio-visual aid *n* 視聴覚教材 shichōkakukyōzai

audit [ɔːd'it] *vt* (COMM: accounts) 監査する kańsa suru

audition [ɔːdiʃ'ən] *n* (CINEMA, THEATER etc) オーディション ōdishòn

auditor [ɔː'dətəːr] *n* (accountant) 監査役 kańsayaku

auditorium [ɔːdiːtəːr'iːəm] *n* (building) 講堂 kōdō; (audience area) 観客席 kańkyakusèki

augment [ɔ:gment'] *vt* (income etc) 増やす fuyásù

augur [ɔ:'gə:r] *vi*: *it augurs well* いい兆しだ íi kizashi da

August [ɔ:g'əst] *n* 8月 hachígatsu

aunt [ænt] *n* 伯(叔)母 obá

auntie [æn'ti:] *n dimin of* **aunt**

aunty [æn'ti:] *n* = **auntie**

au pair [ɔ: pe:r'] *n* (*also*: **au pair girl**) オペア (ガール) opéa(gàru)

aura [ɔ:r'ə] *n* (*fig*: air, appearance) 雰囲気 fuñ-ikì

auspices [ɔ:s'pisiz] *npl*: *under the auspices of* …の後援で …no kōen de

auspicious [ɔ:spiʃ'əs] *adj* (opening, start, occasion) 前途有望な zéñtoyūbō na

austere [ɔ:sti:r'] *adj* (room, decoration) 質素な shíssò na; (person, lifestyle, manner) 厳格な geñkaku na

austerity [ɔ:ste:r'iti:] *n* (simplicity) 質素さ shissōsa; (ECON: hardship) 苦労 kúrō

Australia [ɔ:streil'jə] *n* オーストラリア ōsutorarīa

Australian [ɔ:streil'jən] *adj* オーストラリアの ōsutorarīa no
♦*n* オーストラリア人 ōsutorariajìn

Austria [ɔ:s'tri:ə] *n* オーストリア ōsutorīa

Austrian [ɔ:s'tri:ən] *adj* オーストリアの ōsutorīa no
♦*n* オーストリア人 ōsutoriajìn

authentic [ɔ:θen'tik] *adj* (painting, document, account) 本物の hoñmono no

author [ɔ:'θə:r] *n* (of text) 著者 chóshà; (profession) 作家 sakká; (creator: of plan, character etc) 発案者 hatsúañsha

authoritarian [əθɔ:rite:r'i:ən] *adj* (attitudes, conduct) 独裁的な dokúsaiteki na

authoritative [əθɔ:r'iteitiv] *adj* (person, manner) 権威ありげな kéñ-i aríge na; (source) 信頼できる shiñrai dekirù

authority [əθɔ:r'iti:] *n* (power) 権限 keñgeñ; (expert) 権威 kéñ-i; (government body) 当局 tōkyoku; (official permission) 許可 kyókà
the authorities 当局 tōkyoku

authorize [ɔ:'θə:raiz] *vt* (publication etc)

autistic [ɔ:tis'tik] *adj* 自閉症の jihéishō no

auto [ɔ:'tou] (*US*) *n* (car) 自動車 jídōsha, カーкā

autobiography [ɔ:təbaiɑ:g'rəfi:] *n* 自叙伝 jijódèn

autocratic [ɔ:təkræt'ik] *adj* (government, ruler) 独裁的な dokúsaiteki na

autograph [ɔ:'təgræf] *n* サイン sáîn
♦*vt* (photo etc) …にサインする …ni sáîn suru

automata [ɔ:tɑ:m'ətə] *npl of* **automaton**

automated [ɔ:'təmeitid] *adj* (factory, process) 自動化した jidōka shita

automatic [ɔ:təmæt'ik] *adj* (process, machine) 自動の jidō no; (reaction) 自動的な jidōteki na
♦*n* (gun) 自動ピストル jidōpisùtoru, オートマチック otomachikkù; (*BRIT*: washing machine) 自動洗濯機 jidōsentakùki; (car) オートマチック車 ōtomachikkùsha

automatically [ɔ:təmæt'ikli:] *adv* (*also fig*) 自動的に jidōteki ni

automation [ɔ:təmei'ʃən] *n* (of factory process, office) 自動化 jidōka, オートメーション ōtomēshon

automaton [ɔ:tɑ:m'ətɑ:n] (*pl* **automata**) *n* (robot) ロボット robôtto

automobile [ɔ:təməbi:l'] (*US*) *n* 自動車 jídōsha

autonomous [ɔ:tɑ:n'əməs] *adj* (region, area) 自治の jíchì no; (organization, person) 独立の dokúritsu no

autonomy [ɔ:tɑ:n'əmi:] *n* (of organization, person, country) 独立 dokúritsu

autopsy [ɔ:'tɑ:psi:] *n* (post-mortem) 司法解剖 shihókaìbō, 検死解剖 keñshikaìbō

autumn [ɔ:'təm] *n* (season) 秋 ákì
in autumn 秋に ákì ni

auxiliary [ɔ:gzil'jə:ri:] *adj* (assistant) 補助の hójò no; (back-up) 予備の yóbì no
♦*n* 助手 joshú

avail [əveil'] *vt*: *to avail oneself of* (offer, opportunity, service) …を利用する …wo riyō suru
♦*n*: *to no avail* 無駄に mudá ni

availability [əveiləbiliˈəti:] n (supply: of goods, staff etc) 入手の可能性 nyúshu no kanōsei

available [əveiˈləbəl] adj (obtainable: article etc) 手に入る te ni haíru; (service, time etc) 利用できる riyō dekiru; (person: unoccupied) 手が空いている te ga aíte iru; (: unattached) 相手がいない aíte ga ínái

avalanche [ævˈəlæntʃ] n (of snow) 雪崩 nadáre; (fig: of people, mail, events) 殺到 sattō

avant-garde [ævɑːntgɑːrdˈ] adj 前衛の zeñ-ei no, アバンギャルドの abángyarù-do no

avarice [ævˈəris] n どん欲 dóñ-yoku

Ave. [æv] abbr = avenue

avenge [əvendʒˈ] vt (person, death etc) ...の復しゅうをする ...no fukúshū wò suru

avenue [ævˈənuː] n (street) 通り tōri; (drive) 並木通り namíkidòri; (means, solution) 方法 hōhō

average [ævˈərɪdʒ] n (mean, norm) 平均 heíkin
♦adj (mean) 平均の heíkin no; (ordinary) 並の namí no
♦vt (reach an average of: in speed, output, score) 平均...で...する heíkin ...de ...surú
on average 平均で heíkin de

average out vi: to average out at 平均が...になる heíkin ga ...ni nárù

averse [əvəːrsˈ] adj: to be averse to something/doing ...[...するの]が嫌いである ...[...surú nò] ga kirái de arù

aversion [əvəːrˈʒən] n (to people, work etc) 嫌悪 kéñ-o

avert [əvəːrtˈ] vt (prevent: accident, war) 予防する yobō suru; (ward off: blow) 受け止める ukétomerù; (turn away: one's eyes) そらす sorásù

aviary [eiˈviːeːriː] n 鳥用大型ケージ torí-yō ōgata kèji

aviation [eiviːeiˈʃən] n 航空 kōkū

avid [ævˈid] adj (supporter, viewer) 熱心な nésshìn na

avocado [ævəkɑːdˈou] n (BRIT: also:

avocado pear) アボカド abókado

avoid [əvɔidˈ] vt (person, obstacle, danger) 避ける sakérù

avuncular [əvʌŋˈkjələːr] adj (expression, tone, person) 伯(叔)父の様に優しい ojí no yǒ ni yasáshiì

await [əweitˈ] vt 待つ mátsù

awake [əweikˈ] adj (from sleep) 目が覚めている me ga sámète irú
♦vb (pt awoke, pp awoken or awaked)
♦vt 起す okósù
♦vi 目が覚める me ga samérù
to be awake 目が覚めている me ga samérù

awakening [əweiˈkəniŋ] n (also fig: of emotion) 目覚め mezáme

award [əwɔːrdˈ] n (prize) 賞 shō; (LAW: damages) 賠償 baíshō
♦vt (prize) 与える atáeru; (LAW: damages) 命ずる meízuru

aware [əweiˈr] adj: aware (of) (conscious) (...に)気が付いている (...ni) ki gá tsuíte irù; (informed) (...を)知っている (...wo) shittê iru
to become aware of/that (become conscious of) ...に[...という事に]気が付く ...ni[...to iú koto ni]ki gá tsukù; (learn) ...を[...という事を]知る ...wo[...to iú koto wò]shírú

awareness [əweiˈrnis] n (consciousness) 気が付いている事 ki gá tsuíte irú koto; (knowing) 知っている事 shittê iru koto

awash [əwɑːʃˈ] adj (with water) 水浸しの mizúbitashi no; (fig: awash with) ...だらけの ...daráke no

away [əweiˈ] adv (movement) 離れて hanárète; (position) 離れた所に hanárèta tokóro ni; (not present) 留守で rúsù de; (in time) ...先で ...sáki de; (far away) 遠くに tōku ni
two kilometers away 2キロメートル離れて nikírométoru hanarete
two hours away by car 車で2時間走った所に kurúma de nijíkan hashítta tokoro ni
the holiday was two weeks away 休暇は2週間先だった kyúka wa nishúkan saki dattá

he's away for a week 彼は1週間の予定で留守です kárè wa isshūkan no yotei de rusū desu

to take away (remove) 片付ける katázukerù; (subtract) 引く hikú

to work/pedal etc away 一生懸命に働く〔ペダルを踏む〕etc isshōkenmei ni határakù 〔pedáru wò fumù〕etc

to fade away (color) さめる sameru; (enthusiasm) 冷える samérù; (light, sound) 消えてなくなる kiéte nakunarù

away game n (SPORT) ロードゲーム rōdogēmu

awe [ɔ:] n (respect) い敬 ikéi

awe-inspiring [ɔ:'inspaiə:riŋ] adj (overwhelming: person, thing) い敬の念を抱かせる ikéi no neñ wo idákaserù

awesome [ɔ:'səm] adj = **awe-inspiring**

awful [ɔ:'fəl] adj (frightful: weather, smell) いやな iyá na; (dreadful: shock) ひどい hidóì; (number, quantity): **an awful lot (of)** いやに沢山の iyá ni takusañ no

awfully [ɔ:'fəli:] adv (very) ひどく hídòku

awhile [əwail'] adv しばらく shibáràku

awkward [ɔ:k'wə:rd] adj (clumsy: person, movement) ぎこちない gikóchinaì; (difficult: shape) 扱いにくい atsúkainikuì; (embarrassing: problem, situation) 厄介な yákkai na

awning [ɔ:'niŋ] n 日よけ hiyóke

awoke [əwouk'] pt of **awake**

awoken [əwou'kən] pp of **awake**

awry [ərai'] adv: **to be awry** (order, clothes, hair) 乱れている midárète irú

to go awry (outcome, plan) 失敗する shippái suru

axe [æks] (US: also: **ax**) n 斧 ónò
♦vt (project etc) 廃止する haíshi suru

axes[1] [æk'siz] npl of **ax(e)**

axes[2] [æk'siz] npl of **axis**

axis [æk'sis] (pl **axes**) n (of earth, on graph) 軸 jikú

axle [æk'səl] n (AUT) 車軸 shajíku

aye [ai] excl (yes) はい hấi

azalea [əzeil'jə] n ツツジ tsutsúji

B

B [bi:] n (MUS: note) ロ音 ro-óñ; (: key) ロ調 róchō

B.A. [bi:ei'] abbr = **Bachelor of Arts**

babble [bæb'əl] vi (person, voices) ぺちゃくちゃしゃべる péchàkucha shabérù; (brook) さらさら流れる sárāsara nagárerù

baby [bei'bi:] n (infant) 赤ん坊 ákanbō, 赤ちゃん akáchan; (US: inf: darling) あなた anátà, ベビー bébī

baby carriage (US) n 乳母車 ubáguruma

baby-sit [bei'bi:sit] vi 子守をする komórì wo suru, ベビーシッターをする bebíshittà wo suru

baby-sitter [bei'bi:sitə:r] n 子守役 komóriyaku, ベビーシッター bebíshittà

bachelor [bætʃ'ələ:r] n 独身の男 dokúshin no otóko

Bachelor of Arts/Science (person) 文〔理〕学士 buñ(ri)gakùshi; (qualification) 文〔理〕学士号 buñ(ri)gakùshigō

back [bæk] n (of person, animal) 背中 senáka; (of hand) 甲 kố; (of house, page, book) 裏 urá; (of car, train) 後ろ ushíro, 後部 kōbu; (of chair) 背もたれ semótàre; (of crowd, audience) 後ろの方 ushíro no hố; (SOCCER) バック bákkù
♦vt (candidate: also: **back up**) 支援する shiēn suru; (horse: at races) ...にかける ...ni kakérù; (car) バックさせる bákkù saséru
♦vi (also: **back up**) person) 後ずさりする atózusàri suru; (: : car etc) バックする bákkù suru
♦cpd (payment, rent) 滞納の taínō no; (AUT: seat, wheels) 後部の kōbu no
♦adv (not forward): **he's back** 彼は帰って来た kárè wa kaétte kità; (return): **throw the ball back** ボールを投げ返して下さい bốru wò nagékaeshite kudasaì; (again): **he called back** 彼は電話を掛け直してきた kárè wa deñwa wò kakénao-

shite kita

he ran back 彼は駆け戻った kárè wa kakémodottà

can I have it back? それを返してくれませんか sorè wò kaéshite kuremaseñ ka

backbencher [bæk'bentʃər] (*BRIT*) *n* 平議員 hirágiìn

backbone [bæk'boun] *n* (ANAT) 背骨 sebóne; (*fig*: main strength) 主力 shúryòku; (: courage) 勇気 yúki

backcloth [bæk'klɔːθ] (*BRIT*) *n* = backdrop

backdate [bækdeit'] *vt* (document, pay raise etc) ...にさかのぼって有効にする ...ni sakánobottè yúkō ni suru

back down *vi* 譲る yuzúru

backdrop [bæk'drɑːp] *n* 背景幕 haíkeìmaku

backfire [bæk'faiər] *vi* (AUT) バックファイアする bakkúfaìa suru; (plans) 裏目に出る uráme ni derù

background [bæk'graund] *n* (of picture, events: *also* COMPUT) 背景 haíkei, バック bákkù; (basic knowledge) 予備知識 yobíchishìki; (experience) 経歴 keíreki

family background 家庭環境 kateikankyō

backhand [bæk'hænd] *n* (TENNIS: *also*: **backhand stroke**) バックハンド bakkúhaǹdo

backhanded [bæk'hændid] *adj* (*fig*: compliment) 当てこすりの atékosuri no

backhander [bæk'hændər] (*BRIT*) *n* (bribe) 賄ろ waíro

backing [bæk'iŋ] *n* (*fig*) 支援 shién

backlash [bæk'læʃ] *n* (*fig*) 反動 hañdō

backlog [bæk'lɔːg] *n*: *backlog of work* たまった仕事 tamátta shigoto

back number *n* (of magazine etc) バックナンバー bakkúnaǹbā

back out *vi* (of promise) 手を引く te wo hikú

backpack [bæk'pæk] *n* リュックサック ryukkúsakkù

back pay *n* 未払いの給料 mihárài nò kyúryò

backside [bæk'said] (*inf*) *n* おしり o-shírì

ri

backstage [bæk'steidʒ'] *adv* (THEATER) 楽屋に〔で〕gakúya ni〔de〕

backstroke [bæk'strouk] *n* 背泳ぎ seóyògi

back up *vt* (support: person, theory etc) 支援する shién suru; (COMPUT) バックアップコピーを作る bakkúappukopī wo tsukúrù

backup [bæk'ʌp] *adj* (train, plane) 予備の yóbì no; (COMPUT) バックアップ用の bakkúappu yō no

♦*n* (support) 支援 shién; (*also*: **backup file**) バックアップファイル bakkúappu faìru

backward [bæk'wərd] *adj* (movement) 後ろへの ushíro e no; (person, country) 遅れた okúreta

backwards [bæk'wərdz] *adv* (move, go) 後ろに〔へ〕ushíro ni〔e〕; (read a list) 逆に gyakú nì; (fall) 仰向けに aómuke ni; (walk) 後ろ向きに ushíromuki ni

backwater [bæk'wɔːtər] *n* (*fig*) 後進地 kóshiñchi

backyard [bæk'jɑːrd] *n* (of house) 裏庭 urániwa

bacon [bei'kən] *n* ベーコン bèkon

bacteria [bækti:'ri:ə] *npl* 細菌 saíkin

bad [bæd] *adj* (gen) 悪い warúì; (mistake, accident, injury) 大きな ókina; (meat, food) 悪くなった warúku nattá

his bad leg 彼の悪い方の脚 kárè no warúi hō nò ashí

to go bad (food) 悪くなる warúku narù

bade [bæd] *pt of* bid

badge [bædʒ] *n* (of school etc) 記章 kishō; (of policeman) バッジ bájjì

badger [bædʒ'ər] *n* アナグマ anáguma

badly [bæd'li:] *adv* (work, dress etc) 下手に hetá ni; (reflect, think) 悪く warúku

badly wounded 重傷を負った júshō wò ottá

he needs it badly 彼にはそれがとても必要だ kárè ni wa sorè gà totémo hitsuyō da

to be badly off (for money) 生活が苦しい seíkatsu ga kurushiì

badminton [bæd'mintən] *n* バドミント

ン badómiǹton

bad-tempered [bæd'tem'pə:rd] adj (person: by nature) 怒りっぽい okórippoî; (: on one occasion) 機嫌が悪い kigén gà warúî

baffle [bæf'əl] vt (puzzle) 困惑させる koñwaku saserù

bag [bæg] n (of paper, plastic) 袋 fukúro; (handbag) ハンドバッグ hañdobaggù; (satchel, case) かばん kában

bags of (inf: lots of) 沢山の takúsan no

baggage [bæg'idʒ] n (luggage) 手荷物 teńmotsu

baggy [bæg'i:] adj だぶだぶの dabúdabu no

bagpipes [bæg'paips] npl バグパイプ bagúpaîpu

Bahamas [bəhɑ:m'əz] npl: *the Bahamas* バハマ諸島 bahámashotō

bail [beil] n (LAW: payment) 保釈金 hoshákukin; (: release) 保釈 hosháku

♦vt (prisoner: gen: grant bail to) 保釈する hosháku suru; (boat: also: bail out) ...から水をかい出す ...kará mizú wò kaídasù

on bail (prisoner) 保釈中 (の) hoshákuchū (no)

bailiff [bei'lif] n (LAW: US) 廷吏 teîri; (: BRIT) 執行吏 shíkkòri

bail out vt (prisoner) 保釈させる hosháku saserù ¶ *see also* **bale**

bait [beit] n (for fish, animal) えさ esá; (for criminal etc) おとり otóri

♦vt (hook, trap) ...にえさをつける ...ni esá wò tsukérù; (person: tease) からかう karákaù

bake [beik] vt (CULIN: cake, potatoes) オーブンで焼く ōbun de yakú; (TECH: clay etc) 焼く yakú

♦vi (cook) オーブンに入っている ōbun ni háîtte irù

baked beans [beikt-] npl ベークトビーンズ bēkutobìnzu

baker [bei'kə:r] n パン屋 páñ-ya

bakery [bei'kə:ri:] n (building) パン屋 páñ-ya

baking [bei'kiŋ] n (act) オーブンで焼く事 ōbun de yakú koto; (batch) オーブン

で焼いたもの ōbun de yaíta mono

baking powder n ふくらし粉 fukúrashikò, ベーキングパウダー bēkingupaùdā

balance [bæl'əns] n (equilibrium) 均衡 kiñkō, バランス baránsu; (COMM: sum) 残高 zańdaka; (remainder) 残り nokóri; (scales) 天びん teńbin

♦vt (budget) ...の収入と支出を合せる ...no shūnyū tò shishútsu wò awáserù; (account) ...の決算をする ...no kessán wò suru; (make equal) 釣合を取る tsuríai wo torù

balance of trade 貿易収支 bōekishūshi

balance of payments 国際収支 kokúsaishūshi

balanced [bæl'ənst] adj (report) バランスの良い baránsu no yoî; (personality) 安定した afitei shita

a balanced diet 均衡食 kiñkō shòku

balance sheet n 貸借対照表 taíshakutaishōhyō, バランスシート baránsu shìto

balcony [bæl'kəni:] n バルコニー barúkonī; (in theater) 天井さじき teńjōsajìki

bald [bɔ:ld] adj (head) はげた hágeta; (tire) 坊主になった bōzu ni nattá

bale [beil] n (of paper, cotton, hay) こり korí

baleful [beil'fəl] adj (glance) 邪悪な jaáku na

bale out vi (of a plane) パラシュートで脱出する paráshùto de dasshútsu suru

ball [bɔ:l] n (SPORT) 球 tamá, ボール bōru; (of wool, string) 玉 tamá; (dance) 舞踏会 bútōkai

to play ball (co-operate) 協力する kyōryoku suru

ballad [bæl'əd] n (poem, song) バラード bárādo

ballast [bæl'əst] n (on ship, balloon) バラスト barásùto

ball bearings npl ボールベアリング bōrubeàringu

ballerina [bæləri:'nə] n バレリーナ barérìna

ballet [bælei'] n (art) バレエ bárèe; (an artistic work) バレエ曲 baréekyokù

ballet dancer n バレエダンサー baréedańsā

ballistics [bəlis'tiks] *n* 弾道学 dańdōgaku

balloon [bəlu:n'] *n* (child's) 風船 fūsen; (hot air balloon) 熱気球 netsūkikyū

ballot [bæl'ət] *n* (vote) 投票 tōhyō

ballot paper *n* 投票用紙 tōhyōyōshi

ballpoint (pen) [bɔːl'pɔint] *n* ボールペン bōrupen

ballroom [bɔːl'ruːm] *n* 舞踏の間 butō no ma

balm [bɑːm] *n* バルサム bárùsamu

Baltic [bɔːl'tik] *n*: **the Baltic (Sea)** バルト海 barútokài

balustrade [bæl'əstreid] *n* (on balcony, staircase) 手すり tesúri

bamboo [bæmbu:'] *n* (plant) 竹 také; (material) 竹材 takézai

ban [bæn] *n* (prohibition) 禁止 kiñshi
◆*vt* (prohibit) 禁止する kińshi suru

banal [bənæl'] *adj* (remark, idea, situation) 陳腐な chíñpu na

banana [bənæn'ə] *n* バナナ bánàna

band [bænd] *n* (group) 一団 ichídan; (MUS: jazz, rock, military etc) バンド bańdo; (strip of cloth etc) バンド bańdo; (stripe) 帯状の物 obíjō no mono

bandage [bæn'didʒ] *n* 包帯 hōtai
◆*vt* ...に包帯を巻く ...ni hōtai wò makú

bandaid [bænd'eid'] ® *(US)* n バンドエイド bańdoeìdo ◇ばん創こうの一種 bańsōkō no isshù

bandit [bæn'dit] *n* 盗賊 tōzoku

band together *vi* 団結する dańketsu suru

bandwagon [bænd'wægən] *n*: **to jump on the bandwagon** *(fig)* 便乗する bińjō suru

bandy [bæn'di:] *vt* (jokes, insults, ideas) やり取りする yarítòri surù

bandy-legged [bæn'di:legid] *adj* がにまたの ganímata no

bang [bæŋ] *n* (of door) ばたんという音 bátàn to iú oto; (of gun, exhaust) ばんという音 páñ to iú otò; (blow) 打撃 dagéki
◆*excl* ばんばん páñpaん
◆*vt* (door) ばたんと閉める batán to shimerù; (one's head etc) ぶつける butsúke-

ru
◆*vi* (door) ばたんと閉まる batáñ to shimárù; (fireworks) ばんばん súru
báñban to bakúhatsu suru

bangle [bæŋ'gəl] *n* (bracelet) 腕飾り udékazarì

bangs [bæŋz] *(US) npl* (fringe) 切下げ前髪 kirísagemaegamì

banish [bæn'iʃ] *vt* (exile: person) 追放する tsuíhō suru

banister(s) [bæn'istə:r(z)] *n(pl)* (on stairway) 手すり tesúri

bank [bæŋk] *n* (COMM: building, institution: *also* of blood etc) 銀行 gińkō, バンク báñku; (of river, lake) 岸 kishí; (of earth) 土手 doté
◆*vi* (AVIAT) 傾く katámukù
data bank データバンク dētabańku

bank account *n* 銀行口座 gińkōkòza

bank card *n* ギャランティーカード gyarántīkàdo ◇小切手を使う時に示すカード.カードのサインと小切手のサインが照合される kogíttè wo tsukáù tokí nì shimésu kàdo. kàdo no sáin to kogíttè no sáin ga shōgō sarerù

banker [bæŋk'əːr] *n* 銀行家 gińkōka

banker's card *(BRIT)* n = **bank card**

Bank Holiday *(BRIT)* n 銀行定休日 gińkōteikyūbi

banking [bæŋk'iŋ] *n* 銀行業 gińkōgyò

banknote [bæŋk'nout] *n* 紙幣 shíhèi

bank on *vt fus* ...を頼りにする ...wo táyòri ni suru

bank rate *n* 公定歩合 kōteibuài

bankrupt [bæŋk'rʌpt] *adj* (person, organization) 倒産した tōsan shita
to go bankrupt 倒産する tōsan suru
to be bankrupt 返済能力がない heñsainōryoku ga naí

bankruptcy [bæŋk'rʌptsi:] *n* (COMM) 倒産 tōsan

bank statement *n* 勘定照合表 kañjōshōgōhyō

banner [bæn'əːr] *n* (for decoration, advertising) 横断幕 ōdañmaku; (in demonstration) 手持ち横断幕 temóchi ōdañmaku

banns [bænz] *npl*: **the banns** 結婚予告

kekkón-yokóku

banquet [bæŋ'kwit] *n* 宴会 eñkai

baptism [bæp'tizəm] *n* (REL) 洗礼 seńrei

baptize [bæptaiz'] *vt* ...に洗礼を施す ...ni seńrei wò hodókosù

bar [bɑːr] *n* (place: for drinking) バー bằ; (counter) カウンター kaúntằ; (rod: of metal etc) 棒 bố; (slab: of soap) 1個 ikkố; (*fig:* obstacle) 障害 shốgai; (prohibition) 禁止 kińshi; (MUS) 小節 shốsetsu

♦*vt* (road) ふさぐ fuságu; (person) ...が ...するのを禁止する ...ga ...surú no wò kińshi suru; (activity) 禁止する kińshi suru

a bar of chocolate 板チョコ itáchoko

the Bar (LAW: profession) 弁護士 beñgoshi ◇総称 sốshố

bar none 例外なく reigai nakù

barbaric [bɑːrbær'ik] *adj* (uncivilized, cruel) 野蛮な yabán na

barbarous [bɑːr'bərəs] *adj* (uncivilized, cruel) 野蛮な yabán na

barbecue [bɑːr'bəkjuː] *n* (grill) バーベキューこん炉 bắbekyūkoñro; (meal, party) バーベキューパーティ bắbekyūpằti

barbed wire [bɑːrbd-] *n* 有刺鉄線 yúshitessèn, バラ線 barásen

barber [bɑːr'bər] *n* 理髪師 rihátsushì, 床屋 tokóya

bar code *n* (on goods) バーコード bắkồdo

bare [be:r] *adj* (naked: body) 裸の hadáka no; (: tree) 葉の落ちた ha no óchìta; (countryside) 木のない ki no náì; (minimum: necessities) ほんの hoñno

♦*vt* (one's body, teeth) むき出しにする mukídashi ni suru

bareback [be:r'bæk] *adv* くらなしで kuránashì de

barefaced [be:r'feist] *adj* (lie, cheek) 厚かましい atsúkamashiì

barefoot [be:r'fut] *adj* 裸足の hadáshi no

♦*adv* 裸足で hadáshi de

barely [be:r'li:] *adv* (scarcely) 辛うじて kárõjite

bargain [bɑːr'gin] *n* (deal, agreement) 取引 torfhìki; (good buy) 掘出し物 horídashimono, バーゲン bằgen

♦*vi* (negotiate): *to bargain (with someone)* (...と) 交渉する (...to) kốshố suru; (haggle) 駆引きする kakéhìki suru

into the bargain おまけに o-máke ni

bargain for *vt fus:* *he got more than he bargained for* 彼はそんな結果を予想していなかった kárè wa sofina kekká wò yosố shite inakattà

barge [bɑːrdʒ] *n* (boat) はしけ hashíke

barge in *vi* (enter) いきなり入り込む ikínari hairikomù; (interrupt) 割込む waríkomù

bark [bɑːrk] *n* (of tree) 皮 kawá; (of dog) ほえ声 hoégoe

♦*vi* (dog) ほえる hoérù

barley [bɑːr'liː] *n* 大麦 ốmugi

barley sugar *n* 氷砂糖 kốrizatồ

barmaid [bɑːr'meid] *n* 女性バーテン joséibàten

barman [bɑːr'mən] (*pl* **barmen**) *n* バーテン bằten

barn [bɑːrn] *n* 納屋 náyà

barometer [bərɑːm'itər] *n* (for weather) 気圧計 kiátsukei

baron [bær'ən] *n* (nobleman) 男爵 dańshaku; (of press, industry) 大立て者 ốdatemòno

baroness [bær'ənis] *n* 男爵夫人 dańshakufujìn

barracks [bær'əks] *npl* (MIL) 兵舎 hếisha

barrage [bərɑːʒ'] *n* (MIL) 弾幕 dańmaku; (dam) ダム dámù; (*fig:* of criticism, questions etc) 連発 reńpatsu

barrel [bær'əl] *n* (of wine, beer) たる tarú; (of oil) バレル bárèru; (of gun) 銃身 júshin

barren [bær'ən] *adj* (land) 不毛の fumố no

barricade [bær'əkeid] *n* バリケード barfkèdo

♦*vt* (road, entrance) バリケードでふさぐ barfkèdo de fuságu

to barricade oneself (in) (...に) ろう城する (...ni) rồjố suru

barrier [bær'iːər] *n* (at frontier, entrance) 関門 kańmon; (*fig:* to progress, communication etc) 障害 shṓgai

barring [bɑːr'iŋ] *prep* ...を除いて ...wo nozóite

barrister [bær'istər] (*BRIT*) *n* 法廷弁護士 hōteibengoshì

barrow [bær'ou] *n* (wheelbarrow) 一輪車 ichírinsha

bars [bɑːrz] *npl* (on window etc: grille) 格子 kōshi

behind bars (prisoner) 刑務所に〔で〕 keímushò ni 〔de〕

bartender [bɑːr'tendər] (*US*) *n* バーテンbáten

barter [bɑːr'tər] *vt*: *to barter something for something* ...を...と交換する ...wo ...to kōkan suru

base [beis] *n* (foot: of post, tree) 根元 nemóto; (foundation: of food) 主成分 shuséibun; (: of make-up) ファウンデーション faúndềshon; (center: for military, research) 基地 kichí; (: for individual, organization) 本拠地 honkyochi
◆*vt*: *to base something on* (opinion, belief) ...が...に基づく ...ga ...ni motózukù
◆*adj* (mind, thoughts) 卑しい iyáshiì

baseball [beis'bɔːl] *n* 野球 yakyū, ベースボール bḗsubòru

basement [beis'mənt] *n* 地下室 chikáshìtsu

bases[1] [bei'siz] *npl of* **base**

bases[2] [bei'siz] *npl of* **basis**

bash [bæʃ] (*inf*) *vt* (beat) ぶん殴る buńnagurù

bashful [bæʃ'fəl] *adj* 内気な uchíki na

basic [bei'sik] *adj* (fundamental: principles, problem, essentials) 基本的な kihónteki na; (starting: wage) 基本の kihón no; (elementary: knowledge) 初歩的な shohóteki na; (primitive: facilities) 最小限の saíshōgen no

basically [bei'sikliː] *adv* (fundamentally) 根本的に koñponteki ni; (in fact, put simply) はっきり言って hakkíri itté

basics [bei'siks] *npl*: *the basics* 基本 kihón

basil [bæz'əl] *n* メボウキ mébòki, バジル bájìru

basin [bei'sin] *n* (vessel) たらい tarái;

(*also*: **wash basin**) 洗面台 sefimendai; (GEO: of river, lake) 流域 ryūiki

basis [bei'sis] (*pl* **bases**) *n* (starting point, foundation) 基礎 kisó

on a part-time/trial basis パートタイム〔見習い〕で paátotaìmù(minarai)de

bask [bæsk] *vi*: *to bask in the sun* 日光浴をする nikkōyoku wo suru, 日なたぼっこをする hínátabokkò wo suru

basket [bæs'kit] *n* (container) かご kagó, バスケット basúkettò

basketball [bæs'kitbɔːl] *n* バスケットボール basúkettobòru

bass [beis] *n* (part, instrument) バス básù; (singer) バス歌手 basúkashù

bassoon [bæsuːn'] *n* (MUS) バスーン básùn

bastard [bæs'tərd] *n* (offspring) 私生児 shiséiji; (*inf!*) くそ野郎 kusóyarò

bastion [bæs'tʃən] *n* (of privilege, wealth etc) とりで toríde

bat [bæt] *n* (ZOOL) コウモリ kômori; (for ball games) バット báttò; (*BRIT*: for table tennis) ラケット rakéttò
◆*vt*: *he didn't bat an eyelid* 彼は瞬き1つしなかった kárè wa mabátàki hitótsù shinákàtta

batch [bætʃ] *n* (of bread) 1かま分 hitókamabùn; (of letters, papers) 1山 hitóyàma

bated [bei'tid] *adj*: *with bated breath* 息を殺して íkì wo koróshite

bath [bæθ] *n* (bathtub) 風呂 fúrò, 湯船 yúbùne; (act of bathing) 入浴 nyūyoku
◆*vt* (baby, patient) 風呂に入れる fúrò ni iréru

to have a bath 風呂に入る fúrò ni haíru
¶ *see also* **baths**

bathe [beið] *vi* (swim) 泳ぐ oyógù, 遊泳する yūei suru; (*US*: have a bath) 風呂に入る fúrò ni haíru
◆*vt* (wound) 洗う aráu

bather [beið'ər] *n* 遊泳〔水泳〕する人 yūei〔suíei〕suru hito

bathing [bei'ðiŋ] *n* (taking a bath) 入浴 nyūyoku; (swimming) 遊泳 yūei, 水泳 suíei

bathing cap *n* 水泳帽 suíeìbð

bathing suit (*BRIT* **bathing costume**)

n 水着 mizúgi

bathrobe [bæθ'roub] *n* バスローブ basúrōbu

bathroom [bæθ'ru:m] *n* トイレ tôîre; (without toilet) 浴室 yokúshitsu

baths [bæðz] *npl* (*also*: **swimming baths**) 水泳プール suíeipūru

bath towel *n* バスタオル basútaòru

baton [bætæn'] *n* (MUS) 指揮棒 shikíbō; (ATHLETICS) バトン batón; (policeman's) 警棒 keíbō

battalion [bətæl'jən] *n* 大隊 daítai

batter [bæt'ə:r] *vt* (child, wife) …に暴力を振るう …ni bôryoku wo furúù; (subj: wind, rain) …に強く当たる …ni tsúyòku atáru
♦*n* (CULIN) 生地 kíjì

battered [bæt'ə:rd] *adj* (hat, pan) 使い古した tsukáifurushîta

battery [bæt'ə:ri:] *n* (of flashlight etc) 乾電池 kañdeñchi; (AUT) バッテリー battérī

battle [bæt'əl] *n* (MIL, *fig*) 戦い tatákai
♦*vi* 戦う tatákau

battlefield [bæt'əlfi:ld] *n* 戦場 señjō

battleship [bæt'əlʃip] *n* 戦艦 señkan

bawdy [bɔ:'di:] *adj* (joke, song) わいせつな waísetsu na

bawl [bɔ:l] *vi* (shout: adult) どなる donárù; (wail: child) 泣きわめく nakíwamekù

bay [bei] *n* (GEO) 湾 wáñ
to hold someone at bay …を寄付けない …wo yosétsukenaî

bay leaf *n* ゲッケイジュの葉 gekkéîju no ha, ローリエ rôrie, ベイリーフ beírîfu

bayonet [bei'ənet] *n* 銃剣 júken

bay window *n* 張出し窓 harídashimadò

bazaar [bəza:r'] *n* (market) 市場 íchìba; (fete) バザー bazâ

B. & B. [bi:' ænd bi:'] *n abbr* = **bed and breakfast**

BBC [bi:bi:si:'] *n abbr* (= *British Broadcasting Company*) 英国放送協会 eíkoku hōsō kyôkai

B.C. [bi:si:'] *adv abbr* (= *before Christ*) 紀元前 kigéñzen

be [bi:] (*pt* **was, were**, *pp* **been**) *aux vb* **1** (with present participle: forming continuous tenses) …している …shîte iru
what are you doing? 何をしていますか nánì wo shité imasù ká
it is raining 雨が降っています ámè ga fúttè imasù
they're coming tomorrow 彼らは明日来る事になっています kárèra wa asú kurù koto ni náttè imásù
I've been waiting for you for hours 何時間もあなたを待っていますよ nánjikàn mo anátà wo máttè imásù yo

2 (with *pp*: forming passives) …される …saréru
to be killed 殺される korósareru
the box had been opened 箱は開けられていた hakó wa àkérarete ita
the thief was nowhere to be seen 泥棒はどこにも見当らなかった doróbō wa dókò ni mo mîátaranakàtta

3 (in tag questions) …ね …né, …でしょう …deshô
it was fun, wasn't it? 楽しかったね tanóshikàtta né
he's good-looking, isn't he? 彼は男前だね kárè wa otôkomae da ne
she's back again, is she? 彼女はまた来たのか kánojò wa matá kita nò ká

4 (+ **to** + *infinitive*) …すべきである …subékì de aru
the house is to be sold 家は売る事になっている ié wà urú koto nî náttè iru
you're to be congratulated for all your work 立派な仕事を完成しておめでとう rippá na shigoto wo kansei shite ômédetô
he's not to open it 彼はそれを開けてはならない kárè wa soré wo akete wà naránaî

♦*vb* + *complement* **1** (*gen*) …である …de árù
I'm English 私はイングランド人です watákushi wa íngurandojîn desu
I'm tired/hot/cold 私は疲れた〔暑い, 寒い〕watákushi wa tsùkáretà〔atsúî,

samúî)

he's a doctor 彼は医者です kárè wa ishá desù

2 and 2 are 4 2足す2は4 ní tasù ní wà yón

she's tall/pretty 彼女は背が高い〔きれいです〕kánojò wa sé gà takáî〔kírèi desu〕

be careful/quiet/good! 注意〔静かに, 行儀よく〕して下さい chúî〔shízùka ni, gyógi yokù〕shité kudasài

2 (of health): *how are you?* お元気ですか o-génkì desu ká

he's very ill 彼は重病です kárè wa júbyō desù

I'm better now もう元気になりました mō génkì ni narímashìta

3 (of age) ...才です ...sài desu

how old are you? 何才ですか nànsai desu ka, (お) 幾つですか (ó)ikùtsu desu ka

I'm sixteen (years old) 16才です júrokusài desu

4 (cost): *how much was the meal?* 食事はいくらでしたか shokúji wa ikùra deshita ká

that'll be $5.75, please 5ドル75セント頂きます gódòru nanájùgoséntò itádakimasù

♦*vi* 1 (exist, occur etc) 存在する sónzai suru

the best singer that ever was 史上最高の歌手 shijó saikó no kashù

is there a God? 神は存在するか kámì wa sónzai surù kà

be that as it may それはそれとして sorè wa sore toshite

so be it それでよい sorè de yoî

2 (referring to place) ...にある〔いる〕...ni árù〔írú〕

I won't be here tomorrow 明日はここに来ません asú wa kokó ni kimásèn

Edinburgh is in Scotland エジンバラはスコットランドにある ejínbàra wa sukóttoràndo ni árù

it's on the table それはテーブルにあります sorè wa tēburu ni árìmasù

we've been here for ages 私たちはずっと前からここにいます watákushitàchi wa zuttó maè kara kokó ni ímàsù

3 (referring to movement) 行って来る itté kurù

where have you been? どこへ行っていましたか dókò e itté imashìta ká

I've been to the post office/to China 郵便局〔中国〕へ行って来ました yúbìnkyoku(chūgòku)e itté kimashìta

I've been in the garden 庭にいました niwá ni imashìta

♦*impers vb* 1 (referring to time): *it's 5 o'clock* 5時です gójì desu

it's the 28th of April 4月28日です shigátsu nijùhachínichi dèsu

2 (referring to distance): *it's 10 km to the village* 村まで10キロメーターです murá màde jukkíromètā desu

3 (referring to the weather): *it's too hot* 暑過ぎる atsúsugirù

it's too cold 寒過ぎる samúsugirù

it's windy today 今日は風が強い kyō wà kazé ga tsuyoî

4 (emphatic): *it's only me/the postman* ご心配なく, 私〔郵便屋さん〕です go-shínpai nakù, watákushi〔yúbin-yasan〕desu

it was Maria who paid the bill 勘定を払ったのはマリアでした kánjō wò harátta no wa márìa deshita

beach [bi:tʃ] *n* 浜 hamá

♦*vt* (boat) 浜に引上げる hamá ni hikíagerù

beacon [bi:'kən] *n* (lighthouse) 燈台 tódai; (marker) 信号 shingó

bead [bi:d] *n* (glass, plastic etc) ビーズ bízu; (of sweat) 玉 tamá

beak [bi:k] *n* (of bird) くちばし kuchíbashi

beaker [bi:'kə:r] *n* (cup) コップ koppú, グラス gúràsu

beam [bi:m] *n* (ARCHIT) はり harí; (of light) 光線 kósen

♦*vi* (smile) ほほえむ hohóemù

bean [bi:n] *n* マメ mamé

runner bean サヤインゲン sayáingèn

broad bean ソラマメ sorámàme

coffee bean コーヒーマメ kṓhīmàme

beansprouts [biːnˈsprauts] *npl* マメモヤ
シ mamémoyàshi

bear [beːr] *n* (ZOOL) クマ kumá
♦*vb* (*pt* **bore**, *pp* **borne**)
♦*vt* (carry, support: weight) 支える sasáerù; (: responsibility) 負う oú; (: cost) 払
う haráù; (tolerate: examination, scrutiny, person) ...に耐える ...ni taérù; (produce: children) 産む umú
♦*vi*: *to bear right/left* (AUT) 右〔左〕
に曲る mígì〔hidári〕ni magárù
to bear fruit ...に実がなる ...ni mi ga
narú

beard [biːrd] *n* ひげ higé

bearded [biːrdˈid] *adj* ひげのある higé no
arù

bearer [beːrˈəːr] *n* (of letter, news) 運ぶ
人 hakóbu hito; (of cheque) 持参人 jisán-
nin; (of title) 持っている人 mốttè irú hito

bearing [beːrˈiŋ] *n* (in air) 態度 tǎido; (connection) 関係 kaǹkei
to take a bearing 方角を確かめる hṓgaku wò tashíkamerù
to find one's bearings 自分の位置を確かめる jibún no ichi wò tashíkamerù

bearings [beːrˈiŋz] *npl* (*also:* **ball bearings**) ボールベアリング bōrubeàringu

bear out *vt* (person) ...の言う事を保証する ...no iu koto wo hoshṓ suru; (suspicions etc) ...の事実を証明する ...no jijítsu wo shṓmei suru

bear up *vi* (person) しっかりする shikkárì suru

beast [biːst] *n* (animal) 野獣 yajū́; (*inf:* person) いやなやつ iyá na yatsú

beastly [biːstˈliː] *adj* (awful: weather, child, trick etc) ひどい hídoì

beat [biːt] *n* (of heart) 鼓動 kodṓ; (MUS) 拍子 hyṓshi, ビート bī́to; (of policeman) 巡回区域 juǹkaikuìki
♦*vb* (*pt* **beat**, *pp* **beaten**)
♦*vt* (strike: wife, child) 殴る nagúrù; (eggs, cream) 泡立てる awádaterù, ホイップする hoíppù suru; (defeat: opponent) ...に勝つ ...ni kátsù; (: record) 破る yabúrù
♦*vi* (heart) 鼓動する kodṓ suru; (rain) た

たき付ける様に降る tatákitsukeru yṓ ni
fúrù; (wind) たたき付ける様に吹く tatákitsukeru yṓ ni fúkù; (drum) 鳴る narú
off the beaten track へんぴな所に heń-
pi na tokóro ni
to beat it (*inf*) ずらかる zurákarù

beating [biːtˈiŋ] *n* (punishment with
whip etc) むち打ち muchíuchi; (violence)
殴るけるの暴行 nagurukeru no bōkō

beat off *vt* (attack, attacker) 撃退する
gekítai suru

beat up *vt* (person) 打ちのめす uchínomesù; (mixture) かく拌する kakúhan suru; (eggs, cream) 泡立てる awádaterù, ホ
イップする hoíppù suru

beautiful [bjuːˈtəfəl] *adj* (woman, place)
美しい utsúkushiî; (day, weather) 素晴ら
しい subárashiî

beautifully [bjuːˈtəfəliː] *adv* (play music,
sing, drive etc) 見事に mígòto ni

beauty [bjuːˈtiː] *n* (quality) 美しさ utsú-
kushīsà; (beautiful woman) 美女 bíjò, 美
人 bíjin; (*fig:* attraction) 魅力 miryóku

beauty salon *n* 美容院 bíyṓin

beauty spot *n* (*BRIT:* TOURISM) 景勝
地 keíshōchì

beaver [biːˈvəːr] *n* (ZOOL) ビーバー bī́bā

became [bikeimˈ] *pt of* **become**

because [bikɔːzˈ] *conj* ...だから ...dá kàra, ...であるので ...de árù nodé
because of ...のため ...no tamé, ...のせい
で ...no seí de

beck [bek] *n:* *to be at the beck and
call of* ...の言いなりになっている ...no
iínari ni natté irú

beckon [bekˈən] *vt* (*also:* **beckon to:** person) ...に来いと合図する ...ni kói to aízu
suru

become [bikʌmˈ] (*pt* **became**, *pp* **become**)
vi ...になる ...ni nárù
to become fat 太る futórù
to become thin やせる yasérù

becoming [bikʌmˈiŋ] *adj* (behavior) ふさ
わしい fusáwashiî; (clothes) 似合う niáù

bed [bed] *n* (piece of furniture) ベッド
béddò; (of coal, clay) 層 sṓ; (bottom: of
river, sea) 底 sokó; (of flowers) 花壇 kádàn

to go to bed 寝る nerú

bed and breakfast *n* (place) 民宿 mińshuku; (terms) 朝食付き宿泊 chōshokutsuki shukúhaku

bedclothes [bed'klouz] *npl* シーツと毛布 shītsu to mōfu

bedding [bed'iŋ] *n* 寝具 shíŋgu

bedlam [bed'ləm] *n* 大騒ぎ ōsawàgi

bedraggled [bidræg'əld] *adj* (person, clothes, hair) びしょ濡れの bishōnure no

bedridden [bed'ridən] *adj* 寝たきりの netákiri no

bedroom [bed'ru:m] *n* 寝室 shiñshitsu

bedside [bed'said] *n*: *at someone's bedside* ...の枕元に ...no makúramòto ni

bedsit(ter) [bed'sit(ər)] (*BRIT*) *n* 寝室兼居間 shiñshitsu keñ imá

bedspread [bed'spred] *n* ベッドカバー beddókabà

bedtime [bed'taim] *n* 寝る時刻 nerú jíkòku

bee [bi:] *n* ミツバチ mitsúbachi

beech [bi:tʃ] *n* (tree) ブナ búnà; (wood) ブナ材 bunázai

beef [bi:f] *n* 牛肉 gyúniku

roast beef ローストビーフ rōsutobīfu

beefburger [bi:f'bə:rgə:r] *n* ハンバーガー hañbāgà

Beefeater [bi:f'i:tə:r] *n* ロンドン塔の守衛 rondontō nò shuéi

beehive [bi:'haiv] *n* ミツバチの巣箱 mitsúbachi no súbàko

beeline [bi:'lain] *n*: *to make a beeline for* まっしぐらに...に向かう masshígùra ni ...ni mukáu

been [bin] *pp of* be

beer [bi:r] *n* ビール bīru

beet [bi:t] *n* (vegetable) サトウダイコン satódaìkon, ビート bīto; (*US: also*: **red beet**) ビーツ bītsu

beetle [bi:t'əl] *n* 甲虫 kốchū

beetroot [bi:t'ru:t] (*BRIT*) *n* ビーツ bītsu

before [bifɔ:r'] *prep* (of time, space) ...の前に〔で〕 ...no máè ni〔de〕

♦*conj* ...する前に ...surú maè ni

♦*adv* (time, space) 前に máè ni

before going 行く前に ikú maè ni

before she goes 彼女が行く前に kánòjo ga ikú maè ni

the week before (week past) 1週間前 isshúkan maè

I've never seen it before これまで私はそれを見た事はない koré madè watákushi wà soré wò mitá koto wà nái

beforehand [bifɔ:r'hænd] *adv* あらかじめ arákajime, 前もって maémottè

beg [beg] *vi* (as beggar) こじきをする kojíki wò suru

♦*vt* (*also*: **beg for**: food, money) こい求める koímotomerù; (: forgiveness, mercy etc) 願う negáù

to beg someone to do something ...に...してくれと頼む ...ni ...shité kurè to tanómù ¶ *see also* pardon

began [bigæn'] *pt of* begin

beggar [beg'ə:r] *n* こじき kojíki

begin [bigin'] (*pt* began, *pp* begun) *vt* 始める hajímeru

♦*vi* 始まる hajímaru

to begin doing/to do something ...し始める ...shihajímeru

beginner [bigin'ə:r] *n* 初心者 shoshíñsha

beginning [bigin'iŋ] *n* 始め hajíme

begun [bigʌn'] *pp of* begin

behalf [bihæf'] *n*: *on behalf of* (as representative of) ...を代表して ...wo daíhyō shité; (for benefit of) ...のために ...no tamé ni

on my/his behalf 私〔彼〕のために watákushi〔kárè〕nò tamé ni

behave [biheiv'] *vi* (person) 振舞う furúmaù; (well: *also*: **behave oneself**) 行儀良くする gyógi yokù suru

behavior [biheiv'jə:r] (*BRIT* **behaviour**) *n* 行動 kốdō

behead [bihed'] *vt* ...の首を切る ...no kubí wò kírù

beheld [biheld'] *pt, pp of* behold

behind [bihaind'] *prep* (position: at the back of) ...の後ろに〔で〕 ...no ushíro ni〔de〕; (supporting) ...を支援して ...wo shién shite; (lower in rank, etc) ...に劣って ...ni otótte

♦*adv* (at/towards the back) 後ろに〔の方へ〕 ushíro ni〔no hố e〕; (leave, stay) 後に

átò ni

♦*n* (buttocks) しり shirí

to be behind (schedule) 遅れている okúrete irú

behind the scenes (fig) 非公式に hikóshiki ni

behold [bihould'] (*pt, pp* **beheld**) *vt* 見る mírù

beige [beiʒ] *adj* ベージュ bḗju

Beijing [bei'dʒiŋ'] *n* 北京 pḗkìn

being [bi:'iŋ] *n* (creature) 生き物 ikímonò; (existence) 存在 sońzai

Beirut [beiru:t'] *n* ベイルート beírùto

belated [bilei'tid] *adj* (thanks, welcome) 遅ればせの okúrebase no

belch [beltʃ] *vi* げっぷをする geppú wò suru

♦*vt* (*gen*: belch out: smoke etc) 噴出する fuńshutsu suru

belfry [bel'fri:] *n* 鐘楼 shōrō

Belgian [bel'dʒən] *adj* ベルギーの berúgì no

♦*n* ベルギー人 berúgìjin

Belgium [bel'dʒəm] *n* ベルギー berúgì

belie [bilai'] *vt* (contradict) 隠す kakúsù; (disprove) 反証する hańshō suru

belief [bili:f'] *n* (opinion) 信念 shíñnen; (trust, faith) 信仰 shińkō

believe [bili:v'] *vt* 信じる shiñjirù

♦*vi* 信じる shiñjirù

to believe in (God, ghosts) ...の存在を信じる ...no sońzai wò shiñjirù; (method) ...が良いと考える ...ga yóì to kańgaerù

believer [bili:v'ə:r] *n* (in idea, activity) ...が良いと考える人 ...ga yóì to kańgaeru hito; (REL) 信者 shińja

belittle [bilit'əl] *vt* 軽視する keíshi suru

bell [bel] *n* (of church) 鐘 kané; (small) 鈴 suzú; (on door, *also* electric) 呼び鈴 yobírin, ベル bérù

belligerent [bəlidʒ'ə:rənt] *adj* (person, attitude) けんか腰の keńkagoshi no

bellow [bel'ou] *vi* (bull) 大声で鳴く ồgoe de nakú; (person) どなる donárù

bellows [bel'ouz] *npl* (for fire) ふいご fuígo

belly [bel'i:] *n* (ANAT: of person, animal) 腹 hará

belong [bilɔːŋ'] *vi*: *to belong to* (person) ...の物である ...no monó de arù; (club etc) ...に所属している ...ni shozóku shite irù, ...の会員である ...no kaíiñ de arù

this book belongs here この本はここにしまうことになっている konó hoñ wa kokó ni shimaù kotó ni nattè irú

belongings [bilɔːŋ'iŋz] *npl* 持物 mochímòno

beloved [bilʌv'id] *adj* (person) 最愛の saíai no; (place) 大好きな daísuki na; (thing) 愛用の aíyō no

below [bilou'] *prep* (beneath) ...の下に〔で〕 ...no shitá ni(de); (less than: level, rate) ...より低く ...yórì hikúkù

♦*adv* (beneath) 下に shitá ni

see below (in letter etc) 下記参照 kakísañshō

belt [belt] *n* (of leather etc: *also* TECH) ベルト berúto; (*also*: belt of land) 地帯 chítài

♦*vt* (thrash) 殴る nagúrù

beltway [belt'wei] (*US*) *n* (AUT: ring road) 環状道路 kańjōdòro

bemused [bimju:zd'] *adj* (person, expression) ぼう然とした bōzen to shitá

bench [bentʃ] *n* (seat) ベンチ bénchi; (work bench) 作業台 sagyōdai; (*BRIT*: POL) 議員席 giíñseki

the Bench (LAW: judges) 裁判官 saíbañkan ◇総称 sṓshō

bend [bend] (*pt, pp* **bent**) *vt* (leg, arm, pipe) 曲げる magéru

♦*vi* (person) かがむ kagámu

♦*n* (*BRIT*: in road) カーブ kábu; (in pipe, river) 曲った所 magátta tokoro

bend down *vi* 身をかがめる mi wo kagámeru

bend over *vi* 身をかがめる mi wo kagámeru

beneath [bini:θ'] *prep* (position) ...の下に〔で〕 ...no shitá ni(de); (unworthy of) ...のこけんに関わる ...no kokén ni kakawarù

♦*adv* 下に shitá ni

benefactor [ben'əfæktəːr] *n* (to person, institution) 恩人 ońjin

beneficial [benəfiʃ'əl] *adj* (effect, influence) 有益な yū́eki na

beneficial (to) (...に) 有益な (...ni) yū́eki na

benefit [ben'əfit] *n* (advantage) 利益 ríèki; (money) 手当て tēate

♦*vt* ...の利益になる ...no ríèki ni narù

♦*vi: he'll benefit from it* それは彼のためになるだろう sorè wà kárè no tamé ni narù darò

Benelux [ben'əlʌks] *n* ベネルクス benérukùsu

benevolent [bənev'ələnt] *adj* (person) 温和な ofiwa na; (organization) 慈善の jizén no

benign [binain'] *adj* (person, smile) 優しい yasáshii; (MED) 良性の ryōsei no

bent [bent] *pt, pp of* **bend**

♦*n* 才能 saínō

♦*adj* (*inf*: corrupt) 不正な fuséi na

to be bent on doing ...しようと心掛けている ...shíyò to kokórogakete irù

bequest [bikwest'] *n* (to person, charity) 遺贈 izó

bereaved [biri:vd'] *n: the bereaved* 喪中の人々 mochū no hitóbìto

beret [bərei'] *n* ベレー帽 bérèbō

Berlin [bə:rlin'] *n* ベルリン berúrin

berm [bə:rm] (*US*) *n* (AUT) 路肩 rokáta

Bermuda [bə:rmju:d'ə] *n* バーミューダ bámyùda

berry [be:r'i:] *n* ベリー berí ◇総称 sốshō

berserk [bə:rsə:rk'] *adj: to go berserk* (madman, crowd) 暴れ出す abáredasù

berth [bə:rθ] *n* (on ship or train) 寝台 shifídai; (for ship) バース bāsu

♦*vi* (ship) 接岸する setsúgan suru

beseech [bisi:tʃ'] (*pt, pp* **besought**) *vt* (person, God) ...に嘆願する ...ni tafígan suru

beset [biset'] (*pt, pp* **beset**) *vt* (subj: fears, doubts, difficulties) 襲う osóu

beside [bisaid'] *prep* (next to) ...の横に〔で〕...no yokó ni(de)

to be beside oneself (with anger) 逆上している gyakújō shite irù

that's beside the point それは問題外です sorè wà mofídaigài desu

besides [bisaidz'] *adv* (in addition) それ

に sorè ni, その上 sonó ue; (in any case) とに角 toníkaku

♦*prep* (in addition to, as well as) ...の外に ...no hoká ni

besiege [bisi:dʒ'] *vt* (town) 包囲攻撃する hốikōgeki suru; (*fig*: subj: journalists, fans) ...に押寄せる ...ni oshíyoserù

besought [bisɔ:t'] *pt, pp of* **beseech**

best [best] *adj* (quality, suitability, extent) 最も良い mottómò yoî

♦*adv* 最も良く mottómò yókù

the best part of (quantity) ...の大部分 ...no dafbubun

at best 良くても yókùte mo

to make the best of something ...を出来るだけ我慢する ...wo dekíru dake gamañ suru

to do one's best 最善を尽す saízen wo tsukúsù, ベストを尽くす bésùto wo tsukúsù

to the best of my knowledge 私の知っている限りでは watákushi no shittè irú kagiri de wa

to the best of my ability 私に出来る限り watákushi ni dekírù kagíri

best man *n* 新郎付添い役 shifírōtsukiso-iyàku

bestow [bistou'] *vt* (honor, title): *to bestow something on someone* ...に...を授ける ...ni ...wo sazúkerù

bestseller [best'selə:r] *n* (book) ベストセラー besútoserà

bet [bet] *n* (wager) かけ kaké

♦*vb* (*pt, pp* **bet** *or* **betted**)

♦*vt* (wager): *to bet someone something* ...と...をかける ...to ...wo kakérù

♦*vi* (wager) かける kakérù

to bet money on something ...に金をかける ...ni kané wò kakérù

betray [bitrei'] *vt* (friends, country, trust, confidence) 裏切る urágirù

betrayal [bitrei'əl] *n* (action) 裏切り urágiri

better [bet'ə:r] *adj* (quality, skill, sensation) より良い yorí yoî; (health) 良くなった yókù nattá

♦*adv* より良く yorí yókù

♦*vt* (score) ...より高い得点をする ...yórì

takáî tokúten wo suru; (record) 破る ya-búrù

♦*n*: *to get the better of* ...に勝つ ...ni kátsù

you had better do it あなたはそうした方が良い anátá wa sô shita hô ga yoî

he thought better of it 彼は考え直した kárê wa kañgaenaoshita

to get better (MED) 良くなる yókù naru, 回復する kaífuku suru

better off *adj* (wealthier) ...より金があ る ...yórî kané ga arù; (more comfortable etc) ...の方が良い ...no hô ga yoî

betting [bet'iŋ] *n* (gambling, odds) かけ 事 kakégòto, ギャンブル gyáñburu

betting shop (*BRIT*) *n* 私営馬券売り場 shiéîbaken-urîba

between [bitwi:n'] *prep* (all senses) ...の 間に〔で〕...no aîda ni〔de〕

♦*adv* 間に aîda ni

beverage [bev'ə:ridʒ] *n* 飲物 nomímòno, 飲料 íñryô

beware [biwe:r'] *vi*: *to beware (of)* (dog, fire) (...を) 用心する (...wo) yójin suru

「*beware of the dog*」猛犬注意 môkenchûi

bewildered [biwil'də:rd] *adj* (stunned, confused) 当惑した tôwaku shita

bewitching [biwitʃ'iŋ] *adj* (smile, person) うっとりさせる uttórî saséru

beyond [bi:ɑ:nd'] *prep* (in space) ...より先 に〔で〕...yórî sakí ni〔de〕; (past: understanding) ...を越えて ...wo koéte; (after: date) ...以降に ...îkô ni; (above) ...以上に ...íjô ni

♦*adv* (in space, time) 先に sakí ni

beyond doubt 疑いもなく utágai mo nakú

beyond repair 修理不可能で shûri fukánô de

bias [bai'əs] *n* (prejudice) 偏見 heñken

bias(s)ed [bai'əst] *adj* (jury) 偏見を持っ た heñken wo mottá; (judgement, reporting) 偏見に基づいた heñken ni motózuîta

bib [bib] *n* (child's) よだれ掛け yodárekàke

Bible [bai'bəl] *n* (REL) 聖書 seîsho, バイ ブル baîburu

biblical [bib'likəl] *adj* 聖書の seîsho no

bibliography [bibli:ɑ:g'rəfi:] *n* (in text) 文献目録 buñkenmokûroku

bicarbonate of soda [baikɑ:r'bənit-] *n* 重炭酸ソーダ jûtansansôda, 重曹 jûsô

bicker [bik'ə:r] *vi* (squabble) 口論する kôron suru

bicycle [bai'sikəl] *n* 自転車 jitéñsha

bid [bid] *n* (at auction) 付値 tsukéñe; (in tender) 入札 nyûsatsu; (attempt) 試み kokóromi

♦*vb* (*pt* **bade** *or* **bid**, *pp* **bidden** *or* **bid**)

♦*vi* (at auction) 競りに加わる serî ni kuwawarù

♦*vt* (offer) ...と値を付ける ...to né wò tsukérù

to bid someone good day (hello) ...に今 日はと言う ...ni konnichi wa to iu; (farewell) ...にさようならと言う ...ni sayônara to iu

bidder [bid'ə:r] *n*: *the highest bidder* 最高入札者 saîkônyûsatsùsha

bidding [bid'iŋ] *n* (at auction) 競り serî

bide [baid] *vt*: *to bide one's time* (for opportunity) 時期を待つ jíkì wo mátsù

bidet [bi:dei'] *n* ビデ bídè

bifocals [baifou'kəlz] *npl* 二重焦点眼鏡 nijûshôtenmegâne

big [big] *adj* (gen) 大きい ôkiî, 大きな ôkina

big brother 兄 áni, 兄さん nîisan

big sister 姉 ané, 姉さん nêsan

bigamy [big'əmi:] *n* 重婚 jûkon

big dipper [-dip'ə:r] (*BRIT*) *n* (at fair) ジェットコースター jettôkôsutâ

bigheaded [big'hedid] *adj* うぬぼれた u-núboreta

bigot [big'ət] *n* (on race, religion) 偏狭な 人 heñkyô na hito

bigoted [big'ətid] *adj* (on race, religion) 偏狭な heñkyô na

bigotry [big'ətri:] *n* 偏狭さ heñkyôsà

big top *n* (at circus) 大テント ôteñto

bike [baik] *n* (bicycle) 自転車 jitéñsha

bikini [biki:'ni:] *n* ビキニ bíkìni

bilateral [bailæt'ə:rəl] *adj* (agreement)

双務的な sṓmuteki na
bile [bail] n (BIO) 胆汁 tańjū
bilingual [bailiŋ'gwəl] adj (dictionary) 二か国語の nikákokugo no; (secretary) 二か国語を話せる nikákokugo wò hanáserù
bill [bil] n (account) 勘定書 kańjōgaki; (invoice) 請求書 seíkyūsho; (POL) 法案 hṓan; (US: banknote) 紙幣 shíhèi; (of bird) くちばし kuchíbashi; (THEATER: of show: on the bill) 番組 bańgumi
「post no bills」張紙厳禁 harígamigenkin
to fit/fill the bill (fig) 丁度いい chōdo iî
billboard [bil'bɔːrd] n 広告板 kṓkokuban
billet [bil'it] n (MIL) 軍人宿舎 guńjinshukùsha
billfold [bil'fould] (US) n 財布 saífu
billiards [bil'jəːrdz] n ビリヤード biríyàdo
billion [bil'jən] n (BRIT) 兆 chṓ; (US) 10億 jûoku
bin [bin] n (BRIT: for rubbish) ごみ入れ gomíire, (container) 貯蔵箱 chózōbako, 瓶 bíñ
binary [bai'nəːri:] adj (MATH) 二進法の nishínhō no
bind [baind] (pt, pp bound) vt (tie, tie together) 縛る shibárù; (constrain) 束縛する sokúbaku suru; (book) 製本する seíhon suru
♦n (inf: nuisance) いやな事 iyá na koto
binding [bain'diŋ] adj (contract) 拘束力のある kōsokuryòku no aru
binge [bindʒ] (inf) n: to go on a binge (drink a lot) 酒浸りになる sakébitari ni narù
bingo [biŋ'gou] n ビンゴ bíñgo
binoculars [bənɑːk'jələːrz] npl 双眼鏡 sṓgankyō
biochemistry [baioukem'istri:] n 生化学 seíkagàku
biography [baiɑːg'rəfi:] n 伝記 deñki
biological [baiɑːlɑdʒ'ikəl] adj (science, warfare) 生物学の seíbutsugàku no; (washing powder) 酵素洗剤 kṓsoseñzai
biology [baiɑːl'ədʒi:] n 生物学 seíbutsu-

gàku
birch [bəːrtʃ] n (tree) カバノキ kabá no ki; (wood) カバ材 kabázài
bird [bəːrd] n (ZOOL) 鳥 torí; (BRIT: inf: girl) 女の子 ofina no ko
bird's-eye view [bəːrd'wɑːtʃəːr] n (aerial view) 全景 zeńkei; (overview) 概観 gaíkan
bird-watcher [bəːrd'wɑːtʃəːr] n バードウォッチャー bàdowotchā
bird-watching [bəːrd'wɑːtʃiŋ] n バードウォッチング bàdowotchìngu
Biro [bai'rou] ® n ボールペン bṓrupen
birth [bəːrθ] n (of baby, animal, also fig) 誕生 tańjō
to give birth to (BIO: subj: woman, animal) …を生む …wo umú
birth certificate n 出生証明書 shusshṓ〔shusséi〕shṓmeisho
birth control n (policy) 産児制限 sańjiseìgen; (methods) 避妊 hinín
birthday [bəːrθ'dei] n 誕生日 tańjòbi
♦cpd (cake, card, present etc) 誕生日の tańjòbi no ¶ see also happy
birthplace [bəːrθ'pleis] n (country, town etc) 出生地 shusshṓchì〔shusséichì〕, 生れ故郷 umárekokyò; (house etc) 生家 seíka
birth rate n 出生率 shusshṓritsu〔shussèiritsu〕
Biscay [bis'kei] n: the Bay of Biscay ビスケー湾 bisúkēwan
biscuit [bis'kit] (BRIT) n ビスケット bisúkettò
bisect [baisekt'] vt (angle etc) 二等分する nitṓbun suru
bishop [biʃ'əp] n (REL: Catholic etc) 司教 shíkyò; (: Protestant) 監督 kańtoku; (: Greek Orthodox) 主教 shúkyò; (CHESS) ビショップ bíshòppu
bit [bit] pt of **bite**
♦n (piece) 欠けら kakéra; (COMPUT) ビット bíttò; (of horse) はみ hámì
a bit of 少しの sukóshi no, ちょっとの chottó no
a bit mad ちょっと頭がおかしい chottó atáma ga okáshiì
a bit dangerous ちょっと危ない chottó abúnaì

bit by bit 少しずつ sukóshi zutsù

bitch [bitʃ] *n* (dog) 雌犬 mesúinu; (*inf!*: woman) あま ámà

bite [bait] (*pt* bit, *pp* bitten) *vt* (subj: person) かむ kámù; (: dog etc) ...にかみ付く ...ni kamítsuku; (: insect etc) 刺す sásù
♦*vi* (dog etc) かみ付く kamítsuku; (insect etc) 刺す sásù
♦*n* (insect bite) 虫刺され mushísasàre; (mouthful) 一口 hitókùchi
to bite one's nails つめをかむ tsumé wo kamù
let's have a bite (to eat) (*inf*) 何か食べよう nánì ka tabéyò

bitten [bit'ən] *pp of* **bite**

bitter [bit'əːr] *adj* (person) 恨みを持った urámì wò mottá; (taste, experience, disappointment) 苦い nigáì; (wind) 冷たい tsumétaì; (struggle) 激しい hagéshiì; (criticism) 辛らつな shifiratsu na
♦*n* (*BRIT*: beer) ビター bitá ◇ホップの利いた苦いビール hoppù no kífta nigáì bìru

bitterness [bit'əːrnis] *n* (anger) 恨み urámi; (bitter taste) 苦み nigámi

bizarre [bizɑːr'] *adj* (conversation, contraption) 奇妙な kímyõ na

blab [blæb] (*inf*) *vi* (to the press) しゃべる shabérù

black [blæk] *adj* (color) 黒い kuróì; (person) 黒人の kokújin no; (tea, coffee) ブラックの burákkù no
♦*n* (color) 黒 kúrò; (person): *Black* 黒人 kokújin
♦*vt* (*BRIT*: INDUSTRY) ボイコットする boíkottò suru
black humor ブラックユーモア burákkuyùmoa
to give someone a black eye ...を殴って目にあざを作る ...wo nagútte me ni azá wo tsukúrù
black and blue (bruised) あざだらけのazá daràke no
to be in the black (in credit) 黒字である kuróji de arù

blackberry [blæk'beːriː] *n* ブラックベリー burákkuberì ◇キイチゴの一種 kiíchigo no isshù

blackbird [blæk'bəːrd] *n* (European bird) クロウタドリ kuróutadòri

blackboard [blæk'bɔːrd] *n* 黒板 kokúban

black coffee *n* ブラックコーヒー burákku kòhì

blackcurrant [blækkʌr'ənt] *n* クロスグリ kurósugùri

blacken [blæk'ən] *vt* (*fig*: name, reputation) 汚す kegásù

black ice *n* (on road) 凍結路面 tóketsuromèn

blackleg [blæk'leg] (*BRIT*) *n* (INDUSTRY) スト破り sutóyabùri

blacklist [blæk'list] *n* ブラックリスト burákkurisùto

blackmail [blæk'meil] *n* ゆすり yusúri
♦*vt* ゆする yusúru

black market *n* やみ市 yamíchi

blackout [blæk'aut] *n* (MIL) 灯火管制 tókakañsei; (power cut) 停電 teíden; (TV, RADIO) 放送中止 hósōchūshi; (faint) 一時的意識喪失 ichíjitekiishìkisòshitsu, ブラックアウト burákkuaùto

Black Sea *n*: *the Black Sea* 黒海 kókkài

black sheep *n* (*fig*) 持て余し者 motéamashimono

blacksmith [blæk'smiθ] *n* 鍛冶屋 kajíya

black spot *n* (*BRIT*: AUT) 事故多発地点 jikótahátsuchitèn; (: for unemployment etc) ...が深刻になっている地域 ...ga shifikoku ni nattè irú chiìki

bladder [blæd'əːr] *n* (ANAT) ぼうこう bókō

blade [bleid] *n* (of knife, sword) 刃 hà; (of propeller) 羽根 hané
a blade of grass 草の葉 kusá no ha

blame [bleim] *n* (for error, crime) 責任 sekínin
♦*vt*: *to blame someone for something* ...を...のせいにする ...wo ...no seí ni suru
to be to blame 責任が...にある sekínin ga ...ni arù

blameless [bleim'lis] *adj* (person) 潔白な keppáku na

bland [blænd] *adj* (taste, food) 味気ない ajíke naì

blank [blæŋk] *adj* (paper etc) 空白の kú-

haku no; (look) ぼう然とした bōzen to shitá
♦n (of memory) 空白 kúhaku; (on form) 空所 kúsho; (also: **blank cartridge**) 空包 kúhō
a blank sheet of paper 白紙 hakúshi

blank check n 金額未記入の小切手 kiñgakumiki-nyū no kogíttè

blanket [blæŋ'kit] n (of cloth) 毛布 mófu; (of snow, fog etc) 一面の... ichímen no ...

blare [ble:r] vi (brass band, horns, radio) 鳴り響く narîhibikù

blasé [blɑ:zei'] adj (reaction, tone) 無関心な mukáñshin na

blasphemy [blæs'fəmi:] n (REL) 冒とく bótoku

blast [blæst] n (of wind) 突風 toppú; (of explosive) 爆発 bakúhatsu
♦vt (blow up) 爆破する bakúha suru

blast-off [blæst'ɔ:f] n (SPACE) 発射 hasshá

blatant [blei'tənt] adj (discrimination, bias) 露骨な rokótsu na

blaze [bleiz] n (fire) 火事 kájì; (fig: of color, glory) きらめき kirámeki; (: publicity) 大騒ぎ ōsawàgi
♦vi (fire) 燃え盛る moésakerù; (guns) 続け様に発砲する tsuzúkezama ni happō suru; (fig: eyes) 怒りで燃える ikári de moérù
♦vt: *to blaze a trail* (fig) 先べんを付ける señben wo tsúkerù

blazer [blei'zə:r] n (of school, team etc) ブレザー burézā

bleach [bli:tʃ] n (also: **household bleach**) 漂白剤 hyōhakuzài
♦vt (fabric) 漂白する hyōhaku suru

bleached [bli:tʃt] adj (hair) 漂白した hyōhaku shitá

bleachers [bli:'tʃə:rz] (US) npl (SPORT) 外野席 gaíyasèki

bleak [bli:k] adj (countryside) もの寂しい monósabishiì; (weather) 悪い warúì; (prospect, situation) 暗い kurái; (smile) 悲しそうな kanáshisò na

bleary-eyed [bli:'ri:aid] adj 目がしょぼしょぼしている me ga shobòshobo shité

irù

bleat [bli:t] vi (goat, sheep) 鳴く nakú

bled [bled] pt, pp of **bleed**

bleed [bli:d] (pt, pp bled) vi (MED) 出血する shukkétsu suru
my nose is bleeding 鼻血が出ている hanáji ga dete irù

bleeper [bli:'pə:r] n (device) ポケットベル pokétto berù

blemish [blem'iʃ] n (on skin) 染み shimí; (on fruit) 傷 kizú; (on reputation) 汚点 otéñ

blend [blend] n (of tea, whisky) 混合 kóñgō, ブレンド buréndo
♦vt 混ぜ合せる mázěawaserù, 混合する kóñgō suru
♦vi (colors etc: also: **blend in**) 溶け込む tokékomù

bless [bles] (pt, pp blessed or blest) vt (REL) 祝福する shukúfuku suru
bless you! (after sneeze) お大事に o-dáiji ni

blessing [bles'iŋ] n (approval) 承認 shōnin; (godsend) 恵み megúmi; (REL) 祝福 shukúfuku

blew [blu:] pt of **blow**

blight [blait] vt (hopes, life etc) 駄目にする damé ni suru

blimey [blai'mi:] (BRIT: inf) excl おやおや oyá

blind [blaind] adj (MED) 盲目の mómoku no; (pej) めくら mekúra no; (euphemistically) 目の不自由な me no fujìyū na; (fig): **blind (to)** (...を) 見る目がない (...wo) mirù mé ga naì
♦n (for window) ブラインド buráindo; (: also: **Venetian blind**) ベネシアンブラインド benéshian buraíndo
♦vt (MED) 失明させる shitsúmei saserù; (dazzle) ...の目をくらます ...no me wo kurámasù; (deceive) だます damásù
the blind (blind people) 盲人 mójiñ ◇総称 sōshō

blind alley n (fig) 行き詰り yukízumari

blind corner (BRIT) n 見通しの悪い曲り角 mitōshi no waruì magárikadò

blindfold [blaind'fould] n 目隠し mekákùshi

♦*adj* 目隠しをした mekákùshi wo shitá

♦*adv* 目隠しをして mekákùshi wo shitê

♦*vt* 目隠しする mekákùshi suru

blindly [blaind'li:] *adv* (without seeing) よく見ないで yókù mináide; (without thinking) めくら滅法に mekúrameppó ni

blindness [blaind'nis] *n* (MED) 盲目 mōmoku; (euphemistically) 目の障害 me no shōgai

blind spot *n* (AUT) 死角 shikáku; (*fig*: weak spot) 盲点 mōten

blink [bliŋk] *vi* (person, animal) 瞬く mabátakù; (light) 点滅する tenmetsu suru

blinkers [bliŋk'ə:rz] *npl* 馬の目隠し umá no mekákùshi

bliss [blis] *n* (complete happiness) 至福 shifúku

blister [blis'tə:r] *n* (on skin) 水膨れ mizúbukùre; (in paint, rubber) 気胞 kihō

♦*vi* (paint) 気胞ができる kihô ga dekirù

blithely [blaið'li:] *adv* (proceed, assume) 軽率に keísotsu ni

blitz [blits] *n* (MIL) 空襲 kūshū

blizzard [bliz'ə:rd] *n* 吹雪 fubúki, ブリザード burízàdo

bloated [blou'tid] *adj* (face, stomach: swollen) はれた haréta; (person: full) たらふく食べた taráfùku tabèta

blob [blɑːb] *n* (of glue, paint) 滴 shizúku; (something indistinct) はっきり見えないもの hakkírì miénài monō

bloc [blɑːk] *n* (POL) 連合 reñgō, ブロック burōkkù

block [blɑːk] *n* (of buildings) 街区 gáìku, ブロック burōkkù; (of stone, wood) ブロック burōkkù; (in pipes) 障害物 shōgaìbutsu

♦*vt* (entrance, road) 塞ぐ fuságu; (progress) 邪魔する jamá suru

block of flats (*BRIT*) マンション mañshon

mental block 精神的ブロック seíshinteki burokkù

blockade [blɑːkeid'] *n* 封鎖 fúsa

blockage [blɑːk'idʒ] *n* 閉そく heísoku

blockbuster [blɑːk'bʌstəːr] *n* (film, book) センセーション señsēshon

block letters *npl* 活字体 katsújitai

bloke [blouk] (*BRIT*: *inf*) *n* 男 otóko, 野郎 yárō

blond(e) [blɑːnd] *adj* (hair) 金髪の kiñpatsu no, ブロンドの burōndo no

♦*n* (woman) 金髪の女性 kiñpatsu no joséi, ブロンド burōndo

blood [blʌd] *n* (BIO) 血 chi, 血液 ketsúèki

blood donor *n* 献血者 keñketsùsha

blood group *n* 血液型 ketsúekigata

bloodhound [blʌd'haund] *n* ブラッドハウンド buráddohaùndo

blood poisoning [-poi'zəniŋ] *n* 敗血症 haíketsushō

blood pressure *n* 血圧 ketsúatsu

bloodshed [blʌd'ʃed] *n* 流血 ryūketsu

bloodshot [blʌd'ʃɑːt] *adj* (eyes) 充血した jūketsu shitá

bloodstream [blʌd'striːm] *n* 血流 ketsúryū

blood test *n* 血液検査 ketsúekikeñsa

bloodthirsty [blʌd'θə:rsti:] *adj* (tyrant, regime) 血に飢えた chi ni úèta

blood vessel *n* 血管 kekkán

bloody [blʌd'i:] *adj* (battle) 血みどろの chimídoro no; (nose) 鼻血を出した hanáji wo dashíta; (*BRIT*: *inf!*): *this bloody …* くそったれ… kusóttarè…

bloody strong/good (*inf!*) すごく強い〔良い〕sugókù tsuyóì〔yoì〕

bloody-minded [blʌd'i:main'did] (*BRIT*: *inf*) *adj* 意地悪な ijíwàru na

bloom [bluːm] *n* (BOT: flower) 花 haná

♦*vi* (tree) …の花が咲く … no haná ga sakú; (flower) 咲く sakú

blossom [blɑːs'əm] *n* (BOT) 花 haná

♦*vi* (BOT) 花が咲く haná ga sakú; (*fig*): *to blossom into* 成長して…になる seíchōshite …ni narú

blot [blɑːt] *n* (on text) 染み shimí; (*fig*: on name etc) 傷 kizú

♦*vt* (with ink etc) 汚す yogósu

blotchy [blɑːtʃ'i:] *adj* (complexion) 染みだらけの shimídaràke no

blot out *vt* (view) 見えなくする miénàku suru; (memory) 消す kesú

blotting paper [blɑːt'iŋ-] *n* 吸取り紙 suítorigàmi

blow [blou] n (punch etc: also fig) 打撃 dagéki; (with sword) 一撃 ichígeki

♦vb (pt **blew**, pp **blown**)

♦vi (wind) 吹く fúkù; (person) 息を吹掛ける íkì wo fukíkakerù

♦vt (subj: wind) 吹飛ばす fukítobasù; (instrument, whistle) 吹く fúkù; (fuse) 飛ばす tobásu

to blow one's nose 鼻をかむ haná wo kamú

blow away vt 吹飛ばす fukítobasù

blow down vt (tree) 吹倒す fukítaosù

blow-dry [blou'drai] n (hairstyle) ブロー仕上げ buróshiàge

blowlamp [blou'læmp] (BRIT) n = **blowtorch**

blow off vt (hat etc) 吹飛ばす fukítobasù

blow out vi (fire, flame) 吹消す fukíkesù

blow-out [blou'aut] n (of tire) パンク pañku

blow over vi (storm) 静まる shizúmarù; (crisis) 収まる osámarù

blowtorch [blou'tɔːrtʃ] n ブローランプ burốraǹpu, トーチランプ tốchiraǹpu

blow up vi (storm) 起きる okírù; (crisis) 起る okórù

♦vt (bridge: destroy) 爆破する bakúha suru; (tire: inflate) 膨らます fukúramasu; (PHOT: enlarge) 引延ばす hikínobasù

blue [bluː] adj (color) 青い aóì, ブルーの burū no; (depressed) 憂うつな yū́utsu na

blue film ポルノ映画 porúnoeìga

blue joke わいせつなジョーク waísetsu na jōku

out of the blue (fig) 青天のへきれきの様に seften no hekirekì no yō ni

bluebell [bluː'bel] n ツルボ tsurúbð

bluebottle [bluː'bɑːtəl] n (insect) アオバエ aóbae

blueprint [bluː'print] n (fig): **a blueprint (for)** (...の) 計画 (...no) keíkaku, (...の) 青写真 (...no) aójashìn

blues [bluːz] n: **the blues** (MUS) ブルース búrùsu

bluff [blʌf] vi (pretend, threaten) はった

りを掛ける hattári wo kakérù

♦n (pretense) はったり hattári

to call someone's bluff ...に挑戦する ...ni chősen suru

blunder [blʌn'dəːr] n (political) へま hémà

♦vi (bungle something) へまをする hémà wo suru

blunt [blʌnt] adj (pencil) 先が太い sakí ga futóì; (knife) 切れない kirénài; (person, talk) 率直な sotchóku na

blur [bləːr] n (shape) かすんで見える物 kasúnde mièrú monó

♦vt (vision) くらます kurámasu; (distinction) ぼかす bokásù

blurb [bləːrb] n (for book, concert etc) 宣伝文句 señdenmoñku

blurt out [bləːrt-] vt 出し抜けに言い出す dashínuke ni iídasù

blush [blʌʃ] vi (with shame, embarrassment) 赤面する sekímen suru

♦n 赤面 sekímen

blustering [blʌs'təːriŋ] adj (person) 威張り散らす ibárichirasù

blustery [blʌs'təːriː] adj (weather) 風の強い kazé no tsuyóì

boar [bɔːr] n イノシシ inóshishì

board [bɔːrd] n (cardboard) ボール紙 bốrugami; (wooden) 板 ítà; (on wall: notice board) 掲示板 keíjiban; (for chess etc) ...盤 ...bañ; (committee) 委員会 iíñkai; (in firm) 役員会 yakúiñkai; (NAUT, AVIAT): **on board** ...に乗って ...ni notte

♦vt (ship, train) ...に乗る ...ni norú

full/half board (BRIT) 3食〔2食〕付き sañshoku(nishóku)tsukí

board and lodging 賄い付き下宿 makánaitsuki geshùku

to go by the board (fig) 捨てられる sutérareru

boarder [bɔːr'dəːr] n (SCOL) 寄宿生 kishúkuseì

boarding card [bɔːr'diŋ-] n = **boarding pass**

boarding house n 下宿屋 geshúkuya

boarding pass n (AVIAT, NAUT) 搭乗券 tōjōken

boarding school n 全寮制学校 zeñryōseigakkŏ

board room n 役員会議室 yakúinkaigi-shĩtsu

board up vt (door, window) ...に板を張る ...ni ítä wo harú

boast [boust] vi: *to boast (about/of)* (...を) 自慢する (...wo) jimán suru

boat [bout] n (small) ボート bõto; (ship) 船 fúne

boater [bou'tər] n (hat) かんかん帽 kañkañbō

boatswain [bou'sən] n 甲板長 kõhañchō, ボースン bōsun

bob [ba:b] vi (boat, cork on water: *also*: **bob up and down**) 波に揺れる namí ni yuréru

bobby [ba:b'i:] (*BRIT*: *inf*) n (policeman) 警官 keíkan

bobsleigh [ba:b'slei] n ボブスレー bobùsurê

bob up vi (appear) 現れる aráwarerù

bode [boud] vi: *to bode well/ill (for)* (...にとって) 良い〔悪い〕前兆である (...ni tottè) yoî〔warûi〕zeñchō de arù

bodily [ba:d'əli:] adj (needs, functions) 身体の shíntai no
♦adv (lift, carry) 体ごと karádagoto

body [ba:d'i:] n (ANAT: *gen*) 体 karáda, 身体 shĩntai; (corpse) 死体 shitái; (object) 物体 buttái; (main part) 本体 hôntai; (of car) 車体 shatái, ボディ bódì; (fig: group) 団体 dañtai; (: organization) 組織 sóshìki; (quantity: of facts) 量 ryõ; (of wine) こく kokù

body-building [ba:d'i:bil'diŋ] n ボディービル bodíbirù

bodyguard [ba:d'i:ga:rd] n (of statesman, celebrity) 護衛 goéi, ボディーガード bodígàdo

bodywork [ba:d'i:wə:rk] n (AUT) 車体 shatái

bog [ba:g] n (GEO) 沼沢地 shŏtakùchì
♦vt: *to get bogged down* (fig) 泥沼にはまり込む dorónuma ni hamárikomù

boggle [ba:g'əl] vi: *the mind boggles* 理解できない ríkai dekínai

bogus [bou'gəs] adj (claim, workman etc) 偽の nisé no

boil [bɔil] vt (water) 沸かす wakásu; (eggs, potatoes etc) ゆでる yudéru
♦vi (liquid) 沸く wakú; (fig: with anger) かんかんに怒る kañkan ni okórù; (: with heat) うだるような暑さになる udáru yõ na atsùsa ni narú
♦n (MED) 出来物 dekímonò
to come to a (US)/the (BRIT) boil 沸き始める wakíhajimerù

boil down to vt fus (fig) 要するに...である yõ surù ni ...de arù

boiled egg [bɔild-] n ゆで卵 yudétamà-go

boiled potatoes npl ゆでジャガイモ yu-déjagaìmo

boiler [bɔi'lər] n (device) ボイラー bôīrā

boiler suit (*BRIT*) n つなぎの作業着 tsunági no sagyõgi

boiling point [bɔi'liŋ-] n (of liquid) 沸騰点 fúttōten

boil over vi (kettle, milk) 吹こぼれる fu-kíkoborerù

boisterous [bɔis'tə:rəs] adj (noisy, excitable: person, crowd) 騒々しい sõzōshiĩ

bold [bould] adj (brave) 大胆な daítañ na; (pej: cheeky) ずうずうしい zûzūshiî; (pattern) 際立った kiwádattà; (line) 太い futôi; (color) 派手な hadé na

Bolivia [bouliv'i:ə] n ボリビア boríbia

bollard [ba:l'ə:rd] (*BRIT*) n (AUT) 標識柱 hyŏshikichû ◇安全地帯などを示す añzenchitái nadò wo shimésù

bolster [boul'stər] n (pillow) 長まくら nagámakùra

bolster up vt (case) 支持する shíjì suru

bolt [boult] n (lock) ラッチ rátchì; (with nut) ボルト borúto
♦adv: *bolt upright* 背筋を伸ばして se-súji wo nobáshìte
♦vt (door) ...のラッチを掛ける ...no ratchì wo kakérù; (*also*: **bolt together**) ボルトで止める borúto de tomérù; (food) 丸のみする marúnomi suru
♦vi (run away: horse) 逃出す nigédasu

bomb [ba:m] n (device) 爆弾 bakúdan
♦vt 爆撃する bakúgeki suru

bombard [ba:m'ba:rd] vt (MIL: with big guns etc) 砲撃する hôgeki suru; (: from planes) 爆撃する bakúgeki suru; (*fig*: with questions) ...に浴びせる ...ni abíseru

bombardment [bɑːmbɑːrd'mənt] *n*: *bombardment from guns* 砲撃 hōgeki *bombardment from planes* 爆撃 bakúgeki

bombastic [bɑːmbæs'tik] *adj* (person, language) もったい振った mottáibuttà

bomb disposal *n*: *bomb disposal unit* 爆弾処理班 bakúdanshorihàn

bomber [bɑːm'əːr] *n* (AVIAT) 爆撃機 bakúgekikì

bombshell [bɑːm'ʃel] *n* (*fig*: revelation) 爆弾 bakúdan

bona fide [bou'nəfaid'] *adj* (traveler etc) 本物の hońmono no

bond [bɑːnd] *n* (of affection, *also* gen: link) きずな kizúna; (binding promise) 約束 yakúsoku; (FINANCE) 証券 shōken; (COMM): *in bond* (of goods) 保税倉庫で hozéisōko de

bondage [bɑːn'didʒ] *n* (slavery) 奴隷の身分 doréi no mibùn

bone [boun] *n* (ANAT, gen) 骨 honé
♦*vt* (meat, fish) 骨を抜く honé wò nukú

bone idle *adj* ぐうたらの gútara no

bonfire [bɑːn'faiəːr] *n* たき火 takíbi

bonnet [bɑːn'it] *n* (hat: *also BRIT*: of car) ボンネット boǹnettò

bonus [bou'nəs] *n* (payment) ボーナス bōnasu; (*fig*: additional benefit) おまけ o-máke

bony [bou'niː] *adj* (MED: tissue) 骨の honé no; (arm, face) 骨張った honébattà; (meat, fish) 骨の多い honé no ōi

boo [buː] *excl* (to surprise someone) わっ wá; (to show dislike) ぶー bū
♦*vt* 野次る yajírù

booby trap [buːbiː-] *n* (MIL) 仕掛爆弾 shikákebakùdan

book [buk] *n* (novel etc) 本 hóǹ; (of stamps, tickets) 1つづり hitótsuzùri
♦*vt* (ticket, seat, room) 予約する yoyáku suru; (subj: traffic warden, policeman) ...に違反切符を書く ...ni ihánkippù wo kakù; (: referee) ...に勧告を与える ...ni kańkoku wò atáeru

bookcase [buk'keis] *n* 本棚 hoǹdana

booking office [buk'iŋ-] (*BRIT*) *n* (RAIL, THEATER) 切符売り場 kippú urība

book-keeping [bukki'piŋ] *n* 簿記 bókì

booklet [buk'lit] *n* 小冊子 shōsasshì, パンフレット páǹfurettò

bookmaker [buk'meikəːr] *n* 馬券屋 bakén-ya

books [buks] *npl* (COMM: accounts) 帳簿 chōbo

bookseller [buk'seləːr] *n* 本屋 hóǹ-ya

bookshop [buk'ʃɑːp] *n* = **bookstore**

bookstore [buk'stɔːr] *n* 本屋 hóǹ-ya, 書店 shotén

boom [buːm] *n* (noise) とどろき todóroki; (in prices, population etc) ブーム būmu
♦*vi* (guns, thunder) とどろく todórokù; (voice) とどろく様な声で言う todórokù yō na koè de iú; (business) 繁盛する hańjō suru

boomerang [buː'məːræŋ] *n* ブーメラン būmeran

boon [buːn] *n* (blessing, benefit) 有難い物 arígataì monó

boost [buːst] *n* (to confidence, sales etc) 増す事 masú kotò
♦*vt* (confidence, sales etc) 増す masú; (economy) 促進する sokúshin suru

booster [buːs'təːr] *n* (MED) ブースター būsutā

boot [buːt] *n* (knee-length) 長靴 nagágutsu, ブーツ būtsu; (*also*: **hiking/climbing boots**) 登山靴 tozáǹgutsu; (*also*: **soccer boots**) サッカーシューズ sakkáshùzu; (*BRIT*: of car) トランク toráǹku
♦*vt* (COMPUT) 起動する kidó suru
... to boot (in addition) おまけに o-máke ni

booth [buːθ] *n* (at fair) 屋台 yátaì; (telephone booth, voting booth) ボックス bokkùsu

booty [buː'tiː] *n* 戦利品 seńrihin

booze [buːz] (*inf*) *n* 酒 saké

border [bɔːr'dəːr] *n* (of a country) 国境 kokkyō; (*also*: **flower border**) ボーダー花壇 bōdākadàn; (band, edge: on cloth etc) へり herí
♦*vt* (road: subject: trees etc) ...に沿って

立っている ...ni sottě tattě irú; (another country: also: **border on**) ...ni riñsetsu suru

borderline [bɔːr'dərlain] n (fig): **on the borderline** 際どいところで kiwádoì tokốro de, ボーダーラインすれすれで bốdāraìn surésure de

borderline case n 決めにくいケース kiménikuì kěsu

border on vt fus (fig: insanity, brutality) ...に近い ...ni chikáì

Borders [bɔːr'dərz] n: **the Borders** ボーダーズ州 bốdāzùshū ◇イングランドに隣接するスコットランド南部の1州 iñgurando ni riñsetsu surú sukóttòrando nañbu no isshū

bore [bɔːr] pt of **bear**
◆vt (hole) ...に穴を開ける ...ni aná wo akéru; (oil well, tunnel) 掘る hórù; (person) 退屈させる taíkutsu saséru
◆n (person) 詰まらない話で退屈させる人 tsumáranaì hanáshi de taíkutsu saséru hitő; (of gun) 口径 kőkei
to be bored 退屈する taíkutsu suru

boredom [bɔːr'dəm] n (condition) 退屈 taíkutsu; (boring quality) 詰まらなさ tsumáranasà

boring [bɔːr'iŋ] adj (tedious, unimaginative) 退屈な taíkutsu na

born [bɔːrn] adj: **to be born** 生れる umáreru
I was born in 1960 私は1960年に生れました watákushi wa séñkyūhyakurokújūnen ni umáremashìta

borne [bɔːrn] pp of **bear**

borough [bʌr'ə] n (POL) 区 ku

borrow [bɑːr'ou] vt: **to borrow something** (from someone) ...を借りる ...wo karíru

bosom [buz'əm] n (ANAT) 胸 muné

bosom friend n 親友 shiñ-yū

boss [bɔːs] n (employer) 雇い主 yatőinushi; (supervisor, superior) 上司 jőshi, 親方 oyákata, ボス bốsù
◆vt (also: **boss around**, **boss about**) こき使う kokítsukaù

bossy [bɔːs'iː] adj (overbearing) 威張り散らす ibárichirasù

bosun [bou'sən] n (NAUT) = **boatswain**

botany [bɑːt'əni:] n 植物学 shokúbutsugàku

botch [bɑːtʃ] vt (bungle: also: **botch up**) 不手際で...をしくじる futégiwa de ...wo shikújirù

both [bouθ] adj 両方の ryőhō no
◆pron (things, people) 両方 ryőhō
◆adv: **both A and B** A も B も A mo B mo
both of us went, we both went 私たち2人共行きました watákushitàchi futáritomo ikímashìta

bother [bɑːð'əːr] vt (worry) 心配させる shiñpai saséru; (disturb) ...に迷惑を掛ける ...ni mêìwaku wo kakérù
◆vi (also: **bother oneself**) ...に気付かう ...ni kizúkaù
◆n (trouble) 迷惑 mêìwaku; (nuisance) いやな事 iyá na kotő
to bother doing わざわざ...する wázàwaza ...surú

bottle [bɑːt'əl] n (container: for milk, wine, perfume etc) ビン bíñ; (of wine, whiskey etc) ボトル botőru; (amount contained) 瓶一杯 bíñ ippái; (baby's) 乳瓶 hő-nyūbin
◆vt (beer, wine) 瓶に詰める bíñ ni tsuméru

bottleneck [bɑːt'əlnek] n (AUT: also fig: of supply) ネック nékkù

bottle-opener [bɑːt'əloupənəːr] n 栓抜き señnukì

bottle up vt (emotion) 抑える osáerù

bottom [bɑːt'əm] n (of container, sea etc) 底 sokő; (buttocks) しり shirí; (of page, list) 一番下の所 ichíban shitá no tokőro; (of class) びり bírí
◆adj (lower: part) 下の方の shitá no hő no; (last: rung, position) 一番下の ichíban shitá no

bottomless [bɑːt'əmlis] adj (funds, store) 際限のない saígeñ no naì

bough [bau] n 枝 edá

bought [bɔːt] pt, pp of **buy**

boulder [boul'dəːr] n 大きな丸石 ốkinà marúishi

bounce [bauns] vi (ball) 跳ね返る hané-

kaèru; (check) 不渡りになる fuwátàri ni narù
♦vt (ball) 跳ねさせる hanésaserù
♦n (rebound) 跳ね返る事 hanékaèru kotó

bouncer [baun'sər] (inf) n (at dance, club) 用心棒 yójìnbō

bound [baund] pt, pp of **bind**
♦n (leap) 一跳び hitótòbi; (gen pl: limit) 限界 geňkai
♦vi (leap) 跳ぶ tobú
♦vt (border) ...の境界になる ...no kyṓkai ni narù
♦adj: **bound by** (law, regulation) ...に拘束されている ...ni kṓsoku saréte irù
to be bound to do something (obliged) やむを得ず...しなければならない yamú wo ezú ...shinákereba naranaî; (likely) 必ず...するだろう kanárazu ...surú darð
bound for (NAUT, AUT, RAIL) ...行きの ...yukí no
out of bounds (fig: place) 立入禁止で tachíirikinshi de

boundary [baun'də:ri:] n (border, limit) 境界 kyṓkai

boundless [baund'lis] adj (energy etc) 果てし無い hatéshinaî

bouquet [boukei'] n (of flowers) 花束 hanátàba, ブーケ bũke

bourgeois [bur'ʒwɑ:] adj ブルジョア根性の burújoakoǹjō no

bout [baut] n (of malaria etc) 発作 hossá; (of activity) 発作的にする事 hossáteki ni suru kotó; (BOXING etc) 試合 shiái

boutique [bu:ti:k'] n ブティック butíkku

bow[1] [bou] n (knot) チョウ結び chṓmusùbi; (weapon, MUS) 弓 yumí

bow[2] [bau] n (of the head) 会釈 éshàku; (of the head and body) お辞儀 ojígi; (NAUT: also: **bows**) 船首 señshu, へ先 hesáki
♦vi (with head) 会釈する éshàku suru; (with head and body) お辞儀する ojígi suru; (yield): **to bow to/before** (reason, pressure) ...に屈服する ...ni kuppúku suru

bowels [bau'əlz] npl (ANAT) 腸 chṓ; (of the earth etc) 深い所 fukáî tokóro

bowl [boul] n (container) 鉢 hachí, ボール bṓru; (contents) ボール一杯 bṓru ippái; (ball) 木球 mokkyū́, ボール bṓru
♦vi (CRICKET) 投球する tṓkyū suru

bow-legged [bou'legid] adj がにまたの ganímata no

bowler [bou'lə:r] n (CRICKET) 投手 tṓshu, ボウラー bṓrà; (BRIT: also: **bowler hat**) 山高帽 yamátakabō

bowling [bou'liŋ] n (game) ボーリング bṓringu

bowling alley n (building) ボーリング場 bṓringujō; (track) レーン rḕn

bowling green n ローンボーリング場 rōňbōringujō

bowls [boulz] n (game) ローンボーリング rōňbōringu

bow tie n チョウネクタイ chṓnekùtai

box [bɑ:ks] n (gen) 箱 hakó; (also: **cardboard box**) 段ボール箱 daňbōrubàko; (THEATER) ボックス bókkùsu
♦vt (put in a box) 箱に詰める hakó ni tsumérù
♦vi (SPORT) ボクシングする bókùshingu suru

boxer [bɑ:k'sə:r] n (person) ボクシング選手 bokúshingu señshu, ボクサー bõkùsā

boxing [bɑ:k'siŋ] n (SPORT) ボクシング bókùshingu

Boxing Day (BRIT) n ボクシングデー bokúshingudḕ

boxing gloves npl ボクシンググローブ bokúshingugurồbu

boxing ring n リング riǹgu

box office n 切符売り場 kippú urìba

boxroom [bɑ:ks'ru:m] (BRIT) n 納戸 naňdo

boy [bɔi] n (young) 少年 shṓnen, 男の子 otóko no kð; (older) 青年 seínen; (son) 息子 musúko

boycott [bɔi'kɑ:t] n ボイコット boíkottò
♦vt (person, product, place etc) ボイコットする boíkottò suru

boyfriend [bɔi'frend] n 男友達 otókotomòdachi, ボーイフレンド bṓifureňdo

boyish [bɔi'iʃ] adj (man) 若々しい wakáwakashiî; (looks, smile, woman) 少年の様な shṓnen no yṓ na

B.R. [bi:a:r'] n abbr = **British Rail**

bra [brɑː] n ブラジャー burájā

brace [breis] n (on teeth) 固定器 kotéīki, ブレース burḗsu; (tool) 曲り柄ドリル magáriedorīru
◆vt (knees, shoulders) ...に力を入れる ...ni chikára wo irérù
to brace oneself (for weight) 構えて待つ kamáete matsù; (for shock) 心を静めて待つ kokóro wo shizúmetè matsu

bracelet [breis'lit] n 腕輪 udéwa, ブレスレット burésùretto

braces [breis'iz] (BRIT) npl ズボンつり zubóñtsuri, サスペンダー sasúpeñdā

bracing [brei'siŋ] adj (air, breeze) さわやかな sawáyàka na

bracken [bræk'ən] n ワラビ warábi

bracket [bræk'it] n (TECH) 腕金 udégane; (group) グループ gúrūpu; (range) 層 sō; (also: **brace bracket**) 中括弧 chūkakkò, ブレース búrēsu; (also: **round bracket**) 小括弧 shōkakkò, 丸括弧 marúkakkò, パーレン pāren; (also: **square bracket**) かぎ括弧 kagíkakkò
◆vt (word, phrase) ...に括弧を付ける ...ni kakkò wo tsúkerù

brag [bræg] vi 自慢する jimán suru

braid [breid] n (trimming) モール mṓru; (of hair) お下げ o-ságè

Braille [breil] n 点字 teñji

brain [brein] n (ANAT) 脳 nṓ; (fig) 頭脳 zúnō

brainchild [brein'tʃaild] n (project) 発案 hatsúan; (invention) 発明 hatsúmei

brains [breinz] npl (CULIN) 脳みそ nṓmisò; (intelligence) 頭脳 zúnō

brainwash [brein'wɑːʃ] vt 洗脳する señnō suru

brainwave [brein'weiv] n 脳波 nṓha

brainy [brei'ni:] adj (child) 頭の良い atáma no yoỉ

braise [breiz] vt (CULIN) いためてから煮込む itámete karà nikómù

brake [breik] n (AUT) 制動装置 seídōsōchi, ブレーキ burḗki; (fig) 歯止め hadóme
◆vi ブレーキを掛ける burḗki wo kakérù

brake fluid n ブレーキ液 burḗkièki

brake light n ブレーキライト burḗkiraīto

bramble [bræm'bəl] n (bush) イバラ ibára

bran [bræn] n ふすま fusúma

branch [bræntʃ] n (of tree) 枝 edá; (COMM) 支店 shiten

branch out vi (fig): *to branch out into* ...に手を広げる ...ni te wo hirógeru

brand [brænd] n (trademark: also: **brand name**) 銘柄 meígara, ブランド burándo; (fig: type) 種類 shúrùi
◆vt (cattle) 焼印 yakín

brandish [bræn'diʃ] vt (weapon) 振り回す furímawasù

brand-new [brænd'nu:'] adj 真新しい maátarashiì

brandy [bræn'di:] n ブランデー burándē

brash [bræʃ] adj (forward, cheeky) ずうずうしい zúzūshiì

brass [bræs] n (metal) 真ちゅう shiñchū
the brass (MUS) 金管楽器 kiñkangàkki

brass band n 吹奏楽団 suísōgakùdan, ブラスバンド burásubañdo

brassiere [brəzi:r'] n ブラジャー burájā

brat [bræt] (pej) n (child) がき gakí

bravado [brəvɑː'dou] n 空威張り karáibàri

brave [breiv] adj (attempt, smile, action) 勇敢な yúkan na
◆vt (face up to) ...に立ち向う ...ni tachímukaù

bravery [brei'və:ri:] n 勇気 yúki

bravo [brɑː'vou] excl ブラボー burabō

brawl [brɔːl] n (in pub, street) けんか keñka

brawny [brɔː'ni:] adj (arms etc) たくましい takúmashiì

bray [brei] vi (donkey) 鳴く nakú

brazen [brei'zən] adj (woman) ずうずうしい zúzūshiì; (lie, accusation) 厚かましい atsúkamashiì
◆vt: *to brazen it out* 最後までしらばくれる saígo madè shirábakurerù

brazier [brei'ʒə:r] n (on building site etc) 野外用簡易暖炉 yagáiyō kañ-i dañro

Brazil [brəzil'] n ブラジル burájiru

Brazilian [brəzil'i:ən] adj ブラジルの burájiru no

♦*n* ブラジル人 burájirujìn

breach [bri:tʃ] *vt* (defence, wall) 突破する toppá suru

♦*n* (gap) 突破口 toppákò; (breaking): *breach of contract* 契約不履行 keíyakufurikò

breach of the peace 治安妨害 chiánbògai

bread [bred] *n* (food) パン páǹ

bread and butter *n* バターを塗ったパン bátà wo nuttá páǹ; (*fig:* source of income) 金づる kanézuru

breadbox [bred'bɑ:ks] (*BRIT* **breadbin**) *n* パン入れ paǹ-irè

breadcrumbs [bred'krʌmz] *npl* (gen) パンくず paǹkuzù; (CULIN) パン粉 paǹko

breadline [bred'lain] *n: on the breadline* 貧しい mazúshiì

breadth [bredθ] *n* (of cloth etc) 幅 habá; (*fig:* of knowledge, subject) 広さ hírðsa

breadwinner [bred'winə:r] *n* (in family) 稼ぎ手 kaségite

break [breik] (*pt* **broke**, *pp* **broken**) *vt* (cup, glass) 割る warú; (stick, leg, arm) 折る orù; (machine etc) 壊す kowásù; (promise, law, record) 破る yabúrù; (journey) 中断する chúdan suru

♦*vi* (crockery) 割れる waréru; (stick, arm, leg) 折れる orérù; (machine etc) 壊れる kowárerù; (storm) 起る okórù; (weather) 変る kawáru; (story, news) 報道される hődð saréru; (dawn) *dawn breaks* 夜が明ける yo ga akéru

♦*n* (gap) 途切れた所 togíreta tokóro; (fracture: *gen*) 破損 hasón; (: of limb) 骨折 kossétsu; (pause for rest) 休憩 kyūkei; (at school) 休み時間 yasúmijikàn; (chance) チャンス cháǹsu

to break the news to someone ...に知らせる ...ni shiráseru

to break even (COMM) 収支がとんとんになる shūshi ga tońton ni narú

to break free/loose (person, animal) 逃げ出す nigédasu

to break open (door etc) ...を壊して開ける ...wo kowáshite akéru

breakage [brei'kidʒ] *n* (act of breaking)

壊す事 kowásù kotó; (object broken) 損傷 soǹshō

break down *vt* (figures, data) 分析する buńseki suru

♦*vi* (machine, car) 故障する koshő suru; (person) 取乱す torímidasù; (talks) 物別れになる monówakàre ni narú

breakdown [breik'daun] *n* (AUT) 故障 koshő; (in communications) 中断 chúdan; (of marriage) 破たん hatán; (MED: *also: nervous breakdown*) 神経衰弱 shińkeisuïjaku; (of statistics) 分析 buńseki

breakdown van (*BRIT*) *n* レッカー車 rékkàsha

breaker [brei'kə:r] *n* (wave) 白波 shiránami

breakfast [brek'fəst] *n* 朝ご飯 asá gohàn, 朝食 chőshoku

break in *vt* (horse etc) 慣らす narásù

♦*vi* (burglar) 押入る oshírù; (interrupt) 割込む waríkomù

break-in [breik'in] *n* 押入り oshíiri

breaking and entering [breik'iǹ æ014nd eǹ'tə:riŋ] *n* (LAW) 不法侵入 fuhőshiǹ-nyū

break into *vt fus* (house) ...に押入る ...ni oshírù

break off *vi* (branch) 折れる orérù; (speaker) 話を中断する hanáshi wo chúdan suru

break out *vi* (begin: war) ぼっ発する boppátsu suru; (: fight) 始まる hajímaru; (escape: prisoner) 脱出する dasshútsu suru

to break out in spots/a rash にきび〔湿しん〕になる níkibi〔shisshíǹ〕ni narú

breakthrough [breik'θru:] *n* (*fig:* in technology etc) 躍進 yakúshin

break up *vi* (ship) 分解する buńkai suru; (crowd, meeting) 解散する kaísan suru; (marriage) 離婚に終る rikóǹ ni owáru; (SCOL) 終る owáru

♦*vt* (rocks, biscuit etc) 割る warú; (fight etc) やめさせる yamésaseru

breakwater [breik'wɔ:tə:r] *n* 防波堤 bőhatei

breast [brest] *n* (of woman) 乳房 chíbùsa; (chest) 胸 muné; (of meat) 胸肉 munénĭkù

breast-feed [brest'fi:d] (*pt*, *pp* **breast-fed**) *vt* ...に母乳を飲ませる ...ni bonyū wo nomáserù

♦*vi* 子供に母乳を飲ませる kodómo ni bonyū wo nomáserù

breaststroke [brest'strouk] *n* 平泳ぎ hiráoyõgi

breath [breθ] *n* 息 íkì

   out of breath 息を切らせて íkì wo kirásete

Breathalyser [breθ'əlaizə:r] ® *n* 酒気検査器 shukíkensakì

breathe [bri:ð] *vt* 呼吸する kokyū suru

♦*vi* 呼吸する kokyū suru

breathe in *vt* 吸込む suíkomù

♦*vi* 息を吸込む íkì wo suíkomù

breathe out *vt* 吐出す hakídasu

♦*vi* 息を吐く íkì wo hakù

breather [bri:'ðə:r] *n* (break) 休憩 kyūkei

breathing [bri:'ðiŋ] *n* 呼吸 kokyū

breathless [breθ'lis] *adj* (from exertion) 息を切らせる íkì wo kirásete irú; (MED) 呼吸困難の kokyūkoñnan no

breathtaking [breθ'teikiŋ] *adj* (speed) 息が止る様な íkì ga tomáru yõ na; (view) 息を飲むような íkì wo nomù yõ na

bred [bred] *pt*, *pp of* **breed**

breed [bri:d] (*pt*, *pp* **bred**) *vt* (animals) 繁殖させる hañshoku saséru; (plants) 栽培する saíbai suru

♦*vi* (ZOOL) 繁殖する hañshoku suru

♦*n* (ZOOL) 品種 hiñshu; (type, class) 種類 shúrùi

breeding [bri:'diŋ] *n* (upbringing) 育ち sodáchi

breeze [bri:z] *n* そよ風 soyókàze

breezy [bri:'zi:] *adj* (manner, tone) 快活な kaíkatsu na; (weather) 風の多い kazé no õi

brevity [brev'iti:] *n* (shortness, conciseness) 簡潔さ kañketsusa

brew [bru:] *vt* (tea) 入れる iréru; (beer) 醸造する jõzõ suru

♦*vi* (storm) 起ろうとしている okórō to shité irù; (*fig*: trouble, a crisis) 迫ってい

る semáttè irù

brewery [bru:'ə:ri:] *n* 醸造所 jõzõshò

bribe [braib] *n* 賄ろ waíro

♦*vt* (person, witness) 買収する baíshū suru

bribery [brai'bə:ri:] *n* (with money, favors) 贈賄 zõwai

bric-a-brac [brik'əbræk] *n* 置物類 okímonorùi

brick [brik] *n* (for building) れんが réñga

bricklayer [brik'leiə:r] *n* れんが職人 reñgashokùnin

bridal [braid'əl] *adj* (gown) 花嫁の hanáyòme no; (suite) 新婚者の shiñkoñsha no

bride [braid] *n* 花嫁 hanáyòme, 新婦 shiñpu

bridegroom [braid'gru:m] *n* 花婿 hanámùko, 新郎 shiñrõ

bridesmaid [braidz'meid] *n* 新婦付き添いの女性 shiñputsukísoi no joséi

bridge [bridʒ] *n* (TECH, ARCHIT) 橋 hashí; (NAUT) 船橋 señkyõ, ブリッジ burijjī; (CARDS, DENTISTRY) ブリッジ burijjī

♦*vt* (*fig*: gap, gulf) 乗越える noríkoerù

   bridge of the nose 鼻柱 hanábashira

bridle [braid'əl] *n* くつわ kutsúwa

bridle path *n* 乗馬用の道 jõbayõ no michí

brief [bri:f] *adj* (period of time, description, speech) 短い mijíkaì

♦*n* (LAW) 事件摘要書 jikéntekiyōsho; (*gen*: task) 任務 níñmu

♦*vt* (inform) ...に指示を与える ...ni shijí wo atáeru

briefcase [bri:f'keis] *n* かばん kabán, ブリーフケース burífukèsu

briefing [bri:'fiŋ] *n* (*gen*, PRESS) 説明 setsúmei

briefly [bri:f'li:] *adv* (smile, glance) ちらっと chiráttò; (explain, say) 短く mijíkakù

briefs [bri:fs] *npl* (for men) パンツ pañtsu, ブリーフ burífu; (for women) パンティー pañtī, ショーツ shõtsu

brigade [brigeid'] *n* (MIL) 旅団 ryodán

brigadier [brigədi:'ə:r] *n* (MIL) 准将 juñshõ

bright [brait] *adj* (*gen*) 明るい akárui; (person, idea: clever) 利口な rikó na; (person: lively) 明朗な meírō na

brighten [brait'ən] (*also*: **brighten up**) *vt* (room) 明るくする akáruku suru; (event) 楽しくする tanóshikù suru
♦*vi* 明るくなる akáruku narù

brilliance [bril'jəns] *n* (of light) 明るさ akárusa; (of talent, skill) 素晴らしさ subárashisà

brilliant [bril'jənt] *adj* (person, idea) 天才的な teñsaiteki na; (smile, career) 輝かしい kagáyakashiì; (sunshine, light) 輝く kagáyakù; (*fig*: satisfaction) 素晴らしい subárashiì

brim [brim] *n* (of cup etc) 縁 fuchí; (of hat) つば tsubá

brine [brain] *n* (CULIN) 塩水 shiómizu

bring [briŋ] (*pt, pp* **brought**) *vt* (thing) 持って来る motté kurù; (person) 連れて来る tsuréte kurù; (*fig*: satisfaction) もたらす motárasù; (trouble) 起す okósù

bring about *vt* (cause) 起こす okósù

bring back *vt* (restore: hanging etc) 復帰させる fukkí saséru; (return: thing/person) 持って[連れて]帰る motté[tsuréte]kaèru

bring down *vt* (government) 倒す taósù; (MIL: plane) 撃墜する gekítsui suru; (price) 下げる sagérù

bring forward *vt* (meeting) 繰り上げる kuríagerù; (proposal) 提案する teían suru

bring off *vt* (task, plan) ...に成功する ...ni seíkō suru

bring out *vt* (gun) 取出す torídasu; (meaning) 明らかにする akíraka ni suru; (publish, produce: book) 出版する shuppán suru; (: album) 発表する happyṓ suru

bring round *vt* (unconscious person) 正気付かせる shōkizukaserù

bring up *vt* (carry up) 上に持って来る〔行く〕uế ni motté kurù[ikú]; (educate: person) 育てる sodáterù; (question, subject) 持出す mochídasù; (vomit: food) 吐く hakú

brink [briŋk] *n* (of disaster, war etc) 瀬戸際 setógiwa

brisk [brisk] *adj* (tone, person) きびきびした kíbìkibi shitá; (pace) 早い hayáì; (trade) 盛んな sakán na

bristle [bris'əl] *n* (animal hair, hair of beard) 剛毛 gṓmō; (of brush) 毛 ke
♦*vi* (in anger) 怒る okórù

Britain [brit'ən] *n* (*also*: **Great Britain**) 英国 eíkoku, イギリス igírisu ◇イングランド, スコットランド, ウェールズを含む iñgurañdo, sukóttorañdo, uếruzu wo fukúmù

British [brit'iʃ] *adj* 英国の eíkoku no, イギリスの igírisu no
♦*npl*: **the British** 英国人 eíkokujìn, イギリス人 igírisujìn

British Isles *npl*: **the British Isles** イギリス諸島 igírisushotṓ

British Rail *n* 英国国有鉄道 eíkoku kokúyū tetsùdō

Briton [brit'ən] *n* 英国人 eíkokujìn, イギリス人 igírisujìn

brittle [brit'əl] *adj* (fragile: glass etc) 割れやすい waréyasuì; (: bones etc) もろい moróì

broach [broutʃ] *vt* (subject) 持出す mochídasu

broad [brɔːd] *adj* (street, shoulders, smile, range) 広い hiróì; (general: outlines, distinction etc) 大まかな ṓmakà na; (accent) 強い tsuyóì

in broad daylight 真っ昼間に mappírùma ni

broadcast [brɔːd'kæst] *n* (TV, RADIO) 放送 hṓsō
♦*vb* (*pt, pp* **broadcast**)
♦*vt* (TV, RADIO) 放送する hṓsō suru; (TV) 放映する hṓei suru
♦*vi* (TV, RADIO) 放送する hṓsō suru

broaden [brɔːd'ən] *vt* (scope, appeal) 広くする híròku suru, 広げる hirógeru
♦*vi* (river) 広くなる híròku narú, 広がる hírógaru

to broaden one's mind 心を広くする kokóro wo hiróku suru

broadly [brɔːd'li:] *adv* (in general terms) 大まかに ṓmakà ni

broad-minded [brɔːd'main'did] *adj* 心の広い kokóro no hiroì

broccoli [brɑ:k'əli:] n (BOT, CULIN) ブロッコリー burókkòrī

brochure [brouʃu:r'] n (booklet) 小冊子 shōsasshí, パンフレット pánfuretto

broil [broil] vt (CULIN) じか火で焼く jikábi de yakú

broke [brouk] pt of **break**
♦adj (inf: person, company) 無一文になった muíchimòn ni nattá

broken [brou'kən] pp of **break**
♦adj (window, cup etc) 割れた waréta; (machine: also: **broken down**) 壊れた kowáreta
a **broken leg** 脚の骨折 ashí no kossétsu
in broken English/Japanese 片言の英語〔日本語〕で katákoto no eígo〔nihóngo〕de

broken-hearted [brou'kənhɑ:r'tid] adj 悲嘆に暮れた hitán ni kuréta

broker [brou'kə:r] n (COMM: in shares) 証券ブローカー shōken burōkā; (: insurance broker) 保険代理人 hokén dairinin

brolly [brɑ:l'i:] (BRIT: inf) n 傘 kásà

bronchitis [brɑ:ŋkai'tis] n 気管支炎 kikánshièn

bronze [brɑ:nz] n (metal) 青銅 seídō, ブロンズ burónzu; (sculpture) 銅像 dózo

brooch [broutʃ] n ブローチ burōchi

brood [bru:d] n (of birds) 一腹のひな hitóhàra no hiná
♦vi (person) くよくよする kuyòkuyo suru

brook [bruk] n 小川 ogáwa

broom [bru:m] n (for cleaning) ほうき hōki; (BOT) エニシダ eníshida

broomstick [bru:m'stik] n ほうきの柄 hōki no e

Bros. abbr (= brothers) 兄弟 kyōdai

broth [brɔ:θ] n (CULIN) スープ sūpu

brothel [brɑ:θ'əl] n 売春宿 baíshun-yadò

brother [brʌð'ə:r] n (also: **older brother**) 兄 ani, 兄さん niísan; (also: **younger brother**) 弟 otótò; (REL) 修道士 shūdōshi

brother-in-law [brʌð'ə:rinlɔ:] (p l **brothers-in-law**) n (older) 義理の兄 girí no aní; (younger) 義理の弟 girí no otótò

brought [brɔ:t] pt, pp of **bring**

brow [brau] n (forehead) 額 hitái; (rare: gen: eyebrow) まゆ mayú; (of hill) 頂上 chōjō

brown [braun] adj (color) 褐色の kasshóku no, 茶色の chaíro no; (tanned) 日焼けした hiyáke shitá
♦n (color) 褐色 kasshóku, 茶色 chaíro
♦vt (CULIN) ...に焼き目を付ける ...ni yakíme wo tsukérú

brown bread n 黒パン kurópan

brownie [brau'ni:] n (Brownie guide) ブラウニー buráùnī ◇ガールスカウトの幼年団員 gàrusukaùto no yõnendañ-in; (US: cake) チョコレートクッキーの一種 chokórētokukkī no isshù

brown paper n クラフト紙 kuráfutoshì

brown sugar n 赤砂糖 akázatò

browse [brauz] vi (through book) 拾い読みする hiróiyomi suru; (in shop) 商品を見て回る shōhin wo mitè mawáru

bruise [bru:z] n (on face etc) 打撲傷 dabókushō, あざ azá
♦vt (person) ...に打撲傷を与える ...ni dabókushō wo atáeru

brunch [brʌntʃ] n ブランチ buráñchi

brunette [bru:net'] n (woman) ブルネット burúnettò

brunt [brʌnt] n: **to bear the brunt of** (attack, criticism) ...の矢面に立つ ...no yaómòte ni tatsù

brush [brʌʃ] n (for cleaning, shaving etc) ブラシ buráshi; (for painting etc) 刷毛 haké; (artist's) 筆 fudé, 絵筆 efúde; (quarrel) 小競り合い kozériai
♦vt (sweep etc) ...にブラシを掛ける ...ni búrashi wo kakérù; (clean: teeth etc) 磨く migáku; (groom) ブラシでとかす búrashi de tokásù; (also: **brush against**: person, object) ...に触れる ...ni furéru

brush aside vt (emotion, criticism) 無視する mushí suru

brush up vt (subject, language) 復習する fukúshū suru

brushwood [brʌʃ'wud] n (sticks) しば shibá

brusque [brʌsk] adj (person, manner) 無愛想な buáīsō na; (apology) ぶっきらぼうな bukkírabò na

Brussels [brʌs'əlz] n ブリュッセル buryússèru

Brussels sprout n メキャベツ mekyábètsu

brutal [bru:t'əl] adj (person, actions) 残忍な zańnin na; (honesty, frankness) 厳しい程の kibíshiì hodó no

brutality [bru:tæl'iti:] n 残忍さ zańninsa

brute [bru:t] n (person) 人でなし hitódenashi, けだもの kedámono; (animal) 獣 kemóno

♦adj: **by brute force** 暴力で bóryoku de

B.Sc. [bi:essi:'] abbr = **Bachelor of Science**

bubble [bʌb'əl] n (in liquid, soap) 泡 awá; (of soap etc) シャボン玉 shabóndama

♦vi (liquid) 沸く wakú; (: sparkle) 泡立つ awádatsù

bubble bath n 泡風呂 awáburo

bubble gum n 風船ガム fúsengamù

buck [bʌk] n (rabbit) 雄ウサギ osúusàgi; (deer) 雄ジカ ojíka; (US: inf: dollar) ドル dorù

♦vi (horse) 乗手を振り落そうとする noríte wo furíotosò to surù

to pass the buck (to someone) (...に)責任をなすり付ける (...ni) sekínin wo nasúritsukerù

bucket [bʌk'it] n (pail) バケツ bakétsu; (contents) バケツ一杯 bakétsu ippái

buckle [bʌk'əl] n (on shoe, belt) バックル bakkúru

♦vt (shoe, belt) ...のバックルを締める ...no bakkúru wo shimérù

♦vi (wheel) ゆがむ yugámu; (bridge, support) 崩れる kuzúrerù

buck up vi (cheer up) 元気を出す géńki wo dasù

bud [bʌd] n (of tree, plant, flower) 芽 me

♦vi 芽を出す me wo dasù

Buddhism [bu:'dizəm] n (REL) 仏教 bukkyō

budding [bʌd'iŋ] adj (actor, entrepreneur) 有望な yūbō na

buddy [bʌd'i:] (US) n (friend) 相棒 aíbō

budge [bʌdʒ] vt (object) ちょっと動かす chóttò ugókasù; (fig: person) 譲歩させる

jóho sasérù

♦vi (object, person) ちょっと動く chóttò ugóků; (fig: person) 譲歩する jóho suru

budgerigar [bʌdʒ'ə:ri:gɑ:r] n セキセイインコ sekíseiiñko

budget [bʌdʒ'it] n (person's, government's) 予算 yosáň, 予算案 yosáň-an

♦vi: **to budget for something** ...を予算案に入れる ...wo yosáň-an ni iréru

I'm on a tight budget 台所が苦しい daídokoro ga kúrushiì

budgie [bʌdʒ'i:] n = **budgerigar**

buff [bʌf] adj (color: envelope) 薄茶色 usúchairo

♦n (inf: enthusiast) マニア mánìa

buffalo [bʌf'əlou] (pl **buffalo** or **buffaloes**) n (BRIT) スイギュウ suígyū; (US: bison) バイソン báĭson

buffer [bʌf'ə:r] n (COMPUT) バッファ báffà; (RAIL) 緩衝機 kańshòki

buffet[1] [bufei'] (BRIT) n (in station) ビュッフェ byúffè; (food) 立食 risshóku

buffet[2] [bʌf'it] vt (subj: wind, sea) もみ揺さぶる momíyusaburù

buffet car (BRIT) n (RAIL) ビュッフェ車 byúffēsha

bug [bʌg] n (esp US: insect) 虫 mushí; (COMPUT: of program) バグ bágù; (fig: germ) 風邪 kazé; (hidden microphone) 盗聴器 tóchòki

♦vt (inf: annoy) 怒らせる okóraserù; (room, telephone etc) ...に盗聴器を付ける ...ni tóchòki wo tsukérù

buggy [bʌg'i:] n (baby buggy) 乳母車 ubágurùma

bugle [bju:'gəl] n (MUS) らっぱ rappá

build [bild] n (of person) 体格 taíkaku

♦vb (pt, pp **built**)

♦vt (house etc) 建てる tatérù, 建築する kefíchiku suru; (machine, cage etc) 作る tsukúrù

builder [bil'də:r] n (contractor) 建築業者 kefíchikugyòsha

building [bil'diŋ] n (industry, construction) 建築業 keńchikugyò; (structure) 建物 tatémonò, ビル birú

building society (BRIT) n 住宅金融組合 júttakukin-yūkumìai

build up *vt* (forces, production) 増やす fuyásù; (morale) 高める takámerù; (stocks) 蓄積する chikúseki suru

built [bilt] *pt, pp of* **build**

♦*adj:* **built-in** (oven, wardrobes etc) 作り付けの tsukúritsuke no

built-up area [bilt'ʌp-] *n* 市街化区域 shigáikakuĭki

bulb [bʌlb] *n* (BOT) 球根 kyůkon; (ELEC) 電球 deñkyū

Bulgaria [bʌlgeːr'iːə] *n* ブルガリア burúgaria

Bulgarian [bʌlgeːr'iːən] *adj* ブルガリアの burúgaria no

♦*n* ブルガリア人 burúgariajìn

bulge [bʌldʒ] *n* (bump) 膨らみ fukúrami

♦*vi* (pocket, file, cheeks etc) 膨らむ fukúramu

bulk [bʌlk] *n* (mass: of thing) 巨大な姿 kyodái na sugáta; (: of person) 巨体 kyotái

in bulk (COMM) 大口で ôguchi de

the bulk of (most of) ...の大半 ...no taíhan

bulky [bʌl'kiː] *adj* (parcel) かさばった kasábattà; (equipment) 大きくて扱いにくい ôkikùte atsúkainikuĭ

bull [bul] *n* (ZOOL) 雄牛 oúshi; (male elephant/whale) 雄 osú

bulldog [bul'dɔːg] *n* ブルドッグ burúdoggù

bulldozer [bul'douzəːr] *n* ブルドーザー burúdōzā

bullet [bul'it] *n* 弾丸 dañgan

bulletin [bul'itən] *n* (TV etc: news update) 速報 sokúhō; (journal) 会報 kaíhō, 紀要 kiyô

bulletproof [bul'itpruːf] *adj* (glass, vest, car) 防弾の bôdan no

bullfight [bul'fait] *n* 闘牛 tôgyū

bullfighter [bul'faitəːr] *n* 闘牛士 tôgyūshi

bullfighting [bul'faitiŋ] *n* 闘牛 tôgyū

bullhorn [bul'hɔːrn] (*US*) *n* ハンドマイク hañdomaĭku

bullion [bul'jən] *n* (gold, silver) 地金 jigáne

bullock [bul'ək] *n* 去勢した雄牛 kyoséi shitá oúshi

bullring [bul'riŋ] *n* 闘牛場 tôgyūjō

bull's-eye [bulz'ai] *n* (on a target) 的の中心 matô no chûshin

bully [bul'iː] *n* 弱い者いじめ yowáimonoijĭme

♦*vt* いじめる ijímeru

bum [bʌm] (*inf*) *n* (backside) しり shirí; (esp *US*: tramp) ルンペン ruñpen; (: good-for-nothing) ろくでなし rokúdenashi

bumblebee [bʌm'bəlbiː] *n* クマンバチ kumáñbachi

bump [bʌmp] *n* (in car: minor accident) 衝突 shôtotsu; (jolt) 衝撃 shôgeki; (swelling: on head) こぶ kobú; (on road) 段差 dañsa

♦*vt* (strike) ...にぶつかる ...ni butsúkaru

bumper [bʌm'pəːr] *n* (AUT) バンパー bañpā

♦*adj:* **bumper crop/harvest** 豊作 hôsaku

bumper cars *npl* (in amusement park) バンパーカー bañpākā

bump into *vt fus* (strike: obstacle) ...にぶつかる ...ni butsúkaru; (*inf*: meet: person) ...に出くわす ...ni dekúwasù

bumptious [bʌmp'ʃəs] *adj* (person) うぬぼれた unúboreta

bumpy [bʌm'piː] *adj* (road) 凸凹な dekóboko na

bun [bʌn] *n* (CULIN) ロールパン rôrupan, パン báñ; (of hair) まげ magé, シニヨン shíñîyon

bunch [bʌntʃ] *n* (of flowers, keys) 束 tábà; (of bananas) 房 fusá; (of people) グループ gúrūpu

bunches [bʌntʃ'iz] *npl* (in hair) 左右のポニーテール sáyù no poníteru

bundle [bʌn'dəl] *n* (parcel: of clothes, samples etc) 包み tsutsúmi; (of sticks, papers) 束 tabâ

♦*vt* (*also:* **bundle up**) 厚着させる atsúgi saséru; (put:) *to bundle something/someone into* ...にほうり〔押し込む ...ni hôri(oshí)komù

bungalow [bʌŋ'gəlou] *n* バンガロー bañgarô

bungle [bʌŋ'gəl] *vt* (job, assassination) ...にしくじる ...ni shikújirù

bunion [bʌn'jən] *n* (MED) けん膜りゅう kefímakuryū, バニオン bánîon

bunk [bʌŋk] *n* (bed) 作り付けベッド tsukúritsukebeddò

bunk beds *npl* 二段ベッド nidánbeddð

bunker [bʌŋ'kə:r] *n* (*also*: **coal bunker**) 石炭庫 sekítañko; (MIL) えんぺいごう efípeigō; (GOLF) バンカー bañkā

bunny [bʌn'i:] *n* (*also*: **bunny rabbit**) ウサちゃん usáchan

bunting [bʌn'tiŋ] *n* (flags) 飾り小旗 kazárikobàta

buoy [bu:'i:] *n* (NAUT) ブイ buî

buoyant [bɔi'ənt] *adj* (ship) 浮力のある fúryòku no arù; (economy, market) 活気のある kakkí no arù; (*fig*: person, nature) 朗らかな hogáràka na

buoy up *vt* (*fig*) 元気づける geñkizukerù

burden [bə:r'dən] *n* (responsibility, worry) 負担 fután; (load) 荷物 nímòtsu
♦*vt* (trouble): **to burden someone with** (oppress) ...を打明けて...に心配を掛ける ...wo uchíakete ...ni shifípai wo kakérù

bureau [bjur'ou] (*pl* **bureaux** or **bureaus**) *n* (*BRIT*: writing desk) 書き物机 kakímonozukùe ◇ふたが書く面になる机を指す futá ga kakù meñ ni narù tsukúe wo sasù; (*US*: chest of drawers) 整理だんす seíridañsu; (office: government, travel, information) 局 kyókù, 課 ka

bureaucracy [bjura:k'rəsi:] *n* (POL, COMM) 官僚制 kafíryōsei

bureaucrat [bjur'əkræt] *n* (administrator) 官僚 kafíryō; (*pej*: pen-pusher) 小役人 koyákùnin

bureaux [bjur'ouz] *npl of* **bureau**

burglar [bə:r'glə:r] *n* 押込み強盗 oshíkomigōtō

burglar alarm *n* 盗難警報機 tōnankeihōki

burglary [bə:r'glə:ri:] *n* (crime) 住居侵入罪 jūkyoshifínyūzai

burial [be:r'i:əl] *n* 埋葬 maísō

burly [bə:r'li:] *adj* (figure, workman etc) ごつい gotsúi

Burma [bə:rm'ə] *n* ビルマ bírùma

burn [bə:rn] (*pt, pp* **burned** or **burnt**) *vt* (papers, fuel etc) 燃やす moyásu; (toast, food etc) 焦がす kogásù; (house etc: arson) ...に放火する ...ni hōka suru
♦*vi* (house, wood etc) 燃える moéru; (cakes etc) 焦げる kogérù; (sting) ひりひりする hírìhiri suru
♦*n* やけど yakédo

burn down *vt* 全焼させる zeñshō saséru

burner [bə:r'nə:r] *n* (on cooker, heater) 火口 hígùchi, バーナー bānā

burning [bə:r'niŋ] *adj* (house etc) 燃えている moéte irù; (sand) 焼ける様に熱い yakéru yð ni atsuî; (desert) しゃく熱の shakúnetsu no; (ambition) 熱烈な netsúretsu na

burnt [bə:rnt] *pt, pp of* **burn**

burrow [bə:r'nə:r] *n* (of rabbit etc) 巣穴 suána
♦*vi* (dig) 掘る hórù; (rummage) あさる asáru

bursary [bə:r'sə:ri:] (*BRIT*) *n* (SCOL) 奨学金 shōgakukin

burst [bə:rst] (*pt, pp* **burst**) *vt* (bag, balloon, pipe etc) 破裂させる harétsu saséru; (subj: river: banks etc) 決壊させる kekkái saséru
♦*vi* (pipe, tire) 破裂する harétsu suru
♦*n* (*also*: **burst pipe**) 破裂した水道管 harétsu shita suídōkan

a burst of energy/speed/enthusiasm 突発的なエネルギー〔スピード，熱心さ〕 toppátsuteki na enérugī(supído, nesshíñsa)

a burst of gunfire 連射 reñsha

to burst into flames 急に燃え出す kyū ni moédasù

to burst into tears 急に泣き出す kyū ni nakídasù

to burst out laughing 急に笑い出す kyū ni waráidasù

to be bursting with (subj: room, container) はち切れんばかりに...で一杯になっている hachíkireñbakari ni ...de ippái ni natté irù; (: person: emotion) ...で胸が一杯になっている ...de muné ga ippái ni natté irù

burst into *vt fus* (room etc) ...に飛込む

...ni tobíkomù

bury [berr'i:] vt (gen) 埋める uméru; (at funeral) 埋葬する maísō suru

bus [bʌs] n (vehicle) バス básù

bush [buʃ] n (in garden) 低木 teíboku; (scrubland) 未開地 mikáĭchi, ブッシュ bússhù

   to beat about the bush 遠回しに言う tŏmawàshi ni iú

bushy [buʃ'i:] adj (tail, hair, eyebrows) ふさふさした fúsafusa shitá

busily [biz'ili:] adv (actively) 忙しく isógashikù

business [biz'nis] n (matter, question) 問題 moñdai; (trading) 商売 shŏbai; (firm) 会社 kaísha; (occupation) 仕事 shigóto

   to be away on business 出張して留守である shutchŏ shite rusù de arù

   it's my business to ... ...するのは私の務めです ...surú no wa watákushi no tsutóme desù

   it's none of my business 私の知った事じゃない watákushi no shittá kotó ja naì

   he means business 彼は本気らしい karè wa hoñki rashiì

businesslike [biz'nislaik] adj てきぱきした tekípaki shita

businessman [biz'nismæn] (pl **businessmen**) n 実業家 jitsúgyōka

business trip n 出張 shutchŏ

businesswoman [biz'niswumən] (pl **businesswomen**) n 女性実業家 joséijitsugyōka

busker [bʌs'kə:r] (BRIT) n 大道芸人 daídōgeìnin

bus-stop [bʌs'sta:p] n バス停留所 básùteíryùjo

bust [bʌst] n (ANAT) 乳房 chíbusa, 胸 muné; (measurement) バスト básùto; (sculpture) 胸像 kyŏzō

   ♦adj (inf: broken) 壊れた kowárèta

   to go bust (company etc) つぶれる tsubúreru

bustle [bʌs'əl] n (activity) 雑踏 zattŏ

   ♦vi (person) 忙しく飛回る isógashikù tobímawarù

bustling [bʌs'liŋ] adj (town, place) にぎやかな nígiyàka na

busy [biz'i:] adj (person) 忙しい isógashiì; (shop, street) にぎやかな nígiyàka na; (TEL: line) 話し中の hanáshichū no

   ♦vt: *to busy oneself with* 忙しそうに...する isógashisŏ ni ...suru

busybody [biz'i:bɑ:di:] n でしゃばり屋 deshábariya

busy signal (US) n (TEL) 話中音 wáchūon

KEYWORD

but [bʌt] conj 1 (yet) ...であるが ...de árù ga, ...であるけれども ...de árù keredomo, しかし shikáshì

   he's not very bright, but he's hard-working 彼はあまり頭は良くないが、よく働きます kárè wa amári àtama wà yókùnaì ga, yókù határakimasù

   I'm tired but Paul isn't 私は疲れていますが、ポールは疲れていません watákushi wa tsùkárète imasu ga, pŏrù wa tsukárète imásèn

   the trip was enjoyable but tiring 旅行は楽しかったけれども、疲れました ryokŏ wa tànóshikàtta keredomo, tsukáremashĭta

2 (however) ...であるが ...de árù ga, ...であるけれども ...de árù keredomo, しかし shikáshì

   I'd love to come, but I'm busy 行きたいが、今忙しいんです ikítaì ga, ímà isógashiĭn desu

   she wanted to go, but first she had to finish her homework 彼女は行きたかったけれども、先に宿題を済ます必要がありました kánojo wa ikítakàtta keredomo, sakí ni shùkúdai wo sùmásu hitsúyō ga àrímashĭta

   I'm sorry, but I don't agree 済みませんが、私は同意できません sumímasèn ga, watákushi wa dŏi dekimasèn

3 (showing disagreement, surprise etc) しかし shikáshì

   but that's far too expensive! しかしそれは高過ぎますよ shikáshì soré wa tàkásugimasù yo

   but that's fantastic! しかし素晴らし

いじゃありませんか shikáshì subárashiî ja arímasèn ka
♦*prep* (apart from, except) ...を除いて ...wo nozóite, ...以外に ...ígai ni
he was nothing but trouble 彼は厄介な問題ばかり起していました kárè wa yákkài na móndai bakàri okóshìte imáshìta
we've had nothing but trouble 厄介な問題ばかり起っています yákkài na móndai bakàri okóttè imásù
no one but him can do it 彼を除けば出来る人はいません kárè wo nozókebà dekírù hito wa imásèn
who but a lunatic would do such a thing? 気違いを除けばそんな事をする人はいないでしょう kichígaì wo nozókebà sónna koto wò suru hito wà ináì deshō
but for you あなたがいなかったら anátà ga inákàttara
but for your help あなたが助けてくれなかったら anátà ga tasúketè kurénakàttara
I'll do anything but that それ以外なら何でもします soré ígai nara nán de mo shimasù
♦*adv* (just, only) ただ tádà, ...だけ ...dàkè, ...しか...ない ...shika ...náî
she's but a child 彼女はほんの子供です kánojò wa hón no kòdómo desù
had I but known 私がそれを知ってさえいたら watákushi ga sòrè wo shitte saè itárà
I can but try やってみるしかありません yátte mirù shika arímasèn
all but finished もう少しで出来上りです mó sukoshì de dekíagari desù

butcher [butʃ'ə:r] *n* (tradesman) 肉屋 nikúyà
♦*vt* (cattle etc for meat) と殺する tosátsu suru; (prisoners etc) 虐殺する gyakúsatsu suru
butcher's (shop) [butʃ'ə:rz-] *n* 精肉店 seínikutèn, 肉屋 nikúyà
butler [bʌt'lə:r] *n* 執事 shítsùji
butt [bʌt] *n* (large barrel) たる tarú; (of

pistol) 握り nigíri; (of rifle) 床尾 shōbi; (of cigarette) 吸い殻 suígara; (*fig*: target: of teasing, criticism etc) 的 matō
♦*vt* (subj: goat, person) 頭で突く atáma de tsukù

butter [bʌt'ə:r] *n* (CULIN) バター bátā
♦*vt* (bread) ...にバターを塗る ...ni bátā wo nurú

buttercup [bʌt'ə:rkʌp] *n* キンポウゲ kínpōge

butterfly [bʌt'ə:rflai] *n* (insect) チョウチョウ chōchō; (SWIMMING: *also*: butterfly stroke) バタフライ bátāfurai

butt in *vi* (interrupt) ...に割込む ...ni waríkomù

buttocks [bʌt'əks] *npl* (ANAT) しり shirí

button [bʌt'ən] *n* (on clothes) ボタン botán; (on machine) 押しボタン oshíbotàn; (*US*: badge) バッジ bájjì
♦*vt* (*also*: button up) ...のボタンをはめる ...no botán wo haméru
♦*vi* ボタンで止まる botán de tomáru

buttress [bʌt'tris] *n* (ARCHIT) 控え壁 hikáekàbe

buxom [bʌk'səm] *adj* (woman) 胸の豊かな muné no yutàka na

buy [bai] (*pt, pp* bought) *vt* 買う kaú
♦*n* (purchase) 買物 kaímono
to buy someone something/something for someone ...に...を買って上げる ...ni ...wo katté agéru
to buy something from someone ...から...を買う ...kará ...wo kaú
to buy someone a drink ...に酒をおごる ...ni saké wo ogóru

buyer [bai'ə:r] *n* (purchaser) 買手 kaíte; (COMM) 仕入係 shiíregakàri, バイヤー báíyā

buzz [bʌz] *n* (noise: of insect) ぶんぶんという音 bunbun to iú otó; (: of machine etc) うなり unári; (*inf*: phone call): *to give someone a buzz* ...に電話を掛ける ...ni defiwa wo kakérù
♦*vi* (insect) ぶんぶん羽音を立てる bunbun haóto wo terù; (saw) うなる unárù

buzzer [bʌz'ə:r] *n* (ELEC) ブザー búzā

buzz word (*inf*) *n* 流行語 ryúkōgo

KEYWORD

by [bai] *prep* **1** (referring to cause, agent)
...に（によって）...ni (yotte)
killed by lightning 雷に打たれて死ん
だ kamínari ni ùtárete shínda
surrounded by a fence 塀に囲まれた
heí ni kakomareta
a painting by Picasso ピカソの絵画
pikásò no káîga
it's by Shakespeare シェイクスピアの
作品です sheíkusupìa no sakúhin desù
2 (referring to method, manner, means)
...で ...de
by bus/car/train バス〔車，列車〕で
básù(kurúma, rèssha)de
to pay by check 小切手で払う kogíttè
de haráù
by moonlight/candlelight 月明り〔ろ
うそくの灯〕で tsukíakàri(rósoku no a-
kari)de
by saving hard, he ... 一生懸命に金を
貯めて彼は... isshókènmei ni kané wo
tamete karè wa...
3 (via, through) ...を通って ...wo tóttè,
...経由で ...kéîyu de
we came by Dover ドーバー経由で来ま
した dóbàkeîyu de kimáshìta
he came in by the back door 彼は裏口
から入りました kárè wa uráguchi kara
hairimashìta
4 (close to) ...のそばに〔で〕 ...no sóbà ni
〔de〕, ...の近くに〔で〕 ...no chikákù ni
〔de〕
the house by the river 川のそばにある
家 kawá no sobà ni árù ié
a holiday by the sea 海辺の休暇 umíbe no kyūka
she sat by his bed 彼女は彼のベッドの
そばに座っていました kánojò wa kárè
no béddò no sóbà ni suwátte imashìta
5 (past) ...を通り過ぎて ...wo tórisugíte
she rushed by me 彼女は足早に私の前
を通り過ぎた kánojò wa ashíbaya ni
wàtákushi no maè wo tórisugíta
I go by the post office every day 私
は毎日郵便局の前を通ります watákushi
wa maìnichi yūbìnkyoku no máè wo

tórimasù
6 (not later than) ...までに ...mádè ni
by 4 o'clock 4時までに yójì made ni
by this time tomorrow 明日のこの時間
までに myónichì no konó jikan màdè ni
*by the time I got here it was too
late* 私がここに着いたころにはもう手遅
れでした watákushi ga kòkó ni tsuíta
koro ni wá mŏ teŏkure deshita
7 (during): *by daylight* 日中に nitchū ni
8 (amount) ...単位で ...tàn-i de
by the kilo/meter キロ〔メーター〕単位
で kiró(mētā)tàn-i de
paid by the hour 時給をもらって jikyū
wo moratte
one by one (people) 1人ずつ hitórizutsù;
(animals) 1匹ずつ ippíkizutsù; (things) 1
つずつ hitótsuzutsù
little by little 少しずつ sukóshizutsù
9 (MATH, measure): *to divide by 3* 3
で割る sán de waru
to multiply by 3 3を掛ける sán wo
kakerù
a room 3 meters by 4 3メーター掛ける
4メーターの部屋 sánmētā kakerù yón-
mētā no heyá
it's broader by a meter 1メーターも広
くなっている ichímētà mŏ hiróku náttè
iru
10 (according to) ...に従って ...nì shitágatte
to play by the rules ルールを守る rúrù
wo mamórù
it's all right by me 私は構いませんよ
watákushi wa kàmáimasèn yó
11: *(all) by oneself etc* 一人だけで hitórì dakē dè
he did it (all) by himself 彼は彼1人
だけの力でやりました kárè wa kárè hitóri dake nò chikára dè yarímashìta
*he was standing (all) by himself in
the corner* 彼は1人ぼっちで隅に立って
いました kárè wa hitóribotchì de súmì
ni táttè imáshìta
12: *by the way* ところで tokóro dè
*by the way, did you know Claire
was back?* ところでね，クレアが帰っ
て来たのをご存知? tokóro dè ne, kùrea

ga kâette kita no wo go-zònji?
this wasn't my idea by the way しか
しね、これを提案したのは私じゃないか
らね shikáshí nê, korê wo teian shita nò
wa watákushi ja nài kara nê
♦*adv* 1 *see* go; pass *etc*
2: *by and by* やがて yagáte
*by and by they came to a fork in the
road* やがて道路はY字路になりました
yagáte dòro ha wafjirò ni narímashìta
they'll come back by and by そのう
ち帰って来ますよ sonô uchi kaètte kimásù yo
by and large (on the whole) 大体におい
て dáitaì ni ôite, 往々にして ōō ni shite
*by and large I would agree with
you* 大体あなたと同じ意見です dáitar a-
natá to onáji ikèn desu
*Britain has a poor image abroad, by
and large* 海外における英国のイメージ
は往々にして悪い kâigai ni okéru êîko-
ku no ìmèjì wa ōō ni shite wàrûî

bye(-bye) [bai'(bai')] *n excl* じゃあねじゃ
ね、バイバイ bâîbai
by(e)-law [bai'lɔ:] *n* 条例 jôrei
by-election [bai'ilekʃən] (*BRIT*) *n* 補欠
選挙 hokêtsuseñkyo
bygone [bai'gɔ:n] *adj* (age, days) 昔の
mukáshi no
♦*n*: *let bygones be bygones* 済んだ事を
水に流す sûuda kotô ni mizú ni nagásù
bypass [bai'pæs] *n* (AUT) バイパス baî-
pasu; (MED: operation) 冠状動脈バイパ
ス kańjōdōmyakubaîpasu
♦*vt* (town) ...にバイパスを設ける ...ni baî-
pasu wo môkerù
by-product [bai'prɑːdəkt] *n* (of industrial process) 副産物 fukúsañbutsu; (of
situation) 二次的結果 nijítekikekka
bystander [bai'stændər] *n* (at accident,
crime) 居合せた通行人 iáwasèta tsúkō-
nin
byte [bait] *n* (COMPUT) バイト bâîto
byword [bai'wərd] *n*: *to be a byword
for* ...の代名詞である ...no daîmeîshi de
arù
by-your-leave [baiju:rli:v'] *n*: *without*

so much as a by-your-leave 自分勝手
に jibúnkattè ni

C

C [si:] *n* (MUS: note) ハ音 há-òn; (: key) ハ
調 háchō
C. [si:] *abbr* = centigrade
C.A. [si:ei'] *abbr* = chartered accountant
cab [kæb] *n* (taxi) タクシー tákùshī; (of
truck, tractor etc) 運転台 uñtendai
cabaret [kæbərei'] *n* (nightclub) キャバ
レー kyábàrē; (floor show) フロアショー
furôashō
cabbage [kæb'idʒ] *n* キャベツ kyábètsu
cabin [kæb'in] *n* (on ship) キャビン kyá-
bìn; (on plane) 操縦室 sōjūshìtsu; (house)
小屋 koyá
cabin cruiser *n* 大型モーターボート ô-
gata môtābôto, クルーザー kúrùzā ◊居
室、炊事場などのある物を指す kyôshì-
tsu, suíjiba nádò no árù monó wo sásù
cabinet [kæb'ənit] *n* (piece of furniture)
戸棚 todána, キャビネット kyabínettò;
(*also*: display cabinet) ガラス戸棚 garásu tódàna; (POL) 内閣 naîkaku
cable [kei'bəl] *n* (strong rope) 綱 tsuná;
(ELEC, TEL, TV) ケーブル kêburu
♦*vt* (message, money) 電信で送る defi-
shin de okúru
cable-car [kei'bəlkɑːr] *n* ケーブルカー
kêburukà
cable television *n* 有線テレビ yúsente-
rèbi
cache [kæʃ] *n*: *a cache of drugs* 隠匿さ
れた麻薬 iñtoku saretá mayáku
a weapons cache 隠匿武器 iñtokubùki
cackle [kæk'əl] *vi* (person, witch) 薄気味
悪い声で笑う usúkimiwaruî kôê de waráù; (hen) こここと鳴く kokoko to nákù
cacti [kæk'tai] *npl of* cactus
cactus [kæk'təs] (*pl* cacti) *n* サボテン
sabóten
caddie [kæd'i:] *n* (GOLF) キャディー
kyádì
caddy [kæd'i:] *n* = caddie

cadet [kədet'] *n* (MIL) 士官候補生 shikánkōhosèi; (POLICE) 警察学校の生徒 keísatsugakkō no sēīto

cadge [kædʒ] (*inf*) *vt* (lift, cigarette etc) ねだる nedáru

Caesarean [size:r'i:ən] (*BRIT*) = **Cesarean**

café [kæfei'] *n* (snack bar) 喫茶店 kíssàten

cafeteria [kæfiti:'ri:ə] *n* (in school, factory, station) 食堂 shokúdō

caffein(e) [kæ'fi:n] *n* カフェイン kaféìn

cage [keidʒ] *n* (of animal) おり orí, ケージ kèji; (*also*: **bird cage**) 鳥かご toríkago, ケージ kèji; (of lift) ケージ kèji

cagey [kei'dʒi:] (*inf*) *adj* 用心深い yōjinbukaì

cagoule [kəgu:l'] (*BRIT*) *n* カグール kágūru ◇薄手の雨ガッパ usúde no amágappa

Cairo [kai'rou] *n* カイロ káìro

cajole [kədʒoul'] *vt* 丸め込む marúmekomù

cake [keik] *n* (CULIN: large) デコレーションケーキ dekórēshonkèki; (: small) 洋菓子 yōgashì

a cake of soap 石けん1個 sekkén íkkò

caked [keikt] *adj*: **caked with** (blood, mud etc) ...の塊で覆われた ...no katámari de ōwareta

calamity [kəlæm'iti:] *n* (disaster) 災難 saínan

calcium [kæl'si:əm] *n* (in teeth, bones etc) カルシウム karúshiùmu

calculate [kæl'kjəleit] *vt* (work out: cost, distance, numbers etc) 計算する keísan suru; (: effect, risk, impact etc) 予測する yosóku suru

calculating [kæl'kjəleitiŋ] *adj* (scheming) ずる賢い zurúgashikoì

calculation [kælkjəlei'ʃən] *n* (MATH) 計算 keísan; (estimate) 予測 yosóku

calculator [kæl'kjəleitə:r] *n* 電卓 deñtaku

calculus [kæl'kjələs] *n* (MATH) 微積分学 bisékibungàku

calendar [kæl'əndə:r] *n* (of year) カレンダー káreñdà; (timetable, schedule) 予定表 yotéihyō

calendar month/year *n* 暦月〔年〕 rekígetsu〔nen〕

calf [kæf] (*pl* **calves**) *n* (of cow) 子ウシ koúshi; (of elephant, seal etc) ...の子 ...no ko; (*also*: **calfskin**) 子牛革 koúshigàwa, カーフスキン káfusukiǹ; (ANAT) ふくらはぎ fukúrahàgi

caliber [kæl'əbə:r] (*BRIT* **calibre**) *n* (of person) 能力 nōryoku; (of skill) 程度 téìdo; (of gun) 口径 kōkéi

call [kɔ:l] *vt* (christen, name) 名付ける nazúkerù; (label) ...を...と呼ぶ ...wo...to yobú; (TEL) ...に電話を掛ける ...ni deñwa wo kakérù; (summon: doctor etc) 呼ぶ yobú; (: witness etc) 召喚する shōkan suru; (arrange: meeting) 召集する shōshū suru

♦*vi* (shout) 大声で言う ōgoè de iú; (telephone) 電話を掛ける deñwa wo kakerù; (visit: *also*: **call in**, **call round**) 立寄る tachíyoru

♦*n* (shout) 呼声 yobígoè; (TEL) 電話 deñwa; (of bird) 鳴声 nakígoè

: to be called ... ...と呼ばれる ...to yobárerù, ...という ...to íù

on call (nurse, doctor etc) 待機して taíki shitè

call back *vi* (return) また寄る matá yorú; (TEL) 電話を掛け直す deñwa wo kakénaosù

callbox [kɔ:l'bɑ:ks] (*BRIT*) *n* 電話ボックス deñwabokkùsu

caller [kɔ:l'ə:r] *n* (visitor) 訪問客 hōmoñkyaku; (TEL) 電話を掛けてくる人 deñwa wo kakète kurù hitò

call for *vt fus* (demand) 要求する yōkyū suru; (fetch) 迎えに行く mukáe ni ikú

call girl *n* (prostitute) コールガール kōrugàru

call-in [kɔ:l'in] (*US*) *n* (phone-in) ◇視聴者が電話で参加する番組 shíchōsha ga deñwa de sañka suru bañgumi

calling [kɔ:l'iŋ] *n* (occupation) 職業 shokùgyō; (*also*: **religious calling**) 神のお召し kámí no o-méshi

calling card (*US*) *n* 名刺 meíshi

call off *vt* (cancel) 中止する chúshi suru

call on vt fus (visit) 訪ねる tazúnerù, 訪問する hōmon suru; (appeal to) ...に...を求める ...ni ...wo motómerù

callous [kǽl'əs] adj (heartless) 冷淡な reítañ na

call out vt (name etc) 大声でいう őgoè de iù; (summon for help etc) 呼び出す yobídasu
♦vi (shout) 大声で言う őgoè de iú

call up vt (MIL) 召集する shōshū suru; (TEL) ...に電話をかける ...ni deñwa wo kakérù

calm [kɑːm] adj (unworried) 落着いている ochítsuite irú; (peaceful) 静かな shízùka na; (weather, sea) 穏やかな odáyàka na
♦n (quiet, peacefulness) 静けさ shizúkesà
♦vt (person, child) 落着かせる ochítsukasèru; (fears, grief etc) 鎮める shizúmerù

calm down vi (person) 落着く ochítsukù
♦vt (person) 落着かせる ochítsukasèru

Calor gas [kǽ'lɔːr-] ® n ◇携帯用燃料ガスボンベの商品名 keítaiyō neñryō gasuboñbe no shōhiñmei

calorie [kǽl'əːri:] n カロリー káròrī

calves [kævz] npl of **calf**

camber [kǽm'bəːr] n (of road) 真ん中が高くなっている事 mañnaka ga takakù nattè irú kotó

Cambodia [kæmbou'di:ə] n カンボジア kañbojìa

came [keim] pt of **come**

camel [kǽm'əl] n (ZOOL) ラクダ rakúda

cameo [kǽm'i:ou] n (jewellery) カメオ kámèo

camera [kǽm'əːrə] n (PHOT) 写真機 shashíñki, カメラ kámèra; (CINEMA) 映画カメラ eíga kámèra; (also: **TV camera**) テレビカメラ terébi kamèra
in camera (LAW) 非公開で híkòkai de

cameraman [kǽm'əːrəmæn] (pl **cameramen**) n (CINEMA, TV) カメラマン kaméramàn

camouflage [kǽm'əflɑːʒ] n (MIL) カムフラージュ kamúfuràju; (ZOOL) 隠ぺいの擬態 iñpeitekigitái
♦vt (conceal: also MIL) 隠す kakúsù

camp [kæmp] n (encampment) キャンプ場 kyañpujō; (MIL: barracks) 基地 kichí; (for prisoners) 収容所 shúyōjo; (faction) 陣営 jiñ-ei
♦vi (in tent) キャンプする kyañpu suru
♦adj (effeminate) 女々しい memēshiì

campaign [kæmpein'] n (MIL) 作戦 sakúsen; (POL etc) 運動 uñdō, キャンペーン kyañpèn
♦vi (objectors, pressure group etc) 運動をする uñdō wo suru

camp bed (BRIT) n 折畳みベッド orítatami beddō

camper [kǽm'pəːr] n (person) キャンパー kyañpā; (vehicle) キャンピングカー kyañpingukā

camping [kǽm'piŋ] n 野営 yaéi, キャンピング kyañpiñgu
to go camping キャンピングに行く kyañpiñgu ni iku

campsite [kæmp'sait] n キャンプ場 kyañpujō

campus [kǽm'pəs] n (SCOL) キャンパス kyañpasu

can¹ [kæn] n (container: for foods, drinks, oil etc) 缶 káñ
♦vt (foods) 缶詰にする kañzume ni suru

KEYWORD

can² [kæn] (negative **cannot**, **can't** conditional and pt **could**) aux vb 1 (be able to) 出来る dekírù
you can do it if you try 努力すればできますよ dóryòku surébà dekímasù yo
I'll help you all I can できるだけ力になりましょう dekíru dake chíkára nì narímashō
she couldn't sleep that night その晩彼女は眠れませんでした sonó ban kanòjo wa nemúremasèn deshita
I can't go on any longer 私はもうこれ以上やっていけません watákushi wa mō koré ijō yatté ikemasen
I can't see you あなたの姿が見えません anátà no súgàta ga miémasen
can you hear me? 私の声が聞えますか watákushi no koè ga kikőemasù ká
I can see you tomorrow, if you're

free 明日でよかったらお会いできますよ asú dè yókáttara o-ái dekimasù yó

2 (know how to) ...の仕方が分かる ...no shikáta ga wakarù, ...ができる ...ga dekírù

I can swim/play tennis/drive 私は水泳〔テニス，運転〕ができます watákushi wa sūíei(ténisù, únten)ga dèkímasu

can you speak French? あなたはフランス語ができますか anátā wa furánsugo ga dèkimasù ká

3 (may) ...してもいいですか ...shíté mò íi desu ká

can I use your phone? 電話をお借りしてもいいですか dénwa wo ò-kári shite mò íi desu ká

could I have a word with you? ちょっと話しがあるんですが chóttò hanáshi gà árùn desu ga

you can smoke if you like タバコを吸いたければ遠慮なくどうぞ tabáko wo suitakèreba énryo nakù dōzo

can I help you with that? 手を貸しましょうか té wò kashímashō ka

4 (expressing disbelief, puzzlement): *it can't be true!* うそでしょう úso deshố

what CAN he want? あいつは何をねらっているのだろうね aítsu wa nánì wo neráttè iru dàro né

5 (expressing possibility, suggestion, etc) ...かも知れない ...ká mò shirenai

he could be in the library 彼は図書室にいるかも知れません kárè wa toshóshìtsu ni irú kà mo shiremasen

she been delayed 彼女は何かの原因で出発が遅れたかも知れません kánòjo wa nánìka no gén-in de shùppátsu ga òkúreta kà mo shirémasèn

Canada [kænədə] *n* カナダ kánada
Canadian [kəneiˈdiːən] *adj* カナダの kánàda no
♦*n* カナダ人 kanádajìn
canal [kənælˈ] *n* (for ships, barges, irrigation) 運河 úñga; (ANAT) 管 káñ
canary [kənrˈiː] *n* カナリヤ kanáriya
cancel [kænˈsəl] *vt* (meeting) 中止する chúshi suru; (appointment, reservation,

contract, order) 取消す toríkesu, キャンセルする kyáñseru suru; (cross out: words, figures) 線を引いて消す séñ wo hiíte kesú

the flight was canceled その便は欠航になった sonó bíñ wa kekkố ni nattá

the train was canceled その列車は運休になった sonó resshà wa uñkyū ni nattá

cancellation [kænsəleiˈʃən] *n* (of meeting) 中止 chúshi; (of appointment, reservation, contract, order) 取消し toríkeshi, キャンセル kyáñseru; (of flight) 欠航 kekkố; (of train) 運休 uñkyū
cancer [kænˈsər] *n* (MED) がん gáñ
Cancer (ASTROLOGY) かに座 kaníza
candid [kænˈdid] *adj* (expression, comment) 率直な sotchóku na
candidate [kænˈdideit] *n* (for job) 候補者 kốhoshà; (in exam) 受験者 jukéñsha; (POL) 立候補者 rikkóhoshà
candle [kænˈdəl] *n* ろうそく rốsokù
candlelight [kænˈdəllait] *n*: *by candlelight* ろうそくの明りで rốsokù no akári de
candlestick [kænˈdəlstik] *n* (*also:* **candle holder**: plain) ろうそく立て rốsoku-tàte; (*:* bigger, ornate) しょく台 shokúdai
candor [kænˈdər] (*BRIT* **candour**) *n* (frankness) 率直さ sotchókusà
candy [kænˈdiː] *n* (*also:* **sugar-candy**) 氷砂糖 kốrizatố; (*US*: sweet) あめ amé
candy-floss [kænˈdiːflɔːs] (*BRIT*) *n* 綿あめ watá-àme, 綿菓子 watágashì
cane [kein] *n* (BOT) 茎 kukí ◇竹などの様に中空になっている植物を指す takè nadð no yố ni nakà ga kúdð ni nattě irú shokúbùtsu wo sasù; (for furniture) 藤とう tố; (stick) 棒 bố; (for walking) 杖 tsúě, ステッキ sutékkì
♦*vt* (*BRIT*: SCOL) むち打つ muchífutsu
canine [keiˈnain] *adj* イヌの inú no
canister [kænˈistər] *n* (container: for tea, sugar etc) 容器 yốki ◇茶筒の様な物を指す chazútsu no yố na monó wo sasù; (pressurized container) スプレー缶 supúrēkañ; (of gas, chemicals etc) ボンベ bốñbe

cannabis [kænˈəbis] *n* マリファナ marí-fāna

canned [kænd] *adj* (fruit, vegetables etc) 缶詰の kañzume no

cannibal [kænˈəbəl] *n* (person) 人食い人間 hitókui niñgen; (animal) 共食いする動物 tomógui suru dóbutsu

cannon [kænˈən] (*pl* **cannon** *or* **cannons**) *n* (artillery piece) 大砲 taíhō

cannot [kænˈɑːt] = **can not**

canny [kænˈi] *adj* (quick-witted) 抜け目ない nukémenaì

canoe [kənuːˈ] *n* (boat) カヌー kánû

canon [kænˈən] *n* (clergyman) 司教座聖堂参事会員 shikyózaseídō sañjikàiin; (rule, principle) 規準 kijún

canonize [kænˈənaiz] *vt* (REL) 聖人の列に加える seíjin no retsù ni kuwáerù

can opener *n* 缶切 kañkirì

canopy [kænˈəpi] *n* (above bed, throne etc) 天がい teñgai

can't [kænt] = **can not**

cantankerous [kæntæŋˈkə:rəs] *adj* (fault-finding, complaining) つむじ曲りの tsumújimagàri no

canteen [kæntiːnˈ] *n* (in workplace, school etc) 食堂 shokúdō; (*also:* **mobile canteen**) 移動食堂 idóshokùdō; (*BRIT:* of cutlery) 収納箱 shúnōbàko◊ナイフ、フォークなどを仕舞う箱 naífu, fóku nadò wo shimáu hakò

canter [kæntˈəːr] *vi* (horse) キャンターで走る kyañtā de hashirù

canvas [kænˈvəs] *n* (fabric) キャンバス kyáñbasu; (painting) 油絵 abúraè; (NAUT) 帆 hò ◊総称 sóshō

canvass [kænˈvəs] *vi* (POL): **to canvass for** ...のために選挙運動をする ...no tamè ni senkyoundō wo suru

◆*vt* (investigate: opinions, views) 調査する chōsa surù

canyon [kænˈjən] *n* 峡谷 kyókoku

cap [kæp] *n* (hat) 帽子 bóshi◊主につばのある物を指す ōmò ni tsubà no arù monó wo sásù; (of pen) キャップ kyáppù; (of bottle) ふた futá; (contraceptive) ペッサリー péssàrī; (for toy gun) 紙雷管 kamíraìkan

◆*vt* (outdo) しのぐ shinógù

capability [keipəbilˈəti:] *n* (competence) 能力 nóryoku

capable [keiˈpəbəl] *adj* (person, object): **capable of doing** ...ができる ...ga dekírù; (able: person) 有能な yūnō na

capacity [kəpæsˈiti:] *n* (of container, ship etc) 容積 yōseki; (of stadium etc) 収容力 shūyōryòku; (capability) 能力 nóryoku; (position, role) 資格 shikáku; (of factory) 生産能力 seísannōryòku

cape [keip] *n* (GEO) 岬 misáki; (short cloak) ケープ kèpu

caper [keiˈpəːr] *n* (CULIN: *gen:* capers) ケーパー képā; (prank) いたずら itázura

capital [kæpˈitəl] *n* (*also:* **capital city**) 首都 shútò; (money) 資本金 shihóñkin; (*also:* **capital letter**) 大文字 ómoji

capital gains tax *n* 資本利得税 shihóñritokuzèi

capitalism [kæpˈitəlizəm] *n* 資本主義 shihóñshùgi

capitalist [kæpˈitəlist] *adj* 資本主義の shihóñshùgi no

◆*n* 資本主義者 shihóñshugishà

capitalize [kæpˈitəlaiz]: **capitalize on** *vt fus* (situation, fears etc) 利用する riyō suru

capital punishment 死刑 shikéi

capitulate [kəpitʃˈuleit] *vi* (give in) 降参する kósan suru

capricious [kəpriʃˈəs] *adj* (fickle: person) 気まぐれの kimágure no

Capricorn [kæpˈrikɔːrn] *n* (ASTROLOGY) やぎ座 yagíza

capsize [kæpˈsaiz] *vt* (boat, ship) 転覆させる teñpuku saséru

◆*vi* (boat, ship) 転覆する teñpuku suru

capsule [kæpˈsəl] *n* (MED) カプセル kápùseru; (spacecraft) 宇宙カプセル uchúkapùseru

captain [kæpˈtin] *n* (of ship) 船長 señchō; (of plane) 機長 kichó; (of team) 主将 shushó; (in army) 大尉 taí-i; (in navy) 大佐 taísa; (*US:* in air force) 大尉 taí-i; (*BRIT:* SCOL) 主席の生徒 shuséki no seíto

caption [kæpˈʃən] *n* (to picture) 説明文

setsúmeïbun

captivate [kæp'təveit] vt (fascinate) 魅了する miryō suru

captive [kæp'tiv] adj (person) とりこの toríko no; (animal) 飼育下の shiíkukà no
♦n (person) とりこ toríko; (animal) 飼育下の動物 shiíkukà no dóbutsu

captivity [kæptiv'əti:] n 監禁状態 kañkinjōtai

capture [kæp'tʃə:r] vt (animal, person) 捕まえる tsukámaeru; (town, country) 占領する señryō suru; (attention) 捕える toráerù; (COMPUT) 収納する shūnō suru
♦n (seizure: of animal) 捕獲 hokáku; (: of person: by police) 逮捕 táiho; (: of town, country: by enemy) 占領 señryō; (COMPUT) 収納 shūnō

car [kɑːr] n (AUT) 自動車 jídōsha, 車 kurúma; (: US: carriage) 客車 kyakúsha; (RAIL: BRIT: dining car, buffet car) 特殊車両 tokúshusharyō

carafe [kəræf'] n 水差し mizúsashì

caramel [kær'əməl] n (CULIN: sweet) キャラメル kyarámeru; (: burnt sugar) カラメル karámeru

carat [kær'ət] n (of diamond, gold) カラット karáttò

caravan [kær'əvæn] n (BRIT: vehicle) キャンピングカー kyañpingukà; (in desert) 隊商 taíshò, キャラバン kyáràban

caravan site (BRIT) n オートキャンプ場 ótokyanpujò

carbohydrate [kɑːrbouhai'dreit] n (CHEM, food) 炭水化物 tañsuikabùtsu

carbon [kɑːr'bən] n 炭素 tánso

carbon copy n カーボンコピー káboñ kopī

carbon dioxide [-daiɑːk'said] n 二酸化炭素 nisánkatañso

carbon monoxide [-mənɑːk'said] n 一酸化炭素 issánkatañso

carbon paper n カーボン紙 káboñshi

carburetor [kɑːr'bəreitəːr] (BRIT **carburettor**) n (AUT) キャブレター kyábùretà

carcass [kɑːr'kəs] n (of animal) 死体 shitái

card [kɑːrd] n (cardboard) ボール紙 bórugami; (greetings card, index card etc) カード kādo; (playing card) トランプのカード toráñpu no kādo; (visiting card) 名刺 meíshi

cardboard [kɑːrd'bɔːrd] n ボール紙 bórugami

card game n トランプゲーム toráñpugēmu

cardiac [kɑːr'diːæk] adj (arrest, failure) 心臓の shíñzō no

cardigan [kɑːr'digən] n カーディガン kádigàn

cardinal [kɑːr'dənəl] adj (chief: principle) 重要な júyō na
♦n (REL) 枢機けい sūkikèi
of cardinal importance 極めて重要で kiwámète jūyō de

cardinal number 基数 kisū

card index n カード式索引 kádoshiki sakúin

care [ke:r] n (attention) 注意 chūi; (worry) 心配 shiñpai; (charge) 管理 káñri
♦vi: **to care about** (person, animal) ...を気に掛ける ...wo ki ni kakérù, ...を愛する ...wo aí surù; (thing, idea etc) ...に関心を持つ ...ni kañshin wo motsù
care of (on mail) ...方 ...gatá
in someone's care ...の管理に任せ（られ）て ...no kanri ni makáse(rarè)tè
to take care (to do) ...をするよう心掛ける ...wo suru yō kokórogakerù
to take care of (patient, child etc) ...の世話をする ...no sewá wo suru; (problem, situation) ...の始末を付ける ...no shimátsu wo tsukerù
I don't care 私は構いません watákushi wa kamáimasèn
I couldn't care less 私はちっとも気にしない watákushi wa chittó mò ki ni shinaí

career [kəri:r'] n (job, profession) 職業 shokùgyō; (life: in school, work etc) キャリア kyaría
♦vi (also: **career along**): car, horse) 猛スピードで走る mósupído de hashirù

career woman (pl **career women**) n キャリアウーマン kyaríaùman

care for *vt fus* (look after) ...の世話をする ...no sewá wo suru; (like) ...が好きである ...ga sukí de arū, ...を愛している ...wo aí shité irú

carefree [keːrˈfriː] *adj* (person, attitude) 気苦労のない kigurō no naí

careful [keːrˈfəl] *adj* (cautious) 注意深い chūibukaí; (thorough) 徹底的な tettéiteki na

(be) careful! 気を付けてね ki wo tsukéte ne

carefully [keːrˈfəliː] *adv* (cautiously) 注意深く chūibukakù; (methodically) 念入りに nefi-iri ni

careless [keːrˈlis] *adj* (negligent) 不注意な fuchūi na; (heedless) 軽率な keísotsu na

carelessness [keːrˈlisnis] *n* (negligence) 不注意 fuchūi; (lack of concern) 無とん着 mutoñchaku

caress [kəresˈ] *n* (stroke) 愛ぶ aíbu
♦*vt* (person, animal) 愛ぶする aíbu suru

caretaker [keːrˈteikəːr] *n* (of flats etc) 管理人 kañrinin

car-ferry [kɑːrˈferiː] *n* カーフェリー kāferī

cargo [kɑːrˈgou] (*pl* **cargoes**) *n* (of ship, plane) 積荷 tsumíni, 貨物 kámòtsu

car hire (*BRIT*) *n* レンタカーサービス refitakā sābisu

Caribbean [kærəbiːˈən] *n*: **the Caribbean (Sea)** カリブ海 karíbukaì

caricature [kærˈəkətʃəːr] *n* (drawing) 風刺漫画 fūshimañga, カリカチュア karíkachùa; (description) 風刺文 fūshibùn; (exaggerated account) 真実のわい曲 shiñjitsu no waikyoku

caring [keːrˈiŋ] *adj* (person, society, behavior) 愛情深い aíjōbukaì; (organization) 健康管理の keñkōkañri no

carnage [kɑːrˈnidʒ] *n* (MIL) 虐殺 gyakúsatsu

carnal [kɑːrˈnəl] *adj* (desires, feelings) 肉体的な nikútaiteki na

carnation [kɑːrneiˈʃən] *n* カーネーション káneshon

carnival [kɑːrˈnəvəl] *n* (festival) 謝肉祭 shaníkusài, カーニバル kánibaru; (US:

funfair) カーニバル kánibaru

carnivorous [kɑːrnivˈəːrəs] *adj* (animal, plant) 肉食の nikúshoku no

carol [kærˈəl] *n*: **(Christmas) carol** クリスマスキャロル kurísumasu kyaròru

carp [kɑːrp] *n* (fish) コイ koí

car park (*BRIT*) *n* 駐車場 chūshajō

carp at *vt fus* (criticize) とがめ立てする togámedate suru

carpenter [kɑːrˈpəntəːr] *n* 大工 daíku

carpentry [kɑːrˈpəntriː] *n* 大工仕事 daíkushigòto

carpet [kɑːrˈpit] *n* (in room etc) じゅうたん jūtan, カーペット kápettò; (*fig*: of pine needles, snow etc) じゅうたんの様な... jūtan no yō na...
♦*vt* (room, stairs etc) ...にじゅうたんを敷く ...ni jūtan wo shikú

carpet slippers *npl* スリッパ súrìppa

carpet sweeper [-swiːˈpəːr] *n* じゅうたん掃除機 jūtan sōjikì

carriage [kærˈidʒ] *n* (*BRIT*: RAIL) 客車 kyakúsha; (*also*: **horse-drawn carriage**) 馬車 bashá; (of goods) 運搬 uñpan; (transport costs) 運送料 uñsōryō

carriage return *n* (on typewriter etc) 復帰キー fukkí kī

carriageway [kærˈidʒwei] (*BRIT*) *n* (part of road) 車線 shasén ◇自動車道の上りまたは下り半分を指す jidōshadō no nobóri mata wá kudári hañbuñ wo sasù

carrier [kærˈiːəːr] *n* (transporter, transport company) 運送会社 uñsōgaìsha; (MED) 保菌者 hókìnsha, キャリア kyárìa

carrier bag (*BRIT*) *n* 買い物袋 kaímonobukùro, ショッピングバッグ shoppíngubaggù

carrot [kærˈət] *n* (BOT, CULIN) ニンジン niñjin

carry [kærˈiː] *vt* (take) 携帯する keítai suru; (transport) 運ぶ hakóbu; (involve: responsibilities etc) 伴う tomónaù; (MED: disease, virus) 保有する hoyú suru
♦*vi* (sound) 通る tōru

to get carried away (*fig*: by enthusiasm, idea) 夢中になる muchū ni narū

carrycot [kærˈiːkɑːt] (*BRIT*) *n* 携帯ベビ

一ベッド keítai bebíbèddò

carry on *vi* (continue) 続ける tsuzúkeru
◆*vt* (continue) 続ける tsuzúkeru

carry-on [kær'iːɑːn] (*inf*) *n* (fuss) 大騒ぎ ōsawàgi

carry out *vt* (orders) 実行する jikkō surù; (investigation) 行う okónau

cart [kɑːrt] *n* (for grain, silage, hay etc) 荷車 nígùruma; (*also*: **horsedrawn cart**) 馬車 báshà; (*also*: **handcart**) 手押し車 teóshigurùma
◆*vt* (*inf*: people) 否応なしに連れて行く iyáō nashi ni tsuréte ikú; (objects) 引きずる hikízuru

cartilage [kɑːr'təlidʒ] *n* (ANAT) 軟骨 nañkotsu

carton [kɑːr'tən] *n* (large box) ボール箱 bōrubako; (container: of yogurt, milk etc) 容器 yōki; (of cigarettes) カートン kāton

cartoon [kɑːrtuːn'] *n* (drawing) 漫画 mañga; (*BRIT*: comic strip) 漫画 mañga ◇四こま漫画などを指す yoñkoma manga nadò wo sasù; (CINEMA) アニメ映画 aníme-eìga

cartridge [kɑːr'tridʒ] *n* (for gun) 弾薬筒 dañ-yakutō, 実弾 jitsúdan; (of record-player) カートリッジ kātorijjì; (of pen) インクカートリッジ iñku kātorijjì

carve [kɑːrv] *vt* (meat) 切分ける kiríwakerù, スライスする suráisu surù; (wood, stone) 彫刻する chōkoku suru; (initials, design) 刻む kizámu

carve up *vt* (land, property) 切分ける kiríwakerù

carving [kɑːr'viŋ] *n* (object made from wood, stone etc) 彫刻 chōkoku; (in wood etc: design) 彫物 horímonò; (: art) 彫刻 chōkoku

carving knife *n* カービングナイフ kābingunaìfu

car wash *n* 洗車場 señshajō, カーウォッシュ kāuosshù

cascade [kæskeid'] *n* (waterfall) 小さい滝 chiísaī takí
◆*vi* (water) 滝になって流れ落ちる takí ni natté nagáreochirù; (hair, people, things) 滝の様に落ちる takí no yō ni o-

chirù

case [keis] *n* (situation, instance) 場合 baái; (MED) 症例 shōrei; (LAW) 事件 jíkèn; (container: for spectacles etc) ケース kēsu; (box: of whisky etc) 箱 hakó, ケース kēsu; (*BRIT*: *also*: **suitcase**) スーツケース sūtsukēsu

in case (of) (fire, emergency) ...の場合に ...no baái ni

in any case とにかく toníkaku

just in case 万一に備えて mañ-ichi ni sonáete

cash [kæʃ] *n* (money) 現金 geñkin
◆*vt* (check etc) 換金する kañkin suru

to pay (in) cash 現金で払う geñkin de haraù

cash on delivery 着払い chakúbarài

cash-book [kæʃ'buk] *n* 出納簿 suítōbo

cash card (*BRIT*) *n* (for cash dispenser) キャッシュカード kyasshúkādo

cash desk (*BRIT*) *n* 勘定カウンター kañjōkauñtà

cash dispenser *n* 現金自動支払い機 geñkin jidōshiharaìki, カード kādokí

cashew [kæʃ'uː] *n* (*also*: **cashew nut**) カシューナッツ kashūnattsù

cash flow *n* 資金繰り shikínguri

cashier [kæʃiː'əːr] *n* (in bank) 出納係 suítōgakàri; (in shop, restaurant) レジ係 rejígakàri

cashmere [kæʒ'miːr] *n* (wool, jersey) カシミア kashímia

cash register *n* レジスター réjisutà

casing [kei'siŋ] *n* (covering) 被覆 hífùku

casino [kæsiː'nou] *n* カジノ kájìno

cask [kæsk] *n* (of wine, beer) たる tarú

casket [kæs'kit] *n* (for jewelery) 宝石箱 hōsekibakò; (*US*: coffin) 棺 káñ

casserole [kæs'əroul] *n* (of lamb, chicken etc) キャセロール kyasérōru; (pot, container) キャセロールなべ kyasérōrunabè

cassette [kəset'] *n* (tape) カセットテープ kasétto tēpu

cassette player *n* カセットプレーヤー kasétto purèyā

cassette recorder *n* カセットレコーダー kasétto rekōdā

cast [kæst] (*pt, pp* **cast**) *vt* (throw: light, shadow) 映す utsúsù; (: object, net) 投げる nagérù; (: fishing-line) キャストする kyásùto surù; (: aspersions, doubts) 投掛ける nagékakerù; (glance, eyes) 向ける mukérù; (THEATER) ...に ...の役を振当てる ...ni ...no yakú wo furíaterù; (make: statue) 鋳込む ikómù

♦*n* (THEATER) キャスト kyásùto; (*also*: **plaster cast**) ギプス gípùsu

to cast a spell on (subject: witch etc) ...に魔法を掛ける ...ni mahố wò kakérù

to cast one's vote 投票する tōhyố suru

castaway [kæs'təwei] *n* 難破した人 nanpa shita hitō

caste [kæst] *n* (social class) カースト kásùto; (: **caste system**) 階級制 kaíkyūsei, カースト制 kásutosei

caster [kæs'tə:r] *n* (wheel) キャスター kyásutā

caster sugar (*BRIT*) *n* 粉砂糖 konázatō

casting vote [kæs'tiŋ-] (*BRIT*) *n* 決定票 kettéihyō, キャスティングボート kyásútingubōto

cast iron [kæst'ai'ə:rn] *n* 鋳鉄 chūtetsu

castle [kæs'əl] *n* (building) 城 shirố; (CHESS) 城将 jōshō

cast off *vi* (NAUT) 綱を解く tsuná wo tokù; (KNITTING) 編み終える amíoerù

cast on *vi* (KNITTING) 編み始める amíhajimerù

castor [kæs'tə:r] (*BRIT*) *n* = **caster**

castor oil *n* ひまし油 himáshiyu

castrate [kæs'treit] *vt* (bull, man) 去勢する kyoséi suru

casual [kæʒ'uːəl] *adj* (by chance) 偶然の gūzen no; (irregular: work etc) 臨時の ríñji no; (unconcerned) さりげない sarígenaì; (informal: clothes) 普段用の fudányō no

casually [kæʒ'uːəli] *adv* (in a relaxed way) さりげなく sarígenakù; (dress) 普段着で fudángi de

casualty [kæʒ'uːəltiː] *n* (of war, accident: someone injured) 負傷者 fushōsha; (: someone killed) 死者 shishá; (of situation, event: victim) 犠牲者 giséisha;

(MED: *also*: **casualty department**) 救急病棟 kyúkyūbyōtō

cat [kæt] *n* (pet) ネコ nekố; (wild animal) ネコ科の動物 nekóka no dốbutsu

catalogue [kæt'ələ:g] (*US also*: **catalog**) *n* (COMM: for mail order) カタログ katárogu; (of exhibition, library) 目録 mokúroku

♦*vt* (books, collection, events) ...の目録を作る ...no mokúroku wo tsukurù

catalyst [kæt'əlist] *n* (CHEM, *fig*) 触媒 shokúbai

catapult [kæt'əpʌlt] (*BRIT*) *n* (slingshot) ぱちんこ pachínko

cataract [kæt'ərækt] *n* (MED) 白内障 hakúnaīshō

catarrh [kətɑ:r'] *n* カタル kátàru

catastrophe [kətæs'trəfi:] *n* (disaster) 災害 saígai

catastrophic [kætəstrɑ:f'ik] *adj* (disastrous) 破局的な hakyókuteki na

catch [kætʃ] (*pt, pp* **caught**) *vt* (animal) 捕る tốrù, 捕まえる tsukámaeru; (fish: with net) 捕る tốrù; (: with line) 釣る tsurú; (ball) 捕る tốrù; (bus, train etc) ...に乗る ...ni norú; (arrest: thief etc) 逮捕する taího suru; (surprise: person) びっくりさせる bikkúri sasérù; (attract: attention) 引く hikú; (hear: comment, whisper etc) 聞く kikú; (MED: illness) ...に掛る ...ni kakarù; (person: *also*: **catch up with/to**) ...に追い付く ...ni oítsukù

♦*vi* (fire) 付く tsukù; (become trapped: in branches, door etc) 引っ掛る hikkákarù

♦*n* (of fish etc) 獲物 emóno; (of ball) 捕球 hokyū; (hidden problem) 落し穴 otóshiàna; (of lock) 留金 tomégane; (game) キャッチボール kyátchibòru

to catch one's breath (rest) 息をつく íkì wo tsukù, 一休みする hitoyàsumi surù

to catch fire 燃え出す moédasù

to catch sight of 見付ける mitsúkeru

catching [kætʃ'iŋ] *adj* (infectious) 移る utsurù

catchment area [kætʃ'mənt-] (*BRIT*) (of school) 学区 gakkù; (of hospital) 通院

圏 tsúïnken

catch on vi (understand) 分かる wakarù; (grow popular) 流行する ryūkō suru

catch phrase n キャッチフレーズ kyátchífurēzu

catch up vi (fig: with person, on work) 追付く oítsukù
♦vt (person) ...に追い付く ...ni oítsukù

catchy [kætʃ'i:] adj (tune) 覚え易い obőeyasuï

catechism [kæt'əkizəm] n (REL) 公教要理 kőkyőyőri

categoric(al) [kætəgɔːr'ik(əl)] adj (certain, absolute) 絶対的な zettáiteki na

category [kæt'əgɔːri:] n (set, class) 範ちゅう hańchū

cater [kei'tə:r] vi: **to cater for** (BRIT: person, group) ...向きである ...mukí de arù; (needs) ...を満たす ...wo mitasù; (COMM: weddings etc) ...の料理を仕出しする ...no ryőri wo shidáshi suru

caterer [kei'tə:rə:r] n 仕出し屋 shidáshiya

catering [kei'tə:riŋ] n (trade, business) 仕出し shidáshi

caterpillar [kæt'ə:rpilə:r] n (with hair) 毛虫 kemúshi; (without hair) 芋虫 imomúshi

caterpillar track n キャタピラ kyatápirà

cathedral [kəθi:'drəl] n 大聖堂 daíseidő

catholic [kæθ'əlik] adj (tastes, interests) 広い hiroï

Catholic [kæθ'əlik] adj (REL) カトリック教の katőrikkukyő no
♦n (REL) カトリック教徒 katőrikkukyőto

cat's-eye [kæts'ai'] (BRIT) n (AUT) 反射びょう hańshabyő ◇夜間の目印として道路の中央またはわきに埋込むガラスなどの反射器 yakán no mejírūshi toshitè dőro no chűő mata wà wakí ni umékomù garásu nadò no hańshakī

cattle [kæt'əl] npl ウシ ushí ◇総称 sőshő

catty [kæt'i:] adj (comment, woman) 意地悪な ijíwarù na

caucus [kɔː'kəs] n (POL: group) 実力者会議 jitsúryokusha kaîgi; (: US) 党部会 tő-

bukái

caught [kɔːt] pt, pp of **catch**

cauliflower [kɔː'ləflauə:r] n カリフラワー karífurawà

cause [kɔːz] n (of outcome, effect) 原因 geñ-in; (reason) 理由 riyū; (aim, principle: also POL) 目的 mokúteki
♦vt (produce, lead to: outcome, effect) 引起こす hikíokosù

caustic [kɔːs'tik] adj (CHEM) 腐食性の fushőkusei no; (fig: remark) 辛らつな shiñratsu na

caution [kɔː'ʃən] n (prudence) 慎重さ shiñchōsa; (warning) 警告 keíkoku, 注意 chűi
♦vt (warn: also POLICE) 警告する keíkoku suru

cautious [kɔː'ʃəs] adj (careful, wary) 注意深い chűibukaï

cautiously [kɔː'ʃəsli:] adv 注意深く chűibukakù

cavalier [kævəliə:r'] adj (attitude, fashion) 威張り腐った ibárikusattà

cavalry [kæv'əlri:] n (MIL: mechanized) 装甲部隊 sőkōbutái; (: mounted) 騎兵隊 kihéitai

cave [keiv] n (in cliff, hill) 洞穴 horá-ana

cave in vi (roof etc) 陥没する kañbotsu suru, 崩れる kuzúrerù

caveman [keiv'mæn] (pl **cavemen**) n 穴居人 kékkyojin

cavern [kæv'ə:rn] n どうくつ dőkutsu

caviar(e) [kæv'i:ɑːr] n キャビア kyàbia

cavity [kæv'iti:] n (in wall) 空どう kūdő; (ANAT) 腔 kő; (in tooth) 虫歯の穴 mushíba no aná

cavort [kəvɔːrt'] vi (romp) はしゃぎ回る hashágimawarù

CB [si:'bi:'] n abbr (= Citizens' Band (Radio)) 市民バンド shimínbañdo, シチズンバンド shichízunbañdo

CBI [si:bi:ai'] n abbr (= Confederation of British Industry) 英国産業連盟 eíkokusañgyőreñmei

cc [si:si:'] abbr (= cubic centimeter(s)) 立方センチメートル rippősenchimētoru, cc shíshī; = **carbon copy**

cease [si:s] vt (end, stop) 終える oéru
♦vi (end, stop) 終る owáru, 止る tomáru

ceasefire [si:s'faiə:r'] n (MIL) 停戦 teísen

ceaseless [si:s'lis] adj (chatter, traffic) 絶間ない taéma naí

cedar [si:'də:r] n (tree) ヒマラヤスギ himárayasugí; (wood) シーダー材 shídāzai

cede [si:d] vt (land, rights etc) 譲る yuzúru

ceiling [si:'liŋ] n (in room) 天井 teñjō; (upper limit: on wages, prices etc) 天井 teñjō, 上限 jōgen

celebrate [sel'əbreit] vt (gen) 祝う iwáu; (REL: mass) 挙げる agéru
♦vi お祝いする o-íwai suru

celebrated [sel'əbreitid] adj (author, hero) 有名な yūmei na

celebration [seləbrei'ʃən] n (party, festival) お祝い o-íwai

celebrity [səleb'riti:] n (famous person) 有名人 yūmeíjin

celery [sel'ə:ri:] n セロリ sérðri

celestial [səles'tʃəl] adj (heavenly) 天上的な teñjōteki na

celibacy [sel'əbəsi:] n 禁欲生活 kiñ-yoku seíkatsu

cell [sel] n (in prison: gen) 監房 kañbō; (：solitary) 独房 dokúbō; (in monastery) 個室 koshítsu; (BIO, also of revolutionaries) 細胞 saíbō; (ELEC) 電池 déñchi

cellar [sel'ə:r] n (basement) 地下室 chikáshìtsu; (also: wine cellar) ワイン貯蔵室 waín chozóshìtsu

cello [tʃel'ou] n (MUS) チェロ chérð

cellophane [sel'əfein] n セロハン sérðhan

cellular [sel'jələ:r] adj (BIO: structure, tissue) 細胞の saíbō no; (fabrics) 保温効果の高い hoóňkòka no takaí, 防寒の bôkan no

cellulose [sel'jələous] n (tissue) 繊維素 señ-isò

Celt [selt, kelt] n ケルト人 kerútðjin

Celtic [sel'tik, kel'tik] adj ケルト人の kerútðjin no; (language etc) ケルトの kérùto no

cement [siment'] n (powder) セメント seméNto; (concrete) コンクリート kóñkurī̀to

cement mixer n セメントミキサー seméNto mikisà

cemetery [sem'ite:ri:] n 基地 bóchi

cenotaph [sen'ətæf] n (monument) 戦没者記念碑 señbotsusha kineñhi

censor [sen'sə:r] n (POL, CINEMA etc) 検閲官 keñ-etsúkan
♦vt (book, play, news etc) 検閲する keñetsu suru

censorship [sen'sə:rʃip] n (of book, play, news etc) 検閲 keñ-etsu

censure [sen'ʃə:r] vt (reprove) とがめる togámerù

census [sen'səs] n (of population) 国勢調査 kokúzeichòsa

cent [sent] n (US: also: one-cent coin) 1 セント玉 isséntodamá ¶ see also per

centenary [sen'tənæ:ri:] n (of birth etc) 100周年 hyakúshūnen

center [sen'tə:r] n (BRIT centre) n (of circle, room, line) 中心 chūshin; (of town) 中心部 chūshiñbu, 繁華街 hañkagài; (of attention, interest) 的 matô; (heart: of action, belief etc) 核心 kakúshin; (building: health center, community center) センター séñtā; (POL) 中道 chūdō
♦vt (weight) ...の中心に置く ...no chūshin ni okú; (sights) ...にぴったり合わせる ...ni pittari awaseru; (SOCCER: ball) グランド中央へ飛ばす gurándo chūō e tobásu; (TYP: on page) 中央に合わせる chūō ni awáseru

center forward n (SPORT) センターフォワード señtáfowàdo

center half n (SPORT) センターハーフ señtáhāfu

centigrade [sen'tigreid] adj 摂氏 sesshì

centimeter [sen'təmi:tə:r] n (BRIT centimetre) n センチメートル señchimètoru

centipede [sen'təpi:d] n ムカデ mukáde

central [sen'trəl] adj (in the center) 中心点の chūshiñten no; (near the center) 中心の chūshin no; (committee, government) 中央の chūō no; (idea, figure) 中心の chūshin no

Central America n 中米 chúbei

central heating n セントラルヒーティング señtoraruhītìñgu

centralize [sen'trəlaiz] vt (decision-making, authority) 中央に集中させる chūō ni shūchū saséru

central reservation (BRIT) n (AUT: of road) 中央分離帯 chūōbunritai

centre [sen'tə:r] (etc BRIT) = **center** etc

century [sen'tʃə:ri:] n 世紀 seíki
20th century 20世紀 nijússeíki

ceramic [sərǽm'ik] adj (art, tiles) セラミックの serámikku no

ceramics [sərǽm'iks] npl (objects) 焼物 yakímono

cereal [si:r'i:əl] n (plant, crop) 穀物 kókumotsu; (food) シリアル shiríarù

cerebral [se:r'əbrəl] adj (MED: of the brain) 脳の nō no; (intellectual) 知的な chitéki na

ceremony [se:r'əmouni:] n (event) 式 shikí; (ritual) 儀式 gíshìki; (behavior) 形式 keíshiki
to stand on ceremony 礼儀にこだわる reígi ni kodáwarù

certain [sə:r'tən] adj (sure: person) 確信している kakúshin shité irù; (: fact) 確実な kakújitsu na; (person): **a certain Mr Smith** スミスと呼ばれる男 sumísù to yobareru otóko; (particular): **certain days/places** ある日〔場所〕árù hi 〔bashò〕; (some): **a certain coldness/pleasure** ある程度の冷たさ〔喜び〕árù teido no tsumétasa 〔yorókobi〕
for certain 確実に kakújitsu ni

certainly [sə:r'tənli:] adv (undoubtedly) 間違いなく machígai nakù; (of course) もちろん mochírðn

certainty [sə:r'tənti:] n (assurance) 確実性 kakújitsusei; (inevitability) 必然性 hitsúzensei

certificate [sə:rtif'əkit] n (of birth, marriage etc) 証明書 shómeisho; (diploma) 資格証明書 shikákushōmeisho

certified mail [sə:r'təfaid-] (US) n 配達証明付き書留郵便 haítatsushōmei tsukí kakítome yūbin

certified public accountant (US) n 公認会計士 kónin kaikèishi

certify [sə:r'təfai] vt (fact) 証明する shó-

mei suru; (award a diploma to) ...に資格を与える ...ni shikáku wo atáeru; (declare insane) 精神異常と認定する seíshinijō to niñtei suru

cervical [sə:r'vikəl] adj (smear, cancer) 子宮けい部の shikyűkeîbu no

cervix [sə:r'viks] n (ANAT) 子宮けい部 shikyűkeîbu

Cesarean [size:r'i:ən] (BRIT **Caesarean**) adj: **Cesarean (section)** 帝王切開 teíōsekkài

cesspit [ses'pit] n (sewage tank) 汚水だめ osúidame

cf. abbr = **compare**

ch. abbr = **chapter**

chafe [tʃeif] vt (rub: skin) 擦る súrù

chagrin [ʃəgrin'] n (annoyance) 悔しさ kuyáshisa; (disappointment) 落胆 rakútan

chain [tʃein] n (for anchor, prisoner, dog etc) 鎖 kusári; (on bicycle) チェーン chèn; (jewelery) 首飾り kubíkazàri; (of shops, hotels) チェーン chèn; (of events, ideas) 連鎖 reñsa
♦vt (also: **chain up**: prisoner, dog) 鎖につなぐ kusári ni tsunágu
an island chain/a chain of islands 列島 rettó
a mountain chain/a chain of mountains 山脈 sañmyaku

chain reaction n 連鎖反応 reñsahañnō

chain-smoke [tʃein'smouk] vi 立続けにタバコを吸う tatétsuzuke ni tabáko wo suú

chain store n チェーンストア chénsutoà

chair [tʃe:r] n (seat) いす isú; (armchair) 安楽いす añrakuisù; (of university) 講座 kóza; (of meeting) 座長 zachō; (of committee) 委員長 iíñchō
♦vt (meeting) 座長を務める zachō wo tsutómerù

chairlift [tʃe:r'lift] n リフト rífùto

chairman [tʃe:r'mən] (pl **chairmen**) n (of committee) 委員長 iíñchō; (BRIT: of company) 社長 shachō

chalet [ʃælei'] n 山小屋 yamágoya

chalice [tʃæl'is] n (REL) 聖さん杯 seísañhai

chalk [tʃɔ:k] *n* (GEO) 白亜 hákùa; (for writing) 白墨 hakúboku, チョーク chōku

challenge [tʃǽl'indʒ] *n* (of new job, unknown, new venture etc) 挑戦 chōsen; (to authority, received ideas etc) 反抗 hañkō; (dare) 挑戦 chōsen

♦*vt* (SPORT) ...に試合を申込む ...ni shiái wo mōshikomù; (rival, competitor) 挑戦 する chōsen suru; (authority, right, idea etc) ...に反抗する ...ni hañkō suru

to challenge someone to do something ...に...を...をやれるものならやってみろ と挑戦する ...ni ...wo yaréru monó nara yatté miro to chōsen suru

challenging [tʃǽl'indʒiŋ] *adj* (career, task) やりがいを感じさせる yarígai wo kañjì saséru; (tone, look etc) 挑発的な chōhatsuteki na

chamber [tʃeim'bə:r] *n* (room) 部屋 heyá; (POL: house) 院 íñ; (BRIT: LAW: *gen pl*) 弁護士事務室 beñgoshi jimushītsu; (: of judge) 判事室 hañjishītsu

chamber of commerce 商工会議所 shōkōkaigisho

chambermaid [tʃeim'bə:rmeid] *n* (in hotel) メード mēdo

chamber music *n* 室内音楽 shitsúnai oñgaku

chamois [ʃæm'i:] *n* (ZOOL) シャモア shamòa; (cloth) セーム革 sēmugawa

champagne [ʃæmpein'] *n* シャンペン shañpeñ

champion [tʃæm'pi:ən] *n* (of league, contest, fight) 優勝者 yūshōsha, チャンピオ ン chañpion; (of cause, principle, person) 擁護者 yōgosha

championship [tʃæm'pi:əñʃip] *n* (contest) 選手権決定戦 señshukèn kettéisen; (title) 選手権 señshukèn

chance [tʃæns] *n* (likelihood, possibility) 可能性 kanōsei; (opportunity) 機会 kikái, チャンス cháñsu; (risk) 危険 kikén, か け kakě

♦*vt* (risk): *to chance it* 危険を冒す kikén wo okasù, 冒険をする bōken wo suru

♦*adj* 偶然の gűzen no

to take a chance 危険を冒す kikén wo okasù, 冒険をする bōken wo suru

by chance 偶然に gűzen ni

chancellor [tʃæn'sələ:r] *n* (head of government) 首相 shushō

Chancellor of the Exchequer (BRIT) *n* 大蔵大臣 ōkuradaìjin

chandelier [ʃændəli'ə:r] *n* シャンデリア shañderìa

change [tʃeindʒ] *vt* (alter, transform) 変 える kaéru; (wheel, bulb etc) 取替える toríkaeru; (clothes) 着替える kigáerù; (job, address) 変える kaéru; (baby, diaper) 替える kaéru; (exchange: money) 両 替する ryōgae suru

♦*vi* (alter) 変る kawáru; (change one's clothes) 着替える kigáerù; (change trains, buses) 乗換える noríkaerù; (traffic lights) 変る kawáru; (be transformed): *to change into* ...に変る ...ni kawáru, ...になる ...ni narú

♦*n* (alteration) 変化 héñka; (difference) 違い chigái; (also: **change of clothes**) 着 替え kigáe; (of government, climate, job) 変る事 kawáru kotò; (coins) 小銭 kozéni; (money returned) お釣 o-tsúri

to change one's mind 気が変る ki gá kawarù

for a change たまには tamá ni wa

changeable [tʃeindʒ'əbəl] *adj* 変りやすい kawáriyasuì

change machine *n* 両替機 ryōgaekì

changeover [tʃeindʒ'ouvə:r] *n* (to new system) 切替え kirīkae

changing [tʃein'dʒiŋ] *adj* (world, nature) 変る kawáru

changing room (BRIT) *n* 更衣室 kōishìtsu

channel [tʃæn'əl] *n* (TV) チャンネル cháñneru; (in sea, river etc) 水路 suíro; (groove) 溝 mizó; (fig: means) 手続 tetsúzùki, ルート rūto

♦*vt* (money, resources) 流す nagásù

the (English) Channel イギリス海峡 igírisu kaíkyō

the Channel Islands チャネル諸島 chanéru shotō

chant [tʃænt] *n* (of crowd, fans etc) 掛声 kakégoè; (REL: song) 詠唱歌 eíshōka

♦*vt* (word, name, slogan) 唱える tonáerù

chaos [kei'ɑːs] *n* (disorder) 混乱 końran

chaotic [keiɑːt'ik] *adj* (mess, jumble) 混乱した końran shitá

chap [tʃæp] (*BRIT*: *inf*) *n* (man) やつ yátsu

chapel [tʃæp'əl] *n* (in church) 礼拝堂 reíhaidō; (in hospital, prison, school etc) チャペル cháperu; (*BRIT*: non-conformist chapel) 教会堂 kyōkaidō

chaperone [ʃæp'əroun] *n* (for woman) 付添い tsukísoi, シャペロン shapéroñ

♦*vt* (woman, child) ...に付添う ...ni tsukísoù

chaplain [tʃæp'lin] *n* (REL, MIL, SCOL) 付属牧師 fuzőkubokùshi

chapped [tʃæpt] *adj* (skin, lips) あかぎれのした akágire shitá

chapter [tʃæp'tə:r] *n* (of book) 章 shō; (of life, history) 時期 jíkì

char [tʃɑːr] *vt* (burn) 黒焦げにする kurőkoge ni suru

♦*n* (*BRIT*) = **charwoman**

character [kær'iktəːr] *n* (nature) 性質 seíshitsu; (moral strength) 気骨 kikőtsu; (personality) 人格 jińkaku; (in novel, film) 人物 jińbutsu; (letter) 文字 mőjì

characteristic [kæriktəris'tik] *adj* (typical) 特徴的な tokúchōteki na

♦*n* (trait, feature) 特徴 tokúchō

characterize [kær'iktəraiz] *vt* (typify) ...の特徴である ...no tokúchō de arú; (describe the character of) ...の特徴を描写する ...no tokúchō wo byősha suru

charade [ʃəreid'] *n* (sham, pretence) 装いyosóoi

charcoal [tʃɑːr'koul] *n* (fuel) 炭 sumí, 木炭 mokútañ; (for drawing) 木炭 mokútañ

charge [tʃɑːrdʒ] *n* (fee) 料金 ryőkin; (LAW: accusation) 容疑 yőgi; (responsibility) 責任 sekínin

♦*vt* (for goods, services) ...の料金を取る ...no ryőkin wo torù; (LAW: accuse): *to charge someone (with)* 起訴する kiső suru; (battery) 充電する júden suru; (MIL: enemy) ...に突撃する ...ni totsúgeki suru

♦*vi* (animal) 掛って来る〔行く〕kakáttè

kurù〔ikú〕; (MIL) 突撃する totsúgeki suru

to take charge of (child) ...の面倒を見る ...no meńdō wo mirù; (company) ...の指揮を取る ...no shikí wo torú

to be in charge of (person, machine) ...の責任を持っている ...no sekínin wo mottè irù; (business) ...の責任者である ...no sekíninsha de arù

how much do you charge? 料金はいくらですか ryőkin wa ikúra desù ka

to charge an expense (up) to someone's account ...の勘定に付ける ...no kańjō ni tsukerù

charge card *n* (for particular shop or organization) クレジットカード kurèjittokādo ◇特定の店でしか使えない物を指す tokútei nò mise de shika tsukáenai monò wo sásù

charges [tʃɑːr'dʒiz] *npl* (bank charges, telephone charges etc) 料金 ryőkin

to reverse the charges (TEL) 先方払いにする seńpōbarài ni surù

charisma [kəriz'mə] *n* カリスマ性 karísumasei

charitable [tʃær'itəbəl] *adj* (organization) 慈善の jizén no

charity [tʃær'iti:] *n* (organization) 慈善事業 jizénjigyő; (kindness) 親切さ shińsetsusa; (generosity) 寛大さ kańdaisa; (money, gifts) 施し hodőkoshi

charlady [tʃɑːr'leidi:] (*BRIT*) *n* = **charwoman**

charlatan [ʃɑːr'lətən] *n* 偽者 nísemono

charm [tʃɑːrm] *n* (attractiveness) 魅力 miryőku; (to bring good luck) お守り o-mámori; (on bracelet etc) 飾り kazári

♦*vt* (please, delight) うっとりさせる uttőri sasèru

charming [tʃɑːr'miŋ] *adj* (person, place) 魅力的な miryőkuteki na

chart [tʃɑːrt] *n* (graph) グラフ gúrafu; (diagram) 図 zu; (map) 海図 káìzu

♦*vt* (course) 地図に書く chízù ni kakù; (progress) 図に書く zù ni kakù

charter [tʃɑːr'təːr] *vt* (plane, ship etc) チャーターする chátā surù

♦*n* (document, constitution) 憲章 keńshō; (of university, company) 免許 ménkyo

chartered accountant [tʃɑːˈtəːrd-] (BRIT) n 公認会計士 kṓnin kaikeīshi

charter flight n チャーターフライト chấtâfuraīto

charts [tʃɑːrts] npl (hit parade): **the charts** ヒットチャート hittṓchảto

charwoman [tʃɑːˈwumən] (pl **charwomen**) n 掃除婦 sōjifu

chase [tʃeis] vt (pursue) 追掛ける oíkakerù; (also: **chase away**) 追払う oíharaù
♦n (pursuit) 追跡 tsuíseki

chasm [kæzˈəm] n (GEO) 深い割れ目 fúkai waréme

chassis [ʃæsˈiː] n (AUT) シャシ shashī

chastity [tʃæsˈtitiː] n (REL) 純潔 juńketsu

chat [tʃæt] vi (also: **have a chat**) おしゃべりする o-sháberí surù
♦n (conversation) おしゃべり o-sháberí

chat show (BRIT) n トーク番組 tṓku bańgumi

chatter [tʃætˈəːr] vi (person) しゃべりまくる shabérimakurù; (animal) きゃっきゃっと鳴く kyákkyattṓ nakú; (teeth) がちがち鳴る gachígachi narú
♦n (of people) しゃべり声 shabérigoè; (of birds) さえずり saézuri; (of animals) きゃっきゃっという鳴き声 kyákkyattṓ iú nakígoè

chatterbox [tʃætˈəːrbɑks] (inf) n おしゃべり好き o-sháberizuki

chatty [tʃætˈiː] adj (style, letter) 親しみやすい shitáshimiyasuì; (person) おしゃべりな o-sháberí na

chauffeur [ʃouˈfəːr] n お抱え運転手 okákae-unteñshu

chauvinist [ʃouˈvənist] n (male chauvinist) 男性優越主義者 dańseiyūetsushugishà; (nationalist) 熱狂的愛国主義者 nekkyṓtekiaikokushugishà

cheap [tʃiːp] adj (inexpensive) 安い yasuì; (poor quality) 安っぽい yasúppoì; (behavior, joke) 下劣な gerétsu na
♦adv: **to buy/sell something cheap** 安く買う［売る］yasúkù kaú［urú］

cheaper [tʃiːˈpəːr] adj (less expensive) も

っと安い móttō yasuì

cheaply [tʃiːpˈliː] adv (inexpensively) 安く yasukù

cheat [tʃiːt] vi (in exam) カンニングする kańningu suru; (at cards) いかさまをする ikásama wo suru
♦vt: **to cheat someone (out of something)** ...から ...をだまし取る ...kara ...wo damáshitorù
♦n (person) いかさま師 ikásamashì

check [tʃek] vt (examine: bill, progress) 調べる shiráberù; (verify: facts) 確認する kakúnin suru; (halt: enemy, disease) 食止める kuítomerù; (restrain: impulse, person) 抑える osáerù
♦n (inspection) 検査 kéñsa; (curb) 抑制 yokúsei; (US: bill) 勘定書 kańjōgaki; (BANKING) 小切手 kogittè; (pattern: gen pl) 市松模様 ichímatsumoyō
♦adj (pattern, cloth) 市松模様の ichímatsumoyō no

checkbook [tʃekˈbuk] (US) n 小切手帳 kogittechō

checkerboard [tʃekˈəːrbɔːrd] n チェッカー盤 chekkában

checkered [tʃekˈəːrd] (BRIT **chequered**) adj (fig: career, history) 起伏の多い kifúku no ōì

checkers [tʃekˈəːrz] (US) npl (game) チェッカー chékkā

check in vi (at hotel, airport) チェックインする chekkùin surù
♦vt (luggage) 預ける azúkerù

check-in (desk) [tʃekˈin-] n フロント furónto

checking account [tʃekˈiŋ-] (US) n (current account) 当座預金 tōzayokìn

checkmate [tʃekˈmeit] n (CHESS) 王手 ṓte

check out vi (of hotel) チェックアウトする chekkúaùto surù

checkout [tʃekˈaut] n (in shop) 勘定カウンター kańjō kauñtā

checkpoint [tʃekˈpɔint] n (on border) 検問所 keńmonjo

checkroom [tʃekˈruːm] (US) n (left-luggage office) 手荷物一時預り所 tenímotsu ichíjìazúkarijo

check up vi: to check up on some-thing/someone ...を調べておく ...wo shirábetè okù

checkup [tʃek'ʌp] n (MED) 健康診断 kéñkōshiñdan

cheek [tʃi:k] n (ANAT) ほお hǒ; (impudence) ずうずうしさ zúzūshisà; (nerve) 度胸 dokyǒ

cheekbone [tʃi:k'boun] n ほお骨 hóbone

cheeky [tʃi:ki:] adj (impudent) ずうずうしい zúzūshiì

cheep [tʃi:p] vi (bird) ぴよぴよ鳴く piyópiyo nakú

cheer [tʃi:r] vt (team, speaker) 声援する seíen suru; (gladden) 喜ばす yorókobasù
♦vi (shout) 声援する seíen suru
♦n (shout) 声援 seíen

cheerful [tʃi:r'fəl] adj (wave, smile, person) 朗らかな hogáraka na

cheerio [tʃi:r'i:ou] (BRIT) excl じゃあね jā ne

cheers [tʃi:rz] npl (of crowd etc) 声援 seíen, かっさい kassái
cheers! (toast) 乾杯 kañpai

cheer up vi (person) 元気を出す géñki wo dasù
♦vt (person) 元気づける geñkizukerù

cheese [tʃi:z] n チーズ chízu

cheeseboard [tʃi:z'bourd] n チーズボード chízubòdo ◊チーズを盛り合せる板または皿 chízu wo moríawaserù ità mata wa sará

cheetah [tʃi:'tə] n チーター chītā

chef [ʃef] n (in restaurant, hotel) コック kókkù

chemical [kem'ikəl] adj (fertilizer, warfare) 化学の kágàku no
♦n 化学薬品 kagákuyakùhin

chemist [kem'ist] n (BRIT: pharmacist) 薬剤師 yakúzaìshi; (scientist) 化学者 kagákùsha

chemistry [kem'istri:] n 化学 kágàku

chemist's (shop) [kem'ists-] (BRIT) n 薬局 yakkyóku

cheque [tʃek] (BRIT: BANKING) n = **check**

chequebook [tʃek'buk] (BRIT) n = **checkbook**

cheque card (BRIT) n (to guarantee cheque) 小切手カード kogítte kàdo

chequered [tʃek'ə:rd] (BRIT) adj = **checkered**

cherish [tʃe:r'iʃ] vt (person) 大事にする daíji ni suru; (memory, dream) 心に抱く kokórò ni idakù

cherry [tʃe:r'i:] n (fruit) サクランボウ sakúranbō; (also: cherry tree) サクラ sakúra

chess [tʃes] n チェス chésù

chessboard [tʃes'bo:rd] n チェス盤 chésuban

chest [tʃest] n (ANAT) 胸 muné; (box) ひつ hitsú
chest of drawers 整理だんす seíridañsu

chestnut [tʃes'nʌt] n クリ kurí; (also: chestnut tree) クリの木 kurí no ki

chew [tʃu:] vt (food) かむ kamù

chewing gum [tʃu:'iŋ-] n チューインガム chūiñgamù

chic [ʃi:k] adj (dress, hat etc) スマートな súmàto na; (person, place) 粋な ikí na

chick [tʃik] n (bird) ひな hínà; (inf: girl) べっぴん beppìn

chicken [tʃik'ən] n (bird) ニワトリ niwátori; (meat) 鶏肉 keíniku; (inf: coward) 弱虫 yowamùshi

chicken out (inf) vi おじ気付いて...から手を引く ojíkezuìte ...kara te wo hikú

chickenpox [tʃik'ənpɑ:ks] n 水ぼうそう mizúbōsō

chicory [tʃik'ə:ri:] n チコリ chíkòri

chief [tʃi:f] n (of tribe) しゅう長 shūchō; (of organization, department) ...長 ...chǒ
♦adj (principal) 主な ómò na

chief executive n 社長 shachō

chiefly [tʃi:f'li:] adv (principally) 主に ómò ni

chiffon [ʃifɑ:n'] n (fabric) シフォン shíffòn

chilblain [tʃil'blein] n 霜焼け shimóyake

child [tʃaild] (pl **children**) n 子供 kodómo
do you have any children? お子さんは？ o-kó-san wa?

childbirth [tʃaild'bə:rθ] n お産 osán

childhood [tʃaild'hud] n 子供時分 kodómojíbun

childish [tʃail'diʃ] *adj* (games, attitude, person) 子供っぽい kodómoppoî

childlike [tʃaild'laik] *adj* 無邪気な mújaki na

child minder (*BRIT*) *n* 保母 hóbò

children [tʃil'drən] *npl of* **child**

Chile [tʃil'i:] *n* チリ chírì

Chilean [tʃil:l'eiən] *adj* チリの chírì no
♦*n* チリ人 chírijìn

chill [tʃil] *n* (coldness: in air, water etc) 冷え hié; (MED: illness) 風邪 kazé
♦*vt* (cool: food, drinks) 冷す hiyasù; (person: make cold) 冷す hiyasù; **to be chilled** 体が冷える karáda ga hierù

chilli [tʃil'i:] *n* チリ chírì

chilly [tʃil'i:] *adj* (weather) 肌寒い hadásamuî; (person) 寒気がする samúke ga suru; (response, look) 冷たい tsumétai

chime [tʃaim] *n* (of bell, clock) チャイム cháìmu
♦*vi* チャイムが鳴る chaímu ga narú

chimney [tʃim'ni:] *n* (of house, factory) 煙突 eńtotsu

chimney sweep *n* 煙突掃除夫 eńtotsu sōjifù

chimpanzee [tʃimpænzi:'] *n* チンパンジー chíñpañjī

chin [tʃin] *n* あご agó

China [tʃai'nə] *n* 中国 chūgoku

china [tʃai'nə] *n* (clay) 陶土 tòdo; (crockery) 瀬戸物 setómono

Chinese [tʃaini:z'] *adj* 中国の chūgoku no; (LING) 中国語の chúgokugo no
♦*n inv* (person) 中国人 chúgokujìn; (LING) 中国語 chúgokugo

chink [tʃiŋk] *n* (crack: in door, wall etc) 透き間 sukíma; (clink: of bottles etc) かちん kachín

chip [tʃip] *n* (*BRIT: gen pl*: CULIN) フライドポテト furáidopotèto; (*US: also*: **potato chip**) ポテトチップス potétochìppusu; (of wood, glass, stone) 欠片 kakéra; (COMPUT) チップ chippù
♦*vt*: **to be chipped** (cup, plate) 縁が欠けている fuchí ga kakéte irú

chip in (*inf*) *vi* (contribute) 寄付する kífu surù; (interrupt) 口を挟む kuchí wo

hasamù

chiropodist [kirɑːp'ədist] (*BRIT*) *n* 足治療師 ashí chiryōshi

chirp [tʃəːrp] *vi* (bird) ちゅうちゅう鳴く chūchū nakú

chisel [tʃiz'əl] *n* (for wood) のみ nómì; (for stone) たがね tagáne

chit [tʃit] *n* (note) メモ mémò; (receipt) 領収書 ryōshūsho

chitchat [tʃit'tʃæt] *n* 世間話 sekénbanàshi

chivalrous [ʃiv'əlrəs] *adj* 親切な shíñsetsu na

chivalry [ʃiv'əlri:] *n* (behavior) 親切さ shiñsetsusa; (medieval system) 騎士道 kishídò

chives [tʃaivz] *npl* (herb) チャイブ cháìbu

chlorine [klɔːr'iːn] *n* (CHEM) 塩素 éñso

chock-a-block [tʃɑːk'əblɑːk'] *adj* 一杯で íppaì de

chock-full [tʃɑːk'ful'] *adj* = **chock-a-block**

chocolate [tʃɔːk'əlit] *n* (bar, sweet, cake) チョコレート chokórèto; (drink) ココア kókòa

choice [tʃɔis] *n* (selection) 選んだ物 eránda monò; (option) 選択 seńtaku; (preference) 好み konómi
♦*adj* (fine: cut of meat, fruit etc) 一級の ikkyū no

choir [kwaiəːr] *n* (of singers) 聖歌隊 seíkatai; (area of church) 聖歌隊席 seíkataisèki

choirboy [kwaiəːr'bɔi] *n* 少年聖歌隊員 shóneñ seikataiin

choke [tʃouk] *vi* (on food, drink etc) ...がのどに詰る ...ga nodò ni tsumarù; (with smoke, dust, anger etc) むせる muséru
♦*vt* (strangle) ...ののどを締める ...no nodò wo shimerù; (block): **to be choked (with)** (...で)詰っている (...de) tsumattè irú
♦*n* (AUT) チョーク chóku

cholera [kɑːl'əːrə] *n* コレラ kórèra

cholesterol [kələs'tərɔːl] *n* (fat) コレステロール korésuteròru

choose [tʃuːz] (*pt* **chose**, *pp* **chosen**) *vt* 選

ぶ erábù
to choose to do ...をする事に決める
...wo suru kotó ni kiméru

choosy [tʃuːˈziː] *adj* (difficult to please)
えり好みする erígonomi suru

chop [tʃɑːp] *vt* (wood) 割る warú;
(CULIN: *also*: **chop up**: vegetables, fruit,
meat) 刻む kizámu
◆*n* (CULIN) チョップ chóppù, チャップ
cháppu

chopper [tʃɑːpˈəːr] *n* (helicopter) ヘリコ
プター heríkopùtā

choppy [tʃɑːpˈiː] *adj* (sea) しけの shiké no

chops [tʃɑːps] *npl* (jaws) あご agó

chopsticks [tʃɑːpˈstiks] *npl* はし háshì

choral [kɔːrˈəl] *adj* (MUS) 合唱の gasshō
no

chord [kɔːrd] *n* (MUS) 和音 wáòn

chore [tʃɔːr] *n* (domestic task) 家事 kájì;
(routine task) 毎日の雑用 máìnichi no
zatsúyō

choreographer [kɔːriːˈɑːgˈrəfəːr] *n* 振付
師 furítsukeshì

chortle [tʃɔːrˈtəl] *vi* 楽しそうに笑う tanó-
shisō ni waraù

chorus [kɔːrˈəs] *n* (MUS: group) 合唱隊
gasshōtai, コーラス kōrasu; (: song) 合唱
gasshō; (: refrain) リフレーン rifúrèn; (of
musical play) コーラス kōrasu

chose [tʃouz] *pt of* **choose**

chosen [tʃouˈzən] *pp of* **choose**

Christ [kraist] *n* キリスト kirísuto

christen [krisˈən] *vt* (REL: baby) ...に洗
礼を施す ...ni seírei wo hodókosù; (nickname) ...を...と呼ぶ ...wo ...to yobú

Christian [krisˈtʃən] *adj* キリスト教の
kirísutokyō no
◆*n* キリスト教徒 kirísutokyòto

Christianity [kristʃiːænˈitiː] *n* キリスト
教 kirísutokyō

Christian name *n* ファーストネーム fá-
sutonèmu

Christmas [krisˈməs] *n* (REL: festival)
クリスマス kurísumàsu; (period) クリス
マスの季節 kurísumàsu no kisetsù
Merry Christmas! メリークリスマス！
merí kurisumàsu!

Christmas card *n* クリスマスカード

kurísumasu kàdo

Christmas Day *n* クリスマス kurísumàsu

Christmas Eve *n* クリスマスイブ kurísumasu ibù

Christmas tree *n* クリスマスツリー kurísumasu tsurì

chrome [kroum] *n* クロームめっき kuró-
mumekkì

chromium [krouˈmiːəm] *n* = **chrome**

chromosome [krouˈməsoum] *n* 染色体
seńshokutai

chronic [krɑːnˈik] *adj* (continual: ill-
health, illness etc) 慢性の mańsei no;
(: drunkenness etc) 常習的な jōshūteki
na; (severe: shortage, lack etc) ひどい
hídoì

chronicle [krɑːnˈikəl] *n* (of events) 記録
kiróku ◇年代順または日付順の記録を指
す neńdaijuǹ mata wa hizúkejuǹ no
kiróku wo sasú

chronological [krɑːnələˈdʒikəl] *adj*
(order) 日付順の hizúkejuǹ no

chrysanthemum [krisænˈθəməm] *n* キ
ク kikú

chubby [tʃʌbˈiː] *adj* (cheeks, child) ぽっち
ゃりした potchárì shitá

chuck [tʃʌk] (*inf*) *vt* (throw: stone, ball
etc) 投げる nagerù; (*BRIT*: *also*: **chuck
up**) やめる yaméru

chuckle [tʃʌkˈəl] *vi* くすくす笑う kúsùkusu waraù

chuck out *vt* (person) 追い出す oídasù;
(rubbish etc) 捨てる sutéru

chug [tʃʌg] *vi* (machine, car engine etc)
ぽっぽっと音を立てる póppòtto otó wo
taterù; (car, boat: *also*: **chug along**) ぽっ
ぽっと音を立てて行く poppòtto otó wo
tatète ikú

chum [tʃʌm] *n* (friend) 友達 tomódachi

chunk [tʃʌŋk] *n* (of stone, meat) 塊 katámari

church [tʃəːrtʃ] *n* (building) 教会 kyōkai;
(denomination) 教派 kyōha, ...教 ...kyō

churchyard [tʃəːrtʃˈjɑːrd] *n* 教会墓地
kyōkaibochì

churlish [tʃəːrˈliʃ] *adj* (silence, behavior)
無礼な buréi na

churn [tʃəːrn] n (for butter) かく乳器 kakúnyūki; (BRIT: also: **milk churn**) 大型ミルク缶 ōgata mirukukan

churn out vt (mass-produce: objects, books etc) 大量に作る taíryō ni tsukurù

chute [ʃuːt] n (also: **rubbish chute**) ごみ捨て場 gomísuteba; (for coal, parcels etc) シュート shūto

chutney [tʃʌtniː] n チャツネ chátsùne

CIA [siːaiei'] (US) n abbr (= Central Intelligence Agency) 中央情報局 chūōjōhōkyoku

CID [siːaidiː'] (BRIT) n abbr (= Criminal Investigation Department) 刑事部 keíjibù

cider [sai'dəːr] n リンゴ酒 riŋgoshū

cigar [sigɑːr'] n 葉巻 hamáki

cigarette [sigəret'] n (紙巻) タバコ (kamímaki) tábako

cigarette case n シガレットケース shigárettokèsu

cigarette end n 吸殻 suígara

Cinderella [sindərel'ə] n シンデレラ shiñdererà

cinders [sin'dəːrz] npl (of fire) 燃え殻 moégara

cine-camera [sin'iːkæməːrə] (BRIT) n 映画カメラ eíga kamèra

cine-film [sin'iːfilm] (BRIT) n 映画用フィルム eígayō firùmu

cinema [sin'əmə] n (THEATER) 映画館 eígakàn; (film-making) 映画界 eígakài

cinnamon [sin'əmən] n (CULIN) ニッケイ nikkéi, シナモン shinámoñ

cipher [sai'fəːr] n (code) 暗号 añgō

circle [səːr'kəl] n (shape) 円 éñ; (of friends) 仲間 nakáma; (in cinema, theater) 二階席 nikáisekì
♦vi (bird, plane) 旋回する señkai suru
♦vt (move round) 回る mawáru; (surround) 囲む kakómu

circuit [səːr'kit] n (ELEC) 回路 kaíro; (tour) 1周 isshū; (track) サーキット sākitto; (lap) 1周 isshū, ラップ ráppù

circuitous [səːrkjuː'itəs] adj (route, journey) 遠回りの tōmawàri no

circular [səːr'kjələːr] adj (plate, pond etc) 丸い marúi
♦n (letter) 回状 kaíjō

circulate [səːr'kjəleit] vi (traffic) 流れる nagárerù; (blood) 循環する juñkan suru; (news, rumour, report) 出回る demáwaru; (person: at party etc) 動き回る ugókimawarù
♦vt (report) 回す mawásu

circulation [səːrkjəlei'ʃən] n (of report, book etc) 回される事 mawásareru kotó; (of traffic) 流れ nagáre; (of air, water, also MED: of blood) 循環 juñkan; (of newspaper) 発行部数 hakkōbusū

circumcise [səːr'kəmsaiz] vt (MED) ...の包皮を切除する ...no hōhi wo setsùjo surù; (REL) ...に割礼を行う ...ni katsúrei wo okónau

circumference [səːrkʌm'fəːrəns] n (edge) 周囲 shūi; (distance) 周囲の長さ shūi no nagàsa

circumflex [səːr'kəmfleks] n (also: **circumflex accent**) 曲折アクセント kyokúsetsu akùsento

circumspect [səːr'kəmspekt] adj (cautious, careful) 慎重な shiñchō na

circumstances [səːr'kəmstænsiz] npl (of accident, death) 状況 jōkyō; (conditions, state of affairs) 状態 jōtai; (also: **financial circumstances**) 経済状態 keízaijōtai

circumvent [səːrkəmvent'] vt (regulation) ...に触れない様にする ...ni furénai yō ni surù; (difficulty) 回避する káihi surù

circus [səːr'kəs] n (show) サーカス sākasu; (performers) サーカス団 sākasudañ

CIS [siːaies'] n abbr = **Commonwealth of Independent States**

cistern [sis'təːrn] n (water tank) 貯水タンク chosúitañku; (of toilet) 水槽 suísō

cite [sait] vt (quote: example, author etc) 引用する in-yō suru; (LAW) 召喚する shōkan suru

citizen [sit'əzən] n (gen) 住民 jūmin; (of a country) 国民 kokúmin, 市民 shímìn; (of a city) 市民 shímìn; (of other political divisions) ...民 ...mìn

citizenship [sit'əzənʃip] n (of a country) 市民権 shimíñken

citrus fruit [sit'rəs fruːt] n カンキツ類 kańkitsurùi

city [sit'iː] n 都市 toshì
the City (FINANCE) シティー shitî ◇ ロンドンの金融業の中心地 rondon no kińyūgyō no chūshińchi

civic [siv'ik] adj (leader, duties, pride) 公 民の kômin no; (authorities) 自治体の ji-chítai no

civic centre (BRIT) n 自治体中心部 ji-chítaichūshińbu

civil [siv'əl] adj (gen) 市民の shímin no, 公民の kômin no; (authorities) 行政の gyôsei no; (polite) 礼儀正しい reígitadashiî

civil defense n 民間防衛 mińkanbôei

civil disobedience n 市民的不服従 shi-míntekifufukujù

civil engineer n 土木技師 dobôkugishì

civilian [sivil'jən] adj (attitudes, casu-alties, life) 民間の mińkan no
◆n 民間人 mińkańjin

civilization [sivələzei'ʃən] n (a society) 文明社会 buńmeishakài; (social organi-zation) 文化 buńka

civilized [siv'əlaizd] adj (society) 文明的 な buńmeiteki na; (person) 洗練された seńren saréta

civil law n 民法 mínpō

civil rights npl 公民権 kômińken

civil servant n 公務員 kômuìn

Civil Service n 文官職 buńkanshoku

civil war n 内乱 naíran

clad [klæd] adj: **clad (in)** ...を着た ...wo kitá

claim [kleim] vt (expenses) 請求する sei-kyû suru; (inheritance) 要求する yōkyû suru; (rights) 主張する shuchô suru; (assert): **to claim that/to be** ...である と主張する ...de arù to shuchô suru
◆vi (for insurance) 請求する seikyû suru
◆n (assertion) 主張 shuchô; (for pension, wage rise, compensation) 請求 seíkyū; (to inheritance, land) 権利 kêñri

to claim responsibility (for) (...の) 犯行声明を出す (...no) hańkōseimèi wo dasù

to claim credit (for) (...が) 自分の業績

であると主張する (...ga) jibún no gyôseki de arù to shuchô suru

claimant [klei'mənt] n (ADMIN) 要求者 yôkyûshà; (LAW) 原告 geńkoku

clairvoyant [klɛːrvɔi'ənt] n (psychic) 霊 媒 reíbai

clam [klæm] n (ZOOL, CULIN) ハマグリ hamagùri ◇英語では食用二枚貝の総称とし て使われる eígo de wa shokúyōnimaî-gai no sôshō toshité tsukáwarerù

clamber [klæm'bəːr] vi (aboard vehicle) 乗る norú; (up hill etc) 登る nobôru ◇手 足を使って物に乗ったり登ったりすると いう含みがある teâshi wo tsukátte mo-nô ni nottári nobôttari suru to iú fukúmi ga arù

clammy [klæm'iː] adj (hands, face etc) 冷たくてべとべとしている tsumétakùte betôbeto shité irù

clamor [klæm'əːr] (BRIT **clamour**) vi: **to clamor for** (change, war etc) ...をや かましく要求する ...wo yakámashikù yô-kyū suru

clamp [klæmp] n (device) 留金 tomégà-ne, クランプ kuráñpu
◆vt (two things together) クランプで留 める kuráñpu de tomérù; (put: one thing on another) 締付ける shimétsukerù

clamp down on vt fus (violence, specu-lation etc) 取り締まる toríshimarù

clan [klæn] n (family) 一族 ichízoku

clandestine [klændes'tin] adj (activity, broadcast) 秘密の himítsu no

clang [klæŋ] vi (bell, metal object) かん と鳴る kań to narú

clap [klæp] vi (audience, spectators) 拍手 する hákùshu surù

clapping [klæp'iŋ] n (applause) 拍手 há-kùshu

claret [klær'it] n クラレット kurárett-tô ◇ボルドー産の赤ワイン bôrudōsañ no aká waiñ

clarify [klær'əfai] vt (argument, point) はっきりさせる hakkíri saséru

clarinet [klærənet'] n (MUS: instru-ment) クラリネット kurárinettô

clarity [klær'itiː] n (of explanation, thought) 明りょうさ meíryōsa

clash [klæʃ] *n* (of opponents) 衝突 shṓtotsu; (of beliefs, ideas, views) 衝突 shṓtotsu, 対立 tairitsu; (of colors) 不調和な fuchṓwa; (of styles) つり合わない事 tsuríawanai kotò; (of two events, appointments) かち合い kachíai; (noise) ぶつかる音 butsúkaru otó

♦*vi* (fight: rival gangs etc) 衝突する shṓtotsu suru; (disagree: political opponents, personalities) 角突合いをする tsunótsukiài wo surù; (beliefs, ideas, views) 相容れない afirénai; (colors, styles) 合わない awánai; (two events, appointments) かち合う kachíaù; (make noise: weapons, cymbals etc) 音を立ててぶつかり合う otó wo tatéte butsúkariaù

clasp [klæsp] *n* (hold: with hands) 握る事 nigíru kotó, 握り nigíri; (: with arms) 抱締めること dakíshimerù kotó, 抱擁 hṓyō; (of necklace, bag) 留金 tomégane, クラスプ kurásupù

♦*vt* (hold) 握る nigíru; (embrace) 抱締める dakíshimerù

class [klæs] *n* (SCOL: pupils) 学級 gakkyū́, クラス kurásu; (: lesson) 授業 jugyṓ; (of society) 階級 kaíkyū; (type, group) 種類 shurùi

♦*vt* (categorize) 分類する buńrui suru

classic [klǽsik] *adj* (example, illustration) 典型的な teñkeiteki na; (film, work etc) 傑作の kessáku no; (style, dress) 古典的な kotenteki na

♦*n* (film, novel etc) 傑作 kessáku

classical [klǽsikəl] *adj* (traditional) 伝統的な deńtōteki na; (MUS) クラシックの kuráshikkù no; (Greek, Roman) 古代の kódài no

classification [klæsəfəkei'ʃən] *n* (process) 分類する事 buńrui suru kotó; (category, system) 分類 buńrui

classified [klǽsʼəfaid] *adj* (information) 秘密の himítsu no

classified advertisement *n* 分類広告 buńruikōkoku

classify [klǽsʼəfai] *vt* (books, fossils etc) 分類する buńrui suru

classmate [klǽsʼmeit] *n* 同級生 dṓkyūsei, クラスメート kurásumḕto

classroom [klǽsʼruːm] *n* 教室 kyṓshitsu

clatter [klǽtʼəːr] *n* (of dishes, pots etc) がちゃがちゃ gáchàgacha; (of hooves) かたかた kátàkata

♦*vi* (dishes, pots etc) がちゃがちゃいう gáchàgacha iú; (hooves) かたかた鳴る kátàkata narú

clause [klɔːz] *n* (LAW) 条項 jṓkō; (LING) 文節 buńsetsu

claustrophobia [klɔːstrəfouˈbiːə] *n* (PSYCH) 閉所恐怖症 heíshokyṓfushṓ

claw [klɔː] *n* (of animal, bird) つめ tsumé; (of lobster) はさみ hasámi

claw at *vt fus* (curtains, door etc) 引っかく hikkáku

clay [klei] *n* 粘土 néñdo

clean [kliːn] *adj* (person, animal) きれい好きな kiréizuki na; (place, surface, clothes etc) 清潔な seíketsu na; (fight) 反則のない hańsoku no naì; (record, reputation) 無傷の múkīzu no; (joke, story) 下品でない gehín de naì; (MED: fracture) 単純な tañjun na

♦*vt* (car, hands, face etc) 洗う aráu; (room, house) 掃除する sṓji suru

clean-cut [kliːnˈkʌt] *adj* (person) 品の良いひん no yoì

cleaner [kliːˈnəːr] *n* (person) 掃除係 sṓjigakàri; (substance) 洗剤 señzai

cleaner's [kliːˈnəːrz] *n* (*also:* **dry cleaner's**) クリーニング店 kuríningùten

cleaning [kliːˈniŋ] *n* (of room, house) 掃除 sṓji

cleanliness [klenˈliːnis] *n* 清潔 seíketsu

clean out *vt* (cupboard, drawer) 中身を出してきれいにする nakámì wo dashíte kiréi ni suru

cleanse [klenz] *vt* (purify) 清める kiyómerù; (face, cut) 洗う aráu

cleanser [klenˈzəːr] *n* (for face) 洗顔料 señgañryō

clean-shaven [kliːnˈʃeiˈvən] *adj* ひげのないひげ no naì

cleansing department [klenˈziŋ-] (BRIT) *n* 清掃局 seísōkyoku

clean up *vt* (mess) 片付ける katázukerù; (child) 身ぎれいにする migírei ni surù

clear [kliˈəːr] *adj* (easy to understand:

report, argument) 分かりやすい wakáriyasuǐ; (easy to see, hear) はっきりした hakkíri shitá; (obvious: choice, commitment) 明らかな akíraka na; (glass, plastic) 透明な tōmei na; (water, eyes) 澄んだ súnda; (road, way, floor etc) 障害のない shōgai no naǐ; (conscience) やましい所のない yamashiǐ tokóro no naǐ; (skin) 健康そうな keńkōsō na; (sky) 晴れた haréta

♦vt (space, room) 開ける akéru; (LAW: suspect) 容疑を晴す yōgi wo harasù; (fence, wall) 飛び越える tobíkoerù; (check) 払う haraù

♦vi (weather, sky) 晴れる harerù; (fog, smoke) 消える kierù

♦adv: **clear of** (trouble) ...を避けて ...wo sakéte; (ground) ...から離れて ...kara hanárete

to clear the table 食卓を片付ける shokútaku wo katázukerù

clearance [kli:'rəns] n (removal: of trees, slums) 取払う事 toríharaù kotó; (permission) 許可 kyóka

clear-cut [kli:'ərkʌt'] adj (decision, issue) 明白な meíhaku na

clearing [kli:'riŋ] n (in woods) 開けた所 hiráketà tokóro

clearing bank (BRIT) n 手形交換組合銀行 tegátakōkankumiaigiñkō ◇ロンドンの中央手形交換所を通じて他の銀行との取引を行う銀行 róñdon no chūō tegata kōkañjo wo tsújitè tá no giñkō to no toríhiki wò okónaù giñkō

clearly [kli:'ərli:] adv (distinctly, coherently) はっきりと hakkírì to; (evidently) 明らかに akíraka ni

clear up vt (room, mess) 片付ける katázukerù; (mystery, problem) 解決する kaíketsu suru

clearway [kli:r'wei] (BRIT) n 駐停車禁止道路 chūteíshakinshúroad

cleaver [kli:'vəːr] n 骨割包丁 honéwaribōchō ◇なたに似た物で，肉のブロックをたたき切ったり骨を割ったりするのに使う natá ni nitá monó de, nikú no burokkù wo tatákikittarì honé wo wattárì surù no ni tsukaù

clef [klef] n (MUS) 音部記号 oñbukigō

cleft [kleft] n (in rock) 割れ目 waréme

clemency [klem'ənsi:] n 慈悲 jíhi

clench [klentʃ] vt (fist) 握り締める nigírishimerù; (teeth) 食いしばる kuíshibarù

clergy [klər'dʒi:] n 聖職者 seíshokùsha ◇総称 sōshō

clergyman [klər'dʒi:mən] (pl **clergymen**) n (Protestant) 牧師 bókùshi; (Catholic) 神父 shíñpu

clerical [kler'ikəl] adj (worker, job) 事務の jímù no; (REL) 聖職者の seíshokùsha no

clerk [kləːrk] n (BRIT: office worker) 事務員 jimúìn; (US: sales person) 店員 teñin

clever [klev'əːr] adj (intelligent) 利口な rikō na; (deft, crafty) こうかつな kṓkatsu na; (device, arrangement) 良く工夫した yókù kufū shitá

cliché [kli:ʃei'] n 決り文句 kimárimoñku

click [klik] vt (tongue) 鳴らす narásu; (heels) 打鳴らす uchínarasu

♦vi (device, switch etc) かちっと鳴る kachíttò narú

client [klai'ənt] n (of bank, company) 客 kyakú; (of lawyer) 依頼人 iráinìn

cliff [klif] n (GEO) 断崖 dañgai

climate [klai'mit] n (weather) 気候 kikṓ; (of opinion etc) 雰囲気 fuñ-íkì

climax [klai'mæks] n (of battle, career) 頂点 chōten; (of film, book) クライマックス kuráimakkùsu; (sexual) オルガズム orúgazùmu

climb [klaim] vi (sun, plant) 上がる agáru; (plant) はい上がる haíagarù; (plane) 上昇する jōshō suru; (prices, shares) 上昇する jōshō suru; (move with effort): **to climb over a wall** 塀を乗り越える heí wo noríkoerù

♦vt (stairs, ladder) 上がる agáru, 登る nobóru; (hill) 登る nobóru; (tree) ...に登る ...ni nobóru

♦n (of hill, cliff etc) 登る事 nobóru kotó; (of prices etc) 上昇 jōshō

to climb into a car 車に乗り込む kurúma ni noríkomù

climb-down [klaim'daun] n (retraction)

撤回 tekkái

climber [klai'məːr] *n* (mountaineer) 登山者 tozánsha; (plant) つる性植物 tsurúseishokubùtsu

climbing [klai'miŋ] *n* (mountaineering) 山登り yamánobòri, 登山 tózàn

clinch [klintʃ] *vt* (deal) まとめる matómeru; (argument) ...に決着を付ける ...ni ketcháku wo tsukerù

cling [kliŋ] (*pt, pp* **clung**) *vi*: **to cling to** (mother, support) ...にしがみつく ...ni shigámitsukù; (idea, belief) 固執する koshū suru; (subj: clothes, dress) ...にぴったりくっつく ...ni pittári kuttsùku

clinic [klin'ik] *n* (MED: center) 診療所 shinryōjō

clinical [klin'ikəl] *adj* (MED: tests) 臨床の rińshō no; (: teaching) 臨床の rińshō no; (*fig*: thinking, attitude) 冷淡な reítan na; (: building, room) 潤いのない uruói no naì

clink [kliŋk] *vi* (glasses, cutlery) ちんと鳴る chíñ to narú

clip [klip] *n* (*also*: **paper clip**) クリップ kurippù; (*also*: **hair clip**) 髪留 kamídome; (TV, CINEMA) 断片 dañpen
◆*vt* (fasten) 留める toméru; (cut) はさみで切る hasámi de kíru

clippers [klip'əːrz] *npl* (for gardening) せん定ばさみ señteibasàmi; (*also*: **nail clippers**) つめ切り tsumékiri

clipping [klip'iŋ] *n* (from newspaper) 切抜き kirínuki

clique [kli:k] *n* 徒党 totő

cloak [klouk] *n* (cape) マント máñto
◆*vt* (*fig*: in mist, secrecy) 隠す kakúsù

cloakroom [klouk'ru:m] *n* (for coats etc) クローク kurôku; (*BRIT*: WC) お手洗 o-téarai

clock [kla:k] *n* 時計 tokéi

clock in *vi* (for work) 出勤する shukkín suru

clock off *vi* (from work) 退社する taísha suru

clock on *vi* = **clock in**

clock out *vi* = **clock off**

clockwise [kla:k'waiz] *adv* 時計回りに tokéimawàri ni

clockwork [kla:k'wəːrk] *n* 時計仕掛 tokéijikàke
◆*adj* (model, toy) 時計仕掛の tokéijikàke no

clog [kla:g] *n* (leather) 木底の靴 kizóko no kutsú; (*also*: **wooden clog**) 木靴 kígùtsu
◆*vt* (drain, nose) ふさぐ fuságu
◆*vi* (*also*: **clog up**: sink) 詰る tsumarù

cloister [klɔis'təːr] *n* 回廊 kaírò

clone [kloun] *n* (of animal, plant) クローン kúrồn

close[1] [klous] *adj* (near) 近くの chikákù no; (friend) 親しい shitáshiì; (relative) 近縁の kíñ-en no; (contact) 密な mítsù na; (link, ties) 密接な missétsu na; (examination, watch) 注意深い chūibukaì; (contest) 互角の gokáku no; (weather) 重苦しい omókurushiì
◆*adv* (near) 近くに chikákù ni
close to ...の近くに ...no chikákù ni
close at hand, close by adj 近くの chikákù no
◆*adv* 近くに chikákù ni
to have a close shave (*fig*) 間一髪で助かる kań-ippátsu de tasukaru

close[2] [klouz] *vt* (shut: door, window) しめる shimérù; (finalize: sale) 取決める toríkimerù; (end: case, speech) 終える oéru
◆*vi* (shop etc) 閉店する heíten suru; (door, lid) 閉る shimarù; (end) 終る owáru

closed [klouzd] *adj* (door, window, shop etc) 閉っている shimattè irú

close down *vi* (factory) 廃業する haígyō suru; (magazine) 廃刊する haíkan suru

closed shop *n* (*fig*) クローズドショップ kurốzudo shoppù ◇特定の労働組合員だけしか雇わない事業所 tokútei no rōdōkumiaiìn dake shika yatówanài jigyósho

close-knit [klous'nit'] *adj* (family, community) 堅く結ばれた katáku musúbareta

closely [klous'li:] *adv* (examine, watch) 注意深く chūibukakù; (connected) 密接に missétsu ni; (related) 近縁になって kíñ-en ni nattè; (resemble) そっくり sokkúrì

closet [klɑːz'it] n (cupboard) たんす tañsu

close-up [klous'ʌp] n (PHOT) クローズアップ kurózuappù

closure [klou'ʒəːr] n (of factory) 閉鎖 heísa; (of magazine) 廃刊 haíkan

clot [klɑːt] n (gen: blood clot) 血の塊 chi no katámari; (inf: idiot) ばか bákà
♦vi (blood) 固まる katámaru, 凝固する gyōko suru

cloth [klɔːθ] n (material) 布 nunó; (rag) ふきん fukín

clothe [klouð] vt (dress) ...に服を着せる ...ni fukú wo kiséru

clothes [klouz] npl 服 fukú

clothes brush n 洋服ブラシ yófukubúrashi

clothes line n 物干綱 monóhoshizùna

clothes pin (BRIT **clothes peg**) n 洗濯ばさみ señtakubasàmi

clothing [klou'ðiŋ] n = **clothes**

cloud [klaud] n (in sky) 雲 kúmò
a cloud of smoke/dust もうもうとした煙〔ほこり〕mómò to shita kemúri 〔hokori〕

cloudburst [klaud'bəːrst] n 集中豪雨 shúchūgòu

cloudy [klau'diː] adj (sky) 曇った kumottà; (liquid) 濁った nigottà

clout [klaut] vt (hit, strike) 殴る nagurù

clove [klouv] n (spice) チョウジ chōji, クローブ kurōbu
clove of garlic ニンニクの一粒 nifniku no hitótsubu

clover [klou'vəːr] n クローバー kurōba

clown [klaun] n (in circus) ピエロ píero
♦vi (also: **clown about**, **clown around**) おどける odókeru

cloying [klɔi'iŋ] adj (taste, smell) むかつかせる mukátsukaseru

club [klʌb] n (society, place) クラブ kúràbu; (weapon) こん棒 koñbō; (also: **golf club**) クラブ kúràbu
♦vt (hit) 殴る nagurù
♦vi: *to club together* (BRIT: for gift, card) 金を出し合う kané wo dashiaù

club car (US) n (RAIL) ラウンジカー raúnjikà ◇休憩用客車 kyúkeiyō kyakùsha

clubhouse [klʌb'haus] n (of sports club) クラブハウス kurábuhaùsu ◇スポーツクラブのメンバーが集まる部屋、建物など supótsukuràbu no meñbā ga atsúmarù heyá, tatémono nadò

clubs [klʌbz] npl (CARDS) クラブ kúràbu

cluck [klʌk] vi (hen) こっこっと鳴く kókkòtto nakú

clue [kluː] n (pointer, lead) 手掛かり tégàkari; (in crossword) かぎ kagí
I haven't a clue さっぱり分らない sáppàri wakáranaì

clump [klʌmp] n (gen) 塊 katámari; (buildings etc) 一連 ichíren
a clump of trees 木立 kódàchi

clumsy [klʌm'ziː] adj (person, movement) 不器用な búkìyo na; (object) 扱いにくい atsúkainikuì; (effort, attempt) 下手な hetá na

clung [klʌŋ] pt, pp of **cling**

cluster [klʌs'təːr] n (of people, stars, flowers etc) 塊 katámari
♦vi 固まる katámaru, 群がる murágarù

clutch [klʌtʃ] n (grip, grasp) つかむ事 tsukamù kotó; (AUT) クラッチ kúràtchi
♦vt (purse, hand, stick) しっかり持つ shíkkàri motsù

clutter [klʌt'əːr] vt (room, table) 散らかす chірákasu

cm abbr = **centimeter**

CND [siːendiː'] n abbr (= *Campaign for Nuclear Disarmament*) 核廃絶運動 kakúhaizetsu uñdō

Co. abbr = **county; company**

c/o abbr = **care of**

coach [koutʃ] n (bus) バス bású; (also: **horse-drawn coach**) 馬車 básha; (of train) 客車 kyakùsha; (SPORT: trainer) コーチ kōchi; (tutor) 個人教師 kojínkyōshi
♦vt (sportsman/woman) コーチする kōchi suru; (student) ...に個人指導をする ...ni kojínshidō wo surù

coach trip n バス旅行 basúryokò

coagulate [kouæg'jəleit] vi (blood, paint etc) 凝固する gyōko surù

coal [koul] n (substance) 石炭 sekítañ;

(also: **lump of coal**) 石炭1個 sekítaṅ ikkò

coal face n 石炭切り場 sekítankiríba

coalfield [koul'fiːld] n 炭田 taṅden

coalition [kouəliʃ'ən] n (POL: also: **coalition government**) 連合政権 reṅgōseikèn; (of pressure groups etc) 連盟 reṅmei

coalman [koul'mən] (pl **coalmen**) n 石炭屋 sekítanya

coal merchant n = **coalman**

coalmine [koul'main] n 炭坑 taṅkō

coarse [kɔːrs] adj (texture: rough) 荒い aráì; (person: vulgar) 下品な gehìn na

coast [koust] n 海岸 kaígan
♦vi (car, bicycle etc) 惰力走行する daryókusōkō suru

coastal [kous'təl] adj (cities, waters) 海岸沿いの kaíganzòi no

coastguard [koust'gɑːrd] n (officer) 沿岸警備隊員 eṅgankeibitáiin; (service) 沿岸警備隊 eṅgankeibitái

coastline [koust'lain] n 海岸線 kaígansen

coat [kout] n (overcoat) コート kòto; (of animal) 毛 ke; (of paint) 塗り nurí
♦vt: **coated with** ...で覆われた ...de ōwarèta

coat hanger n ハンガー háṅgā

coating [kou'tiŋ] n (of dust, mud etc) 覆う物 ōù monó; (of chocolate, plastic etc) 被覆 hifúku

coat of arms n 紋 móṅ

coax [kouks] vt (person: persuade) 説得する settóku suru

cob [kɑːb] n see **corn**

cobbler [kɑːb'lər] n (maker/repairer of shoes) 靴屋 kutsúyà

cobbles [kɑːb'əlz] npl 敷石 shikíishi

cobblestones [kɑːb'əlstounz] npl = **cobbles**

cobweb [kɑːb'web] n クモの巣 kúmò no su

cocaine [koukein'] n コカイン kókàin

cock [kɑːk] n (rooster) おん鳥 oṅdori; (male bird) 鳥の雄 torí no osú
♦vt (gun) ...の撃鉄を起す ...no gekítetsu wo okosù

cockerel [kɑːk'əːrəl] n 雄のひな鳥 osú no hinàdori

cock-eyed [kɑːk'aid] adj (fig: idea, method) ばかな bákà na

cockle [kɑːk'əl] n ホタテガイ hotátègai

cockney [kɑːk'niː] n コックニー kókkùnī ◇ロンドンのEast End地区生れの人 roṅdon no Eást End chikú umáre no hitó

cockpit [kɑːk'pit] n (in aircraft) 操縦室 sōjūshitsu, コックピット kokkúpittò; (in racing car) 運転席 uṅteṅseki, コックピット kokkúpittò

cockroach [kɑːk'routʃ] n ゴキブリ gokíburi

cocktail [kɑːk'teil] n (drink) カクテル kákùteru; (mixture: fruit cocktail, prawn cocktail etc) ...カクテル ...kakùteru

cocktail cabinet n ホームバー hōmubà

cocktail party n カクテルパーティ kakúterupàti

cocoa [kou'kou] n (powder, drink) ココア kókòa

coconut [kou'kənʌt] n (fruit) ヤシの実 yáshì no mi; (flesh) ココナッツ kokónattsu

cocoon [kəkuːn'] n (of butterfly) 繭 máyù

cod [kɑːd] n タラ tárà

C.O.D. [siːoudiː'] abbr (= cash or also (US) collect on delivery) 着払い chakúbarài

code [koud] n (of practice, behavior) 規定 kitéi; (cipher) 暗号 aṅgō; (dialling code, post code) 番号 baṅgō

cod-liver oil [kɑːd'livəːr-] n 肝油 kaṅyu

coercion [kouəːr'ʃən] n (pressure) 強制 kyōsei

coffee [kɔːf'iː] n (drink, powder) コーヒー kóhì; (cup of coffee) コーヒー一杯 kóhì ippái

coffee bar (BRIT) n 喫茶店 kissáten

coffee bean n コーヒー豆 kóhìmame

coffee break n コーヒーブレーク kóhìburèku

coffeepot [kɔːf'iːpɑːt] n コーヒーポット kóhìpottò

coffee table n コーヒーテーブル kóhìtēburu

coffin [kɔː'fin] *n* ひつぎ hitsúgi

cog [kɑːg] *n* (TECH: wheel) 歯車 hágùruma; (: tooth) 歯車の歯 hágùruma no há

cogent [kou'dʒənt] *adj* (argument etc) 説得力ある settőkuryóku arù

cognac [koun'jæk] *n* コニャック kőnyàkku

coherent [kouhi:'rənt] *adj* (answer, theory, speech) 筋の通った sují no tőtta; (person) 筋の通った事を言う sují no tőtta kotő wo iú

cohesion [kouhi:'ʒən] *n* (political, ideological etc) 団結 dañketsu

coil [kɔil] *n* (of rope, wire) 一巻 hitőmaki; (ELEC) コイル kőîru; (contraceptive) 避妊リング hinînrìñgu
♦*vt* (rope) 巻く makú

coin [kɔin] *n* (money) 硬貨 kőka, コイン kőîn
♦*vt* (word, slogan) 造る tsukúru

coinage [kɔi'nidʒ] *n* 貨幣制度 kahéiseìdo

coin-box [kɔin'bɑːks] (*BRIT*) *n* コイン電話 koíndeñwa でカードだけしか使えない物に対比して言う kőshūdeñwa de kàdo daké shìká tsukáenai monő ni taíhi shité iú

coincide [kouinsaid'] *vi* (events) 同時に起る dőji ni okőru; (ideas, views) 一致する itchí suru

coincidence [kouin'sidəns] *n* 偶然の一致 gűzen no itchí

Coke [kouk] ® *n* (drink) コカコーラ kokákòra

coke [kouk] *n* (coal) コークス kőkusu

colander [kɑː'ləndər] *n* 水切り mizúkiri ◇ボール型で穴の比較的大きい物を指す bőrugata de aná no hikákuteki őkiì monő wo sasù

cold [kould] *adj* (water, food) 冷たい tsumétai; (weather, room) 寒い samúî; (person, attitude: unemotional) 冷たい tsumétai, 冷淡な reítan na
♦*n* (weather) 寒さ samúsa; (MED) 風邪 kazé

it's cold 寒い samui

to be cold (person, object) 冷たい tsumétai

to catch (a) cold 風邪を引く kazé wo hikú

in cold blood (kill etc) 冷酷に reíkoku ni

coldly [kould'li:] *adv* (speak, behave) 冷たく tsumétaku, 冷淡に reítan ni

cold-shoulder [kould'ʃouldər] *vt* 冷たくあしらう tsumétaku ashíraù

cold sore *n* 口角炎 kőkakuèn

coleslaw [koul'slɔː] *n* コールスロー kőrusurō

colic [kɑː'lik] *n* (MED) 腹痛 fukútsū

collaborate [kəlæb'əreit] *vi* (on book, research) 協同する kyődō suru; (with enemy) 協力する kyőryoku suru

collaboration [kəlæbərei'ʃən] *n* 協力 kyőryoku

collage [kəlɑ:ʒ'] *n* コラージュ kőràju

collapse [kəlæps'] *vi* (building, system, resistance) 崩れる kuzúrerù, 崩壊する hőkai suru; (government) 倒れる taőrerù; (MED: person) 倒れる taőrerù; (table) 壊れる kowárerù, つぶれる tsubúrerù; (company) つぶれる tsubúrerù, 破産する hasán suru
♦*n* (of building, system, government, resistance) 崩壊 hőkai; (MED: of person) 倒れる事 taőreru kotő; (of table) 壊れる〔つぶれる〕事 kowáreru(tsubureru)kotő; (of company) 破産 hasán

collapsible [kəlæps'əbəl] *adj* (seat, bed, bicycle) 折畳みの orítatami no

collar [kɑː'lər] *n* (of coat, shirt) 襟 erí, カラー kárà; (of dog, cat) 首輪 kubíwa, カラー kárà

collarbone [kɑː'lə:rboun] *n* (ANAT) 鎖骨 sakótsu

collateral [kəlæt'ə:rəl] *n* (COMM) 担保 táñpo

colleague [kɑː'li:g] *n* 同僚 dőryō

collect [kəlekt'] *vt* (gather: wood, litter etc) 集める atsúmerù; (as a hobby) 収集する shűshū suru; (*BRIT*: call and pick up: person) 迎えに行く mukáe ni ikú; (: object) 取りに行く torí ni ikú; (for charity, in church) 募金する bokín suru; (debts, taxes etc) 集金する shűkin suru; (mail) 取集する shushū suru

♦*vi* (crowd) 集る atsúmarù

to call collect (*US*: TEL) コレクトコールする korékutokòru suru

collection [kəlek'1ʃən] *n* (of art, stamps etc) コレクション kórèkushon; (of poems, stories etc) ...集...shū; (from place, person) 受取る事 ukétoru kotó; (for charity) 募金 bokín; (of mail) 取集 shushū

collective [kəlek'tiv] *adj* (farm, decision) 共同の kyódō no

collector [kəlek'tə:r] *n* (of art, stamps etc) 収集家 shūshūka; (of taxes etc) 集金人 shūkìnnin

college [ka:l'idʒ] *n* (SCOL: of university) 学寮 gakúryō; (: of agriculture, technology) 大学 daígaku

collide [kəlaid'] *vi* (cars, people) ぶつかる butsúkaru, 衝突する shótotsu suru

collie [ka:l'i:] *n* コリー犬 koríken

colliery [ka:l'jə:ri:] (*BRIT*) *n* 炭坑 tañkō

collision [kəliʒ'ən] *n* (of vehicles) 衝突 shótotsu

colloquial [kəlou'kwi:əl] *adj* (LING: informal) 口語の kógo no

collusion [kəlu:'ʒən] *n* (collaboration) 結託 kettáku

colon [kou'lən] *n* (punctuation mark) コロン kóròn; (ANAT) 大腸 daíchō

colonel [kə:r'nəl] *n* 大佐 taísa

colonial [kəlou'ni:əl] *adj* 植民地の shokúmiñchi no

colonize [ka:l'ənaiz] *vt* (country, territory) 植民地にする shokúmiñchi ni surù

colony [ka:l'əni:] *n* (subject territory) 植民地 shokúmiñchi; (of people) ...人街 ...jiñgai; (of animals) 個体群 kotáigùn

color [kʌl'ə:r] (*BRIT* **colour**) *n* (*gen*) 色 iro

♦*vt* (paint) ...に色を塗る ...ni iró wo nurú; (dye) 染める soméru; (*fig*: account) ...に色を付ける ...ni iró wo tsukerù; (judgment) ゆがめる yugámerù

♦*vi* (blush) 赤面する sekímen suru

in color 天然色で teñneñshoku de, カラーで kárā de

color bar *n* 人種差別 jiñshusabètsu ◇有色人種, 特に黒人に対する差別を指す yúshokujiñshu, tokù ni kokújin ni taí suru sabètsu wo sasù

color-blind [kʌl'ə:rblaind] *adj* 色盲の shikímō no

colored [kʌl'ə:rd] *adj* (person) 有色の yúshoku no; (illustration etc) カラーの kárā no

color film *n* カラーフィルム karáfirùmu

colorful [kʌl'ə:rfəl] *adj* (cloth) 色鮮やかな iró azáyaka na; (account, story) 華やかな hanáyaka na; (personality) 華々しい hanábanashiì

color in *vt* (drawing) ...に色を塗る ...ni iró wo nurú

coloring [kʌl'ə:riŋ] *n* (complexion) 肌の色合い hadà no iróai; (*also*: **food coloring**) 着色料 chakúshokùryō

colors [kʌl'ə:rz] *npl* (of party, club etc) 色 iró

color scheme *n* 配色計画 haíshokukeìkaku

color television *n* カラーテレビ karáterèbi

colossal [kəla:s'əl] *adj* 巨大な kyodái na

colour [kʌl'ə:r] *etc* (*BRIT*) *n* = **color** *etc*

colt [koult] *n* 子ウマ koúma

column [ka:l'əm] *n* (ARCHIT) 円柱 eñchū; (of smoke) 柱 hashíra; (of people) 縦隊 jútai; (gossip column, sports column) コラム kóràmu

columnist [ka:l'əmist] *n* コラムニスト korámunisùto

coma [kou'mə] *n* (MED) こん睡状態 koñsuijōtai

comb [koum] *n* くし kushí

♦*vt* (hair) くしでとかす kushí de tokasù; (*fig*: area) 捜索する sósaku suru

combat [*n* ka:m'bæt *vb* kəmbæt'] *n* (MIL: fighting) 戦闘 señtō; (fight, battle) 戦い tatákai

♦*vt* (oppose) 反抗する hañkō suru

combination [ka:mbənei'ʃən] *n* (mixture) 組合せ kumíawase; (for lock, safe etc) 組合せ番号 kumíawasebañgō

combine [*vb* kəmbain' *n* ka:m'bain] *vt*: *to combine something with something* ...を...と組合せる ...wo ...to kumía-

waserù; (qualities) 兼備える kanésonae-
rù; (two activities) 兼任する keñnin suru
♦*vi* (people, groups) 合併する gappéi suru
♦*n* (ECON) 連合 reñgō

combine (harvester) [kɑ:m'baɪn(hɑːr'-
vestəːr)] *n* コンバイン koñbaìn

combustion [kəmbʌs'tʃən] *n* (act, process) 燃焼 neñshō

| KEYWORD |

come [kʌm] (*pt* **came**, *pp* **come**) *vi* **1**
(movement towards) 来る kúrù

come here! ここにおいで kokó ni oide

I've only come for an hour 1時間しか
いられません ichíjikàn shika iráremasèn

come with me ついて来て下さい tsúìte
kite kudasai

are you coming to my party? 私のパ
ーティに来てくれますね watákushi no
pátī ni kité kuremasu né

to come running 走って来る hashíttè
kúrù

2 (arrive) 着く tsúkù, 到着する tóchaku
suru, 来る kúrù

he's just come from Aberdeen 彼はア
バーディーンから来たばかりです kárè
wa abádìn kara kitá bakàri desu

he's come here to work 彼はここに
働きに来ました kárè wa kokó ni wà
határaki ni kimashìta

they came to a river 彼らは川に着きま
した kárèra wa kawá nì tsukímashìta

to come home 家に戻って来る ié nì
modóttè kurù

3 (reach): *to come to* ...に届く ...ni todókù, ...になる ...ni nárù

the bill came to £40 勘定は計40ポン
ドだった kánjō wa kéì yónjuppòndo datta

her hair came to her waist 彼女の髪
の毛は腰まで届いていた kánojò no kamí
no ke wa koshí madè todóìte ita

to come to power 政権を握る seíken
wo nigiru

to come to a decision 結論に達する
ketsúron ni tassuru

4 (occur): *an idea came to me* いい考え

が浮かびました fi kángaè ga ukábima-
shìta

5 (be, become) なる nárù

to come loose/undone etc 外れる hazúreru

I've come to like him 彼が好きになり
ました kárè ga sukí nì narímashìta

---

come about *vi* 起る okórù

come across *vt fus* (person, thing) ...に
出会う ...ni deáù

come away *vi* (leave) 帰る káeru, 出て
来る détè kure; (become detached) 外れ
る hazúreru

come back *vi* (return) 帰って来る káètte
kuru

comeback [kʌm'bæk] *n* (of film star
etc) 返り咲き kaérizaki, カムバック ka-
múbakkù

come by *vt fus* (acquire) 手に入れる té
nì iréru

comedian [kəmiː'diːən] *n* (THEATER,
TV) コメディアン kómèdian

comedienne [kəmiːdiːen'] *n* 女性コメデ
ィアン joséi komèdian

come down *vi* (price) 下がる sagárù;
(tree) 倒れる taórerù; (building) 崩れ落ち
る kuzúreochirù

comedy [kɑːm'idiː] *n* (play, film) 喜劇 kígèki, コメディー kómèdī; (humor) 喜劇
性 kigékisei, ユーモア yūmoa

come forward *vi* (volunteer) 進んで...す
る susúnde ...sùrù

come from *vt fus* (place, source etc)
...から来る ...kara kúrù

come in *vi* (visitor) 入る háìru; (on deal
etc) 加わる kuwáwarù; (be involved) 関
係する kánkei suru

come in for *vt fus* (criticism etc) 受け
る ukérù

come into *vt fus* (money) 相続する só-
zoku suru; (be involved) ...に関係する
...ni kánkei suru

to come into fashion 流行する ryūkō
suru

come off *vi* (button) 外れる hazúreru;
(attempt) 成功する seíkō suru

come on *vi* (pupil, work, project) 進歩す

る shínpo suru; (lights, electricity) つく tsukú

   come on! さあさあ sāsā

come out *vi* (fact) 発覚する hakkáku suru; (book) 出版される shúppan sareru; (stain) 取れる torérù, 落ちる ochírù; (sun) 出る dérù

come round *vi* (after faint, operation) 正気に返る shóki ni kaèru, 目が覚める mé gà samérù, 気が付く ki gá tsukù

comet [ka:m'it] *n* すい星 suísei

come to *vi* (regain consciousness) 正気に戻る shóki ni modorù, 目が覚める mé gà samérù

come up *vi* (sun) 出る dérù; (problem) 起る okórù, 出る dérù; (event) 起る okórù; (in conversation) 出る dérù

come up against *vt fus* (resistance, difficulties) ぶつかる butsúkaru

come upon *vt fus* (find) 見付ける mitsúkeru

comeuppance [kʌm'ʌp'əns] *n*: *to get one's comeuppance* 当然の罰を受ける tözen no batsù wo ukerù

come up with *vt fus* (idea) 持出す mochídasù; (money) 出す dásù

comfort [kʌm'fə:rt] *n* (well-being: physical, material) 安楽 áñraku; (relief) 慰め nagúsame

   ♦*vt* (console) 慰める nagúsamerù

comfortable [kʌm'fə:rtəbəl] *adj* (person: physically) 楽な rákù na; (: financially) 暮しに困らない kuráshi ni komáranaì; (furniture) 座り心地の良い suwárigokochi nò yoì; (room) 居心地のよい igókochi nò yói; (patient) 苦痛のない kutsú no naì; (easy: walk, climb etc) 楽な rákù na

comfortably [kʌm'fə:rtəbli:] *adv* (sit, live etc) 楽に rákù ni

comforts [kʌm'fə:rts] *npl* (of home etc) 生活を楽にするもの seíkatsu wo rakú ni suru monò

comfort station (*US*) *n* お手洗 o-téaraì

comic [ka:m'ik] *adj* (*also*: **comical**) こっけいな kokkéi na

   ♦*n* (comedian) コメディアン kómèdian; (*BRIT*: magazine) 漫画(雑誌) mañ-ga(zasshì)

comic strip *n* 連続漫画 reñzokumaṅga

coming [kʌm'iŋ] *n* (arrival) 到着 tóchaku

   ♦*adj* (event, attraction) 次の tsugí no, これからの koré kara no

coming(s) and going(s) *n(pl)* 行き来 yukíki, 往来 ōrai

comma [ka:m'ə] *n* コンマ kóñma

command [kəmænd'] *n* (order) 命令 meírei; (control, charge) 指揮 shikí; (MIL: authority) 司令部 shírèibu; (mastery: of subject) マスターしていること masútà shité irú kotó

   ♦*vt* (give orders to): *to command someone to do something* ...に...をする様に命令する ...ni ...wo suru yō ni meírei suru; (troops) ...の司令官である ...no shirēikan de arù

commandeer [ka:məndi:r'] *vt* (requisition) 徴発する chóhatsu suru; (*fig*) 勝手に取って使う katté ni totté tsukáù

commander [kəmæn'də:r] *n* (MIL) 司令官 shírèikan

commandment [kəmænd'mənt] *n* (REL) 戒律 kaíritsu

commando [kəmæn'dou] *n* (group) コマンド部隊 komándobùtai; (soldier) コマンド隊員 komándotaìin

commemorate [kəmem'ə:reit] *vt* (with statue, monument, celebration, holiday) 記念する kinén suru

commence [kəmens'] *vt* (begin, start) 始める hajímeru

   ♦*vi* 始まる hajímaru

commend [kəmend'] *vt* (praise) ほめる homérù; (recommend) ゆだねる yudánerù

commensurate [kəmen'sərit] *adj*: *commensurate with* ...に相応した ...ni sōō shitá

comment [ka:m'ent] *n* (remark: written or spoken) コメント koméñto

   ♦*vi*: *to comment (on)* (...について) コメントする ...ni tsuité koméñto surù

   no comment ノーコメント nókomento

commentary [ka:m'ənte:ri:] *n* (TV, RADIO) 実況放送 jikkyöhōsō; (book, article) 注解 chūkai

commentator [kɑːm'ənteitə:r] *n* (TV, RADIO) 解说者 kaísetsùsha

commerce [kɑːm'ə:rs] *n* 商業 shōgyō

commercial [kəmə:r'ʃəl] *adj* (organization, activity) 商業 の shōgyō no; (success, failure) 商業上の shōgyōjō no
♦*n* (TV, RADIO: advertisement) コマーシャル kómàsharu, CM shíemu

commercialized [kəmə:r'ʃəlaizd] (*pej*) *adj* (place, event etc) 営利本意の eírihoñi no

commercial radio/television *n* 民間 ラジオ〔テレビ〕放送 miñkan rajio(terebi) hōsō, 民放 míñpō

commiserate [kəmiz'əreit] *vi*: **to commiserate with** ...をいたわる ...wo itáwarù

commission [kəmiʃ'ən] *n* (order for work: esp of artist) 依頼 irái; (COMM) 歩合 buái, コミッション kómìsshon; (committee) 委員会 iñkai
♦*vt* (work of art) 依頼する irái suru
out of commission (not working) 故障 して koshō shité

commissionaire [kəmiʃənə:r'] (*BRIT*) *n* ドアマン dóàman

commissioner [kəmiʃ'ənə:r] *n* (POLICE) 長官 chōkan

commit [kəmit'] *vt* (crime, murder etc) 犯す okásu; (money, resources) 充当する jūtō suru; (to someone's care) 任せる makáserù
to commit oneself (to do) (...する事を)約束する (...surú kotó wo) yakúsoku suru
to commit suicide 自殺する jisátsu suru

commitment [kəmit'mənt] *n* (to ideology, system) 献身 keñshin; (obligation) 責任 sekínin; (undertaking) 約束 yakúsoku

committee [kəmit'iː] *n* (of organization, club etc) 委員会 iñkai

commodity [kəmɑ:d'itiː] *n* (saleable item) 商品 shōhin

common [kɑːm'ən] *adj* (shared by all: knowledge, property, good) 共同の kyō-

dō no; (usual, ordinary: event, object, experience etc) 普通の futsū no; (vulgar: person, manners) 下品な gehín na
♦*n* (area) 共有地 kyōyúchi
in common 共通で kyótsū de

commoner [kɑːm'ənə:r] *n* 庶民 shomín

common law *n* コモン・ロー komón rō ◇成文化されてない慣習に基づく英米の一般法を指す seíbunka saréte naí kañshū ni motőzukù eíbei no ippánhō wo sasú

commonly [kɑːm'ənliː] *adv* (usually) 通常 tsūjō

Common Market *n* ヨーロッパ共同市場 yőroppa kyődōshijō

commonplace [kɑːm'ənpleis] *adj* 平凡な heíbon na

common room *n* (SCOL) 談話室 dañwashìtsu

Commons [kɑːm'ənz] (*BRIT*) *npl*: **the Commons** 下院 ká-ìn

common sense *n* 常識 jōshiki, コモンセンス komónseñsu

Commonwealth [kɑːm'ənwelθ] *n* (British Commonwealth): **the Commonwealth** イギリス連邦 igírisureñpō
the Commonwealth of Independent States 独立国家共同体 dokúritsu kòkka kyődōtai

commotion [kəmou'ʃən] *n* (uproar) 騒ぎ sáwàgi

communal [kəmjuː'nəl] *adj* (shared) 共同の kyōdō no

commune [*n* kɑːm'juːn *vb* kəmjuːn'] *n* (group) コミューン komyūñ
♦*vi*: **to commune with** (nature, God) ...に親しむ ...ni shitáshimù

communicate [kəmjuː'nikeit] *vt* (idea, decision, feeling) 伝える tsutáerù
♦*vi*: **to communicate (with)** ...と通信する ...to tsūshin suru

communication [kəmjuːnikei'ʃən] *n* (process) 通信 tsūshin; (letter, call) 連絡 refraku

communication cord (*BRIT*) *n* (on train) 非常通報装置 hijótsūhōsōchi

communion [kəmjuːn'jən] *n* (*also*: **Holy Communion**) 聖体拝領 seítaihaìryō

communiqué [kəmju:nikei'] n (POL, PRESS) コミュニケ kómyùnike

communism [ka:m'jənizəm] n 共産主義 kyōsanshùgi

communist [ka:m'jənist] adj 共産主義の kyōsanshùgi no

♦n 共産主義者 kyōsanshugishà

community [kəmju:'niti:] n (group of people) 共同体 kyōdōtai; (within larger group) 社会 shákài

community center n 公民館 kōmìñkan

community chest (US) n 共同募金 kyōdōbòkin

community home (BRIT) n 養育施設 yōikushisètsu

commutation ticket [ka:mjətei'(ʃ)ən-] (US) n 定期券 teíkìkèn

commute [kəmju:t'] vi (to work) 通う kayóu

♦vt (LAW: sentence) 減刑する geñkei suru

commuter [kəmju:t'ə:r] n 通勤者 tsūkìñsha

compact [ka:m'pækt] adj (taking up little space) 小型の kogáta no

♦n (also: powder compact) コンパクト kóñpakuto

compact disk n コンパクトディスク koñpakuto disùku

companion [kəmpæn'jən] n 相手 aíte

companionship [kəmpæn'jənʃip] n つきあい tsukíai

company [kʌm'pəni:] n (COMM) 会社 kaísha; (THEATER) 劇団 gekídan; (companionship) 付合い tsukíai

to keep someone company ...の相手になる ...no aíte ni narù

company secretary (BRIT) n 総務部長 sōmubùchō

comparable [ka:m'pə:rəbəl] adj (size, style, extent) 匹敵する hittéki suru

comparative [kəmpær'ətiv] adj (peace, stranger, safety) 比較的 hikákuteki; (study) 比較の hikáku no

comparatively [kəmpær'ətivli:] adv (relatively) 比較的に hikákuteki ni

compare [kəmpe:r'] vt: *to compare someone/something with/to* (set side

by side) ...を...と比較する ...wo ...to hikáku suru; (liken) ...を...に例える ...wo ...ni tatóerù

♦vi: *to compare (with)* (...に) 匹敵する (...ni) hittéki suru

comparison [kəmpær'isən] n (setting side by side) 比較 hikáku; (likening) 例え tatóe

in comparison (with) ...と比較して ...to hikáku shité

compartment [kəmpa:rt'mənt] n (RAIL) 客室 kyakúshitsu, コンパートメント koñpātomènto; (section: of wallet, fridge etc) 区画 kukáku

compass [kʌm'pəs] n (instrument: NAUT, GEO) 羅針盤 rashíñban, コンパス kóñpasu

compasses [kʌm'pəsiz] npl (MATH) コンパス koñpasu

compassion [kəmpæʃ'ən] n (pity, sympathy) 同情 dōjō

compassionate [kəmpæʃ'ənit] adj (person, look) 情け深い nasákebukaì

compatible [kəmpæt'əbəl] adj (people) 気が合う ki ga aù; (ideas etc) 両立できる ryōritsu dekírù; (COMPUT) 互換性のある gokáñsei no arù

compel [kəmpel'] vt (force) 強制する kyōsei suru

compelling [kəmpel'iŋ] adj (fig: argument, reason) 止むに止まれぬ yamú ni yamárenù

compensate [ka:m'pənseit] vt (employee, victim) ...に補償する ...ni hoshō suru

♦vi: *to compensate for* (loss, disappointment, change etc) ...を埋め合せる ...wo uméawaserù

compensation [ka:mpənsei'(ʃ)ən] n (to employee, victim) 補償 hoshō; (for loss, disappointment, change etc) 埋め合せ uméawase

compère [ka:m'pe:r] (BRIT) n (TV, RADIO) 司会者 shíkàisha

compete [kəmpi:t'] vi (companies, rivals): *to compete (with)* (...と) 競り合う (...to) seríaù; (in contest, game) 参加する sañka suru

competence [ka:m'pitəns] n (of worker

etc) 能力 nṓryoku

competent [ka:m'pitənt] *adj* 有 能 な yū́nō na

competition [ka:mpitiʃ'ən] *n* (between firms, rivals) 競争 kyṓsō; (contest) コンクール koṅkū́ru; (ECON) ライバル商品 raíbaru shṓhin

competitive [kəmpet'ətiv] *adj* (industry, society) 競争の激しい kyṓsō no hagéshiĩ; (person) 競争心の強い kyṓsōshin no tsuyóĩ; (price, product) 競争できる kyṓsō dekírù

competitive sports 競技 kyṓgi

competitor [kəmpet'itə:r] *n* (rival) 競争相手 kyṓsōaìte; (participant) 参加者 saṅkashà

compile [kəmpail'] *vt* (book, film, report) 編集する heñshū suru

complacency [kəmplei'sənsi:] *n* (smugness) 自己満足 jikṓmaṅzoku

complacent [kəmplei'sənt] *adj* (smug) 自己満足にふける jikṓmaṅzoku ni fukérù

complain [kəmplein'] *vi* (grumble) 不平不満を言う fuhéifùman wo iú; (protest: to authorities, shop etc) 訴える uttaèru

to complain of (pain) ...を訴える ...wo uttaérù

complaint [kəmpleint'] *n* (objection) 訴え uttáe; (criticism) 非難 hínàn; (MED: illness) 病気 byṓki

complement[*n* ka:m'pləmənt *vb* ka:m'pləmənt] *n* (supplement) 補う物 ogínaù monó; (esp ship's crew) 人員 jiñ-in

♦*vt* (enhance) 引立たせる hikítataserù

complementary [ka:mpləmen'tə:ri:] *adj* (mutually supportive) 補足し合う hosóku shiaù

complete [kəmpli:t'] *adj* (total, whole) 完全な kaṅzen na; (finished: building, task) 完成した kaṅsei shitá

♦*vt* (finish: building, task) 完成する kaṅsei suru; (: set, group etc) そろえる soróerù; (fill in: a form) ...に記入する ...ni kinyū suru

completely [kəmpli:t'li:] *adv* (totally) 全く mattáku, 完全に kaṅzen ni

completion [kəmpli:'ʃən] *n* (of building)

完成 kaṅsei; (of contract) 履行 rikṓ

complex [*adj* kəmpleks' *n* ka:m'pleks] *adj* (structure, problem, decision) 複雑な fukúzatsu na

♦*n* (group: of buildings) 団地 daṅchi; (PSYCH) コンプレックス koṅpurekkùsu

complexion [kəmplek'ʃən] *n* (of face) 顔の肌 kaó no hadà

complexity [kəmplek'siti:] *n* (of problem, law) 複雑さ fukúzatsuùsa

compliance [kəmplai'əns] *n* (submission) 服従 fukújū; (agreement) 同意 dṓi

in compliance with ...に従って ...ni shitágatte

complicate [ka:m'pləkeit] *vt* (matters, situation) 複雑にする fukúzatsu ni suru

complicated [ka:m'pləkeitid] *adj* (explanation, system) 複雑な fukúzatsu na

complication [ka:mpləkei'ʃən] *n* (problem) 問題 moñdai; (MED) 合併症 gappéishō

complicity [kəmplis'əti:] *n* (in crime) 共犯 kyṓhan

compliment [*n* ka:m'pləmənt *vb* ka:m'pləmənt] *n* (expression of admiration) ほめ言葉 homékotòba

♦*vt* (express admiration for) ほめる homérù

to pay someone a compliment ...をほめる ...wo homéru

complimentary [ka:mpləmen'tə:ri:] *adj* (remark) 賛辞の sañji no; (ticket, copy of book etc) 無料の muryṓ no

compliments [ka:m'pləmənts] *npl* (regards) 挨拶 aîsatsu

comply [kəmplai'] *vi*: *to comply with* (law, ruling) ...に従う ...ni shitágaù

component [kəmpou'nənt] *adj* (parts, elements) 構成している kṓsei shité irù

♦*n* (part) 部分 búbùn

compose [kəmpouz'] *vt* (form): *to be composed of* ...から出来ている ...kará dekítè irú; (write: music, poem, letter) 書く kákù

to compose oneself 心を落着かせる kokṓrò wo ochítsukaserù

composed [kəmpouzd'] *adj* (calm) 落着いている ochítsuite irù

composer [kəmpou'zə:r] *n* (MUS) 作曲家 sakkyókuka

composition [kɑ:mpəzi'ʃən] *n* (of substance, group etc) 構成 kósei; (essay) 作文 sakúbun; (MUS) 作曲 sakkyóku

compost [kɑːm'poust] *n* たい肥 taíhi

composure [kəmpou'ʒə:r] *n* (of person) 落着き ochítsuki

compound [kɑːm'paund] *n* (CHEM) 化合物 kágōbutsu; (enclosure) 囲い地 kakóichi; (LING) 複合語 fukúgōgo
♦*adj* (fracture) 複雑な fukúzatsu na
compound interest 複利 fúkùri

comprehend [kɑ:mprihend'] *vt* (understand) 理解する rikái suru

comprehension [kɑ:mprihen'ʃən] *n* (understanding) 理解 ríkài

comprehensive [kɑ:mprihen'siv] *adj* (description, review, list) 包括的な hókatsuteki na; (INSURANCE) 総合的な sógōteki na

comprehensive (school) (*BRIT*) *n* 総合中等学校 sógōchūtōgakkō ◇あらゆる能力の子供に適した課程のある中等学校 aráyuru nőryoku no kodőmo ni tekí shita katéi no arù chútōgakkō

compress [*vb* kɑ:mpres' *n* kɑ:m'pres] *vt* (air, cotton, paper etc) 圧縮する asshúku suru; (text, information) 要約する yőyaku suru
♦*n* (MED) 湿布 shippú

comprise [kəmpraiz'] *vt* (*also*: **be comprised of**) ...からなる ...kará narù; (constitute) 構成する kósei suru

compromise [kɑːm'prəmaiz] *n* 妥協 dakyő
♦*vt* (beliefs, principles) 傷つける kizú tsukerù
♦*vi* (make concessions) 妥協する dakyő suru

compulsion [kəmpʌl'ʃən] *n* (desire, impulse) 強迫観念 kyőhakukaňnen; (force) 強制 kyősei

compulsive [kəmpʌl'siv] *adj* (liar, gambler etc) 病的な byőteki na; (viewing, reading) 止められない yamérarenãi

compulsory [kəmpʌl'sə:ri:] *adj* (attendance, retirement) 強制的な kyőseiteki

na

computer [kəmpju:'tə:r] *n* コンピュータ kofipyúta

computerize [kəmpju:'təraiz] *vt* (system, filing, accounts etc) コンピュータ化する kofipyútaka surù; (information) コンピュータに覚えさせる kofipyúta ni obóesaserù

computer programmer *n* プログラマー purőgurāmã

computer programming *n* プログラミング purőguramiňgu

computer science *n* コンピュータ科学 kofipyúta kagáku

computing [kəmpju:'tiŋ] *n* (activity, science) コンピュータ利用 kofipyúta riyő

comrade [kɑ:m'ræd] *n* (POL, MIL) 同志 dőshi; (friend) 友人 yújin

comradeship [kɑ:m'rədʃip] *n* 友情 yújō

con [kɑ:n] *vt* (deceive) だます damásù; (cheat) ぺてんに掛ける petén ni kakérù
♦*n* (trick) いかさま ikásama

concave [kɑ:nkeiv'] *adj* 凹面の őmen no

conceal [kənsi:l'] *vt* (hide: weapon, entrance) 隠す kakúsù; (keep back: information) 秘密にする himítsu ni surù

concede [kənsi:d'] *vt* (admit: error, point, defeat) 認める mitómeru

conceit [kənsi:t'] *n* (arrogance) うぬぼれ unúbore

conceited [kənsi:'tid] *adj* (vain) うぬぼれた unúboreta

conceivable [kənsi:v'əbəl] *adj* (reason, possibility) 考えられる kafigaerarerù

conceive [kənsi:v'] *vt* (child) はらむ harámù; (plan, policy) 考え出す kafigaedasù
♦*vi* (BIO) 妊娠する niňshin suru

concentrate [kɑ:n'səntreit] *vi* (on problem, activity etc) 専念する seńnen suru; (in one area, space) 集中する shúchū suru
♦*vt* (energies, attention) 集中させる shúchū saséru

concentration [kɑ:nsəntrei'ʃən] *n* (on problem, activity etc) 専念 seńnen; (in one area, space) 集中 shúchū; (attention) 注意 chūi; (CHEM) 濃縮 nőshuku

concentration camp n 強制収容所 kyṓseishūyōjo

concept [ka:n'sept] n (idea, principle) 概念 gáinen

conception [kənsep'ʃən] n (idea) 概念 gáinen; (of child) 妊娠 nińshin

concern [kənsə:rn'] n (affair) 責任 sekínin; (anxiety, worry) 心配 shińpai; (COMM: firm) 企業 kígyð

♦vt (worry) 心配させる shińpai saséru; (involve, relate to) ...に関係がある ...ni kańkē ga arù

to be concerned (about) (person, situation etc) (...について) 心配する (...ni tsuitḗ) shińpai suru

concerning [kənsə:r'niŋ] prep (regarding) ...について ...ni tsuitḗ

concert [ka:n'sə:rt] n (MUS) 演奏会 eńsōkai, コンサート końsāto

concerted [kənsə:r'tid] adj (effort etc) 共同の kyṓdō no

concert hall n コンサートホール końsātohòru

concertina [ka:nsə:rti:'nə] n (MUS: instrument) コンサーティーナ końsātīna ◇六角形の小型アコーディオン rokkákkèi no kogáta akòdion

concerto [kəntʃe:r'tou] n 協奏曲 kyṓsōkyoku, コンチェルト kóńcheruto

concession [kənseʃ'ən] n (compromise) 譲歩 jðho; (COMM: right) 特権 tokkén

tax concession 減税 geńzei

conciliatory [kənsil'i:ətɔ:ri:] adj (gesture, tone) 懐柔的な kaíjūteki na

concise [kənsais'] adj (description, text) 簡潔な kańketsu na

conclude [kənklu:d'] vt (finish: speech, chapter) 終える oéru; (treaty) 締結する teíketsu suru; (deal etc) まとめる matómeru; (decide) (...だと) 結論する (...da to) ketsúron suru

conclusion [kənklu:'ʒən] n (of speech, chapter) 終り owári; (of treaty) 締結 teíketsu; (of deal etc) まとめる事 matómeru kotó; (decision) 結論 ketsúron

conclusive [kənklu:'siv] adj (evidence, defeat) 決定的な kettéiteki na

concoct [kənka:kt'] vt (excuse) でっち上

げる detchíagerù; (plot) 企てる kuwádaterù; (meal, sauce) 工夫して作る kufú shitḗ tsukúrù

concoction [kənka:k'ʃən] n (mixture) 調合物 chṓgòbutsu

concourse [ka:n'kɔ:rs] n (hall) 中央ホール chūōhòru, コンコース końkōsu

concrete [ka:n'kri:t] n コンクリート końkurīto

♦adj (block, floor) コンクリートの końkurīto no; (proposal, idea) 具体的な gutáiteki na

concur [kənkə:r'] vi 同意する dói suru

concurrently [kənkə:r'əntli:] adv (happen, run) 同時に dóji ni

concussion [kənkʌʃ'ən] n (MED) 脳震とう nóshintð

condemn [kəndem'] vt (denounce: action, report etc) 非難する hínàn suru; (sentence: prisoner) ...に...刑を宣告する ...ni...keÌ wo seńkoku suru; (declare unsafe: building) 使用に耐えない物と決定する shiyṓ ni taénài monð to kettéi suru

condemnation [ka:ndemnei'ʃən] n (criticism) 非難 hínàn

condensation [ka:ndensei'ʃən] n (on walls, windows) 結露 kétsùro

condense [kəndens'] vi (vapor) 液化する ekíka suru

♦vt (report, book) 要約する yṓyaku suru

condensed milk [kəndenst'-] n 練乳 reńnyū

condescending [ka:ndisen'diŋ] adj (reply, attitude) 恩着せがましい ońkisegamashiì

condition [kəndiʃ'ən] n (state: gen) 状態 jṓtai; (MED: of illness) 病状 byōjō; (requirement) 条件 jōken; (MED: illness) 病気 byðki

♦vt (person) 慣れさせる narésaserù

on condition that ...という条件で ...to iú jōken de

conditional [kəndiʃ'ənəl] adj 条件付きの jōkentsuki no

conditioner [kəndiʃ'ənə:r] n (also: hair conditioner) ヘアコンディショナー heákondishònā; (for fabrics) 柔軟剤 jūnańzai

conditions [kəndiʃ'ənz] *npl* (circumstances) 状況 jōkyō

condolences [kəndou'lənsiz] *npl* お悔みo-kúyami

condom [ka:n'dəm] *n* コンドーム koňdōmu, スキン sukín

condominium [ka:ndəmin'i:əm] (*US*) *n* 分譲マンション buňjōmaňshon

condone [kəndoun'] *vt* (misbehavior, crime) 容認する yōnín suru

conducive [kəndu:'siv] *adj*: **conducive to** (rest, study) …を助ける …wo tasúkerù

conduct [*n* ka:n'dʌkt *vb* kəndʌkt'] *n* (of person) 振舞 furúmai
♦*vt* (survey, research etc) 行う okónaù; (orchestra, choir etc) 指揮する shikí suru; (heat, electricity) 伝導する deńdō suru

to conduct oneself (behave) 振舞う furúmaù

conducted tour [kəndʌk'tid-] *n* ガイド付き見物 gaídotsuki keńbutsu

conductor [kəndʌk'tə:r] *n* (of orchestra) 指揮者 shikíshà; (*BRIT*: on bus, *US*: on train) 車掌 shashō; (ELEC) 伝導体 deńdōtai

conductress [kəndʌk'tris] *n* (on bus) 女性車掌 joséishashō, バスガール basúgāru

cone [koun] *n* (shape) 円すい形 eńsuikei; (on road) カラーコーン karákòn, セーフティコーン sēfutikòn; (BOT) 松かさ matsúkasa; (ice cream cornet) コーン kōn

confectioner [kənfek'ʃənə:r] *n* (person) 菓子職人 kashíshokùnin

confectioner's (shop) [kənfek'ʃənə:rz-] *n* (sweet shop) 菓子屋 kashíyà

confectionery [kənfek'ʃəne:ri:] *n* (sweets, candies) 菓子類 kashírui

confederation [kənfedərei'ʃən] *n* (POL, COMM) 連合 reńgō

confer [kənfə:r'] *vt*: **to confer something (on someone)** (honor, degree, advantage) (…に) …を与える (…ni) …wo atáerù
♦*vi* (panel, team) 協議する kyōgi suru

conference [ka:n'fə:rəns] *n* (meeting) 会議 kái̇gi

confess [kənfes'] *vt* (sin, guilt, crime) 白状する hákùjō suru; (weakness, ignorance) 認める mitómeru
♦*vi* (admit) 認める mitómeru

confession [kənfeʃ'ən] *n* (admission) 白状 hákùjō; (REL) ざんげ zánge

confetti [kənfet'i:] *n* コンフェティ kóňfeti ◇紙吹雪き用に細かく切った色紙 kamífubuki yō ni komákaku kittá irógami

confide [kənfaid'] *vi*: **to confide in** …に打明ける …ni uchíakerù

confidence [ka:n'fidəns] *n* (faith) 信用 shiń-yō; (*also*: **self-confidence**) 自信 jishín; (secret) 秘密 himítsu

in confidence (speak, write) 内緒で naísho de

confidence trick *n* いかさま ikásama

confident [ka:n'fidənt] *adj* (self-assured) 自信のある jishín no arù; (positive) 確信している kakúshin shitē irù

confidential [ka:nfiden'ʃəl] *adj* (report, information) 秘密の himítsu no; (tone) 親しげな shitáshige na

confine [kənfain'] *vt* (limit) 限定する geńtei suru; (shut up) 閉じ込める tojíkomerù

confined [kənfaind'] *adj* (space) 限られた kagíraretà

confinement [kənfain'mənt] *n* (imprisonment) 監禁 kańkin

confines [ka:n'fainz] *npl* (of area) 境 sakái

confirm [kənfə:rm'] *vt* (belief, statement) 裏付ける urázukerù; (appointment, date) 確認する kakúnin suru

confirmation [ka:nfə:rmei'ʃən] *n* (of belief, statement) 裏付け urázuke; (of appointment, date) 確認 kakúnin; (REL) 堅信礼 keńshiňrei

confirmed [kənfə:rmd'] *adj* (bachelor, teetotaller) 常習的な jōshūteki na

confiscate [ka:n'fiskeit] *vt* (impound, seize) 没収する bosshú suru

conflict [*n* ka:n'flikt *vb* kənflikt'] *n* (disagreement) 論争 rońsō; (difference: of interests, loyalties etc) 対立 taíritsu; (fighting) 戦闘 seńtō
♦*vi* (opinions) 対立する taíritsu suru; (research etc) 矛盾する mujún suru

conflicting [kənflik'tiŋ] *adj* (reports) 矛盾する mujún suru; (interests etc) 対立する taíritsu suru

conform [kənfɔ:rm'] *vi* (comply) 従う shitágaù

to conform to (law, wish, ideal) ...に従う ...ni shitágaù

confound [kənfaund'] *vt* (confuse) 当惑させる tówaku saséru

confront [kənfrʌnt'] *vt* (problems, task) ...と取組む ...to toríkumù; (enemy, danger) ...に立向かう ...ni tachímukaù

confrontation [kɑːnfrəntei'ʃən] *n* (dispute, conflict) 衝突 shótotsu

confuse [kənfju:z'] *vt* (perplex: person) 当惑させる tówaku saséru; (mix up: two things, people etc) 混同する kondō suru; (complicate: situation, plans) 混乱させる kofiran saséru

confused [kənfju:zd'] *adj* (bewildered) 当惑した tówaku shitá; (disordered) 混乱した kofiran shitá

confusing [kənfju:'ziŋ] *adj* (plot, instructions) 分かりにくい wakárinikuî

confusion [kənfju:'ʒən] *n* (perplexity) 当惑 tówaku; (mix-up) 混同 kondō; (disorder) 混乱 kofiran

congeal [kəndʒi:l'] *vi* (blood, sauce) 凝結する gyóketsu suru

congenial [kəndʒi:n'jəl] *adj* (person) 気の合った ki no attá; (atmosphere etc) 楽しい tanóshiî

congenital [kəndʒen'itəl] *adj* (MED: defect, illness) 先天性の sefitensei no

congested [kəndʒes'tid] *adj* (MED: with blood) うっ血した ukkétsu shitá; (: with mucus: nose) 詰まった tsumátta; (road) 渋滞した jūtai shitá; (area) 人口密集の jinkōmisshū no

congestion [kəndʒes'tʃən] *n* (MED: with blood) うっ血 ukkétsu; (: with mucus) 鼻詰まり hanázumàri; (of road) 渋滞 jūtai; (of area) 人口密集 jinkōmisshū

conglomerate [kəngla'mʼərit] *n* (COMM) 複合企業 fukūgōkigyõ, コングロマリット kofiguromarítto

conglomeration [kəngla:mʼərei'ʃən] *n* (group, gathering) 寄せ集め yoséatsume

congratulate [kəngrætʃ'uleit] *vt* (parents, bridegroom etc) ...にお祝いを言う ...ni o-íwai wo iú

congratulations [kəngrætʃulei'ʃənz] *npl* 祝詞 shukúji

congratulations! おめでとうございます omédetō gozáimasù

congregate [kɑːŋ'grəgeit] *vi* (people) 集まる atsúmarù; (animals) 群がる murágarù

congregation [kɑːŋgrəgei'ʃən] *n* (of a church) 会衆 kaíshū

congress [kɑːŋ'gris] *n* (conference) 大会 taíkai; (US): **Congress** 議会 gikái

congressman [kɑːŋ'grismən] (*US*: *pl* **congressmen**) *n* 下院議員 ka-íngiìn

conical [kɑːn'ikəl] *adj* (shape) 円すい形の efisuikei no

conifer [kou'nifər] *n* 針葉樹 shiñ-yõju

conjecture [kəndʒek'tʃər] *n* (speculation) 憶測 okúsoku

conjugal [kɑːn'dʒəgəl] *adj* 夫婦間の fúfùkàn no

conjugate [kɑːn'dʒəgeit] *vt* (LING) ...の活用形を挙げる ...no katsúyōkei wo agérù

conjunction [kəndʒʌŋk'ʃən] *n* (LING) 接続詞 setsúzokushi

conjunctivitis [kəndʒʌŋktəvai'tis] *n* (MED) 結膜炎 ketsúmakuèn

conjure [kɑːn'dʒəːr] *vi* (magician) 奇術をする kijútsu wo suru

conjurer [kɑːn'dʒəːrəːr] *n* (magician) 奇術師 kijútsushì, マジシャン majíshan

conjure up *vt* (ghost, spirit) 呼出す yobídasù; (memories) 思い起す omóiokosù

conk out [kɑːŋk-] (*inf*) *vi* (machine, engine) 故障する koshō suru

con man [kɑːn'mən] (*pl* **con men**) *n* ぺてん師 peténshì

connect [kənekt'] *vt* (join, *also* TEL) つなぐ tsunágù; (ELEC) 接続する setsúzoku suru; (*fig*: associate) 関係付ける kañkeizūkeru

◆*vi*: *to connect with* (train, plane etc) ...に連絡する ...ni refíraku suru

to be connected with (associated) 関係付ける kañkeizūkeru

connection [kənek'ʃən] n (joint, link) つなぎ tsunági; (ELEC, TEL) 接続 setsúzoku; (train, plane etc) 連絡 refiraku; (fig: association) 関係 kañkei

connive [kənaiv'] vi: **to connive at** (misbehavior) ...を容認する ...wo yónin suru

connoisseur [kɑːnisəːr'] n (of food, wine, art etc) 通 tsū

connotation [kɑːnətei'ʃən] n (implication) 含み fukúmi

conquer [kɑːŋ'kəːr] vt (MIL: country, enemy) 征服する seífuku suru; (fear, feelings) 克服する kokúfuku suru

conqueror [kɑːŋ'kəːrəːr] n (MIL) 征服者 seífukushā

conquest [kɑːn'kwest] n (MIL) 征服 seífuku; (prize) 勝得た物 kachíeta monð; (mastery: of space etc) 征服 seífuku

cons [kɑːnz] npl see **convenience; pro**

conscience [kɑːn'ʃəns] n (sense of right and wrong) 良心 ryðshin

conscientious [kɑːnʃiːen'ʃəs] adj (worker) 良心的な ryðshinteki na

conscious [kɑːn'ʃəs] adj (aware): **conscious (of)** (...に) 気が付いている (...ni) ki ga tsuíte irù; (deliberate) 意識的な ishíkiteki na; (awake) 目が覚めている me ga saméte irù

consciousness [kɑːn'ʃəsnis] n (awareness, mentality: also MED) 意識 ishíki

conscript [kɑːn'skript] n (MIL) 徴集兵 chōshūhei

conscription [kənskrip'ʃən] n (MIL) 徴兵 chōhei

consecrate [kɑːn'səkreit] vt (building, place) 奉献する hōken suru

consecutive [kənsek'jətiv] adj (days, wins) 連続の refizoku na

consensus [kənsen'səs] n 合意 gōi

consent [kənsent'] n (permission) 許可 kyoká
♦vi: **to consent to** ...に同意する ...ni dōi suru

consequence [kɑːn'səkwens] n (result) 結果 kekká; (significance) 重要さ júyōsa

consequently [kɑːn'səkwentliː] adv (as a result, so) 従って shitágattè

conservation [kɑːnsəːrvei'ʃən] n (of the environment) 保護 hogð, 保全 hozén; (of energy) 節約 setsúyaku; (of paintings, books) 保全 hozén

conservative [kənsəːr'vətiv] adj (traditional, conventional: person, attitudes) 保守的な hoshúteki na; (cautious: estimate etc) 控え目の hikáeme no; (BRIT: POL): **Conservative** 保守党の hoshútō no
♦n (BRIT: POL): **Conservative** 保守党員 hoshútōin

conservatory [kənsəːr'vətɔːriː] n (greenhouse) 温室 oñshitsu; (MUS) 音楽学校 oñgaku gakkð

conserve [vb kənsəːrv' n kɑːn'səːrv] vt (preserve) 保護する hogð suru; (supplies, energy) 節約する setsúyaku suru
♦n (jam) ジャム jámù

consider [kənsid'əːr] vt (believe) ...だと思う ...da to omðù; (study) 熟考する jukkð suru; (take into account) 考慮に入れる kōryo ni irérù
to consider doing something ...しようかと考える ...shiyð ka to kángaerù

considerable [kənsid'əːrəbəl] adj (amount, expense, difference etc) かなりの kanári no

considerably [kənsid'əːrəbliː] adv (improve, deteriorate) かなり kanári

considerate [kənsid'əːrit] adj (person) 思いやりのある omóiyari no arù

consideration [kənsidərei'ʃən] n (deliberation) 熟考 jukkð; (factor) 考慮すべき点 kōryo subeki tén; (thoughtfulness) 思いやり omóiyarì

considering [kənsid'əːriŋ] prep (bearing in mind) ...を考慮すると ...wo kōryo suru to

consign [kənsain'] vt (something unwanted): **to consign to** (place) ...にしまっておく ...ni shimátte okù; (person): **to consign to** (someone's care etc) ...に委ねる ...ni yudánerù; (poverty etc) ...に追込む ...ni oíkomù

consignment [kənsain'mənt] n (COMM) 輸送貨物 yusōkamòtsu

consist [kənsist'] vi: **to consist of** (comprise) ...から成る ...kará narù

consistency [kənsis'tənsi:] *n* (of actions, policies etc) 一貫性 ikkánsei; (of yoghurt, cream etc) 固さ katása

consistent [kənsis'tənt] *adj* (person) 変らない kawáranaî; (argument, idea) 一貫性のある ikkánsei no arù

consolation [kɑːnsəlei'ʃən] *n* (comfort) 慰め nagúsame

console [*vb* kənsoul' *n* kɑːn'soul] *vt* (comfort) 慰める nagúsamerù
♦*n* (panel) コンソール koñsòru

consolidate [kənsɑːl'ideit] *vt* (position, power) 強化する kyőka suru

consommé [kɑːnsəmei'] *n* (CULIN) コンソメ koñsome

consonant [kɑːn'sənənt] *n* (LING) 子音 shíin

consortium [kənsɔːr'ʃiːəm] *n* (COMM) 協会 kyőkai

conspicuous [kənspik'juːəs] *adj* (noticeable: person, feature) 目立つ medátsu

conspiracy [kənspir'əsiː] *n* (plot) 陰謀 iñbő

conspire [kənspai'əːr] *vi* (criminals, revolutionaries etc) 共謀する kyőbō suru; (events) 相重なる aíkasanarù

constable [kɑːn'stəbəl] (*BRIT*) *n* 巡査 juñsa
chief constable (*BRIT*) 警察本部長 keísatsu hoñbuchó

constabulary [kənstæb'jələːriː] (*BRIT*) *n* 警察 keísatsu ◇一地区の警察隊を指す ichíchiku no keísatsutai wo sasù

constant [kɑːn'stənt] *adj* (continuous: criticism, pain) 絶えない taénài; (fixed: temperature, level) 一定の ittéi no

constantly [kɑːn'stəntliː] *adv* (continually) 絶間なく taémanàku

constellation [kɑːnstəlei'ʃən] *n* (ASTRONOMY) 星座 seíza

consternation [kɑːnstəːrnei'ʃən] *n* (dismay) ろうばい rőbai

constipated [kɑːn'stəpeitid] *adj* (MED) 便秘している beñpi shité irù

constipation [kɑːnstəpei'ʃən] *n* (MED) 便秘 beñpi

constituency [kənstitʃ'uːənsiː] *n* (POL: area) 選挙区 señkyokù; (: electors) 選挙民 señkyomìn

constituent [kənstitʃ'uːənt] *n* (POL) 有権者 yűkeñsha; (component) 部分 búbùn

constitute [kɑːn'stitut] *vt* (represent: challenge, emergency) ...である ...de arù; (make up: whole) 構成する kősei suru

constitution [kɑːnstitu'ʃən] *n* (of country) 憲法 keñpō; (of club etc) 会則 kaísoku; (health) 体質 taíshitsu; (make-up: of committee etc) 構成 kősei

constitutional [kɑːnstitu'ʃənəl] *adj* (government, reform etc) 憲法の keñpō no

constraint [kənstreint'] *n* (restriction) 制限 seígen; (compulsion) 強制 kyősei

construct [kɑːn'strʌkt] *vt* (building) 建てる tatérù; (bridge, road etc) 建設する keñsetsu suru; (machine) 作る tsukúrù

construction [kənstrʌk'ʃən] *n* (of building etc) 建築 keñchiku; (of bridge, road etc) 建設 keñsetsu; (of machine) 製作 seísaku; (structure) 構造物 kőzōbùtsu

constructive [kənstrʌk'tiv] *adj* (remark, criticism) 建設的な keñsetsuteki na

construe [kənstru:'] *vt* (statement, event) 解釈する kaíshaku suru

consul [kɑːn'səl] *n* 領事 ryőji

consulate [kɑːn'səlit] *n* 領事館 ryőjikàn

consult [kənsʌlt'] *vt* (doctor, lawyer, friend) ...に相談する ...ni sődan suru; (reference book) 調べる shiráberù

consultant [kənsʌl'tənt] *n* (MED) 顧問医 komón-i; (other specialist) 顧問 kőmòn, コンサルタント koñsarùtanto

consultation [kɑːnsəltei'ʃən] *n* (MED) 診察 shiñsatsu; (discussion) 協議 kyőgi

consulting room [kənsʌl'tiŋ-] (*BRIT*) *n* 診察室 shiñsatsushìtsu

consume [kənsu:m'] *vt* (food) 食べる tabérù; (drink) 飲む nőmù; (fuel, energy, time etc) 消費する shőhi suru

consumer [kənsu:'məːr] *n* (COMM) 消費者 shőhishà

consumer goods *npl* 消費財 shőhizài

consumerism [kənsu:'mərizəm] *n* 消費者運動 shőhishauñdō

consumer society n 消費社会 shōhisha-kai

consummate [kɑːnˈsəmeit] vt (ambition etc) 全うする mattō suru

to consummate a marriage 床入りする tokó-iri suru

consumption [kənsʌmpˈʃən] n (of food) 食べる事 tabérù kotó; (of drink) 飲む事 nómù kotó; (of fuel, energy, time etc) 消費活動 shṓhi; (amount consumed) 消費量 shōhiryō; (buying) 消費 shōhi

cont. abbr (= continued) 続く tsuzúku

contact [kɑːnˈtækt] n (communication) 連絡 reñraku; (touch) 接触 sesshóku; (person) 連絡相手 reñrakuaîte

♦vt (by phone, letter) ...に連絡する ...ni reñraku suru

contact lenses npl コンタクトレンズ koñtakutoreñzu

contagious [kənteiˈdʒəs] adj (MED: disease) 伝染性の deñsensei no; (fig: laughter, enthusiasm) 移りやすい utsúriyasuî

contain [kənteiˈn] vt (hold: objects) ...に...が入っている ...ni ...ga haítte irù; (have: component, ingredient etc) ...に...が含まれている ...ni ...ga fukúmarète irù; (subj: piece of writing, report etc) ...に...が書いてある ...ni ...ga kaíte arù; (curb: growth, spread, feeling) 抑える osáerù

to contain oneself 自制する jiséi suru

container [kənteiˈnəːr] n (box, jar etc) 入れ物 irémono; (COMM: for shipping etc) コンテナー kóñtenā

contaminate [kəntæmˈəneit] vt (water, food, soil etc) 汚染する osén suru

contamination [kəntæmənˈeiʃən] n (of water, food, soil etc) 汚染 osén

cont'd abbr (= continued) 続く tsuzúku

contemplate [kɑːnˈtəmpleit] vt (idea, subject, course of action) じっくり考える jikkúrî kañgaerù; (person, painting etc) 眺める nagámerù

contemporary [kəntemˈpəreːriː] adj (present-day) 現代の geñdai no; (belonging to same time) 同時代の dōjidai no

♦n (person) 同時代の人 dōjidai no hitó

contempt [kəntempˈt] n (scorn) 軽べつ keîbetsu

contempt of court (LAW) 法廷侮辱罪 hōteibujokuzai

contemptible [kəntempˈtəbəl] adj (conduct) 卑劣な hirétsu na

contemptuous [kəntempˈtʃuːəs] adj (attitude) 軽べつ的な keîbetsuteki na

contend [kəntendˈ] vt (assert): **to contend that** ...だと主張する ...da to shuchō suru

♦vi (struggle): **to contend with** (problem, difficulty) ...と戦う ...to tatákaù; (compete): **to contend for** (power etc) ...を争う ...wo arásoù

contender [kəntenˈdəːr] n (in competition) 競争者 kyṓsōshà; (POL) 候補者 kōhoshà; (SPORT) 選手 séñshu

content [adj, vb kəntentˈ n kɑːnˈtent] adj (happy and satisfied) 満足して mañzoku shitē

♦vt (satisfy) 満足させる mañzoku saséru

♦n (of speech, novel) 内容 naíyō; (fat content, moisture content etc) 含有量 gañ-yūryō

contented [kəntenˈtid] adj (happy and satisfied) 満足して mañzoku shitē

contention [kəntenˈʃən] n (assertion) 主張 shuchṓ; (disagreement, argument) 論争 roñsō

contentment [kəntentˈmənt] n (happiness, satisfaction) 満足 mañzoku

contents [kɑːnˈtents] npl (of bottle, packet) 中身 nakámî; (of book) 内容 naíyō

(table of) contents 目次 mokúji

contest [n kɑːnˈtest vb kəntestˈ] n (competition) コンテスト kóñtesuto, コンクール kóñkūru; (struggle: for control, power etc) 争い arásoî

♦vt (election, competition) ...で競う ...de kisóu; (statement, decision: also LAW) ...に対して異議を申立てる ...ni taíshite igî wo mōshítaterù

contestant [kəntesˈtənt] n (in quiz, competition) 参加者 sañkashà; (in fight) 競争者 kyṓsōshà

context [kɑːnˈtekst] n (circumstances: of events, ideas etc) 背景 haíkei; (of word, phrase) 文脈 buñmyaku

continent [kɑ:n'tənənt] *n* (land mass) 大陸 taíriku

the Continent (*BRIT*) ヨーロッパ大陸 yóroppa taíriku

continental [kɑ:ntənen'təl] *adj* 大陸の taíriku no

continental quilt (*BRIT*) *n* 掛布団 kakébuton

contingency [kəntin'dʒənsi:] *n* 有事 yúji

contingent [kəntin'dʒənt] *n* (group of people: *also* MIL) 一団 ichídan

continual [kəntin'ju:əl] *adj* (movement, process, rain etc) 絶間ない taémanài

continually [kəntin'ju:əli:] *adv* 絶間なく taémanàku

continuation [kəntinju:ei'ʃən] *n* 継続 keízoku

continue [kəntin'ju:] *vi* 続く tsuzúkù
♦*vt* 続ける tsuzúkerù

continuity [kɑ:tənu:'iti:] *n* (in policy, management etc) 連続性 reńzokusei; (TV, CINEMA) 撮影台本 satsúeidaìhon, コンテ kóñte

continuous [kəntin'ju:əs] *adj* (process, growth etc) 絶間ない taémanài; (line) 途切れのない togíre no naì; (LING) 進行形の shiñkōkei no

continuous stationery *n* 連続用紙 reńzokuyōshi

contort [kəntɔ:rt'] *vt* (body) ねじる nejírù; (face) しかめる shikámerù

contortion [kəntɔ:r'ʃən] *n* (of body) ねじれ nejíre; (of face) こわばり kowábari

contour [kɑ:n'tu:r] *n* (on map: *also*: **contour line**) 等高線 tōkōsen; (shape, outline: *gen pl*) 輪郭 rińkaku

contraband [kɑ:n'trəbænd] *n* 密輸品 mitsúyuhìn

contraception [kɑ:ntrəsep'ʃən] *n* 避妊 hinín

contraceptive [kɑ:ntrəsep'tiv] *adj* (method, technique) 避妊の hinín no
♦*n* (device) 避妊用具 hinín yōgu; (pill etc) 避妊薬 hinín-yaku

contract [*n* kɑ:n'trækt *vb* kəntrækt'] *n* (LAW, COMM) 契約 keíyaku
♦*vi* (become smaller) 収縮する shúshuku suru; (COMM): *to contract to do*

something ...をする契約をする ...wo suru keíyaku wo suru
♦*vt* (illness) ...に掛る ...ni kakárù

contraction [kəntræk'ʃən] *n* (of metal, muscle) 収縮 shúshuku; (of word, phrase) 短縮形 tańshukukei

contractor [kɑ:n'træktə:r] *n* (COMM) 請負人 ukéoinìn

contradict [kɑ:ntrədikt'] *vt* (person) ...の言う事を否定する ...no iú kotò wo hitéi suru; (statement etc) 否定する hitéi suru

contradiction [kɑ:ntrədik'ʃən] *n* (inconsistency) 矛盾 mujún

contradictory [kɑ:ntrədik'tə:ri:] *adj* (ideas, statements) 矛盾する mujún suru

contraption [kəntræp'ʃən] (*pej*) *n* (device, machine) 珍妙な機械 chiñmyō na kikái

contrary[1] [kɑ:n'tre:ri:] *adj* (opposite, different) 反対の hañtai no
♦*n* (opposite) 反対 hañtai

on the contrary それどころか sorédokoro ka

unless you hear to the contrary そうではないと聞かされない限り số de wa nài to kikásarenài kagíri

contrary[2] [kəntre:r'i:] *adj* (perverse) つむじ曲りな tsumújimagàri na, へそ曲りな hesómagari na

contrast [*n* kɑ:n'træst *vb* kəntræst'] *n* (difference) 相違 sối, コントラスト koñtorasùto
♦*vt* (techniques, texts etc) 対照する taíshō suru

in contrast to ...と違って ...to chigátte

contrasting [kəntræs'tiŋ] *adj* (colors, attitudes) 対照的な taíshōteki na

contravene [kɑ:ntrəvin:'] *vt* (law) ...に違反する ...ni ihán suru

contribute [kəntrib'ju:t] *vi* (give) 寄付する kifú suru
♦*vt*: *to contribute an article to* (commissioned) ...に記事を寄稿する ...ni kíjì wo kikố suru; (unsolicited) ...に記事を投稿する ...ni kíjì wo tốkō suru: *to contribute $10* 10ドルを寄付する júdòru wo kifú suru

to contribute to (charity) ...に寄付する ...ni kífu suru; (newspaper: commissioned) ...に寄稿する ...ni kikō suru; (unsolicited) ...に投稿する ...ni tṓkō suru; (discussion) 意見を言う ikén wo iú; (problem etc) ...を悪くする ...wo warúkù surù

contribution [kɑːntrəbjuːʹʃən] n (donation) 寄付 kifu; (BRIT: for social security) 掛金 kakékin; (to debate, campaign) 貢献 kṓken; (to journal: commissioned) 寄稿 kikō; (: unsolicited) 投稿 tṓkō

contributor [kəntribʹjətəːr] n (to appeal) 寄付者 kifúshà; (to newspaper) 投稿者〔寄稿者〕tṓkōshà 〔kikṓshà〕

contrive [kəntraivʹ] vi: **to contrive to do** 努力して...に成功する doryóku shite ...ni seíkō suru

control [kəntroulʹ] vt (country, organization) 支配する shiháî suru; (machinery, process) 制御する seígyo suru; (wages, prices) 規制する kiséi suru; (temper) 自制する jiséi suru; (disease) 抑制する yokúsei suru
♦n (of country, organization) 支配 shiháî; (of oneself, emotions) 自制心 jiséishin
to be in control of (situation) ...を掌握している ...wo shōaku shité irù; (car etc) ...を思いのままに動かしている ...wo o-móî no mamá ni ugókashite irù
under control (crowd) 指示に従って shijî ni shitágatte; (situation) 収拾が付いて shúshū ga tsuíte; (dog) 言う事を聞いて iú kotò wo kíîte
out of control (crowd) 制止が利かなくなって seíshi ga kikánakù nattě; (situation) 手に負えなくなって te ni oénakù nattě; (dog) 言う事を聞かなくなって iú kotò wo kikánakù nattě
control panel n 制御盤 seígyoban
control room n 制御室 seígyoshìtsu
controls [kəntroulzʹ] npl (of vehicle) ハンドル hándoru ◇ブレーキ，クラッチなど全ての運転制御装置を含む burěki, kurátchî nadò subéte no uñtenseígyosōchì wo fukúmù; (on radio, television etc) コントロール盤 koñtorōruban ◇全てのス

イッチ，調節用つまみ，ボタンなどを含む subete no suítchì, chōsetsu yō tsumami, botán nadò wo fukúmù; (governmental) 規制 kiséi

control tower n (AVIAT) 管制塔 kañseitō

controversial [kɑːntrəvəːrʹʃəl] adj (topic, person) 論争の的になっている roñsō no matō ni nattě irù

controversy [kɑːnʹtrəvəːrsiː] n 論争 roñsō

conurbation [kɑːnəːrbeiʹʃən] n 大都市圏 daítoshikèn

convalesce [kɑːnvəlesʹ] vi (MED) 回復する kaífuku suru

convalescence [kɑːnvəlesʹəns] n (MED) 回復期 kaífukukì

convector [kənvekʹtəːr] n (heater) 対流式暖房器 taíryūshikidanbōkì, コンベクター koñbekūtā

convene [kənviːnʹ] vt (meeting, conference) 召集する shōshū suru
♦vi (parliament, inquiry) 開会する kaíkai suru

convenience [kənviːnʹjəns] n (easiness: of using something, doing something) 便利 bénri; (suitability: of date, meeting, house etc) 好都合 kōtsugō; (advantage, help) 便宜 béngi
at your convenience ご都合の良い時に go-tsúgō no yoî tokí ni
all modern conveniences, (BRIT) all mod cons 近代設備完備 kiñdaisetsubi-kañbi ◇不動産の広告などに使われる語句 fudṓsan no kṓkoku nadò ni tsukáwarerù gokù

convenient [kənviːnʹjənt] adj (handy) 便利な bénri na; (suitable) 都合の良い tsugō no yoî

convent [kɑːnʹvent] n (REL) 女子修道院 joshíshūdōìn

convention [kənvenʹʃən] n (custom) 慣例 kañrei; (conference) 大会 taíkai; (agreement) 協定 kyōtei

conventional [kənvenʹʃənəl] adj (person) 型にはまった katá ni hamátta; (method) 伝統的な deñtōteki na

converge [kənvəːrdʒʹ] vi (roads) 合流す

る gốryū suru; (people): *to converge on* (place, person) ...に集まる ...ni atsúmarù

conversant [kənvər'sənt] *adj*: *to be conversant with* (problem, requirements) ...に通じている ...ni tsūjite irù

conversation [kɑːnvəːrseiʹʃən] *n* (talk) 会話 kaíwa

conversational [kɑːnvəːrseiʹʃənəl] *adj* (tone, language, skills) 会話的な kaíwateki na

converse [*n* kɑːnʹvəːrs *vb* kənvəːrsʹ] *n* (of statement) 逆 gyakú
♦*vi* (talk): *to converse (with someone)* (...と) 話をする (...to) hanáshi wo suru

conversely [kənvəːrsʹliː] *adv* 逆 に gyakú ni

conversion [kənvəːrʹʒən] *n* (of weights, substances etc) 変換 henkan; (REL) 改宗 kaíshū

convert [*vb* kənvəːrtʹ *n* kɑːnʹvəːrt] *vt* (change): *to convert something into/ to* ...を...に変換する ...wo ...ni henkan suru; (person: REL) 改宗させる kaíshū saséru; (: POL) 党籍を変えさせる tōseki wo kaésaserù
♦*n* (REL) 改宗者 kaíshūsha; (POL) 党籍を変える人 tōseki wo kaéru hitő

convertible [kənvəːrʹtəbəl] *n* (AUT) コンバーチブル konbāchiburù ◊ 畳込み式屋根を持つ乗用車 tatámikomishiki yané wo motsú jōyōsha

convex [kɑːnveksʹ] *adj* 凸面の totsúmen no

convey [kənveiʹ] *vt* (information, idea, thanks) 伝える tsutáerù; (cargo, traveler) 運ぶ hakóbu

conveyor belt [kənveiʹəːr-] *n* ベルトコンベヤー berútokonbeyà

convict [*vb* kənviktʹ *n* kɑːnʹvikt] *vt* (of a crime) ...に有罪の判決を下す ...ni yūzai no hañketsu wo kudásù
♦*n* (person) 囚人 shūjin

conviction [kənvikʹʃən] *n* (belief) 信念 shíñnen; (certainty) 確信 kakúshin; (LAW) 有罪判決 yūzaihañketsu

convince [kənvinsʹ] *vt* (assure) 分からせる wakáraserù; (persuade) 納得させる

nattóku saséru

convinced [kənvinstʹ] *adj*: *convinced of/that* ...を〔だと〕確信している ...wo 〔dátò〕 kakúshin shité irù

convincing [kənvinʹsiŋ] *adj* (case, argument) 納得のいく nattóku no ikú

convoluted [kɑːnʹvəluːtid] *adj* (statement, argument) 込入った komíittà

convoy [kɑːnʹvɔi] *n* (of trucks) 護衛付き輸送車隊 goéitsuki yusōshatai; (of ships) 護衛付き輸送船団 goéitsukiyusōseñdan

convulse [kənvʌlsʹ] *vt*: *to be convulsed with laughter* 笑いこける waráikokerù
to be convulsed with pain もだえる modáerù

convulsion [kənvʌlʹʃən] *n* (MED) けいれん keíren

coo [kuː] *vi* (dove, pigeon) くーく ー鳴く kūkū nakú; (person) 優しい声で言う yasáshii koè de iú

cook [kuk] *vt* (food, meal) 料理する ryốri suru
♦*vi* (person) 料理する ryṓri suru; (meat, pie etc) 焼ける yakéru
♦*n* 料理人 ryốrinìn, コック kokkù

cookbook [kukʹbuk] *n* 料理の本 ryṓri no hoñ

cooker [kukʹəːr] *n* (stove) レンジ réñji

cookery [kukʹəːriː] *n* 料理する事 ryṓri suru kotő

cookery book (*BRIT*) *n* = **cookbook**

cookie [kukʹiː] (*US*) *n* ビスケット bisúkettò, クッキー kúkkì

cooking [kukʹiŋ] *n* (activity) 料理すること ryṓri suru kotő; (food) 料理 ryṓri

cool [kuːl] *adj* (temperature, clothes) 涼しい suzúshiì; (drink) 冷たい tsumétai; (person: calm) 落着いている ochítsuite irù; (: unfriendly) そっけない sokkénaì
♦*vt* (make colder: tea) 冷ます samásù; (: room) 冷やす hiyásù
♦*vi* (become colder: water) 冷たくなる tsumétaku narù; (: air) 涼しくなる suzúshiku narù

coolness [kuːlʹnis] *n* (of temperature, clothing) 涼しさ suzúshisà; (of drink) 冷たさ tsumétasà; (calm) 落着き ochítsuki;

coop [kuːp] n (*also*: **rabbit coop**) ウサギ小屋 uságigoya; (*also*: **hen coop**) ニワトリ小屋 niwátorigoya

◆vt: **to coop up** (*fig*: imprison) 閉込める tojíkomerù

cooperate [kouɑːpˈəreit] vi (collaborate) 協同する kyódō suru; (assist) 協力する kyóryoku suru

cooperation [kouɑːpəreiˈʃən] n (collaboration) 協同 kyódō; (assistance) 協力 kyóryoku

cooperative [kouɑːpˈrətiv] adj (farm, business) 協同組合の kyódōkùmiai no; (person) 協力的な kyóryokuteki na

◆n (factory, business) 協同組合 kyódōkùmiai

coordinate [vb kouɑːrˈdəneit n kouɑːrˈdənit] vt (activity, attack) 指揮する shikí suru; (movements) 調整する chósei suru

◆n (MATH) 座標 zahyó

coordinates [kouɑːrˈdənits] npl (clothes) コーディネートされた服 kódinèto saréta fukú

coordination [kouɑːrˈdəneiˈʃən] n (of services) 指揮 shikí; (of one's movements) 調整 chósei

co-ownership [kouou'nəːrʃip] n 協同所有 kyódōshoyū

cop [kɑːp] (*inf*) n (policeman/woman) 警官 keíkan

cope [koup] vi: **to cope with** (problem, situation etc) …に対応する …ni taíō suru

copious [kouˈpiːəs] adj (helpings) たっぷりの táppùri no

copious amounts of 多量の taryó no

copper [kɑːpˈəːr] n (metal) 銅 dó; (*inf*: policeman/woman) 警官 keíkan

coppers [kɑːpˈəːrz] npl (small change, coins) 小銭 kozéni

coppice [kɑːpˈis] n 木立 kodáchi

copse [kɑːps] n = **coppice**

copulate [kɑːpˈjəleit] vi (people) 性交する seíkō suru; (animals) 交尾する kóbi suru

copy [kɑːpˈiː] n (duplicate) 複写 fukúsha, コピー kópī; (of book) 1冊 issátsu; (of record) 1枚 ichímaì; (of newspaper) 1部 ichíbù

◆vt (person, idea etc) まねる manérù; (something written) 複写する fukúsha suru, コピーする kópī suru

copyright [kɑːpˈiːrait] n 著作権 chosákukèn

coral [kɔːrˈəl] n (substance) さんご sángo

coral reef n さんご礁 sángoshò

cord [kɔːrd] n (string) ひも himó; (ELEC) コード kódo; (fabric) コールテン kóruten

cordial [kɔːrˈdʒəl] adj (person, welcome) 暖かい atátakaì; (relationship) 親密な shińmitsu na

◆n (*BRIT*: drink) フルーツシロップ furútsu shiròppu

cordon [kɔːrˈdən] n (MIL, POLICE) 非常線 hijósen

cordon off vt 非常線を張って…への立入りを禁止する hijósen wo hatté …e no tachíiri wo kińshi suru

corduroy [kɔːrˈdəroi] n コールテン kóruten

core [kɔːr] n (of fruit) しん shiń; (of organization, system, building) 中心部 chúshinbu; (heart: of problem) 核心 kakúshin

◆vt (an apple, pear etc) …のしんをくりぬく …no shiń wo kurínukù

coriander [kɔːriːænˈdəːr] n (spice) コリアンダー koríandà

cork [kɔːrk] n (stopper) 栓 séń; (bark) コルク kóruku

corkscrew [kɔːrkˈskruː] n 栓抜き sefinuki

corn [kɔːrn] n (*US*: maize) トウモロコシ tómorokoshi; (*BRIT*: cereal crop) 穀物 kokúmòtsu; (on foot) 魚の目 uó no me

corn on the cob 軸付きトウモロコシ jikútsuki tómorokoshi

cornea [kɔːrˈniːə] n (of eye) 角膜 kakúmaku

corned beef [kɔːrnd-] n コーンビーフ kóñbīfu

corner [kɔːrˈnəːr] n (outside) 角 kádò; (inside) 隅 súmì; (in road) 角 kádò; (SOCCER) コーナーキック kónakikkù; (BOXING) コーナー kónā

◆vt (trap) 追詰める oítsumerù, 袋のネズ

ミにする fukúro no nezumi ni suru;
(COMM: market) 独占する dokúsen suru

♦*vi* (in car) コーナリングする kŏnariñgu
surù

cornerstone [kɔːr'nəːrstoun] *n* (*fig*) 土台
dodái

cornet [kɔːr'net] *n* (MUS) コルネット
korúnettò; (*BRIT*: of ice-cream) アイス
クリームコーン aísukurīmukòn

cornflakes [kɔːrn'fleiks] *npl* コーンフレ
ーク kŏnfurēku

cornflour [kɔːrn'flauə:r] (*BRIT*) *n* =
cornstarch

cornstarch [kɔːrn'staːrtʃ] (*US*) *n* コーン
スターチ kŏnsutāchi

Cornwall [kourn'wɔːl] *n* コーンウォール
kŏn-uòru

corny [kɔːr'niː] (*inf*) *adj* (joke) さえない
saénai

corollary [kɔːr'əle:riː] *n* (of fact, idea) 当
然の結果 tŏzen no kekká

coronary [kɔːr'əne:riː] *n* (*also*: **coronary
thrombosis**) 肝動脈血栓症 kañdōmyaku-
kessénshō

coronation [kɔːrənei'ʃən] *n* たい冠式 taíkañshiki

coroner [kɔːr'ənəːr] *n* (LAW) 検死官 keñ-
shikàn

coronet [kɔːr'ənit] *n* コロネット koró-
nettò ◇貴族などがかぶる小さな冠 kizó-
ku nadò ga kabúrù chíisana kañmuri

corporal [kɔːr'pəːrəl] *n* (MIL) ご長 gŏ-
chŏ

♦*adj*: **corporal punishment** 体罰 taíba-
tsu

corporate [kɔːr'pəːrit] *adj* (action,
effort, ownership) 共同の kyŏdō no;
(finance, image) 企業の kigyŏ no

corporation [kɔːrpərei'ʃən] *n* (COMM)
企業 kigyŏ; (of town) 行政部 gyŏseibù

corps [kɔːr *pl* kɔːrz] (*pl* **corps**) *n* (MIL)
兵団 heídan; (of diplomats, journalists)
...団 ...dàn

corpse [kɔːrps] *n* 遺体 itái

corpuscle [kɔːr'pəsəl] *n* (BIO) 血球 kek-
kyū

corral [kəræl'] *n* (for cattle, horses) 囲い

kakói

correct [kərekt'] *adj* (right) 正しい tadáshiì; (proper) 礼儀正しい reígitadashiì

♦*vt* (mistake, fault) 直す naósù; (exam)
採点する saíten suru

correction [kərek'ʃən] *n* (act of correcting) 直す事 naósù kotó; (instance) 直し
naóshi

correlation [kɔːrəlei'ʃən] *n* (link) 相互関
係 sŏgokañkei

correspond [kɔːrəspaːnd'] *vi* (write): **to
correspond (with)** (...と) 手紙のやり
取りをする (...to) tegámi no yarítòri
wo surù; (be equivalent): **to correspond
(to)** (...に) 相当する (...ni) sŏtō suru;
(be in accordance): **to correspond
(with)** (...と) 一致する (...to) itchí
suru

correspondence [kɔːrəspaːn'dəns] *n*
(letters) 手紙 tegámi; (communication
by letters) 文通 buñtsū; (relationship) 一
致 itchí

correspondence course *n* (SCOL) 通
信講座 tsūshinkōza

correspondent [kɔːrəspaːn'dənt] *n*
(journalist) 特派員 tokúhaìn

corridor [kɔːr'idəːr] *n* (in house, building
etc) 廊下 rŏka; (in train) 通路 tsūro

corroborate [kərɑːb'əreit] *vt* (facts,
story) 裏付ける urázukerù

corrode [kəroud'] *vt* (metal) 浸食する
shiñshoku suru

♦*vi* (metal) 腐食する fushóku suru

corrosion [kərou'ʒən] *n* 腐食 fushóku

corrugated [kɔːr'əgeitid] *adj* (roof,
cardboard) 波型の namígata no

corrugated iron *n* なまこ板 namákoi-
tà

corrupt [kərʌpt'] *adj* (person) 腐敗した
fuhái shitá; (COMPUT: data) 化けた ba-
kétà, 壊れた kowáretà

♦*vt* (person) 買収する baíshū suru;
(COMPUT: data) 化けさせる bakésase-
rù

corruption [kərʌp'ʃən] *n* (of person) 汚
職 oshóku; (COMPUT: of data) 化ける事
bakérù kotó

corset [kɔːr'sit] *n* (undergarment: *also*

MED) コルセット kórùsetto

Corsica [kɔːr'sikə] *n* コルシカ島 korúshikatō

cosh [kaːʃ] (*BRIT*) *n* (cudgel) こん棒 kóñbō

cosmetic [kɑːzmet'ik] *n* (beauty product) 化粧品 keshōhin
♦*adj* (*fig*: measure, improvement) 表面的な hyṓmenteki na

cosmic [kɑːz'mik] *adj* 宇宙の uchū no

cosmonaut [kɑːz'mənɔːt] *n* 宇宙飛行士 uchūhikōshi

cosmopolitan [kɑːzmɑːpɑːl'itən] *adj* (place, person) 国際的な kokúsaiteki na

cosmos [kɑːz'məs] *n* 宇宙 uchū

cosset [kɑːs'it] *vt* (person) 甘やかす amáyakasù

cost [kɔːst] *n* (price) 値段 nedáñ; (expenditure) 費用 híyò
♦*vt* (*pt, pp* **cost**) (be priced at) ...の値段である ...no nedán de arù; (find out cost of: project, purchase etc: *pt, pp* **costed**) ...の費用を見積る ...no hiyṓ wo mitsúmorù

how much does it cost? いくらですか ikùra desu ká

to cost someone time/effort ...に時間〔労力〕を要する ...ni jikán 〔rōryoku〕 wo yō surù

it cost him his life そのために彼は命をなくした sono tamé ni kárè wa íñochi wo nákù shitá

at all costs 何があっても naní ga atté mò

co-star [kou'stɑːr] *n* (TV, CINEMA) 共演者 kyōeñsha

cost-effective [kɔːstifek'tiv] *adj* 費用効果比の高い hiyōkōkahi no takáì

costly [kɔːst'liː] *adj* (high-priced) 値段の高い nedán no takáì; (involving much expenditure) 費用の掛かる hiyṓ no kakárù

cost-of-living [kɔːstəvliv'iŋ] *adj* (allowance, index) 生計費の sefkeíhi no

cost price (*BRIT*) *n* 原価 géñka

costs [kɔːsts] *npl* (COMM: overheads) 経費 kéihì; (LAW) 訴訟費用 soshōhiyò

costume [kɑːs'tuːm] *n* (outfit, style of dress) 衣装 íshò; (*BRIT*: also: **swimming costume**) 水着 mizúgi

costume jewelry *n* 模造宝石類 mozṓhōsekirùi

cosy [kou'ziː] (*BRIT*) *adj* = **cozy**

cot [kɑːt] *n* (*BRIT*: child's) ベビーベッド bebíbeddò; (*US*: campbed) キャンプベッド kyañpubeddò

cottage [kɑːt'idʒ] *n* (house) 小さな家 chíisa na ie, コッテージ kottḗji

cottage cheese *n* カッテージチーズ kattḗji chízù

cotton [kɑːt'ən] *n* (fabric) 木綿 moméñ, コットン kóttòn; (*BRIT*: thread) 縫い糸 nuí-itò

cotton batting [-bæt'iŋ] *n* (*US*) 脱脂綿 dasshíméñ

cotton candy (*US*) *n* (candy floss) 綿菓子 watágashì, 綿あめ watá-àme

cotton on to (*inf*) *vt fus* ...に気が付く ...ni kí ga tsúkù

cotton wool (*BRIT*) *n* = **cotton batting**

couch [kautʃ] *n* (sofa) ソファー sófà; (doctor's) 診察台 shiñsatsudai

couchette [kuːʃet'] *n* (on train, boat) 寝台 shiñdai ◇昼間壁に畳み掛けるか普通の座席に使う物を指す hiráma kabé ni tatámikakerù ka futsú no zasékì ni tsukáù monò wo sasù

cough [kɔːf] *vi* (person) せきをする sekí wo surù
♦*n* (noise) せき sekí; (illness) せきの多い病気 sekí no ōi byṓki

cough drop *n* せき止めドロップ sekídome dorōppu

could [kud] *pt of* **can**

couldn't [kud'ənt] = **could not**

council [kaun'səl] *n* (committee, board) 評議会 hyōgikài

city/town council 市〔町〕議会 shi 〔chō〕 gíkai

council estate (*BRIT*) *n* 公営住宅団地 kōeijūtakudañchi

council house (*BRIT*) *n* 公営住宅 kōeijūtaku

councillor [kaun'sələːr] *n* 議員 gíiñ

counsel [kaun'səl] *n* (advice) 助言 jogéñ;

(lawyer) 弁護人 beńgonin

♦vt (advise) ...に助言する ...ni jogén suru

counsel(l)or [kaun'sələr] n (advisor) カ
ウンセラー káùnserā; (US: lawyer) 弁護
人 beńgonin

count [kaunt] vt (add up: numbers,
money, things, people) 数える kazóerù;
(include) 入れる iréru, 含む fukúmù

♦vi (enumerate) 数 え る kazóerù; (be
considered) ...と見なされる ...to minasa-
reru; (be valid) 効果をもつ kōka wo mótsù

♦n (of things, people, votes) 数 kazù;
(level: of pollen, alcohol etc) 値 atái, 数
値 sūchi; (nobleman) 伯爵 hakúshaku

countdown [kaunt'daun] n (to launch)
秒読み byóyomi

countenance [kaun'tənəns] n (face) 顔
kaó

♦vt (tolerate) 容認する yōnin suru

counter [kaun'tər] n (in shop, café,
bank etc) カウンター kaúntā; (in game)
こま komá

♦vt (oppose) ...に対抗する ...ni taikō suru

♦adv: **counter to** ...に反して ...ni hań
shite

counteract [kauntə:rækt'] vt (effect,
tendency) 打消す uchíkesu

counter-espionage [kauntə:res'pi:ə-
nɑ:ʒ] n 対抗的スパイ活動 taíkōteki supá-
ikatsudò

counterfeit [kaun'tə:rfit] n (forgery) 偽
物 nisémono

♦vt (forge) 偽造する gizō suru

♦adj (coin) 偽物の nisémono no

counterfoil [kaun'tə:rfɔil] n (of check,
money order) 控え hikáe

countermand [kauntə:rmænd'] vt
(order) 取消す toríkesu

counterpart [kaun'tə:rpɑːrt] n; **counterpart of** (person) ...に相当する人 ...ni
sōtō suru hitó; (thing) ...に相当するもの
...ni sōtō suru mono

counterproductive [kauntə:rprədʌk'-
tiv] adj (measure, policy etc) 逆効果的な
gyakúkōkateki na

countersign [kaun'tə:rsain] vt (document) ...に副署する ...ni fukúsho surù

countess [kaun'tis] n 伯爵夫人 hakúsha-
kufújin

countless [kaunt'lis] adj (innumerable)
無数の músū no

country [kʌn'tri:] n (state, nation) 国 kuní; (native land) 母国 bókòku; (rural
area) 田舎 ináka; (region) 地域 chíìka

country dancing (BRIT) n 英国郷土舞
踊 eíkokukyōdòbuyō

country house n 田舎の大邸宅 ináka
no daíteitàku

countryman [kʌn'tri:mən] (pl countrymen) n (compatriot) 同国人 dókokujìn;
(country dweller) 田舎者 inákamòno

countryside [kʌn'tri:said] n 田舎 ináka

county [kaun'ti:] n (POL, ADMIN) 郡
gúñ

coup [ku:] (pl coups) n (MIL, POL: also:
coup d'état) ク ー デ タ ー kū́detà;
(achievement) 大成功 daíseikō

coupé [ku:pei'] n (AUT) クーペ kū́pe

couple [kʌp'əl] n (also: **married couple**)
夫婦 fūfu; (cohabiting etc) カップル káp-
pūru; (of things) 一対 ittsúi

a couple of (two people) 2人の futári
no; (two things) 2つの futátsu no; (a few
people) 数人の sū́nin no; (a few things) 幾
つかの ikùtsuka no

coupon [ku:'pɑn] n (voucher) クーポン券
kū́poñken; (detachable form) クーポン
kū́pon

courage [kə:r'idʒ] n (bravery) 勇気 yū́ki

courageous [kərei'dʒəs] adj (person,
attempt) 勇敢な yū́kan na

courgette [kur3et'] (BRIT) n ズッキー
ニ zúkkìni

courier [kə:r'i:ə:r] n (messenger) メッセ
ンジャー mésseñjā; (for tourists) 添乗員
teńjōin

course [kɔːrs] n (SCOL) 課程 katéi;
(process: of life, events, time etc) 過程
katéi; (of treatment) クール kū́ru; (direction: of argument, action) 方針 hōshin; (:
of ship) 針路 shíñro; (part of meal) 一品
ippín, コース kōsu; (for golf) コース kōsu

court [kɔːt] *n* (royal) 宮殿 kyúden; (LAW) 法廷 hôtei; (for tennis, badminton etc) コート kôto

♦*vt* (woman) 妻にしようとして...と交際する tsumà ni shiyô to shitè ...to kôsai suru

to take someone to court (LAW) ...を相手取って訴訟を起す ...wo aítedottè soshô wo okôsù

courteous [kəːrˈtiːəs] *adj* (person, conduct) 丁寧な teínei na

courtesan [kɔːrˈtizən] *n* 宮廷しょう婦 kyúteishōfu

courtesy [kəːrˈtisiː] *n* (politeness) 礼儀正しさ reígitadashìsa

(by) courtesy of (thanks to) ...のお陰で ...no okâge de

court-house [kɔːrtˈhaus] (*US*) *n* 裁判所 saíbansho

courtier [kɔːrˈtiːər] *n* 廷臣 teíshin

court-martial [kɔːrtˈmɑːrˈʃəl] (*pl* **courts-martial**) *vt* (MIL) 軍法会議 guńpōkaĩgi

courtroom [kɔːrtˈruːm] *n* 法廷 hôtei

courtyard [kɔːrtˈjɑːrd] *n* (of castle, house) 中庭 nakániwa

cousin [kʌzˈin] *n* (relative) 親せき shínseki

first cousin いとこ itôkò

second cousin はとこ hatôkò, またいとこ mata-itoko

cove [kouv] *n* (bay) 入江 iríe

covenant [kʌvˈənənt] *n* (promise) 契約 keíyaku

cover [kʌvˈəːr] *vt* (hide: face, surface, ground): *to cover (with)* ...で覆う ...de oû; (hide: feelings, mistake): *to cover (with)* ...で隠す ...de kakúsù; (shield: book, table etc): *to cover (with)* ...に(...を)掛ける ...ni (...wo) kakérù; (with lid): *to cover (with)* ...にふたをする ...ni futá wo suru; (travel: distance) 行く ikú; (protect: *also* INSURANCE) カバーする kábà suru; (discuss: topic, subject: *also* PRESS) 取上げる toríagerù; (include) 含む fukúmù

♦*n* (for furniture) 覆い oî; (lid) ふた futá; (on bed) 上掛 uwágake; (of book, magazine) 表紙 hyôshi; (shelter: for hiding) 隠れ場所 kakúrebasho; (: from rain) 雨宿りの場所 amáyadòri no bashò; (INSURANCE) 保険 hokén; (of spy) 架空の身分 kakû no míbun

to take cover (shelter: from rain) 雨宿りをする amáyadòri wo suru; (: from gunfire etc) 隠れる kakúrerù

under cover (indoors) 屋根の下で〔に〕 yané no shitá de 〔ni〕

under cover of darkness やみに紛れて yamí ni magírete

under separate cover (COMM) 別便で betsúbin de

coverage [kʌvˈəːridʒ] *n* (TV, PRESS) 報道 hôdō

cover charge *n* (in restaurant) サービス料 sâbisuryô

covering [kʌvˈəːriŋ] *n* (layer) 覆い oî; (of snow, dust etc) 覆う物 oû monò

covering letter (*US also*: **cover letter**) *n* 添状 soéjō

cover note (*BRIT*) *n* (INSURANCE) 仮保険証 karíhokeñshō

covert [kouˈvəːrt] *adj* (glance, threat) 隠れた kakúretà

cover up *vi*: *to cover up for someone* ...をかばう ...wo kabáù

cover-up [kʌvˈəːrʌp] *n* もみ消し momíkeshi

covet [kʌvˈit] *vt* (desire) 欲しがる hoshígarù

cow [kau] *n* (animal) 雌ウシ meúshi; (*inf!*: woman) あま amâ

♦*vt* (oppress): *to be cowed* おびえる obíerù

coward [kauˈəːrd] *n* おく病者 okúbyōmono

cowardice [kauˈəːrdis] *n* おく病 okúbyō

cowardly [kauˈəːrdliː] *adj* おく病な okúbyō na

cowboy [kauˈbɔi] *n* (in US) カウボーイ kaúbòi

cower [kauˈəːr] *vi* い縮する ishúku suru

coxswain [kɑːkˈsin] *n* (ROWING: abbr:

cox) コックス kókkùsu

coy [kɔi] *adj* (demure, shy) はにかんでみせる haníkañde misérù

coyote [kaiout'i:] *n* コヨーテ kóyòte

cozy [kou'zi:] (*BRIT* **cosy**) *adj* (room, house) こじんまりした kojíñmarì shita; (person) 心地よい kokóchi yoì

CPA [si:pi:ei'] (*US*) *abbr* = **certified public accountant**

crab [kræb] *n* カニ kaní

crab apple *n* ヒメリンゴ himériñgo

crack [kræk] *n* (noise: of gun) バン páñ; (: of thunder) ばりばり barîbari; (: of twig) ぽっきり pokkíri; (: of whip) バン ban; (gap) 割れ目 waréme; (in bone, dish, glass, wall) ひび hibí

♦*vt* (whip, twig) 鳴らす narásù; (bone, dish, glass, wall) ひびを入れる hibí wo irérù; (nut) 割る warú; (solve: problem) 解決する kaíketsu suru; (: code) 解く tókù; (joke) 飛ばす tobásu

♦*adj* (expert) 優秀な yúshū na

crack down on *vt fus* (crime, expenditure etc) 取り締る toríshimarù

cracker [kræk'ə:r] *n* (biscuit, Christmas cracker) クラッカー kurákkā

crackle [kræk'əl] *vi* (fire) ぱちぱちと音を立てる páchìpachi to otó wo tatérù; (twig) ぽきぽきと音を立てる pókìpoki to otó wo tatérù

crack up *vi* (PSYCH) 頭がおかしくなる atáma ga okáshikù nárù

cradle [krei'dəl] *n* (baby's) 揺りかご yuríkago

craft [kræft] *n* (skill) 芸術 geíjutsu; (trade) 職業 shokúgyò; (boat: *pl inv*) 船 fúnè; (plane: *pl inv*) 飛行機 hikóki

craftsman [kræfts'mən] (*pl* **craftsmen**) *n* (artisan) 職人 shokúnin

craftsmanship [kræfts'mənʃip] *n* (quality) 芸術 geíjutsu

crafty [kræf'ti:] *adj* (sneaky) 腹黒い haráguroì, こうかつな kókatsu na

crag [kræg] *n* 険しい岩山 kewáshiì iwáyama

cram [kræm] *vt* (fill): **to cram something with** ...を...で一杯にする ...wo ...de ippái ni surù; (put): **to cram something into** ...を...に詰込む ...wo ...ni tsumékomù

♦*vi*: **to cram for exams** 一夜漬の試験勉強をする ichíyazuke no shikénbenkyò wo suru

cramp [kræmp] *n* (MED) けいれん keíren

cramped [kræmpt] *adj* (accommodation) 窮屈な kyúkutsu na

crampon [kræm'pɑːn] *n* (CLIMBING) アイゼン áīzen

cranberry [kræn'be:ri:] *n* (berry) コケモモ kokémòmo, クランベリー kuránberì

crane [krein] *n* (machine) クレーン kúrèn; (bird) ツル tsúrù

crank [kræŋk] *n* (person) 変人 heñjiñ; (handle) クランク kuráñku

crankshaft [kræŋk'ʃæft] *n* (AUT) クランクシャフト kuránkushafùto

cranny [kræn'i:] *n see* **nook**

crash [kræʃ] *n* (noise) 大音響 daíoñkyò ◇物が落ちる、ぶつかるなどの大きな音を指す monó ga ochírù, butsúkarù nádò no ōkina otó wo sásù; (of car, train etc) 衝突 shótotsu; (of plane) 墜落 tsuíraku; (COMM: of stock-market) 暴落 bóraku; (COMM: of business etc) 倒産 tōsan

♦*vt* (car etc) 衝突させる shótotsu saséru; (plane) 墜落させる tsuíraku saséru

♦*vi* (car) 衝突する shótotsu suru; (plane) 墜落する tsuíraku suru; (COMM: market) 暴落する bóraku suru; (COMM: firm) 倒産する tōsan suru

crash course *n* 速成コース sokúseikòsu

crash helmet *n* ヘルメット herúmettò

crash landing *n* (AVIAT) 不時着陸 fujíchakùriku

crass [kræs] *adj* (behavior, comment, person) 露骨な rokótsu na

crate [kreit] *n* (box) 箱 hakó; (for bottles) ケース kèsu

crater [krei'tə:r] *n* (of volcano) 噴火口 fuñkakò; (on moon etc) クレーター kuré̀tā

bomb crater 爆弾坑 bakúdankò

cravat [krəvæt'] *n* アスコットタイ asúkottotaì

crave [kreiv] *vt, vi*: **to crave for** ...を強く欲しがる ...wo tsuyókù hoshígarù

crawl [krɔ:l] *vi* (person) 四つんばいには
う yotsúnbai ni háù; (insect) は う háù;
(vehicle) のろのろと進む nórónoro to susúmù
♦*n* (SWIMMING) クロール kúróru

crayfish [krei'fiʃ] *n inv* (freshwater) ザ
リガニ zarígani; (saltwater) エビガニ e-
bígani

crayon [krei'ɑ:n] *n* クレヨン kuréyòn

craze [kreiz] *n* (fashion) 大流行 dáiryūkō

crazy [krei'zi:] *adj* (insane) 正気でない
shōki de náì; (*inf*: keen): **crazy about**
someone/something ...が大好きである
...ga daísuki de arù

crazy paving (*BRIT*) *n* 不ぞろい舗装
fuzóroi hosō ◊不ぞろいの敷石からなる
舗装 fuzóroi no shikíishi kara narù hosō

creak [kri:k] *vi* (floorboard, door etc) き
しむ kishímù

cream [kri:m] *n* (of milk) (生)クリーム
(namá)kúrīmu; (*also*: **artificial cream**)
人造クリーム jínzòkurìmu; (cosmetic) 化
粧クリーム keshōkurìmu; (élite) 名士た
ち meíshi tachì
♦*adj* (color) クリーム色の kúrìmuírò no

cream cake *n* クリームケーキ kurímu-
kèki

cream cheese *n* クリームチーズ kurí-
muchìzu

creamy [kri:'mi:] *adj* (color) クリーム色
の kurímuirò no; (taste) 生クリームたっ
ぷりの namákurìmu táppùri no

crease [kri:s] *n* (fold) 折り目 oríme; (wrinkle) しわ shiwá; (in trousers) 折目 oríme
♦*vt* (wrinkle) しわくちゃにする shiwákucha ni suru
♦*vi* (wrinkle up) しわくちゃになる shi-
wakucha ni naru

create [kri:eit'] *vt* (cause to happen,
exist) 引起こす hikíokosù; (produce,
design) 作る tsukúrù

creation [kri:ei'ʃən] *n* (causing to happen, exist) 引起こす事 hikíokosù kotó;
(production, design) 作る事 tsukúrù kotó; (REL) 天地創造 teńchisōzō

creative [kri:ei'tiv] *adj* (artistic) 芸術的
な geíjutsuteki na; (inventive) 創造性の
ある sōzōsei no árù

creator [kri:ei'tə:r] *n* (maker, inventor)
作る人 tsukúrù hitó

creature [kri:'tʃə:r] *n* (living animal) 動
物 dōbutsu; (person) 人 hitó

crèche [kreʃ] *n* 託児所 takújisho

credence [kri:d'əns] *n*: **to lend cre-**
dence to (prove) ...を信じさせる ...wo
shiñji saséru
to give credence to (prove) ...を信じさ
せる ...wo shiñji saséru; (believe) 信じる
shiñjirù

credentials [kriden'ʃəlz] *npl* (refer-
ences) 資格 shikáku; (identity papers) 身
分証明証 mibúnshōmeishō

credibility [kredəbil'əti:] *n* (of person,
fact) 信頼性 shiñraisei

credible [kred'əbəl] *adj* (believable) 信じ
られる shiñjirarerù; (trustworthy) 信用
できる shiñ-yō dekírù

credit [kred'it] *n* (COMM: loan) 信用 shiñ-
yō; (recognition) 名誉 meíyo
♦*vt* (COMM) ...の入金にする ...no nyúkin
ni suru; (believe: *also*: **give credit to**) 信
じる shiñjirù
to be in credit (person, bank account)
黒字になっている kuróji ni nattě irù
to credit someone with (*fig*) ...に...の美
徳があると思う ...ni...no bitóku ga arù to
omóù

credit card *n* クレジットカード kuréjit-
tokàdo

creditor [kred'itə:r] *n* (COMM) 債権者
saíkeñsha

credits [kred'its] *npl* (CINEMA) クレジ
ット kuréjittò

creed [kri:d] *n* (REL) 信条 shíñjō

creek [kri:k] *n* (*US*: stream) 小川 ogáwa;
(*BRIT*: inlet) 入江 iríe

creep [kri:p] (*pt, pp* **crept**) *vi* (person,
animal) 忍び足で歩く shinóbiàshi de arú-
kù

creeper [kri:'pi:r] *n* (plant) つる tsurú

creepy [kri:'pi:] *adj* (frightening: story,
experience) 薄気味悪い usúkimiwaruì

cremate [kri:'meit] *vt* (corpse) 火葬にす
る kasō ni surú

cremation [krimei'ʃən] *n* 火葬 kasō

crematoria [kri:mətɔ:r'i:ə] *npl of* **cre-**

matorium

crematorium [kri:mətə:r'i:əm] (*pl* **crematoria**) *n* 火葬場 kasóba

crêpe [kreip] *n* (fabric) クレープ kúrēpu; (rubber) クレープゴム kurépugomù ◇靴底に使う表面がしわ状のゴム kutsúzoko ni tsukáù hyómen ga shiwájō no gómù

crêpe bandage (*BRIT*) *n* 伸縮性包帯 shińshukuseihōtai

crept [krept] *pt, pp* of **creep**

crescent [kres'ənt] *n* (shape) 三日月形 mikázukigata; (street) ...通り ...dōri ◇特にカーブになっている通りの名前に使う tókù ni kâbu ni natté irù tôri no namáe ni tsukáù

cress [kres] *n* (BOT, CULIN) クレソン kurésoñ

crest [krest] *n* (of hill) 頂上 chôjō; (of bird) とさか tosáka; (coat of arms) 紋 móñ

crestfallen [krest'fɔ:lən] *adj* しょんぼりした shoñborì shitá

Crete [kri:t] *n* クレタ kurétà

crevice [krev'is] *n* (gap, crack) 割れ目 waréme

crew [kru:] *n* (NAUT) 乗組員 norîkumiñ; (AVIAT) 乗員 jóiñ; (TV, CINEMA) カメラ班 kamérahàn ◇3つの意味とも総称として使う mittsú no imî to mo sôshō toshité tsukáù

crew-cut [kru:'kʌt] *n* 角刈り kakúgari

crew-neck [kru:'nek] *n* (of jersey) 丸首 marúkubi

crib [krib] *n* (cot) ベビーベッド bebíbeddò

◆*vt* (*inf*: copy: during exam etc) カンニングする kañningu suru; (: from writings etc of others) 盗用する tôyō suru

crick [krik] *n*: **to have a crick in one's neck** 首が痛い kubî ga itái

cricket [krik'it] *n* (game) クリケット kuríkettò; (insect) コオロギ kôrogi

crime [kraim] *n* (no pl: illegal activities) 犯罪 hañzai; (illegal action) 犯罪 (行為) hañzai(kôi); (*fig*) 罪悪 zaîaku no

criminal [krim'ənəl] *n* 犯罪者 hañzaîsha

◆*adj* (illegal) 違法の ihô no; (morally wrong) 罪悪の zaîaku no

crimson [krim'zən] *adj* 紅色の beníiro no

cringe [krindʒ] *vi* (in fear, embarrassment) 縮こまる chijíkomarù

crinkle [kriŋ'kəl] *vt* (crease, fold) しわくちゃにする shiwákucha ni suru

cripple [krip'əl] *n* (MED) 身障者 shiñshô-sha

◆*vt* (person) 不具にする fúgù ni suru

crises [krai'si:z] *npl of* **crisis**

crisis [krai'sis] (*pl* **crises**) *n* 危機 kikî

crisp [krisp] *adj* (vegetables) ぱりぱりした párìpari shitá; (bacon) かりかりした kárìkari shitá; (weather) からっとした karáttò shitá; (manner, tone, reply) 無愛想な buáisō na

crisps [krisps] (*BRIT*) *npl* ポテトチップ potétochippù

criss-cross [kris'krɔ:s] *adj* (pattern, design) 十字模様の jújimoyò no

criteria [kraiti:'ri:ə] *npl of* **criterion**

criterion [kraiti:r'i:ən] (*pl* **criteria**) *n* (standard) 規準 kijúñ

critic [krit'ik] *n* (of system, policy etc) 反対者 hañtaîsha; (reviewer) 評論家 hyôronka

critical [krit'ikəl] *adj* (time, situation) 重大な júdai na; (opinion, analysis) 批判的な hihyôteki na; (person: fault-finding) 粗捜し好きな arásagashizùki na; (illness) 危険な kikén na

critically [krit'ikli:] *adv* (speak, look etc) 批判的に hihánteki ni

critically ill 重症で jóshō de

criticism [krit'isizəm] *n* (disapproval, complaint) 非難 hínàn; (of book, play etc) 批評 hihyô

criticize [krit'əsaiz] *vt* (find fault with) 非難する hínàn suru

croak [krouk] *vi* (frog) げろげろ鳴く gérògero nakú; (bird etc) かーかー鳴く kâkā nakú; (person) がらがら声で言う garágaragoe de iu

crochet [krou'ʃei] *n* かぎ針編み kagíbariami

crockery [krɑ:k'ə:ri:] *n* (dishes) 皿類 saráruì

crocodile [krɑ:k'ədail] *n* ワニ wánì

crocus [krou'kəs] *n* クロッカス kurókkāsu

croft [krɔːft] (*BRIT*) *n* (small farm) 小農場 shōnōjō

crony [krou'niː] (*inf: pej*) *n* 仲間 nakáma

crook [kruk] *n* (criminal) 悪党 akútō; (*also*: **shepherd's crook**) 羊飼のつえ hitsújikai no tsúe ◇片端の曲った物を指す katáhashi no magátta monó wo sásù

crooked [kruk'id] *adj* (bent, twisted) 曲った magátta; (dishonest) 不正の fuséi no

crop [krɑːp] *n* (of fruit, cereals, vegetables) 作物 sakúmotsu; (harvest) 収穫 shúkaku; (riding crop) むち múchi ◇乗馬用の物を指す jōbayō no monó wo sásù
♦*vt* (hair) 刈込む karíkomù

crop up *vi* (problem, topic) 持ち上る mochíagarù

croquet [kroukei'] *n* クロッケー kurókkē ◇複雑なゲートボールに似た球技 fukúzatsu na gētobōru ni nitá kyūgi

croquette [krouket'] *n* (CULIN) コロッケ kórōkke

cross [krɔːs] *n* (shape) 十字 jūji; (REL) 十字架 jūjika; (mark) ばつ(印) bátsù(jírùshi); (hybrid) 合の子 aínoko
♦*vt* (street, room etc) 横断する ōdan suru; (arms, legs) 組む kúmù; (animal, plant) 交雑する kōzatsu suru
♦*adj* (angry) 不機嫌な fukígen na
to cross a check 線引小切手にする señbiki kogíttè ni suru

crossbar [krɔːs'bɑːr] *n* (SPORT) ゴールの横棒 gōru no yokóbō

cross country (race) *n* クロスカントリーレース kurósukantorīrēsu

cross-examine [krɔːs'igzæm'in] *vt* (LAW) 反対尋問する hañtaijiñmon suru

cross-eyed [krɔːs'aid] *adj* 寄り目の yoríme no

crossfire [krɔːs'faiər] *n* 十字射撃 jūjishagèki

crossing [krɔːs'iŋ] *n* (sea passage) 船旅 funátabi; (*also*: **pedestrian crossing**) 横断歩道 ōdanhodō

crossing guard (*US*) *n* 交通指導員 kōtsūshidōin ◇交通事故を防ぐために横断歩道に立って学童などの横断を助ける係員 kōtsūjikò wo fuségù tamé ni ōdanhodō ni tattě gakúdō nádò no ōdan wo tasúkerù kakáriìn

cross out *vt* (delete) 線を引いて消す séñ wo hiíte kesú

cross over *vi* (move across) 横断する ōdan suru

cross-purposes [krɔːs'pəːr'pəsiz] *npl*: *to be at cross-purposes* 話が食違っている hanáshi ga kuíchigatte irù

cross-reference [krɔːs'ref'əːrəns] *n* 相互参照 sōgosañshō

crossroads [krɔːs'roudz] *n* 交差点 kōsatèn

cross section *n* (of an object) 断面 dañmeñ; (sketch) 断面図 dañmeñzu
cross section of the population 国民を代表する人々 kokumin wo daíhyō suru hitóbìto

crosswalk [krɔːs'wɔːk] (*US*) *n* 横断歩道 ōdanhodō

crosswind [krɔːs'wind] *n* 横風 yokókaze

crossword [krɔːs'wəːrd] *n* クロスワードパズル kurósuwādopazùru

crotch [krɑːtʃ] *n* (ANAT, of garment) また matá

crotchet [krɑːtʃ'it] *n* (MUS) 四分音符 shibúoñpu

crotchety [krɑːtʃ'ətiː] *adj* (person) 気難しい kimúzukashiì

crouch [krautʃ] *vi* (person, animal) うずくまる uzúkumarù

croupier [kruːp'iːːr] *n* (in casino) とばく台の元締 tobákudai no motójime, ディーラー dīrā

crow [krou] *n* (bird) カラス kárāsu; (of cock) 鳴き声 nakígoè
♦*vi* (cock) 鳴く nakú

crowbar [krou'bɑːr] *n* バール bāru

crowd [kraud] *n*: *crowd of people* 群衆 guñshū
♦*vt* (fill: room, stadium etc) ...にぎっしり入る ...ni gisshírì haírù
♦*vi* (gather): *to crowd round* ...の回りに群がる ...no mawári ni muragarù; (cram): *to crowd in* ...の中へ詰めかける ...no nákà e tsumékakerù

a crowd of fans 大勢のファン ōzei nð fán

crowded [krau'did] *adj* (full) 込入った komſitta; (densely populated) 人口密度の高い jínkōmitsúdo no takáî

crown [kraun] *n* (gen) 冠 kańmuri; (of monarch) 王冠 ōkan; (monarchy): *the Crown* 国王 kokúō; (of head, hill) てっぺん téppeň; (of tooth) 歯冠 shikáň

◆*vt* (monarch) 王位に就かせる ði ni tsukáserù; (fig: career, evening) ...に有終の美を飾る ...ni yūshū no bí wo kazárù

crown jewels *npl* 王位の象徴 ōshố-chō ◇王冠、しゃくなど国家的儀式で王または女王が王位の象徴として用いる物を指す ōkan, shákù nádð kokkáteki gishíki de ð matá wa jóō ga ði no shóchō toshité mochíirù monó wo sásù

crown prince *n* 皇太子 kốtaîshi

crow's feet *npl* 目じりの小じわ méjîri no kojíwa, カラスの足跡 kárāsu no ashíatð

crucial [kru:'ʃəl] *adj* (decision, vote) 重大な júdai na

crucifix [kru:'səfiks] *n* (REL) 十字架像 jújikazð

crucifixion [kru:səfik'ʃən] *n* (REL) キリストのはりつけ kirísuto no harítsuke

crude [kru:d] *adj* (materials) 原... geń...; (fig: basic) 原始的な geńshiteki na; (: vulgar) 露骨な rokótsu na

crude (oil) *n* 原油 geń-yu

cruel [kru:'əl] *adj* (person, action) 残酷な zańkoku na; (situation) 悲惨な hisán na

cruelty [kru:'əlti:] *n* (of person, action) 残酷さ zańkokusa; (of situation) 悲惨さ hisánsa

cruise [kru:z] *n* (on ship) 船旅 funátabi

◆*vi* (ship) 巡航する juńkō suru; (car) 楽に走行する rákù ni sōkō suru

cruiser [kru:'zə:r] *n* (motorboat) 大型モーターボート ōgata mótābòto, クルーザー kurūzà; (warship) 巡洋艦 juń-yōkan

crumb [krʌm] *n* (of bread, cake) くず kúzù

crumble [krʌm'bəl] *vt* (bread, biscuit etc) 崩す kuzúsù

◆*vi* 崩れる kuzúrerù

crumbly [krʌm'bli:] *adj* (bread, biscuits etc) 崩れやすい kuzúreyasùi, ぼろぼろした pórðporo shitá

crumpet [krʌm'pit] *n* クランペット kuránpettð ◇マフィンの一種 mafín no isshù

crumple [krʌm'pəl] *vt* (paper, clothes) しわくちゃにする shiwákucha ni suru

crunch [krʌntʃ] *vt* (food etc) かみ砕く kamíkudakù; (underfoot) 踏み砕く fumíkudakù

◆*n* (fig: moment of truth) いざという時 izá to iú tokí

crunchy [krʌn'tʃi:] *adj* (food) ぱりぱりした parípari shitá

crusade [kru:seid'] *n* (campaign) 運動 uńdō

crush [krʌʃ] *n* (crowd) 人込み hitógomi; (love): *to have a crush on someone* ...にのぼせる ...ni noboseru; (drink): *lemon crush* レモンスカッシュ remónsukasshù

◆*vt* (press, squeeze) 押しつぶす oshítsubusù; (crumple: paper, clothes) しわくちゃにする shiwákucha ni suru; (defeat: army, opposition) 圧倒する attō suru; (devastate: hopes) 台無しにする daínashi ni suru; (: person) 落胆させる rakútan saséru

crust [krʌst] *n* (of bread, pastry) 皮 kawá; (of snow, ice) アイスバーン aísubàn; (of the earth) 地殻 chikáku

crutch [krʌtʃ] *n* (support, stick) 松葉づえ matsúbazùe

crux [krʌks] *n* (of problem, matter) 核心 kakúshin

cry [krai] *vi* (weep) 泣く nakú; (shout: *also*: **cry out**) 叫ぶ sakébù

◆*n* (shriek) 悲鳴 himéi; (shout) 叫び声 sakébigoè; (of bird, animal) 鳴き声 nakígoè

cry off *vi* (change one's mind, cancel) 手を引く te wo hikú

crypt [kript] *n* 地下室 chikáshitsu ◇特に納骨堂などに使われる教会の地下室を指す tókù ni nốkotsudō nadð ni tsukáwarerù kyōkai no chikáshitsu wo sásù

cryptic [krip'tik] *adj* (remark, clue) なぞめいた nazómeità

crystal [kris'təl] *n* (mineral) 結晶 kesshō; (in jewelery) 水晶 suíshō; (glass) クリスタル kurísùtaru

crystal-clear [kris'təlkli'ə:r] *adj* (transparent) よく澄んだ yōkù súnda; (*fig*: easy to understand) 明白な meíhaku na

crystallize [kris'təlaiz] *vt* (opinion, thoughts) まとめる matómeru
♦*vi* (sugar etc) 結晶する kesshō suru

cub [kʌb] *n* (of lion, wolf etc) ...の子 ...no ko; (*also*: **cub scout**) カブスカウト kabúsukaùto

Cuba [kju:'bə] *n* キューバ kyūba

Cuban [kju:'bən] *adj* キューバの kyūba no
♦*n* キューバ人 kyūbajìn

cubbyhole [kʌb'i:houl] *n* 小さな納戸 chíìsa na nañdo

cube [kju:b] *n* (shape) 立方体 rippótai; (MATH: of number) ...の3乗 ...no sañjō
♦*vt* (MATH) 三乗する sañjō suru

cube root *n* (MATH) 立方根 ríppōkon

cubic [kju:'bik] *adj* (volume) 立方の rippó no

cubic capacity *n* 体積 taíseki

cubicle [kju:'bikəl] *n* (at pool) 更衣室 kóishìtsu ◊小さい個室について言う chíìsaí koshìtsu ni tsuíte iú; (in hospital) カーテンで仕切った1病床分のスペース kấten de shikítta ichíbyōshōbùn no supēsu

cuckoo [ku'ku:] *n* カッコウ kákkð

cuckoo clock *n* はと時計 hatódokèi

cucumber [kju:'kʌmbə:r] *n* キューリ kyūri

cuddle [kʌd'əl] *vt* (baby, person) 抱締める dakíshimerù
♦*vi* (lovers) 抱合う dakíaù

cue [kju:] *n* (snooker cue) キュー kyū; (THEATER etc) 合図 aízu, キュー kyū

cuff [kʌf] *n* (of sleeve) カフス káfùsu; (*US*: of trousers) 折返し oríkaeshi; (blow) 平手打ち hiráteuchi
off the cuff (impromptu) 即座に(の) sókùza ni (no)

cufflinks [kʌf'liŋks] *npl* カフスボタン kafúsubotàn

cuisine [kwizi:n'] *n* (of country, region) 料理 ryōri

cul-de-sac [kʌl'dəsæk'] *n* (road) 行き止り yukídomari

culinary [kju:'lənе:ri:] *adj* 料理の ryōri no

cull [kʌl] *vt* (story, idea) えり抜く erínukù
♦*n* (of animals) 間引き mabíki

culminate [kʌl'məneit] *vi*: *to culminate in* (*gen*) 遂に...となる tsuí ni ...to narù; (unpleasant outcome) 挙句の果てに...となってしまう agéku no haté ni ...to nattё shimáù

culmination [kʌlmənei'ʃən] *n* (of career, process etc) 頂点 chōten

culottes [kju:lots'] *npl* キュロット kyúròtto

culpable [kʌl'pəbəl] *adj* (blameworthy) とがむべき togámùbeki

culprit [kʌl'prit] *n* (of crime) 犯人 hañnin

cult [kʌlt] *n* (REL: worship) 崇拝 sūhai; (: sect, group) 宗派 shūha; (fashion) 流行 ryūkō

cultivate [kʌl'təveit] *vt* (land) 耕す tagáyasù; (crop) 栽培する saíbai suru; (person) 近付きになろうとする chikázuki ni nárò to suru

cultivation [kʌltəvei'ʃən] *n* (AGR) 耕作 kōsaku

cultural [kʌl'tʃə:rəl] *adj* (traditions etc) 文化文明の buñkabúnmei no; (activities etc) 芸術の geíjutsu no

culture [kʌl'tʃə:r] *n* (of a country, civilization) 文明 buñmei, 文化 buñka; (the arts) 芸術 geíjutsu; (BIO) 培養 baíyō

cultured [kʌl'tʃə:rd] *adj* (individual) 教養のある kyōyō no arù

cumbersome [kʌm'bə:rsəm] *adj* (object) 扱いにくい atsúkainikui ◊かさ張る物, 重い物, 大きくて不格好な物などについて言う kasábarù monó, omói monó, ōkikùte bukákkō na monó nadð ni tsuíte iú; (process) 面倒な meñdð na

cumulative [kju:m'fələtiv] *adj* (effect, result) 累積する ruíseki suru

cunning [kʌn'iŋ] *n* (craftiness) こうかつさ kōkatsusa
♦*adj* (crafty) こうかつな kōkatsu na

cup [kʌp] *n* (for drinking) カップ káppù;

(as prize) 賞杯 shṓhai, カップ káppù; (of bra) カップ káppù

cupboard [kʌb'ərd] *n* 戸棚 todána

Cupid [kju:'pid] *n* キューピッド kyūpiddo

cup-tie [kʌp'tai] (*BRIT*) *n* (SOCCER) トーナメント tònamento

curate [kju:'rit] *n* 助任牧師 jonínbokùshi

curator [kjurei'tə:r] *n* (of museum, gallery) キューレーター kyūrētā ◊学芸員の管理職に相当する人を指す gakúgeìn no kañrishòku ni sṓtō suru hitó wo sásù

curb [kə:rb] *vt* (powers, expenditure) 制限する seígen suru; (person) 抑える osáerù

◆*n* (restraint) 抑制 yokúsei; (*US*: kerb) 縁石 fuchíishi

curdle [kə:r'dəl] *vi* (milk) 凝結する gyṓketsu suru

cure [kju:r] *vt* (illness, patient) 治す naósù; (CULIN) 保存食にする hozónshoku ni suru

◆*n* (MED) 治療法 chiryṓhō; (solution) 解決 kaíketsu

curfew [kə:r'fju:] *n* (MIL, POL) 夜間外出禁止令 yakán gaíshutsu kiñshirei

curio [kju:'ri:ou] *n* 骨とう品 kottóhin

curiosity [kju:ri:əs'əti:] *n* (of person) 好奇心 kṓkishìn; (object) 珍しい物 mezúrashiì monó

curious [kju:'ri:əs] *adj* (person: interested) 好奇心がある kṓkishìn ga arù; (: nosy) せん索好きな señsakuzùki na; (thing: strange, unusual) 変った kawátta

curl [kə:rl] *n* (of hair) カール kāru

◆*vt* (hair) カールする kāru suru

◆*vi* (hair) カールになっている kāru ni natté irù

curler [kə:r'lə:r] *n* (for hair) カーラー kārā

curl up *vi* (person, animal) 縮こまる chijíkomarù

curly [kə:r'li:] *adj* 巻毛の makíge no

currant ◊ [kə:r'ənt] *n* (dried fruit) レーズン rēzun ◊小型の種無しブドウから作った物を指す kogáta no tanénashibùdō kara tsukútta monó wo sásù; (bush, fruit: blackcurrant, redcurrant) スグリ

súgùri

currency [kə:r'ənsi:] *n* (system) 通貨 tsūka; (money) 貨幣 káhèi

to gain currency (*fig*) 通用する様になる tsūyō suru yṓ ni nárù

current [kə:r'ənt] *n* (of air, water) 流れ nagáre; (ELEC) 電流 dénryū

◆*adj* (present) 現在の geñzai no; (accepted) 通用している tsūyō shité irù

current account (*BRIT*) *n* 当座預金 tṓzayokìn

current affairs *npl* 時事 jiji

currently [kə:r'əntli:] *adv* 現在は geñzai wa

curricula [kərik'jələ] *npl of* **curriculum**

curriculum [kərik'jələm] (*pl* **curriculums** *or* **curricula**) *n* (SCOL) 指導要領 shidṓyōryō

curriculum vitae [-vi:'tai] *n* 履歴書 rirékisho

curry [kə:r'i:] *n* (dish) カレー karé

◆*vt*: *to curry favor with* ...にへつらう ...ni hetsuraù

curry powder *n* カレー粉 karéko

curse [kə:rs] *vi* (swear) 悪態をつく akútai wo tsukù

◆*vt* (swear at) のゝしる nonóshirù; (bemoan) のろう norou

◆*n* (spell) 呪い norói; (swearword) 悪態 akútai; (problem, scourge) 災の元 wazáwai no motó

cursor [kə:r'sə:r] *n* (COMPUT) カーソル kāsoru

cursory [kə:r'sə:ri:] *adj* (glance, examination) 何気ない nanígenài

curt [kə:rt] *adj* (reply, tone) 無愛想な buáisō na

curtail [kə:rteil'] *vt* (freedom, rights) 制限する seígen suru; (visit etc) 短くする mijíkakù suru; (expenses etc) 減らす herásu

curtain [kə:r'tən] *n* (at window) カーテン kāten; (THEATER) 幕 makú

curts(e)y [kə:rt'si:] *vi* (woman, girl) ひざを曲げて御辞儀をする hizá wo magéte ojígi wo suru

curve [kə:rv] *n* (bend: in line etc) 曲線 kyokúsen; (: in road) カーブ kâbu

♦*vi* 曲る magáru

cushion [ku⁷ʃən] *n* (on sofa, chair) クッション kusshòn, 座布団 zabútòn; (*also*: **air cushion**) エアクッション eákusshòn ◇ホバークラフトなどを支える空気の事 hobákurafùto nádò wo sasáeru kůki no kotó

♦*vt* (collision, fall) ...の衝撃を和らげる ...no shṓgeki wo yawárageru; (shock, effect) 和らげる yawárageru

custard [kʌs⁷tərd] *n* カスタード kasútàdo

custodian [kʌstou⁷diːən] *n* (of building, collection) 管理人 kaṅrinìn

custody [kʌs⁷tədiː] *n* (LAW: of child) 親権 shiṅken

to take into custody (suspect) 逮捕する taího suru

custom [kʌs⁷təm] *n* (tradition) 伝統 deṅtō; (convention) 慣習 kaṅshū; (habit) 習慣 shúkan; (COMM) ひいき hiìki

customary [kʌs⁷təmeːriː] *adj* (behavior, method, time) いつもの itsùmo no, 相変らずの aíkawarazu no

customer [kʌs⁷təmər] *n* (of shop, business etc) 客 kyakú

customized [kʌs⁷təmaizd] *adj* (car etc) 改造した kaízō shitá

custom-made [kʌs⁷təmmeid⁷] *adj* (shirt, car etc) あつらえの atsúraè no, オーダーメードの ṓdāmèdo no

customs [kʌs⁷təmz] *npl* (at border, airport etc) 税関 zeíkan

customs duty *n* 関税 kaṅzei

customs officer *n* 税関吏 zeíkaṅri

cut [kʌt] (*pt, pp* **cut**) *vt* (bread, meat, hand etc) 切る kirù; (shorten: grass, hair) 刈る karú; (: text, program) 短くする mijíkaku suru; (reduce: prices, spending, supply) 減らす herásù

♦*vi* (knife, scissors) 切れる kirérù

♦*n* (in skin) 切り傷 kiríkìzu; (in salary) 減給 geṅkyū; (in spending etc) 削減 sakúgen; (of meat) ブロック burókkù; (of garment) カット káttò

to cut a tooth 歯が生える há ga haérù

cutback [kʌt⁷bæk] *n* 削減 sakúgen

cut down *vt* (tree) 切り倒す kirítaosù;

(consumption) 減らす herásu

cute [kjuːt] *adj* (*US*: pretty) かわいい kawáiì; (sweet) 陳腐な chíñpu na

cuticle [kjuː⁷tikəl] *n* (of nail) 甘皮 amákawa

cutlery [kʌt⁷ləːriː] *n* ナイフとフォークとスプーン naífu to fṓku to súpūn ◇総称 sṓshō

cutlet [kʌt⁷lit] *n* (piece of meat) カツ(レツ) katsú(retsu); (vegetable cutlet, nut cutlet) コロッケ kóròkke

cut off *vt* (limb) 切断する setsúdan suru; (piece) 切る kirù, 切分ける kiríwakerù; (person, village) 孤立させる korítsu saséru; (supply) 遮断する shadán suru; (TEL) 切る kirù

cut out *vt* (shape, article from newspaper) 切抜く kirínukù; (stop: an activity etc) やめる yaméru; (remove) 切除する setsùjo suru

cutout [kʌt⁷aut] *n* (switch) 非常遮断装置 hijṓshadansṑchi, 安全器 aṅzeňki; (shape) 切抜き kirínuki

cut-rate [kʌt⁷reit] (*BRIT* **cut-price**) *adj* 安売りの yasúuri no

cutthroat [kʌt⁷θrout] *n* (murderer) 人殺し hitógoroshi

♦*adj* (business, competition) 殺人的な satsújinteki na

cutting [kʌt⁷iŋ] *adj* (remark) 辛らつな shiíratsu na

♦*n* (from newspaper) 切抜き kirínuki; (from plant) 穂木 hogí, さし穂 sashího

cut up *vt* (paper, meat) 刻む kizámu

CV [siː⁷viː⁷] *n abbr* = **curriculum vitae**

cwt *abbr* = **hundredweight(s)**

cyanide [sai⁷ənaid] *n* 青酸化物 seísankabùtsu

cyclamen [sik⁷ləmən] *n* シクラメン shikúramèn

cycle [sai⁷kəl] *n* (bicycle) 自転車 jitéñsha; (series: of events, seasons etc) 周期 shúki; (: TECH) サイクル sáìkuru; (: of songs etc) 一連 ichíren

♦*vi* (on bicycle) 自転車で行く jitéñsha de ikú

cycling [saik⁷liŋ] *n* サイクリング sáìkuringu

cyclist [saik'list] n サイクリスト sáikurisuto

cyclone [saik'loun] n (storm) サイクロン sáikuron

cygnet [sig'nit] n 若いハクチョウ wakáí hakúchō

cylinder [sil'indər] n (shape) 円柱 eńchū; (of gas) ボンベ bóňbe; (in engine, machine etc) 気筒 kitő, シリンダー shíriňdā

cylinder-head gasket [sil'indər:rhed-] n (AUT) シリンダーヘッドのパッキング shiríndāheddð no pakkíngu

cymbals [sim'bəlz] npl (MUS) シンバル shíňbaru

cynic [sin'ik] n 皮肉屋 hiníkuya, シニック shínìkku

cynical [sin'ikəl] adj (attitude, view) 皮肉な hiníku na, シニカルな shínìkaru na

cynicism [sin'əsizəm] n シニカルな態度 shínìkaru na táìdo

cypress [sai'pris] n (tree) イトスギ itósùgi

Cypriot [sip'ri:ət] adj キプロスの kípùrosu no
♦n キプロス人 kipúrosujin

Cyprus [saip'rəs] n キプロス kípùrosu

cyst [sist] n (MED) のうしゅ nôshu

cystitis [sistai'tis] n (MED) ぼうこう炎 bókōen

czar [zɑ:r] n = **tsar**

Czech [tʃek] adj チェコスロバキアの chékðsurðbakia no
♦n (person) チェコスロバキア人 chékðsurðbakìajìn; (language) チェコスロバキア語 chékðsurðbakiago

Czechoslovak [tʃekəslou'væk] adj, n = **Czechoslovakian**

Czechoslovakia [tʃekəsləvɑːˈkiːə] n チェコスロバキア chékðsurðbakìa

Czechoslovakian [tʃekəsləvɑːˈkiːən] adj チェコスロバキアの chékðsurðbakìa no
♦n (person) チェコスロバキア人 chékðsurðbakìajìn

D

D [di:] n (MUS: note) ニ音 níðn; (: key) ニ調 níchð

dab [dæb] vt (eyes, wound) 軽くふく karúku fùkú; (paint, cream) 軽く塗る karúku nurú

dabble [dæb'əl] vi: **to dabble in** (politics, antiques etc) 趣味でやる shúmì de yarú

dad [dæd] (inf) n 父ちゃん tôchàn

daddy [dæd'i:] (inf) n = **dad**

daffodil [dæf'ədil] n スイセン suísen

daft [dæft] adj (silly) ばかな bákà ná

dagger [dæg'ə:r] n 短刀 tántō

daily [dei'li:] adj (dose, wages, routine etc) 毎日の maínichi no
♦n (also: **daily paper**) 日刊新聞 nikkanshíńbun
♦adv (pay, see) 毎日 maínichi

dainty [dein'ti:] adj (petite) 繊細な séńsai na

dairy [de:r'i:] n (BRIT: shop) 牛乳店 gyúnyūten; (on farm) 牛乳小屋 gyúnyūgoya◇酪農場で牛乳を置いたり加工したりする小屋 rakúnōjō dè gyúnyū wò oítarì kakő shitarì suru koyá

dairy farm n 酪農場 rakúnōjō

dairy products npl 乳製品 nyúseihin

dairy store (US) n 牛乳店 gyúnyūten

dais [dei'is] n 演壇 eńdan

daisy [dei'zi:] n デイジー deíjī

daisy wheel n (on printer) デイジーホイール deíjīhoírù

dale [deil] n (valley) 谷 tàní

dam [dæm] n (on river) ダム dámù
♦vt (river, stream) ...にダムを造る ...ni dámù wo tsukúrù

damage [dæm'idʒ] n (harm: also fig) 害 gaí; (dents etc) 損傷 sońshō
♦vt (harm: reputation etc) 傷付ける kizutsukérù; (spoil, break: toy, machine etc) 壊す kowásù

damages [dæm'idʒiz] npl (LAW) 損害賠償 sóńgaibaìshō

damn [dæm] vt (curse at) ...に悪態を浴びせる ...ni akútai wo ábìseru; (condemn) 非難する hínàn suru
♦n (inf): **I don't give a damn** おれの知った事じゃない oré no shíttá koto jà náì

♦*adj* (*inf*: *also*: **damned**) くそったれの kusóttare no, 畜生の chikúshō no

damn (it)! 畜生 chikúshō

damning [dæm'iŋ] *adj* (evidence) 動かぬ ugókanù

damp [dæmp] *adj* (building, wall) 湿っぽい shiméppoi; (cloth) 湿った shimétta

♦*n* (in air, in walls) 湿り気 shimérike

♦*vt* (*also*: **dampen**: cloth, rag) 湿らす shimérasu; (: enthusiasm etc) ...に水を差す ...ni mizú wo sasù

damson [dæm'zən] *n* (fruit) ダムソンスモモ damúsonsumòmo

dance [dæns] *n* (movements, MUS, dancing) 踊り odóri, ダンス dànsu; (social event) 舞踏会 butōkai, ダンスパーティ dánsupāti

♦*vi* (person) 踊る odóru

dance hall *n* ダンスホール dánsuhòru

dancer [dæn'sə:r] *n* (for pleasure) 踊る人 odóru hito; (professional) ダンサー dànsā

dancing [dæn'siŋ] *n* (skill, performance) 踊り odóri, ダンス dànsu

dandelion [dæn'dəlaiən] *n* タンポポ tànpopo

dandruff [dæn'drəf] *n* ふけ fuké

Dane [dein] *n* デンマーク人 dénmākujìn

danger [dein'dʒə:r] *n* (hazard, risk) 危険 kikén; (possibility): *there is a danger of ...* ...の恐れがある ...no kikén ga arù

「*danger!*」 (on sign) 危険 kikén

in danger 危険にさらされて kikén ni sàràsaretē

to be in danger of (risk, be close to) ...される危険がある ...saréru kikén ga arù

dangerous [dein'dʒə:rəs] *adj* 危険な kikén na

dangle [dæŋ'gəl] *vt* (keys, toy) ぶら下げる burásageru; (arms, legs) ぶらぶらさせる buràbura saséru

♦*vi* (earrings, keys) ぶら下がる burásagaru

Danish [dei'niʃ] *adj* デンマークの dénmāku no; (LING) デンマーク語の dénmākugo no

♦*n* (LING) デンマーク語 dénmākugo

dapper [dæp'ə:r] *adj* (man, appearance) きびきびした kíbìkibi shitá

dare [de:r] *vt*: *to dare someone to do* 出来るものならしてみろと...にけし掛ける dekírù monó nàrà shité mirò to ...ni keshíkakerù

♦*vi*: *to dare (to) do something* 敢えて...する áète ...surú

I dare say (I suppose) 多分 tábùn

daredevil [de:r'devəl] *n* 無謀な人 mubō na hito

daring [de:r'iŋ] *adj* (escape, person, dress, film, raid, speech) 大胆な daítàn na

♦*n* 大胆さ daítànsa

dark [dɑ:rk] *adj* (room, night) 暗い kurái; (hair) 黒っぽい kuróppoì; (complexion) 浅黒い aságuroì; (color: blue, green etc) 濃い kôì

♦*n*: *in the dark* やみの中で〔に〕yamí no nakà de〔ni〕

to be in the dark about (fig) ...について何も知らない ...ni tsúìte naní mo shíránai

after dark 暗くなってから kuráku nattè kará

darken [dɑ:r'kən] *vt* (color) 濃くする kôkù suru

♦*vi* (sky, room) 暗くなる kuráku narù

dark glasses *npl* サングラス sánguràsu

darkness [dɑ:rk'nis] *n* (of room, night) 暗やみ kuráyami

darkroom [dɑ:rk'ru:m] *n* (PHOT) 暗室 ánshitsu

darling [dɑ:r'liŋ] *adj* (child, spouse) 愛する aí surù

♦*n* (dear) あなた anátà; (favorite) ひいきの人 híìki no hitó

darn [dɑ:rn] *vt* (sock, jersey) 繕う tsukúroù

dart [dɑ:rt] *n* (in game) 投げ矢 nagéya, ダート dàto; (in sewing) ダツ dátsu

♦*vi* 素早く走る subáyakù hashírù

to dart away/along 素早く走っていく subáyakù hashíttè ikú

dartboard [dɑ:rt'bɔ:rd] *n* ダーツの的 dàtsu no mató

darts [dɑ:rts] *n* (game) ダーツ dàtsu

dash [dæʃ] n (small quantity) 少々 shōshō; (sign) ダッシュ dásshù

♦vt (throw) 投げ付ける nagétsukerù; (hopes) くじく kujíkù

♦vi 素早く行く subáyakù ikú

dash away vi 走って行く hashíttè ikú

dashboard [dæʃ'bɔːrd] n (AUT) ダッシュボード dasshúbòdò

dashing [dæʃ'iŋ] adj さっそうとした sàssō to shita

dash off vi = **dash away**

data [dei'tə] npl (ADMIN, COMPUT) 情報 jōhō, データ dèta

database [dei'təbeis] n データベース dḗtabèsu

data processing n 情報処理 jōhōshorì

date [deit] n (day) 日にち hiníchi; (with boy/girlfriend) デート dèto; (fruit) ナツメヤシの実 natsúmeyashì no mí

♦vt (event) ...の年代を決める ...no néndai wo kìmérù; (letter) ...に日付を書く ...ni hizúke wo kakù; (person) ...とデートをする ...to dèto wo suru

date of birth 生年月日 seínengàppi

to date (until now) 今まで imá madè

dated [dei'tid] adj (expression, style) 時代遅れの jidáiokùre no

daub [dɔːb] vt (mud, paint) 塗付ける nurítsukerù

daughter [dɔːt'əːr] n 娘 musúme

daughter-in-law [dɔː'təːrinlɔː] (pl **daughters-in-law**) n 嫁 yomé

daunting [dɔːn'tiŋ] adj (task, prospect) しりごみさせる様な shirígomì saséru yō na, たじろがせる様な hirúmaserù yō nà

dawdle [dɔːd'əl] vi (go slow) ぐずぐずする gúzùguzu suru

dawn [dɔːn] n (of day) 夜明け yoáke; (of period, situation) 始まり hajímari

♦vi (day) 夜が明ける yó gà akérù; (fig):

it dawned on him that ... 彼は...だと気が付いた kárè wa ...da tò ki gá tsuìta

day [dei] n (period) 日 hi, 1日 ichínichi; (daylight) 昼間 hirúma; (heyday) 全盛期 zenséiki

the day before 前の日 maé no hi, 前日 zénjitsu

the day after 翌日 yokújitsu

the day after tomorrow 明後日 asáttè

the day before yesterday 一昨日 otótoi

the following day 次の日 tsugí nò hi, 翌日 yokújitsu

by day 昼間に hirúma nì

daybreak [dei'breik] n 明け方 akégata, 夜明け yoáke

daydream [dei'driːm] vi 空想にふける kūsō ni fūkérù

daylight [dei'lait] n (sunlight) 日光 níkkō; (daytime) 昼間 hirúma, 日中 nítchū

day return (BRIT) n (ticket) 往復券 ōfukukèn

daytime [dei'taim] n 昼間 hirúma

day-to-day [deitu:dei'] adj (life, organization) 日常の nichíjo no

daze [deiz] vt (stun) ぼう然とさせる bōzen to sàséru

♦n: *in a daze* (confused, upset) ぼう然として bōzen to shite

dazzle [dæz'əl] vt (bewitch) 感嘆させる kántan sàséru; (blind) ...の目をくらます ...no mé wò kurámasu

DC [di:si:'] abbr (= direct current) 直流 chokúryū

D-day [di:'dei] n 予定日 yotéïbi

dead [ded] adj (not alive: person, animal) 死んだ shínda; (flowers) 枯れた karéta; (numb) しびれた shibírèta; (telephone) 通じない tsūjinai; (battery) 上がった agátta

♦adv (completely) 全く máttaku; (directly, exactly) 丁度 chōdo

♦npl: *the dead* 死者 shíshà

to shoot someone dead 射殺す uchíkorosù

dead tired へとへとに疲れた hetóheto ni tsúkàreta

to stop dead 突然止る totsúzen tòmáru

deaden [ded'ən] vt (blow, pain) 和らげる yawáragerù; (sound) 鈍くする nibúkù suru

dead end n (street) 行き止り ikídomari

dead heat n (SPORT) 同着 dóchaku

deadline [ded'lain] n (PRESS etc) 締切り shimékiri

deadlock [ded'lɑːk] n (POL, MIL) 行き詰

り ikízumari

dead loss (inf) n: **to be a dead loss** (person) 役立たず yakútatàzu

deadly [ded'li:] adj (lethal: poison) 致命的な chiméiteki na; (devastating: accuracy) 恐ろしい osóroshiì; (: insult) 痛烈な tsúretsu na

deadpan [ded'pæn] adj (look, tone) 無表情の muhyójò no

Dead Sea n: **the Dead Sea** 死海 shikái

deaf [def] adj (totally) 耳の聞えない mimí no kikóenai

deafen [def'ən] vt ...の耳を聞えなくする ...no mimí wo kikóenaku súrù

deafness [def'nis] n 難聴 nànchō

deal [di:l] n (agreement) 取引 toríhikì
♦vt (pt, pp **dealt**) (card) 配る kubárù
a great deal (of) 沢山(の) takúsan (nò)

dealer [di:'lə:r] n (COMM) 販売業者 hánbaigyōsha, ディーラー dírà

deal in vt fus (COMM) 取扱う toríatsukau

dealings [di:'liŋz] npl (business) 取引 toríhikì; (relations) 関係 kañkei

dealt [delt] pt, pp of **deal**

deal with vt fus (person) ...と取引をする ...to toríhikì wo suru; (problem) 処理する shórì suru; (subject) 取扱う toríatsukau

dean [di:n] n (REL) 主任司祭 shuníñshisài; (SCOL) 学部長 gakúbuchò

dear [di:r] adj (person) 愛しい itóshiì; (expensive) 高価な kókà na
♦n: **my dear** あなた anátà, お前 omáe
♦excl: **dear me!** おや oyá ◇驚きを表す odóroki wo àráwasù
Dear Sir/Madam (in letter) 拝啓 hàikei
Dear Mr/Mrs X 親愛なる...さん shín-ai narù ...sàn

dearly [di:r'li:] adv (love) 深く fukákù
to pay dearly for one's carelessness 自らの不注意が高く付く mízùkara no fuchúi gà tákàku tsukú

death [deθ] n (BIO) 死 shí, 死亡 shibó; (fig) 死 shí

death certificate n 死亡証明書 shibóshōmeisho

deathly [deθ'li:] adj (color) 死人の様な shinín no yō na; (silence) 不気味な bukími na

death penalty n 死刑 shikéi

death rate n 死亡率 shibórìtsu

death toll n 死者の数 shíshà no kázù

debacle [dəba:k'əl] n 大失敗 daíshippài

debar [diba:r'] vt: **to debar someone from doing** ...が...をするのを禁止する ...gà ...wo súrú nò wo kíñshi suru

debase [dibeis'] vt (value, quality) 下げる sagérù

debatable [dibei'təbəl] adj (decision, assertion) 疑問のある gímòn no arù

debate [dibeit'] n (discussion, also POL) 討論 tóròn
♦vt 討議する tógì suru

debauchery [dəbɔ:'tʃə:ri:] n (drunkenness, promiscuity) 放とう hótō

debilitating [dibil'əteitiŋ] adj (illness etc) 衰弱させる suíjaku sàseru

debit [deb'it] n (COMM) 支払額 shiháraigàku
♦vt: **to debit a sum to someone/to someone's account** ...の口座から落す ...no kóza kara òtósù ¶ see **direct**

debris [dəbri:'] n (rubble) がれき garéki

debt [det] n 借金 shakkíñ
to be in debt 借金がある shakkíñ gà árù

debtor [det'ə:r] n 負債者 fusáìsha

debunk [dibʌŋk'] vt (myths, ideas) ...の正体をあばく ...no shótaì wo abákù

début [deibju:'] n (THEATER, SPORT) デビュー débyù

decade [dek'eid] n 10年間 júnènkan

decadence [dek'ədəns] n (moral, spiritual) 堕落 daráku

decaffeinated [di:kæf'əneitid] adj カフェインを取除いた kaféiñ wo torínozoìta

decanter [dikæn'tə:r] n (for wine, whiskey) デカンター dekántà

decay [dikei'] n (of meat, fish etc) 腐敗 fuhái; (of building) 老朽 rókyū; (of tooth) カリエス kárìesu
♦vi (rot: body, leaves etc) 腐敗する fuhái suru; (teeth) 虫歯になる mushíba ni narù

deceased [disi:st'] n: **the deceased** 故人

kójìn

deceit [disi:t'] n (duplicity) 偽り itsúwari

deceitful [disi:t'fəl] adj 不正な fuséi na

deceive [disi:v'] vt (fool) だます damásù

December [disem'bə:r] n 12月 júnigatsu

decency [di:'sənsi:] n (propriety) 上品さ jóhìnsa; (kindness) 親切さ shínsetsusa

decent [di:'sənt] adj (proper) 上品な jóhìn na; (kind) 親切な shínsetsu na

deception [disep'ʃən] n ごまかし gomákashi

deceptive [disep'tiv] adj (appearance) 見掛けによらない mikáke ni yōránai

decibel [des'əbəl] n デシベル déshìberu

decide [disaid'] vt (person: persuade) 納得させる nattóku sàséru; (question, argument: settle) 解決する káìketsu suru
♦vi 決める kiméru
to decide to do/that ...する〔...だ〕と決める ...sùrú 〔...da〕to kìméru
to decide on something (choose something) ...を選ぶ ...wo erábù

decided [disai'did] adj (resolute) 決意の固い kétsùi no katái; (clear, definite) はっきりした hakkírì shita

decidedly [disai'didli:] adv (distinctly) はっきりと hakkírì to; (emphatically: act, reply) き然と kizén to

deciduous [disidʒ'u:əs] adj (tree, bush) 落葉の rakúyō no

decimal [des'əmal] adj (system, currency) 十進法 jisshínhō
♦n (fraction) 小数 shōsū

decimal point n 小数点 shōsūten

decimate [des'əmeit] vt (population) 多数の...を死なせる tasú nò ...wo shináseru

decipher [disai'fə:r] vt (message, writing) 解読する kaídoku sùrú

decision [disiʒ'ən] n (choice) 決定した事 kettéi shita koto; (act of choosing) 決定 kettéi; (decisiveness) 決断力 ketsudànryoku

decisive [disai'siv] adj (action, intervention) 決定的な kettéiteki na; (person) 決断力のある ketsudánryoku no árù

deck [dek] n (NAUT) 甲板 kánpàn, デッキ dekkí; (of bus) 階 káì; (record deck)

デッキ dékkì; (of cards) 一組 hitókùmi

deckchair [dek'tʃe:r] n デッキチェア dekkíchea

declaration [deklərei'ʃən] n (statement) 断言 dangèn; (public announcement) 布告 fùkóku

declare [dikler'] vt (truth, intention, result) 発表する happyō suru; (reveal: income, goods at customs etc) 申告する shínkoku suru

decline [diklain'] n: *decline in/of* (drop, lowering) ...の下落 ...no gèráku; (lessening) ...の減少 ...no génshō
♦vt (turn down: invitation) 辞退する jítài suru
♦vi (strength, old person) 弱る yowárù; (business) 不振になる fushín ni narù

decode [di:koud'] vt (message) 解読する káìdoku suru

decompose [di:kəmpouz'] vi (organic matter, corpse) 腐敗する fùhái suru

décor [deikour'] n (of house, room) 装飾 shóshoku; (THEATER) 舞台装置 butáisòchi

decorate [dek'ə:reit] vt (adorn): *to decorate (with)* (...で) 飾る (...de) kazáru; (paint and paper) ...の室内を改装する ...no shitsúnài wo kaísō suru

decoration [dekərei'ʃən] n (on tree, dress etc) 飾り kazári; (act) 飾る事 kazáru koto; (medal) 勲章 kúnshō

decorative [dek'ə:rətiv] adj 装飾の shóshoku no

decorator [dek'ə:reitə:r] n (BRIT: painter) ペンキ屋 pénkiya

decorum [dikɔ:r'əm] n (propriety) 上品さ jóhìnsa

decoy [di:'kɔi] n (person, object) おとり otóri

decrease [n di:'kri:s vb dikri:s'] n (reduction, drop): *decrease (in)* 減少 génshō
♦vt (reduce, lessen) 減らす herásu
♦vi (drop, fall) 減る herú

decree [dikri:'] n (ADMIN, LAW) 命令 meírei

decree nisi [-nai'sai] n 離婚の仮判決 rikón no kàríhànketsu

decrepit [dikrep'it] *adj* (run-down: shack) おんぼろの ónboro no; (person) よぼよぼの yòbóyobo no

dedicate [ded'ikeit] *vt* (time, effort etc): *to dedicate to* ...につぎ込む ...ni tsugíkomù; (oneself): *to dedicate to* ...に専念する ...ni sénnèn suru; (book, record): *to dedicate to* ...に捧げる ...ni saságeru

dedication [dedikei'ʃən] *n* (devotion) 献身 kénshin; (in book, on radio) 献辞 kénji

deduce [didus'] *vt* 推測する suísoku suru

deduct [didʌkt'] *vt* (subtract) 差し引く sashíhikù

deduction [didʌk'ʃən] *n* (act of deducing) 推測 suísoku; (act of deducting) 差引 sashíhìki; (amount) 差し引く分 sashíhikù bùn

deed [di:d] *n* (feat) 行為 kói; (LAW: document) 証書 shósho

deem [di:m] *vt* (judge, consider) ...だと判断する ...dá tò hándàn suru

deep [di:p] *adj* (hole, water) 深い fukáî; (in measurements) 奥行の okúyuki no; (voice) 太い futóî; (color) 濃い kóî
♦*adv*: *the spectators stood 20 deep* 観衆は20列に並んで立っていた kánshū wa nijūretsu ni naránde tàtte ita
a deep breath 深呼吸 shínkokyū
to be 4 meters deep 深さは4メータである fukásà wa yón mèta de árù

deepen [di:'pən] *vt* (hole, canal etc) 深くする fukáku suru
♦*vi* (crisis, mystery) 深まる fukámarù

deep-freeze [di:p'fri:z'] *n* 冷凍庫 réitōkò, フリーザー furîzâ

deep-fry [di:p'frai'] *vt* 揚げる agéru

deeply [di:p'li:] *adv* (breathe) 深く fukáku; (interested, moved, grateful) 非常に hijó ni

deep-sea diving [di:p'si:'-] *n* 深海ダイビング shínkaidàibingu

deep-seated [di:p'si:'tid] *adj* (beliefs, fears, dislike etc) 根の深い né nò fukáî

deer [di:r] *n inv* (ZOOL) シカ shiká

deerskin [di:r'skin] *n* シカ皮 shikágawa

deface [difeis'] *vt* (wall, notice) 汚すyogósu

defamation [defəmei'ʃən] *n* (LAW) 名誉

毀損 méîyokisòn

default [difɔ:lt'] *n* (COMPUT) デフォルト値 défòrutone
by default (win) 不戦勝で fusénshō de

defeat [difi:t'] *n* (of enemy) 敗北 háiboku; (failure) 失敗 shippái
♦*vt* (enemy, opposition) 破る yabúrù

defeatist [difi:'tist] *adj* 敗北主義の háibokushugî no
♦*n* 敗北主義者 háibokushùgísha

defect [*n* di:'fekt *vb* difekt'] *n* (flaw, imperfection: in machine etc) 欠陥 kekkán; (: in person, character etc) 欠点 kettén
♦*vi*: *to defect to the enemy* 敵側に亡命する tekígawa ni bōmei suru

defective [difek'tiv] *adj* (goods) 欠陥のある kekkán no arù

defence [difens'] (*BRIT*) *n* = **defense**

defend [difend'] *vt* (protect, champion) 守る mamórù; (justify) 釈明する shákúmei suru; (LAW) 弁護する bèngo suru; (SPORT: goal) 守る mamórù; (: record, title) 防衛する bóei suru

defendant [difen'dənt] *n* (LAW: in criminal case) 被告人 hîkókunin; (: in civil case) 被告 hîkóku

defender [difen'də:r] *n* (*also fig*, SPORT) 防衛者 bóeisha

defense [difens'] (*BRIT* **defence**) *n* (protection, assistance) 防衛 bóei; (justification) 釈明 shákúmei

defenseless [difens'lis] *adj* (helpless) 無防備の mùbóbì no

defensive [difen'siv] *adj* (weapons, measures) 防御の bógyo no; (behavior, manner) 釈明的な shàkúmeiteki na
♦*n*: *on the defensive* 守勢に立って shuséi ni tattè

defer [difə:r'] *vt* (postpone) 延期する ènki suru

deference [def'ə:rəns] *n* (consideration) 丁重さ téîchōsa

defiance [difai'əns] *n* (challenge, rebellion) 反抗 hánkō
in defiance of (despite: the rules, someone's orders etc) ...を無視して ...wo múshì shite

defiant [difai'ənt] *adj* (challenging,

rebellious: tone, reply, person) 反抗的な hánkōteki na

deficiency [difiʃ'ənsi:] n (lack) 欠如 kétsùjo; (defect) 欠点 kettén

deficient [difiʃ'ənt] adj (inadequate): **deficient in** ...が不足している ...ga fùsóku shìté iru; (defective) 欠点の多い kettén no ôī

deficit [def'isit] n (COMM) 赤字 akáji

defile [difail'] vt (memory, statue etc) 汚す kegásu

define [difain'] vt (limits, boundaries) 明らかにする akírakà ni suru; (expression, word) 定義する teígi suru

definite [def'ənit] adj (fixed) 決まった kimátta; (clear, obvious) 明白な mêîhaku na; (certain) 確実な kakújitsu na **he was definite about it** 彼はその事をはっきり言った kárè wa sonó koto wò hakkírì ittá

definitely [def'ənitli:] adv (positively, certainly) 確実に kakújitsu ni

definition [defəniʃ'ən] n (of word) 定義 teígi; (clearness of photograph etc) 鮮明さ sénmeisa

definitive [difin'ətiv] adj (account, version) 決定的な kèttéiteki na

deflate [difleit'] vt (tire, balloon) ...の空気を抜く ...no kûkî wo nukú

deflect [diflekt'] vt (fend off: attention, criticism) 回避する kaîhi suru; (divert: shot, light) 横へそらす yokó e sōrásù

deform [difɔ:rm'] vt (distort) 変形させる hénkei sàséru

deformed [difɔ:rmd'] adj 変形した hénkei shita

deformity [difɔ:r'miti:] n 奇形 kîkéi

defraud [difrɔ:d'] vt: **to defraud someone (of something)** ...から (...を) だまし取る ...kárà (...wo) dàmáshitorù

defrost [difrɔ:st'] vt (fridge, windshield) ...の霜取りをする ...no shímotori wò suru; (food) 解凍する kaítō suru

defroster [difrɔs'tə:r] (US) n 霜取り装置 shimótorisòchi

deft [deft] adj (movement, hands) 器用な kíyò na

defunct [difʌŋkt'] adj (industry, organi-

zation) 現存しない génzon shìnáî

defuse [di:fju:z'] vt (bomb) ...の信管を外す ...no shínkan wo hàzúsu; (fig: crisis, tension) 緩和する kánwa suru

defy [difai'] vt (resist) ...に抵抗する ...ni teíkō suru; (challenge) 挑発する chōhatsu suru; (fig: description, explanation) ...の仕様がない ...no shíyō ga naī

degenerate
[vb didʒen'ə:reit adj didʒen'ə:rit] vi (condition, health) 悪化する ákká suru
♦adj (depraved) 堕落した dáráku shita

degrading [digrei'diŋ] adj (conduct, activity) 恥ずべき hàzúbekì; (task etc) 誇りを傷つけられる様な hokóri wo kîzútsukerárerù yó na

degree [digri:'] n (extent) 度合 doái; (of temperature, angle, latitude) 度 do; (SCOL) 学位 gákùi
a degree in science 科学の学位 súgaku no gákùi
by degrees (gradually) 徐々に jójò ni
to some degree ある程度 arú teîdo

dehydrated [di:hai'dreitid] adj (MED) 脱水状態の dassúijōtai no; (milk) エバミルク ebámirùku

de-ice [di:ais'] vt (windshield) ...の霜取りをする ...no shímotori wò suru

deign [dein] vi: **to deign to do** ...をしてくれてやる ...wo shîté kurete yaru

deity [di:'iti:] n 神 kámî

dejected [didʒek'tid] adj (depressed) がっかりした gakkárì shita

delay [dilei'] vt 遅らせる okúraseru
♦vi (linger) 待つ mátsù; (hesitate) ためらう tameráù
♦n (waiting period) 待つべき期間 mátsùbeki kikàn; (postponement) 延期 énki
to be delayed (person, flight, departure etc) 遅れる ôkúreru
without delay 直ちに tádàchi ni

delectable [dilek'təbəl] adj (person) 美しい ùtsúkushiî; (food) おいしい ôíshiî

delegate [n del'əgit vb del'əgeit] n 代表 dáîhyō
♦vt (person) 任命する nínmei suru; (task) 任せる màkáserù

delegation [deləgei'ʃən] n (group) 代表団

dáîhyòdan; (by manager, leader) 任命 nín-mei

delete [dili:t'] *vt* (cross out, *also* COMPUT) 消す kèsú, 削除する sákùjo suru

deliberate [*adj* dilib'ə:rit *vb* dilib'ə:reit] *adj* (intentional) 故意の kóî no; (slow) 落着いた òchítsuita
◆*vi* (consider) 熟考する jukkő suru

deliberately [dilib'ə:ritli:] *adv* (on purpose) 故意に kóî ni, わざと wáza to

delicacy [del'əkəsi:] *n* (of movement) しとやかさ shitóyakasà; (of material) 繊細さ sénsaisa; (of problem etc) 微妙さ bĭmyősa; (choice food) 珍味 chînmi

delicate [del'əkit] *adj* (movement) しとやかな shitóyakà na; (taste, smell, color) 淡い awáì; (material) 繊細な sénsai na; (approach, problem) 微妙な bimyố na; (health) 弱い yowáì

delicatessen [deləkətes'ən] *n* 総菜屋 sốzaiya, デリカテッセン dèríkatessèn

delicious [diliʃ'əs] *adj* (food) おいしい òîshìî; (smell) おいしそうな òîshisồ na; (feeling) 心地好い kòkóchiyoî; (person) 魅力的な mìryókuteki na

delight [dilait'] *n* 喜び yòrókobi
◆*vt* (please) 喜ばす yòrókobasu
to take (a) delight in ...するのが大好きである ...surú nò ga dáîsuki de aru

delighted [dilai'tid] *adj*: **delighted (at/with)** (...で) 喜んでいる (...de) yòrókòn-de iru
delighted to do 喜んで...する yòrókòn-de ...suru

delightful [dilait'fəl] *adj* (evening, house, person etc) 楽しい tànóshiî

delinquency [diliŋ'kwənsi:] *n* 非行 hikố

delinquent [diliŋ'kwint] *adj* (boy/girl) 非行の hikố no
◆*n* (youth) 非行少年〔少女〕hikốshònen 〔shòjo〕

delirious [dili:r'i:əs] *adj*: **to be delirious** (with fever) うわ言を言う ùwágoto wo iu; (with excitement) 夢中になっている mùchú ni nattè irú

deliver [diliv'ə:r] *vt* (distribute) 配達する háîtatsu suru; (hand over) 引渡す hǐkí-

watasù; (message) 届ける tòdőkeru; (MED: baby) ...の出産を助ける ...no shùssan wo tàsúkerù
to deliver a speech 演説をする ènzetsu wo sùrú

delivery [diliv'ə:ri:] *n* (distribution) 配達 háîtatsu; (of speaker) 演説振り ènzetsu-buri; (MED) 出産 shùssán
to take delivery of ...を受取る ...wo ùkétorù

delta [del'tə] *n* (of river) デルタ地帯 dè-rútachitài

delude [dilu:d'] *vt* (deceive) だます damásù

deluge [del'ju:dʒ] *n* (*also*: **deluge of rain**) 大雨 óamè; (*fig*: of petitions, requests) 殺到 sàttố

delusion [dilu:'ʒən] *n* (false belief) 錯覚 sàkkáku

de luxe [dilʌks'] *adj* (car, holiday) 豪華な gốkà na

delve [delv] *vi*: **to delve into** (subject) ...を探求する ...wo tánkyū suru; (cupboard, handbag) ...の中を捜す ...no nákà wo sagásu

demand [dimænd'] *vt* 要求する yốkyu suru
◆*n* 要求 yốkyu; (ECON) 需要 juyố
to be in demand ...の需要がある ...no jùyố ga arú
on demand (available, payable) 請求次第 sèîkyushìdài

demanding [dimænd'iŋ] *adj* (boss, child) 気難しい kìmúzukashiì; (work) きつい kìtsuî

demarcation [di:mɑ:rkei'ʃən] *n* (of areas) 境 sàkáî; (of tasks) 区分 kúbùn

demean [dimi:n'] *vt*: **to demean oneself** 軽べつを招く事をする kèîbetsu wo mà-nékù kotó wò suru

demeanor [dimi:'nə:r] (*BRIT* **demeanour**) *n* 振舞 fùrúmai

demented [dimen'tid] *adj* 気の狂った kì-nố kurúttà

demise [dimaiz'] *n* (end) 消滅 shốmetsu; (death) 死亡 shibố

demister [dimis'tə:r] (*BRIT*) *n* (AUT) 霜取り装置 shimótorisòchi

demo [dem'ou] (*BRIT: inf*) *n abbr* = **demonstration**

democracy [dimə:k'rəsi:] *n* (POL: system) 民主主義 mínshushugî; (country) 民主主義国 mínshushùgîkòku

democrat [dem'əkræt] *n* (*gen*) 民主主義者 mínshushugìshà; (*US*) 民主党員 mínshutôin

democratic [deməkræt'ik] *adj* (*gen*) 民主的な mínshuteki na; (*US*) 民主党の mínshutô no

demolish [dimɑ:l'iʃ] *vt* (building) 取壊す toríkowasù; (*fig*: argument) 論破する rónpà suru

demolition [deməliʃ'ən] *n* (of building) 取壊し toríkowashi; (of argument) 論破 rònpa

demon [di:'mən] *n* (evil spirit) 悪魔 ákùma

demonstrate [dem'ənstreit] *vt* (prove: theory) 立証する rìsshő suru; (show: skill, appliance) 見せる misérù
♦*vi* (POL) デモをする démò wo suru

demonstration [demənstrei'ʃən] *n* (POL) デモ démò; (proof) 立証 risshő; (exhibition) 実演 jitsúen

demonstrator [dem'ənstreitə:r] *n* (POL) デモの参加者 démò no sánkashà; (COMM) 実演をする店員 jitsúen wo sùrú tén-in

demoralize [dimɔ:r'əlaiz] *vt* (dishearten) がっかりさせる gàkkárì saséru

demote [dimout'] *vt* (*also* MIL) 降格する kőkaku sùrú

demure [dimjur'] *adj* (smile, dress, little girl) しとやかな shitóyàka ná

den [den] *n* (of animal) 巣穴 sùána; (of thieves) 隠れ家 kàkúregà, アジト ájìto; (room) 書斎 shòsái

denatured alcohol [di:nei'tʃə:rd-] (*US*) *n* 変性アルコール hénseiàrúkòru

denial [dinai'əl] *n* (refutation) 否定 hìtéi; (refusal) 拒否 kyóhì

denim [den'əm] *n* (fabric) デニム dénìmu

denims [den'əmz] *npl* ジーパン jípan, ジーンズ jínzù

Denmark [den'mɑ:rk] *n* デンマーク dénmàkù

denomination [dinɑ:mənei'ʃən] *n* (of money) 額面 gakúmen; (REL) 宗派 shúhà

denominator [dinɑ:m'əneitə:r] *n* (MATH) 分母 búnbò

denote [dinout'] *vt* (indicate, represent) 示す shimésù

denounce [dinauns'] *vt* (person, action) 非難する hínàn suru

dense [dens] *adj* (crowd) 密集した mìsshú shita; (smoke, fog etc) 濃い kôî; (foliage) 密生した mìsséi shita; (*inf*: person) 鈍い nibúî

densely [dens'li:] *adv*: **densely populated** 人口密度の高い jínkōmitsùdo no takâî

density [den'siti:] *n* (of population: *also* PHYSICS) 密度 mítsùdo
single / double-density disk (COMPUT) 単〔倍〕密度ディスク tán(bâi)mitsùdo disuku ◇日本語では廃語 nihón go de wà haígo

dent [dent] *n* (in metal or wood) へこみ hèkômi
♦*vt* (*also*: **make a dent in**) へこませる hèkômaseru

dental [den'təl] *adj* (treatment, hygiene etc) 歯科の shíkà no

dental surgeon *n* 歯医者 háisha

dentist [den'tist] *n* 歯医者 háisha

dentistry [den'tistri:] *n* 歯科医学 shíkáigàku

dentures [den'tʃə:rz] *npl* 入れ歯 iréba

denunciation [dinʌnsi:ei'ʃən] *n* (condemnation) 非難 hínàn

deny [dinai'] *vt* (charge, allegation, involvement) 否定する hitéi suru; (refuse: permission, chance) 拒否する kyóhî suru

deodorant [di:ou'də:rənt] *n* 防臭剤 bőshùzai

depart [dipɑ:rt'] *vi* (visitor) 帰る kâèru; (plane) 出発する shùppátsu suru; (bus, train) 発車する hàsshá suru
to depart from (*fig*: stray from) ...を離れる ...wo hànárerù

department [dipɑ:rt'mənt] *n* (COMM) 部 bú; (SCOL) 講座 kőza; (POL) 省 shő

department store n (COMM) デパート depåtò

departure [dipɑ:r'tʃər] n (of visitor) 帰る事 káeru koto; (of plane) 出発 shùppátsu; (of bus, train) 発車 hàsshá; (of employee, colleague) 退職 tàíshoku

a new departure (in or from policy etc) 新方針 shínhòshin

departure lounge n (at airport) 出発ロビー shùppátsurobì

depend [dipend'] vi: **to depend on** (be supported by) ...に頼っている ...ni tàyőttè irú; (rely on, trust) 信用する shínyō suru

it depends 時と場合によりけりだ tòkí tò baái ni yòríkeri dá

depending on the result ... 結果次第で... kèkkà shidài dé

dependable [dipen'dəbəl] adj (person) 頼りになる táyòri ni nárù; (watch, car etc) 信頼性の高い shínraisei no tàkái

dependant [dipen'dənt] n 扶養家族 fuyōkazòku

dependence [dipen'dəns] n (on drugs, systems, partner) 依存 izón

dependent [dipen'dənt] adj: **to be dependent on** (person, decision) ...に頼っている ...ni tàyòttè iru
♦n = **dependant**

depict [dipikt'] vt (in picture) 描く egákù; (describe) 描写する byősha suru

depleted [diplit'id] adj (stocks, reserves) 減少した génshō shita

deplorable [diplɔːr'əbəl] adj (conditions) 悲惨な hìsán na; (lack of concern) 嘆かわしい nàgèkawashiì

deplore [diplɔːr'] vt (condemn) 非難する hínàn suru

deploy [diplɔi'] vt (troops, resources) 配置する hàíchi suru

depopulation [dipɑ:pjəlei'ʃən] n 人口減少 jínkōgenshò

deport [dipɔːrt'] vt (criminal, illegal immigrant) 強制送還する kyōseisòkan suru

deportment [dipɔːrt'mənt] n (behavior, way of walking etc) 態度 tàído

depose [dipouz'] vt (ruler) 退位させる tàí
sàséru

deposit [dipɑːz'it] n (money: in account) 預金 yòkín; (: down payment) 手付金 tètsúkekin; (on bottle etc) 保証金 hòshókin; (CHEM) 沈殿物 chíndènbutsu; (of ore) 鉱床 kőshō; (of oil) 石油埋蔵量 sèkíyumàīzōryò
♦vt (money) 預金する yòkín suru; (case, bag) 預ける azúkerù

deposit account n 普通預金口座 fùtsűyokinkôzà

depot [di:'pou] n (storehouse) 倉庫 sőkò; (for vehicles) 車庫 shákò; (US: station) 駅 ékì

depraved [dipreivd'] adj (conduct, person) 邪悪な jàáku na

depreciate [dipri:'ʃiːeit] vi (currency, property, value etc) 値下がりする nèságari suru

depreciation [dipri:ʃiːei'ʃən] n 値下がり nèságari

depress [dipres'] vt (PSYCH) 憂うつにさせる yűutsu ni sàséru; (price, wages) 下落させる gèráku saseru; (press down: switch, button etc) 押える osáerù; (: accelerator) 踏む fùmú

depressed [diprest'] adj (person) 憂うつな yűutsu na; (price, industry) 下落した gèráku shita

depressing [dipres'iŋ] adj (outlook, time) 憂うつな yűutsu na

depression [dipreʃ'ən] n (PSYCH) 憂うつ yűutsu; (ECON) 不況 fùkyő; (of weather) 低気圧 tèíkiatsù; (hollow) くぼみ kùbőmi

deprivation [deprəvei'ʃən] n (poverty) 貧乏 bínbò

deprive [dipraiv'] vt: **to deprive someone of** (liberty, life) ...から奪う ...kárà ubáu

deprived [dipraivd'] adj 貧しい màzúshiì

depth [depθ] n (of hole, water) 深さ fùkásà; (of cupboard etc) 奥行 òkúyuki; (of emotion, feeling) 強さ tsúyðsa; (of knowledge) 豊富さ hőfusa

in the depths of despair 絶望のどん底に zètsúbō no dònzoko ní

out of one's depth (in water) 背が立た

ない sé ga tatánài; (*fig*) 力が及ばない chǐkára ga òyóbanai

deputation [depjətei'ʃən] *n* (delegation) 代表団 dàíhyōdàn

deputize [dep'jətaiz] *vi*: *to deputize for someone* (stand in) ...の代りに...する ...no kàwári ni ...sùrú

deputy [dep'jəti:] *adj*: *deputy head* (BRIT: SCOL: primary/secondary) 副校長 fùkúkôchò
◆*n* (assistant) 代理 dâíri; (POL) (下院) 議員 (kàin)gíin; (: *also*: **deputy sheriff**) 保安官代理 hóànkàndàíri

derail [direil'] *vt*: *to be derailed* 脱線する dàssén suru

derailment [direil'mənt] *n* 脱線 dàssén

deranged [direindʒd'] *adj* (person) 精神病の sêíshinbyô no

derby [də:r'bi:] (*US*) *n* (bowler hat) 山高帽 yàmátakabò

derelict [de:r'əlikt] *adj* (building) 廃虚になった háíkyo ni nàttà

deride [diraid'] *vt* (mock, ridicule) ばかにする bàká ni suru

derisory [dirai'sə:ri:] *adj* (sum) 笑うべきwàráubekì; (laughter, person) ばかにする bàká ni suru

derivative [diriv'ətiv] *n* (CHEM) 派生物 hàsêíbutsú; (LING) 派生語 hàséigo

derive [diraiv'] *vt* (pleasure, benefit) 受ける ùkérù
◆*vi*: *to derive from* (originate in) ...に由来する ...ni yùrái suru

dermatitis [də:rmətai'tis] *n* 皮膚炎 hǐfúèn

derogatory [dirɑːg'ətɔːriː] *adj* (remark) 中傷的な chûshōteki na

derv [də:rv] (*BRIT*) *n* 軽油 kéíyu

descend [disend'] *vt* (stairs, hill) 降りる òrírù
◆*vi* (go down) 降りる òrírù
to descend from ...から降りる ...kárà orírù
to descend to (lying, begging etc) ...するまでに成り下がる ...surú madè ni narísagarù

descendant [disen'dənt] *n* 子孫 shísòn

descent [disent'] *n* (of stairs, hill, by person etc) 降りる事 òrírù koto; (AVIAT) 降下 kôkà; (origin) 家系 kàkéi

describe [diskraib'] *vt* (event, place, person, shape) 描写する byôsha suru

description [diskrip'ʃən] *n* (account) 描写 byôsha; (sort) 種類 shúrùi

descriptive [diskrip'tiv] *adj* (writing, painting) 写実的な shàjítsuteki na

desecrate [des'əkreit] *vt* (altar, cemetery) 汚す kegásu

desert [*n* dez'ə:rt *vb* dizə:rt'] *n* (GEO) 砂漠 sàbáku; (*fig*: wilderness) 殺風景な所 sàppúkèi na tòkóro
◆*vt* (place, post) 放置して逃亡する hôchi shite tôbô sùrú; (partner, family) 見捨てる mísùteru
◆*vi* (MIL) 脱走する dàssô suru

deserter [dizə:r'tə:r] *n* (MIL) 脱走兵 dassôhei

desertion [dizə:r'ʃən] *n* (MIL) 脱走 dassô; (LAW) 遺棄 íkí

desert island *n* 熱帯の無人島 nèttái no mùjíntô

deserts [dizə:rts'] *npl*: *to get one's just deserts* 天罰を受ける tènbatsu wo ukérù

deserve [dizə:rv'] *vt* (merit, warrant) ...に値する ...ni àtái suru

deserving [dizə:r'ving] *adj* (person) 援助に値する énjò ni atái suru; (action, cause) 立派な rïppá na

design [dizain'] *n* (art, process) 意匠 ishô; (sketch) スケッチ sùkétchì; (layout, shape) デザイン dèzâîn; (pattern) 模様 mòyô; (intention) 意図 ítô
◆*vt* (house, kitchen, product etc) 設計する sèkkéi suru; (test etc) ...の案を作る ...no àn wo tsùkúrù

designate [*vb* dez'igneit *adj* dez'ignit] *vt* (nominate) 任命する nínmei suru
◆*adj* (chairman etc) 任命された nínmei sàréta

designer [dizai'nə:r] *n* (ART) デザイナー dèzâínā; (TECH) 設計者 sèkkéisha; (*also*: **fashion designer**) ファッションデザイナー fàsshôndezàínā

desirable [dizai'ə:rəbəl] *adj* (proper) 望ましい nòzómashìi; (attractive) 魅力的な

mǐryōkuteki na

desire [dizai'ə:r] *n* (urge) 望 み nòzómi; (*also*: **sexual desire**) 性欲 séiyoku
♦*vt* (want) 欲しがる hòshígarù; (lust after) ...とセックスをしたがる ...to sékkùsu wo shìtágarù

desk [desk] *n* (in office, for pupil) 机 tsùkúe, デスク désùku; (in hotel) フロント fùrónto; (at airport) カウンター kâuntā; (*BRIT*: in shop, restaurant) 勘定カウンター kánjōkàuntā

desolate [des'əlit] *adj* (place) 物寂しい mònósabishíi; (person) 惨めな míjìme na

desolation [desəlei'ʃən] *n* (of place) 物寂しさ mònósabishìsà; (of person) 惨めさ míjímesà

despair [dispe:r'] *n* (hopelessness) 絶望 zètsúbō
♦*vi*: **to despair of** (give up on) ...をあきらめる ...wo àkíramerù

despatch [dispætʃ'] *n, vt* = **dispatch**

desperate [des'pə:rit] *adj* (s c r e a m, shout) 恐怖の kyōfù no; (situation, shortage) 絶望的な zètsúbōteki na; (fugitive) 必死の hìsshí no
to be desperate for something/to do 必死の思いで...を欲しがって[したがって]いる hìsshí no òmóî dé ...wó hòshígattè [shìtágattè]irú

desperately [des'pə:ritli:] *adv* (in despair, frantically: struggle, shout etc) 必死になって hìsshí ni nattè; (very) とても tòtémo

desperation [despərei'ʃən] *n* (recklessness) 必死の思い hìsshí no òmóî
in (sheer) desperation 必死の思いで hìsshí no òmóî dé, 死に物狂いで shìnímonogurùi dé

despicable [des'pikəbəl] *adj* (action, person) 卑劣な hìrétsu na

despise [dispaiz'] *vt* 軽べつする kèîbetsu suru

despite [dispait'] *prep* (in spite of) ...にもかかわらず ...nî mò kakáwarazu

despondent [dispɑ:n'dənt] *adj* (downcast) 意気消沈している íkîshōchin shìté iru

despot [des'pət] *n* 暴君 bôkùn

dessert [dizə:rt'] *n* (CULIN) デザート dèzấtò

dessertspoon [dizə:rt'spu:n] *n* (object) 小さじ kòsáji; (quantity) 小さじ一杯 kòsáji íppài

destination [destənei'ʃən] *n* (of traveler) 目的地 mòkútekìchi; (of mail) 宛先 átésaki

destined [des'tind] *adj*: **to be destined to do/for** ...する〔される〕事になっている ...sùrú (sareru)koto nì náttè iru

destiny [des'təni:] *n* (fate) 運命 ùnméì

destitute [des'titu:t] *adj* (person) 一文無しの íchímon nàshi no

destroy [distrɔi'] *vt* (demolish, wreck, *also fig*) 破壊する hàkái suru; (animal) 安楽死させる ánrakùshi sasérù

destroyer [distrɔi'ə:r] *n* (NAUT) 駆逐艦 kùchíkukan

destruction [distrʌk'ʃən] *n* (act, state) 破壊 hàkái

destructive [distrʌk'tiv] *adj* (capacity, force) 破壊的な hàkáiteki na; (child) 暴れん坊の àbárenbō no; (not constructive: criticism etc) 建設的でない kénsetsuteki de náî

detach [ditætʃ'] *vt* (remove, unclip, unstick) 外す hàzúsu

detachable [ditætʃ'əbəl] *adj* (removable) 外せる hàzúseru

detached [ditætʃt'] *adj* (attitude, person) 無とん着な mútònchaku ná
a detached house 一軒家 íkkén-yà

detachment [ditætʃ'mənt] *n* (aloofness) 無関心 mùkánshìn; (MIL: detail) 分遣隊 bùnkèntái

detail [diteil'] *n* (fact, feature) 詳細 shṓsai; (no pl: in picture, one's work etc) 細かい事 kòmákaï kotó; (trifle) ささいな事 sásàι na kòtó
♦*vt* (list) 詳しく話す kùwáshìku hanásù
in detail 細かく kòmákakù

detailed [diteild'] *adj* (account, description) 細かい kòmákaì

detain [ditein'] *vt* (keep, delay) 引留める hìkítomerù; (in captivity) 監禁する kánkin sùrú; (in hospital) 入院させる nyǔín saserù

detect [ditekt'] vt (sense) ...に感付く ...ni kánzukù; (MED) 発見する hàkkén suru; (MIL, POLICE, RADAR, TECH) 関知する kànchi suru

detection [ditek'ʃən] n (discovery) 発見 hàkkén

detective [ditek'tiv] n (POLICE) 刑事 kéìji

private detective 私立探偵 shírítsutántei

detective story n 探偵小説 tànteishōsetsù

detector [ditek'tər] n (TECH) 探知機 tánchikì

détente [deitɑnt'] n (POL) 緊張緩和 kínchōkanwa, デタント dètánto

detention [diten'tʃən] n (arrest) 監禁 kánkin; (SCOL) 居残り ìnókori

deter [ditər'] vt (discourage, dissuade) 阻止する sóshì suru

detergent [ditər'dʒənt] n 洗剤 sénzai

deteriorate [diti:'ri:əreit] vi (health, sight, weather) 悪くなる wárùku nárù; (situation) 悪化する àkká suru

deterioration [diti:ri:ərei'ʃən] n 悪化 àkká

determination [ditə:rmənei'ʃən] n (resolve) 決意 kétsùi; (establishment) 決定 kèttéi

determine [ditə:r'min] vt (facts) 確認する kàkúnin suru; (limits etc) 決める kìméru

determined [ditə:r'mind] adj (person) 意志の強い íshì no tsùyóì

determined to do どうしても...すると決心している dōshitemó ...sùrú tò késshìn shité iru

deterrent [ditə:r'ənt] n (MIL, LAW) 抑止する物 yókùshi suru mònó

detest [ditest'] vt 嫌う kìráu

detonate [det'əneit] vi 爆発する bàkúhatsu suru
♦vt 爆発させる bàkúhatsu sàséru

detour [di:'tu:r] n (from route) 回り道 màwárimìchí; (US: AUT: diversion) う回路 ùkáîro

detract [ditrækt'] vi: *to detract from* (effect, achievement) ...を損なう ...wo sò-

kónaù

detriment [det'rəmənt] n: *to the detriment of* ...に損害を与えて ...ni sóngai wo àtáete

detrimental [detrəmen'təl] adj: *detrimental to* 損害になる sóngai ni nárù

devaluation [di:vælju:ei'ʃən] n (ECON) 平価切下げ hêîkakirîsage

devalue [di:væl'ju:] vt (work, person) 見くびる mìkúbirù; (currency) ...の平価を切り下げる ...no hêîka wo kírîsagerù

devastate [dev'əsteit] vt (destroy) さんざん荒らす sánzan àrásu; (fig: shock): *to be devastated by* ...に大きなショックを受ける ...ni ōkîna shókkù wo ùkérù

devastating [dev'əsteitiŋ] adj (weapon, storm etc) 破壊力の大きい hàkáîryoku no ōkiî; (announcement, news, effect) 衝撃的な shṓgekiteki na, ショッキングな shókkìngu ná

develop [divel'əp] vt (business, land, idea, resource) 開発する kàîhatsu sùrú; (PHOT) 現像する génzo sùrú; (disease) ...にかかる ...ni kàkárù; (fault, engine trouble) ...が発生する ...ga hàsséi sùrú
♦vi (advance) 発展する hàttén sùrú; (evolve: situation, disease) 発生する hàsséi sùrú; (appear: facts, symptoms) 現れる àráwarerù

developer [divel'əpə:r] n (also: **property developer**) 開発業者 kàîhatsugyōsha

developing country [divel'əpiŋ-] n 発展途上国 hàtténtojōkokù

development [divel'əpmənt] n (advance) 発展 hàttén; (of affair, case) 新事実 shínjijitsù; (of land) 開発 kàîhatsu

deviate [di:'vi:eit] vi: *to deviate (from)* (...から) それる (...kára) sòrérù

deviation [di:vi:ei'ʃən] n 脱線 dàssén

device [divais'] n (apparatus) 仕掛け shìkáke

devil [dev'əl] n (REL, fig) 悪魔 ákùma

devilish [dev'əliʃ] adj (idea, action) 悪魔的な ákùmateki na

devious [di:'vi:əs] adj (person) 腹黒い hàráguroì

devise [divaiz'] vt (plan, scheme, machine) 発案する hàtsúan sùrú

devoid [divɔid'] *adj*: **devoid of** (lacking) ...が全くない ...ga màttáku naî

devolution [devəlu:'ʃən] *n* (POL) 権限委譲 kéngenìjǒ

devote [divout'] *vt*: **to devote something to** (dedicate) ...に...をつぎ込む ...nî ...wo tsùgíkomù

devoted [divout'id] *adj* (loyal: service, friendship) 忠実な chújitsu na; (: admirer, partner) 熱心な nésshìn na
to be devoted to someone ...を熱愛している ...wo nètsúai shǐté iru
the book is devoted to politics その本は政治の専門書である sonó hòn wa seìji no sénmonsho dè árù

devotee [devouti:'] *n* (fan) ファン fàn; (REL) 信徒 shíntǒ

devotion [divou'ʃən] *n* (affection) 愛情 àijō; (dedication: to duty etc) 忠誠 chǔsei; (REL) 信心 shínjìn

devour [divau'ə:r] *vt* (meal, animal) むさぼり食う mùsáborikúù

devout [divaut'] *adj* (REL) 信心深い shínjinbùkaî

dew [du:] *n* (on grass) 露 tsúyù

dexterity [dekste:r'iti:] *n* (manual, mental) 器用さ kìyósa

diabetes [daiəbi:'tis] *n* 糖尿病 tónyóbyō

diabetic [daiəbet'ik] *adj* 糖尿病の tónyóbyō no
♦*n* 糖尿病患者 tónyóbyōkànja

diabolical [daiəbɑ:l'ikəl] *adj* (behavior) 悪魔的な àkúmateki na; (weather) ひどい hìdôî

diagnose [daiəgnous'] *vt* (illness, problem) 診断する shíndàn sùrú

diagnoses [daiəgnou'si:z] *npl of* **diagnosis**

diagnosis [daiəgnou'sis] (*pl* **diagnoses**) *n* 診断 shíndàn

diagonal [daiæg'ənəl] *adj* (line) 斜めの nànámè nó
♦*n* (MATH) 対角線 taīkakùsen

diagram [dai'əgræm] *n* 図 zu

dial [dail] *n* (of phone, radio etc) ダイヤル daîyaru; (on instrument, clock etc) 文字盤 mòjíban
♦*vt* (number) ダイヤルする daîyaru sùrú

dial code (*BRIT* **dialling code**) *n* 市外番号 shìgáibàngǒ

dialect [dai'əlekt] *n* 方言 hǒgèn

dialogue [dai'əlɔ:g] (*US also*: **dialog**) *n* (communication) 対話 taîwa; (conversation) 会話 kaîwa

dial tone (*BRIT* **dialling tone**) *n* 発信音 hàsshín-òn, ダイヤルトーン daîyarutōn

diameter [daiæm'itə:r] *n* 直径 chòkkéi

diamond [dai'mənd] *n* (gem) ダイヤモンド daîyamòndo, ダイヤ daîya; (shape) ひし形 hìshígata

diamonds [dai'məndz] *npl* (CARDS) ダイヤ daîya

diaper [dai'pə:r] (*US*) *n* おむつ òmútsù

diaphragm [dai'əfræm] *n* (ANAT) 横隔膜 ŏkakumàkú; (contraceptive) ペッサリー péssarî

diarrhea [daiəri:'ə] (*BRIT* **diarrhoea**) *n* げり gèrí

diary [dai'ə:ri:] *n* (engagements book) 手帳 tèchǒ; (daily account) 日記 nîkkí

dice [dais] *n inv* (in game) さいころ saîkorð
♦*vt* (CULIN) 角切りにする kàkúgiri ni sùrú

dichotomy [daikɑ:t'əmi:] *n* 二分化 nîbúnkǎ

Dictaphone [dik'təfoun]® *n* ディクタフォーン dîkútafòn ◇一種の録音機の商品名 îsshù no ròkúonkî no shóhinmeî

dictate [dik'teit] *vt* (letter) 書取らせる kàkítoraserù; (conditions) 指図する sáshizu sùrú

dictation [diktei'ʃən] *n* (of letter: *also* SCOL) 書取り kàkítori; (of orders) 指図 sáshizu

dictator [dik'teitə:r] *n* (POL, MIL, *fig*) 独裁者 dòkúsaìsha

dictatorship [dikteit'ə:rʃip] *n* 独裁政権 dòkúsaisélken

diction [dik'ʃən] *n* (in speech, song) 発音 hàtsúon

dictionary [dik'ʃəne:ri:] *n* (monolingual, bilingual etc) 辞書 jíshǒ, 字引 jîbíki

did [did] *pt of* **do**

didactic [daidæk'tik] *adj* (teaching, purpose, film) 教育的な kyóikuteki na

didn't [dɪd'ənt] = **did not**

die [daɪ] vi (person, animal) 死ぬ shīnú; (plant) 枯れる karéru; (fig: cease) やむ yámù; (: fade) 次第に消える shīdái ni kiéru

to be dying for something/to do something 死ぬ程...が欲しい〔...をしたい〕 shīnú hodo ...ga hōshíi〔...wo shitái〕

die away vi (sound, light) 次第に消える shīdái ni kiéru

die down vi (wind) 弱まる yowámarù; (fire) 小さくなる chiísakù nárù; (excitement, noise) 静まる shizúmarù

diehard [daɪ'hɑːrd] n 頑固な保守派 gànko na hōshúha

die out vi (activity) 消えてなくなる kiéte nákù narù; (animal, bird) 絶滅する zetsúmetsu sùrú

diesel [diː'zəl] n (vehicle) ディーゼル車 dízerushà; (also: **diesel oil**) 軽油 kéíyu

diesel engine n ディーゼルエンジン dízeruènjin

diet [daɪ'ət] n (food intake) 食べ物 tabémònò; (restricted food: MED, when slimming) 減食 génshoku, ダイエット daíetto
◆vi (also: **be on a diet**) 減食する génshoku sùrú, ダイエットする daíetto sùrú

differ [dɪf'əːr] vi (be different): *to differ (from)* (...と) 違う (...to) chigáu; (disagree): *to differ (about)* (...について) 意見が違う (...ni tsúíte) íkèn ga chigáu

difference [dɪf'əːrəns] n (dissimilarity) 違い chigái; (disagreement) 意見の相違 íkèn no sói

different [dɪf'əːrənt] adj 別の bétsu no

differentiate [dɪfəːren'tʃiːeit] vi: *to differentiate (between)* (...を) 区別する (...wo) kúbetsu sùrú

differently [dɪf'əːrəntliː] adv 違う風に chigáu fū ni

difficult [dɪf'əkʌlt] adj (task, problem) 難しい mùzúkashiī; (person) 気難しい kímúzukashiī

difficulty [dɪf'əkʌltiː] n (困難) kònnàn; (problem) 問題 móndai

diffident [dɪf'idənt] adj (hesitant, self-effacing) 気の小さい kì nó chíisaī

diffuse [adj dɪfjuːs' vb dɪfjuːz'] adj (idea, sense) 不鮮明な fùsénmèi na
◆vt (information) 広める hirómerù

diffuse light 反射光 hánshakō

dig [dɪg] (pt, pp **dug**) vt (hole, garden) 掘る hórù
◆n (prod) 小突く事 kozúkù kotó; (archeological) 発掘現場 hàkkútsugènba; (remark) 当てこすり àtékosuri

digest [daɪ'dʒest] vt (food: *also fig*: facts) 消化する shōka suru
◆n (book) 要約 yóyaku, ダイジェスト版 dáíjesutoban

digestion [dɪdʒes'tʃən] n (process) 消化 shōka; (system) 消化器系 shōkakikei

digestive [dɪdʒes'tiv] adj (juices, system) 消化の shōka no

dig into vt (savings) 掘り出す hòrídasù
to dig one's nails into 引っかく hìkkákù

digit [dɪdʒ'it] n (number) 数字 sújì; (finger) 指 yùbí

digital [dɪdʒ'itəl] adj (clock, watch) デジタルの déjītaru nó

digital computer n デジタルコンピュータ dèjítarukònpyútā

dignified [dɪg'nəfaid] adj (person, manner) 品のある hín no arù

dignity [dɪg'nitiː] n (poise, self-esteem) 気品 kíhìn

digress [dɪgres'] vi: *to digress (from)* (topic, subject) (...から) それる (...kárà) sòrérù

digs [dɪgz] (BRIT: inf) npl 下宿 geshúku

dig up vt (plant) 掘り起す hòríokosù; (information) 探り出す sàgúridasù

dike [daik] n = **dyke**

dilapidated [dɪlæp'ədeitid] adj (building) 老朽した rōkyū shitá

dilate [daileit'] vi (eyes) 見張る míharu

dilemma [dilem'ə] n (political, moral) 板挟み itábasamí, ジレンマ jírénma

diligent [dɪl'idʒənt] adj (worker, research) 勤勉な kínben na

dilute [dɪluːt'] vt (liquid) 薄める usúmeru, 希釈する kisháku sùrú

dim [dim] adj (light, room) 薄暗い ùsúguraì; (outline, figure) ぼんやりした bónyarì shitá; (inf: person) 頭の悪い àtáma no wàrúî

♦*vt* (light) 暗くする kùráku sùrú; (AUT: headlights) 下向きにする shìtámuki ni sùrú

dime [daim] (*US*) *n* 10セント玉 jùssénto-dàmá

dimension [dimen'tʃən] *n* (aspect) 面 mèn; (measurement) 寸法 súnpō; (*also* pl: scale, size) 大きさ ókisa

diminish [dimin'iʃ] *vi* (size, effect) 小さくなる chíisakù nárù

diminutive [dimin'jətiv] *adj* (tiny) 小型の kògáta no
♦*n* (LING) 指小辞 shìshóJì

dimmers [dim'ə:rz] (*US*) *npl* (AUT: dipped headlights) 下向きのヘッドライト shìtámuki no hèddóraìtò; (: parking lights) 車幅灯 shafúkutō

dimple [dim'pəl] *n* (on cheek, chin) えくぼ ékùbo

din [din] *n* (row, racket) 騒音 sóon

dine [dain] *vi* 食事する shokúji suru

diner [dain'ə:r] *n* (person) レストランの客 résùtoran no kyakú; (*US*: restaurant) 簡易食堂 kañ-ishokùdō

dinghy [diŋ'i:] *n* ボート bóto
rubber dinghy ゴムボート gomúbòto

dingy [din'dʒi:] *adj* (streets, room) 薄暗い usúgurài; (clothes, curtains etc) 薄汚い usúgitanaì

dining car [dain'iŋ-] *n* (RAIL) 食堂車 shokúdòsha

dining room [dain'iŋ-] *n* (in house, hotel) 食堂 shokúdō

dinner [din'ə:r] *n* (evening meal) 夕食 yúshoku; (lunch) 昼食 chúshoku; (banquet) 宴会 eñkai

dinner jacket *n* タキシード takíshìdo

dinner party *n* 宴会 eñkai

dinner time *n* (midday) 昼食時 chúshokudòki; (evening) 夕食時 yúshokudòki

dinosaur [dai'nəsɔ:r] *n* 恐竜 kyóryū

dint [dint] *n*: *by dint of* ...によって ...ni yottě

diocese [dai'əsi:s] *n* 司教区 shikyókù

dip [dip] *n* (slope) 下り坂 kudárizaka; (in sea) 一泳ぎ hitóoyògi; (CULIN) ディップ díppù

♦*vt* (in water etc) ...に浸す ...ni hitásù; (ladle etc) 入れる irérù, (*BRIT*: AUT: lights) 下向きにする shitámuki nì suru

♦*vi* (ground, road) 下り坂になる kudári-zaka ni narù

diphthong [dif'θɔ:ŋ] *n* 二重母音 nijúboìn

diploma [diplou'mə] *n* 卒業証書 sotsú-gyōshósho

diplomacy [diplou'məsi:] *n* (POL) 外交 gaíkō; (*gen*) 如才なさ josáinasà

diplomat [dip'ləmæt] *n* (POL) 外交官 gaíkōkan

diplomatic [dipləmæt'ik] *adj* (mission, corps) 外交の gaíkō no; (person, answer, behavior) 如才ない josáinaì

dipstick [dip'stik] *n* (AUT) 油量計 yuryókèi, オイルゲージ oírugèji

dipswitch [dip'switʃ] (*BRIT*) *n* (AUT) ヘッドライト切替えスイッチ heddóraìto kiríkaesuìtchi

dire [dai'ə:r] *adj* (consequences, effects) 恐ろしい osóroshiì

direct [direkt'] *adj* (route) 直行の chok-kō no; (sunlight, light) 直射の chokúsha no; (control, payment) 直接の chokúsetsu no; (challenge) あからさまな akárasàma na; (person) 率直な sotchóku na

♦*vt* (address: letter) 宛てる atérù; (aim: attention, remark) 向ける mukérù; (manage: company, project etc) 管理する káñri suru; (play, film, programme) 監督する kañtoku suru; (order): *to direct someone to do something* ...に...する様に命令する ...ni ...surú yō ni meírei suru

♦*adv* (go, write) 直接 chokúsetsu
can you direct me to ...? ...に行くにはどう行けばいいんですか ...ni ikú nì wa dō ikeba iñ desu ká

direct debit (*BRIT*) *n* 自動振替 jidófùrikae

direction [direk'ʃən] *n* (way) 方向 hókō; (TV, RADIO, CINEMA) 演出 eñshutsu
sense of direction 方向感覚 hókōkañkaku

directions [direk'ʃənz] *npl* (instructions) 指示 shíJì
directions for use 取扱い説明 toríatsu-

kaisetsúmei

directly [direkt'li:] *adv* (in a straight line) 真っ直ぐに massúgu ni; (at once) 直ぐに súgu ni

director [direk'tə:r] *n* (COMM) 取締役 toríshimariyàku; (of project) 責任者 sekíninsha; (TV, RADIO, CINEMA) 監督 kañtoku

directory [direk'tə:ri:] *n* (TEL) 電話帳 deñwachō; (COMPUT) ディレクトリー dírékutòrī; (COMM) 名簿 meíbo

dirt [də:rt] *n* (stains, dust) 汚れ yogóre; (earth) 土 tsuchí

dirt-cheap [də:rt'tʃi:p'] *adj* べら安の beráyàsu no

dirty [də:r'ti:] *adj* (clothes, face) 汚い kitánai, 汚れた yogóretà; (joke) わいせつな waísetsu na
♦*vt* (clothes, face) 汚す yogósù

dirty trick *n*: **to play a dirty trick on someone** ...に汚いまねをする ...ni hirétsu na manè wo suru

disability [disəbil'əti:] *n* (*also*: **physical disability**) 身体障害 shiñtaishōgai; (*also*: **mental disability**) 精神障害 seíshinshōgai

disabled [disei'bəld] *adj* (physically) 身体障害のある shiñtaishōgai no aru; (mentally) 精神障害のある seíshinshōgai no árù
♦*npl*: **the disabled** 身体傷害者 shiñtaishōgaishà ◊総称 sōshō

disadvantage [disædvæn'tidʒ] *n* (drawback) 不利な点 fúrì na teñ; (detriment) 不利な立場 fúrì na tachíba

disaffection [disəfek'ʃən] *n* (with leadership etc) 不満 fumáñ

disagree [disəgri:'] *vi* (differ) 一致しない itchí shinaî; (be against, think otherwise): **to disagree (with)** (...と) 意見が合わない (...to) íken ga awánaî

disagreeable [disəgri:'əbəl] *adj* (encounter, person, experience) 嫌な iyá na

disagreement [disəgri:'mənt] *n* (lack of consensus) 不一致 fuítchì; (argument) けんか keñka

disallow [disəlau'] *vt* (LAW: appeal) 却下する kyákkà suru

disappear [disəpiə:r'] *vi* (person, object, vehicle: from sight) 消える kiérù, 見えなくなる miénaku narù; (: deliberately) 姿を消す súgata wo kesú; (custom etc) 消えてなくなる kiéte naku narù

disappearance [disəpiə:r'əns] *n* (from sight) 消える事 kiéru kotð; (deliberate) 失そう shissṓ; (of custom etc) なくなる事 nakú naru kotð

disappoint [disəpoint'] *vt* (person) がっかりさせる gakkárì saserù

disappointed [disəpoin'tid] *adj* がっかりしている gakkárì shité irù

disappointing [disəpoin'tiŋ] *adj* (outcome, result, book etc) 期待外れの kitáihazùre no

disappointment [disəpoint'mənt] *n* (emotion) 落胆 rakútan; (cause) 期待外れ kitáihazùre

disapproval [disəpru:'vəl] *n* 非難 hínàn

disapprove [disəpru:v'] *vi*: **to disapprove (of)** (person, thing) (...を) 非難の目で見る (...wo) hínàn no mê dè mírù

disarm [disɑ:rm'] *vt* (MIL) 武装解除する busṓkaìjo suru

disarmament [disɑ:r'məmənt] *n* (MIL, POL) 軍備縮小 guñbishukushō

disarming [disɑ:rm'iŋ] *adj* (smile, friendliness) 心を和ませるような kokórð wo nagómaseru yð na

disarray [disərei'] *n*: **in disarray** (army, organization) 混乱して koñran shitè; (hair, clothes) 乱れて midáretè

disaster [dizæs'tə:r] *n* (*also*: **natural disaster**) 天災 teñsai; (AVIAT etc) 災害 saígai; (*fig*: mess) 大失敗 daíshippài

disastrous [dizæs'trəs] *adj* (mistake, effect, results) 悲惨な hisán na

disband [disbænd'] *vt* (regiment, group) 解散する kaísan suru
♦*vi* (regiment, group) 解散する kaísan suru

disbelief [disbili:f'] *n* 信じられない事 shiñjirarenai kotð

disc [disk] *n* (ANAT) つい間板 tsuíkanbañ; (record) レコード rekṓdð; (COMPUT) = **disk**

discard [diskɑːrdʹ] *vt* (old things: *also fig*) 捨てる sutérù

discern [disəːrnʹ] *vt* (see) 見分ける miwákerù; (identify) 理解する ríkài suru

discerning [disəːrʹniŋ] *adj* (judgement, look, listeners etc) 理解のある ríkài no árù

discharge [*vb* distʃɑːrdʒʹ *n* dis'tʃɑːdʒ] *vt* (duties) 履行する rikṓ suru; (waste) 放出する hṓshutsu suru; (patient) 退院させる taíin saserù; (employee) 解雇する káìko suru; (soldier) 除隊にする jotái ni surù; (defendant) 釈放する shakúhō suru

♦*n* (CHEM, ELEC) 放電 hṓden; (MED) 排出 haíshutsu; (of employee) 解雇 káìko; (of soldier) 除隊 jotái; (of defendant) 釈放 shakúhō

disciple [disaiʹpəl] *n* (REL: *also fig*: follower) 弟子 deshí

discipline [disʹəplin] *n* (control) 規律 kirítsu; (self-control) 自制心 jiséishìn; (branch of knowledge) 分野 búñ-ya

♦*vt* (train) 訓練する kúñren suru; (punish) 罰する bassúrù

disc jockey [disk'-] *n* ディスクジョッキー disúkujokkī

disclaim [diskleimʹ] *vt* (knowledge, responsibility) 否定する hitéi suru

disclose [disklouzʹ] *vt* (interest, involvement) 打明ける uchíakerù

disclosure [disklouʹʒəːr] *n* (revelation) 打明け話 uchíakebanàshi

disco [disʹkou] *n abbr* (event) ディスコダンス disúkodañsu; (place) = **discotheque**

discolored [diskʌlʹəːrd] (*BRIT* **discoloured**) *adj* (teeth, pots) 変色した heñshoku shità

discomfort [diskʌmʹfəːrt] *n* (unease) 不安 fuáñ; (physical) 不便 fúbèn

disconcert [diskənsəːrtʹ] *vt* どぎまぎさせる dṓgìmagi saséru

disconnect [diskənektʹ] *vt* (pipe, tap) 外す hazúsu; (ELEC) 切断する setsúdan suru; (TEL) 切る kírù

discontent [diskəntentʹ] *n* 不満 fumáñ

discontented [diskəntentʹid] *adj* 不満の fumáñ no

discontinue [diskəntinʹjuː] *vt* (visits) やめる yamérù; (payments) 止める tomérù

discontinued (COMM) 生産中止 seísanchūshi

discord [disʹkɔːrd] *n* (quarrelling) 不和 fúwà; (MUS) 不協和音 fukyṓwaòn

discordant [diskɔːrʹdənt] *adj* (*fig*) 不協和音の fukyṓwaòn no

discotheque [disʹkoutek] *n* (place) ディスコ dísùko

discount [*n* disʹkaunt *vb* diskauntʹ] *n* (for students, employees etc) 割引 waríbiki

♦*vt* (COMM) 割引く waríbikù; (idea, fact) 無視する múshì suru

discourage [diskəːrʹidʒ] *vt* (dishearten) 落胆させる rakútan saserù; (advise against): *to discourage something* ...を阻止する ...wo sóshì suru

to discourage someone from doing ...するのを...に断念させようとする ...surú no wò ...ni dañnen saseyṓ to suru

discouraging [diskəːrʹidʒiŋ] *adj* (remark, response) がっかりさせる様な gakkárì saséru yṓ na

discourteous [diskəːrʹtiːəs] *adj* 失礼な shitsúrei na

discover [diskʌvʹəːr] *vt* 発見する hakkén suru

to discover that (find out) ...だと発見する ...dá tò hakkén suru

discovery [diskʌvʹəːriː] *n* 発見 hakkén

discredit [diskredʹit] *vt* (person, group) ...の信用を傷付ける ...no shiñyō wò kizútsukerù; (claim, idea) ...に疑問を投げ掛ける ...ni gimón wò nagékakerù

discreet [diskriːtʹ] *adj* (tactful, careful) 慎重な shiñchō na; (unremarkable) 目立たない medátanaì

discrepancy [diskrepʹənsiː] *n* (difference) 不一致 fuítchì

discretion [diskreʹʃən] *n* (tact) 慎重さ shiñchōsa

at the discretion of ...の判断次第で ...no hañdan shidài de

discriminate [diskrimʹəneit] *vi*: *to discriminate between* ...と...を区別する ...to ...wo kúbètsu suru *to discriminate against* ...を差別する ...wo sábètsu suru

discriminating [diskrim'əneitiŋ] *adj* (public, audience) 理解のある ríkài no árù

discrimination [diskrimənei'ʃən] *n* (bias) 差別 sábètsu; (discernment) 理解 ríkài

discuss [diskʌs'] *vt* (talk over) 話し合う hanáshiaù; (analyze) 取上げる toríageru

discussion [diskʌʃ'ən] *n* (talk) 話し合い hanáshiai; (debate) 討論 tóròn

disdain [disdein'] *n* 軽べつ keíbetsu

disease [dizi:z'] *n* (MED, *fig*) 病気 byóki

disembark [disembɑːrk'] *vt* (goods) 陸揚げする rikúagè suru; (passengers: from boat) 上陸させる jóriku saserù; (: from plane, bus) 降ろす orósù

♦*vi* (passengers: from boat) 上陸する jóriku suru; (: from plane, bus) 降りる orírù

disenchanted [disentʃæn'tid] *adj*: *disenchanted (with)* (...の) 魅力を感じなくなった (...no) miryóku wò kańjinaku nattà

disengage [disengeidʒ'] *vt* (AUT: clutch) 切る kírù

disentangle [disentæŋ'gəl] *vt* ほどく hodókù

disfigure [disfig'jəːr] *vt* (person) ...の美ぼうを損なう ...no bibó wò sokónaù; (object, place) 汚す yogósù

disgrace [disgreis'] *n* (shame, dishonor) 恥 hají; (cause of shame, scandal) 恥ずべき事 hazúbeki kotò

♦*vt* (one's family, country) ...の恥になる ...no hají ni narù; (one's name) 汚す kegásù

disgraceful [disgreis'fəl] *adj* (behavior, condition, state) 恥ずべき hazúbeki

disgruntled [disgrʌn'təld] *adj* (supporter, voter) 不満の fumán no

disguise [disgaiz'] *n* (make-up, costume) 変装の道具 heńsō no dògu; (art) 変装 heńsō

♦*vt* (person, object): *to disguise (as)* (...に) 見せ掛ける (...ni) misékakerù

in disguise 変装して heńsō shitè

disgust [disgʌst'] *n* (aversion, distaste) 嫌悪 kéñ-o

♦*vt* うんざりさせる uñzarí saserù

disgusting [disgʌs'tiŋ] *adj* (revolting: food etc) むかつかせる mukátsukaserù; (unacceptable: behavior etc) いやな iyá nà

dish [diʃ] *n* (piece of crockery) 皿 sará; (food) 料理 ryóri

to do/wash the dishes 皿洗いをする saráarài wo suru

dishcloth [diʃ'klɔːθ] *n* (for washing) 皿洗いのふきん saráarài no fukíñ

dishearten [dishɑːr'tən] *vt* がっかりさせる gakkárì saserù

disheveled [diʃev'əld] (*BRIT* **dishevelled**) *adj* (hair, clothes) 乱れた midáretà

dishonest [disɑːn'ist] *adj* (person, means) 不正な fuséi na

dishonesty [disɑːn'isti:] *n* 不正 fuséi

dishonor [disɑːn'əːr] (*BRIT* **dishonour**) *n* 不名誉 fuméiyo

dishonorable [disɑːn'əːrəbəl] *adj* 不名誉な fuméiyo na

dish out *vt* (distribute) 配る kubárù

dishtowel [diʃ'tauəl] *n* 皿ぶきん sarábukiñ

dish up *vt* (food) 皿に盛る sará ni morù

dishwasher [diʃ'wɑːʃəːr] *n* (machine) 皿洗い機 saráaraikì

disillusion [disilu:'ʒən] *vt* ...の迷いを覚ます ...no mayói wo samásù

disincentive [disinsen'tiv] *n* (to work, investment) 阻害要因 sogáiyòin

disinfect [disinfekt'] *vt* 消毒する shódoku suru

disinfectant [disinfek'tənt] *n* 消毒剤 shódokuzài

disintegrate [disin'təgreit] *vi* (object) 分解する buńkai suru

disinterested [disin'tristid] *adj* (impartial: advice, help) 私欲のない shiyóku no naì

disjointed [disdʒɔint'id] *adj* (thoughts, words) まとまりのない matómari no naì

disk [disk] *n* (COMPUT) ディスク dísùku

disk drive *n* ディスクドライブ disúkudoraîbu

diskette [disket'] *n* = **disk**

dislike [dislaik'] *n* (feeling) 嫌悪 kén·o; (*gen pl*: object of dislike) 嫌いな物 kírái na monò
♦*vt* 嫌う kiráù

dislocate [dis'loukeit'] *vt* (joint) 脱きゅうさせる dakkyū saserù

dislodge [disla:dʒ'] *vt* (boulder etc) 取除く torínozokù

disloyal [disloi'əl] *adj* (to country, family) 裏切り者の urágirimono no

dismal [diz'məl] *adj* (depressing: weather, song, person, mood) 陰気な iñki na; (very bad: prospects, failure) 最低の saítei no

dismantle [dismæn'təl] *vt* (machine) 分解する buñkai suru

dismay [dismei'] *n* 困惑 koñwaku
♦*vt* 困惑させる koñwaku saserù

dismiss [dismis'] *vt* (worker) 解雇する káíko suru; (pupils, soldiers) 解散させる kaísan saseru; (LAW: case) 却下する kyákkà suru; (possibility, idea) 考えない様にする kañgaenai yō ni suru

dismissal [dismis'əl] *n* (sacking) 解雇 káíko

dismount [dismaunt'] *vi* (from horse, bicycle) 降りる orírù

disobedience [disəbi:'di:əns] *n* 不服従 fufúkujū

disobedient [disəbi:'di:ənt] *adj* (child, dog) 言う事を聞かない iú koto wò kikánaì

disobey [disəbei'] *vt* (person, order) 違反する ihán suru

disorder [diso:r'də:r] *n* (untidiness) 乱雑さ rañzatsu; (rioting) 騒動 sōdō; (MED) 障害 shōgai

disorderly [diso:r'də:rli:] *adj* (untidy: room etc) 整理されていない seíri sarete inaì; (meeting) 混乱の koñran no; (behavior) 治安を乱す chián wò midásù

disorganized [diso:r'gənaizd] *adj* (person, event) 支離滅裂な shírìmetsúretsu na

disorientated [diso:'ri:inteitid] *adj* (person: after journey, deep sleep) 頭が混乱

している atáma gà koñran shite irù

disown [disoun'] *vt* (action) ...との関係を否定する ...tó nò kañkei wò hitéi suru; (child) 勘当する kañdō suru

disparaging [dispær'idʒiŋ] *adj* (remarks) 中傷的な chūshōteki na

disparate [dis'pə:rit] *adj* (levels, groups) 異なった kotónattà

disparity [dispær'iti:] *n* 差異 sáí

dispassionate [dispæʃ'ənit] *adj* (approach, reaction) 客観的な kyakkánteki na

dispatch [dispætʃ'] *vt* (send: message, goods, mail) 送る okúrù; (: messenger) 派遣する hakén suru
♦*n* (sending) 送付 sōfu; (PRESS, MIL) 派遣 hakén

dispel [dispel'] *vt* (myths, fears) 払いのける haráinokerù

dispense [dispens'] *vt* (medicines) 調剤する chōzai suru

dispenser [dispen'sə:r] *n* (machine) 自動販売機 jidōhanbaikì

dispense with *vt fus* (do without) ...なしで済ませる ...náshì de sumáserù

dispensing chemist [dispens'iŋ-] (*BRIT*) *n* (shop) 薬屋 kusúriya

dispersal [dispə:r'səl] *n* (of objects, group, crowd) 分散 buñsan

disperse [dispə:rs'] *vt* (objects, crowd etc) 散らす chirásù
♦*vi* (crowd) 散って行く chitté ikù

dispirited [dispir'itid] *adj* 意気消沈した íkìshōchin shita

displace [displeis'] *vt* (shift) 押し出す oshídasù

displaced person [displeist'-] *n* (POL) 難民 nañmin

display [displei'] *n* (in shop) 陳列 chiñretsu; (exhibition) 展示 teñji; (of feeling) 表現 hyṓgen; (COMPUT, TECH) ディスプレー disúpurè, モニター mónìtā
♦*vt* (show) 展示する teñji suru; (ostentatiously) 見せびらかす misébirakasù

displease [displi:z'] *vt* (offend, annoy) 怒らせる okóraserù

displeased [displi:zd'] *adj*: *displeased with* (unhappy, disappointed) ...にがっか

りしている ...ni gakkárî shité irù

displeasure [displɛʒ'ə:r] n 怒り ikári

disposable [dispou'zəbl] adj (lighter, bottle) 使い捨ての tsukáisute no; (income) 自由に使える jiyū ni tsukáerù

disposable nappy (BRIT) n 紙おむつ kamfomutsû

disposal [dispou'zəl] n (of goods for sale) 陳列 chifiretsu; (of property) 売却 baíkyaku; (of rubbish) 処分 shóbùn

at one's disposal ...の自由になる ...no jiyū ni narù

dispose [dispouz'] vi: *to dispose of* (get rid of: body, unwanted goods) 始末する shímatsu suru; (deal with: problem, argument) 片付ける katázukerù

disposed [dispouzd'] adj: *disposed to do* (inclined, willing) ...する気がある ...surú ki gà árù

to be well disposed towards someone ...に好意を寄せている ...ni kôî wo yoséte irù

disposition [dispəziʃ'ən] n (nature) 性質 seíshitsu; (inclination) 傾向 keíkô

disproportionate [disprəpɔːr'ʃənit] adj (amount, effect) 過剰な kajô na

disprove [dispruːv'] vt (belief, assertion) 反証する hafishô suru

dispute [dispjuːt'] n (domestic) けんか kefika; (also: **industrial dispute**) 争議 sôgi; (POL) 論議 rôngi

◆vt (fact, statement) 反ばくする hafibaku suru; (ownership etc) 争う arásoù

territorial dispute 領土紛争 ryôdofufisô

border dispute 国境紛争 kokkyôfufisô

disqualify [diskwɑːl'əfai] vt (SPORT) ...の資格を取り上げる ...no shíkaku wò toríageru

to disqualify someone for something/from doing something ...から ...の〔...する〕資格を取上げる ...kárà ...no 〔...surú〕 shíkaku wò toríageru

disquiet [diskwai'it] n (anxiety) 不安 fuán

disregard [disrigɑːrd'] vt (ignore, pay no attention to) 無視する múshi suru

disrepair [disripeːr'] n: *to fall into*

disrepair (machine, building) ひどく痛んでしまう hídòku itánde shimaù

disreputable [disrep'jətəbəl] adj (person, behavior) いかがわしい ikágawashiî

disrespectful [disrispekt'fəl] adj (person, conduct) 無礼な búrèi na

disrupt [disrʌpt'] vt (plans) 邪魔する jamá suru; (conversation, proceedings) 妨害する bôgai suru

disruption [disrʌp'ʃən] n (interruption) 中断 chúdan; (disturbance) 妨害 bôgai

dissatisfaction [dissætisfæk'ʃən] n 不満 fumán

dissatisfied [dissæt'isfaid] adj 不満な fumán na

dissect [disekt'] vt (dead person, animal) 解剖する kaíbô suru

disseminate [disem'əneit] vt 普及させる fukyû saserù

dissent [disent'] n (disagreement, protest) 反対 hafitai

dissertation [disərtei'ʃən] n (also SCOL) 論文 rofibun

disservice [disəːr'vis] n: *to do someone a disservice* (person: harm) ...に迷惑を掛ける ...ni mêîwaku wo kakérù

dissident [dis'idənt] adj (faction, voice) 反対の hafitai no

◆n (POL, REL) 反対分子 hafitaibufishi

dissimilar [disim'ilər] adj 異なる kotónarù

dissipate [dis'əpeit] vt (heat) 放散する hôsan suru; (clouds) 散らす chirásù; (money, effort) 使い果す tsukáihatasù

dissociate [disou'ʃieit] vt ...との関係を否定する ...tô nò kafikei wò hitéî suru

to dissociate oneself from ...との関係を否定する ...tô nò kafikei wò hitéî suru

dissolute [dis'əluːt] adj (individual, behavior) 道楽ざんまいの dôrakuzafimai no

dissolution [disəluː'ʃən] n (of organization, POL) 解散 kaísan; (of marriage) 解消 kaíshô

dissolve [dizɑːlv'] vt (in liquid) 溶かす tokású; (organization, POL) 解散させる kaísan saserù; (marriage) 解消する kaíshô suru

♦*vi* (material) 溶ける tokérù

to dissolve in(to) tears 泣崩れる nakíkuzurerù

dissuade [disweid'] *vt*: *to dissuade someone (from)* (...を) 思い止まる様 ...を説得する (...wo) omóitodomaru yō ...wo settóku suru

distance [dis'təns] *n* (gap: in space) 距離 kyórì; (: in time) 隔たり hedátarì

in the distance ずっと向うに zúttò mukō nì

distant [dis'tənt] *adj* (place, time, relative) 遠い tōì; (manner) よそよそしい yosósyoshìì

distaste [disteist'] *n* (dislike) 嫌悪 kén-o

distasteful [disteist'fəl] *adj* (offensive) いやな iyá nà

distended [distend'id] *adj* (stomach) 膨らんだ fukúraǹda

distill [distil'] (*BRIT* **distil**) *vt* (water, whiskey) 蒸留する jōryū suru

distillery [distil'ə:ri:] *n* 醸造所 jōzōjò

distinct [distiŋkt'] *adj* (different) 別個の békkò no; (clear) はっきりした hakkírì shita; (unmistakable) 明白な meíhaku na

as distinct from (in contrast to) ...ではなくて ...dé wà nákùte

distinction [distiŋk'ʃən] *n* (difference) 区別 kúbetsu; (honor) 名誉 meíyo; (in exam) 優等の成績 yútō no seíseki

distinctive [distiŋk'tiv] *adj* 独特な dokútoku na

distinguish [distiŋ'gwiʃ] *vt* (differentiate) 区別する kúbetsu suru; (identify: details etc: by sight) 見分ける miwákerù; (: by sound) 聞分ける kikíwakerù

to distinguish oneself (in battle etc) 見事な活躍をする mígòto na katsúyaku wo surù

distinguished [distiŋ'gwiʃt] *adj* (eminent) 有名な yūmei na; (in appearance) 気品のある kihín no arù

distinguishing [distiŋ'gwiʃiŋ] *adj* (feature) 特徴的な tokúchōteki na

distort [distɔːrt'] *vt* (argument) 曲げる magérù; (sound) ひずませる hizúmaserù; (shape, image) ゆがめる yugámerù

distortion [distɔːr'ʃən] *n* (of argument

etc) わい曲 waíkyoku; (of sound, image, shape etc) ひずみ hizúmi

distract [distrækt'] *vt* (sb's attention) 散らす chirásù; (person) ...の気を散らす ...no ki wo chirásù

distracted [distræk'tid] *adj* (dreaming) ぼんやりした boń-yarì shita; (anxious) 気が動転している ki ga dṓten shite irù

distraction [distræk'ʃən] *n* (inattention) 気を散らす事〔物〕ki wo chirásù kotó 〔monó〕; (confusion) 困惑 koñwaku; (amusement) 気晴らし kibárashi

distraught [distrɔːt'] *adj* (with pain, worry) 気が動転している ki ga dṓten shite irù

distress [distres'] *n* (anguish) 苦痛 kutsū

♦*vt* (cause anguish) 苦しめる kurúshimerù

distressing [distres'iŋ] *adj* (experience, time) 苦しい kurúshiì

distress signal *n* (AVIAT, NAUT) 遭難信号 sōnanshiñgō

distribute [distrib'jut] *vt* (hand out: leaflets, prizes etc) 配る kubárù; (share out: profits) 分ける wakérù; (spread out: weight) 分布する búñpu suru

distribution [distrəbju:'ʃən] *n* (of goods) 流通 ryútsū; (of profits etc) 分配 buñpai

distributor [distrib'jətə:r] *n* (COMM) 流通業者 ryútsūgyōsha; (AUT, TECH) ディストリビュータ disútoribyūta

district [dis'trikt] *n* (of country) 地方 chihṓ; (of town, ADMIN) 地区 chíkù

district attorney (*US*) *n* 地方検事 chihṓkeñji

district nurse (*BRIT*) *n* 保健婦 hokéñfu

distrust [distrʌst'] *n* 不信感 fushíñkan

♦*vt* 信用しない shiń-yō shinaì

disturb [distəːrb'] *vt* (interrupt) 邪魔する jamá suru; (upset) 心配させる shiñpai saserù; (disorganize) 乱す midásù

disturbance [distəːr'bəns] *n* (upheaval) 邪魔 jamá; (political etc) 騒動 sōdō; (violent event) 動乱 dṓran; (of mind) 心配 shiñpai

disturbed [distəːrbd'] *adj* (person: worried, upset) 不安な fuán na; (childhood)

乱れた midáretà

emotionally disturbed 情緒障害の jōchoshŏgai no

disturbing [distəːrbʼiŋ] *adj* (experience, moment) 動転させる dŏten saserù

disuse [disjuːsʼ] *n: to fall into disuse* (be abandoned: methods, laws etc) 廃れる sutárerù

disused [disjuːzdʼ] *adj* (building, airfield) 使われていない tsukáwarete inaì

ditch [ditʃ] *n* (at roadside) どぶ dobú; (also: **irrigation ditch**) 用水路 yŏsuirò

♦*vt* (inf: person) …と縁を切る …to én wo kírù; (: plan, car etc) 捨てる sutérù

dither [diðʼəːr] (*pej*) *vi* (hesitate) ためらう taméraù

ditto [ditʼou] *adv* 同じく onájìku

divan [divænʼ] *n* (also: **divan bed**) ソファベッド sofábeddò

dive [daiv] (*pt* **dived** also *US* **dove**, *pp* **dived**) *n* (from board) 飛込み tobíkomi; (underwater) 潜水 seńsui, ダイビング dáibingu; (of submarine) 潜水 seńsui

♦*vi* (swimmer: into water) 飛込む tobíkomù; (under water) 潜水する seńsui suru, ダイビングする dáibingu suru; (fish) 潜る mogúrù; (bird) 急降下する kyúkōka suru; (submarine) 潜水する seńsui suru

to dive into (bag, drawer etc) …に手を突っ込む …ni té wò tsukkómù; (shop, car etc) …に飛込む …ni tobíkomù

diver [daiʼvəːr] *n* (person) ダイバー dáibā

diverge [divəːrdʒʼ] *vi* (paths, interests) 分かれる wakárerù

diverse [divəːrsʼ] *adj* 様々な samázàma na

diversify [divəːrʼsəfai] *vi* (COMM) 多様化する tayóka suru

diversion [divəːrʼʒən] *n* (*BRIT*: AUT) う回路 ukáirò; (distraction) 気分転換 kibúnteñkan; (of funds) 流用 ryúyō

diversity [divəːrʼsiti] *n* (range, variety) 多様性 tayósei

divert [divəːrtʼ] *vt* (funds) 流用する ryúyō suru; (someone's attention) 反らす soråsù; (re-route) う回させる ukái saserù

divide [divaidʼ] *vt* (separate) 分ける wakérù; (MATH) 割る warú; (share out) 分

ける wakérù, 分配する buńpai suru

♦*vi* (cells etc) 分裂する buńretsu suru; (road) 分岐する búñki suru; (people, groups) 分裂する buńretsu suru

8 divided by 4 is 2 8割る4は2 hachí warù 4 yôn wa ni

divided highway [divaidʼid-] (*US*) *n* 中央分離帯のある道路 chūōbuñritai no árù dŏrò

dividend [divʼidend] *n* (COMM) 配当金 haítōkin; (*fig*): *to pay dividends* 利益になる rîeki ni narú

divine [divainʼ] *adj* (REL) 神の kámì no; (*fig*: person, thing) 素晴らしい subárashiì

diving [daivʼiŋ] *n* (underwater) 飛込み tobíkomi; (SPORT) 潜水 seńsui, ダイビング dáibingu

diving board *n* 飛込み台 tobíkomidài

divinity [divinʼəti] *n* (nature) 神性 shiñsei; (god) 神 kámì; (subject) 神学 shiñgàku

division [diviʒʼən] *n* (of cells etc) 分裂 buńretsu; (MATH) 割算 warízan; (sharing out) 分配 buńpai; (disagreement) 分裂 buńretsu; (COMM) 部門 búmòn; (MIL) 師団 shídàn; (especially SOCCER) 部 bú

divorce [divoːrsʼ] *n* 離婚 rîkòn

♦*vt* (spouse) …と離婚する …to rîkòn suru; (dissociate) 別々に扱う betsúbetsu nì atsúkaù

divorcé [divoːrsiːʼ] *n* 離婚男性 rikóndañsei

divorced [divoːrstʼ] *adj* 離婚した rîkònshita

divorcée [divoːrsiːʼ] *n* 離婚女性 rikónjòsei

divulge [divʌldʒʼ] *vt* (information, secret) 漏らす morásù

D.I.Y. [diːaiwaiʼ] (*BRIT*) *n abbr* = **do-it-yourself**

dizzy [dizʼiː] *adj: a dizzy spell/turn* めまい memái

to feel dizzy めまいがする memái ga suru

DJ [diːʼdʒei] *n abbr* (= *disk jockey*) ディスクジョッキー disúkujokkî

KEYWORD

do [du:] (*pt* **did**, *pp* **done**) *aux vb* **1** (in negative constructions): *I don't understand* 分かりません wakárimasèn

she doesn't want it 彼女はそれを欲しがっていません kánòjo wa sorè wo hòshígattè imásèn

he didn't seem to care 彼はどうでもいい様でした kárè wa dò de mo iî yō deshita

2 (to form questions): *didn't you know?* 知りませんでしたか shirímasèn deshita ká

why didn't you come? どうして来てくれなかったのですか dòshíte kitè kùrénakatta no desu ká

what do you think? どう思いますか dò omóimasù ká

3 (for emphasis, in polite expressions): *people do make mistakes sometimes* だれだって間違いをしますよ dárè datte machígaì wo shimásù yo

she does seem rather late そう言える彼女は本当に遅い様ですね sò iebà kánòjo wa hóntò ni òsói yò desu nè

do sit down/help yourself どうぞお掛け〔お召し上がり〕下さい dòzo o-káke〔o-méshiagari〕kudasaì

do take care! くれぐれもお気をつけて kurégurè mo o-kí wo tsuketè

oh do shut up! いい加減に黙ってくれませんか iíkagen ni dàmáttè kurémasèn ká

4 (used to avoid repeating vb): *she swims better than I do* 彼女は私より泳ぎがうまい kánòjo wa watákushi yorì oyógi gà umaî

do you agree? - yes, I do/no, I don't 賛成しますか-はい、します〔いいえ、しません〕sánsei shimasù ká - haî, shimásù〔iíe, shimásèn〕

she lives in Glasgow - so do I 彼女はグラスゴーに住んでいます-私もそうです kánòjo wa gurásugò ni súndè imásù - watákushi mo sò dèsu

he didn't like it and neither did we 彼はそれを気に入らなかったし、私たち

もそうでした kárè wa sorè wo kì nì iranakàtta shi, watákushitàchi mó sò deshita

who made this mess? - I did だれだ、ここを汚したのは-私です dárè da, kokó wo yògòshita nò wa - watákushi desù

he asked me to help him and I did 助けてくれと彼に頼まれたのでそうしました tasúketè kure to kárè ni tanómarè-ta no de sò shimashita

5 (in question tags): *you like him, don't you?* あなたは彼を好きでしょう？ anátà wa kárè wo sukí dèshò?

he laughed, didn't he? 彼は笑ったでしょう？ kárè wa warátta dèshò?

I don't know him, do I? 私の知らない人でしょう？ watákushi no shìránai hito dèshò?

♦*vt* **1** (*gen*: carry out, perform etc) する sùrú, やる yàrú

what are you doing tonight? 今夜のご予定は? kòn-ya no gò-yótei wá?

have you done your homework? 宿題をしましたか shùkúdai wo shìmáshìta ká

I've got nothing to do 何もする事がありません nàní mo sùrú koto gà arímasèn

what can I do for you? どんなご用でしょうか dònna go-yò dèshò ka

to do the cooking/washing-up 料理〔皿洗い〕をする ryòrì〔saráaraì〕wo sùrú

to do one's teeth/hair/nails 歯を磨く〔髪をとかす、つめにマニキュアをする〕há wò migáku〔kàmí wò tokásù, tsùmé ni mànîkyua wo sùrú〕

we're doing "Othello" at school (studying it) 学校で今オセロを勉強しています gàkkò de ímà òsèro wo bénkyò shite imasù; (performing it) 学校で今オセロを上演しています gàkkò de ímà ò-sèro wo jòén shite imasù

2 (AUT etc) 走る hàshírù

the car was doing 100 車は時速100マイルを出していた kurúma wa jisóku hyàkúmaìru wo dáshìte ita

we've done 200 km already 私tachiはもう200キロメーター走ってきました watákushitàchi wa mò nihyákukiromètā hashítte kimáshìta

he can do 100 mph in that car あの車で彼は時速100マイル出せます anó kuruma de karè wa jísòku hyàkúmaìru dasémasù

♦*vi* **1** (act, behave) する sùrú

do as I do 私のする通りにしなさい watákushi no sùrú tòrí ni shinásaì

do as I tell you 私の言う通りにしなさい watákushì no iu tòrí ni shinásaì

you did well to come so quickly すぐに来てくれて良かったよ súgù ni kité kùrete yókàtta yó

2 (get on, fare): *he's doing well/badly at school* 彼は学校の成績がいい〔良くない〕 kárè wa gakkō no seiseki ga ií 〔yokúnaì〕

the firm is doing well 会社は繁盛しています kaísha wa hànjō shité imasù

how do you do? 初めまして hajímemashìte

3 (suit) 適当である tekítō de arù

will it do? 役に立ちますか yakú nì tachímasù ká

will this dress do for the party? パーティにはこのドレスでいいかしら paátì ni wa konó dorèsu de íi kashira

4 (be sufficient) 十分である júbùn de árù

will £ 10 do? 10ポンドで間に合いますか júppòndo de ma ní aimasù ká

that'll do 十分です júbùn desu

that'll do! (in annoyance) いい加減にしなさい íikagen ni shínàsaì

to make do (with) (...で) 間に合せる (...dé) mà ní awaserù

you'll have to make do with $15 15ドルで間に合せなさい júgòdòru de ma ní awasenasài

♦*n* (*inf*: party etc) パーティ pátì

we're having a little do on Saturday 土曜日にちょっとしたパーティをしようと思っています doyóbì ni chótto shita pátì wo shiyó tò omótte imásù

it was rather a do なかなかいいパーティだった nakánaka íi pátì datta

---

do away with *vt fus* (kill) 殺す korósu; (abolish: law etc) なくす nakúsu

docile [dɑːsˈəl] *adj* (person) 素直な súnào na; (beast) 大人しい otónashii

dock [dɑːk] *n* (NAUT) 岸壁 gañpeki; (LAW) 被告席 hikókuseki

♦*vi* (NAUT) 接岸する setsúgan suru; (SPACE) ドッキングする dokkíngu suru

docker [dɑːkˈəːr] *n* 港湾労働者 kōwanrō-dōsha

docks [dɑːks] *npl* (NAUT) 係船きょ keíseñkyo

dockyard [dɑːkˈjɑːrd] *n* 造船所 zōseñjo

doctor [dɑːkˈtəːr] *n* (MED) 医者 ishá; (PhD etc) 博士 hákàse

♦*vt* (drink etc) ...に薬物をこっそり混ぜる ...ni yakúbùtsu wo kossórì mazérù

Doctor of Philosophy *n* 博士号 hákàsegō

doctrine [dɑːkˈtrin] *n* (REL) 教義 kyógi; (POL) 信条 shíñjō

document [dɑːkˈjəmənt] *n* 書類 shorúi

documentary [dɑːkjəmənˈtɑːri:] *adj* (evidence) 書類による shorúi ni yorù

♦*n* (TV, CINEMA) ドキュメンタリー dokyúmeñtarī

documentation [dɑːkjəməntei'ʃən] *n* (papers) 書類 shorúi

dodge [dɑːdʒ] *n* (trick) 策略 sakúryaku

♦*vt* (question) はぐらかす hagúrakasù; (tax) ごまかす gomákasù; (blow, ball) 身を交して避ける mi wò kawáshite sakérù

dodgems [dɑːdʒˈəmz] (*BRIT*) *npl* ドジェム dojému ◇遊園地の乗り物の一種: 相手にぶっつけたりして遊ぶ小型電気自動車 yúeñchi no norímono no isshù: aíte nì buttsúketàri shité asobù kogáta denki jidósha

doe [dou] *n* (deer) 雌 ジカ mesújikà; (rabbit) 雌ウサギ mesúusàgi

does [dʌz] *vb see* **do**

doesn't [dʌzˈnt] = **does not**

dog [dɔːg] *n* (ZOOL) イヌ inú

♦*vt* (subj: person) ...の後を付ける ...no átò wo tsukérù; (: bad luck) ...に付きまとう ...ni tsukímatoù

dog collar *n* (of dog) 首輪 kubiwa, カラー kárā; (REL) ローマンカラー rōmankarā

dog-eared [dɔːgˈiːrd] *adj* (book, paper)

手擦れした tezúre shitá

dogged [dɔːg'id] *adj* (determination, spirit) 根気強い kónkizuyóì

dogma [dɔːg'mə] *n* (REL) 教理 kyóri; (POL) 信条 shínjō

dogmatic [dɔːgmæt'ik] *adj* (attitude, assertion) 独断的な dokúdanteki na

dogsbody [dɔːgz'bɑːdiː] (*BRIT*: *inf*) *n* 下っ端 shitáppa

doings [duː'iŋz] *npl* (activities) 行動 kódō

do-it-yourself [duː'itjurself'] *n* 日曜大工 nichíyōdaíku

doldrums [doul'drəmz] *npl*: **to be in the doldrums** (person) ふさぎ込んでいる fuságikonde irù; (business) 沈滞している chiñtai shite irù

dole [doul] (*BRIT*) *n* (payment) 失業手当 shitsúgyōteàte

on the dole 失業手当を受けて shitsúgyōteàte wo úkète

doleful [doul'fəl] *adj* (voice, expression) 悲しげな kanáshige na

dole out *vt* (food, money) 配る kubárù

doll [dɑːl] *n* (toy) 人形 ningyō; (*US*: *inf*: woman) 美人 bijín

dollar [dɑːl'əːr] (*US etc*) *n* ドル dórù

dolled up [dɑːld^p'] (*inf*) *adj* おめかしした o-mékashi shita

dolphin [dɑːl'fin] *n* イルカ irúka

domain [doumein'] *n* (sphere) 分野 búñya; (empire) 縄張 nawábari

dome [doum] *n* (ARCHIT) 円がい eñgai, ドーム dómu

domestic [dəmes'tik] *adj* (of country: trade, situation) 国内の kokúnai no; (of home: tasks, appliances) 家庭の katéi no

domestic animal 家畜 kachíku

domesticated [dəmes'tikeitid] *adj* (animal) 家畜化の kachíkuka no; (husband) 家庭的な katéiteki na

dominant [dɑːm'ənənt] *adj* (share, part, role) 主な ómò na; (partner) 支配的な shiháiteki na

dominate [dɑːm'əneit] *vt* (discussion) ...の主な話題になる ...no ómò na wadái ni narù; (people) 支配する shíhài suru; (place) ...の上にそびえ立つ ...no ué nì so-

bíetatsù

domineering [dɑːməniːr'iŋ] *adj* (overbearing) 横暴な óbò na

dominion [dəmin'jən] *n* (authority) 支配権 shiháiken; (territory) 領土 ryódò

domino [dɑːm'ənou] (*pl* **dominoes**) *n* (block) ドミノ dómìno

dominoes [dɑːm'ənouz] *n* (game) ドミノ遊び dómìnoasòbi

don [dɑːn] (*BRIT*) *n* (SCOL) 大学教官 daígakukyōkan

donate [dou'neit] *vt* 寄付する kifú suru

donation [dou'neiʃən] *n* 寄付 kifú

done [d^n] *pp of* do

donkey [dɑːŋ'kiː] *n* (ZOOL) ロバ róbà

donor [dou'nəːr] *n* (MED: of blood, heart etc) 提供者 teíkyōsha; (to charity) 寄贈者 kizóshà

don't [dount] = do not

doodle [duː'd'əl] *vi* 落書する rakúgaki suru

doom [duːm] *n* (fate) 悲運 hfun

♦*vt*: **to be doomed to failure** 失敗するに決っている shippái suru ní kimátte irù

doomsday [duːmz'dei] *n* 世の終り yó nò owári

door [dɔːr] *n* 戸 to, 扉 tobíra, ドア dóà

doorbell [dɔːr'bel] *n* 呼び鈴 yobírin

door handle *n* (*gen*) 取っ手 tottě; (of car) ドアハンドル doáhañdoru

doorman [dɔːr'mæn] (*pl* **doormen**) *n* (in hotel) ドアマン doáman

doormat [dɔːr'mæt] *n* (mat) 靴ふき kutsúfùki, マット máttò

doorstep [dɔːr'step] *n* 玄関階段 geñkankaídan

door-to-door [dɔːr'tədɔːr'] *adj* (selling, salesman) 訪問販売の hómonhañbai no

doorway [dɔːr'wei] *n* 戸口 tógùchi

dope [doup] *n* (*inf*: illegal drug) 麻薬 mayáku; (: person) ばか bákà

♦*vt* (horse, person) ...に麻薬を与える ...ni mayáku wò atáerù

dopey [dou'piː] (*inf*) *adj* (groggy) ふらふらになっている furáfura nì natté irù; (stupid) ばかな bákà na

dormant [dɔːr'mənt] *adj* (plant) 休眠中の kyúminchū no

a dormant volcano 休火山 kyūkazàn

dormice [dɔːrˈmais] *npl of* **dormouse**

dormitory [dɔːrˈmitɔːri] *n* (room) 共同寝室 kyōdōshiñshitsu; (*US*: building) 寮 ryō

dormouse [dɔːrˈmaus] (*pl* **dormice**) *n* ヤマネ yamáne

DOS [dous] *n abbr* (COMPUT) (= *disk operating system*) ディスク・オペレーティング・システム disúku operētingu shisutèmu

dosage [douˈsidʒ] *n* 投薬量 tốyakuryò

dose [dous] *n* (of medicine) 一回量 ikkái-ryō

doss house [dɑːs-] (*BRIT*) *n* 安宿 yasúyado, どや doyá

dossier [dɑːsˈiːei] *n* (POLICE etc) 調書一式 chốsho isshìki

dot [dɑːt] *n* (small round mark) 点 teñ; (speck, spot) 染み shimí
♦*vt*: **dotted with** ...が点々とある ...ga teñten tò árù
on the dot (punctually) きっかり kikkárì

dote [dout]: *to dote on vt fus* (child, pet, lover) でき愛する dekíai suru

dot-matrix printer [dɑːtmeitˈriks-] *n* (COMPUT) ドットプリンタ dottốpuriñta

dotted line [dɑːtˈid-] *n* 点線 teñsen

double [dʌbˈəl] *adj* (share, size) 倍の baí no; (chin etc) 二重の nijū no; (yolk) 二つある futátsu arù
♦*adv* (twice): *to cost double* 費用は二倍掛かる híyō wa nibái kakarù
♦*n* (twin) そっくりな人 sokkúrì na hitô
♦*vt* (offer) 二倍にする nibái ni surù; (fold in two: paper, blanket) 二つに折る futátsu nì órù
♦*vi* (population, size) 二倍になる nibái ni narù
on the double, (*BRIT*) *at the double* 駆け足で kakéashi de

double bass *n* コントラバス koñtorabasù

double bed *n* ダブルベッド dabúrubeddò

double bend (*BRIT*) *n* S-カーブ esúkā-bu

double-breasted [dʌbˈəlbresˈtid] *adj* (jacket, coat) ダブルの dabúru no

doublecross [dʌbˈəlkrɔːsˈ] *vt* (trick, betray) 裏切る urágirù

doubledecker [dʌbˈəldekˈəːr] *n* (*also*: **doubledecker bus**) 二階建てバス nikáidatebasù

double glazing [-gleizˈiŋ] (*BRIT*) *n* 二重ガラス nijūgaràsu

double room *n* ダブル部屋 dabúrubeya

doubles [dʌbˈəlz] *n* (TENNIS) ダブルス dábùrusu

doubly [dʌbˈliː] *adv* (especially) 更に sárà ni

doubt [daut] *n* (uncertainty) 疑問 gimón
♦*vt* (disbelieve) 信じない shiñjinaì; (mistrust, suspect) 信用しない shiñ-yō shinaì
to doubt that ... ...だとは思わない ...dá tò wa omówanaì

doubtful [dautˈfəl] *adj* (fact, provenance) 疑わしい utágawashiì; (person) 疑っている utágatte irù

doubtless [dautˈlis] *adv* (probably, almost certainly) きっと ...だろう kíttò ...darô

dough [dou] *n* (CULIN) 生地 kíjì

doughnut [douˈnʌt] *n* ドーナッツ dốnattsu

do up *vt* (laces) 結ぶ musúbu; (buttons) かける kakérù; (dress) しめる shimérù; (renovate: room, house) 改装する kaísō suru

douse [daus] *vt* (drench) ...に水を掛ける ...ni mízù wò kakérù; (extinguish) 消す kesú

dove [dʌv] *n* (bird) ハト hátò

Dover [douˈvəːr] *n* ドーバー dôbā

dovetail [dʌvˈteil] *vi* (*fig*) 合う áù

dowdy [dauˈdiː] *adj* (clothes, person) 野暮な yábò na

do with *vt fus* (need) いる irú; (want) 欲しい hòshíì; (be connected) ...と関係がある ...to káñkei ga árù
I could do with a drink 一杯飲みたい íppai nomítaì
I could do with some help だれかに手伝ってもらいたい darèka ni tetsúdattè

moráitaì

what has it got to do with you? あなたとはどういう関係ですか anáta to wa dô ìu kánkei desù ká

I won't have anything to do with it その件にはかかわりたくない sonô kèn ni wa kakáwaritakùnaì

it has to do with money 金銭関係の事です kínsen kànkei no kotô desù

do without *vi* なしで済ます náshì de sumásù

♦*vt fus* ...なしで間に合せる ...náshì de ma nî awaserù

if you're late for lunch then you'll do without 昼食の時間に遅れたら何もなしだからね chûshoku no jikan ni òkúretarà nanî mo nashì da kara nê

I can do without a car 私には車はいりません watákushi ni wà kurúma wa ìrímasèn

we'll have to do without a holiday this year 私たちは今年休暇を取るのは無理な様です watákushitàchi wa kotôshi kyûka wo torù no wa múrî na yô desù

down [daun] *n* (feathers) 羽毛 ùmô

♦*adv* (downwards) 下へ shitâ e; (on the ground) 下に shitâ ni

♦*prep* (towards lower level) ...の下へ ...no shitâ e; (movement along) ...に沿って ...ni sôttè

♦*vt* (*inf*: drink) 飲む nômù

down with X! 打倒X! datô X!

down-and-out [daun'ənaut] *n* 浮浪者 furôshà, ルンペン rûñpen

down-at-heel [daunæthi:l'] *adj* (shoes etc) 使い古した tsukáifurushità; (appearance, person) 見すぼらしい misúborashiî

downcast [daun'kæst] *adj* がっかりした gakkárî shita

downfall [daun'fɔ:l] *n* 失脚 shikkyáku

downhearted [daun'hɑ:r'tid] *adj* 落胆した rakútan shita

downhill [daun'hil'] *adv*: *to go downhill* (road, person, car) 坂を下る sakâ wò kudárù; (*fig*: person, business) 下り坂になる kudárizàka ni narù

down payment *n* (first payment of

series) 頭金 atámakin; (deposit) 手付金 tetsúkekin

downpour [daun'pɔ:r] *n* 土砂降 dosháburi

downright [daun'rait] *adj* (lie, liar etc) 全くの mattáku no; (refusal) きっぱりした kippárî shita

a downright lie 真っ赤なうそ makká nà úsò

downstairs [daun'ste:rz'] *adv* (below) 下の階に〔で〕 shitâ nò kâî ni〔de〕; (downwards: go, run etc) 下の階へ shitâ nò kâî e

downstream [daun'stri:m'] *adv* (be) 川下に kawáshimo ni; (go) 川下へ kawáshimo e

down-to-earth [dauntuə:rθ'] *adj* (person, solution) 現実的な geñjitsuteki na

downtown [daun'taun'] *adv* 繁華街に〔で, へ〕 hañkagai ni〔de, e〕

down under *adv* (Australia etc) オーストラリア〔ニュージーランド〕に〔で〕ôsutorarìa〔nyûjīrañdo〕ni〔de〕

downward [daun'wə:rd] *adv* 下へ shitâ e

♦*adj* 下への shitâ e nò

downwards [daun'wə:rdz] *adv* 下へ shitâ e

dowry [dau'ri:] *n* (bride's) 持参金 jisáñkin

doz. *abbr* = **dozen**

doze [douz] *vi* 居眠りする inémurì suru

dozen [dʌz'ən] *n* 1ダース ichî dāsu

a dozen books 本12冊 hôñ jûni sàtsu

dozens of 幾つもの îkùtsu mo no

doze off *vi* (nod off) まどろむ madóromù

Dr. *abbr* = **doctor** (in street names) = **drive**

drab [dræb] *adj* (weather, building, clothes) 陰気な iñki nà

draft [dræft] *n* (first version) 草案 sôan; (POL: of bill) 原案 geñ-an; (*also*: **bank draft**) 小切手 kogîtte; (*US*: call-up) 徴兵 chôhei; (of air: *BRIT*: **draught**) すきま風 sukîmakaze; (NAUT: *BRIT*: **draught**) 喫水 kissûi

♦*vt* (plan) 立案する ritsúan suru; (write roughly) ...の下書きをする ...no shitágaki wo surù

draft beer 生ビール namábîru

draftsman [dræfts'mən] (*pl* **draftsmen**: *BRIT* **draughtsman**) *n* 製図工 seízukō

drag [dræg] *vt* (bundle, person) 引きずる hikízurù; (river) さらう saráù

♦*vi* (time, a concert etc) 長く感じられる nágàku kañjirarerù

♦*n* (*inf*: bore) 退屈な人 taíkutsu na hitò; (women's clothing): **in drag** 女装して josō shite

drag on *vi* (case, concert etc) だらだらと長引く dáràdara to nagábikù

dragon [dræg'ən] *n* 竜 ryū

dragonfly [dræg'ənflai] *n* トンボ tóñbo

drain [drein] *n* (in street) 排水口 haísuikō; (on resources, source of loss) 負担 fután

♦*vt* (land, marshes, pond) 干拓する kañtaku suru; (vegetables) ...の水切りをする ...no mizúkiri wò suru

♦*vi* (liquid) 流れる nagárerù

drainage [drei'nidʒ] *n* (system) 排水 haísui; (process) 水はけ mizúhake

drainboard [drein'bɔːrd] (*BRIT* **draining board**) *n* 水切り板 mizúkiribàn

drainpipe [drein'paip] *n* 排水管 haísuikan

drama [drɑːm'ə] *n* (art) 劇文学 gekíbuñgaku; (play) 劇 gékì, ドラマ dórāma; (excitement) ドラマ dórāma

dramatic [drəmæt'ik] *adj* (marked, sudden) 劇的な gekíteki na; (theatrical) 演劇の eñgeki no

dramatist [dræm'ətist] *n* 劇作家 gekísakka

dramatize [dræm'ətaiz] *vt* (events) 劇的に描写する gekíteki nì byṓsha suru; (adapt: for TV, cinema) 脚色する kyakúshoku suru

drank [dræŋk] *pt of* **drink**

drape [dreip] *vt* (cloth, flag) 掛ける kakérù

drapes [dreips] (*US*) *npl* (curtains) カーテン kāten

drastic [dræs'tik] *adj* (measure) 思い切った omóikittà; (change) 抜本的な bappóñteki na

draught [dræft] (*BRIT*) = **draft**

draughtboard [dræft'bɔːrd] (*BRIT*) = **checkerboard**

draughts [dræfts] (*BRIT*) = **checkers**

draughtsman [dræfts'mən] (*BRIT*) = **draftsman**

draw [drɔː] (*pt* **drew**, *pp* **drawn**) *vt* (ART, TECH) 描く kákù; (pull: cart) 引く hikú; (: curtain) 引く hikú, 閉じる tojírù, 閉める shimérù; (take out: gun, tooth) 抜く nukú; (attract: admiration, attention) 引く hikú, 引付ける hikítsukerù; (money) 引出す hikídasù; (wages) もらう moráù

♦*vi* (SPORT) 引分けになる hikíwake ni narù

♦*n* (SPORT) 引分け hikíwake; (lottery) 抽選 chūsen

to draw near (approach: person, event) 近付く chikázukù

drawback [drɔː'bæk] *n* 欠点 kettéñ

drawbridge [drɔː'bridʒ] *n* 跳ね橋 hanébàshi

drawer [drɔː'əːr] *n* (of desk etc) 引出し hikídashi

drawing [drɔː'iŋ] *n* (picture) 図 zu, スケッチ sukétchi; (skill, discipline) 製図 seízu

drawing board *n* 製図板 seízuban

drawing pin (*BRIT*) *n* 画びょう gábyō

drawing room *n* 居間 imá

drawl [drɔːl] *n* のろい話振り noróì hanáshibùri

drawn [drɔːn] *pp of* **draw**

draw out *vi* (lengthen) 引延ばす hikínobasù

♦*vt* (money: from bank) 引出す hikídasù, 下ろす orósù

draw up *vi* (stop) 止まる tomárù

♦*vt* (document) 作成する sakúsei suru; (chair etc) 引寄せる hikíyoserù

dread [dred] *n* (great fear, anxiety) 恐怖 kyṓfu

♦*vt* (fear) 恐れる osórerù

dreadful [dred'fəl] *adj* (weather, day, person etc) いやな iyá nà

dream [driːm] *n* (PSYCH, fantasy, ambition) 夢 yumé

♦*vb* (*pt*, *pp* **dreamed** *or* **dreamt**)

◆*vt* 夢に見る yumé ni mirù

◆*vi* 夢を見る yumé wo mirù

dreamer [dri:'mə:r] *n* 夢を見る人 yumé wo miru hitò; (*fig*) 非現実的な人 hígeñjitsuteki na hitò

dreamt [dremt] *pt, pp* of **dream**

dreamy [dri:'mi:] *adj* (expression, person) うっとりした uttórì shita; (music) 静かな shízùka na

dreary [dri:'i:] *adj* (weather, talk, time) 陰気な iñki na

dredge [dredʒ] *vt* (river, harbor) しゅんせつする shuñsetsu suru

dregs [dregz] *npl* (of drink) かす kásù, おり orí; (of humanity) くず kúzù

drench [drentʃ] *vt* (soak) びしょ濡れにする bishónùre ni suru

dress [dres] *n* (frock) ドレス dóresu; (no pl: clothing) 服装 fukúsō

◆*vt* (child) ...に服を着せる ...ni fukú wò kisérù; (wound) ...の手当をする ...no téàte wo suru

◆*vi* 服を着る fukú wò kirú

to get dressed 服を着る fukú wò kirú

dress circle (*BRIT*) *n* (THEATER) 2階席 nikáìsèki

dresser [dres'ə:r] *n* (*BRIT*: cupboard) 食器戸棚 shokkítodàna; (*US*: chest of drawers) 整理だんす seírìdañsu

dressing [dres'iŋ] *n* (MED) 包帯 hótai; (CULIN: for salad) ドレッシング dorésshiñgu

dressing gown (*BRIT*) *n* ガウン gáùn

dressing room *n* (THEATER) 楽屋 gakúya; (SPORT) 更衣室 kôishìtsu

dressing table *n* 鏡台 kyōdai

dressmaker [dres'meikə:r] *n* 洋裁師 yō-saishì, ドレスメーカー doręsuměkā

dress rehearsal *n* (THEATER) ドレスリハーサル doręsurihāsaru ◇衣装を着けて本番並に行う舞台げいこ íshō wo tsukétè hoñbannami nì okónaù butáìgeìko

dress up *vi* (wear best clothes) 盛装する seísō suru; (in costume) 仮装する kasō suru

dressy [dres'i:] (*inf*) *adj* (smart: clothes) スマートな sumátò na

drew [dru:] *pt* of **draw**

dribble [drib'əl] *vi* (baby) よだれを垂らす yodáre wò tarásu

◆*vt* (ball) ドリブルする doríbùru suru

dried [draid] *adj* (fruit) 干した hóshìta, 干し... hoshí...; (eggs, milk) 粉末の fuñmatsu no

drier [drai'ə:r] *n* = **dryer**

drift [drift] *n* (of current etc) 方向 hōkō; (of snow) 吹きだまり fukídamarì; (meaning) 言わんとする事 iwán tò suru kotò, 意味 ímì

◆*vi* (boat) 漂流する hyōryū suru; (sand, snow) 吹寄せられる fukíyoserarerù

driftwood [drift'wud] *n* 流木 ryūboku

drill [dril] *n* (*also*: **drill bit**) ドリル先 dorírusaki, ドリル dórìru; (machine: for DIY, dentistry, mining etc) ドリル dórìru; (MIL) 教練 kyōren

◆*vt* (troops) 教練する kyōren suru

◆*vi* (for oil) ボーリングする bőriñgu suru

to drill a hole in something ドリルで...に穴を開ける dórìru de ...ni aná wò akérù

drink [driŋk] *n* (*gen*) 飲物 nomímono, ドリンク doríñku; (alcoholic drink) 酒 saké; (sip) 一口 hitókùchi

◆*vb* (*pt* **drank**, *pp* **drunk**)

◆*vt* 飲む nómù

◆*vi* 飲む nómù

to have a drink 1杯飲む íppaì nómù

a drink of water 水1杯 mizú íppaì

drinker [driŋ'kə:r] *n* (of alcohol) 酒飲み sakénomì

drinking water [driŋ'kiŋ-] *n* 飲料水 iñryōsui

drip [drip] *n* (dripping, noise) 滴り shitátari; (one drip) 滴 shizúku; (MED) 点滴 tefíteki

◆*vi* (water, rain) 滴る shitátarù; (tap) ...から水が垂れる ...kara mizú gà tarérù

drip-dry [drip'drai] *adj* (shirt) ドリップドライの doríppudorài no

dripping [drip'iŋ] *n* (CULIN) 肉汁 nikújū

drive [draiv] *n* (journey) ドライブ doráìbu; (*also*: **driveway**) 車道 shadō ◇私有地内を通って公道と家などをつなぐ私道を

指す shiyúchinaì wo tôtte kôdō tò ié nadò wo tsunágù shidô wo sásù; (energy) 精力 sêīryoku; (campaign) 運動 uñdô; (COMPUT: also: **disk drive**) ディスクドライブ disúkudoraìbu

♦*vb* (*pt* **drove**, *pp* **driven**)

♦*vt* (car) 運転する uñten suru; (push: *also* TECH: motor etc) 動かす ugókasù; (nail): *to drive something into* ...を...に 打込む ...wo ...ni uchíkomù

♦*vi* (AUT: at controls) 運転する uñten suru; (travel) 車で行く kurúma de ikù

left-/right-hand drive 左〔右〕ハンドル hidári〔migî〕hañdoru

to drive someone mad ...をいらいら させる ...wo íraira saséru

drivel [driv'əl] (*inf*) *n* 与太話 yotábanàshi

driven [driv'ən] *pp of* drive

driver [drai'və:r] *n* (of own car) 運転者 uñteñsha, ドライバー doráìbā; (chauffeur) お抱え運転手 o-kákae unteñshu; (of taxi, bus) 運転手 uñteñshu; (RAIL) 運転士 uñteñshi

driver's license (*US*) *n* 運転免許証 uñtenmenkyoshō

driveway [draiv'wei] *n* 車道 shadô ◇ 私有地内を通って公道と家などをつなぐ私道を指す shiyúchinaì wo tôtte kôdō tò ié nadò wo tsunágù shidô wò sásù

driving [drai'viŋ] *n* 運転 uñten

driving instructor *n* 運転指導者 uñtenshidōsha

driving lesson *n* 運転教習 uñtenkyōshū

driving licence (*BRIT*) *n* 運転免許証 uñtenmenkyoshō

driving mirror *n* バックミラー bakkúmirà

driving school *n* 自動車教習所 jidôsha-kyōshùjo

driving test *n* 運転免許試験 uñtenmenkyoshikèn

drizzle [driz'əl] *n* 霧雨 kirísame

drone [droun] *n* (noise) ぶーんという音 bûñ to iú otò; (male bee) 雄バチ osúbàchi

drool [dru:l] *vi* (dog etc) よだれを垂らす yodáre wo tarásù

droop [dru:p] *vi* (flower) しおれる shióre-

rù; (of person: shoulders) 肩を落とす kátà wo otósù; (: head) うつむく utsúmukù

drop [drɑ:p] *n* (of water) 滴 shizúku; (lessening) 減少 geñshō; (fall) 落差 rákùsa

♦*vt* (allow to fall: object) 落す otósù; (voice) 潜める hisómerù; (eyes) 落す otósù; (reduce: price) 下げる sagérù; (set down from car) 降ろす orósù; (omit: name from list etc) 削除する sakújo suru

♦*vi* (object) 落ちる ochírù; (wind) 弱まる yowámarù

drop off *vi* (go to sleep) 眠る nemúrù

♦*vt* (passenger) 降ろす orósù

drop out *vi* (withdraw) 脱退する dattái suru

drop-out [drɑ:p'aut] *n* (from society) 社会からの脱落者 shákài kara no datsúrakushà; (SCOL) 学校からの中退者 gakkô kara nò chútaishà

dropper [drɑ:p'ə:r] *n* スポイト supóìto

droppings [drɑ:p'iŋz] *npl* (of bird, mouse) ふん fúñ

drops [drɑ:ps] *npl* (MED: for eyes) 点眼剤 teñgañzai; (: for ears) 点耳薬 teñjiyàku

drought [draut] *n* かんばつ kañbatsu

drove [drouv] *pt of* drive

drown [draun] *vt* (kill: person, animal) 水死させる suíshi saserù; (*fig*: voice, noise) 聞えなくする kikóenakù suru, 消す kesú

♦*vi* (person, animal) おぼれ死ぬ obóreshinù

drowsy [drau'zi:] *adj* (sleepy) 眠い nemúì

drudgery [drʌdʒ'ə:ri:] *n* (uninteresting work) 骨折り仕事 honéorishigòto

drug [drʌg] *n* (MED) 薬剤 yakúzai, 薬 kusúri; (narcotic) 麻薬 mayáku

♦*vt* (sedate: person, animal) 薬で眠らせる kusúri dè nemúraserù

to be on drugs 麻薬を打って〔飲んで〕いる mayáku wò útte〔nôñde〕irù

hard/soft drugs 中毒性の強い〔弱い〕麻薬 chúdokusei nò tsuyôî〔yowáî〕mayáku

drug addict *n* 麻薬常習者 mayákujō-shūsha

druggist [drʌg'ist] (*US*) *n* (person) 薬剤師 yakúzaìshi; (store) 薬屋 kusúriya

drugstore [drʌg'stɔːr] (*US*) *n* ドラッグストア dorággusutòa

drum [drʌm] *n* (MUS) 太鼓 taíko, ドラム dóràmu; (for oil, petrol) ドラム缶 dorámukaǹ

drummer [drʌm'əːr] *n* ドラマー dorámà

drums [drʌmz] *npl* ドラム dóràmu

drunk [drʌŋk] *pp of* drink
♦*adj* (with alcohol) 酔っ払った yoppárattà
♦*n* (*also*: **drunkard**) 酔っ払い yoppárai

drunken [drʌŋ'kən] *adj* (laughter, party) 酔っ払いの yoppárai no; (person) 酔っ払った yoppárattà

dry [drai] *adj* (ground, climate, weather, skin) 乾いた kawáita, 乾燥した kañsō shita; (day) 雨の降らない ámè no furánaì; (lake, riverbed) 干上がった hiágattà; (humor) 皮肉っぽい hiníkuppòi; (wine) 辛口の karákuchi no
♦*vt* (ground, clothes etc) 乾かす kawákasù; (tears) ふく fukú
♦*vi* (paint etc) 乾く kawákù

dry-cleaner's [drai'kliːnəːrz] *n* ドライクリーニング屋 doráikurīninguyà

dry-cleaning [drai'kliːniŋ] *n* ドライクリーニング doráikurīnìgu

dryer [drai'əːr] *n* (*also*: **hair dryer**) ヘアドライヤー heádoraìyà; (for laundry) 乾燥機 kañsōki; (*US*: spin-drier) 脱水機 dassúiki

dryness [drai'nis] *n* (of ground, climate, weather, skin) 乾燥 kañsō

dry rot *n* 乾腐病 kañpubyò

dry up *vi* (river, well) 干上がる hiágarù

DSS [diːeses'] (*BRIT*) *n abbr* (= *Department of Social Security*) 社会保障省 sha-káihoshòshō

dual [duː'əl] *adj* 二重の nijū no

dual carriageway (*BRIT*) *n* 中央分離帯のある道路 chūōbuñritai no árù dōrò

dual nationality *n* 二重国籍 nijūkoku-sèki

dual-purpose [duː'əlpəːr'pəs] *adj* 二重目的の nijūmokutèki no

dubbed [dʌbd] *adj* (CINEMA) 吹き替えの fukíkae no

dubious [duː'biːəs] *adj* (claim, reputation, company) いかがわしい ikágawashiì; (person) 疑っている utágatte irù

Dublin [dʌb'lin] *n* ダブリン dábùrin

duchess [dʌtʃ'is] *n* 公爵夫人 kōshakufujìn

duck [dʌk] *n* (ZOOL, CULIN: domestic bird) アヒル ahíru; (wild bird) カモ kámò
♦*vi* (*also*: **duck down**) かがむ kagámù

duckling [dʌk'liŋ] *n* (ZOOL, CULIN: domestic bird) アヒルの子 ahíru no kò; (: wild bird) カモの子 kámò no ko

duct [dʌkt] *n* (ELEC, TECH) ダクト dákùto; (ANAT) 管 kán

dud [dʌd] *n* (bomb, shell etc) 不発弾 fuhátsudàn; (object, tool etc) 欠陥品 kekkáñhin
♦*adj*: **dud cheque** (*BRIT*) 不渡り小切手 fuwátarikogittè

due [duː] *adj* (expected: meeting, publication, arrival) 予定した yotéi shita; (owed: money) 払われるべき haráware-rubeki; (proper: attention, consideration) 当然の tōzen no
♦*n*: **to give someone his (or her) due** ...に当然の物を与える ...ni tōzen no monò wo atáerù
♦*adv*: **due north** 真北に ma-kítà ni
in due course (when the time is right) 時が来たら tokí ga kitarà; (eventually) やがて yagáte
due to (owing to) ...が原因で ...ga señ-in de
to be due to do ...する事になっている ...surú kotò ni natté irù

duel [duː'əl] *n* (*also fig*) 決闘 kettó

dues [duːz] *npl* (for club, union) 会費 káìhi; (in harbor) 使用料 shiyóryō

duet [duːet'] *n* (MUS) 二重唱 nijūshō, デュエット dúètto

duffel bag [dʌf'əl-] *n* 合切袋 gassáibukùro

duffel coat [dʌf'əl-] *n* ダッフルコート daffúrukòto ◇丈夫なフード付き防寒コート jōbu nà fúdotsuki bōkan kòto

dug [dʌg] *pt*, *pp of* **dig**

duke [duːk] *n* 公爵 kōshaku

dull [dʌl] *adj* (weak: light) 暗い kuráì;

(intelligence, wit) 鈍い nibúī; (boring: event) 退屈な taíkutsu na; (sound, pain) 鈍い nibúī; (gloomy: weather, day) 陰気な iñki na

♦*vt* (pain, grief) 和らげる yawáragerù; (mind, senses) 鈍くする nfbùku suru

duly [du:'li:] *adv* (properly) 正当に seítō ni; (on time) 予定通りに yotéidòri ni

dumb [dʌm] *adj* (mute, silent) 話せない hanásenaī; (*pej*: stupid) ばかな bákà na

dumbfounded [dʌmfaund'id] *adj* あぜんとした azén tò shita

dummy [dʌm'i:] *n* (tailor's model) 人台 jiñdai; (TECH, COMM: mock-up) 模型 mokéi; (*BRIT*: for baby) おしゃぶり o-shábùri

♦*adj* (bullet) 模擬の mógì no; (firm) ダミーの dámì no

dump [dʌmp] *n* (*also*: rubbish dump) ごみ捨て場 gomísuteba; (*inf*: place) いやな場所 iyá na bashò

♦*vt* (put down) 落す otósù; (get rid of) 捨てる sutérù; (COMPUT: data) 打ち出す uchídasù, ダンプする dáñpu suru

dumpling [dʌm'pliŋ] *n* (CULIN: with meat etc) 団子 dañgo

dumpy [dʌm'pi:] *adj* (person) ずんぐりした zuñgurí shita

dunce [dʌns] *n* (SCOL) 劣等生 rettősei

dune [du:n] *n* (in desert, on beach) 砂丘 sakyū

dung [dʌŋ] *n* (AGR, ZOOL) ふん fúñ

dungarees [dʌŋgəri:z'] *npl* オーバーオール ōbāòru

dungeon [dʌn'dʒən] *n* 地下ろう chikárò

duo [du:'ou] *n* (*gen*, MUS) ペア péà

dupe [du:p] *n* (victim) かも kámò

♦*vt* (trick) だます damásù

duplex [du:'pleks] (*US*) *n* (house) 2世帯用住宅 nisétaiyōjūtaku; (apartment) 複層式アパート fukúsōushikiapàto

duplicate [*n* du:'plikit *vb* du:'plikeit] *n* (of document, key etc) 複製 fukúsei

♦*vt* (copy) 複製する fukúsei suru; (photocopy) ...のコピーを取る ...no kópī wo to-rù, ...をコピーする ...wo kópī suru; (repeat) 再現する saígen suru

in duplicate 2部で níbù de

duplicity [du:plis'əti:] *n* (deceit) いかさま ikásama

durable [dur'əbəl] *adj* (goods, materials) 丈夫な jōbu na

duration [durei'ʃən] *n* (of process, event) 継続期間 keízokukikan

duress [dures'] *n*: *under duress* (moral, physical) 強迫 kyōhaku

during [dur'iŋ] *prep* ...の間に ...no aída ni

dusk [dʌsk] *n* 夕暮 yúgure

dust [dʌst] *n* ほこり hokóri

♦*vt* (furniture) ...のほこりを拭く ...no hokóri wò fukù; (cake etc): *to dust with* ...に... を振掛ける ...ni ...wo furíkakerù

dustbin [dʌst'bin] (*BRIT*) *n* ごみ箱 gomíbàko

duster [dʌs'tə:r] *n* (cloth) 雑きん zőkin

dustman [dʌst'mæn] (*BRIT* *pl* **dustmen**) *n* ごみ収集人 gomíshūshūnin

dusty [dʌs'ti:] *adj* (road) ほこりっぽい hokórippoī; (furniture) ほこりだらけの hokóridaràke no

Dutch [dʌtʃ] *adj* オランダの oráñda no; (LING) オランダ語の orándagò no

♦*n* (LING) オランダ語 orándagò

♦*npl*: *the Dutch* オランダ人 orándajìn

to go Dutch (*inf*) 割勘にする waríkan ni surù

Dutchman/woman [dʌtʃ'mən/wumən] (*pl* **Dutchmen/Dutchwomen**) *n* オランダ人男性〔女性〕orándajin dañsei 〔joséi〕

dutiful [du:'tifəl] *adj* (son, daughter) 従順な jūjun na

duty [du:'ti:] *n* (responsibility) 義務 gímù; (tax) 税金 zeíkin

on/off duty (policeman, nurse) 当番〔非番〕で tōban 〔híban〕de

duty-free [du:'ti:fri:'] *adj* (drink, cigarettes) 免税の meñzei no

duvet [du:'vei] (*BRIT*) *n* 掛布団 kakébutòn

dwarf [dwɔ:rf] (*pl* **dwarves**) *n* (person) 小人 kobíto; (animal, plant) わい小種 waíshōshù

♦*vt* 小さく見せる chíisaku misérù

dwarves [dwɔ:rvz] *npl of* **dwarf**

dwell [dwel] (*pt*, *pp* **dwelt**) *vi* (reside,

stay) 住む súmù

dwelling [dwel'iŋ] *n* (house) 住居 júkyò

dwell on *vt fus* (brood on) 長々と考える naganaga tò kañgaerù

dwelt [dwelt] *pt, pp of* **dwell**

dwindle [dwin'dəl] *vi* (interest, attendance) 減る hérù

dye [dai] *n* (for hair, cloth) 染料 señryò
♦*vt* 染める somérù

dying [dai'iŋ] *adj* (person, animal) 死に掛かっている shiníkakatte irù

dyke [daik] (*BRIT*) *n* (wall) 堤防 teíbō

dynamic [dainæm'ik] *adj* (leader, force) 力強い chikárazuyoì

dynamite [dai'nəmait] *n* ダイナマイト daínamaìto

dynamo [dai'nəmou] *n* (ELEC) 発電機 hatsúdeñki, ダイナモ daínamo

dynasty [dai'nəsti:] *n* (family, period) 王朝 ốchō

dyslexia [dislek'si:ə] *n* 読書障害 dokúshoshōgai

E

E [i:] *n* (MUS: note) ホ音 hó-oñ; (: key) ホ調 hóchō

each [i:tʃ] *adj* (thing, person, idea etc) それぞれの sorézòre no
♦*pron* (each one) それぞれ sorézòre
each other 互いを(に) tagái wò (nì)
they hate each other 彼らは互いに憎み合っている kárèra wa tagái nì nikúmiatte irù
they have 2 books each 彼らはそれぞれ2冊の本を持っている kárèra wa sorézòre nísàtsu no hốñ wo motté irù

eager [i:'gə:r] *adj* (keen) 熱心な nesshín na
to be eager to do something 一生懸命に...をしたがっている isshôkeñmei ni ...wo shitágatte irù
to be eager for とても...をほしがっている totémo ...wo hoshígatte irù

eagle [i:'gəl] *n* ワシ washí

ear [i:r] *n* (ANAT) 耳 mimí; (of corn) 穂 hó

earache [i:r'eik] *n* 耳の痛み mimí nò itámi

eardrum [i:r'drʌm] *n* 鼓膜 komáku

earl [ə:rl] (*BRIT*) *n* 伯爵 hakúshaku

earlier [ə:r'li:ə:r] *adj* (date, time, edition etc) 前の máè no
♦*adv* (leave, go etc) もっと早く mốttò háyàku

early [ə:r'li:] *adv* (in day, month etc) 早く háyàku; (ahead of time) 早めに hayáme ni
♦*adj* (near the beginning: work, hours) 早朝の sốchō no; (Christians, settlers) 初期の shốkì no; (sooner than expected: departure) 早めの hayáme no; (quick: reply) 早期の sốki no
an early death 早死に hayájinì
to have an early night 早めに寝る hayáme nì nérù
in the early/early in the spring 春先に harúsaki ni
in the early/early in the 19th century 19世紀の初めに júkyūseìki no hajíme ni

early retirement *n* 早めの引退 hayáme nò iñtai

earmark [i:r'ma:rk] *vt*: *to earmark (for)* (...に) 当てる (...ni) atérù

earn [ə:rn] *vt* (salary etc) 稼ぐ kaségù; (COMM: interest) 生む umú; (praise) 受ける ukérù

earnest [ə:r'nist] *adj* (wish, desire) 心からの kokórò kara no; (person, manner) 真剣な shiñken na
in earnest 真剣に shiñken ni

earnings [ə:r'niŋz] *npl* (personal) 収入 shúnyū; (of company etc) 収益 shōeki

earphones [i:r'founz] *npl* イヤホーン iyáhòñ

earring [i:r'riŋ] *n* イヤリング íyàringu

earshot [i:r'ʃɑt] *n*: *within earshot* 聞える範囲に kikóerù háñ-i ni

earth [ə:rθ] *n* (planet) 地球 chikyú; (land surface) 地面 jímèn; (soil) 土 tsuchí; (*BRIT*: ELEC) アース ầsu
♦*vt* (*BRIT*: ELEC) アースに落す ầsu ni otósù

earthenware [ə:r'θənwe:r] *n* 土器 dókì

earthquake [ə:rθ'kweik] *n* 地震 jishín

earthy [ə:r'θi:] *adj* (*fig*: humor: vulgar) 下品な gehín na

ease [i:z] *n* (easiness) 容易さ yóisà; (comfort) 楽 rakú

♦*vt* (lessen: problem, pain) 和らげる yawáragerù; (: tension) 緩和する kańwa suru

to ease something in/out ゆっくりと ...を入れる〔出す〕yukkúrì to ...wo irérù 〔dásù〕

at ease! (MIL) 休め! yasúmè!

easel [i:'zəl] *n* 画架 gáká, イーゼル ízèru

ease off *vi* (lessen: wind) 弱まる yowámarù; (: rain) 小降りになる kobúri ni narù; (slow down) スピードを落す supídò wo otósù

ease up *vi* = **ease off**

easily [i:'zili:] *adv* (with ease) 容易に yói ni; (in comfort) 楽に rakú ni

east [i:st] *n* (direction) 東 higáshi; (of country, town) 東部 tóbù

♦*adj* (region) 東の higáshi no; (wind) 東からの higáshi karà no

♦*adv* 東に〔へ〕higáshi ni 〔e〕

the East (Orient) 東洋 tóyò; (POL) 東欧 tóò, 東ヨーロッパ higáshi yòroppa

Easter [i:s'tə:r] *n* 復活祭 fukkátsusài, イースター ísutā

Easter egg *n* イースターエッグ ísutaeggù ◇復活祭の飾り、プレゼントなどに使う色や模様を塗ったゆで卵 fukkátsusài no kazári, purézènto nádò ni tsukáu irò ya moyó wo nuttá yudétamàgo

easterly [i:s'tə:rli:] *adj* (to the east: direction, point) 東への higáshi e nò; (from the east: wind) 東からの higáshi kara nò

eastern [i:s'tə:rn] *adj* (GEO) 東の higáshi no; (oriental) 東洋の tóyò no; (communist) 東欧の tóò no, 東ヨーロッパの higáshi yòroppa no

East Germany *n* 東ドイツ higáshi dóìtsu

eastward(s) [i:st'wə:rd(z)] *adv* 東へ higáshi e

easy [i:'zi:] *adj* (simple) 簡単な kańtan na; (relaxed) 寛いだ kutsúroìda; (com-

fortable) 楽な rakú na; (victim) だまされやすい damásareyasuì; (prey) 捕まりやすい tsukámariyasuì

♦*adv*: *to take it/things easy* (go slowly) 気楽にやる kiráku ni yarù; (not worry) 心配しない shíñpai shinaì; (rest) 休む yasúmù

easy chair *n* 安楽いす añrakuisù

easy-going [i:'zi:gou'iŋ] *adj* 穏やかな o-dáyàka na

eat [i:t] (*pt* **ate**, *pp* **eaten**) *vt* (breakfast, lunch, food etc) 食べる tabérù

♦*vi* 食べる tabérù

eat away *vt fus* = **eat into**

eat into *vt fus* (metal) 腐食する fushóku suru; (savings) ...に食込む ...ni kuíkomù

eau de Cologne [ou' də kəloun'] *n* オーデコロン ódekoròn

eaves [i:vz] *npl* (of house) 軒 nokí

eavesdrop [i:vz'dra:p] *vi*: *to eavesdrop (on)* (person, conversation) (...を) 盗み聞きする (...wo) nusúmigiki suru

ebb [eb] *n* (of sea, tide) 引く事 hikú kotò

♦*vi* (tide, sea) 引く hikú; (*fig*: *also*: **ebb away**: strength, feeling) 段々なくなる dańdan nakùnaru

ebony [eb'əni:] *n* (wood) 黒たん kokútan

EC [i:'si:'] *n abbr* (= *European Community*) 欧州共同体 óshūkyódòtai

eccentric [iksen'trik] *adj* (choice, views) 風変りな fúgawàri na

♦*n* (person) 変り者 kawárimono

ecclesiastical [ikli:zi:æs'tikəl] *adj* 教会の kyókai no

echo [ek'ou] (*pl* **echoes**) *n* (of noise) こだま kodáma, 反響 hańkyō

♦*vt* (repeat) 繰返す kuríkaesù

♦*vi* (sound) 反響する hańkyō suru; (place) ...で鳴り響く ...de naríhibikù

echoes [ek'ouz] *npl* of **echo**

éclair [ikler'] *n* (cake) エクレア ekúrea

eclipse [iklips'] *n* (*also*: **eclipse of the sun**) 日食 nisshóku; (*also*: **eclipse of the moon**) 月食 gesshóku

ecology [ika:l'ədʒi:] *n* (environment) 環境 kańkyō, エコロジー ekórojì; (SCOL) 生態学 seítaigàku

economic [i:kəna:m'ik] *adj* (system, history) 経済の keízai no; (BRIT: profitable: business etc) もうかる mōkarù

economical [i:kənə'mikəl] *adj* (system, car, machine) 経済的な keízaiteki na; (person) 倹約な keń-yaku na

economics [i:kənə'miks] *n* (SCOL) 経済学 keízaigàku
◆*npl* (of project, situation) 経済問題 kefzaimoñdai

economist [ika:n'əmist] *n* 経済学者 keízaigakùsha

economize [ika:n'əmaiz] *vi* (make savings) 節約する setsúyaku suru

economy [ika:n'əmi:] *n* (of country) 経済 keízai; (financial prudence) 節約 setsúyaku

economy class *n* (AVIAT) エコノミークラス ekónomíkuràsu

economy size *n* (COMM) お買い得サイズ o-káidoku saìzu

ecstasy [ek'stəsi:] *n* (rapture) 狂喜 kyōki, エクスタシー ekúsutashī

ecstatic [ekstæt'ik] *adj* (welcome, reaction) 熱烈な netsúretsu na; (person) 無我夢中になった múgàmuchū ni nattà

ecumenical [ekju:men'ikəl] *adj* 超宗派の chóshūha no

eczema [ek'səmə] *n* (MED) 湿しん shisshín

edge [edʒ] *n* (border: of lake, table, chair etc) 縁 fuchí; (of knife etc) 刃 há
◆*vt* (trim) 縁取りする fuchídori suru
on edge (fig) = **edgy**
to edge away from じりじり...から離れる jfrìjiri ...kara hanárerù

edgeways [edʒ'weiz] *adv*: **he couldn't get a word in edgeways** 何一つ発言出来なかった nanihitótsu hatsúgen dekinakattà

edgy [edʒ'i:] *adj* (nervous, agitated) いらいらした fràira shita

edible [ed'əbəl] *adj* (mushroom, plant) 食用の shokúyō no

edict [i:'dikt] *n* (order) 政令 seírei

edifice [ed'əfis] *n* (building, structure) 大建造物 daíkenzōbùtsu

Edinburgh [ed'ənbə:rə] *n* エジンバラ ejínbara

edit [ed'it] *vt* (text, report) 校正する kōsei suru; (book, film, newspaper etc) 編集する heñshū suru

edition [idiʃ'ən] *n* (of book) 版 háñ; (of newspaper, magazine) 号 gō; (TV, RADIO) 回 kaí

editor [ed'itə:r] *n* (of newspaper) 編集局長 heñshūkyokuchō, デスク désùku; (of magazine) 編集長 heñshūchō; (of column: foreign/political editor) 編集主任 heñshūshuniñ; (of book) 編集者 heñshūsha

editorial [editɔ:r'i:əl] *adj* (staff, policy, control) 編集の heñshū no
◆*n* (of newspaper) 社説 shasétsu

educate [edʒ'u:keit] *vt* (teach) 教育する kyōiku suru; (instruct) ...に教える ...ni oshíerù

education [edʒu:kei'ʃən] *n* (schooling, teaching) 教育 kyōiku; (knowledge, culture) 教養 kyōyō

educational [edʒu:kei'ʃənəl] *adj* (institution, policy etc) 教育の kyōiku no; (experience, toy) 教育的な kyōikuteki na

EEC [i:i:si:'] *n abbr* (= *European Economic Community*) 欧州経済共同体 ōshūkeizaikyōdōtai

eel [i:l] *n* ウナギ unági

eerie [i:'ri:] *adj* (strange, mysterious) 不気味な bukími na

effect [ifek'] *n* (result, consequence) 結果 kekká; (impression: of speech, picture etc) 効果 kōka
◆*vt* (repairs) 行う okónau; (savings etc) ...に成功する ...ni seíkō suru
to take effect (law) 実施される jisshí sarerù; (drug) 効き始める kikíhajimerù
in effect 要するに yō surù ni

effective [ifek'tiv] *adj* (successful) 効果的な kōkateki na; (actual: leader, command) 実際の jissái no

effectively [ifek'tivli:] *adv* (successfully) 効果的に kōkateki ni; (in reality) 実際には jissái ni wa

effectiveness [ifek'tivnis] *n* (success) 有効性 yūkōsei

effeminate [ifem'ənit] *adj* (boy, man) 女々しい meméshiǐ

effervescent [efə:rves'ənt] *adj* (drink) 炭酸ガス入りの tańsangasuirī no

efficacy [ef'ikəsi:] *n* (effectiveness) 有効性 yūkōsei

efficiency [ifiʃ'ənsi:] *n* (of person, organization) 能率 nōritsu; (of machine) 効率 kōritsu

efficient [ifiʃ'ənt] *adj* (person, organization) 能率的な nōritsuteki na; (machine) 効率の良い kōritsu no yoî

effigy [ef'idʒi:] *n* (image) 像 zō

effort [ef'ə:rt] *n* (endeavor) 努力 dóryoku; (determined attempt) 試み kokóromì, 企て kuwádate; (physical/mental exertion) 苦労 kúrò

effortless [ef'ə:rtlis] *adj* (achievement) 楽な rakú nà; (style) ごく自然な gókù shizén na

effrontery [ifrʌn'tə:ri:] *n* (cheek, nerve) ずうずうしさ zūzúshisà

effusive [ifju:'siv] *adj* (handshake, welcome) 熱烈な netsúretsu na

e.g. [i:dʒi:'] *adv abbr* (= *exempli gratia*) 例えば tatóeba

egg [eg] *n* 卵 tamágò
hard-boiled/soft-boiled egg 堅ゆで〔半熟〕卵 katáyude(hanjuku)tamâgo

eggcup [eg'kʌp] *n* エッグカップ eggúkappù

egg on *vt* (in fight etc) そそのかす sosónokasù

eggplant [eg'plænt] (*esp US*) *n* (aubergine) ナス násù

eggshell [eg'ʃel] *n* 卵の殻 tamágò no kará

ego [i:'gou] *n* (self-esteem) 自尊心 jisóñshin

egotism [i:'gətizəm] *n* 利己主義 rikóshugì

egotist [i:'gətist] *n* 利己主義者 rikóshugishà, エゴイスト egóisùto

Egypt [i:'dʒipt] *n* エジプト ejíputo

Egyptian [idʒip'ʃən] *adj* エジプトの ejíputo no
◆*n* エジプト人 ejíputojîn

eiderdown [ai'də:rdaun] *n* (quilt) 羽布団 hanébutòn

eight [eit] *num* 八 (の) hachî(no), 八つ (の) yattsú no

eighteen [ei'ti:n'] *num* 十八 (の) júhachi (no)

eighth [eitθ] *num* 第八の dáîhachi no

eighty [ei'ti:] *num* 八十 (の) hachî-jù(no)

Eire [e:r'ə] *n* アイルランド aîrurañdo

either [i:'ðə:r] *adj* (one or other) どちらかの dóchìraka no; (both, each) 両方の ryóhō no
◆*pron: either (of them)* どちらも...ない dóchìra mo ...nai
◆*adv* ...も...ない ...mo ...nâî
◆*conj: either yes or no* はいかいいえかはî ka iîe kà
on either side 両側に ryógawa ni
I don't like either どちらも好きじゃない dóchìra mo sukî ja naî
no, I don't either いいえ、私もしない iîe, watákushi mò shinâî

eject [idʒekt'] *vt* (object) 放出する hōshutsu suru; (tenant) 立ちのかせる tachínokaserù; (gatecrasher etc) 追出す oídasù

eke [i:k]: *to eke out vt* (make last) 間に合せる ma nî awaserù

elaborate [*n* ilæb'ə:rit *vb* ilæb'ə:reit] *adj* (complex: network, plan, ritual) 複雑な fukúzatsu na
◆*vt* (expand) 拡張する kakúchō suru; (refine) 洗練する señren suru
◆*vi: to elaborate (on)* (idea, plan etc) (...を) 詳しく説明する (...wo) kuwáshikù setsúmei suru

elapse [ilæps'] *vi* (time) 過ぎる sugírù

elastic [ilæs'tik] *n* (material) ゴムひも gomúhimo
◆*adj* (stretchy) 弾力性のある dañryokusei no arù; (adaptable) 融通の利く yūzū no kikù

elastic band (*BRIT*) *n* 輪ゴム wagómu

elated [ilei'tid] *adj: to be elated* 大喜びになっている ōyorðkobi ni natté irù

elation [ilei'ʃən] *n* (happiness, excitement) 大喜び ōyorðkobi

elbow [el'bou] *n* (ANAT: *also* of sleeve) ひじ hijî

elder [el'də:r] *adj* (brother, sister etc) 年上の toshíue no

♦*n* (tree) ニワトコ niwátoko; (older person: *gen pl*) 年上の人々 toshíue no hitobìto

elderly [el'də:rli:] *adj* (old) 年寄の toshíyorì no

♦*npl: the elderly* 老人 rójin

eldest [el'dist] *adj* 最年長の saínenchō no

♦*n* 最年長の人 saínenchō no hitó

the eldest child/son/daughter 長子〔長男，長女〕chóshì(chónàn, chójò)

elect [ilekt'] *vt* (government, representative, spokesman etc) 選出する seńshutsu suru

♦*adj: the president elect* 次期大統領 jíkìdaítòryō ◇当選したものの，まだ就任していない人について言う tósen shita mono nò, mádà shúnin shite inaî hitó nì tsúìte iú

to elect to do (choose) ...する事にする ...surú kotò ni suru

election [ilek'ʃən] *n* (voting) 選挙 séñkyo; (installation) 当選 tósen

electioneering [ilekʃəni:'riŋ] *n* (campaigning) 選挙運動 seńkyouńdō

elector [ilek'tə:r] *n* (voter) 有権者 yúkeñsha

electoral [ilek'tə:rəl] *adj* (register, roll) 有権者の yúkeñsha no

electorate [ilek'tə:rit] *n* (of constituency, country) 有権者 yúkeñsha ◇総称 sóshō

electric [ilek'trik] *adj* (machine, current, power) 電気の déñki no

electrical [ilek'trikəl] *adj* (appliance, system, energy) 電気の déñki no

electric blanket *n* 電気毛布 deńkimōfu

electric chair (*US*) *n* 電気いす deńkiîsu

electric fire *n* 電気ヒーター deńkihītā

electrician [ilektriʃ'ən] *n* 電気屋 deńkiyà

electricity [ilektris'əti:] *n* 電気 déñki

electrify [ilek'trəfai] *vt* (fence) 帯電させる taíden saserù; (rail network) 電化する deńka suru; (audience) ぎょっとさせる gyóttō saserù

electrocute [ilek'trəkju:t] *vt* 感電死させる kańdeñshi saserù

electrode [ilek'troud] *n* 電極 deńkyoku

electron [ilek'trɑ:n] *n* (PHYSICS) 電子 denshi

electronic [ilektrɑ:n'ik] *adj* (device, equipment) 電子の déñshi no

electronic mail *n* 電子郵便 deńshiyùbin

electronics [ilektrɑ:n'iks] *n* (industry, technology) 電子工学 deńshikōgaku

elegance [el'əgəns] *n* (of person, building) 優雅さ yúgàsa, エレガンス éregansu; (of idea, plan) 見事さ migótosà

elegant [el'əgənt] *adj* (person, building) 優雅な yúga na; (idea, plan) 洗練された seńren saretà

element [el'əmənt] *n* (part: of whole, job, process) 要素 yóso; (CHEM) 元素 geñso; (of heater, kettle etc) ヒーター素子 hítàsoshi

elementary [elimen'tə:ri:] *adj* (basic) 基本的な kihónteki na; (primitive) 原始的な geńshiteki na; (school, education) 初等の shotó no

elephant [el'əfənt] *n* ゾウ zõ

elevation [eləvei'ʃən] *n* (raising, promotion) 向上 kójō; (height) 海抜 kaíbatsu

elevator [el'əveitə:r] *n* (*US*: lift) エレベーター erébētā

eleven [ilev'ən] *num* 十一 (の) júichi no

elevenses [ilev'ənsiz] (*BRIT*) *npl* (coffee-break) 午前のおやつ gózèn no o-yátsu

eleventh [ilev'ənθ] *num* 第十一の dáìjúichi no

elf [elf] (*pl* **elves**) *n* 小妖精 shóyōsei

elicit [ilis'it] *vt: to elicit (from)* (information, response, reaction) ...(から)...を引出す (...kará)...wò hikídasù

eligible [el'idʒəbəl] *adj* (qualified, suitable) 資格のある shikáku no arù; (man, woman) 好ましい結婚相手である konómashiî kekkón aìte de árù

to be eligible for something (qualified, suitable) ...する資格がある ...suru shikáku ga arù

eliminate [əlim'əneit] *vt* (eradicate: poverty, smoking) 無くす nakúsù; (candidate, team, contestant) 除外する jogái suru

elimination [əlimənei'ʃən] *n* (eradication) 根絶 koɲzetsu; (of candidate, team etc) 除外 jogái

élite [iliːt'] n エリート eríto

elm [elm] n (tree) ニレ niré; (wood) ニレ 材 nirézai

elocution [eləkjuː'ʃən] n 話術 wájutsu

elongated [iloːŋ'geitid] adj (body, shadow) 細長い hosónagaì

elope [iloup'] vi 駆落ちする kakéochi suru

elopement [iloup'mənt] n 駆落ち kakéochi

eloquence [el'əkwəns] n (of person, description, speech) 雄弁 yúben

eloquent [el'əkwənt] adj (person, description, speech) 雄弁な yúben na

else [els] adv (other) 外に hoká ni

something else 外の物 hoká no monò

somewhere else 外の場所 hoká no ba-shò

everywhere else 外はどこも hoká wà dókò mo

where else? 外にどこ? hoká nì dókò?

there was little else to do 外にする事 はなかった hoká nì suru kotò wa nákàtta

nobody else spoke 外にだれもしゃべら なかった hoká nì daré mò shabéranakattà

elsewhere [els'weːr] adv (be) 外の所に hoká no tokorò ni; (go) 外の所へ hoká no tokorò e

elucidate [iluː'sideit] vt (argument, point) 解明する kaímei suru

elude [iluːd'] vt (subj: fact, idea: not realized) 気付かれない kizúkarenaì; (: : not remembered) 思い出せない omóidasenaì; (: : not understood) 理解されない ríkai sarénaì; (captor) ...から逃げる ...kara nigérù; (capture) 免れる manúgarerù

elusive [iluː'siv] adj (person, animal) 見付けにくい mitsúkenikuì; (quality) 分か りにくい wakárinikuì

elves [elvz] npl of elf

emaciated [imei'ʃiːeitid] adj (person, animal) 衰弱した suíjaku shita

emanate [em'əneit] vi: **to emanate from** (idea, feeling) ...から放たれる ...ka-

ra hanatárerù; (sound) ...から聞える ...kara kikóerù; (light) ...から放射される ...kara hṓsha sarerù

emancipate [imæn'səpeit] vt (poor, slave, women) 解放する kaíhō suru

emancipation [imænsəpei'ʃən] n (of poor, slaves, women) 解放 kaíhō

embankment [embæŋk'mənt] n (of road, railway) 土手 dotè; (of river) 堤防 teíbō

embargo [embaːr'gou] (pl **embargoes**) n (POL, COMM) 通商停止 tsúshōteìshi

embark [embaːrk'] vi (NAUT): **to embark (on)** (...に) 乗船する (...ni) jṓsen suru

♦vt (passengers, cargo) 乗せる nosérù

to embark on (journey) ...に出発する ...ni shuppátsu surù; (task, course of action) ...に乗出す ...ni norídasù

embarkation [embaːrkei'ʃən] n (of people) 乗船 jṓsen; (of cargo) 船積み funázumi

embarrass [embær'əs] vt (emotionally) 恥をかかせる hají wò kakáserù; (politician, government) 困らせる komáraserù

embarrassed [embær'əst] adj (laugh, silence) 極り悪そうな kimáriwarusṑ na

embarrassing [embær'əsiŋ] adj (statement, situation, moment) 恥ずかしい ha-zúkashiì

embarrassment [embær'əsmənt] n (shame) 恥 hajî; (embarrassing problem) 厄介な問題 yákkài na moñdai

embassy [em'bəsiː] n (diplomats) 使節団 shisétsudàn; (building) 大使館 taíshikàn

embedded [embed'id] adj (object) 埋め込 まれた umékomaretà

embellish [embel'iʃ] vt (place, dress) 飾 る kazáru; (account) 潤色する juñshoku suru

embers [em'bəːrz] npl: **the embers (of the fire)** 残り火 nokóribì

embezzle [embez'əl] vt (LAW) 横領する ṓryō suru

embezzlement [embez'əlmənt] n 横領 ṓ-ryō

embitter [embit'əːr] vt (fig: sour) 世の中 を憎ませる yo nò nàka wo nikúmaserù

emblem [em'bləm] *n* (design) 標章 hyṓshō, マーク mãku; (symbol) 象徴 shṓchō

embody [əmbɑːd'iː] *vt* (idea, principle) 現す aráwasù; (features: include, contain) 含む fukúmù

embossed [embɔːst'] *adj* (design, word) 浮き出しの ukídashi no

embrace [embreis'] *vt* (hug) 抱く dakú; (include) 含む fukúmù
♦*vi* (hug) 抱合う dakíaù
♦*n* (hug) 抱擁 hṓyō

embroider [embrɔi'dəːr] *vt* (cloth) 刺繍する shishū suru

embroidery [embrɔi'dəːriː] *n* 刺しゅう shishū

embryo [em'briːou] *n* (BIO) はい haí

emerald [em'əːrəld] *n* エメラルド eméraldo

emerge [iməːrdʒ'] *vi*: *to emerge (from)* (...から) 出て来る (...kara) détè kuru; (fact: from discussion etc) (...で) 明らかになる (...de) akíraka ni nárù; (new idea, industry, society) 現れる aráwarerù
to emerge from sleep 目が覚める mé gà samérù
to emerge from prison 釈放される shakúhō sarerù

emergency [iməːr'dʒənsiː] *n* (crisis) 非常時 hijōjì
in an emergency 緊急の場合 kiñkyū no baài
state of emergency 緊急事態 kiñkyūjìtài

emergency cord (*US*) *n* 非常の際に引くコード hijṓ no saí ni hikú kṓdo

emergency exit *n* 非常口 hijṓgùchi

emergency landing *n* (AVIAT) 不時着陸 fujíchakùriku

emergency services *npl* (fire, police, ambulance) 非常時のサービス機関 hijōjì no sắbisukìkàn

emergent [iməːr'dʒənt] *adj* (nation) 最近独立した saíkin dokúritsu shità; (group) 最近創立された saíkin sṓritsu saretà

emery board [iː'məːriː-] *n* つめやすり tsuméyasùri ◇ボール紙製の物を指す bṓrugamisei no monò wo sásù

emigrant [em'əgrənt] *n* (from native country) 移住者 ijúshà

emigrate [em'əgreit] *vi* (from native country) 移住する ijū suru

emigration [eməgrei'ʃən] *n* 移住 ijū

eminent [em'ənənt] *adj* (scientist, writer) 著名な chómei na

emission [imiʃ'ən] *n* (of gas) 放出 hṓshutsu; (of radiation) 放射 hṓsha

emit [imit'] *vt* (smoke, smell, sound) 出す dásù; (light, heat) 放射する hṓsha suru

emotion [imou'ʃən] *n* 感情 kañjō

emotional [imou'ʃənəl] *adj* (needs, exhaustion, person, issue etc) 感情的な kañjōteki na; (scene etc) 感動的な kañdōteki na

emotive [imou'tiv] *adj* (subject, language) 感情に訴える kañjō nì uttáerù

emperor [em'pəːrəːr] *n* (gen) 皇帝 kṓtei; (of Japan) 天皇 teñnō

emphases [em'fəsiːz] *npl of* **emphasis**

emphasis [em'fəsis] (*pl* **emphases**) *n* (importance) 重点 jūten; (stress) 強調 kyṓchō

emphasize [em'fəsaiz] *vt* (word, point) 強調する kyṓchō suru; (feature) 浮彫にする ukíbori ni surù

emphatic [əmfæt'ik] *adj* (statement, denial, manner, person) 断固とした dáñko to shita

emphatically [əmfæt'ikliː] *adv* (forcefully) 断固として dáñko to shité; (certainly) 絶対に zéttai ni

empire [em'paiəːr] *n* (*also fig*) 帝国 teíkoku

empirical [empir'ikəl] *adj* (knowledge, study) 経験的な keíkenteki na

employ [emplɔi'] *vt* (workforce, person) 雇う yatóù; (tool, weapon) 使用する shiyṓ suru

employee [emplɔiː'] *n* 雇用人 koyṓnìn

employer [emplɔi'əːr] *n* 雇い主 yatóinùshi

employment [emplɔi'mənt] *n* (work) 就職 shūshoku

employment agency *n* 就職あっ旋会社 shūshokuassengaìsha

empower [empau'əːr] *vt*: *to empower*

someone to do something (LAW, ADMIN) ...に...する権限を与える ...ni ...suru keńgen wò atáerù

empress [em'pris] *n* (woman emperor) 女帝 jotéi; (wife of emperor) 皇后 kốgō

emptiness [emp'ti:nis] *n* (of area, region etc) 何もない事 naní mo naì kotó; (of life etc) むなしさ munáshìsa

empty [emp'ti:] *adj* (container) 空の kará no, 空っぽの karáppò no; (place, street) だれもいない daré mò inaì; (house, room, space) 空きの akí no
♦*vt* 空にする kará ni suru
♦*vi* (house, container) 空になる kará nì nárù; (liquid) 注ぐ sosógù
an empty threat こけおどし kokéodòshi
an empty promise 空約束 karáyakùsoku

empty-handed [empti:hæn'did] *adj* 手ぶらの tebúra no

emulate [em'jəleit] *vt* (hero, idol) まねる manérù

emulsion [imʌl'ʃən] *n* (liquid) 乳剤 nyǘzai; (*also*: **emulsion paint**) 水溶ペンキ suíyōpeñki

enable [enei'bəl] *vt*: *to enable someone to do* (permit, allow) ...が...する事を許可する ...ga ...surú kotò wo kyóka suru; (make possible) ...が...する事を可能にする ...ga ...surú kotò wo kanő ni surù

enact [enækt'] *vt* (law) 制定する seítei suru; (play, role) 上演する jően suru

enamel [inæm'əl] *n* (for decoration) エナメル塗料 enámeru tòryō; (*also*: **enamel paint**) エナメルペイント enámerupeìnto; (of tooth) エナメル質 enámerushìtsu

enamored [enæm'ɔːrd] *adj*: *to be enamored of* (person, pastime, idea, belief) ...に惚れる ...ni horérù

encased [enkeist'] *adj*: *encased in* (plaster, shell) ...に覆われた ...ni ốwaretà

enchant [entʃænt'] *vt* (delight) 魅了する miryő suru

enchanted [entʃæn'tid] *adj* (castle, island) 魔法の mahő no

enchanting [entʃæn'tiŋ] *adj* (appearance, behavior, person) 魅力的な miryő-

kuteki na

encircle [ensər'kəl] *vt* (place, prisoner) 囲む kakómù

encl. *abbr* (= *enclosed*) 同封の dốfū no

enclave [en'kleiv] *n* 飛び地 tobíchi

enclose [enklouz'] *vt* (land, space) 囲む kakómù; (object) 閉じ込める tojíkomerù; (letter etc): *to enclose (with)* (...に) 同封する (...ni) dốfū suru
please find enclosed ...を同封します ...wo dốfū shimasù

enclosure [enklou'ʒər] *n* (area of land) 囲い kakói

encompass [enkʌm'pəs] *vt* (include: subject, measure) 含む fukúmù

encore [ɑːŋ'koːr] *excl* アンコール ańkōru
♦*n* (THEATER) アンコール ańkōru

encounter [enkaun'tər] *n* (with person etc) 出会い deáì; (with problem etc) 直面 chokúmen
♦*vt* (person) ...に出会う ...ni deáù; (new experience, problem) 直面する chokúmen suru

encourage [enkə'ridʒ] *vt* (person): *to encourage someone (to do something)* (...する事を) ...に勧める (...surú kotò wo) ...ni susúmerù; (activity, attitude) 激励する gekírei suru; (growth, industry) 刺激する shigéki suru

encouragement [enkər'idʒmənt] *n* (to do something) 勧め susúme; (of activity, attitude) 激励 gekírei; (of growth, industry) 刺激 shigéki

encroach [enkroutʃ'] *vi*: *to encroach (up)on* (rights) ...を侵す ...wo okásù; (property) ...に侵入する ...ni shińnyū suru; (time) ...の邪魔をする ...no jamá wo surù

encrusted [enkrʌs'tid] *adj*: *encrusted with* (gems) ...をちりばめられた ...wo chiríbameraretà; (snow, dirt) ...に覆われた ...ni ốwaretà

encumber [enkʌm'bəːr] *vt*: *to be encumbered with* (suitcase, baggage etc) ...が邪魔になっている ...ga jamá nì natté irù; (debts) ...を背負っている ...wo seótte irù

encyclop(a)edia [ensaikləpi:'di:ə] *n* 百

科辞典 hyakkájīten

end [end] *n* (of period, event, book etc) 終り owári; (of table, street, line, rope) 端 hashí; (of town) 外れ hazúre; (of pointed object) 先 sakí; (aim) 目的 mokúteki

♦*vt* (finish) 終える oérù; (stop: activity, protest etc)

JPNや止める yamérù

♦*vi* (situation, activity, period etc) 終る owárù

in the end 仕舞いには shimái ni wà
on end (object) 縦になって táté ni natté
to stand on end (hair) よだつ yodátsù
for hours on end ぶっ続けで何時間も buttsúzuke dè nańjikàn mo

endanger [endein'dʒər] *vt* (lives, prospects) 危険にさらす kikén nì sarásù

endearing [endi:r'iŋ] *adj* (personality, conduct) 愛敬のある aíkyō no arù

endeavor [endev'əːr] (*BRIT* **endeavour**) *n* (attempt) 試み kokóromi; (effort) 努力 dóryòku

♦*vi: to endeavor to do* (attempt) ...しようとする ...shiyó tò surù; (strive) ...しようと努力する ...shiyó tò dóryòku suru

endemic [endem'ik] *adj* (poverty, disease) 地方特有の chihótokuyū no

ending [en'diŋ] *n* (of book, film, play etc) 結末 ketsúmatsu; (LING) 語尾 góbì

endive [en'daiv] *n* (curly) エンダイブ eńdaìbu; (smooth: chicory) チコリ chikórì

endless [end'lis] *adj* (argument, search) 果てし無い hatéshinaì; (forest, beach) 延々と続く eń-en tò tsuzúkù

endorse [endɔːrs'] *vt* (check) ...に裏書きする ...ni urágaki suru; (approve: proposal, plan, candidate) 推薦する suísen suru

endorsement [endɔːrs'mənt] *n* (approval) 推薦 suísen; (*BRIT*: on driving licence) 違反記録 ihánkiròku

endow [endau'] *vt* (provide with money) ...に金を寄付する ...ni kané wò kifú suru
to be endowed with (talent, quality) ...の持主である ...no mochínushi de árù

end up *vi: to end up in* (place) ...に行ってしまう ...ni itté shimaù; (condition)

...になってしまう ...ni natté shimaù

endurance [endu:r'əns] *n* (stamina) 耐久力 taíkyūryòku; (patience) 忍耐強さ nińtaizuyòsa

endure [endu:r'] *vt* (bear: pain, suffering) 耐える taérù

♦*vi* (last: friendship, love etc) 長続きする nagátsuzùki suru

an enduring work of art 不朽の名作 fukyū no meísaku

enemy [en'əmi:] *adj* (forces, strategy) 敵の tekí no

♦*n* 敵 tekí

energetic [enəːrdʒet'ik] *adj* (person, activity) 精力的な seíryokuteki na

energy [en'əːrdʒi:] *n* (strength, drive) 精力 seíryoku; (power: nuclear energy etc) エネルギー enérùgī

enforce [enfɔːrs'] *vt* (LAW) 実施する jisshí suru

engage [engeidʒ'] *vt* (attention, interest) 引く hikú; (employ: consultant, lawyer) 雇う yatóù; (AUT: clutch) つなぐ tsunágù

♦*vi* (TECH) 掛る kakárù

to engage in (commerce, study, research etc) ...に従事する ...ni jūji suru
to engage someone in conversation ...に話し掛ける ...ni hanáshikakerù

engaged [engeidʒd'] *adj* (betrothed) 婚約している koń-yaku shite irù; (*BRIT*: busy, in use) 使用中 shiyóchū

to get engaged 婚約する koń-yaku suru

engaged tone (*BRIT*) *n* (TEL) 話し中の信号音 hanáshichū no shíngōon

engagement [engeidʒ'mənt] *n* (appointment) 約束 yakúsoku; (booking: for musician, comedian etc) 仕事 shigóto; (to marry) 婚約 koń-yaku

engagement ring *n* 婚約指輪 koń-yaku yubíwa, エンゲージリング eńgejiriñgu

engaging [engei'dʒiŋ] *adj* (personality, trait) 愛敬のある aíkyō no arù

engender [endʒen'dəːr] *vt* (feeling, sense) 生む umú

engine [en'dʒən] *n* (AUT) エンジン eńjin; (RAIL) 機関車 kikáñsha

engine driver n (RAIL) 運転手 uñteñshu

engineer [endʒəniːr'] n (designer) 技師 gíshì; (BRIT: for repairs) 修理工 shúrikō; (US: RAIL) 運転手 uñteñshu; (on ship) 機関士 kikáñshì

engineering [endʒəniːr'iŋ] n (science) 工学 kōgaku; (design, construction: of roads, bridges) 建設 keñsetsu; (: of cars, ships, machines) 製造 seízō

England [iŋ'glənd] n イングランド íñgurando

English [iŋ'gliʃ] adj イングランドの íñgurando no; (LING) 英語の eígo no
♦n (LING) 英語 eígo
♦npl: the English イングランド人 íñgurandojìn ◇総称 sōshō

English Channel n: the English Channel イギリス海峡 igírisukaíkyō

Englishman/woman [iŋ'gliʃmən/wumən] (pl Englishmen/women) n イングランド人男性〔女性〕íñgurandojin dañsei〔jòsei〕

engraving [engrei'viŋ] n (picture, print) 版画 hañga

engrossed [engroust'] adj: engrossed in (book, program) ...に夢中になった ...ni muchū ni nattà

engulf [engʌlf'] vt (subj: fire) 巻込む makíkomù; (water) 飲込む nomíkomù; (: panic, fear) 襲う osóù

enhance [enhæns'] vt (enjoyment, reputation) 高める takámerù; (beauty) 増す masú

enigma [enig'mə] n (mystery) なぞ nazó

enigmatic [enigmæt'ik] adj (smile) なぞめいた nazómeìta; (person) 得体の知れない etái no shirenaì

enjoy [endʒɔi'] vt (like) ...が好きである ...ga sukí de arù; (take pleasure in) 楽しむ tanóshimù; (have benefit of: health, fortune, success) ...に恵まれる ...ni megúmarerù
to enjoy oneself 楽しむ tanóshimù

enjoyable [endʒɔi'əbəl] adj (pleasant) 楽しい tanóshiì

enjoyment [endʒɔi'mənt] n (feeling of pleasure) 楽しさ tanóshìsa; (activity) 楽しみ tanóshimì

enlarge [enlɑːrdʒ'] vt (size, scope) 拡大する kakúdai suru; (PHOT) 引伸ばす hikínobasù
♦vi: to enlarge on (subject) 詳しく話す kuwáshikù hanásù

enlargement [enlɑːrdʒ'mənt] n (PHOT) 引伸ばし hikínobashi

enlighten [enlait'ən] vt (inform) ...に教える ...ni oshíerù

enlightened [enlait'ənd] adj (person, policy, system) 聡明な sōmei na

enlightenment [enlait'ənmənt] n: the Enlightenment (HISTORY) 啓もう運動 keímōuñdō

enlist [enlist'] vt (soldier) 入隊させる nyūtai saserù; (person) ...の助けを借りる ...no tasúke wò karírù; (support, help) 頼む tanómù
♦vi: to enlist in (army, navy etc) ...に入隊する ...ni nyūtai suru

enmity [en'mitiː] n (hostility) 恨み urámi

enormity [inɔːr'mitiː] n (of problem, danger) 物すごさ monósugòsa

enormous [inɔːr'məs] adj (size, amount) 巨大な kyodái na; (delight, pleasure, success etc) 大きな ōkìna

enough [inʌf'] adj (time, books, people etc) 十分な jūbuñ na
♦pron 十分 jūbuñ
♦adv: big enough 十分に大きい jūbuñ ni ōkìi
he has not worked enough 彼の努力が足りない kárè no dóryòku ga tarínaì
have you got enough? 足りましたか tarímashìta ká
enough to eat 食べ物が足りる tabémonò ga tarírù
enough! もういい! mō iì!
that's enough, thanks もう沢山です. 有難う. mō takusañ desu. arígàtō.
I've had enough of him 彼にはもううんざりだ kárè ni wa mō uñzari dá
... which, funnily/oddly enough ... おかしいけれども，それは... okáshii kerèdomo, soré wà ...

enquire [enkwai'əːr] vt, vi = inquire

enrage [enreidʒ'] vt (anger, madden) 激

怒させる gékìdo saseru

enrich [enritʃ'] vt (morally, spiritually) 豊かにする yútàka ni suru; (financially) 金持にする kanémochi ni surù

enroll [enroul'] (BRIT: **enrol**) vt (at school, university) 入学させる nyúgaku saserù; (on course) 登録する tōroku suru; (in club etc) 入会させる nyúkai saserù

♦vi (at school, university) 入学する nyúgaku suru; (on course) 参加手続きをする sañkatetsuzūki wo suru; (in club etc) 入会する nyúkai suru

enrollment [enroul'mənt] (BRIT: **enrolment**) n (registration) 登録 tōroku

en route [ɔːn ruːt'] adv (on the way) 途中で tochū dè

ensue [ensuː'] vi (follow) ...の結果として起る ...no kekká toshitè okórù

ensure [enʃuːr'] vt (result, safety) 確実にする kakújitsu ni surù

entail [enteil'] vt (involve) 要する yō suru

entangled [entæŋ'gəld] adj: **to become entangled (in)** (in net, rope etc) ...に絡まる ...ni karámarù

enter [en'təːr] vt (room, club) ...に入る ...ni háìru; (race, competition) ...に参加する ...ni sañkà suru, ...に出場する ...ni shutsújō suru; (someone for a competition) ...に...の参加を申込む ...ni ...no sañka wò mōshikomù; (write down) 記入する kinyū suru; (COMPUT: data) 入力する nyúryòku suru

♦vi (come or go in) 入る háìru

enter for vt fus (race, competition, examination) ...に参加を申込む ...ni sañka wò mōshikomù

enter into vt fus (discussion, correspondence, negotiations) 始める hajímerù; (agreement) 結ぶ musúbù

enterprise [en'təːrpraiz] n (company, business) 企業 kigyō; (undertaking) 企画 kikáku; (initiative) 進取の気 shíñshu no ki

free enterprise 自由企業 jiyúkigyò

private enterprise (private company) 民間企業 míñkankigyò, 私企業 shikígyò

enterprising [en'təːrpraiziŋ] adj (adventurous) 進取の気に富んだ shíñshu no ki ni tóñda

entertain [entəːrtein'] vt (amuse) 楽しませる tanóshimaserù; (invite: guest) 接待する séttài suru; (idea, plan) 考える kañgaerù

entertainer [entəːrtein'əːr] n (TV etc) 芸能人 geínōjìn

entertaining [entəːrtei'niŋ] adj 面白い omóshiroì

entertainment [entəːrtein'mənt] n (amusement) 娯楽 goráku; (show) 余興 yokyō

enthralled [enθrɔːld'] adj (engrossed, captivated) 魅せられた miséraretà

enthusiasm [enθuː'ziæzəm] n (eagerness) 熱心さ nesshíñsa

enthusiast [enθuː'ziæst] n (fan) マニア mánìa

enthusiastic [enθuːzi:æs'tik] adj (excited, eager) 熱心な nesshíñ na

to be enthusiastic about ...に夢中になっている ...ni muchū ni natté irù

entice [entais'] vt (lure, tempt) 誘惑する yúwaku suru

entire [entai'əːr] adj (whole) 全体の zeñtai no

entirely [entaiəːr'liː] adv (completely) 全く mattákù

entirety [entai'əːrtiː] n: **in its entirety** 全体に zeñtai ni

entitle [entait'əl] vt: **to entitle someone to something** ...に...に対する権利を与える ...ni ...ni taísùru keñri wò atáerù

entitled [entait'əld] adj (book, film etc) ...という題の ...to iú daì no

to be entitled to do (be allowed) ...する権利がある ...suru keñri ga árù

entity [en'titi:] n 物 monó

entourage [ɑːnturɑːʒ'] n (of celebrity, politician) 取巻き連 torímakireñ

entrails [en'treilz] npl (ANAT, ZOOL) 内臓 naízō

entrance [n en'trəns vb entræns'] n (way in) 入口 irígùchi; (arrival) 登場 tōjō

♦vt (enchant) 魅惑する miwáku suru

to gain entrance to (university, profession etc) ...に入る ...ni háīru

entrance examination n 入学試験 nyúgakushikeñ, 入試 nyúshi

entrance fee n 入場料 nyújŏryŏ

entrance ramp (*US*) n (AUT) 入口ランプ irīguchiraňpu

entrant [en'trənt] n (in race, competition etc) 参加者 sañkashà; (*BRIT*: in exam) 受験者 jukéñsha

entreat [entri:t'] vt (implore) 嘆願する tañgan suru

entrenched [entrentʃt'] adj (position, power) 固められた katámeraretà; (ideas) 定着した teíchakushità

entrepreneur [ɑːntrəprənəːr'] n (COMM) 企業家 kigyŏka

entrust [entrast'] vt: **to entrust something to someone** ...を...に預ける ...wo ...ni azúkerù

entry [en'tri:] n (way in) 入口 irīguchi; (in competition) 参加者 sañkashà; (in register, account book) 記入 kinyú; (in reference book) 記事 kíji; (arrival) 登場 tójŏ; (to country) 入国 nyúkoku
「**no entry**」 (to room etc) 立入禁止 tachíirikiñshi; (AUT) 進入禁止 shíñnyūkiñshi

entry form n (for club etc) 入会申込書 nyúkaimŏshikomishò; (for competition etc) 参加申込書 sañkamŏshikomishò

entry phone n 玄関のインターホン géñkan no iñtàhon

enumerate [inuː'məːreit] vt (list) 列挙する rékkyo suru

enunciate [inʌn'siːeit] vt (word) はっきりと発音する hakkírì to hatsúon suru; (principle, plan etc) 明確に説明する meíkaku nì setsúmei suru

envelop [envel'əp] vt (cover, enclose) 覆い包む óitsutsumù

envelope [en'vəloup] n 封筒 fútŏ

envious [en'viːəs] adj (person, look) うらやましい uráyamashiì

environment [envai'rənmənt] n (surroundings) 環境 kañkyō; (natural world): **the environment** 環境 kañkyō

environmental [envairənmen'təl] adj 環境の kañkyō no

envisage [enviz'idʒ] vt (foresee) 予想す

る yosŏ suru

envoy [en'vɔi] n (diplomat) 特使 tókùshi

envy [en'viː] n (jealousy) せん望 señbŏ
♦vt うらやましく思う uráyamashìku omóù
to envy someone something ...の...をうらやましく思う ...no ...wo uráyamashìku omóù

enzyme [en'zaim] n (BIO, MED) 酵素 kŏso

ephemeral [ifem'əːrəl] adj (fashion, fame) つかの間の tsuká no mà no

epic [ep'ik] n (poem) 叙事詩 jojíshì; (book, film) 大作 taisaku
♦adj (journey) 歴史的な rekíshiteki na

epidemic [epidem'ik] n (of disease) 流行病 ryúkŏbyŏ

epilepsy [ep'əlepsiː] n (MED) てんかん teñkan

epileptic [epəlep'tik] adj てんかんの teñkan no
♦n てんかん患者 teñkankañja

episode [ep'isoud] n (period, event) 事件 jíkeñ; (TV, RADIO: installment) 1回 ikkái

epistle [ipis'əl] n (letter: *also* REL) 書簡 shokán

epitaph [ep'itæf] n 墓碑銘 bohímei

epithet [ep'əθet] n 形容語句 keíyŏgokù

epitome [ipit'əmiː] n (model, archetype) 典型 teñkei

epitomize [ipit'əmaiz] vt (characterize, typify) ...の典型である ...no teñkei dè árù

epoch [ep'ək] n (age, era) 時代 jídai

equable [ek'wəbəl] adj (climate) 安定した añteishità; (temper, reply) 落着いた ochítsuità

equal [iː'kwəl] adj (size, number, amount) 等しい hitóshì; (intensity, quality) 同様な dŏyŏ na; (treatment, rights, opportunities) 平等な byŏdŏ na
♦n (peer) 同輩 dŏhai
♦vt (number) イコール ikŏrù; (quality) ...と同様である ...to dŏyŏ dè árù
to be equal to (task) ...を十分出来る ...wo júbuñ dekírù

equality [ikwaːl'itiː] n 平等 byŏdŏ

equalize [iː'kwəlaiz] vi (SPORT) 同点に

する dṓten ni surù

equally [i:'kwəli:] *adv* (share, divide etc) 平等 に byṓdō ni; (good, brilliant, bad etc) 同様に dṓyō ni

equanimity [i:kwənim'iti:] *n* (calm) 平静 さ heíseisà

equate [ikweit'] *vt*: *to equate something with* ...を...と同等視する ...wo ...to dṓtōshi suru

equation [ikwei'ʒən] *n* (MATH) 方程式 hṓteishiki

equator [ikwei'tə:r] *n* 赤道 sekídō

equestrian [ikwes'tri:ən] *adj* 乗馬 の jṓbà no

equilibrium [i:kwəlib'ri:əm] *n* (balance) 均衡 kiñkō; (composure) 平静さ heíseisà

equinox [i:'kwənɑ:ks] *n*: *spring/autumn equinox* 春〔秋〕分 の 日 shuñ〔shū〕bun no hì

equip [ikwip'] *vt* (person, army, car etc) ...に...を装備させる ...ni ...wo sōbi saserù; (room) ...に...を備え付ける ...ni ...wo sonáetsukerù

to be well equipped 装備が十分である sōbi gà jûbuñ de árù

to be equipped with ...を装備している ...wo sōbi shite irù

equipment [ikwip'mənt] *n* (tools, machinery) 設備 sétsùbi

equitable [ek'witəbəl] *adj* (settlement, agreement) 公正な kōsei na

equities [ek'witi:z] (*BRIT*) *npl* (COMM) 普通株 futsūkàbu

equivalent [ikwiv'ələnt] *adj*: *equivalent (to)* (...に)相当する (...ni) sōtō suru
◆*n* (equal) 相当の物 sōtō no monò

equivocal [ikwiv'əkəl] *adj* (ambiguous) あいまいな aímai na; (open to suspicion) いかがわしい ikágawashiì

era [i:'rə] *n* (age, period) 時代 jidái

eradicate [iræd'ikeit] *vt* (disease, problem) 根絶する koñzetsu suru

erase [ireis'] *vt* (tape, writing) 消す kesú

eraser [irei'sə:r] *n* (for pencil etc) 消しゴム keshígomu; (*US*: for blackboard etc) 黒板消し kokúbankeshì

erect [irekt'] *adj* (posture) 直立の chokúritsu no; (tail, ears) ぴんと立てた piñ tò

tatétà
◆*vt* (build) 建てる tatérù; (assemble) 組立てる kumítaterù

erection [irek'ʃən] *n* (of building) 建築 keñchiku; (of statue) 建立 kofíryū; (of tent) 張る事 harú kotò; (of machinery etc) 組立て kumítate; (PHYSIOL) ぼっ起 bokkî

ermine [ə:r'min] *n* (fur) アーミン ámìn

erode [iroud'] *vt* (soil, rock) 侵食する shiñshoku suru; (metal) 腐食する fushóku suru; (confidence, power) 揺るがす yurúgasù

erosion [irou'ʒən] *n* (of soil, rock) 侵食 shiñshoku; (of metal) 腐食 fushóku; (of confidence, power) 揺るがされる事 yurúgasarerù kotó

erotic [irɑt'ik] *adj* (activities) 性的な seíteki na; (dreams, books, films) 扇情的な señjōteki na, エロチックな eróchikkù na

eroticism [irɑt'isizəm] *n* 好色 kōshoku, エロチシズム eróchishizùmu

err [ə:r] *vi* (formal: make a mistake) 過ちを犯す ayámachi wo okásù

errand [er'ənd] *n* お使い o-tsúkai

erratic [iræt'ik] *adj* (behavior) 突飛な toppí na; (attempts, noise) 不規則な fukísoku na

erroneous [irou'ni:əs] *adj* (belief, opinion) 間違った machígattà

error [er'ə:r] *n* (mistake) 間違い machígaì, エラー èrà

erudite [er'judait] *adj* (person) 博学な hakúgaku na

erupt [irʌpt'] *vi* (volcano) 噴火する fuñka suru; (war, crisis) ぼっ発する boppátsu suru

eruption [irʌp'ʃən] *n* (of volcano) 噴火 fuñka; (of fighting) ぼっ発 boppátsu

escalate [es'kəleit] *vi* (conflict, crisis) 拡大する kakúdai suru, エスカレートする esúkarēto suru

escalator [es'kəleitə:r] *n* エスカレーター esúkarētā

escapade [es'kəpeid] *n* (adventure) 冒険 bṓken

escape [iskeip'] *n* (from prison) 脱走 dassṓ; (from person) 逃げる事 nigéru ko-

tð; (of gas) 漏れる事 moréru kotð
♦*vi* (get away) 逃げる nigérù; (from jail) 脱走する dassô suru; (leak) 漏れる morérù
♦*vt* (consequences, responsibility etc) 回避する kaíhi suru; (elude): *his name escapes me* 彼の名前を思い出せない kárè no namáe wò omóidasenaì
to escape from (place) ...から脱出する ...kara dasshútsu suru; (person) ...から逃げる ...kara nigérù

escapism [eskei'pizəm] *n* 現実逃避 geñjitsutōhi

escort [*n* es'kɔ:rt *vb* eskɔ:rt'] *n* (MIL, POLICE) 護衛 goéi; (companion) 同伴者 dóhañsha
♦*vt* (person) ...に同伴する ...ni dôhan suru

Eskimo [es'kəmou] *n* エスキモー人 esúkimòjìn

esoteric [esəte:r'ik] *adj* 難解な nañkai na

especially [espeʃ'əli:] *adv* (above all, particularly) 特に tókù ni

espionage [es'pi:ənɑ:ʒ] *n* (POL, MIL, COMM) スパイ行為 supáikòi

esplanade [esplənæd'] *n* (by sea) 海岸の遊歩道 kaígan nò yûhodò

espouse [espauz'] *vt* (policy) 採用する saíyō suru; (idea) 信奉する shiñpô suru

Esq. *abbr* = **Esquire**

Esquire [es'kwaiə:r] *n*: *J. Brown, Esquire* J.ブラウン様 jê buráùn samá

essay [es'ei] *n* (SCOL) 小論文 shôroñbun; (LITERATURE) 随筆 zuíhitsu, エッセーéssè

essence [es'əns] *n* (soul, spirit) 本質 hoñshitsu; (CULIN) エキス ékìsu, エッセンス éssènsu

essential [əsen'tʃəl] *adj* (necessary, vital) 不可欠な fukáketsu na; (basic) 根本的な koñponteki na
♦*n* (necessity) 不可欠な事柄 fukáketsu nà kotógarà

essentially [əsen'tʃəli:] *adv* (basically) 根本的に koñponteki ni

establish [əstæb'liʃ] *vt* (organization, firm) 創立する sôritsu suru; (facts,

proof) 確認する kakúnin suru; (relations, contact) 樹立する jurítsu suru; (reputation) 作り上げる tsukúriagerù

established [əstæb'liʃt] *adj* (business) 定評のある teíhyō no arù; (custom, practice) 定着した teíchaku shità

establishment [əstæb'liʃmənt] *n* (of organization etc) 創立 sôritsu; (of facts etc) 確認 kakúnin; (of relations etc) 樹立 jurítsu; (of reputation) 作り上げる事 tsukúriageru kotð; (shop etc) 店 misé; (business, firm) 会社 kaísha; (institution) 施設 shísètsu

the Establishment 体制 taísei

estate [əsteit'] *n* (land) 屋敷 yashíki; (BRIT: also: **housing estate**) 住宅団地 jútakudañchi; (LAW) 財産 zaísan

estate agent (BRIT) *n* 不動産屋 fudôsan-yà

estate car (BRIT) *n* ステーションワゴン sutêshonwagòn

esteem [əsti:m'] *n*: *to hold someone in high esteem* (admire, respect) ...を尊敬する ...wo soñkei suru

esthetic [esθet'ik] (US) *adj* = **aesthetic**

estimate [*n* es'təmit *vb* es'təmeit] *n* (calculation) 概算 gaísan; (assessment) 推定 suítei; (COMM: builder's etc) 見積 mitsúmori
♦*vt* (reckon, calculate) 推定する suítei suru

estimation [estəmei'ʃən] *n* (opinion) 意見 íkèn; (calculation) 推定 suítei

estranged [estreind3d'] *adj* (from spouse) ...と別居している ...to bekkyô shite irù; (from family, friends) ...と仲たがいしている ...to nakátagai shite irù

estuary [es'tʃuə:ri:] *n* 河口 kakô

etc *abbr* (= *et cetera*) など nádò

etching [etʃ'iŋ] *n* 版画 hañga, エッチング etchíngu

eternal [itə:r'nəl] *adj* (everlasting, unceasing) 永遠の eíen no; (unchanging: truth, value) 不変的な fuhénteki na

eternity [itə:r'niti:] *n* 永遠 eíen

ether [i:'θə:r] *n* (CHEM) エーテル êteru

ethical [eθ'ikəl] *adj* (question, problem) 道徳的な dôtokuteki na

ethics [eθ'iks] *n* (science) 倫理学 ríñrigàku
♦*npl* (morality) 道徳 dôtoku

Ethiopia [i:θi:ou'pi:ə] *n* エチオピア echíopìa

ethnic [eθ'nik] *adj* (population, music, culture etc) 民族の míñzoku no

ethos [i:'θɑːs] *n* 気風 kifū

etiquette [et'əkit] *n* (manners, conduct) 礼儀作法 reígisahò, エチケット échìketto

eucalyptus [ju:kəlip'təs] *n* (tree) ユーカリ yūkari

euphemism [ju:'fəmizəm] *n* えん曲表現 eñkyokuhyôgen

euphoria [ju:fɔːr'iːə] *n* (elation) 幸福感 kôfukukañ

Eurocheque [ju:'rout∫ek] *n* ユーロチェック yūrochekkù ◊ヨーロッパ諸国で通用する小切手 yôroppa shokùku de tsúyō surù kogíttè

Europe [ju:'rəp] *n* 欧州 ôshū, ヨーロッパ yôroppà

European [ju:rəpi:'ən] *adj* 欧州の ôshū no, ヨーロッパの yôroppà no
♦*n* ヨーロッパ人 yôroppajìn

euthanasia [ju:θənei'ʒə] *n* 安楽死 añrakushì

evacuate [ivæk'ju:eit] *vt* (people) 避難させる hínan saserù; (place) ...から避難させる ...kara hínan saserù

evacuation [ivækju:ei'ʃən] *n* 避難 hínan

evade [iveid'] *vt* (tax, duty) 脱税する datsúzei suru; (question) 言逃れる iínogarerù; (responsibility) 回避する kaîhi suru; (person) 避ける sakérù

evaluate [ivæl'ju:eit] *vt* (importance, achievement, situation etc) 評価する hyôka suru

evaporate [ivæp'əreit] *vi* (liquid) 蒸発する jôhatsu suru; (feeling, attitude) 消えてなくなる kíète nakunarù

evaporated milk [ivæp'əreitid-] *n* エバミルク ebámirùku

evasion [ivei'ʒən] *n* (of responsibility, situation etc) 回避 kaîhi
tax evasion 脱税 datsúzei

evasive [ivei'siv] *adj* (reply, action) 回避

的な kaîhiteki na

eve [i:v] *n*: *on the eve of* ...の前夜に ...no zéñ-ya ni

even [i:'vən] *adj* (level) 平らな taîra na; (smooth) 滑らかな naméràka na; (equal) 五分五分の gobúgobu no
♦*adv* (showing surprise) ...さえ ...sáè; (introducing a comparison) 更に sárà ni
an even number 偶数 gûsū
even if 例え...だとしても tatôe ...dá tò shité mò
even though 例え...だとしても tatôe ...dá tò shité mò
even more なおさら naôsara
even so それにしても soré ni shite mò
not even ...さえも...ない ...sáè mo ...naî
even he was there 彼さえもいた kárè sáè mo ità
even on Sundays 日曜日にも nichíyòbi ni mo
to get even with someone ...に復しゅうする ...ni fukúshū suru

evening [i:v'niŋ] *n* (early) 夕方 yūgata; (late) 夜 yórù; (whole period, event) ...の夕べ ...no yūbe
in the evening 夕方に yūgata ni

evening class *n* 夜間学級 yakángakkyù

evening dress *n* (no pl: formal clothes) 夜会服 yakáifùku; (woman's) イブニングドレス ibúningu dorèsu

even out *vi* (ground) 平らになる taîra ni narù; (prices etc) 安定する añtei suru

event [ivent'] *n* (occurrence) 事件 jíkèn; (SPORT) イベント ibéñto
in the event of ...の場合 ...no baái

eventful [ivent'fəl] *adj* (day) 忙しい isôgashiî; (life, game) 波乱の多い hárañ no ôî

eventual [iven't∫u:əl] *adj* (outcome, goal) ゆくゆくの yukúyuku no

eventuality [iven't∫uæl'iti:] *n* (possibility) 可能性 kanôsei

eventually [iven't∫u:əli:] *adv* (finally) 結局 kekkyóku; (in time) やがて yagáte

ever [ev'əːr] *adv* (always) 常に tsúnè ni; (at any time) いつか ítsù ka; (in question): *why ever not?* どうしてまたしないのか dôshite matá shinaî no ká

the best ever 絶対に一番良い物 zettái
nì ichíban yoī monó

have you ever seen it? それを見た事が
ありますか soré wò mítà kotó gà arímà-
sù ká

better than ever なお一層良くなった
náò issó yokù náttà

ever since adv それ以来 soré iraì
♦*conj* …して以来 …shité iraì

evergreen [ev'ə:rgri:n] n (tree, bush) 常
緑樹 jőryokujù

everlasting [evə:rlæs'tiŋ] adj (love, life
etc) 永遠の eîen no

KEYWORD

every [ev'ri:] adj 1 (each) すべての sùbè-
te no, 皆の miná no

every one of them (persons) 彼らは
〔を〕皆 karèra wa 〔wo〕miná; (objects)
それらは〔を〕皆 sorèra wa〔wo〕miná

I interviewed every applicant 私は応
募者全員に面接しました watákushi wa
őboshà zén-in ni ménsetsu shimashìta

every shop in the town was closed 町
中の店が閉っていました machíjū no mi-
se gà shimáttè imáshìta

2 (all possible) 可能な限りすべての kanő
na kagíri súbète no

I gave you every assistance 私は可能
な限りあなたを助けました watákushi
wa kanó na kagíri anátà wo tasúkema-
shìta

I have every confidence in him 私は
完全に彼を信用しています watákushi
wa kánzen ni karè wo shín-yōshite imasù

we wish you every success ご成功を祈
ります go-seíkō wo inőrimasù

*he's every bit as clever as his
brother* 才能に関しては彼は彼の兄に少
しも引けを取りません saínō ni kàn shite
wa kárè wa kárè no ánī ni sukőshi mo
hike wo tòrímasèn

3 (showing recurrence) 毎… maî…

every day/week 毎日〔週〕maínichi
〔shū〕

every Sunday 毎日曜日 máinichiyőbì

every other car (had been broken

into) 車は2台に1台ドアが壊されていた
kurúma wa nidái ni ichídai doa ga ko-
wásarète ita

she visits me every other/third day
彼女は1日〔2日〕置きに面会に来てくれま
す kánðjo wa ichínichi〔futsúka〕oki nì
ménkai ni kite kùrémasù

every now and then 時々 tokídoki

everybody [ev'ri:bɑ:di:] pron (gen) だれ
も dáre mo; (form of address) 皆さん
minásàn

everyday [ev'ri:dei] adj (daily) 毎日の
maínichi no; (usual, common) 平凡な heíbon na

everyone [ev'ri:wʌn] pron = **everybody**

everything [ev'ri:θiŋ] pron 何もかも nánì mo ká mò

everywhere [ev'ri:hwe:r] adv (all over)
いたる所に itárù tokoro ni; (wherever)
どこにでも dőkð ni de mo

evict [ivikt'] vt (squatter, tenant) 立ちの
かせる tachínokaserù

eviction [ivik'ʃən] n (from house, land)
立ちのかせる事 tachínokaseru kotð

evidence [ev'idəns] n (proof) 証拠 shőko;
(of witness) 証言 shőgen; (sign, indication) 印 shirúshi

to give evidence 証言する shőgen suru

evident [ev'idənt] adj (obvious) 明らかな
akíraka na

evidently [ev'idəntli:] adv (obviously) 明
らかに akíraka ni; (apparently) …らしい
…rashìì

evil [i:'vəl] adj (person, system, influence) 悪い warúì

♦n (wickedness, sin) 罪悪 zaíaku; (unpleasant situation or activity) 悪 ákù

evocative [ivɑ:k'ətiv] adj (description,
music) 想像を刺激する sőzō wò shigéki
suru

evoke [ivouk'] vt (feeling, memory,
response) 呼び起す yobíokosù

evolution [evəlu:'ʃən] n (BIO: process)
進化 shíñka; (also: **theory of evolution**)
進化論 shiñkarðn; (development) 発展
hattén

evolve [ivɑ:lv'] vt (scheme, style) 練上げ

る neríagerù

♦vi (animal, plant etc) 進化する shínka suru; (plan, idea, style etc) 展開する teñkai suru

ewe [ju:] n 雌ヒツジ mesúhitsùji

ex- [eks] prefix 元... mótò...

exacerbate [igzæs'ə:rbeit] vt (crisis, problem) 悪化させる akká saserù

exact [igzækt'] adj (correct: time, amount, word etc) 正確な seíkaku na; (person, worker) き帳面な kichốmen na

♦vt: to exact something (from) (obedience, payment etc) (...に) ...を強要する (...ni) ...wo kyốyō suru

exacting [igzæk'tiŋ] adj (task, conditions) 難しい muzúkashiî; (person, master etc) 厳しい kibíshiî

exactly [igzækt'li:] adv (precisely) 正確 に seíkaku ni, 丁度 chốdo; (indicating emphasis) 正に másà ni; (indicating agreement) その通り sonố tőri

exaggerate [igzædʒ'əreit] vt (difference, situation, story etc) 大げさに言う ốgesa ni iú

♦vi 大げさな事を言う ốgesa na kotố wo iú

exaggeration [igzædʒəreiʃ'ən] n 大げさ ốgesa

exalted [igzɔ:l'tid] adj (prominent) 著名 な chomếi na

exam [igzæm'] n abbr (SCOL) = **examination**

examination [igzæməneiʃ'ən] n (of object, accounts etc) 検査 kéñsa; (of idea, plan etc) 検討 keñtố; (SCOL) 試験 shikéñ; (MED) 診察 shíñsatsu

examine [igzæm'in] vt (inspect: object, idea, plan, accounts etc) 調べる shiráberù; (SCOL: candidate) 試験する shikéñ suru; (MED: patient) 診察する shíñsatsu suru

examiner [igzæm'inə:r] n (SCOL) 試験 官 shikéñkan

example [igzæm'pəl] n (typical illustration) 例 reí; (model: of good behavior etc) 手本 tehốn

for example 例えば tatőèba

exasperate [igzæs'pəreit] vt (annoy,

frustrate) 怒らせる okốraserù

exasperating [igzæs'pəreitiŋ] adj いら いらさせる íraira sasérù

exasperation [igzæspəreiʃ'ən] n いらだ ち irádachi

excavate [eks'kəveit] vt (site) 発掘する hakkútsu suru

excavation [eks'kəveiʃ'ən] n (act) 発掘 hakkútsu; (site) 発掘現場 hakkútsugeñba

exceed [iksi:d'] vt (number, amount, budget) 越える koérù; (speed limit etc) 越す kosú; (powers, hopes) 上回る uwámawarù

exceedingly [iksi:'diŋli:] adv (enormously) 極めて kiwámète

excel [iksel'] vi: to excel (in/at) (sports, business etc) (...に) 優れる (...ni) sugúrerù

excellence [ek'sələns] n 優れる事 sugúreru kotố

Excellency [ek'selənsi:] n: His Excellency 閣下 kákkà

excellent [ek'sələnt] adj (idea, work etc) 優秀な yűshū na

except [iksept'] prep (apart from: also: except for, excepting) ...を除いて ...wo nozőite

♦vt: to except someone (from) (attack, criticism etc) (...から) ...を除く (...kara) ...wo nozőkù

except if/when ...する場合を除いて ...suru baái wò nozőite

except that がしかし... ga shikáshì...

exception [iksep'ʃən] n (special case) 例外 reígai

to take exception to ...が気に食わない ...ga ki ní kuwanaî

exceptional [iksep'ʃənəl] adj (person, talent) 優れた sugúretà; (circumstances) 例外的な reígaiteki na

excerpt [ek'sə:rpt] n (from text, film) 抜粋 bassúi

excess [ek'ses] n (surfeit) 過剰 kajő

excess baggage n 超過手荷物 chốkatenimòtsu

excesses [ekses'iz] npl (of cruelty, stupidity etc) 極端な行為 kyokútan na kối

excess fare (*BRIT*) *n* (RAIL) 乗越し運賃 noríkoshi uńchin

excessive [iksesʼiv] *adj* (amount, extent) 過剰の kajṓ no

exchange [ikstʃeindʒʼ] *n* (of presents, prisoners etc) 交換 kṓkan; (conversation) 口論 kṓron; (*also*: **telephone exchange**) 電話局 deńwakyòku
♦*vt*: **to exchange (for)** (goods etc) (...と) 交換する (...to) kṓkan suru

exchange rate *n* 為替相場 kawásesòba

Exchequer [ekstʃʼekər] (*BRIT*) *n*: **the Exchequer** 大蔵省 ōkurashṓ

excise [ekʼsaiz] *n* (tax) 消費税 shōhizèi

excite [iksait] *vt* (stimulate) 興奮させる kṓfun saserù; (arouse) 性的に刺激する seíteki nì shigékì suru
to get excited 興奮する kṓfun suru

excitement [iksaitʼmənt] *n* (agitation) 興奮 kṓfun; (exhilaration) 喜び yorókobî

exciting [iksaiʼtiŋ] *adj* (time, event, place) 興奮の kṓfun no, エキサイティングな ekísaitìŋgu na

exclaim [ikskleimʼ] *vi* (cry out) 叫ぶ sakébù

exclamation [ekskləmeiʼʃən] *n* (cry) 叫び sakébì

exclamation mark *n* 感嘆符 kańtañfu

exclude [ikskluːdʼ] *vt* (fact, possibility, person) 除外する jogái suru

exclusion [ikskluːʼʒən] *n* 除外 jogái

exclusive [ikskluːʼsiv] *adj* (club, district) 高級な kṓkyū na; (use, story, interview) 独占の dokúsen no
exclusive of tax 税別の zeíbetsu no

exclusively [ikskluːʼsivli:] *adv* (only, entirely) 独占的に dokúsenteki ni

excommunicate [ekskəmjuːʼnəkeit] *vt* (REL) 破門する hamón suru

excrement [eksʼkrəmənt] *n* ふん fúñ

excruciating [ikskruːʼʃiːeitiŋ] *adj* (pain, agony, embarrassment etc) 極度の kyókùdo no, 耐えがたい taégatàì; (noise) 耳をつんざくような mimí wò tsuńzaku yō na

excursion [ikskəːrʼʒən] *n* (tourist excursion, shopping excursion) ツアー tsúā

excuse [*n* ekskjuːsʼ *vb* ekskjuːzʼ] *n* (justification) 言訳 iíwake
♦*vt* (justify: personal fault, mistake) ...の言訳をする ...no iíwake wo suru; (forgive: someone else's mistake) 許す yurúsù

to excuse someone from doing something ...する義務を...に免除する ...suru gímù wo ...ni mêñjo suru

excuse me! (attracting attention) 済みません sumímaseñ; sumímaseñ (ga)...; (as apology) 済みません sumímaseñ

if you will excuse me ... ちょっと失礼します chóttò shitsúrei shimasù

ex-directory [eksdirekʼtəːriː] (*BRIT*) *adj* 電話帳に載っていない deńwachò ni notté inaì

execute [ekʼsəkjuːt] *vt* (person) 死刑にする shikéi ni surù; (plan, order) 実行する jikkṓ suru; (maneuver, movement) する surú

execution [eksəkjuːʼʃən] *n* (of person) 死刑 shikéi; (of plan, order, maneuver etc) 実行 jikkṓ

executioner [eksəkjuːʼʃənəːr] *n* 死刑執行人 shikéishikkōnìn

executive [igzekʼjətiv] *n* (person: of company) 重役 júyaku; (committee: of organization, political party etc) 執行委員会 shikkṓiñkai
♦*adj* (board, role) 幹部の káñbu no

executor [igzekʼjətəːr] *n* (LAW) 執行人 shikkṓnìn

exemplary [igzemʼpləːriː] *adj* (conduct) 模範的な mohánteki na; (punishment) 見せしめの miséshime no

exemplify [igzemʼpləfai] *vt* (typify) ...の典型である ...no teñkei dè árù; (illustrate) ...の例を挙げる ...no reí wò agérù

exempt [igzemptʼ] *adj*: **exempt from** (duty, obligation) ...を免除された ...wo mêñjo sarétà
♦*vt*: **to exempt someone from** (duty, obligation) ...の...を免除する ...no ...wo mêñjo suru

exemption [igzempʼʃən] *n* 免除 mêñjo

exercise [ekʼsəːrsaiz] *n* (no pl: keep-fit) 運動 uñdō; (energetic movement) 体操 taísō; (SCOL) 練習問題 reńshūmoñdai;

(MUS) 練習曲 reńshūkyoku; (MIL) 軍事演習 guńjieńshū; (of authority etc) 行使 kóshī

♦vt (right) 行使する kóshī suru; (dog) ...に運動をさせる ...ni uńdō wò sasérù; (mind) 働かせる határakaserù

♦vi (also: **to take exercise**) 運動する uńdō suru

to exercise patience 我慢する gámàn suru

exercise book n (SCOL) ノート nōto

exert [igzə:rt'] vt (influence) 及ぼす oyóbosù; (authority) 行使する kóshī suru

to exert oneself 努力する dóryòku suru

exertion [igzə:r'ʃən] n 努力 dóryòku

exhale [eksheil'] vt (air, smoke) 吐き出す hakídasù

♦vi (breathe out) 息を吐く íkì wò hákù

exhaust [igzɔ:st'] n (AUT: also: **exhaust pipe**) 排気管 haíkikàn; (: fumes) 排気ガス haíkigasù

♦vt (person) へとへとに疲れさせる hetóhetò ni tsukáresaserù; (money, resources etc) 使い果す tsukáihatasù; (topic) ...について語り尽す ...ni tsúìte katáritsukusù

exhausted [igzɔ:s'tid] adj (person) へとへとに疲れた hetóhetò ni tsukáretà

exhaustion [igzɔ:s'tʃən] n (tiredness) 極度の疲労 kyókùdo no hirő

nervous exhaustion 神経衰弱 shińkeisuijàku

exhaustive [igzɔ:s'tiv] adj (search, study) 徹底的な tettéiteki na

exhibit [igzib'it] n (ART) 展示品 teńjihìn; (LAW) 証拠品 shőkohìn

♦vt (quality, ability, emotion) 見せる misérù; (paintings) 展示する teńji suru

exhibition [eksəbiʃ'ən] n (of paintings etc) 展示会 teńjikai; (of ill-temper etc) 極端な態度 kyokútàn na táido; (of talent etc) 素晴らしい例 subárashiì reí

exhibitionist [eksəbiʃ'ənist] n (show-off) 気取り屋 kidőriya

exhilarating [igzil'əreitiŋ] adj (experience, news) 喜ばしい yorőkobashiì

exhort [igzɔ:rt'] vt 訓戒する kuńkai suru

exile [eg'zail] n (condition, state) 亡命 bőmei; (person) 亡命者 bőmeìsha

♦vt 追放する tsuíhō suru

exist [igzist'] vi (be present) 存在する sońzai suru; (live) 生活する seíkatsu suru

existence [igzis'təns] n (reality) 存在 sońzai; (life) 生活 seíkatsu

existing [igzis'tiŋ] adj (present) 現存の geńzon no, geńzon no

exit [eg'zit] n (from room, building, motorway etc) 出口 déguchi; (departure) 出ていく事 dété ikú kotð

♦vi (THEATER) 退場する taíjō suru; (COMPUT) プログラムを終了する purőgurāmu wo shūryō suru

exit ramp (US) n (AUT) 出口ランプ déguchiranpu

exodus [ek'sədəs] n 大脱出 daídasshùtsu

exonerate [igzɑːn'əreit] vt: **to exonerate someone from something** (blame, guilt etc) ...について...の容疑を晴らす ...ni tsúìte ...no yőgi wò harásù

exorbitant [igzɔ:r'bətənt] adj (prices, rents) 法外な hőgai na

exorcize [ek'sɔ:rsaiz] vt (spirit) 追い払う oíharaù; (person, place) ...から悪魔を追い払う ...kara ákùma wo oíharaù

exotic [igzɑt'ik] adj (food, place) 異国的な ikőkuteki na, エキゾチックな ekízochikkù na

expand [ikspænd'] vt (business etc) 拡張する kakúchō suru; (staff, numbers etc) 増やす fuyásù

♦vi (population etc) 増える fuérù; (business etc) 大きくなる őkìku nárù; (gas, metal) 膨張する bőchō suru

expanse [ikspæns'] n (of sea, sky etc) 広がり hirőgarì

expansion [ikspæn'tʃən] n (of business, population, economy etc) 増大 ződai

expatriate [ekspei'tri:it] n 国外在住者 kokúgai zaijùsha

expect [ikspekt'] vt (anticipate) 予想する yoső suru; (await) 待つ mátsù; (require) 要求する yőkyū suru; (suppose) ...だと思う ...dá tð omőù

♦vi: **to be expecting** (be pregnant) 妊娠している nińshin shite irù

expectancy [ikspek'tənsi:] n (anticipation) 期待 kitái

life expectancy 寿命 jumyố

expectant mother [ikspek'tənt-] n 妊婦 nínpu

expectation [ekspektei'ʃən] n (hope, belief) 期待 kitái

expedience [ikspi:'di:əns] n (convenience) 便宜 béñgi, 都合 tsugố

expediency [ikspi:'di:ənsi:] n = **expedience**

expedient [ikspi:'di:ənt] adj (useful, convenient) 都合の良い tsugố no yoí
♦n (measure) 便法 beñpố

expedition [ekspədiʃ'ən] n (for exploration) 探検 旅行 tañkenryokố; (for shopping etc) ツアー tsûấ

expel [ikspel'] vt (person: from school) 退学させる taígaku saserù; (: from organization, place) 追出す oídasù; (gas, liquid) 排出する haíshutsu suru

expend [ikspend'] vt (money, time, energy) 費やす tsuíyasù

expendable [ikspen'dəbəl] adj (person, thing) 消耗品的な shốmōhinteki na

expenditure [ikspen'ditʃər] n (of money, energy, time) 消費 shốhi

expense [ikspens'] n (cost) 費用 híyồ; (expenditure) 出費 shuppí

at the expense of ...を犠牲にして ...wo giséi ni shité

expense account n 交際費 kốsaíhi

expenses [ikspen'siz] npl (traveling expenses, hotel expenses etc) 経費 keíhi

expensive [ikspen'siv] adj (article) 高価な kốka na; (mistake, tastes) 高く付く tákàku tsukú

experience [ikspi:r'i:əns] n 経験 keíken
♦vt (situation, feeling etc) 経験する keíken suru

experienced [ikspi:r'i:ənst] adj (in job) 熟練した jukúren shità

experiment [ikspe:r'əmənt] n (trial: also SCIENCE) 実験 jikkén
♦vi: *to experiment (with/on)* (...を使って) 実験する (...wo tsukátté) jikkén suru

experimental [ikspe:rəmen'təl] adj 実験

的な jikkénteki na

expert [ek'spə:rt] adj (opinion, help) 専門家の señmonka no; (driver etc) 熟練した jukúren shità
♦n (specialist) 専門家 señmonka, エキスパート ekísupàto

expertise [ekspə:rti:z'] n (know-how) 技術 gíjutsu, ノーハウ nốhaù

expire [ikspai'ə:r] vi (passport, licence etc) 切れる kirérù

expiry [ikspaiə:r'i:] n (of passport, lease etc) 満期 máñki

explain [ik(s)plein'] vt 説明する setsúmei suru

explanation [eksplənei'ʃən] n 説明 setsúmei

explanatory [iksplæn'ətɔ:ri:] adj (statement, comment) 説明の setsúmei no

explicit [iksplis'it] adj (clear) 明白な meíhaku na; (frank) 隠し立てしない kakúshidate shinaí

explode [iksploud'] vi (bomb) 爆発する bakúhatsu suru; (population) 爆発的に増える bakúhatsuteki nī fuérù; (person: with rage etc) 激怒する gékìdo suru

exploit [n eks'plɔit vb iksplɔit'] n (deed, feat) 手柄 tegára
♦vt (workers) 搾取する sákùshu suru; (person, idea) 私利私欲に利用する shírìshíyòku ni riyố suru; (opportunity, resources) 利用する riyố suru

exploitation [eksplɔitei'ʃən] n (of workers) 搾取 sákùshu; (of person, idea, resources, opportunity etc) 利用 riyố

exploration [eksplərei'ʃən] n (of place, space) 探検 tañken; (with hands etc) 探る事 sagúru kotố; (of idea, suggestion) 検討 keñtố

exploratory [iksplɔ:r'ətɔ:ri:] adj (expedition) 探検の tañken no; (talks, operation) 予備的な yobíteki na

explore [iksplɔ:r'] vt (place, space) 探検する tañken suru; (with hands etc) 探る sagúrù; (idea, suggestion) 検討する keñtố suru

explorer [iksplɔ:r'ə:r] n (of place, country etc) 探検家 tañkenka

explosion [iksplou'ʒən] n (of bomb) 爆発

bakúhatsu; (increase: of population etc)
爆発的増加 bakúhatsutekizóka; (outburst: of rage, laughter etc) 激怒 gékído

explosive [iksplou'siv] *adj* (device, effect) 爆発の bakúhatsu no; (situation, temper) 爆発的な bakúhatsuteki na
♦*n* (substance) 爆薬 bakúyaku; (device) 爆弾 bakúdañ

exponent [ekspou'nent] *n* (of idea, theory) 擁護者 yōgoshà; (of skill, activity) 達人 tatsújin

export [*vb* ekspɔːrt' *n* eks'pɔːrt] *vt* (goods) 輸出する yushútsu suru
♦*n* (process) 輸出 yushútsu; (product) 輸出品 yushútsuhiñ
♦*cpd* (duty, permit) 輸出... yushútsu...

exporter [ekspɔːr'təːr] *n* 輸出業者 yushútsugyōsha

expose [ikspouz'] *vt* (reveal: object) むき出しにする mukídashi ni surù; (unmask: person) ...の悪事を暴く ...no ákùji wo abákù

exposed [ikspouzd'] *adj* (house, place etc) 雨風にさらされた ámèkaze ni sarásareta

exposure [ikspou'ʒəːr] *n* (to heat, cold, radiation) さらされる事 sarásareru kotò; (publicity) 報道 hōdō; (of person) 暴露 bákùro; (PHOT) 露出 roshútsu
to die from exposure (MED) 低体温症で死ぬ teítaioñshō de shinú

exposure meter *n* (PHOT) 露出計 roshútsukei

expound [ikspaund'] *vt* (theory, opinion) 説明する setsúmei suru

express [ikspres'] *adj* (clear: command, intention etc) 明白な meíhaku na; (BRIT: letter etc) 速達の sokútatsu no
♦*n* (train, bus, coach) 急行 kyúkō
♦*vt* (idea, view) 言表わす iíarawasù; (emotion, quantity) 表現する hyōgen suru

expression [ikspreʃ'ən] *n* (word, phrase) 言方 iíkata; (of idea, emotion) 表現 hyōgen; (on face) 表情 hyōjō; (of actor, singer etc: feeling) 表現力 hyōgeñryoku

expressive [ikspres'iv] *adj* (glance) 意味ありげな ímìarige na; (ability) 表現の hyōgen no

expressly [ikspres'liː] *adv* (clearly, intentionally) はっきりと hakkírì to

expressway [ikspres'wei] (*US*) *n* (urban motorway) 高速道路 kōsokudōro

expulsion [ikspʌl'ʃən] *n* (SCOL) 退学処分 taígakushobùn; (from organization etc) 追放 tsuíhō; (of gas, liquid etc) 排出 haíshutsu

expurgate [eks'pəːrgeit] *vt* (text, recording) 検閲する keñ-etsu suru

exquisite [ekskwiz'it] *adj* (perfect: face, lace, workmanship, taste) 見事な mígòto na

extend [ikstend'] *vt* (visit) 延ばす nobásù; (street) 延長する eñchō suru; (building) 増築する zōchiku suru; (arm, hand) 伸ばす nobásù
♦*vi* (land) 広がる hirógarù; (road) 延びる nobírù; (period) 続く tsuzúkù
to extend an offer of help 援助を申出る eñjo wo mōshiderù
to extend an invitation to ... ...を招待する ...wo shōtai suru

extension [iksten'ʃən] *n* (of building) 増築 zōchiku; (of time) 延長 eñchō; (of campaign, rights) 拡大 kakúdai; (ELEC) 延長コード eñchōkōdo; (TEL: in private house, office) 内線 naísen

extensive [iksten'siv] *adj* (area) 広い hirōi; (effect, damage) 甚大な jiñdai na; (coverage, discussion) 広範囲の kōhañ-i no

extensively [iksten'sivliː] *adv*: *he's traveled extensively* 彼は広く旅行している kárè wa híròku ryokō shite irù

extent [ikstent'] *n* (size: of area, land etc) 広さ híròsa; (: of problem etc) 大きさ ōkìsa
to some extent ある程度 árù teído
to the extent of ... ...までも ...mádè mo
to such an extent that ... ...という程 ...to iú hodò
to what extent? どのぐらい? donó guraî?

extenuating [iksten'juːeitiŋ] *adj*: *extenuating circumstances* 酌量すべき情状 shakúryō subèki jōjō

exterior [iksti:r'i:ər] *adj* (external) 外部 の gáíbu no
♦*n* (outside) 外 部 gáíbu; (appearance) 外 見 gáíken

exterminate [ikstər'məneit] *vt* (animals) 撲滅する bokúmetsu suru; (people) 根絶する kofizetsu suru

external [ikstə:r'nəl] *adj* (walls etc) 外部 の gáíbu no; (examiner, auditor) 部外の búgái no
external evidence 外的証拠 gaítekishō-ko
「*for external use*」外用薬 gaíyōyaku

extinct [ikstiŋk'] *adj* (animal, plant) 絶 滅した zetsúmetsu shitá
an extinct volcano 死火山 shikázàn

extinction [ikstiŋk'ʃən] *n* (of species) 絶 滅 zetsúmetsu

extinguish [ikstiŋ'gwiʃ] *vt* (fire, light) 消 す kesú

extinguisher [ikstiŋ'gwiʃə:r] *n* 消 火 器 shōkakì

extort [ikstɔ:rt'] *vt* (money) ゆすり取る yusúritorù; (confession) 強要する kyōyō suru

extortion [ikstɔ:r'ʃən] *n* (of money etc) ゆすり yusúri; (confession) 強要 kyōyō

extortionate [ikstɔ:r'ʃənit] *adj* (price, demands) 法外な hōgai na

extra [eks'trə] *adj* (thing, person, amount) 余分の yobún no
♦*adv* (in addition) 特別に tokúbetsu ni
♦*n* (luxury) 特別の物 tokúbetsu no mo-nò, 余分の物 yobún no monò; (surcharge) 追加料金 tsuíkaryōkin; (CINEMA, THEATER) エキストラ ekísutòra

extra-... [eks'trə] *prefix* 特別に...tokúbetsu ni ...

extract [*vt* ikstrækt' *n* eks'trækt] *vt* (take out: object) 取出す toridasù; (: tooth) 抜く nukú, 抜歯する basshí suru; (mineral: from ground) 採掘する saíkutsu suru, 抽出する chūshutsu suru; (money) 強要して取る kyōyō shitè tórù; (promise) 無理強いする muríjii suru
♦*n* (of novel, recording) 抜粋 bassúi; (malt extract, vanilla extract etc) エキ ス ékìsu, エッセンス éssènsu

extracurricular [ekstrəkərik'jələ:r] *adj* (activities) 課外の kagái no

extradite [eks'trədait] *vt* (from country) 引渡す hikíwatasù; (to country) ...の引渡 しを受ける ...no hikíwatashi wò ukérù

extradition [ekstrədiʃ'ən] *n* 外国への犯 人引渡し gaíkoku e nò háñnin hikíwata-shi

extramarital [ekstrəmær'itəl] *adj* (affair, relationship) 婚外の koñgai no, 不倫の furín no

extramural [ekstrəmju:r'əl] *adj* (lectures, activities) 学外の gakúgai no

extraordinary [ikstrɔ:r'dəne:ri:] *adj* (person) 抜きん出た nukíndetà; (conduct, situation) 異常な ijō na; (meeting) 臨時の ríñji no

extravagance [ikstræv'əgəns] *n* (no pl: spending) 浪費 rōhi; (example of spending) ぜいたく zeítaku

extravagant [ikstræv'əgənt] *adj* (lavish: person) 気前の良い kimáe no yoì; (: gift) ぜいたくな zeítaku na; (wasteful: person) 金遣いの荒い kanézukaì no arai; (: machine) 不経済な fukéizai na

extreme [ikstri:m'] *adj* (cold, poverty etc) 非常な hijō na; (opinions, methods etc) 極端な kyokútan na; (point, edge) 末 端の mattán no
♦*n* (of behavior) 極端 kyokútan

extremely [ikstri:m'li:] *adv* 非常に hijō ni

extremity [ikstrem'iti:] *n* (edge, end) 端 hashí; (of situation) 極端 kyokútan

extricate [eks'trikeit] *vt*: *to extricate someone/something (from)* (trap, situation) (...から)...を救い出す (...kara) ...wo sukúidasù

extrovert [ek'strouvə:rt] *n* 外向的な人 gaíkōteki na hitò

exuberant [igzu:'bə:rənt] *adj* (person etc) 元気一杯の geñkiíppaì no; (imagination etc) 豊かな yútàka na

exude [igzu:d'] *vt* (liquid) にじみ出させる nijímidasaserù; (smell) 放つ hanátsu
to exude confidence 自信満々である jishín mañman dè árù
to exude enthusiasm 意気込む ikígo-

mù

exult [igzʌlt'] *vi* (rejoice) 喜び勇む yorókobiisamù

eye [ai] *n* (ANAT) 目 mé

♦*vt* (look at, watch) 見詰める mitsúmerù

the eye of a needle 針の目 hárì no mé

to keep an eye on ...を見張る ...wo miháru

eyeball [ai'bɔːl] *n* 眼球 gańkyū

eyebath [ai'bæθ] *n* 洗眼カップ sengankappù

eyebrow [ai'brau] *n* 眉毛 máyùge

eyebrow pencil *n* アイブローペンシル aíburōpeñshiru

eyedrops [ai'drɑːps] *npl* 点眼薬 teńgañyaku

eyelash [ai'læʃ] *n* まつげ mátsùge

eyelid [ai'lid] *n* まぶた mábùta

eyeliner [ai'lainəːr] *n* アイライナー aíraìnā

eye-opener [ai'oupənəːr] *n* (revelation) 驚くべき新事実 odórokubèki shiñjijîtsu

eyeshadow [ai'ʃædou] *n* アイシャドー aíshadõ

eyesight [ai'sait] *n* 視力 shírỳoku

eyesore [ai'sɔːr] *n* (building) 目障り mezáwàri

eye witness *n* (to crime, accident) 目撃者 mokúgekishà

F

F [ef] *n* (MUS: note) ヘ音 hé-òn; (: key) ヘ調 héchõ

F. *abbr* (= *Fahrenheit*) 華氏 káshì

fable [fei'bəl] *n* (story) ぐう話 gū́wa

fabric [fæb'rik] *n* (cloth) 生地 kíjì

fabrication [fæbrikei'ʃən] *n* (lie) うそ úsò; (making) 製造 seízõ

fabulous [fæb'jələs] *adj* (*inf*: super) 素晴らしい subárashiì; (extraordinary) 途方もない tohṍ mo nài; (mythical) 伝説的な deńsetsuteki na

facade [fəsɑːd'] *n* (of building) 正面 shṍmen; (*fig*: pretence) 見せ掛け misékake

face [feis] *n* (ANAT) 顔 kaó; (expression) 表情 hyṍjō; (of clock) 文字盤 mojíban; (of cliff) 面 mêñ; (of building) 正面 shṍmen

♦*vt* (particular direction) ...に向かう ...ni mukáù; (facts, unpleasant situation) 直視する chókushi suru

face down (person) 下向きになって shitámuki ni nattè; (card) 伏せてあって fuséte attè

to lose face 面目を失う meñboku wo ushínaù

to make/pull a face 顔をしかめる kaó wo shikámerù

in the face of (difficulties etc) ...にめげず ...ni megézù

on the face of it (superficially) 表面は hyṍmen wa

face to face (with person, problem) 面と向かって meñ to mukattè

face cloth (*BRIT*) *n* フェースタオル fésutaòru

face cream *n* フェースクリーム fésukurīmu

face lift *n* (of person) 顔のしわ取り手術 kaó no shiwátori shujùtsu; (of building etc) 改造 kaízõ

face powder *n* フェースパウダー fésupaùdā

face-saving [feis'seiviŋ] *adj* (compromise, gesture) 面子を立てる méñtsu wo tatérù

facet [fæs'it] *n* (of question, personality) 側面 sokúmen; (of gem) 切子面 kiríkomèn

facetious [fəsi:'ʃəs] *adj* (comment, remark) ふざけた fuzáketà

face up to *vt fus* (obligations, difficulty) ...に立ち向かう ...ni tachímukaù

face value *n* (of coin, stamp) 額面 gakúmen

to take something at face value (*fig*) そのまま信用する sonṍ mama shiñ-yō suru

facial [fei'ʃəl] *adj* (hair, expression) 顔の kaó no

facile [fæs'əl] *adj* (comment, reaction) 軽々しい karúgarushì

facilitate [fəsil'əteit] *vt* 助ける tasúkerù

facilities [fəsil'əti:z] *npl* (buildings,

equipment) 設備 setsúbi

credit facilities 分割払い取扱い buńkatsubarái toríatsukai

facing [fei'siŋ] *prep* (opposite) ...の向い側の ...no mukáigawa no

facsimile [fæksim'əli:] *n* (exact replica) 複製 fukúsei; (*also*: **facsimile machine**) ファックス fákkùsu; (transmitted document) ファックス fákkùsu

fact [fækt] *n* (true piece of information) 事実 jijítsu; (truth) 真実 shińjitsu
in fact 事実は jijítsu wa

faction [fæk'ʃən] *n* (group: *also* REL, POL) 派 há

factor [fæk'tə:r] *n* (of problem, decision etc) 要素 yóso

factory [fæk'tə:ri:] *n* (building) 工場 kójō

factual [fæk'tʃu:əl] *adj* (analysis, information) 事実の jijítsu no

faculty [fæk'əlti:] *n* (sense, ability) 能力 nōryoku; (of university) 学部 gakúbu; (*US*: teaching staff) 教職員 kyōshokuin ◇総称 sōshō

fad [fæd] *n* (craze) 一時的流行 ichíjitekiryūkō

fade [feid] *vi* (color) あせる asérù; (light, sound) 次第に消える shidái ni kiérù; (flower) しぼむ shibómù; (hope, memory, smile) 消える kiérù

fag [fæg] (*BRIT*: *inf*) *n* (cigarette) もく mokú

fail [feil] *vt* (exam) 落第する rakúdai surù; (candidate) 落第させる rakúdai saserù; (subj: leader) ...の期待を裏切る ...no kitái wo urágirù; (: courage, memory) なくなる nakúnarù
♦*vi* (candidate, attempt etc) 失敗する shippái suru; (brakes) 故障する koshō surù; (eyesight, health) 衰える otóroerù; (light) 暗くなる kuráku narù
to fail to do something (be unable) ...する事が出来ない ...surú koto gà dekínai; (neglect) ...する事を怠る ...surú koto wò okótarù
without fail 必ず kánarazu

failing [fei'liŋ] *n* (weakness) 欠点 kettéñ
♦*prep* ...がなければ ...ga nakéreba

failure [feil'jə:r] *n* (lack of success) 失敗 shippái; (person) 駄目人間 daméniñgen; (mechanical etc) 故障 koshō

faint [feint] *adj* かすかな kásùka na
♦*n* (MED) 気絶 kizétsu
♦*vi* (MED) 気絶する kizétsu suru
to feel faint 目まいがする memái ga suru

fair [fe:r] *adj* (reasonable, right) 公平な kōhei na; (quite large) かなりな kánari na; (quite good) 悪くない warúkunài; (skin) 白い shirói; (hair) 金色の kiñ-iro no; (weather) 晴れの haré no
♦*adv* (play) 正々堂々と seíseidōdō to
♦*n* (*also*: **trade fair**) トレードフェアー torédofeà; (*BRIT*: funfair) 移動遊園地 idōyūeñchi

fairly [fe:r'li:] *adv* (justly) 公平に kōhei ni; (quite) かなり kánàri

fairness [fe:r'nis] *n* (justice, impartiality) 公平さ kōheisa

fair play *n* 公平さ kōheisa

fairy [fe:r'i:] *n* (sprite) 妖精 yōsei

fairy tale *n* おとぎ話 otógibanàshi

faith [feiθ] *n* (trust) 信用 shiń-yō; (religion) 宗教 shūkyō; (religious belief) 信仰 shiñkō

faithful [feiθ'fəl] *adj* 忠実な chūjitsu na

faithfully [feiθ'fəli:] *adv* 忠実に chūjitsu ni
yours faithfully (*BRIT*: in letters) 敬具 keígu

fake [feik] *n* (painting etc) 偽物 nisémono; (person) ぺてん師 petéñshi
♦*adj* (phoney) いんちきの íñchiki no
♦*vt* (painting etc) 偽造する gizō suru; (illness, emotion) ...だと見せ掛ける ...da to misékakerù

falcon [fæl'kən] *n* ハヤブサ hayábusa

fall [fɔːl] *n* (of person, object: from height) 転落 teñraku; (of person, horse: from standing position) 転倒 teñtō; (of price, temperature, dollar) 下がる事 sagáru kotò; (of government, leader, country) 倒れる事 taóreru kotò; (*US*: autumn) 秋 ákì
♦*vi* (*pt* **fell**, *pp* **fallen**) (person, object: from height) 落ちる ochírù; (person,

horse: from standing position) 転ぶ koróbù; (snow, rain) 降る fúrù; (price, temperature, dollar) 下がる sagárù; (government, leader, country) 倒れる taórerù; (night, darkness) (...に) なる (...ni) nárù

snowfall 降雪 kōsetsu

rainfall 降雨 kōu

the fall of darkness 暗くなる事 kuráku naru kotò

the fall of night 夜になる事 yórù ni náru kotò

to fall flat (on one's face) うつぶせに倒れる utsúbuse ni taórerù; (plan) 失敗する shippái suru; (joke) 受けない ukénaî

fallacy [fæl'əsi:] *n* (misconception) 誤信 goshín

fall back *vt fus* (retreat) 後ずさりする atózusàri suru; (MIL) 後退する kōtaisuru

fall back on *vt fus* (remedy etc) ...に頼る ...ni tayórù

fall behind *vi* 遅れる okúrerù

fall down *vi* (person) 転ぶ koróbù; (building) 崩壊する hōkai suru

fallen [fɔːl'ən] *pp of* fall

fall for *vt fus* (trick) ...にだまされる ...ni damásarerù; (person) ...にほれる ...ni horérù

fallible [fæl'əbəl] *adj* (person, memory) 間違いをしがちな machígaî wo shigáchi na

fall in *vi* (roof) 落込む ochíkomù; (MIL) 整列する sefretsu suru

fall off *vi* (person, object) 落ちる ochírù; (takings, attendance) 減る herú

fall out *vi* (hair, teeth) 抜ける nukérù; (friends etc) けんかする kefika suru

fallout [fɔːl'aut] *n* (radiation) 放射性落下物 hōshaseirákkabutsu, 死の灰 shí nò hai

fallout shelter *n* 放射性落下物待避所 hōshaseirákkabutsu taíhijò

fallow [fæl'ou] *adj* (land, field) 休閑中の kyūkaňchū no

falls [fɔːlz] *npl* (waterfall) 滝 takí

fall through *vi* (plan, project) 失敗に終る shippái ni owarù

false [fɔːls] *adj* (untrue: statement, accusation) うその usó no; (wrong: impres-

sion, imprisonment) 間違った machígattà; (insincere: person, smile) 不誠実な fuséijitsu na

false alarm *n* 誤った警報 ayámattà keíhō

false pretenses *npl*: *under false pretenses* うその申立てで usó nò mōshitate de

false teeth *npl* 入れ歯 iréba

falter [fɔːl'təːr] *vi* (engine) 止りそうになる tomárisō ni narù; (person: hesitate) ためらう taméraù; (: stagger) よろめく yorómekù

fame [feim] *n* 名声 meísei

familiar [fəmil'jəːr] *adj* (well-known: face, voice) おなじみの onájimi no; (intimate: behavior, tone) 親しい shitáshiî

to be familiar with (subject) よく知っている yókù shitté iru

familiarize [fəmil'jəraiz] *vt*: *to familiarize oneself with* ...になじむ ...ni najímù

family [fæm'li:] *n* (relations) 家族 kázòku; (children) 子供 kodómo ◇総称 sōshō

family business *n* 家族経営の商売 kazókukeîei no shōbai

family doctor *n* 町医者 machí-îsha

famine [fæm'in] *n* 飢餓 kíga

famished [fæm'iʃt] *adj* (hungry) 腹がぺこぺこの hará gà pekópeko no

famous [fei'məs] *adj* 有名な yūmei na

famously [fei'məsli:] *adv* (get on) 素晴らしく subárashikù

fan [fæn] *n* (person) ファン fáñ; (folding) 扇子 séňsu; (ELEC) 扇風機 señpūki

◆*vt* (face, person) あおぐ aógù; (fire, quarrel) あおる aórù

fanatic [fənæt'ik] *n* (extremist) 熱狂者 nekkyōshà; (enthusiast) マニア mánià

fan belt *n* (AUT) ファンベルト faňberùto

fanciful [fæn'sifəl] *adj* (notion, idea) 非現実的な hígeňjitsuteki na; (design, name) 凝った kóttà

fancy [fæn'si:] *n* (whim) 気まぐれ kimágurè; (imagination) 想像 sōzō; (fantasy) 夢 yumé

◆*adj* (clothes, hat, food) 凝った kóttà;

(hotel etc) 高級の kṓkyū no

♦*vt* (feel like, want) 欲しいなと思う hoshíi na to omóu; (imagine) 想像する sṓzō suru; (think) ...だと思う ...da to omóu

to take a fancy to ...を気に入る ...wo kí ni irú

he fancies her (*inf*) 彼は彼女が好きだ kárè wa kanójo ga sukí dà

fancy dress *n* 仮装の衣裳 kasṓ no ishṓ

fancy-dress ball *n* 仮装舞踏会 kasṓbutōkai

fanfare [fæn'feːr] *n* ファンファーレ fanfáre

fang [fæŋ] *n* (tooth) きば kibá

fan out *vi* 扇形に広がる ṓgigata nì hirógarù

fantastic [fæntæs'tik] *adj* (enormous) 途方もない tohṓmonāi; (strange, incredible) 信じられない shiṅjirarenài; (wonderful) 素晴らしい subá rashíi

fantasy [fæn'təsiː] *n* (dream) 夢 yumé; (unreality, imagination) 空想 kūsō

far [fɑːr] *adj* (distant) 遠い tṓi

♦*adv* (a long way) 遠く tṓku; (much) はるかに hárùka ni

far away/off 遠く tṓku

far better ...の方がはるかにいい ...no hṓ ga hárùka ni ii

far from 決して...でない kesshíte ...de náì ◇強い否定を表す tsuyói hitéi wo aráwasù

by far はるかに hárùka ni

go as far as the farm 農場まで行って下さい nṓjō madè itté kudasaì

as far as I know 私の知る限り watákushi nò shirú kagirî

how far? (distance) どれぐらいの距離 doré gurai no kyòri; (referring to activity, situation) どれ程 doré hodò

faraway [fɑːr'əweì] *adj* (place) 遠くの tṓku no; (look) 夢見る様な yumémiru yṑ na; (thought) 現実離れの geñjitsubanare no

farce [fɑːrs] *n* (THEATER) 笑劇 shṓgeki, ファース fásù; (*fig*) 茶番劇 chabáñgeki

farcical [fɑːr'sikəl] *adj* (situation) ばかげた bakágèta

fare [feːr] *n* (on trains, buses) 料金 ryṓkin; (*also*: **taxi fare**) タクシー代 takúshìdai; (food) 食べ物 tabémòno

half/full fare 半(全)額 hañ(zeñ)gàku

Far East *n*: *the Far East* 極東 kyokútō

farewell [feːr'wel'] *excl* さようなら sayṓnarà

♦*n* 別れ wakáre

farm [fɑːrm] *n* 農場 nṓjō

♦*vt* (land) 耕す tagáyasù

farmer [fɑːr'məːr] *n* 農場主 nṓjōshù

farmhand [fɑːrm'hænd] *n* 作男 sakúotðko

farmhouse [fɑːrm'haus] *n* 農家 nṓka

farming [fɑːr'miŋ] *n* (agriculture) 農業 nṓgyō; (of crops) 耕作 kṓsaku; (of animals) 飼育 shíku

farmland [fɑːrm'lænd] *n* 農地 nṓchi

farm worker *n* = **farmhand**

farmyard [fɑːr'jɑːrd] *n* 農家の庭 nṓka no niwà

far-reaching [fɑːr'riː'tʃiŋ] *adj* (reform, effect) 広範囲の kṓhañ-i no

fart [fɑːrt] (*inf!*) *vi* おならをする onára wo surù

farther [fɑːr'ðəːr] *compar of* **far**

farthest [fɑːr'ðist] *superl of* **far**

fascinate [fæs'əneit] *vt* (intrigue, interest) うっとりさせる uttóri saserù

fascinating [fæs'əneitiŋ] *adj* (story, person) 魅惑的な miwákuteki na

fascination [fæsənei'ʃən] *n* 魅惑 miwáku

fascism [fæʃ'izəm] *n* (POL) ファシズム fashízùmu

fashion [fæʃ'ən] *n* (trend: in clothes, thought, custom etc) 流行 ryū́kō, ファッション fásshòn; (*also*: **fashion industry**) ファッション業界 fasshòn gyòkai; (manner) やり方 yaríkata

♦*vt* (make) 作る tsukúrù

in fashion 流行して ryū́kō shite

out of fashion 廃れて sutárete

fashionable [fæʃ'ənəbəl] *adj* (clothes, club, subject) 流行の ryū́kō no

fashion show *n* ファッションショー fasshòn shṓ

fast [fæst] *adj* (runner, car, progress) 速い hayáî; (clock): *to be fast* 進んでいる susúnde irù; (dye, color) あせない asénai
♦*adv* (run, act, think) 速く hayákù; (stuck, held) 固く katáku
♦*n* (REL etc) 断食 dañjiki
♦*vi* (REL etc) 断食する dañjiki suru
fast asleep ぐっすり眠っている gussúrî nemútte irù

fasten [fæs'ən] *vt* (tie, join) 縛る shibárù; (buttons, belt etc) 締める shimérù
♦*vi* 締まる shimárù

fastener [fæs'ənəːr] *n* (button, clasp, pin etc) ファスナー fásùnā

fastening [fæs'əniŋ] *n* = **fastener**

fast food *n* (hamburger etc) ファーストフード fásùtofūdo

fastidious [fæstid'iːəs] *adj* (fussy) やかましい yakámashiî

fat [fæt] *adj* (person, animal) 太った futótta; (book, profit) 厚い atsúi; (wallet) 金がたんまり入った kané gà tañmarî haîttà; (profit) 大きな ōkina
♦*n* (on person, animal: *also* CHEM) 脂肪 shibō; (on meat) 脂身 abúramî; (for cooking) ラード rādo

fatal [feit'əl] *adj* (mistake) 重大な jūdai na; (injury, illness) 致命的な chiméiteki na

fatalistic [feitəlis'tik] *adj* (person, attitude) 宿命論的な shukúmeironteki na

fatality [feitæl'itiː] *n* (road death etc) 死亡事故 shibōjikò

fatally [feit'əliː] *adv* (mistaken) 重大に jūdai ni; (injured etc) 致命的に chiméiteki ni

fate [feit] *n* (destiny) 運命 úñmei; (of person) 安否 áñpi

fateful [feit'fəl] *adj* (moment, decision) 決定的な kettéiteki na

father [fɑː'ðəːr] *n* 父 chichî, 父親 chichíoya, お父さん o-tốsan

father-in-law [fɑː'ðəːrinlɔː] *n* しゅうと shūto

fatherly [fɑː'ðəːliː] *adj* (advice, help) 父親の様な chichíoya no yố na

fathom [fæð'əm] *n* (NAUT) 尋 hírò ◇水深の単位, 約1.83メーター suíshin no táñ-i,

yákù 1.83mếtằ
♦*vt* (understand: mystery, reason) 理解する rikái suru

fatigue [fətiːg'] *n* (tiredness) 疲労 hirō
metal fatigue 金属疲労 kiñzokuhirō

fatten [fæt'ən] *vt* (animal) 太らせる futóraserù
♦*vi* 太る futórù

fatty [fæt'iː] *adj* (food) 脂肪の多い shibố no ōi
♦*n* (*inf*: person) でぶ débù

fatuous [fætʃ'uːəs] *adj* (idea, remark) ばかな bákà na

faucet [fɔː'sit] (*US*) *n* (tap) 蛇口 jagúchi

fault [fɔːlt] *n* (blame) 責任 sekínin; (defect: in person) 欠点 kettén; (: in machine) 欠陥 kekkán; (GEO: crack) 断層 dañsố; (TENNIS) フォールト fốrùto
♦*vt* (criticize) 非難する hínàn suru
it's my fault 私が悪かった watákushi gà warúkattà
to find fault with ...を非難する ...wo hínàn suru
at fault ...のせいで ...no séî de

faulty [fɔːl'tiː] *adj* (machine) 欠陥のある kekkán no arù

fauna [fɔːn'ə] *n* 動物相 dốbutsusố

faux pas [fou pɑː'] *n inv* 非礼 hiréi

favor [fei'vəːr] (*BRIT* **favour**) *n* (approval) 賛成 sañsei; (help) 助け tasúke
♦*vt* (prefer: solution etc) ...の方に賛成する ...no hố nî sañsei surù; (: pupil etc) ひいきする hiîki suru; (assist: team, horse) ...に味方する ...ni mikáta suru
to do someone a favor ...の頼みを聞く ...no tánòmi wo kîkù
to find favor with ...の気に入る ...no kî ni irù
in favor of ...に賛成して ...ni sañsei shite

favorable [fei'vəːrəbəl] *adj* (gen) 有利な yūri na; (reaction) 好意的な kốiteki na; (impression) 良い yối; (comparison) 賞賛的な shốsanteki na; (conditions) 好適な kốteki na

favorite [fei'vəːrit] *adj* (child, author etc) 一番好きな ichíban suki na
♦*n* (of teacher, parent) お気に入り o-kí-

niiri; (in race) 本命 hoñmei

favoritism [feiʹvəːritizəm] n えこひいき ekóhiìki

favour [feiʹvər] etc = **favor** etc

fawn [fɔːn] n (young deer) 子ジカ kojíka
♦adj (also: **fawn-colored**) 薄茶色 usúcha-iro
♦vi: **to fawn (up)on** ...にへつらう ...ni hetsúraù

fax [fæks] n (machine, document) ファックス fákkùsu
♦vt (transmit document) ファックスで送る fákkùsu de okúrù

FBI [efbiːaiʹ] (US) n abbr (= Federal Bureau of Investigation) 連邦捜査局 reñpōsōsakyòku

fear [fiːr] n (being scared) 恐怖 kyófu; (worry) 心配 shiñpai
♦vt (be scared of) 恐れる osórerù; (be worried about) 心配する shiñpai suru
for fear of (in case) ...を恐れて ...wo osóretè

fearful [fiːrʹfəl] adj (person) 怖がっている kowágatte irù; (risk, noise) 恐ろしい osóroshiì

fearless [fiːrʹlis] adj (unafraid) 勇敢な yūkan na

feasible [fiːʹzəbəl] adj (proposal, idea) 可能な kanó na

feast [fiːst] n (banquet) 宴会 eñkai; (delicious meal) ごちそう gochísò; (REL: also: **feast day**) 祝日 shukújitsu
♦vi (take part in a feast) ごちそうを食べる gochísō wò tabérù

feat [fiːt] n (of daring, skill) 目覚しい行為 mezámashiì kói

feather [feðʹəːr] n (of bird) 羽根 hané

feature [fiːʹtʃəːr] n (characteristic) 特徴 tokúchō; (of landscape) 目立つ点 medátsu tèn; (PRESS) 特別記事 tokúbetsukijì; (TV) 特別番組 tokúbetsu bañgumi
♦vt (subj: film) 主役とする shuyáku to surù
♦vi: **to feature in** (situation, film etc) ...で主演する ...de shuén suru

feature film n 長編映画 chóhen eìga

features [fiːʹtʃəːrz] npl (of face) 顔立ち kaódachi

February [febʹjəweːriː] n 2月 nigátsu

fed [fed] pt, pp of **feed**

federal [fedʹəːrəl] adj (system, powers) 連邦の reñpō no

federation [fedəreiʹʃən] n (association) 連盟 reñmei

fed up [fed ʌpʹ] adj: **to be fed up** うんざりしている uñzarì shite iru

fee [fiː] n (payment) 料金 ryókin; (of doctor, lawyer) 報酬 hóshū; (for examination, registration) 手数料 tesúryō
school fees 授業料 jugyóryō

feeble [fiːʹbəl] adj (weak) 弱い yowáì; (ineffectual: attempt, joke) 効果的でない kókateki dè náì

feed [fiːd] n (of baby) ベビーフード bebífūdo; (of animal) えさ esá; (on printer) 給紙装置 kyúshisòchi
♦vt (pt, pp **fed**) (person) ...に食べさせる ...ni tabésaserù; (baby) ...に授乳する ...ni junyú suru; (horse etc) ...にえさをやる ...ni esá wò yárù; (machine) ...に供給する ...ni kyókyū suru; (data, information): **to feed into** ...に入力する ...ni nyúryoku suru

feedback [fiːdʹbæk] n (response) フィードバック fídobàkku

feeding bottle [fiːʹdiŋ-] (BRIT) n ほ乳瓶 honyūbiñ

feed on vt fus (gen) ...を食べる ...wo tabérù, ...を常食とする ...wo jóshoku to suru; (fig) ...にはぐくまれる ...ni hagúkumarerù

feel [fiːl] n (sensation, touch) 感触 kañshoku; (impression) 印象 iñshó
♦vt (pt, pp **felt**) (touch) ...に触る ...ni sawárù; (experience: desire, anger) 覚える obóerù; (: cold, pain) 感じる kañjirù; (think, believe) ...だと思う ...da to omóù
to feel hungry おなかがすく onáka gà sukú
to feel cold 寒がる samúgarù
to feel lonely 寂しがる sabíshigarù
to feel better 気分がよくなる kíbùn ga yóku narù
I don't feel well 気分が悪い kíbùn ga warúì
it feels soft 柔らかい感じだ yawárakai

kañji da

to feel like (want) ...が欲しい ...ga hoshíi

feel about/around vi ...を手探りで捜す ...wo teságuri de sagásù

feeler [fi:'lə:r] n (of insect) 触角 shokkáku

to put out a feeler/feelers (fig) 打診 する dashín suru

feeling [fi:'liŋ] n (emotion) 感情 kañjō; (physical sensation) 感触 kañshoku; (impression) 印象 iñshō

feet [fi:t] npl of **foot**

feign [fein] vt (injury, interest) 見せ掛け る misékakerù

feline [fi:'lain] adj (cat-like) ネコの様な nékò no yṓ na

fell [fel] pt of **fall**

♦vt (tree) 倒す taósù

fellow [fel'ou] n (man) 男 otóko; (comrade) 仲間 nakáma; (of learned society) 会員 kaíin

fellow citizen n 同郷の市民 dókyō nò shímin

fellow countryman (pl **countrymen**) n 同国人 dókokujin

fellow men npl 外の人間 hoká no niñgen

fellowship [fel'ouʃip] n (comradeship) 友情 yújō; (society) 会 káì; (SCOL) 大学特別研究員 daígaku tokubetsu kenkyúin

felony [fel'əni:] n 重罪 júzai

felt [felt] pt, pp of **feel**

♦n (fabric) フェルト férùto

felt-tip pen [felt'tip-] n サインペン saínpen

female [fi:'meil] n (ZOOL) 雌 mesú; (pej: woman) 女 ofina

♦adj (BIO) 雌の mesú no; (sex, character, child) 女の ofina no, 女性の joséi no; (vote etc) 女性たちの joséitachi no

feminine [fem'ənin] adj (clothes, behavior) 女らしい joséi rashíì; (LING) 女性の joséi no

feminist [fem'ənist] n 男女同権論者 dañjodōkenroñsha, フェミニスト femínisùto

fence [fens] n (barrier) 塀 heí

♦vt (also: **fence in**: land) 塀で囲む heí de kakómù

♦vi (SPORT) フェンシングをする féñshingu wo suru

fencing [fen'siŋ] n (SPORT) フェンシング féñshingu

fend [fend] vi: **to fend for oneself** 自力 でやっていく jíriki dè yatté ikù

fender [fen'də:r] n (of fireplace) 火格子 higóshi; (on boat) 防げん物 bōgenbùtsu; (US: of car) フェンダー feñdā

fend off vt (attack etc) 受流す ukénagasù

ferment [vb fə:rment' n fə:r'ment] vi (beer, dough etc) 発酵する hakkō suru

♦n (fig: unrest) 動乱 dóran

fern [fə:rn] n シダ shídà

ferocious [fərou'ʃəs] adj (animal, behavior) どう猛な dṓmō na; (competition) 激しい hagéshiì

ferocity [fərɑs'iti:] n (of animal, behavior) どう猛さ dṓmōsa; (of competition) 激しさ hagéshisà

ferret [fe:r'it] n フェレット férètto

ferret out vt (information) 捜し出す sagáshidasù

ferry [fe:r'i:] n (also: **ferry boat**) フェリー férī, フェリーボート feríbòto

♦vt (transport: by sea, air, road) 輸送する yusō suru

fertile [fə:r'təl] adj (land, soil) 肥よくな hiyṓku na; (imagination) 豊かな yútàka na; (woman) 妊娠可能な niñshinkanō na

fertility [fə:rtil'əti:] n (of land) 肥よくさ hiyṓkusa; (of imagination) 独創性 dokúsōsei; (of woman) 繁殖力 hañshokuryòku

fertilize [fə:r'təlaiz] vt (land) ...に肥料を やる ...ni hiryō wò yárù; (BIO) 受精させる jusei saserù

fertilizer [fə:r'təlaizə:r] n (for plants, land) 肥料 hiryō

fervent [fə:r'vənt] adj (admirer, belief) 熱心な nesshín na

fervor [fə:r'və:r] n 熱心さ nesshíñsa

fester [fes'tə:r] vi (wound) 化のうする kanō suru

festival [fes'təvəl] n (REL) 祝日 shukújitsu; (ART, MUS) フェスティバル fésùtibaru

festive [fes'tiv] *adj* (mood, atmosphere) お祭気分の o-mátsurikibùn no
the festive season (BRIT: Christmas) クリスマスの季節 kurísùmasu no kisétsù

festivities [festiv'iti:z] *npl* (celebrations) お祝い o-íwai

festoon [festu:n'] *vt*: *to festoon with* ...で飾る ...de kazárù

fetch [fetʃ] *vt* (bring) 持って来る notté kurù; (sell for) ...の値で売れる ...no ne de urérù

fetching [fetʃ'iŋ] *adj* (woman, dress) 魅惑的な miwákuteki na

fête [feit] *n* (at church, school) バザー bazā

fetish [fet'iʃ] *n* (obsession) 強迫観念 kyóhakukaňnen

fetus [fi:'təs] (BRIT **foetus**) *n* (BIO) 胎児 táiji

feud [fju:d] *n* (quarrel) 争い arásoì

feudal [fju:d'əl] *adj* (system, society) 封建的な hőkenteki na

fever [fi:'vəɪr] *n* (MED) 熱 netsú

feverish [fi:'vəːriʃ] *adj* (MED) 熱がある netsú ga arù; (emotion) 激しい hageshiì; (activity) 慌ただしい awátadashiì

few [fju:] *adj* (not many) 少数の shósū no; (some): *a few* 幾つかの íkùtsuka no
◆*pron* (not many) 少数 shósū; (some): *a few* 幾つかの íkùtsuka

fewer [fju:'əːr] *adj compar of* **few**

fewest [fju:'ist] *adj superl of* **few**

fiancé [fi:ɑːnsei'] *n* 婚約者 koň-yakushà, フィアンセ fiáňse ◇男性 dańsei

fiancée [fi:ɑːnsei'] *n* 婚約者 koň-yakushà, フィアンセ fiáňse ◇女性 joséi

fiasco [fi:æs'kou] *n* (disaster) 失敗 shippái

fib [fib] *n* (lie) うそ úsò

fiber [fai'bəːr] (BRIT **fibre**) *n* (thread, roughage) 繊維 séñ-i; (cloth) 生地 kíjì; (ANAT: tissue) 神経繊維 shiňkeiseň-i

fiber-glass [fai'bəːrglæs] *n* ファイバーグラス faíbāguràsu

fickle [fik'əl] *adj* (person) 移り気な utsúrigi na; (weather) 変りやすい kawáriyasuì

fiction [fik'ʃən] *n* (LITERATURE) フィクション fíkùshon; (invention) 作り事 tsukúrigoto; (lie) うそ úsò

fictional [fik'ʃənəl] *adj* (character, event) 架空の kakū́ no

fictitious [fiktiʃ'əs] *adj* (false, invented) 架空の kakū́ no

fiddle [fid'əl] *n* (MUS) バイオリン baíorin; (*inf*: fraud, swindle) 詐欺 ságì
◆*vt* (BRIT: accounts) ごまかす gomákasù

fiddle with *vt fus* (glasses etc) いじくる ijíkurù

fidelity [fidel'iti:] *n* (faithfulness) 忠誠 chūsei

fidget [fidʒ'it] *vi* (nervously) そわそわする sówàsowa suru; (in boredom) もぞもぞする mózòmozo suru

field [fi:ld] *n* (on farm) 畑 hatáke; (SPORT: ground) グランド guráňdo; (*fig*: subject, area of interest) 分野 búň-ya; (range: of vision) 視野 shíyà; (: of magnet: *also* ELEC) 磁場 jíbà

field marshal *n* (MIL) 元帥 geñsui

fieldwork [fi:ld'wəːrk] *n* (research) 現地調査 géňchichòsa, 実地調査 jitchíchòsa, フィールドワーク fírudowàku

fiend [fi:nd] *n* (monster) 怪物 kaíbutsu

fiendish [fi:n'diʃ] *adj* (person, problem) 怪物の様な kaíbutsu no yṓ na; (problem) ものすごく難しい monósugokù muzúkashiì

fierce [fi:rs] *adj* (animal, person) どう猛な dő̀mo na; (fighting) 激しい hageshiì; (loyalty) 揺るぎない yurúginài; (wind) 猛烈な mő̀retsu na; (heat) うだる様な udáru yṑ na

fiery [fai'əːri:] *adj* (burning) 燃え盛る moésakarù; (temperament) 激しい hageshiì

fifteen [fif'ti:n'] *num* 十五（の）jū́go (no)

fifth [fifθ] *num* 第五（の）dáigo (no)

fifty [fif'ti:] *num* 五十（の）gojū́ (no)

fifty-fifty [fif'ti:fif'ti:] *adj* (deal, split) 五分五分の gobúgobu no
◆*adv* 五分五分に gobúgobu ni

fig [fig] *n* (fruit) イチジク ichíjiku

fight [fait] n 戦い tatákai
♦vb (pt, pp **fought**)
♦vt (person, enemy, cancer etc: also MIL) ...と戦う ...to tatákaù; (election) ...に出馬する ...ni shutsúba suru; (emotion) 抑える osáerù
♦vi (people: also MIL) 戦う tatákaù

fighter [fai'tə:r] n (combatant) 戦う tatákaù hitò; (plane) 戦闘機 señtóki

fighting [fai'tiŋ] n (battle) 戦い tatákai; (brawl) けんか kéñka

figment [fig'mənt] n: **a figment of the imagination** 気のせい kí nò séi

figurative [fig'jə:rativ] adj (expression, style) 比ゆ的な hiyúteki na

figure [fig'jə:r] n (DRAWING, GEOM) 図 zu; (number, statistic etc) 数字 súji; (body, shape, outline) 形 katáchi; (person, personality) 人 hitó
♦vt (think: esp US) (...だと) 思う (...da to) omóù
♦vi (appear) 見える miérù

figurehead [fig'jə:rhed] n (NAUT) 船首像 señshuzō; (pej: leader) 名ばかりのリーダー na bákarī no rīdā

figure of speech n 比ゆ híyù

figure out vt (work out) 理解する rikái suru

filament [fil'əmənt] n (ELEC) フィラメント fīrámento

filch [filtʃ] (inf) vt (steal) くすねる kusúnerù

file [fail] n (dossier) 資料 shiryố; (folder) 書類ばさみ shorúibàsami; (COMPUT) ファイル fáiru; (row) 列 rétsù; (tool) やすり yasúrì
♦vt (papers) 保管する hokán suru; (LAW: claim) 提出する teíshutsu suru; (wood, metal, fingernails) ...にやすりを掛ける ...ni yasúrì wo kakérù

file in/out vi 1列で入る〔出る〕ichíretsu dè haírù〔dérù〕

filing cabinet [fai'liŋ-] n ファイルキャビネット faíru kyabínètto

fill [fil] vt (container, space): **to fill (with)** (...で) 一杯にする (...de) ippái ni surù; (vacancy) 補充する hojū suru; (need) 満たす mitásù

fill in vt (hole) うめる umérù; (time) つぶす tsubúsù; (form) ...に書き入れる ...ni kakíirerù

filling [fil'iŋ] n (for tooth) 充てん jūten; (CULIN) 中身 nakami

filling station n (AUT) ガソリンスタンド gasórinsutàndo

fill up vt (container, space) 一杯にする ippái ni surù
♦vi (AUT) 満タンにする mañtan ni surù

film [film] n (CINEMA, TV) 映画 eíga; (PHOT) フィルム fírùmu; (of powder, liquid etc) 膜 makú
♦vt (scene) 撮影する satsúei suru
♦vi 撮影する satsúei suru

film star n 映画スター eígasutā

film strip n (slide) フィルムスライド firúmusuraìdo

filter [fil'tə:r] n (device) ろ過装置 rokásōchi, フィルター fírùta; (PHOT) フィルター fírùta
♦vt (liquid) ろ過する rokấ suru

filter lane (BRIT) n (AUT) 右〔左〕折車線 u〔sa〕sétsu shasèn

filter-tipped [fil'tə:rtipt] adj フィルター付きの fírùtàtsuki no

filth [filθ] n (dirt) 汚物 obútsu

filthy [fil'θi:] adj (object, person) 不潔な fukétsu na; (language) みだらな mídàra na

fin [fin] n (of fish) ひれ hiré

final [fai'nəl] adj (last) 最後の saígo no; (ultimate) 究極の kyūkyoku no; (definitive: answer, decision) 最終的な saíshūteki na
♦n (SPORT) 決勝戦 kesshốsen

finale [finæl'i:] n フィナーレ fínāre

finalist [fai'nəlist] n (SPORT) 決勝戦出場選手 kesshốsen shutsujố señshu

finalize [fai'nəlaiz] vt (arrangements, plans) 最終的に決定する saíshūteki nì kettéi suru

finally [fai'nəli:] adv (eventually) ようやく yōyaku; (lastly) 最後に saígo ni

finals [fai'nəlz] *npl* (SCOL) 卒業試験 sotsúgyōshikén

finance [*n* fai'næns *vb* finæns'] *n* (money, backing) 融資 yúshi; (money management) 財政 zaísei
♦*vt* (back, fund) 融資する yúshi suru

finances [finæn'siz] *npl* (personal finances) 財政 zaísei

financial [finæn'tʃəl] *adj* (difficulties, year, venture) 経済的な keízaiteki na

financial year *n* 会計年度 kaíkeinèndo

financier [finænsi:r'] *n* (backer, funder) 出資者 shusshíshà

find [faind] (*pt*, *pp* **found**) *vt* (person, object, answer) 見付ける mitsúkeru; (discover) 発見する hakkén suru; (think) ...だと思う ...da to omóù
♦*n* (discovery) 発見 hakkén
to find someone guilty (LAW) ...に有罪判決を下す ...ni yúzaihañketsu wo kudásù

findings [fain'diŋz] *npl* (LAW, of report) 調査の結果 chósa no kekkà

find out *vt* (fact, truth) 知る shírù; (person) ...の悪事を知る ...no ákùji wo shírù
to find out about (subject) 調べる shiráberù; (by chance) 知る shírù

fine [fain] *adj* (excellent: quality, performance etc) 見事な mígòto na; (thin: hair, thread) 細い hosóì; (not coarse: sand, powder etc) 細かい komákaì; (subtle: detail, adjustment etc) 細かい komákaì
♦*adv* (well) うまく úmàku
♦*n* (LAW) 罰金 bakkín
♦*vt* (LAW) ...に罰金を払わせる ...ni bakkín wð haráwaserù
to be fine (person) 元気である géñki de árù; (weather) 良い天気である yóî téñki de árù

fine arts *npl* 美術 bíjùtsu

finery [fai'nə:ri:] *n* (dress) 晴着 harégi; (jewelry) 取って置きの装身具 tottéoki nð sóshiñgu

finesse [fines'] *n* 手腕 shúwàn

finger [fiŋ'gə:r] *n* (ANAT) 指 yubí
♦*vt* (touch) ...に指で触る ...ni yubí dè sawárù
little/index finger 小〔人指し〕指 ko

〔hitósashi〕yúbi

fingernail [fiŋ'gə:rneil] *n* つめ tsumé

fingerprint [fiŋ'gə:rprint] *n* (mark) 指紋 shimón

fingertip [fiŋ'gə:rtip] *n* 指先 yubísaki

finicky [fin'iki:] *adj* (fussy) 気難しい kimúzukashiî

finish [fin'iʃ] *n* (end) 終り owári; (SPORT) ゴール gðru; (polish etc) 仕上り shiágari
♦*vt* (work, eating, book etc) 終える oérù
♦*vi* (person, course, event) 終る owáru
to finish doing something ...し終える ...shi oérù
to finish third (in race etc) 3着になる sañchaku ni naru

finishing line [fin'iʃiŋ-] *n* ゴールライン gðruraiñ

finishing school [fin'iʃiŋ-] *n* 花嫁学校 hanáyomegàkkō

finish off *vt* (complete) 仕上げる shiágerù; (kill) 止めを刺す todóme wo sasú

finish up *vt* (food, drink) 平らげる taíragerù
♦*vi* (end up) 最後に...に行ってしまう sáîgo ni ...ni itté shimaù

finite [fai'nait] *adj* (time, space) 一定の ittéi no; (verb) 定形の teíkei no

Finland [fin'lənd] *n* フィンランド fíñrando

Finn [fin] *n* フィンランド人 fiñrandojîn

Finnish [fin'iʃ] *adj* フィンランドの fíñrando no; (LING) フィンランド語の fíñrandogo no
♦*n* (LING) フィンランド語 fíñrandogo

fiord [fjourd] = **fjord**

fir [fə:r] *n* モミ mómî

fire [fai'ə:r] *n* (flames) 火 hî; (in hearth) たき火 takíbi; (accidental) 火事 kají; (gas fire, electric fire) ヒーター hîtā
♦*vt* (shoot: gun etc) うつ útsù; (: arrow) 射る írù; (stimulate: imagination, enthusiasm) 刺激する shigéki suru; (*inf*: dismiss: employee) 首にする kubí ni surù
♦*vi* (shoot) 発砲する happó suru
on fire 燃えて moéte

fire alarm *n* 火災警報装置 kasáikeihōsòchi

firearm [faiə:r'ɑ:rm] *n* 銃砲 júhō ◇ 特に

ピストルを指す tókù ni pisútoru wò sásù

fire brigade n 消防隊 shōbōtai

fire department (US) n = **fire brigade**

fire engine n 消防自動車 shōbōjidōsha

fire escape n 非常階段 hijōkaīdan

fire extinguisher n 消化器 shōkakì

fireman [faiər'mən] (pl **firemen**) n 消防士 shōbōshi

fireplace [faiər'pleis] n 暖炉 dáñro

fireside [faiər'said] n 暖炉のそば dáñro no sóbà

fire station n 消防署 shōbōsho

firewood [faiər'wud] n まき makī

fireworks [faiər'wərks] npl 花火 hánabi

firing squad [faiər'iŋ-] n 銃殺隊 jūsatsutai

firm [fərm] adj (mattress, ground) 固い katái; (grasp, push, tug) 強い tsuyóī; (decision) 断固とした dáñko to shita; (faith) 固い katái; (measures) 強固な kyōko na; (look, voice) しっかりした shikkárī shita

♦n (company) 会社 kaísha

firmly [fərm'li:] adv (grasp, pull, tug) 強く tsuyóku; (decide) 断固として dáñko to shite; (look, speak) しっかりと shikkárī to

first [fərst] adj (before all others) 第一の dáīchi no, 最初の saísho no

♦adv (before all others) 一番に ichíbaǹ ni, 一番最初に ichíbaǹ saísho ni; (when listing reasons etc) 第一に dáīchi ni

♦n (person: in race) 1着 itchákù; (AUT) ローギヤ rōgiya; (BRIT SCOL: degree) 1級優等卒業学位 íkkyū yūtō sotsugyō gakùi ◊英国では優等卒業学位は成績の高い順に1級, 2級, 3級に分けられる eíkoku de wà yūtō sotsugyō gakùi wa seísèki no takái jùn ni ikkyū, nikyū, sankyū nì wakérarerù

at first 最初は saísho wa

first of all まず第一に mázù dáīchi ni

first aid n 応急手当 ōkyūteàte

first-aid kit n 救急箱 kyūkyūbako

first-class [fərst'klæs'] adj (excellent: mind, worker) 優れた sugúretà; (carriage, ticket, post) 1等の ittō no

first-hand [fərst'hænd'] adj (account, story) 直接の chokúsetsu no

first lady (US) n 大統領夫人 daítōryōfujìn

firstly [fərst'li:] adv 第一に daíichi ni

first name n 名 na, ファーストネーム fásutonēmu

first-rate [fərst'reit'] adj (player, actor etc) 優れた sugúretà

fiscal [fis'kəl] adj (year) 会計の kaíkei no; (policies) 財政の zaísei no

fish [fiʃ] n inv 魚 sakána

♦vt (river, area) ...で釣をする ...de tsurí wo surù

♦vi (commercially) 漁をする ryō wo surù; (as sport, hobby) 釣をする tsurí wo surù

to go fishing 釣に行く tsurí ni ikù

fisherman [fiʃ'ərmən] (pl **fishermen**) n 漁師 ryōshi

fish farm n 養魚場 yōgyojō

fish fingers (BRIT) npl = **fish sticks**

fishing boat [fiʃ'iŋ-] n 漁船 gyosén

fishing line n 釣糸 tsuríìto

fishing rod n 釣ざお tsurízao

fishmonger's (shop) [fiʃ'mʌŋgərz-] n 魚屋 sakánaya

fish sticks (US) npl フィッシュスティック fisshúsutikkù ◊細長く切った魚にパン粉をまぶして揚げた物 hosónagaku kittà sakána ni páñko wo mabúshite agéta monò

fishy [fiʃ'i:] (inf) adj (tale, story) 怪しい ayáshiī

fission [fiʃ'ən] n 分裂 buñretsu

fissure [fiʃ'ər] n 亀裂 kirétsu

fist [fist] n こぶし kóbùshi, げんこつ geñkotsu

fit [fit] adj (suitable) 適当な tekítō na; (healthy) 健康な keñkō na

♦vt (subj: clothes, shoes) ...にぴったり合う ...ni pittárī au; (put in) ...に入れる ...ni irérù; (attach, equip) ...に取付ける ...ni torítsukeru; (suit) ...に合う ...ni áù

♦vi (clothes) ぴったり合う pittárī áù; (parts) 合う áù; (in space, gap) ぴったりはいる pittárī haírù

♦*n* (MED) 発作 hossá; (of coughing, giggles) 発作的に...する事 hossáteki ni ...suru kotó

fit to (ready) ...出来る状態にある ...dekirù jótai ni arù

fit for (suitable for) ...に適当である ...ni tekítò de arù

a fit of anger かんしゃく kańshaku

this dress is a good fit このドレスはぴったり体に合う konó doresu wa pittárì karáda ni aù

by fits and starts 動いたり止ったりして ugóitarì tomáttarì shité

fitful [fit'fəl] *adj* (sleep) 途切れ途切れの togíretogíre no

fit in *vi* (person) 溶込む tokékomù

fitment [fit'mənt] *n* (in room, cabin) 取付け家具 torítsukekagù ◇つり戸棚など壁などに固定した家具を指す tsurítodàna nádò kabé nadò ni kotéi shita kagù wo sásù

fitness [fit'nis] *n* (MED) 健康 keńkō

fitted carpet [fit'id-] *n* 敷込みじゅうたん shikíkomijūtan

fitted kitchen [fit'id-] *n* システムキッチン shisútemu kitchiñ

fitter [fit'əːr] *n* (of machinery, equipment) 整備工 seíbikō

fitting [fit'iŋ] *adj* (compliment, thanks) 適切な tekísetsu na

♦*n* (of dress) 試着 shicháku; (of piece of equipment) 取付け torítsuke

fitting room *n* (in shop) 試着室 shichákushìtsu

fittings [fit'iŋz] *npl* (in building) 設備 sétsubi

five [faiv] *num* 五 (の) gó (no), 五つ (の) itsútsu (no)

fiver [fai'vəːr] *n* (*inf*: *BRIT*: 5 pounds) 5ポンド札 gópondo satsù; (*US*: 5 dollars) 5ドル札 gódoru satsù

fix [fiks] *vt* (attach) 取付ける torítsukerù; (sort out, arrange) 手配する tehái surù; (mend) 直す naósù; (prepare: meal, drink) 作る tsukúrù

♦*n*: **to be in a fix** 困っている komátte irù

fixation [fiksei'ʃən] *n* 固着 kocháku

fixed [fikst] *adj* (price, amount etc) 一定の ittéi no

a fixed idea 固定観念 kotéikaňnen

a fixed smile 作り笑い tsukúriwarài

fixture [fiks'tʃəːr] *n* (bath, sink, cupboard etc) 設備 sétsubi; (SPORT) 試合の予定 shiái no yotéi

fix up *vt* (meeting) 手配する tehái surù

to fix someone up with something ...のために...を手に入れる ...no tamé ni ...wo té ni irerù

fizzle out [fiz'əl-] *vi* (event) しりすぼみに終ってしまう shirísùbomi ni owátte shimàu; (interest) 次第に消えてしまう shidái ni kiète shimáù

fizzy [fiz'i:] *adj* (drink) 炭酸入りの tańsan-iri no

fjord [fjourd] *n* フィヨルド fíyòrudo

flabbergasted [flæb'əːrgæstid] *adj* (dumbfounded, surprised) あっけにとられた akké ni toraretá

flabby [flæb'i:] *adj* (fat) 締まりのない shimárì no náì

flag [flæg] *n* (of country, organization) 旗 hatá; (for signalling) 手旗 tebáta; (*also*: **flagstone**) 敷石 shikíishi

♦*vi* (person, spirits) 弱る yowárù

to flag someone down (taxi, car etc) 手を振って...を止める té wo futté ...wo tomérù

flagpole [flæg'poul] *n* 旗ざお hatázao

flagrant [fleig'rənt] *adj* (violation, injustice) 甚だしい hanáhadashiî

flagship [flæg'ʃip] *n* (of fleet) 旗艦 kikáñ; (*fig*) 看板施設 kańbanshisètsu

flair [fleːr] *n* (talent) 才能 saínō; (style) 粋なセンス ikí na señsu

flak [flæk] *n* (MIL) 対空砲火 taíkūhòka; (*inf*: criticism) 非難 hínàn

flake [fleik] *n* (of rust, paint) はげ落ちた欠けら hagéochità kakéra; (of snow, soap powder) 一片 ippéñ

♦*vi* (*also*: **flake off**) paint, enamel) はげ落ちる hagéochirù

flamboyant [flæmbɔi'ənt] *adj* (dress, design) けばけばしい kebákebashiî; (person) 派手な hadé na

flame [fleim] *n* (of fire) 炎 honó-ð

flamingo [fləmiŋ'gou] n フラミンゴ fu-ráminĝo

flammable [flæm'əbəl] adj (gas, fabric) 燃えやすい moéyasuì

flan [flæn] (BRIT) n フラン fúràn ◊菓子の一種 kashí no isshū

flank [flæŋk] n (of animal) わき腹 wakí-bàra; (of army) 側面 sokúmèn
♦vt ...のわきにある〔いる〕 ...no wakí ni arù (iru)

flannel [flæn'əl] n (fabric) フランネル furánneru; (BRIT: also: **face flannel**) フェースタオル fésutaòru

flannels [flæn'əlz] npl フランネルズボン furánneruzubòn

flap [flæp] n (of pocket, envelope, jacket) ふた futá
♦vt (arms, wings) ばたばたさせる bátà-bata saserù
♦vi (sail, flag) はためく hátamekù; (inf: also: **be in a flap**) 興奮している kốfun shite irù

flare [fle:r] n (signal) 発煙筒 hatsúentō; (in skirt etc) フレア furéa

flare up vi (fire) 燃え上る moéagarù; (fig: person) 怒る okórù; (: fighting) ぼっ発する boppátsu suru

flash [flæʃ] n (of light) 閃光 seńkō; (also: **news flash**) ニュースフラッシュ nyúsu-furasshù; (PHOT) フラッシュ furásshù
♦vt (light, headlights) 点滅させる teńmetsu saserù; (send: news, message) 速報する sokúhō suru; (: look, smile) 見せる misérù
♦vi (lightning, light) 光る hikárù; (light on ambulance etc) 点滅する teńmetsu suru

in a flash 一瞬にして isshún nì shite
to flash by/past (person) 走って通り過ぎる hashíttè tŏrisugirù

flashback [flæʃ'bæk] n (CINEMA) フラッシュバック furásshubakkù

flashbulb [flæʃ'bʌlb] n フラッシュバルブ furásshubarùbu

flashcube [flæʃ'kju:b] n フラッシュキューブ furásshukyùbu

flashlight [flæʃ'lait] n 懐中電灯 kaíchū-deñtō

flashy [flæʃ'i:] (pej) adj 派手な hadé na

flask [flæsk] n (bottle) 瓶 bíñ; (also: **vacuum flask**) 魔法瓶 máhōbin, ポット pótto

flat [flæt] adj (ground, surface) 平な taíra na; (tire) パンクした páñku shita; (battery) 上がった agáttà; (beer) 気が抜けた ki gá nùketa; (refusal, denial) きっぱりした kippárì shita; (MUS: note) フラットの furáttō; (: voice) そっけない sokkénài; (rate, fee) 均一の kiń-itsu no
♦n (BRIT: apartment) アパート ápàto; (AUT) パンク páñku; (MUS) フラット furáttō
to work flat out 力一杯働く chikára ippài hataraku

flatly [flæt'li:] adv (refuse, deny) きっぱりと kippárì to

flatten [flæt'ən] vt (also: **flatten out**) 平にする taíra ni surù; (building, city) 取壊す toríkowasù

flatter [flæt'ə:r] vt (praise, compliment) ...にお世辞を言う ...ni oséji wò iú

flattering [flæt'ə:riŋ] adj (comment) うれしい uréshiì; (dress) よく似合う yókù niáù

flattery [flæt'ə:ri:] n お世辞 oséji

flaunt [flɔ:nt] vt (wealth, possessions) 見せびらかす misébirakasù

flavor [flei'və:r] (BRIT **flavour**) n (of food, drink) 味 ajî; (of ice-cream etc) 種類 shúrùi
♦vt ...に味を付ける ...ni ajî wo tsukerù
strawberry-flavored イチゴ味の ichí-goajì no

flavoring [flei'və:riŋ] n 調味料 chốmi-ryŏ

flaw [flɔ:] n (in argument, policy) 不備な点 fúbì na teñ; (in character) 欠点 kettén; (in cloth, glass) 傷 kízù

flawless [flɔ:'lis] adj 完璧な kañpeki na

flax [flæks] n 亜麻 amá

flaxen [flæk'sən] adj (hair) ブロンドの buróñdo no

flea [fli:] n (human, animal) ノミ nomí

fleck [flek] n (mark) 細かいはん点 ko-mákaì hañten

fled [fled] pt, pp of **flee**

flee [fli:] (*pt*, *pp* **fled**) *vt* (danger, famine, country) 逃れる nogárerù, ...から逃げる ...kara nigérù
♦*vi* (refugees, escapees) 逃げる nigérù

fleece [fli:s] *n* (sheep's wool) 羊毛一頭分 yōmōittōbun; (sheep's coat) ヒツジの毛 hitsúji no kè
♦*vt* (*inf*: cheat) ...から大金をだまし取る ...kara taíkin wò dámashitorù

fleet [fli:t] *n* (of ships: for war) 艦隊 kańtai; (: for fishing etc) 船団 seńdan; (of trucks, cars) 車両団 sharyōdan

fleeting [fli:tiŋ] *adj* (glimpse) ちらっと 見える chiráttò miérù; (visit) 短い mijíkaì; (happiness) つかの間の tsuká no mà no

Flemish [flem'iʃ] *adj* フランダースの furándāsu no; (LING) フランダース語の furándāsugo no
♦*n* (LING) フランダース語 furándāsugo

flesh [fleʃ] *n* (ANAT) 肉 nikú; (skin) 肌 hadá; (of fruit) 果肉 kaníku

flesh wound *n* 軽傷 keíshō

flew [flu:] *pt of* **fly**

flex [fleks] *n* (of appliance) コード kōdo
♦*vt* (leg, muscles) 曲げたり伸したりする magétarì nobáshitarì suru

flexibility [fleksəbil'əti:] *n* (of material) しなやかさ shináyakasà; (of response, policy) 柔軟性 jūnañsei

flexible [flek'səbəl] *adj* (material) 曲げ やすい magéyasuì; (response, policy) 柔 軟な jūnan na

flick [flik] *n* (of hand, whip etc) 一振り hitófurì
♦*vt* (with finger, hand) はじき飛ばす ha-jíkitobasù; (towel, whip) ぴしっと振る pishíttò furú; (switch: on) 入れる iréru; (: off) 切る kírù

flicker [flik'ə:r] *vi* (light) ちらちらする chírāchira suru; (flame) ゆらゆらする yúrāyura suru; (eyelids) まばたく mabá-takù

flick through *vt fus* (book) ぱらぱらと ...のページをめくる párapara to ...no pèji wo mekúru

flier [flai'ə:r] *n* (pilot) パイロット paírot-tò

flight [flait] *n* (action: of birds, plane) 飛 行 hikō; (AVIAT: journey) 飛行機旅行 hikōkiryokō; (escape) 逃避 tōhi; (*also*: **flight of steps/stairs**) 階段 kaídan

flight attendant (*US*) *n* 乗客係 jōkya-kugakàri

flight deck *n* (AVIAT) 操縦室 sōjūshì-tsu; (NAUT) 空母の飛行甲板 kūbo no hikōkanpan

flimsy [flim'zi:] *adj* (shoes) こわれやすい kowáreyasuì; (clothes) 薄い usúi; (building) もろい morói; (excuse) 見え透いた miésuità

flinch [flintʃ] *vi* (in pain, shock) 身震いす る mibúrùi suru
to flinch from (crime, unpleasant duty) ...するのをしり込みする ...surú no wò shirígomi surù

fling [fliŋ] (*pt*, *pp* **flung**) *vt* (throw) 投げ る nagérù

flint [flint] *n* (stone) 火打石 hiúchiishì; (in lighter) 石 ishí

flip [flip] *vt* (switch) はじく hajíkù; (coin) トスする tōsù suru

flippant [flip'ənt] *adj* (attitude, answer) 軽率な keísotsu na

flipper [flip'ə:r] *n* (of seal etc) ひれ足 hi-réashì; (for swimming) フリッパー furíp-pā

flirt [flə:rt] *vi* (with person) いちゃつく ichátsuku
♦*n* 浮気者 uwákimono

flit [flit] *vi* (birds, insects) ひょいと飛ぶ hyoí tò tobú

float [flout] *n* (for swimming, fishing) 浮 き ukí; (vehicle in parade) 山車 dashí; (money) つり用の小銭 tsuríyō nò kozéni
♦*vi* 浮く ukú

flock [flɑ:k] *n* 群れ muré; (REL) 会衆 ka-íshū
♦*vi*: **to flock to** (place, event) ぞくぞく 集まる zókùzoku atsúmarù

flog [flɑ:g] *vt* (whip) むち打つ múchìutsu

flood [flʌd] *n* (of water) 洪水 kōzui; (of letters, imports etc) 大量 taíryō
♦*vt* (subj: water) 水浸しにする mizúbità-shi ni suru; (: people) ...に殺到する ...ni sattō suru

♦*vi* (place) 水浸しになる mizúbitàshi ni nárù; (people): *to flood into* ...に殺到する ...ni sattō suru

flooding [flʌd'iŋ] *n* 洪水 kōzui

floodlight [flʌd'lait] *n* 照明灯 shōmeitō

floor [flɔːr] *n* (of room) 床 yuká; (storey) 階 káì; (of sea, valley) 底 sókò

♦*vt* (subj: blow) 打ちのめす uchínomesù; (: question) 仰天させる gyōten saserù

ground floor 1階 ikkái

first floor (*US*) 1階 ikkai (*BRIT*) 2階 nikái

floorboard [flɔːr'bɔːrd] *n* 床板 yuká-ita

floor show *n* フロアショー furóashō

flop [flɑːp] *n* (failure) 失敗 shippái

♦*vi* (fail) 失敗する shippái suru; (fall: into chair, onto floor etc) どたっと座り込む dotáttò suwárikomù

floppy [flɑːp'iː] *adj* ふにゃふにゃした fúnyafunya shita

floppy (disk) *n* (COMPUT) フロッピー（ディスク）furóppì(dìsùku)

flora [flɔːr'ə] *n* 植物相 shokúbutsusò

floral [flɔːr'əl] *adj* (dress, wallpaper) 花柄の hanágara no

florid [flɔːr'id] *adj* (style) ごてごてした gótègote shitá; (complexion) 赤らんだ akáraǹda

florist [flɔːr'ist] *n* 花屋 hanáyà

florist's (shop) *n* 花屋 hanáyà

flounce [flauns] *n* (frill) 縁飾り fuchíkazarì

flounce out *vi* 怒って飛び出す okóttè tobídasù

flounder [flaun'dər] *vi* (swimmer) もがく mogákù; (fig: speaker) まごつく magótsukù; (economy) 停滞する teítai suru

♦*n* (ZOOL) ヒラメ hiráme

flour [flau'ər] *n* (gen) 粉 koná; (also: **wheat flour**) 小麦粉 komúgiko

flourish [flər'iʃ] *vi* (business) 繁栄する haṅ-ei suru; (plant) 生い茂る oíshigerù

♦*n* (bold gesture): *with a flourish* 大げさな身振りで ōgesa na mibùri de

flourishing [flər'iʃiŋ] *adj* (company) 繁栄する haṅ-ei suru; (trade) 盛んな sakán na

flout [flaut] *vt* (law, rules) 犯す okásù

flow [flou] *n* 流れ nagáre

♦*vi* 流れる nagárerù

flow chart *n* 流れ図 nagárezù, フローチャート furōchāto

flower [flau'ər] *n* 花 haná

♦*vi* (plant, tree) 咲く sakú

flower bed *n* 花壇 kádàn

flowerpot [flau'ə:rpɑːt] *n* 植木鉢 uékibàchi

flowery [flau'ə:riː] *adj* (perfume) 花の様な haná no yō na; (pattern) 花柄の hanágara no; (speech) 仰々しい gyōgyōshìì

flown [floun] *pp* of **fly**

flu [fluː] *n* (MED) 流感 ryūkan

fluctuate [flʌk'tʃuːeit] *vi* (price, rate, temperature) 変動する heńdō suru

fluctuation [flʌktʃuːei'ʃən] *n*: *fluctuation (in)* (...の) 変動 (...no) heńdō

fluent [fluː'ənt] *adj* (linguist) 語学たん能な gogákutaǹnō na; (speech, writing etc) 滑らかな naméràka na

he speaks fluent French, he's fluent in French 彼はフランス語が堪能だ kárè wa furánsugo gà taǹnō da

fluently [fluː'əntliː] *adv* (speak, read, write) 流ちょうに ryūchō ni

fluff [flʌf] *n* (on jacket, carpet) 毛羽 kebá; (fur: of kitten etc) 綿毛 watáge

fluffy [flʌf'iː] *adj* (jacket, toy etc) ふわふわした fúwàfuwa shitá

fluid [fluː'id] *adj* (movement) しなやかな shináyàka na; (situation, arrangement) 流動的な ryūdōteki na

♦*n* (liquid) 液 ékì

fluke [fluːk] *n* (inf) まぐれ magúrè

flung [flʌŋ] *pt, pp* of **fling**

fluorescent [fluːres'ənt] *adj* (dial, paint, light etc) 蛍光の keíkō no

fluoride [fluː'əraid] *n* フッ化物 fukkábùtsu

flurry [flər'iː] *n*: *a snow flurry* にわか雪 niwákayùki

flurry of activity 慌ただしい動き awátadashìì ugóki

flush [flʌʃ] *n* (on face) ほてり hotéri; (fig: of youth, beauty etc) 輝かしさ kagáyakashisà

♦*vt* (drains, pipe) 水を流して洗う mizú

wǒ nagáshite araù

♦*vi* (become red) 赤くなる akáku narù

♦*adj*: **flush with** (level) ...と同じ高さの

...to onáji takasà no

to flush the toilet トイレの水を流す tóire no mizú wo nagasù

flushed [flʌʃt] *adj* 赤らめた akárametà

flush out *vt* (game, birds) 茂みから追出す shigémi kàra oídasù

flustered [flʌs'tə:rd] *adj* (nervous, confused) まごついた magótsuità

flute [fluːt] *n* フルート fúrùto

flutter [flʌt'ə:r] *n* (of wings) 羽ばたき habátaki; (of panic, excitement, nerves) うろたえ urótae

♦*vi* (bird) 羽ばたきする habátaki suru

flux [flʌks] *n*: **in a state of flux** 流動的状態で ryūdōtekijōtai de

fly [flai] *n* (insect) ハエ haé; (on trousers: *also*: **flies**) ズボンの前 zubón no máè

♦*vb* (*pt* **flew**, *pp* **flown**)

♦*vt* (plane) 操縦する sōjū suru; (passengers, cargo) 空輸する kū́yu suru; (distances) 飛ぶ tobú

♦*vi* (bird, insect, plane) 飛ぶ tobú; (passengers) 飛行機で行く hikṓki de ikú; (escape) 逃げる nigérù; (flag) 掲げられる kakágerarerù

fly away *vi* (bird, insect) 飛んで行く tońde ikù

flying [flai'iŋ] *n* (activity) 飛行機旅行 hikṓkiryokṓ; (action) 飛行 hikṓ

♦*adj*: **a flying visit** ほんの短い訪問 hoń-no mijíkaì hṓmon

with flying colors 大成功で daíseikō de

flying saucer *n* 空飛ぶ円盤 sórà tobú eñban

flying start *n*: **to get off to a flying start** 好調な滑りだしをする kṓchō na suberidáshi wo suru

fly off *vi* = **fly away**

flyover [flai'ouvə:r] (*BRIT*) *n* (overpass) 陸橋 rikkyṓ

flysheet [flai'ʃiːt] *n* (for tent) 入口の垂れ布 iríguchi nò tarénuno

foal [foul] *n* 子ウマ koúma

foam [foum] *n* (of surf, water, beer) 泡

awá; (*also*: **foam rubber**) フォームラバー fṓmurabā

♦*vi* (liquid) 泡立つ awádàtsu

to foam at the mouth (person, animal) 泡をふく awá wo fukù

fob [faːb] *vt*: **to fob someone off** ...をだます ...wo damásù

focal point [fou'kəl-] *n* (of room, activity etc) 中心 chū́shin

focus [fou'kəs] *n* (PHOT) 焦点 shṓten; (of attention, storm etc) 中心 chū́shin

♦*vt* (field glasses etc) ...の焦点を合せる ...no shṓten wò awáserù

♦*vi*: **to focus (on)** (with camera) (...に) カメラを合せる (...ni) kámèra wò awáserù; (person) (...に) 注意を向ける (...ni) chū́i wo mukérù

in/out of focus 焦点が合っている〔いない〕shṓten ga attè irú〔inái〕

fodder [faːd'ə:r] *n* (food) 飼葉 kaíba

foe [fou] *n* (rival, enemy) 敵 tekí

foetus [fiː'təs] *n* (*BRIT*) = **fetus**

fog [fɔːg] *n* 霧 kirí

foggy [fɔːg'iː] *adj*: **it's foggy** 霧が出ている kirí ga detè irú

fog light (*BRIT* **fog lamp**) *n* (AUT) フォッグライト fóggùraito

foil [fɔil] *vt* (attack, plan) くじく kujíkù

♦*n* (metal foil, kitchen foil) ホイル hóìru; (complement) 引立てる物 hikítaterù monő; (FENCING) フルーレ furúrè

fold [fould] *n* (bend, crease) 折目 oríme; (of skin etc) しわ shiwá; (in cloth, curtain etc) ひだ hidá; (AGR) ヒツジの囲い hitsúji nò kakőì; (*fig*) 仲間 nakáma

♦*vt* (clothes, paper) 畳む tatámu; (arms) 組む kúmù

folder [foul'də:r] *n* (for papers) 書類挟み shorúibasàmi

folding [foul'diŋ] *adj* (chair, bed) 折畳み式の orítatamishiki no

fold up *vi* (map, bed, table) 折畳める orítatamerù; (business) つぶれる tsubúrerù

♦*vt* (map, clothes etc) 畳む tatámu

foliage [fou'liːidʒ] *n* (leaves) 葉 ha ◇総称 sṓshō

folk [fouk] *npl* (people) 人々 hitobito

◆*adj* (art, music) 民族の miñzoku no
folks (parents) 両親 ryōshin

folklore [fouk'lɔːr] *n* 民間伝承 miñka-ndeñshō

folk song *n* 民謡 miñ-yō

follow [fɑːl'ou] *vt* (person) ...について行く ...ni tsúíte ikú; (suspect) 尾行する bikō suru; (event) ...に注目する ...ni chúmoku suru; (story) 注意して聞く chúí shite kikú; (leader, example, advice, instructions) ...に従う ...ni shitágaù; (route, path) たどる tadórù
◆*vi* (person, period of time) 後に来る〔いく〕átò ni kúru(ikú); (result) ...という結果になる ...to iú kekka ni nárù

to follow suit (*fig*) (...と) 同じ事をする (...to) onáji kotò wo suru

follower [fɑːl'ouəːr] *n* (of person) 支持者 shijíshà; (of belief) 信奉者 shiñpōsha

following [fɑːl'ouiŋ] *adj* 次の tsugí no
◆*n* (of party, religion, group etc) 支持者 shijíshà ◇総称 sōshō

follow up *vt* (letter, offer) ...に答える ...ni kotárerù; (case) 追及する tsuíkyū suru

folly [fɑːl'iː] *n* (foolishness) ばかな事 bákà na kotó

fond [fɑːnd] *adj* (memory) 楽しい tanóshiî; (smile, look) 愛情に満ちた añjō ni michita; (hopes, dreams) 愚かな órðka na

to be fond of ...が好きである ...ga sukí de arù

fondle [fɑːn'dəl] *vt* 愛ぶする aíbù suru

font [fɑːnt] *n* (in church) 洗礼盤 señreîban; (TYP) フォント fôñto

food [fuːd] *n* 食べ物 tabémonð

food mixer *n* ミキサー míkîsā

food poisoning [-pɔi'zəniŋ] *n* 食中毒 shokuchūdoku

food processor [-prɑːs'esəːr] *n* ミキサー míkîsā ◇食べ物を混ぜたりひいたりおろしたりする家庭電気製品 tabemono wo mazetari hiitari oroshitari suru tame no katei denki seihin

foodstuffs [fuːd'stʌfs] *npl* 食料 shokúryō

fool [fuːl] *n* (idiot) ばか bákà; (CULIN)

フール fûru ◇果物入りムースの一種 kudámono-iri mûsu no ísshù
◆*vt* (deceive) だます damásù
◆*vi* (*also*: **fool around**: be silly) ふざける fuzákerù

foolhardy [fuːl'hɑːrdiː] *adj* (conduct) 無謀な mubō na

foolish [fuːl'iʃ] *adj* (stupid) ばかな bákà na; (rash) 無茶な muchá na

foolproof [fuːl'pruːf] *adj* (plan etc) 絶対確実な zettáikakùjitsu na

foot [fut] (*pl* **feet**) *n* (of person, animal) 足 ashí; (of bed, cliff) ふもと fumóto; (measure) フィート fîto
◆*vt* (bill) 支払う shiháraù

on foot 徒歩で tóhò de

footage [fut'idʒ] *n* (CINEMA) 場面 bámèn

football [fut'bɔːl] *n* (ball: round) サッカーボール sakkáboru; (: oval) フットボール futtóbŏru; (sport: BRIT) サッカー sakká; (: US) フットボール futtóbōru

football player *n* (BRIT: *also*: **footballer**) サッカー選手 sakká señshu; (US) フットボール選手 futtóbōru señshu

footbrake [fut'breik] *n* 足ブレーキ ashíburèki

footbridge [fut'bridʒ] *n* 橋 hashí ◇歩行者しか渡れない狭い物を指す hokōshà shika watárenài semâî monð wo sasù

foothills [fut'hilz] *npl* 山ろくの丘陵地帯 sañroku nð kyûryōchītai

foothold [fut'hould] *n* 足場 ashíba

footing [fut'iŋ] *n* (*fig*: position) 立場 tachíba

to lose one's footing 足を踏み外す ashí wo fumihazusù

footlights [fut'laits] *npl* (THEATER) フットライト futtóraîto

footman [fut'mən] (*pl* **footmen**) *n* (servant) 下男 genán

footnote [fut'nout] *n* 脚注 kyakúchū

footpath [fut'pæθ] *n* 遊歩道 yūhodð

footprint [fut'print] *n* (of person, animal) 足跡 ashíato

footstep [fut'step] *n* (sound) 足音 ashíoto; (footprint) 足跡 ashíato

footwear [fut'weəːr] *n* (shoes, sandals

etc) 履物 hakímono

KEYWORD
---

for [fɔːr] *prep* **1** (indicating destination, intention) ...行きの ...yuki no, ...に向かって ...ni mùkátte, ...のために〔の〕...notámèní[no]
the train for London ロンドン行きの電車 róndonyuki no densha
he left for Rome 彼はローマへ出発しました kárè wa rốmà e shúppatsu shimashìta
he went for the paper 彼は新聞を取りに行きました kárè wa shínbun wo torí ni ikímashìta
is this for me? これは私に? koré wa wàtákushi ní?
there's a letter for you あなた宛の手紙が来ています ànáta ate no tegami ga kìté imasu
it's time for lunch 昼食の時間です chúshoku no jikan desù

2 (indicating purpose) ...のために〔の〕...no tamé nì[no]
what's it for? それは何のためですか soré wa nàn no tamé dèsu ká
give it to me - what for? それをよこせ-何で? soré wo yòkóse - nàndé?
clothes for children 子供服 kodómofùku
to pray for peace 平和を祈る héiwa wo inorú

3 (on behalf of, representing) ...の代理として ...no daíri toshite
the MP for Hove ホープ選出の議員 hōbùsénshutsu no gíìn
he works for the government/a local firm 彼は政府〔地元の会社〕に雇われています kárè wa séìfu(jimóto no kaisha)ni yatówarète imasù
I'll ask him for you あなたに代って私が彼に聞きましょう ànátà ni kawátte wàtákushi ga karè ni kikímashò
G for George GはジョージのG G wà jóji no G

4 (because of) ...の理由で ...no riyú de, ...のために ...no tamé nì
for this reason このため kònó tame

for fear of being criticized 批判を恐れて hìhán wo òsórète
the town is famous for its canals 町は運河で有名です machí wà úngà de yūmei desù

5 (with regard to) ...にしては ...ni shité wà
it's cold for July 7月にしては寒い shichígatsu nì shité wà samúì
he's mature for his age 彼はませている kárè wa másète iru
a gift for languages 語学の才能 gógàku no saínō
for everyone who voted yes, 50 voted no 賛成1に対して反対50だった sánsei íchì nì táì shite hántaihyò gojú dàtta

6 (in exchange for) ...と交換して ...to kókan shite
I sold it for $5 5ドルでそれを売りました gódòru de soré wo ùrímashìta
to pay $2.50 for a ticket 切符を2ドル50セントで買う kíppú wo nídòru gojússeñto de kaú

7 (in favor of) ...に賛成して ...ni sánsei shite
are you for or against us? あなたは我々に賛成なのか反対なのかはっきり言いなさい ànátà wa waréware ni sánsei na nò ka hántai na nò ka hakkírì fìnasaì
I'm all for it 私は無条件で賛成です watákushi wa mùjókèn de sánsei desù
vote for X Xに投票する ékkùsu ni tóhyò suru

8 (referring to distance): *there are roadworks for 5 km* 5キロもの区間が工事中です gókìro mo no kúkàn ga kójichū desù
we walked for miles 何マイルも歩きました nánmaìru mo arúkimashìta

9 (referring to time) ...の間 ...no aída
he was away for 2 years 彼は2年間家を離れていました kárè wa nínèñkan ié wò hanárete imashìta
she will be away for a month 彼女は1か月出掛ける事になっています kánòjo wa ikkágetsukàn dekákeru kotò ni natté imasù

it hasn't rained for 3 weeks 雨は3週間も降っていません ámè wa sañshūkan mo futté imaseñ

I have known her for years 何年も前から彼女とは知り合いです náñnen mo máè kara kánòjo to wa shiríai desù

can you do it for tomorrow? 明日までに出来ますか asú madè ni dekímasù ká

10 (with infinitive clause): *it is not for me to decide* 私が決める事ではありません watákushi gà kiméru kotò de wa arímaseñ

it would be best for you to leave あなたは帰った方がいい anátà wa káètta hō ga íi

there is still time for you to do it あなたはまだまだそれをする時間があります anátà wa mádàmada sorè wò suru jikañ ga arímasù

for this to be possible ... これが可能になるのには... korè gà kanō ni narù no ni wa...

11 (in spite of) ...にもかかわらず ...ní mò kakáwarazù

for all his complaints, he is very fond of her 彼は色々と文句を言うが、結局彼女を愛しています kárè wa iróiro tò móñku wo iú gà, kekkyóku kanòjo wo áì shite imásù

for all he said he would write, in the end he didn't 手紙を書く書くと言っていましたけれども、結局書いてくれませんでした tegámi wò kákù kákù to itté imashità keredomo, kekkyóku kaitè kurémasen deshìta

♦*conj* (since, as: rather formal) なぜならば...だから názènaraba ...dá kàra

she was very angry, for he was late again 彼女はかんかんになっていました、というのは彼はまたも遅刻したからです kánòjo wa kañkañ ni natté imashìta, to iú no wà kárè wa matá mò chikóku shita kara desù

---

forage [fɔːr'idʒ] *vi* (search: for food, interesting objects etc) ...をあさる ...wo **asárù**

foray [fɔːr'ei] *n* (raid) 侵略 shiñryaku

forbad(e) [fər'bæd'] *pt of* **forbid**

forbid [fər'bid'] (*pt* **forbad(e)**, *pp* **forbidden**) *vt* (sale, marriage, event etc) 禁ずる kiñzurù

to forbid someone to do something ...に...するのを禁ずる ...ni ...surú no wò kiñzurù

forbidden [fər'bid'ən] *pp of* **forbid**

forbidding [fər'bid'iŋ] *adj* (look, prospect) 怖い kowáì

force [fɔːrs] *n* (violence) 暴力 bṓryoku; (PHYSICS, *also* strength) 力 chikára

♦*vt* (compel) 強制する kyṓsei suru; (push) 強く押す tsúyòku osú; (break open: lock, door) こじ開ける kojíakerù

in force (in large numbers) 大勢で ōzei de; (LAW) 有効で yūkō de

to force oneself to do 無理して...する múrì shite ...suru

forced [fɔːrst] *adj* (labor) 強制的な kyṓseiteki na; (smile) 作りの tsukúri no

forced landing (AVIAT) 不時着 fujíchaku

force-feed [fɔːrs'fiːd] *vt* (animal, prisoner) ...に強制給餌をする ...ni kyṓseikyūji wo suru

forceful [fɔːrs'fəl] *adj* (person) 力強い chikárazuyoì; (attack) 強烈な kyṓretsu na; (point) 説得力のある settókuryoku no arù

forceps [fɔːr'səps] *npl* ピンセット piñsettò

forces [fɔːrs'iz] (*BRIT*) *npl*: *the Forces* (MIL) 軍隊 guñtai

forcibly [fɔːr'səbliː] *adv* (remove) 力ずくで chikárazukù de; (express) 力強く chikárazuyokù

ford [fɔːrd] *n* (in river) 浅瀬 asáse ◇船を使わないで川を渡れる場所を指す fúnè wo tsukáwanaìde kawá wò watáreru bashò wo sásù

fore [fɔːr] *n*: *to come to the fore* 前面に出て来る zeñmen ni dete kurù

forearm [fɔːr'ɑːrm] *n* 前腕 maéude

foreboding [fɔːrbou'diŋ] *n* (of disaster) 不吉な予感 fukítsu na yokañ

forecast [fɔːr'kæst] *n* (of profits, prices,

weather) 予報 yohō

♦*vt* (*pt, pp* **forecast**) (predict) 予報する yohō suru

forecourt [fɔːr'kɔːrt] *n* (of garage) 前庭 maéniwa

forefathers [fɔːr'fɑːðəːrz] *npl* (ancestors) 先祖 señzo

forefinger [fɔːr'fiŋgəːr] *n* 人差指 hitósashiyùbi

forefront [fɔːr'frʌnt] *n*: *in the forefront of* (industry, movement) ...の最前線で ...no saízeñsen de

forego [fɔːrgou'] (*pt* **forewent** *pp* **foregone**) *vt* (give up) やめる yamérù; (go without) ...なしで我慢する ...náshi de gámàn suru

foregone [fɔːrgɔːn'] *adj*: *it's a foregone conclusion* 結果は決まっている kekká wa kimattè irú

foreground [fɔːr'graund] *n* (of painting) 前景 zeñkei

forehead [fɔːr'hed] *n* 額 hitái

foreign [fɔːr'in] *adj* (country) 外国の gaíkoku no; (trade) 対外の taígai no; (object, matter) 異質の ishítsu no

foreigner [fɔːr'ənəːr] *n* 外国人 gaíkokujìn

foreign exchange *n* 外国為替 gaíkokukawàse; (currency) 外貨 gaíka

Foreign Office (*BRIT*) *n* 外務省 gaímushò

Foreign Secretary (*BRIT*) *n* 外務大臣 gaímudaìjin

foreleg [fɔːr'leg] *n* (of animal) 前足 maéàshi

foreman [fɔːr'mən] (*pl* **foremen**) *n* (in factory, on building site etc) 現場監督 geñbakañtoku

foremost [fɔːr'moust] *adj* (most important) 最も大事な mottómò dáìji na

♦*adv*: *first and foremost* 先ず第一に mázu dáìchi ni

forensic [fəren'sik] *adj* (medicine, test) 法医学的な hōigakuteki na

forerunner [fɔːr'rʌnəːr] *n* 先駆者 señkushà

foresee [fɔːrsiː'] (*pt* **foresaw** *pp* **foreseen**) *vt* (problem, development) 予想す

る yosō suru

foreseeable [fɔːrsiː'əbəl] *adj* (problem, development) 予想出来る yosō dekirù

foreshadow [fɔːrʃæd'ou] *vt* (event) ...の前兆となる ...no zeñchō to narù

foresight [fɔːr'sait] *n* 先見の明 señken nò meí

forest [fɔːr'ist] *n* 森 mórì

forestall [fɔːrstɔːl'] *vt* (person) 出し抜く dashínuku; (discussion) 防ぐ fuségù

forestry [fɔːr'istriː] *n* 林業 riñgyō

foretaste [fɔːr'teist] *n* 前兆 zeñchō

foretell [fɔːrtel'] (*pt, pp* **foretold**) *vt* (predict) 予言する yogén suru

forever [fɔːrev'əːr] *adv* (for good) 永遠に eíen ni; (continually) いつも ítsùmo

forewent [fɔːrwent'] *pt* of **forego**

foreword [fɔːr'wəːrd] *n* (in book) 前書 maégaki

forfeit [fɔːr'fit] *vt* (lose: right, friendship etc) 失う ushínaù

forgave [fərgeiv'] *pt* of **forgive**

forge [fɔːrdʒ] *n* (smithy) 鍛冶屋 kajíyà

♦*vt* (signature, money) 偽造する gizō súru; (wrought iron) 鍛えて作る kitáetè tsukúrù

forge ahead *vi* (country, person) 前進する zeñshin suru

forger [fɔːr'dʒəːr] *n* 偽造者 gizōshà

forgery [fɔːr'dʒəːriː] *n* (crime) 偽造 gizō; (object) 偽物 nisémono

forget [fərget'] (*pt* **forgot**, *pp* **forgotten**) *vt* (fact, face, skill, appointment) 忘れる wasúrerù; (leave behind: object) 置き忘れる okíwasurerù; (put out of mind: quarrel, person) 考えない事にする kañgaeñai kotó ni surù

♦*vi* (fail to remember) 忘れる wasúrerù

forgetful [fərget'fəl] *adj* (person) 忘れっぽい wasúreppòi

forget-me-not [fərget'miːnɑːt] *n* ワスレナグサ wasúrenagùsa

forgive [fərgiv'] (*pt* **forgave**, *pp* **forgiven**) *vt* (pardon) 許す yurúsù

to forgive someone for something (excuse) ...の...を許す ...wo yurúsù

forgiveness [fərgiv'nis] *n* 許し yurúshi

forgo [fɔːrgou'] *vt* = **forego**

forgot [fəːrgɑːt'] *pt of* **forget**

forgotten [fəːrgɑːt'ən] *pp of* **forget**

fork [fɔːrk] *n* (for eating) フォーク fôku; (for gardening) ホーク hôku; (in road, river, railway) 分岐点 bufíkiten
♦*vi* (road) 分岐する bufíki suru

fork-lift truck [fɔːrk'lift-] *n* フォークリフト fôkurifûto

fork out (*inf*) *vt* (pay) 払う haráù

forlorn [fəːrlɔːrn'] *adj* (person, place) わびしい wabíshiî; (attempt) 絶望的な zetsúbôteki na; (hope) 空しい munáshiî

form [fɔːrm] *n* (type) 種類 shúrùi; (shape) 形 katáchi; (SCOL) 学年 gakúnen; (questionnaire) 用紙 yôshi
♦*vt* (make: shape, queue, object, habit) 作る tsukúrù; (make up: organization, group) 構成する kósei suru; (idea) まとめる matómerù

in top form 調子が最高で chôshi gà saíkō de

formal [fɔːr'məl] *adj* (offer, statement, occasion) 正式な seíshiki na; (person, behavior) 堅苦しい katágurushiî; (clothes) 正装の seísō no; (garden) 伝統的な defítōteki na ◇極めて幾何学的な配置の庭園について言う kiwámetè kikágakuteki na haíchi nò teien ni tsuite iú; (education) 正規の seíki no

formalities [fɔːrmæl'itiːz] *npl* (procedures) 手続き tetsúzzki

formality [fɔːrmæl'itiː] *n* (procedure) 形式 keíshiki

formally [fɔːr'məliː] *adv* (make offer etc) 正式に seíshiki ni; (act) 堅苦しく katágurushikù; (dress): *to dress formally* 正装する seísō suru

format [fɔːr'mæt] *n* (form, style) 形式 keíshiki
♦*vt* (COMPUT: disk) 初期化する shókìka suru, フォーマットする fômatto suru

formation [fɔːrmei'ʃən] *n* (creation: of organization, business) 創立 sóritsu; (: of theory) 考案 kôan; (pattern) 編隊 heńtai; (of rocks, clouds) 構造 kôzō

formative [fɔːr'mətiv] *adj* (years, influence) 形成的な keíseiteki na

former [fɔːr'məːr] *adj* (one-time) かつて

の kátsùte no; (earlier) 前の máè no

the former ... the latter ... 前者...後者... zeńshà... kôshà...

formerly [fɔːr'məːrliː] *adv* (previously) 前は máè wa

formidable [fɔːr'midəbəl] *adj* (task, opponent) 手ごわい tegówaì

formula [fɔːr'mjələ] (*pl* **formulae** *or* **formulas**) *n* (MATH, CHEM) 公式 kôshiki; (plan) 方式 hôshiki

formulate [fɔːr'mjəleit] *vt* (plan, strategy) 練る nérù; (opinion) 表現する hyôgen suru

forsake [fɔːrseik'] (*pt* **forsook**, *pp* **forsaken**) *vt* (abandon: person) 見捨てる misúterù; (: belief) 捨てる sutérù

forsook [fɔːrsuk'] *pt of* **forsake**

fort [fɔːrt] *n* (MIL) とりで toríde

forte [fɔːr'tei] *n* (strength) 得意 tokúi

forth [fɔːrθ] *adv* (out) 外へ sótò e

back and forth 行ったり来たりして ittárì kitárì shité

and so forth など nádò

forthcoming [fɔːrθ'kʌm'iŋ] *adj* (event) 今度の końdò no; (help, evidence) 手に入る té ni hairù; (person) 率直な sotchóku na

forthright [fɔːrθ'rait] *adj* (condemnation, opposition) はっきりとした hakkírì to shitá

forthwith [fɔːrθwiθ'] *adv* 直ちに tádàchi ni

fortify [fɔːr'təfai] *vt* (city) ...の防備を固める ...no bôbi wo katámerù; (person) 力付ける chikárazukerù

fortitude [fɔːr'tətuːd] *n* 堅忍 keńnin

fortnight [fɔːrt'nait] *n* (two weeks) 2週間 nishúkan

fortnightly [fɔːrt'naitliː] *adj* (payment, visit, magazine) 2週間置きの nishúkan-oki no
♦*adv* (pay, meet, appear) 2週間置きに nishúkan-oki ni

fortress [fɔːr'tris] *n* 要塞 yôsai

fortuitous [fɔːrtuː'itəs] *adj* (discovery, result) 偶然の gûzen no

fortunate [fɔːr'tʃənit] *adj* (person) 運のいい úń no ìi; (event) 幸運な kôun na *it is fortunate that ...* 幸いに... saíwai ni ...

fortunately [fɔːr'tʃənitli:] *adv* (happily, luckily) 幸いに saíwai ni

fortune [fɔːr'tʃən] *n* (luck) 運 úñ; (wealth) 財産 zaísan

fortune-teller [fɔːr'tʃəntelər] *n* 易者 e-kísha

forty [fɔːr'ti:] *num* 40 (の) yóñjū (no)

forum [fɔːr'əm] *n* フォーラム fōramu

forward [fɔːr'wərd] *adj* (in position) 前方の zeñpō no; (in movement) 前方への zeñpō e no; (in time) 将来のための shōrai nò tame no; (not shy) 出過ぎた desúgità

♦*n* (SPORT) フォワード fowádo

♦*vt* (letter, parcel, goods) 転送する teñsō suru; (career, plans) 前進させる zeñshin saserù

to move forward (progress) 進歩する shíñpo suru

forward(s) [fɔːr'wərd(z)] *adv* 前へ máè e

fossil [fɑːs'əl] *n* 化石 kaséki

foster [fɔːs'tər] *vt* (child) 里親として育てる satóoya toshitè sodáterù; (idea, activity) 助成する joséi suru

foster child *n* 里子 satógo

fought [fɔːt] *pt, pp of* **fight**

foul [faul] *adj* (state, taste, smell, weather) 悪い warúì; (language) 汚い kitánaì; (temper) ひどい hidôî

♦*n* (SPORT) 反則 hañsoku, ファウル fáùru

♦*vt* (dirty) 汚す yogósù

foul play *n* (LAW) 殺人 satsújin

found [faund] *pt, pp of* **find**

♦*vt* (establish: business, theater) 設立する setsúritsu suru

foundation [faundei'ʃən] *n* (act) 設立 setsúritsu; (base) 土台 dodái; (organization) 財団 zaídan; (*also:* **foundation cream**) ファンデーション fañdḕshon

foundations [faundei'ʃənz] *npl* (of building) 土台 dodái

founder [faun'dər] *n* (of firm, college) 設立者 setsúritsushà

♦*vi* (ship) 沈没する chíñbotsu suru

foundry [faun'dri:] *n* 鋳造工場 chūzōkō-

fountain [faun'tin] *n* 噴水 fuñsui

fountain pen *n* 万年筆 mañneñhitsu

four [fɔːr] *num* 4 (の) yóñ (no), 四つ (の) yotsu (no)

on all fours 四つんばいになって yotsúñbai ni nattè

four-poster [fɔːr'pous'tər] *n* (*also:* **four-poster bed**) 天がい付きベット teñgaitsukibetto

foursome [fɔːr'səm] *n* 4人組 yoníñgumi

fourteen [fɔːr'tiːn'] *num* 14 (の) jǘyon (no)

fourth [fɔːrθ] *num* 第4(の) daíyon (no)

fowl [faul] *n* 家きん kakín

fox [fɑːks] *n* キツネ kitsúne

♦*vt* (baffle) 困らす komárasu

foyer [fɔi'əːr] *n* (of hotel, theater) ロビー róbī

fraction [fræk'ʃən] *n* (portion) 一部 ichíbù; (MATH) 分数 buñsū

fracture [fræk'tʃər] *n* (of bone) 骨折 kossétsu

♦*vt* (bone) 折る órù

fragile [frædʒ'əl] *adj* (breakable) 壊れやすい kowáreyasuì

fragment [fræg'mənt] *n* (small piece) 破片 hahén

fragrance [freig'rəns] *n* (scent) 香り kaóri

fragrant [freig'rənt] *adj* 香り高い kaóritakaì

frail [freil] *adj* (person, invalid) か弱い kayówaì; (structure) 壊れやすい kowáreyasuì

frame [freim] *n* (of building, structure) 骨組 honégumi; (of human, animal) 体格 taíkaku; (of door, window) 枠 wakú; (of picture) 額縁 gakúbuchi; (of spectacles: *also:* **frames**) フレーム fúrēmu

♦*vt* (picture) 額縁に入れる gakúbuchi ni irerù

frame of mind *n* 気分 kibúñ

framework [freim'wərk] *n* (structure) 骨組 honégumi

France [fræns] *n* フランス furáñsu

franchise [fræn'tʃaiz] *n* (POL) 参政権 sañseikèn; (COMM) フランチャイズ fu-

furánchaìzu

frank [fræŋk] adj (discussion, look) 率直な sotchóku na, フランクな furáñku na
♦vt (letter) ...に料金別納の判を押す ...ni ryókinbetsunó no háñ wo osú

frankly [fræŋk'li:] adv (honestly) 正直に shójikí ni; (candidly) 率直に sotchóku ni

frankness [fræŋk'nis] n (honesty) 正直さ shójikisà; (candidness) 率直さ sotchókusa

frantic [fræn'tik] adj (distraught) 狂乱した kyóran shita; (hectic) てんてこ舞いの teñtekomài no

fraternal [frətər'nəl] adj (greetings, relations) 兄弟の様な kyódai no yó na

fraternity [frətər'niti:] n (feeling) 友愛 yúai; (group of people) 仲間 nakáma

fraternize [fræt'ə:rnaiz] vi 付き合う tsukíaù

fraud [frɔːd] n (crime) 詐欺 sagí; (person) ぺてん師 peteñshi

fraudulent [frɔ:'dʒələnt] adj (scheme, claim) 不正な fuséi na

fraught [frɔːt] adj: **fraught with** (danger, problems) ...をはらんだ ...wo haráñda

fray [frei] n (battle, fight) 戦い tatákai
♦vi (cloth, rope) 擦切れる suríkirerù; (rope end) ほつれる hotsúrerù
tempers were frayed 皆短気になっていた miná táñki ni nátte itá

freak [fri:k] n (person: in attitude, behavior) 変人 heñjin; (: in appearance) 奇形 kikéi
♦adj (event, accident) まぐれの mágùre no

freckle [frek'əl] n そばかす sobákasù

free [fri:] adj (person, press, movement) 自由な jíyù na; (not occupied: time) 暇なhímà na; (: seat) 空いている afte irù; (costing nothing: meal, pen etc) 無料のmuryó no
♦vt (prisoner etc) 解放する kaíhō suru; (jammed object) 動ける様にする ugókeru yó ni suru
free (of charge) 無料で muryó de
for free = free of charge

freedom [fri:'dəm] n (liberty) 自由 jíyù

free-for-all [fri:'fə:rɔ:l'] n 乱闘 rañtō

free gift n 景品 keíhin

freehold [fri:'hould] n (of property) 自由保有権 jiyúhoyùken

free kick n (SPORT) フリーキック furíkikkù

freelance [fri:'læns] adj (journalist, photographer, work) フリーランサーの furírañsā no

freely [fri:'li:] adv (without restriction, limits) 自由に jíyù ni; (liberally) 気ままに kimáma ni

Freemason [fri:'meisən] n フリーメーソン furímèson

Freepost [fri:'poust] (® BRIT) n (postal service) 料金受取人払い ryókin uketorininbaraì

free-range [fri:'reind3] adj 放し飼いのhanáshigai no ◊特にニワトリやその卵について言う tóku ni niwátori yà sonó tamagò ni tsúíte iú

free trade n 自由貿易 jiyúbōeki

freeway [fri:'wei] (US) n 高速道路 kósokudòro

free will n 自由意志 jiyúishì
of one's own free will 自発的に jihátsuteki ni

freeze [fri:z] (pt **froze**, pp **frozen**) vi (weather) 氷点下になる hyóteñka ni nárù; (liquid, pipe) 凍る kórù; (person: with cold) 冷える hiérù; (: stop moving) 立ちすくむ tachísukumù
♦vt (water, lake) 凍らせる kóraserù; (food) 冷凍にする reftó ni surú; (prices, salaries) 凍結する tóketsu suru
♦n (weather) 氷点下の天気 hyóteñka no téñki; (on arms, wages) 凍結 tóketsu

freeze-dried [fri:z'draid'] adj 凍結乾燥の tóketsukañsō no

freezer [fri:'zə:r] n フリーザー fúrīzā

freezing [fri:'ziŋ] adj (wind, weather, water) 凍る様な kóru yó na
3 degrees below freezing 氷点下3度 hyóteñka sáñdo

freezing point n 氷点 hyóten

freight [freit] n (goods) 貨物 kámòtsu; (money charged) 運送料 uñsōryó

freight train (US) n (goods train) 貨物

列車 kamótsuresshà

French [frentʃ] *adj* フランス の furánsu no; (LING) フランス語の furánsugo no
♦*n* (LING) フランス語 furánsugo
♦*npl*: **the French** (people) フランス人 furánsujìn

French bean *n* サヤインゲン sayá-iñgen

French fried potatoes *npl* フレンチフライ（ポテト）furénchifurài(pótèto)

French fries [-fraiz] (*US*) *npl* = **French fried potatoes**

Frenchman/woman [fren'tʃmən /wumən] (*pl* **Frenchmen/women**) *n* フランス人男性〔女性〕furánsujin dañsei〔jòsei〕

French window *n* フランス窓 furánsu madò

frenetic [frənet'ik] *adj* (activity, behavior) 熱狂的な nekkyōteki na

frenzy [fren'zi:] *n* (of violence) 逆上 gyakújō; (of joy, excitement) 狂乱 kyōran

frequency [fri:'kwənsi:] *n* (of event) 頻度 híndo; (RADIO) 周波数 shūhasū

frequent [*adj* fri:'kwint *vb* frikwent'] *adj* (intervals, visitors) 頻繁な hiñpan na
♦*vt* (pub, restaurant) ...に よく 行 く ...ni yōkù ikú

frequently [fri:'kwintli:] *adv* (often) しばしば shíbàshiba

fresco [fres'kou] *n* フレスコ画 furésukoga

fresh [freʃ] *adj* (food, vegetables, bread, air etc) 新鮮な shiñsen na; (memories, footprint) 最近の saíkin no; (instructions) 新たな aráta na; (paint) 塗立ての nurítate no; (new: approach, start) 新しい atárashiì; (cheeky: person) 生意気な namáìki na

freshen [freʃ'ən] *vi* (wind) 強くなる tsuyóku narù; (air) 涼しくなる suzúshiku narù

freshen up *vi* (person) 化粧直しをする keshōnaòshi wo suru

fresher [freʃ'ə:r] (*BRIT*: *inf*) *n* = **freshman**

freshly [freʃ'li:] *adv* (made, cooked, painted) ...されたばかりで ...saréta bakàri de

freshman [freʃ'mən] (*pl* **freshmen**) *n* (*US*: SCOL) 1年生 ichínensei ◇大学生や高校生について言う daígakùsei ya kōkōsei ni tsuitè iú

freshness [freʃ'nis] *n* 新鮮さ shiñsensà

freshwater [freʃ'wɔ:tə:r] *adj* (lake, fish) 淡水の tañsui no

fret [fret] *vi* (worry) 心配する shiñpai suru

friar [frai'ə:r] *n* (REL) 修道士 shūdōshì

friction [frik'ʃən] *n* (resistance, rubbing) 摩擦 masátsu; (between people) 不仲 fúnàka

Friday [frai'dei] *n* 金曜日 kiñ-yòbi

fridge [fridʒ] (*BRIT*) *n* 冷蔵庫 reízòko

fried [fraid] *adj* (steak, eggs, fish etc) 焼いた yaítà; (chopped onions etc) いためた itámetà; (in deep fat) 揚げた agétà, フライした furái shita

friend [frend] *n* 友達 tomódachi

friendly [frend'li:] *adj* (person, smile) 愛想のいい aíso nò íi; (government) 友好的な yūkōteki na; (place, restaurant) 居心地の良い igókochi no yoì; (game, match) 親善の shiñzen no

friendship [frend'ʃip] *n* 友情 yújō

frieze [fri:z] *n* フリーズ fúrīzu ◇壁の一番高い所に付ける細long い飾り、彫刻などを指す kabé no ichíban takáì tokórò ni tsukérù hosónagaì kazárì, chōkoku nadò wo sásù

frigate [frig'it] *n* フリゲート艦 furígètokan

fright [frait] *n* (terror) 恐怖 kyōfu; (scare) 驚き odóroki
to take fright 驚く odórokù

frighten [frait'ən] *vt* 驚かす odórokasù

frightened [frait'ənd] *adj* (afraid) 怖がった kowágattà; (worried, nervous) 不安に駆られた fúàn ni karáreta

frightening [frait'niŋ] *adj* (experience, prospect) 恐ろしい osóroshiì

frightful [frait'fəl] *adj* (dreadful) 恐ろしい osóroshiì

frightfully [frait'fəli:] *adv* 恐ろしく osóroshikù

frigid [fridʒ'id] *adj* (woman) 不感症の fukánshō no

frill [fril] n (of dress, shirt) フリル fúrìru

fringe [frindʒ] n (BRIT: of hair) 前髪 maégami; (decoration: on shawl, lampshade etc) 縁飾り fuchíkazàri; (edge: of forest etc) へり herí

fringe benefits npl 付加給付 fukákyùfu

frisk [frisk] vt (suspect) ボディーチェックする bodíchekkù suru

frisky [fris'ki:] adj (animal, youngster) はつらつとした hatsúratsu to shità

fritter [frit'ə:r] n (CULIN) フリッター furíttā

fritter away vt (time, money) 浪費する róhi suru

frivolous [friv'ələs] adj (conduct, person) 軽率な keísotsu na; (object, activity) 下らない kudáranaì

frizzy [friz'i:] adj (hair) 縮れた chijíretà

fro [frou] see **to**

frock [fra:k] n (dress) ドレス dórèsu

frog [fro:g] n カエル kaérù

frogman [fro:g'mæn] (pl **frogmen**) n ダイバー dáibā

frolic [fra:l'ik] vi (animals, children) 遊び回る asóbimawarù

KEYWORD

from [frʌm] prep 1 (indicating starting place) ...から ...kárà

where do you come from?, where are you from? (asking place of birth) ご出身はどちらですか go-shússhìn wa dóchìra désù ka

from London to Glasgow ロンドンからグラスゴーへ róndon kara gurásugò e

to escape from something/someone ...から逃げる ...kárà nigérù

2 (indicating origin etc) ...から ...kárà

a letter/telephone call from my sister 妹からの手紙〔電話〕imóto kàra no tegámi〔deñwa〕

tell him from me that ... 私からの伝言で彼に ...と言って下さい watákushi kárà no deñgon dè kárè ni ...to itté kudasaì

a quotation from Dickens ディケンズからの引用 díkènzu kara no iñyō

to drink from the bottle 瓶から飲む bíñ kara nómù

3 (indicating time) ...から ...kárà

from one o'clock to/until/till two 1時から2時まで ichíji karà níji madè

from January (on) 1月から(先) ichígatsu karà (sakí)

4 (indicating distance) ...から ...kárà

the hotel is 1 km from the beach ホテルは浜辺から1キロ離れています hótèru wa hamabé kàrà ichíkiro hanaréte imásù

we're still a long way from home まだまだ家まで遠い mádamada ié madè tói

5 (indicating price, number etc) ...から ...kárà, ...ないし... ...nàishi

prices range from $10 to $50 値段は10ドルないし50ドルです nédan wà júdòru nàishi gojúdòru désù

there were from 20 to 30 people there 20ないし30人いました níjù nàishi sañjūnìn imáshìta

the interest rate was increased from 9% to 10% 公定歩合は9パーセントから10パーセントに引き上げられました kóteibùai wa kyúpāsèñto kara juppásèñto ni hikíageraremashìta

6 (indicating difference) ...と ...tò

he can't tell red from green 彼は赤と緑の区別ができません kárè wa ákà to mídòri no kúbètsu ga dekímaseñ

to be different from someone/something ...と違っている ...tò chigátte irù

7 (because of, on the basis of) ...から ...kárà, ...によって ...ni yottè

from what he says 彼の言う事によると kárè no iú kotò ni yórù tò

from what I understand 私が理解したところでは watákushi gà ríkài shita tokóro de wà

to act from conviction 確信に基づいて行動する kakúshin ni motozuìte kódo suru

weak from hunger 飢えでぐったりになって uế dè guttárì ni náttè

front [frʌnt] n (of house, dress) 前面 zeñmeñ; (of coach, train, car) 最前部 saízeñ-bu; (promenade: *also*: **sea front**) 海岸沿いの遊歩道 kaígañzoi no yúhodō; (MIL) 戦線 señsen; (METEOROLOGY) 前線 zeñsen; (*fig*: appearances) 外見 gaíken

◆*adj* (*gen*) 前の máe no, 一番前の ichíban-maè no; (gate) 正面の shōmeñ no

in front (of) (...の) 前に (...no) máe ni

front tooth 前歯 máeba

frontage [frʌn'tidʒ] *n* (of building) 正面 shōmen

frontal [frʌn'təl] *adj* 真っ向からの makkō kara no

front door *n* 正面玄関 shōmengeñkan

frontier [frʌnti:r'] *n* (between countries) 国境 kokkyō

front page *n* (of newspaper) 第一面 dáiichimen

front room (*BRIT*) *n* 居間 imá

front-wheel drive [frʌnt'wi:l-] *n* (AUT) 前輪駆動 zeñrinkùdō

frost [frɔːst] *n* (weather) 霜が降りる事 shimō ga oríru koto; (*also*: **hoarfrost**) 霜 shimó

frostbite [frɔːst'bait] *n* 霜焼け shimóyake

frosted [frɔːs'tid] *adj* (glass) 曇の kumóri no

frosty [frɔːs'tiː] *adj* (weather, night) 寒い samúi ◇気温が氷点下であるが雪が降っていない状態について言う kíon ga hyṓtenka de arù ga yukí ga futte inài jōtai ni tsuīte iú; (welcome, look) 冷たい tsumétaì

froth [frɔːθ] *n* (on liquid) 泡 awá

frown [fraun] *vi* 顔をしかめる káo wo shikámerù

froze [frouz] *pt of* **freeze**

frozen [frou'zən] *pp of* **freeze**

frugal [fruː'gəl] *adj* (person) 倹約的な keñ-yakuteki na; (meal) つましい tsumáshiì

fruit [fruːt] *n inv* (AGR, BOT) 果物 kudámono; (*fig*: results) 成果 seíka

fruiterer [fruː'tə:rə:r] (*BRIT*) *n* 果物屋 kudámonoyà

fruiterer's (shop) [fruː'tə:rə:rz-] (*BRIT*) *n* 果物屋 kudámonoyà

fruitful [fruːt'fəl] *adj* (meeting, discussion) 有益な yūeki na

fruition [fruːiʃ'ən] *n*: *to come to fruition* 実る minórù

fruit juice *n* 果汁 kajū́, フルーツジュース furū́tsujùsu

fruit machine (*BRIT*) *n* スロットマシン surốttomashiñ

fruit salad *n* フルーツサラダ furū́tsusa-ràda

frustrate [frʌs'treit] *vt* (upset) ...に欲求不満を起させる ...ni yokkyū́fumàn wo okósaserù; (block) ざ折させる zasétsu saserù

frustration [frʌstreiʃ'ən] *n* (irritation) 欲求不満 yokkyū́fumàn; (disappointment) がっかり gakkárì

fry [frai] (*pt, pp* **fried**) *vt* (CULIN: steak, eggs etc) 焼く yákù; (: chopped onions etc) いためる itámerù; (: in deep fat) 揚げる agérù ¶ *see also* **small fry**

frying pan [frai'iŋ-] *n* フライパン furáipan

ft. *abbr* = **foot**; **feet**

fuddy-duddy [fʌd'iːdʌdiː] (*pej*) *n* 古臭い人 furúkusaì hitó

fudge [fʌdʒ] *n* (CULIN) ファッジ fájjī

fuel [fjuː'əl] *n* 燃料 neñryō

fuel oil *n* 重油 jū́yu

fuel tank *n* 燃料タンク neñryōtaǹku

fugitive [fjuː'dʒətiv] *n* (runaway, escapee) 逃亡者 tōbṓsha

fulfil [fulfil'] *vt* (function) 果す hatásù; (condition) 満たす mitásù; (request, wish, desire) かなえる kanáerù; (order) 実行する jikkṓ suru

fulfilment [fulfil'mənt] *n* (satisfaction) 満足 máñzoku; (of promise, desire) 実現 jitsúgen

full [ful] *adj* (container, cup, car, cinema) 一杯の ippái no; (maximum: use, volume) 最大限の saídaìgen no; (complete: details, information) 全ての súbète no; (price) 割引なしの waríbikinashì no; (skirt) ゆったりした yuttárì shitá

◆*adv*: *to know full well that* ...という事を重々承知している ...to iú kotò wo jū́jū shóchi shite irù

I'm full (up) 満腹だ manpuku da
a full two hours 2時間も nijíkàn mo
at full speed 全速力で zeńsokuryòku de
in full (reproduce, quote, pay) 完全に kańzen ni

full employment n 100パーセントの就業率 hyakú pàseǹto no shūgyōrìtsu

full-length [ful'leŋkθ'] adj (film, novel etc) 長編の chōheǹ no; (coat) 長い nágài; (portrait) 全身の zeńshin no

full moon n 満月 mańgetsu

full-scale [ful'skeil'] adj (attack, war) 全面的な zeńmenteki na; (model) 実物大の jitsúbutsudai no

full stop n 終止符 shūshifù, ピリオド pírìodo

full-time [ful'taim] adj (work, study) 全時間制の zeńjikansei no
♦adv 全時間で zeńjikàn de

fully [ful'i:] adv (completely) 完全に kańzen ni; (at least): *fully as big as* 少なくとも...と同じぐらいの大きさの sukúnàkutomo ...to onaji gurai no ōkisa no

fully-fledged [ful'i:fledʒd'] adj (teacher, barrister) 一人前の ichíninmaè no

fulsome [ful'səm] (pej) adj (praise, compliments) 大げさな ōgesa na

fumble [fʌm'bəl] vi: *to fumble with* (key, catch) ...でもたもたする ...de mótàmota suru

fume [fju:m] vi (rage) かんかんに怒る káńkan ni okórù
fumes (of fire, fuel, car) ガス gásù

fun [fʌn] n (amusement) 楽しみ tanóshimi
to have fun 楽しむ tanóshimù
for fun 冗談として jōdan toshitè
to make fun of (ridicule, mock) ばかにする bákà ni suru

function [fʌŋk'ʃən] n (role) 役割 yakúwari, 機能 kinō; (product) ...による ...ni yórù monó; (social occasion) 行事 gyōji
♦vi (operate) 作動する sadō suru

functional [fʌŋk'ʃənəl] adj (operational) 作動できる sadō dekirù; (practical) 機能的な kinōteki na

fund [fʌnd] n (of money) 基金 kikíñ;
(source, store) 貯蓄 chochíku

fundamental [fʌndəmen'təl] adj (principle, change, mistake) 基本的な kihóntekì na

fundamentalist [fʌndəmen'təlist] n 原理主義者 geńrishugìshà

funds [fʌndz] npl (money) 資金 shikíñ

funeral [fju:'nərəl] n 葬式 sōshiki

funeral parlor n 葬儀屋 sōgiya

funeral service n 葬式 sōshiki

funfair [fʌn'fe:r] (BRIT) n 移動遊園地 idōyūeǹchi

fungi [fʌn'dʒai] npl of fungus

fungus [fʌŋ'gəs] (pl fungi) n (plant) キノコ kínòko; (mold) かび kabí

funnel [fʌn'əl] n (for pouring) じょうご jōgo; (of ship) 煙突 eńtotsu

funny [fʌn'i:] adj (amusing) こっけいな kokkéi na; (strange) 変な héñ na

fur [fə:r] n (on animal) 毛 ke; (animal skin for clothing etc) 毛皮 kegáwa; (BRIT: in kettle etc) 湯あか yuáka

fur coat n 毛皮コート kegáwakòto

furious [fju:r'i:əs] adj (person) 猛烈な mōretsu na

furlong [fə:r'lɔːŋ] n (HORSE-RACING) ハロン háròn ◊距離の単位で，約201メーター kyórì no táń-i de, yakú 201 mḕtà

furlough [fə:r'lou] n (MIL: leave) 休暇 kyūka

furnace [fə:r'nis] n (in foundry) 炉 ro; (in power plant) ボイラー bóìrā

furnish [fə:r'niʃ] vt (room, building) ...に家具調度を備える ...ni kagúchòdo wo sonáerù; (supply) ...に供給する ...ni kyōkyū suru

furnishings [fə:r'niʃiŋz] npl 家具と設備 kágù to sétsùbi

furniture [fə:r'nitʃər] n 家具 kágù
piece of furniture 家具一点 kágù itteñ

furrow [fə:r'ou] n (in field) 溝 mizó; (in skin) しわ shiwá

furry [fə:r'i:] adj 毛で覆われた ke de ōwaretà

further [fə:r'ðə:r] adj (additional) その上の sonō ue no, 追加の tsuíka no
♦adv (farther) もっと遠くに móttò tōku ni; (more) 以上 soré ijō; (moreover) 更に sárà ni, なお náò

♦*vt* (career, project) 促進する sokúshin suru

further education (*BRIT*) *n* 成人教育 seíjin kyőiku

furthermore [fəːr'ðəːrmɔːr] *adv* (moreover) 更に sárà ni, なお nao

furthest [fəːr'ðist] *superl of* **far**

furtive [fər'tiv] *adj* (glance, movement) こっそりとする kossőrī to surù

fury [fjuːr'iː] *n* (anger, rage) 憤慨 fuńgai

fuse [fjuːz] *n* (ELEC: in plug, circuit) ヒューズ hyűzu; (for bomb etc) 導火線 dőkasen

♦*vt* (metal) 融合させる yűgő saserù; (*fig*: ideas, systems) 混合する końgő suru

♦*vi* (metal: *also fig*) 融合する yűgő suru
  to fuse the lights (*BRIT*: ELEC) ヒューズを飛ばす hyűzu wo tobásu

fuse box *n* (ELEC) ヒューズ箱 hyűzubàko

fuselage [fjuː'səlɑːʒ] *n* (AVIAT) 胴体 dőtai

fusion [fjuː'ʒən] *n* (of ideas, qualities) 混合 końgő; (*also*: **nuclear fusion**) 核融合 kakúyűgő

fuss [fʌs] *n* (anxiety, excitement) 大騒ぎ ősawàgi; (complaining, trouble) 不平 fuhéi
  to make a fuss 大騒ぎをする ősawàgi wo suru
  to make a fuss of someone ...をちやほやする ...wo chíyàhoya suru

fussy [fʌs'iː] *adj* (person) 小うるさい koúrusaì; (clothes, rooms etc) 凝った kőttà

futile [fjuː'təl] *adj* (attempt, comment, existence) 無駄な mudá na

future [fjuː'tʃər] *adj* (date, generations) 未来の mírai no; (president, spouse) 将来の shőrai no

♦*n* (time to come) 未来 mírài; (prospects) 将来 shőrai; (LING) 未来形 miráikei
  in future 将来に shőrai ni

fuze [fjuːz] (*US*) = **fuse**

fuzzy [fʌz'iː] *adj* (PHOT) ぼやけた boyáketà; (hair) 縮れた chijíretà

G

G [dʒiː] *n* (MUS: note) ト音 to-óñ; (: key) ト調 tőchő

g. abbr = **gram(s)**

gabble [gæb'əl] *vi* ぺちゃくちゃしゃべる péchàkucha shábèru

gable [gei'bəl] *n* (of building) 切妻 kiŕízùma

gadget [gædʒ'it] *n* 装置 sőchi

Gaelic [gei'lik] *adj* ゲール語の gérugo no
♦*n* (LING) ゲール語 gérugo

gaffe [gæf] *n* (in words) 失言 shitsúgen; (in actions) 失態 shittái

gag [gæg] *n* (on mouth) 猿ぐつわ sarúgutsùwa; (joke) ギャグ gyágù

♦*vt* (prisoner) ...に猿ぐつわをはめる ...ni sarúgutsùwa wo hamérù

gaiety [gei'əti:] *n* お祭り騒ぎ o-mátsuri sawàgi

gaily [gei'li:] *adv* (talk, dance, laugh) 楽しそうに tanóshiső ni; (colored) 華やかに hanáyàka ni

gain [gein] *n* (increase) 増加 zőka; (improvement) 進歩 shíñpo; (profit) 利益 ríeki

♦*vt* (speed, weight, confidence) 増す masú

♦*vi* (benefit): *to gain from something* ...から利益を得る ...kara ríeki wo érù; (clock, watch) 進む susúmù
  to gain on someone ...に迫る ...ni semárù
  to gain 3lbs (in weight) (体重が) 3 ポンド増える (taíjū ga) sañpoñdo fuérù

gait [geit] *n* 歩調 hochő

gal. abbr = **gallon**

gala [gei'lə] *n* (festival) 祝祭 shukúsai

galaxy [gæl'əksi:] *n* (SPACE) 星雲 sefun

gale [geil] *n* (wind) 強風 kyőfū

gallant [gæl'ənt] *adj* (brave) 勇敢な yűkan na; (polite) 紳士的な shiñshiteki na

gallantry [gæl'əntri:] *n* (bravery) 勇気 yűki; (politeness) 礼儀正しさ reígitadashìsa

gall bladder [gɔːl-] *n* 胆のう tańnő

gallery [gǽl'əːriː] *n* (*also*: **art gallery**: public) 美術博物館 bijútsu hakubutsukàn; (: private) 画廊 garô; (in hall, church, theater) 二階席 nikáiseki

galley [gǽl'iː] *n* (ship's kitchen) 調理室 chôrishītsu

gallon [gǽl'ən] *n* (= 8 pints; *BRIT* = 4.5 l; *US* = 3.8 l) ガロン gáròn

gallop [gǽl'əp] *n* ギャロップ gyárôppu
♦*vi* (horse) ギャロップで走る gyárôppu de hashírù

gallows [gǽl'ouz] *n* 絞首台 kôshudai

gallstone [gɔːl'stoun] *n* (MED) 胆石 tañseki

galore [gəlɔːr'] *adv* どっさり dossárì

galvanize [gǽl'vənaiz] *vt* (audience) ぎょっとさせる gyóttò sasérù; (support) 求める motómerù

gambit [gǽm'bit] *n* (*fig*): **(opening) gambit** 皮切り kawákiri

gamble [gǽm'bəl] *n* (risk) かけ kaké
♦*vt* (money) かける kakérù
♦*vi* (take a risk) 冒険をする bôken wo surù; (bet) ばくちをする bakúchi wo surù, ギャンブルをする gyáñburu wo suru
to gamble on something (horses, race, success etc) ...にかける ...ni kakérù

gambler [gǽm'bləːr] *n* (punter) ばくち打ち bakúchiuchi

gambling [gǽm'bliŋ] *n* (betting) ばくち bakúchi, ギャンブル gyáñburu

game [geim] *n* (activity, sport) 遊び asôbi; (match) 試合 shiái; (part of match: esp TENNIS: *also*: **board game**) ゲーム gêmu; (strategy, scheme) 策略 sakúryaku; (HUNTING) 猟鳥獣 ryôchōjū; (CULIN) 猟鳥獣の肉 ryôchōjū no nikú
♦*adj* (willing): **game (for)** (...をする) 気がある (...wo suru) kí ga arù
big game 大型猟獣 ôgataryōjū

gamekeeper [geim'kiːpəːr] *n* 猟番 ryôban

gammon [gǽm'ən] *n* (bacon) ベーコン bêkon; (ham) スモークハム sumôkuhamù

gamut [gǽm'ət] *n* (range) 範囲 háñ-i

gang [gǽŋ] *n* (of criminals, hooligans) 一味 ichímì; (of friends, colleagues) 仲間 nakama; (of workmen) 班 háñ

gangrene [gǽŋ'griːn] *n* (MED) えそ ésò

gangster [gǽŋ'stəːr] *n* (criminal) 暴力団員 bôryokudañ-in, ギャング gyáñgu

gang up *vi*: **to gang up on someone** 寄ってたかって...をやっつける yotté takatte ...wo yattsukeru

gangway [gǽŋ'wei] *n* (from ship) タラップ taráppù; (*BRIT*: in cinema, bus, plane etc) 通路 tsûro

gaol [dʒeil] (*BRIT*) *n*, *vt* = **jail**

gap [gǽp] *n* (space) すき間 sukíma, ギャップ gyappu; (: in time) 空白 kúhaku; (difference): **gap (between)** (...の) 断絶 (...no) dañzetsu

gape [geip] *vi* (person) ぽかんと口を開けて見詰める pokáñ to kuchí wo aketé mitsúmerù; (shirt, hole) 大きく開いている ôkiku aîte irù

gaping [gei'piŋ] *adj* (shirt, hole) 大きく開いた ôkiku aîtà

garage [gərɑːʒ'] *n* (of private house) 車庫 shákò; (for car repairs) 自動車修理工場 jidôshashūrikōjō

garbage [gɑːr'bidʒ] *n* (*US*: rubbish) ごみ gomí; (*inf*: nonsense) でたらめ detárame

garbage can (*US*) *n* ごみ容器 gomíyðki

garbled [gɑːr'bəld] *adj* (account, message) 間違った machígattà

garden [gɑːr'dən] *n* (private) 庭 niwá

gardener [gɑːr'dnəːr] *n* 庭師 niwáshi

gardening [gɑːr'dəniŋ] *n* 園芸 éñgei

gardens [gɑːr'dənz] *npl* (public park) 公園 kôen

gargle [gɑːr'gəl] *vi* うがいする ugái suru

garish [geːr'iʃ] *adj* けばけばしい kebákebashiì

garland [gɑːr'lənd] *n* (*also*: **garland of flowers**) 花輪 hanáwa

garlic [gɑːr'lik] *n* (BOT, CULIN) ニンニク niñniku

garment [gɑːr'mənt] *n* (dress) 衣服 ífuku

garnish [gɑːr'niʃ] *vt* (food) 飾る kazárù

garrison [gǽr'isən] *n* (MIL) 守備隊 shubítai

garrulous [gǽr'ələs] *adj* (talkative) 口数の多い kuchíkazu no ôi

garter [gɑːr'təːr] *n* (for sock etc) 靴下止

め kutsúshitadome, ガーター gātā; (US: suspender) ガーターベルト gátāberùto

gas [gæs] n (CHEM) 気体 kítāi; (fuel) ガス gásù; (US: gasoline) ガソリン gasórin
♦vt (kill) ガスで殺す gásù de korósù

gas cooker (BRIT) n ガスレンジ gasúrenji

gas cylinder n ガスボンベ gasúboñbe

gas fire (BRIT) n ガスストーブ gasúsutōbu

gash [gæʃ] n (wound) 切り傷 kiríkizu; (tear) 裂け目 sakéme
♦vt (wound) 傷を負わせる kizú wo owáserù

gasket [gæs'kit] n (AUT) ガスケット gasúkettò

gas mask n ガスマスク gasúmasùku

gas meter n ガスメーター gasúmētā

gasoline [gæsəli:n'] (US) n ガソリン gasórin

gasp [gæsp] n (breath) 息切れ ikígire; (of shock, horror) はっとする事 háttò suru kotó
♦vi (pant) あえぐ aégù

gasp out vt (say) あえぎながら言う aéginagàra iú

gas station (US) n ガソリンスタンド gasórinsutàndo

gassy [gæs'i:] adj (beer etc) 炭酸ガスの入った tañsangasù no haítta

gastric [gæs'trik] adj 胃の í no

gastroenteritis [gæstrouentərai'tis] n 胃腸炎 ichóen

gate [geit] n (of garden, field, grounds) 門 mon; (at airport) ゲート gēto

gatecrash [geit'kræʃ] (BRIT) vt ...に押し掛ける ...ni oshíkakerù

gateway [geit'wei] n (entrance: also fig) 入口 iríguchi

gather [gæð'əːr] vt (flowers, fruit) 摘む tsúmù; (pick up) 拾う hiróù; (assemble, collect: objects, information) 集める atsúmerù; (understand) 推測する suísoku suru; (SEWING) ...にギャザーを寄せる ...ni gyázā wo yosérù
♦vi (assemble) 集まる atsúmerù
to gather speed スピードを上げる supído wo agerù

gathering [gæð'əːriŋ] n 集まり atsúmarì

gauche [gouʃ] adj (adolescent, youth) ぎこちない gigóchinài

gaudy [gɔːd'i:] adj 派手な hadé na

gauge [geidʒ] n (instrument) 計器 keíkì
♦vt (amount, quantity) 計る hakárù; (fig: feelings, character etc) 判断する hañdan suru

gaunt [gɔːnt] adj (haggard) やせこけた yasékoketà; (bare, stark) 荒涼とした kóryō to shita

gauntlet [gɔːnt'lit] n (glove) 長手袋 nagátebukùro; (fig): **to run the gauntlet** 方々からやられる hōbō kara yarárerù
to throw down the gauntlet 挑戦する chósen suru

gauze [gɔːz] n (fabric: also MED) ガーゼ gāze

gave [geiv] pt of **give**

gay [gei] adj (homosexual) 同性愛の dóseīai no, ホモの hómò no; (cheerful) 陽気な yóki na; (color, music, dress etc) 華やかな hanáyàka na

gaze [geiz] n (look, stare) 視線 shisén
♦vi: **to gaze at something** ...をじっと見る ...wo jíttò mírù

gazelle [gəzel'] n ガゼル gázèru

gazetteer [gæziti:r'] n (index) 地名辞典 chiméijitèn

gazumping [gəzʌm'piŋ] (BRIT) n (of house buyer) 詐欺 ságì

GB [dʒi:bi:'] abbr = **Great Britain**

GCE [dʒi:si:i:'] (BRIT) n abbr (= General Certificate of Education) 普通教育証書 futsúkyōikushōsho ◊16才の時に受けるOレベルと大学入学前に受けるAレベルの2種類がある jūrokusai no tokí nì ukérù O rébèru to daígaku nyūgaku máè ni ukérù A rébèru no nishúrui ga arù

GCSE [dʒi:si:si:i:'] (BRIT) n abbr (= General Certificate of Secondary Education) ◊1988年からGCEのOレベルはGCSEに置換えられた señkyūhyakuhachijūhachi nèn ni GCE no O rébèru wa GCSE ni okíkaeraretà

gear [gi:r] n (equipment) 道具 dōgu; (TECH) 歯車 hagúrùma; (AUT) ギヤ gíyà

♦*vt* (*fig*: adapt): *to gear something to* ...に...を適応させる ...ni ...wo tekíō saserù

high (*US*) *or top* (*BRIT*) / *low gear* ハイ〔ロー〕ギヤ haí[rō]giyà

in gear ギヤを入れて gíyà wo iréte

gear box *n* ギヤボックス giyábokkùsu

gear shift (*BRIT* **gear lever**) *n* シフトレバー shífùtorebā

geese [gi:s] *npl of* **goose**

gel [dʒel] *n* (for hair) ジェル jérù; (CHEM) ゲル gérù

gelatin(e) [dʒel'ətin] *n* (CULIN) ゼラチン zeráchìn

gelignite [dʒel'ignait] *n* (explosive) ゼリグナイト zerígunaìto

gem [dʒem] *n* (stone) 宝石 hōseki

Gemini [dʒem'ənai] *n* (ASTROLOGY) 双子座 futágoza

gender [dʒen'də:r] *n* (sex: *also* LING) 性 seí

gene [dʒi:n] *n* (BIO) 遺伝子 idénshi

general [dʒen'ə:rəl] *n* (MIL) 大将 taíshō

♦*adj* (overall, non-specific, miscellaneous) 一般の ippán no, 一般的の ippánteki na; (widespread: movement, interest) 全面的な zenmenteki na

in general 一般に ippán ni

general delivery (*US*) *n* (poste restante) 局留 kyokúdome

general election *n* 総選挙 sōseñkyo

generalization [dʒenə:rələzei'ʃən] *n* 一般化 ippáñka

generally [dʒen'ə:rəli:] *adv* (in general) 一般に ippán ni; (usually) 普通は futsū wa

general practitioner *n* 一般開業医 ippán kaigyōi

generate [dʒen'ə:reit] *vt* (power, energy) 発生させる hasséi saserù; (jobs, profits) 生み出す umídasù

to generate electricity 発電する hatsúden suru

generation [dʒenərei'ʃən] *n* (period of time) 世代 sedái; (of people, family) 同じ世代の人々 onáji sedài no hitobito; (of heat, steam, gas etc) 発生 hasséi; (of electricity) 発電 hatsúden

generator [dʒen'ə:reitə:r] *n* (ELEC) 発電機 hatsúdeñki

generosity [dʒenərɑ:s'əti:] *n* 寛大さ kańdaisa

generous [dʒen'ə:rəs] *adj* (person, measure, remuneration etc) 寛大な kańdai na

genetics [dʒənet'iks] *n* (science) 遺伝学 idéngàku

Geneva [dʒəni:'və] *n* ジュネーブ júnèbu

genial [dʒi:'ni:əl] *adj* (host, smile) 愛想の良い aíso no yoì

genitals [dʒen'itəlz] *npl* (ANAT) 性器 seíki

genius [dʒi:n'jəs] *n* (ability, skill, person) 天才 teñsai

genocide [dʒen'əsaid] *n* 民族虐殺 miñzokugyakusàtsu, ジェノサイド jénòsaido

gent [dʒent] *n abbr* = **gentleman**

genteel [dʒenti:l'] *adj* (person, family) 家柄の良い iégara no yoì

gentle [dʒen'təl] *adj* (person) 優しい yasáshiì; (animal) 大人しい otónashiì; (movement, shake) 穏やかな odáyàka na, 静かな shizúkà na; (slope, curve) 緩やかな yurúyàka na

a gentle breeze そよ風 soyókàze

gentleman [dʒen'təlmən] (*pl* **gentlemen**) *n* (man) 男の方 otóko no katà; (referring to social position: *also* well-mannered man) 紳士 shiñshì, ジェントルマン jéñtoruman

gentleness [dʒen'təlnis] *n* (of person) 優しさ yasáshisà; (of animal) 大人しさ otónashisà; (of movement, breeze, shake) 穏やかさ odáyàkasa, 静かさ shizúkàsa; (of slope, curve) 緩やかさ yurúyàkasa

gently [dʒen'tli:] *adv* (subj: person) 優しく yasáshikù; (: animal) 大人しく otónashikù; (: breeze etc) 穏かに shizúkàni (: slope, curve) 緩やかに yurúyàka ni

gentry [dʒen'tri:] *n* 紳士階級 shiñshikaìkyū

gents [dʒents] (*BRIT*) *n* (men's toilet) 男性トイレ dañseitoirè

genuine [dʒen'ju:in] *adj* (real) 本物の hoñmonò no; (person) 誠実な seíjitsu na

geographic(al) [dʒiːəgræfˈik(əl)] adj 地理の chírì no

geography [dʒiːɑːgˈrəfiː] n (of town, country etc: also SCOL) 地理 chírì

geological [dʒiːələdʒˈikəl] adj 地質学の chishítsugàku no

geologist [dʒiːɑːlˈədʒist] n 地質学者 chishítsugakushà

geology [dʒiːɑːlˈədʒiː] n (of area, rock etc) 地質 chíshìtsu; (SCOL) 地質学 chishítsugàku

geometric(al) [dʒiːəmetˈrik(əl)] adj (problem, design) 幾何学的な kikágakuteki na

geometry [dʒiːɑːmˈətriː] n (MATH) 幾何学 kikágaku

geranium [dʒəreiˈniːəm] n ゼラニウム zerániumu

geriatric [dʒeːriːætˈrik] adj (of old people) 老人の rôjin no

germ [dʒəːrm] n ばい菌 baíkin

German [dʒəːrˈmən] adj (of Germany) ドイツの dóìtsu no; (LING) ドイツ語の doítsugo no
♦n ドイツ人 doítsujin; (LING) ドイツ語 doítsugo

German measles n (rubella) 風しん fúshin

Germany [dʒəːrˈməniː] n ドイツ dóìtsu

germination [dʒəːrməneiˈʃən] n (of seed) 発芽 hatsúga

gesticulate [dʒestikˈjəleit] vi (with arms, hands) 手振りをする tébùri wo suru

gesture [dʒesˈtʃəːr] n (movement) 手振り tébùri, ジェスチャー jésùchā; (symbol, token) ジェスチャー jésùchā

| KEYWORD |

get [get] (pt, pp **got**, (US) pp **gotten**) vi **1** (become, be) ...になる ...ni narù
to get old (thing) 古くなる fúrùku naru; (person) 年を取る toshí wò toru
to get cold 寒くなる sámùku naru
to get annoyed/bored/tired 怒る〔退屈する, 疲れる〕okórù〔taíkutsu surù, tsukárerù〕
to get drunk 酔っ払う yopparau

to get dirty 汚れる yogórerù
to get killed 殺される korósarerù
to get married 結婚する kekkón surù
when do I get paid? 金はいつ払ってくれますか kané wà ítsù harátte kuremasù ká
it's getting late 遅くなってきました osóku nattè kimáshìta

2 (go): **to get to/from** ...へ〔から〕行く ...é〔kará〕ikù
to get home 家に帰る ié ni kaerù
how did you get here? あなたはどうやってここへ来ましたか anátà wa dô yattè kokó è kimáshìtà ká

3 (begin): **to get to know someone** ...と親しくなる ...tò shitáshikù naru
I'm getting to like him 彼を好きになってきました kárè wo sukí ni nattè kimáshìta
let's get going/started さあ, 行きましょう sâ, ikímashô
♦**modal aux vb: you've got to do it** あなたはどうしてもそれをしなければなりません anátà wa dôshite mò soré wò shinákereba narimaseñ
I've got to tell the police 警察に知らせなければなりません keísatsu nì shirásenakereba narimaseñ
♦**vt 1: to get something done** (do) ...を済ます ...wò sumásù; (have done) ...をしてもらう ...wò shité moraù
to get the washing/dishes done 洗濯〔皿洗い〕を済ます señtaku〔saráarài〕wò sumásù
to get one's hair cut 散髪してもらう sañpatsu shite moraù
to get the car going/to go 車のエンジンをかける kurúma no eñjin wo kakérù
to get someone to do something ...に...をさせる ...nì ...wò saserù
to get something ready ...を用意する ...wò yôì suru
to get someone ready ...に用意をさせる ...nì yôì wo saserù
to get someone drunk/into trouble ...を酔っ払わせる〔困らせる〕...wò yoppárawaserù〔komáraserù〕

2 (obtain: money) 手に入れる té ni irerù;

(: permission, results) 得る ērù; (find: job, flat) 見付ける mitsúkerù; (fetch: person, doctor) 呼んで来る yoñde kuru; (: object) 持って来る motté kurù

to get something for someone ...のために...を持って来る ...no tamé nî ...wò motté kurù

he got a job in London 彼はロンドンに仕事を見付けました kárè wa rôñdon ni shigóto wò mitsúkemashìta

get me Mr Jones, please (TEL) ジョーンズさんをお願いしたいんですが jôñzu san wo o-négai shitaiñ dèsù ga

I think you should get the doctor 医者を呼んだ方がいいと思います ishá wò yoñda hồ ga íi to omóimasù

can I get you a drink? 何か飲みませんか nánìka nomímaseñ ka

3 (receive: present, letter) 受ける ukérù; (acquire: reputation, prize) 得る ērù, 獲得する kakútoku suru

what did you get for your birthday? お誕生日に何をもらいましたか o-táñjòbi ni nánì wo moráimashìta ká

he got a prize for French 彼はフランス語の成績で賞をもらいました kárè wa furáñsugò no seíseki dè shổ wò moráimashìta

how much did you get for the painting? 絵画はいくらで売れましたか kâíga wa íkùra de urémashìta kà

4 (catch) つかむ tsukámù; (hit: target etc) ...に当る ...ni atárù

to get someone by the arm/throat ...の腕(のど)をつかむ ...no udé(nôdò)wò tsukámù

get him! やつを捕まえろ yátsù wo tsukámaerò

the bullet got him in the leg 弾丸は彼の脚に当った dañgan wà kárè no ashí ni atattà

5 (take, move) 連れて〔持って〕いく tsuréte〔motté〕ikù, 移動する idō suru

to get something to someone ...に...を持って行く ...nî ...wo motté ikù

do you think we'll get it through the door? それは戸口から入ると思いますか soré wà tógùchi kara háìru to omó-

imasù ká

I'll get you there somehow 何とかしてあなたを連れて行きます náñ to ka shite anátà wo tsuréte ikimasù

we must get him to (US the) hospital どうしても彼を病院に連れて行かなくちゃ dồshité mo kárè wo byôìn ni tsuréte ikanakùcha

6 (catch, take: plane, bus etc) 乗る norú

where do I get the train - Birmingham? 電車はどこで乗ればいいんですか-バーミンガムですか deñsha wà dôkò de norébà iiñ desù ká - bâmìñgamu desu ká

7 (understand) 理解する ríkài suru; (hear) 聞き取る kikítorù

I've got it 分かった wakáttà

I don't get your meaning あなたが言おうとしている事が分かりません anátà ga iố to shite iru kotò ga wakárimaseñ

I'm sorry, I didn't get your name 済みませんが，お名前を聞き取れませんでした sumímaseñ ga, o-námae wò kikítoremasen deshìta

8 (have, possess): *to have got* 持つ môtsù

how many have you got? いくつ持っていますか íkùtsu motté imasù ká

---

get about *vi* 動き回る ugókimawarù; (news) 広まる hirómarù

get along *vi* (agree) 仲良くする nákàyoku suru; (depart) 帰る káèru; (manage) = **get by**

get at *vt fus* (attack, criticize) 批判する hiháñ suru; (reach) ...に手が届く ...ni té gà todókù

get away *vi* (leave) 帰る káèru; (escape) 逃げる nigérù

get away with *vt fus* ...をうまくやりおおせる ...wò úmàku yaríỗseru

get back *vi* (return) 帰る káèru
♦*vt* 返す káèsu

get by *vi* (pass) 通る tổrù; (manage) やって行く yatté ikù

get down *vi* 降りる orírù
♦*vt fus* 降りる orírù
♦*vt* 降ろす orósù; (depress: person) がっかりさせる gakkárì saseru

get down to vt fus (work) ...に取り掛る ...ni toríkakarù

get in vi 入る háiru; (train) 乗る norú; (arrive home) 帰って来る káette kurù

get into vt fus ...に入る ...ni háiru; (vehicle) ...に乗る ...ni norú; (clothes) 着る kirú

to get into bed ベッドに入る béddò ni háiru

to get into a rage かんかんに怒る kañkan nì okóru

get off vi (from train etc) 降りる orírù; (depart: person, car) 出発する shuppátsu suru; (escape punishment etc) 逃れる nogárerù

♦vt (remove: clothes) 脱ぐ núgù; (: stain) 消す kesú, 落す otósù; (send off) 送る okúrù

♦vt fus (train, bus) 降りる orírù

get on vi (at exam etc) how are you getting on? 万事うまく行っていますか báñji úmàku itté imasù ká; (agree): *to get on (with)* (...と) 気が合う (...tò) ki gá aù

♦vt fus ...に乗る ...ni norú

get out vi 出る dérù; (of vehicle) 降りる orírù

♦vt 取り出す torídasù

get out of vt fus ...から出る ...kara dérù; (vehicle) ...から降りる ...kara orírù; (bed) ...から起きる ...kara okírù; (duty etc) 避ける sakérù, 逃れる nogárerù

get over vt fus (illness) ...が直る ...ga naórù

get round vt fus (problem, difficulty) 避ける sakérù; (law, rule) ...に触れないようにする ...ni furénai yō ni suru; (fig: person) 言いくるめる iíkurumerù

get through vi (TEL) 電話が通じる deñwa gà tsūjiru

get through to vt fus (TEL) ...に電話が通じる ...ni deñwa gà tsūjiru

get together vi (people) 集まる atsúmarù

♦vt 集める atsúmerù

get up vi (rise) 起きる okírù

♦vt fus 起す okósù

get up to vt fus (reach) ...に着く ...ni

tsukú; (BRIT: prank etc) 仕出かす shidékasù

geyser [gai'zəːr] n (GEO) 間欠温泉 kañketsu oñsen; (BRIT: water heater) 湯沸かし器 yuwákashikì

Ghana [gɑːn'ə] n ガーナ gāna

ghastly [gæst'liː] adj (horrible: person, behavior, situation) いやな fyá na, ひどい hídòi; (: building, appearance) 薄気味悪い usúkimiwaruì; (pale: complexion) 青白い aójiroì

gherkin [gəːr'kin] n キュウリのピクルス kyūri no píkùrusu

ghetto [get'ou] n (ethnic area) ゲットー géttò

ghost [goust] n (spirit) 幽霊 yūrei, お化け o-báke

giant [dʒai'ənt] n (in myths, children's stories) 巨人 kyojín, ジャイアント jáìanto; (fig: large company) 大企業 daíkigyō

♦adj (enormous) 巨大な kyodái na

gibberish [dʒib'əːriʃ] n (nonsense) でたらめ detárame

gibe [dʒaib] n = jibe

giblets [dʒib'lits] npl 鳥の内臓 torí nò naízō

Gibraltar [dʒibrɔːl'təːr] n ジブラルタル jíbùrarutaru

giddy [gid'iː] adj (dizzy) めまいがする memái ga suru

gift [gift] n (present) 贈り物 okúrimonò, プレゼント purézènto, ギフト gíftùto; (ability) 才能 saínō

gifted [gif'tid] adj (actor, sportsman, child) 才能ある saínō arù

gift token n ギフト券 gifútokèn

gift voucher n = gift token

gigantic [dʒaigæn'tik] adj 巨大な kyodái na

giggle [gig'əl] vi くすくす笑う kusúkusu waráù

gill [dʒil] n (= 0.25 pints; BRIT = 0.15 l; US = 0.12 l) ギル gírù

gills [gilz] npl (of fish) えら erá

gilt [gilt] adj (frame, jewelery) 金めっきした kiñmekkī shita

♦n 金めっき kiñmekkī

gilt-edged [gilt'edʒd] adj (stocks, securities) 優良な yúryō na

gimmick [gim'ik] *n* (sales, electoral) 仕掛け shikáke

gin [dʒin] *n* ジン jín

ginger [dʒin'dʒər] *n* (spice) ショウガ shōga

ginger ale *n* ジンジャーエール jińjáèru

ginger beer *n* ジンジャービール jińjábìru

gingerbread [dʒin'dʒə:rbred] *n* (cake) ジンジャーブレッドケーキ jińjábureddokèki; (biscuit) ジンジャーブレッドクッキー jińjábureddokukkī

gingerly [dʒin'dʒə:rli:] *adv* (tentatively) 慎重に shíńchō ni

gipsy [dʒip'si:] *n* = **gypsy**

giraffe [dʒəræf'] *n* キリン kirín

girder [gə:r'də:r] *n* 鉄骨 tekkótsu

girdle [gə:r'dəl] *n* (corset) ガードル gádoru

girl [gə:rl] *n* (child) 女の子 ońna nò ko, 少女 shōjo; (young unmarried woman) 若い女性 wakái joséi, ガール gáru; (daughter) 娘 musúme

　an English girl 若いイングランド人女性 wakái ińgurandojìn joséi

girlfriend [gə:rl'frend] *n* (of girl) 女友達 ońna tomodàchi; (of boy) ガールフレンド gárufureńdo

girlish [gə:r'liʃ] *adj* 少女の様な shōjo nó yō na

giro [dʒai'rou] *n* (also: **bank giro**) 銀行振替為替 gińkōfurikaekawàse; (also: **post office giro**) 郵便振替為替 yūbinfurikaekawàse; (BRIT: welfare check) 生活保護の小切手 seíkatsuhogò no kogíttè

girth [gə:rθ] *n* (circumference) 周囲 shūi; (of horse) 腹帯 haráobi

gist [dʒist] *n* (of speech, program) 骨子 kósshì

KEYWORD

give [giv] (*pt* **gave**, *pp* **given**) *vt* **1** (hand over): *to give someone something, give something to someone* ...に...を与える ...nī ...wò atáerù, ...に...を渡す ...nī ...wò watásu

　I gave David the book, I gave the book to David 私は本をデービッドに渡しました watákushi wà hón wò débìddo ni watáshinashìta

　give him your key あなたのかぎを彼に渡しなさい anátá no kagí wò kárè ni watáshinasaì

　he gave her a present 彼は彼女にプレゼントをあげた kárè wa kánòjo ni purézeñto wo agétá

　give it to him, give him it それを彼に渡しなさい soré wò kárè ni watáshi nasaì

　I'll give you £5 for it それを5ポンドで私に売ってくれませんか soré wò gopóñdo de watákushi nì utté kuremaseñ ká

2 (used with noun to replace a verb): *to give a sigh* ため息をつく taméikì wo tsuku

　to give a cry/shout 叫ぶ sakébù

　to give a push 押す osú

　to give a groan うめく umékù

　to give a shrug 肩をすくめる kátá wo sukúmerù

　to give a speech/a lecture 演説〔講演〕をする eñzetsu(kōeñ)wo surú

　to give three cheers 万歳三唱をする bañzaisañshō wo suru

3 (tell, deliver: news, advice, message etc) 伝える tsutáerù, 言う iú, 与える atáerù

　did you give him the message/the news? 彼にメッセージ〔ニュース〕を伝えましたか kárè ni méssèji(nyúsù)wo tsutáemashìta ká

　let me give you some advice ちょっと忠告をあげよう chóttò chūkoku wo ageyō

　he gave me his new address over the phone 彼は電話で新しい住所を教えてくれました kárè wa deńwa dè atárashii jūsho wo oshíete kuremashìta

　to give the right/wrong answer 正しい〔間違った〕答を言う tadáshii(machígatta)kotáe wo iú

4 (supply, provide: opportunity, surprise, job etc) 与える atáerù, 提供する teíkyō suru; (bestow: title) 授与する júyò suru;

(: honor, right) 与える atáerù

I gave him the chance to deny it それを否定するチャンスを彼に与えました soré wò hitéi suru chañsu wo kárè nì atáemashìta

the sun gives warmth and light 太陽は熱と光を我々に与えてくれる táiyō wa netsú tò hikári wò waréware nì atáete kurerù

what gives you the right to do that? 何の権利でそんな事をするのか nán no keñri de sofina kotò wo suru nò ka

that's given me an idea あれでいい事を思い付いたんですが arê de ii kotò wo omóitsuitan desù ga

5 (dedicate: time) 当てる atérù; (: one's life) 捧げる saságerù; (: attention) 払う haráu

you'll need to give me more time もっと時間を下さい móttò jikán wo kudasaì

she gave it all her attention 彼女はそれに専念した kánòjo wa soré nì sefinen shitá

6 (organize): *to give a party/dinner etc* パーティ[晩さん会]を開催する pātì [bañsañkai] wo kaísai suru

◆*vi* **1** (*also*: **give way**: break, collapse) 崩れる kuzúrerù

his legs gave beneath him 彼は突然立てなくなった kárè wa totsúzen taténaku nattà

the roof/floor gave as I stepped on it 私が踏んだとたん屋根[床]が抜け落ちた watákushi ga funda totañ yánè [yuká] ga nukéochitá

2 (stretch: fabric) 伸びる nobírù

give away *vt* (money) 人にやる hitó nì yarú; (opportunity) 失う ushínaù; (secret, information) 漏らす morásù; (bride) 新郎に渡す shiñrō nì watásu

give back *vt* 返す káèsu

give in *vi* (yield) 降参する kõsan suru

◆*vt* (essay etc) 提出する teíshutsu suru

give off *vt* (heat) 放つ hanátsù; (smoke) 出す dásù

give out *vt* (distribute: prizes, books,

drinks etc) 配る kubárù; (make known: news etc) 知らせる shiráserù

give up *vi* (surrender) 降参する kõsan suru

◆*vt* (renounce: job, habit) やめる yamérù; (boyfriend) …との交際をやめる …to no kõsai wò yamérù; (abandon: idea, hope) 捨てる sutérù

to give up smoking タバコをやめる tabáko wò yamérù

to give oneself up 自首する jishú suru

give way *vi* (yield) 譲る yuzúru; (break, collapse: floor, ladder etc) 崩れる kuzúrerù, 壊れる kowárerù; (: rope) 切れる kirérù; (*BRIT*: AUT) 道を譲る michí wò yuzúru

glacier [glei'ʒəːr] *n* 氷河 hyőga

glad [glæd] *adj* (happy, pleased) うれしい uréshiì

gladly [glæd'liː] *adv* (willingly) 喜んで yorókoñde

glamorous [glæm'əːrəs] *adj* 魅惑的な miwákuteki na

glamour [glæm'əːr] *n* 魅惑 miwáku

glance [glæns] *n* (look) ちらっと見る事 chiráttò mírù koto

◆*vi*: *to glance at* …をちらっと見る …wo chiráttò mírù

glance off *vt fus* …に当って跳ね返る …ni attátè hanékaerù

glancing [glæn'siŋ] *adj* (blow) かすめる kasúmerù

gland [glænd] *n* せん séñ

glare [gleːr] *n* (of anger) にらみ nirámi; (of light) まぶしさ mabúshisà; (of publicity) 脚光 kyakkő

◆*vi* (light) まぶしく光る mabúshikù hikárù

to glare at (glower) …をにらみ付ける …wo nirámitsukerù

glaring [gleːr'iŋ] *adj* (mistake) 明白な meſhaku na

glass [glæs] *n* (substance) ガラス garásu; (container) コップ koppù, グラス gúràsu; (contents) コップ一杯 koppú ippái

glasses [glæs'iz] *npl* 眼鏡 mégàne

glasshouse [glæs'haus] *n* 温室 oñshitsu

glassware [glæs'weːr] *n* グラス類 gurásurui

glassy [glæs'i:] *adj* (eyes) うつろな utsúro na

glaze [gleiz] *vt* (door, window) ...にガラスをはめる ...ni garásu wò hamérù; (pottery) ...にうわぐすりを掛ける ...ni uwágusùri wo kakérù
♦*n* (on pottery) うわぐすり uwágusùri

glazed [gleizd] *adj* (eyes) うつろな utsúro na; (pottery) うわぐすりを掛けた uwágusùri wo kakéta

glazier [glei'ʒəːr] *n* ガラス屋 garásuyà

gleam [gli:m] *vi* (shine: light, eyes, polished surface) 光る hikárù

glean [gli:n] *vt* (information) かき集める kakíatsumerù

glee [gli:] *n* (joy) 喜び yorókobi

glen [glen] *n* 谷間 taníaĩ

glib [glib] *adj* (person) 口達者な kuchídasshà na; (promise, response) 上辺だけの uwábe dake no

glide [glaid] *vi* (snake, dancer, boat etc) 滑る様に動く subéru yõ ni ugókù; (AVIAT, birds) 滑空する kakkū suru

glider [glai'dəːr] *n* (AVIAT) グライダー gurấidā

gliding [glai'diŋ] *n* (AVIAT) 滑空 kakkū

glimmer [glim'əːr] *n*: *a glimmer of light* かすかな光 kásùka na hikári
a glimmer of interest かすかな表情 kásùka na hyójō
a glimmer of hope かすかな希望 kásùka na kibō

glimpse [glimps] *n* (of person, place, object) ちらっと見える事 ...ga chiráttò miérù koto
♦*vt* ...がちらっと見える ...ga chiráttò miérù

glint [glint] *vi* (flash: light, eyes, shiny surface) ぴかっと光る pikáttò hikárù

glisten [glis'ən] *vi* (with sweat, rain etc) ぎらぎらする gíràgira suru

glitter [glit'əːr] *vi* (sparkle: light, eyes, shiny surface) 輝く kagáyakù

gloat [glout] *vi*: *to gloat (over)* (exult) ...にほくそえむ ...ni hokúsoemu

global [glou'bəl] *adj* (worldwide) 世界的な sekáiteki na

globe [gloub] *n* (world) 地球 chikyū; (model) 地球儀 chikyūgĩ; (shape) 球 kyū

gloom [glu:m] *n* (dark) 暗やみ kuráyami; (sadness) 失望 shitsúbō

gloomy [glu:'mi:] *adj* (dark) 薄暗い usúguraì; (sad) 失望した shitsúbō shita

glorious [glɔːr'i:əs] *adj* (sunshine, flowers, weather) 素晴らしい subárashiĩ; (victory, future) 栄光の eíkō no

glory [glɔːr'i:] *n* (prestige) 栄光 eíkō; (splendor) 華々しさ hanábanashisà

gloss [glɔːs] *n* (shine) つや tsuyá; (*also*: **gloss paint**) つや出しペイント tsuyádashipeìnto

glossary [glɑːs'əːri:] *n* 用語集 yōgoshū

gloss over *vt fus* (error) 言繕う iítsukuroù; (problem) 言いくるめる iíkurumerù

glossy [glɑːs'i:] *adj* (hair) つやつやした tsuyátsùya shitá; (photograph) つや出しの tsuyádashi no; (magazine) アート紙の átoshī no

glove [glʌv] *n* (gen) 手袋 tebúkùro; (in baseball) グローブ gúròbu, グラブ gúràbu

glove compartment *n* (AUT) グローブボックス gurốbubokkùsu

glow [glou] *vi* (embers) 赤く燃える akákù moérù; (stars) 光る hikárù; (face, eyes) 輝く kagáyakù

glower [glau'əːr] *vi*: *to glower at* ...をにらみ付ける ...wo nirámitsukerù

glucose [glu:'kous] *n* ブドウ糖 budōtō, グルコース gurúkòsu

glue [glu:] *n* (adhesive) 接着剤 setcháku-zài
♦*vt* 接着する setchákù suru

glum [glʌm] *adj* (miserable) ふさぎ込んだ fuságikoñda

glut [glʌt] *n* (of oil, goods etc) 生産過剰 seísankajō

glutton [glʌt'ən] *n* 大食らい ōgurai
a glutton for work 仕事の鬼 shigóto nò oní

gluttony [glʌt'əni:] *n* 暴食 bōshoku

glycerin(e) [glis'əːrin] *n* グリセリン guríserìn

gnarled [nɑːrld] *adj* (tree, hand) 節くれだった fushíkuredattà

gnat [næt] n ブヨ búyò

gnaw [nɔ:] vt (bone) かじる kajírù

gnome [noum] n 地の小鬼 chi no koôni

KEYWORD

---

go [gou] (pt **went**, pp **gone**) vi **1** (travel, move) 行く ikú

she went into the kitchen 彼女は台所に行った kánòjo wa daídokoro ni ittá

shall we go by car or train? 車で行きましょうか，それとも電車で行きましょうか kuruma dè ikímashò ka, sorétomò deñsha dè ikímashò ka

a car went by 車が通り過ぎた kuruma gà tòri sugitá

to go round the back 裏へ回る urá e mawárù

to go by the shop 店の前を通る misé no maè wo tòrù

he has gone to Aberdeen 彼はアバーディーンへ行きました kárè wa abádìn e ikímashìta

2 (depart) 出発する shuppátsu suru, たつ tátsù, 帰る kaéru, 行ってしまう itté shimaù

"I must go," she said 「帰ります」と彼女は言った "kaérimasù" to kánòjo wa ittá

our plane went at 6 pm 我々の飛行機は夕方6時に出発しました waréware no hikòki wa yùgata rokuji ni shuppátsu shimashìta

they came at 8 and went at 9 彼らは8時に来て9時に帰った kárèra wa hachìji ni kitè kùji ni kaérimashìta

3 (attend) 通う kayóu

she went to university in Aberdeen 彼女はアバーディーンの大学に通った kánòjo wa abádìn no daígaku nì kayóu

she goes to her dancing class on Tuesdays 彼女がダンス教室に通うのは火曜日です kánòjo ga dañsukyòshitsu ni kayóu no wa kayòbi desu

he goes to the local church 彼は地元の教会に通っています kárè wa jimóto no kyòkai ni kayótte imasù

4 (take part in an activity) ...に行く ...ni ikú, ...する ...surù

to go for a walk 散歩に行く safipo ni ikù, 散歩する sanpo suru

to go dancing ダンスに行く dáñsu ni iku

5 (work) 作動する sadó suru

the clock stopped going 時計が止りました tokéi gà tomárimashìta

is your watch going? あなたの時計は動いていますか anátà no tokéi wà ugòite imasù ká

the bell went just then 丁度その時ベルが鳴りました chòdo sono tokì bèru ga narímashìta

the tape recorder was still going テープレコーダーはまだ回っていました tèpurekòda wa màdà mawátte imashìta

6 (become) ...になる ...ni nárù

to go pale 青白くなる aójiroku narù

to go moldy かびる kabíru

7 (be sold): *to go for $10* 10ドルで売れる jùdòru de urérù

8 (fit, suit) 合う áù

to go with ...に合う ...ni áù

that tie doesn't go with that shirt そのネクタイはシャツと合いません sonó nekùtai wa shàtsù to aímaseñ

9 (be about to, intend to): *he's going to do it* 彼は今それをやる所です kárè wa ímà soré wò yarú tokorò desu

we're going to leave in an hour 1時間したら出発します ichíjikan shitarà shuppátsu shimasù

are you going to come? あなたも一緒に来ますか anátà mo isshó nì kimasù ká

10 (time) 経つ tátsù

time went very slowly/quickly 時間が経つのがとても遅く〔早く〕感じられました jikán ga tatsù no ga totémò osóku 〔hàyàku〕 kanjiraremashìta

11 (event, activity) 行く ikú

how did it go? うまく行きましたか úmàku ikímashìta ka

12 (be given) 与えられる atáerarerù

the job is to go to someone else そのポストは他の人のところへいきました sonó posùto wa hoká no hito no tokorò e ikímashìta

13 (break etc: glass etc) 割れる warérù;

(: stick, leg, pencil etc) 折れる orérù;
(: thread, rope, chain etc) 切れる kirérù
the fuse went ヒューズが切れた〔飛ん
だ〕hyúzù ga kirēta(tónda)
the leg of the chair went いすの脚が
折れた isú no ashī ga órēta
14 (be placed) ...にしまう事になっている
...ni shimáu kotō ni nátte irù
where does this cup go? このカップは
どこにしまうのですか konó kappù wa
dókò ni shimáù no desu ká
the milk goes in the fridge ミルクは
冷蔵庫にしまう事になっています mírù-
ku wa reízōko ni shimáu kotō ni nátte
imasù

♦*n* (*pl* **goes**) **1** (try): *to have a go (at)*
(...を) やってみる (...wo) yatté mirù
2 (turn) 番 bán
whose go is it? だれの番ですか dáre no
bán desu ká
3 (move): *to be on the go* 忙しくする
isógashiku surù

---

go about *vi* (*also*: **go around**: rumor) 流
れる nagárerù
♦*vt fus*: *how do I go about this?* どう
いう風にやればいいんですか dō iu fū ni
yareba íin desu ká

goad [goud] *vt* 刺激する shigéki suru

go ahead *vi* (make progress) 進歩する
shínpo suru; (get going) 取り掛る toríkakarù

go-ahead [gou'əhed] *adj* (person, firm)
進取の気に富んだ shínshu no ki ni tónda
♦*n* (for project) 許可 kyóka, ゴーサイン
gōsaín

goal [goul] *n* (SPORT) ゴール gṓru;
(aim) 目標 mokúhyō

goalkeeper [goul'ki:pə:r] *n* ゴールキー
パー gōrukīpā

go along *vi* ついて行く tsúite ikú
♦*vt fus* ...を行く ...wò ikú
to go along with (agree with: plan,
idea, policy) ...に賛成する ...ni sańsei surù

goalpost [goul'poust] *n* ゴールポスト gṓ-
rupòsùto

goat [gout] *n* ヤギ yágì

go away *vi* (leave) どこかへ行く dókò
ka e ikú

go back *vi* (return) 帰る káèru; (go
again) また行く matá ikù

go back on *vt fus* (promise) 破る yabúrù

gobble [ga:b'əl] *vt* (*also*: **gobble down**,
gobble up) むさぼり食う musáborikuù

go-between [gou'bitwi:n] *n* 仲介者 chū-
kaishà

go by *vi* (years, time) 経つ tátsù
♦*vt fus* (book, rule) ...に従う ...ni shitágaù

God [ga:d] *n* (REL) 神 kámì

god [ga:d] *n* (MYTHOLOGY, *fig*) 神 kámì

godchild [ga:d'tʃaild] *n* 名付け子 nazúke-
gò

goddaughter [ga:d'dɔ:tə:r] *n* 名付け娘
nazúkemusùme

goddess [ga:d'is] *n* (MYTHOLOGY,
REL, *fig*) 女神 mégàmi

godfather [ga:d'fa:ðə:r] *n* 名付け親 na-
zúkeðya, 代父 daìfù, 教父 kyṓfù

godforsaken [ga:d'fɔ:rsei'kən] *adj*
(place, spot) 荒れ果てた aréhatetà

godmother [ga:d'mʌðə:r] *n* 名付け親 na-
zúkeðya, 代母 daìbò, 教母 kyṓbò

go down *vi* (descend) 降りる orírù;
(ship) 沈む shizúmu, 沈没する chiñbotsu
suru; (sun) 沈む shizúmu
♦*vt fus* (stairs, ladder) ...を降りる ...wo
orírù

godsend [ga:d'send] *n* (blessing) 天の恵
み teñ no megúmi

godson [ga:d'sʌn] *n* 名付け息子 nazúke-
musùko

go for *vt fus* (fetch) 取りに行く tórì ni
ikú; (like) 気に入る ki ní irù; (attack)
...に襲い掛る ...ni osóikakarù

goggles [ga:g'əlz] *npl* (for skiing, motor-
cycling) ゴーグル gōguru

go in *vi* (enter) 入る háìru

go in for *vt fus* (competition) ...に参加
する ...ni sańka suru; (like) ...が好きであ
る ...ga sukí de arù, ...を気に入る ...wò ki
ní irù

going [gou'iŋ] *n* (conditions) 状況 jṓkyō

♦*adj*: *the going rate* 相場 sṓba

go into *vt fus* (enter) ...に入る ...ni háiru; (investigate) 調べる shiráberù; (embark on) ...に従事する ...ni jū́ji suru

gold [gould] *n* (metal) 金 kíñ

♦*adj* (jewelery, watch, tooth etc) 金の kíñ no

gold reserves 金の正貨準備 kíñ no séíka juñbi

golden [goul'dən] *adj* (made of gold) 金の kíñ no; (gold in color) 金色の kiñ-iro no

goldfish [gould'fiʃ] *n* 金魚 kíñgyo

goldmine [gould'main] *n* 金山 kíñzan; (*fig*) ドル箱 dorúbako

gold-plated [gouldplei'tid] *adj* 金めっきの kíñmekkī no

goldsmith [gould'smiθ] *n* 金細工師 kíñzaikushī

golf [gɑːlf] *n* ゴルフ górufu

golf ball *n* (for game) ゴルフボール gorúfubṓru; (on typewriter) 電動タイプライターのボール deñdōtaipuraītā no bṓru

golf club *n* (organization, stick) ゴルフクラブ gorúfukurabu

golf course *n* ゴルフコース gorúfukōsu

golfer [gɑːl'fəːr] *n* ゴルファー górùfā

gondola [gɑːn'dələ] *n* (boat) ゴンドラ goñdora

gone [gɔːn] *pp of* go

gong [gɔːŋ] *n* どら dorá, ゴング góñgu

good [gud] *adj* (pleasant, satisfactory etc) 良い yóì; (high quality) 高級な kṓkyū na; (tasty) おいしい oíshiī; (kind) 親切な shiñsetsu na; (well-behaved: child) 行儀の良い gyṓgi no yoì; (morally correct) 正当な seítō na

♦*n* (virtue, morality) 善 zéñ; (benefit) 利益 ríeki

good! よろしい！ yoróshiì!

to be good at ...が上手である ...ga jṓzu dè árù

to be good for (useful) ...に使える ...ni tsukáerù

it's good for you あなたのためにいい anáta no tamè ni íi

would you be good enough to ...? 済みませんが...して下さいませんか sumí-

masêñ ga ...shite kudásaimaseñ ká

a good deal (of) 沢山 (の) takúsan (no)

a good many 沢山の takúsañ no

to make good (damage, loss) 弁償する beñshō suru

it's no good complaining 不平を言ってもしようがない fuhéi wo ittè mo shiyō ga nái

for good (forever) 永久に eíkyū ni

good morning! お早うございます o-háyō gozaimasù

good afternoon! 今日は koñnichi wa

good evening! 今晩は koñban wa

good night! お休みなさい o-yásumi nasaì

goodbye [gudbai'] *excl* さようなら sayṓnarà

to say goodbye 別れる wakárerù

Good Friday *n* (REL) 聖金曜日 seíkin-yōbi

good-looking [gud'luk'iŋ] *adj* (woman) 美人の bijíñ no; (man) ハンサムな háñsamu na

good-natured [gud'nei'tʃərd] *adj* (person, pet) 気立ての良い kidáte no yoì

goodness [gud'nis] *n* (of person) 優しさ yasáshisà

for goodness sake! 後生だから goshṓ da kara

goodness gracious! あらまあ! ará mā

goods [gudz] *npl* (COMM) 商品 shṓhin

goods train (*BRIT*) *n* 貨物列車 kamótsuresshā

goodwill [gud'wil'] *n* (of person) 善意 zéñ-i

go off *vi* (leave) どこかへ行く dókò ka é ikù; (food) 悪くなる warúku naru; (bomb) 爆発する bakúhatsu suru; (gun) 暴発する bṓhatsu suru; (event): *to go off well* うまくいく úmàku iku

♦*vt fus* (person, place, food etc) 嫌いになる kirái ni narù

go on *vi* (continue) 続く tsuzúku; (happen) 起る okórù

to go on doing something ...をし続ける ...wò shitsuzúkerù

goose [guːs] (*pl* **geese**) *n* ガチョウ gachṓ

gooseberry [guːsˈbeːriː] *n* (tree, fruit) ス

グリ súgùri

to play gooseberry (*BRIT*) アベックの邪魔をする abékkù no jamá wo surù

gooseflesh [guːs'fleʃ] *n* 鳥肌 toríhada

goose pimples *npl* = **gooseflesh**

go out *vi* (leave: room, building) 出る dérù; (for entertainment): *are you going out tonight?* 今夜どこかへ出掛けますか kôn-ya dókòka e dekákemasù ká; (couple): *they went out for 3 years* 彼らは3年交際した kárèra wa sañnen kōsai shita; (fire, light) 消える kiérù

go over *vi* (ship) 転覆する teñpuku suru

◆*vt fus* (check) 調べる shiráberù

gore [goːr] *vt* (subj: bull, buffalo) 角で刺す tsunó dè sásù

◆*n* (blood) 血のり chinóri

gorge [gɔːrdʒ] *n* (valley) 峡谷 kyōkoku

◆*vt*: *to gorge oneself (on)* (...を) たらふく食う (...wo) taráfuku kúù

gorgeous [gɔːr'dʒəs] *adj* (necklace, dress etc) 豪華な gṓka na; (weather) 素晴らしい subárashiǐ; (person) 美しい utsúkushiǐ

gorilla [gəril'ə] *n* ゴリラ górìra

gorse [gɔːrs] *n* ハリエニシダ haríenishìda

gory [gɔːr'iː] *adj* (details, situation) 血みどろの chimídoro no

go-slow [gou'slou'] (*BRIT*) *n* 遵法闘争 juñpōtōsō

gospel [gɑːs'pəl] *n* (REL) 福音 fukúìn

gossip [gɑːs'əp] *n* (rumors) うわさ話 uwásabanashi, ゴシップ goshíppù; (chat) 雑談 zatsúdan; (person) おしゃべり o-sháberi, ゴシップ屋 goshíppuyà

◆*vi* (chat) 雑談する zatsúdan suru

got [gɑːt] *pt, pp of* **get**

go through *vt fus* (town etc) ...を通る ...wð tṓrù; (search through: files, papers) ...を一つ一つ調べる ...wð hitótsu hitotsù shiráberù; (examine: list, book, story) 調べる shiráberù

gotten [gɑːt'ən] (*US*) *pp of* **get**

go up *vi* (ascend) 登る nobóru; (price, level) 上がる agáru

gout [gaut] *n* 通風 tsúfū

govern [gʌv'əːrn] *vt* (country) 統治する tṓchi suru; (event, conduct) 支配する shi-

hái suru

governess [gʌv'əːrnis] *n* (children's) 女性家庭教師 joséikateikyōshì

government [gʌv'əːrnmənt] *n* (act of governing) 政治 seíji; (governing body) 政府 seífu; (*BRIT*: ministers) 内閣 naíkaku

governor [gʌv'əːrnəːr] *n* (of state) 知事 chíjì; (of colony) 総督 sōtoku; (of bank, school, hospital) 理事 ríjì; (*BRIT*: of prison) 所長 shochō

go without *vt fus* (food, treats) ...無しで済ます ...náshì de sumásù

gown [gaun] *n* (dress: *also* of teacher) ガウン gáùn; (*BRIT*: of judge) 法服 hōfuku

GP [dʒiːpiː'] *n abbr* = **general practitioner**

grab [græb] *vt* (seize) つかむ tsukámù

◆*vi*: *to grab at* ...をつかもうとする ...wo tsukámō to suru

grace [greis] *n* (REL) 恩恵 oñkei; (gracefulness) しとやかさ shitóyakasà

◆*vt* (honor) ...に栄誉を与える ...ni éìyo wo atáerù; (adorn) 飾る kazárù

5 days' grace 5日間の猶予 itsúkakañ no yūyo

graceful [greis'fəl] *adj* (animal, athlete) しなやかな shináyàka na; (style, shape) 優雅な yūga na

gracious [grei'ʃəs] *adj* (person) 親切な shiñsetsu na

grade [greid] *n* (COMM: quality) 品質 hiñshitsu; (in hierarchy) 階級 kaíkyū; (SCOL: mark) 成績 seíseki; (*US*: school class) 学年 gakûnen

◆*vt* (rank, class) 格付けする kakúzuke suru; (exam papers etc) 採点する saíten suru

grade crossing (*US*) *n* 踏切 fumíkiri

grade school (*US*) *n* 小学校 shōgakkō

gradient [grei'diːənt] *n* (of road, slope) こう配 kōbai

gradual [grædʒ'uːəl] *adj* (change, evolution) 少しずつの sukóshizutsù no

gradually [grædʒ'uːəliː] *adv* 徐々に jójò ni

graduate [*n* grædʒ'uːit *vb* grædʒ'uːeit] *n* (*also*: **university graduate**) 大学の卒

業生 daígaku nò sotsúgyòsei; (US: also: **high school graduate**) 高校の卒業生 kókò nò sotsúgyòsei
♦vi 卒業する sotsúgyō suru

graduation [grædʒuːeiˈʃən] n (also: **graduation ceremony**) 卒業式sotsúgyòshiki

graffiti [grəfiːˈtiː] npl 落書 rakúgaki

graft [græft] n (AGR) 接 木 tsugíki; (MED) 移植 ishóku; (BRIT: inf: hard work) 苦労 kúrō; (bribery) 汚職 oshóku
♦vt (AGR) 接木する tsugíki suru; (MED) 移植する ishóku suru

grain [grein] n (of rice, wheat, sand, salt) 粒 tsúbù; (no pl: cereals) 穀物 kokúmòtsu; (of wood) 木目 mokúme

gram [græm] n グラム gúràmu

grammar [græmˈəːr] n (LING) 文法 buñpō; (book) 文法書 buñpòsho

grammar school (BRIT) n 公立高等学校 kóritsukōtōgakkò◇大学進学教育をする公立高校 daígakushingakukyòiku wo suru kóritsukōkō; (US) 小学校 shógakkò

grammatical [grəmætˈikəl] adj (LING) 文法の buñpō no

gramme [græm] n = **gram**

gramophone [græmˈəfoun] n 蓄音機 chikúoñki

grand [grænd] adj (splendid, impressive) 壮大な sódai na; (inf: wonderful) 素晴らしい subárashiì; (also humorous: gesture etc) 大げさな ógesa na

grandchildren [grænˈtʃildrən] npl 孫 mágó

granddad [grænˈdæd] n (inf) おじいちゃん ojíichan

granddaughter [grænˈdɔːtəːr] n 孫 娘 magómusùme

grandeur [grænˈdʒəːr] n (of scenery etc) 壮大さ sódaisa

grandfather [grænˈfɑːðəːr] n 祖父 sófù

grandiose [grænˈdiːous] adj (scheme, building) 壮大な sódai na; (pej) 大げさな ógesa na

grandma [græmˈə] n (inf) おばあちゃん obáachan

grandmother [grænˈmʌðəːr] n 祖母 só-

bò

grandpa [grænˈpə] n (inf) = **granddad**

grandparents [grænˈpeːrənts] npl 祖父母 sófùbo

grand piano n グランドピアノ gurándopiàno

grandson [grænˈsʌn] n 孫息子 magómusùko

grandstand [grænˈstænd] n (SPORT) 観覧席 kañrañseki, スタンド sutáñdo

granite [grænˈit] n 御影石 mikágeìshi

granny [grænˈiː] n (inf) おばあちゃん obáachan

grant [grænt] vt (money) 与 え る atáerù; (request etc) かなえる kanáerù; (visa) 交付する kófu suru; (admit) 認める mitómerù
♦n (SCOL) 助 成 金 joséìkin; (ADMIN: subsidy) 交付金 kófùkin
to take someone/something for granted ...を軽く見る ...wo karúkù mírù

granulated sugar [grænˈjəleitid-] n グラニュー糖 gurányūtō

granule [grænˈjuːl] n (of coffee, salt) 粒 tsúbù

grape [greip] n ブドウ budó

grapefruit [greipˈfruːt] (pl **grapefruit** or **grapefruits**) n グレープフルーツ gurḗpufurùtsu

graph [græf] n (diagram) グラフ gúràfu

graphic [græfˈik] adj (account, description) 写実的な shajítsuteki na; (art, design) グラフィックの guráfikkù no

graphics [græfˈiks] n (art, process) グラフィックス guráfikkùsu
♦npl (drawings) グラフィックス guráfikkùsu

grapple [græpˈəl] vi: **to grapple with someone** ...ともみ合う ...to momíaù
to grapple with something (problem etc) ...と取組む ...to toríkumù

grasp [græsp] vt (hold, seize) 握る nigírù; (understand) 理解する rikái suru
♦n (grip) 握り nigírì; (understanding) 理解 rikái

grasping [græsˈpiŋ] adj (money-grabbing) 欲深い yokúfukaì

grass [grɑːs] *n* (BOT) 草 kusá; (lawn) 芝生 shibáfu

grasshopper [grɑːs'hɑːpər] *n* バッタ battá

grass-roots [grɑːs'ruːts] *adj* (level, opinion) 一般人の ippánjìn no

grate [greit] *n* (for fire) 火格子 higóshi
♦*vi* (metal, chalk): **to grate (on)** (...にすれて) きしる (...ni suréte) kishírù
♦*vt* (CULIN) すりおろす suríorosù

grateful [greit'fəl] *adj* (thanks) 感謝の kánsha no; (person) 有難く思っている arígatakù omótte irù

grater [grei'təːr] *n* (CULIN) 卸し金 oróshigàne

gratifying [græt'əfaiiŋ] *adj* (pleasing, satisfying) 満足な mánzoku na

grating [grei'tiŋ] *n* (iron bars) 鉄格子 tetsúgōshi
♦*adj* (noise) きしる kishírù

gratitude [græt'ətuːd] *n* 感謝 kánsha

gratuity [grətuː'itiː] *n* (tip) 心付け kokórozùke, チップ chíppù

grave [greiv] *n* (tomb) 墓 haká
♦*adj* (decision, mistake) 重大な júdai na; (expression, person) 重々しい omóomoshiì

gravel [græv'əl] *n* 砂利 jarí

gravestone [greiv'stoun] *n* 墓石 hakáishi

graveyard [greiv'jɑːrd] *n* 墓場 hakába, 墓地 bóchi

gravity [græv'itiː] *n* (PHYSICS) 引力 ínryoku; (seriousness) 重大さ júdaisa

gravy [grei'viː] *n* (juice of meat) 肉汁 nikújū; (sauce) グレービーソース gurébīsōsu

gray [grei] *adj* = **grey**

graze [greiz] *vi* (animal) 草を食う kusá wo kuù
♦*vt* (touch lightly) かすめる kasúmerù; (scrape) こする kosúrù
♦*n* (MED) かすり傷 kasúrikìzu

grease [griːs] *n* (lubricant) グリース gurísù; (fat) 脂肪 shibó
♦*vt* ...にグリースを差す ...ni gurísù wo sásù

greaseproof paper [griːs'pruːf-] (*BRIT*)

n パラフィン紙 paráfìnshi

greasy [griː'siː] *adj* (food) 脂っこい abúrakkoì; (tools) 油で汚れた abúra dè yogóretà; (skin, hair) 脂ぎった abúragittà

great [greit] *adj* (large: area, amount) 大きい ōkii; (intense: heat, pain) 強い tsuyói; (important, famous: city, man) 有名な yūmei na; (*inf*: terrific) 素晴らしい subárashiì

Great Britain *n* 英国 eíkoku, イギリス igírisu

great-grandfather [greit'græn'fɑːðəːr] *n* そう祖父 sōsofù

great-grandmother [greit'græn'mʌðəːr] *n* そう祖母 sōsobò

greatly [greit'liː] *adv* とても totémo

greatness [greit'nis] *n* (importance) 偉大さ idáisa

Greece [griːs] *n* ギリシア gírìshia

greed [griːd] *n* (*also*: **greediness**) どん欲 dón-yoku

greedy [griː'diː] *adj* どん欲な dón-yoku na

Greek [griːk] *adj* ギリシアの gírìshia no; (LING) ギリシア語の giríshiago no
♦*n* (person) ギリシア人 giríshiajìn; (LING) ギリシア語 giríshiago

green [griːn] *adj* (color) 緑 (色) の mídòri(iro) no; (inexperienced) 未熟な mijúku na; (POL) 環境保護の kańkyōhogò no
♦*n* (color) 緑 (色) mídòri(iro); (stretch of grass) 芝生 shibáfu; (on golf course) グリーン gurín

green belt *n* (round town) 緑地帯 ryokúchitài, グリーンベルト gurínberùto

green card *n* (*BRIT*: AUT) グリーンカード gurínkàdo ◇海外自動車保険証 kaígai jidōsha hokeñshō; (*US*: ADMIN) グリーンカード gurínkàdo ◇外国人入国就労許可書 gaíkokujìn nyūkoku shūrō kyokasho

greenery [griː'nəːriː] *n* 緑 mídòri ◇ 主に人為的に植えた樹木などを指す ómò ni jiń-iteki ni ueta júmòku nádà wo sásù

greengrocer [griːn'grousəːr] (*BRIT*) *n* 八百屋 yaóya

greenhouse [griːn'haus] *n* 温室 ońshitsu

greenish [griː'niʃ] *adj* 緑がかった midórigakattā

Greenland [griːnˈlənd] n グリーンランド gurīnrando

greens [griːnz] npl (vegetables) 葉物 hamóno, 葉菜 yōsai

greet [griːt] vt (welcome: person) ...にあいさつする ...ni áisatsu suru, 歓迎する kañgei suru; (receive: news) 受けとめる ukétomerù

greeting [griːtiŋ] n (welcome) あいさつ áisatsu, 歓迎 kañgei

greeting(s) card n グリーティングカード gurītingukádo

gregarious [grigeˈriːəs] adj (person) 社交的な shakōteki na

grenade [grineidˈ] n (also: hand grenade) 手りゅう弾 teryūdan, shuryūdan

grew [gruː] pt of **grow**

grey [grei] adj (color) 灰色 haíro; (dismal) 暗い kuráì

grey-haired [greiˈheːrd] adj 白髪頭の shirágaatàma no, 白髪の hakúhatsu no

greyhound [greiˈhaund] n グレーハウンド gurēhaùndo

grid [grid] n (pattern) 碁盤の目 gōban no me; (ELEC: network) 送電網 sōdenmō

grief [griːf] n (distress, sorrow) 悲しみ kanáshimì

grievance [griːˈvəns] n (complaint) 苦情 kujō

grieve [griːv] vi (feel sad) 悲しむ kanáshimù

♦vt (cause sadness or distress to) 悲しませる kanáshimaserù

to grieve for (dead spouse etc) ...を嘆く ...wo nagékù

grievous [griːˈvəs] adj: *grievous bodily harm* (LAW) 重傷 jūshō

grill [gril] n (on cooker) グリル gúrìru; (grilled food: also: mixed grill) グリル料理 gurír-uryòri

♦vt (BRIT: food) グリルで焼く gúrìru de yákù; (inf: question) 尋問する jiñmon suru

grille [gril] n (screen: on window, counter etc) 鉄格子 tetsúgōshi; (AUT) ラジエーターグリル rajétāgùriru

grim [grim] adj (unpleasant: situation)

厳しい kibíshiì; (unattractive: place) 陰気な iñki na; (serious, stern) 険しい kewáshiì

grimace [grimˈəs] n (ugly expression) しかめっ面 shikámettsura

♦vi しかめっ面をする shikámetsura wo surù

grime [graim] n (dirt) あか aká

grin [grin] n (smile) にやにや笑い níyàni-yawarai

♦vi にやにやと笑う níyàniya to waráù

grind [graind] (pt, pp **ground**) vt (crush) もみつぶす momítsubusù; (coffee, pepper etc: also US: meat) 挽く hikú; (make sharp: knife) 研ぐ tógù

♦n (work) 骨折れ仕事 honéoreshigòto

grip [grip] n (hold) 握り nigíri; (control, grasp) 支配 shihái; (of tire, shoe) グリップ guríppù; (handle) 取っ手 tottè; (holdall) 旅行かばん ryokôkabàn

♦vt (object) つかむ tsukámù, 握る nigírù; (audience, attention) 引付ける hikítsukerù

to come to grips with (problem, difficulty) ...と取組む ...to toríkumù

gripping [gripˈiŋ] adj (story, film) 引付ける hikítsukerù

grisly [grizˈliː] adj (death, murder) ひどい hidóì

gristle [grisˈəl] n (on meat) 軟骨 nánkotsu

grit [grit] n (sand, stone) 砂利 jarí; (determination, courage) 根性 koñjō

♦vt (road) ...に砂利を敷く ...ni jarí wo shíkù

to grit one's teeth 歯を食いしばる há wo kuíshibarù

groan [groun] n (of person) うめき声 umékigoè

♦vi うめく umékù

grocer [grouˈsəːr] n 食料品商 shokúryō-hìnshō

groceries [grouˈsəːriːz] npl (provisions) 食料品 shokúryōhìn

grocer's (shop) [grouˈsəːrz-] n 食料品店 shokúryōhìnten

groggy [grɑːgˈiː] adj ふらふらする fúrà-fura suru, グロッキーの gurókkì no

groin [grɔin] n そけい部 sokéibu

groom [gru:m] n (for horse) 馬丁 batéi; (also: **bridegroom**) 花婿 hanámukò

♦vt (horse) ...の手入れをする ...no teíre wò suru; (fig): **to groom someone for** (job) 仕込む shikómù

well-groomed (person) 身だしなみのいい midáshinami no íi

groove [gru:v] n 溝 mizó

grope [group] vi (fumble): **to grope for** 手探りで探す teságuri de sagásù

gross [grous] adj (flagrant: neglect, injustice) 甚だしい hanáhadashiì; (vulgar: behavior, building) 下品な gehín na; (COMM: income, weight) 全体の zeñtai no

grossly [grous'li:] adv (greatly) 甚だしく hanáhadashikù

grotesque [groutesk'] adj (exaggerated, ugly) 醜悪な shūaku na, グロテスクな gurótesùku na

grotto [gra:t'ou] n (cave) 小さな洞穴 chíisana horáana

grotty [gra:t'i:] adj (BRIT inf) adj (dreadful) ひどい hídòi

ground [graund] pt, pp of **grind**

♦n (earth, soil) 土 tsuchí; (land) 地面 jímèn; (SPORT) グランド gurándo; (US: also: **ground wire**) アース線 ásùsen; (reason: gen pl) 根拠 koñkyo

♦vt (plane) 飛べない様にする tobénai yò ni suru; (US: ELEC) ...のアースを取付ける ...no ásu wò torítsukerù

on the ground 地面に〔で〕 jímèn ni 〔de〕

to the ground 地面へ jímèn e

to gain/lose ground 前進〔後退〕する zeñshin〔kòtai〕surù

ground cloth (US) n = **groundsheet**

grounding [graun'diŋ] n (in education) 基礎 kisó

groundless [graund'lis] adj (fears, suspicions) 根拠のない koñkyo no nài

grounds [graundz] npl (of coffee etc) かす kásù; (gardens etc) 敷地 shikíchi

groundsheet [graund'ʃi:t] n グラウンドシート guráundoshìto

ground staff n (AVIAT) 整備員 seíbiìn

◇総称 sṓshō

ground swell n (of opinion) 盛り上がり moríagarì

groundwork [graund'wə:rk] n (preparation) 準備 júñbi

group [gru:p] n (of people) 集団 shūdan, グループ gúrūpu; (of trees etc) 一群れ hitómùre; (of cars etc) 一団 ichídan; (also: **pop group**) グループ gúrūpu; (COMM) グループ gúrūpu

♦vt (also: **group together**: people, things etc) 一緒にする ísshò ni suru, グループにする gúrūpu ni suru

♦vi (also: **group together**) 群がる murágarù, グループになる gúrūpu ni nárù

grouse [graus] n inv (bird) ライチョウ ráichō

♦vi (complain) 不平を言う fuhéi wò iú

grove [grouv] n 木立 kodáchì

grovel [grʌv'əl] vi (fig): **to grovel (before)** (boss etc) (...に) ぺこぺこする (..ni) pékòpeko suru

grow [grou] (pt **grew**, pp **grown**) vi (plant, tree) 生える haérù; (person, animal) 成長する seíchō suru; (increase) 増える fuérù; (become) なる nárù; (develop): **to grow (out of/from)** (...から) 発生する (...kara) hasséi suru

♦vt (roses, vegetables) 栽培する saíbai suru; (beard) 生やす hayásù

grower [grou'ə:r] n (BOT, AGR) 栽培者 saíbaishà

growing [grou'iŋ] adj (fear, awareness, number) 増大する zṓdai suru

growl [graul] vi (dog, person) うなる unárù

grown [groun] pp of **grow**

grown-up [groun'ʌp'] n (adult) 大人 otóna

growth [grouθ] n (development, increase: of economy, industry) 成長 seíchō; (what has grown: of weeds, beard etc) 生えた物 haéta monò; (growing: of child, animal etc) 発育 hatsúiku; (MED) しゅよう shuyṓ

grow up vi (child) 育つ sodátsu

grub [grʌb] n (larva) 幼虫 yṓchū; (inf: food) 飯 meshí

grubby [grʌb'i:] *adj* (dirty) 汚い kitánaì

grudge [grʌdʒ] *n* (grievance) 恨み urámì

♦*vt*: **to grudge someone something** (be unwilling to give) ...に...を出し惜しみする ...ni ...wo dashíoshimi suru; (envy) ...の...をねたむ ...no ...wo netámù

to bear someone a grudge ...に恨みがある ...ni urámi ga arù

gruelling [gru:'əliŋ] *adj* (trip, journey, encounter) きつい kitsúì

gruesome [gru:'səm] *adj* (tale, scene) むごたらしい mugótarashiì

gruff [grʌf] *adj* (voice, manner) ぶっきらぼうな bukkírabò na

grumble [grʌm'bəl] *vi* (complain) 不平を言う fuhéi wò iú

grumpy [grʌm'pi:] *adj* (bad-tempered) 機嫌が悪い kigén ga warúì

grunt [grʌnt] *vi* (pig) ぶーぶー言う bûbū iú; (person) うなる unáru

G-string [dʒi:'striŋ] *n* (garment) バタフライ bátàfurai

guarantee [gærənti:'] *n* (assurance) 保証 hoshő; (COMM: warranty) 保証書 hoshōshò

♦*vt* 保証する hoshő suru

guard [gɑːrd] *n* (one person) 警備員 keíbiìn, ガードマン gâdoman; (squad) 護衛隊 goéitai; (BRIT: RAIL) 車掌 shashő; (on machine) 安全カバー añzenkabà; (also: **fireguard**) 安全格子 añzenkòshi

♦*vt* (protect: place, person, secret etc) **to guard (against)** (...から)守る (...kara) mamőrù; (prisoner) 見張る mihárù

to be on one's guard 警戒する keíkai suru

guard against *vt fus* (prevent: disease, damage etc) 防ぐ fuségù

guarded [gɑːr'did] *adj* (statement, reply) 慎重な shiñchō na

guardian [gɑːr'di:ən] *n* (LAW: of minor) 保護者 hógòsha; (defender) 監視人 kañshinìn

guard's van (BRIT) *n* (RAIL) 乗務員車 jőmuìnsha

guerrilla [gəril'ə] *n* ゲリラ gérìra

guess [ges] *vt, vi* (estimate: number, dis-

tance etc) 推定する suítei suru; (correct answer) 当ててみる atétè mírù; (US: think) ...だと思う ...da to omőù

♦*n* (attempt at correct answer) 推定 suítei

to take/have a guess 推定する suítei suru, 当ててみる atétè mírù

guesswork [ges'wəːrk] *n* (speculation) 当て推量 atézuiryò

guest [gest] *n* (visitor) 客 kyákù; (in hotel) 泊り客 tomárikyàku

guest-house [gest'haus] *n* 民宿 mínshuku

guest room *n* 客間 kyakúma

guffaw [gʌfɔː'] *n* ばか笑い bakáwaraì

guidance [gaid'əns] *n* (advice) 指導 shidő

guide [gaid] *n* (person: museum guide, tour guide, mountain guide) 案内人 annáinìn, ガイド gaído; (book) ガイドブック gaídobukkù; (BRIT: also: **girl guide**) ガールスカウト gârusukaùto

♦*vt* (round city, museum etc) 案内する annái suru; (lead) 導く michíbikù; (direct) ...に道を教える ...ni michí wò oshíerù

guidebook [gaid'buk] *n* ガイドブック gaídobukkù

guide dog *n* 盲導犬 mődőkèn

guidelines [gaid'lainz] *npl* (advice) 指針 shishín, ガイドライン gaídoraìn

guild [gild] *n* (association) 組合 kumíaì, 協会 kyőkai

guile [gail] *n* (cunning) 悪意 akúì

guillotine [gil'ətiːn] *n* (for execution) 断頭台 dañtődai, ギロチン giróchin; (for paper) 裁断機 saídañki

guilt [gilt] *n* (remorse) 罪の意識 tsumí nò ishíki; (culpability) 有罪 yűzai

guilty [gil'tiː] *adj* (person) 有罪の yűzai no; (expression) 後ろめたそうな ushírometasò na; (secret) やましい yamáshiì

guinea [gin'iː] *n* (BRIT) (old money) ギニー gínì

guinea pig *n* (animal) モルモット morúmottò; (fig: person) 実験台 jikkéñdai

guise [gaiz] *n*: **in/under the guise of** ...の装いで ...no yosóoì de

guitar [gitɑːʳ] *n* ギター gítā

gulf [gʌlf] *n* (GEO) 湾 wán; (abyss: *also fig*: difference) 隔たり hedátarì

gull [gʌl] *n* カモメ kamóme

gullet [gʌl'it] *n* 食道 shokúdō

gullible [gʌl'əbəl] *adj* (naive, trusting) だまされやすい damásareyàsui

gully [gʌl'iː] *n* (ravine) 峡谷 kyókoku

gulp [gʌlp] *vi* (swallow) 息を飲み込む íkì wo nomíkomù

◆*vt* (*also*: **gulp down**: drink) がぶがぶ飲み込む gábùgabu nomíkomù; (: food) 急いで食べる isóìde tabérù

gum [gʌm] *n* (ANAT) 歯茎 hágùki; (glue) アラビア糊 arábia nòri; (sweet: *also*: **gumdrop**) ガムドロップ gamúdoroppù; (*also*: **chewing-gum**) チューインガム chúingaðamu, ガム gámù

◆*vt* (stick): **to gum (together)** 張り合わせる haríawaserù

gumboots [gʌm'buːts] (*BRIT*) *npl* ゴム靴 gomúgðutsu

gumption [gʌmp'ʃən] *n* (sense, wit) 度胸 dokyō

gun [gʌn] *n* (small: revolver, pistol) けん銃 keñjū, ピストル písùtoru, ガン gáñ; (medium-sized: rifle) 銃 jū, ライフル raífùru; (: *also*: **airgun**) 空気銃 kūkijū; (large: cannon) 大砲 taíhō

gunboat [gʌn'bout] *n* 砲艦 hōkan

gunfire [gʌn'faiəːr] *n* 銃撃 jūgeki

gunman [gʌn'mən] (*pl* **gunmen**) *n* (criminal) ガンマン gáñman

gunpoint [gʌn'point] *n*: **at gunpoint** (pointing a gun) ピストルを突付けて písùtoru wo tsukítsuketè; (threatened with a gun) ピストルを突付けられて písùtoru wo tsukítsukerarète

gunpowder [gʌn'paudəːr] *n* 火薬 kayákù

gunshot [gʌn'ʃɑːt] *n* (act) 発砲 happō; (sound) 銃声 jūsei

gurgle [gəːr'gəl] *vi* (baby) のどを鳴らす nodó wò narásù; (water) ごぼごぼ流れる góbògobo nagárerù

guru [guː'ruː] *n* (REL: *also fig*) 教師 kyōshi

gush [gʌʃ] *vi* (blood, tears, oil) どっと流れ出る dóttò nagárederù; (person) 大げさに言う ógesa ni iu

gusset [gʌs'it] *n* (SEWING) まち máchì

gust [gʌst] *n* (*also*: **gust of wind**) 突風 toppū; (of smoke) 渦巻 uzúmàki

gusto [gʌs'tou] *n* (enthusiasm) 楽しみ tanóshimì

gut [gʌt] *n* (ANAT: intestine) 腸 chō

guts [gʌts] *npl* (ANAT: of person, animal) 内臓 naízō; (*inf*: courage) 勇気 yúki, ガッツ gáttsū

gutter [gʌt'əːr] *n* (in street) どぶ dobu; (of roof) 雨どい amádòi

guttural [gʌt'əːrəl] *adj* (accent, sound) のどに絡まった様な nódò ni karámatta yō na

guy [gai] *n* (*inf*: man) 野郎 yarō, やつ yátsù; (*also*: **guyrope**) 支線 shisén; (figure) ガイフォークスの人形 gaífōkusu no niñgyō

guzzle [gʌz'əl] *vt* (drink) がぶがぶ飲む gábùgabu nómù; (food) がつがつ食う gátsùgatsu kúù

gym [dʒim] *n* (building, room: *also*: **gymnasium**) 体育館 taíikukàn; (activity: *also*: **gymnastics**) 体操 taísō

gymnast [dʒim'næst] *n* 体操選手 taísō-señshu

gymnastics [dʒimnæs'tiks] *n* 体操 taísō

gym shoes *npl* 運動靴 uñdōgùtsu, スニーカー súnìkā

gym slip (*BRIT*) *n* (tunic) スモック su-mókkù ◆そで無しの上っ張りでかつて女子学童の制服として使われた物. sodénashi no uwáppari de katsútè joshí gakudō no seífuku toshite tsukáwaretà monó.

gynecologist [gainəkɑːl'ədʒist] (*BRIT* **gynaecologist**) *n* 婦人科医 fujíñka-i

gypsy [dʒip'siː] *n* ジプシー jípùshī

gyrate [dʒai'reit] *vi* (revolve) 回転する kaíten suru

H

haberdashery [hæb'əːrdæʃəːriː] *n* (*US*) 紳士服店 shiñshifukutèn; (*BRIT*) 小間物店 komámonotèn

habit [hǽb'it] n (custom, practice) 習慣 shúkan; (addiction) 中毒 chúdoku; (REL: costume) 修道服 shúdōfùku

habitable [hǽb'itəbəl] adj 住める suméru

habitat [hǽb'itæt] n 生息地 seísokuchì

habitual [həbitʃ'u:əl] adj (action) 習慣的な shúkanteki na; (drinker, liar) 常習的な jōshūteki na

hack [hæk] vt (cut, slice) ぶった切る buttágirù

♦n (pej: writer) 三文文士 saǹmonbuǹshi

hacker [hæk'ə:r] n (COMPUT) コンピュータ破り coǹpyūtayaburì, ハッカー hákkā

hackneyed [hæk'ni:d] adj 陳腐な chíǹpu na

had [hæd] pt, pp of **have**

haddock [hæd'ək] (pl **haddock** or **haddocks**) n タラ tárà

hadn't [hæd'ənt] = **had not**

haemorrhage [hem'ə:ridʒ] (BRIT) n = **hemorrhage**

haemorrhoids [hem'ə:rɔidz] (BRIT) npl = **hemorrhoids**

haggard [hæg'ə:rd] adj (face, look) やつれた yatsúretà

haggle [hæg'əl] vi (bargain) 値切る negírù

Hague [heig] n: **The Hague** ハーグ hāgù

hail [heil] n (frozen rain) ひょう hyṑ; (of objects, criticism etc) 降り注ぐ物 furísosogù monó

♦vt (call: person) 呼ぶ yobú; (flag down: taxi) 呼止める yobítomerù; (acclaim: person, event etc) ほめる homérù

♦vi (weather) ひょうが降る hyṑ ga fúrù

hailstone [heil'stoun] n ひょうの粒 hyṑ no tsubù

hair [he:r] n (of animal: also gen) 毛 ke; (of person's head) 髪の毛 kamí no kè

to do one's hair 髪をとかす kamí wò tokásu

hairbrush [he:r'brʌʃ] n ヘアブラシ heáburashì

haircut [he:r'kʌt] n (action) 散髪 saǹpatsu; (style) 髪型 kamígata, ヘアスタイル heásutaìru

hairdo [he:r'du:] n 髪型 kamígata, ヘアスタイル heásutaìru

hairdresser [he:r'dresə:r] n 美容師 biyṓshì

hairdresser's [he:r'dresə:rz] n (shop) 美容院 biyṓiǹ

hair dryer n ヘアドライヤー heádoraìyā

hairgrip [he:r'grip] n 髪止め kamídome

hairnet [he:r'net] n ヘアネット heánettò

hairpin [he:r'pin] n ヘアピン heápiǹ

hairpin curve (BRIT **hairpin bend**) n ヘアピンカーブ heápinkàbu

hair-raising [he:r'reiziŋ] adj (experience, tale) ぞっとする様な zóttò suru yṑ na

hair remover [-rimu:'və:r] n (cream) 脱毛クリーム datsúmōkurìmù

hair spray n ヘアスプレー heásupurè

hairstyle [he:r'stail] n 髪型 kamígata, ヘアスタイル heásutaìru

hairy [he:r'i:] adj (person, animal) 毛深い kebúkài; (inf: situation) 恐ろしい osóroshìi

hake [heik] (pl inv or **hakes**) n タラ tárà

half [hæf] (pl **halves**) n (of amount, object) 半分 haǹbuǹ; (of beer etc) 半パイント haǹpaìnto; (RAIL, bus) 半額 haǹgaku

♦adj (bottle, fare, pay etc) 半分の haǹbuǹ no

♦adv (empty, closed, open, asleep) 半ば nakábà

two and a half 2と2分の1 ní tò nibún no ichi

two and a half years/kilos/hours 2年〔キロ, 時間〕半 ninén(kíro, jíkan) hàn

half a dozen 半ダース haǹdāsu

half a pound 半ポンド haǹpoǹdo

to cut something in half ...を半分に切る ...wo haǹbuǹ ni kírù

half-baked [hæf'beikt] adj (idea, scheme) ばかげた bakágetà

half-caste [hæf'kæst] n 混血児 koǹketsujì, ハーフ hāfu

half-hearted [hæf'hɑ:r'tid] adj (attempt) いい加減な iíkagen na

half-hour [hæf'au'ə:r] n 半時間 hañjikàn

half-mast [hæf'mæst']: *a flag at half-mast* 半旗 háñki

halfpenny [hei'pəni] (*BRIT*) n 半ペニー hañpenī

half-price [hæf'prais'] adj 半額の hañgaku no
♦adv 半額で hañgaku de

half term (*BRIT*) n (SCOL) 中間休暇 chūkankyùka

half-time [hæf'taim'] n (SPORT) ハーフタイム háfutaimù

halfway [hæf'wei'] adv (between two points in place, time) 中途で chūto de

halibut [hæl'əbət] n inv オヒョウ ohyő

hall [hɔ:l] n (entrance way) 玄関ホール geñkanhòru; (for concerts, meetings etc) 講堂 kődò, ホール hőru

hall of residence (*BRIT*) n 学生寮 gakúseiryő

hallmark [hɔ:l'mɑ:rk] n (on metal) 太鼓判 taíkoban; (of writer, artist etc) 特徴 tokúchō

hallo [həlou'] excl = **hello**

Hallowe'en [hæləwi:n'] n ハロウィーン harőuìn

hallucination [həlu:sənei'ʃən] n 幻覚 geñkaku

hallway [hɔ:l'wei] n (entrance hall) 玄関ホール geñkanhòru

halo [hei'lou] n (of saint) 後光 gokő

halt [hɔ:lt] n (stop) 止る事 tomáru kotò
♦vt (progress, activity, growth etc) 止める tomérù
♦vi (stop) 止る tomárù

halve [hæv] vt (reduce) 半分に減らす hañbuñ ni herásù; (divide) 半分に切る hañbuñ ni kírù

halves [hævz] pl of **half**

ham [hæm] n (meat) ハム hámù

hamburger [hæm'bə:rgə:r] n ハンバーガー hañbāgā

hamlet [hæm'lit] n (village) 小さな村 chíisana murá

hammer [hæm'ə:r] n (tool) 金づち kanázuchì, とんかち toñkàchi
♦vt (nail) たたく tatákù
♦vi (on door, table etc) たたく tatákù

to hammer an idea into someone ...にある考え方をたたき込む ...ni árù kañgàekata wo tátakikomù

to hammer a message across ある考えを繰返し強調する aru kañgaè wo kuríkaeshì kyőchō suru

hammock [hæm'ək] n (on ship, in garden) ハンモック hañmokkù

hamper [hæm'pə:r] vt (person, movement, effort) 邪魔する jamá suru
♦n (basket) ふた付きバスケット futátsukibasukettð

hamster [hæm'stə:r] n ハムスター hámùsutā

hand [hænd] n (ANAT) 手 tế; (of clock) 針 hárì; (handwriting) 筆跡 hisséki; (worker) 使用人 shíyònin; (of cards) 持札 mochífùda
♦vt (pass, give) 渡す watásù

to give/lend someone a hand ...の手伝いをする ...no tetsúdaì wo suru

at hand 手元に temóto nì

in hand (time) 空いていて aíte itè; (job, situation) 当面の tőmen no

on hand (person, services etc) 利用できる ríyò dekirù

to hand (information etc) 手元に temóto nì

on the one hand ..., on the other hand ... 一方では...他方では... ippő de wa ..., táhð de wa ...

handbag [hænd'bæg] n ハンドバッグ hañdobaggù

handbook [hænd'buk] n (manual) ハンドブック hañdobukkù

handbrake [hænd'breik] n (AUT) サイドブレーキ saídoburèki

handcuffs [hænd'kʌfs] npl (POLICE) 手錠 tejő

handful [hænd'ful] n (of soil, stones) 一握り hitónigirì

a handful of people 数人 sűnin

handicap [hæn'di:kæp] n (disability) 障害 shőgai; (disadvantage) 不利 fúrì; (SPORT) ハンデ háñde
♦vt (hamper) 不利にする fúrì ni suru

mentally/physically handicapped 精神的〔身体〕障害のある seíshinteki〔shiñtai) shōgai no árù

handicraft [hæn'di:kræft] n (activity) 手芸の活動 shugéi; (object) 手芸品 shugéihiǹ

hand in vt (essay, work) 提出する teí-shutsu suru

handiwork [hæn'di:wə:rk] n やった事 yattá kotð

handkerchief [hæn'kə:rtʃif] n ハンカチ hañkachi

handle [hæn'dəl] n (of door, window, drawer etc) 取っ手 tottě; (of cup, knife, brush etc) 柄 e; (for winding) ハンドル hañdðru

◆vt (touch: object, ornament etc) いじる ijírù; (deal with: problem, responsibility etc) 処理する shórì suru; (treat: people) 扱う atsúkaù

「*handle with care*」取扱い注意 toríatsukai chûi

to fly off the handle 怒る okórù

handlebar(s) [hæn'dəlbɑ:r(z)] n(pl) ハンドル hañdðru

hand luggage n 手荷物 tenímòtsu

handmade [hænd'meid'] adj (clothes, jewellery, pottery etc) 手作りの tezúkùri no

hand out vt (object, information) 配る kubárù; (punishment) 与える atáerù

handout [hænd'aut] n (money, clothing, food) 施し物 hodókoshimono; (publicity leaflet) パンフレット páñfuretto; (summary: of lecture) 講演の要約 kóen nð yóyaku

hand over vt (thing) 引渡す hikíwatasù; (responsibility) 譲る yuzúrù

handrail [hænd'reil] n (on stair, ledge) 手すり tesúri

handshake [hænd'ʃeik] n 握手 ákùshu

handsome [hæn'səm] adj (man) 男前の otókomaè no, ハンサムな háñsamu na; (woman) きりっとした kiríttð shita; (building) 立派な rippá na; (fig: profit, return) 相当な sótð na

handwriting [hænd'raitiŋ] n (style) 筆跡 hisséki

handy [hæn'di:] adj (useful) 便利な béñri na; (skilful) 手先の器用な tesáki nò kíyð na; (close at hand) 手元にある temóto nì

árù

handyman [hæn'di:mæn] (pl **handymen**) n (at home) 手先の器用な人 te-sáki nð kíyð na hitð; (in hotel etc) 用務員 yőmuin

hang [hæŋ] (pt, pp **hung**) vt (painting, coat etc) 掛ける kakérù; (criminal: pt, pp hanged) 絞首刑にする kőshukei ni surù

◆vi (painting, coat, drapery etc) 掛っている kakátte irù; (hair etc) 垂れ下がる tarésagarù

to get the hang of something (inf) ...のこつが分かる ...no kótsù ga wakárù

hang about vi (loiter) ぶらつく burátsukù

hangar [hæŋ'ə:r] n (AVIAT) 格納庫 ka-kúnòko

hang around vi = hang about

hanger [hæŋ'ə:r] n (for clothes) 洋服掛け yőfukukàke, ハンガー háñgà

hanger-on [hæŋ'ə:rɑ:n'] n (parasite) 取巻き torímaki

hang-gliding [hæŋ'glaidiŋ] n (SPORT) ハンググライダー hañguguraídā

hang on vi (wait) 待つ mátsù

hangover [hæŋ'ouvə:r] n (after drinking) 二日酔い futsúkayoì

hang up vi (TEL) 電話を切る deñwa wò kírù

◆vt (coat, painting etc) 掛ける kakérù

hang-up [hæŋ'ʌp] n (inhibition) ノイローゼ noíròze

hanker [hæŋ'kə:r] vi: *to hanker after* (desire, long for) 渇望する katsúbō suru

hankie [hæŋ'ki:] n abbr = **handkerchief**

hanky [hæŋ'ki:] n abbr = **handkerchief**

haphazard [hæp'hæz'ə:rd] adj (system, arrangement) いい加減な iíkagen na

happen [hæp'ən] vi (event etc: occur) 起る okórù; (chance): *to happen to do something* 偶然に...する gūzen ni ...surù

as it happens 実は jitsú wà

happening [hæp'əniŋ] n (incident) 出来事 dekígòto

happily [hæp'ili:] adv (luckily) 幸い saíwai; (cheerfully) 楽しそうに tanóshisò ni

happiness [hæp'i:nis] n (contentment) 幸せ shiáwase

happy [hæp'i:] adj (pleased) うれしい uréshiî; (cheerful) 楽しい tanóshiî

  to be happy (with) (content) (...に)満足する (...ni) mañzoku suru

  to be happy to do (willing) 喜んで...する yorókonde ...surù

  happy birthday! 誕生日おめでとう! tañjōbi omédetó!

happy-go-lucky [hæp'i:goulʌk'i:] adj (person) のんきな nóñki na

harangue [həræŋ'] vt (audience, class) ...に向かって熱弁を振るう ...ni mukáttè netsúben wò furúù

harass [həræs'] vt (annoy, pester) ...にいやがらせをする ...ni iyágarase wo surù

harassment [həræs'mənt] n (hounding) 嫌がらせ iyágarase

harbor [hɑːr'bəːr] (BRIT **harbour**) n (NAUT) 港 mináto

  ♦vt (hope, fear etc) 心に抱く kokórò ni idákù; (criminal, fugitive) かくまう kakúmaù

hard [hɑːrd] adj (surface, object) 堅い katái; (question, problem) 難しい muzúkashiî; (work) 骨の折れる honé no orérù; (life) 苦しい kurúshiî; (person) 非情な hijō na; (facts, evidence) 確実な kakújitsu na

  ♦adv (work, think, try) 一生懸命に isshōkeñmei ni

  to look hard at ...を見詰める ...wo mitsúmerù

  no hard feelings! 悪く思わないから warúkù omówanài kará

  to be hard of hearing 耳が遠い mimí ga tòi

  to be hard done by 不当な扱いを受けた futō na atsukái wo ukétà

hardback [hɑːrd'bæk] n (book) ハードカバー hádokabā

hard cash n 現金 geñkin

hard disk n (COMPUT) ハードディスク hádodisùku

harden [hɑːr'dən] vt (wax, glue, steel) 固める katámerù; (attitude, person) かたくなにする katákùna ni suru

  ♦vi (wax, glue, steel) 固まる katámarù; (attitude, person) かたくなになる katákùna ni nárù

hard-headed [hɑːrd'hed'id] adj (businessman) 現実的な geñjitsuteki na

hard labor n (punishment) 懲役 chóeki

hardly [hɑːrd'li:] adv (scarcely) ほとんど...ない hotóndo ...nài; (no sooner) ...するや否や ...surú ya inà ya

  hardly ever ほとんど...しない hotóndo ...shinài

hardship [hɑːrd'ʃip] n (difficulty) 困難 kofínañ

hard up (inf) adj (broke) 金がない kané ga naî, 懐が寂しい fuíokoro ga sabishiî

hardware [hɑːrd'weːr] n (ironmongery) 金物 kanámono; (COMPUT) ハードウエア hádoueà; (MIL) 兵器 héiki

hardware shop n 金物屋 kanámonoya

hard-wearing [hɑːrd'weːr'iŋ] adj (clothes, shoes) 丈夫な jōbu na

hard-working [hɑːrd'wəːr'kiŋ] adj (employee, student) 勤勉な kiñben na

hardy [hɑːr'di:] adj (plants, animals, people) 丈夫な jōbu na

hare [heːr] n ノウサギ noúsàgi

hare-brained [heːr'breind] adj (scheme, idea) バカげた bakágetà

harem [heːr'əm] n (of wives) ハーレム háremu

harm [hɑːrm] n (injury) 害 gái; (damage) 損害 sofígai, ダメージ daméjì

  ♦vt (person) ...に危害を加える ...ni kígài wo kuwáerù; (thing) 損傷する sofíshō suru

  out of harm's way 安全な場所に añzen na bashò ni

harmful [hɑːrm'fəl] adj (effect, toxin, influence etc) 有害な yúgai na

harmless [hɑːrm'lis] adj (animal, person) 無害な mugái na; (joke, pleasure, activity) たわいのない tawai no nai

harmonica [hɑːrmɑːn'ikə] n ハーモニカ hámonika

harmonious [hɑːrmou'ni:əs] adj (discussion, relationship) 友好的な yúkōteki na; (layout, pattern) 調和の取れた chówa no torétà; (sound, tune) 調子の良い chóshi no yoï

harmonize [hɑːr'mənaiz] vi (MUS) ハーモニーを付ける hāmonī wo tsukérù; (colors, ideas): **to harmonize (with)** (...と)調和する (...to) chōwa suru

harmony [hɑːr'məni:] n (accord) 調和 chōwa; (MUS) ハーモニー hāmonī

harness [hɑːr'nis] n (for horse) 馬具 bágù; (for child, dog) 胴輪 dṓwa, ハーネス hānesù; (safety harness) 安全ハーネス añzenhānesu

♦vt (resources, energy etc) 利用する riyō suru; (horse) ...に馬具をつける ...ni bágù wo tsukérù; (dog) ...にハーネスを付ける ...ni hānesù wo tsukérù

harp [hɑːrp] n (MUS) たて琴 tatégòto, ハープ hāpu

♦vi: **to harp on about** (pej) ...の事をくどくどと話し続ける ...no kotó wò kúdòkudo to hanáshitsuzukerù

harpoon [hɑːrpuːn'] n もり mórì

harrowing [hær'ouiŋ] adj (experience, film) 戦りつの señritsu no

harsh [hɑːrʃ] adj (sound) 耳障りな mimízawàri na; (light) どぎつい dogítsui; (judge, criticism) か酷な kakókù na; (life, winter) 厳しい kibíshìï

harvest [hɑːr'vist] n (harvest time) 収穫期 shūkakukì; (of barley, fruit etc) 収穫 shūkaku

♦vt (barley, fruit etc) 収穫する shūkaku suru

has [hæz] vb see **have**

hash [hæʃ] n (CULIN) ハッシュ hásshù; (fig: mess) めちゃめちゃな有様 mechámecha na arisama

hashish [hæʃ'iːʃ] n ハシシ háshìshi

hasn't [hæz'ənt] = **has not**

hassle [hæs'əl] (inf) n (bother) 面倒 meńdṓ

haste [heist] n (hurry) 急ぎ isógi

hasten [hei'sən] vt (decision, downfall) 早める hayámerù

♦vi (hurry): **to hasten to do something** 急いで...する isóide ...surù

hastily [heis'tili:] adv (hurriedly) 慌ただしく awátadashikù; (rashly) 軽はずみに karúhazùmi ni

hasty [heis'ti:] adj (hurried) 慌ただしい awátadashìï; (rash) 軽はずみの karúhazùmi no

hat [hæt] n (headgear) 帽子 bōshi

hatch [hætʃ] n (NAUT: also: **hatchway**) 倉口 sōkō, ハッチ hátchì; (also: **service hatch**) サービス口 sābisugùchi, ハッチ hátchì

♦vi (bird) 卵からかえる tamágò kara kaérù; (egg) かえる kaérù, ふ化する fuká suru

hatchback [hætʃ'bæk] n (AUT) ハッチバック hatchíbakkù

hatchet [hætʃ'it] n (axe) おの ónò

hate [heit] vt (wish ill to: person) 憎む nikúmù; (dislike strongly: person, thing, situation) 嫌う kiráu

♦n (illwill) 増悪 zōō; (strong dislike) 嫌悪 kéñ-o

hateful [heit'fəl] adj ひどい hidóï

hatred [hei'trid] n (illwill) 増悪 zōō; (strong dislike) 嫌悪 kéñ-o

haughty [hɔː'ti:] adj (air, attitude) 尊大な sońdai na

haul [hɔːl] vt (pull) 引っ張る hippáru

♦n (of stolen goods etc) 獲物 emóno; (also: **a haul of fish**) 漁獲 gyokáku

haulage [hɔː'lidʒ] n (business, costs) 運送 uñsō

hauler [hɔːl'əːr] (BRIT **haulier**) n 運送屋 uñsōya

haunch [hɔːntʃ] n (ANAT) 腰 koshí; (of meat) 腰肉 koshíniku

haunt [hɔːnt] vt (subj: ghost) (place) ...に出る ...ni dérù; (person) ...に付きまとう ...ni tsukímatou; (: problem, memory etc) 悩ます nayámasù

♦n (of crooks, childhood etc) 行き付けの場所 ikítsuke nò bashó

haunted house お化け屋敷 obákeyashìki

| KEYWORD |

have [hæv] (pt, pp **had**) aux vb **1** (gen) **to have arrived/gone/eaten/slept** 着いた〔行った, 食べた, 眠った〕tsúita〔ittá, tábèta, nemúttà〕

he has been kind/promoted 彼は親切

だった〔昇格した〕kárè wa shínsetsu dáttà〔shōkaku shita〕

has he told you? 彼はあなたにそれを話しましたか kárè wa anátà ni soré wò hanáshimashìta ká

having finished/when he had finished, he left 仕事が済むと彼は帰った shigóto ga sumù to kárè wa káètta

2 (in tag questions): *you've done it, haven't you?* あなたはその仕事をやったんでしょう anátà wa sonó shigòto wo yattáñ deshő

he hasn't done it, has he? 彼は仕事をやらなかったんでしょう kárè wa shigőto wò yaránakattàñ deshő

3 (in short answers and questions): *you've made a mistake - no I haven't/so I have* あなたは間違いをしました-違いますよ〔そうですね〕anátà wa machígaì wo shimáshìta - chigáimasù yő〔ső desu né〕

we haven't paid - yes we have! 私たちはまだ金を払っていません-払いましたよ watákushitàchi wa mádà kané wo harátte imaseñ - haráimashìta yő

I've been there before, have you? 私は前にあそこへ行った事がありますが、あなたは? watákushi wà máè ni asóko è ittá kotò ga arímasù ga, anátà wá?

♦*modal aux vb* (be obliged): *to have (got) to do something* ...をしなければならない ...wò shinákereba naraì

she has (got) to do it 彼女はどうしてもそれをしなければなりません kánòjo wa dőshite mo soré wò shinákereba narimaseñ

I have (got) to finish this work 私はこの仕事を済まさなければなりません watákushi wà konó shigòto wo sumásasanakereba narimaseñ

you haven't to tell her 彼女に言わなくてもいい〔言ってはならない〕kánòjo ni iwánakute mò íi〔itté wa naránaì〕

I haven't got/I don't have to wear glasses 私は眼鏡を掛けなくてもいい watákushi wà mégàne wò kakénakute mò íi

this has to be a mistake これは何かの

間違いに違いない koré wa nánìka no machígaì ni chigái naì

♦*vt* 1 (possess) 持っている mótte iru, ...がある ...gá arù

he has (got) blue eyes/dark hair 彼は目が青い〔髪が黒い〕kárè wa mé ga aóì〔kamí gà kuróì〕

do you have/have you got a car/phone? あなたは車〔電話〕を持っていますか anátà wa kurúma〔deñwa〕wò mőttè imasu ká

I have (got) an idea いい考えがあります íi kañgaè ga arímasù

have you any more money? もっとお金がありませんか mőttò o-káne gà arímaseñ ká

2 (take: food) 食べる tabérù; (: drink) 飲む nómù

to have breakfast/lunch/dinner 朝食〔昼食, 夕食〕を食べる chőshoku〔chűshoku, yűshoku〕wò tabérù

to have a drink 何かを飲む nánìka wo nómù

to have a cigarette タバコを吸う tabáko wo suù

3 (receive, obtain etc) 受ける ukérù, 手に入れる té ni irérù

may I have your address? ご住所を教えて頂けますか go-júsho wò oshíete itadakemasù ká

you can have it for $5 5ドルでそれを譲ります gődòru de soré wò yuzúrimasù

I must have it by tomorrow どうしても明日までにそれをもらいたいのです dőshite mò ashíta made nì soré wò móraitai no desù

to have a baby 子供を産む kodómo wo umù

4 (maintain, allow) 主張する shuchő suru, 許す yurúsù

he will have it that he is right 彼は自分が正しいと主張している kárè wa jibún gà tadáshiì to shuchő shite irù

I won't have it/this nonsense! それ〔こんなばかげた事〕は許せません soré〔koñna bakageta kotò〕wà yurúsemaseñ

we can't have that そんな事は許せません soñna kotò wa yurúsemaseñ

5: *to have something done* ...をさせる ...wò sasérù, ...をしてもらう ...wò shité mòrau

to have one's hair cut 散髪をしてもらう sañpatsu wò shité moraù

to have a house built 家を建てる ié wò tatérù

to have someone do something ...に ...をさせる ...ní ...wò sasérù

he soon had them all laughing/ working まもなく彼は皆を笑わせて〔働かせて〕いた ma mó nàku kárè wa miná wò waráwasete〔hátarakasete〕ità

6 (experience, suffer) 経験する keíken suru

to have a cold 風邪を引いている kazé wò hifte irù

to have (the) flu 感冒にかかっている kañbō nì kakátte irù

she had her bag stolen/her arm broken 彼女はハンドバッグを盗まれた〔腕を折った〕kánòjo wa hañdobaggù wo nusúmaretà〔udé wo ottá〕

to have an operation 手術を受ける shújùtsu wo ukérù

7 (+ noun: take, hold etc) ...する ... suru

to have a swim/walk/bath/rest 泳ぐ〔散歩する、風呂に入る、ひと休みする〕oyógù〔sañpo suru, fúrò ni háìru, hitóyàsumi suru〕

let's have a look 見てみましょう mítè mimashō

to have a meeting/party 会議〔パーティ〕を開く kaígi〔pátì〕wo hirákù

let me have a try 私に試させて下さい watákushi nì tamésasete kudasaì

8 (*inf*: dupe) だます damásù

he's been had 彼はだまされた kárè wa damásaretà

haven [hei'vən] *n* (harbor) 港 mináto; (safe place) 避難所 hináñjo

haven't [hæv'ənt] = **have not**

have out *vt*: *to have it out with someone* (settle a problem etc) ...と決着をつける ...tò ketcháku wò tsukérù

haversack [hæv'ə:rsæk] *n* (of hiker, soldier) リュックサック ryukkúsakkù

havoc [hæv'ək] *n* (chaos) 混乱 koñran

Hawaii [həwai'ji:] *n* ハワイ háwài

hawk [hɔːk] *n* タカ taká

hay [hei] *n* 干草 hoshíkusa

hay fever *n* 花粉症 kafúñshō

haystack [hei'stæk] *n* 干草の山 hoshíkusa no yama

haywire [hei'waiə:re] (*inf*) *adj*: *to go haywire* (machine etc) 故障する koshő suru; (plans etc) とんざする tóñza suru

hazard [hæz'ə:rd] *n* (danger) 危険 kikén
♦*vt* (risk: guess, bet etc) やってみる yatté mirù

hazardous [hæz'ə:rdəs] *adj* (dangerous) 危険な kikén na

hazard (warning) lights *npl* (AUT) 非常点滅灯 hijőtenmetsutő

haze [heiz] *n* (of heat, smoke, dust) かすみ kasúmi

hazelnut [hei'zəlnʌt] *n* ヘーゼルナッツ hēzerunattsù

hazy [hei'zi:] *adj* (sky, view) かすんだ kasúnda; (idea, memory) ぼんやりとした boñ-yarì to shita

he [hi:] *pron* 彼は〔が〕kárè wa〔ga〕

he who ... ...する人は ...surú hitò wa

head [hed] *n* (ANAT, mind) 頭 atáma; (of table) 上席 jőseki; (of queue) 先頭 señtō; (of company, organization) 最高責任者 saíkōsekiniñsha; (of school) 校長 kő-chō
♦*vt* (list, queue) ...の先頭にある〔いる〕...no señtō ni arù〔irù〕; (group, company) 取仕切る toríshikirù

heads (or tails) 表か（裏か）omóte kà (urá kà)

head first (fall) 真っ逆様に massákasama ni; (rush) 向こう見ずに mukő mìzu ni

head over heels (in love) ぞっこん zokkón

to head a ball ボールをヘディングで飛ばす bőru wo hedíñgu de tobásu

headache [hed'eik] *n* 頭痛 zutsū

headdress [hed'dres] (*BRIT*) *n* (of bride) ヘッドドレス heddődoresù

head for *vt fus* (place) ...に向かう ...ni mukáù; (disaster) ...を招く ...wo manékù

heading [hed'iŋ] *n* (of chapter, article)

表題 hyṓdai, タイトル tāĭtoru

headlamp [hed'læmp] (*BRIT*) n = headlight

headland [hed'lænd] n 岬 misáki

headlight [hed'lait] n ヘッドライト heddṓraĭto

headline [hed'lain] n (PRESS, TV) 見出し midáshi

headlong [hed'lɔːŋ] adv (fall) 真っ逆様に massákàsama ni; (rush) 向こう見ずに mukṓ mĭzu ni

headmaster [hed'mæs'tər] n 校長 kṓchō◇男性の場合 dañsei nṍ baái

headmistress [hed'mis'tris] n 校長 kṓchō◇女性の場合 joséi nṍ baái

head office n (of company etc) 本社 hoñsha

head-on [hed'ɑːn'] adj (collision, confrontation) 正面の shṓmen no

headphones [hed'founz] npl ヘッドホン heddṓhoñ

headquarters [hed'kwɔːrtə:rz] npl (of company, organization) 本部 hóñbu; (MIL) 司令部 shiréĭbu

headrest [hed'rest] n (AUT) ヘッドレスト heddṓrèsuto

headroom [hed'ruːm] n (in car) 天井の高さ teñjō no takàsa; (under bridge) 通行可能な高さ tsúkōkanŏ na takàsa

headscarf [hed'skɑːrf] n スカーフ sukáfù

headstrong [hed'strɔːŋ] adj (determined) 強情な gṓjō na

head waiter n (in restaurant) 給仕頭 kyúyigashira

headway [hed'wei] n: **to make headway** 進歩する shíñpo suru

headwind [hed'wind] n 向かい風 mukáikaze

heady [hed'iː] adj (experience, time) 陶酔の tṓsui no; (drink, atmosphere) 酔わせる yowáserù

heal [hiːl] vt (injury, patient) 治す naósù
♦vi (injury, damage) 治る naórù

health [helθ] n (condition: also MED) 健康状態 keñkōjṓtai; (good health) 健康 keñkō

health food n 健康食品 keñkōshokùhin

Health Service (*BRIT*) n: **the Health Service** 公共衛生機構 kṓkyōeiseikikṓ

healthy [hel'θiː] adj (person, appetite etc) 健康な keñkō na; (air, walk) 健康に良い keñkō ni yoĭ; (economy) 健全な keñzen na; (profit etc) 大いなる ṓi naru

heap [hiːp] n (pile: of clothes, papers, sand etc) 山 yamá
♦vt (stones, sand etc): **to heap (up)** 積み上げる tsumfagerù
to heap something with (plate) ...に...を山盛りする ...ni ...wo yamámori suru; (sink, table etc) ...に...を山積みする ...ni ...wo yamázumi suru
to heap something on (food) ...を...に山盛りする ...wo ...ni yamámori suru; (books etc) ...を...に山積みする ...wo ...ni yamázumi suru
heaps of (inf: time, money, work etc) 一杯の ippái no

hear [hiːr] (pt, pp **heard**) vt (sound, voice etc) ...を聞く ...wo kikú, ...が聞える ...ga kikóeru; (news, information) ...を聞く ...wo kikú, ...で聞いて知る ...de kiĭte shirú; (LAW: case) 審理する shiñri suru
to hear about (event, person) ...の事を聞く ...no kotó wo kikú
to hear from someone ...から連絡を受ける ...kara reñraku wŏ ukérù

heard [həːrd] pt, pp of **hear**

hearing [hiː'riŋ] n (sense) 聴覚 chṓkaku; (of facts, witnesses etc) 聴聞会 chṓmoñkai

hearing aid n 補聴器 hochṓkì

hearsay [hiːr'sei] n (rumor) うわさ uwása

hearse [həːrs] n 霊きゅう車 reíkyùsha

heart [hɑːrt] n (ANAT) 心臓 shiñzō; (fig: emotions, character) 心 kokórō; (of problem) 核心 kakúshin; (of city) 中心部 chúshiñbu; (of lettuce) しん shíñ; (shape) ハート形 hátogata
to lose heart (courage) 落胆する rakútan suru
to take heart (courage) 勇気を出す yúki wŏ dásù
at heart (basically) 根は... né wà ...
by heart (learn, know) 暗記で añki de

heart attack n (MED) 心臓発作 shiñzō-hossà

heartbeat [hɑ:rt'bi:t] n 心拍 shiñpaku

heartbreaking [hɑ:rt'breikiŋ] adj (news, story) 悲痛な hitsū na

heartbroken [hɑ:rt'broukən] adj: **to be heartbroken** 悲嘆に暮れている hitán ni kurete irù

heartburn [hɑ:rt'bə:rn] n (indigestion) 胸焼け muñéyake

heart failure n (MED) 心不全 shiñfùzen

heartfelt [hɑ:rt'felt] adj (prayer, wish) 心からの kokórò kara no

hearth [hɑ:rθ] n (fireplace) 炉床 roshō

heartland [hɑ:rt'lænd] n (of country, region) 中心地 chūshiñchi

heartless [hɑ:rt'lis] adj (person, attitude) 非情な hijō na

hearts [hɑ:rts] npl (CARDS) ハート hāto

hearty [hɑ:r'ti:] adj (person) 明朗な meírō na; (laugh) 大きな ōkina; (appetite) おう盛な ōsei na; (welcome) 熱烈な netsúretsu na; (dislike) 絶対的な zettáiteki na; (support) 心からの kokórò kara no

heat [hi:t] n (warmth) 暑さ átsùsa; (temperature) 温度 óñdo; (excitement) 熱気 nekkí; (SPORT: also: **qualifying heat**) 予選 yosén

♦vt (water) 沸かす wákasù; (food) ...に火を通す ...ni hí wò tōsù; (room, house) 暖める atátamerù

heated [hi:'tid] adj (pool) 温水の oñsui no; (room etc) 暖房した dañbō shita; (argument) 激しい hagéshiì

heater [hi:'tə:r] n ヒーター hītā

heath [hi:θ] (BRIT) n 荒野 aréno

heathen [hi:'ðən] n (REL) 異教徒 ikyōtò

heather [heð'ə:r] n エリカ érìka, ヒース hīsù

heating [hi:'tiŋ] n (system, equipment) 暖房 dáñbō

heatstroke [hi:t'strouk] n (MED) 熱射病 nesshábyō

heat up vi (water, room) 暖まる atátamarù

♦vt (food, water, room) 暖める atátamerù

heatwave [hi:t'weiv] n 熱波 néppà

heave [hi:v] vt (pull) 強く引く tsúyòku hikú; (push) 強く押す tsúyòku osú; (lift) ぐいと持上げる gúì to mochíagerù

♦vi (vomit) 吐く hákù; (feel sick) むかつく mukátsukù

♦n (of chest) あえぎ aégi; (of stomach) むかつき mukátsuki

to heave a sigh ため息をつく taméiki wo tsukú

his chest was heaving 彼はあえいでいた kárè wa aéide itá

heaven [hev'ən] n (REL: also fig) 天国 téñgoku

heavenly [hev'ənli:] adj (REL) 天からの téñ kara no; (fig: day, place) 素晴らしい subárashiì

heavily [hev'ili:] adv (land, fall) どしんと dóshìn to; (drink, smoke) 大量に taíryō ni; (sleep) ぐっすりと gussúrì to; (sigh) 深く fukákù; (depend, rely) すっかり sukkárì

heavy [hev'i:] adj (person, load, responsibility) 重い omói; (clothes) 厚い atsúi; (rain, snow) 激しい hagéshiì; (of person: build, frame) がっしりした gasshírì shita; (blow) 強い tsúyòi; (breathing) 荒い aráì; (sleep) 深い fukáì; (schedule, week) 過密な kamítsu na; (work) きつい kitsúi; (weather) 蒸し暑い mushíatsuì; (food, meal) もたれる motárerù

a heavy drinker 飲兵隊 nóñbē

a heavy smoker ヘビースモーカー hebísumōkā

heavy goods vehicle (BRIT) n 大型トラック ōgatatoràkku

heavyweight [hev'i:weit] n (SPORT) ヘビー級選手 hebíkyūseñshu

Hebrew [hi:'bru:] adj ヘブライの hebúrài no; (LING) ヘブライ語の hebúraigo no

♦n (LING) ヘブライ語 hebúraigo

Hebrides [heb'ridi:z] npl: **the Hebrides** ヘブリディーズ諸島 hebúridìzushotō

heckle [hek'əl] vt (speaker, performer) 野次る yajírù

hectic [hek'tik] adj (event, week) やたらに忙しい yatára ni isogáshiì

he'd [hi:d] = **he would; he had**

hedge [hedʒ] n (in garden, on roadside)

生け垣 ikégàki
♦*vi* (stall) あいまいな態度を取る aímai nà táìdo wo tórù
to hedge one's bets (*fig*) 失敗に備える shippái nì sonáerù

hedgehog [hedʒ'hɑːg] *n* ハリネズミ harínezùmi

heed [hiːd] *vt* (*also:* **take heed of**: advice, warning) 聞き入れる kikírerù

heedless [hiːd'lis] *adj:* **heedless (of)** (...を) 無視して (...wo) múshì shité

heel [hiːl] *n* (of foot, shoe) かかと kakáto
♦*vt:* **to heel shoes** 靴のかかとを修理する kutsú nò kakáto wò shúri suru

hefty [hef'tiː] *adj* (person) がっしりした gasshírì shita; (parcel etc) 大きくて重い ōkikute omóì; (profit) 相当な sōtō na

heifer [hef'əːr] *n* 若い雌ウシ wakáì méùshi ◊ まだ子を生んだ事のない物を指す mádà ko wo uńda kotò no náì monó wo sásù

height [hait] *n* (of tree, building, mountain) 高さ takása; (of person) 身長 shińchō; (of plane) 高度 kṓdo; (high ground) 高地 kṓchi; (*fig*: of powers) 絶頂期 zetchṓkì; (: of season) 真っ最中 massáìchū; (: of luxury, stupidity) 極み kiwámi

heighten [hait'ən] *vt* (fears, uncertainty) 高める takámerù

heir [eːr] *n* (to throne) 継承者 keíshōshà; (to fortune) 相続人 sōzokunìn

heiress [eːr'is] *n* 大遺産の相続人 daísan no sṓzokunìn ◊ 女性について言う joséi ni tsuité iú

heirloom [eːr'luːm] *n* 家宝 kahṓ

held [held] *pt, pp* of **hold**

helicopter [hel'əkɑːptəːr] *n* (AVIAT) ヘリコプター heríkopùtā

heliport [hel'əpɔːrt] *n* (AVIAT) ヘリポート herípòto

helium [hiː'liːəm] *n* ヘリウム heríùmu

he'll [hiːl] = **he will, he shall**

hell [hel] *n* (life, situation: *also* REL) 地獄 jigóku
hell! (*inf*) 畜生！ chikúshṓ!, くそ！ kusó!

hellish [hel'iʃ] (*inf*) *adj* (traffic, weather, life etc) 地獄の様な jigóku no yṓ na

hello [helou'] *excl* (as greeting) や あ yá, 今日は końnichi wa; (to attract attention) おい ói; (on telephone) もしもし móshìmoshi; (expressing surprise) おや oyá

helm [helm] *n* (NAUT: stick) かじ棒 kajíbò, チラー chirá; (: wheel) だ輪 daríñ

helmet [hel'mit] *n* (*gen*) ヘルメット herúmettò

help [help] *n* (assistance, aid) 助け tasúke, 手伝い tetsúdaì; (charwoman) お手伝いさん o-tétsùdaisan
♦*vt* (person) 助ける tasúkerù, 手伝う tétsùdau; (situation) ...に役に立つ ...ni yakú ni tatsù
help! 助けてくれ！ tasúketè kurè!
help yourself (to) (...を) 自由に取って下さい (...wo) jiyú ni tottè kudásai
he can't help it 彼はそうせざるを得ない kárè wa sō sezarù wo énài

helper [hel'pəːr] *n* (assistant) 助手 joshú, アシスタント ashísùtanto

helpful [help'fəl] *adj* (person, advice, suggestion etc) 役に立つ yakú ni tatsù

helping [hel'piŋ] *n* (of food) 一盛り hitómòri
a second helping お代り o-káwarì

helpless [help'lis] *adj* (incapable) 何もできない naní mo dekinài; (defenceless) 無防備の mubṓbi no

hem [hem] *n* (of skirt, dress) すそ susó
♦*vt* (skirt, dress etc) ...のすそ縫いをする ...no susónui wo suru

hem in *vt* 取囲む toríkakomù

hemisphere [hem'isfiːr] *n* 半球 hańkyū

hemorrhage [hem'əːridʒ] (*BRIT* **haemorrhage**) *n* 出血 shukkétsu

hemorrhoids [hem'əːrɔidz] (*BRIT* **haemorrhoids**) *npl* じ jí

hen [hen] *n* (female chicken) メンドリ meńdori; (female bird) 雌の鳥 mesú no torí

hence [hens] *adv* (therefore) 従って shitágattè
2 years hence 今から2年先 ímà kara nínen saki

henceforth [hens'fɔːrθ] *adv* (from now on) 今後 kóñgo; (from that time on) その

後 sonō go

henchman [hentʃ'mən] (*pej*: *pl* **henchmen**) *n* (of gangster, tyrant) 手下 teshíta, 子分 kóbun

henpecked [hen'pekt] *adj* (husband) 妻 のしりに敷かれた tsúmā no shirí ni shikaretá

hepatitis [hepətai'tis] *n* (MED) 肝炎 kánen

her [həːr] *pron* (direct) 彼女を kánōjo wo; (indirect) 彼女に kánōjo ni
◆*adj* 彼女の kánōj no ¶ *see also* **me**; **my**

herald [he:r'əld] *n* (forerunner) 兆し kizáshi
◆*vt* (event, action) 予告する yokóku suru

heraldry [he:r'əldri:] *n* (study) 紋章学 mońshōgáku; (coat of arms) 紋章 mońshō ◇総称 sōshō

herb [əːrb] *n* (*gen*) ハーブ hā̀bu; (BOT, MED) 薬草 yakúsō; (CULIN) 香草 kōsō

herd [həːrd] *n* (of cattle, goats, zebra etc) 群れ muré

here [hiːr] *adv* (this place): *she left here yesterday* 彼女は昨日ここを出ました kánōjo wa kínō kokó wò demáshita; (beside me): *I have it here* ここに持っています kokó ni mottè imásù; (at this point): *here he stopped reading ...* その時彼は読むのをやめて... sonō tokì kárè wa yómù no wo yaméte ...
here! (I'm present) はい! hái!; (take this) はいどうぞ hái dòzo
here is/are はい, ...です hái, ...désù
here she is! 彼女はここにいました! kánōjo wa kokó ni imáshita!

hereafter [hi:ræf'təːr] *adv* (in the future) 今後 kóngo

hereby [hi:rbai'] *adv* (in letter) これをもって koré wo mottè

hereditary [həred'ite:ri:] *adj* (disease) 先天的な señtenteki na; (title) 世襲の seshū no

heredity [həred'iti:] *n* (BIO) 遺伝 idén

heresy [he:r'isi:] *n* (opposing belief: *also* REL) 異端 itán

heretic [he:r'itik] *n* 異端者 itáñsha

heritage [he:r'itidʒ] *n* (of country, nation) 遺産 isán

hermetically [həːrmet'ikli:] *adv*: *hermetically sealed* 密閉した mippéi shita

hermit [həːr'mit] *n* 隠とん者 iñtoñsha

hernia [həːr'niːə] *n* (MED) 脱腸 datchṑ

hero [hiːrou] (*pl* **heroes**) *n* (in book, film) 主人公 shujíñkō, ヒーロー hírò ◇男性を指す dansei wo sasu; (of battle, struggle) 英雄 eíyū; (idol) アイドル áĩdoru

heroic [hirou'ik] *adj* (struggle, sacrifice, person) 英雄的な eíyūteki na

heroin [he:r'ouin] *n* ヘロイン herōĩn

heroine [he:r'ouin] *n* (in book, film) 女主人公 oñnashujíñkō, ヒロイン hirōĩn; (of battle, struggle) 英雄的女性 eíyūtekijosei; (idol) アイドル áĩdoru

heroism [he:r'ouizəm] *n* (bravery, courage) 勇敢さ yūkansa

heron [he:r'ən] *n* アオサギ aósagi

herring [he:r'iŋ] *n* (fish) ニシン níshìn

hers [həːrz] *pron* 彼女の物 kánōjo no mono ¶ *see also* **mine**

herself [hə:rself'] *pron* 彼女自身 kánōjojishìn ¶ *see also* **oneself**

he's [hi:z] = **he is**; **he has**

hesitant [hez'ətənt] *adj* (smile, reaction) ためらいがちな taméraigachi na

hesitate [hez'əteit] *vi* (pause) ためらう taméraù; (be unwilling) 後込みする shirígomì suru

hesitation [hezətei'ʃən] *n* (pause) ためらい tamérai; (unwillingness) 後込み shirígomì

heterosexual [hetə:rəsek'ʃuəl] *adj* (person, relationship) 異性愛の iséiai no

hew [hju:] *vt* (stone, wood) 刻む kizámu

hexagonal [heksæg'ənəl] *adj* (shape, object) 六角形の rokkákukei no

heyday [hei'dei] *n*: *the heyday of* ...の全盛時代 ...no zeñseijidài

HGV [eitʃgi:vi:'] (*BRIT*) *n abbr* = **heavy goods vehicle**

hi [hai] *excl* (as greeting) やあ yǎ, 今日は koñnichi wa; (to attract attention) おい ồi

hiatus [haiei'təs] *n* (gap: in manuscript etc) 脱落個所 datsúrakukashò; (pause)

中断 chūdan

hibernate [hai'bə:rneit] *vi* (animal) 冬眠 する tōmin suru

hiccough [hik'ʌp] *vi* しゃっくりする shákkùri suru

hiccoughs [hik'ʌps] *npl* しゃっくり shákkùri

hiccup [hik'ʌp] *vi* = **hiccough**

hiccups [hik'ʌps] *npl* = **hiccoughs**

hid [hid] *pt of* **hide**

hidden [hid'ən] *pp of* **hide**

hide [haid] *n* (skin) 皮 kawá
♦*vb* (*pt* **hid**, *pp* **hidden**)
♦*vt* (person, object, feeling, information) 隠す kakúsù; (obscure: sun, view) 覆い隠す ōikakusù
♦*vi: to hide (from someone)* (...に見つからない様に) 隠れる (...ni mitsúkaranai yō ni) kakúrerù

hide-and-seek [haid'ənsi:k'] *n* (game) 隠れん坊 kakúreñbō

hideaway [haid'əwei] *n* (retreat) 隠れ家 kakúregà

hideous [hid'i:əs] *adj* (painting, face) 醜い miníkuì

hiding [hai'diŋ] *n* (beating) むち打ち muchíuchi
to be in hiding (concealed) 隠れている kakúrete irù

hierarchy [hai'ərɑːrki:] *n* (system of ranks) 階級制 kaíkyūsei; (people in power) 幹部 káñbu ◊総称 sōshō

hi-fi [hai'fai'] *n* ステレオ sutéreo
♦*adj* (equipment, system) ステレオの sutéreo no

high [hai] *adj* (gen) 高い takáì; (speed) 速い hayáì; (wind) 強い tsuyóì; (quality) 上等な jōtō na; (principles) 崇高な sūkō na
♦*adv* (climb, aim etc) 高く tákàku
it is 20 m high その高さは20メーターです sonó takàsa wa nijū mētā desu
high in the air 空高く sóratakaku

highbrow [hai'brau] *adj* (intellectual) 知的な chitéki na

highchair [hai'tʃe:r] *n* (for baby) ベビーチェア bebíchèa

higher education [hai'ə:r-] *n* 高等教育 kótōkyōiku

high-handed [hai'hæn'did] *adj* (decision, rejection) 横暴な ōbō na

high-heeled [hai'hi:ld] *adj* (shoe) ハイヒールの haíhìru no

high jump *n* (SPORT) 走り高飛び hashíritakàtobi

highlands [hai'ləndz] *npl: the High-lands* スコットランド高地地方 sukóttorañdo kőchichihō

highlight [hai'lait] *n* (*fig*: of event) 山場 yamába, ハイライト haíraìto; (of news etc) 要点 yōten, ハイライト haíraìto; (in hair) 光る部分 hikárù búbùn, ハイライト haíraìto
♦*vt* (problem, need) ...に焦点を合せる ...ni shōten wò awáserù

highly [hai'li:] *adv* (critical, confidential) 非常に hijō ni; (a lot): *to speak highly of* ...をほめる ...wo homérù
to think highly of ...を高く評価する ...wo tákàku hyōka suru
highly paid 高給取りの kókyūtòri no

highly strung (*BRIT*) *adj* = **high-strung**

highness [hai'nis] *n: Her (or His) Highness* 陛下 hếìka

high-pitched [hai'pitʃt'] *adj* (voice, tone, whine) 調子の高い chōshi no tákaì

high-rise block [hai'raiz'-] *n* 摩天楼 matêñrō

high school *n* (*US*: for 14-18 year-olds) 高等学校 kótōgakkō, ハイスクール haísùkūru; (*BRIT*: for 11-18 year-olds) 総合中等学校 sōgōchūtōgakkō

high season (*BRIT*) *n* 最盛期 saiseiki, シーズン shízun

high street (*BRIT*) *n* 本通り hoñdòri

high-strung [hai'strʌŋ] (*US*) *adj* 神経質な shiñkeishitsu na

highway [hai'wei] *n* 幹線道路 kañsendō-ro, ハイウエー haíwè

Highway Code (*BRIT*) *n* 道路交通法 dōrokōtsūhō

hijack [hai'dʒæk] *vt* (plane, bus) 乗っ取る nottórù, ハイジャックする haíjakkù suru

hijacker [hai'dʒækə:r] *n* 乗っ取り犯 nottórihañ

hike [haik] *vi* (go walking) ハイキングする haíkingu suru
♦*n* (walk) ハイキング haíkingu

hiker [hai'kər] *n* ハイカー haíkā

hilarious [hiler'i:əs] *adj* (account, adventure) こっけいな kokkéi na

hill [hil] *n* (small) 丘 oká; (fairly high) 山 yamá; (slope) 坂 saká

hillside [hil'said] *n* 丘の斜面 oká no shamèn

hilly [hil'i:] *adj* 丘の多い oká no ōî
a hilly area 丘陵地帯 kyūryōchitài

hilt [hilt] *n* (of sword, knife) 柄 e
to the hilt (fig: support) とことんまで tokóton made

him [him] *pron* (direct) 彼を kárè wo; (indirect) 彼に kárè ni ¶ *see also* **me**

himself [himself'] *pron* 彼自身 kárèjishin ¶ *see also* **oneself**

hind [haind] *adj* (legs, quarters) 後ろの ushíro no

hinder [hin'dər] *vt* (progress, movement) 妨げる samátagerù

hindrance [hin'drəns] *n* 邪魔 jamá

hindsight [haind'sait] *n:* *with hindsight* 後になってみると áto ni nátte mirù to

Hindu [hin'du:] *adj* ヒンズーの hiñzū no

hinge [hindʒ] *n* (on door) ちょうつがい chōtsugài
♦*vi* (fig): *to hinge on* …による …ni yorú

hint [hint] *n* (suggestion) 暗示 añji, ヒント híñto; (advice) 勧め susúme, 提言 teígen; (sign, glimmer) 兆し kizáshi
♦*vt:* *to hint that* (suggest) …だとほのめかす …da to honómekasù
♦*vi:* *to hint at* (suggest) ほのめかす honómekasù

hip [hip] *n* (ANAT) 腰 koshí, ヒップ híppù

hippopotamus [hipəpɑ:t'əməs] (*pl* **hippopotamuses** *or* **hippopotami**) *n* カバ kábà

hire [haiər] *vt* (BRIT: car, equipment, hall) 賃借りする chíñgari suru; (worker) 雇う yatóù
♦*n* (BRIT: of car, hall etc) 賃借り chíñgari

for hire (taxi, boat) 賃貸し用の chíñgashiyō no

hire purchase (BRIT) *n* 分割払い購入 buñkatsubaraikōnyū

his [hiz] *pron* 彼の物 kárè no monó
♦*adj* 彼の kárè no ¶ *see also* **my; mine**

hiss [his] *vi* (snake, gas, roasting meat) しゅーっと言う shūtto iú; (person, audience) しーっと野次る shītto yajírù

historian [histɔːr'i:ən] *n* 歴史学者 rekíshigakushà

historic(al) [histɔːr'ik(əl)] *adj* (event, person) 歴史上の rekíshijō no, 歴史的な rekíshiteki na; (novel, film) 歴史に基づく rekíshi ni motózukù

history [his'tə:ri:] *n* (of town, country, person: *also* SCOL) 歴史 rekíshi

hit [hit] (*pt, pp* **hit**) *vt* (strike: person, thing) 打つ utsú, たたく tatáku; (reach: target) …に当る …ni atárù; (collide with: car) …にぶつかる …ni butsúkarù; (affect: person, services, event etc) …に打撃を与える …ni dagéki wò atáerù
♦*n* (knock) 打撃 dagéki; (success: play, film, song) 大当り ōatàri, ヒット híttò
to hit it off with someone …と意気投合する …to íkitōgō suru

hit-and-run driver [hit'ənran'-] *n* ひき逃げ運転者 hikínige unteñsha

hitch [hitʃ] *vt* (fasten) つなぐ tsunágù; (*also:* **hitch up**: trousers, skirt) 引上げる hikíagerù
♦*n* (difficulty) 問題 mońdai
to hitch a lift ヒッチハイクをする hitchíhaìku wo suru

hitch-hike [hitʃ'haik] *vi* ヒッチハイクをする hitchíhaìku wo suru

hitch-hiker [hitʃ'haikər] *n* ヒッチハイクをする人 hitchíhaìku wo suru hitò

hi-tech [hai'tek'] *adj* ハイテクの haíteku no
♦*n* ハイテク haíteku

hitherto [hið'ə:rtu:] *adv* (until now) 今まで imá madè

hive [haiv] *n* (of bees) ミツバチの巣箱 mitsúbàchi no súbako

hive off (*inf*) *vt* (company) …の一部を切り放す …no ichíbu wo kiríhanasù

HMS [eitʃemes'] *abbr* (= *Her/His Majesty's Ship*) 軍艦...号 guńkaǹ ...gǒ ◇英国海軍の軍艦の名前の前に付ける eíkokukaigùn no guńkaǹ no namáè no máè ni tsukérù

hoard [hɔːrd] *n* (of food etc) 買いだめ kaídame; (of money, treasure) 蓄え takúwaè

♦*vt* (food etc) 買いだめする kaídamesuru

hoarding [hɔːr'diŋ] (*BRIT*) *n* (for posters) 掲示板 keíjiban

hoarfrost [hɔːr'frɔːst] *n* (on ground) 霜 shimó

hoarse [hɔːrs] *adj* (voice) しわがれた shiwágaretà

hoax [houks] *n* (trick) いんちき íńchiki, いかさま ikásama

hob [hɑːb] *n* (of cooker, stove) レンジの上部 reńji no jôbu

hobble [hɑːb'əl] *vi* (limp) びっこを引く bíkkò wo hikú

hobby [hɑːb'iː] *n* (pastime) 趣味 shúmì

hobby-horse [hɑːb'iːhɔːrs] *n* (*fig*: favorite topic) 十八番の話題 oháko nò wadái

hobo [hou'bou] (*US*) *n* (tramp) ルンペン rúńpen

hockey [hɑːk'iː] *n* (game) ホッケー hókkē

hoe [hou] *n* (tool) くわ kuwá, ホー hǒ

hog [hɔːg] *n* (pig) ブタ butá ◇去勢した雄ブタを指す kyoséi shita osubùta wo sasu

♦*vt* (*fig*: road, telephone etc) 独り占めにする hitórijime ni suru

to go the whole hog とことんまでやる tokóton made yarú

hoist [hɔist] *n* (apparatus) 起重機 kijǔkì, クレーン kurěn

♦*vt* (heavy object) 引上げる hikíagerù; (flag) 掲げる kakágerù; (sail) 張る harú

hold [hould] (*pt, pp* **held**) *vt* (bag, umbrella, someone's hand etc) 持つ mótsù; (contain: subj: room, box etc) ...に...が入っている ...ni ...ga háìtte iru; (have: power, qualification, opinion) ...を持っている ...wo móttè iru, ...がある ...ga árù; (meeting) 開く hirákù; (detain: prisoner,

hostage) 監禁する kańkin suru; (consider): *to hold someone responsible/liable etc* ...の責任と見なす ...no sekínin tò minású; (keep in certain position): *to hold one's head up* 頭を上げる atáma wò agérù

♦*vi* (withstand pressure) 持ちこたえる mochíkotaeru; (be valid) 当てはまる atéhamarù

♦*n* (grasp) 握り nigíri; (of ship) 船倉 seńsō; (of plane) 貨物室 kamótsushìtsu; (control): *to have a hold over* ...の急所を握っている ...no kyǔsho wò nigítte irù

to hold a conversation with ...と話し合う ...to hanáshiaù

hold the line! (TEL) 少々お待ち下さい shôshō o-máchi kudasai

hold on! ちょっと待って chótto máttè

to hold one's own (*fig*) 引けを取らない hiké wò toránaî, 負けない makénaî

to catch/get (a) hold of ...に捕まる ...ni tsukámarù

holdall [hould'ɔːl] (*BRIT*) *n* 合切袋 gassáibukùro

hold back *vt* (person, thing) 制止する seíshi suru; (thing, emotion) 押さえる osáerù; (secret, information) 隠す kakúsù

hold down *vt* (person) 押さえつける o-sáetsukerù; (job) ...についている ...ni tsúîte iru

holder [houl'dəːr] *n* (container) 入れ物 irémono, ケース kěsu, ホールダー hôrudā; (of ticket, record, title) 保持者 hojísha; (of office) 在職者 zaíshokusha

holding [houl'diŋ] *n* (share) 持株 mochíkabu; (small farm) 小作農地 kosákunôchi

hold off *vt* (enemy) ...に持ちこたえる ...ni mochíkotaerù

hold on *vi* (hang on) 捕まる tsukámarù; (wait) 待つ mátsù

hold on to *vt fus* (for support) ...に捕まる ...ni tsukámarù; (keep) 預かる azúkarù

hold out *vt* (hand) 差伸べる sashínoberù; (hope, prospect) 持たせる motáserù

♦*vi* (resist) 抵抗する teíkō suru

hold up *vt* (raise) 上げる agérù; (sup-

port) 支える sasáerù; (delay) 遅らせる o-
kúraserù; (rob: person, bank) 武器を突付
けて...から金を奪う búkì wo tsukítsuketè ...kara kané wò ubáù

hold-up [hould'ʌp] *n* (robbery) 強盗 gṓ-
tō; (delay) 遅れ okúre; (*BRIT*: in traffic)
渋滞 jūtai

hole [houl] *n* 穴 aná
♦*vt* (ship, building etc) ...に穴を開ける
...ni aná wò akéru

holiday [hɑːl'idei] *n* (*BRIT*: vacation) 休
暇 kyūka; (day off) 休暇の日 kyūka no
hi; (public holiday) 祝日 shukújitsu
on holiday 休暇中 kyūkachū

holiday camp (*BRIT*) *n* (*also*: **holiday
centre**) 休暇村 kyūkamùra

holiday-maker [hɑːl'ideimeikəːr]
(*BRIT*) *n* 行楽客 kōrakukyàku

holiday resort *n* 行楽地 kōrakuchì, リ
ゾート rizótò

holiness [hou'liːnis] *n* (of shrine, person)
神聖さ shińseisa

Holland [hɑːl'ənd] *n* オランダ oráňda

hollow [hɑːl'ou] *adj* (container) 空っぽの
karáppo no; (log, tree) うろのある uró
no arù; (cheeks, eyes) くぼんだ kubóňda;
(laugh) わざとらしい wazátorashiì;
(claim) 根拠のない końkyo no naì;
(sound) うつろな utsúro na
♦*n* (in ground) くぼみ kubómi
♦*vt*: **to hollow out** (excavate) がらんど
うにする garándō ni surù

holly [hɑːl'iː] *n* (tree, leaves) ヒイラギ híi-
ragi

holocaust [hɑːl'əkɔːst] *n* 大虐殺 daígyakùsatsu

hologram [hou'ləgræm] *n* ホログラム
horógurãmu

holster [houl'stəːr] *n* (for pistol) ホルス
ター horúsutā

holy [hou'liː] *adj* (picture, place, person)
神聖な shińsei na
holy water 聖水 seísui

homage [hɑːm'idʒ] *n* (honor, respect) 敬
意 kéìi
to pay homage to (hero, idol) ...に敬意
を表す ...ni kéìi wo aráwasù

home [houm] *n* (house) 家 ié, 住い sumáì;

(area, country) 故郷 kokyṓ; (institution)
収容施設 shūyōshisètsu
♦*cpd* (domestic) 家庭の katéi no; (ECON,
POL) 国内の kokúnài no;
(SPORT: team, game) 地元の jimóto no
♦*adv* (go, come, travel etc) 家に ié ni
at home (in house) 家に〔で〕 ié ni 〔de〕;
(in country) 本国に〔で〕 hóňgoku ni 〔de〕;
(in situation) ...に通じて ...ni tsújite
make yourself at home どうぞお楽に
dṓzo o-ráku ni
to drive something home (nail etc) ...を
打込む ...wo uchíkomù; (*fig*: point etc)
...を強調する ...wo kyōchō suru

home address *n* 自宅の住所 jitáku no
jūsho

home computer *n* パーソナルコンピュ
ータ pāsonarukonpyùta, パソコン pasó-
kon

homeland [houm'lænd] *n* 母国 bókòku

homeless [houm'lis] *adj* (family, refugee) 家のない ié no naì

homely [houm'liː] *adj* (simple, plain) 素
朴な sobóku na; (*US*: not attractive: person) 不器量な bukíryò na

home-made [houm'meid'] *adj* (bread,
bomb) 手製の teséi no, 自家製の jikásei
no

Home Office (*BRIT*) *n* 内務省 naímu-
shṓ

homeopathy [houmiːɑːp'əθiː] (*BRIT*
homoeopathy) *n* (MED) ホメオパシー
homéopashī

home rule *n* (POL) 自治権 jichíkèn

Home Secretary (*BRIT*) *n* 内務大臣
naímudaìjin

homesick [houm'sik] *adj* ホームシック
の hōmushikkù no

hometown [houmtaun'] *n* 故郷 kokyṓ

homeward [houm'wəːrd] *adj* (journey)
家に帰る ié ni kaerù

homework [houm'wəːrk] *n* (SCOL) 宿題
shukúdai

homicide [hɑːm'isaid] (*US*) *n* 殺人 satsújin

homoeopathy [houmiːɑːp'əθiː] (*BRIT*)
n = **homeopathy**

homogeneous   [houmədʒiː'niːəs]   *adj*

(group, class) 均質の kínshitsu no

homosexual [houmǝsek'ʃuːǝl] *adj* (person, relationship: *gen*) 同性愛の dōseiai no; (man) ホモの hómò no; (woman) レズの rézù no

♦*n* (man) 同性愛者 dōseiaìsha, ホモ hómò; (woman) 同姓愛者 dōseiaìsha, レズ rézù

honest [ɑːn'ist] *adj* (truthful, trustworthy) 正直な shōjiki na; (sincere) 率直な sotchóku na

honestly [ɑːn'istliː] *adv* (truthfully) 正直に shōjiki ni; (sincerely, frankly) 率直に sotchóku ni

honesty [ɑːn'istiː] *n* (truthfulness) 正直 shōjiki; (sincerity, frankness) 率直さ sotchókusa

honey [hʌn'iː] *n* (food) はちみつ hachímitsu

honeycomb [hʌn'iːkoum] *n* (of bees) ミツバチの巣 mitsúbàchi no su

honeymoon [hʌn'iːmuːn] *n* (holiday, trip) 新婚旅行 shiñkonryokō, ハネムーン hanémùn

honeysuckle [hʌn'iːsʌkǝl] *n* (BOT) スイカズラ suíkazùra

honk [hɑːŋk] *vi* (AUT: horn) 鳴らす narásu

honorary [ɑːn'ǝːreriː] *adj* (unpaid: job, secretary) 無給の mukyū no; (title, degree) 名誉の meíyo no

honor [ɑːn'ǝːr] (*BRIT* **honour**) *vt* (hero, author) ほめたたえる hométataerù; (commitment, promise) 守る mamórù

♦*n* (pride, self-respect) 名誉 meíyo; (tribute, distinction) 光栄 kóei

honorable [ɑːn'ǝːrǝbǝl] *adj* (person, action, defeat) 名誉ある meíyo aru

honors degree [ɑːn'ǝːrz-] *n* (SCOL) 専門学士号 señmongakushigō

hood [hud] *n* (of coat, cooker etc) フードfūdo; (*US*: AUT: engine cover) ボンネット boñnettò; (*BRIT*: AUT: folding roof) 折畳み式トップ orftatamishiki toppù

hoodlum [huːd'lǝm] *n* (thug) ごろつき gorótsuki, 暴力団員 bóryokudan-ìn

hoodwink [hud'wiŋk] *vt* (con, fool) だます damásù

hoof [huf] (*pl* **hooves**) *n* ひずめ hizúme

hook [huk] *n* (for coats, curtains etc) かぎ kagí, フック fúkkù; (on dress) ホック hókkù; (*also*: **fishing hook**) 釣針 tsurfbàri

♦*vt* (fasten) 留める tomérù; (fish) 釣る tsurú

hooligan [huː'ligǝn] *n* ちんぴら chiñpira

hoop [huːp] *n* (ring) 輪 wá

hooray [hǝrei'] *excl* = **hurrah**, **hurray**

hoot [hut] *vi* (AUT: horn) クラクションを鳴らす kurákùshon wo narásù; (siren) 鳴る narú; (owl) ほーほーと鳴く hōhō to nakú

hooter [huː'tǝːr] *n* (*BRIT*: AUT) クラクション kurákùshon, ホーン hōn; (NAUT, factory) 警報機 keíhōkì

hoover [huː'vǝːr] Ⓡ(*BRIT*) *n* (vacuum cleaner) (真空) 掃除機 (shiñkū)sōjikì

♦*vt* (carpet) ...に掃除機を掛ける ...ni sōjikì wo kakérù

hooves [huvz] *npl of* **hoof**

hop [hɑːp] *vi* (on one foot) 片足で跳ぶ katáashi de tobù; (bird) ぴょんぴょん跳ぶ pyóñpyon tobù

hope [houp] *vt*: **to hope that/to do** ...だと〔する事を〕望む ...da to〔surú kotò wo〕nozómù

♦*vi* 希望する kibō suru

♦*n* (desire) 望み nozómi; (expectation) 期待 kitái; (aspiration) 希望 kibō

I hope so/not そうだ〔でない〕といいが sō dà〔de naí〕to íi ga

hopeful [houp'fǝl] *adj* (person) 楽観的な rakkánteki na; (situation) 見込みのある mikómi no arù

hopefully [houp'fǝliː] *adv* (expectantly) 期待して kitái shite; (one hopes) うまくいけば úmaku ikébà

hopeless [houp'lis] *adj* (grief, situation, future) 絶望的な zetsúbōteki na; (person: useless) 無能な munóna

hops [hɑːps] *npl* (BOT) ホップ hóppù

horde [hɔːrd] *n* (of critics, people) 大群 taígun

horizon [hǝrai'zǝn] *n* (skyline) 水平線 suíheìsen

horizontal [hɔːrizɑːn'tǝl] *adj* 水平の suíhei no

hormone [hɔːr'moun] n (BIO) ホルモン hórùmon

horn [hɔːrn] n (of animal) 角 tsunó; (material) 角質 kakúshitsu; (MUS: *also*: **French horn**) ホルン hórùn; (AUT) クラクション kurákùshon, ホーン hòn

hornet [hɔːr'nit] n (insect) スズメバチ suzúmebàchi

horny [hɔːr'niː] (*inf*) adj (aroused) セックスをしたがっている sékkùsu wo shitágatte irù

horoscope [hɔːr'əskoup] n (ASTROLOGY) 星占い hoshíuranài

horrendous [hɔːren'dəs] adj (crime) 恐ろしい osóroshiì; (error) ショッキングな shókkìngu na

horrible [hɔːr'əbəl] adj (unpleasant: color, food, mess) ひどい hidóì; (terrifying: scream, dream) 恐ろしい osóroshiì

horrid [hɔːr'id] adj (person, place, thing) いやな iyá na

horrify [hɔːr'əfai] vt (appall) ぞっとさせる zóttò sasérù

horror [hɔːr'əːr] n (alarm) 恐怖 kyófù; (abhorrence) 憎悪 zòo; (of battle, warfare) むごたらしさ mugótarashisà

horror film n ホラー映画 horáeìga

hors d'oeuvre [ɔːr dəːrv'] n (CULIN: *gen*) 前菜 zeñsai; (: Western food) オードブル ódobùru

horse [hɔːrs] n 馬 umá

horseback [hɔːrs'bæk]: **on horseback** adj 乗馬の jòba no
◆adv 馬に乗って umá ni nottè

horse chestnut n (tree) トチノキ tochí no kì; (nut) とちの実 tochí no mì

horseman/woman [hɔːrs'mən/wumən] (pl **horsemen/women**) n (rider) 馬の乗り手 umá nò norítè

horsepower [hɔːrs'pauəːr] n (of engine, car etc) 馬力 baríki

horse-racing [hɔːrs'reisiŋ] n (SPORT) 競馬 keíba

horseradish [hɔːrs'rædiʃ] n (BOT, CULIN) ワサビダイコン wasábidaìkon, セイヨウワサビ seíyowasàbi

horseshoe [hɔːrs'ʃuː] n てい鉄 teítetsu

horticulture [hɔːr'təkʌltʃəːr] n 園芸 eñgei

hose [houz] n ホース hòsu

hosiery [hou'ʒəːriː] n (in shop) 靴下類 kutsúshitarùi

hospice [hɑːs'pis] n (for the dying) ホスピス hósùpisu

hospitable [hɑːspit'əbəl] adj (person) 持て成しの良い moténashi no yoì; (behavior) 手厚い teátsuì

hospital [hɑːs'pitəl] n 病院 byóin

hospitality [hɑːspətæl'itiː] n (of host, welcome) 親切な持て成し shiñsetsu nà moténashi

host [houst] n (at party, dinner etc) 主人 shújìn, ホスト hósùto; (TV, RADIO) 司会者 shikáìsha; (REL) 御聖体 go-séitai; (large number): **a host of** 多数の tasú no

hostage [hɑːs'tidʒ] n (prisoner) 人質 hitójichi

hostel [hɑːs'təl] n (for homeless etc) 収容所 shúyòjo; (*also*: **youth hostel**) ユースホステル yúsuhosùteru

hostess [hous'tis] n (at party, dinner etc) 女主人 ofnashujìn, ホステス hósùtesu; (*BRIT*: air hostess) スチュワーデス suchúwàdesu; (TV, RADIO) (女性) 司会者 (joséi)shikáìsha

hostile [hɑːs'təl] adj (person, attitude: aggressive) 敵対する tekítai suru, 敵意のある tékì-i no árù; (: unwelcoming): **hostile to** ...に対して排他的な ...ni táìshite haítateki na; (conditions, environment) か酷な kakóku na

hostilities [hɑːstil'ətiːz] npl (fighting) 戦闘 señto

hostility [hɑːstil'ətiː] n (antagonism) 敵対 tekítai, 敵意 tékì-i; (lack of welcome) 排他的態度 haítatekitàìdo; (of conditions, environment) か酷さ kakókusa

hot [hɑːt] adj (moderately warm) 暖かい atátakaì; (very hot) 熱い atsúì; (weather, room etc) 暑い atsúì; (spicy: food) 辛いkaráì; (fierce: temper, contest, argument) 激しい hagéshiì

it is hot (weather) 暑い atsúì; (object) 熱い atsúì

I am hot (person) 私は暑い watákushi wà atsuî

he is hot 彼は暑がっている kárè wa atsúgatte irù

hotbed [hɑːt'bed] *n* (*fig*) 温床 ońshō

hot dog *n* (snack) ホットドッグ hottódoggù

hotel [houtel'] *n* ホテル hôtèru

hotelier [ɔːteljei'] *n* (owner) ホテルの経営者 hôtèru no kéîêisha; (manager) ホテルの支配人 hôtèru no shihâinin

hotheaded [hɑːt'hedid] *adj* (impetuous) 気の早い kí no hayaî

hothouse [hɑːt'haus] *n* (BOT) 温室 oń-shitsu

hot line *n* (POL) ホットライン hottóraìn

hotly [hɑːt'liː] *adv* (speak, contest, deny) 激しく hagéshikù

hotplate [hɑːt'pleit] *n* (on cooker) ホットプレート hottópurèto

hot-water bottle [hɑːtwɔːt'əːr-] *n* 湯たんぽ yutáñpo

hound [haund] *vt* (harass, persecute) 迫害する hakúgai suru
♦*n* (dog) 猟犬 ryóken, ハウンド haúndo

hour [au'əːr] *n* (sixty minutes) 1時間 ichí jikàn; (time) 時間 jíkàn

hourly [auəːr'liː] *adj* (service, rate) 1時間当りの ichí jikan atàri no

house [*n* haus *vb* hauz] *n* (home) 家 iê, うち uchî; (household) 家族 kázòku; (company) 会社 kaísha; (POL) 議院 gíìn; (THEATER) 客席 kyakúseki; (dynasty) ...家 ...ké
♦*vt* (person) ...に住宅を与える ...ni jútaku wò atáerù; (collection) 収容する shúyō suru

on the house (*fig*) サービスで sâbisu de

house arrest *n* (POL, MIL) 軟禁 nañkin

houseboat [haus'bout] *n* 屋形船 yakáta-bunè, ハウスボート haúsubòto ◊住宅用の船を指す jútakuyō no funè wo sásù

housebound [haus'baund] *adj* (invalid) 家から出られない iê kara derárenaî

housebreaking [haus'breikiŋ] *n* 家宅侵入 kátakushiñnyū

housecoat [haus'kout] *n* 部屋着 heyági

household [haus'hould] *n* (inhabitants) 家族 kázoku; (home) 家 iê

housekeeper [haus'kiːpəːr] *n* (servant) 家政婦 kaséifù

housekeeping [haus'kiːpiŋ] *n* (work) 家事 kájì; (money) 家計費 kakéihi

house-warming party [haus'wɔːrmiŋ-] *n* 新居祝いのパーティ shiñkyo-iwaì no pâti

housewife [haus'waif] (*pl* **housewives**) *n* 主婦 shúfù

housework [haus'wəːrk] *n* (chores) 家事 kájì

housing [hau'ziŋ] *n* (houses) 住宅 jútaku; (provision) 住宅供給 jútakukyōkyū

housing development *n* 住宅団地 jútaku-kudañchi

housing estate (*BRIT*) *n* 住宅団地 jútaku-kudañchi

hovel [hʌv'əl] *n* (shack) あばら屋 abára-ya

hover [hʌv'əːr] *vi* (bird, insect) 空中に止まる kúchū ni tomarù

hovercraft [hʌv'əːrkræft] *n* (vehicle) ホバークラフト hobâkurafùto

how [hau] *adv* **1** (in what way) どう dô, どの様に donó yō ni, どうやって dô yattè
how did you do it? どうやってそれができたんですか dô yattè soré gà dekítan desù kâ

I know how you did it あなたがどの様にしてそれができたか私には分かっています anátà ga donó yō ni shite soré gà dekíta kà watákushi ni wà wakátte imasù

to know how to do something ...の仕方を知っている ...no shikáta wò shitté irù

how is school? 学校はどうですか gakkô wa dô desu kâ

how was the film? 映画はどうでしたか eíga wa dô deshita kâ

how are you? お元気ですか o-géñki desu kâ

2 (to what degree) どのくらい donó kurai

how much milk? どのくらいのミルク

donó kurai nò mírùku

how many people? 何人の人々 náñnin
no hitóbito

how much does it cost? 値段はいくら
ですか nedán wà íkùra desu ká

how long have you been here? いつか
らここにいますか ítsù kara kokó nì imásù ká

how old are you? お幾つですか o-íkù-
tsu desu ká

how tall is he? 彼の身長はどれくらい
ですか kárè no shiñchō wà doré gùrai
desu ká

how lovely/awful! なんて美しい〔ひど
い〕nánte utsúkushiì〔hidóì〕

howl [haul] *vi* (animal) 遠ぼえする tóboe
suru; (baby, person) 大声で泣く ógoè de
nakú; (wind) うなる unárù

H.P. [eitʃpiː'] *abbr* = **hire purchase**

h.p. *abbr* = **horsepower**

HQ [eitʃkjuː'] *abbr* = **headquarters**

hub [hʌb] *n* (of wheel) ハブ hábù; (*fig*:
centre) 中心 chúshin

hubbub [hʌb'ʌb] *n* (din, commotion) どよ
めき doyómeki

hubcap [hʌb'kæp] *n* (AUT) ホイールキ
ャップ hoírukyappù

huddle [hʌd'əl] *vi*: ***to huddle together***
(for heat, comfort) 体を寄せ合う karáda
wò yoséaù

hue [hjuː] *n* (color) 色 iró; (shade of color)
色合い iróaì

hue and cry *n* (outcry) 騒ぎ sáwàgi

huff [hʌf] *n*: ***in a huff*** (offended) 怒って
okóttè

hug [hʌg] *vt* (person, thing) 抱締める dakíshimerù

huge [hjuːdʒ] *adj* (enormous) ばく大な
bakúdai na

hulk [hʌlk] *n* (ship) 廃船 haísen; (person)
図体ばかり大きい人 zūtai bakari ókìi
hitó, うどの大木 udo no taiboku; (building etc) ばかでかい物 bakádekai monò

hull [hʌl] *n* (of ship) 船体 señtai, ハル hárù

hullo [həlou'] *excl* = **hello**

hum [hʌm] *vt* (tune, song) ハミングで歌

う hamingu de utau

♦*vi* (person) ハミングする hámìngu suru;
(machine) ぶーんと鳴る bún to narú;
(insect) ぶんぶんいう búñbun iu

human [hjuː'mən] *adj* (existence, body)
人の hitó no, 人間の niñgen no; (weakness, emotion) 人間的な niñgenteki na

♦*n* (person) 人 hitó, 人間 niñgen

humane [hjuːmein'] *adj* (treatment,
slaughter) 苦痛を与えない kutsū wò atá-
enai

humanitarian [hjuːmænite:r'iːən] *adj*
(aid, principles) 人道的な jiñdōteki na

humanity [hjuːmæn'itiː] *n* (mankind) 人
類 jíñrui, 人間 niñgen; (human nature) 人
間性 niñgensei; (humaneness, kindness)
思いやり omóiyari

humble [hʌm'bəl] *adj* (modest) 謙虚な
kéñkyo na; (lowly: background) 身分の
低い míbùn no hikúì

♦*vt* (humiliate, crush) ...の高慢な鼻を折
る ...no kōman na haná wò órù

humbug [hʌm'bʌg] *n* (of statement,
writing) でたらめ detárame; (*BRIT*:
sweet) はっかあめ hakká-ame

humdrum [hʌm'drʌm] *adj* (dull, boring)
退屈な taíkutsu na

humid [hjuː'mid] *adj* (atmosphere, climate) 湿度の高い shitsúdò no takáì

humidity [hjuːmid'ətiː] *n* 湿度 shitsúdò

humiliate [hjuːmil'iːeit] *vt* (rival, person)
...の高慢な鼻を折る ...no kōman na haná
wò órù

humiliation [hjuːmiliːei'ʃən] *n* (embarrassment) 恥 hají; (situation, experience)
恥辱 chijóku

humility [hjuːmil'ətiː] *n* (modesty) 謙そ
ん keñson

humor [hjuː'məːr] (*BRIT* **humour**) *n*
(comedy, mood) ユーモア yūmoa

♦*vt* (child, person) ...の機嫌を取る ...no
kigén wò tórù

humorous [hjuː'məːrəs] *adj* (remark,
book) おどけた odóketa; (person) ユーモ
アのある yūmoa no árù

hump [hʌmp] *n* (in ground) 小山 koyá-
ma; (of camel: *also* deformity) こぶ kobú

humpbacked [hʌmp'bækt] *adj*: ***hump-***

backed bridge 反り橋 soríhàshi

hunch [hʌntʃ] *n* (premonition) 直感 chokkán

hunchback [hʌntʃˈbæk] *n* せむしの人 semúshi nò hitó◇べっ称 besshố

hunched [hʌntʃt] *adj* (bent, stooped: shoulders) 曲げた magéta; (: person) 肩を落とした kátá wo otóshità

hundred [hʌnˈdrid] *num* 百 (の) hyakú (no); (before *n*): *a/one hundred books* 100冊の本 hyakúsatsu nò hôn: *a/one hundred people* 100人の人 hyakúnin nò hitó: *a/one hundred dollars* 100ドル hyakú doru

hundreds of 何百もの nañbyaku mo no

hundredweight [hʌnˈdridweit] *n* (US = 45.3 kg, 100 lb; BRIT = 50.8 kg, 112 lb)

hung [hʌŋ] *pt, pp of* **hang**

Hungarian [hʌŋgeːrˈiːən] *adj* ハンガリーの hañgarī no; (LING) ハンガリー語の hañgarígo no

◆*n* (person) ハンガリー人 hañgarījin; (LING) ハンガリー語 hañgarígo

Hungary [hʌŋˈgəːriː] *n* ハンガリー hañgarī

hunger [hʌŋˈgəːr] *n* (lack of food) 空腹 kúfuku; (starvation) 飢餓 kígà

◆*vi*: *to hunger for* (desire) ...に飢える ...ni uérù

hunger strike *n* ハンガーストライキ hañgāsutoraìki, ハンスト hañsuto

hungry [hʌŋˈgriː] *adj* (person, animal) 空腹な kúfuku na; (keen, avid): *hungry for* ...に飢えた ...ni uétà

to be hungry おなかがすいた onáka ga suità

hunk [hʌŋk] *n* (of bread etc) 塊 katámari

hunt [hʌnt] *vt* (for food: subj: animal) 捜し求める sagáshimotomerù, あさる asárù; (SPORT) 狩る kárù, ...の狩りをする ...no kárî wo suru; (criminal, fugitive) 捜す sagásu, 捜索する sósaku suru

◆*vi* (search): *to hunt (for)* (...を) 捜す (...wo) sagásu; (SPORT) (...の) 狩りをする (...no) kárî wo suru

◆*n* (for food: *also* SPORT) 狩り kárî; (search) 捜す事 sagásu kotò; (for criminal) 捜索 sósaku

hunter [hʌnˈtəːr] *n* (sportsman) ハンター hâñtā

hunting [hʌnˈtiŋ] *n* (for food: *also* SPORT) 狩り kárî

hurdle [həːrˈdəl] *n* (difficulty) 障害 shốgai; (SPORT) ハードル hấdoru

hurl [həːrl] *vt* (object) 投げる nagérù; (insult, abuse) 浴びせ掛ける abísekakerù

hurrah [hərɑ̄ː] *n* (as cheer) 歓声 kañsei

hurray [həreiˈ] *n* = **hurrah**

hurricane [həːrˈəkein] *n* (storm) ハリケーン haríkēn

hurried [həːrˈiːd] *adj* (hasty, rushed) 大急ぎの ōisògi no

hurriedly [həːrˈiːdliː] *adv* 大急ぎで ōisògi de

hurry [həːrˈiː] *n* (haste, rush) 急ぎ isógi

◆*vi* (*also*: **hurry up**: hasten, rush) 急ぐ isógù

◆*vt* (*also*: **hurry up**: person) 急がせる isógaserù; (: work) 急いでする isóide suru

to be in a hurry 急いでいる isóide irù

hurt [həːrt] (*pt, pp* **hurt**) *vt* (cause pain to) 痛める itámerù; (injure, *fig*) 傷付ける kizútsukerù

◆*vi* (be painful) 痛む itámù

it hurts! 痛い！itái!

hurtful [həːrtˈfəl] *adj* (remark) 傷付ける様な kizútsukeru yố na

hurtle [həːrˈtəl] *vi*: *to hurtle past* (train, car) 猛スピードで通り過ぎる mốsupîdo de tôrisugirù

to hurtle down (fall) 落ちる ochírù

husband [hʌzˈbənd] *n* 夫 ottó

hush [hʌʃ] *n* (silence) 沈黙 chiñmoku; (stillness) 静けさ shizúkesà

◆*vt* (silence) 黙らせる damáraserù

hush! 静かに shízùka ni

hush up *vt* (scandal etc) もみ消す momíkesù

husk [hʌsk] *n* (of wheat, rice) 殻 kará; (of maize) 皮 kawá

husky [hʌsˈkiː] *adj* (voice) しわがれた shiwágaretà, ハスキーな hásùkī na

◆*n* (dog) ハスキー hásùkī

hustle [hʌsˈəl] *vt* (hurry) 急がせる isógaserù

◆*n*: *hustle and bustle* 雑踏 zattố

hut [hʌt] *n* (house) 小屋 koyá; (shed) 物置 monó-oki

hutch [hʌtʃ] *n* (*also*: **rabbit hutch**) ウサギ小屋 uságigoya

hyacinth [hai'əsinθ] *n* ヒヤシンス hiyáshiñsu

hybrid [hai'brid] *n* (plant, animal) 交雑種 kốzatsushù, ハイブリッド haíbɯriddò; (mixture) 混成物 koñseibùtsu

hydrant [hai'drənt] *n* (*also*: **fire hydrant**) 消火栓 shốkasen

hydraulic [haidrɔ:'lik] *adj* (pressure, system) 油圧の yuátsu no

hydroelectric [haidrouilek'trik] *adj* (energy, complex) 水力発電の suíryokuhatsùden no

hydrofoil [hai'drəfɔil] *n* (boat) 水中翼船 suíchūyokùsen

hydrogen [hai'drədʒən] *n* (CHEM) 水素 suíso

hyena [haii:'nə] *n* ハイエナ haíena

hygiene [hai'dʒi:n] *n* (cleanliness) 衛生 eísei

hygienic [haidʒi:en'ik] *adj* 衛生的な eíseiteki na

hymn [him] *n* 賛美歌 sañbika

hype [haip] (*inf*) *n* 売込み口上 uríkomikōjò

hypermarket [hai'pə:rmɑ:rkit] (*BRIT*) *n* 大型スーパー ốgatasūpā

hyphen [hai'fən] *n* (dash) ハイフン haífun

hypnosis [hipnou'sis] *n* 催眠 saímin

hypnotic [hipnɑt'ik] *adj* (trance) 催眠術の saímiñjutsu no; (rhythms) 催眠的な saímiñteki na

hypnotism [hip'nətizəm] *n* 催眠術 saímiñjutsu

hypnotist [hip'nətist] *n* (person) 催眠術師 saíminjutsushì

hypnotize [hip'nətaiz] *vt* (MED etc) ...に催眠術を掛ける ...ni saímiñjutsu wo kakérù; (*fig*: mesmerise) 魅惑する miwáku suru

hypochondriac [haipəkɑ:n'dri:æk] *n* 心気症患者 shiñkishōkàñja

hypocrisy [hipɑ:k'rəsi:] *n* (falseness, in-

sincerity) 偽善 gizén

hypocrite [hip'əkrit] *n* (phoney) 偽善者 gizéñsha

hypocritical [hipəkrit'ikəl] *adj* (person) 偽善の gizén no; (behavior) 偽善者的な gizéñshateki na

hypothermia [haipəθə:r'mi:ə] *n* (MED) 低体温症 teítaioñshō

hypothesis [haipɑ:θ'əsis] (*pl* **hypotheses**) *n* (theory) 仮説 kasétsu

hypothetic(al) [haipəθet'ik(əl)] *adj* (question, situation) 仮定の katéi no

hysteria [histi:'ri:ə] *n* (panic: *also* MED) ヒステリー hisúterī

hysterical [histe:r'ikəl] *adj* (person, rage) ヒステリックな hisúterikkù na; (situation: funny) 笑いが止らない様な warái gà tomáranai yố na

hysterical laughter ばか笑い bakáwarài

hysterics [histe:r'iks] *npl* (anger, panic) ヒステリー hisúterī; (laughter) 大笑い ốwarài

I

I [ai] *pron* 私は〔が〕watákushi wa〔ga〕

ice [ais] *n* (frozen water) 氷 kốri; (*also*: **ice cream**) アイスクリーム aísukurīmu

◆*vt* (cake) ...にアイシングを掛ける ...ni aíshingu wo kakérù

◆*vi* (*also*: **ice over**, **ice up**): road, window etc) 氷に覆われる kốri nì ốwarerù

iceberg [ais'bə:rg] *n* 氷山 hyốzan

icebox [ais'bɑ:ks] *n* (*US*: fridge) 冷蔵庫 reízōko; (*BRIT*: compartment) 冷凍室 reítōshitsu; (insulated box) クーラー kūrā

ice cream *n* アイスクリーム aísukurīmu

ice cube *n* 角氷 kakúgòri

iced [aist] *adj* (cake) アイシングを掛けた aíshingu wo kákèta; (beer) 冷した hiyáshìta

iced tea アイスティー aísutī

ice hockey *n* (SPORT) アイスホッケー aísuhokkē

Iceland [ais'lənd] *n* アイスランド **aísurañ-**

do

ice lolly [-lɑ:l'i:] (*BRIT*) n アイスキャンディー aísukyandī

ice rink n スケートリンク sukétoriñku

ice-skating [ais'skeitiŋ] n アイススケート aísusukéto

icicle [ai'sikəl] n (on gutter, ledge etc) つらら tsurára

icing [ai'siŋ] n (CULIN) 砂糖衣 satógoròmo, アイシング áishingu

icing sugar (*BRIT*) n 粉砂糖 konázatò

icon [ai'kɑm] n (REL) 聖像画 seízòga, イコン íkòn

icy [ai'si:] adj (air, water, temperature) 冷たい tsumétai; (road) 氷に覆われた kóri ni ówareta

I'd [aid] = I would; I had

idea [aidi:'ə] n (scheme, notion) 考え kañgaè; (opinion) 意見 íkèn; (objective) つもり tsumóri

ideal [aidi:'əl] n (principle) 理想 risó; (epitome) 模範 mohán

♦adj (perfect) 理想的な risóteki na

idealist [aidi:'əlist] n 理想主義者 risóshugìshà

identical [aiden'tikəl] adj 同一の dóitsu no

identification [aidentəfəkei'ʃən] n (process) 識別 shikíbetsu; (of person, dead body) 身元の確認 mimóto nò kakúnin

(means of) identification 身分証明書 mibúnshōmeìsho

identify [aiden'təfai] vt (recognize) 見分ける miwákerù; (distinguish) 識別する shikíbetsu suru; (associate): **to identify someone/something (with)** ...を (...と) 関連付ける ...wo (...to) kañrenzukerù

Identikit [aiden'təkit] ® n: **Identikit (picture)** モンタージュ写真 moñtājushashìn

identity [aiden'titi:] n (of person, suspect etc) 身元 mimóto, 正体 shótai; (of group, culture, nation etc) 特性 tokúsei

identity card n 身分証明書 mibúnshōmeìsho

ideology [aidi:ɑ:l'ədʒi:] n (beliefs) 思想 shisó, イデオロギー idéorògī

idiom [id'i:əm] n (style) 作風 sakúfū; (phrase) 熟語 jukúgo, イディオム ídīomu

idiomatic [idi:əmæt'ik] adj 熟語的な jukúgoteki na

idiosyncrasy [idi:əsiŋ'krəsi:] n (foible) 特異性 tokúisei

idiot [id'i:ət] n (fool) ばか bákà

idiotic [idi:ɑ:t'ik] adj (stupid) ばかな bákà na

idle [ai'dəl] adj (inactive) 暇な himá na; (lazy) 怠惰な taída na; (unemployed) 失業中の shitsúgyōchū no; (machinery) 動いていない ugóite inái; (factory) 休業中の kyúgyōchū no; (question, conversation) 無意味な muími na; (pleasure) むなしい munáshiì

♦vi (machine, engine) 空回りする káramawàri suru, アイドリングする aídoriñgu suru

idle away vt: **to idle away the time** のらくらする nórakura suru

idol [ai'dəl] n (hero) アイドル áidoru; (REL) 偶像 gúzō

idolize [ai'dəlaiz] vt ...に心酔する ...ni shiñsui suru

idyllic [aidil'ik] adj のどかな nódòka na

i.e. [aii:'] abbr (= id est: that is) 即ち sunáwàchi

KEYWORD

---

if [if] conj 1 (conditional use: given that, providing that etc) (もし)...すれば[するならば] (móshī) ...suréba(surú naràba)

I'll go if you come with me あなたが一緒に来れば、私は行ってもいいです anátà ga isshó ni kuréba watákushi wà itté mò íi desu

I'd be pleased if you could do it あなたがそれをやって下されば私は助かりますが anátà ga soré wò yatté kudasarèba watákushi wà tasúkarimasù ga

if anyone comes in だれかが入って来れば dárèka ga háitte kuréba

if necessary 必要であれば hitsúyō de aréba

if I were you 私があなただったら watákushi gà anátà dáttàra

2 (whenever) ...の時 ...no tókì

if we are in Scotland, we always go to see her スコットランドにいる時私たちは必ず彼女に会いに行きます sukóttoraǹdo ni irú tokì watákushitàchi wa kanárazù kánòjo ni áì ni ikímasù

3 (although): *(even) if* たとえ...でも tatôè ...dé mò

I am determined to finish it, (even) if it takes all week たとえ今週いっぱいかかっても私はこの仕事を片付けたい tatôè kòńshū ippái kakátte mò watákushi wà konó shigoto wò katázuketaì

I like it, (even) if you don't あなたがいやでも、私はこれが好きです anátà ga iyá de mò, watákushi wà koré gà sukí desù

4 (whether) ...かどうか ...ka dò ka

I don't know if he is here 彼がここにいるかどうか私には分かりません kárè ga kokó nì irú ka dòka watákushi ni wà wakárimaseǹ

ask him if he can come 来られるかどうか彼に聞いて下さい koráreru ka dò ka kárè ni kíìte kudasaì

5: *if so/not* そうであれば〔なければ〕sô de arèba〔nakerèba〕

if only ...であったらなあ ...dè áttara ná

if only I could 私にそれができたらなあ watákushi nì soré gà dékìtara ná

¶ *see also* **as**

---

igloo [ig'lu:] *n* イグルー ígùrū

ignite [ignait'] *vt* (set fire to) ...に火をつける ...ni hí wò tsukérù

♦*vi* 燃出す moédasù

ignition [igniʃ'ən] *n* (AUT: process) 点火 teńka; (: mechanism) 点火装置 teńkasôchi

to switch on/off the ignition エンジンスイッチを入れる〔切る〕eńjinsuìtchi wo irérù〔kírù〕

ignition key *n* (AUT) カーキー kákì

ignorance [ig'nɔːrəns] *n* (lack of knowledge) 無知 múchì

ignorant [ig'nɔːrənt] *adj* (uninformed, unaware) 無学な múgàku na, 無知な múchì na

to be ignorant of (subject, events) ...を知らない ...wo shiránaì

ignore [ignɔːr'] *vt* (person, advice, event, fact) 無視する mushí suru

I'll [ail] = **I will; I shall**

ill [il] *adj* (sick) 病気の byóki no; (harmful: effects) 悪い warúì

♦*n* (evil) 悪 ákù; (trouble) 凶兆 kyóchō

♦*adv*: *to speak ill of someone* ...の悪口を言う ...no warúgùchi wo iú

to think ill (of someone) (...を) 悪く思う (...wo) warúkù omóù

to be taken ill 病気になる byóki ni narù, 倒れる taórerù

ill-advised [il'ædvaizd'] *adj* (decision) 軽率な keísatsu na; (person) 無分別な mufúnbetsu na

ill-at-ease [il'əti:z'] *adj* (awkward, uncomfortable) 落着かない ochítsukanaì

illegal [ili:'gəl] *adj* (not legal: activity, organization, immigrant etc) 不法の fuhô no

illegible [iledʒ'əbəl] *adj* (writing) 読めない yoménaì

illegitimate [ilidʒit'əmit] *adj*: *an illegitimate child* 私生児 shiséiji

ill-fated [il'fei'tid] *adj* (doomed) 不運な fûǹ na

ill feeling *n* (animosity, bitterness) 恨み urámi

illicit [ilis'it] *adj* (unlawful: sale, association, substance) 不法の fuhô no

illiterate [ilit'ə:rit] *adj* (person) 文盲の mofímō no; (letter) 無学な múgàku na

ill-mannered [il'mæn'əːrd] *adj* (rude: child etc) 行儀の悪い gyôgi no warùi

illness [il'nis] *n* 病気 byóki

illogical [ila:dʒ'ikəl] *adj* (fear, reaction, argument) 不合理な fugôri na

ill-treat [il'tri:t] *vt* (child, pet, prisoner) 虐待する gyakútai suru

illuminate [ilu:'məneit] *vt* (light up: room, street) 明るくする akárukù suru; (decorate with lights: building, monument etc) ライトアップする raítoappù suru; (shine light on) 照らす terásù

illumination [ilu:mənei'ʃən] *n* (lighting) 照明 shômei

illuminations [ilu:mənei'ʃənz] *npl* (decorative lights) 電飾 deńshoku, イルミネーション irúmineshon

illusion [ilu:'ʒən] *n* (false idea, belief) 錯覚 sakkáku; (trick) いんちき iñchiki, トリック toríkkù

illusory [ilu:'sɔ:ri:] *adj* (hopes, prospects) 錯覚の sakkáku no

illustrate [il'əstreit] *vt* (point) 例を挙げて説明する rei wò agétè setsúmei suru; (book) …に挿絵を入れる …ni sashíe wo irérù; (talk) …にスライド（など）を使う …ni suráido (nádò) wo tsukáù

illustration [iləstrei'ʃən] *n* (act of illustrating) 図解 zukái; (example) 例 reí; (in book) 挿絵 sashíe

illustrious [ilʌs'tri:əs] *adj* (career) 輝かしい kagáyakashiì; (predecessor) 著名な choméi na

ill will *n* (hostility) 恨み urámi

I'm [aim] = **I am**

image [im'idʒ] *n* (picture) 像 zṓ; (public face) イメージ ímēji; (reflection) 姿 sugáta

imagery [im'idʒri:] *n* (in writing, painting etc) 比ゆ híyù

imaginary [imædʒ'əne:ri:] *adj* (being, danger) 想像上の sṓzōjō no

imagination [imædʒənei'ʃən] *n* (part of the mind) 想像 sṓzō; (inventiveness) 想像力 sṓzōryoku

imaginative [imædʒ'ənətiv] *adj* (person) 想像力に富んだ sṓzōryoku ni toñdà; (solution) 奇抜な kibátsu na

imagine [imædʒ'in] *vt* (visualise) 想像するsṓzō suru; (dream) …だと錯覚する …da to sakkáku suru; (suppose) …だと思う …da to omóù

imbalance [imbæl'əns] *n* (inequality) 不均等 fukíñtō, アンバランス añbarànsu

imbecile [im'bəsil] *n* (idiot) ばか bákà

imbue [imbju:'] *vt*: **to imbue someone/something with** …に …を吹き込む …ni …wo fukíkomù

imitate [im'əteit] *vt* (copy) まねる manérù; (mimic) …の物まねをする …no monómane wò suru

imitation [imətei'ʃən] *n* (act of copying)

まね manḕ; (act of mimicking) 物まね monómane; (copy) 偽物 nisémono

immaculate [imæk'jəlit] *adj* (room) 汚れ一つない yogóre hitotsù náì; (appearance) 清潔な seíketsu na; (piece of work) 完璧な kañpeki na; (REL) 原罪のない geñzai nò náì

immaterial [imæti:'ri:əl] *adj* (unimportant) どうでもいい dṓ dè mo íi

immature [imətu:r'] *adj* (fruit, cheese) 熟していない jukú shite inái; (organism) 未成熟の miséijuku no; (person) 未熟な mijúku na

immediate [imi:'di:it] *adj* (reaction, answer) 即時の sokúji no; (pressing: need) 緊迫した kiñpaku shita; (nearest: neighborhood, family) 最も近い mottó-mò chikáì

immediately [imi:'di:itli:] *adv* (at once) 直ぐに súgù ni, 直ちに tádàchi ni; (directly) 真っ直ぐに massúgù ni

immediately next to …の直ぐ隣に …no súgù tonári ni

immense [imens'] *adj* (huge: size) 巨大な kyodái na; (: progress, importance) 大変な taíhen na

immerse [imə:rs'] *vt* (submerge) 浸す hitásù

to be immersed in (fig: work, study etc) …に熱中している …ni netchū shite irú

to be immersed in thought 考え込んでいる kañgaekoñde irú

immersion heater [imə:r'ʒən-] (*BRIT*) *n* 投込み式湯沸かし器 tṓnyūshiki yuwakashikì

immigrant [im'əgrənt] *n* 移民 imín

immigration [iməgrei'ʃən] *n* (process) 移住 ijū; (control: at airport etc) 入国管理局 nyū́koku kañrikyoku

imminent [im'ənənt] *adj* (arrival, departure) 差迫った sashísematta

immobile [imou'bəl] *adj* (motionless) 動かない ugókanaì

immobilize [imou'bəlaiz] *vt* (person, machine) 動けなくする ugókenakù suru

immoral [imɔ:r'əl] *adj* (person, behavior, idea etc) 不道徳な fudṓtoku na

immorality [iməræl'iti:] *n* 不道徳 fudó-
toku

immortal [imɔːr'təl] *adj* (living for ever:
god) 永遠に生きる eíen ni ikírù; (unforgettable: poetry, fame) 不滅の fumétsu
no

immortalize [imɔːr'təlaiz] *vt* (hero,
event) ...に不朽の名声を与える ...ni fu-
kyū no meísei wo atáerù

immune [imjuːn'] *adj*: **immune (to)** (disease) (...に) 免疫がある (...ni) meń-eki
ga arù; (flattery) (...が) ...に通じない
(...ga) ...ni tsūjínaì; (criticism, attack)
...に (...の) しようがない ...ni (...no) shí-
yò ga nai

immunity [imjuː'niti:] *n* (to disease etc)
免疫 meń-eki; (from prosecution, taxation etc) 免除 meńjo

diplomatic immunity 外交特権 gaíko-
utokkèn

immunize [im'jənaiz] *vt* (MED: *gen*) ...に
免疫性を与える ...ni meń-ekisei wò atáe-
rù; (with injection) ...に予防注射をする
...ni yobốchūsha wo suru

imp [imp] *n* (small devil) 小鬼 ko-óni;
(child) いたずらっ子 itázurakkò

impact [im'pækt] *n* (of bullet, crash) 衝
撃 shốgeki, インパクト íhpakuto; (of
law, measure) 影響 eíkyō

impair [impeːr'] *vt* (vision, judgement) 損
なう sokónaù

impale [impeil'] *vt* くし刺しにする kushí-
zashi ni suru

impart [impɑːrt'] *vt* (make known: information) 与える atáerù; (bestow: flavor)
添える soérù

impartial [impɑːr'ʃəl] *adj* (judge,
observer) 公平な kốhei na

impassable [impæs'əbəl] *adj* (river) 渡れ
ない watárenaì; (road, route etc) 通行不
可能な tsūkốfukanò na

impasse [im'pæs] *n* (in war, negotiations) 行き詰り ikízumari

impassive [impæs'iv] *adj* (face, expression) 無表情な muhyốjō na

impatience [impei'ʃəns] *n* (annoyance
due to waiting) じれったさ jiréttasà;
(irritation) 短気 táñki; (eagerness) 意欲 í-
yòku

impatient [impei'ʃənt] *adj* (annoyed by
waiting) じれったい jiréttaì; (irritable)
短気な táñki na; (eager, in a hurry): *impatient to ...* ...従っている ...shitágatte
irù

to get/grow impatient もどかしがる
modókashigarù

impeccable [impek'əbəl] *adj* (perfect:
manners, dress) 申分のない mōshibùn no
náì

impede [impiːd'] *vt* (progress, development etc) 妨げる samátagerù

impediment [impe'dəmənt] *n* (to
growth, movement) 障害 shốgai; (*also*:
speech impediment) 言語障害 geńgoshố-
gai

impending [impen'diŋ] *adj* (arrival,
catastrophe) 差し迫る sashísemarù

impenetrable [impen'itrəbəl] *adj* (wall,
jungle) 通れない tốrenaì; (*fig*: law, text)
難解な nañkai na

imperative [imper'ətiv] *adj* (need) 緊急
の kiñkyū no; (tone) 命令的な meíreiteki
na

♦*n* (LING) 命令形 meíreikei

imperceptible [impərsep'təbəl] *adj*
(change, movement) 気付かれない kizúkarenaì

imperfect [impəːr'fikt] *adj* (goods, system etc) 不完全な fukáñzen na

♦*n* (LING: *also*: **imperfect tense**) 過去進
行形 kakóshinkōkei

imperfection [impəːrfek'ʃən] *n* (failing,
blemish) 欠点 kettéñ

imperial [impiːr'iːəl] *adj* (history, power)
帝国の teíkoku no; (*BRIT*: measure) ヤ
ードポンド法の yárdopondohố no

imperialism [impiːr'iːəlizəm] *n* 帝国主義
teíkokushùgi

impersonal [impəːr'sənəl] *adj* (place,
organization) 人間味のない niñgeñmi no
náì

impersonate [impəːr'səneit] *vt* (another
person, police officer etc) ...の名をかた
る ...no ná wò katárù, ...に成り済ます
...ni narísumasù; (THEATER) ...にふん
する ...ni fuñ surù

impertinent [ɪmˈpəːrˈtənənt] *adj* (pupil, question) 生意気な namáiki na

impervious [ɪmˈpəːrˈviːəs] *adj* (*fig*): **impervious to** (criticism etc) …に影響されない …ni eíkyō sarenái

impetuous [ɪmˈpetʃʹuːəs] *adj* (impulsive) 無鉄砲な mutéppō na

impetus [ɪmˈpɪtəs] *n* (momentum: of flight, runner) 惰性 daséi; (*fig*: driving force) 原動力 geńdōryoku

impinge [ɪmˈpɪndʒ]: **to impinge on** *vt fus* (person) …の行動を制限する …no kṓdō wò seígen suru; (rights) 侵害する shiñgai suru

implacable [ɪmˈplækʹəbəl] *adj* (hatred, anger etc) なだめがたい nadámegàtai; (opposition) 執念深い shúnenbùkai

implement
[*n* ɪmˈpləmənt *vb* ɪmˈplɛmənt] *n* (tool: for farming, gardening, cooking etc) 道具 dṓgu
♦*vt* (plan, regulation) 実行する jikkṓ suru

implicate [ɪmˈplɪkeit] *vt* (in crime, error) …のかかわり合いを立証する …no kakáwariaì wo risshṓ suru

implication [ɪmplɪkeiʹʃən] *n* (inference) 含み fukúmi; (involvement) 係り合い kakáwariai

implicit [ɪmplɪsʹit] *adj* (inferred: threat, meaning etc) 暗黙の añmoku no; (unquestioning: belief, trust) 盲目的な mṓmokuteki na

implore [ɪmˈplɔːr] *vt* (beg) …に嘆願する …ni tañgan suru

imply [ɪmplaiʹ] *vt* (hint) …の意味を含む …no ímì wo fukúmù; (mean) …を意味する …wo ímì suru

impolite [ɪmpəlaitʹ] *adj* (rude, offensive) 失礼な shitsúrei na

import [*vb* ɪmpɔːrtʹ *n* ɪmˈpɔːrt] *vt* (goods etc) 輸入する yunyū suru
♦*n* (COMM: article) 輸入品 yunyū́hin; (: importation) 輸入 yunyū́

importance [ɪmpɔːrˈtəns] *n* (significance) 重大さ júdaisa; (of person) 有力 yū́ryoku

important [ɪmpɔːrˈtənt] *adj* (significant: decision, difference etc) 重要な júyō na, 重大な júdai na; (influential: person) 偉い erái
it's not important 大した事じゃない taíshita kotò ja náî

importer [ɪmpɔːrˈtər] *n* (COMM) 輸入業者 yunyū́gyòsha

impose [ɪmpouzʹ] *vt* (sanctions, restrictions, discipline etc) 負わせる owáserù
♦*vi*: **to impose on someone** …に付込む …ni tsukékomù, …に迷惑を掛ける …ni méîwaku wo kakérù

imposing [ɪmpouʹzɪŋ] *adj* (building, person, manner) 貫ろくある kañroku arù

imposition [ɪmpəziʹʃən] *n* (of tax etc) 賦課 fukā
to be an imposition on (person) …に付込む …ni tsukékomù, …に迷惑を掛ける …ni méîwaku wo kakérù

impossible [ɪmpɑːsʹəbəl] *adj* (task, demand etc) 不可能な fukánō na; (situation) 厄介な yakkáî na; (person) どうしようもない dṓ shiyò mo nai

impostor [ɪmpɑːsʹtər] *n* 偽者 nisémono

impotence [ɪmˈpətəns] *n* (lack of power) 無力 múryòku; (MED) 性交不能 seíkōfùnō, インポテンツ iñpoteñtsu

impotent [ɪmˈpətənt] *adj* (powerless) 無力な múryòku na; (MED) 性交不能の seíkōfùnō no

impound [ɪmpaundʹ] *vt* (belongings, passports) 没収する bosshū suru

impoverished [ɪmpɑːvʹəːriʃt] *adj* (country, person etc) 貧しくなった mazúshiku nattá

impracticable [ɪmprækʹtikəbəl] *adj* (idea, solution) 実行不可能な jikkōfukanṓ na

impractical [ɪmprækʹtikəl] *adj* (plan) 実用的でない jitsúyōteki de naî; (person) 不器用な bukíyò na

imprecise [ɪmprisaisʹ] *adj* (inexact) 不正確な fuseíkaku na

impregnable [ɪmpregʹnəbəl] *adj* (castle, fortress) 難攻不落の nañkōfuràku no

impregnate [ɪmpregʹneit] *vt* (saturate) …に染込ませる …ni shimīkomaserù

impresario [ɪmprəsɑːˈriːou] *n* (THEA-

TER) 興業師 kốgyōshì

impress [impres'] *vt* (person) ...に印象を与える ...ni iñshō wǒ atáerù; (mark) ...に押付ける ...ni oshítsukerù

to impress something on someone ...に...を強く言い聞かす ...ni ...wo tsuyókù ifkikasu

impression [impreʃ'ən] *n* (of place, situation, person) 印象 iñshō; (of stamp, seal) 刻印 kokúiñ, 刻印 kokúiñ; (idea) 思い込み omóikomi; (effect) 効果 kốka; (mark) 跡 átò; (imitation) 物まね monómane

to be under the impression that ...だと思い込んでいる ...da to omóikoñde irú

impressionable [impreʃ'ənəbəl] *adj* (child, person) 感じやすい kañjiyasui

impressionist [impreʃ'ənist] *n* (entertainer) 物真似芸人 monómanegeìnin; (ART): *Impressionist* 印象派画家 iñshōhagaka

impressive [impres'iv] *adj* (reputation, collection) 印象的な iñshōteki na

imprint [im'print] *n* (outline: of hand etc) 跡 ato; (PUBLISHING) 奥付 okúzuke

imprison [impriz'ən] *vt* (criminal) 拘置する kốchi suru, 刑務所に入れる keímushò ni irérù

imprisonment [impriz'ənmənt] *n* 拘置 kốchi

improbable [imprɑ:b'əbəl] *adj* (unlikely: outcome) ありそうもない arísō mò naí; (: explanation, story) 本当らしくない hoñtōrashikù naí

impromptu [imprɑ:mp'tu:] *adj* (celebration, party) 即席の sokúseki no

improper [imprɑ:p'ə:r] *adj* (unsuitable: conduct, procedure) 不適切な futékisetsu na; (dishonest: activities) 不正な fuséi na

improve [impru:v'] *vt* (make better: character, housing, result) 改善する kaízen suru

◆*vi* (get better: weather, pupil, patient, health etc) 良くなる yốku naru

improvement [impru:v'mənt] *n* (making better) 改善 kaízen; (getting better) 良くなる事 yốkù naru kotó: *improve-*

ment (in) (making better) (...を) 改善する事 (...wo) kaízen surù kotó; (getting better) (...が) 良くなる事 (...ga) yốkù naru kotó

improvise [im'prəvaiz] *vt* (meal, bed etc) 有り合せの物で作る aríawase no mono dè tsukúrù

◆*vi* (THEATER, MUS) 即興的にしゃべる〔演奏する〕sokkyốteki nì shabérù〔eñsō suru〕, アドリブする adóribu suru

imprudent [impru:d'ənt] *adj* (unwise) 賢明でない keñmei de naí

impudent [im'pjədənt] *adj* (child, comment, remark) 生意気な namáiki na

impulse [im'pʌls] *n* (urge: *gen*) 衝動 shốdō; (: to do wrong) 出来心 dekígokòro; (ELEC) 衝撃 shốgeki, インパルス îñparusu

to act on impulse 衝動的に行動する shốdōteki nì kốdō suru

impulsive [impʌl'siv] *adj* (purchase, gesture, person) 衝動的な shốdōteki na

impunity [impju:'niti:] *n*: *with impunity* 罰せられずに bassérarezù ni

impure [impju:r'] *adj* (adulterated) 不純な fujún na; (sinful) みだらな mídàra na

impurity [impju:r'iti:] *n* (foreign substance) 不純物 fujúñbutsu

---

KEYWORD

in [in] *prep* 1 (indicating place, position) ...に〔で〕 ... nì〔dè〕

in the house/garden 家〔庭〕に〔で〕 ié〔niwá〕nì〔dè〕

in the box/fridge/drawer 箱〔冷蔵庫, 引き出し〕に〔で〕hakó〔reízōko, hikídashi〕nì〔dè〕

I have it in my hand 手に持っています té nì mốttè imasu

to spend a day in town/the country 町〔田舎〕で1日を過ごす machí〔ináka〕dè ichínichi wò sugósù

in school 学校に〔で〕gakkố nì〔dè〕

in here/there ここ〔あそこ〕に〔で〕kokó〔asóko〕nì〔dè〕

2 (with place names: of town, region, country) ...に〔で〕 ... nì〔dè〕

in London ロンドンに〔で〕róñdon ni

〔de〕

*in England/Japan/Canada/the
United States* 英国〔日本, カナダ, ア
メリカ〕に〔で〕 eîkoku(nippóñ, kánàda,
amérîka) nî〔dè〕

in Burgundy バーガンディーに〔で〕 bá-
gañdì ni(de)

3 (indicating time: during) ...に ...nî

in spring/summer 春〔夏〕に háru(natsú)ni

in 1998 1998年 に señkyūhyakukyūjū-
hachi néñ ni

in May 5月に gógàtsu ni

I'll see you in July 7月に会いましょう
shichígatsu ni aîmashò

in the afternoon 午後に gógò ni

at 4 o'clock in the afternoon 午後4時
に gógò yójì ni

4 (indicating time: in the space of) ...で
...dè

I did it in 3 hours/days 3時間〔3日〕
でやりました sañjikan(mìkkà)de yarímashìta

*I'll see you in 2 weeks/in 2 weeks'
time* 2週間したらまた会いましょう ni-
shūkan shitara matá aimashò

5 (indicating manner etc) ...で ...dè

in a loud/soft voice 大きな〔小さな〕声
で ōkìna(chîsana)kôè de

in pencil/ink 鉛筆〔インク〕で eñpitsu
〔íñku〕de

in English/French 英語〔フランス語〕で
eîgo〔furánsugo〕dè

the boy in the blue shirt 青いシャツの
少年 aôî shátsù no shôñen

6 (indicating circumstances): *in the sun*
直射日光に当って chokúshanikkò ni a-
táttè, 日なたに hinátà ni

in the rain 雨の中で áme no nákà

in the shade 日陰で hikáge de

a change in policy 政策の変更 seîsaku
nô heñkô

a rise in prices 物価の上昇 búkkà no
jôshò

7 (indicating mood, state): *in tears* 泣い
て naîte

in anger 怒って okóttè

in despair 失望して shitsúbò shìtè

in good condition 無事に bujî nî

to live in luxury ぜいたくに暮す zeîtaku
ni kurâsu

8 (with ratios, numbers): *1 in 10
households has a second car, 1
household in 10 has a second car* 10
世帯中1世帯は車を2台持っている jussé-
taichū issétai wà kurúma wò nídài
môtte irù

6 months in the year 1年の内6か月
ichíñen no uchî rokkágètsu

they lined up in twos 彼らは2人ずつ並
んだ kárèra wa futárizùtsu naráñda

9 (referring to people, works): *the disease is common in children* この病気
は子供によく見られる konô byôki wa
kodómo nì yókù mirárerù

in (the works of) Dickens ディケンズ
の作品の中に díkenzu no sakúhin no
nakâ ni

she has it in her to succeed 彼女には
成功する素質がある kánjo ni wa seîkō
suru soshitsù ga árù

they have a good leader in him 彼ら
にとって彼は素晴らしいリーダーです
kárèra ni tôttè kárè wa subárashiî rîdà
desu

10 (indicating profession etc): *to be in
teaching* 教員である kyôîñ de árù

to be in publishing 出版関係の仕事を
している shuppánkañkei no shigôto wò
shitê irù

to be in the army 軍人である guñjiñ de
árù

11 (after superlative): *the best pupil in
the class* クラスで最優秀の生徒 kúràsu
de saîyūshū no seîto

the biggest/smallest in Europe ヨー
ロッパ中で最も大きな〔小さな〕物 yôrop-
pajū de mottômò ōkìna(chîsana)monô

12 (with present participle): *in saying
this* こう言って kô ittè

*in doing things the way she did, she
alienated everyone* 彼女のやり方は皆
の反感を買った kánjo no yaríkata wà
minâ nò hañkan wò kattâ

◆*adv*: *to be in* (person: at home) 在宅で
ある zaîtaku de arù; (: at work) 出社して

いる shusshá shite irù; (train, plane) 到着 している tôchaku shite irù; (ship) 入港 している nyûkō shite irù; (in fashion) 流行 している ryûkō shite irù

he'll be in later today 2-3時間したら 出社すると思います nisánjikàn shitárá shusshá suru tò omôimasù

miniskirts are in again this year 今 年ミニスカートが再び流行しています kotóshi minísukàto ga fútàtabî ryûkō shite imasù

to ask someone in ...を家に上がらせる ...wò ié nì agáraserù

to run/limp etc in 走って〔びっこを引 いて〕入って来る hashîttè〔bîkkò wo hiî tè〕hâitte kurù

♦*n: the ins and outs* (of proposal, situation etc) 詳細 shôsai

he explained all the ins and outs of the deal to me 彼は私に取引の詳細を 説明してくれました kâre wa watákushi nî torîhiki no shôsai wo setsúmei shite kuremashîta

in. *abbr* = **inch**

inability [inəbil'əti:] *n* (incapacity): *in-ability (to do)* (...surú kotò ga) dekínai kotó

inaccessible [inækses'əbəl] *adj* (place) 入りにくい haírinikùi, 近付きにくい chi-kázukinikùi; (*fig*: text, music) 難解な nañka-i na

inaccurate [inæk'jəːrit] *adj* (account, answer, person) 不正確な fuséikaku na

inactivity [inæktiv'iti:] *n* (idleness) 活動 しない事 katsúdōshìnai kotó

inadequate [inæd'əkwit] *adj* (income, amount, reply) 不十分な fujûbùn na; (person) 無能な munô na

inadvertently [inədvəːr'təntli:] *adv* (un-intentionally) うっかり ukkárì

inadvisable [inədvai'zəbəl] *adj* 得策でな い tokúsaku de naî

inane [inein'] *adj* (smile, remark) 愚かな ôrôka na

inanimate [inæn'əmit] *adj* 生命のない seímei no naî

inappropriate [inəprou'pri:it] *adj* (un-suitable) 不適切な futékisetsu na; (im-proper: word, expression) 非難すべき hi-nánsubeki

inarticulate [inɑːrtik'jəlit] *adj* (person) 口下手な kuchîbeta na; (speech) 分かり にくい wakárinikuî

inasmuch as [inəzmʌtʃ'-] *adv* (in that) ...という点で ...to iú teñ de; (insofar as) できる限り dekíru kagiri

inaudible [inɔː'dəbəl] *adj* (voice, aside) 聞取れない kikítorenaî

inaugural [inɔː'gjəːrəl] *adj* (speech) 就 任の shûnin no; (meeting) 発 会の hakkái no

inaugurate [inɔː'gjəːreit] *vt* (president, official) ...の就任式を行う ...no shûniñshiki wo okonau; (system, measure) 始 める hajímeru; (organization) 発足させ る hossóku saserù

inauguration [inɔːgjəːrei'ʃən] *n* (of presi-dent, official) 就任式 shûniñshiki; (of system, measure) 開始 kaíshi; (of organi-zation) 発足 hossóku

in-between [in'bitwiːn] *adj* (intermedi-ate) 中間的な chûkanteki na

inborn [in'bɔːrn] *adj* (quality) 生れ付きの umáretsuki no

inbred [in'bred] *adj* (quality) 生まれつき の umaretsuki no; (family) 近親配合の kíñshinkôhai no

Inc. *abbr* = **incorporated**

incalculable [inkæl'kjələbəl] *adj* (effect, loss) 途方もない tohô mo naî

incapable [inkei'pəbəl] *adj* (helpless) 無 能な munô na; (unable to): *to be in-capable of something/doing some-thing* ...が〔する事が〕できない ...ga〔surú kotò ga〕dekínaî

incapacitate [inkəpæs'əteit] *vt* 不具に する fúgù ni suru

incapacity [inkəpæs'iti:] *n* (weakness) 弱さ yówàsa; (inability) 不能 funô

incarcerate [inkɑːr'səːrit] *vt* 拘置する kôchi suru, 刑務所に入れる keímushò ni irérù

incarnation [inkɑːrnei'ʃən] *n* (of beauty) 化身 késhìn; (of evil) 権化 gôñge; (REL) 神が人間の姿を取る事 kámì ga niñgen no sugatá wo tórù kotó

incendiary [insen'di:e:rri:] *adj* (device) 放火の hōka no

an incendiary bomb 焼い弾 shóidàn

incense [*n* in'sens *vb* insens'] *n* (perfume: *also* REL) 香 kō

♦*vt* (anger) 怒らせる okóraserù

incentive [insen'tiv] *n* (inducement) 動機 dōkì, 刺激 shigéki

incessant [inses'ənt] *adj* (bickering, criticism) 引っ切り無しの hikkíri nashì no

incessantly [inses'əntli:] *adv* 引っ切り無しに hikkíri nashì ni

incest [in'sest] *n* 近親相かん kinshinsōkan

inch [intʃ] *n* (measurement) インチ fñchi

to be within an inch of doing 危うく ...するところである ayáuku ...surú tokoro de árù

he didn't give an inch (*fig*: back down, yield) 一寸も譲ろうとしなかった issúñ mo yuzúrō to shinákatta

inch forward *vi* 一寸刻みに進む issúñkizami ni susúmù

incidence [in'sidəns] *n* (of crime, disease) 発生率 hasséiritsu

incident [in'sidənt] *n* (event) 事件 jíkèn

incidental [insiden'təl] *adj* (additional, supplementary) 付随的な fuzúiteki na

incidental to ...に対して二次的な ...ni táìshite nijíteki na

incidentally [insiden'təli:] *adv* (by the way) ところで tokóro dè

incinerator [insin'ə:reitər] *n* (for waste, refuse) 焼却炉 shōkyakurò

incipient [insip'i:ənt] *adj* (baldness, madness) 初期の shókì no

incision [insiʒ'ən] *n* (cut: *also* MED) 切開 sékkài

incisive [insai'siv] *adj* (comment, criticism) 痛烈な tsúretsu na

incite [insait'] *vt* (rioters, violence) 扇動する señdō suru; (hatred) あおりたてる aóritatèru

inclination [inklənei'ʃən] *n* (tendency) 傾向 keíkō; (disposition, desire) 望み nozómi

incline [in'klain] *n* (slope) 坂 saká

♦*vt* (bend: head) 下げる sagérù

♦*vi* (surface) 傾斜する keísha suru

to be inclined to (tend) ...する傾向がある ...suru keíkō ga arù

include [inklu:d'] *vt* (incorporate: in plan, team etc) 入れる irérù; (: in price) 含む fukúmù

including [inklu:d'iŋ] *prep* ...を含めて ...wo fukúmète

inclusion [inklu:'ʒən] *n* (incorporation: in plan etc) 入れる事 irérù kotó; (: in price) 含む事 fukúmù kotó

inclusive [inklu:'siv] *adj* (price, terms) 含んでいる fukúnde iru

inclusive of ...を含めて ...wo fukúmète

incognito [inka:gni:'tou] *adv* (travel) 御忍びで o-shínobi de

incoherent [inkouhi:'rənt] *adj* (argument, speech, person) 分かりにくい wakárinikuì

income [in'kʌm] *n* 収入 shúnyū

income tax *n* 所得税 shotókuzèi

incoming [in'kʌmiŋ] *adj* (flight, passenger) 到着の tōchaku no; (call, mail) 着信の chakúshin no; (government, official) 新任の shifinin no; (wave) 寄せて来る yosête kurù

the incoming tide 上げ潮 agéshio

incomparable [inka:m'pə:rəbəl] *adj* (genius, efficiency etc) 類のない rúì no náì

incompatible [inkəmpæt'əbəl] *adj* (lifestyles, systems, aims) 相容れない áìrenai

incompetence [inka:m'pitəns] *n* 無能 munō

incompetent [inka:m'pitənt] *adj* (person) 無能な munō na; (job) 下手な hetá na

incomplete [inkəmpli:t'] *adj* (unfinished: book, painting etc) 未完成の mikánsei no; (partial: success, achievement) 部分的な bubúnteki na

incomprehensible [inka:mprihen'səbəl] *adj* (conduct) 不可解な fukákai na; (language) 分からない wakáranaì

inconceivable [inkənsi:'vəbəl] *adj* (unthinkable) 考えられない kañgaerarenaì

incongruous [inkɑ:ŋ'gru:əs] *adj*
(strange: situation, figure) 変った kawátta; (inappropriate: remark, act) 不適
当な futékitō na

inconsiderate [inkənsid'ə:rit] *adj* (person, action) 心ない kokóronaì

inconsistency [inkənsis'tənsi:] *n* (of
behavior, person etc) 一貫しない事 ikkán
shinai koto; (in work) むら murá; (in
statement, action) 矛盾 mujún

inconsistent [inkənsis'tənt] *adj* (behavior, person) 変りやすい kawáriyasuì;
(work) むらの多い murá no ōi; (statement, action) 矛盾した mujún shita

inconsistent with (beliefs, values) ...と
矛盾する ...to mujún suru

inconspicuous [inkənspik'ju:əs] *adj*
(person, color, building etc) 目立たない
medátanaì

incontinent [inkɑ:n'tənənt] *adj* (MED)
失禁の shikkín no

inconvenience [inkənvi:n'jəns] *n* (problem) 問題 mońdai; (trouble) 迷惑 meíwaku

♦*vt* ...に迷惑を掛ける ...ni meíwaku wò
kakérù

inconvenient [inkənvi:n'jənt] *adj* (time,
place, house) 不便な fubén na; (visitor,
incident etc) 厄介な yakkái na

incorporate [inkɔ:r'pə:rit] *vt* (make
part of) 取入れる toríirerù; (contain) 含
む fukúmù

incorporated company [inkɔ:r'-
pə:reitid-] (*US*) *n* (*abbr* **Inc.**) 会社 kaísha

incorrect [inkərekt'] *adj* (information,
answer, attitude etc) 間違った machígattà

incorrigible [inkɔ:r'idʒəbəl] *adj* (liar,
crook) 救い様のない sukúiyō no naì

incorruptible [inkərʌp'təbəl] *adj* (not
open to bribes) 買収のできない baíshū
no dekínaì

increase [*n* in'kri:s *vb* inkri:s'] *n* (rise):
increase (in/of) (...の) 増加 (...no) zō-
ka

♦*vi* (: price, level, productivity etc) 増す
masú

♦*vt* (make greater: price, knowledge

etc) 増す masú

increasing [inkri:s'iŋ] *adj* (number, use)
増加する zōka suru

increasingly [inkri:s'iŋli:] *adv* (more
intensely, more often) ますます masúmàsu

incredible [inkred'əbəl] *adj* (unbelievable) 信じられない shiñjirarenaì; (enormous) ばく大な bakúdai na

incredulous [inkredʒ'ələs] *adj* (tone,
expression) 半信半疑の hańshiñhangi no

increment [in'krəmənt] *n* (in salary) 定
期昇給 teíkishōkyū

incriminate [inkrim'əneit] *vt* (LAW)
...の罪を立証する ...no tsúmì wo risshō
suru

incubation [inkjəbei'ʃən] *n* (of eggs) ふ
卵 furán; (of illness) 潜伏期間 señpukuki-
kàn

incubator [in'kjəbeitə:r] *n* (for babies)
保育器 hoíkukì

incumbent [inkʌm'bənt] *n* (official:
POL, REL) 現役 gén-eki

♦*adj*: *it is incumbent on him to ...*
...するのが彼の義務である ...surú no gà
kárè no gímù de árù

incur [inkə:r'] *vt* (expenses) ...が掛る ...ga
kakárù; (loss) 受ける ukérù; (debt) こし
らえる koshíraerù; (disapproval, anger)
被る kōmurù

incurable [inkju:r'əbəl] *adj* (disease) 不
治の fújì no

incursion [inkə:r'ʒən] *n* (MIL: invasion)
侵入 shiñnyū

indebted [indet'id] *adj*: *to be indebted
to someone* (grateful) ...に感謝している
...ni kánsha shitè irù

indecent [indi:'sənt] *adj* (film, book) み
だらな mídàra na

indecent assault (*BRIT*) *n* 強制わいせ
つ罪 kyōsei waisetsuzài

indecent exposure *n* 公然わいせつ罪
kōzen waisetsuzài

indecisive [indisai'siv] *adj* (person) 決断
力のない ketsúdanryoku no naì

indeed [indi:d'] *adv* (certainly) 確かに táshìka ni, 本当に hoñtō ni; (in fact) 実は
jitsú wà; (furthermore) なお náò

yes indeed! 確かにそうだ! táshĭka ni sŏ dă!

indefinite [indef'ənit] *adj* (answer, view) 不明確な fuméikaku na; (period, number) 不定の futéi no

indefinitely [indef'ənitli:] *adv* (continue, wait) いつまでも ítsŭ made mo

indelible [indel'əbəl] *adj* (mark, stain, ink) 消せない kesénaï

indelible pen 油性フェルトペン yuséi ferútopen

indemnity [indem'niti:] *n* (insurance) 賠償保険 baíshōhokèn; (compensation) 賠償 baíshō

independence [indipen'dəns] *n* (of country, person etc) 独立 dokúritsu; (of thinking etc) 自主性 jishúsei

independent [indipen'dənt] *adj* (country, business etc) 独立した dokúritsu shita; (person, thought) 自主的な jishúteki na; (school) 私立の shírītsu no; (broadcasting company) 民間の miñkan no; (inquiry) 独自の dokúji no

indestructible [indistrʌk'təbəl] *adj* 破壊できない hakái dekinaï

indeterminate [inditə:r'mənit] *adj* (number, nature) 不明の fuméi no

index [in'deks] (*pl* indexes) *n* (in book) 索引 sakúin, インデックス iñdekkŭsu; (in library etc) 蔵書目録 zóshomokùroku; (*pl*: indices: ratio) 率 rítsù, 指数 shísū; (: sign) 印 shírushi

index card *n* インデックスカード iñdekkusukădo

indexed [in'dekst] (*BRIT* index-linked) *adj* (income, payment) スライド制のsuráidosei no

index finger *n* 人差指 hitósashiyùbi

India [in'di:ə] *n* インド íñdo

Indian [in'di:ən] *adj* インドの íñdo no

Red Indian アメリカインディアン amérika iñdian

Indian Ocean *n*: *the Indian Ocean* インド洋 iñdoyŏ

indicate [in'dikeit] *vt* (show) 示す shimésù; (point to) 指す sásù; (mention) 示唆する shisá suru

indication [indikei'ʃən] *n* (sign) しるし shirúshi

indicative [indik'ətiv] *adj*: *indicative of* ...のしるしである ...no shirúshi de aru ♦*n* (LING) 直接法 chokúsetsuhŏ

indicator [in'dikeitə:r] *n* (marker, signal) しるし shirúshi; (AUT) 方向指示器 hŏkōshijìki, ウインカー uíñkā

indices [in'disi:z] *npl of* index

indictment [indait'mənt] *n* (denunciation) 避難 hínàn; (charge) 起訴 kisŏ

indifference [indif'ə:rəns] *n* (lack of interest) 無関心 mukánshin

indifferent [indif'ə:rənt] *adj* (uninterested: attitude) 無関心な mukánshin na; (mediocre: quality) 平凡な heíbon na

indigenous [indidʒ'ənəs] *adj* (wildlife) 固有の koyŭ no

the indigenous population 原住民 geñjūmin

indigestion [indidʒes'tʃən] *n* 消化不良 shŏkafuryŏ

indignant [indig'nənt] *adj*: *to be indignant at something/with someone* (angry) ...に怒っている ...ni okŏtte irù

indignation [indignei'ʃən] *n* (outrage, resentment) 立腹 rippúku

indignity [indig'niti:] *n* (humiliation) 侮辱 bujóku

indigo [in'dəgou] *n* (color) あい áî

indirect [indirekt'] *adj* (way, route) 遠回しの tŏmawashĭ no; (answer, effect) 間接的な kañsetsuteki na

indirectly [indirekt'li:] *adv* (responsible) 間接的に kañsetsuteki ni

indiscreet [indiskri:t'] *adj* (person, behavior, comment) 軽率な keísotsu na

indiscriminate [indiskrim'ənit] *adj* (bombing) 無差別の musábetsu no; (taste) はっきりしない hakkírî shinaî

indispensable [indispen'səbəl] *adj* (tool, worker) 掛替えのない kakégae no naï

indisposed [indispouzd'] *adj* (unwell) 体調の悪い taíchō no warûî

indisputable [indispju:'təbəl] *adj* (undeniable) 否めない inámenaî

indistinct [indistiŋkt'] *adj* (image, memory) ぼんやりした boñ-yarî shita; (noise) かすかな kásùka na

individual [indəvidʒ'u:əl] n (person: different from all others) 個人 kójîn; (: with adj) 人 hitô, 人物 jinbutsu
♦adj (personal) 個人個人の kojínkôjin no; (single) それぞれの sorézòre no; (particular: characteristic) 独特な dokûtoku na

individualist [indəvidʒ'u:əlist] n 個人主義者 kojínshugishà

individually [indəvidʒ'u:əli:] adv (singly: persons) 一人一人で hitórihitorî de; (: things) 一つ一つで hitótsuhitotsù de

indivisible [indəviz'əbəl] adj (matter, power) 分割できない buñkatsu dekinâi

indoctrinate [indɑ:k'trəneit] vt ...に ...を教え込む ...ni ...wo oshíekomù, 洗脳する señnő suru

indoctrination [indɑ:ktrənei'ʃən] n 教え込む事 oshíekomù kotô, 洗脳 señnő

indolent [in'dələnt] adj (lazy) 怠惰な tâida na

Indonesia [indəni:'ʒə] n インドネシア iñdoneshìa

indoor [in'dɔ:r] adj 屋内の okûnai no

indoors [indɔ:rz'] adv (inside) 屋内で okûnai de

induce [indu:s'] vt (bring about) 引起こす hikíokosù; (persuade) 説得する settôku suru; (MED: birth) 誘発する yûhatsu suru

inducement [indu:s'mənt] n (incentive) 動機 dôki, 刺激 shigéki; (pej: bribe) 賄ろ wâîro

indulge [indʌldʒ'] vt (desire, whim) 満たす mitásù; (person, child) 気ままにさせる kimáma ni saserù
♦vi: **to indulge in** (vice, hobby) ...にふける ...ni fukérù

indulgence [indʌl'dʒəns] n (pleasure) 楽しみ tanóshimi; (leniency) 寛大さ kañdaisa

indulgent [indʌl'dʒənt] adj (parent, smile) 甘やかす amáyakasù

industrial [indʌs'tri:əl] adj 産業の sañgyō no, 工業の kốgyō no

industrial action (BRIT) n 争議行為 sốgikồi

industrial estate (BRIT) n = **industrial park**

industrialist [indʌs'tri:əlist] n 実業家 jitsúgyồka

industrialize [indʌs'tri:əlaiz] vt (country, society) 工業化する kốgyōka suru

industrial park (US) n 工業団地 kốgyōdañchi

industrious [indʌs'tri:əs] adj (student, worker) 勤勉な kiñben na

industry [in'dəstri] n (manufacturing) 産業 sañgyō, 工業 kốgyō; (oil industry, textile industry etc) ...業界 ...gyốkai; (diligence) 勤勉さ kiñbensa

inebriated [ini:'bri:eitid] adj (drunk) 酔っ払った yoppáratta

inedible [ined'əbəl] adj (disgusting) 食べられない tabérarenaì; (poisonous) 食用に適さない shokúyō nì tekísanaì

ineffective [inifek'tiv] adj (policy, government) 効果のない kôka no naì

ineffectual [inifek'tʃu:əl] adj = **ineffective**

inefficiency [inifiʃ'ənsi:] n 非能率 hinốritsu

inefficient [inifiʃ'ənt] adj (person, machine, system) 能率の悪い nốritsu no waruî

inept [inept'] adj (politician, management) 無能な munố na

inequality [inikwɑ:l'iti:] n (of system) 不平等 fubyôdō; (of amount, share) 不等 futồ

inert [inə:rt'] adj (immobile) 動かない ugốkanaì; (gas) 不活性の fukássei no

inertia [inə:r'ʃə] n (apathy) 物臭 monốgusa; (PHYSICS) 惰性 daséi

inescapable [inəskei'pəbəl] adj (conclusion, impression) 避けられない sakérarenaì

inevitable [inev'itəbəl] adj (outcome, result) 避けられない sakérarenaì, 必然的な hitsúzenteki na

inevitably [inev'itəbli:] adv 必然的に hitsúzenteki ni

inexcusable [inikskju:'zəbəl] adj (behavior, error) 許されない yurúsarenaì

inexhaustible [inigzɔ:s'təbəl] adj (wealth, resources) 無尽蔵の mujîñzō no

inexorable [inek'sə:rəbəl] *adj* (progress, decline) 止め様のない toméyō no naì

inexpensive [inikspen'siv] *adj* (cheap) 安い yasúì

inexperience [inikspi:'ri:əns] *n* (of person) 不慣れ fúnàre

inexperienced [inikspi:'ri:ənst] *adj* (swimmer, worker) 不慣れの fúnàre no

inexplicable [ineks'plikəbəl] *adj* (decision, mistake) 不可解な fukákài na

inextricably [ineks'trikəbli:] *adv* (entangled, linked) 分けられない程 wakérarenài hodo

infallible [infæl'əbəl] *adj* (person, guide) 間違いのない machígaì no naì

infamous [in'fəməs] *adj* (crime, murderer) 悪名高い akúmeidakaì

infamy [in'fəmi:] *n* (notoriety) 悪評 akúhyō

infancy [in'fənsi:] *n* (of person) 幼年時代 yōnenjidài

infant [in'fənt] *n* (baby) 赤ちゃん ákàchan; (young child) 幼児 yōjì

infantile [in'fəntail] *adj* (disease) 幼児の yōjì no; (foolish) 幼稚な yōchì na

infantry [in'fəntri:] *n* (MIL) 歩兵隊 hoheitai

infant school (*BRIT*) *n* 幼稚園 yōchien

infatuated [infæt∫'u:eitid] *adj*: **to be infatuated with** ...にのぼせている ...ni nobósete irù

infatuation [infæt∫u:ei'∫ən] *n* (passion) ...にのぼせる事 ...ni nobóseru koto

infect [infekt'] *vt* (person, animal) ...に感染させる ...ni kafisen saserù; (food) 汚染する osén suru

infection [infek'∫ən] *n* (MED: disease) 感染 kafisen; (contagion) 伝染 defisen

infectious [infek'∫əs] *adj* (person, animal) 伝染病にかかった defisenbyō ni kakáttà; (disease) 伝染性の defisensei no; (*fig*: enthusiasm, laughter) 移りやすい utsúriyasuì

infer [infə:r'] *vt* (deduce) 推定する suítei suru; (imply) ...の意味を含む ...no ímì wo fukúmù

inference [in'fə:rəns] *n* (deduction) 推定 suítei; (implication) 含み fukúmi

inferior [infi:'ri:ə:r] *adj* (in rank) 下級の kakyū no; (in quality, quantity) 劣った otóttà
♦*n* (subordinate) 下の者 shitá no monò; (junior) 年下の者 toshíshita no monò

inferiority [infi:ri:ɔːr'iti:] *n* (in rank) 下級である事 kakyū de arù kotó; (in quality) 品質の悪さ hiñshitsu nò wárùsa

inferiority complex *n* (PSYCH) 劣等感 rettókan

infernal [infə:r'nəl] *adj* (racket, temper) ひどい hidóì

inferno [infə:r'nou] *n* (blaze) 大火事 ōkajì

infertile [infə:r'təl] *adj* (soil) 不毛の fumō no; (person, animal) 不妊の funín no

infertility [infə:rtil'əti:] *n* (of soil) 不毛 fumō; (of person, animal) 不妊症 funínshō

infested [infes'tid] *adj*: **infested with** (vermin, pests) ...がうじゃうじゃいる ...ga újàuja irú

infidelity [infidel'iti:] *n* (unfaithfulness) 浮気 uwáki

in-fighting [in'faitiŋ] *n* 内紛 naífun, 内ゲバ uchígeba

infiltrate [infil'treit] *vt* ...に潜入する ...ni seínyū suru

infinite [in'fənit] *adj* (very great: variety, patience) ばく大な bakúdai na; (without limits: universe) 無限の mugén no

infinitive [infin'ətiv] *n* (LING) 不定詞 futéishi

infinity [infin'əti:] *n* (infinite number) 無限大 mugéndai; (infinite point) 無限 mugén

infirm [infə:rm'] *adj* (weak) 虚弱な kyojáku na; (ill) 病弱な byójaku na

infirmary [infə:r'mə:ri:] *n* (hospital) 病院 byōin

infirmity [infə:r'miti:] *n* (weakness) 虚弱さ kyojákusa; (being ill) 病弱さ byójakusa; (specific illness) 病気 byōki

inflamed [infleimd'] *adj* (tongue, appendix) 炎症を起した efishō wò okóshità

inflammable [inflæm'əbəl] *adj* (fabric, chemical) 可燃性の kanénsei no, 燃えや

すい moﾞeyasuﾞ

inflammation [infləmei'ʃən] *n* (of throat, appendix etc) 炎症 eﾞnshō

inflatable [inflei'təbəl] *adj* (life jacket, dinghy, doll) 膨らます事のできる fukúramasu kotò no dekírù

inflate [infleit'] *vt* (tire, balloon) 膨らます fukúramasù; (price) つり上げる tsurfageù

inflation [inflei'ʃən] *n* (ECON) インフレ iﾞnfure

inflationary [inflei'ʃəne:ri:] *adj* (spiral) インフレの iﾞnfure no; (demand) インフレを引起こす iﾞnfure wò hikíokosù

inflexible [inflek'səbəl] *adj* (rule, timetable) 融通が利かない yúzū ga kikánai; (person) 譲らない yuzúranaì

inflict [inflikt'] *vt*: **to inflict something on someone** (damage, suffering) ...に...を加える ...ni ...wo kuwáerù

influence [in'flu:əns] *n* (power) 実力 jitsúryoku; (effect) 影響 eﾞkyō
♦*vt* (person, situation, choice etc) 左右する sáyū suru
under the influence of alcohol 酒に酔って saké ni yottè

influential [influ:en'tʃəl] *adj* (politician, critic) 有力な yúryoku na

influenza [influ:en'zə] *n* (MED) 流感 ryúkan

influx [in'flʌks] *n* (of refugees, funds) 流入 ryúnyū

inform [infɔ:rm'] *vt*: **to inform someone of something** (tell) ...に...を知らせる ...ni ...wo shiráserù
♦*vi*: **to inform on someone** (to police, authorities) ...を密告する ...wo mikkóku suru

informal [infɔ:r'məl] *adj* (manner, discussion, party) 寛いだ kutsúroidà; (clothes) 普段の fúdàn no; (unofficial: visit, meeting) 非公式の hikóshiki no

informality [infɔ:rmæl'iti:] *n* (of manner, party etc) 寛いだ雰囲気 kutsúroida fuﾞn-iki

informant [infɔ:r'mənt] *n* (source) 情報提供者 jōhōteikyòsha, インフォーマント iﾞnfōmaﾞnto

information [infə:rmei'ʃən] *n* 情報 jōhō
a piece of information 1つの情報 hitótsù no jōhō

information office *n* 案内所 aﾞnnaijo

informative [infɔ:r'mətiv] *adj* (report, comment) 有益な yúeki na

informer [infɔ:r'mər] *n* (also: **police informer**) 密告者 mikkókushà, スパイ supáì

infra-red [in'frəred] *adj* (rays, light) 赤外線の sekígaisen no

infrastructure [in'frəstrʌk'tʃər] *n* (of system etc) 下部構造 kabúkòzō, インフラストラクチャー iﾞnfurasutorakùchā

infrequent [infri:'kwint] *adj* (visits) 間遠な madò na; (buses) 本数の少ない hoﾞnsū nò sukúnaì

infringe [infrind3'] *vt* (law) 破る yabúrù
♦*vi*: **to infringe on** (rights) ...を侵す ...wo okású

infringement [infrind3'mənt] *n* (of law) 違反 ihán; (of rights) 侵害 shiﾞngai

infuriating [infju:r'i:eitiŋ] *adj* (habit, noise) いらいらさせる iﾞraira saséru

ingenious [ind3i:n'jəs] *adj* (idea, solution) 巧妙な kómyō na

ingenuity [ind3ənu:'iti:] *n* (cleverness, skill) 才能 saínō

ingenuous [ind3en'ju:əs] *adj* (innocent, trusting) 無邪気な mújàki na

ingot [iŋ'gət] *n* (of gold, platinum) 延べ棒 nobébō, インゴット iﾞngòtto

ingrained [ingreind'] *adj* (habit, belief) 根深い nebúkaì

ingratiate [ingrei'ʃi:eit] *vt*: **to ingratiate oneself with** ...に取入る ...ni toríiru

ingratitude [ingræt'ətu:d] *n* (of beneficiary, heir) 恩知らず oﾞnshirázu

ingredient [ingri:'di:ənt] *n* (of cake) 材料 zaíryò; (of situation) 要素 yóso

inhabit [inhæb'it] *vt* (town, country) ...に住む ...ni súmù

inhabitant [inhæb'ətənt] *n* (of town, street, house, country) 住民 júmin

inhale [inheil'] *vt* (breathe in: smoke, gas etc) 吸込む suﾞkkomu
♦*vi* (breathe in) 息を吸う íkì wo suu; (when smoking) 煙を吸込む kemúri wò

suíkomù

inherent [inhe:r'ent] *adj*: *inherent in* ...に固有の ...ni koyú no

inherit [inhe:r'it] *vt* (property, money) 相続する sōzoku suru; (characteristic) 遺伝で受継ぐ idén de ukétsugù

inheritance [inhe:r'itəns] *n* (property, money etc) 相続財産 sōzoku zaisàn; (characteristics etc) 遺伝 idén

inhibit [inhib'it] *vt* (growth: *also* PSYCH) 抑制 yokúsei

inhibited [inhib'itid] *adj* (PSYCH) 抑制の多い yokúsei no ōi

inhibition [inibi'ʃən] *n* 抑制 yokúsei

inhospitable [inha:spit'əbəl] *adj* (person) もてなしの悪い moténashi nò warui; (place, climate) 住みにくい sumínikuì

inhuman [inhju:'mən] *adj* (behavior) 残忍な zañnin na; (appearance) 非人間的な hiníngenteki na

inimitable [inim'itəbəl] *adj* (tone, style) まねのできない mané no dekinài

iniquity [inik'witi:] *n* (wickedness) 悪ákù; (injustice) 不正 fuséi

initial [iniʃ'əl] *adj* (stage, reaction) 最初の saísho no
◆*n* (letter) 頭文字 kashíramojì
◆*vt* (document) ...に頭文字で署名する ...ni kashíramojì de shoméi surù

initials [iniʃ'əlz] *npl* (of name) 頭文字 kashíramojì; (as signature) 頭文字の署名 kashíramojì no shoméi

initially [iniʃ'əli:] *adv* (at first) 最初は saísho wa; (first) まず最初に mázù saísho ni

initiate [iniʃ'i:it] *vt* (begin: talks, process) 始める hajímerù; (new member) 入会させる nyúkai saséru
to initiate someone into a secret ...に秘密を教える ...ni himítsu wò oshíerù
to initiate proceedings against someone (LAW) ...を起訴する ...wo kisó suru

initiation [iniʃi:ei'ʃən] *n* (beginning) 開始 kaíshi; (into organization etc) 入会式 nyúkaìshiki; (into secret etc) 伝授 déñju

initiative [iniʃ'i:ətiv] *n* (move) 企画 kikáku; (enterprise) 進取の気 shíñshu no kí
to take the initiative 先手を打つ señte

wð útsù

inject [indʒekt'] *vt* (drugs, poison) 注射する chúsha suru; (patient): *to inject someone with something* ...に...を注射する ...ni ...wo chúsha suru; (funds) つぎ込む tsugíkomù

injection [indʒek'ʃən] *n* (of drugs, medicine) 注射 chúsha; (of funds) つぎ込む事 tsugíkomù kotó

injunction [indʒʌŋk'ʃən] *n* (LAW) 差止め命令 sashítomemeìrei

injure [in'dʒə:r] *vt* (hurt: person, leg etc) 傷付ける kizútsukerù; (: feelings, reputation) 害する gaí surù

injured [in'dʒə:rd] *adj* (person, arm) 傷付いた kizútsuità; (feelings) 害された gaí sareà; (tone) 感情を害された kañjō wð gaí sareta

injury [in'dʒə:ri:] *n* (wound) 傷 kizú, けが kegá

injury time *n* (SPORT) 延長時間 eñchōjikàn ◇傷の手当てなどに使った分の延長時間 kizú no teàte nádò ni tsukátta buñ no eñchōjikàn

injustice [indʒʌs'tis] *n* (unfairness) 不公平 fukóhei

ink [iŋk] *n* (in pen, printing) インク íñku

inkling [iŋk'liŋ] *n* (idea, clue) 薄々と気付く事 usúusu tð kizúku kotð

inlaid [in'leid] *adj* (with gems, wood etc) ...をちりばめた ...wo chiríbametà

inland [in'lænd] *adj* (port, sea, waterway) 内陸の naíriku no
◆*adv* (travel) 内陸へ naíriku e

Inland Revenue (BRIT) *n* 国税庁 kokúzeichō

in-laws [in'lɔ:z] *npl* 義理の親せき girí nð shíñseki, 姻せき íñseki

inlet [in'let] *n* (GEO) 入江 iríe

inmate [in'meit] *n* (in prison) 受刑者 jukéisha; (in asylum) 入院患者 nyúinkañja

inn [in] *n* 旅館 ryokán

innate [ineit'] *adj* (skill, quality, characteristic) 生来の seírai no

inner [in'ə:r] *adj* (office, courtyard) 内側の uchígawa no; (calm, feelings) 内心の naíshin no

inner city *n* インナーシティー íñnāshìti ◊スラム化した都心部を指す súramuka shita toshíñbu wo sásù

inner tube *n* (of tire) チューブ chúbu

inning [in'iŋ] *n* (BASEBALL) イニング íníngu

innings [in'iŋz] *n* (CRICKET) イニング íníngu

innocence [in'əsəns] *n* (LAW) 無罪 múzài; (naivety: of child, person) 純真さ juñshínsa

innocent [in'əsənt] *adj* (not guilty: of crime etc) 無罪の múzài no, 潔白な keppáku na; (naive: child, person) 純真な juñshin na; (not involved: victim) 罪のない tsúmì no náì; (remark, question) 無邪気な mújàki na

innocuous [inɑ:k'ju:əs] *adj* (harmless) 無害の múgai no

innovation [inəvei'ʃən] *n* (change) 刷新 sasshín

innuendo [inju:en'dou] (*pl* **innuendoes**) *n* (insinuation) 当てこすり atékosuri

innumerable [inu:'mə:rəbəl] *adj* (countless) 無数の musû no

inoculation [inɑ:kjəlei'ʃən] *n* (MED) 接種 sesshú

inopportune [inɑ:pə:rtu:n'] *adj* (event, moment) 都合の悪い tsugó no warúi

inordinately [inɔ:r'dənitli:] *adv* (proud, long, large etc) 極度に kyokúdò ni

in-patient [in'peiʃənt] *n* (in hospital) 入院患者 nyúinkañja

input [in'put] *n* (information) 情報 jóhō; (resources etc) つぎ込む事 tsugíkomù kotó; (COMPUT) 入力 nyúryoku, インプット íñputtò

inquest [in'kwest] *n* (on someone's death) 検死審問 keñshishimòn

inquire [inkwaiə:r'] *vi* (ask) 尋ねる tazúnerù, 聞く kíkù
♦*vt* (ask) ...に尋ねる ...ni tazúnerù, ...に聞く ...ni kíkù
  to inquire about (person, fact) ...について問い合せする ...ni tsúìte toíawase surù

inquire into *vt fus* (death, circumstances) 調べる shirábèrù

inquiry [inkwaiə:r'i:] *n* (question) 質問 shitsúmon; (investigation) 調査 chósa

inquiry office (*BRIT*) *n* 案内所 añnaijò

inquisitive [inkwiz'ətiv] *adj* (curious) せん索好きな señsakuzuki na

inroads [in'roudz] *npl*: *to make inroads into* (savings, supplies) ...を消費する ...wo shóhi suru

ins *abbr* = **inches**

insane [insein'] *adj* (foolish, crazy) 気違い染みた kichígaijimità; (MED) 狂気の kyóki no

insanity [insæn'iti:] *n* (foolishness) 狂気のさた kyóki nò satá; (MED) 狂気 kyóki

insatiable [insei'ʃəbəl] *adj* (greed, appetite) 飽く事のない akú kotò no nái

inscription [inskrip'ʃən] *n* (on gravestone, memorial etc) 碑文 hibún; (in book) 献呈の言葉 keñtei no kotóba

inscrutable [inskru:'təbəl] *adj* (comment, expression) 不可解な fukákài na

insect [in'sekt] *n* 虫 mushi, 昆虫 koñchū

insecticide [insek'tisaid] *n* 殺虫剤 satchúzai

insecure [insikju:r'] *adj* (structure, lock, door: weak) 弱い yówài; (: unsafe) 安全でない añzen de naì; (person) 自信のない jishín no naì

insecurity [insikju:r'iti:] *n* (of structure, lock etc: weakness) 弱さ yówàsa; (: lack of safety) 安全でない事 añzen de naì kotó; (of person) 自信欠如 jishínketsujò

insemination [inseminei'ʃən] *n*: *artificial insemination* (AGR, MED) 人工授精 jiñkōjùsei

insensible [insen'səbəl] *adj* (unconscious) 意識を失った íshìki wo ushínattà

insensitive [insen'sətiv] *adj* (uncaring, indifferent) 思いやりのない omóiyarì no náì

inseparable [insep'ə:rəbəl] *adj* (ideas, elements) 分離できない buñri dekinài; (friends) いつも一緒の ítsùmo isshó no

insert [insə:rt'] *vt* (between two things) ...の間に入れる ...no áìda ni irérù; (into something) 差込む sashíkomù, 挿入する sóñyū suru

insertion [insə:r'ʃən] *n* (of needle, comment, peg etc) 差込む事 sashíkomù kotó, 挿入 sóñyū

in-service [in'sər'vis] *adj* (training, course) 現職の geńshoku no

inshore [in'ʃɔːr] *adj* (fishing, waters) 近海の kiǹkai no
♦*adv* (be) 岸の近くに kishí no chikakù ni; (move) 岸の近くへ kishí no chikakù e

inside [in'saíd] *n* (interior) 中 nákà, 内側 uchígawa
♦*adj* (interior) 中〔内側〕nákà〔uchigawa〕no
♦*adv* (go) 中〔内側〕へ nákà〔uchigawa〕e; (be) 中〔内側〕に nákà〔uchigawa〕ni
♦*prep* (of location) ...の中へ〔に〕...no nákà e〔ni〕; (of time): *inside 10 minutes* 10分以内に juppún inài ni

inside forward *n* (SPORT) インサイドフォワード iǹsaidofowàdo

inside information *n* 内部情報 naíbujōhò

inside lane *n* (AUT) 内側車線 uchígawashaseǹ

inside out *adv* (be, turn) 裏返しで urágaèshi de; (know) すっかり sukkárì

insides [in'saidz] *npl* (*inf*: stomach) おなか onáka

insidious [insid'i:əs] *adj* (effect, power) 潜行的な seńkōteki na

insight [in'sait] *n* (into situation, problem) 洞察 dōsatsu

insignia [insig'ni:ə] *npl* 記章 kishō

insignificant [insignif'ikənt] *adj* (extent, importance) ささいな sasái na

insincere [insinsi:r'] *adj* (smile, welcome) 偽りの itsúwari no

insinuate [insin'ju:eit] *vt* (imply) 当てこする atékosurù

insipid [insip'id] *adj* (person, activity, color) 面白くない omóshirokunài; (food, drink) 風味のない fūmi no nái

insist [insist'] *vi* (maintain) 主張する shuchō suru, 言い張る iíharù
to insist on (demand) ...を要求する ...wo yōkyū suru
to insist that (demand) ...する様要求する ...surú yō yōkyū suru; (claim) ...だと言い張る ...da to iíharù

insistence [insis'təns] *n* (determination) 強要 kyōyō

insistent [insis'tənt] *adj* (determined: person) しつこい shitsúkoì; (continual: noise, action) 絶間ない taémanaì

insole [in'soul] *n* (of shoe) 敷皮 shikíkawa

insolence [in'sələns] *n* (rudeness) 横柄さ ōheisa

insolent [in'sələnt] *adj* (attitude, remark) 横柄な ōhei na

insoluble [insɑ:l'jəbəl] *adj* (problem) 解決のできない kaíketsu nō dekínaì

insolvent [insɑ:l'vənt] *adj* (bankrupt) 破産した hasán shita

insomnia [insɑ:m'ni:ə] *n* 不眠症 fumíňshō

inspect [inspekt'] *vt* (examine: gen) 調べる shiráberù; (premises) 捜査する sōsa suru; (equipment) 点検する teńken suru; (troops) 査閲する saétsu suru; (*BRIT*: ticket) 改札する kaísatsu suru

inspection [inspek'ʃən] *n* (examination: gen) 検査 keńsa; (of premises) 捜査 sōsa; (of equipment) 点検 teńken; (of troops) 査閲 saétsu; (*BRIT*: of ticket) 改札 kaísatsu

inspector [inspek'tə:r] *n* (ADMIN) 検査官 keńsakàn; (*BRIT*: on buses, trains) 車掌 shashō; (: POLICE) 警部 keibu

inspiration [inspərei'ʃən] *n* (encouragement) 発憤 happún; (influence, source) 発憤させる物 happún saserù mono; (idea) 霊感 reíkan, インスピレーション iǹsupirēshon

inspire [inspaiə:r'] *vt* (workers, troops) 奮い立たせる furúitataserù; (confidence, hope etc) 持たせる motáserù

instability [instəbil'əti:] *n* (of place, person, situation) 不安定 fuáńtei

install [instɔ:l'] *vt* (machine) 取付ける torítsukerù; (official) 就任させる shūnin saserù

installation [instəlei'ʃən] *n* (of machine, equipment) 取付け torítsuke, 設置 sétchi; (plant: INDUSTRY) 工場施設 kōjōshisètsu, プラント puráǹto; (: MIL) 基地 kichí

installment [instɔ:l'mənt] (*BRIT* **instalment**) *n* (of payment, story, TV

serial etc) 1回分 ikkáìbun
in installments (pay, receive) 分割払い
で buñkatsubarài de
instance [in'stəns] *n* (example) 例 réì
for instance 例えば tatóèba
in the first instance まず最初に mázù
saìsho ni
instant [in'stənt] *n* (moment) 瞬間 shuñ-
kan
♦*adj* (reaction, success) 瞬間的な shuñ-
kanteki na; (coffee, food) 即席の sokúseki no, インスタントの íñsutanto no
instantaneous [instəntei'ni:əs] *adj*
(immediate) 即時の sokúji no
instantly [in'stəntli:] *adv* (immediately)
即時に sokúji ni
instead [insted'] *adv* (in place of) (そ
の) 代りに (sonó) kawári ni
instead of ...の代りに ...no kawári ni
instep [in'step] *n* (of foot) 足の甲 ashí no
kő; (of shoe) 靴の甲 kutsú no kő
instigate [in'stəgeit] *vt* (rebellion etc) 起
させる okősaserù; (talks etc) 始めさせる
hajímesaserù
instil(l) [instil'] *vt*: *to instil something
into* (confidence, fear etc) ...を...に吹込
む ...wo ...ni fukíkomù
instinct [in'stiŋkt] *n* 本能 hoñnő
instinctive [instiŋk'tiv] *adj* (reaction,
feeling) 本能的な hoñnőteki na
institute [in'stitu:t] *n* (for research,
teaching) 施設 shisétsu; (professional
body: of architects, planners etc) 協会
kyőkai
♦*vt* (system, rule, course of action) 設け
る mőkerù; (proceedings, inquiry) 始める
hajímerù
institution [institu:'ʃən] *n* (of system
etc) 開設 kaísetsu; (custom, tradition) 伝
統 deñtő; (organization: financial, religious, educational) 協会 kyőkai; (hospital, mental home) 施設 shisétsu
instruct [instrʌkt'] *vt*: *to instruct
someone in something* (teach) ...に...を
教える ...ni ...wo oshíerù
to instruct someone to do something
(order) ...する様...に命令する ...surú yő
...ni meírei suru

instruction [instrʌk'ʃən] *n* (teaching) 教
育 kyőiku
instructions [instrʌk'ʃənz] *npl* (orders)
命令 meírei
instructions (for use) 取扱い説明 toríatsukai setsúmei
instructive [instrʌk'tiv] *adj* (lesson,
response) 有益な yűeki na
instructor [instrʌk'tə:r] *n* (teacher) 先
生 señsei; (for skiing, driving etc) 指導者
shidőshà
instrument [in'strəmənt] *n* (tool) 道具
dőgu; (measuring device etc) 計器 keíki;
(MUS) 楽器 gakkí
instrumental [instrəmen'təl] *adj* (MUS)
器楽の kígaku no
to be instrumental in ...に大きな役割
を果す ...ni őkina yakúwari wo hatasù
instrument panel *n* 計器盤 keíkiban
insubordination [insəbɔːrdənei'ʃən] *n*
(disobedience) 不服従 fufúkujù
insufferable [insʌf'ə:rəbəl] *adj* (arrogance, laziness) 耐えがたい taégataì;
(person) 我慢のならない gámàn no naránaì
insufficient [insəfiʃ'ənt] *adj* (funds,
data, research) 不十分な fujűbun na
insular [in'sələ:r] *adj* (outlook, person)
狭量な kyőryo na
insulate [in'səleit] *vt* (protect: person,
group) 孤立させる korítsu saserù;
(against cold: house, body) 断熱する daň-
netsu suru; (against sound) 防音にする
bőon ni suru; (against electricity) 絶縁す
る zetsúen suru
insulating tape [in'səleitiŋ-] *n* (ELEC)
絶縁テープ zetsúeñtèpu
insulation [insəlei'ʃən] *n* (of person,
group) 孤立させる事 korítsu saserù ko-
tő; (against cold) 断熱材 daňnetsuzài;
(against sound) 防音材 bőonzài; (against
electricity) 絶縁材 zetsúenzài
insulin [in'səlin] *n* (MED) インシュリン iñ-
shurin
insult [*n* in'sʌlt *vb* insʌlt'] *n* (offence) 侮
辱 bujóku
♦*vt* (offend) 侮辱する bujóku suru
insulting [insʌl'tiŋ] *adj* (attitude, lan-

guage) 侮辱的な bujókuteki na

insuperable [insuː'pəːrəbəl] *adj* (obstacle, problem) 乗越えられない noríkoerarenaì

insurance [inʃə:r'əns] *n* (on property, car, life etc) 保険 hokén

fire/life insurance 火災〔生命〕保険 kasái〔seímei〕hokén

insurance agent *n* 保険代理店 hokéndairitèn

insurance policy *n* 保険証書 hokénshòsho

insure [inʃu:r'] *vt* (life, property): *to insure (against)* ...に (...の) 保険を掛ける ...ni (...no) hokén wò kakérù

to insure (oneself) against (disappointment, disaster) ...に備える ...ni sonáerù

insurrection [insərek'ʃən] *n* (uprising) 反乱 hañran

intact [intækt'] *adj* (whole) 元のままの mótò no mamá no; (unharmed) 無傷の múkìzu no

intake [in'teik] *n* (gen) 取込み toríkomi; (of food etc) 摂取 sésshù; (of air) 吸入 kyúnyù; (BRIT: SCOL): *an intake of 200 a year* 毎年の新入生は200人 maítoshi nò shíñnyùsei wa nihyákunìn

intangible [intæn'dʒəbəl] *adj* (quality, idea, benefit) ばく然とした bakúzen to shita

integral [in'təgrəl] *adj* (feature, element) 不可欠な fukáketsu na

integrate [in'təgreit] *vt* (newcomer) 溶け込ませる tokékomaserù; (ideas, systems) 取入れる toríirerù

♦*vi* (groups, individuals) 溶け込む tokékomù

integrity [integ'riti:] *n* (morality: of person) 誠実さ seíjitsusa

intellect [in'təlekt] *n* (intelligence) 知性 chiséi; (cleverness) 知能 chinō

intellectual [intələk'tʃuːəl] *adj* (activity, interest, pursuit) 知的な chitéki na

♦*adj* (intelligent person) 知識人 chishíkijìn, インテリ iñteri

intelligence [intel'idʒəns] *n* (cleverness, thinking power) 知能 chinō; (MIL etc) 情報 jōhō

intelligence service *n* 情報部 jōhōbu

intelligent [intel'idʒənt] *adj* (person) 知能の高い chinō no takaì; (decision) 利口な rikó na; (machine) インテリジェントの iñterijeñto no

intelligentsia [intelidʒen'tsi:ə] *n* 知識階級 chishíkikaìkyū, インテリ階級 iñterikaìkyū

intelligible [intel'idʒəbəl] *adj* (clear, comprehensible) 分かりやすい wakáriyasuì

intend [intend'] *vt* (gift etc): *to intend something for* ...を...に上げようと思っている ...wo ...ni agéyò to omótte irù

to intend to do something (mean) ...する決心でいる ...suru kesshíñ de irú; (plan) ...するつもりである ...suru tsumóri de arù

intended [inten'did] *adj* (effect, insult) 意図した ítò shita; (journey) 計画した keíkaku shita; (victim) ねらった nerátta

intense [intens'] *adj* (heat, effort, anger, joy) 猛烈な mõretsu na; (person) 情熱的な jōnetsuteki na

intensely [intens'li:] *adv* (extremely) 激しく hagéshikù

intensify [inten'səfai] *vt* (efforts, pressure) 増す mású

intensity [inten'siti:] *n* (of heat, anger, effort) 激しさ hagéshisa

intensive [inten'siv] *adj* (concentrated) 集中的な shūchūteki na

intensive care unit *n* (MED) 集中治療室 shūchūchiryōshitsu, ICU aishīyū

intent [intent'] *n* (intention) 意図 ítò; (LAW) 犯意 hán-i

♦*adj* (absorbed): *intent (on)* (...しようとして) 余念がない (...shíyò to shite) yonén ga naì; (attentive) 夢中な muchū na

to all intents and purposes 事実上 jijítsujò

to be intent on doing something (determined) ...しようとして余念がない ...shíyò to shite yonén ga naì

intention [inten'tʃən] *n* (purpose) 目的 mokúteki; (plan) 意図 ítò

intentional [inten't∫ənəl] *adj* (deliberate) 意図的な ítòteki na

intentionally [inten't∫ənəli:] *adv* (deliberately) 意図的に ítòteki ni, わざと wázà to

intently [intent'li:] *adv* (listen, watch) 熱心に nesshín ni

inter [intəːr'] *vt* (bury) 埋葬する maísō suru

interact [intəːrækt'] *vi*: **to interact (with)** (people, things, ideas) (...と) 相互に反応し合う (...to) sōgo ni hañnō shiaù

interaction [intəːræk'∫ən] *n* 相互反応 sōgohañnō

intercede [intəːrsiːd'] *vi*: **to intercede (with)** (...に) 取りなしをする (...ni) torínashi wo surù

intercept [in'təːrsept] *vt* (person, car) 途中で捕まえる tochū de tsukamaerù; (message) 傍受する bōju suru

interchange [in'təːrt∫eindʒ] *n* (exchange) 交換 kōkan; (on motorway) インターチェンジ íntāchieñji

interchangeable [intəːrt∫ein'dʒəbəl] *adj* (terms, ideas, things) 置換えられる okíkaerarerù

intercom [in'təːrkɑːm] *n* (in office etc) インターホーン íntāhōn

intercourse [in'təːrkɔːrs] *n* (*also*: **sexual intercourse**) 性交 seíkō

interest [in'trist] *n* (in subject, idea, person etc) 興味 kyōmi; (pastime, hobby) 趣味 shúmì; (advantage, profit) 利益 ríèki; (COMM: in company) 株 kábù; (: sum of money) 利息 risòku
♦*vt* (subj: work, subject, idea etc) ...の興味をそそる ...no kyōmi wo sosórù
to be interested in ...に興味がある ...ni kyōmi ga árù

interesting [in'tristiŋ] *adj* (idea, place, person) 面白い omóshiroì

interest rate *n* 利率 rirítsu

interface [in'təːrfeis] *n* (COMPUT) インターフェース íntāfèsu

interfere [intəːrfiːr'] *vi*: **to interfere in** (quarrel, other people's business) ...に干渉する ...ni kañshō suru
to interfere with (object) ...をいじる

...wo ijírù; (plans, career, duty, decision) ...を邪魔する ...wo jamá suru

interference [intəːrfiːr'əns] *n* (in someone's affairs etc) 干渉 kañshō; (RADIO, TV) 混信 koñshin

interim [in'təːrim] *adj* (agreement, government) 暫定的な zañteiteki na
♦*n*: **in the interim** (meanwhile) その間 sonó aìda

interior [intiːr'iːəːr] *n* (of building, car, box etc) 内部 náìbu; (of country) 内陸 naíriku
♦*adj* (door, window, room etc) 内部の náìbu no; (minister, department) 内務の náìmu no

interior designer *n* インテリアデザイナー íñteriadezaìnā

interjection [intəːrdʒek'∫ən] *n* (interruption) 野次 yájì; (LING) 感嘆詞 kañtañshi

interlock [in'təːrlɑːk] *vi* かみ合う kamíaù

interloper [intəːrlou'pəːr] *n* (in town, meeting etc) ちん入者 chíñnyūsha

interlude [in'təːrluːd] *n* (break) 休憩 kyūkei; (THEATER) 休憩時間 kyūkeijikàn

intermarry [intəːrmæːr'iː] *vi* 交婚する kōkon suru

intermediary [intəːrmiː'diːeːriː] *n* 仲介者 chūkaìsha

intermediate [intəːrmiː'diːit] *adj* (stage, student) 中間の chūkan no

interminable [intəːr'mənəbəl] *adj* (process, delay) 果てし無い hatéshinaì

intermission [intəːrmi∫'ən] *n* (pause) 休止 kyūshi; (THEATER, CINEMA) 休憩時間 kyūkeijikàn

intermittent [intəːrmit'ənt] *adj* (noise, publication etc) 断続的な dañzokuteki na

intern [in'təːrn] *vt* (imprison) 拘置する kōchi suru
♦*n* (*US*: houseman) 研修医 keñshūì

internal [intəːr'nəl] *adj* (layout, structure, memo etc) 内部の náìbu no; (pipes etc) 埋め込みの umékomi no; (bleeding, injury) 体内の taínai no; (security, politics) 国内の kokúnài no

internally [intə:r'nəli:] *adv*: 「*not to be taken internally*」 内服外用薬 naífukugaiyŏyaku

Internal Revenue Service (*US*) *n* 国税庁 kokúzeichŏ

international [intə:rnæʃ'ənəl] *adj* (trade, agreement etc) 国際的な kokúsaiteki na, 国際... kokúsai...
♦*n* (*BRIT*: SPORT: match) 国際試合 kokúsaijiài

interplay [in'tə:rplei] *n*: *interplay (of/ between)* (...の) 相互反応 (...no) sŏgohañnō

interpret [intə:r'prit] *vt* (explain, understand) 解釈する kaíshaku suru; (translate) 通訳する tsŭyaku suru
♦*vi* (translate) 通訳する tsŭyaku suru

interpretation [intə:rpritei'ʃən] *n* (explanation) 解釈 kaíshaku; (translation) 通訳 tsŭyaku

interpreter [intə:r'pritə:r] *n* (translator) 通訳（者）tsŭyaku(sha)

interrelated [intə:rilei'tid] *adj* (causes, factors etc) 相互関係のある sŏgokankèi no aru

interrogate [inter'r'əgeit] *vt* (question: witness, prisoner, suspect) 尋問する jiñmon suru

interrogation [intə:rəgei'ʃən] *n* (of witness, prisoner etc) 尋問 jiñmon

interrogative [intərɑ:g'ətiv] *adj* (LING) 疑問の gímòn no

interrupt [intərʌpt'] *vt* (speaker) ...の話に割込む ...no hanáshi nì waríkomù; (activity) 邪魔する jamá suru
♦*vi* (during someone's conversation etc) 話に割込む hanáshi ni waríkomù; (during activity) 邪魔する jamá suru

interruption [intərʌp'ʃən] *n* (act) 邪魔する事 jamá suru kotò; (instance) 邪魔 jamá

intersect [intə:rsekt'] *vi* (roads) 交差する kŏsa suru

intersection [intə:rsek'ʃən] *n* (of roads) 交差点 kŏsatèn

intersperse [intə:rspə:rs'] *vt*: *to intersperse with* ...を所々に入れる ...wo tokŏrodokòro ni irérù

intertwine [intə:rtwain'] *vi* 絡み合う karámiaù

interval [in'tə:rvəl] *n* (break, pause) 間隔 kañkaku; (*BRIT*: SCOL: *also* THEATER, SPORT) 休憩時間 kyŭkeijikàn
at intervals (periodically) 時々 tokídoki

intervene [intə:rvi:n'] *vi* (person: in situation: interfere) 介入する kaínyu suru; (: : to help) 仲裁に入る chŭsai ni hairù; (: in speech) 割込む waríkomù; (event) 間に起る aída ni okorù; (time) 経つ tátsù

intervention [intə:rven'tʃən] *n* (of person: interference) 介入 kaínyū; (help) 仲裁 chŭsai

interview [in'tə:rvju:] *n* (for job etc) 面接 meñsetsu; (RADIO, TV etc) インタビュー íñtabyū
♦*vt* (for job etc) ...と面接する ...to meñsetsu suru; (RADIO, TV etc) ...にインタビューする ...ni íñtabyū suru

interviewer [in'tə:rvju:ə:r] *n* (of candidate, job applicant) 面接者 meñsetsushà; (RADIO, TV etc) インタビューア íñtabyùa

intestine [intes'tin] *n* 腸 chŏ

intimacy [in'təməsi:] *n* (closeness) 親しみ shitáshimi

intimate [*adj* in'təmit *vb* in'təmeit] *adj* (friendship, relationship) 親しい shitáshiì; (detail) 知られざる shirárezarù; (restaurant, dinner, atmosphere) こじんまりした kojínmarì shita; (knowledge) 詳しい kuwáshiì
♦*vt* (announce) ほのめかす honōmekasù

intimidate [intim'ideit] *vt* (frighten) 脅す odósu

intimidation [intimidei'ʃən] *n* 脅し odóshi

KEYWORD

---

into [in'tu:] *prep* **1** (indicating motion or direction) ...の中に〔へ〕 ...no nákà ni〔e〕
come into the house/garden 家〔庭〕に入って来て下さい ié(niwá)nì háitte kitè kudasaì
go into town 町に出掛ける machí ni dekakerù

he got into the car 彼は車に乗った kárè wa kurúma ni nottà

throw it into the fire 火の中へ捨てて下さい hí no nakà e sutéte kudasaì

research into cancer がんの研究 gáñ no keñkyū

he worked late into the night 彼は夜遅くまで働いた kárè wa yórù osóku madè határaìta

the car bumped into the wall 車は塀にぶつかった kurúma wà heí nì butsúkattà

she poured tea into the cup 彼女は紅茶をカップについだ kánòjo wa kőcha wò káppù ni tsuídà

2 (indicating change of condition, result): *she burst into tears* 彼女は急に泣き出した kánòjo wa kyū nì nakídashìta

he was shocked into silence 彼はショックで物も言えなかった kárè wa shőkkù de monő mò iénakattà

it broke into pieces ばらばらに割れたbarábara nì waréta

she translated into French 彼女はフランス語に訳した kánòjo wa furánsugo nì yakúshìta

they got into trouble 彼らは問題を起した kárèra wa moñdai wò okóshita

intolerable [intɑːˈləˈrəbəl] *adj* (extent, quality) 我慢できない gámàn dekínaì

intolerance [intɑːˈlərəns] *n* (bigotry, prejudice) 偏狭さ heñkyōsa

intolerant [intɑːˈlərənt] *adj*: *intolerant (of)* (...に対して) 偏狭な (...ni táìshite) heñkyō na

intonation [intouneiˈʃən] *n* (of voice, speech) 抑揚 yokúyō, イントネーション iñtonēshon

intoxicated [intɑːˈksikeitid] *adj* (drunk) 酔っ払った yoppárattà

intoxication [intɑːksikeiˈʃən] *n* 泥酔 deísui

intractable [intrækˈtəbəl] *adj* (child, problem) 手に負えない té ni oenài

intransigent [intrænˈsidʒənt] *adj* (attitude) 頑固な gañko na

intransitive [intrænˈsətiv] *adj* (LING): *intransitive verb* 自動詞 jidőshì

intravenous [intrəviːˈnəs] *adj* (injection, drip) 静脈内の jőmyakunài no

in-tray [inˈtrei] *n* (in office) 着信のトレー chakúshin nò torế

intrepid [intrepˈid] *adj* (adventurer, explorer) 勇敢な yūkan na

intricate [inˈtrəkit] *adj* (pattern, design) 複雑な fukúzatsu na

intrigue [intriːˈgʔ] *n* (plotting) 策略 sakúryàku

♦*vt* (fascinate) ...の好奇心をそそる ...no kőkishin wò sosórù

intriguing [intriːˈgiŋ] *adj* (fascinating) 面白い omóshiroì

intrinsic [intrinˈsik] *adj* (quality, nature) 本質的な hoñshitsuteki na

introduce [intrəduːˈs] *vt* (new idea, measure etc) 導入する dőnyū suru; (speaker, TV show etc) 紹介する shőkai suru

to introduce someone (to someone) (...に) ...を紹介する (...ni) ...wo shőkai suru

to introduce someone to (pastime, technique) ...に...を初めて経験させる ...ni ...wo hajímète keíken saserù

introduction [intrədʌkˈʃən] *n* (of new idea, measure etc) 導入 dőnyū; (of person) 紹介 shőkai; (to new experience) 初めて経験させる事 hajímète keíken saserù kotő; (to book) 前書 maégaki

introductory [intrədʌkˈtəriː] *adj* (lesson) 導入の dőnyū no; (offer) 初回の shokái no

introspective [intrəspekˈtiv] *adj* (person, mood) 内省的な naíseiteki na

introvert [inˈtrəvəːrt] *n* 内向性の人 naíkōsei no hitő

♦*adj* (also: **introverted**: behavior, child etc) 内向性の naíkōsei no

intrude [intruːˈd] *vi* (person) 邪魔する jamá suru

to intrude on (conversation, grief, party etc) ...のところを邪魔する ...no tokőro wò jamá suru

intruder [intruːˈdəːr] *n* (into home, camp) 侵入者 shiñnyūshà

intrusion [intru:'ʒən] *n* (of person, outside influences) 邪魔 jamá

intuition [intu:iʃ'ən] *n* (feeling, hunch) 直感 chokkán

intuitive [intu:'ətiv] *adj* (instinctive) 直感的な chokkánteki na

inundate [invʌd'] *vt*: *to inundate with* (calls, letters etc) ...が殺到する ...ga sattő suru

invade [inveid'] *vt* (MIL) ...を侵略する ...wo shińryaku suru

invalid [*n* in'vəlid *adj* invæ'lid] *n* (MED: disabled person) 身障者 shińshōsha; (: sick and weak person) 病弱な人 byőjaku na hitő

◆*adj* (not valid) 無効の mukő no

invaluable [invæl'ju:əbəl] *adj* (person, thing) 貴重な kichő na

invariable [inve:r'i:əbəl] *adj* 変らない kawáranaî, 不変の fuhén no

invariably [inve:r'i:əbli:] *adv* 必ず kanárazù

invasion [invei'ʒən] *n* (MIL) 侵略 shińryaku

invent [invent'] *vt* (machine, game, phrase etc) 発明する hatsúmei suru; (fabricate: lie, excuse) でっち上げる detchiagerù

invention [inven'tʃən] *n* (machine, system) 発明品 hatsúmeihin; (untrue story) 作り話 tsukúribanàshi; (act of inventing: machine, system) 発明 hatsúmei

inventor [inven'tər] *n* (of machines, systems) 発明家 hatsúmeika

inventory [in'vəntɔ:ri:] *n* (of house, ship etc) 物品目録 buppínmokùroku

inverse [invə:rs'] *adj* (relationship) 逆の gyakú no

invert [invə:rt'] *vt* (turn upside down) 逆さにする sakása ni surù

invertebrate [invə:r'təbrit] *n* 無せきつい動物 musékitsuidōbutsu

inverted commas [invə:r'tid-] (*BRIT*) *npl* 引用符 ińyōfù

invest [invest'] *vt* (money) 投資する tőshi suru; (*fig*: time, energy) つぎ込む tsugíkomù

◆*vi*: *invest in* (COMM) ...に投資する

...ni tőshi suru; (*fig*: something useful) 購入する kőnyū suru

investigate [inves'təgeit] *vt* (accident, crime, person) 取調べる toríshiraberù, 捜査する sősa suru

investigation [inves'təgeiʃən] *n* 取調べ toríshirabe, 捜査 sősa

investigator [inves'təgeitər] *n* (of events, situations, people) 捜査官 sősakàn

investiture [inves'tit'ər] *n* (of chancellor) 就任式 shűniñshiki; (of prince) たい冠式 taíkañshiki

investment [invest'mənt] *n* (activity) 投資 tőshi; (amount of money) 投資額 tőshigàku

investor [inves'tər] *n* (COMM) 投資者 tőshishà

inveterate [invet'ə:rit] *adj* (liar, cheat etc) 常習的な jőshūteki na

invidious [invid'i:əs] *adj* (task, job: unpleasant) 憎まれ役の nikúmareyàku no; (comparison, decision: unfair) 不公平な fukőhei na

invigilator [invidʒ'əleitər] (*BRIT*) *n* (in exam) 試験監督 shikénkañtoku

invigorating [invig'ə:reitiŋ] *adj* (air, breeze etc) さわやかな sawáyàka na; (experience etc) 元気が出る様な geńki ga deru yő na

invincible [invin'səbəl] *adj* (army, team: unbeatable) 無敵の mútèki no

invisible [inviz'əbəl] *adj* 目に見えない mé ni mienài

invitation [invitei'ʃən] *n* (to party, meal, meeting etc) 招待 shőtai; (written card, paper) 招待状 shőtaîjō

invite [in'vait] *vt* (to party, meal, meeting etc) 招く manékù, 招待する shőtai suru; (encourage: discussion, criticism) 求める motőmerù

to invite someone to do ...に...するよう求める ...ni ...surú yő motőmerù

inviting [invai'tiŋ] *adj* (attractive, desirable) 魅力的な miryőkuteki na

invoice [in'vɔis] *n* (COMM) 請求書 seíkyūsho

◆*vt* ...に請求書を送る ...ni seíkyūsho wo

okúrù

invoke [invouk'] vt (law, principle) ...に 訴える ...ni uttáerù

involuntary [invɑː'lʌntəriː] adj (action, reflex etc) 反射的な hañshateki na

involve [invɑːlv'] vt (person, thing: include, use) 伴う tomónaù, 必要とする hitsúyō to surù; (: concern, affect) ...に関 係する ...ni kañkei suru
to involve someone (in something) (...に) ...を巻込む (...ni) ...wo makíkomù

involved [invɑːlvd'] adj (complicated) 複 雑な fukúzatsu na
to be involved in (take part: in activity etc) ...にかかわる ...ni kakáwarù; (be en-grossed) ...に夢中になっている ...ni mu-chū ni nattè irú

involvement [invɑːlv'mənt] n (partici-pation) 参加 sañka; (concern, enthusi-asm) 感情的かかわり合い kañjōteki nà kakáwariaì

inward [in'wərd] adj (thought, feeling) 内心の naíshin no; (movement) 中の方へ の náka no hố e no

inward(s) [in'wərd(z)] adv (move, face) 中の方へ náka no hố e

I/O [ai/ou'] abbr (COMPUT: = input/output) 入出力 nyūshutsuryòku

iodine [ai'ədain] n (chemical element) ヨ ウ素 yốso, ヨード yốdo; (disinfectant) ヨ ードチンキ yốdochiñki

ion [ai'ən] n イオン iòn

iota [aiou'tə] n: *not one/an iota* 少しも ...ない sukóshì mo ...naī

IOU [aiouju'] n abbr (= *I owe you*) 借用 証 shakúyōshō

IQ [aikju'] n abbr (= *intelligence quo-tient*) 知能指数 chinóshisù, IQ aikyū

IRA [aiɑːrei'] n abbr (= *Irish Republi-can Army*) アイルランド共和国軍 aíru-rando kyōwakakugùn

Iran [iræn'] n イラン irán

Iranian [irei'niːən] adj イランの irán no
◆n イラン人 iránjìn

Iraq [iræk'] n イラク íràku

Iraqi [irɑːk'iː] adj イラクの íràku no
◆n イラク人 irákujìn

irascible [iræs'əbəl] adj 怒りっぽい okó-

rippoì

irate [aireit'] adj 怒っている okótte irú

Ireland [aiə'r'lənd] n アイルランド aíru-rando

iris [ai'ris] (pl **irises**) n (ANAT) こう彩 kōsai; (BOT) アヤメ ayáme, アイリス aí-risu

Irish [ai'riʃ] adj アイルランドの aíruràn-do no
◆npl: *the Irish* アイルランド人 aíruran-dojìn ◇総称 sōshō

Irishman/woman [ai'riʃmən/wumən] (pl **Irishmen/women**) n アイルランド人 男性〔女性〕aírurandojìn dañsei〔joséi〕

Irish Sea n: *the Irish Sea* アイリッシ ュ海 aírisshukài

irksome [ə:rk'səm] adj いらいらさせる í-raira saséru

iron [ai'ə:rn] n (metal) 鉄 tetsú; (for clothes) アイロン aíron
◆cpd (bar, railings) 鉄の tetsú no; (will, discipline etc) 鉄の様な tetsú no yố na
◆vt (clothes) ...にアイロンを掛ける ...ni aíron wò kakérù

Iron Curtain n: *the Iron Curtain* 鉄 のカーテン tetsú no kấten

ironic(al) [airɑːn'ik(əl)] adj (remark, gesture, situation) 皮肉な híniku na

ironing [ai'ə:rniŋ] n (activity) アイロン 掛け aíronkake; (clothes) アイロンを掛 けるべき衣類 aíron wố kakérubeki irùi

ironing board n アイロン台 aírondai

ironmonger [ai'ə:rnmʌŋgəːr] (BRIT) n 金物屋 kanámonoya ◇人を指す hitó wð sásù

ironmonger's (shop) [ai'ə:rnmʌŋgəːrz-] n 金物屋 kanámono-ya ◇店を指す misé wò sásù

iron out vt (fig: problems) 打開する da-kái suru

irony [ai'rəniː] n 皮肉 híniku

irrational [iræʃ'ənəl] adj (feelings, behavior) 不合理な fugốri na

irreconcilable [irek'ənsailəbəl] adj (ideas, views) 両立しない ryōritsu shina-ì; (disagreement) 調和不可能な chốwafu-kanð na

irrefutable [irifjuː'təbəl] adj (fact) 否め

られない inámerarenaì; (argument) 反ば
くできない hañbaku dekinaì

irregular [ireg'jələr] adj (surface) 凸凹
の dekóboko no; (pattern, action, event
etc) 不規則な fukísoku na; (not acceptable: behavior) 良くない yókunai; (verb,
noun, adjective) 不規則変化の fukísoku-
heñka no

irregularity [iregjələr'iti:] n (of surface) 凸凹 dekóboko; (of pattern, action
etc) 不規則 fukísoku; (instance of behavior) 良くない行為 yókunai kôì

irrelevant [irel'əvənt] adj (fact, information) 関係のない kañkei no naì

irreparable [irep'ərəbəl] adj (harm,
damage etc) 取返しの付かない toríkae-
shi no tsukanaì

irreplaceable [iriplei'səbəl] adj 掛替え
のない kakégae no naì

irrepressible [iripres'əbəl] adj 陽気な
yôki na

irresistible [irizis'təbəl] adj (force) 抵抗
できない teíkō dekinaì; (urge, desire) 抑
えきれない osáekirenaì; (person, thing)
とても魅惑的な totémð miwákuteki na

irresolute [irez'əlu:t] adj 決断力のない
ketsúdanryòku no naì

irrespective [irispek'tiv]: **irrespective
of** prep ...と関係なく ...to kañkei nakù

irresponsible [irispɑ:n'səbəl] adj (person, action) 無責任な musékinin na

irreverent [irev'ə:rənt] adj 不敬な fukéi
na

irrevocable [irev'əkəbəl] adj (action,
decision) 変更できない heñkō dekinaì

irrigate [ir'igeit] vt (AGR) かんがいする
kañgai suru

irrigation [irigei'ʃən] n (AGR) かんがい
kañgai

irritable [ir'itəbəl] adj 怒りっぽい okó-
rippoì

irritate [ir'əteit] vt (annoy) いらいらさ
せる íraira saséru; (MED) 刺激する shigéki suru

irritating [ir'əteitiŋ] adj (person, sound
etc) いらいらさせる íraira saséru

irritation [iritei'ʃən] n (feeling of annoyance) いら立ち irádachi; (MED) 刺激 shi-

géki; (annoying thing) いら立ちの元 irádachi no motò

IRS [aiɑ:res'] (US) n abbr = **Internal
Revenue Service**

is [iz] vb see **be**

Islam [iz'lɑ:m] n イスラム教 isúramukyō

Islamic [izlɑ:m'ic] adj イスラム教の isúramukyō no

island [ai'lənd] n (GEO) 島 shimá

islander [ai'ləndə:r] n 島の住民 shimá no
júmin

isle [ail] n (GEO) 島 shimá

isn't [iz'ənt] = **is not**

isolate [ai'səleit] vt (physically, socially:
set apart) 孤立させる korítsu saséru;
(substance) 分離する buñri suru; (sick
person, animal) 隔離する kakúri suru

isolated [ai'səleitid] adj (place) へんぴな
heñpi na; (person) 孤立した korítsu shita; (incident) 単独の tañdoku no

isolation [aisəlei'ʃən] n 孤立 korítsu

isotope [ai'sətoup] n (PHYSICS) 同位体
dôitai, アイソトープ aísotôpu

Israel [iz'reiəl] n イスラエル isúraèru

Israeli [izrei'li:] adj イスラエルの isúraèru no
♦n イスラエル人 isúraerujìn

issue [iʃ'u:] n (problem, subject, most
important part) 問題 mońdai; (of newspaper, magazine etc) 号 gô; (of book) 版
hâñ; (of stamp) 発行部数 hakkôbūsu
♦vt (statement) 発表する happyô suru;
(rations, equipment, documents) 配給す
る kaíkyū suru
at issue 問題は〔の〕mońdai wa〔no〕
to take issue with someone (over)
(...について) ...と争う (...ni tsuîte) ...to
arásoù

isthmus [is'məs] n (GEO) 半島 hañtō

---

it [it] pron 1 (specific: subject) それは
〔が〕soré wà〔ga〕; (: direct object) それ
を soré wò; (: indirect object) それに soré
nî ◇通常日本語では表現しない tsūjō ni-
hongo de wa hyōgen shínaì
where's my book? - it's on the table
私の本はどこですか-テーブルにあります

watákushi no hoñ wa dókò desu ká - tébùru ni arímasù

I can't find it 見当りません miátari-maseñ

give it to me それを私に渡して下さい soré wò watákushi nî watashite kudasaî

about/from/in/of/to it それについて〔から、の中に、の、の方へ〕soré ni tsuîte〔kárà, no nákà ni, nó, no hô é〕

I spoke to him about it その件について私は彼に話しました sonó keñ ni tsúîte watákushi wà kárè ni hanáshimashìta

what did you learn from it? その事からあなたは何を学びましたか sonó kotò kara anátà wa nánî wo manábimashìta ká

what role did you play in it? その件に関してあなたはどんな役割をしましたか sonó keñ ni kárì shite anátà wa doñna yakùwari wo shimáshìta ká

I'm proud of it それを誇りに思っています soré wò hokóri nî omótte imasù

did you go to it? (party, concert etc) 行きましたか ikímashìta ká

2 (impersonal): *it's raining* 雨が降っている ámè ga futté irù

it's cold today 今日は寒い kyô wà samúî

it's Friday tomorrow 明日は金曜日です asú wà kiñ-yôbi desu

it's 6 o'clock/the 10th of August 6時〔8月10日〕です rokújî〔hachígàtsu tôkà〕desu

how far is it? - it's 10 miles/2 hours on the train そこまでどのぐらいありますか-10マイルあります〔列車で2時間です〕sokó madè donó gurai arimasù ká - júmaìru arímasù〔resshá dè nijíkàn desu〕

who is it? - it's me どなたですか-私です dónàta desu ká - watákushi desù

Italian [itæl'jən] *adj* イタリアの itária no; (LING) イタリア語の itáriago no
♦*n* (person) イタリア人 itáriajìn; (LING) イタリア語 itáriago

italics [itæl'iks] *npl* (TYP) 斜体文字 shatáimòji, イタリック体 itárikkutai

Italy [it'əli:] *n* イタリア itária

itch [itʃ] *n* (irritation) かゆみ kayúmi
♦*vi* (person) かゆがる kayúgarù; (part of body) かゆい kayúî

to itch to do something …をしたくてむずむずしている …wo shitákutè múzùmuzu shité irù

itchy [itʃ'i:] *adj* (person) かゆがっている kayúgatte irù; (skin etc) かゆい kayúî

it'd [it'əd] = **it would; it had**

item [ai'təm] *n* (one thing: of list, collection) 品目 hiñmoku; (on agenda) 項目 kômoku; (*also:* **news item**) 記事 kíjì

itemize [ai'təmaiz] *vt* (list) 明細に書く meísai ni kakù, リストアップする risúto-appù suru

itinerant [aitin'ə:rənt] *adj* (laborer, salesman, priest etc) 巡回する juñkai suru

itinerary [aitin'ə:re:ri:] *n* 旅程 ryotéi

it'll [it'əl] = **it will; it shall**

its [its] *adj* それ〔あれ〕の soré〔aré〕no

it's [its] = **it is; it has**

itself [itself'] *pron* それ〔あれ〕自身 soré〔aré〕jishìñ

ITV [ait:vi:'] *n abbr* (*BRIT:* = *Independent Television*) 民間テレビ放送 miñkan terebi hôsô

IUD [aiju:di:'] *n abbr* (= *intra-uterine device*) 子宮内避妊具 shikyúnaihininˌgu, IUD aiyúdî

I've [aiv] = **I have**

ivory [ai'və:ri:] *n* (substance) 象げ zôge; (color) アイボリー áîborî

ivory tower *n* (*fig*) 象げの塔 zôge no tô

ivy [ai'vi:] *n* (BOT) キツタ kízùta, アイビー áîbî

J

jab [dʒæb] *vt* (poke: with elbow, stick) 突く tsukú
♦*n* (*inf*: injection) 注射 chúsha

to jab something into something …を…に突っ込む …wo…ni tsukkómù

jabber [dʒæb'ə:r] *vi* (*also:* **jabber away**) ぺちゃくぺちゃしゃべる péchàkucha shabérù

jack [dʒæk] *n* (AUT) ジャッキ jákkì; (CARDS) ジャック jákkù

jackal [dʒæk'əl] *n* ジャッカル jákkàru

jackdaw [dʒæk'dɔ:] *n* コクマルガラス kokúmarugaràsu

jacket [dʒæk'it] *n* (garment) ジャケット jákètto; (of book) ジャケット jákètto, カバー kábà

potatoes in their jackets 皮ごと料理 したジャガイモ kawágòto ryōri shita jagáimo

jack-knife [dʒæk'naif] *vi* (trailer truck) ジャックナイフ現象を起す jakkúnaifu geñshō wo okósù ◇鋭角に折り曲って動 けなくなる eíkaku ni orímagatte ugokenáku nárù

jack plug *n* (ELEC: for headphones etc) プラグ purágù

jackpot [dʒæk'pɑ:t] *n* 大賞金 daíshōkin

to hit the jackpot 大賞金を当てる daíshōkin wo atérù, 大当りする óatàri suru

jack up *vt* (AUT) ジャッキで持上げる jákkì de mochíagerù

jade [dʒeid] *n* (stone) ひすい hisúi

jaded [dʒei'did] *adj* (tired) 疲れ切った tsukárekittà; (fed-up) うんざりした uñzaríshita

jagged [dʒæg'id] *adj* (outline, edge) ぎざ ぎざの gízàgiza no

jail [dʒeil] *n* 刑務所 keímusho

◆*vt* 刑務所に入れる keímusho ni irérù

jam [dʒæm] *n* (food) ジャム jámù; (also: **traffic jam**) 交通渋滞 kōtsūjūtai; (inf: difficulty): *to be in a jam* 困っている komátte irù

◆*vt* (passage etc) ふさぐ fuságù; (mechanism, drawer etc) 動けなくする ugokenáku suru; (RADIO) 妨害する bōgai suru

◆*vi* (mechanism, drawer etc) 動けなくな る ugókenàku nárù

to jam something into something (cram, stuff) ...に...を押込む ...ni...wo oshíkomù

Jamaica [dʒəmei'kə] *n* ジャマイカ jámaìka

jangle [dʒæŋ'gəl] *vi* (keys, bracelets etc) じゃらじゃら鳴る járàjara narú

janitor [dʒæn'itə:r] *n* (caretaker: of building) 管理人 kañrinin

January [dʒæn'ju:we:ri:] *n* 1月 ichígatsu

Japan [dʒəpæn'] *n* 日本 nihóñ(nippóñ)

Japanese [dʒæpəni:z'] *adj* 日本の nihóñ 〔nippóñ〕no; (LING) 日本語の nihóngo no

◆*n inv* (person) 日本人 nihóñ〔nippóñ〕jiñ; (LING) 日本語 nihóngo

jar [dʒɑ:r] *n* (container: glass with wide mouth) 瓶 bíñ; (: stone, earthenware) つ ぼ tsubó, かめ kamé

◆*vi* (sound) 耳ざわりである mimízawàri de aru, きしる kishírù; (colors) 釣合わな い tsuríawanài

jargon [dʒɑ:r'gən] *n* 専門用語 señmon-yōgo, 隠語 iñgo

jasmine [dʒæz'min] *n* ジャスミン jásùmin

jaundice [dʒɔ:n'dis] *n* (MED) 黄だん ódan

jaundiced [dʒɔ:n'dist] *adj* *to view with a jaundiced eye* 白い目で見る shiróì me de mírù

jaunt [dʒɔ:nt] *n* (trip, excursion) 遠足 eñsoku

jaunty [dʒɔ:n'ti:] *adj* (attitude, tone) 陽気 な yōki na; (step) 軽やかな karóyàka na

javelin [dʒæv'lin] *n* (SPORT) やり投げ yaʹrínage

jaw [dʒɔ:] *n* (ANAT) あご agó

jay [dʒei] *n* カケス kakésu

jaywalker [dʒei'wɔ:kə:r] *n* ◇交通規則を 無視して道路を横断する人 kōtsūkisòku wo mushí shite dōro wo ódan surù hitó

jazz [dʒæz] *n* (MUS) ジャズ jázù

jazz up *vt* (liven up: party) 活気付ける kakkízukerù; (: taste) ぴりっとさせる pi-ríttò sasérù; (: image) 派手にする hadé ni surù

jazzy [dʒæz'i:] *adj* (shirt, pattern) 派手な hadé na

jealous [dʒel'əs] *adj* (suspicious: husband etc) 嫉妬深い shittóbukài; (envious: person) うらやましい uráyamashiì, うらや ましがっている uráyamashigàtte irú; (look etc) うらやましそうな uráyamashi-sōna

jealousy [dʒel'əsi:] *n* (resentment) ねた

み netámi; (envy) うらやむ事 uráyamù kotó

jeans [dʒi:nz] *npl* (trousers) ジーパン jípaǹ

jeep [dʒi:p] *n* (AUT, MIL) ジープ jípù

jeer [dʒi:r] *vi* (mock, scoff): **to jeer (at)** 野次る yajírù

jelly [dʒel'i:] *n* (CULIN) ゼリー zérì

jellyfish [dʒel'i:fiʃ] *n* クラゲ kuráge

jeopardize [dʒep'ə:rdaiz] *vt* 危険にさらす kikén ni sarásù

jeopardy [dʒep'ə:rdi:] *n*: **to be in jeopardy** 危険にさらされる kikén ni sarásarerù

jerk [dʒə:rk] *n* (jolt, wrench) ◇急な動き kyū́ na ugóki; (*inf*: idiot) 間抜け manúke
♦*vt* (pull) ぐいと引っ張る guí to hippárù
♦*vi* (vehicle, person, muscle) 急に動く kyū́ ni ugókù

jerkin [dʒə:r'kin] *n* チョッキ chokkí

jersey [dʒə:r'zi:] *n* (pullover) セーター sétā; (fabric) ジャージ jā́jì

jest [dʒest] *n* 冗談 jōdaǹ

Jesus [dʒi:'səs] *n* イエス iésù

jet [dʒet] *n* (of gas, liquid) 噴射 funshá, ジェット jéttò; (AVIAT) ジェット機 jéttoki

jet-black [dʒet'blæk'] *adj* 真っ黒な makkúrò na

jet engine *n* ジェットエンジン jétto eǹjin

jet lag *n* 時差ぼけ jisáboke

jettison [dʒet'əsən] *vt* (fuel, cargo) 捨てる sutérù

jetty [dʒet'i:] *n* 波止場 hatóba

Jew [dʒu:] *n* ユダヤ人 yudáyajiǹ

jewel [dʒu:'əl] *n* (*also fig*) 宝石 hóseki; (in watch) 石 ishí

jeweler [dʒu:'ələ:r] (*BRIT* **jeweller**) *n* (dealer in jewelery) 宝石商 hósekishō; (dealer in watches) 時計屋 tokéiya

jeweler's [dʒu:'ələ:rz-] (*jewelery shop*) 宝石店 hósekitèn; (watch shop) 時計店 tokéitèn

jewelry [dʒu:'əlri:] (*BRIT* **jewellery**) *n* 装身具 sōshiǹgu

Jewess [dʒu:'is] *n* ユダヤ人女性 yudáyajin jòsei

Jewish [dʒu:'iʃ] *adj* ユダヤ人の yudáyajiǹ no

jibe [dʒaib] *n* 野次 yájì

jiffy [dʒif'i:] (*inf*) *n*: **in a jiffy** 直ぐ súgù

jig [dʒig] *n* (dance) ジグ jígù ◇動きの早い活発なダンス ugóki nò hayáì kappátsu na dáǹsu

jigsaw [dʒig'sɔ:] *n* (*also*: **jigsaw puzzle**) ジグソーパズル jígùsō-pazuru

jilt [dʒilt] *vt* (lover etc) 振る furú

jingle [dʒiŋ'gəl] *n* (for advert) コマーシャルソング komásharu soǹgu
♦*vi* (bells, bracelets) ちりんちりんと鳴る chírìnchirin to narú

jinx [dʒiŋks] *n* ジンクス jíǹkusu

jitters [dʒit'ə:rz] (*inf*) *npl*: **to get the jitters** びびる bibírù

job [dʒɑ:b] *n* (chore, task) 仕事 shigóto; (post, employment) 職 shokú
it's not my job (duty, function) それは私の仕事ではない soré wà watákushi nò shigóto de wa naì
it's a good job that ... (*BRIT*) ...して良かったね ...shite yókàtta né
just the job! (*BRIT*: *inf*) おあつらえ向きだ o-átsurae muki da, 丁度いい chōdo iì

job centre (*BRIT*) *n* 公共職業安定所 kókyōshokugyō anteishò

jobless [dʒɑ:b'lis] *adj* (ECON) 失業の shitsúgyō no

jockey [dʒɑ:k'i:] *n* (SPORT) 騎手 kíshù
♦*vi*: **to jockey for position** (rivals, competitors) 画策する kakúsaku suru

jocular [dʒɑ:k'jələ:r] *adj* (person, remark) ひょうきんな hyókiǹ na

jog [dʒɑ:g] *vt* (bump) 小突く kozúkù
♦*vi* (run) ジョギングする jógiǹgu suru
to jog someone's memory ...に...を思い起させる ...ni...wo omói okosaserù

jog along *vi* (person, vehicle) のんびりと進む noǹbiri to susúmù

jogging [dʒɑ:g'iŋ] *n* ジョギング jógiǹgu

join [dʒɔin] *vt* (queue) ...に加わる ...ni kuwáwarù; (party) ...に参加する ...ni saṅka suru; (club etc) ...に入会する ...ni nyūkai suru; (put together: things, places) つなぐ tsunágu; (meet: group of people) 一緒

になる isshō ni narù
♦*vi* (roads, rivers) 合流する gṓryū suru
♦*n* つなぎ目 tsunágimè

joiner [dʒɔi'nər] (*BRIT*) *n* 建具屋 tatéguya

joinery [dʒɔi'nəːri:] *n* 建具職 tatégushōku

join in *vi* 参加する sañka suru
♦*vt fus* (work, discussion etc) …に参加する …ni sañka surù

joint [dʒɔint] *n* (TECH: in woodwork, pipe) 継目 tsugíme; (ANAT) 関節 kañsetsu; (of meat) ブロック肉 búrŏkku niku; (*inf*: nightclub, pub, cheap restaurant etc) 店 misé; (: of cannabis) マリファナタバコ marífana tabakó
♦*adj* (common) 共通の kyṓtsū no; (combined) 共同の kyṓdō no

joint account *n* (at bank etc) 共同預金口座 kyṓdō yokin kōza

join up *vi* (meet) 一緒になる isshō ni narù; (MIL) 入隊する nyútai suru

joist [dʒɔist] *n* はり harí

joke [dʒouk] *n* (gag) 冗談 jṓdañ; (*also*: **practical joke**) いたずら itázura
♦*vi* 冗談を言う jṓdañ wo iú
to play a joke on …をからかう …wo karákaù

joker [dʒou'kəːr] *n* (*inf*) 冗談を言う人 jṓdañ wo iu hitṓ; (*pej*: person) 野郎 yárŏ; (cards) ジョーカー jṓkā

jolly [dʒɑl'iː] *adj* (merry) 陽気な yṓki na; (enjoyable) 楽しい tanóshiī
♦*adv* (*BRIT*: *inf*) とても totémo

jolt [dʒoult] *n* (physical) 衝撃 shṓgeki; (emotional) ショック shókkù
♦*vt* (physically) …に衝撃を与える …ni shṓgeki wǒ atáerù; (emotionally) ショックを与える shókkù wo atáerù

Jordan [dʒɔːr'dʌn] *n* ヨルダン yórùdan

jostle [dʒɑːsʼəl] *vt*: **to be jostled by the crowd** 人込みにもまれる hitógomi ni momárerù

jot [dʒɑːt] *n*: **not one jot** 少しも…ない sukóshī mo …náī

jot down *vt* (telephone number etc) 書留める kakítomerù

jotter [dʒɑːtʼəːr] (*BRIT*) *n* (notebook,

pad) ノート（ブック）nṓto(búkkù), メモ帳 memóchō

journal [dʒəːr'nəl] *n* (magazine, periodical) 雑誌 zasshí; (diary) 日記 nikkí

journalese [dʒəːrnəliːzʼ] *n* (*pej*) 大衆新聞調 taíshūshinbunchō

journalism [dʒəːr'nəlizəm] *n* ジャーナリズム jănarizùmu

journalist [dʒəːr'nəlist] *n* ジャーナリスト jănarisùto

journey [dʒəːr'niː] *n* (trip, route) 旅行 ryokṓ; (distance covered) 道のり michínori

jovial [dʒou'viːəl] *adj* (person, air) 陽気な yṓki na

joy [dʒɔi] *n* (happiness, pleasure) 喜び yorókobi

joyful [dʒɔi'fəl] *adj* (news, event) うれしい uréshiī; (look) うれしそうな uréshisō na

joyride [dʒɔi'raid] *n* (AUT: *US*) 無謀運転のドライブ mubṓuñten no doráibù; (: *BRIT*) 盗難車でのドライブ tṓnanshà de no doráibù

joystick [dʒɔi'stik] *n* (AVIAT) 操縦かん sṓjūkan; (COMPUT) 操縦レバー sṓjū rebǎ, ジョイスティック joísutikku

JP [dʒeipiːʼ] *n abbr* = **Justice of the Peace**

Jr *abbr* = **junior**

jubilant [dʒuː'bələnt] *adj* 大喜びの ṓyorokobi no

jubilee [dʒuː'bəliː] *n* (anniversary) …周年記念日 …shúnen kinènbi

judge [dʒʌdʒ] *n* (LAW) 裁判官 saíbankan; (in competition) 審査員 shiñsa-in; (*fig*: expert) 通 tsū
♦*vt* (LAW) 裁く sabákù; (competition) 審査する shiñsa suru; (person, book etc) 評価する hyṓka suru; (consider, estimate) 推定する suítei suru

judg(e)ment [dʒʌdʒ'mənt] *n* (LAW) 判決 hañketsu; (REL) 審判 shiñpan; (view, opinion) 意見 ikén; (discernment) 判断力 hañdañryoku

judicial [dʒuːdiʃʼəl] *adj* (LAW) 司法の shihṓ no

judiciary [dʒuːdiʃʼiːəːriː] *n* 司法部 shihṓ

bù

judicious [dʒuːdíʃˈəs] adj (action, decision) 分別のある funbetsu no árù

judo [dʒuːˈdou] n 柔道 júdõ

jug [dʒʌg] n 水差し mizúsashi

juggernaut [dʒʌgˈəːrnɔːt] (BRIT) n (huge truck) 大型トラック ōgata torakkù

juggle [dʒʌgˈəl] vi 品玉をする shinádama wo surù ◊幾つもの玉などを投上げて受止める曲芸 íkùtsu mo no tamá nadò wo nagéagetè ukétomerù kyokúgei

juggler [dʒʌgˈləːr] n 品玉をする曲芸師 shinádama wo suru kyokúgeishì

Jugoslav [juːˈgouslɑːv] etc = **Yugoslav** etc

juice [dʒuːs] n (of fruit, plant, meat) 汁 shírù; (beverage) ジュース júsu

juicy [dʒuːˈsiː] adj (food) 汁の多い shírù no ōi; (inf: story, details) エッチな étchì na

jukebox [dʒuːkˈbɑːks] n ジュークボックス júkùbokkusu

July [dʒuːlaiˈ] n 7月 shichí gatsu

jumble [dʒʌmˈbəl] n (muddle) ごたまぜ gotámaze
♦vt (also: **jumble up**) ごたまぜにする gotámaze ni suru

jumble sale (BRIT) n 慈善バザー jizén bazā

jumbo (jet) [dʒʌmˈbou] n ジャンボジェット機 jánbo jettókì

jump [dʒʌmp] vi (into air) 飛び上る tobíagarù; (with fear, surprise) ぎくっとする gíkùtto surù; (increase: price etc) 急上昇する kyūjōshō suru; (: population etc) 急増する kyūzō suru
♦vt (fence) 飛び越える tobíkoeru
♦n (into air etc) 飛び上る事 tobíagarù kotó; (increase: in price etc) 急上昇 kyūjōshō; (: in population etc) 急増 kyūzō
to jump the queue (BRIT) 列に割込む rétsù ni waríkomù

jumper [dʒʌmˈpəːr] n (BRIT: pullover) セーター sētā; (US: dress) ジャンパースカート janpásukāto

jumper cables npl (US) ブースターケーブル būsutākēburu ◊外のバッテリーから

電気を得るために用いるコード hoká nò báttèrī kara dénki wo érù tamé nì mochíirù kõdo

jump leads (BRIT) [-liːdz] npl = **jumper cables**

jumpy [dʒʌmˈpiː] adj (nervous) びくびくしている bíkùbiku shité írù

Jun. abbr = **junior**

junction [dʒʌŋkˈʃən] n (BRIT: of roads) 交差点 kōsatèn; (RAIL) 連絡駅 renrakueki

juncture [dʒʌŋkˈtʃəːr] n: *at this juncture* この時点で konó tokì

June [dʒuːn] n 6月 rokúgatsu

jungle [dʒʌŋˈgəl] n ジャングル jángùru; (fig) 弱肉強食の世界 jakúniku kyōshoku nò sékài

junior [dʒuːnˈjəːr] adj (younger) 年下の toshíshita no; (subordinate) 下位の kái no; (SPORT) ジュニアの jùnia no
♦n (office junior) 後輩 kōhai; (young person) 若者 wakámono
he's my junior by 2 years 彼は私より2才年下です kárè wa watákushi yorì nísaì toshíshita desu

junior school (BRIT) n 小学校 shōgakkō

junk [dʒʌŋk] n (rubbish, cheap goods) がらくた garákuta; (ship) ジャンク jánku

junk food n ジャンクフード jánku fūdo ◊ポテトチップス，ファーストフードなど高カロリーだが低栄養のスナック食品 potétochippùsu, fāsuto fūdo nádò kōkarorī da ga teíeiyō no sunákku shokùhin

junkie [dʒʌŋˈkiː] (inf) n ペイ中 peichū

junk shop n 古物商 kobútsushō

Junr. abbr = **junior**

jurisdiction [dʒuːrisdikˈʃən] n (LAW) 司法権 shihókèn; (ADMIN) 支配権 shiháikèn

juror [dʒuːˈrəːr] n (person on jury) 陪審員 baíshiñ-in

jury [dʒuːˈriː] n (group of jurors) 陪審員 baíshiñ-in

just [dʒʌst] adj (fair: decision) 公正な kōsei na; (: punishment) 適切な tekísetsu na

◆*adv* (exactly) 丁度 chŏdo; (only) ただ tádǎ; (barely) ようやく yŏyaku

he's just done it ついさっきそれをやったばかりだ tsuí sakkí sore wo yatta bákàri da

he's just left ついさっき出た〔帰った〕ばかりだ tsuí sakkí détà〔kaéttà〕bákàri da

just right 丁度いい chŏdo iî

just two o'clock 丁度2時 chŏdo nîji

she's just as clever as you 彼女はあなたに負けないぐらい頭がいい kánòjo wa anátà ni makénai gurài atáma ga iî

just as well that ... ...して良かった ...shîtè yokátta

just as he was leaving 丁度出掛けるところに丁度 chŏdo dekákerù tokóro ni

just before 丁度前に chŏdo máè ni

just enough 辛うじて間に合って káròjite ma ní attè

just here ぴったりここに pittárî kokó ni

he just missed わずかの差で外れた wázùka no sá de hazúreta

just listen ちょっと聞いて chottó kiite

justice [dʒʌs'tis] *n* (LAW: system) 司法 shihŏ; (rightness: of cause, complaint) 正当さ seftŏsa; (fairness) 公正さ kŏseisa; (US: judge) 裁判官 safbankan

to do justice to (*fig*: task) ...をやりこなす ...wo yaríkonasù; (: meal) ...を平らげる ...wo taíragerù; (: person) ...を正当に扱う ...wo seftŏ ni atsúkaù

Justice of the Peace *n* 治安判事 chían hañji

justifiable [dʒʌs'tifaiəbəl] *adj* (claim, statement etc) もっともな móttòmo na

justification [dʒʌstəfəkei'ʃən] *n* (reason) 正当とする理由 seftŏ to suru riyú

justify [dʒʌs'təfai] *vt* (action, decision) 正当である事を証明する seftŏ de arù kotŏ wo shŏmei suru; (text) 行の長さをそろえる gyŏ no nágàsa wo soróerù

justly [dʒʌst'li:] *adv* (with reason) 正当に seftŏ ni; (deservedly) 当然 tŏzen

jut [dʒʌt] *vi* (*also*: **jut out**: protrude) 突出る tsukíderù

juvenile [dʒu:'vənəl] *adj* (court) 未成年の miséìnen no; (books) 少年少女向きの shŏnen shŏjo mukí no; (humor, mentality) 子供っぽい kodŏmoppoî

◆*n* (LAW, ADMIN) 未成年者 miséìneñsha

juxtapose [dʒʌkstəpouz'] *vt* (things, ideas) 並べておく narábete okù

K

K [kei] *abbr* (= *one thousand*) 1000 señ = *kilobyte*

kaleidoscope [kəlai'dəskoup] *n* 万華鏡 mañgekyŏ

Kampuchea [kæmpu:tʃi:'ə] *n* カンプチア kâñpuchia

kangaroo [kæŋgəru:'] *n* カンガルー kañgarû

karate [kərɑ:'ti:] *n* 空手 karáte

kebab [kəbɑ:b'] *n* くし刺の焼肉 kushísashi nò yakíniku, シシカバブ shishikababu

keel [ki:l] *n* 竜骨 ryúkotsu

on an even keel (*fig*) 安定して añtei shite

keen [ki:n] *adj* (eager) やりたがっている yarítagattè írù; (intense: interest, desire) 熱心な nesshín na; (acute: eye, intelligence) 鋭い surúdoî; (fierce: competition) 激しい hagéshiî; (sharp: edge) 鋭い surúdoî

to keen to do/on doing something (eager, anxious) ...をやりたがっている ...wo yarítagattè írù

to be keen on something/someone ...に熱を上げている ...ni netsú wò agéte irù

keep [ki:p] (*pt, pp* **kept**) *vt* (retain: receipt etc) 保管する hokán suru; (: money etc) 自分の物にする jíbùn no monŏ ni surù; (: job etc) なくさない様にする nakúsanai yŏ ni suru, 守る mamórù; (preserve, store) 貯蔵する chozŏ suru; (maintain: house, garden etc) 管理する kâñri suru; (detain) 引留める hikítomerù; (run: shop etc) 経営する keféi suru; (chickens, bees etc) 飼育する shiíku suru; (accounts, diary etc) ...を付ける ...wo tsukérù; (support: family etc) 養う yashínaù; (fulfill: promise) 守る mamórù; (prevent): **to keep someone from doing something** ...が...をできない様に阻止する ...ga ...wo dekínài yō ni soshí surù

♦vi (remain: in a certain state) ...でいる 〔ある〕...de irú 〔árù〕; (: in a certain place) ずっと...にいる zuttó ...ni irú; (last: food) 保存がきく hozón ga kikù

♦n (cost of food etc) 生活費 seíkatsuhì; (of castle) 本丸 hofimaru

to keep doing something ...をし続ける ...wo shitsúzukerù

to keep someone happy ...の期限をとる ...no kígen wo torú

to keep a place tidy ある場所をきちんとさせておく árù bashó wo kichín to sasète okú

to keep something to oneself ...について黙っている ...ni tsúite damátte irù

to keep something (back) from someone ...の事を...に隠す ...no kotó wo ...ni kakúsù

to keep time (clock) 時間を正確に計る jíkan wo seíkaku ni hakárù

for keeps (inf) 永久に eíkyū ni

keeper [ki:'pə:r] n (in zoo, park) 飼育係 shi-íkugakàri, キーパー kípà

keep-fit [ki:p'fit'] n (BRIT) 健康体操 keńkōtaìsō

keeping [ki:'piŋ] n (care) 保管 hokán

in keeping with ...に合って ...ni áttè, ...に従って ...ni shitagatte

keep on vi (continue): **to keep on doing** ...し続ける ...shitsúzukerù

to keep on (about something) (...を話題に) うるさくしゃべる (...wo wadái ni) urúsakù shabérù

keep out vt (intruder etc) 締出す shimédasù

「**keep out**」立入禁止 tachíiri kinshi

keepsake [ki:p'seik] n 形見 katámi

keep up vt (maintain: payments etc) 続ける tsuzúkerù; (: standards etc) 保持する hojí suru

♦vi: **to keep up (with)** (match: pace)

(...と) 速度を合せる (...to) sókùdo wo awáserù; (: level) (...に) 遅れない様にする (...ni) okúrenai yō ni suru

keg [keg] n たる tarú

kennel [ken'əl] n イヌ小屋 inúgoya

kennels [ken'əlz] npl (establishment) イヌ屋 inúya

Kenya [ken'jə] n ケニア kénìa

Kenyan [ken'jən] adj ケニアの kénìa no

♦n ケニア人 kenfajìn

kept [kept] pt, pp of **keep**

kerb [kə:rb] (BRIT) n = **curb**

kernel [kə:r'nəl] n (BOT: of nut) 実 mi; (fig: of idea) 核 kákù

kerosene [ke:r'əsi:n] n 灯油 tóyu

ketchup [ketʃ'əp] n ケチャップ kecháppù

kettle [ket'əl] n やかん yakán

kettle drum n ティンパニ tífìpani

key [ki:] n (for lock etc) かぎ kagí; (MUS: scale) 調 chó; (of piano, computer, typewriter) キー kí

♦adj (issue etc) 重要な jūyō na

♦vt (also: **key in**: into computer etc) 打込む uchíkomù, 入力する nyūryoku suru

keyboard [ki:'bɔ:rd] n (of computer, typewriter) キーボード kíbòdo; (of piano) けん盤 keńban, キーボード kíbòdo

keyed up [ki:d-] adj (person) 興奮している kófun shite irù

keyhole [ki:'houl] n 鍵穴 kagíana

keynote [ki:'nout] n (MUS) 主音 shúòn; (of speech) 基調 kichó

key ring n キーホルダー kíhorùdā

kg abbr = **kilogram**

khaki [kæk'i:] n (color) カーキ色 kákì iro; (also: **khaki cloth**) カーキ色服地 kákì iro fukùji

kibbutz [kibuts'] n キブツ kíbùtsu ◇イスラエルの農業共同体 ísùraeru no nógyō kyōdōtai

kick [kik] vt (person, table, ball) ける kérù; (inf: habit, addiction) やめる yamérù; (also: **khaki cloth**) ける kérù

♦vi ける kérù

♦n (from person, animal) けり kéri; (to ball) キック kíkkù; (thrill): **he does it for kicks** 彼はそんな事をやるのはスリ

ルのためだ kárě wa sofina kotó wo yárù no wa surírù no tamé dà

kick off vi (FOOTBALL, SOCCER) 試合を開始する shiái wò kaíshi suru

kick-off [kik'ɔːf] n (FOOTBALL, SOCCER) 試合開始 shiái kaishi, キックオフ kíkkùofu

kid [kid] n (inf: child) がき gakí, じゃり jarí; (animal) 子ヤギ koyágì; (also: **kid leather**) キッド革 kíddògawa
♦vi (inf) 冗談を言う jṓdaǹ wo iú

kidnap [kid'næp] vt 誘拐する yúkai suru

kidnapper [kid'næpə:r] n 誘拐犯人 yúkai haǹnin

kidnapping [kid'næpiŋ] n 誘拐事件 yúkai jikèn

kidney [kid'ni:] n (ANAT) じん臓 jiǹzō; (CULIN) キドニー kídònī

kill [kil] vt (person, animal) 殺す korósù; (plant) 枯らす karásù; (murder) 殺す korosu, 殺害する satsúgai suru
♦n 殺し koróshi
to kill time 時間をつぶす jíkàn wo tsubúsù

killer [kil'ə:r] n 殺し屋 koróshiya

killing [kil'iŋ] n (action) 殺す事 korósu kotò; (instance) 殺人事件 satsújin jikèn
to make a killing (inf) 大もうけする ṓmòke suru

killjoy [kil'dʒɔi] n 白けさせる人 shirákesaserù hitó

kiln [kiln] n 窯 kamá

kilo [ki:'lou] n キロ kírò

kilobyte [kil'əbait] n (COMPUT) キロバイト kiróbaìto

kilogram(me) [kil'əgræm] n キログラム kirógurāmu

kilometer [kil'əmitə:r] (BRIT **kilometre**) n キロメーター kirómèta

kilowatt [kil'əwɑːt] n キロワット kiró-wattò

kilt [kilt] n キルト kirúto

kimono [kimou'nou] n 着物 kimóno, 和服 wafúku

kin [kin] n see kith; next-of-kin

kind [kaind] adj 親切な shíñsetsu na
♦n (type, sort) 種類 shúrùi; (species) 種 shú

to pay in kind 現物で支払う geñbutsu de shiháraù

a kind of ...の一種 ...no ísshù

to be two of a kind 似たり寄ったりする nitári yottárì suru, 似た者同志である nitá mono dṓshi de árù

kindergarten [kin'də:rgɑːrtən] n 幼稚園 yōchìen

kind-hearted [kaind'hɑːr'tid] adj 心の優しい kokórò no yasáshiì

kindle [kin'dəl] vt (light: fire) たく takú, つける tsukeru; (arouse: emotion) 起す okósù, そそる sosórù

kindly [kaind'li:] adj 親切な shíñsetsu na
♦adv (smile) 優しく yasáshikù; (behave) 親切に shíñsetsu ni
will you kindly ... ...して下さいませんか ...shítè kudásaìmasen ká

kindness [kaind'nis] n (personal quality) 親切 shíñsetsu; (helpful act) 親切な行為 shíñsetsu na kṓi

kindred [kin'drid] adj: **kindred spirit** 自分と気の合った人 jíbùn to kí no attà hitó

kinetic [kinet'ik] adj 動的な dṓteki na

king [kiŋ] n (monarch) 国王 kokúṓ; (CARDS, CHESS) キング kíñgu

kingdom [kiŋ'dəm] n 王国 ṓkoku

kingfisher [kiŋ'fiʃə:r] n カワセミ kawásemi

king-size [kiŋ'saiz] adj 特大の tokúdai no

kinky [kiŋ'ki:] (pej) adj (person, behavior) へんてこな heñteko na, 妙な myṓ na; (sexually) 変態気味の heñtaigimi no

kiosk [ki:ɑːsk'] n (shop) キオスク kiósùku; (BRIT: TEL) 電話ボックス deñwa bokkùsu

kipper [kip'ə:r] n 薫製ニシン kuñsei nishín

kiss [kis] n キス kísù
♦vt ...にキスする ...ni kísù suru
to kiss (each other) キスする kísù suru

kiss of life n 口移しの人工呼吸 kuchútsushi no jíñkōkokyū

kit [kit] n (clothes: sports kit etc) 運動服一式 uñdófùku isshíki; (equipment, set of tools: also MIL) 道具一式 dṓgu isshíki; (for assembly) キット kíttð

kitchen [kitʃ'ən] *n* 台所 daídokoro, キッチン kítchin

kitchen sink *n* 台所 の 流し daídokoro no nagáshi

kite [kait] *n* (toy) たこ takð

kith [kiθ] *n*: **kith and kin** 親せき知人 shíñsekichijin

kitten [kit'ən] *n* 子ネコ konékð

kitty [kit'i:] *n* (pool of money) お金の蓄え o-káne no takúwae; (CARDS) 総掛金 sókakekîn

kleptomaniac [kleptəmei'ni:æk] *n* 盗 癖のある人 tốheki no árù hitð

km *abbr* = **kilometer**

knack [næk] *n*: **to have the knack of doing something** ...をするのが上手である ...wo suru nð ga jōzu de arù

knapsack [næp'sæk] *n* ナップサック nappúsakkù

knead [ni:d] *vt* (dough, clay) 練る nérù

knee [ni:] *n* ひざ hizá

kneecap [ni:'kæp] *n* ひざ 頭 hizágashìra, ひざ小僧 hizákozð

kneel [ni:l] (*pt, pp* **knelt**) *vi* (*also:* **kneel down**) ひざまずく hizámazukù

knelt [nelt] *pt, pp of* **kneel**

knew [nu:] *pt of* **know**

knickers [nik'ə:rz] (*BRIT*) *npl* パンティー pấñtî

knife [naif] (*pl* **knives**) *n* ナイフ náìfu
♦*vt* ナイフで刺す náìfu de sásù

knight [nait] *n* (HISTORY) 騎士 kishí; (*BRIT*) ナイト náìto; (CHESS) ナイト náìto

knighthood [nait'hud] (*BRIT*) *n* (title): **to get a knighthood** ナイト爵位を与えられる naíto shakùi wo atáerarerù

knit [nit] *vt* (garment) 編む ámù
♦*vi* (with wool) 編物をする amímòno wo suru; (broken bones) 治る naórù
to knit one's brows まゆをひそめる máyù wo hisómerù

knitting [nit'iŋ] *n* 編物 amímòno

knitting machine *n* 編機 amíkì

knitting needle *n* 編棒 amíbð

knitwear [nit'we:r] *n* ニット・ウェアー nittð ueâ

knives [naivz] *npl of* **knife**

knob [na:b] *n* (handle: of door) 取っ手 tottê, つまみ tsumámi; (: of stick) 握り nigíri; (on radio, TV etc) つまみ tsumámi

knock [na:k] *vt* (strike) たたく tatákù; (*inf*: criticize) 批判する hihán suru
♦*vi* (at door etc): **to knock at/on** ...にノックする ...ni nókku surù
♦*n* (blow, bump) 打撃 dagéki; (on door) ノック nókkù

knock down *vt* (subj: person) 殴り倒す nagúritaosù; (: car) ひき倒す hikítaosù

knocker [na:k'ə:r] *n* (on door) ノッカー nokkâ

knock-kneed [na:k'ni:d] *adj* X脚の ekúsukyaku no

knock off *vi* (*inf*: finish) やめる yamérù, 終りにする owári ni surù
♦*vt* (from price) 値引きする nebíki suru; (*inf*: steal) くすねる kusúnerù

knock out *vt* (subj: drug etc) 気絶させる kizétsu saserù, 眠らせる nemúraserù; (BOXING, *also fig*) ノックアウトする nokkúaùto suru; (defeat: in game, competition) ...に勝つ ...ni kátsù, 敗退させる haítai saserù

knockout [na:k'aut] *n* (BOXING) ノックアウト nokkúaùto
♦*cpd* (competition etc) 決定的な kettéiteki na

knock over *vt* (person, object) 倒す taósù

knot [na:t] *n* (in rope) 結び目 musúbime; (in wood) 節目 fushíme; (NAUT) ノット nóttð
♦*vt* 結ぶ musúbù

knotty [na:t'i:] *adj* (*fig*: problem) 厄介な yakkái na

know [nou] (*pt* **knew**, *pp* **known**) *vt* (facts, dates etc) 知っている shitté irù; (language) できる dekírù; (be acquainted with: person, place, subject) 知っている shitté irù; (recognize: by sight) 見て分かる mítè wakárù; (: by sound) 聞いて分かる kiite wakaru

to know how to swim 泳げる oyógerù
to know about/of something/some-

one ...の事を知っている ...no kotó wò shitté irù

know-all [nou'ɔːl] *n* 知ったか振りの人 shittákaburi no hitó

know-how [nou'hau] *n* 技術知識 gijútsuchíshìki, ノウハウ nóùháù

knowing [nou'iŋ] *adj* (look: of complicity) 意味ありげな imfarige na

knowingly [nou'iŋliː] *adv* (purposely) 故意に kóì ni; (smile, look) 意味ありげに ímìarige ni

knowledge [nɑːl'idʒ] *n* (understanding, awareness) 認識 nínshiki; (learning, things learnt) 知識 chíshìki

knowledgeable [nɑːl'idʒəbəl] *adj* 知識のある chíshìki no árù

known [noun] *pp of* **know**

knuckle [nʌk'əl] *n* 指関節 yubí kañsetsu ◊特に指の付根の関節を指す tókù ni yubí no tsukéne no kañsetsu wò sásù

KO [kei'ou'] *n abbr* = **knockout**

Koran [kɔːrɑːn] *n* コーラン kôran

Korea [kɔːriː'ə] *n* 韓国 káñkoku, 朝鮮 chôsèn

Korean [kɔːriː'ən] *adj* 韓国の káñkoku no, 朝鮮の chôsèn no; (LING) 韓国語の kañkokugo no, 朝鮮語の chôsengo no ◊*n* (person) 韓国人 kañkokujìn, 朝鮮人 chôsenjìn; (LING) 韓国語 kañkokugo, 朝鮮語 chôsengo

kosher [kou'ʃər] *adj* 適法の tekíhò no ◊ユダヤ教の戒律に合った食物などについて言う yudáyakyō no kaíritsu ni attá shokúmòtsu nádò ni tsuíte iú

L

L (*BRIT*) *abbr* = **learner driver**

l. *abbr* = **liter**

lab [læb] *n abbr* = **laboratory**

label [leiˈbəl] *n* (on suitcase, merchandise etc) ラベル rábèru ◊*vt* (thing) ...にラベルを付ける ...ni rábèru wo tsukérù

labor [lei'bər] (*BRIT* **labour**) *n* (hard work) 労働 rôdō; (work force) 労働者 rôdôshà ◊総称 sōshō; (work done by work force) 労働 rôdō; (MED): *to be in labor* 陣痛が始まっている jińtsū ga hajímatte irù ◊*vi*: *to labor (at something)* (...に) 苦心する (...ni) kushín suru ◊*vt*: *to labor a point* ある事を余計に強調する árù kotó wò yokéi nì kyốchō suru

laboratory [læb'rətɔːriː] *n* (scientific: building, institution) 研究所 keñkyūjo; (: room) 実験室 jikkéñshitsu; (school) 理科教室 rikákyōshitsu

labored [lei'bərd] *adj* (breathing: one's own) 苦しい kurúshiì; (: someone else's) 苦しそうな kurúshisò na

laborer [lei'bə:rə:r] *n* (industrial) 労働者 rôdôshà

farm laborer 農場労務者 nôjōrōmushà

laborious [ləbɔːr'iːəs] *adj* 骨の折れる honé no orérù

labour [lei'bə:r] *etc n* = **labor** *etc*

Labour, the Labour Party (*BRIT*) 労働党 rōdôtō

labyrinth [læb'ə:rinθ] *n* 迷路 mêîro

lace [leis] *n* (fabric) レース rêsu; (of shoe etc) ひも himó ◊*vt* (shoe etc: *also*: **lace up**) ...のひもを結ぶ ...no himó wo musúbù

lack [læk] *n* (absence) 欠如 kétsùjo ◊*vt* (money, confidence) ...が無い ...ga náì; (intelligence etc) 欠いている kaíte irù

through/for lack of ...が無いために ...ga náì tamé ni

to be lacking ...がない ...ga náì

to be lacking in (intelligence, generosity etc) ...を欠いている ...wo kaíte iru

lackadaisical [lækədei'zikəl] *adj* (lacking interest, enthusiasm) 気乗りしない kinóri shinaì

laconic [ləkɑːn'ik] *adj* 言葉数の少ない kotóbakazù no sukúnaì

lacquer [læk'əːr] *n* (paint) ラッカー rákkã; (*also*: **hair lacquer**) ヘアスプレー heásupurê

lad [læd] *n* (boy) 少年 shônen; (young man) 若者 wakámonò

ladder [læd'ə:r] *n* (metal, wood, rope) は

しご子 hashígo子; (*BRIT*: in tights) 伝線 densen

laden [lei'dən] *adj*: *laden (with)* (ship, truck etc) (...を) たっぷり積んだ (...wo) tappúrí tsuńda; (person) (...を) 沢山抱 えている (...wo) takúsan kakáete irù

laden with fruit (tree) 実をたわわに付けている mi wo tawáwa ni tsukéte irù

ladle [lei'dəl] *n* 玉じゃくし tamájakùshi

lady [lei'di:] *n* (woman) 女性 joséi; (: dignified, graceful etc) 淑女 shukújò, レディー rédī; (in address): *ladies and gentlemen ...* 紳士淑女の皆様 shińshishukujò no mínásàma

young lady 若い女性 wakái joseì

the ladies' (room) 女性用トイレ joséiyòtoìre

ladybird [lei'di:bə:rd] *n* テントウムシ teńtōmushi

ladybug [lei'debʌg] (*US*) *n* = **ladybird**

ladylike [lei'di:laik] *adj* (behavior) レディーらしい rédīrashii

ladyship [lei'di:ʃip] *n*: *your ladyship* 奥様 ókùsama

lag [læg] *n* (period of time) 遅れ okúre
♦*vi* (*also*: **lag behind**: person, thing) ...に遅れる ...ni okúrerù; (: trade, investment etc) ...の勢いが衰える ...no ikfoì ga otóroerù
♦*vt* (pipes etc) ...に断熱材を巻く ...ni dańnetsuzai wo makù

lager [lɑ:'gə:r] *n* ラガービール ragábìru

lagoon [ləgu:n'] *n* 潟 katá, ラグーン rágūn

laid [leid] *pt, pp of* **lay**[3]

laid back (*inf*) *adj* のんびりした nońbirī shitá

laid up *adj*: *to be laid up (with)* (...で) 寝込んでいる (...de) nekónde irù

lain [lein] *pp of* **lie**

lair [le:r] *n* (ZOOL) 巣穴 suána

lake [leik] *n* 湖 mizú-umì

lamb [læm] *n* (animal) 子ヒツジ kohítsujì; (meat) ラム rámù

lamb chop *n* ラムチャップ ramúchappù, ラムチョップ ramúchoppù

lambswool [læmz'wul] *n* ラムウール ramúùru

lame [leim] *adj* (person, animal) びっこの bíkkò no; (excuse, argument, answer) 下手な hetá na

lament [ləment'] *n* 嘆き nagéki
♦*vt* 嘆く nagékù

laminated [læm'əneitid] *adj* (metal, wood, glass) 合板の góhan no; (covering, surface) プラスチック張りの purásuchikkubari no

lamp [læmp] *n* (electric, gas, oil) 明り akári, ランプ ráñpu

lamppost [læmp'poust] *n* 街灯 gaítō

lampshade [læmp'ʃeid] *n* ランプの傘 ráñpu no kasá, シェード shèdo

lance [læns] *n* やり yarí
♦*vt* (MED) 切開する sekkái suru

land [lænd] *n* (area of open ground) 土地 tochí; (property, estate) 土地 tochí, 所有地 shoyúchì; (as opposed to sea) 陸 rikú; (country, nation) 国 kuní
♦*vi* (from ship) 上陸する jóriku suru; (AVIAT) 着陸する chakúriku suru; (*fig*: fall) 落ちる ochírù
♦*vt* (passengers, goods) 降ろす orósù

to land someone with something (*inf*) ...に...を押付ける ...ni ...wo oshítsukerù

landing [læn'diŋ] *n* (of house) 踊り場 odóriba; (AVIAT) 着陸 chakúriku

landing gear *n* (AVIAT) 着陸装置 chakúrikusōchi

landing strip *n* 滑走路 kassórò

landlady [lænd'leidi:] *n* (of rented house, flat, room) 女大家 ofinaðya; (of pub) 女主人 ofinashujìn, おかみ okámi

landlocked [lænd'lɑ:kt] *adj* 陸地に囲まれた rikúchi ni kakómareta

landlord [lænd'lɔ:rd] *n* (of rented house, flat, room) 大家 ōya; (of pub) 主人 shujìn

landmark [lænd'mɑ:rk] *n* (building, hill etc) 目標 mokúhyō; (*fig*) 歴史的な事件 rekíshiteki na jíkèn

landowner [lænd'ounə:r] *n* 地主 jinúshi

landscape [lænd'skeip] *n* (view over land, buildings etc) 景色 késhìki; (ART) 風景画 fūkeiga

landscape gardener *n* 造園家 zóenka

landslide [lænd'slaid] *n* (GEO) 地滑り jisúbèri; (*fig*: electoral) 圧勝 asshó

land up *vi*: *to land up in/at* 結局...に行くはめになる kekkyókù ...ni ikú hame ni narù

lane [lein] *n* (in country) 小道 komíchi; (AUT: of carriageway) 車線 shasén; (of race course, swimming pool) コース kṓsu

language [læŋ'gwidʒ] *n* (national tongue) 国語 kokúgo; (ability to communicate verbally) 言語 géngo; (specialized terminology) 用語 yṓgo; (style: of written piece, speech etc) 言葉遣 kotóbazukài; (SCOL) 語学 gógàku

bad language 下品な言葉 gehín na kotóba

he is studying languages 彼は外国語を勉強している kare wa gaikokugo wo benkyō shite iru

language laboratory *n* ランゲージラボラトリー rañgḗjiraboratòrī, エルエル érùeru

languid [læŋ'gwid] *adj* (person, movement) 元気のない géñki no náī

languish [læŋ'gwiʃ] *vi* 惨めに生きる míjìme ni ikírù

lank [læŋk] *adj* (hair) 長くて手入れしないい nagákutè tefre shinai

lanky [læŋ'ki:] *adj* ひょろっとした hyorottṓ shita

lantern [læn'tərn] *n* カンテラ kañtera

lap [læp] *n* (of person) ひざの上 hizá nò ué; (in race) 1周 ísshū, ラップ ráppù
♦*vt* (*also*: **lap up**: drink) ぴちゃぴちゃ飲む pichápìcha nómu
♦*vi* (water) ひたひたと打寄せる hitáhìta to uchíyoserù

lapel [ləpel'] *n* 折えり oríeri, ラペル rápèru

Lapland [læp'lænd] *n* ラップランド ráppùrando

lapse [læps] *n* (bad behavior) 過失 kashítsu; (of memory) 喪失 sṓshitsu; (of time) 経過 keíka
♦*vi* (law) 無効になる mukṓ ni narù; (contract, membership, passport) 切れる kirérù

a lapse of concentration 不注意 fuchúì

to lapse into bad habits (of behavior) 堕落する daráku suru

lap up *vt* (*fig*: flattery etc) 真に受ける ma ni ukérù

larceny [lɑːr'səni:] *n* (LAW) 窃盗罪 settōzai

larch [lɑːrtʃ] *n* (tree) カラマツ karámàtsu

lard [lɑːrd] *n* ラード rấdo

larder [lɑːr'dəːr] *n* 食料貯蔵室 shokúryōchozòshitsu

large [lɑːrdʒ] *adj* (big: house, person, amount) 大きい ōkii

at large (as a whole) 一般に ippán ni; (at liberty) 捕まらないで tsukámaranaì de ¶ *see also* **by**

largely [lɑːrdʒ'li:] *adv* (mostly) 大体 daítai; (mainly: introducing reason) 主に ṓmò ni

large-scale [lɑːrdʒ'skeil'] *adj* (action, event) 大規模の daíkibo no; (map, diagram) 大縮尺の daíshukùshaku no

largesse [lɑːrdʒes'] *n* (generosity) 気前良さ kimáeyosà; (money etc) 贈り物 okúrimonò

lark [lɑːrk] *n* (bird) ヒバリ hibári; (joke) 冗談 jṓdan

lark about *vi* ふざけ回る fuzákemawaru

larva [lɑːr'və] (*pl* **larvae**) *n* 幼虫 yṓchū

larvae [lɑːr'vi:] *npl of* **larva**

laryngitis [lærəndʒai'tis] *n* こうとう炎 kṓtōen

larynx [lær'iŋks] *n* (ANAT) こうとう kṓtō

lascivious [ləsiv'i:əs] *adj* (person, conduct) みだらな midára na

laser [lei'zəːr] *n* レーザー rḕzā

laser printer *n* レーザープリンター rḗzāpuriñtā

lash [læʃ] *n* (eyelash) まつげ mátsùge; (blow of whip) むち打ち muchíuchi
♦*vt* (whip) むち打つ muchíutsù; (subj: rain) 激しくたたく hagéshikù tatákú; (: wind) 激しく揺さぶる yusáburù; (tie): *to lash to/together* ...を...に (...と一緒に)縛る ...wo ...ni (...to isshō ni)

shibárù

lash out vi: *to lash out (at someone)* (hit) (...に) 打ち掛る (...ni) uchíkakarù

to lash out against someone (criticize) ...を激しく非難する ...wo hagéshikù hínan suru

lass [læs] n (girl) 少女 shòjo; (young woman) 若い女性 wakáì joséi

lasso [læs'ou] n 投縄 nagénawa

last [læst] adj (latest: period of time, event, thing) 前の máè no; (final: bus, hope etc) 最後の saígo no; (end: of series, row) 一番後の ichíban atò no; (remaining: traces, scraps etc) 残りの nokórì no

♦adv (most recently) 最近 saíkin; (finally) 最後に saígo ni

♦vi (continue) 続く tsuzúkù; (: in good condition) もつ mótsù; (money, commodity) ...に足りる ...ni taríru

last week 先週 señshū

last night 昨晩 sakúban, 昨夜 sakúyà

at last (finally) とうとう tòtō

last\ but one 最後から2番目 saígo kara nibánme

last-ditch [læst'ditʃ'] adj (attempt) 絶体絶命の zettáizetsumei no

lasting [læs'tiŋ] adj (friendship, solution) 永続的な eízokuteki na

lastly [læst'li:] adv 最後に saígo ni

last-minute [læst'min'it] adj (decision, appeal etc) 土壇場の dotánba no

latch [lætʃ] n (on door, gate) 掛け金 kakégàne, ラッチ rátchi

late [leit] adj (far on in time, process, work etc) 遅い osói; (not on time) 遅れた okúreta; (former) 前の máè no, 前... zéñ...

♦adv (far on in time, process, work etc) 遅く osóku; (behind time, schedule) 遅れて okúrete

of late (recently) 最近 saíkin

in late May 5月の終り頃 gógàtsu no owári gorò

the late Mr X (deceased) 故Xさん ko ékusu san

latecomer [leit'kʌmə:r] n 遅れて来る人 okúrete kurù hitó

lately [leit'li:] adv 最近 saíkin

latent [lei'tənt] adj (energy, skill, ability) 表に出ない omóte nì dénài

later [lei'tə:r] adj (time, date, meeting etc) もっと後の móttò átò no; (version etc) もっと新しい móttò atárashiì

♦adv 後で átò de

later on 後で átò de

lateral [læt'ə:rəl] adj (position) 横のyokô no; (direction) 横への yokô e no

latest [lei'tist] adj (train, flight etc) 最後の saígo no; (novel, film, news etc) 最新の saíshin no

at the latest 遅くとも osókùtomo

lathe [leið] n (for wood, metal) 旋盤 señban

lather [læð'ə:r] n 石けんの泡 sekkén nò awá

♦vt ...に石けんの泡を塗る ...ni sekkén no awá wò nurú

Latin [læt'in] n (LING) ラテン語 raténgo

♦adj ラテン語の raténgo no

Latin America n ラテンアメリカ raténamèrika

Latin American adj ラテンアメリカの ratén-amèrika no

♦n ラテンアメリカ人 ratén-amerikajìn

latitude [læt'ətu:d] n (GEO) 緯度 ídò; (fig: freedom) 余裕 yoyú

latrine [lətri:n'] n 便所 beñjo

latter [læt'ə:r] adj (of two) 後者の kôsha no; (recent) 最近の saíkin no; (later) 後の方の átò no hô no

♦n: *the latter* (of two people, things, groups) 後者 kôsha

latterly [læt'ə:rli:] adv 最近 saíkin

lattice [læt'is] n (pattern, structure) 格子 kôshi

laudable [lɔː'dəbəl] adj (conduct, motives etc) 感心な kañshin na

laugh [læf] n 笑い waráì

♦vi 笑う waráù

(to do something) for a laugh 冗談として (...をする) jôdañ toshitè (...wo suru)

laugh at vt fus ...をばかにする ...wo bakâ ni surù

laughable [læf'əbəl] adj (attempt, quality etc) ばかげた bakágeta

laughing stock [læfˈiŋ-] *n*: *to be the laughing stock of* ...の笑い者になる ...no waráimono ni narù

laugh off *vt* (criticism, problem) 無視する mushí suru

laughter [læfˈtər] *n* 笑い声 waráigoè

launch [lɔːntʃ] *n* (of rocket, missile) 発射 hasshá; (of satellite) 打上げ uchíage; (COMM) 新発売 shiñhatsubai; (motorboat) ランチ ráñchi

◆*vt* (ship) 進水させる shiñsui saséru; (rocket, missile) 発射する hasshá suru; (satellite) 打上げる uchíagerù; (*fig*: start) 開始する kaíshi suru; (COMM) 発売する hatsúbai suru

launch into *vt fus* (speech, activity) 始める hajímerù

launch(ing) pad [lɔːntʃ(iŋ)-] *n* (for missile, rocket) 発射台 hasshádai

launder [lɔːnˈdər] *vt* (clothes) 洗濯する señtaku suru

launderette [lɔːndəret'] (*BRIT*) *n* コインランドリー koíñrañdorī

Laundromat [lɔːnˈdrəmæt] (℞) *US* *n* コインランドリー koíñrañdorī

laundry [lɔːnˈdriː] *n* (dirty, clean) 洗濯物 señtakumono; (business) 洗濯屋 señtakuya ◇ドライクリーニングはしない doráikurīningu wa shináî; (room) 洗濯場 señtakuba

laureate [lɔːˈriːit] *adj see* **poet laureate**

laurel [lɔːrˈəl] *n* (tree) ゲッケイジュ gekkéîju

lava [lɑːvˈə] *n* 溶岩 yōgan

lavatory [lævˈətɔːriː] *n* お手洗い otéaraì

lavender [lævˈəndər] *n* (BOT) ラベンダー rabéñda

lavish [lævˈiʃ] *adj* (amount) たっぷりの tappúrî no; (meal) 多量の taryō no; (person): *lavish with* ...を気前良く与える ...wo kimáeyokù atáerù

◆*vt*: *to lavish something on someone* ...に...を気前よく与える ...ni ...wo kimáeyokù atáerù

law [lɔː] *n* (system of rules: of society, government) 法 hố; (a rule) 法律 hốritsu; (of nature, science) 法則 hốsoku; (lawyers) 弁護士の職 beñgoshi no shokú;

(police) 警察 keísatsu; (SCOL) 法学 hốgaku

law-abiding [lɔːˈəbaidiŋ] *adj* 法律を遵守する hốritsu wò júñshu suru

law and order *n* 治安 chíañ

law court *n* 法廷 hốtei

lawful [lɔːfˈəl] *adj* 合法の gốhō no

lawless [lɔːˈlis] *adj* (action) 不法の fuhố no

lawn [lɔːn] *n* 芝生 shibáfu

lawnmower [lɔːnˈmouər] *n* 芝刈機 shibákarikì

lawn tennis *n* ローンテニス rőntenisu

law school (*US*) *n* (SCOL) 法学部 hốgakùbu

lawsuit [lɔːˈsuːt] *n* 訴訟 soshố

lawyer [lɔːˈjər] *n* (*gen*) 弁護士 beñgoshì; (solicitor) 事務弁護士 jimúbeñgoshi; (barrister) 法廷弁護士 hốteibeñgoshi

lax [læks] *adj* (behavior, standards) いい加減な iíkagen na

laxative [lækˈsətiv] *n* 下剤 gezái

lay¹ [lei] *pt of* **lie**

lay² [lei] *adj* (REL) 俗人の zokújin no; (not expert) 素人の shíroto no

lay³ [lei] (*pt, pp* **laid**) *vt* (place) 置く okú; (table) ...に食器を並べる ...ni shokkí wo náraberù; (carpet etc) 敷く shikú; (cable, pipes etc) 埋設する maísetsu suru; (ZOOL: egg) 産む úmù

layabout [leiˈəbaut] (*BRIT*: *inf*) *n* のらくら者 norákuramono

lay aside *vt* (put down) わきに置く wakí ni okù; (money) 貯蓄する chochíku suru; (belief, prejudice) 捨てる sutérù

lay by *vt* = **lay aside**

lay-by [leiˈbai] (*BRIT*) *n* 待避所 taíhijo

lay down *vt* (object) 置く okú; (rules, laws etc) 設ける mốkerù

to lay down the law (*pej*) 威張り散らす ibárichirasu

to lay down one's life (in war etc) 命を捨てる inóchi wo sutérù

layer [leiˈər] *n* 層 số

layman [leiˈmən] (*pl* **laymen**) *n* (nonexpert) 素人 shíroto

lay off *vt* (workers) 一時解雇にする i-chíjikaĭko ni suru, レイオフにする reíoffū ni suru

lay on vt (meal, entertainment etc) 提供する teíkyō suru

lay out vt (spread out: things) 並べて置く narábete okù

layout [lei'aut] n (arrangement: of garden, building) 配置 haíchi; (: of piece of writing etc) レイアウト reíaùto

laze [leiz] vi (also: **laze about**) ぶらぶらする búrabura suru

laziness [lei'zi:nis] n 怠惰 taída

lazy [lei'zi:] adj (person) 怠惰な taída na; (movement, action) のろい noróì

lb abbr = **pound (weight)**

lead[1] [li:d] n (front position: SPORT, fig) 先頭 seńtō; (piece of information) 手掛り tegákari; (in play, film) 主演 shuén; (for dog) 引綱 hikízuna; (ELEC) リード線 rídosen

♦vb (pt, pp **led**)

♦vt (walk etc in front) 先導する seńdō suru; (guide): **to lead someone somewhere** ...を...に案内する ...wo ...ni ańnai suru; (group of people, organization) ...のリーダーになる ...no rídā ni narù; (start, guide: activity) ...の指揮を取る ...no shikí wo torù

♦vi (road, pipe, wire etc) ...に通じる ...ni tsūjiru; (SPORT) 先頭に立つ seńtō ni tatsù

in the lead (SPORT, fig) 先頭に立って seńtō ni tatte

to lead the way (also fig) 先導する seńdō suru

lead[2] [led] n (metal) 鉛 namári; (in pencil) しん shíñ

lead away vt 連れ去る tsurésarù

lead back vt 連れ戻す tsurémodosù

leaden [led'ən] adj (sky, sea) 鉛色の namáriiro no

leader [li:'də:r] n (of group, organization) 指導者 shidōshà, リーダー rídā; (SPORT) 先頭を走る選手 seńtō wo hashírù seńshu

leadership [li:'də:rʃip] n (group, individual) 指導権 shidōkèn; (position, quality) リーダーシップ rídāshìppu

lead-free [ledfri:'] adj (petrol) 無鉛の

muén no

leading [li:'diŋ] adj (most important: person, thing) 主要な shuyō na; (role) 主演の shuén no; (first, front) 先頭の seńtō no

leading lady n (THEATER) 主演女優 shuénjoyū

leading light n (person) 主要人物 shuyōjinbutsu

leading man (pl **leading men**) n (THEATER) 主演男優 shuéndañ-yū

lead on vt (tease) からかう karákaù

lead singer n (in pop group) リードシンガー rídoshiñgā, リードボーカリスト rídobōkarisuto

lead to vt fus ...の原因になる ...no geń-in ni narù

lead up to vt fus (events) ...の原因になる ...no geń-in ni narù; (in conversation) 話題を...に向ける wadái wo ...ni mukérù

leaf [li:f] (pl **leaves**) n (of tree, plant) 葉 ha

♦vi: **to leaf through** (book, magazine) ...にさっと目を通す ...ni sátto me wò tōsù

to turn over a new leaf 心を入れ換える kokórò wo irékaerù

leaflet [li:f'lit] n ビラ birá, 散らし chiráshi

league [li:g] n (group of people, clubs, countries) 連盟 reńmei, リーグ rígu

to be in league with someone ...と手を組んでいる ...to te wo kuńdè irú

leak [li:k] n (of liquid, gas) 漏れ moré; (hole: in roof, pipe etc) 穴 aná; (piece of information) 漏えい rôei

♦vi (shoes, ship, pipe, roof) ...から...が漏れる ...kara ...ga moreru; (liquid, gas) 漏れる morérù

♦vt (information) 漏らす mōrasù

the news leaked out そのニュースが漏れた sonó nyūsu ga moréta

lean [li:n] adj (person) やせた yaséta; (meat) 赤身の akámi no

♦vb (pt, pp **leaned** or **leant**)

♦vt: **to lean something on something** ...を...にもたせかける ...wo ...ni motásekakerù

♦*vi* (slope) 傾く katámukù

to lean against ...にもたれる ...ni motárerù

to lean on ...に寄り掛る ...ni yoríkakerù

lean back *vi* 後ろへもたれる ushíro e motárerù

lean forward *vi* 前にかがむ máè ni kagámù

leaning [li:'niŋ] *n: leaning (towards)* (tendency, bent) (...する) 傾向 (...surú) keíkō

lean out *vi* ...から体を乗出す ...kara karáda wò norídasù

lean over *vi* ...の上にかがむ ...no ué nì kagámù

leant [lent] *pt, pp of* **lean**

leap [li:p] *n* (jump) 跳躍 chóyaku; (in price, number etc) 急上昇 kyū́jōshō

♦*vi* (*pt, pp* **leaped** *or* **leapt**) (jump: high) 跳ね上がる hanéagarù; (: far) 跳躍する chóyaku suru; (price, number etc) 急上昇する kyū́jōshō suru

leapfrog [li:p'frɔːg] *n* 馬跳び umátobi

leapt [lept] *pt, pp of* **leap**

leap year *n* うるう年 urū́doshi

learn [lə:rn] (*pt, pp* **learned** *or* **learnt**) *vt* (facts, skill) 学ぶ manábù; (study, repeat: poem, play etc) 覚える obóerù, 暗記する aṅki suru

♦*vi* 習う naráù

to learn about something (hear, read) ...を知る ...wo shírù

to learn to do something ...の仕方を覚える ...no shikáta wò obóerù

learned [lə:r'nid] *adj* (person) 学識のある gakúshiki no arù; (book, paper) 学術の gakújùtsu no

learner [lə:r'nə:r] (*BRIT*) *n* (*also*: **learner driver**) 仮免許運転者 karímenkyo unteṅsha

learning [lə:r'niŋ] *n* (knowledge) 学識 gakúshiki

learnt [lə:rnt] *pt, pp of* **learn**

lease [li:s] *n* (legal agreement, contract: to borrow something) 賃借契約 chiṅshakukeíyaku, リース rī́su; (: to lend something) 賃貸契約 chiṅtaikeíyaku, リース rī́su

♦*vt* (borrow) 賃借する chiṅshaku suru; (lend) 賃貸する chiṅtai suru

leash [li:ʃ] *n* (for dog) ひも himó

least [li:st] *adj: the least* (+noun: smallest) 最も小さい móttòmo chíísaì; (: smallest amount of) 最も少ない móttòmo sukúnaì

♦*adv* (+verb) 最も ...しない móttòmo ...shináì; (+adjective): *the least* 最も ...でない móttòmo ...de náì

the least possible effort 最小限の努力 saíshōgen no dóryòku

at least 少なくとも sukúnakùtomo

you could at least have written 少なくとも手紙をくれたら良かったのに sukúnakùtomo tegámi wò kurétara yokàtta no ni

not in the least ちっとも...でない chíttò mo ...de náì

leather [leð'ə:r] *n* なめし革 naméshigàwa, 革 kawá

leave [li:v] (*pt, pp* **left**) *vt* (place: go away from) 行ってしまう itté shimaù, 帰る kaérù; (place, institution: permanently) 去る sárù, 辞める yamérù; (leave behind: person) 置去りにする okízari ni surù, 見捨てる misúterù; (: thing: accidentally) 置忘れる okíwasurerù; (: deliberately) 置いて行く oíte ikù; (husband, wife) ...と別れる ...to wakárerù; (allow to remain: food, space, time etc) 残す nokósù

♦*vi* (go away) 去る sárù, 行ってしまう itté shimaù; (: permanently) 辞める yamérù; (bus, train) 出発する shuppátsu suru, 出る dérù

♦*n* 休暇 kyū́ka

to leave something to someone (money, property etc) ...に...を残して死ぬ ...ni ...wo nokóshite shinù; (responsibility etc) ...に...を任せる ...ni ...wo makáserù

to be left 残る nokórù

there's some milk left over ミルクは少し残っている mírùku wa sukóshì nokótte irù

on leave 休暇中で kyū́kachū de

leave behind *vt* (person, object) 置いて

行く oíte ikù; (object: accidentally) 置忘れる okíwasurerù

leave of absence n 休暇 kyúka, 暇 himá

leave out vt 抜かす nukásù

leaves [li:vz] npl of **leaf**

Lebanon [leb'ənən] n レバノン rebánòn

lecherous [letʃ'ə:rəs] (pej) adj 助平な sukébē na

lecture [lek'tʃə:r] n (talk) 講演 kóen; (SCOL) 講義 kógi
♦vi (talk) 講演する kóen suru; (SCOL) 講義する kógi sùru
♦vt (scold): **to lecture someone on/about something** ...の事で...をしかる ...no kotó de ...wo shikárù
to give a lecture on ...について講演する ...ni tsúite kóen suru

lecturer [lek'tʃə:rə:r] (BRIT) n (at university) 講師 kóshi

led [led] pt, pp of **lead**¹

ledge [ledʒ] n (of mountain) 岩棚 iwádana; (of window) 桟 sán; (on wall) 棚 taná

ledger [ledʒ'ə:r] n (COMM) 台帳 dáichō

lee [li:] n 風下 kazáshimo

leech [li:tʃ] n ヒル hírù

leek [li:k] n リーキ ríki, リーク ríku

leer [li:r] vi: **to leer at someone** ..をいん乱な目で見る ..wo ifran na me de mirù

leeway [li:'wei] n (fig): **to have some leeway** 余裕がある yoyú ga arù

left [left] pt, pp of **leave**
♦adj (direction, position) 左の hidári no
♦n (direction, side, position) 左 hidári
♦adv (turn, look etc) 左に〔へ〕hidári ni〔e〕
on the left 左に〔で〕hidári ni〔de〕
to the left 左に〔へ〕hidári ni〔e〕
the Left (POL) 左翼 sáyoku

left-handed [left'hæn'did] adj 左利きの hidárikiki no, ぎっちょの gítchò no

left-hand side [left'hænd'-] n 左側 hidárigawa

left-luggage (office) [leftlʌg'idʒ-] (BRIT) n 手荷物預かり所 tenímotsu azukarishò

leftovers [left'ouvə:rz] npl (of meal) 残り物 nokórimono

left-wing [left'wiŋ] adj (POL) 左翼の sáyoku no

leg [leg] n (gen) 脚 ashí; (CULIN: of lamb, pork, chicken) もも mómò; (part: of journey etc) 区切り kugíri

legacy [leg'əsi:] n (of will: also fig) 遺産 isán

legal [li:'gəl] adj (of law) 法律の hóritsu no; (action, situation) 法的な hóteki na

legal holiday (US) n 法定休日 hóteikyūjitsu

legality [li:gæl'iti:] n 合法性 góhōsei

legalize [li:'gəlaiz] vt 合法化する góhōka suru

legally [li:'gəli:] adv (by law) 法的に hóteki ni

legal tender n (currency) 法定通貨 hóteitsūka, 法貨 hóka

legend [ledʒ'ənd] n (story) 伝説 deñsetsu; (fig: person) 伝説的人物 deñsetsutekijinbutsu

legendary [ledʒ'əndeːriː] adj (of legend) 伝説の deñsetsu no; (very famous) 伝説的な deñsetsuteki na

legible [ledʒ'əbəl] adj 読める yomérù

legion [li:'dʒən] n (MIL) 軍隊 guñtai

legislation [ledʒislei'ʃən] n 法律 hóritsu

legislative [ledʒ'isleitiv] adj 立法の rippō no

legislature [ledʒ'isleitʃə:r] n (POL) 議会 gíkai

legitimate [lidʒit'əmit] adj (reasonable) 正当な seítō na; (legal) 合法な góhō na

leg-room [leg'ru:m] n (in car, plane etc) 脚を伸ばせる空間 ashí wo nobáserù kúkan

leisure [li:'ʒə:r] n (period of time) 余暇 yoká, レジャー rejá
at leisure ゆっくり yukkúrì

leisure centre (BRIT) n レジャーセンター rejásentà ◇スポーツ施設, 図書室, 会議室, 喫茶店などを含んだ文化施設 supótsushisetsù, toshóshitsu, kaígishìtsu, kissátèn nádò wo fukúnda buñkashisetsù

leisurely [li:'ʒə:rli:] adj (pace, walk) ゆっくりした yukkúrì shitá

lemon [lem'ən] n (fruit) レモン rémòn

lemonade [leməneid'] n (BRIT: fizzy drink) ラムネ rámùne; (with lemon juice) レモネード remónèdo

lemon tea n レモンティー remóñtī

lend [lend] (pt, pp lent) vt: **to lend something to someone** (money, thing) ...に...を貸す ...ni ...wo kásù

lending library [len'diŋ-] n 貸出し図書館 kashídashitoshokàn

length [leŋθ] n (measurement) 長さ nagása; (distance): **the length of** ...の端から端まで ...no hashí kara hashi madè; (of swimming pool) プールの長さ pūru no nagása; (piece: of wood, string, cloth etc) 1本 ippóñ; (amount of time) 時間 jikáñ

at length (at last) とうとう tôtō; (for a long time) 長い間 nagáì aídà

lengthen [leŋk'θən] vt 長くする nágàku suru

◆vi 長くなる nágàku naru

lengthways [leŋkθ'weiz] adv (slice, fold, lay) 縦に tátè ni

lengthy [leŋk'θi:] adj (meeting, explanation, text) 長い nagáì

lenient [li:'ni:ənt] adj (person, attitude) 寛大な kañdai na

lens [lenz] n (of spectacles, camera) レンズ réñzu; (telescope) 望遠鏡 bôenkyō

Lent [lent] n 四旬節 shijúñsetsu

lent [lent] pt, pp of **lend**

lentil [len'təl] n ヒラマメ hirámame

Leo [li:'ou] n (ASTROLOGY) しし座 shishíza

leopard [lep'ə:rd] n (ZOOL) ヒョウ hyồ

leotard [li:'əta:rd] n レオタード reótàdo

leprosy [lep'rəsi:] n らい病 raíbyō, ハンセン病 hañsenbyō

lesbian [lez'bi:ən] n 女性同性愛者 joséidōseiaishà, レスビアン resúbiàn

less [les] adj (in size, degree) ...より小さい ...yórì chíisài; (in amount, quality) ...より少ない ...yórì sukúnaì

◆pron ...より少ないもの ...yórì sukúnaì monò

◆adv ...より少なく ...yórì sukúnakù

◆prep: **less tax/10% discount** ...から税金〔1割り〕を引いて ...kara zeíkin〔ichí-

wàri〕wo hiíte

less than half 半分以下 hañbùn íkà

less than ever 更に少なく sárà ni sukúnàku

less and less ますます少なく masúmàsu sukúnàku

the less he talks the better ... 彼はできるだけしゃべらない方がいい kárè wa dekíru dake shabéranai hồ ga íi

lessen [les'ən] vi 少なくなる sukúnaku narù

◆vt 少なくする sukúnàku suru

lesser [les'ə:r] adj (smaller: in degree, importance, amount) 小さい〔少ない〕方の chíisài〔sukúnài〕hồ no

to a lesser extent ...も それ程ではないが ...mo soré hodò de wa naí ga ...mo

lesson [les'ən] n (class: history etc) 授業 jugyỗ; (: ballet etc) けいこ kéìko, レッスン réssùn; (example, warning) 見せしめ miséshime

to teach someone a lesson (fig) ...に思い知らせてやる ...ni omóishirasete yarù

lest [lest] conj ...しない様に ...shinái yồ ni

let [let] (pt, pp let) vt (allow) 許す yurúsù; (BRIT: lease) 賃貸する chiñtai suru

to let someone do something ...に...するのを許す ...ni ...surú no wò yurúsù

to let someone know something ...に...を知らせる ...ni ...wo shiráserù

let's go 行きましょう ikímashō

let him come (permit) 彼が来るのを邪魔しないで下さい kárè ga kúrù no wo jamá shinàide kudásaì

「**to let**」貸し家 kashíya

let down vt (tire etc) ...の空気を抜く ...no kùki wo nuku; (person) がっかりさせる gakkárì saséru

let go vi (stop holding: thing, person) 手を放す te wo hanásù

◆vt (release: person, animal) 放す hanásu

lethal [li:'θəl] adj (chemical, dose etc) 致命的な chiméiteki na

a lethal weapon 凶器 kyỗki

lethargic [ləθɑ:r'dʒik] adj 無気力の mukíryòku no

let in vt (water, air) ...が漏れる ...ga mo-

let off *vt* (culprit) 許す yurúsù; (firework, bomb) 爆発させる bakúhatsu saseru; (gun) 撃つ útsù

let on *vi* 漏らす morásù

let out *vt* (person, dog) 外に出す sótò ni dásù; (breath) 吐く hákù; (water, air) 抜く núkù; (sound) 出す dásù

letter [let'ə:r] *n* (correspondence) 手紙 tegámi; (of alphabet) 文字 mójì

letter bomb *n* 手紙爆弾 tegámibakúdan

letterbox [let'ə:rba:ks] (*BRIT*) *n* (for receiving mail) 郵便受け yūbiñ-uke; (for sending mail) 郵便ポスト yūbinposúto, ポスト pósùto

lettering [let'ə:riŋ] *n* 文字 mójì

lettuce [let'is] *n* レタス rétàsu

let up *vi* (cease) やむ yámù; (diminish) 緩む yurúmù

let-up [let'ʌp] *n* (of violence, noise etc) 減少 geñshō

leukemia [lu:ki:'mi:ə] (*BRIT* **leukaemia**) *n* 白血病 hakkétsubyō

level [lev'əl] *adj* (flat) 平らな taíra na
♦*adv*: **to draw level with** (person, vehicle) ...に追い付く ...ni oítsukù
♦*n* (point on scale, height etc) 高さ tákàsa, レベル rébèru; (of lake, river) 水位 súìi
♦*vt* (land: make flat) 平らにする taíra ni suru; (building, forest etc: destroy) 破壊する hakái suru
to be level with ...と同じぐらいである ...to onáji guraí de árù
"A" levels (*BRIT*) 学科の上級試験 gakká no jōkyū shikeñ ◇大学入学資格を得るための試験 daígakunyūgaku shikakù wo érù tamé nò shikeñ
"O" levels (*BRIT*) 学科の普通級試験 gakká no futsúkyū shikeñ ◇中等教育を5年受けた後に受ける試験 chūtōkyōiku wò gonén ukéta nochi ni ukérù shikeñ
on the level (*fig*: honest) 正直で shōjiki de

level crossing (*BRIT*) *n* 踏切 fumíkiri

level-headed [lev'əlhed'id] *adj* (calm) 分別のある fúñbetsu no árù

level off *vi* (prices etc) 横ばい状態にな

る yokóbaijōtai ni nárù

level out *vi* = **level off**

lever [lev'ə:r] *n* (to operate machine) レバー rébà; (bar) バール bárù; (*fig*) 人を動かす手段 hitó wò ugókasù shúdàn, てこ tékò

leverage [lev'ə:ridʒ] *n* (using bar, lever) てこの作用 tékò no sáyò; (*fig*: influence) 影響力 eíkyōryòku

levity [lev'iti:] *n* (frivolity) 不真面目さ fumájimesa

levy [lev'i:] *n* (tax, charge) 税金 zeíkin
♦*vt* 課する ka súrù

lewd [lu:d] *adj* (look, remark etc) わいせつな waísetsu na

liabilities [laiəbil'əti:z] *npl* (COMM) 債務 sáìmu

liability [laiəbil'əti:] *n* (person, thing) 負担 fután; (LAW: responsibility) 責任 sekínin

liable [lai'əbəl] *adj* (subject): **liable to** ...の罰則が適用される ...no bassóku ga tekíyō sarerù; (responsible): **liable for** ...の責任を負うべきである ...no sekínin wò oúbeki de arù; (likely): **liable to do** ...しがちである ...shigáchi de arù

liaise [li:eiz'] *vi*: **to liaise (with)** (...と) 連携する (...to) reñkei suru

liaison [li:ei'zɑ:n] *n* (cooperation, coordination) 連携 reñkei; (sexual relationship) 密通 mittsū

liar [lai'ə:r] *n* うそつき usótsùki

libel [lai'bəl] *n* 名誉毀損 meíyokisòn
♦*vt* 中傷する chūshō suru

liberal [lib'ə:rəl] *adj* (tolerant) 開放的な kaíhōteki na; (large: offer, amount etc) 寛大な kañdai na

liberate [lib'ə:reit] *vt* 解放する kaíhō suru

liberation [libərei'ʃən] *n* 解放 kaíhō

liberty [lib'ə:rti:] *n* (*gen*) 自由 jiyū; (criminal): **to be at liberty** 捕まらないでいる tsukámaranàide írù, 逃走中である tōsōchū de arù
to be at liberty to do 自由に...できる jiyū ni ...dekírù
to take the liberty of doing something 勝手に...する katté ni ...surú

Libra [liːˈbrə] n (ASTROLOGY) 天びん座 teñbinza

librarian [laibreːrˈiːən] n (worker) 図書館員 toshōkáň-in; (qualified) 司書 shíshō

library [laiˈbreːriː] n (institution, SCOL: building) 図書館 toshōkáṅ; (: room) 図書室 toshōshítsu; (private collection) 蔵書 zōsho

libretto [libretˈou] n (OPERA) 脚本 kyakúhon

Libya [libˈiːə] n リビア ríbìa

Libyan [libˈiːən] adj リビアの ríbìa no
♦n リビア人 ribìajìn

lice [lais] npl of **louse**

licence [laiˈsəns] (US also: **license**) n (official document) 免許 méñkyo; (AUT) 運転免許証 uńtenmeńkyoshō

license [laiˈsəns] n (US) = **licence**
♦vt (person, organization, activity) 認可する níňka suru

licensed [laiˈsənst] adj (driver, pilot etc) 免許 を 持った méňkyo wo mottá; (for alcohol) 酒類販売許可を持った sakéruihanbaikyòka wo mottá

license plate (US) n ナンバープレート nañbāpurèto

licentious [laisenˈtʃəs] adj いん乱な iñran na

lichen [laiˈkən] n 地衣 chíi

lick [lik] vt (stamp, fingers etc) なめる namérù; (inf: defeat) ...に 楽勝する ...ni rakúshō suru

to lick one's lips (also fig) 舌なめずりする shitánamèzuri suru

licorice [likˈəris] (US) n カンゾウあめ kañzōame

lid [lid] n (of box, case, pan) ふた futá; (eyelid) まぶた mábùta

lie [lai] (pt lay, pp lain) vi (person) 横になる yokó ni narù; (be situated: place, object: also fig) ...に ある ...ni árù; (be placed: in race, league etc) 第...位である daí ...í de arù; (tell lies: pt, pp **lied**) うそをつく usó wo tsúkù
♦n (untrue statement) うそ usó

to lie low (fig) 人目を避ける hitóme wo sakérù

lie about/around vi (things) 散らばって

いる chirábatte iru; (people) ごろりと寝ている gorórì to neté iru

lie-down [laiˈdaun] (BRIT) n: *to have a lie-down* 昼寝する hirúne suru

lie-in [laiˈin] (BRIT) n: *to have a lie-in* 寝坊する nebō suru

lieu [luː]: *in lieu of* prep ...の代りに ...no kawári ni

lieutenant [luːtenˈənt] n (MIL) (also: **first lieutenant**) 中尉 chūi; (also: **second lieutenant**) 小尉 shōi

life [laif] (pl **lives**) n (quality of being alive) 生命 seímeì; (live things) 生物 seíbùtsu; (state of being alive) 命 ínòchi; (lifespan) 一生 isshō; (events, experience, activities) 生活 seíkatsu

to come to life (fig: person, party etc) 活気付く kakkízukù

life assurance (BRIT) n = **life insurance**

lifebelt [laifˈbelt] n 救命具 kyūmeìgu

lifeboat [laifˈbout] n (rescue launch) 巡視艇 juñshitèi; (on ship) 救命ボート kyūmeibòto

lifeguard [laifˈgɑːrd] n (at beach, swimming pool) 看視員 kañshiìn

life imprisonment n 無期懲役 mukíchòeki

life insurance n 生命保険 seímeihokèn

life jacket n 救命胴衣 kyūmeidòi

lifeless [laifˈlis] adj (dead: person, animal) 死んだ shíňda; (fig: person) 元気のない géñki no naì; (: party etc) 活気のない kakkí no naì

lifelike [laifˈlaik] adj (model, dummy, robot etc) 生きている様な íkìte irú yòna; (realistic: painting, performance) 写実的な shajítsuteki na

lifeline [laifˈlain] n (means of surviving) 命綱 inóchizùna

lifelong [laifˈlɔːŋ] adj (friend, ambition etc) 一生の isshō no

life preserver (US) n = **lifebelt**; **life jacket**

life sentence n 無期懲役 mukíchòeki

life-size(d) [laifˈsaiz(d)] adj (painting, model etc) 実物大の jitsúbutsudaì no

life-span [laifˈspæn] n (of person, animal, plant: also fig) 寿命 jumyō

life style n 生き方 ikíkata, ライフスタイル raífusutaîru

life support system n (MED) 生命維持装置 seímeiijisōchi

lifetime [laif'taim] n (of person) 生涯 shōgai; (of thing) 寿命 jumyō

lift [lift] vt (raise: thing, part of body) 上げる agéru; (end: ban, rule) 撤廃する teppái suru

♦vi (fog) 晴れる harérù

♦n (BRIT: machine) エレベーター erébētā

to give someone a lift (AUT) ...を車に乗せて上げる ...wo kurúma ni noséte agerù

lift-off [lift'ɔːf] n (of rocket) 離昇 rishō

ligament [lig'əmənt] n じん帯 jíntai

light [lait] n (brightness: from sun, moon, lamp, fire) 光 hikári; (ELEC) 電気 deńki; (AUT) ライト ráito; (for cigarette etc): **have you got a light?** 火をお持ちですか hí wò o-móchi desu ká

♦vt (pt, pp **lit**) (fire) たく takú; (candle, cigarette) ...に火を付ける ...ni hí wo tsukérù; (room): **to be lit by** ...で照明されている ...de shōmei saréte irù

♦adj (pale) 淡い awái; (not heavy: object) 軽い karúí; (: rain) 細かい komákaì; (: traffic) 少ない sukúnaì; (not strenuous: work) 軽い karúí; (bright: building, room) 明るい akárui; (graceful, gentle: movement, action) 軽やかな karóyàka na; (not serious: book, play, film, music) 肩の凝らない katá no koránaì

to come to light 明るみに出る akárumi ni derù

in the light of (discussions, new evidence etc) ...を考慮して ...wo kōryo shite

light bulb n 電球 deńkyū

lighten [lait'ən] vt (make less heavy) 軽くする karúku surù

lighter [lait'əːr] n (also: **cigarette lighter**) ライター ráitā

light-headed [lait'hed'id] adj (dizzy) 頭がふらふらする atáma ga fúràfura suru; (excited) 浮わついた uwátsuita

light-hearted [lait'hɑːr'tid] adj (person)

陽気な yōki na; (question, remark etc) 気楽な kiráku na

lighthouse [lait'haus] n 燈台 tōdai

lighting [lai'tiŋ] n (system) 照明 shōmei

lightly [lait'li:] adv 軽く karúku; (thoughtlessly) 軽率に keísotsu ni; (slightly) 少し sukóshì

to get off lightly 軽い罰だけで逃れる karúi bátsù dáke de nogárerù

lightness [lait'nis] n (in weight) 軽さ karúsa

lightning [lait'niŋ] n (in sky) 稲妻 inázùma

lightning conductor (BRIT) n = **lightning rod**

lightning rod (US) n 避雷針 hiráíshin

light pen n ライトペン raítopeñ

lights [laits] npl (AUT: traffic lights) (交通)信号 (kōtsū)shiñgō

light up vi (face) 輝く kagáyakù

♦vt (illuminate) 明るくする akáruku suru

lightweight [lait'weit] adj (suit) 薄いusúi

♦n (BOXING) ライト級のボクサー raítokyū no bókùsā

light year n (PHYSICS) 光年 kōnen

like [laik] vt (find pleasing, attractive, acceptable: person, thing) ...が好きである ...ga sukí de arù

♦prep (similar to) ...の様な ...no yō na; (in comparisons) ...の様に ...no yō ni; (such as) 例えば..などの様な〔に〕 tatóèba ...nádò no yō na〔ni〕

♦adj 似た nitá

♦n: **and the like** など nádò

his likes and dislikes 彼の好きな物と嫌いな物 kárè no sukí na monò to kirái na monò

I would like, I'd like ...が欲しいのですが ...ga hoshíi no desu gà

would you like a coffee? コーヒーはいかがですか kōhī wa ikágà desu ká

to be/look like someone/something ...に似ている ...ni nité irù

what does it look/taste/sound like? どんな格好〔味, 音〕ですか dóñna kákkō〔ají, otó〕dèsu ká

that's just like him 彼らしいね karé rashīi né

do it like this やり方はこうです yari-kata wa kō desu

it is nothing like ... ...とは全く違います ...to wa mattáku chigaìmasu

likeable [lai'kəbəl] *adj* (person) 人好きのする hitózuki no suru

likelihood [laik'li:hud] *n* 可能性 kanōsei

likely [laik'li:] *adj* (probable) ありそうな arísō na

to be likely to do ...しそうである ...shi-sō de arū

not likely! 何があっても...しない nánì ga atté mo ...shínai, とんでもない toñdemonai

likeness [laik'nis] *n* (similarity) 似ている事 nité irú kotó

that's a good likeness (photo, portrait) 実物そっくりだ jitsúbùtsu sokkúrì da

likewise [laik'waiz] *adv* (similarly) 同じく onájiku

to do likewise 同じ様にする onáji yō ni suru

liking [lai'kiŋ] *n*: **to have a liking for** (person, thing) ...が好きである ...ga sukí de arū

to be to someone's liking ...の気に入っている ...no kí ni itte irū

lilac [lai'lək] *n* (BOT: tree, flower) ライラック raírakkù, リラ rírà

lily [lil'i:] *n* (plant, flower) ユリ yurí

lily of the valley *n* スズラン suzúrañ

limb [lim] *n* (ANAT) 手足 tēàshi, 肢 shí

limber up [lim'bə:r-] *vi* (SPORT) 準備運動をする juñbiuñdò wo suru, ウオーミングアップする uōminguappù suru

limbo [lim'bou] *n*: **to be in limbo** (*fig*) 忘れ去られている wasúresararete irù

lime [laim] *n* (fruit) ライム raímu; (*also*: **lime tree**) ライムの木 raímu no ki; (*also*: **lime juice**) ライムジュース raímujùsu; (for soil) 石灰 sèkkái; (rock) 石灰岩 sek-káìgan

limelight [laim'lait] *n*: **to be in the limelight** 注目を浴びている chúmoku wò abíte irù

limerick [lim'ə:rik] *n* 五行わい歌 gogyō-waìka

limestone [laim'stoun] *n* 石灰岩 sekkáìgan

limit [lim'it] *n* (greatest amount, extent, degree) 限界 geñkai; (restriction: of time, money etc) 制限 seígen; (of area) 境界 kyōkai

♦*vt* (production, expense etc) 制限する seígen suru

limitation [limitei'ʃən] *n* (control, restriction) 制限 seígen; (of person, thing) 限界 geñkai

limited [lim'itid] *adj* (small: choice, resources etc) 限られた kagírarèta

to be limited to ...に限られる ...ni kagírarerù

limited (liability) company (*BRIT*) *n* 有限会社 yūgeñgaìsha

limousine [lim'əzi:n] *n* リムジン rímùjin

limp [limp] *n*: **to have a limp** びっこを引く bíkkò wo hikú

♦*vi* (person, animal) びっこを引く bíkkò wo hikú

♦*adj* (person) ぐにゃぐにゃの gúnyàgu-nya no

limpet [lim'pit] *n* カサガイ kaságai

line [lain] *n* (long thin mark) 線 séñ; (wrinkle: on face) しわ shiwá; (row: of people, things) 列 rétsù; (of writing, song) 行 gyō; (rope) 綱 tsuná, ロープ rōpu; (*also*: **fishing line**) 釣糸 tsuríito; (*also*: **power line**) 送電線 sōdensen; (*also*: **telephone line**) 電話線 deñwasen; (TEL) 回線 kaísen; (railway track) 線路 séñro; (bus, coach, team route) ...線 ...séñ; (*fig*: attitude, policy) 方針 hōshin; (: business, work) 分野 búñ-ya; (COMM: of product's) シリーズ shírīzu

♦*vt* (road, room) ...に並ぶ ...ni narábù; (subj: person: container) ...の内側に...を張る ...no uchigawa ni ...wo hárù; (: clothing) ...に裏地を付ける ...ni uráji wo tsukérù

to line something with ...に...の裏を付ける ...ni ...no urá wo tsukérù

to line the streets 道路の両側に並ぶ dōro no ryōgawa ni narábù

in line (in a row) 1列に ichíretsu ni

in line with (according to) …に従って …ni shitágatte

linear [lin'i:ər] *adj* (process, sequence) 一直線の itchókusen no; (shape, form) 線形の señkei no

lined [laind] *adj* (face) しわのある shiwá no arú; (paper) 線を引いた sén wo hiíta

linen [lin'ən] *n* (cloth) リンネル rínneru, リネン rínen; (tablecloths, sheets etc) リネン rínen

liner [lai'nər] *n* (ship) 豪華客船 gókakyakùsen; (for bin) ごみ袋 gomíbukuro

linesman [lainz'mən] (*pl* **linesmen**) *n* (SPORT) 線審 señshin, ラインズマン raínzuman

line up *vi* 列を作る rétsu wo tsukúru
♦*vt* (people) 1列に並ばせる ichíretsu ni narábaserù; (prepare: event, celebration) 手配する tehái suru

line-up [lain'ʌp] *n* (US: queue) 行列 gyóretsu; (SPORT) ラインアップ raín-appù

linger [liŋ'gər] *vi* (smell, tradition etc) 残る nokórù; (person) ぐずぐずする gúzuguzu suru

lingerie [lɑːn'dʒərei] *n* 女性下着類 joséishitagirùi, ランジェリー ránjerī

lingo [liŋ'gou] (*pl* **lingoes**: *inf*) *n* (language) 言葉 kotóba

linguist [liŋ'gwist] *n* (person who speaks several languages) 数カ国語を話せる人 súkakokùgo wo hanáserù hitó

linguistic [liŋgwis'tik] *adj* (studies, developments, ideas etc) 語学の gógaku no

linguistics [liŋgwis'tiks] *n* 語学 gógaku

lining [lai'niŋ] *n* (cloth) 裏地 uráji; (ANAT) 粘膜 néñmaku

link [liŋk] *n* (relationship) 関係 kañkei; (of a chain) 輪 wá
♦*vt* (join) つなぐ tsunágu; (associate): **to link with/to** …と関連付ける …to kañren-zukerù

links [liŋks] *npl* (GOLF) ゴルフ場 gorúfujð

link up *vt* (machines, systems) つなぐ tsunágu
♦*vi* 合流する góryū suru

lino [lai'nou] *n* = **linoleum**

linoleum [linou'li:əm] *n* リノリウム rínoriumu

lion [lai'ən] *n* (ZOOL) ライオン raíon

lioness [lai'ənis] *n* 雌ライオン mesúraion

lip [lip] *n* (ANAT) 唇 kuchíbiru

lip-read [lip'ri:d] *vi* 読唇する dokúshin suru

lip salve *n* 唇の荒れ止め kuchíbiru no arédome

lip service *n*: **to pay lip service to something** (*pej*) 上辺だけ…に賛成する uwábe dake …ni sañsei suru

lipstick [lip'stik] *n* 口紅 kuchíbeni

liqueur [likər'] *n* リキュール ríkyūru

liquid [lik'wid] *adj* (state) 液体の ekítai no
♦*n* 液 ékì, 液体 ekítai

liquidate [lik'wideit] *vt* (opponents, rivals) 消す késù, 殺す korósù; (company) つぶす tsubúsù

liquidize [lik'widaiz] *vt* (CULIN) ミキサーに掛ける míkìsā ni kakérù

liquidizer [lik'widaizər] (*BRIT*) *n* ミキサー míkìsā

liquor [lik'ər] *n* 酒 saké

liquorice [lik'əːris] (*BRIT*) *n* = **licorice**

liquor store (*US*) *n* 酒屋 sákayà

Lisbon [liz'bən] *n* リスボン rísùbon

lisp [lisp] *n* 舌足らずの発音 shitátaràzu no hatsúon
♦*vi* 舌足らずに発音する shitátaràzu ni hatsúon suru

list [list] *n* (catalog: of things) 目録 mokúroku, リスト rísùto; (: of people) 名簿 meíbo, リスト rísùto
♦*vt* (mention) 並べてあげる narábete agerù; (put on list) …のリストを作る …no rísùto wo tsukúrù

listed building [lis'tid-] (*BRIT*) *n* 指定建造物 shitéikenzòbutsu

listen [lis'ən] *vi* 聞く kikú
to listen to someone/something …を〔…の言う事を〕聞く …wo〔…no iú kotð wo〕kikú

listener [lis'ənər] *n* (person listening to speaker) 聞いている人 kiíte irù hitó; (RADIO) 聴取者 chóshushà

listless [list'lis] *adj* 物憂い monóuì

lit [lit] *pt, pp of* **light**

liter [li:'tə:r] (*US*) *n* (unit of volume) リットル rīttoru

literacy [lit'ə:rəsi:] *n* 識字 shikíji

literal [lit'ə:rəl] *adj* (exact: sense, meaning) 厳密な geńmitsu na; (word for word: translation) 逐語的な chikúgoteki na

literally [lit'ə:rəli:] *adv* (in fact) 本当に hoñtó ni; (really) 文字通りに mojídōri ni

literary [lit'ə:re:ri:] *adj* 文学の buńgàku no

literate [lit'ə:rit] *adj* (able to read etc) 読み書きできる yomíkaki dekirù; (educated) 教養のある kyóyō no arù

literature [lit'ə:rətʃə:r] *n* (novels, plays, poetry) 文学 buńgàku; (printed information: scholarly) 文献 buńken; (: brochures etc) 印刷物 iñsatsubùtsu, カタログ katárogu

lithe [laið] *adj* (person, animal) しなやかな shináyàka na

litigation [litəgei'ʃən] *n* 訴訟 soshō

litre [li:'tə:r] (*BRIT*) *n* = **liter**

litter [lit'ə:r] *n* (rubbish) 散らばっているごみ chirábatte irù gomi; (young animals) 一腹 hitóhara

litter bin (*BRIT*) *n* ごみ入れ gomíire

littered [lit'ə:rd] *adj*: **littered with** (scattered) ...を散らかされた ...wo chirákasareta

little [lit'əl] *adj* (small: thing, person) 小さい chiísaì; (young: child) 幼い osánaì; (short: distance) 近い chikáì; (time, event) 短い mijíkaì

♦*adv* 少ししか...ない sukóshì shika ...náì

a little (amount) 少し(の) sukóshì (no)

a little bit 少し sukóshì

little brother/sister 弟〔妹〕otóto(imóto)

little by little 少しずつ sukóshizutsu

little finger *n* 小指 koyúbi

live [*vb* liv *adj* laiv] *vi* (reside: in house, town, country) 住む sūmù; (lead one's life) 暮す kurásù; (be alive) 生きている ikíte irù

♦*adj* (animal, plant) 生きている ikíte irù; (TV, RADIO) 生の namá no, ライブの ráibu no; (performance) 実演の jitsúen

no; (ELEC) 電流が通じている deńryū ga tsūjíte irù, 生きている ikíte irù; (bullet, bomb, missile) 使用可能状態の shiyókanōjōtai no, 実の jitsú no

to live with someone (cohabit) ...と同せいする ...to dōsei suru

live down *vt* (defeat, error, failure): *I'll never live it down* 一生の恥だ isshō no hájì da

livelihood [laiv'li:hud] *n* (income source) 生計 seíkei

lively [laiv'li:] *adj* (person) 活発な kappátsu na; (interesting: place etc) 活気に満ちた kakkí ni michítà; (: event) にぎやかな nigíyaka na; (: book) 面白い omóshiroì; (enthusiastic: interest, admiration etc) 熱心な nesshín na

liven up [laiv'ən-] *vt* (person) ...に元気を付ける ...ni géñki wo tsukérù; (discussion, evening etc) 面白くする omóshirokù suru

♦*vi* (person) 元気になる géñki ni nárù; (discussion, evening etc) 面白くなる omóshirokù nárù

live on *vt fus* (food) ...を食べて暮す ...wo tábète kurásu

liver [liv'ə:r] *n* (ANAT) 肝臓 kańzō; (CULIN) レバー rébā

livery [liv'ə:ri:] *n* (of servant) お仕着せ o-shíkise

lives [laivz] *npl of* **life**

livestock [laiv'sta:k] *n* (AGR) 家畜 kachíku

live together *vi* (cohabit) 同せいする dōsei suru

live up to *vt fus* (fulfil) 守る mamórù

livid [liv'id] *adj* (color: of bruise) 青黒い aóguroì; (: of angry face) どす黒い dosúguroì; (: of sky) 鉛色の namáiiro no; (furious: person) 激怒した gékìdo shitá

living [liv'iŋ] *adj* (alive: person, animal) 生きている ikíte iru

♦*n: to earn/make a living* 生計を立てる seíkei wo tatérù

living conditions *npl* 暮しの状況 kuráshi no jōkyō

living room *n* 居間 imá

living standards *npl* 生活水準 seíkatsusuijùn

living wage n 生活賃金 seíkatsuchiǹgin

lizard [liz'ə:rd] n トカゲ tokáge

load [loud] n (thing carried: of person) 荷物 nímòtsu; (: of animal) 荷 ní; (: of vehicle) 積荷 tsumíni; (weight) 負担 fután

♦vt (also: **load up**: vehicle, ship etc): *to load (with)* (...を) ...に積む (...wo) ...ni tsúmù; (COMPUT: program) メモリーに読込む mémòrī ni yomíkomù, ロードする rōdo suru; (gun) ...に弾丸を込める ...ni dañgan wo komérù; (camera) ...にフィルムを入れる ...ni fírùmu wo irérù; (tape recorder) ...にテープを入れる ...ni tḗpu wo irérù

a load of rubbish (inf) でたらめ detárame

loads of/a load of (fig) 沢山の takúsaǹ no

loaded [lou'did] adj (vehicle): *to be loaded with* ...を積んでいる ... wo tsuǹde irù; (question) 誘導的な yúdòteki na; (inf: rich) 金持の kanémochi no

loaf [louf] (pl **loaves**) n 一かたまりのパン hitókàtamari no pan

loan [loun] n (sum of money) 貸付金 kashítsukekin, ローン rôn

♦vt (money, thing) 貸す kasú

on loan (borrowed) 借りている karíte irù

loath [louθ] adj: *to be loath to do something* ...をしたくない ...wo shitáku naì

loathe [louð] vt (person, activity) ...が大嫌いである ...ga daíkiraì de árù

loaves [louvz] npl of **loaf**

lobby [lɑːb'iː] n (of building) ロビー robī; (POL: pressure group) 圧力団体 atsúryokudaǹtai

♦vt (POL) ...に圧力を掛ける ...ni atsúryoku wò kakérù

lobe [loub] n (also: **earlobe**) 耳たぶ mimítabù

lobster [lɑːb'stəːr] n ロブスター róbùsutā

local [lou'kəl] adj (council, paper, police station) 地元の jimóto no

♦n (BRIT: pub) 地元のパブ jimóto no pábù

local anesthetic n (MED) 局部麻酔 kyokúbumasùi

local authority n 地方自治体 chihójichitài

local call n (TEL) 市内通話 shináitsùwa

local government n 地方自治体 chihójichitài

locality [loukæl'iti:] n 場所 basho

locally [lou'kəli:] adv 地元で jimóto de

locals [lou'kəlz] npl: *the locals* (local inhabitants) 地元の住民 jimóto no júmìn

locate [lou'keit] vt (find: person, thing) 見付ける mitsúkeru; (situate): *to be located in* ...にある〔いる〕...ni árù〔irú〕

location [loukei'ʃən] n (particular place) 場所 basho

on location (CINEMA) ロケで roké de

loch [lɑːk] n 湖 mizúumì

lock [lɑːk] n (of door, drawer, suitcase) 錠 jṓ; (on canal) こう門 kṓmon; (also: **lock of hair**) 髪の一房 kamí no hitófùsa

♦vt (door, drawer, suitcase: with key) ...のかぎを掛ける ...no kagí wo kakérù

♦vi (door etc) かぎが掛る kagí ga kakárù; (wheels) 回らなくなる mawáranaku narù

locker [lɑːk'əːr] n (in school, railway station etc) ロッカー rôkkā

locket [lɑːk'it] n ロケット rokéttò

lock in vt 閉じ込める tojíkomerù

lock out vt (person) 閉出す shimédasu

locksmith [lɑːk'smiθ] n 錠前師 jṓmaeshì

lock up vt (criminal) 刑務所に入れる keímushò ni irérù; (mental patient) 施設に預ける shisétsu ni azúkerù; (house) ...のかぎを掛ける ...no kagí wo kakérù

♦vi ...のかぎを掛ける ...no kagí wo kakérù

lockup [lɑːk'ʌp] n (jail) 刑務所 keímushò

locomotive [loukəmou'tiv] n 機関車 kikáñsha

locum tenens [lou'kəm ti:'nenz] (BRIT **locum**) n (MED) 代診 daíshin

locust [lou'kəst] n イナゴ inágo

lodge [lɑːdʒ] n (small house) 守衛室 shuéishìtsu; (hunting lodge) 山小屋 yamágoya

◆vi (person): **to lodge (with)** (...の家に) 下宿する (...no iɛ ni) geshúku suru; (bullet, bone etc) ...に支える ...ni tsukáerù

◆vt (complaint, protest etc) 提出する teíshutsu suru

lodger [lɑ:dʒə:r] n 下宿人 geshúkunin

lodgings [lɑ:dʒɪŋz] npl 下宿 geshúku

loft [lɔ:ft] n (attic) 屋根裏部屋 yanéurabèya

lofty [lɔ:fti:] adj (noble: ideal, aim) 高尚な kōshō na; (self-important: manner) 横柄な őhei na

log [lɔ:g] n (piece of wood) 丸太 marúta; (written account) 日誌 nisshí

◆vt (event, fact) 記録する kiróku suru

logarithm [lɔ:gˈərɪðəm] n (MATH) 対数 taísū

logbook [lɔ:gˈbuk] n (NAUT) 航海日誌 kōkainisshí; (AVIAT) 航空日誌 kōkūnisshí; (BRIT: of car) 登録帳 tōrokuchō

loggerheads [lɔ:gˈə:rhedz] npl: **to be at loggerheads** 対立している taíritsu shite iru

logic [lɑ:dʒik] n (method of reasoning) 論理学 roñrigàku; (process of reasoning) 論理 róñri

logical [lɑ:dʒikəl] adj (argument, analysis) 論理的な roñriteki na; (conclusion, result) 当然な tōzen na; (course of action) 合理的な gōriteki na

logistics [loudʒisˈtiks] n (planning and organization) 仕事の計画と実行 shigóto nò keíkaku tò jikkō

logo [lou'gou] n (of firm, organization) シンボルマーク shíñborumàku, ロゴ rógò

loin [lɔin] n (of meat) 腰肉 koshíniku

loiter [lɔiˈtə:r] vi (linger) ぶらつく burátsuku

loll [lɑ:l] vi (person: also: **loll about**) ごろ寝している goróne suru

lollipop [lɑ:liˈpɑ:p] n 棒あめ bōame

lollipop lady (BRIT) n 緑のおばさん midóri no obasàn ◇学童道路横断監視員 gakúdō dōroōdan kañshiin

lollipop man (BRIT: pl **lollipop men**) n ◇緑のおばさんの仕事をする男性 midó-

ri no obasàn no shigóto wò suru dansei

London [lʌnˈdən] n ロンドン róñdon

Londoner [lʌnˈdənə:r] n ロンドンっ子 roñdonkko

lone [loun] adj (person) たったひとりのtattá hitóri no; (thing) たったひとつの tattá hitótsu ŋo

loneliness [lounˈliːnis] n 孤独 kodóku

lonely [lounˈliː] adj (person) 寂しい sabíshiì; (situation) 孤独な kodóku na; (place) 人気のない hitóke no naì

long [lɔ:ŋ] adj 長い nagáì

◆adv 長く nágàku

◆vi: **to long for something** ...を恋しがる ...wo koíshigarù

so/as long as ...さえすれば ...sáè suréba

don't be long! 早く帰って来て下さいね háyàku kaétte kite kudásai né

how long is the street? この道の端から端までどのぐらいありますか konó michí no hashí kara hashí madè donó guraì arímasù ká

how long is the lesson? レッスンの時間はどのぐらいですか réssùn no jíkàn wa donó guraì desu ká

6 meters long 長さは6メーター nágàsa wa rokú mētā

6 months long 期間は6か月 kíkàn wa rokkágetsu

all night long ひと晩中 hitóbanjū

he no longer comes 彼はもう来ない kárè wa mō kónai

long before ずっと前に zuttó máè ni

before long (+future, +past) まもなく mamónàku

at long last やっと yattó

long-distance [lɔ:ŋˈdisˈtəns] adj (travel, phone call) 長距離の chōkyori no

longevity [lɑ:ndʒevˈiti:] n 長生き nagáiki

long-haired [lɔ:ŋˈheːrd] adj (person) 長髪の chōhatsu no

longhand [lɔ:ŋˈhænd] n 普通の書き方 futsū no kakíkata

longing [lɔ:ŋˈiŋ] n あこがれ akógare

longitude [lɑ:nˈdʒətuːd] n 経度 keído

long jump n 走り幅跳び hashírihabàtobi

long-life [lɔː'laif] *adj* (batteries etc) 寿命の長い jumyō no nagáĩ; (milk) ロングライフの erúpīrekōdo

long-lost [lɔː'lɔːst] *adj* (relative, friend) 長年会わなかった nagánen awánakattà

long-playing record [lɔːŋ'plei'iŋ-] *n* L Pレコード erúpīrekōdo

long-range [lɔːŋ'reindʒ] *adj* (plan, forecast) 長期の chōki no; (missile, plane etc) 長距離の chōkyori no

long-sighted [lɔːŋ'saitid] *adj* (MED) 遠視の eñshi no

long-standing [lɔːŋ'stæn'diŋ] *adj* 長年にわたる nagánen ni watárù

long-suffering [lɔːŋ'sʌf'əːriŋ] *adj* (person) 忍耐強い niñtaizuyoi

long-term [lɔːŋ'təːrm] *adj* (project, solution etc) 長期の chōki no

long wave *n* (RADIO) 長波 chōha

long-winded [lɔːŋ'win'did] *adj* (speech, text) 長たらしい nagátarashiĩ

loo [luː] (*BRIT: inf*) *n* トイレ tôîre

look [luk] *vi* (see) 見る mírù; (seem, appear) ...に見える ...ni miérù; (building etc): **to look south/(out) onto the sea** 南〔海〕に面している minámi〔úmi〕ni méñ shite irú

♦*n* (*gen*): **to have a look** 見る mírù; (glance: expressing disapproval etc) 目付き métsùki; (appearance, expression) 様子 yōsu

look (here)! (expressing annoyance etc) おい ôî

look! (expressing surprise: male language) 見てくれ mítè kuré; (: female language) 見て mítê

look after *vt fus* (care for) ...の面倒を見る ...no meñdō wo mírù; (deal with) 取扱う toríatsukaù

look at *vt fus* (see) ...を見る ...wo mírù; (read quickly) ...にさっと目を通す ...ni sattó me wo tōsù; (study: problem, subject etc) 調べる shiráberù

look back *vi* (remember) 振返ってみる furíkaette mirù

look down on *vt fus* (*fig*) 軽べつする keíbetsu suru

look for *vt fus* (person, thing) 捜す sagásu

gásu

look forward to *vt fus* ...を楽しみにする ...wo tanóshimi ni suru; (in letters): *we look forward to hearing from you* ご返事をお待ちしております go-héñji wo o-máchi shitè orímasù

look into *vt* (investigate) ...を調べる ...wo shiráberù

look on *vi* (watch) 傍観する bōkan suru

look out *vi* (beware): **to look out (for)** (...に) 注意する (...ni) chūĩ suru

lookout [luk'aut] *n* (tower etc) 看視所 kañshijō; (person) 見張り人 mihárinin

to be on the lookout for something ...を警戒する ...wo keíkai suru

look out for *vt fus* (seek) 捜す sagásu

look round *vi* 見回す mimáwasù

looks [luks] *npl* (good looks) 容ぼう yṓbō

look through *vt fus* (examine) ...を調べる ...wo shiráberù

look to *vt fus* (rely on) ...を頼りにする ...wo tayóri ni surù

look up *vi* (with eyes) 見上げる miágerù; (situation) ...の見通しがよくなる ...no mitōshi ga yokù naru

♦*vt* (piece of information) 調べる shiráberù

look up to *vt fus* (hero, idol) ...を尊敬する ...wo soñkei suru

loom [luːm] *vi* (*also*: **loom up**: object, shape) ぼんやりと姿を現す boñ-yarí to sugáta wò aráwasù; (: event: approach) 迫っている semátte irù

♦*n* (for weaving) 機織機 hatáorikì

loony [luː'niː] (*inf*) *adj* 狂っている kurútte irù

♦*n* 気違い kichígaì

loop [luːp] *n* (in string, ribbon etc) 輪 wá

♦*vt*: **to loop something round something** ...を...に...を巻付ける ...ni ...wo makítsukerù

loophole [luːp'houl] *n* (*fig*) 抜け穴 nukéana

loose [luːs] *adj* (not firmly fixed) 緩い yurúĩ; (not close fitting: clothes etc) ゆったりした yuttárî shita; (not tied back: long hair) 縛ってない shibátte naĩ; (promiscuous: life, morals) ふしだらな fushídàra na

♦*n: to be on the loose* (prisoner, maniac) 逃亡中である tōbōchū de arù

loose change *n* 小銭 kozéni

loose chippings [-tʃip'iŋz] *npl* (on road) 砂利 jarí

loose end *n: to be at loose ends* (US) *or a loose end* (BRIT) 暇を持て余している himá wo motéamashite irù

loosely [luːs'liː] *adv* 緩く yúrùku

loosen [luː'sən] *vt* 緩める yurúmerù

loot [luːt] *n* (*inf*) 分捕り品 buńdorihìn

♦*vt* (steal from: shops, homes) 略奪する ryakúdatsu suru

lop off [lɑ:p-] *vt* (branches etc) 切り落す kiríotosù

lopsided [lɑ:p'sai'did] *adj* (crooked) 偏った katáyottà

lord [lɔːrd] *n* (BRIT: peer) 貴族 kízòku

Lord Smith スミス卿 sumísukyō

the Lord (REL) 主 shú

my lord (to bishop, noble, judge) 閣下 kákkà

good Lord! えっ ét

the (House of) Lords (BRIT) 上院 jōin

lordship [lɔːrd'ʃip] *n: your Lordship* 閣下 kákkà

lore [lɔːr] *n* (of particular culture) 伝承 deńshō

lorry [lɔːr'iː] (BRIT) *n* トラック torákkù

lorry driver (BRIT) *n* トラック運転手 torákku unteñshu

lose [luːz] (*pt, pp* lost) *vt* (object) 紛失する fuńshitsu suru、なくす nakúsù; (job) 失う ushínaù; (weight) 減らす herásù; (friend, relative through death) 失う ushínaù、なくす nakusu; (waste: time) 無駄にする mudá ni surù; (: opportunity) 逃す nogásù; (money) 損する sóñ suru

♦*vi* (competition, argument) ...に負ける ...ni makérù

to lose (time) (clock) 遅れる okúrerù

loser [luː'zəːr] *n* (in game, contest) 敗者 háìsha; (*inf*: failure: person, thing) 出来損ない dekísokonai

loss [lɔːs] *n* (act of losing something) 紛失 fuńshitsu; (occasion of losing some-

thing) 喪失 sōshitsu; (death) 死亡 shibō; (COMM): *to make a loss* 損する sóñ suru

heavy losses (MIL) 大きな損害 ōkina sońgai

to be at a loss 途方に暮れる tohō ni kurèru

lost [lɔːst] *pt, pp of* lose

♦*adj* (person, animal: in unknown place) 道に迷った michí ni mayóttà; (: missing) 行方不明の yukúe fumèi no; (object) なくした nakúshita

lost and found (US) *n* 遺失物 ishítsubùtsu

lost property (BRIT) *n* = lost and found

lot [lɑːt] *n* (set, group: of things) ひと組 hitókùmi; (at auctions) ロット róttò

the lot (everything) 全部 zéñbu

a lot (large number, amount) 沢山 takusan

a lot of 沢山の takusan no

lots of (things, people) 沢山の takúsañ no

I read a lot 私は沢山の本を読みます watákushi wa takúsañ no hoñ wò yomímasù

to draw lots (for something) (...のために) くじを引く (...no tamé nì) kújì wo hīkù

lotion [lou'ʃən] *n* (for skin, hair) ローション rōshon

lottery [lɑ:t'əːriː] *n* (game) 宝くじ takárakùji

loud [laud] *adj* (noise, voice, laugh) 大きい ōkii; (support, condemnation) 強い tsuyóì; (clothes) 派手な hadé na

♦*adv* (speak etc) 大きな声で ōkina kóè de

out loud (read, laugh, pray etc) 声を出して kóè wo dáshìte

loudhailer [laud'heilə:r] (BRIT) *n* = bullhorn

loudly [laud'liː] *adv* 大きな声で ōkina kóè de

loudspeaker [laud'spi:kə:r] *n* 拡声器 kakúseìki、スピーカー súpìkā

lounge [laundʒ] *n* (BRIT: in house) 居間

imá; (in hotel, at airport, station) ロビー
rôbî; (BRIT: also: **lounge bar**) ラウンジ
バー raúnjibâ
♦*vi* ぐったりもたれる guttárì motárerù

lounge about *vi* ぶらぶらする búràbura
suru

lounge around *vi* = **lounge about**

lounge suit (*BRIT*) *n* 背広 sebíro, スー
ツ sûtsu

louse [laus] (*pl* **lice**) *n* (insect) シラミ shi-
rámi

lousy [lau'zi:] *adj* (*inf*: bad quality: show,
meal etc) 最低の saítei no; (: ill) 気持が悪
い kimóchi gà warúì

lout [laut] *n* ちんぴら chíñpira

lovable [lʌv'əbəl] *adj* 愛らしい aíràshiî

love [lʌv] *n* (*gen*) 愛 aî, 愛情 aíjō; (romantic) 恋愛 reñ-ai; (sexual) 性愛 seíai;
(strong liking: for music, football, animals etc) 愛着 aíchaku, 好み konômi
♦*vt* (*gen*) 愛する aí surù; (thing, activity
etc) ...が大好きである ...ga daísuki de
arù

love (from) Anne (on letter) 愛を込め
て, アン（より）aî wo kométe, áñ (yórì)

to love to do ...するのが大好きである
...surú nò ga daísuki de arù

to be in love with ...にほれている ...ni
horéte irù, ...が好きである ...ga sukí de
arù

to fall in love with ...と恋に落ちる ...to
kôî ni ochírù, ...が好きになる ...ga sukí ni
narù

to make love (have sex) 性交する seíkō
suru, セックスする sékkùsu suru

15 love (TENNIS) 15対0 jûgo taî zérò,
フィフティーンラブ fífùtīn rabu

I love chocolate 私はチョコレートが大
好きです watákushi wà chokórèto ga
daísuki desù

love affair *n* 情事 jôji

love letter *n* ラブレター rábùretā

love life *n* 性生活 seíseikàtsu

lovely [lʌv'li:] *adj* (beautiful) 美しい utsúkushiî; (delightful) 楽しい tanóshiî

lover [lʌv'ə:r] *n* (sexual partner) 愛人 aíjin; (person in love) 恋人 koíbito

a lover of art/music 美術〔音楽〕の愛

好者 bíjùtsu〔óñgaku〕no aíkòsha

loving [lʌv'iŋ] *adj* (person) 愛情深い aíjō-
bukaî; (actions) 愛情のこもった aíjō no
komôtta

low [lou] *adj* (*gen*) 低い hikuì; (income,
price etc) 安い yasûî; (quality) 粗悪な so-
áku na; (sound: deep) 深い fukâî; (: quiet)
低い hikuî
♦*adv* (sing) 低音で teíon de; (fly) 低く hikúkù
♦*n* (METEOROLOGY) 低気圧 teíkiàtsu

to be low on (supplies etc) ...が少なくな
っている ...ga sukúnàku natté irù

to feel low (depressed) 元気がない géñki ga naî

low-alcohol [lou'æl'kəhɔ:l] *adj* (wine,
beer) 度の低い do no hikûî

low-cut [lou'kʌt'] *adj* (dress) 襟ぐりの深
い erîguri no fukâî, ローカットの rôkat-
tò no

lower [lou'ə:r] *adj* (bottom, less important) 下の shitá no
♦*vt* (object, price etc) 下げる sagérù;
(voice) 低くする hikûkù suru; (eyes) 下に
向ける shitá ni mukéru

low-fat [lou'fæt'] *adj* 低脂肪の teíshibō
no, ローファットの rôfattò no

lowlands [lou'ləndz] *npl* (GEO) 低地 teí-
chi

lowly [lou'li:] *adj* (position, origin) 卑し
い iyáshiî

loyal [lɔi'əl] *adj* (friend, support etc) 忠実
な chûjitsu na

loyalty [lɔi'əlti:] *n* 忠誠 chûsei

lozenge [lɑ:z'indʒ] *n* (MED) ドロップ dô-
ròppu

LP [el'pi:'] *n abbr* = **long-playing
record**

L-plates [el'pleits] (*BRIT*) *npl* 仮免許運
転中の表示プレート karímenkyo unten-
chū no hyójipurèto

Ltd *abbr* (COMM) = **limited (liability)
company**

lubricate [lu:b'rikeit] *vt* (part of
machine, chain etc) ...に油を差す ...ni a-
búra wo sásù

lucid [lu:'sid] *adj* (writing, speech) 分かり
やすい wakáriyasuî; (able to think clear-

ly) 正気な shṓki na

luck [lʌk] *n* (*also*: **good luck**) 運 úñ
bad luck 悪運 akúuñ
good luck! 成功を祈るよ seíkō wò inṓrù yo
bad/hard/tough luck! 残念だね zañneñ da né

luckily [lʌk'ili:] *adv* 幸いに saíwai ni

lucky [lʌk'i:] *adj* (person: fortunate) 運の良い úñ no yóì; (: at cards etc) ...に強い ...ní tsuyói; (situation, event) まぐれの magúrê no; (object) 好運をもたらす kṓùn wo motárasù

lucrative [lu:'krətiv] *adj* もうかる mṓkarù

ludicrous [lu:'dəkrəs] *adj* (feeling, situation, price etc) ばかばかしい bakábakashii

lug [lʌg] (*inf*) *vt* (heavy object, suitcase etc) 引きずる hikízuru

luggage [lʌg'idʒ] *n* 手荷物 tenímòtsu

luggage rack *n* (on car) ルーフラック rūfurakku; (in train) 網棚 amidana

lukewarm [lu:k'wɔ:rm'] *adj* (liquid) ぬるい nurúî; (person, reaction etc) 気乗りしない kinóri shinai

lull [lʌl] *n* (break: in conversation, fighting etc) 途切れる事 togíreru kotó
◆*vt*: *to lull someone to sleep* ゆすって ...を寝付かせる yusútte ...wo netsúkaserù
to be lulled into a false sense of security 油断する yudán suru

lullaby [lʌl'əbai] *n* 子守歌 komóriuta

lumbago [lʌmbei'gou] *n* (MED) 腰痛 yōtsū

lumber [lʌm'bə:r] *n* (wood) 材木 zaímoku; (*BRIT*: junk) 粗大ごみ sodáigomi

lumberjack [lʌm'bə:rdʒæk] *n* きこり kikóri

lumber with *vt*: *to be lumbered with something* ...を押付けられる ...wo oshítsukerarerù

luminous [lu:'minəs] *adj* (fabric, color, dial, instrument etc) 蛍光の keíkō no

lump [lʌmp] *n* (of clay, butter etc) 塊 katámari; (on body) しこり shikóri; (on head) こぶ kobú; (*also*: **sugar lump**) 角砂糖 kakúzatō
◆*vt*: *to lump together* 一緒くたに扱う isshókuta ni atsúkaù
a lump sum 一時払い金額 ichíjibaraikíngaku

lumpy [lʌm'pi:] *adj* (sauce) 塊だらけの katámaridaràke no; (bed) ごつごつの gotsúgotsuno

lunar [lu:'nə:r] *adj* (landscape, module, landing etc) 月の tsukí no

lunatic [lu:'nətik] *adj* (behavior) 気違い染みた kichígaijimità

lunch [lʌntʃ] *n* 昼食 chūshoku

luncheon [lʌn'tʃən] *n* (formal meal) 昼食会 chūshokukai

luncheon meat *n* ランチョンミート rañchonmīto

luncheon voucher (*BRIT*) *n* 昼食券 chūshokukèn

lunch time *n* 昼食時 chūshokudoki

lung [lʌŋ] *n* (ANAT) 肺 haí

lunge [lʌndʒ] *vi* (*also*: **lunge forward**) 突進する tosshín suru
to lunge at ...を目掛けて突っ掛る ...wo megákete tsukkákarù

lurch [lə:rtʃ] *vi* (person) よろめく yorómekù; (vehicle) 揺れる yurérù
◆*n* (movement: of person) よろめき yorómeki; (: of vehicle) 揺れる事 yurérù kotó
to leave someone in the lurch 見捨てる misúterù

lure [lu:r] *n* (attraction) 魅惑 miwáku
◆*vt* (entice, tempt) 魅惑する miwáku suru

lurid [lu:'rid] *adj* (violent, sexually graphic: story etc) どぎつい dogítsuī; (*pej*: brightly colored: dress etc) けばけばしい kebákebashiì

lurk [lə:rk] *vi* (animal, person) 待ち伏せする machíbuse surù

luscious [lʌʃ'əs] *adj* (attractive: person, thing) 魅力的な miryókuteki na; (food) おいしそうな oíshisō na

lush [lʌʃ] *adj* (fields, gardens) 生茂った oíshigettà

lust [lʌst] (*pej*) *n* (sexual desire) 性欲 seíyoku; (desire for money, power etc) 欲望

yokúbō

lust after *vt fus* (desire: strongly) ...の欲に駆られる ...no yokú ni karárerù; (: sexually) ...とセックスをしたがる ...to sekkúsù wo shitágarù

luster [lʌs'tər] (*BRIT* **lustre**) *n* (shining: of metal, polished wood etc) つや tsuyá

lust for *vt fus* = **lust after**

lusty [lʌs'ti:] *adj* (healthy, energetic) 元気一杯の geñkiippaì no

Luxembourg [lʌk'səmbə:rg] *n* ルクセンブルク rukúseñburuku

luxuriant [lugʒu:r'i:ənt] *adj* (plants, trees) 生茂った oíshigettà; (gardens) 植込みの生茂った uékomi no oíshigettà; (hair) 豊富な hōfu na

luxurious [lugʒu:r'i:əs] *adj* (hotel, surroundings etc) 豪華な gōka na

luxury [lʌk'ʃə:ri:] *n* (great comfort) ぜいたく zeítaku; (expensive extra) ぜいたく品 zeítakuhìn; (infrequent pleasure) 得難い楽しみ egátaì tanóshimì

◆*cpd* (hotel, car etc) 豪華... gōka...

lying [lai'iŋ] *n* うそをつく事 usó wo tsúkù kotó

◆*adj* うそつきの usótsuki no

lynch [lintʃ] *vt* (prisoner, suspect) 勝手に絞り首にする katté ni shibárikùbi ni suru

lyrical [lir'ikəl] *adj* (poem) 叙情の jojó no; (*fig*: praise, comment) 叙情的な jojóteki na

lyrics [lir'iks] *npl* (of song) 歌詞 káshì

M

m. *abbr* = **meter; mile; million**

M.A. [emei'] *abbr* = **Master of Arts**

mac [mæk] (*BRIT*) *n* = **mackintosh**

macabre [məka:'brə] *adj* 背筋の凍る様な sesúji no kōru na

macaroni [mækərou'ni:] *n* マカロニ makároni

machine [məʃi:n'] *n* (piece of equipment) 機械 kikái; (*fig*: party machine, war machine etc) 組織 sóshìki

◆*vt* (TECH) 機械で作る kikái de tsukú-

rù; (dress etc) ミシンで作る míshìn de tsukúrù

machine gun *n* 機関銃 kikánjū

machine language *n* (COMPUT) 機械語 kikáigò

machinery [məʃi:'nə:ri:] *n* (equipment) 機械類 kikáirùi; (*fig*: of government) 組織 sóshìki

macho [mɑ:'tʃou] *adj* (man, attitude) 男っぽい otókoppoi

mackerel [mæk'ə:rəl] *n inv* サバ sabá

mackintosh [mæk'intɑ:ʃ] (*BRIT*) *n* レーンコート rḗnkòto

mad [mæd] *adj* (insane) 気の狂った ki no kurúttà; (foolish) ばかげた bakágetà; (angry) 怒っている okótte irù; (keen): **to be mad about** (person, football etc) ...に夢中になっている ...ni muchū ni nátte iru

madam [mæd'əm] *n* (form of address) 奥様 ṓkùsama

madden [mæd'ən] *vt* 怒らせる okóraserù

made [meid] *pt, pp* of **make**

Madeira [mədei'rə] *n* (GEO) マデイラ madéira; (wine) マデイラ madéira

made-to-measure [meid'təmeʒ'ə:r] (*BRIT*) *adj* = **made-to-order**

made-to-order [meid'tu:ɔ:r'də:r] (*US*) *adj* オーダーメードの ṓdāmèdo no

madly [mæd'li:] *adv* (frantically) 死物狂いで shinímonogurùi de

madly in love ぞっこんほれ込んで zokkón horékonde

madman [mæd'mæn] (*pl* **madmen**) *n* 気違い kichígaì

madness [mæd'nis] *n* (insanity) 狂気 kyōki; (foolishness) 気違い沙汰 kichígaizata

Madrid [mədrid'] *n* マドリード madórīdo

Mafia [mɑ:f'i:ə] *n* マフィア máfìa

magazine [mægəzi:n'] *n* (PRESS) 雑誌 zasshí; (RADIO, TV) 放送ジャーナル hōsō jānarù

maggot [mæg'ət] *n* ウジムシ ujímùshi

magic [mædʒ'ik] *n* (supernatural power) 魔法 mahō; (conjuring) 手品 tejína, マジック májìkku

♦*adj* (powers, ritual) 魔法の mahō no

magical [mædʒ'ikəl] *adj* (powers, ritual) 魔法の mahō no; (experience, evening) 夢の様な yumé no yō na

magician [mədʒiʃ'ən] *n* (wizard) 魔法使い mahōtsukaí; (conjurer) マジシャン májīshan

magistrate [mædʒ'istreit] *n* 軽犯罪判事 keíhanzai hañji

magnanimous [mægnæn'əməs] *adj* (person, gesture) 寛大な kañdai na

magnate [mæg'neit] *n* 大立者 ódatemóno, ...王...ō

magnesium [mægni:'zi:əm] *n* マグネシウム magúneshiùmu

magnet [mæg'nit] *n* 磁石 jíshaku

magnetic [mægnet'ik] *adj* (PHYSICS) 磁石の jíshaku no; (personality) 魅力的な miryókuteki na

magnetic tape *n* 磁気テープ jikí tèpu

magnetism [mæg'nitizəm] *n* 磁気 jíkì

magnificent [mægnif'əsənt] *adj* 素晴らしい subárashiì

magnify [mæg'nəfai] *vt* (enlarge: object) 拡大する kakúdai suru; (increase: sound) 大きくする ōkiku suru

magnifying glass [mæg'nəfaiiŋ-] *n* 拡大鏡 kakúdaikyō

magnitude [mæg'nətu:d] *n* (size) 大きさ ōkisa; (importance) 重要性 jūyōsei

magnolia [mægnoul'jə] *n* マグノリア magúnorìa ◊ モクレン, コブシ, タイサンボクを含む植物の類 mókùren, kóbùshi, taísañboku wo fukúmù shokúbùtsu no ruí

magpie [mæg'pai] *n* カササギ kasásagi

mahogany [məhɑ:g'əni:] *n* マホガニー mahóganī

maid [meid] *n* (servant) メイド meídò
  old maid (*pej*: spinster) ハイミス haímīsu

maiden [meid'ən] *n* (literary: girl) 少女 shōjo
  ♦*adj* (aunt etc) 未婚の mikón no; (speech, voyage) 処女... shójò ...

maiden name *n* 旧姓 kyūsei ◊既婚女性について使う kikónjosei ni tsuíte tsukáù

mail [meil] *n* (postal service) 郵便 yūbin;

(letters etc) 郵便物 yūbiñbutsu

♦*vt* (post) 投かんする tōkan suru

mailbox [meil'bɑ:ks] (*US*) *n* ポスト pósùto

mailing list [mei'liŋ-] *n* 郵送先名簿 yūsōsaki meíbo

mail-order [meil'ɔ:rdə:r] *n* (system) 通信販売 tsūshinhañbai

maim [meim] *vt* 重傷を負わせる jūshō wo owáserù ◊その結果不具になる場合について言う sónò kekká fúgù ni nárù baái ni tsuíte iú

main [mein] *adj* 主な ómò na, 主要な shuyō na, メーンの mèn no
  ♦*n* (pipe) 本管 hoñkan
  in the main (in general) 概して gái shite

mainframe [mein'freim] *n* (COMPUT) メインフレーム meínfurèmu

mainland [mein'lənd] *n* 本土 hóñdo

mainly [mein'li:] *adv* 主に ómò ni

main road *n* 幹線道路 kañsendōro

mains [meinz] *npl*: *the mains* (gas, water) 本管 hoñkan; (ELEC) 本線 hoñsen

mainstay [mein'stei] *n* (*fig*: prop) 大黒柱 daíkokubàshira

mainstream [mein'stri:m] *n* (*fig*) 主流 shuryū

maintain [meintein'] *vt* (preserve: contact, friendship, system) 続ける tsuzúkeru, 保持する hojí suru; (keep up: momentum, output) 維持する ijí suru; (provide for: dependant) 養う yashínaù; (look after: building) 管理する káñri suru; (affirm: belief, opinion) 主張する shuchō suru

maintenance [mein'tənəns] *n* (of contact, friendship, system) 保持 hojí; (of momentum, output) 維持 ijí; (provision for dependent) 扶養 fuyō; (looking after building) 管理 káñri; (affirmation: of belief, opinion) 主張する事 shuchō suru koto; (*BRIT*: LAW: alimony) 離婚手当 rikónteate

maize [meiz] *n* トウモロコシ toúmorðkoshi

majestic [mədʒes'tik] *adj* (splendid: scenery etc) 壮大な sodái na; (dignified)

堂々とした dōdō to shitá

majesty [mædʒ'isti:] n (title): *Your Majesty* 陛下 hêīka; (sovereignty) 王位 ôi; (splendor) 威厳 igén

major [mei'dʒər] n (MIL) 少佐 shốsa
◆*adj* (important, significant: event, factor) 重要な jūyō na; (MUS: key) 長調の chôchō no

Majorca [məjɔːr'kə] n マジョルカ majórūka

majority [mədʒɔːr'iti:] n (larger group: of people, things) 過半数 kahânsū; (margin: of votes) 得票差 tokúhyòsa

make [meik] (pt, pp **made**) vt (produce, form: object, clothes, cake) 作る tsukúrù; (: noise) 立てる tatérù; (: speech, mistake) する surú; (: remark) 言う iú; (manufacture: goods) 作る tsukúrù, 製造する seízō suru; (cause to be): *to make someone sad* ...を悲しくさせる ...wo kanáshikù saséru; (force): *to make someone do something* ...に...をさせる ...ni ...wo saseru; (earn: money) もうける mốkerù; (equal): *2 and 2 make 4* 2足す2は4 2 tásù 2 wà 4
◆*n* (brand): *it's a Japanese make* 日本製です nihônsei desu

to make the bed ベッドを整える béddò wo totônoerù

to make a fool of someone ...をばかにする ...wo bákà ni suru

to make a profit 利益を得る riéki wò érù

to make a loss 損をする sôn wo suru

to make it (arrive on time) 間に合う ma ní aù; (achieve something) 成功する seíkō suru

what time do you make it? 今何時ですか imá nânji desu kà

to make do with ...で間に合せる ...de ma ní awaserù

make-believe [meik'bili:v] n (pretense) 見せ掛け misékake

make for vt fus (place) ...に向かう ...ni mukâù

make out vt (decipher) 解読する kaídoku suru; (understand) 分かる wakárù; (see) 見る mírù; (write: cheque) 書く kákù

maker [mei'kər] n (of program, film etc) 制作者 seísakushà; (manufacturer) 製造者 seízōshà, メーカー mḗkā

makeshift [meik'ʃift] adj (temporary) 間に合せの ma ní awase no

make up vt (constitute) 構成する kốsei suru; (invent) でっち上げる detchîagerù; (prepare: bed) 用意する yồi suru; (: parcel) 包む tsutsúmù
◆*vi* (after quarrel) 仲直りする nakánaori suru; (with cosmetics) 化粧する keshố suru

make-up [meik'ʌp] n (cosmetics) メーキャップ mḗkyappù

make up for vt fus (loss, disappointment) ...の埋め合せをする ...no umêawase wò suru

make-up remover n 化粧落し keshố otòshi

making [mei'kiŋ] n (fig): *a doctor etc in the making* 医者の卵 ishá no tamâgo

to have the makings of ...の素質がある ...no soshîtsu ga arù

malaise [mæleiz'] n 倦怠 keńtai

malaria [məleːr'iːə] n マラリア marária

Malaya [məlei'jə] n マラヤ márāya

Malaysia [məlei'ʒə] n マレーシア marḗshìa

male [meil] n (BIOL: not female) 雄 osú
◆*adj* (animal) 雄の osú no; (human) 男の otôko no, 男性の dańsei no; (attitude etc) 男性的な dańseiteki na

malevolent [məlev'ələnt] adj (evil, harmful: person, intention) 悪魔の様な ákùma no yồ na

malfunction [mælfʌŋk'ʃən] n (of computer, machine) 故障 koshố

malice [mæl'is] n (ill will) 悪意 ákùi; (rancor) 恨み urámi

malicious [məliʃ'əs] adj (spiteful: person, gossip) 悪意に満ちた ákùi ni michíta

malign [məlain'] vt (slander) 中傷する chūshō suru

malignant [məlig'nənt] adj (MED: tumor, growth) 悪性の akúsei no

mall [mɔːl] n (also: **shopping mall**) ショ

ッピング・モール shoppíngu mòru

mallet [mæl'it] *n* 木づち kízuchi

malnutrition [mælnu:triʃ'ən] *n* 栄養失調 eíyōshītchō

malpractice [mælpræk'tis] *n* (MED) 医療過誤 iryōkagò; (LAW) 不正行為 fuséikòi

malt [mɔːlt] *n* (grain) もやし moyáshi, モルト mórùto; (*also*: **malt whisky**) モルトウイスキー morúto uisùkī

Malta [mɔːl'tə] *n* マルタ márùta

Maltese [mɔːlti:z'] *adj* マルタの márùta no
♦*n inv* マルタ人 marútajìn

maltreat [mæltri:t'] *vt* (treat badly, violently: child, animal) 虐待する gyakútai suru

mammal [mæm'əl] *n* ほ乳類 honyúrùi

mammoth [mæm'əθ] *n* (animal) マンモス mánmosu
♦*adj* (colossal, enormous: task) ばく大な bakúdai na

man [mæn] (*pl* **men**) *n* (adult male) 男 otóko, 男性 dañsei; (mankind) 人類 jínrui
♦*vt* (NAUT: ship) 乗組ませる norfkumaserù; (MIL: gun, post) 配置につく haíchi ni tsúkù; (operate: machine) 操作する sṓsa suru
　an old man 老人 rṓjìn
　man and wife 夫婦 fū́fu

manage [mæn'idʒ] *vi* (succeed) うまくなんとかする úmàku nántoka suru; (get by financially) なんとかして暮す nántoka shite kurásù
♦*vt* (be in charge of: business, shop, organization) 管理する kánri suru; (control: ship) 操縦する sṓjū suru; (: person) うまくあしらう úmàku ashír`aù

manageable [mæn'idʒəbəl] *adj* (task, number) 扱いやすい atsúkaiyasuì

management [mæn'idʒmənt] *n* (of business etc: control, organization) 管理 kánri; (: persons) 管理職 kanríshòku

manager [mæn'idʒəːr] *n* (of business etc) 支配人 shiháinin; (of pop star) マネージャー manéjà; (SPORT) 監督 kantóku

manageress [mæn'idʒəːris] *n* (of business etc) 女性支配人 joséishihaìnin; (of pop star) 女性マネージャー josei manèjā; (SPORT) 女性監督 josei kantóku

managerial [mænidʒi:'riəl] *adj* (role, skills) 管理職の kanríshòku no

managing director [mæn'idʒiŋ-] *n* 専務取締役 sénmutoríshimariyàku

mandarin [mæn'dərin] *n* (*also*: **mandarin orange**) みかん mīkàn; (high-ranking bureaucrat) 高級官僚 kōkyū kañryō

mandate [mæn'deit] *n* (authority) 権限 kengen; (task) 任務 nínmu

mandatory [mæn'dətɔ:ri:] *adj* (obligatory) 義務的な gimúteki na

mane [mein] *n* (of horse, lion) たてがみ tatégami

maneuver [mənu:'vəːr] (*US*) *vt* (move: car, bulky, object) 巧みに動かす tákùmi ni ugókasù; (manipulate: person, situation) 操る ayátsuru
♦*vi* (move: car, plane) 巧みに動く tákùmi ni ugókù; (MIL) 軍事演習を行う guñjieñshū wo okonau
♦*n* 巧みな動き tákùmi na ugóki

manfully [mæn'fəli:] *adv* (valiantly) 勇ましく isámashikù

mangle [mæŋ'gəl] *vt* (crush, twist) めちゃくちゃにする mechákucha ni suru

mango [mæŋ'gou] (*pl* **mangoes**) *n* マンゴー mángo

mangy [mein'dʒi:] *adj* (animal) 汚らしい kitánarashiì

manhandle [mæn'hændəl] *vt* (mistreat) 手荒に扱う teára ni atsúkaù

manhole [mæn'houl] *n* マンホール mańhòru

manhood [mæn'hud] *n* (age) 成人時代 seíjin jidài; (state) 成人である事 seíjin de arù kotó ◊男性のみについて言う dañsei nomí ni tsúìte iú

man-hour [mæn'auəːr] *n* (time) 人時 nínji

manhunt [mæn'hʌnt] *n* (POLICE) 人間狩り niñgengari

mania [mei'ni:ə] *n* (craze) ...狂 ...kyõ; (illness) そう病 sōbyō

maniac [mei'ni:æk] *n* (lunatic) 狂人 kyõjin; (*fig*) 無謀な人 mubō na hitò

manic [mæn'ik] *adj* (behavior, activity) 猛烈な mōretsu na

manic-depressive [mæn'ikdipres'iv] *n* そううつ病患者 sōutsubyō kañja

manicure [mæn'əkju:r] *n* マニキュア maníkyùa

manicure set *n* マニキュア・セット maníkyua settò

manifest [mæn'əfest] *vt* (show, display) 表す aráwasù

◆*adj* (evident, obvious) 明白な meíhaku na

manifestation [mænəfestei'(ən] *n* 現れ aráware

manifesto [mænəfes'tou] *n* 声明書 seímeisho

manipulate [mənip'jəleit] *vt* (people) 操る ayátsurù; (system, situation) 操作する sōsa suru

mankind [mæn'kaind'] *n* (human beings) 人類 jiñrui

manly [mæn'li:] *adj* (masculine) 男らしい otókorashiǐ

man-made [mæn'meid] *adj* (environment, satellite etc) 人工の jiñkō no; (fiber, lake etc) 人造の jiñzō no

manner [mæn'ə:r] *n* (way) やり方 yaríkata; (behavior) 態度 taído; (type, sort): **all manner of things** あらゆる物 aráyuru monò

mannerism [mæn'ə:rizəm] *n* 癖 kusé

manners [mæn'ə:rz] *npl* (conduct) 行儀 gyógi, マナー mánā
bad manners 行儀の悪い事 gyógi no warúǐ kotó

manoeuvre [mənu:'və:r] (*BRIT*) = **maneuver**

manor [mæn'ə:r] *n* (*also*: **manor house**) 屋敷 yashíki

manpower [mæn'pauə:r] *n* (workers) 人手 hitóde

mansion [mæn't(ən] *n* 豪邸 gōtei

manslaughter [mæn'slɔ:tə:r] *n* (LAW) 殺意なき殺人 satsúinaki satsújin

mantelpiece [mæn'təlpi:s] *n* マントルピース mañtorupīsu

manual [mæn'ju:əl] *adj* (work, worker) 肉体の nikútai no; (controls) 手動の shu-

dó no

◆*n* (book) マニュアル mányùaru

manufacture [mænjəfæk't(ə:r] *vt* (make, produce: goods) 製造する seízō suru

◆*n* (making) 製造 seízō

manufacturer [mænjəfæk't(ə:rə:r] *n* 製造業者 seízōgyōsha, メーカー mḗkā

manure [mənu:r'] *n* 肥やし koyáshi

manuscript [mæn'jəskript] *n* (of book, report) 原稿 geñkō; (old document) 写本 shahón

many [men'i:] *adj* (a lot of: people, things, ideas) 沢山の takúsañ no

◆*pron* (several) 多数 tasú
a great many 非常に沢山の hijō ni takúsañ no
many a time 何回も nañkai mo

map [mæp] *n* (of town, country) 地図 chízù

maple [mei'pəl] *n* (tree) カエデ kaéde; (wood) カエデ材 kaédezài

map out *vt* (plan, task) 計画する keíkaku suru

mar [ma:r] *vt* (spoil: appearance) 損なう sokónaù; (: day, event) ぶち壊す buchíkowasù

marathon [mær'əθɑ:n] *n* (race) マラソン maráson

marauder [mərɔ:d'ə:r] *n* (robber, killer)◇殺人、略奪などを繰返しながら荒し回る無法者 satsújin, ryakúdatsu nado wo kuríkaeshinagara arashimawarù muhōmòno

marble [mɑ:r'bəl] *n* (stone) 大理石 daírisèki; (toy) ビー玉 bídama

March [mɑ:rt(] *n* 3月 sáñgatsu

march [mɑ:rt(] *vi* (MIL: soldiers) 行進する kōshin suru; (*fig*: protesters) デモ行進をする demó kōshin wo suru; (walk briskly) 足音も高く歩く ashíoto mo takakù arúkù

◆*n* (MIL) 行進 kōshin; (demonstration) デモ行進 demó kōshin

mare [me:r] *n* 牝ウマ mesú uma

margarine [mɑ:r'dʒə:rin] *n* マーガリン māgarin

margin [mɑ:r'dʒin] *n* (difference: of

votes) 差 sa; (extra amount) 余裕 yoyú; (COMM: profit) 利ざや rizáya, マージン májin; (space: on page) 余白 yoháku; (edge: of area, group) 外れ hazúre

marginal [mɑ'r'dʒinəl] *adj* (unimportant) 二次的な nijíteki na

marginal (seat) *n* (POL) 不安定な議席 fuántei na giséki ◇わずかな票の差で得たので，次の選挙で失う可能性のある議席 wázùka na hyố nò sá de etá node, tsugí nò señkyo de ushínaù kanôsei no arú giséki

marigold [mær'əgould] *n* マリーゴールド marígorudo

marijuana [mærəwɑː'nə] *n* マリファナ marífàna

marina [məri'nə] *n* (harbor) マリーナ marína

marinate [mær'əneit] *vt* (CULIN) マリネにする márìne ni suru

marine [məriːn'] *adj* (life, plant, biology) 海の umí no; (engineer, engineering) 船舶の señpaku no

♦*n* (US: sailor) 海兵隊員 kaíheitaìin; (BRIT: soldier) 海兵隊員 kaíheitaìin

marital [mær'itəl] *adj* (problem, relations) 夫婦の fúfu no

marital status ◇未婚，既婚，離婚を尋ねる時に使う言葉 mikón, kikón, ríkon wo tazúnerù tokí ni tsukaú kotôba

maritime [mær'itaim] *adj* 海事の kálji no

marjoram [mɑː'dʒəːrəm] *n* マヨラナ mayónàra, マージョラム májòramu

mark [mɑːrk] *n* (symbol: cross, tick etc) 印 shirúshi; (stain) 染み shimí; (of shoes, fingers, tires: in snow, mud etc) 跡 átò; (sign: of friendship, respect etc) 印 shirúshi; (SCOL) 成績 seíseki; (level, point): *the halfway mark* 中間点の目印 chůkanteñ no mejírùshi; (currency) マルク márùku

♦*vt* (make a mark on: with pen etc) 印を書く shirúshi wo kákù; (: with shoes, tires etc) 跡を残す átò wo nokósù; (damage: furniture etc) 傷を付ける kizú wo tsukérù; (stain: clothes, carpet etc) 染みを付ける shimí wo tsukérù; (indicate:

place, time, price) 示す shimésù; (commemorate: event) 記念する kinén suru; (BRIT: SCOL) 成績をつける seíseki wò tsukérù

to mark time (MIL, *fig*) 足踏みする ashíbumi suru

marked [mɑːrkt] *adj* (obvious) 著しい ichíjirushìi

marker [mɑːr'kəːr] *n* (sign) 目印 mejírùshi; (bookmark) しおり shióri

marker pen サインペン saíñpen

market [mɑːr'kit] *n* (for fish, cattle, vegetables etc) 市場 íchìba; (in proper names) 市場 íchìba, 市場 shijố; (COMM: business and trading activity) 市場 shijố; (: demand) 需要 juyố

♦*vt* (COMM: sell) 市場に出す shijố ni dásù

market garden (BRIT) *n* 野菜農園 yasáiñoen ◇主に市場向けの野菜や果物を栽培する小規模農場 ómò ni shijố muke nò yasái ya kudámono wò saíbai surù shố kibo nôjò

marketing [mɑːr'kitiŋ] *n* (COMM) 販売 hañbai

marketplace [mɑːr'kitpleis] *n* (area, site: also COMM) 市場 íchìba

market research *n* 市場調査 shijốchōsa

marksman [mɑːrks'mən] (*pl* **marksmen**) *n* 射撃の名手 shagéki no meíshù

marmalade [mɑːr'məleid] *n* マーマレード mámaredò

maroon [məruːn'] *vt*: *to be marooned* (shipwrecked) 遭難で置去りになる sốnan dè okízari ni narù; (*fig*: abandoned) 置去りにされる okízari ni saréru

♦*adj* (color) クリ色 kurírio

marquee [mɑːrkiː'] *n* (tent) テント téñto ◇運動会，野外パーティなどで使う幕を指す uñdókai, yagái pàti nádò de tsukáù monó wo sásù

marquess [mɑːr'kwis] *n* 侯爵 kôshaku

marquis [mɑːr'kwis] *n* = **marquess**

marriage [mær'idʒ] *n* (relationship, institution) 結婚 kekkón; (wedding) 結婚式 kekkôñshiki

marriage bureau *n* 結婚相談所 kekkónsōdanjo

marriage certificate *n* 結婚証明書 kekkónshōmeishō

married [mær'i:d] *adj* (man, woman) 既婚の kikón no; (life, love) 結婚の kekkón no

marrow [mær'ou] *n* (vegetable) セイヨウカボチャ seíyokabòcha; (*also*: **bone marrow**) 骨髄 kotsúzui

marry [mær'i:] *vt* (man, woman) ...と結婚する ...to kekkón surù; (subj: father, priest etc) ...の結婚式を行う ...no kekkónshiki wo okónaù

♦*vi* (*also*: **get married**) 結婚する kekkón suru

Mars [ma:rz] *n* (planet) 火星 kaséi

marsh [ma:rʃ] *n* (bog) 沼沢地 shōtakùchi; (*also*: **salt marsh**) 塩性沼沢地 eñsei shōtakuchi

marshal [ma:r'ʃəl] *n* (MIL: *also*: **field marshal**) 陸軍元帥 rikúgun geñsui; (official: at sports meeting etc) 役員 yakúin; (*US*: of police, fire department) 長官 chōkan

♦*vt* (organize: thoughts) 整理する seíri suru; (: support) 集める atsúmerù; (: soldiers) 整列させる seíretsu saserù

marshy [ma:r'ʃi:] *adj* 沼沢の多い shōtaku nō ōì

martial [ma:r'ʃəl] *adj* (military) 軍の gúñ no

martial arts *npl* 武術 bújùtsu

martial law *n* 戒厳令 kaígenrei

martyr [ma:r'tə:r] *n* (for beliefs) 殉教者 juñkyōsha

martyrdom [ma:r'tə:rdəm] *n* 殉教 juñkyō

marvel [ma:r'vəl] *n* (wonder) 驚異 kyōi

♦*vi*: **to marvel (at)** 驚嘆する kyōtan suru

marvelous [ma:r'vələs] (*BRIT* **marvellous**) *adj* 素晴らしい subárashiî

Marxism [ma:rk'sizəm] *n* マルクス主義 marúkusushùgi

Marxist [ma:r'ksist] *adj* マルクス主義の marúkusushùgi no

♦*n* マルクス主義者 marúkusushùgisha

marzipan [ma:r'zəpæn] *n* マジパン mají-

pan

mascara [mæskæ:r'ə] *n* マスカラ masúkara

mascot [mæs'kɔ:t] *n* マスコット masúkòtto

masculine [mæs'kjəlin] *adj* (male: characteristics, pride) 男性の dañsei no; (: atmosphere) 男性的な dañseiteki na; (woman) 男の様な otóko no yō na; (LING: noun, pronoun etc) 男性の dañsei no

mash [mæʃ] *vt* つぶす tsubúsu

mashed potatoes [mæʃt-] *npl* マッシュポテト masshú potèto

mask [mæsk] *n* (disguise) 覆面 fukúmen; (shield: gas mask, face mask) マスク másùku

♦*vt* (cover: face) 覆い隠す ōikakùsu; (hide: feelings) 隠す kakúsù

masochist [mæs'əkist] *n* マゾヒスト mazóhisùto

mason [mei'sən] *n* (*also*: **stone mason**) 石屋 ishíya; (*also*: **freemason**) フリーメーソン furímèson

masonic [məsa:n'ik] *adj* (lodge, dinner) フリーメーソンの furímèson no

masonry [mei'sənri:] *n* (stonework) 石造部 sekízòbu ◇建物の石やれんがなどで造られた部分 tatémòno no ishí yà reñga nadò de tsukúrarèta búbùn

masquerade [mæskəreid'] *vi*: **to masquerade as** ...を装う ...wo yosóoù

mass [mæs] *n* (large number: of papers, people etc) 多数 tasú; (large amount: of detail, hair etc) 大量 taíryò; (amount: of air, liquid, land) 集団 shúdan; (PHYSICS) 物量 butsúryò; (REL) ミサ聖祭 misá seisài

♦*cpd* (communication, unemployment etc) 大量の taíryo no

♦*vi* (troops, protesters) 集合する shúgō suru

massacre [mæs'əkə:r] *n* 大虐殺 daígyakùsatsu

massage [məsa:ʒ'] *n* マッサージ massájì

♦*vt* (rub) マッサージする massájì suru

masses [mæs'iz] *npl*: **the masses** (ordinary people) 大衆 taíshū

masses of (*inf*: food, money, people) 一杯の ippái no

masseur [mæsəːr'] *n* マッサージ師 mas-sájìshì

masseuse [məsuːs'] *n* マッサージ嬢 mas-sájijô

massive [mæs'iv] *adj* (large and heavy: furniture, door, person) どっしりした dosshírì shita; (huge: support, changes, increase) 膨大な bôdai na

mass media [-mi:'di:ə] *npl* マスメディア masúmèdia

mass production (*BRIT* **mass-production**) *n* 大量生産 taíryōseisan, マスプロ masúpuro

mast [mæst] *n* (NAUT) マスト másùto; (RADIO etc) 放送アンテナ hôsō añtena

master [mæs'təːr] *n* (of servant, slave) 主人 shujíñ; (in secondary school) 先生 señseì; (title for boys): ***Master X*** X君 ékusu kùn

♦*vt* (control: situation) 掌握する shôaku suru; (: one's feelings etc) 抑える osáerù; (learn: skills, language) 修得する shútoku suru, マスターする masútā suru

to be master of the situation (*fig*) 事態を掌握している jítài wo shôaku shite irù

master key *n* マスターキー masútā kī

masterly [mæs'təːrli:] *adj* あっぱれな appárè na

mastermind [mæs'təːrmaind] *n* (of crime etc) 首謀者 shubôshà, 黒幕 kurómaku

♦*vt* 計画を練って実行させる keíkaku wo néttè jikkô saserù

Master of Arts/Science *n* (person) 文学〔理学〕修士 buñgaku (rigáku) shūshi; (qualification) 文学〔理学〕修士号 buñgaku (rigáku) shūshigō

masterpiece [mæs'təːrpiːs] *n* 傑作 kessáku

mastery [mæs'təːriː] *n* (of skill, language) 修得 shútoku

masturbate [mæs'təːrbeit] *vi* マスターベーション〔オナニー〕をする masútābèshon(onánī)wo suru

masturbation [mæstəːrbei'ʃən] *n* マスタ

ーベーション masútābèshon, オナニー onánī

mat [mæt] *n* (on floor) マット máttò; (at door: *also*: **doormat**) ドアマット doámattò; (on table: *also*: **table mat**) テーブルマット têburumattò

♦*adj* = **matt**

match [mætʃ] *n* (game: of football, tennis etc) 試合 shiái, マッチ mátchì; (for lighting fire, cigarette) マッチ mátchì; (equal) 力が同等な人 chikára ga dôtô na hitô

♦*vt* (go well with: subj: colors, clothes) ...に合う ...ni áù; (equal) ...と同等である ...to dôtô de arù; (correspond to) ...に合う ...ni áù; (pair: *also*: **match up**) ...と合せる ...to awáserù, ...と組ませる ...to kumáserù

♦*vi* (colors, materials) 合う áù

to be a good match (colors etc) よく合う yokù áù; (couple) 似合いの...である niái no ...de arù

matchbox [mætʃ'bɑːks] *n* マッチ箱 matchíbàko

matching [mætʃ'iŋ] *adj* (clothes etc) そろいの soróì no

mate [meit] *n* (workmate) 仲間 nakáma; (*inf*: friend) 友達 tomódachi; (animal) 相手 aíte; (in merchant navy: first, second) ...等航海士 ...tô kōkaishì

♦*vi* (animals) 交尾する kôbi suru

material [məti:'ri:əl] *n* (substance) 物質 busshítsu; (cloth) 生地 kijí; (information, data) 情報 jôhō

♦*adj* (possessions, existence) 物質的な busshítsuteki na

materialistic [məti:ri:əlis'tik] *adj* 唯物主義的な yuíbutsushugiteki na

materialize [məti:'ri:əlaiz] *vi* (happen) 起る okórù; (appear) 現れる aráwarerù

materials [məti:'ri:əlz] *npl* (equipment) 材料 zaíryō

maternal [mətəːr'nəl] *adj* (feelings, role) 母性の boséi no

maternity [mətəːr'niti:] *n* 母性 boséi

maternity dress *n* マタニティドレス matánitidorèsu

maternity hospital *n* 産院 sañ-in

math [mæθ] (BRIT **maths**) n 数学 sūgaku

mathematical [mæθəmæt'ikəl] adj (formula) 数学の sūgaku no; (mind) 数学的な sūgakuteki na

mathematician [mæθəmətiʃ'ən] n 数学者 sūgakushā

mathematics [mæθəmæt'iks] n 数学 sūgaku

maths [mæθs] (BRIT) n = **math**

matinée [mætənei'] n マチネー machínē

mating call [mei'tiŋ-] n (of animals) 求愛の声 kyūai nò kóè

matrices [meit'risi:z] npl of **matrix**

matriculation [mətrikjəlei'ʃən] n (enrollment) 大学入学 daígakunyūgaku

matrimonial [mætrəmou'ni:əl] adj 結婚の kekkón no

matrimony [mæt'rəmouni:] n (marriage) 結婚 kekkón

matrix [mei'triks] (pl **matrices**) n (context, environment) 環境 kańkyō

matron [mei'trən] n (in hospital) 婦長 fuchō; (in school) 養護員 yōgoiñ

mat(t) [mæt] adj つや消しの tsuyákeshi no

matted [mæt'id] adj もつれた motsúretà

matter [mæt'əːr] n (event) 事件 jikén; (situation) 事情 jijō; (problem) 問題 mońdai; (PHYSICS) 物質 busshítsu; (substance, material) 素材 sozái; (written material: reading matter etc) 印刷物 iñsatsubùtsu, 本 hóñ; (MED: pus) うみ umí
♦vi (be important: family, job etc) 大切である taísetsu de arù

it doesn't matter 構わない kamáwanài

what's the matter? どうしましたか dō shimashita ká

no matter what (whatever happens) 何があっても nánì ga atté mo

as a matter of course (automatically) 当然ながら tōzen nagara

as a matter of fact 実は jitsú wa

matter-of-fact [mæt'əːrʌvfækt'] adj 無味乾燥な mumíkañsō na

matters [mæt'əːrz] npl (affairs) 物事 monógòto; (situation) 状況 jōkyō

mattress [mæt'ris] n マットレス mattórēsu

mature [mətu:r'] adj (person) 成熟した seíjuku shita; (cheese, wine etc) 熟成した jukúsei shita
♦vi (develop: child, style) 成長する seíchō suru; (grow up: person) 成熟する seíjuku suru; (ripen, age: cheese, wine etc) 熟成する jukúsei suru

maturity [mətu:'riti:] n (adulthood) 成熟 seíjuku; (wisdom) 分別 fúñbetsu

maul [mɔːl] vt ...に大けがをさせる ...ni ōkega wò saséru

mausoleum [mɔːsəli:'əm] n 納骨堂 nōkotsudō

mauve [mouv] adj フジ色の fujíiro no

maverick [mæv'əːrik] n 一匹オオカミ ippíki ōkami

maxim [mæk'sim] n 格言 kakúgen

maximum [mæk'səməm] (pl **maxima**) adj (efficiency, speed, dose) 最大の saídai no
♦n 最大限 saídaigen

May [mei] n 5月 gógàtsu

may [mei] (conditional: **might**) vi (indicating possibility): *he may come* 彼は来るかも知れない kárè wa kurú ka mo shirenài; (be allowed to): *may I smoke?* タバコをすってもいいですか tabáko wo sutté mò íi desu ká; (wishes): *may God bless you!* 神の祝福をあなたに！ kamí nò shukúfuku wò anáta ni; *you may as well go* 行ってもいいかも知れない itté mò íi ka mo shirenai; (dismissive) 行った方がいいかも知れない itta hō ga íi ka mo shirénài

maybe [mei'bi:] adv 事によると kotó ni yorù to

May Day n メーデー mḗdē

mayhem [mei'hem] n 混乱 końran

mayonnaise [meiəneiz'] n マヨネーズ mayónēzu

mayor [mei'əːr] n (of city, town) 市〔町, 村〕長 shi〔chō, son〕chō

mayoress [mei'əːris] n (partner) 市〔町, 村〕長夫人 shi〔chō, son〕chō fujín

maze [meiz] n (labyrinth, puzzle) 迷路 mēiro

M.D. [emdi:ʳ] *abbr* = **Doctor of Medicine**

KEYWORD

me [mi:] *pron* **1** (direct) 私 を watákushi wo

can you hear me? 私の声が聞えますか watákushi no koè ga kikóemasù ká

he heard me 彼は私の声を聞いた kárè wa watákushi no koè wo kiítà

he heard ME! (not anyone else) 彼が聞いたのは私の声だった kárè ga kiítà no wa watákushi no koè dáttà

it's me 私です watákushi desù

2 (indirect) 私に watákushi nì

he gave me the money, he gave the money to me 彼は私に金を渡した kárè wa watákushi nì kané wò watáshità

give them to me それらを私に下さい sorérà wo watákushi nì kudásaì

3 (after prep): *the letter's for me* 手紙は私宛てです tegámi wà watákushi ate dèsù

with me 私と一緒に watákushi tò isshò nì

without me 私抜きで watákushi nukì de

meadow [med'ou] *n* 草原 kusáhara
meager [mi:'gə:r] (*BRIT* **meagre**) *adj* 乏しい tobóshiì
meal [mi:l] *n* (occasion, food) 食事 shokúji; (flour) 粉 koná
mealtime [mi:l'taim] *n* 食事時 shokújidòki
mean [mi:n] *adj* (with money) けちな kechí na; (unkind: person, trick) 意地悪な ijíwarù na; (shabby: street, lodgings) 見すぼらしい misúborashiì; (average: height, weight) 中位の chúgurai no
♦*vt* (*pt, pp* **meant**) (signify) 意味する ímì suru; (refer to): *I thought you meant her* あなたは彼女の事を言っていると私は思った anátà wa kanójò no kotò wo itté irù to watákushi wà omótta; (intend): *to mean to do something* …をするつもりでいる …wo suru tsumóri de irú

♦*n* (average) 平均 heíkin
do you mean it? 本当ですか hoñtó desù ká
what do you mean? それはどういう事ですか sorè wa dó iú kotò desu ká
to be meant for someone/something …に当てた物である …ni atéta monò de árù

meander [mi:æn'də:r] *vi* (river) 曲がりくねって流れる magárikunettè nagárerù
meaning [mi:'niŋ] *n* (of word, gesture, book) 意味 ímì; (purpose, value) 意義 ígì
meaningful [mi:'niŋfəl] *adj* (result) 意味のある ímì no árù; (explanation) 納得できる nattóku dekirù; (glance, remark) 意味ありげな imíarige na; (relationship, occasion) 意味深い imíbùkai
meaningless [mi:'niŋlis] *adj* 無意味な muími na
meanness [mi:n'nis] *n* (with money) けち kechí; (unkindness) 意地悪 ijíwarù; (shabbiness) 見すぼらしさ misúborashisà
means [mi:nz] *npl* (way) 方法 hóhō; (money) 財政 zaísan
by means of …を使って …wo tsukátte
by all means! ぜひどうぞ zéhì dózò
meant [ment] *pt, pp of* **mean**
meantime [mi:n'taim] *adv* (also: **in the meantime**) その間に sonó aìda ni
meanwhile [mi:n'wail] *adv* (meantime) その間に sonó aìda ni
measles [mi:'zəlz] *n* はしか hashíka
measly [mi:z'li:] (*inf*) *adj* ちっぽけな chippókè na
measure [meʒ'əːr] *vt* (size, weight, distance) 計る hakárù
♦*vi* (room, person) …だけの寸法がある …daké nò suñpō ga arù
♦*n* (amount: of protection etc) ある程度 árù teídò; (: of whisky etc) 定量 teíryō; (ruler, *also*: **tape measure**) 巻尺 makíjaku, メジャー mejá; (action) 処置 shochí
measured [meʒ'əːrd] *adj* 慎重な shiñchō na
measurements [meʒ'əːrmənts] *npl* (size) 寸法 suñpō
meat [mi:t] *n* 肉 nikú

cold meat コールドミート kṓrudomìto

meatball [miːtˈbɔːl] *n* ミートボール mī́toborù

meat pie *n* ミートパイ mī́topaì

Mecca [mekˈə] *n* (city) メッカ mékkà; (*fig*) あこがれの地 akṓgare nò chí

mechanic [məkænˈik] *n* 自動車整備士 jidṓsha seībishi

mechanical [məkænˈikəl] *adj* 機械仕掛の kikáijikakè no

mechanics [məkænˈiks] *n* (PHYSICS) 力学 rikígaku
♦*npl* (of reading, government etc) 機構 kikṓ

mechanism [mekˈənizəm] *n* (device) 装置 sṓchi; (procedure) 方法 hṓhō; (automatic reaction) 反応 hańnō

mechanization [mekənizeiˈʃən] *n* 機械化 kikáika

medal [medˈəl] *n* (award) メダル médàru

medallion [mədælˈjən] *n* メダリオン medáriòn

medalist [medˈlist] (*BRIT* **medallist**) *n* (SPORT) メダリスト medárisùto

meddle [medˈəl] *vi*: **to meddle in** ...にちょっかいを出す ...ni chokkáî wo dásù
to meddle with something ...をいじる ...wo ijírù

media [miˈdiːə] *npl* マスメディア masúmedìa

mediaeval [miːdiːˈvəl] *adj* = **medieval**

median [miˈdiən] (*US*) *n* (*also*: **median strip**) 中央分離帯 chūō buńritai

mediate [miˈdiːit] *vi* (arbitrate) 仲裁する chūsai suru

mediator [miˈdiːeitəːr] *n* 仲裁者 chūsaishà

Medicaid [medˈəkeid] (*US*) *n* メディケイド medíkeìdo ◇低所得者への医療扶助 teíshotòkusha e no iryṓfùjo

medical [medˈikəl] *adj* (treatment, care) 医学的な igákuteki na
♦*n* (*BRIT*: examination) 健康診断 keńkōshindan

Medicare [medˈəkeːr] (*US*) *n* メディケア medíkèa ◇高齢者への医療扶助 kṓreishà e no iryṓfujo

medicated [medˈikeitid] *adj* 薬用の ya-

kúyō no

medication [medikeiˈʃən] *n* (drugs etc) 薬 kusúri

medicinal [mədisˈənəl] *adj* 薬効のある yakkṓ no arù

medicine [medˈisin] *n* (science) 医学 ígàku; (drug) 薬 kusúri

medieval [miːdiːˈvəl] *adj* 中世の chūsei no

mediocre [miːdiːoukəːr] *adj* (play, artist) 粗末な sómàtsu na

mediocrity [miːdiːɑːkˈritiː] *n* (poor quality) 粗末さ sómàtsusà

meditate [medˈəteit] *vi* (think carefully) 熟考する jukkṓ suru; (REL) めい想する meísō suru

meditation [mediteiˈʃən] *n* (thinking) 熟考 jukkṓ; (REL) めい想 meísō

Mediterranean [meditəreiˈniːən] *adj* 地中海の chichūkai no
the Mediterranean (Sea) 地中海 chichūkai

medium [miˈdiːəm] *adj* (average: size, color) 中位の chūgurai no
♦*n* (*pl* **media**: means) 手段 shúdàn; (*pl* **mediums**: people) 霊媒 reíbai

medium wave *n* 中波 chūha

medley [medˈliː] *n* (mixture) ごったまぜ gottámaze; (MUS) メドレー médòrē

meek [miːk] *adj* 穏和な ońwa na

meet [miːt] (*pt, pp* **met**) *vt* (friend: accidentally) ...に出会う ...ni deáù; (: by arrangement) ...に会う ...ni áù; (stranger: for the first time) ...と知合いになる ...to shíriai ni naru; (go and fetch: at station, airport) 出迎える demúkaerù; (opponent) ...と試合をする ...to shiái wo surù; (obligations) 果す hatásù; (problem, need) 解決する kaíketsu suru
♦*vi* (friends: accidentally) 出会う deáù; (: by arrangement) 会う áù; (strangers: for the first time) 知合いになる shiríai ni narù; (for talks, discussion) 会合する kaígō suru; (join: lines, roads) 合流する gṓryū suru

meeting [miˈtin] *n* (assembly: of club, committee etc) 会合 kaígō; (: of people) 集会 shūkai; (encounter: with friend) 出

会い deáī; (COMM) 会議 káīgi; (POL) 集会 shúkai

meet with *vt fus* (encounter: difficulty) 合う áū

to meet with success 成功する seíkō suru

megabyte [meg'əbait] *n* (COMPUT) メガバイト megábaīto

megaphone [meg'əfoun] *n* メガホン megáhòn

melancholy [mel'ənka:li:] *n* (sadness) 憂うつ yúutsu, メランコリー meránkorī

◆*adj* (sad) 憂鬱な yúutsu na

mellow [mel'ou] *adj* (sound, light, color) 柔らかい yawárakaì; (wine) 芳じゅんな hōjun na

◆*vi* (person) 角が取れる kádò ga torérù

melodrama [mel'ədræmə] *n* メロドラマ meródòrama

melody [mel'ədi:] *n* 旋律 seńritsu, メロディー méròdī

melon [mel'ən] *n* メロン méròn

melt [melt] *vi* (metal, snow) 溶ける tokérù

◆*vt* (metal, snow, butter) 溶かす tokásù

melt down *vt* (metal) 溶かす tokásù

meltdown [melt'daun] *n* (in nuclear reactor) メルトダウン merútodàun

melting pot [melt'iŋ-] *n* (*fig*: mixture) るつぼ rútsùbo

member [mem'bə:r] *n* (of group, family) 一員 ichí-in; (of club) 会員 kaíin, メンバー méñbā; (ANAT) 体の一部 karáda no íchìbu

Member of Parliament (*BRIT*) 国会議員 kokkái giìn

Member of the European Parliament (*BRIT*) 欧州議会議員 ōshūgikai giìn

membership [mem'bə:rʃip] *n* (members) 会員一同 kaíin ichídò; (state) 会員である事 kaíin de arù kotó

membership card *n* 会員証 kaíiñshō

membrane [mem'brein] *n* 膜 makú

memento [məmen'tou] *n* 記念品 kinéñhin

memo [mem'ou] *n* 覚書 obóegaki, メモ mémò

memoirs [mem'wa:rz] *npl* 回顧録 kaíko-

ròku

memorable [mem'ə:rəbəl] *adj* 記念すべき kinéñsubeki

memorandum [meməræn'dəm] (*pl* **memoranda**) *n* (official note) 覚書 obóegaki; (order to employees etc) 社内通達 shanái tsūtatsu

memorial [məmɔ:'ri:əl] *n* (statue, monument) 記念碑 kinéñhi

◆*adj* (service) 追悼の tsuítō no; (prize) 記念の kinén no

memorize [mem'ə:raiz] *vt* (learn) 暗記する ańki suru

memory [mem'ə:ri:] *n* (ability to remember) 記憶 kióku; (things one remembers) 思い出 omóide; (instance) 思い出 omóide; (of dead person): *in memory of* ...を記念して ...wo kinén shitè; (COMPUT) 記憶装置 kiókusòchi, メモリー mémòrī

men [men] *pl of* **man**

menace [men'is] *n* (threat) 脅威 kyói; (nuisance) 困り者 komárimono

◆*vt* (threaten) 脅かす odókasu; (endanger) 危険にさらす kikén ni sarásu

menacing [men'isiŋ] *adj* (person, gesture) 脅迫的な kyóhakuteki na

mend [mend] *vt* (repair) 修理する shúri suru; (darn: socks etc) 繕う tsukúroù, 修繕する shúzen suru

◆*n*: *to be on the mend* 回復に向かっている kaífuku nì mukátte irù

to mend one's ways 心を入替える kokórò wo irékaerù

mending [mend'iŋ] *n* (repairing) 修繕 shúzen; (clothes) 繕い物 tsukúroimòno

menial [mi:'ni:əl] *adj* (lowly: often *pej*) 卑しい iyáshiì

meningitis [menindʒai'tis] *n* 脳膜炎 nómakuèn

menopause [men'əpɔ:z] *n* 更年期 kōneñki

menstruation [menstru:ei'ʃən] *n* 月経 gekkéi, 生理 seíri, メンス méñsu

mental [men'təl] *adj* (ability, effort) 精神的な seíshinteki na; (illness, health) 精神の seíshin no

mental arithmetic/calculation 暗算 ańzan

mentality [mentæl'iti:] n (attitude) 考え方 kańgaekàta

menthol [men'θɔːl] n メントール meńtồru

mention [men'tʃən] n (reference) 言及 geńkyū
♦vt (speak of) ...に言及する ...ni geńkyū suru
don't mention it! どういたしまして dồ itáshimashitè

mentor [men'tɔːr] n 良き指導者 yokí shidồsha

menu [men'juː] n (set menu) 献立 końdate; (printed) 献立表 końdatehyồ, メニュー ményū; (COMPUT) メニュー ményū

MEP [emiːpiːʔ] (BRIT) n abbr = **Member of the European Parliament**

mercenary [mərːʔsəneriː] adj 金銭ずくの kińsenzuku no
♦n (soldier) よう兵 yồhei

merchandise [mərːʔtʃəndais] n 商品 shồhin

merchant [mərːʔtʃənt] n (trader) 貿易商 bồekishồ

merchant bank (BRIT) n マーチャントバンク mắchantobańku

merchant marine (BRIT **merchant navy**) n 商船 shồsen ◇一国の全商船を集合的に指す ikkóku no zeńshosen wồ shūgồteki ni sasù

merciful [mərːʔsifəl] adj (kind, forgiving) 情け深い nasákebukaì; (fortunate): *merciful release* 苦しみからの解放 kurúshimì kara no kaíhō ◇重病人などの死亡について言う jūbyṓnin nado no shibṓ ni tsuitè iú

merciless [mərːʔsilis] adj (person, regime) 冷酷な reíkoku na

mercury [mərːʔkjəriː] n 水銀 suígin

mercy [mərːʔsiː] n (clemency: also REL) 情け nasáke, 慈悲 jihí
at the mercy of ...のなすがままになって ...no násù ga mamá ni nattè

mere [miːr] adj (emphasizing insignificance: child, trifle, amount) ほんの hoń no; (emphasizing significance): *his mere presence irritates her* 彼がそこにいるだけで彼女は頭に来る kárè ga sokó ni irù daké de kánòjo wa atáma ni kurù

merely [miːrˈliː] adv ただ...だけ tádà ...daké

merge [məːrdʒ] vt (combine: companies, institutions etc) 合併させる gappéi saserù
♦vi (COMM) 合併する gappéi suru; (colors, sounds, shapes) 次第に溶け合う shidái ni tokéaù; (roads) 合流する gồryū suru

merger [məːrˈdʒəːr] n (COMM) 合併 gappéi

meringue [məræŋˈ] n メレンゲ meréňge

merit [mer'it] n (worth, value) 価値 kachí; (advantage) 長所 chồsho, 利点 ritén
♦vt ...に値する ...ni atái suru

mermaid [məːrˈmeid] n 人魚 níńgyo

merry [mer'iː] adj (happy: laugh, person) 陽気な yồki na; (cheerful: music) 活気ある kakkí arù
Merry Christmas! メリークリスマス merí kurisùmasu

merry-go-round [mer'iːgouraund] n 回転木馬 kaíteńmokuba

mesh [meʃ] n (net) メッシュ mésshù

mesmerize [mezˈməːraiz] vt 魅惑する miwáku suru

mess [mes] n (muddle: in room) 散らかしっ放し chirákashippanashi, めちゃくちゃ mechákucha; (: of situation) 混乱 końran; (dirt) 汚れ yogóre; (MIL) 食堂 shokúdō

mess about/around (inf) vi (fool around) ぶらぶらする búràbura suru

mess about/around with vt fus (play around with) いじる ijírù

message [mesˈidʒ] n (piece of information) 伝言 deńgon, メッセージ mésseːji; (meaning: of play, book etc) 教訓 kyồkun

messenger [mesˈindʒəːr] n 使者 shíshà, メッセンジャー messéňjā

Messrs. [mesˈəːrz] abbr (on letters) ◇Mr. の複数形 Mr. no fukúsūkei

mess up vt (spoil) 台無しにする daínashi ni suru; (dirty) 汚す yogósù

messy [mesˈiː] adj (dirty) 汚れた yogóreta; (untidy) 散らかした chirákashita

met [met] pt, pp of **meet**

metabolism [mətæb'əlizəm] *n* 新陳代謝 shifichintaīsha

metal [met'əl] *n* 金属 kiñzoku

metallic [mitæl'ik] *adj* (made of metal) 金属の kiñzoku no; (sound, color) 金属的な kiñzokuteki na

metallurgy [met'ələ:rdʒi:] *n* や 金 学 yakiñgaku

metamorphosis [metəmɔ:r'fəsis] (*p l* **metamorphoses**) *n* 変態 heñtai

metaphor [met'əfɔ:r] *n* 隠 ゆ iñ-yu, メタファー metáfā

mete [mi:t] *vt: to mete out* (punishment, justice) 与える atáerù, 加える kuwáerù

meteor [mi:'ti: our] *n* 流れ星 nagárebòshi

meteorite [mi:'ti:ərait] *n* いん石 íñseki

meteorology [mi:ti:ərɑ:l'ədʒi:] *n* 気象学 kishőgàku

meter [mi:'tə:r] *n* (instrument: gas meter, electricity meter) ...計 ...kéi, メーター mếtā; (*also: parking meter*) パーキングメーター pákiñgumètā; (*US:* unit) メートル mếtðru

method [meθ'əd] *n* (way) 方法 hőhō

methodical [məθɑ:d'ikəl] *adj* (careful, thorough) 慎重な shiñchō na

Methodist [meθ'ədist] *n* メソジスト教徒 mesőjisuto kyőto

methodology [meθədɑ:l'ədʒi:] *n* 方法論 hőhōròn

meths [meθs] (*BRIT*) *n* = **methylated spirit**

methylated spirit [meθ'əleitid-] (*BRIT*) *n* 変性アルコール heñsei arukðru

meticulous [mətik'jələs] *adj* 厳密な geñmitsu na

metre [mi:'tə:r] (*BRIT*) *n* (unit) = **meter**

metric [met'rik] *adj* メートル法の mếtoruhð no

metropolis [mitrɑ:p'əlis] *n* 大都会 daítokai

metropolitan [metrəpɑ:l'itən] *adj* 大都会の daítokai no

Metropolitan Police (*BRIT*) *n: the Metropolitan Police* ロンドン市警察 roñdon shikeīsatsu

mettle [met'əl] *n* (spirit, courage): *to be on one's mettle* 張切っている haríkitte

irù

mew [mju:] *vi* (cat) にゃあと鳴く nyá tò nakú

mews [mju:z] *n* (*BRIT*): *mews flat* アパート apáto ◇昔の馬屋をアパートに改造した物を指す mukáshi nò umáya wò apátð ni kaízo shita monð wo sásù

Mexican [mek'səkən] *adj* メキシコの mekíshiko no

♦*n* メキシコ人 mekíshikojìn

Mexico [mek'səkou] *n* メキシコ mekíshiko

Mexico City *n* メキシコ市 mekíshiko-shi

miaow [mi:au'] *vi* (cat) にゃあと鳴く nyá tò nakú

mice [mais] *pl of* **mouse**

micro- [mai'krou] *prefix* 微小... bishő ...

microbe [mai'kroub] *n* 細菌 saíkin

microchip [mai'krətʃip] *n* マイクロチップ maíkurochippù

micro(computer) [maikrou(kəmpju:'-tə:r)] *n* マイクロコンピュータ maíkuro-kompyùta, パソコン pasőkon

microcosm [mai'krəkɑ:zəm] *n* 小宇宙 shőuchū, ミクロコスモス mikúrokosu-mðsu

microfilm [mai'krəfilm] *n* マイクロフィルム maíkurofirùmu

microphone [mai'krəfoun] *n* マイクロホン maíkurohòn

microprocessor [maikroupro:s'esə:r] *n* マイクロプロセッサー maíkuropurosessà

microscope [mai'krəskoup] *n* 顕微鏡 keñbikyõ

microscopic [mai'krəskɑ:p'ik] *adj* 微小の bishő no

microwave [mai'krouweiv] *n* (*also: microwave oven*) 電子レンジ deñshi reñji

mid [mid] *adj: in mid May* 5月半ばに gogátsu nakàba ni

in mid afternoon 昼下がりに hirúsagari ni

in mid air 空中に kúchū ni

midday [mid'dei] *n* 正午 shőgo

middle [mid'əl] *n* (center) 真ん中 mañnaka, 中央 chǔõ; (half-way point) 中間 chǔkan; (waist) ウエスト uésùto

◆*adj* (of place, position) 真ん中の mañnaka no; (average: quantity, size) 中位の chǔgurai no

in the middle of the night 真夜中に mayónaka ni

middle-aged [mid'əleid3d'] *adj* 中年の chǔnen no

Middle Ages *npl*: *the Middle Ages* 中世 chǔsei

middle-class [mid'əlklæs] *adj* 中流の chǔryū no

middle class(es) [mid'əlklæs(iz)] *n(pl)*: *the middle class(es)* 中流階級 chǔryūkaīkyū

Middle East *n*: *the Middle East* 中東 chǔtō

middleman [mid'əlmæn] (*pl* **middlemen**) *n* 仲買人 nakágainin

middle name *n* ミドルネーム midórunèmu

middle-of-the-road [mid'ələvðəroud'] *adj* (politician, music) 中道の chǔdō no

middleweight [mid'əlweit] *n* (BOXING) ミドル級の midórukyū no

middling [mid'liŋ] *adj* 中位の chǔgurai no

midge [mid3] *n* ブヨ búyò ◇ブヨの様な小さい虫の総称 búyò no yō na chíīsaì mushí no sōshō

midget [mid3'it] *n* 小人 kobíto

Midlands [mid'ləndz] (*BRIT*) *npl*: *the Midlands* イングランド中部地方 iñgurañdo chūbu chihō

midnight [mid'nait] *n* 真夜中 mayónaka

midriff [mid'rif] *n* おなか onáka ◇ウエストから胸までの部分を指す uésùto kara muné madè no búbùn wo sásù

midst [midst] *n*: *in the midst of* (crowd, group) ...の中に〔で〕...no nákà ni 〔de〕; (situation, event) ...のさなかに ...no sanákà ni; (action) ...をしている所を ...wo shité irù tokóro

midsummer [mid'sʌm'əːr] *n* 真夏 manátsu

midway [mid'wei] *adj*: *midway (between/through)* ...の途中で ...no to-

chū de

◆*adv*: *midway (between/through)* ...の途中に〔で〕...no tochū ni 〔de〕

midweek [mid'wi:k] *adv* 週半ば shū nakabà

midwife [mid'waif] (*pl* **midwives**) *n* 助産婦 josáñpu

midwinter [mid'win'təːr] *n*: *in midwinter* 真冬に mafúyu ni

might[1] [mait] *see* **may**

might[2] [mait] *n* (power) 力 chikára

mighty [mai'ti:] *adj* 強力な kyóryoku na

migraine [mai'grein] *n* 偏頭痛 heñzutsū

migrant [mai'grənt] *adj*: *migrant bird* 渡り鳥 watáridòri

migrant worker 渡り季節労働者 watári kisetsurōdōsha

migrate [mai'greit] *vi* (bird etc) 移動する idō suru; (person) 移住する ijū suru

migration [maigrei'ʃən] *n* (bird etc) 移動 idō; (person) 移住 ijū

mike [maik] *n abbr* = **microphone**

Milan [milæn'] *n* ミラノ miránò

mild [maild] *adj* (gentle: character) 大人しい otónashiï; (climate) 穏やかな odáyàka na; (slight: infection, illness) 軽い karúi; (: interest) 少しの sukóshì no; (taste) 甘口の amákuchi no

mildew [mil'du:] *n* かび kabí

mildly [maild'li:] *adv* (gently) 優しく yasáshikù; (somewhat) 少し sukóshì

to put it mildly 控え目に言って hikáeme ni ittè

mile [mail] *n* (unit) マイル maírù

mileage [mai'lid3] *n* (number of miles) マイル数 maírùsū

mileometer [maila:m'itəːr] (*BRIT*) *n* = **odometer**

milestone [mail'stoun] *n* (marker) 一里塚 ichírizùka; (*fig*: important event) 画期的な出来事 kakkíteki na dekígòto

milieu [mi:lju:'] *n* 環境 kañkyō

militant [mil'ətənt] *adj* 戦闘的な señtōteki na

military [mil'iteːri:] *adj* 軍隊の gúñtai no

militate [mil'əteit] *vi*: *to militate against* (prevent) 邪魔する jamá suru

militia [miliʃ'ə] *n* 民兵 miñpei

milk [milk] *n* (of any mammal) 乳 chichí; (of cow) 牛乳 gyúnyū, ミルク mírùku
♦*vt* (cow, goat): ...の乳を搾る ...no chichí wo shibórù; (*fig*: situation, person) 食い物にする kuímonò ni suru

milk chocolate *n* ミルクチョコレート mírùkuchokorēto

milkman [milk'mæn] (*pl* **milkmen**) *n* 牛乳配達人 gyúnyūhaitatsunìn

milkshake [milk'ʃeik] *n* ミルクセーキ mírùkusēki

milky [mil'ki:] *adj* (color) 乳白色の nyúhakùshoku no; (drink) ミルク入りの mírùku iri no

Milky Way *n* 銀河 gínga

mill [mil] *n* (windmill etc: for grain) 製粉機 seífunki; (*also*: **coffee mill**) コーヒーひき kōhīhikí; (factory: steel mill, saw mill) 製...工場 seí...kōjō
♦*vt* (grind: grain, flour) ひく híkù
♦*vi* (*also*: **mill about**: people, crowd) 右往左往する uősaő suru

woolen mill 織物工場 orímonokōjo

miller [mil'əːr] *n* 製粉業者 seífungyōsha

milligram(me) [mil'əgræm] *n* ミリグラム mirígurāmu

millimeter [mil'əmiːtəːr] (*BRIT* **millimetre**) *n* ミリメートル mirímētoru

millinery [mil'əneːri:] *n* 婦人帽子店 fujínbōshiten

million [mil'jən] *n* 100万 hyakúman
a million times 何回も nañkai mo

millionaire [miljəneːr'] *n* 大富豪 daífugō

milometer [mai'loumi:təːr] *n* = **mileometer**

mime [maim] *n* (action) パントマイム pañtomaìmu; (actor) パントマイム役者 pañtomaimu yakùsha
♦*vt* (act) 身振り手振りでまねる mibúritebùri de manérù
♦*vi* (act out) パントマイムを演ずる pañtomaìmu wo eñzurù

mimic [mim'ik] *n* 物まね師 monómaneshì
♦*vt* (imitate) ...のまねをする ...no mané wo surù

min. *abbr* = minute(s); minimum

minaret [minəret'] *n* ミナレット miná-

rètto ◇モスクのせん塔 mósùku no señtō

mince [mins] *vt* (meat) ひく híkù
♦*vi* (in walking) 気取って歩く kidótte arukù
♦*n* (*BRIT*: CULIN) ひき肉 hikíniku

mincemeat [mins'miːt] *n* (fruit) ミンスミート miñsumìto ◇ドライフルーツなどの細切り doráifurūtsu nádò no komágiri; (*US*: meat) ひき肉 hikíniku

mincemeat pie (*US*) *n* (sweet) ミンスミートパイ miñsumītopaì

mince pie (*BRIT*) *n* (sweet) = **mincemeat pie**

mincer [min'səːr] *n* 肉ひき器 nikúhikikì

mind [maind] *n* (thoughts) 考え kañgaè; (intellect) 頭脳 zunő; (opinion): **to my mind** 私の意見では watákushi no ikên de wa; (sanity): **to be out of one's mind** 気が狂っている ki ga kurútte irù
♦*vt* (attend to, look after: shop, home etc) ...の番をする ...no báñ wo suru; (: children, pets etc) ...の面倒を見る ...no mefïdō wò mírù; (be careful of) ...に注意する ...ni chûî suru; (object to): **I don't mind the noise** その音を気にしません sonő otő wo kî ni shimásen
it is on my mind 気に掛っている kî ni kakátte irù
to keep/bear something in mind ...を気にする ...wo kî ni suru
to make up one's mind 決心する kesshín suru
I don't mind 構いませんよ kamáimasèn yó
mind you, ... でもこれだけ言っておく ... de mo koré dakè itté okù ...
never mind! (it makes no odds) 気にしないで下さい kî ni shináide kudásaì; (don't worry) ほうっておきなさい hőtte oki nasaì, 心配しないで下さい shiñpai shinaìde kudásaì
「**mind the step**」階段に注意 kaídan ni chûî

minder [maind'əːr] *n* (childminder) ベビーシッター bebíshittà; (*BRIT inf*: bodyguard) ボディーガード bodígādo

mindful [maind'fəl] *adj*: **mindful of** ...を気に掛ける ...wo kî ni kakérù

mindless [maind'lis] *adj* (violence) 愚かな óroka na, 愚劣な gurétsu na; (boring: job) 退屈な taíkutsu na

---

KEYWORD

mine[1] [main] *pron* 私の物 watákushi no monò

that book is mine その本は私のです sonó hoñ wa watákushi no dèsu

these cases are mine それらのケースは私のです sorérà no kḗsù wa watákushi no dèsu

this is mine これは私の物です koré wà watákushi no monò desu

yours is red, mine is green あなたのは赤いが，私のは緑色です anátà no wa akáì ga, watákushi no wà midóri irò desu

a friend of mine 私のある友達 watákushi nò árù tomódàchi

---

mine[2] [main] *n* (gen) 鉱山 kǒzan; (also: land mine) 地雷 jiréi; (bomb in water) 機雷 kiréi

♦*vt* (coal) 採掘する saíkutsu suru; (beach) 地雷を敷設する jiréi wo fusétsu suru; (harbor) 機雷を敷設する kiréi wo fusétsu suru

coal mine 炭坑 tañkō

gold mine 金坑 kiñkō

minefield [main'fi:ld] *n* (area: land) 地雷原 jiráigeñ; (: water) 機雷敷設水域 kiréi-fusetsu suìki; (*fig*: situation) 危険をはらんだ事態 kikén wò haráñda jítai

miner [main'ə:r] *n* 鉱山労働者 kǒzanrōdōsha

mineral [min'ə:rəl] *adj* (deposit, resources) 鉱物の kǒbutsu no

♦*n* (in earth) 鉱物 kǒbutsu; (in food) ミネラル mineraru

minerals [min'ə:rəlz] (BRIT) *npl* (soft drinks) 炭酸飲料水 tañsan-inryòsui

mineral water *n* ミネラルウォーター mineraru uồta

mingle [min'gəl] *vi: to mingle with* ...と交わる ...to majíwaru ◇特にパーティなどで多くの人に声を掛けて回るなどの意味で使う tókù ni pàti nádò de ókù no

hitò ni kóè wo kakéte mawárù nádò no ímì de tsukáù

miniature [min'iətʃər] *adj* (small, tiny) ミニチュアの miníchùa no

♦*n* ミニチュア miníchùa

minibus [min'i:bʌs] *n* マイクロバス maíkurobàsu

minim [min'əm] *n* (MUS) 二分音符 níbun oñpu

minimal [min'əməl] *adj* 最小限(度)の saíshōgen(do) no

minimize [min'əmaiz] *vt* (reduce: risks, disease) 最小限(度)に抑える saíshōgen (do) ni osáerù; (play down: role) 見くびる mikúbirù; (: weakness) 問題にしない mofídai ni shinái, 避けて通る sakéte tòru

minimum [min'əməm] (*pl* **minima**) *n* 最小限(度) saíshōgeñ(do)

♦*adj* 最小限(度)の saíshōgeñ(do) no

mining [mai'niŋ] *n* 鉱業 kǒgyō

miniskirt [min'i:skə:rt] *n* ミニスカート minísukàto

minister [min'istə:r] *n* (POL) 大臣 dáijin; (REL) 牧師 bókùshi

♦*vi: to minister to* (people, needs) ...に仕える ...ni tsukáerù

ministerial [ministi:r'i:əl] (BRIT) *adj* (POL) 大臣の dáijin no

ministry [min'istri:] *n* (POL) ...省 ...shǒ; (REL) 聖職 seíshoku

mink [miŋk] *n* (fur) ミンクの毛皮 míñku no kegàwa; (animal) ミンク míñku

mink coat *n* ミンクのコート míñku no kồto

minnow [min'ou] *n* 小魚 kozákàna

minor [mai'nə:r] *adj* (unimportant: repairs) ちょっとした chottó shità; (: injuries) 軽い karúi; (: poet) 二流の niryū no; (MUS) 短調の tanchō no

♦*n* (LAW) 未成年 miséneñ

minority [minɔ:r'iti:] *n* (less than half: of group, society) 少数派 shǒsùha

mint [mint] *n* (plant) ハッカ hakká; (sweet) ハッカあめ hakká amè

♦*vt* (coins) 鋳造する chǔzō suru

the (US) Mint (US), *the (Royal) Mint* (BRIT) 造幣局 zốheìkyoku

in mint condition 新品同様で shiñpindôyō de

minus [mai'nəs] n (also: **minus sign**) マ
イナス記号 maínasu kigô
♦prep: **12 minus 6 equals 6** 12引く6は
6 júni hikú rokú wà rokú; (temperature):
minus 24 零下24度 reíka nijûyon do

minuscule [min'əskju:l] adj 微々たる bí-
bìtaru

minute [min'it] n (unit) 分 fún; (fig: short
time) ちょっと chottó
♦adj (search, detail) 細かい komákaì
at the last minute 土壇場に dotánba
ni

minutes [min'its] npl (of meeting) 会議
録 kaígiròku

miracle [mir'əkəl] n (REL, fig) 奇跡 ki-
sèki

miraculous [miræk'jələs] adj 奇跡的な
kisékiteki na

mirage [mira:ʒ'] n しん気楼 shíñkirò

mirror [mir'ər] n (in bedroom, bathroom) 鏡 kagámi, ミラー mírà; (in car)
バックミラー bakkûmirà

mirth [mə:rθ] n (laughter) 笑い warái

misadventure [misədven't(ə:r] n 災難
saínañ

misapprehension [misæprihen't(ən] n
誤解 gokái

misappropriate [misəprou'pri:eit] vt
(funds, money) 横領する ôryô suru

misbehave [misbiheiv'] vi 行儀悪くする
gyôgiwarukù suru

miscalculate [miskæl'kjəleit] vt 見込み
違いする mikômichigài suru

miscarriage [miskær'idʒ] n (MED) 流産
ryûzan; (failure): **miscarriage of justice** 誤審 goshín

miscellaneous [misəlei'ni:əs] adj (collection, group: of tools, people) 雑多な zattá na; (subjects, items) 種々の shujú no

mischance [mist(æns'] n (misfortune) 不
運 fúùn

mischief [mis't(if] n (naughtiness: of
child) いたずら itázura; (playfulness,
fun) いたずら itázura; (maliciousness) 悪
さ wárùsa

mischievous [mis't(əvəs] adj (naughty,
playful) いたずらな itázura na

misconception [miskənsep'(ən] n 誤解
gokái

misconduct [miska:n'dʌkt] n (behavior)
非行 hikô
♦professional misconduct 背任 haínin,
職権乱用 shokkén rañyô

misdemeanor [misdimi:'nə:r] (BRIT
misdemeanour) n 軽犯罪 keíhañzai

miser [mai'zə:r] n けちん坊 kéchìnbō, 守
銭奴 shuséndo

miserable [miz'ə:rəbəl] adj (unhappy:
person, expression) 惨めな míjìme na, 不
幸な fukô na; (wretched: conditions) 哀
れな áwàre na; (unpleasant: weather,
person) いやな iyá na; (contemptible:
offer, donation) ちっぽけな chippókè na;
(: failure) 情けない nasákenaì

miserly [mai'zə:rli] adj けちな kechí na

misery [miz'ə:ri:] n (unhappiness) 惨めさ
mijímesà, 不幸せ fushiawase; (wretched-
ness) 哀れな状態 áwàre na jôtai

misfire [misfair'] vi (plan etc) 失敗する
shippái suru

misfit [mis'fit] n (person) 適応不能者 te-
kíôfunôsha

misfortune [misfɔ:r't(ən] n (bad luck) 不
運 fúùn

misgiving [misgiv'iŋ] n (apprehension)
心もとなさ kokóromotonasà, 疑念 ginén
to have misgivings about something
...を疑問に思う ...wo gimón nì omóù

misguided [misgai'did] adj (opinion,
view) 心得違いの kokóroechigài no

mishandle [mishæn'dəl] vt (mismanage:
problem, situation) ...の処置を誤る ...no
shôchì wo ayámarù

mishap [mis'hæp] n 事故 jíkò

misinform [misinfɔ:rm'] vt ...にうそを伝
える ...ni úsò wo tsutáerù

misinterpret [misintə:r'prit] vt 誤解す
る gokái suru

misjudge [misdʒʌdʒ'] vt ...の判断を誤る
...no hañdañ wo ayámarù

mislay [mislei'] (pt, pp **mislaid**) vt (lose)
なくす nakúsù, 置忘れる okíwasurerù

mislead [misli:d'] (pt, pp **misled**) vt うそ
を信じ込ませる úsò wo shiñjikomaserù

misleading [misli:'diŋ] adj (information)

誤解させる gokái saserù

mismanage [mismǽnidʒ] vt (manage badly: business, institution) 下手な管理をする hétà na kâñri wo suru; (: problem, situation) ...の処置を誤る ...no shóchì wo ayámarù

misnomer [misnou'mə:r] n (term) 誤った名称 ayámattà meíshō

misogynist [misɑ:dʒ'ənist] n 女嫌い onnágirai

misplace [mispleis'] vt (lose) なくす nakúsù, 置忘れる okíwasurerù

misprint [mis'print] n 誤植 goshóku

Miss [mis] n ...さん ...sán ◊未婚の女性に対する敬称 míkòn no joséi ni taí surù keíshō

miss [mis] vt (train, bus etc) ...に乗遅れる ...ni noríokurerù; (fail to hit: target) ...に当て損なう ...ni atésokonaù; (fail to see): *you can't miss it* 見落しっこない míòtoshikkònai; (regret the absence of) ...が恋しい ...ga koíshiì, ...が懐かしい ...ga natsúkashiì; (chance, opportunity) 逃す nigásù, のがす nogásù; (class, meeting) ...に欠席する ...ni kesséki suru

◆vi (fail to hit) 当り損なう atárisokonaù, それる sorérù

◆n (failure to hit) 当て損ない atésokonài, ミス mísù

misshapen [misʃei'pən] adj 不格好な bukákkō na

missile [mis'əl] n (weapon: MIL) ミサイル misáiru; (: object thrown) 飛道具 tobídōgu

missing [mis'iŋ] adj (lost: person, pupil) 行方不明の yukúefumèi no; (: object) なくなっている nakúnatte irù; (removed: tooth) 抜かれた nukáretà; (: wheel) 外された hazúsaretà; (MIL) 行方不明の yukúefumèi no

to be missing 行方不明である yukúefumèi de aru

mission [miʃ'ən] n (task) 任務 nínmu; (official representatives) 代表団 daíhyōdan; (MIL) 出撃 shutsúgeki ◊特に爆撃機について言う tôkù ni bakúgekikì ni tsuite iú; (REL: activity) 伝道 deñdō; (: building) 伝道所 deñdōjò

missionary [miʃ'əne:ri:] n 伝道師 deñdōshi

miss out (BRIT) vt (leave out) 落す otósù

misspent [misspent'] adj: *his misspent youth* 浪費した彼の青春 rôhi shità kárè no seíshun

mist [mist] n (light) もや móyà; (heavy) 濃霧 nômu

◆vi (also: **mist over, mist up**) (eyes) 涙ぐむ namídagùmu; (windows) 曇る kumórù

mistake [misteik'] n (error) 間違い machígaì

◆vt (pt **mistook**, pp **mistaken**) (be wrong about) 間違える machígaerù

by mistake 間違って machígattè

to make a mistake 間違いをする machígaì wo suru

to mistake A for B AをBと間違える A wo B to machígaerù

mistaken [mistei'kən] (pp of **mistake**) adj (idea, belief etc) 間違った machígattà

to be mistaken 間違っている machígattè irú

mister [mis'tə:r] (inf) n ◊男性への呼び掛け dañsei e no yobíkake ¶ see **Mr.**

mistletoe [mis'əltou] n ヤドリギ yadórigì

mistook [mistuk'] pt of **mistake**

mistress [mis'tris] n (lover) 愛人 aíjin; (of house, servant) 女主人 ofína shùjin; (in primary, secondary schools) 先生 señsei

to be mistress of the situation (fig) 事態を掌握している jítai wo shôaku shite irú

mistrust [mistrʌst'] vt 信用しない shiñyō shinái

misty [mis'ti:] adj (day etc) もやった moyáttà; (glasses, windows) 曇った kumóttà

misunderstand [misʌndə:rstǽnd'] (irreg) vt (fail to understand: person, book) 誤解する gokái suru

◆vi (fail to understand) 誤解する gokái suru

misunderstanding [misʌndə:rstǽn'diŋ]

n (failure to understand) 誤解 gokái; (disagreement) 口げんか kuchígeñka

misuse [misju:s'] *n* (of power) 乱用 rañyō; (of funds) 悪用 akúyō

◆*vt* (power) 乱用する rañ-yō suru; (funds) 悪用する akúyō suru

mitigate [mit'əgeit] *vt* 和らげる yawáragerù

mitt(en) [mit('ən)] *n* ミトン mítòn

mix [miks] *vt* (combine: liquids, ingredients, colors) 混ぜる mazérù; (cake, cement) こねる konérù; (drink, sauce) 作る tsukúrù

◆*vi* (people): **to mix (with)** ...と交わる ...to majíwarù ◇特にパーティなどで多くの人に声を掛けて回るなどの意味で使う tókù ni páti nádò de ōku no hitó nī kóè wo kakéte máwarù nádò no ímì de tsukáù

◆*n* (combination) 混合物 koñgōbùtsu; (powder) ミックス míkkùsu

mixed [mikst] *adj* (salad) コンビネーションの koñbinéshon no; (grill) 盛り合せの moríawase no; (feelings, reactions) 複雑な fukúzatsu na; (school, education etc) 共学の kyōgaku no

a mixed marriage (religion) 異なった宗教の信徒間の結婚 kotónatta shúkyō no shinto kan no kekkon; (race) 異なった人種間の結婚 kotónatta jiñshu kan no kekkon

mixed-up [mikst'ʌp] *adj* (confused) 混乱している koñran shite irù

mixer [mik'sə:r] *n* (for food) ミキサー míkisā; (person): **to be a good mixer** 付合い上手である tsukíaijōzu de aru

mixture [miks't'fə:r] *n* (combination) 混合物 koñgōbùtsu; (MED: for cough etc) 飲薬 nomígusùri

mix up *vt* (confuse: people, things) 混同する koñdō suru

mix-up [miks'ʌp] *n* (confusion) 混乱 koñran

mm *abbr* = **millimeter**

moan [moun] *n* (cry) うめき umḗki

◆*vi* (*inf*: complain): **to moan (about)** (...について) 愚痴を言う (...ni tsúite) guchí wo iù

moat [mout] *n* 堀 horí

mob [ma:b] *n* (crowd) 群衆 guñshū

◆*vt* (person) ...の回りにわっと押し寄せる ...no mawári ni wáttò oshíyoserù

mobile [mou'bəl] *adj* (able to move) 移動式の idóshiki no

◆*n* (decoration) モビール móbīru

mobile home *n* モビールハウス mobíruhaùsu

mobility [moubil'əti:] *n* 移動性 idósei

mobilize [mou'bəlaiz] *vt* (friends, work force) 動員する dóin suru; (MIL: country, army) 戦時態勢を取らせる señji taísei wo toráserù

moccasin [ma:k'əsin] *n* モカシン mokáshìn

mock [ma:k] *vt* (ridicule) ばかにする bákà ni suru; (laugh at) あざ笑う azáwaraù

◆*adj* (fake) 見せ掛けの misékake no; (exam, battle) 模擬の mógì no

mockery [ma:k'ə:ri:] *n* (derision) あざけり azákeri

to make a mockery of ...をばかにする ...wo bákà ni suru

mock-up [ma:k'ʌp] *n* (model) 模型 mokḗi

mod [ma:d ka:nz] *adj see* **convenience**

mode [moud] *n* (form: of life) 様式 yōshiki; (: of transportation) 手段 shūdan

model [ma:d'əl] *n* (representation: of boat, building etc) 模型 mokéi; (fashion model, artist's model) モデル módèru; (example) 手本 tehón

◆*adj* (excellent) 模範的な mohánteki na

◆*vt* (clothes) ...のモデルをする ...no módèru wo suru; (with clay etc) ...の模型を作る ...no mokéi wo tsukúrù; (copy): **to model oneself on** ...の模範に習う ...no móhàn ni naráù

◆*vi* (for designer, photographer etc) モデルをする módèru wo suru

model railway *n* 模型鉄道 mokḗi tetsudō

modem [mou'dem] *n* (COMPUT) モデム módèmu

moderate [*adj* ma:d'ə:rit *vb* ma:d'ə:reit] *adj* (views, opinion) 穏健な oñken na; (amount) 中位の chūgurai no; (change)

ある程度の arú teído no
◆*vi* (storm, wind etc) 弱まる yawámarù
◆*vt* (tone, demands) 和らげる yawárageru

moderation [mɑːdəreiʃ'ən] *n* 中庸 chúyō

modern [mɑːd'ərn] *adj* 現代的な geńdaiteki na, 近代的な kińdaiteki na, モダンな modán na

modernize [mɑːd'ə:rnaiz] *vt* 現代的にする geńdaiteki ni suru

modest [mɑːd'ist] *adj* (small: house, budget) 質素な shíssò na; (unassuming: person) 謙虚な keńkyo na

modesty [mɑːd'isti:] *n* 慎み tsutsúshimi

modicum [mɑːd'əkəm] *n*: *a modicum of* ちょっとだけの... chóttò dake no ...

modification [mɑːdəfəkei'ʃən] *n* (alteration: of law) 改正 kaísei; (: of building) 改修 kaíshū; (: of car, engine etc) 改造 kaízō

modify [mɑːd'əfai] *vt* (law) 改正する kaísei suru; (building, car, engine) 改造する kaízō suru

module [mɑːdʒ'uːl] *n* (unit, component, SPACE) モジュール mojúrù

mogul [mou'gəl] *n* (*fig*) 大立者 ódatemòno

mohair [mou'he:r] *n* モヘア móheà

moist [mɔist] *adj* (slightly wet: earth, eyes, lips) 湿った shiméttà

moisten [mɔis'ən] *vt* (lips, sponge) 湿らす shimérasù

moisture [mɔis'tʃə:r] *n* 湿り気 shimérike

moisturizer [mɔis'tʃə:raizə:r] *n* (cream) モイスチュアクリーム moísuchua kurímu; (lotion) モイスチュアローション moísuchua rōshon

molar [mou'lə:r] *n* きゅう歯 kyúshi

mold [mould] (*BRIT* **mould**) *n* (cast: for jelly, metal) 型 katá; (mildew) かび kabí
◆*vt* (shape: plastic, clay etc) ...で...の形を作る ...de ...no katáchi wò tsukúrù; (*fig*: influence: public opinion, character) 作り上げる tsukúriagerù

moldy [moul'di:] (*BRIT* **mouldy**) *adj* (bread, cheese) かびた kabítà; (smell) かび臭い kabíkusaì

mole [moul] *n* (spot) ほくろ hokúro; (animal) モグラ mogúra; (*fig*: spy) 秘密工作員 himítsukōsakuìn

molecule [mɑːl'əkjuːl] *n* 分子 búnshi

molest [məlest'] *vt* (assault sexually) ...にいたずらをする ...ni itázura wo surù; (harass) いじめる ijímerù

mollycoddle [mɑːl'iːkɑːdəl] *vt* (pamper) 甘やかす amáyakasù

molt [moult] (*BRIT* **moult**) *vi* (animal, bird) 換毛する kańmō suru

molten [moul'tən] *adj* (metal, rock) 溶解の yókai no

mom [mɑːm] (*US*: *inf*) *n* かあちゃん kàchan, ママ mámà

moment [mou'mənt] *n* (period of time): *for a moment* ちょっと chóttò; (point in time): *at that moment* 丁度その時 chódò sonó tokì

at the moment 今の所 imá no tokòro

momentary [mou'mənte:ri:] *adj* (brief: pause, glimpse) 瞬間的な shuńkanteki na

momentous [moumen'təs] *adj* (occasion, decision) 重大な júdai na

momentum [moumen'təm] *n* (PHYSICS) 運動量 uńdōryò; (*fig*: of events, movement, change) 勢い ikíòi, 惰性 daséi

to gather momentum (*lit*, *fig*) 勢いが付く ikíòi ga tsúkù

mommy [mɑːm'iː] (*US*) *n* ママ mámà ◇幼児用語 yójiyògo

Monaco [mɑːn'əkou] *n* モナコ mónàko

monarch [mɑːn'ə:rk] *n* 君主 kúnshu

monarchy [mɑːn'ə:rki:] *n* (system) 王制 ósei; (royal family) 王室 óshitsu, 王族 ózoku

monastery [mɑːn'əste:ri:] *n* 修道院 shúdòin

Monday [mʌn'dei] *n* 月曜日 getsúyòbi

monetary [mɑːn'ite:ri:] *adj* (system, policy, control) 金融の kiń-yū no

money [mʌn'iː] *n* (coins and notes) 金 kané; (currency) 通貨 tsúka

to make money (earn) 金をもうける kané wo mókerù

money order *n* 郵便為替 yúbinkawàse

money-spinner [mʌn'i:spinə:r] (*BRIT*:

inf) *n* (person, idea, business) ドル箱 do-rúbako

mongol [maːŋ'gəl] *adj* モンゴルの móñ-goru no

♦*n* (MED) ダウン症候群患者 daúnshōkō-gun kañja

mongrel [mʌŋ'grəl] *n* (dog) 雑種 zasshú

monitor [maːn'itəːr] *n* (machine) モニター装置 moñítāsōchi; (screen: *also*: **television monitor**) ブラウン管 buráuñkan; (of computer) モニター móñìtā

♦*vt* (broadcasts) 傍受する bṓju suru; (heartbeat, pulse) モニターする móñìtā suru; (progress) 監視する kañshi suru

monk [mʌŋk] *n* 修道師 shúdòshi

monkey [mʌŋ'ki:] *n* (animal) サル sarú

monkey nut (*BRIT*) *n* ピーナッツ pī-nattsu

monkey wrench *n* モンキーレンチ moñ-kīreñchi

mono [maːn'ou] *adj* (recording) モノラルの móñoraru no

monochrome [maːn'əkroum] *adj* (film, photograph) 白黒の shírōkuro no, モノクロの monōkùro no

monogram [maːn'əgræm] *n* モノグラム monōgùramu

monologue [maːn'ɔːg] *n* 会話の独占 kaíwa no dokúsen; (THEATER) 独白 dokúhaku, モノローグ monōrōgu

monopolize [mənaːp'əlaiz] *vt* 独占する dokúsen suru

monopoly [mənaːp'əli:] *n* (domination) 独占 dokúsen; (COMM) 専売 señbai, モノポリー monṓpòrī

monosyllable [maːn'əsiləbəl] *n* 単音節語 tañ-onsetsugò

monotone [maːn'ətoun] *n*: **to speak in a monotone** 単調な声で話す tañchō na kòè de hanásù

monotonous [mənaːt'ənəs] *adj* (life, job etc) 退屈な taíkutsu na; (voice, tune) 単調な tañchō na

monotony [mənaːt'əni:] *n* 退屈 taíkutsu

monsoon [maːnsuːn'] *n* モンスーン móñ-sūn

monster [maːn'stəːr] *n* (animal, plant: misshapen) 奇形 kikéi; (: enormous) 怪物

kaíbùtsu, お化け obáke; (imaginary creature) 怪物 kaíbùtsu; (person: cruel, evil) 怪物 kaíbùtsu

monstrosity [maːnstraːs'əti:] *n* (hideous object, building) 見るに堪えない代物 mí-rù ni taénài shirómòno

monstrous [maːn'strəs] *adj* (huge) 巨大な kyodái na; (ugly) 見るに堪えない mí-rù ni taénài; (atrocious) 極悪な gokúaku na

month [mʌnθ] *n* 月 tsukí

monthly [mʌnθ'li:] *adj* (ticket etc) 一カ月の ikkágètsu no; (magazine) 月刊の gekkán no; (payment etc) 毎月の maítsu-ki no; (meeting) 月例の getsúrei no

♦*adv* 毎月 maítsuki

monument [maːn'jəmənt] *n* (memorial) 記念碑 kinéñhi; (historical building) 史的記念物 shitékikineñbutsu

monumental [maːnjəmen'təl] *adj* (large and important: building, statue) 歴史的な rekíshiteki na; (important: book, piece of work) 画期的な kakkíteki na; (terrific: storm, row) すごい sugóì, すさまじい susámajiì

moo [muː] *vi* (cow) もーと鳴く mṓ tò na-kú

mood [muːd] *n* (humor: of person) 機嫌 kigén; (: of crowd, group) 雰囲気 fuñ-ikì, ムード mùdo

to be in a good/bad mood (temper) 機嫌がいい〔悪い〕kigén gà íi〔warúì〕

moody [muː'di:] *adj* (variable) むら気な muráki na; (sullen) 不機嫌な fukígén na

moon [muːn] *n* 月 tsukí

moonlight [muːn'lait] *n* 月光 gekkṓ

moonlighting [muːn'laitiŋ] *n* (work) アルバイト arúbaito ◇本職の外にする仕事で, 特に規定, 規則違反の仕事を指す hoñshoku no hoká nì suru shigóto dè, tôkù ni kitéi, kisóku ihàn no shigóto wò sásù

moonlit [muːn'lit] *adj*: **a moonlit night** 月夜 tsukíyò

moor [muːr] *n* (heath) 荒れ野 aréno

♦*vt* (ship) つなぐ tsunágù

♦*vi* 停泊する teíhaku suru

moorland [muːr'lænd] *n* 荒れ野 aréno

moose [muːs] *n inv* アメリカヘラジカ a-mérikaherajīka

mop [maːp] *n* (for floor) モップ moppú; (for dishes) スポンジたわし supónjitawashi ◊短い柄の付いた皿洗い用を指す mijíkaì e no tsuíta saráarai yố wo sásù
◆*vt* (floor) モップでふく moppú de fukú; (eyes, face) ふく fukú, ぬぐう nugúù
a mop of hair もじゃもじゃ頭 mojámoja atáma

mope [moup] *vi* ふさぎ込む fuságikomù

moped [mou'ped] *n* モペット mopéttò ◊ペダルで動かす事も出来る小型オートバイ pedárù de ugókasù kotó mo dekirù kogáta ốtobaì

mop up *vt* (liquid) ふく fukú

moral [mɔːr'əl] *adj* 倫理的な ríñriteki na
◆*n* (of story etc) 教訓 kyốkun
moral support (encouragement) 精神的支え seíshinteki sasáe

morale [məræl'] *n* (of army, staff) 士気 shikí

morality [məræl'itiː] *n* (good behavior) 品行 hiñkố; (of morals: *also* correctness, acceptability) 倫理 ríñri

morals [mɔːr'əlz] *npl* (principles, values) 倫理 ríñri

morass [məræs'] *n* (lit, fig) 泥沼 dorónuma

morbid [mɔːr'bid] *adj* (imagination, ideas) 陰気な íñki na

KEYWORD
---

more [mɔːr] *adj* **1** (greater in number etc) より多くの yorí ồku no
more people/work/letters than we expected 私たちが予定していたより多くの人々〔仕事, 手紙〕watákushitāchi ga yotéi shite ita yorí ồku no hitôbito 〔shigôto, tegámi〕
I have more books/money than you 私はあなたより沢山の本〔金〕を持っています watákushi wa anátà yorí takúsan nồ hốñ〔kané〕wo mótte imasù
this store has more wine than beer この店はビールよりワインが沢山あります konó mise wà bírù yori wáìn ga takúsan arimasù

2 (additional) もっと móttò
do you want (some) more tea? もっと紅茶をいかがですか móttò kốcha wò ikága desù ká
is there any more wine? ワインはまだありますか wáìn wa mádà arímasù ká
I have no/I don't have any more money お金はもうありません o-káne wa mố arímaseñ
it'll take a few more weeks あと数週間掛ります átò sūshűkàn kakárimasù
◆*pron* **1** (greater amount) もっと沢山 móttò takúsan
more than 10 10以上 júijồ ◊この成句の英語には「10」が含まれないが、日本語の場合「10」も含まれる konó seíku no eígo ni wà "jū" gà fukúmarenaì ga, nihóñgo no baài "jū" mồ fukúmarerù. (Note: the English phrase indicates a quantity of 11 and above, but the Japanese indicates 10 and above.)
it cost more than we expected 予想以上に金が掛りました yosố ijồ ni kané gà kakárimashìta

2 (further or additional amount) もっと沢山 móttò takúsan
is there any more? まだありますか mádà arímasù ká
there's no more もうありません mố arímaseñ
a little more もう少し mố sukoshí
many/much more ...よりずっと沢山 ...yorí zuttò takúsan
◆*adv* ...よりもっと... ...yorí mottò...
more dangerous/difficult etc (than) ...より危ない〔難しい〕...yorí abúnaì(muzükashi)
more easily/economically/quickly (than) ...よりたやすく〔経済的に, 早く〕...yorí tayasukù〔keizaíteki ni, hayáku〕
more and more ますます masúmasù
more and more excited/friendly/expensive ますます興奮して〔親しくなって, 高くなって〕masúmasù kốfun shitè〔shitáshiku nattè, tákàku natte〕
he grew to like her more and more 彼はますます彼女が好きになった kárè wa masúmasù kánòjo ga sukí ni nattà

more or less 大体 daítai, およそ óyoso
the job's more or less finished 仕事は大体できています shigóto wà daítai dékìte imasu
it should cost £500, more or less 大よそ500ポンド掛りそうです óyoso go-hyákupoňdo kakárisò desu
more than ever ますます masúmàsu, より一層 yorí issò
more beautiful than ever ますます美しい masúmàsu utsúkushìi
more quickly than ever ますます早く masúmàsu háyàku
he loved her more than ever 彼はより一層彼女を愛する様になった kárè wa yorí issò káňdjo wo aí suru yò ni náttà

moreover [mɔːrouˈvəːr] *adv* なお nâô

morgue [mɔːrg] *n* 死体保管所 shitáihokaňjo, モルグ morúgù

moribund [mɔːrˈəbʌnd] *adj* (organization, industry) 斜陽の shayò no

Mormon [mɔːrˈmən] *n* モルモン教徒 morúmon kyòto

morning [mɔːrˈniŋ] *n* (period after daybreak) 朝 asá; (from midnight to noon) 午前 gózeñ
in the morning 朝に asá ni, 午前中に gozéňchū ni
7 o'clock in the morning 午前7時 gózeň shichíji
morning paper 朝刊 chókan
morning sun 朝日 ásàhi
morning walk 朝の散歩 ásà no saňpo

morning sickness *n* つわり tsuwári

Morocco [mərɑːkˈou] *n* モロッコ morókkò

moron [mɔːrˈɑːn] *(inf)* *n* ばか bákà

morose [mərousˈ] *adj* (miserable) 陰気な íñki na

morphine [mɔːrˈfiːn] *n* モルヒネ morúhine

Morse [mɔːrs] *n* (*also*: **Morse code**) モールス信号 mórusu shiňgō

morsel [mɔːrˈsəl] *n* (of food) 一口 hitókùchi

mortal [mɔːrˈtəl] *adj* (man) いつか死ぬ ítsùka shinú; (wound) 致命的な chiméite-

ki na; (danger) 命にかかわる ínòchi ni kakáwarù
♦*n* (human being) 人間 niňgen
mortal combat 死闘 shitò
mortal enemy 宿敵 shukúteki
mortal remains 遺骨 ikótsu
mortal sin 大罪 taízai

mortality [mɔːrtælˈitiː] *n* いつか死ぬ事 ítsùka shinú kotò; (number of deaths) 死亡率 shibòrìtsu

mortar [mɔːrˈtəːr] *n* (cannon) 迫撃砲 hakúgekihò; (CONSTR) モルタル morútaru; (bowl) 乳鉢 nyúbachi

mortgage [mɔːrˈgidʒ] *n* 住宅ローン jútakuròn
♦*vt* (house, property) 抵当に入れて金を借りる teítò ni irète kanè no karírù

mortify [mɔːrˈtəfai] *vt*: *to be mortified* 恥を感じる hají wo kaňjirù

mortuary [mɔːrˈtʃuːeːriː] *n* 霊安室 reíaňshitsu

mosaic [mouzeiˈik] *n* モザイク mozáìku

Moscow [mɑːsˈkau] *n* モスクワ mosúkuwa

Moslem [mɑːzˈləm] *adj, n* = **Muslim**

mosque [mɑːsk] *n* イスラム教寺院 isúramukyō jìin, モスク mósùku

mosquito [məskiːˈtou] *(pl* **mosquitoes**) *n* 蚊 ká

moss [mɔːs] *n* (plant) コケ koké

KEYWORD

most [moust] *adj* 1 (almost all: people, things etc) ほとんどの hotóňdo no
most people ほとんどの人 hotóňdo no hitò
most men/dogs behave like that ほとんどの男性〔イヌ〕はそういう振舞をする hotóňdo no dañsei〔inú〕wà sò iù furúmai wo surù
most houses here are privately owned ここのほとんどの家は個人所有の物です kokó nò hotóňdo no iè wà kojínshoyù nò monó desù
2 (largest, greatest: interest, money etc) 最も沢山の mottómo takúsañ no
who has (the) most money? 最も多くの金を持っているのは誰でしょう mottó-

mò ōku no kane wo motte iru no wa dare deshō

he derived the most pleasure from her visit 最も彼を喜ばせたのは彼女の訪問だった mottómò kárè wo yorókobaseta no wà kánòjo no hōmon dattà

♦*pron* (greatest quantity, number) ほとんど hotôñdo

most of it/them それ〔それら〕のほとんど soré〔sorérà〕no hotôñdo

most of the money/her friends 金〔彼女の友達〕のほとんど kanế〔kánòjo no tomódàchi〕nò hotôñdo

most of the time ほとんどの場合 hotôñdo no baái

do the most you can できるだけの事をして下さい dekíru dakè no kotó wò shité kudasaì

I saw the most 私が一番沢山見ました watákushi gà ichíban takùsan mimáshìta

to make the most of something ...を最大限に利用する ...wò saídaìgen ni riyố surù

at the (very) most 最大に見積っても saídai nì mitsúmotte mò

♦*adv* (+ verb: spend, eat, work etc) 最も多く mottómò ốkù; (+ adjective): **the most intelligent/expensive etc** 最も利口〔高価〕な mottómò rikố〔kốka〕nà; (+ adverb: carefully, easily etc) 最も注意深く〔たやすく〕mottómò chūibukakù〔tayásukù〕; (very: polite, interesting etc) とても totémo

a most interesting book とても面白い本 totémo omoshiroî hôñ

mostly [moust'li:] *adv* (chiefly) 主に ốmò ni; (usually) 普段は fúdàn wa, 普通は futsû wa

MOT [emouti:'] *n abbr* = **Ministry of Transport: the MOT (test)** (*BRIT*) 車検 shakêñ

motel [moutel'] *n* モーテル mốteru

moth [mɔ:θ] *n* (insect) ガ gá; (clothes moth) イガ igá

mothball [mɔ:θ'bɔ:l] *n* 防虫剤 bốchūzài

mother [mʌð'ə:r] *n* 母 háhà, 母親 haháoya, お母さん o-káasan

♦*adj*: **mother country** 母国 bôkòku

♦*vt* (act as mother to) 母親として育てる haháoya toshitè sodáterù; (pamper, protect) 甘やかす amáyakasù

mother company 親会社 oyágaìsha

motherhood [mʌð'ə:rhud] *n* 母親である事 hahâoya de arù kotô

mother-in-law [mʌð'ə:rinlɔ:] (*pl* **mothers-in-law**) *n* しゅうと shûto

motherly [mʌð'ə:rli:] *adj* 母の様な háhà no yố na

mother-of-pearl [mʌð'ə:rəvpə:rl'] *n* 真珠母 shíñjùbo

mother-to-be [mʌð'ə:rtəbi:'] (*pl* **mothers-to-be**) *n* 妊婦 nîñpu

mother tongue *n* 母国語 bokókugò

motif [mouti:f'] *n* (design) 模様 moyố

motion [mou'ʃən] *n* (movement) 動き ugóki; (gesture) 合図 aízù; (at meeting) 動議 dốgi

♦*vt*: **to motion (to) someone to do something** ...する様に...に合図をする ...surú yố ni ...ni aízù wo suru

motionless [mou'ʃənlis] *adj* 動かない ugókanaì

motion picture *n* (film) 映画 eîgà

motivated [mou'təveitid] *adj* (enthusiastic) 張り切っている haríkitte irù; (impelled): **motivated by** (envy, desire) ...の動機で...no dốki de

motivation [moutəvei'ʃən] *n* (drive) 動機 dốki

motive [mou'tiv] *n* (aim, purpose) 目標 mokúhyò

motley [mɑ:t'li:] *adj* 雑多で奇妙な zattá dè kimyố na

motor [mou'tə:r] *n* (of machine) 原動機 geñdốki, モーター mốtā; (of vehicle) エンジン êñjin; (*BRIT*: *inf*: vehicle) 車 kurúma

♦*cpd* (industry, trade) 自動車の jídòsha no

motorbike [mou'tə:rbaik] *n* オートバイ ốtòbai

motorboat [mou'tə:rbout] *n* モーターボート mốtàbōto

motorcar [mou'tə:rkɑ:r] (*BRIT*) *n* 自動

車 jídōsha

motorcycle [mou'tə:rsai'kəl] n オートバイ ōtōbai

motorcycle racing n オートバイレーシング ōtōbairēshingu

motorcyclist [mou'tə:rsaiklist] n オートバイのライダー ōtōbai no raídā

motoring [mou'tə:riŋ] (BRIT) n 自動車運転 jidōsha uńten

motorist [mou'tə:rist] n 運転者 uńteńsha

motor racing (BRIT) n カーレース kárēsu

motor vehicle n 自動車 jídōsha

motorway [mou'tə:rwei] (BRIT) n ハイウェー haíuē

mottled [ma:'təld] adj ぶちの buchí no

motto [ma:'tou] (pl mottoes) n 標語 hyōgo, モットー mottō

mould [mould] (BRIT) n, vt = mold

mouldy [moul'di:] (BRIT) adj = moldy

moult [moult] (BRIT) vi = molt

mound [maund] n (heap: of blankets, leaves, earth etc) 一山 hitóyama

mount [maunt] n (mountain in proper names): *Mount Carmel* カルメル山 karúmeruzàn

◆vt (horse) ...に乗る ...ni norú; (exhibition, display) 開催する kaísai suru; (fix: jewel) 台座にはめる daíza ni hamérù; (: picture) 掛ける kakérù; (staircase) 昇る nobórù

◆vi (increase: inflation) 上昇する jōshō suru; (: tension) つのる tsunoru; (: problems) 増える fuérù

mountain [maun'tən] n (GEO) 山 yamá

◆cpd (road, stream) 山の yamá no

mountaineer [mauntəni:r'] n 登山家 tozáňka

mountaineering [mauntəni:'riŋ] n 登山 tōzàn

mountainous [maun'tənəs] adj (country, area) 山の多い yamá no ōi

mountain rescue team n 山岳救助隊 sańgaku kyūjotai

mountainside [maun'tənsaid] n 山腹 sańpuku

mount up vi (bills, costs, savings) たまる tamárù

mourn [mɔ:rn] vt (death) 悲しむ kanáshimù

◆vi: *to mourn for* (someone) ...の死を悲しむ ...no shí wo kanáshimù

mourner [mɔ:r'nə:r] n 会葬者 kaísōsha

mournful [mɔ:r'fəl] adj (sad) 悲しそうな kanáshisō na

mourning [mɔ:r'niŋ] n 喪 mo
in mourning 喪中で mochú de

mouse [maus] (pl mice) n (animal) ハツカネズミ hatsúkanezùmi; (COMPUT) マウス máusu

mousetrap [maus'træp] n ネズミ取り nezúmitòri

mousse [mu:s] n (CULIN) ムース mūsu; (also: hair mousse) ヘアムース heámūsu

moustache [məstæʃ'] (BRIT) n = mustache

mousy [mau'si:] adj (hair) 薄汚い茶色の usugitanai cha-íro no

mouth [mauθ] (pl mouths) n (ANAT) 口 kuchí; (of cave, hole) 入口 iríguchi; (of river) 河口 kakō

mouthful [mauθ'ful] n (amount) 口一杯 kuchí ippai

mouth organ n ハーモニカ hámonika

mouthpiece [mauθ'pi:s] n (of musical instrument) 吹口 fukíguchi; (spokesman) スポークスマン supōkusumàn

mouthwash [mauθ'wɔ:ʃ] n マウスウォッシュ máusu uósshū ◇口臭防止洗口液 kōshūbōshi senkōeki

mouth-watering [mauθ'wɔ:tə:riŋ] adj おいしそうな oíshisō na

movable [mu:'vəbəl] adj 可動な kadō na

move [mu:v] n (movement) 動き ugóki; (in game: change of position) 手 té; (: turn to play) 番 báñ; (change: of house) 引っ越し hikkóshi; (: of job) 転職 teńshoku

◆vt (change position of: furniture, car, curtains etc) 動かす ugókasù; (chessmen etc: in game) 動かす ugókasù; (emotionally) 感動させる kańdō saserù; (POL: resolution etc) 提議する teígi suru

◆vi (person, animal) 動く ugókù; (traffic) 流れる nagárerù; (also: move house)

引っ越す hikkósù; (develop: situation, events) 進展する shiñten suru
to get a move on 急ぐ isógù
to move someone to do something ...に ...をする気を起こさせる ...ni ...wo suru ki wò okósaserù

moveable [muːˈvəbəl] *adj* = movable

move about/around *vi* (change position) そわそわする sówàsowa suru; (travel) 頻繁に旅行する hiñpan ni ryokó suru; (change: residence) 頻繁に引っ越す hiñpan ni hikkósù; (: job) 頻繁に転職する hiñpan ni teñshoku suru

move along *vi* 立ち去る tachísarù
move along! 立ち止まるな tachídomarù ná

move away *vi* (leave: town, area) よそへ引っ越す yosó e hikkósù

move back *vi* (return) 元の所へ引っ越す mótò no tokóro e hikkósù

move forward *vi* (advance) 前進する zeñshin suru

move in *vi* (to a house) 入居する nyúkyo suru; (police, soldiers) 攻撃を加える kógeki wò kuwáerù

movement [ˈmuːvmənt] *n* (action: of person, animal) 動き ugóki, 動作 dósa; (: of traffic) 流れ nagáre; (gesture) 合図 aízu; (transportation: of goods etc) 運搬 úñ-yu; (shift: in attitude, policy) 変化 heñka; (group of people: esp REL, POL) 運動 uñdó; (MUS) 楽章 gakúshō

move on *vi* 立ち去る tachísarù
move on! 立ち止まるな tachídomarù ná

move out *vi* (of house) 引っ越す hikkósù

move over *vi* (to make room) 横へどいて場所を空ける yokó è dóite bashó wò akérù

move up *vi* (employee, deputy) 昇進する shóshin suru; (pupil) 進級する shiñkyū suru

movie [ˈmuːviː] *n* 映画 eíga
to go to the movies 映画を見に行く eíga wo mí ni ikù

movie camera *n* 映画カメラ eíga kaméra

moving [ˈmuːviŋ] *adj* (emotional) 感動的

に感動的 ni kañdóteki ni; (that moves) 動く ugókù

mow [mou] (*pt* **mowed**, *pp* **mowed** *or* **mown**) *vt* (grass, corn) 刈る karú

mow down *vt* (kill) なぎ払う様に殺す nagíharaù yó nì korósù

mower [ˈmouˈəːr] *n* (*also:* **lawnmower**) 芝刈機 shibákarikì

MP [empiːˈ] (*BRIT*) *n abbr* = **Member of Parliament**

m.p.h. [empieitʃ] *abbr* (= *miles per hour*) 時速...マイル jísoku ...maíru

Mr, Mr. [ˈmisˈtəːr] *n*: *Mr. Smith* スミスさん sumisu sán ◇男性の敬称 dañsei no keíshō

Mrs, Mrs. [ˈmisˈiz] *n*: *Mrs Smith* スミスさん sumisu sán ◇既婚女性の敬称 kíkònjosei no keíshō

Ms, Ms. [miz] *n*: *Ms. Smith* スミスさん sumisu sán ◇既婚・未婚を問わず女性の敬称 kíkòn, míkòn wo towázù josei no keíshō

M.Sc. [emessiːˈ] *abbr* = **Master of Science**

KEYWORD
---

much [mʌtʃ] *adj* (time, money, effort) 沢山の takúsan no, 多くの ókù no
we haven't got much time/money あまり多くの時間〔金〕はありません amári ókù no jikán〔kané〕wà arímaseñ
much effort was expended on the project その企画に多くの努力を費やした sonó kikáku ni ókù no dóryòku wo tsuíyashìta
how much money/time do you need? お金〔時間〕はどのぐらい必要ですか o-káne〔jikán〕wà dóño gurai hitsúyō desù ká
he's done so much work for the charity その慈善事業のために彼は様々な仕事をしてくれました sonó jizéñjigyò no tamé nì kárè wa samázàma na shigó-to wò shité kuremashìta
it's too much あんまりだ añmarî da
it's not much 大した事じゃない taíshita kotó jà nai
to have too much money/free time 金

〔暇〕が有り余る kané〔himá〕gà aríamarù

as much as ...と同じぐらい ...to onáji gurái

I have as much money/intelligence as you 私はあなたと同じぐらいの金〔知識〕を持っています watákushi wà anátà to onáji gurài no kané〔chíshìki〕wò móttè imasu

◆*pron* 沢山の物 takúsan no monò

there isn't much to do あまりする事はありません amári suru kotò wa arímaseǹ

much has been gained from our discussions 我々の話し合いは多くの成果を産みました waréware no hanáshiai wà ốkù no seíka wò umímashìta

how much does it cost? - too much 値段はいくらですか - べらぼうさ nedán wà íkùra desu ká - berábó sà

how much is it? いくらですか íkùra desu ká

◆*adv* **1** (greatly, a great deal) とても totémo

thank you very much 大変有難うございます taíhen arígatố gozáimasù

much bigger (than) (...より) はるかに大きい (...yori) haruka ni ōkii

we are very much looking forward to your visit あなたが来られるのを首を長くして待っております anátà ga korárerù no wo kubí wò nágaku shite matté orimasù

he is very much the gentleman/politician 彼はれっきとした紳士〔政治家〕です kárè wa rekkí tò shita shínshi〔seíji-ka〕desu

however much he tries 彼はどんなに努力しても kárè wa dónna ni doryóku shite mò

as much as ...と同じぐらい沢山 ...tò o-náji gurài takúsaǹ

I read as much as ever 私はいつもと同じぐらい沢山の本を読んでいます watákushi wà ítsumo to onáji gurài no takúsaǹ no hóñ wo yóñde imasù

I read as much as possible/as I can 私はできるだけ沢山の本を読む事にしています watákushi wà dekíru dakè takú-saǹ no hóñ wo yómù koto ni shité imasù

he is as much a part of the community as you 彼はあなたと同様ここの社会の一員です kárè wa anátà to dốyō kokó no shakài no ichíin desù

2 (by far) ずっと zúttò

I'm much better now 私はずっと元気になっています watákushi wà zúttò gé-ǹki ni natté imasu

much reduced in price ずっと安くなって zuttó yasúku natte

it's much the biggest publishing company in Europe あれは断然ヨーロッパ最大の出版社です arè wà dañzen yốroppasaidài no shuppáñsha desu

3 (almost) ほとんど hotóñdo

the view is much as it was 10 years ago 景色は10年前とほとんど変っていません késhìki wa jûnen maè to hotóñdo kawátte imaseñ

the 2 books are much the same その2冊の本はどちらも同じ様な物です sonó nisàtsu no hóñ wa dốchìra mo onáji yố na monó desu

how are you feeling? - much the same ご気分はいかがですか-大して変りません go-kíbuñ wa ikága dèsu ká - taíshite kawárimaseñ

---

muck [mʌk] *n* (dirt) 泥 doró; (excrement) くそ kusó

muck about/around *vi* (*inf*: fool about) ぶらぶらする búrabura suru

muck up *vt* (*inf*: ruin) 台無しにする daí-nashi ni suru

mucus [mjuːˈkəs] *n* 粘液 néñ-eki

mud [mʌd] *n* 泥 doró

muddle [mʌdˈəl] *n* (mess, mix-up) めちゃくちゃ mechákucha, 混乱 koñran

◆*vt* (*also*: **muddle up**) (confuse: person, things) 混乱させる koñran saserù; (: story, names) ごちゃごちゃにする go-chágocha ni suru

muddle through *vi* (get by) どうにかして切抜ける dố ni ka shite kirínukerù

muddy [mʌdˈiː] *adj* (floor, field) どろどろの doródoro no

mudguard [mʌdˈgɑːrd] *n* フェンダー féñ-dā

muesli [mju:z'li:] *n* ムースリ mūsuri ◊ 朝食用のナッツ，ドライフルーツ，穀物の混合 chōshoku yō no nāttsu, doráifurū-tsu, kokúmotsu no kofigō

muffin [mʌf'in] *n* (US) マドレーヌ madórēnu; (BRIT) マフィン máfìn

muffle [mʌf'əl] *vt* (sound) 弱める yowámerù; (against cold) ...に防寒具を付ける ...ni bōkañgu wo tsukérù

muffled [mʌf'əld] *adj* (sound) 弱い yowáì

muffler [mʌf'lə:r] (US) *n* (AUT) マフラー máfùrā

mug [mʌg] *n* (cup) マグ mágù; (for beer) ジョッキ jókkì; (inf: face) 面 tsurá; (: BRIT: fool) ばか bákà
◆*vt* (assault) 襲う osóù ◊特に強盗行為について言う tókù ni gōtōkōi ni tsúìte iú

mugging [mʌg'iŋ] *n* 強盗事件 gōtōjikèn

muggy [mʌg'i:] *adj* (weather, day) 蒸暑い mushíatsuì

mule [mju:l] *n* ラバ rábà

mull [mʌl] *vt*: **to mull over** ...について考え込む ...ni tsúìte kañgaekomù

multi... [mʌl'ti:] *prefix* 複数の ... fukúsū no ...

multicolored [mʌl'tikʌlə:rd] (BRIT **multicoloured**) *adj* 多色の tashóku no

multilateral [mʌlti:læt'ə:rəl] *adj* (disarmament, talks) 多国間の takōkuman no

multi-level [mʌlti:lev'əl] (US) *adj* = **multistory**

multinational [mʌltənæʃ'ənəl] *adj* (company, business) 多国籍の takōkuseki no

multiple [mʌl'təpəl] *adj* (collision) 玉突きの tamátsuki no; (interests) 複数の fukúsū no
◆*n* (MATH) 倍数 baísū

multiple sclerosis [-sklirou'sis] *n* 多発性硬化症 tahátsusei kōkashō

multiplication [mʌltəpləkei'ʃən] *n* (MATH) 掛算 kakézan; (increase) 増加 zōka

multiply [mʌl'təplai] *vt* (MATH): **4 multiplied by 2 is 8** 4掛ける2は8 yóñ kakérù ní wa hachí
◆*vi* (increase) 増える fuérù

multistory [mʌlti:stɔːr'i:] (BRIT **multistorey**) *adj* (building etc) 高層の kōsō no

multitude [mʌl'tətu:d] *n* (crowd) 群衆 guñshū; (large number): **a multitude of** (reasons, ideas) 沢山の takúsan no

mum [mʌm] (BRIT: inf) *n* = **mom**
◆*adj*: **to keep mum** 黙っている damátte irù

mumble [mʌm'bəl] *vt* (speak indistinctly) もぐもぐ言う mógùmogu iú
◆*vi* ぶつぶつ言う bútsùbutsu iú

mummy [mʌm'i:] *n* (embalmed) ミイラ mīira; (BRIT: mother) = **mommy**

mumps [mʌmps] *n* おたふく風邪 otáfukukàze

munch [mʌntʃ] *vt* (chew) かむ kámù
◆*vi* かむ kámù

mundane [mʌndein'] *adj* (task, life) 平凡な heñbon na

municipal [mju:nis'əpəl] *adj* 市の shí no

munitions [mju:niʃ'ənz] *npl* 兵器弾薬 heíkidañ-yaku

mural [mju:r'əl] *n* 壁画 hekíga

murder [mə:r'də:r] *n* (killing) 殺人 satsújin
◆*vt* (kill) 殺す korósù

murderer [mə:r'də:rə:r] *n* 人殺し hitógoroshi

murderous [mə:r'də:rəs] *adj* (person) 殺人も辞さない satsújin mo jisanáì; (attack) 殺しを目的とする koróshi wò mokúteki ni surù

murky [mə:r'ki:] *adj* (street, night) 暗い kurái; (water) 濁った nigótta

murmur [mə:r'mə:r] *n*: **a murmur of voices** かすかな人声 kásùkana hitógoè; (of wind, waves) さざめき sazámeki
◆*vt* (speak quietly) 声をひそめて言う kóè wo hisómetè iú
◆*vi* 声をひそめて話す kóè wo hisómetè hanásù

muscle [mʌs'əl] *n* (ANAT) 筋肉 kíñniku; (fig: strength) 力 chikára

muscle in *vi* 割込む waríkomù

muscular [mʌs'kjələ:r] *adj* (pain) 筋肉の kíñniku no; (build) たくましい takúmashìĩ; (person) 強そうな tsuyósō na

muse [mju:z] vi (think) 考え込む kañgae-komù
♦n (MYTHOLOGY) ミューズ myūzu ◇ 人間の知的活動をつかさどるという女神 nigen no chitékikatsudō wo tsukásadorù to iú mégami

museum [mju:zi:'əm] n 博物館 hakúbùtsukan

mushroom [mʌʃ'ru:m] n (fungus: edible, poisonous) キノコ kínòko
♦vi (fig: town, organization) 急速に成長する kyūsoku ni seíchō suru

music [mju:'zik] n (sound, art) 音楽 óñgaku; (written music, score) 楽譜 gakúfu

musical [mju:'zikəl] adj (career, skills, person) 音楽の óñgaku no; (sound, tune) 音楽的な oñgákuteki na
♦n (show, film) ミュージカル myūjikaru

musical instrument n 楽器 gakkí

music hall n (place) ボードビル劇場 bódobiru gekijō

musician [mju:ziʃ'ən] n ミュージシャン myūjishàn

musk [mʌsk] n じゃ香 jakó

Muslim [mʌz'lim] adj イスラム教の isúramukyō no
♦n イスラム教徒 isúramukyōto

muslin [mʌz'lin] n モスリン mósùrin

mussel [mʌs'əl] n ムールガイ mūrugai

must [mʌst] aux vb (necessity, obligation): *I must do it* 私はそれをしなければならない watákushi wa soré wo shinákereba naranài; (probability): *he must be there by now* もう彼はあそこに着いているでしょう mō kárè wa asóko ni tsuíte írù deshō; (suggestion, invitation): *you must come and see me soon* そのうち是非遊びに来て下さい sonó uchi zéhî asóbi ni kite kudasaî; (indicating something unwelcome): *why must he behave so badly?* どうしてまたあの子はそんなに行儀悪くするのだろう dōshite mata anó ko wa sofína ni gyōgiwarukù suru no darō
♦n (necessity): *it's a must* 必需品だ hitsújuhin da

mustache [məstæʃ'] (US) n 鼻ひげ hanáhige

mustard [mʌs'tə:rd] n (Japanese) 辛子 karáshi, 和辛子 wagáràshi; (Western) 辛子 karáshi, 洋辛子 yógaràshi, マスタード masútàdo

muster [mʌs'tə:r] vt (support) 求める motómerù; (energy, strength) 奮い起す furúiokosù; (MIL) 召集する shōshū suru

mustn't [mʌs'ənt] = **must not**

musty [mʌs'ti:] adj かび臭い kabíkusaì

mutation [mju:tei'ʃən] n (alteration) 変化 heñka

mute [mju:t] adj (silent) 無言の mugón no

muted [mju:'tid] adj (color) 地味な jimí na; (reaction) ひそめた hisómeta

mutilate [mju:'təleit] vt (person, thing) 傷付ける kizútsukerù ◇特に体の部分を切断する場合に使う tókù ni karáda no búbùn wo setsúdan suru baáî ni tsukáù

mutiny [mju:'təni:] n (rebellion: of soldiers, sailors) 反乱 hañran
♦vi 反乱を起す hañran wo okósù

mutter [mʌt'ə:r] vt (speak quietly) つぶやく tsubúyakù
♦vi ぶつぶつ不平を言う bútsùbutsu fuhéi wo iú

mutton [mʌt'ən] n (meat) マトン mátòn

mutual [mju:'tʃu:əl] adj (shared: benefit, interest) 共通の kyótsū no; (reciprocal: feeling, attraction) 相互の sōgo no

mutually [mju:'tʃu:əli:] adv 相互に sōgo ni

muzzle [mʌz'əl] n (mouth: of dog) ふんふん hanázura, 鼻づら hanázura; (: of gun) 銃口 jū-kō; (guard: for dog) 口輪 kuchíwa
♦vt (dog) ...に口輪をはめる ...ni kuchíwa wo hamérù

KEYWORD

my [mai] adj 私の watákushi nò
this is my house/car/brother これは私の家〔車、兄〕です koré wa watákushi nò ié〔kurúma, ánî〕desu
I've washed my hair/cut my finger 私は髪を洗いました〔指を切りました〕 watákushi wa kamí wo aráimashìta〔yubí wo kirímashìta〕
is this my pen or yours? これは私の

ペンですか, それともあなたのですか koré wà watákushi nò péń desu ká, sorétomò anátà no desu ká

Myanmar [maiˈænmɑːr] *n* ミャンマー myáńmā

myopic [maiɑːpˈik] *adj* 近眼の kińgan no

myriad [mirˈiːəd] *n* (of people, things) 無数 musú

myself [maiselˈf] *pron* 私自身 watákushi-jishìn ¶ *see also* **oneself**

mysterious [mistiˈrˈiːəs] *adj* (strange) なぞの nazó no

mystery [misˈtəːriː] *n* (puzzle) なぞ nazó
shrouded in mystery (place) なぞに包まれた nazó nì tsutsúmaréta

mystic [misˈtik] *n* (person) 神秘主義者 shińpishùgisha

mystic(al) [misˈtik(əl)] *adj* 神秘的な shińpiteki na

mystify [misˈtəfai] *vt* (perplex) ...の理解を越える ...no rikái wò koérù

mystique [mistiːkˈ] *n* 神秘 shińpi

myth [miθ] *n* (legend, story) 神話 shińwa; (fallacy) 俗信 zokúshin

mythology [miθɑːlˈədʒiː] *n* 神話集 shińwàshū

N

n/a *abbr* (= *not applicable*) ◇申請用紙などで空欄にしておく場合に書く shińsei yòshi nádð de kúran ni shite oku baài ni kákù

nag [næg] *vt* (scold) がみがみ言う gámì-gami iú

nagging [nægˈiŋ] *adj* (doubt) 晴れない harénaì; (pain) しつこい shitsúkoì

nail [neil] *n* (on fingers, toes) つめ tsumé; (metal) くぎ kugí
♦*vt*: *to nail something to something* ...を...にくぎで留める ...wo ...ni kugí dè toméru
to nail someone down to doing something ...を...をさせる kyōseiteki ni ...ni ...wò saséru

nailbrush [neilˈbrʌʃ] *n* つめブラシ tsu-

mēburàshi

nailfile [neilˈfail] *n* つめやすり tsuméya-sùri

nail polish *n* マニキュア maníkyùa

nail polish remover *n* 除光液 jokóeki, マニキュア落し maníkyua otðshi

nail scissors *npl* つめ切りばさみ tsumé-kiribasàmi

nail varnish (*BRIT*) *n* = **nail polish**

naive [naiiːvˈ] *adj* (person, ideas) 無邪気な mújàki na, ナイーブな naíbù na

naked [neiˈkid] *adj* 裸の hadáka no

name [neim] *n* (of person, animal, place) 名前 namáe; (surname) 名字 myốjì, 姓 séì; (reputation) 評判 hyõban
♦*vt* (child) ...に名前を付ける ...ni namáe wð tsukérù; (identify: accomplice, criminal) 名指す nazásù; (specify: price, date etc) 指定する shitéi suru
what's your name? お名前は何とおっしゃいますか o-námae wà nánto ósshái-masù ká
by name 名指しで nazáshi dè
in the name of (*fig*) ...の名において ...no ná ni oìte
to give one's name and address (to police etc) 名前と住所を知らせる namáe tð jũshð wo shiráserù

nameless [neimˈlis] *adj* (unknown) 無名の muméi no; (anonymous: witness, contributor) 匿名の tokúmei no

namely [neimˈliː] *adv* 即ち sunáwàchi

namesake [neimˈseik] *n* 同姓同名の人 dõseidõmei no hitð

nanny [nænˈiː] *n* 養育係 yõikugakàri

nap [næp] *n* (sleep) 昼寝 hirúne
to be caught napping (*fig*) 不意を突かれる fuí wð tsukárerù

napalm [neiˈpɑːm] *n* ナパーム napámù

nape [neip] *n*: *nape of the neck* えり首 eríkùbi

napkin [næpˈkin] *n* (*also*: **table napkin**) ナプキン nápùkin

nappy [næpˈiː] (*BRIT*) *n* おむつ o-mútsù

nappy rash (*BRIT*) *n* おむつかぶれ o-mútsukabùre

narcissus [nɑːrsisˈəs] (*pl* **narcissi**) *n* (BOT) スイセン suísen

narcotic [nɑːrkɑːt'ik] *adj* 麻酔性の masúisei no
♦*n* 麻薬 mayáku

narrative [nær'ətiv] *n* 物語 monógatàri

narrator [nær'eitər] *n* (in book) 語り手 katárite; (in film etc) ナレーター narḗtā

narrow [nær'ou] *adj* (space, road etc) 狭い semáî; (fig: majority, advantage) ぎりぎりの girígiri no; (: ideas, attitude) 狭量な kyốryo na
♦*vi* (road) 狭くなる sémàku naru; (gap, difference: diminish) 小さくなる chíìsaku naru

to have a narrow escape 間一髪で逃れる káñ-ippátsu de nogárerù

to narrow something down to (choice, possibility) ...を...に絞る ...wo ...ni shibórù

narrowly [nær'ouli:] *adv* (miss) 辛うじて karốjìte, 間一髪で káñ-ippátsu dè

narrow-minded [nær'oumain'did] *adj* 狭量な kyốryo na

nasal [nei'zəl] *adj* (of the nose) 鼻のhaná no; (voice, sound) 鼻にかかった haná ni kakattà

nasty [næs'ti:] *adj* (unpleasant: remark, person) いやな iyá nà; (malicious) 腹黒い haráguroî; (rude) 無礼な búrèi na; (revolting: taste, smell) むかつかせる mukátsukaserù; (wound, disease etc) ひどい hidôî

nation [nei'ʃən] *n* (country) 国 kuní, 国家 kókkà; (people) 国民 kokúmin

national [næʃ'ənəl] *adj* 国の kuní no
♦*n: a foreign national* 外国人 gaíkokujìn

national dress *n* 民族衣装 miñzokuishố

National Health Service (*BRIT*) *n* 国民医療制度 kokúmin iryōseīdo

National Insurance (*BRIT*) *n* 国民保険 kokúminhokèn

nationalism [næʃ'ənəlizəm] *n* 国家主義 kokkáshugì, 民族主義 míñzokushugì

nationalist [næʃ'nəlist] *adj* 国家主義の kokkáshugì no, 民族主義 míñzokushugì no
♦*n* 国家主義者 kokkáshugishà, 民族主義者 miñzokushugishà

nationality [næʃənæl'əti:] *n* 国籍 kokúseki

nationalization [næʃ(ə)nəlozei'ʃən] *n* 国有化 kokúyùka, 国営化 kokúeika

nationalize [næʃ'nəlaiz] *vt* 国営にする kokúei ni surù

nationally [næʃ'nəli:] *adv* (nationwide) 全国的に zeñkokuteki ni; (as a nation) 国として kuní toshite

nationwide [nei'ʃənwaid'] *adj* (problem, campaign) 全国的な zeñkokuteki na
♦*adv* (campaign, search) 全国的に zeñkokuteki ni

native [nei'tiv] *n* (local inhabitant) 地元の人 jimóto no hitò; (of tribe etc) 原住民 geñjūmin
♦*adj* (indigenous) 地元の jimóto no, 地元生れの jimóto umàre no; (of one's birth) 生れの umàre no; (innate) 生れつきの umáretsuki no

a native of Russia ロシア生れの人 roshía umare no hitò

a native speaker of French フランス語を母国語とする人 furánsugo wò bokốkugo to suru hitò

native language *n* 母国語 bokốkugo

Nativity [nətiv'əti:] *n: the Nativity* キリストの降誕 kirísuto nð kốtan

NATO [nei'tou] *n abbr* (= *North Atlantic Treaty Organization*) 北大西洋条約機構 kitátaiseiyō jōyaku kikō

natural [nætʃ'ə:rəl] *adj* (gen) 自然の shizén no; (innate) 生れつきの umáretsuki no

natural gas *n* 天然ガス teñnengasù

naturalist [nætʃ'ə:rəlist] *n* 博物学者 hakúbutsugakushà

naturalize [nætʃ'ə:rəlaiz] *vt: to become naturalized* (person, plant) 帰化する kiká suru

naturally [nætʃ'ə:rəli:] *adv* (gen) 自然に shizén ni; (of course) もちろん mochírðn, 当然 tőzen

nature [nei'tʃə:r] *n* (also: *Nature*) 自然 shizén, 大自然 daíshizèn; (character) 性質 sefshitsu; (type, sort) 種類 shúrùi

by nature 生れつき umáretsuki

naught [nɔːt] *n* 零 réî, ゼロ zérð

naughty [nɔːˈtiː] *adj* (child) 行儀の悪い gyṓgi no warúī

nausea [nɔːˈziːə] *n* 吐気 hakíke

nauseate [nɔːˈziːeit] *vt* むかつかせる mukátsukaserù, 吐気を起させる hakíke wò okósaserù; (*fig*) いやな感じを与える iyá na kanji wo atáerù

nautical [nɔːˈtikəl] *adj* (uniform) 船員の señ-in no; (people) 海洋の kaíyō no
  a nautical mile 海里 káīri

naval [neiˈvəl] *adj* (uniform, academy) 海軍の kaígun no
  a naval battle 海戦 kaísen
  naval forces 海軍力 kaígunryòku

naval officer *n* 海軍将校 kaígunshōkò

nave [neiv] *n* 外陣 gaíjin

navel [neiˈvəl] *n* へそ hesó

navigate [nævˈəgeit] *vi* (NAUT, AVIAT) 航行する kṓkō suru; (AUT) 道案内する michíannai suru

navigation [nævəˈgeiʃən] *n* (action) 航行 kókō; (science) 航海術 kókaijùtsu

navigator [nævˈəgeitər] *n* (NAUT) 航海長 kōkaichō; (AVIAT) 航空士 kókū-shi; (AUT) 道案内をする人 michíannai wo suru hitò

navvy [nævˈiː] (*BRIT*) *n* 労働者 rōdōsha

navy [neiˈviː] *n* 海軍 kaígun

navy(-blue) *adj* 濃紺の nókon no

Nazi [nɑːtˈsiː] *n* ナチ náchi

NB [enˈbiː] *abbr* (= *nota bene*) 注 chū◇脚注などに使う略語 kyakuchū nadò ni tsukáù ryakúgo

near [niːr] *adj* (place, time, relation) 近い chikáī
  ◆*adv* 近く chikákù
  ◆*prep* (*also*: **near to**: space, time) ...の近くに ...no chikákù ni
  ◆*vi* (place, event) ...に近づく ...ni chikázukù

nearby [niːrˈbaiˈ] *adj* 近くの chikákù no
  ◆*adv* 近くに chikákù ni

nearly [niːrˈliː] *adv* (not totally) ほとんど hotóndo; (on the point of) 危うく ayáukù
  I nearly fell 危うく転ぶところだった ayáukù koróbu tokoro dattà

near miss *n* (narrow escape) ニアミス niámisù; (of planes) 異常接近 ijṓsekkìn,

ニアミス niámisù; (of cars etc): *that was a near miss!* 危ないところだった abúnai tokoro dattà

nearside [niːrˈsaid] *n* (AUT: in Britain, Japan) 左側 hidárigawa; (: in US, Europe etc) 右側 migígawa

near-sighted [niːrˈsaitid] *adj* 近眼の kíngan no, 近視の kíshishi no

neat [niːt] *adj* (place, person) きちんとした kichín to shita; (skillful: work, plan) 上手な józu na; (spirits) ストレートの sutórēto no

neatly [niːtˈliː] *adv* (tidily) きちんと kichín to; (skillfully) 上手に józu ni

necessarily [nesəsˈerˈiliː] *adv* (inevitably) 必然的に hitsúzenteki ni
  not necessarily (not automatically) 必ずしも...でない kanárazushìmo ...de naì

necessary [nesˈiseːriː] *adj* (required: skill, quality, measure) 必要な hitsúyō na; (inevitable: result, effect) 必然の hitsúzen no
  it is necessary to/that ...する必要がある ...suru hitsúyō ga arù

necessitate [nəsesˈəteit] *vt* 必要とする hitsúyō to surù

necessities [nəsesˈitiːz] *npl* (essentials) 必需品 hitsújuhin

necessity [nəsesˈitiː] *n* (thing needed) 必需品 hitsújuhin; (compelling circumstances) 必然 hitsúzen

neck [nek] *n* (of person, animal, garment, bottle) 首 kubí
  ◆*vi* (*inf*) ペッティングする pettíngu suru
  neck and neck 接戦して sessén shite

necklace [nekˈlis] *n* ネックレス nékkùresu

neckline [nekˈlain] *n* ネックライン nekkúraìn

necktie [nekˈtai] (*US*) *n* ネクタイ nékùtai

née [nei] *adj*: *née Scott* 旧姓スコット kyūsei sukóttò

need [niːd] *n* (lack) 欠乏 ketsúbō; (necessity) 必要 hitsúyō; (thing needed) 必需品 hitsújuhin
  ◆*vt* (require) ...を必要とする ...wo hitsú-

yō to surù
I need to do it 私はそれをしなければ
ならない watákushi wà soré wò shinákereba naranaì, 私はそれをする必要があ
る watákushi wà soré wò suru hitsúyō
ga arù
you don't need to go 行かなくてもい
い ikánakute mo iî

needle [niːdəl] *n* (*gen*) 針 hárî; (for knitting) 編棒 amíbô
♦*vt* (*fig: inf*) からかう karákaù

needless [niːdʹlis] *adj* (criticism, risk) 不
必要な fuhítsuyō na
needless to say 言うまでもなく iú made mo nakù

needlework [niːdʹəlwəːrk] *n* (item(s) of
needlework) 縫い物 nuímonò; (activity)
針仕事 haríshigòto

needn't [niːdʹənt] = **need not**

needy [niːdi] *adj* 貧しい mazúshiì

negation [nigeiʹʃən] *n* 否定 hitéi

negative [negʹətiv] *adj* (answer) 否定の
hitéi no; (attitude) 否定的な hitéiteki na;
(reaction) 消極的な shókyokuteki na;
(ELEC) 陰極の iñkyoku no, マイナスの
maínasu no
♦*n* (LING) 否定形 hitéikei; (PHOT) 陰画
iñga, ネガ négà

neglect [niglektʹ] *vt* (child) 放任する hônin suru, ほったらかす hottárakasù;
(one's duty) 怠る okótarù
♦*n* (of child) 放任 hônin; (of area, house,
garden) ほったらかす事 hottárakasu ko-
tò; (of duty) 怠る事 okótaru kotò

negligee [negʹləzei] *n* (dressing gown) ネ
グリジェ negúrijè

negligence [negʹlidʒəns] *n* (carelessness)
不注意 fuchûî

negligible [negʹlidʒəbəl] *adj* (cost, difference) わずかな wázùka na

negotiable [nigouʹʃəbəl] *adj* (check) 譲渡
できる jôto dekirù

negotiate [nigouʹʃieit] *vi*: *to negotiate
(with)* (...と) 交渉する (...to) kôshō suru
♦*vt* (treaty, transaction) 協議して決める
kyôgi shite kimerù; (obstacle) 乗越える
noríkoerù; (bend in road) 注意して通る

chúī shite tôrù

negotiation [nigouʃiːeiʹʃən] *n* 交渉 kôshō

negotiator [nigouʹʃiːeitəːr] *n* 交渉する人
kôshō suru hitò

Negress [niːgʹris] *n* 黒人女性 kokújinjo-
seì

Negro [niːgʹrou] *adj* 黒人の kokújin no
♦*n* 黒人 kokújin

neigh [nei] *vi* いななく inánakù

neighbor [neiʹbəːr] (*BRIT* **neighbour**) *n*
(next door) 隣の人 tonári no hitò; (in
vicinity) 近所の人 kîñjo no hitò

neighborhood [neiʹbəːrhud] *n* (place) 近
所 kîñjo, 界隈 kaíwai; (people) 近所の
人々 kîñjo no hitòbito

neighboring [neiʹbəːriŋ] *adj* (town,
state) 隣の tonári no

neighborly [neiʹbəːrliː] *adj* (person, attitude) 親切な shíñsetsu na

neighbour [neiʹbəːr] *etc* (*BRIT*) *n* =
neighbor *etc*

neither [niːʹðəːr] *adj* どちらの...も...でな
い dôchìra no ...mo ...de naî
neither story is true どちらの話も本当
ではない dôchìra no hanáshi mò hoñtô
de wa naî
♦*conj*: *I didn't move and neither did
John* 私も動かなかったしジョンも動か
なかった watákushi mò ugókanakattà
shi, jôñ mo ugókanakattà
♦*pron* どちらも...でない dôchìra mo ...de
naî
neither is true どちらも本当でない dôchìra mo hoñtô de naî
♦*adv*: *neither good nor bad* よくも悪
くもない yókù mo warúkù mo naî

neon [niːʹɑːn] *n* ネオン néòn; (*also*: **neon
sign**) ネオンサイン neóñsaìn

neon light *n* ネオン灯 neóñtò

nephew [nefʹjuː] *n* おい oí

nerve [nəːrv] *n* (ANAT) 神経 shíñkei;
(courage) 勇気 yûkî; (impudence) 厚かま
しさ atsúkamashisà, 図々しさ zúzūshisà
to have a fit of nerves 神経質になる
shíñkeishitsu ni narù

nerve-racking [nəːrvʹrækiŋ] *adj* いらい
らさせる íraira saserù

nervous [nəːrˈvəs] adj (ANAT) 神経の shíñkei no; (anxious) 神経質な shíñkeishitsu na; (timid: person) 気の小さい ki no chíisai; (: animal) おく病な okúbyò na

nervous breakdown n 神経衰弱 shíñkeisuijàku

nest [nest] n 巣 sú
♦vi 巣を作る sú wò tsukúrù

nest egg n (fig) へそくり hesókuri

nestle [nesˈəl] vi: **to nestle in a valley／the mountains** (village etc) 谷間〔山あい〕に横たわる tanímà〔yamá-aì〕nì yokótawarù

net [net] n (gen) 網 amí; (fabric) レース résù; (TENNIS, VOLLEYBALL etc) ネット néttò; (fig) わな wánà
♦adj (COMM) 正味の shómi no
♦vt (fish, game) 網で取る amí dè tórù; (profit) 得る érù

netball [netˈbɔːl] n ネットボール nettóbòru ◇英国で行われるバスケットボールに似た球技 eíkoku de okonawarerù basúkettobòru ni nítà kyúgì

net curtains npl レースのカーテン résù no kâten

Netherlands [neðˈərləndz] npl: **the Netherlands** オランダ oránda

nett [net] (BRIT) adj = **net**

netting [netˈiŋ] n 網 amí

nettle [netˈəl] n イラクサ irákusa

network [netˈwəːrk] n (of roads, veins, shops) ネットワーク nettówàku; (TV, RADIO) 放送網 hósòmò, ネットワーク nettówàku

neurotic [nuraːtˈik] adj 神経過敏な shíñkeikabìn na, ノイローゼの noíròze no
♦n ノイローゼの人 noírôze no hitò

neuter [nuːˈtəːr] adj (LING) 中性の chúsei no
♦vt (cat etc) 去勢する kyoséi suru

neutral [nuːˈtrəl] adj (person) 中立の chúritsu no; (color etc) 中間色の chúkañshoku no; (ELEC) 中性の chúsei no
♦n (AUT) ニュートラル nyútòraru

neutrality [nuːtrælˈitiː] n 中立 chúritsu

neutralize [nuːˈtrəlaiz] vt (acid, poison etc) 中和する chúwa suru; (campaign, goodwill) 台無しにする daínashi ni surù

never [nevˈəːr] adv どんな時でも ...ない dóñna toki de mo ...naî
I never went 行かなかった ikánakattà
never in my life ...したことがない ...shitá kotò ga naî ¶ see also **mind**

never-ending [nevˈəːrenˈdiŋ] adj 終りのない owári no naì, 果てしない hatéshinaì

nevertheless [nevəːrðəlesˈ] adv それにもかかわらず soré ni mò kakáwarazù, それでもやはり soré de mò yahárì

new [nuː] adj (brand new) 新しい atárashiî; (recent) 最近の saíkin no; (different) 今までになかった imá madè ni nákatta; (inexperienced) 新入りの shiñ-iri no

newborn [nuːˈbɔːrn] adj 生れたばかりの umáreta bakàri no

newcomer [nuːˈkʌməːr] n 新顔 shiñgao, 新入り shiñ-iri

new-fangled [nuːˈfæŋˈgəld] (pej) adj 超モダンな chômodàn na

new-found [nuːˈfaund] adj (enthusiasm, confidence) 新たに沸いた árata ni waîta; (friend) 新しくできた atárashikù dékìta

newly [nuːˈliː] adv 新しく atárashikù

newly-weds [nuːˈliːwedz] npl 新婚者 shiñkoñsha

new moon n 新月 shíñgetsu

news [nuːz] n ニュース nyúsu
a piece of news ニュース項目 nyúsukômoku, ニュース nyúsu
the news (RADIO, TV) ニュース nyúsu

news agency n 通信社 tsúshìñsha

newsagent [nuːzˈeidʒənt] (BRIT) n = **newsdealer**

newscaster [nuːzˈkæstəːr] n ニュースキャスター nyúsukyasùtà

newsdealer [nuːzˈdiːləːr] (US) n (shop) 新聞販売店 shiñbunhanbaitèñ; (person) 新聞販売業者 shiñbunhanbaigyòsha

newsflash [nuːzˈflæʃ] n ニュース速報 nyúsusokuhò

newsletter [nuːzˈletəːr] n ニュースレター nyúsuretà

newspaper [nuːzˈpeipəːr] n 新聞 shiñbun

newsprint [nuːzˈprint] n 新聞印刷用紙 shiñbun insatsuyòshi

newsreader [nuːzˈriːdəːr] n = **newscaster**

newsreel [nu:z'ri:l] *n* ニュース映画 nyūsueiga

newsstand [nu:z'stænd] *n* (in station etc) 新聞スタンド shifibun sutafido

newt [nu:t] *n* イモリ imórì

New Year *n* 新年 shífinen

New Year's Day *n* 元旦 gafitan, 元日 gafijitsu

New Year's Eve *n* 大みそ日 ốmisòka

New York [-jɔ:rk] *n* ニューヨーク nyū́yòku

New Zealand [-zi:'lənd] *n* ニュージーランド nyū́jirando

New Zealander [-zi:'ləndə:r] *n* ニュージーランド人 nyū́jirandojìn

next [nekst] *adj* (in space) 隣の tonári no; (in time) 次の tsugí no

♦*adv* (place) 隣に tonári ni; (time) 次に tsugí ni; (next time) 今度 kốndo

the next day 次の日 tsugí no hì, 翌日 yokújitsu

next time 次回に jíkai ni, 今度 kốndo

next year 来年 raínen

next to ...の隣に ...no tonári ni

to cost next to nothing ただ同然である tádà dốzen de arù

to do next to nothing ほとんど何もしない hotóndo naní mo shinài

next please! (at doctor's etc) 次の方 tsugí no katà

next door *adv* 隣の家に tonári nò ié nì

♦*adj* (neighbor, flat) 隣の tonári no

next-of-kin [nekst'əvkin'] *n* 最も近い親せき mottómo chikaì shifiseki

NHS [eneitʃes'] *n abbr* = **National Health Service**

nib [nib] *n* ペン先 peñsakì

nibble [nib'əl] *vt* 少しずつかじる sukóshizutsù kajírù, ちびちび食べる chíbichibi tabérù

Nicaragua [nikərɑ:g'wə] *n* ニカラグア nikáragua

nice [nais] *adj* (likeable) 感じのよい kańji no yoì; (kind) 親切な shífisetsu na; (pleasant) 天気のよい tếnki no yoî; (attractive) 魅力的な miryốkuteki na

nicely [nais'li:] *adv* (pleasantly) 気持よく kimóchi yokù; (kindly) 親切に shífisetsu

ni; (attractively) 魅力的に miryốkuteki ni

niceties [nai'səti:z] *npl* 細かい点 komákaì teñ

nick [nik] *n* (wound) 切傷 kiríkizu; (cut, indentation) 刃の跡 há no atò

♦*vt* (*BRIT inf*: steal) かっ払う kappáraù

in the nick of time 際どい時に kiwádoì tókì ni, 危ういところで ayáui tokoro dè

nickel [nik'əl] *n* (metal) ニッケル nikkéru; (*US*) 5セント玉 5 señto dama

nickname [nik'neim] *n* あだ名 adána, 愛称 aîshō, ニックネーム nikkúnèmu

♦*vt* ...に...のあだ名をつける ...ni ...no adána wò tsukérù

nicotine [nik'əti:n] *n* ニコチン nikóchin

niece [ni:s] *n* めい meî

Nigeria [naidʒi:'ri:ə] *n* ナイジェリア naíjeria

Nigerian [naidʒi:'ri:ən] *adj* ナイジェリアの naíjeria no

♦*n* ナイジェリア人 naíjeriajìn

nigger [nig'ə:r] (*inf*) *n* (highly offensive) 黒人坊 kurốnbō

niggling [nig'lin] *adj* (trifling) つまらない tsumáranaì; (annoying) いらいらさせる íraira sasérù

night [nait] *n* (period of darkness) 夜 yórù; (evening) 夕方 yū́gata

the night before last おとといの夜 otótoì no yórù

at night 夜（に） yórù (ni)

by night 夜に yórù ni

nightcap [nait'kæp] *n* (drink) 寝酒 nezáke, ナイトキャップ naítokyappù

nightclub [nait'klʌb] *n* ナイトクラブ naítokurabu

nightdress [nait'dres] *n* 寝巻 nemáki ◊女性用のを指す joséiyō no wò sásù

nightfall [nait'fɔ:l] *n* 夕暮 yū́gure

nightgown [nait'gaun] *n* = **nightdress**

nightie [nai'ti:] *n* = **nightdress**

nightingale [nai'təngeil] *n* ヨナキウグイス yonákiuguìsu, サヨナキドリ sayónakidòri, ナイチンゲール naíchingèru

nightlife [nait'laif] *n* 夜の生活 yórù no seîkatsu

nightly [nait'li:] *adj* 毎晩の máiban no
◆*adv* 毎晩 máiban

nightmare [nait'me:r] *n* 悪夢 ákumu

night porter *n* 夜間のフロント係 yákàn
no furóntogakàri

night school *n* 夜間学校 yakángakkò

night shift *n* 夜間勤務 yakánkìnmu

night-time [nait'taim] *n* 夜 yórù

night watchman *n* 夜警 yakéi

nil [nil] *n* ゼロ zérò; (*BRIT*: *SPORT*) 零
点 reíten, ゼロ zérò

Nile [nail] *n*: **the Nile** ナイル川 naírugà-
wa

nimble [nim'bəl] *adj* (agile) 素早い subá-
yaì, 軽快な keíkai na; (skillful) 器用な
kíyò na

nine [nain] *num* 9 (の) kyū́ (no), 九つ
(の) kokónòtsu (no)

nineteen [nain'ti:n'] *num* 19 (の) jū́ku
(no)

ninety [nain'ti:] *num* 90 (の) kyū́jù
(no)

ninth [nainθ] *adj* 第9 (の) dáiku (no)

nip [nip] *vt* (pinch) つねる tsunérù; (bite)
かむ kámù

nipple [nip'əl] *n* (ANAT) 乳首 chikúbì

nitrogen [nai'trədʒən] *n* 窒素 chíssò

KEYWORD
---

no [nou] (*pl* **noes**) *adv* (opposite of "yes")
いいえ iíe

are you coming? - no (I'm not) 一緒
に来ませんか–いいえ (行きません) is-
shó ni kimaseñ ká - iíe (ikímaseñ)

*would you like some? - no thank
you* いりませんか–いいえ, 結構です irímaseñ ká - iíe, kékkō desu

◆*adj* (not any) 何も...ない naní mó ...náì

I have no money/time/books 私には
金 [時間, 本] がありません watákushi ni
wà kané [jikán, hóñ] ga arimaseñ

no other man would have done it 他
の人ならだれもそれをしてくれなかった
でしょう hoká no hitò nara daré mò
soré wò shité kurenakatta deshò

「*no parking*」 立入禁止 tachíirikìnshi

「*no smoking*」 禁煙 kiñ-en

◆*n* 反対意見 hañtai ikèn, 反対票 hañtai-

hyò

*there were 20 noes and one "don't
know"* 反対意見20に対し, 「分からな
い」は1つだった hañtai ikèn níjù ni tai-
shi, "wakáranaì" wa hitótsu dattà

---

nobility [noubil'əti:] *n* (dignity) 気高い
kedákasà; (social class) 貴族 kízòku

noble [nou'bəl] *adj* (person, character:
worthy) 気高い kedákaì; (title, family:
of high social class) 貴族の kízòku no

nobody [nou'ba:di:] *pron* だれも...ない
daré mò ...náì

nocturnal [nɑ:ktə:r'nəl] *adj* (tour, visit)
夜の yórù no, 夜間の yákàn no; (animal)
夜行性の yakósei no

nod [nɑ:d] *vi* (gesture) 頭で合図する atáma dè áìzu suru; (*also*: **nod in agreement**) うなずく unázukù; (doze) うとう
とする útòuto suru

◆*vt*: **to nod one's head** うなずく unázukù

◆*n* うなずき unazuki

nod off *vi* 居眠りする inémuri suru

noise [nɔiz] *n* (sound) 音 otó; (din) 騒音
sóon

noisy [nɔi'zi:] *adj* (audience, child,
machine) うるさい urúsaì

nomad [nou'mæd] *n* 遊牧民 yúbokumìn

nominal [nɑ:m'ənəl] *adj* (leader) 名目上
の meímokujò no; (rent, price) わずかな
wázùka na

nominate [nɑ:m'əneit] *vt* (propose) 推薦
する suísen suru; (appoint) 任命する niñmei suru

nomination [nɑ:mənei'ʃən] *n* (proposal)
推薦 suísen; (appointment) 任命 niñmei

nominee [nɑ:məni:'] *n* (proposed person)
推薦された人 suísen sareta hitò;
(appointed person) 任命された人 niñmei
sareta hitò

non... [nɑ:n] *prefix* 非... hí..., 無... mú..., 不
... fú...

non-alcoholic [nɑ:nælkəhɔ:l'ik] *adj* ア
ルコールを含まない arúkōru wò fukú-
manaì

non-aligned [nɑ:nəlaind'] *adj* 非同盟の
hidómei no

nonchalant [naːnʃələˈnt'] *adj* 平然とした heízen to shitá

noncommittal [naːnkəmitˈəl] *adj* (person, answer) どっちつかずの dotchí tsukazù no

nondescript [naːnˈdɪskrɪpt] *adj* (person, clothes, color) 特徴のない tokúchō no naî

none [nʌn] *pron* (person) だれも...ない daré mò ...náì; (thing) どれも...ない dórè mo ...náì
none of you あなたたちの1人も...ない anátatàchi no hitóri mò ...náì
I've none left 何も残っていません naní mò nokótte imaseñ
he's none the worse for it それでも彼は大丈夫です soré de mò kare wa daíjōbu desu

nonentity [naːnenˈtitiː] *n* 取るに足らない人 tórù ni taránai hitô

nonetheless [nʌnˈðəlès] *adv* それにもかかわらず soré ni mò kakáwarazù, それでもやはり soré de mò yahárî

non-existent [naːnɪgzisˈtənt] *adj* 存在しない soñzai shinaî

non-fiction [naːnfikˈʃən] *n* ノンフィクション nofifikúshon

nonplussed [naːnplʌsˈt'] *adj* 困惑した kofiwaku shita, 困った komáttà

nonsense [naːnˈsens] *n* でたらめ detárame, ナンセンス náñsensu
nonsense! そんな事はない sofina koto wà naî, ナンセンス náñsensu

non-smoker [naːnsmouˈkəːr] *n* タバコを吸わない人 tabáko wò suwánai hitô, 非喫煙者 hñkitsueñsha

non-stick [naːnstikˈ] *adj* (pan, surface) こげつかない kogétsukanaî

non-stop [naːnstaːp'] *adj* (conversation) 止らない tomáranaî; (flight, train) 直行の chokkō no, ノンストップの nofisutoppù no
♦*adv* 止らずに tomárazu ni

noodles [nuːˈdəlz] *npl* ヌードル núdòru

nook [nuk] *n: every nook and cranny* 隅々 sumízùmi

noon [nuːn] *n* 正午 shōgò

no one (*BRIT* **no-one**) *pron* = **nobody**

noose [nuːs] *n* (loop) 引結び hikímusùbi
hangman's noose 絞首刑用の縄 kōshukeiyō no nawà

nor [nɔːr] *conj* = **neither**
♦*adv see* **neither**

norm [nɔːrm] *n* (convention) 慣習 kañshū; (rule, requirement) ノルマ nórùma

normal [nɔːrˈməl] *adj* (usual, ordinary: life, behavior, result) 普通の futsū no; (child: not abnormal) 異常のない ijō no naî, ノーマルな nōmaru na

normally [nɔːrˈməliː] *adv* 普通は futsū wa, 普通に futsū ni

north [nɔːrθ] *n* 北 kitá
♦*adj* 北の kitá no
♦*adv* 北へ kitá e

North America *n* 北米 hokúbei

north-east [nɔːrθiːsˈt'] *n* 北東 hokútō

northerly [nɔːrˈðəːrliː] *adj* (point) 北方の hoppō no; (direction) 北方への hoppō e nô
a northerly wind 北からの風 kitá kara nò kazé

northern [nɔːrˈðəːrn] *adj* 北の kitá no
the northern hemisphere 北半球 kitáhañkyū

Northern Ireland *n* 北アイルランド kitá airurañdo

North Pole *n* 北極 hokkyōku

North Sea *n* 北海 hokkái

northward(s) [nɔːrθˈwəːrd(z)] *adv* 北へ kitá e

north-west [nɔːrθwesˈt'] *n* 北西 hokúsei

Norway [nɔːrˈwei] *n* ノルウェー norúuè

Norwegian [nɔːrwiːˈdʒən] *adj* ノルウェーの norúuè no; (LING) ノルウェー語の norúuēgo no
♦*n* (person) ノルウェー人 norúuējìn; (LING) ノルウェー語 norúuēgo

nose [nouz] *n* (ANAT, ZOOL) 鼻 haná; (sense of smell) きゅう覚 kyūkaku
♦*vi: nose about* せん索する señsaku suru

nosebleed [nouzˈbliːd] *n* 鼻血 hanáji

nose-dive [nouzˈdaiv] *n* (of plane) 急降下 kyūkōka

nosey [nouˈziː] (*inf*) *adj* = **nosy**

nostalgia [nəstælˈdʒə] *n* 郷愁 kyōshū, ノ

スタルジア nosútarùjia

nostalgic [nəstǽl'dʒik] *adj* (person, book, film) 懐かしい natsúkashiì

nostril [nɑːs'trəl] *n* (of person, animal) 鼻のあな haná no anà, 鼻孔 bikố

nosy [nou'zi:] (*inf*) *adj* せん索好きな señsakuzùki na

KEYWORD
---

not [nɑːt] *adv* ...でない ...de náì

he is not/isn't here 彼はいません kárè wa imáseñ

you must not/you mustn't do that それをしてはいけません soré wò shité wà ikémaseñ

it's too late, isn't it? 遅過ぎますよね osósugimasù yo né, 遅過ぎるでしょう osósugirù deshô

he asked me not to do it それをしないで下さいと彼に頼まれました soré wò shináide kudasaì to kárè ni tanómaremashìta

not that I don't like him/he isn't interesting 彼を嫌い[面白くない]というのではないが kárè wo kiráì(omóshirokùnai)tò iú no de wa naì gá

not yet まだ mádà

not now とは駄目 ímà wa damé ¶ *see also* all; only

---

notably [nou'təbli:] *adv* (particularly) 特に tốkù ni; (markedly) 著しく ichíjirushikù

notary [nou'tə:ri:] *n* 公証人 kõshōnin

notch [nɑːtʃ] *n* (in wood, blade, saw) 刻み目 kizámime, ノッチ notchí

note [nout] *n* (record) 覚書 obôegaki, ノート nôto, メモ mêmò; (letter) 短い手紙 mijíkaì tegámi; (banknote) 紙幣 shíhèi, 札 satsú; (MUS) 音符 oñpu; (tone) 音 otố
◆*vt* (observe) ...に気が付く ...ni ki gá tsukù; (write down) 書留める kakítomerù

notebook [nout'buk] *n* 帳面 chốmen, ノート nôto

noted [nou'tid] *adj* (famous) 有名な yū́mei na

notepad [nout'pæd] *n* メモ用紙 memóyòshi ◇糊などでつづった物を指す norí

nadò de tsuzútta mono wò sásù

notepaper [nout'peipə:r] *n* 便せん biñsen

nothing [nʌθ'iŋ] *n* (not anything) 何も...ない naní mò ...náì; (zero) ゼロ zérò

he does nothing 彼は何もしない kárè wa naní mò shináì

nothing new/much/special 目新しい〔大した，特別な〕ことはない meátarashiì(táìshita, tokúbetsu nà)kotó wa naì

for nothing (free) 無料で muryố de, ただで tádà ḍe; (in vain) 無駄に mudá ni

notice [nou'tis] *n* (announcement) 通知 tsúchi; (warning) 通告 tsúkoku; (dismissal) 解雇通知 kaíkotsùchi; (resignation) 辞表 jihyố; (period of time) 予告 yokốku
◆*vt* (observe) ...に気が付く ...ni ki gá tsukù

to bring something to someone's notice (attention) ...を...に知らせる ...wo ...ni shiráserù

to take notice of ...に気が付く ...ni ki gá tsukù

at short notice 急に kyú̄ ni

until further notice 追って通知があるまで otté tsúchi ga aru madè

to hand in one's notice 辞表を出す jihyố wo dásù

noticeable [nou'tisəbəl] *adj* (mark, effect) はっきりした hakkírì shita

noticeboard [nou'tisbo:rd] (*BRIT*) *n* 掲示板 keíjiban

notify [nou'təfai] *vt*: *to notify someone (of something)* (...を) ...に知らせる (...wo) ...ni shiráserù

notion [nou'ʃən] *n* (idea) 考え kañgaè, 概念 gaínen; (opinion) 意見 íkèn

notorious [noutɔ:r'i:əs] *adj* (criminal, liar, place) 悪名高い akúmeitakaì

notwithstanding [nɑːtwiθstæn'diŋ] *adv* ...にもかかわらず ...ní mò kakáwarazù
◆*prep* ...にもかかわらず ...ní mò kakáwarazù

nougat [nuː'gət] *n* ヌガー núgầ ◇クルミなどの入ったキャラメル風のお菓子 kurúmi nadò no haítta kyarámerufù no o-káshì

nought [nɔːt] *n* = **naught**

noun [naun] *n* 名詞 meíshi

nourish [nəːrˈiʃ] *vt* (feed) 養う yashínaù; (*fig*: foster) 心中にはぐくむ shíñchū ni hagúkumù

nourishing [nəːrˈiʃiŋ] *adj* (food) 栄養のある eíyō no arù

nourishment [nəːrˈiʃmənt] *n* (food) 栄養 eíyō

novel [nɑːvˈəl] *n* 小説 shôsetsu
♦*adj* (new, fresh: idea, approach) 目新しい meátarashiî, 新鮮な shiñsen na

novelist [nɑːvˈəlist] *n* 小説家 shôsetsuka

novelty [nɑːvˈəlti] *n* (newness) 新鮮さ shiñsensa; (object) 変ったもの kawátta monò

November [nouvemˈbəːr] *n* 11月 júichigatsu

novice [nɑːvˈis] *n* (beginner) 初心者 shoshíñsha; (REL) 修練者 shúreñsha

now [nau] *adv* 今 ímà
♦*conj*: **now (that)** ...であるから ...de árù kara
right now (immediately) 今すぐ ímà súgù; (at the moment) 今の所 imá no tokoro
by now 今ごろはもう imágoro wà mô
just now 今の所 imá no tokoro
now and then, now and again 時々 tokídoki
from now on 今後 kôñgo

nowadays [nauˈədeiz] *adv* このごろ(は) konôgoro (wa)

nowhere [nouˈweːr] *adv* (be, go) どこにも...ない dôkò ni mo ...naî

nozzle [nɑːzˈəl] *n* (of hose, fire extinguisher etc) ノズル nôzùru; (of vacuum cleaner) 吸口 suíkuchi

nuance [nuːˈɑːns] *n* ニュアンス nyúànsu

nubile [nuːˈbail] *adj* (woman) セクシーな sékùshì na

nuclear [nuːˈkliːəːr] *adj* (fission, weapons) 核... kákù...
the nuclear industry 原子力産業界 geñshiryoku sangyôkai
nuclear physics 原始物理学 geñshibutsurigàku, 核物理学 kakúbutsurigàku
nuclear power 原子力 geñshiryòku

nucleus [nuːˈkliːəs] (*pl* **nuclei**) *n* (of atom, cell) 核 kákù; (of group) 中心 chúshin

nude [nuːd] *adj* 裸の hadáka no
♦*n* ヌード nûdo
in the nude (naked) 裸で hadáka de

nudge [nʌdʒ] *vt* (person) 小突く kozúkù

nudist [nuːˈdist] *n* 裸体主義者 ratáishugishà, ヌーディスト nûdisùto

nudity [nuːˈditi] *n* 裸 hadáka

nuisance [nuːˈsəns] *n* (state of affairs) 厄介な事情 yákkài na jijô; (thing) 厄介な物 yákkài na monò; (person: irritating) 迷惑な人 meíwaku na hitò
what a nuisance! 困ったもんだ komátta moñ da

null [nʌl] *adj*: **null and void** (contract, agreement) 無効な mukô na

numb [nʌm] *adj*: **numb (with)** (with cold etc) ...でしびれた ...de shibíretà; (*fig*: with fear etc) ...で気が動転した ...de ki ga dôten shità

number [nʌmˈbəːr] *n* (MATH) 数字 súji; (quantity) 数 kázù; (of house, bank account etc) 番号 bañgô
♦*vt* (pages etc) ...に番号を付ける ...ni bañgô wo tsukérù; (amount to) 総数は...である sôsū wa ...de árù
to be numbered among ...の1人である ...no hitôrì de árù
a number of (several) 数... sū... no
they were ten in number (people) 彼らは10人だった kárèra wa jûnin datta; (things) 10個あった júkkò atta

number plate (*BRIT*) *n* (AUT) ナンバープレート nañbāpurèto

numeral [nuːˈməːrəl] *n* 数詞 súshi

numerate [nuːˈməːreit] *adj* 数学ができる súgaku gà dekírù

numerical [numeːrˈikəl] *adj* (value) 数字で表した súji dè aráwashità; (order) 数字の súji no

numerous [nuːˈməːrəs] *adj* (many, countless) 多くの ôkù no, 多数の tasú no

nun [nʌn] *n* (Christian) 修道女 shûdòjo; (Buddhist) 尼 ámà

nurse [nəːrs] *n* (in hospital) 看護婦 kañgofù; (*also*: **nursemaid**) 保母 hóbò

♦*vt* (patient) 看護する káñgo suru; (baby) ...に乳を飲ませる ...ni chichí wò nomáserù

nursery [nəːrʹsəːriː] *n* (institution) 保育園 hoíkuèn; (room) 育児室 ikújishìtsu; (for plants: commercial establishment) 種苗園 shubyóèn

nursery rhyme *n* 童謡 dóyò

nursery school *n* 保育園 hoíkuèn

nursery slope (*BRIT*) *n* (SKI) 初心者用ゲレンデ shoshìnshayō gereñde

nursing [nəːrsʹiŋ] *n* (profession) 看護職 kañgoshòku; (care) 看病 káñbyō

nursing home *n* (*gen*) 療養所 ryóyòjo; (for old people) 老人ホーム rójinhòmu

nursing mother *n* 授乳している母親 junyū shite irū haháoya

nurture [nəːrʹtʃəːr] *vt* (child, plant) 育てる sodáterù

nut [nʌt] *n* (TECH) ナット náttò; (BOT) 木ノ実 kínòmi(kònòmi), ナッツ náttsù

nutcracker [nʌtʹkrækəːr] *npl* クルミ割り kurúmiwarì

nutmeg [nʌtʹmeg] *n* ニクズク nikúzùku, ナツメッグ natsúmeggù ◇香辛料の一種 kōshiñryō no ísshù

nutrient [nuːʹtriːənt] *n* 養分 yóbùn

nutrition [nuːtriʃʹən] *n* (diet, nourishment) 栄養 eíyō; (proteins, vitamins etc) 養分 yóbùn

nutritious [nuːtriʃʹəs] *adj* (food) 栄養価の高い eíyōka no takáì

nuts [nʌts] (*inf*) *adj* 頭がおかしい atáma gà okáshiì

nutshell [nʌtʹʃel] *n* クルミの殻 kurúmi no karà

in a nutshell (*fig*) 簡単に言えば kañtan nî iébà

nylon [naiʹlɑːn] *n* ナイロン náìron

♦*adj* ナイロンの náìron no

O

oak [ouk] *n* オーク ōkù

♦*adj* (table) オークの ōkù no

O.A.P. [oueipiːʹ] (*BRIT*) *n abbr* = **old-age pensioner**

oar [ɔːr] *n* かい kaí, オール ōrú

oasis [oueiʹsis] (*pl* **oases**) *n* (in desert) オアシス oáshìsu

oath [ouθ] *n* (promise) 誓い chikái; (swear word) 悪態 akútaì

under or on (BRIT) oath 宣誓して señsei shite

oatmeal [outʹmiːl] *n* オートミール ōtómīru

oats [outs] *n* カラスムギ karásumugì

obedience [oubiːʹdiːəns] *n* 服従 fukújù

obedient [oubiːʹdiːənt] *adj* (child, dog etc) 素直な sunáo na, よく言う事を聞く yokú iú koto wo kikù

obesity [oubiːʹsitiː] *n* 肥満 hímàn

obey [oubeiʹ] *vt* (instructions, person) ...に従う ...ni shitágau; (regulations) 守る mamóru

obituary [oubitʃʹuːeːriː] *n* 死亡記事 shibó- kijì

object [*n* ɑːbʹdʒikt *vt* əbdʒektʹ] *n* (thing) 物 monó; (aim, purpose) 目的 mokúteki; (of affection, desires) 対象 taishō; (LING) 目的語 mokútekigo

♦*vi*: *to object to* ...に反対する ...ni hañtai suru

to object that ...だと言って反対する ...da to itté hañtai suru

expense is no object 費用にはこだわらない hiyő ni wa kodáwaranaì

I object! 反対です hañtai dèsu

objection [əbdʒekʹʃən] *n* 異議 igî

I have no objection to ... ...に異議はありません ...ni igî wa arímasèn

objectionable [ədʒekʹʃənəbəl] *adj* (person, language, conduct) いやな iyá na

objective [əbdʒekʹtiv] *adj* (impartial: person, information) 客観的な kyákúkan- teki na

♦*n* (aim, purpose) 目的 mokúteki

obligation [ɑːbləgeiʹʃən] *n* (duty, commitment) 義務 gimù

without obligation (COMM) 買う義務なしで kaú gimù nashi de

obligatory [əbligʹətɔːriː] *adj* 強制的な kyōseiteki na

oblige [əblaidʒʹ] *vt* (force): *to oblige someone to do something* 強制的に

...に..をさせる kyṓseiteki ni ...ni ...wo saserù; (do a favor for) ...の頼みを聞く ...no tanómi wo kikú

to be obliged to someone for something (grateful) ...の事で...に感謝している ...no kotṓ de ...ni kañsha shité irù

obliging [əblai'dʒiŋ] *adj* (helpful) 親切な shíñsetsu na

oblique [əbli:k'] *adj* (line) 斜めの nanámè no; (comment, reference) 間接的な kañsetsuteki na

obliterate [əblit'ə:reit] *vt* 跡形もなくする atókata mo nakúsuru

oblivion [əbliv'i:ən] *n* (unawareness) 無意識 muíshìki; (being forgotten) 忘却 bṓkyaku

oblivious [əbliv'i:əs] *adj: oblivious of/to* ...を意識していない ...wo ishíki shité inai

oblong [ɑ:b'lɔ:ŋ] *adj* 長方形の chṓhṑkei no
◆*n* 長方形 chṓhṑkei

obnoxious [əbnɑ:k'ʃəs] *adj* (unpleasant: behavior, person) 不愉快な fuyúkài na; (: smell) いやな iyá na

oboe [ou'bou] *n* オーボエ ṓbòe

obscene [əbsi:n'] *adj* (gesture, remark, behavior) わいせつな waísetsu na

obscenity [əbsen'iti:] *n* (of book, behavior etc) わいせつ waísetsu; (offensive word) 卑語 higò

obscure [əbskju:r'] *adj* (little known: place, author etc) 無名の muméi no; (difficult to understand) 難解な nañkai na
◆*vt* (obstruct: view, sun etc) 覆い隠す ṓikakusù; (conceal: truth, meaning etc) 隠す kakúsù

obsequious [əbsi:'kwi:əs] *adj* ぺこぺこする péḳpeko suru

observance [əbzə:r'vəns] *n* (of law) 遵守 juñshu; (of custom) 守る事 mamórù koto

observant [əbzə:r'vənt] *adj* (person) 観察力の優れた kañsatsuryòku no sugureta; (remark) 鋭い surúdoì

observation [ɑ:bzə:rvei'ʃən] *n* (remark) 意見 ikèn; (of observing) 観察 kañsatsu; (MED) 監視 kañshi

observatory [əbzə:r'vətɔ:ri:] *n* 観測所 kañsokujo

observe [əbzə:rv'] *vt* (watch) 観察する kañsatsu suru; (comment) 述べる ikèn wo nobérù; (abide by: rule) 守る mamórù, 遵守する juñshu suru

observer [əbzə:r'və:r] *n* 観察者 kañsatsushà

obsess [əbses'] *vt* ...に取付く ...ni torítsuku

obsession [əbseʃ'ən] *n* 強迫観念 kyṓhakukannen

obsessive [əbses'iv] *adj* (person, tendency, behavior) 妄想に取付かれた様な mṓsō ni torítsukareta yṓ na

obsolescence [ɑ:bsəles'əns] *n* 旧式化 kyṓshikika

obsolete [ɑ:bsəli:t'] *adj* (out of use: word etc) 廃れた sutáreta; (: machine etc) 旧式の kyṓshiki no

obstacle [ɑ:b'stəkəl] *n* (obstruction) 障害物 shṓgaibutsù; (fig: problem, difficulty) 障害 shṓgai

obstacle race *n* 障害物競走 shṓgaibutsukyōsō

obstetrics [əbstet'riks] *n* 産科 sañka

obstinate [ɑ:b'stənit] *adj* (determined: person, resistance) 頑固な gañko na

obstruct [əbstrʌkt'] *vt* (block) ふさぐ fuságu; (fig: hinder) 妨害する bṓgai suru

obstruction [əbstrʌk'ʃən] *n* (action) 妨害 bṓgai; (object) 障害物 shṓgaibutsu

obtain [əbtein'] *vt* (get) 手に入れる te nì ireru, 獲得する kakútoku suru; (achieve) 達成する tasséi suru

obtainable [əbtein'əbəl] *adj* (object) 入手できる nyūshu dekírù

obvious [ɑ:b'vi:əs] *adj* (clear) 明かな akíràka na; (self-evident) 分かり切った wakárikitta

obviously [ɑ:b'vi:əsli:] *adv* 明らかに akíràka ni

obviously not 明らかに...でない akíràka ni ...de nai

occasion [əkei'ʒən] *n* (point in time) 時 tokí, 時点 jitén; (event, celebration etc) 行事 gyṓji, イベント ibénto; (opportunity) 機会 kikái, チャンス chañsu

occasional [əkei'ʒənəl] *adj* (infrequent)

時々の tokídokĩ no

occasionally [əkei'ʒənəli:] *adv* 時々 to-kídokĩ

occult [əkʌlt'] *n*: *the occult* 超自然 chō-shizen, オカルト okáruto

occupant [ɑːk'jəpənt] *n* (long-term: of house etc) 居 住 者 kyojũshã; (of office etc) テナント tenánto; (temporary: of car, room etc) 中にいる人 nakã ni iru hitõ

occupation [ɑ:kjəpei'ʃən] *n* (job) 職業 shokúgyõ; (pastime) 趣味 shumĩ; (of building, country etc) 占領 señryo

occupational hazard [ɑ:kjəpei'ʃənəl-] *n* 職業上の危険 shokúgyojõ no kikén

occupier [ɑ:k'jəpaiə:r] *n* 居 住 者 kyojũ-shã

occupy [ɑ:k'jəpai] *vt* (inhabit: house) ...に住む ...ni sumũ; (take: seat, place etc) ...に居る ...ni irú; (take over: building, country etc) 占領する señryo suru; (take up: time) ...が掛る ...ga kakárũ; (: attention) 奪う ubáũ; (: space) 取る torũ
to occupy oneself in doing (to be busy with) ...に専念する ...ni sennen suru

occur [əkə:r'] *vi* (event: take place) 起る okórũ; (phenomenon: exist) 存在する soñ-zai suru
to occur to someone ...の頭に浮ぶ ...no atáma ni ukábu

occurrence [əkə:r'əns] *n* (event) 出来事 dekigoto; (existence) 存在 soñzai

ocean [ou'ʃən] *n* 海 umi
Indian Ocean インド洋 iñdoyõ ¶ *see also* **Atlantic; Pacific**

ocean-going [ou'ʃəngouiŋ] *adj* 外洋の gaíyõ no

ocher [ou'kə:r] (*BRIT*: **ochre**) *adj* (color) 黄土色の ōdõiro no, オークルの ōkũru no

o'clock [əklɑːk'] *adv*: *it is 5 o'clock* 5時です gojĩ desu

OCR [ousiːɑːr'] *n abbr* (COMPUT: = *optical character recognition*) 光学読取り kõgakuyomitorĩ (: = *optical character reader*) 光学読取り装置 kõgakuyomisõ-chĩ

octagonal [ɑ:ktæg'ənəl] *adj* 八角形の hákkakukeĩ no

octave [ɑːk'tiv] *n* (MUS) オクターブ o-kútãbũ

October [ɑːktou'bə:r] *n* 10月 jũgatsu

octopus [ɑːk'təpəs] *n* タコ takõ

odd [ɑːd] *adj* (strange: person, behavior, expression) 変な heñ na, 妙な myõ na; (uneven: number) 奇数の kĩsũ no; (not paired: sock, glove, shoe etc) 片方の kã-tahõ no
60-odd 60幾つ rokújũ ikutsu
at odd times 時々 tokídokĩ
to be the odd one out 例外である ref-gai de aru

oddity [ɑ:d'iti:] *n* (person) 変り者 kawa-rimono; (thing) 変った物 kawatta mono

odd-job man [ɑ:dʒɑ:b'-] *n* 便利屋 beñ-riya

odd jobs *npl* 雑用 zatsúyo

oddly [ɑːd'li:] *adv* (strangely: behave, dress) 変な風に heñ na fū ni ¶ *see also* **enough**

oddments [ɑːd'mənts] *npl* (COMM) 残り物 nokõrimono

odds [ɑːdz] *npl* (in betting) かけ率 kaké-rĩtsu, オッズ ozzũ
it makes no odds 構いません kamáĩ-masen
at odds 仲たがいして nakátagãishite

odds and ends *npl* 半端物 hañpamono

ode [oud] *n* しょう歌 shōkã, オード ōdõ

odious [ou'di:əs] *adj* 不快な fukái na

odometer [oudɑːm'itə:r] *n* 走行距離計 sõkōkyorikeĩ

odor [ou'də:r] (*BRIT* **odour**) *n* (smell) におい niõĩ; (: unpleasant) 悪臭 akúshū

KEYWORD

of [ʌv] *prep* 1 (gen) ...の ...nõ
the history of France フランスの歴史 furánsu no rekíshi
a friend of ours 私たちのある友達 wa-tákushitãchi no árũ tomõdachi
a boy of 10 10才の少年 jússài no shõ-nen
that was kind of you ご親切にどうも go-shíñsetsu ni dõmo
a man of great ability 才能抜群の人 saínõ batsugũn no hitõ

the city of New York ニューヨーク市 nyúyōkushì

south of Glasgow グラスゴーの南 gurásugō no mínámi

2 (expressing quantity, amount, dates etc): *a kilo of flour* 小麦粉1キロ komúgiko ichíkiro

how much of this do you need? これはどのぐらい要りますか koré wà donó gurai irimasù ká

there were 3 of them (people) 3人いました saṅniṅ imáshìta; (objects) 3個ありました sáṅko arímashìta

3 of us went 私たちの内から3人行きました watákushitàchi no uchí karà sáṅnin ikímashìta

the number of road accidents is increasing 交通事故の数が増えています kōtsūjikò no kázù ga fúète imásù

a cup of tea お茶1杯 o-chá ippài

a vase of flowers 花瓶に生けた花 kabín nī ikèta haná

the 5th of July 7月5日 shichígatsu itsúkà

the winter of 1987 1987年の冬 seṅkyúhyakuhachíjūnánánèn no fuyú

3 (from, out of): *a bracelet of solid gold* 純金の腕輪 juṅkin nò udéwa

a statue of marble 大理石の彫像 daírisèki no chōzō

made of wood 木製の mokúsei no

KEYWORD

off [ɔːf] *adv* 1 (referring to distance, time) 離れて hanárète

it's a long way off あれは遠い aré wà tōi

the game is 3 days off 試合は3日先です shiái wà mikká saki desù

2 (departure) 出掛けて dekáketè

to go off to Paris/Italy パリ〔イタリア〕へ出掛ける párì〔itária〕e dekákerù

I must be off そろそろ出掛けます soròsoro dekákemasù

3 (removal) 外して hazúshitè

to take off one's hat/coat/clothes 帽子〔コート，服〕を脱ぐ bōshi〔kōto, fu-

kú〕wo núgù

the button came off ボタンが取れた botán gà tóreta

10% off (COMM) 10パーセント引き juppásentobiki

4 (not at work: on holiday) 休暇中で kyúkachū dè; (: due to sickness) 欠勤して kekkín shitè

I'm off on Fridays 私の休みは金曜日です watákushi nò yasúmi wa kiṅ-yōbi desu

he was off on Friday (on holiday) 金曜日には彼は休みでした kiṅ-yōbi ni wa kárè wa yasúmi deshìta; (sick etc) 金曜日には彼は欠勤しました kiṅ-yōbi ni wa kárè wa kékkin shimashìta

to have a day off (from work) 1日の休みを取る ichínichi no yasúmi wò tórù

to be off sick 病欠する byóketsu suru

♦*adj* 1 (not turned on: machine, engine, water, gas etc) 止めてある tomète arù; (: tap) 締めてある shiméte arù; (: light) 消してある keshíte arù

2 (cancelled: meeting, match, agreement) 取消された toríkesàreta

3 (BRIT: not fresh: milk, cheese, meat etc) 悪くなった wárùku natta

4: *on the off chance* (just in case) ...の場合に備えて ...no baái ni sonaetè

to have an off day (not as good as usual) 厄日である yakúbì de árù

♦*prep* 1 (indicating motion, removal etc) ...から ...kárà

to fall off a cliff 崖から落ちる gakè kará ochírù

the button came off my coat コートのボタンが取れた kōtò no botán gà tóreta

to take a picture off the wall 壁に掛けてある絵を降ろす kabé nī kákète aru é wò orósù

2 (distant from) ...から離れて ...kárá hanárète

it's just off the M1 国道M1を降りて直ぐの所にあります kokúdō emúwaṅ wo órite súgù no tokórò ni arímasù

it's 5 km off the main road 幹線道路から5キロの所にあります kaṅsendòro

kara gókìro no tokórò ni arímasù

an island off the coast 沖合の島 okíai nò shimá

to be off meat (no longer eat it) 肉をやめている nikú wò yaméte irù; (no longer like it) 肉が嫌いになっている nikú gà kirái nì natté irù

offal [ɔ:f'əl] *n* (CULIN) もつ motsù

off-color [ɔ:f'kʌl'ə:r] (*BRIT* **off-colour**) *adj* (ill) 病気の byóki no

offend [əfend'] *vt* (upset: person) 怒らせる okórasèru

offender [əfen'də:r] *n* (criminal) 犯罪者 hañzaìsha, 犯人 hañnin, ...犯 ...hañ

offense [əfens'] (*BRIT* **offence**) *n* (crime) 犯罪 hañzaí

to take offense at ...に怒る ...ni okóru

offensive [əfen'siv] *adj* (remark, gesture, behavior) 侮辱的な bujókuteki na; (smell etc) いやな iyá na; (weapon) 攻撃用の kốgekiyò no

♦*n* (MIL) 攻撃 kốgeki

offer [ɔ:f'ə:r] *n* (proposal: to help etc) 申出 mốshide; (: to buy) 申込み mốshikomi

♦*vt* (advice, help, information) ...すると申出る ...surú to mốshideru; (opportunity, service, product) 提供する teíkyo suru

on offer (*BRIT*: COMM) 値下げ品で neságehin de

offering [ɔ:f'ə:riŋ] *n* (of a company: product) 売物 urímono; (REL) 供物 sonáemono

off-hand [ɔ:f'hænd'] *adj* (behavior etc) いい加減な iíkagen na

♦*adv* 即座に sokúza ni

office [ɔ:f'is] *n* (place) 事務所 jimúshò, オフィス ofisu; (room) 事務室 jimúshìtsu; (position) 職 shokú

doctor's office (*US*) 医院 iîn

to take office 職に就く shokú ni tsuku

office automation *n* オフィスオートメーション ofisu ōtōmêshon

office building (*BRIT* **office block**) *n* オフィスビル ofísubiru

office hours *npl* (COMM) 業務時間 gyốmujikan; (*US*: MED) 診察時間 shiñ-satsujikan

officer [ɔ:f'isə:r] *n* (MIL etc) 将校 shốkò; (*also*: **police officer**) 警官 keíkan; (of organization) 役員 yakuín

office worker *n* 事務員 jimúin

official [əfiʃ'əl] *adj* (authorized) 公認の kốnin no; (visit, invitation, letter etc) 公式の kốshiki no

♦*n* (in government) 役人 yakúnin; (in trade union etc) 役員 yakuín

official residence 官邸 kañtei

officialdom [əfiʃ'əldəm] (*pej*) *n* 官僚の世界 kañryo no sekai

officiate [əfiʃ'i:eit] *vi* 司会する shikái suru

officious [əfiʃ'əs] *adj* (person, behavior) 差出がましい sashídegamashiì

offing [ɔ:f'iŋ] *n*: *in the offing* (*fig*: imminent) 差迫って sashísemattè

off-licence [ɔ:f'laisəns] *BRIT* *n* (shop selling alcohol) 酒屋 sakáya

off-line [ɔ:f'lain'] *adj* (COMPUT) オフラインの ofúrain no

♦*adv* オフラインで ofúrain de

off-peak [ɔ:f'pi:k'] *adj* (heating) オフピークの ofúpìku no; (train, ticket) 混んでいない時の koñde inai tokí no

off-putting [ɔ:f'put'iŋ] (*BRIT*) *adj* (person, remark etc) 気を悪くさせる kì wo warúku saseru

off-season [ɔ:f'si:zən] *adj* (holiday, ticket) オフシーズンの ofúshizun no

♦*adv* (travel, book etc) オフシーズンに ofúshizun ni

offset [ɔ:fset'] (*pt*, *pp* **offset**) *vt* (counteract) 補う ogínaù

offshoot [ɔ:f'ʃu:t] *n* (*fig*) 副産物 fukúsanbutsu

offshore [ɔ:f'ʃɔ:r'] *adj* (breeze) 陸からの rikú kara no; (oilrig, fishing) 沖合の okíai no

offside [ɔ:f'said'] *adj* (SPORT) オフサイドの ofúsaido no; (AUT: with right-hand drive) 右の migí no; (: with left-hand drive) 左の hidári no

offspring [ɔ:f'spriŋ] *n inv* 子孫 shisón

offstage [ɔ:f'steidʒ] *adv* 舞台裏に〔で〕butáiura ni〔de〕

off-the-rack [ɔːf'ðəræk'] (BRIT **off-the-peg**) adj (clothing) 出来合いの dekíai no, 既製の kiséi no

off-white [ɔːf'fwait'] adj (grayish white) 灰色がかった白の haírogakatta shirō no; (yellowish white) 黄色がかった白の kiírogakatta shirō no

often [ɔːf'ən] adv (frequently) よく yokú, しょっちゅう shotchū, 度々 tabítabi

how often do you go? どのぐらい行きますか donō gurai ikímasu ká

ogle [ou'gəl] vt 色目で見る irómè de mirú

oh [ou] excl あっ át

oil [ɔil] n (gen) 油 abúra, オイル oírù; (CULIN) サラダ油 sarádayu; (petroleum) 石油 sekíyu; (crude) 原油 geñyu; (for heating) 石油 sekíyu, 灯油 tōyu

♦vt (lubricate: engine, gun, machine) ...に油を差す ...ni abúra wo sasù

oilcan [ɔil'kæn] n 油差し abúrasashi

oilfield [ɔil'fiːld] n 油田 yudén

oil filter n (AUT) オイルフィルター oírufirutā

oil painting n 油絵 abúrae

oil refinery [-ri:fain'ə:ri:] n 精油所 seíyujo

oil rig n 石油掘削装置 sekíyu kússaku-sōchi

oilskins [ɔil'skinz] npl 防水服 bōsuifuku

oil tanker n (ship) オイルタンカー oírutankā; (truck) タンクローリー tañkurōrī

oil well n 油井 yuséi

oily [ɔi'li:] adj (rag) 油染みた abúrajimità; (substance) 油の様な abúra no yō na; (food) 脂っこい abúrakkoi

ointment [ɔint'mənt] n 軟こう nañkō

O.K., okay [oukei'] (inf) excl (agreement: alright) よろしい yoróshii, オーケー ōkè; (: don't fuss) 分かったよ wakáttà yo

♦adj (average: film, book, meal etc) まあまあの mā mā no

♦vt (approve) 承認する shōnin suru

old [ould] adj (aged: person) 年寄の toshíyori no; (: thing) 古い furúi; (former: school, home etc) 元の motò no, 前の maè no

how old are you? お幾つですか o-íkutsu desu ká

he's 10 years old 彼は10才です karè wa jussái desu

older brother (one's own) 兄 ani; (person spoken to) お兄さん o-níisan; (of third party) 兄さん níisan

old age n 老齢 rōrei

old-age pensioner [ould'eidʒ-] (BRIT) n 年金で生活する老人 neñkin dè seíkatsu surù rōjìn, 年金暮しの人 neñkingurāshi no hitð

old-fashioned [ould'fæʃ'ənd] adj (style, design) 時代遅れの jidáiokùre no, 古くさい furúkusai; (person, values) 保守的な hoshùteki na

olive [ɑːl'iv] n (fruit) オリーブ oríbù; (also: **olive tree**) オリーブの木 oríbù no ki

♦adj (also: **olive-green**) オリーブ色の o-ríbùiro no

olive oil n オリーブ油 oríbùyu

Olympic [oulim'pik] adj 五輪の gorín no, オリンピックの orínpikkù no

Olympic Games npl: *the Olympic Games* 五輪 gorín, オリンピック orínpikkù

the Olympics 五輪 gorín, オリンピック orínpikkù

omelet(te) [ɑːm'lit] n オムレツ omúretsu

omen [ou'mən] n (sign) 兆し kizáshi, 前触れ maèbure

ominous [ɑːm'ənəs] adj (worrying) 不気味な bukìmi na

omission [oumiʃ'ən] n 省略 shōryaku

omit [oumit'] vt (deliberately) 省略する shōryaku suru; (by mistake) うっかりして抜かす ukkárì shite nukásu

---

KEYWORD

on [ɑːn] prep 1 (indicating position) ...(の上)に(で) ...(no uè) ni(de)

on the wall 壁に kabé ni

it's on the table テーブル(の上)にあります tèburu (no uè) nì arímasù

on the left 左に hidári nì

the house is on the main road 家は幹線道路に面しています ié wà kañsendōro ni mếñ shite imásù

2 (indicating means, method, condition etc) ...で ...dè

on foot (go, be) 歩いて arúìte

on the train/plane (go) 電車〔飛行機〕で déñsha(hikôkì)de; (be) 電車〔飛行機〕に乗って déñsha(hikôkì)ni notté

on the telephone/radio/television 電話〔ラジオ，テレビ〕で déñwa(rájìo, térèbi)de

she's on the telephone 彼女は電話に出ています〔電話中です〕kánòjo wa déñwa ni dété imasu(deñwachū desù)

I heard it on the radio/saw him on television 私はラジオで聞きました〔テレビで彼を見ました〕watákushi wà rájìo de kikímashìta(térèbi de kárè wo mimáshìta)

to be on drugs 麻薬をやっている mayáku wò yatté irù

to be on holiday 休暇中である kyúkachū de arù

to be away on business 商用で出掛けている shôyō dè dekákete irù

3 (referring to time) ...に ...ni

on Friday 金曜日に kiñ-yôbì ni

on Fridays 金曜日に kiñ-yôbì ni, 毎週金曜日に maíshū kiñ-yôbì ni, 金曜日毎に kiñ-yôbì gótò ni

on June 20th 6月20日に rokúgatsu hatsúka ni

on Friday, June 20th 6月20日金曜日に rokúgatsu hatsúka kiñ-yôbì ni

a week on Friday 来週の金曜日に raíshū nò kiñ-yôbì ni

on arrival he went straight to his hotel 到着すると彼は真っ直ぐにホテルへ行きました tôchaku suru tò kárè wa massúgù ni hôtèru e ikímashìta

on seeing this これを見ると koré wò mírù to

4 (about, concerning) ...について ...ni tsúìte, ...に関して ...ni kâñ shite

information on train services 列車に関する情報 resshá nì kañ surù jôhô

a book on physics 物理の本 bútsùri no hôñ

◆*adv* **1** (referring to dress) 身につけて

mi nî tsukète

to have one's coat on コートを着ている kôto wo kité irù

what's she got on? 彼女は何を着ていますか kánòjo wa nánì wo kité imasù ká

she put her boots/gloves/hat on 彼女はブーツを履いた〔手袋をはめた，帽子をかぶった〕kánòjo wa bûtsu wo haíta(tebúkuro wò haméta, bôshì wo kabúttà)

2 (referring to covering): ***screw the lid on tightly*** ふたをしっかり締めて下さい futá wò shikkárì shímete kudásaì

3 (further, continuously) 続けて tsuzúketè

to walk/drive/go on 歩き〔車で走り，行き〕続ける arúkì(kurúma dè hashíri, ikî)tsuzukèru

to read on 読み続ける yomítsuzukèru

◆*adj* **1** (functioning, in operation: machine) 動いている ugôite irù; (: radio, TV, light) ついている tsúìte iru; (: faucet) 水が出ている mizú gà deté irù; (: brakes) かかっている kakátte irù; (: meeting) 始まっている tsuzúite irù

is the meeting still on? (in progress) まだ会議中ですか mádà kaígichū desù ká; (not cancelled) 会議は予定通りにやるんですか kâìgi wa yotéi dòri ni yarún desù ká

there's a good film on at the cinema 映画館で今いい映画をやっています eígakàn de ímà iî eíga wò yatté imasù

2: ***that's not on!*** (*inf*: of behavior) それはいけません soré wà ikémaseñ

once [wʌns] *adv* (on one occasion) 一度 ichído, 一回 ikkái; (formerly) 前 は maè wa, かつて katsúte

◆*conj* (immediately afterwards) ...した後 ...shitá ato, ...してから ...shité kara

once he had left/it was done 彼が出て〔事が済んで〕から karè ga deté(kotó ga suñde)kara

at once (immediately) 直ちに tadáchi ni, 直ぐに sugù ni; (simultaneously) 同時に dôji ni

once a week 週一回 shū ikkái

once more もう一度 mô ichído

once and for all 断然 dañzen

once upon a time 昔々 mukáshi mukashi

oncoming [ɑːnˈkʌmiŋ] *adj* (approaching: traffic etc) 向ってくる mukátte kurù

KEYWORD

one [wʌn] *num* 一（の）ichí (no), 1つ（の）hitótsù (no)

one hundred and fifty 150 hyakúgojù

I asked for two coffees, not one 注文したのは1つじゃなくて2つのコーヒーです chûmon shita no wà hitótsu jànakutè futatsu nò kôhî desu

one day there was a sudden knock at the door ある日突然だれかがドアをノックした árù hi totsúzen dárèka ga dóà wo nókkù shita

one by one 1つずつ hitótsu zùtsu

♦*adj* 1 (sole) ただ一つの tádà hitótsu no, 唯一の yuîitsu no

it's the one book which interests me 私が興味を感じる唯一の本です watákushi gà kyômi wo kañjiru yuîitsu no hôñ desu

that is my one worry 私が心配しているのはそれだけです watákushi gà shiñpai shite iru nò wa soré dake dèsu

the one man who ... ...する唯一の人 ...suru yuîitsu no hitò

2 (same) 同じ onáji

they came in the one car 彼らは皆同じ車で来ました kárèra wa mínà onáji kurùma de kimáshìta

they all belong to the one family 彼らは皆内です kárèra wa mínà miúchi desù

♦*pron* 1 物 monó

this one これ koré

that one それ soré, あれ aré

I've already got one/a red one 私は既に1つ〔赤いのを〕持っています watákushi wà súde ni hitótsu〔akái nò wo〕môtte imasu

2: *one another* お互いに o-tágai nì

do you two ever see one another? お二人は付合っていますか o-fútari wa tsu-kíattè imasu ká

the boys didn't dare look at one another 少年たちはあえて顔を合せる事ができなかった shônentàchi wa áète ka-ó wò awáseru kotò ga dekínakattà

3 (impersonal): *one never knows* どうなるか分かりませんね dô naru ka waká-rimaseñ né

to cut one's finger 指を切る yubí wò kírù

one needs to eat 人は食べる必要がある hitó wà tabérù hitsúyò ga arù

one-day excursion [wʌnˈdei-] (*US*) *n* (day return) 日帰り往復券 higáeri ôfuku-ken

one-man [wʌnˈmæn] *adj* (business) 1人だけの hitóri dake no, ワンマンの wañman no

one-man band *n* ワンマンバンド wañ-manbando

one-off [wʌnˈɔːf] (*BRIT*: *inf*) *n* 一つだけの物 hitótsù dake no mono

KEYWORD

oneself [wʌnselfˈ] *pron* (reflexive) 自分自身を jibúnjishìn wo; (after prep) 自分自身に jibúnjishìn ni; (alone: often after prep) 自分一人で jibún hitòri de; (emphatic) 自分で jibún dè

to hurt oneself けがする kegá surù

to keep something for oneself 自分のために...を取って置く jibún no tamè ni ...wò tôtte oku

to talk to oneself 独り言を言う hitóri-gotò wo iú

one-sided [wʌnˈsaidid] *adj* (argument) 一方的な ippôteki na

one-to-one [wʌnˈtəwʌn] *adj* (relationship) 一対一の ittáiichi no

one-upmanship [wʌnʌpˈmənʃip] *n* 自分の方が一枚上だと見せ付ける事 jibún no hō ga ichímai ué da to misétsukerù koto

one-way [wʌnˈwei] *adj* (street, traffic) 一方通行の ippôtsūkō no

ongoing [ɑːnˈɡouiŋ] *adj* (project, situation etc) 進行中の shiñkōchū no

onion [ʌn'jən] n タマネギ tamánegī

on-line [ɑːn'lain] adj (COMPUT) オンラインの oñraín no
♦adv (COMPUT) オンラインで oñraín de

onlooker [ɑːn'lukəːr] n 見物人 keñbutsunín

only [oun'liː] adv ...だけ ...dake
♦adj (sole, single) ただ一つ〔一人〕の tada hitótsù〔hitórī〕no
♦conj (but) しかし shikáshī
an only child 一人っ子 hitórikkò
not only ... but also ... ...ばかりでなく...も ...bakàri de naku ...mo

onset [ɑːn'set] n (beginning: of war, winter, illness) 始まり hajímari, 始め hajíme

onshore [ɑːn'ʃɔːr] adj (wind) 海からの umí kara no

onslaught [ɑːn'slɔːt] n 攻撃 kōgeki

onto [ɑːn'tuː] prep = **on to**

onus [ou'nəs] n 責任 sekínin

onward(s) [ɑːn'wəːrd(z)] adv (forward: move, progress) 先へ sakí e
from that time onward(s) それ以後 soré igo

onyx [ɑːn'iks] n オニキス oníkisu

ooze [uːz] vi (mud, water, slime) にじみでる nijímideru

opal [ou'pəl] n オパール opárù

opaque [oupeik'] adj (substance) 不透明な futómèi na

OPEC [ou'pek] n abbr (= Organization of Petroleum-Exporting Countries) 石油輸出国機構 sekíyu yushutsukoku kikō

open [ou'pən] adj (not shut: window, door, mouth etc) 開いた aíta; (: shop, museum etc) 営業中の eígyōchū no, 開いている aíte iru; (unobstructed: road) 開通している kaítsū shite iru; (: view) 開けた hiráketa; (not enclosed: land) 囲いのない kakói no nai; (fig: frank: person, manner, face) 率直な sótchoku na; (unrestricted: meeting, debate, championship) 公開の kōkai no
♦vt 開ける akéru, 開く hiráku
♦vi (flower, eyes, door, shop) 開く akú, 開く hiráku; (book, debate etc: commence) 始まる hajímaru

in the open (air) 野外に yagái ni
an open car オープンカー ōpunkā

opening [ou'pəniŋ] adj (commencing: speech, remarks etc) 開会の kaíkai no, 冒頭の bōtō no
♦n (gap, hole) 穴 aná; (start: of play, book etc) 始め hajíme, 冒頭 bōtō; (opportunity) 機会 kikái, チャンス chañsu

openly [ou'pənliː] adv (speak, act) 公然と kōzen to; (cry) 人目をはばからず hitóme wo habákarazu

open-minded [ou'pənmain'did] adj 偏見のない heñken no nai

open-necked [ou'pənnekt'] adj (shirt) 開きんの kaíkin no

open on to vt fus (subj: room, door) ...に面している ...ni mén shite iru

open-plan [ou'pənplæn'] adj 間仕切のない majíkiri no nai

open up vt (building, room: unlock) 開ける akéru; (blocked road) ...の障害物を取除く ...no shōgaìbutsu wo torínozokù
♦vi (COMM: shop, business) 開く akú

opera [ɑːp'rə] n 歌劇 kagèki, オペラ opèra

opera singer n オペラ歌手 opèrakashu

operate [ɑːp'əːreit] vt (machine) 操作する sōsà suru; (vehicle) 運転する uñten suru
♦vi (machine) 動く ugókù; (vehicle) 走る hashiru, 動く ugókù; (company, organization) 営業する eígyō suru
to operate on someone (for) (MED) ...に (...の) 手術をする ...ni (...no) shujútsu wo suru

operatic [ɑːpəræt'ik] adj 歌劇の kagèki no, オペラの opèra no

operating [ɑːp'əːreitiŋ] adj: **operating table** 手術台 shujútsudai
operating theater 手術室 shujútsushitsu

operation [ɑːpərei'ʃən] n (of machine etc) 操作 sōsà; (of vehicle) 運転 uñten; (MIL, COMM etc) 作戦 sakúsen; (MED) 手術 shujútsu
to be in operation (law, regulation) 実施されている jisshí sarete iru
to have an operation (MED) 手術を受

ける shujútsu wo ukérù

operational [ɑːpəreiʃ'ənəl] *adj* (working: machine, vehicle etc) 使用可能な shíyōkanō na

operative [ɑːp'ə:rətiv] *adj* (law, measure, system) 実施されている jisshí sarete iru

operator [ɑːp'ə:reitə:r] *n* (TEL) 交換手 kōkanshu, オペレーター opérētā; (of machine) 技師 gishí

ophthalmic [ɑːfθæl'mik] *adj* 眼科の ganka no

opinion [əpin'jən] *n* (point of view, belief) 意見 ikén
in my opinion 私の意見では watákushi no ikén de wa

opinionated [əpin'jəneitid] (*pej*) *adj* 独善的な dokúzenteki na

opinion poll *n* 世論調査 yorónchōsa

opium [ou'pi:əm] *n* あへん ahén

opponent [əpou'nənt] *n* (person not in favor) 反対者 hantaisha; (MIL) 敵 tekí; (SPORT) 相手 aíte

opportunism [ɑːpə:rtu:'nizəm] (*pej*) *n* 日和見主義 hiyórimishugí

opportunist [ɑːpə:rtu:'nist] (*pej*) *n* 日和見主義者 hiyórimishugishà

opportunity [ɑːpə:rtju:'niti:] *n* 機会 kíkái, チャンス chañsu
to take the opportunity of doing 折角の機会を利用して...する sekkáku no kikái wo riyō shite ...suru

oppose [əpouz'] *vt* (object to: wish, opinion, plan) ...に反対する ...ni hantai suru
to be opposed to something ...に反対である ...ni hantai de aru
as opposed to ...ではなくて ...de wa nakutè

opposing [əpouz'iŋ] *adj* (side, ideas) 反対の hantai no; (team) 相手の aíte no

opposite [ɑːp'əzit] *adj* (house) 向かい側の mukáigawa no; (end, direction, side) 反対の hantai no; (point of view, effect) 逆の gyakú no
♦*adv* (live, stand, work, sit) 向い側に〔で〕mukáigawa ni(de)
♦*prep* (in front of) ...の向い側に〔で〕...no ...awa ni(de)

♦*n*: *the opposite* (say, think, do etc) 反対 hantai
the opposite sex 異性 iséi

opposition [ɑːpəziʃ'ən] *n* (resistance) 反対 hantai; (those against) 反対勢力 hantaiseiryokù; (POL) 野党 yatō

oppress [əpres'] *vt* 抑圧する yokúatsu suru

oppression [əpreʃ'ən] *n* 抑圧 yokúatsu

oppressive [əpres'iv] *adj* (political regime) 抑圧的な yokúatsuteki na; (weather, heat) 蒸し暑い mushíatsuì

opt [ɑːpt] *vi*: *to opt for* ...を選ぶ ...wo erábù
to opt to do ...する事にする ...surú koto ni suru

optical [ɑːp'tikəl] *adj* (instrument, device etc) 光学の kōgaku no

optical illusion *n* 目の錯覚 mé no sakkáku

optician [ɑːptiʃ'ən] *n* 眼鏡屋 megáneya

optimism [ɑːp'təmizəm] *n* 楽観 rakkán, 楽天主義 rakútenshugì

optimist [ɑːp'təmist] *n* 楽天家 rakútenka

optimistic [ɑːptəmis'tik] *adj* 楽観的な rakkánteki na

optimum [ɑːp'təməm] *adj* (conditions, number, size) 最良の saíryō no, 最善の saízen no

option [ɑːp'ʃən] *n* (choice) 選択 seřitaku, オプション opúshon

optional [ɑːp'ʃənəl] *adj* (not obligatory) 自由選択の jiyūsentakuno

opt out *vi*: *to opt out of* ...から手を引く ...kara te wò hiku

opulent [ɑːp'jələnt] *adj* (very wealthy: person, society etc) 大金持の ōganèmochi no

or [ɔːr] *conj* (linking alternatives: up or down, in or out etc) それとも sorétomð, または matá wa; (otherwise) でないと de naî to, さもないと sa mð naì to; (with negative): *he hasn't seen or heard anything* 彼は何一つ見ても聞いてもいない karè wa nanî hitótsu mitè mo kiíte mo inai
or else (otherwise) でないと de naî to

oracle [ɔːˈrəkəl] n 予言者 yogénsha

oral [ɔːrəl] adj (spoken: test, report) 口頭の kótō no; (MED: vaccine, medicine) 経口の keíkō no
♦n (spoken examination) 口頭試問 kótō-shimon

orange [ɔːˈrindʒ] n (fruit) オレンジ orénji
♦adj (color) だいだい色の daídaiiro no, オレンジ色の orénjiiro no

orator [ɔːˈrətəːr] n 雄弁家 yúbenka

orbit [ɔːˈrbit] n (SPACE) 軌道 kidó
♦vt (circle: earth, moon etc) ...の周囲を軌道を描いて回る ...no shūí wo kidó wo egaite mawaru

orchard [ɔːˈrtʃəːrd] n 果樹園 kajúen

orchestra [ɔːˈrkistrə] n (MUS) 楽団 gakúdan, オーケストラ ókesùtora; (US: THEATER: seating) 舞台前の特等席 butáimae no tokútōseki

orchestrate [ɔːˈrkistreit] vt (stage-manage) 指揮する shikí suru

orchid [ɔːˈrkid] n ラン rań

ordain [ɔːrdein'] vt (REL) 聖職に任命する seíshoku ni niñmei suru

ordeal [ɔːrdiːl'] n 試練 shíren

order [ɔːˈrdəːr] n (command) 命令 meírei; (COMM: from shop, company etc: also in restaurant) 注文 chúmon; (sequence) 順序 juñjo; (good order) 秩序 chitsújò; (law and order) 治安 chiàn
♦vt (command) 命ずる mèizuru; (COMM: from shop, company etc: also in restaurant) 注文する chúmon suru; (also: put in order) 整理する seíri suru
in order (gen) 整理されて seíri sarete; (of document) 規定通りで kitéidōri de
in (working) order 整備されて seíbi sarete
in order to do/that ...するために ...surú tame ni
on order (COMM) 発注してあって hatchú shite atte
out of order (not in correct order) 順番が乱れて juñban ga midáretè; (not working) 故障して koshó shite
to order someone to do something ...に...する様に命令する ...ni ...suru yō ni meírei suru

order form n 注文用紙 chúmon yōshi

orderly [ɔːˈrdəːrli] n (MIL) 当番兵 tōbanhei; (MED) 雑役夫 zatsúekifu
♦adj (well-organized: room) 整とんされた seíton sarete; (: person, system etc) 規則正しい kisókutadashii

ordinary [ɔːˈrdəneːri] adj (everyday, usual) 普通の futsū no; (pej: mediocre) 平凡な heíbon na
out of the ordinary (exceptional) 変った kawátta

Ordnance Survey [ɔːrdˈnəns-] (BRIT) n 英国政府陸地測量局 eíkokuseifù rikúchi sokuryókyoku

ore [ɔːr] n 鉱石 kóseki

organ [ɔːˈrgən] n (ANAT: kidney, liver etc) 臓器 zóki; (MUS) オルガン orúgan

organic [ɔːrgænˈik] adj (food, farming etc) 有機の yúki no

organism [ɔːˈrgənizəm] n 有機体 yūkítai, 生物 seíbutsu

organist [ɔːˈrgənist] n オルガン奏者 orúgansōsha, オルガニスト orúganisuto

organization [ɔːrgənəzeiˈʃən] n (business, club, society) 組織 soshíki, 機構 kikó, オーガニゼーション óganizēshon

organize [ɔːˈrgənaiz] vt (arrange: activity, event) 企画する kikáku suru

organizer [ɔːˈrgənaizəːr] n (of conference, party etc) 主催者 shusáisha

orgasm [ɔːˈrgæzəm] n オルガズム orúgazumù

orgy [ɔːˈrdʒiː] n 乱交パーティ rańkōpati

Orient [ɔːrˈiːənt] n: *the Orient* 東洋 tóyō

oriental [ɔːriːenˈtəl] adj 東洋の tōyō no

orientate [ɔːrˈiːenteit] vt: *to orientate oneself* (in place) 自分の居場所を確認する jibún no ibásho wo kakúnin suru; (in situation) 環境になれる kañkyō ni naréru

origin [ɔːrˈidʒin] n (beginning, source) 起源 kígen; (of person) 生れ umare

original [əridʒˈənəl] adj (first: idea, occupation) 最初の saísho no; (genuine: work of art, document etc) 本物の hoñmono no; (fig: imaginative: thinker, writer, artist) 独創的な dokúsōteki na

♦*n* (genuine work of art, document) 本物 honmono

originality [ərɪdʒənæl'iti:] *n* (imagination: of artist, writer etc) 独創性 dokúsōsei

originally [ərɪdʒ'ənəli:] *adv* (at first) 最初は saísho wa, 当初 tōsho

originate [ərɪdʒ'əneit] *vi*: *to originate from* (person, idea, custom etc) ...から始まる ...kará hajímaru

to originate in ...で始まる ...dè hajímaru

Orkneys [ɔːrk'niːz] *npl*: *the Orkneys* (*also*: **the Orkney Islands**) オークニー諸島 ōkùnīshotō

ornament [ɔːr'nəmənt] *n* (*gen*) 飾りかざり kazári, 装飾 sōshoku; (to be worn) 装身具 sōshingu

ornamental [ɔːrnəmen'təl] *adj* (decorative: garden, pond) 装飾的な sōshokuteki na

ornate [ɔːrneit'] *adj* (highly decorative: design, style) 凝った kottà

ornithology [ɔːrnəθɑːl'ədʒiː] *n* 鳥類学 chōruigaku

orphan [ɔːr'fən] *n* 孤児 kojì

orphanage [ɔːr'fənɪdʒ] *n* 孤児院 kojìin

orthodox [ɔːr'θədɑːks] *adj* (REL: *also fig*) 正統派の seítōha no

orthodoxy [ɔːr'θədɑːksiː] *n* (traditional beliefs) 正統思想 seítōshisō

orthopedic [ɔːrθəpiː'dik] (*BRIT* **orthopaedic**) *adj* 整形外科の seíkeigeka no

oscillate [ɑːs'əleit] *vi* (ELEC) 発振する hasshín suru; (PHYSICS) 振動する shiñdō suru; (*fig*: mood, person, ideas) 頻繁に変る hiñpan ni kawáru

ostensibly [ɑːsten'səbliː] *adv* 表面上 hyómeñjō

ostentatious [ɑːstentei'ʃəs] *adj* (showy: building, car etc) 派手な hadé na; (: person) 万事に派手な bañji ni hadé na

osteopath [ɑːs'tiːəpæθ] *n* 整骨療法医 seíkotsuryōhōī

ostracize [ɑːs'trəsaiz] *vt* のけ者にする nokémono ni suru

ostrich [ɔːs'tritʃ] *n* ダチョウ dachō

other [ʌð'əːr] *adj* (that which has not been mentioned: person, thing) 外の hoká no; (second of 2 things) もう一つの mō hitotsu no

♦*pron*: *the other (one)* 外の物 hoká no mono

♦*adv*: *other than* ...を除いて ...wo nozóite

others (other people) 他人 tanín

the other day (recently) 先日 señjitsu, この間 konó aida

otherwise [ʌð'əːrwaiz] *adv* (in a different way) 違ったやり方で chígatta yarikata dè; (apart from that) それを除けば soré wo nozókeba

♦*conj* (if not) そうでないと sō dè nai to

otter [ɑːt'əːr] *n* カワウソ kawáuso

ouch [autʃ] *excl* 痛い itáĩ

ought [ɔːt] (*pt* ought) *aux vb*: *she ought to do it* 彼女はそれをやるべきです kanòjo wa soré wo yarubeki desu

this ought to have been corrected これは直すべきだった koré wa naósubeki datta

he ought to win (probability) 彼は勝つはずです karè wa katsù hazu desu

ounce [auns] *n* (unit of weight) オンス oñsu

our [au'əːr] *adj* 私たちの watákushitachi no ¶ *see also* **my**

ours [au'əːrz] *pron* 私たちの物 watákushitachi no mono ¶ *see also* **mine**

ourselves [auəːrselvz'] *pron* 私たち自身 watákushitachi jishìn ¶ *see also* **oneself**

oust [aust] *vt* (forcibly remove: government, MP etc) 追放する tsuíhō suru

---

KEYWORD

---

out [aut] *adv* 1 (not in) 外に〔で、へ〕sótð ni(de, e)

they're out in the garden 彼らは庭にいます kárèra wa niwá ni imasù

(to stand) out in the rain/snow 雨〔雪〕の降る中に立っている áme(yukí)no fúrù nákà ni tátte irù

it's cold out here/out in the desert 外〔砂漠〕は寒い sótð(sabáku)wa samúî

out here/there ここ〔あそこ〕だ-外の方に kokó(asóko)dà - sótð no hõ nî *to go/come etc out* 出て行く〔来る〕déte iku(kuru)

(to speak) out loud 大きな声で言う ōkina koè de iú

2 (not at home, absent) 不在で fuzái de, 留守で rúsù de

Mr Green is out at the moment グリーンさんはただ今留守ですが gurīn san wa tadáìma rúsù desu ga

to have a day/night out 1日〔1晩〕外出して遊ぶ ichínichi(hitóbàn)gaíshutsu shitè asóbù

3 (indicating distance): *the boat was 10 km out* 船は10キロ沖にあった fúnè wa jukkírò okí ni attà

3 days out from Plymouth プリマスを出発して3日の所 purímàsu wo shukkó shitè mikká no tokorò

4 (SPORT) アウトで áùto de

the ball is/has gone out ボールはアウトだ〔出た〕bōru wa áùto da(détà)

out! (TENNIS etc) アウト áùto

♦*adj* **1**: *to be out* (person: unconscious) 気絶〔失神〕している kizétsu(shisshín) shite irù; (: SPORT) アウトである áùto de árù; (out of fashion: style) 流行遅れである ryūkōokùre de árù, 廃れている sutárete irù; (: singer) 人気がなくなった niñki gà nakúnattà

2 (have appeared: flowers): *to be out* 咲いている saíte irù; (: news) 報道されている hōdō sarete irù; (: secret) ばれた báretà, 発覚した hakkáku shità

3 (extinguished: fire, light, gas) 消えた kiétà

before the week was out (finished) その週が終わらない内に sonó shū ga owáranai uchi nì

4: *to be out to do something* (intend) ...しようとしている ...shiyó tò shité irù

to be out in one's calculations (wrong) 計算が間違っている keísan gà machígatte irù

---

out-and-out [aut'əndaut'] *adj* (liar, thief etc) 全くの mattáku no, 根っからの nekkára no

outback [aut'bæk] *n* (in Australia) 奥地 okùchi

outboard [aut'bɔːrd] *adj*: *outboard motor* アウトボードエンジン aùtobōdoenjin

outbreak [aut'breik] *n* (of war, disease, violence etc) ぼっ発 boppátsu

outburst [aut'bəːrst] *n* (sudden expression of anger etc) 爆発 bakúhatsu

outcast [aut'kæst] *n* のけ者 nokémono

outcome [aut'kʌm] *n* (result) 結果 kekká

outcrop [aut'krɑːp] *n* (of rock) 露頭 rotó

outcry [aut'krai] *n* 反発 hañpatsu

outdated [autdei'tid] *adj* (old-fashioned) 時代遅れの jidáiokùre no

outdo [autdu:'] (*pt* **outdid** *pp* **outdone**) *vt* しのぐ shinógu

outdoor [aut'dɔːr] *adj* (open-air: activities, games etc) 野外の yagái no, 屋外の okúgai no; (clothes) 野外用の yagáiyō no

outdoors [autdɔːrz'] *adv* (play, stay, sleep: in the open air) 野外に〔で〕yagái ni(de)

outer [aut'əːr] *adj* (exterior: door, wrapping, wall etc) 外側の sotógawa no

outer space *n* 宇宙空間 uchūkūkan

outfit [aut'fit] *n* (set of clothes) 衣装 i-shō

outgoing [aut'gouiŋ] *adj* (extrovert) 外向性の gaíkōsei no; (retiring: president, mayor etc) 退陣する taíjin suru

outgoings [aut'gouiŋz] (*BRIT*) *npl* 出費 shuppí

outgrow [autgrou'] (*pt* **outgrew** *pp* **outgrown**) *vt* (one's clothes) 大きくなって...が着られなくなる ōkiku natte ...ga kirárenaku naru

outhouse [aut'haus] *n* 納屋 nayà; (*US*) 屋外便所 okùgaibenjo

outing [aut'iŋ] *n* (excursion: family outing, school outing) 遠足 eñsoku

outlandish [autlæn'diʃ] *adj* (strange: looks, behavior, clothes) 奇妙な kimyó na

outlaw [aut'lɔː] *n* 無法者 muhómono

♦*vt* (person, activity, organization) 禁止する kiñshi suru

outlay [aut'lei] *n* (expenditure) 出費 shuppí

shuppí

outlet [aut'let] *n* (hole, pipe) 排水口 haísuíkō; (*US*: ELEC) コンセント koñseñto; (COMM: *also*: retail outlet) 販売店 hañbaíten

outline [aut'lain] *n* (shape: of object, person etc) 輪郭 rińkaku, アウトライン aútoraìn; (brief explanation: of plan) あらまし arámashi, アウトライン aútoraìn; (rough sketch) 略図 ryakúzu

♦*vt* (*fig*: theory, plan etc) ...のあらましを説明する ...no arámashi wo setsúmei suru

outlive [autliv'] *vt* (survive: person) ...より長生きする ...yórí naga-ikí suru; (: war, era) 生き延びる ikínobiru

outlook [aut'luk] *n* (view, attitude) 見方 mikáta; (: for future) 見通し mitóshi; (: for weather) 予報 yohṓ

outlying [aut'laiiŋ] *adj* (away from main cities: area, town etc) 中心部を離れた chúshinbu wo hanáreta

outmoded [autmou'did] *adj* (oldfashioned: custom, theory) 時代遅れの jidáiokùre no

outnumber [autnʌm'bə:r] *vt* ...より多い ...yórí ōi

───────────
| KEYWORD |
───────────

out of *prep* 1 (outside, beyond) ...の外へ〔に, で〕...no sótò e(ni, de)

to go out of the house 家から外へ出る ié karà sótò e dérù

to look out of the window 窓から外を見る mádò kara sótò wo mírù

to be out of danger (safe) 危険がなくなった kikén gà nakúnattà

2 (cause, motive) ...に駆られて ...ni karáretè

out of curiosity/fear/greed 好奇心〔恐怖, どん欲〕に駆られて kṓkishìn〔kyṓfu, dóñ-yoku〕ni karáretè

3 (origin) ...から ...kara

to drink something out of a cup コップから...を飲む káppù kara ...wo nomù

to copy something out of a book 本から...を写す hóñ kara ...wò utsúsù

4 (from among) ...の中から ...no nákà

kara, ...の内 ...no uchí

1 out of every 3 smokers 喫煙者3人に1人 kitsúeñsha safinin nì hitórì

out of 100 cars sold, only one had any faults 売れた100台の車の内, 1台だけに欠陥があった uréta hyakúdài no kurúma no uchi, íchìdai dake ni kekkán ga atta

5 (without) ...が切れて ...ga kírète, ...がなくなって ...ga nakúnattè

to be out of milk/sugar/gas (US)/petrol (BRIT) etc ミルク〔砂糖, ガソリン〕が切れている mírùku(satṓ, gasórin〕ga kírète iru

out-of-date [autəvdeit'] *adj* (passport) 期限の切れた kigén no kiréta; (clothes etc) 時代遅れの jidáiokùre no

out-of-the-way [autəvðəwei'] *adj* (place) へんぴな heñpi na

outpatient [aut'peiʃənt] *n* (MED) 外来患者 gaíraikanja

outpost [aut'poust] *n* (MIL, COMM) 前しょう zeñshō; (COMM) 前進基地 zeñshinkichi

output [aut'put] *n* (production: of factory, mine etc) 生産高 seísañdaka; (: of writer) 作品数 sakúhinsū; (COMPUT) 出力 shutsúryoku, アウトプット aútoputto

outrage [aut'reidʒ] *n* (action: scandalous) 不法行為 fuhṓkōī; (: violent) 暴力行為 bṓryokukōī; (anger) 激怒 gekído

♦*vt* (shock, anger) 激怒させる gekído saseru

outrageous [autrei'dʒəs] *adj* 非難すべき hinánsubeki

outright [*adv* autrait' *adj* aut'rait] *adv* (absolutely: win) 圧倒的に attṓteki ni; (at once: kill) 即座に sokúza ni; (openly: ask, deny, refuse) はっきりと hakkíri to

♦*adj* (absolute: winner, victory) 圧倒的な attṓteki na; (open: refusal, denial, hostility) 明白な meñhaku na

outset [aut'set] *n* (start) 始め hajíme

outside [aut'said'] *n* (exterior: of container, building) 外側 sotōgawa

♦*adj* (exterior) 外側の sotōgawa no

♦*adv* (away from the inside: to be, go,

wait) 外に〔で〕sotò ni(de)
◆*prep* (not inside) ...の外に〔で〕...no sotò ni(de); (not included in) ...の外に ...no hoká ni; (beyond) ...を越えて ...wo koétè
at the outside (*fig*) せいぜい seízei

outside lane *n* (AUT) 追越し車線 oíkoshishasen

outside line *n* (TEL) 外線 gaísen

outsider [autsai'dər] *n* (stranger) 部外者 bugàisha

outside-left/-right [aut'saidleft'/rait] *n* (SOCCER) レフト〔ライト〕ウイング refùto〔raìto〕uíngu

outsize [aut'saiz] *adj* (clothes) キングサイズの kíngusaìzu no

outskirts [aut'skə:rts] *npl* (of city, town) 外れ hazúre

outspoken [aut'spou'kən] *adj* (statement, opponent, reply) 遠慮のない efiryo no nai

outstanding [autstæn'diŋ] *adj* (exceptional) 並外れた namíhazureta, 優れた sugúretà; (remaining: debt, work etc) 残っている nókottè iru

outstay [autstei'] *vt*: *to outstay one's welcome* 長居して嫌われる nagái shite kiráwareru

outstretched [autstretʃt'] *adj* (hand) 伸ばした nobáshìta; (arms) 広げた hirógetà

outstrip [autstrip'] *vt* (competitors, demand) 追抜く oínuku

out-tray [aut'trei] *n* 送信のトレー sóshin no torè

outward [aut'wə:rd] *adj* (sign, appearances) 外部の gaíbu no; (journey) 行きの ikí no

outwardly [aut'wə:rdli:] *adv* 外部的に gaíbuteki ni

outweigh [autwei'] *vt* ...より重要である ...yorí jùyô de aru

outwit [autwit'] *vt* ...の裏をかく ...no urá wo kaku

oval [ou'vəl] *adj* (table, mirror, face) だ円形の daénkei no
◆*n* だ円形 daénkei

ovary [ou'və:ri:] *n* 卵巣 ransô

ovation [ouvei'ʃən] *n* 大喝さい daíkassai

oven [ʌv'ən] *n* (CULIN) 天火 teñpi, オーブン ōbùn; (TECH) 炉 ro

ovenproof [ʌv'ənpru:f] *adj* (dish etc) オーブン用の ōbùn yō no

KEYWORD

over [ou'və:r] *adv* 1 (across: walk, jump, fly etc) ...を越えて ...wò koétè
to cross over to the other side of the road 道路を横断する dòro wo ōdan suru
over here/there ここ〔あそこ〕に〔で〕kokò(asòko) nì(dè)
to ask someone over (to one's house) ...を家に招く ...wò iè nì manékù

2 (indicating movement from upright: fall, knock, turn, bend etc) 下へ shitá è, 地面へ jímèn e

3 (excessively: clever, rich, fat etc) 余り amári, 過度に kádò ni
she's not over intelligent, is she? 彼女はあまり頭が良くないね kánòjo wa amári atáma gà yőkùnai né

4 (remaining: money, food etc) 余って amáttè, 残って nokóttè
there are 3 over 3個が残っている sáñko ga nokótte irù
is there any cake (left) over? ケーキが残っていませんか kěki ga nokótte imaseñ ká

5: *all over* (everywhere) 至る所に〔で〕itárù tokoro ni(de), どこもかしこも dókò mo káshikò mo
over and over (again) (repeatedly) 何度〔何回, 何返〕も náñdo〔náñkai, náñben〕mo
◆*adj* (finished): *to be over* (game, life, relationship etc) 終りである owári de arù
◆*prep* 1 (on top of) ...の上に〔で〕...no uè nì(de); (above) ...の上方に〔で〕...no jôhō nì(de)
to spread a sheet over something ...の上にシーツを掛ける ...no uè nì shìtsu wo kakérù
there's a canopy over the bed ベッドの上に天がいがある béddò no uè nì teñgai ga arù

2 (on the other side of) ...の向こう側に

〔で〕...no mukṓgawa nǐ〔dè〕
the pub over the road 道路の向こう側
にあるパブ dṓro no mukṓgawa ni arù
pábù
he jumped over the wall 彼は塀を飛
越えた kárè wa heí wò tobíkoèta
3 (more than) 以上 ijō
over 200 people came 200人以上の人
が来ました nihyákunìn íjṓ no hitṓ gà
kimáshità
over and above ...の外に ...no hṓkà ni,
...に加えて ...ni kuwáetè
*this order is over and above what
we have already ordered* この注文は
これまでの注文への追加です konṓ chū-
mon wa koré madè no chūṃòn e no
tsuíka desù
4 (during) ...の間 ...no aída
over the last few years 過去数年の間
kákò sūnèn no aída
over the winter 冬の間 fuyú nò aída
let's discuss it over dinner 夕食をし
ながら話し合いましょう yūshoku wò
shinágàra hanáshiaimashṓ

---

overall [*adj, n* ou'vǝ:rɔ:l *adv* ouvǝ:rɔ:l']
adj (length, cost etc) 全体の zeítai no;
(general: study, survey) 全面的な zeímen-
teki na
♦*adv* (view, survey etc) 全面的に zeímen-
teki ni; (measure, paint) 全体に zeítai ni
♦*n* (BRIT: woman's, child's, painter's)
上っ張り uwáppari

overalls [ou'vǝ:rɔ:lz] *npl* オーバーオール
ōbāōrù

overawe [ouvǝ:rɔ:'] *vt* 威圧する iátsu suru

overbalance [ouvǝ:rbæl'ǝns] *vi* バラン
スを失う baránsu wo ushínau

overbearing [ouvǝ:rber'riŋ] *adj* (person,
behavior, manner) 横暴な ōbō na

overboard [ou'vǝ:rbɔ:rd] *adv* (NAUT):
to fall overboard 船から水に落ちる fu-
nè kara mizú ni ochírù

overbook [ou'vǝ:rbuk] *vt* 予約を取り過
ぎる yoyáku wo torísugiru

overcast [ou'vǝ:rkæst] *adj* (day, sky) 曇
った kumóttà

overcharge [ou'vǝ:rtʃɑ:rdʒ] *vt* ...に不当
な金額を請求する ...ni futṓ na kíngaku
wo seíkyū suru

overcoat [ou'vǝ:rkout] *n* オーバーコー
ト ōbākōto, オーバー ōbā

overcome [ouvǝ:rkʌm'] (*pt* **overcame** *pp*
overcome) *vt* (defeat: opponent, enemy)
...に勝つ ...ni katsù; (*fig*: difficulty, problem) 克服する kokúfuku suru

overcrowded [ouvǝ:rkrau'did] *adj*
(room, prison) 超満員の chōman-in no;
(city) 過密な kamítsu na

overdo [ouvǝ:rdu:'] (*pt* **overdid** *pp* **over-
done**) *vt* (exaggerate: concern, interest)
誇張する kochō suru; (overcook) 焼き過
ぎる yakísugiru
to overdo it (work etc) やり過ぎる yarí-
sugirù

overdose [ou'vǝ:rdous] *n* (MED: dangerous dose) 危険量 kikénryō; (: fatal dose)
致死量 chíshìryō

overdraft [ou'vǝ:rdræft] *n* 当座借越 tṓ-
zakarikoshi

overdrawn [ouvǝ:rdrɔ:n'] *adj* (account)
借越した karíkoshi shita

overdue [ouvǝ:rdu:'] *adj* (late: person,
bus, train) 遅れている okúrete iru;
(change, reform) 待望の taíbō no

overestimate [ouvǝ:res'tǝmeit] *vt* (cost,
importance, time) 高く見積りすぎる ta-
kàku mitsúmorisugirù; (person's ability,
skill etc) 買いかぶる kaíkaburu

overexcited [ouvǝ:riksai'tid] *adj* 過度に
興奮した kadò ni kṓfun shita

overflow [*vb* ouvǝ:rflou' *n* ou'vǝ:rflou]
vi (river) はん濫する hañran suru; (sink,
vase etc) あふれる afúreru
♦*n* (also: **overflow pipe**) 放出パイプ hṓ-
shutsupaipu

overgrown [ouvǝ:rgroun'] *adj* (garden)
草がぼうぼうと生えた kusa ga bṓbō to
haèta

overhaul [*vb* ouvǝ:rhɔ:l' *n* ou'vǝ:rhɔ:l]
vt (engine, equipment etc) 分解検査する
buñkaikensa suru, オーバーホールする
ōbāhōru suru
♦*n* オーバーホール ōbāhōru

overhead [*adv* ouvǝ:rhed' *adj, n*

ou'və:rhed] *adv* (above) 頭上に〔で〕zujṓ ni〔de〕; (in the sky) 上空に〔で〕jōkū ni〔de〕

♦*adj* (lighting) 上からの ué kara no; (cables, railway) 高架の kōkā no

♦*n* (*US*) = **overheads**

overheads [ou'və:rhedz] *npl* (expenses) 経費 keíhi

overhear [ouvə:rhiə:r'] *(pt, pp* **overheard)** *vt* 耳にする mimí ni suru

overheat [ouvə:rhi:t'] *vi* (engine) 過熱する kanétsu suru, オーバーヒートする ōbāhīto suru

overjoyed [ouvə:rdʒɔic'] *adj* 大喜びした óyŏrokobi shita

overkill [ou'və:rkil] *n* やり過ぎ yarísugi

overland [ou'və:rlænd] *adj* (journey) 陸路の rikúro no

♦*adv* (travel) 陸路で rikúro de

overlap [ouvə:rlæp'] *vi* (edges) 部分的に重なる bubúnteki ni kasánaru, オーバーラップする ōbārappu suru; (*fig*: ideas, activities etc) 部分的に重複する bubúnteki ni chófuku suru, オーバーラップする ōbārappu suru

overleaf [ou'və:rli:f] *adv* ページの裏に péji no urá ni

overload [ou'və:rloud] *vt* (vehicle) ...に積み過ぎる ...ni tsumísugiru; (ELEC) ...に負荷を掛け過ぎる ...ni fuká wo kakésugiru; (*fig*: with work, problems etc) ...に負担を掛け過ぎる ...ni fután wo kakésugiru

overlook [ou'və:rluk] *vt* (have view over) 見下ろす miórosu; (miss: by mistake) 見落す miótosu; (excuse, forgive) 見逃す minógasu

overnight [*adv* ouvə:rnait' *adj* ou'və:rnait] *adv* (during the whole night) 一晩中 hitóbānjū; (*fig*: suddenly) いつの間にか itsú no ma ni ka

♦*adj* (bag, clothes) 1泊用の ippákuyō no

to **stay overnight** 一泊する ippáku suru

overpass [ou'və:rpæs] *n* 陸橋 ríkkyō

overpower [ouvə:rpau'ə:r] *vt* (person) 腕力で抑え込む waṅryoku de osáekomù; (subj: emotion, anger etc) 圧倒する attṓ

suru

overpowering [ouvə:rpau'ə:riŋ] *adj* (heat, stench) 圧倒する様な attṓ suru yṓ na

overrate [ouvə:rreit'] *vt* (person, film, book) 高く評価し過ぎる takáku hyŏka shisúgiru

override [ouvə:raid'] *(pt* **overrode** *pp* **overridden)** *vt* (order) 無効にする mukṓ ni suru; (objection) 無視する mushí suru

overriding [ouvə:raid'iŋ] *adj* (importance) 最大の saídai no; (factor, consideration) 優先的な yūsénteki na

overrule [ouvə:ru:l'] *vt* (decision, claim, person) 無効にする mukṓ ni suru; (person) ...の提案を退ける ...no teían wo shirízokerù

overrun [ou'və:rʌn] *(pt* **overran** *pp* **overrun)** *vt* (country) 侵略する shiṅryaku suru; (time limit) 越える koéru

overseas [*adv* ouvə:rsi:z' *adj* ou'və:rsi:z] *adv* (live, travel, work: abroad) 海外に〔で〕kaígai ni〔de〕

♦*adj* (market, trade) 海外の kaígai no; (student, visitor) 外国人の gaíkokujīn no

overshadow [ouvə:rʃæd'ou] *vt* (throw shadow over: place, building etc) ...の上にそびえる ...no ué ni sobíerù; (*fig*) ...の影を薄くさせる ...no kagé wo usúku saseru

overshoot [ouvə:rʃu:t'] *(pt, pp* **overshot)** *vt* (subj: plane, train, car etc) ...に止らずに行き過ぎる ...ni tomárazu ni ikísugirù

oversight [ou'və:rsait] *n* 手落ち teóchi

oversleep [ouvə:rsli:p'] *(pt, pp* **overslept)** *vi* 寝過ごす nesúgòsu, 寝坊する nebṓ suru

overstate [ouvə:rsteit'] *vt* (exaggerate: case, problem, importance) 誇張する kochṓ suru

overstep [ouvə:rstep'] *vt*: *to* **overstep** *the* **mark** (go too far) 行き過ぎをやる ikísugi wo yaru

overt [ouvə:rt'] *adj* あからさまな akárasama na

overtake [ouvə:rteik'] *(pt* **overtook** *pp* **overtaken)** *vt* (AUT) 追越す oíkosu

overthrow [ouvə:rθrou'] *vt* (government, leader) 倒す taósù

overtime [ou'və:rtaim] *n* 残業 zańgyō

overtone [ou'və:rtoun] *n* (*fig*) 含 み fukúmì

overture [ou'və:rtʃə:r] *n* (MUS) 序曲 jokyőku; (*fig*) 申出 mőshide

overturn [ouvə:rtə:rn'] *vt* (car, chair) 引っ繰り返す hikkúrikaèsu; (*fig*: decision, plan, ruling) 翻す hirúgaèsu; (: government, system) 倒す taósù

♦*vi* (car, train, boat etc) 転覆する teńpuku suru

overweight [ouvə:rweit'] *adj* (person) 太り過ぎの futórìsugi no

overwhelm [ouvə:rwelm'] *vt* 圧倒する attő suru

overwhelming [ouvə:rwel'miŋ] *adj* (victory, heat, feeling) 圧倒的な attőteki na

overwork [ouvə:rwə:rk'] *n* 働き過ぎ határakisugì, 過労 karő

overwrought [ou'vərɔ:t'] *adj* 神経が高ぶった shińkei ga tákabuttà

owe [ou] *vt*: **to owe someone something, to owe something to someone** (money) ...に...を借りている ...ni ...wo karíte iru, ...に...を払う義務がある ...ni ...wo haráù gìmu ga aru; (*fig*: gratitude, respect, loyalty) ...に...しなければならない ...ni ...shinákereba naranaì; (: life, talent, good looks etc) ...は...のおかげである ...wa ...no o-kagé de aru

owing to [ou'iŋ tu:] *prep* (because of) ...のために ...no tamé nì

owl [aul] *n* フクロウ fukúrō, ミミズク mimízuku

own [oun] *vt* (possess: house, land, car etc) 所有する shoyú suru, 保有する hoyú suru

♦*adj* (house, work, style etc) 自分の jibún no, 自分自身の jubúnjishin no

a room of my own 自分の部屋 jibún no heyá

to get one's own back (take revenge) 復しゅうする fukushū suru

on one's own (alone) 自分で jibun de, 自分の力で jibún no chikára de

owner [ou'nə:r] *n* (*gen*) 所有者 shoyúsha, 持主 mőchìnushi, オーナー ōnà; (of shop)

主人 shujìn, 経営者 kéieìsha; (of pet) 飼主 kaínushi

ownership [ou'nə:rʃip] *n* (possession) 所有 shoyú

own up *vi* (admit: guilt, error) ...を認める ...wo mitőmeru

ox [ɑ:ks] (*pl* **oxen**) *n* ウシ ushí ◇通常去勢した牡ウシを指す tsūjő kyoséi shita oùshi wo sasu

oxtail [ɑ:ks'teil] *n*: **oxtail soup** オックステールスープ okkùsutērusūpu

oxygen [ɑ:k'sidʒən] *n* 酸素 sańso

oxygen mask/tent *n* 酸素マスク〔テント〕sańsomasuku(tento)

oyster [ɔis'tə:r] *n* カキ kaki

oz. *abbr* = **ounce(s)**

ozone [ou'zoun] *n* オゾン ozòn

ozone layer *n* オゾン層 ozòńsō

P

p [pi:] *abbr* = **penny; pence**

P.A. [pi:ei'] *n abbr* = **personal assistant; public address system**

p.a. *abbr* = **per annum**

pa [pɑ:] (*inf*) *n* 父ちゃん tőchan, パパ pápà

pace [peis] *n* (step) 1歩 íppồ; (distance) 歩幅 hohába; (speed) 早さ háyàsa, 速度 sőkùdo, ペース pḗsu

♦*vi*: **to pace up and down** (walk around angrily or impatiently) うろうろする úròuro suru

to keep pace with (person) ...と足並をそろえる ...to ashínami wò soròerù

pacemaker [peis'meikə:r] *n* (MED) ペースメーカー pḗsumèkà; (SPORT: *also*: **pacesetter**) ペースメーカー pḗsumèkà

Pacific [pəsif'ik] *n*: **the Pacific (Ocean)** 太平洋 taíheìyō

pacifist [pæs'əfist] *n* 平和主義者 heíwashugishà

pacify [pæs'əfai] *vt* (soothe: person) なだめる nadámerù; (: fears) 鎮める shizúmerù

pack [pæk] *n* (packet) 包み tsutsúmi; (*US*: of cigarettes) 1箱 hitóhàko; (group:

of hounds) 群れ muré; (: of people) グループ gúrūpu; (back pack) リュックサック ryukkúsakkù; (of cards) 1組 hitókùmi

♦*vt* (fill: box, container, suitcase etc) ...に詰込む ...ni tsumékomù; (cram: people, objects) ...をに詰込む ...wo ...ni tsumékomù

to pack (one's bags) 荷造りをする nizúkùri wo suru

to pack someone off ...を追出す ...wo oídasù

pack it in! (*inf*: stop it!) やめなさい! yaménasaì!

package [pæk'idʒ] *n* (parcel) 小包 kozútsumi; (*also*: **package deal**) 一括取引 ikkátsutorihìki

package holiday *n* = **package tour**

package tour *n* パッケージツアー pakkéjitsuā, パックツアー pakkútsuā

packed lunch [pækt-] *n* 弁当 bentō

packet [pæk'it] *n* (box) 1箱 hitóhàko; (bag) 1袋 hitófùkuro

packing [pæk'iŋ] *n* (act) 詰込む事 tsumékomù kotó; (external: paper, plastic etc) 包装 hōsō

packing case *n* 木箱 kíbàko

pact [pækt] *n* 協定 kyōtei

pad [pæd] *n* (block of paper) 一つづり hitótsùzuri; (to prevent friction, damage) こん包材 koñpōzài; (in shoulders of dress, jacket etc) パッド páddò; (*inf*: home) 住い súmài

♦*vt* (SEWING: cushion, soft toy etc) ...に詰物をする ...ni tsumémòno wo suru

padding [pæd'iŋ] *n* (material) 詰物 tsumémòno

paddle [pæd'əl] *n* (oar) かい kái, パドル páddoru; (*US*: for table tennis) ラケット rakéttò

♦*vt* (boat, canoe etc) こぐ kógù

♦*vi* (with feet) 水の中を歩く mizú no nakà wo arúkù

paddle steamer *n* (on river) 外輪船 gaírinsen

paddling pool [pæd'liŋ-] (*BRIT*) *n* (children's) 子供用プール kodómoyō pūru

paddock [pæd'ək] *n* (for horse: small field) 放牧場 hōbokujō; (: at race course)

パドック pádòkku

paddy field [pæd'i:-] *n* 水田 suíden, 田んぼ tañbo

padlock [pæd'lɑːk] *n* (on door, bicycle etc) 錠 (前) jō(mae)

paediatrics [piːdiːæt'riks] (*BRIT*) *n* = **pediatrics**

pagan [pei'gən] *adj* (gods, festival, worship) 異教の ikyō no ◇キリスト教, ユダヤ教, イスラム教以外の宗教をさげすんで言う語 kirísutokyō, yudáyakyō, isúramukyō igài no shūkyō wo sagésuñde iú go

♦*n* (worshipper of pagan gods) 異教徒 ikyōto

page [peidʒ] *n* (of book, magazine, newspaper) ページ pēji; (*also*: **page boy**) 花嫁付添いの少年 hanáyòmetsukisoi no shōnen

♦*vt* (in hotel etc) ボーイ bōi

pageant [pædʒ'ənt] *n* (historical procession, show) ページェント pèjento

pageantry [pædʒ'əntri:] *n* 見世物 misémono

paid [peid] *pt, pp* of **pay**

♦*adj* (work) 有料の yūryō no; (staff, official) 有給の yūkyū no; (gunman, killer) 雇われた yatówareta

a paid holiday 有給休暇 yūkyūkyūka

to put paid to (*BRIT*: end, destroy) ...を台無しにする ...wo daínashi ni surù

pail [peil] *n* (for milk, water etc) バケツ bakétsu

pain [pein] *n* (unpleasant physical sensation) 痛み itámi, 苦痛 kutsū; (*fig*: unhappiness) 苦しみ kurúshimi, 心痛 shiñtsū

to be in pain (person, animal) 苦痛を感じている kutsū wo kañjite irù, 苦しんでいる kurúshinde irù

to take pains to do something (make an effort) 苦心して...する kushín shite ...surù

pained [peind] *adj* (expression) 怒った okóttà

painful [pein'fəl] *adj* (back, wound, fracture etc) 痛い itái, 痛む itámù; (upsetting, unpleasant: sight etc) 痛々しい itáitashii; (memory) 不快な fukái na; (decision) 苦しい kurúshiĩ; (laborious: task, progress etc) 骨の折れる honé no orerù

painfully [pein'fəli:] adv (fig: very) 痛い程 itáihodo

painkiller [pein'kilər] n (aspirin, paracetamol etc) 鎮痛剤 chíntsūzai

painless [pein'lis] adj (operation, childbirth) 無痛の mutsū no

painstaking [peinz'teikiŋ] adj (work) 骨折れの honéore no; (person) 勤勉な kínben na

paint [peint] n (decorator's: for walls, doors etc) 塗料 toryō, ペンキ peñki, ペイント peínto; (artist's: oil paint, watercolor paint etc) 絵の具 e nő gu

♦vt (wall, door, house etc) ...にペンキを塗る ...ni peñki wo nurù; (picture, portrait) 描く kákù

to paint the door blue ドアに水色のペンキを塗る dóa ni mizúiro nò peñki wò núrù

paintbrush [peint'brʌʃ] n (decorator's) 刷毛 haké, ブラシ búrashi; (artist's) 絵筆 éfùde

painter [pein'tər] n (artist) 画家 gaká; (decorator) ペンキ屋 peñkiya

painting [pein'tiŋ] n (activity: decorating) ペンキ塗り peñkinùri; (: art) 絵描き ekáki; (picture) 絵画 kái ga

an oil painting 油絵 abúraè

paintwork [peint'wərk] n (painted parts) 塗装の部分 tosō no bubùn

pair [pe:r] n (of shoes, gloves etc) 対 tsuí

a pair of scissors はさみ hasámi

a pair of trousers ズボン zubóñ

pajamas [pədʒɑ:m'əz] (US) npl パジャマ pájàma

Pakistan [pæk'istæn] n パキスタン pakísùtan

Pakistani [pæk'əstæn'i:] adj パキスタンの pakísùtan no

♦n パキスタン人 pakísutanjìn

pal [pæl] (inf) n (friend) 友達 tomódachi

palace [pæl'is] n (residence: of monarch) 宮殿 kyúden; (: of president etc) 官邸 kañtei;(: of Japanese emperor) 皇居 kókyo, 御所 góshò

palatable [pæl'ətəbəl] adj (food, drink)

おいしい oíshiĩ

palate [pæl'it] n 口がい kógai

palatial [pəlei'ʃəl] adj (surroundings, residence) 豪華な gōka na

palaver [pəlæv'ər] n (US) 話し合い hanáshiai; (BRIT: inf: fuss) 大騒ぎ ósawàgi

pale [peil] adj (whitish: color) 白っぽい shíroppoĩ; (: face) 青白い aójiroĩ, 青ざめた aózametà; (: light) 薄暗い usúguraĩ

♦n: *beyond the pale* (unacceptable) 容認できない yónin dekinái

Palestine [pæl'istain] n パレスチナ parésùchina

Palestinian [pælistin'i:ən] adj パレスチナの parésùchina no

♦n パレスチナ人 parésuchinajìn

palette [pæl'it] n (ART: paint mixing board) パレット paréttò

palings [pei'liŋz] npl (fence) さく sakú

pall [pɔ:l] n: *a pall of smoke* 一面の煙 ichímen no kemuri

♦vi ...が詰まらなくなる ...ga tsumáranakù naru, ...に飽きる ...ni akírù

pallet [pæl'it] n (for goods) パレット paréttò

pallid [pæl'id] adj (person, complexion) 青白い aójiroĩ

pallor [pæl'ər] n そう白 sóhaku

palm [pɑ:m] n (also: **palm tree**) ヤシ yáshĩ; (of hand) 手のひら tenóhìra

♦vt: *to palm something off on someone* (inf) ...に ...をつかませる ...ni ...wo tsukámaserù

Palm Sunday n 枝の主日 edá nò shujítsu

palpable [pæl'pəbəl] adj (obvious: lie, difference etc) 明白な meíhaku na

palpitations [pælpitei'ʃənz] npl (MED) 動き dóki

paltry [pɔ:l'tri:] adj (amount: tiny, insignificant) ささいな sásài na

pamper [pæm'pə:r] vt (cosset: person, animal) 甘やかす amáyakasù

pamphlet [pæm'flit] n (political, literary etc) 小冊子 shōsasshì, パンフレット páñfuretto

pan [pæn] n (CULIN: also: **saucepan**) 片

手なべ katátenabè; (: *also*: **frying pan**) フライパン furáipan

panacea [pænəsi:'ə] *n* 万能薬 baǹnōyàku

panache [pənæʃ'] *n* 気取り kidóri

Panama [pæn'əmɑ:] *n* パナマ pánama

Panama Canal *n*: *the Panama Canal* パナマ運河 pánama uǹga

pancake [pæn'keik] *n* パンケーキ paǹkēki, ホットケーキ hottókèki

pancreas [pæn'kri:əs] *n* すい臓 suízō

panda [pæn'də] *n* (ZOOL) ジャイアントパンダ jaíantopaǹda

panda car (*BRIT*) *n* (police car) パトカー patókā

pandemonium [pændəmou'ni:əm] *n* (noisy confusion) 大混乱 daíkoǹran

pander [pæn'də:r] *vi*: *to pander to* (person, whim, desire etc) ...に迎合する ...ni geígō suru

pane [pein] *n* (of glass) 窓ガラス madógarāsu

panel [pæn'əl] *n* (oblong piece: of wood, metal, glass etc) 羽目板 haméita, パネル pánèru; (group of judges, experts etc) ...の一団 ...no ichídàn, パネル pánèru

paneling [pæn'əliŋ] (*BRIT* **panelling**) *n* 羽目板 haméita ◇総称 sṓshō

pang [pæŋ] *n*: *a pang of regret* 悔恨の情 kaíkon nò jṓ

hunger pangs (physical pain) 激しい空腹感 hagéshii kūfukukan

panic [pæn'ik] *n* (uncontrollable terror, anxiety) パニック pánìkku

◆*vi* (person) うろたえる urótaerù; (crowd) パニック状態になる paníkkujōtai ni nárù

panicky [pæn'iki:] *adj* (person) うろたえる urótaerù

panic-stricken [pæn'ikstrikən] *adj* (person, face) パニックに陥った pánìkku ni ochíttà

panorama [pænəræm'ə] *n* (view) 全景 zeńkei, パノラマ panórama

pansy [pæn'zi:] *n* (BOT) サンシキスミレ sañshikisumìre, パンジー páǹjī; (*inf*: *pej*) 弱虫 yowámùshi

pant [pænt] *vi* (gasp: person, animal) あえぐ aégù

panther [pæn'θə:r] *n* ヒョウ hyṓ

panties [pæn'ti:z] *npl* パンティー páǹtī

pantomime [pæn'təmaim] (*BRIT*) *n* クリスマスミュージカル kurísumasu myū̀jikaru

pantry [pæn'tri:] *n* 食料室 shokúryōshìtsu, パントリー páǹtorī

pants [pænts] *n* (*BRIT*: underwear: woman's) パンティー páǹtī; (: man's) パンツ páǹtsu; (*US*: trousers) ズボン zubóń

panty hose *n* パンティーストッキング paǹtīsutokkiǹgu

papal [pei'pəl] *adj* ローマ法王の rṓmahṓō no

paper [pei'pə:r] *n* (*gen*) 紙 kamí; (*also*: **newspaper**) 新聞 shiǹbun; (exam) 試験 shikéǹ; (academic essay) 論文 roǹbun, ペーパー pḗpā; (*also*: **wallpaper**) 壁紙 kabégami

◆*adj* (made from paper: hat, plane etc) 紙の kamí no

◆*vt* (room: with wallpaper) ...に壁紙を張る ...ni kabégami wò hárù

paperback [pei'pə:rbæk] *n* ペーパーバック pḗpābakku

paper bag *n* 紙袋 kamíbukùro

paper clip *n* クリップ kuríppù

paper hankie *n* ティッシュ tísshù

papers [pei'pə:rz] *npl* (documents) 書類 shōrùi; (*also*: **identity papers**) 身分証明書 mibúnshōmeishò

paperweight [pei'pə:rweit] *n* 文鎮 buńchin

paperwork [pei'pə:rwə:rk] *n* (in office: dealing with letters, reports etc) 机上の事務 kijṓ no jimù, ペーパーワーク pḗpāwàku

papier-mâché [pei'pə:rməʃei'] *n* 張り子 haríko

paprika [pɑ:pri:'kə] *n* パプリカ papúrìka

par [pɑ:r] *n* (equality of value) 同等 dṓtō; (GOLF) 基準打数 kijúndasù, パー pā

to be on a par with (be equal with) ...と同等である ...to dṓtō de arù

parable [pær'əbəl] *n* たとえ話 tatóebanàshi

parachute [pær'əʃu:t] *n* 落下傘 rakkásàn, パラシュート paráshùto

parade [pəreid'] *n* (public procession) パレード parḗdò
♦*vt* (show off: wealth, knowledge etc) 見せびらかす misébirakasù
♦*vi* (MIL) 行進する kṓshin suru

paradise [pær'ədais] *n* (REL: heaven, nirvana etc: *also fig*) 天国 teñgoku, 極楽 gokúraku

paradox [pær'ədɑks] *n* (thing, statement) 逆説 gyakúsetsu

paradoxically [pærədɑːk'sikli:] *adv* 逆説的に言えば gyakúsetsuteki nì iébà

paraffin [pær'əfin] (*BRIT*) *n* (*also*: **paraffin oil**) 灯油 tṓyu

paragon [pær'əgɑn] *n* (of honesty, virtue etc) 模範 mohán, かがみ kagámi

paragraph [pær'əgræf] *n* 段落 dañrakù, パラグラフ parágùrafu

Paraguay [pær'əgwei] *n* パラグアイ parágùai

parallel [pær'əlel] *adj* (lines, walls, streets etc) 平行の heíkō no; (*fig*: similar) 似た nitá
♦*n* (line) 平行線 heíkōsen; (surface) 平行面 heíkōmen; (GEO) 緯度線 idòsen; (*fig*: similarity) 似た所 nitá tokoro

paralysis [pəræl'isis] *n* (MED) 麻ひ máhì

paralyze [pær'əlaiz] *vt* (MED) 麻ひさせる máhì saséru; (*fig*: organization, production etc) 麻ひ状態にする mahíjōtai ni suru

parameters [pəræm'itəːrz] *npl* (*fig*) 限定要素 geñteiyòso

paramilitary [pærəmil'ite:ri:] *adj* (organization, operations) 準軍事的な juñguñjiteki na

paramount [pær'əmaunt] *adj*: **of paramount importance** 極めて重要な kiwámète jṻyṓ na

paranoia [pærənɔi'ə] *n* 被害妄想 higáimòsō

paranoid [pær'ənɔid] *adj* (person, feeling) 被害妄想の higáimòsō no

parapet [pær'əpit] *n* 欄干 rañkan

paraphernalia [pærəfəːrneil'jə] *n* (gear) 道具 dṓgu

paraphrase [pær'əfreiz] *vt* (poem, arti-

cle etc) やさしく言替える yasáshikù iíkaerù

paraplegic [pærəpli:'dʒik] *n* 下半身麻ひ患者 kahánshinmahi kañja

parasite [pær'əsait] *n* (insect: *also fig*: person) 寄生虫 kiséichū; (plant) 寄生植物 kiséishokùbutsu

parasol [pær'əsɔ:l] *n* 日傘 higasa, パラソル páràsoru

paratrooper [pær'ətru:pəːr] *n* (MIL) 落下傘兵 rakkásanhei

parcel [pɑːr'səl] *n* (package) 小包 kozútsùmi
♦*vt* (object, purchases: *also*: **parcel up**) 小包にする kozútsùmi ni suru

parch [pɑːrtʃ] *vt* (land) 干上がらす hiágarasu; (crops) からからに枯らす karákara ni karasù

parched [pɑːrtʃt] *adj* (person) のどがからからの nódò ga karákara no

parchment [pɑːrtʃ'mənt] *n* (animal skin) 羊皮紙 yṓhishì; (thick paper) 硫酸紙 ryṻsanshì

pardon [pɑːr'dən] *n* (LAW) 赦免 shamén
♦*vt* (forgive: person, sin, error etc) 許す yurúsù

pardon me!, I beg your pardon! (I'm sorry) 済みません sumímaseñ, 失礼しました shitsúrèi shimashita, ご免なさい gomén nasaì

(I beg your) pardon?, pardon me? (what did you say?) もう一度言って下さい mṓ ichido ittè kudásaì

parent [pe:r'ənt] *n* (mother or father) 親 oyá; (mother) 母親 haháoya; (father) 父親 chichíoya

parental [pəren'təl] *adj* (love, control, guidance etc) 親の oyá no

parenthesis [pəren'θəsis] (*pl* **parentheses**) *n* 括弧 kákkò

parents [pe:r'ənts] *npl* (mother and father) 両親 ryṓshin

Paris [pær'is] *n* パリ párì

parish [pær'iʃ] *n* (REL) 教区 kyṓkù; (*BRIT*: civil) 行政教区 gyṓseikyòku

Parisian [pəri:'ʒən] *adj* パリの párì no
♦*n* パリっ子 paríkkò

parity [pæri:ti:] *n* (equality: of pay, conditions etc) 平等 byōdō

park [pɑːrk] n (public) 公園 kōen
♦vt (AUT) 駐車させる chū́sha saséru
♦vi (AUT) 駐車する chū́sha suru

parka [pɑːrˈkə] n パーカ pā́ka, アノラック anórakkù

parking [pɑːrˈkiŋ] n 駐車 chū́sha
「**no parking**」駐車禁止 chū́shakinshi

parking lot (US) n 駐車場 chū́shajō

parking meter n パーキングメーター pā́kingumḕtā

parking ticket n (fine) 駐車違反切符 chū́shaihan kippù

parlance [pɑːrˈləns] n 用語 yṓgo

parliament [pɑːrˈləmənt] (BRIT) n (institution) 議会 gíkài

parliamentary [pɑːrləmenˈtɑːriː] adj (business, behavior etc) 議会の gíkài no

parlor [pɑːrˈlər] (BRIT **parlour**) n (in house) 居間 imá, 応接間 ṓsetsuma

parochial [pərouˈkiːəl] (pej) adj (person, attitude) 偏狭な heńkyō na

parody [pærˈədiː] n (THEATER, LITERATURE, MUS) パロディー párōdī

parole [pərouˈl] n: **on parole** (LAW) 仮釈放で karíshakuhō de

paroxysm [pærˈəksizəm] n (of rage, jealousy, laughter) 爆発 bakúhatsu

parquet [pɑːrkeiˈ] n: **parquet floor(ing)** 寄せ木張りの床 yoségibari nò yuká

parrot [pærˈət] n オウム ṓmu

parry [pærˈiː] vt (blow) かわす kawásu

parsimonious [pɑːrsəmouˈniːəs] adj けちな kechí na

parsley [pɑːrzˈliː] n パセリ pásèri

parsnip [pɑːrsˈnip] n 白にんじん shironinjin, パースニップ pā́sunippù

parson [pɑːrˈsən] n (REL) 牧師 bókùshi

part [pɑːrt] n (section, division) 部分 búbùn; (of machine, vehicle) 部品 buhín; (THEATER, CINEMA etc: role) 役 yakú; (PRESS, RADIO, TV: of serial) 第 …部 dáì…bù; (US: in hair) 分け目 wakéme
♦adv = **partly**
♦vt (separate: people, objects, hair) 分ける wakérù

♦vi (people: leave each other) 別れる wákarerù; (crowd) 道を開ける michí wo akerù

to take part in (participate in) …に参加する …ni sańka suru

to take something in good part …を怒らない …wo okóranaì

to take someone's part (support) …の肩を持つ …no kátà wo mótsù

for my part 私としては watákushi toshite wa

for the most part (usually, generally) ほとんどは hotóndo wa

part exchange n: **in part exchange** (BRIT: COMM) 下取りで shitádòri de

partial [pɑːrˈʃəl] adj (not complete: victory, support, solution) 部分的な bubúnteki na

to be partial to (like: person, food, drink etc) …が大好きである …ga daísuki de arù

participant [pɑːrtisˈəpənt] n (in competition, debate, campaign etc) 参加者 sańkashà

participate [pɑːrtisˈəpeit] vi: **to participate in** (competition, debate, campaign etc) …に参加する …ni sańka suru

participation [pɑːrtisəpeiˈʃən] n (in competition, debate, campaign etc) 参加 sańka

participle [pɑːrˈtisipəl] n (LING) 分詞 búnshi

particle [pɑːrˈtikəl] n (tiny piece: gen) 粒子 ryū́shi; (: of dust) 一片 ippén; (of metal) 砕片 saíhen; (of food) 粒 tsúbù

particular [pərtikˈjələr] adj (distinct from others: person, time, place etc) 特定の tokútei no; (special) 特別な tokúbetsu na; (fussy, demanding) やかましい yakámashiì

in particular 特に tókù ni

particularly [pərtikˈjələːrliː] adv 特に tókù ni

particulars [pərtikˈjələːrz] npl (facts) 詳細 shōsai; (personal details) 経歴 keíreki

parting [pɑːrˈtiŋ] n (action) 分ける事 wakérù kotó; (farewell) 別れ wakáre;

(BRIT: hair) 分け目 wakéme
◆adj (words, gift etc) 別れの wakáre no

partisan [pɑːr'tizən] adj (politics, views) 党派心の tōhashiñ no
◆n (supporter) 支援者 shiéñsha; (fighter) パルチザン parúchizàn

partition [pɑːrtiʃ'ən] n (wall, screen) 間仕切 majíkiri; (POL: of country) 分割 buñkatsu

partly [pɑːrt'liː] adv (to some extent) 幾分か ikúbun ka

partner [pɑːrt'nəːr] n (wife, husband) 配偶者 haígūsha; (girlfriend, boyfriend) 交際の相手 kōsai nò aíte; (COMM) 共同経営者 kyōdōkeieisha; (SPORT) パートナー pātònā; (at dance) 相手 aíte

partnership [pɑːrt'nəːrʃip] n (COMM) 共同経営事業 kyōdōkeieijigyō; (POL etc) 協力 kyōryoku

partridge [pɑːr'tridʒ] n ウズラ uzúra

part-time [pɑːrt'taim] adj (work, staff) 非常勤の hijōkin no, パートタイムの pātotaìmu no
◆adv (work, study) パートタイムで pātotaìmu de

part with vt fus (money, possessions) ...を手放す ...wo tebánasù

party [pɑːr'tiː] n (POL) 政党 seítō; (celebration, social event) パーティ pàti; (group of people) 一行 ikkō, パーティ pàti; (LAW) 当事者 tōjìsha; (individual) 人 hitó
◆cpd (POL) 党の tō no

party dress n パーティドレス pátidòresu

party line n (TEL) 共線線 kyōdōsen

pass [pæs] vt (spend: time) 過ごす sugósù; (hand over: salt, glass, newspaper etc) 渡す watásù; (go past: place) 通り過ぎる tōrisugirù; (overtake: car, person etc) 追越す oíkosù; (exam) ...に合格する ...ni gōkaku suru; (approve: law, proposal) 可決する kakétsu suru
◆vi (go past) 通る tōru; (in exam) 合格する gōkaku suru, パスする pásù suru
◆n (permit) 許可証 kyokáshò; (membership card) 会員証 kaíinshò; (in mountains) 峠 tōge; (SPORT) パス pásù;

(SCOL: also: **pass mark**): **to get a pass in** ...で及第する ...de kyūdai suru, ...でパスする ...de pásù suru
to pass something through something ...を...に通す ...wo ...ni tōsu
to make a pass at someone (inf) ...にモーションを掛ける ...ni mōshon wo kakérù

passable [pæs'əbəl] adj (road) 通行できる tsūkō dekirù; (acceptable: work) まずまずの mázùmazu no

passage [pæs'idʒ] n (also: **passageway**: indoors) 廊下 rōka; (: outdoors) 通路 tsūro; (in book) 一節 issétsu; (ANAT): **the nasal passages** 鼻こう bikō; (act of passing) 通過 tsūka; (journey: on boat) 船旅 funátabi

pass away vi (die) 死ぬ shinú

passbook [pæs'buk] n 銀行通帳 giñkōtsūchō

pass by vi (go past) ...のそばを通る ...no sóbà wo tōru
◆vt (ignore) 無視する múshì suru

passenger [pæs'indʒəːr] n (in car, boat, plane etc) 乗客 jōkyaku

passer-by [pæsəːrbai'] n 通行人 tsūkōnin

pass for vt fus ...で通る ...de tōru

passing [pæs'iŋ] adj (fleeting: moment, glimpse, thought etc) 束の間の tsuká no ma no
in passing (incidentally) ついでに tsuíde ni

passing place n (AUT) 待避所 taíhijò

passion [pæʃ'ən] n (love: for person) 情欲 jōyoku; (fig: for cars, football, politics etc) 熱狂 nekkyō, マニア máñia

passionate [pæʃ'ənit] adj (affair, embrace, person etc) 情熱的な jōnetsuteki na

passive [pæs'iv] adj (person, resistance) 消極的な shōkyokuteki na; (LING) 受動態の judōtai no, 受け身の ukémi no

pass on vt (news, object) 伝える tsutáerù; (illness) 移す utsúsù

pass out vi (faint) 気絶する kizétsu suru

Passover [pæs'ouvəːr] n 過越し祭 sugíkoshisai

passport [pæs'pɔːrt] n (official document) 旅券 ryokén, パスポート pasúpòto

passport control n 出入国管理所 shutsúnyūkoku kañrijo

pass up vt (opportunity) 逃す nogásù

password [pǽs'wə:rd] n (secret word, phrase) 合言葉 aíkotòba, パスワード pasúwàdo

past [pæst] prep (drive, walk, run: in front of) ...を通り過ぎて ...wo tórisugite; (: beyond: also in time: later than) ...を過ぎて ...wo sugíte

♦adj (previous: government, monarch etc) 過去の kákò no; (: week, month etc) この前の konó maè no, 先...no, señ...

♦n (period and events prior to the present: also of person) 過去 kákò

he's past forty (older than 40) 彼は40才を過ぎている kárè wa yoñjussaì wo sugíte irù

ten/quarter past eight 8時10分〔15分〕過ぎ hachíji juppùn〔jūgofun〕sugí

for the past few/3 days この数日〔3日〕の間 konó sūjitsu(mikkà) no aída

pasta [pɑːsˈtə] n パスタ pásùta

paste [peist] n (wet mixture) 練り物 nerímòno; (glue) のり norí; (CULIN: fish, meat, tomato etc paste) ペースト pêsuto

♦vt (stick: paper, label, poster etc) 張る harú

pastel [pæstel'] adj (color) パステルの pásùteru no

pasteurized [pǽsˈtʃə:raizd] adj (milk, cream) 低温殺菌された teíonsakkìn sareta

pastille [pæsti:l'] n (sweet) ドロップ dóròppu

pastime [pǽs'taim] n (hobby) 趣味 shúmì

pastoral [pǽsˈtə:rəl] adj (REL: duties, activities) 牧師としての bókùshi toshite no

pastry [peisˈtri:] n (dough) 生地 kíjì; (cake) 洋菓子 yōgashi, ケーキ kèki

pasture [pǽsˈtʃə:r] n (grassland) 牧場 bokújō

pasty [n pæsˈti: adj peisˈti:] n (meat and vegetable pie) ミートパイ mītopài

♦adj (complexion, face) 青ざめた aózameta

metà

pat [pæt] vt (with hand: dog, someone's back etc) 軽くたたく karúkù tatákù

patch [pætʃ] n (piece of material) 継ぎ tsugí; (also: **eye patch**) 眼帯 gañtai; (area: damp, bald, black etc) 一部 ichíbù; (repair: on tire etc) 継ぎはぎ tsugíhagi

♦vt (clothes) ...に継ぎを当てる ...ni tsugí wo atèrù

to go through a bad patch 不運の時期に合う fúùn no jíkì ni áù

patch up vt (mend temporarily) 応急的に直す ōkyūteki ni naosù; (quarrel) ...をやめて仲直りする ...wo yamétè nakánaori surù

patchwork [pætʃ'wə:rk] n (SEWING) パッチワーク patchíwàku

patchy [pætʃi:] adj (uneven: color) むらの多い murá no ōi; (incomplete: information, knowledge etc) 不完全な fukánzen na

pâté [pɑːtei'] n パテ pátè ◇肉、魚などを香辛料とすり合せて蒸焼きにして冷ました物 nikú, sakana nadò wo kōshiñryō to surísawasetè mushíyaki ni shitè samáshita monò

patent [pæt'ənt] n (COMM) 特許 tókkyo

♦vt (COMM) ...の特許を取る ...no tókkyo wo tórù

♦adj (obvious) 明白な meíhaku na

patent leather n: *patent leather shoes* エナメル靴 enámerugùtsu

paternal [pətə:r'nəl] adj (love, duty) 父親の chichíoya no; (grandmother etc) 父方の chichígata no

paternity [pətə:r'niti:] n 父親である事 chichíoya de arù kotó

path [pæθ] n (trail, track) 小道 kómìchi; (concrete path, gravel path etc) 道 michí; (of planet, missile) 軌道 kidó

pathetic [pəθet'ik] adj (pitiful: sight, cries) 哀れな áwàre na; (very bad) 哀れな程悪い áwàre na hodò warui

pathological [pæθəlɑːdʒ'ikəl] adj (liar, hatred) 病的な byóteki na; (of pathology: work) 病理の byóri no

pathology [pəθɑːl'ədʒi:] n (medical field) 病理学 byórigàku

pathos [pei'θɑːs] *n* 悲哀 hiái

pathway [pæθ'wei] *n* (path) 歩道 hodő

patience [pei'ʃəns] *n* (personal quality) 忍耐 níňtai; (*BRIT*: CARDS) 一人トランプ hitóritoraňpu

patient [pei'ʃənt] *n* (MED) 患者 kaňja
♦*adj* (person) 忍耐強い níňtaizuyoî

patio [pæt'iːou] *n* テラス térasu

patriot [pei'triːət] *n* 愛国者 aíkokushâ

patriotic [peitriːɑt'ik] *adj* (person) 愛国心の強い aíkokushîn no tsuyôî; (song, speech etc) 愛国の aíkoku no

patriotism [pei'triːətizəm] *n* 愛国心 aíkokushîn

patrol [pətroul'] *n* (MIL, POLICE) 巡回 juňkai, パトロール patőrôru
♦*vt* (MIL, POLICE: city, streets etc) 巡回する juňkai suru, パトロールする patőrôru suru

patrol car *n* (POLICE) パトカー patőkâ

patrolman [pətroul'mən] (*pl* **patrolmen**: *US*) *n* (POLICE) 巡査 juňsa

patron [pei'trən] *n* (customer, client) 客 kyakú; (benefactor: of charity) 後援者 kőeňsha
patron of the arts 芸術のパトロン geíjùtsu no pátòron

patronage [pei'trənidʒ] *n* (of artist, charity etc) 後援 kően

patronize [pei'trənaiz] *vt* (*pej*: look down on) 尊大にあしらう soňdai nî ashírau; (artist, writer, musician) 後援する kően suru; (shop, club, firm) ひいきにする hiíki ni surù

patron saint *n* (REL) 守護聖人 shugőseijìn

patter [pæt'əːr] *n* (sound: of feet) ぱたぱたという音 pátàpata to iú oto; (of rain) パラパラという音 páràpara to iú otò; (sales talk) 売込み口上 uríkomikôjò
♦*vi* (footsteps) ぱたぱたと歩く pátàpata to arúkù; (rain) ぱらぱらと降る páràpara to fúrù

pattern [pæt'əːrn] *n* (design) 模様 moyő; (SEWING) 型紙 katágami, パターン patáàn

paunch [pɔːntʃ] *n* 太鼓腹 taíkobara

pauper [pɔː'pəːr] *n* 貧乏人 biňbônin

pause [pɔːz] *n* (temporary halt) 休止 kyűshi, ポーズ pőzu
♦*vi* (stop temporarily) 休止する kyűshi suru; (: while speaking) 間を置く má wò okú

pave [peiv] *vt* (street, yard etc) 舗装する hoső suru
to pave the way for (*fig*) ...を可能にする ...wo kanő ni suru

pavement [peiv'mənt] *n* (*US*) 路面 romén; (*BRIT*) 歩道 hodő

pavilion [pəvil'jən] *n* (*BRIT*: SPORT) 選手更衣所 seňshukôijò

paving [pei'viŋ] *n* (material) 舗装材 hosőzài

paving stone *n* 敷石 shikíishi

paw [pɔː] *n* (of animal) 足 ashî

pawn [pɔːn] *n* (CHESS) ポーン pőn; (*fig*) 操り人形 ayátsuriníňgyō
♦*vt* 質に入れる shichî ni irerù

pawnbroker [pɔːn'broukəːr] *n* 質屋 shichíyâ

pawnshop [pɔːn'ʃɑːp] *n* 質屋 shichíyâ

pay [pei] *n* (wage, salary etc) 給料 kyűryō
♦*vb* (*pt*, *pp* **paid**)
♦*vt* (sum of money, debt, bill, wage) 払う haráù
♦*vi* (be profitable) 利益になる ríèki ni nárù
to pay attention (to) (...に) 注意する (...ni) chűi suru
to pay someone a visit ...を訪問する ...wo hőmon suru
to pay one's respects to someone ...にあいさつをする ...ni aísatsu wo suru

payable [pei'əbəl] *adj* (sum of money) 支払うべき shiháraubeki
payable to bearer (check) 持参人払いの jisánninbaraî no

pay back *vt* (money) 返す kaésù; (person) ...に仕返しをする ...ni shikáeshi wò suru

payday [pei'dei] *n* 給料日 kyűryòbi

payee [peiiː'] *n* (of check, postal order) 受取人 ukétorinîn

pay envelope (*US*) *n* 給料袋 kyűryōbukùro

pay for vt fus (purchases) ...の代金を払う ...no daíkin wò haráù; (fig) 償う tsugúnaù

pay in vt (money, check etc) 預け入れる azúkeirerù, 入金する nyúkin suru

payment [pei'mənt] n (act) 支払い shihárài; (amount of money) 支払い金額 shiháraikiñgaku

a monthly payment 月賦 géppù

pay off vt (debt) 返済する heñsai suru; (person: with bribe etc) 買収する baíshū suru

♦vi (scheme, decision) 成功する seíkō suru

pay packet (BRIT) n = **pay envelope**

pay phone n 公衆電話 kóshūdeñwa

payroll [pei'roul] n 従業員名簿 júgyōinmeìbo

pay slip n 給料明細書 kyúryōmeisaishò

pay up vt 払う haráù

PC [pi:si:'] n abbr = **personal computer**; (BRIT: = **police constable**) 巡査 júñsa

p.c. abbr = **per cent**

pea [pi:] n エンドウマメ eñdōmame

peace [pi:s] n (not war) 平和 heíwa; (calm: of place, surroundings) 静けさ shizúkesà; (: personal) 心の平和 kokórò no heíwa

peaceful [pi:s'fəl] adj (calm: place, time) 静寂な seíjaku na; (: person) 穏和な oñwa na

peach [pi:tʃ] n モモ momó

peacock [pi:'kɑːk] n クジャク kujáku

peak [pi:k] n (of mountain: top) 頂上 chójō; (of cap) つば tsúbà; (fig: physical, intellectual etc) 頂点 chóten, ピーク pīku

peak hours npl ピーク時 pīkuji

peak period n ピーク時 pīkuji

peal [pi:l] n (of bells) 響き hibíki

peal of laughter 大きな笑い声 ōkina waráigoè

peanut [pi:'nʌt] n 落花生 rakkásèi, ピーナッツ pínattsù

peanut butter n ピーナッツバター pínattsubatā

pear [per] n セイヨウナシ seíyōnashì

pearl [pəːrl] n 真珠 shiñju, パール pàru

peasant [pez'ənt] n 百姓 hyakúshō, 農夫

nófu

peat [pi:t] n 泥炭 deítan

pebble [peb'əl] n 小石 koíshi

peck [pek] vt (also: **peck at**: subj: bird) つつく tsutsúkù

♦n (of bird) つつく事 tsutsúkù kotò; (kiss) 軽いキス karúi kísù

pecking order [pek'iŋ-] n (fig: hierarchy) 序列 jorétsu

peckish [pek'iʃ] (BRIT: inf) adj (hungry): *to be peckish* おなかがすいた onáka ga suità

peculiar [pikju:l'jəːr] adj (strange: person, taste, shape etc) 変った kawátta; (belonging exclusively): *peculiar to* 独特な dokútoku na

peculiarity [pikju:li:ær'iti:] n (strange habit, characteristic) 癖 kusé; (distinctive feature: of person, place etc) 特徴 tokúchō

pedal [ped'əl] n (on bicycle, car, machine) ペダル pédàru

♦vi (on bicycle) こぐ kógù

pedantic [pədæn'tik] adj げん学的な geñgakuteki na

peddler [ped'ləːr] n (also: **drug peddler**) 麻薬の売人 mayáku nò baíniñ

pedestal [ped'istəl] n 台座 daíza

pedestrian [pədes'tri:ən] n 歩行者 hokóshà

♦adj 歩行者の hokóshà no

pedestrian crossing (BRIT) n 横断歩道 ōdanhodō

pediatrics [pi:di:æt'riks] (BRIT **paediatrics**) n (hospital department) 小児科 shónika; (subject) 小児科学 shónikagàku

pedigree [ped'əgri:] n (of animal) 血統 kettő; (fig: background) 経歴 keíreki

♦cpd (animal) 純血の juñketsu no

pee [pi:] (inf) vi おしっこする o-shíkkò suru

peek [pi:k] vi のぞく nozóku

peel [pi:l] n (of orange, apple, potato) 皮 kawá

♦vt (vegetables, fruit) ...の皮をむく ...no kawá wo mukú

♦vi (paint, wallpaper) はげる hagérù; (skin) むける mukérù

peep [pi:p] *n* (look) のぞき見 nozókimi; (sound) 鳴き声 nakígoè
♦*vi* (look) のぞく nozóku

peephole [pi:p'houl] *n* のぞき穴 nozókiàna

peep out *vi* (be visible) のぞく nozóku

peer [pi:r] *vi*: **to peer at** ...をじっと見る ...wo jíttò mírù
♦*n* (noble) 貴族 kízoku; (equal) 同等の人 dôtō nò hitő; (contemporary) 同輩 dôhai

peerage [pi:'ridʒ] *n* (rank) 貴族の地位 kízoku no chíi

peeved [pi:vd] *adj* (annoyed) 怒った okóttà

peevish [pi:'viʃ] *adj* (bad-tempered) 機嫌の悪い kigén nò warúî

peg [peg] *n* (hook, knob: for coat etc) フック fúkkù; (BRIT: also: **clothes peg**) 洗濯ばさみ señtakubasàmi

pejorative [pidʒɔːr'ətiv] *adj* (word, expression) 軽べつ的な keíbetsuteki na

Peking [pi:kiŋ'] *n* 北京 pékìn

Pekin(g)ese [pi:kəni:z'] *n* (dog) ペキニーズ pekíniìzu

pelican [pel'ikən] *n* (ZOOL) ペリカン períkàn

pelican crossing (BRIT) *n* (AUT) 押しボタン式信号 oshíbotanshiki shiñgō

pellet [pel'it] *n* (of paper, mud etc) 丸めた球 marúmeta tamà; (also: **shotgun pellet**) 散弾銃の弾 sañdañjū no tamá

pelt [pelt] *vt*: **to pelt someone with something** ...に ...を浴びせ掛ける ...ni ...wo abísekakerù
♦*vi* (rain) 激しく降る hagéshikù fúrù; (inf: run) 駆ける kakérù
♦*n* (animal skin) 毛皮 kegáwa

pelvis [pel'vis] *n* 骨盤 kotsúbàn

pen [pen] *n* (for writing: fountain pen, ballpoint pen) ペン péñ; (: felt-tip pen etc) サインペン saíñpen; (enclosure: for sheep, pigs etc) 囲い kakói

penal [pi:'nəl] *adj* (colony, institution) 刑罰の keíbatsu no; (system, code, reform) 刑法の keíhō no

penalize [pi:'nəlaiz] *vt* (punish) 罰する bassúrù; (: SPORT) ...にペナルティーを科する ...ni penárutî wo kasúrù

penalty [pen'əlti:] *n* (punishment) 罰ばtsù; (fine) 罰金 bakkín; (SPORT) ペナルティー penárutî

penalty (kick) *n* (RUGBY, SOCCER) ペナルティーキック penárutî kikkù

penance [pen'əns] *n* 償い tsugúnai

pence [pens] *pl of* **penny**

pencil [pen'səl] *n* (for writing, drawing) 鉛筆 eñpitsu

pencil case *n* 筆入れ fudêîre

pencil sharpener *n* 鉛筆削り eñpitsukezúri, シャープナー shāpunā

pendant [pen'dənt] *n* ペンダント péñdanto

pending [pen'diŋ] *prep* ...を待つ間 ...wo mátsù aîda
♦*adj* (business) 未決の mikétsu no; (lawsuit) 審理中の shiñrichū no; (exam) 差迫った sashísemattà

pendulum [pen'dʒələm] *n* (of clock) 振子 furíko

penetrate [pen'itreit] *vt* (subj: person: enemy territory) ...に侵入する ...ni shiñnyū suru; (forest etc) ...に入り込む ...ni haírikomù; (: water etc) 染込む shimíkomù; (: light) 通る tôru

penetrating [pen'itreitiŋ] *adj* (sound, glance, mind, observation) 鋭い surúdoî

penetration [penitrei'ʃən] *n* (action) 入り込む事 haírikomù kotó

penfriend [pen'frend] (BRIT) *n* = **pen pal**

penguin [pen'gwin] *n* ペンギン péñgin

penicillin [penisil'in] *n* ペニシリン peníshirin

peninsula [pənin'sələ] *n* 半島 hañtō

penis [pi:'nis] *n* 陰茎 iñkei, ペニス péñis

penitent [pen'itənt] *adj* (person: very sorry) 後悔している kôkai shite irú

penitentiary [peniten'tʃəːri:] (US) *n* 刑務所 keímushò

penknife [pen'naif] *n* ペンナイフ peñnaífu

pen name *n* ペンネーム peñnêmu

penniless [pen'i:lis] *adj* (person) 一文無しの ichímoñnashi no

penny [pen'i:] (*pl* **pennies** or BRIT **pence**) *n* (US) ペニ péni, セント séñto;

(*BRIT*: after 1971: = one hundredth of a pound) ペニ péni

pen pal *n* ペンパル pénparu, ペンフレンド penfureňdo

pension [pen'tʃən] *n* (state benefit) 年金 neňkin; (company pension etc) 恩給 oňkyū

pensioner [pen'tʃənər] (*BRIT*) *n* (old-age pensioner) 年金で生活する老人 neňkin dè seřkatsu surù rōjìn, 年金暮らしの人 neňkinguràshi no hitò

pension fund *n* 年金基金 neňkinkikiň

pensive [pen'siv] *adj* (person, expression etc) 考え込んだ kaňgaekoňda

pentagon [pen'təgɑːn] *n*: **the Pentagon** (*US*: POL) 国防総省 kokúbōsōshò, ペンタゴン peñtàgon

Pentecost [pen'təkɔːst] *n* 聖霊降臨祭 seřreikōriñsai

penthouse [pent'haus] *n* (flat) 屋上階 okújōkai

pent-up [pent'ʌp'] *adj* (feelings) たまった tamáttà

penultimate [pinʌl'təmit] *adj* 最後から2番目の saîgo kara nibáňme no

people [piː'pəl] *npl* (persons) 人々 hitóbìto; (inhabitants) 住民 jùmin; (citizens) 市民 shímìn; (POL): **the people** 国民 kokúmin
♦*n* (nation) 国民 kokúmin; (race) 民族 mìňzoku
several people came 数人来ました sùnin kimashità
people say that ... ...だと言われている ...da to iwárete irù, ...だそうだ ...da sō dà

pep [pep] (*inf*) *n* (energy, vigor) 元気 geňkì

pepper [pep'əːr] *n* (spice) こしょう koshò; (hot pepper) トウガラシ tōgàrashi; (sweet pepper) ピーマン pìman
♦*vt* (*fig*): **to pepper with** ...を振掛ける ...wo furíkakerù

peppermint [pep'əːrmint] *n* (sweet) ハッカあめ hakkáamè

peptalk [pep'tɔːk] (*inf*) *n* (encouraging talk) 激励演説 gekíreienzetsù

pep up *vt* (enliven) 活気付ける kakkízukerù

per [pəːr] *prep* (of amounts, prices etc: for each) ...につき ...ni tsukí
per day/person 1日〈1人〉につき... ichínichi〈hitòri〉ni tsukí...
per annum 1年につき... ichíneň ni tsukí...

per capita [-kæp'itə] *adj* (income) 一人当りの hitóri atarì no
♦*adv* 一人当り hitóri atarì

perceive [pəːrsiːv'] *vt* (sound) 聞く kíkù; (light) 見る mírù; (difference) 認識する niňshiki suru; (notice) ...に気が付く ...ni ki gá tsukù; (realize, understand) 分かる wakárù

per cent *n* パーセント pásentò

percentage [pəːrsen'tidʒ] *n* (amount) 割合 waříai, 率 rítsù

perception [pəːrsep'ʃən] *n* (insight) 洞察力 dōsatsuryðku; (opinion, understanding) 理解 rikái; (faculty) 知覚 chikáku

perceptive [pəːrsep'tiv] *adj* (person) 洞察力のある dōsatsuryðku no árù, 鋭敏な eíbin na; (analysis, assessment) 鋭い surúdoì

perch [pəːrtʃ] *n* (for bird) 止り木 tomárígì; (fish) パーチ pàchi ◇スズキに似た淡水魚 suzúki ni nità tañsuigyò
♦*vi*: **to perch (on)** (bird) (...に) 止る (...ni) tomárù; (person) (...に) 腰掛ける (...ni) koshíkakerù

percolator [pəːr'kəleitəːr] *n* (*also*: **coffee percolator**) パーコレーター pákorètā

percussion [pəːrkʌʃ'ən] *n* 打楽器 dagákkì ◇総称 sōshō

peremptory [pəremp'təːriː] (*pej*) *adj* (person) 横柄な ōhei na; (order, instruction) 断固たる dañkotarù

perennial [pəren'iːəl] *adj* (flower, plant) 多年生の tanénsei no; (*fig*: problem, feature etc) ありがちな arígachi na

perfect [*adj, n* pəːr'fikt *vb* pəːrfekt'] *adj* (without fault: person, weather, behavior etc) 完璧な kañpeki na; (utter: nonsense, stranger etc) 全くの mattáku no
♦*n* (*also*: **perfect tense**) 完了形 kañryōkei

◆*vt* (technique) 仕上げる shiágerù

perfection [pərˈfekʃən] *n* (faultlessness) 完璧さ kañpekisa

perfectionist [pərˈfekʃənist] *n* 完璧主義者 kañpekishugishà

perfectly [pəˈrˈfiktliː] *adv* (emphatic) 全く mattáku; (faultlessly: perform, do etc) 完璧に kañpeki ni; (completely: understand etc) 完全に kañzen ni

perforate [pəˈrˈfəreit] *vt* ...に穴を開ける ...ni aná wò akérù

perforations [pəˈrforeiˈʃənz] *npl* (series of small holes) ミシン目 mishíñme

perform [pəˈrˈfɔːrm] *vt* (carry out: task, operation, ceremony etc) 行う okónaù, する surú; (piece of music) 演奏する eñsō suru; (play etc) 上演する jōen suru
◆*vi* (well, badly) する surú, やる yarú

performance [pəˈrforˈməns] *n* (of actor) 演技 eñgi; (of dancer) 踊り odóri; (of musician) 演奏 eñsō; (of singer) 歌い方 utáikata; (of play, show) 上演 jōen; (of car, engine) 性能 seínō; (of athlete, company, economy) 成績 seíseki

performer [pəˈrfɔːrˈmər] *n* (actor, dancer, singer etc) 芸能人 geínōjin

perfume [pəˈrˈfjuːm] *n* (cologne, toilet water, essence) 香水 kōsui; (pleasant smell: of flowers etc) 香り kaórì

perfunctory [pəˈrfʌŋkˈtəːriː] *adj* (kiss, remark etc) いい加減な iíkagen na

perhaps [pəˈrhæps] *adv* (maybe) たぶん ...だろう tábùn ...daró

peril [peˈrəl] *n* (great danger) 危険 kikén

perimeter [pəˈrimiˈtəːr] *n* 周辺 shūhen

period [piˈrˈiːəd] *n* (length of time) 期間 kikán; (SCOL) 時限 jigén; (full stop) 終止符 shūshifū, ピリオド píriodo; (MED) 月経 gekkéi, メンス méñsu, 生理 seíri
◆*adj* (costume, furniture) 時代の jidái no

periodic(al) [piˈriːɑːˈdik(əl)] *adj* (event, occurrence) 周期的な shūkiteki na, 定期的な teíkiteki na

periodical [piˈriːɑːˈdikəl] *n* (magazine) 雑誌 zasshí

periodically [piˈriːɑːˈdikliː] *adv* 定期的に teíkiteki ni

peripheral [pəriˈfˈəːrəl] *adj* 二次的な nijí-

teki na; (on the edge: also COMPUT) 周辺の shūhen no
◆*n* (COMPUT) 周辺機器 shūhenkikì

periphery [pəriˈfˈəːriː] *n* (edge) 周辺 shūhen

periscope [peˈrˈiskoup] *n* 潜望鏡 señbōkyō

perish [peˈrˈiʃ] *vi* (die) 死ぬ shinú; (die out) 滅びる horóbirù; (rubber, leather etc) 腐る kusárù

perishable [peˈrˈiʃəbəl] *adj* (food) いたみやすい itámiyasuì

perjury [pəˈrˈdʒəːriː] *n* (LAW) 偽証 gishō

perk [pəˈrk] (*inf*) *n* (extra) 役得 yakútoku

perk up *vi* (cheer up) 元気を出す génki wo dásù

perky [pəˈrˈkiː] *adj* (cheerful) 朗らかな hogáraka na

perm [pəˈrm] *n* (for hair) パーマ pàma

permanent [pəˈrˈmənənt] *adj* 永久的な eíkyūteki na

permeate [pəˈrˈmiːeit] *vi* (pass through) 浸透する shiñtō suru; (*fig*: spread) 広がる hirógarù
◆*vt* (subj: liquid) ...に染込む ...ni shimíkomù; (: idea) ...に広まる ...ni hirómarù

permissible [pəˈrmisˈəbəl] *adj* (action, behavior) 許される yurúsarerù

permission [pəˈrmiʃˈən] *n* (consent, authorization) 許可 kyókà

permissive [pəˈrmisˈiv] *adj* (person, behavior, society) 甘い amáì

permit [*n* pəˈrˈmit *vb* pəˈrmit] *n* (official authorization) 許可証 kyokáshō
◆*vt* (allow) 許可する kyókà suru; (make possible) 可能にする kanó ni surù

permutation [pəˈrmjəteiˈʃən] *n* 置換え o-kíkae

pernicious [pəˈrniʃˈəs] *adj* (very harmful: attitude, influence etc) 有害な yūgai na; (MED) 悪性の akúsei no

perpendicular [pəˈrpəndikˈjələr] *adj* (line, surface) 垂直の suíchoku no; (cliff, slope) 険しい kewáshiì

perpetrate [pəˈrˈpitreit] *vt* (commit: crime) 犯す okásù

perpetual [pəˈrpetʃˈuəl] *adj* (constant:

motion, darkness) 永久の eīkyū no; (: noise, questions) 年がら年中の neñgaraneñjū no

perpetuate [pə:rpetʃ'u:eit] vt (situation, custom, belief etc) 永続させる eīzoku saserù

perplex [pə:rpleks'] vt (person) まごつかせる magótsukaserù

persecute [pə:r'səkju:t] vt (harass, oppress: minorities etc) 迫害する hakúgai suru

persecution [pə:rsəkju:'ʃən] n (of minorities etc) 迫害 hakúgai

perseverance [pə:rsəvi:r'əns] n 根気 koñki

persevere [pə:rsəvi:r'] vi 辛抱強く続ける shiñbōzuyokù tsuzúkerù

Persian [pə:r'ʒən] adj ペルシアの pérùshia no
♦n ペルシア人 perúshiajìn
the (Persian) Gulf ペルシア湾 perúshiawàn

persist [pə:rsist'] vi: *to persist (in doing something)* (...を) し続ける (...wo shi)tsuzúkerù

persistence [pə:rsis'təns] n (determination) 根気強さ koñkizuyòsa

persistent [pə:rsis'tənt] adj (noise, smell, cough etc) いつまでも続く ítsùmademo tsuzúkù; (person: determined) 根気強い koñkizuyoì

person [pə:r'sən] n 人 hitó
in person (appear, sing, recite etc) 本人が hoñnin ga

personal [pə:r'sənəl] adj (belongings, phone etc) 個人の kojín no; (opinion, life, habits etc) 個人的な kojínteki na; (in person: visit) 本人自身の hoñninjishiñ no

personal assistant n 秘書 hishò

personal call n (TEL) 私用の電話 shiyő no deñwa

personal column n 私信欄 shishíñrañ

personal computer n パーソナルコンピュータ pāsonarukoñpyūta, パソコン pasókòn

personality [pə:rsənæl'iti:] n (character) 人格 jiñkaku; (famous person) 有名人 yūmeijìn

personally [pə:r'sənəli:] adv (for my etc part) 個人的には kojínteki ni wà; (in person) 本人が hoñnin ga
to take something personally ...を個人攻撃と受止める ...wo kojíñkōgeki to ukétomerù

personal organizer n 予定帳 yotéichō

personify [pə:rsɑn'əfai] vt (evil) ...の権化である ...no góñge de árù; (good) ...の化身である ...no késhìn de árù

personnel [pə:rsənel'] n 職員 shokúin ◇総称 sōshō

perspective [pə:rspek'tiv] n (ARCHIT, ART) 遠近法 eñkinhō; (way of thinking) 見方 mikáta
to get something into perspective (fig) 事情を考えて...を見る jijō wò kañgaetè ...wo mírù

Perspex [pə:rs'peks] ® n アクリル ákùriru

perspiration [pə:rspərei'ʃən] n 汗 ásè

persuade [pə:rsweid'] vt: *to persuade someone to do something* ...する様に...を説き伏せる ...surú yò ni ...wo tokífuserù

persuasion [pə:rswei'ʒən] n (act) 説得 settóku; (creed) 信条 shiñjō

persuasive [pə:rswei'siv] adj (person, argument) 説得力のある settókuryòku no árù

pertaining [pə:rtein'iŋ]: *pertaining to prep* (relating to) ...に関する ...ni kañ suru

pertinent [pə:r'tənənt] adj (answer, remark) 適切な tekísetsu na

perturb [pə:rtə:rb'] vt (person) 不安にする fuán ni surù

Peru [pəru:'] n ペルー pérù

peruse [pəru:z'] vt (newspaper, documents etc) ...に目を通す ...ni mé wo tòsù

Peruvian [pəru:'vi:ən] adj ペルーの pérù no
♦n ペルー人 perújìn

pervade [pə:rveid'] vt (subj: smell, feeling) ...に充満する ...ni júman suru

perverse [pə:rvə:rs'] adj (contrary: behavior) 天のじゃくの amá no jàku no

perversion [pə:rvə:r'ʒən] n (sexual) 変態

heñtai; (of truth) 曲解 kyokkái; (of justice) 悪用 akúyō

pervert [n pə:r'və:rt vb pə:rvə:rt'] n (sexual pervert) 変態 heñtai

♦vt (person, mind) 堕落させる daráku saseru; (truth, someone's words) 曲解する kyokkái suru

pessimism [pes'əmizəm] n 悲観主義 hikánshùgi, ペシミズム peshímizùmu

pessimist [pes'əmist] n 悲観主義者 hikánshugisha, ペシミスト peshímisùto

pessimistic [pesəmis'tik] adj (person) 悲観的な hikánteki na, ペシミスティックな peshímisutikkù na

pest [pest] n (insect) 害虫 gaíchū; (fig: nuisance) うるさいやつ urúsai yatsù

pester [pes'tə:r] vt (bother) 悩ませる nayámaserù

pesticide [pes'tisaid] n 殺虫剤 satchúzài

pet [pet] n (domestic animal) 愛がん動物 aígandòbùtsu, ペット péttò

♦cpd (theory, hate etc) 十八番の oháko no

♦vt (stroke: person, animal) 愛ぶする aíbu suru

♦vi (inf: sexually) ペッティングする pettíngu suru

teacher's pet (favorite) 先生のお気に入り señsei nò o-kí ni irì

petal [pet'əl] n 花びら hanábirà

peter [pi:'tə:r]: *peter out* vi (road, stream etc) だんだんなくなる dañdañ nakúnarù; (conversation, meeting) しりすぼまりに終る shiŕisubomarì ni owárù

petite [pəti:t'] adj (referring to woman: small) 小柄な kogára na

petition [pətiʃ'ən] n (signed document) 陳情書 chíñjōshò; (LAW) 請願 seígan

petrified [pet'rəfaid] adj (fig: terrified) 恐怖に駆られた kyōfu ni karáretà

petrol [pet'rəl] (BRIT) n (fuel) ガソリン gasórin

two/four-star petrol レギュラー〔ハイオク〕ガソリン regyúrà〔haíoku〕gasórin

petrol can n ガソリン缶 gasóriñkan

petroleum [pətrou'li:əm] n 石油 sekíyu

petrol pump (BRIT) n (in garage) ガソリンポンプ gasórinpoñpu

petrol station (BRIT) n ガソリンスタンド gasórinsutañdo

petrol tank (BRIT) n ガソリンタンク gasórintañku

petticoat [pet'i:kout] n (underskirt) ペチコート péchìkōto

petty [pet'i:] adj (small, unimportant) さ さいな sásài na; (small-minded) 狭量な kyóryō na

petty cash n (in office) 小口現金 kogúchigeñkin

petty officer n (in navy) 下士官 kashíkañ

petulant [petʃ'ələnt] adj せっかちな sekkáchi na

pew [pju:] n (in church) 長いす nagáisu

pewter [pju:'tə:r] n しろめ shíròme

phallic [fæl'ik] adj (object, symbol) 陰茎状の iñkeijō no

phantom [fæn'təm] n (ghost) お化け o-bákè

pharmaceutical [fɑːrməsuː'tikəl] adj 製薬の seíyaku no

pharmacist [fɑːr'məsist] n 薬剤師 yakúzaishì

pharmacy [fɑːr'məsi:] n 薬局 yakkyókù

phase [feiz] n (stage) 段階 dañkai

♦vt: *to phase something in/out* …を段階的に取入れる〔なくす〕…wo dañkaiteki nì torírerù〔nakúsù〕

Ph.D. [pi:'eitʃ'di:'] abbr = **Doctor of Philosophy**

pheasant [fez'ənt] n キジ kijí

phenomena [finɑːm'ənə] npl of **phenomenon**

phenomenal [finɑːm'ənəl] adj 驚異的な kyóiteki na

phenomenon [finɑːm'ənɑːn] (pl **phenomena**) n 現象 geñshō

philanthropist [filæn'θrəpist] n 慈善家 jizéñka

Philippines [fil'ipi:nz] npl: *the Philippines* フィリピン fírìpin

philosopher [filɑːs'əfə:r] n (scholar) 哲学者 tetsúgakushà

philosophical [filəsɑːf'ikəl] adj (ideas, conversation etc) 哲学的な tetsúgakuteki na; (fig: calm, resigned) 冷静な reísei na

philosophy [filəːsˈəfiː] n (SCOL) 哲学 tetsúgàku; (set of ideas: of philosopher) ...の哲学 ...no tetsúgàku; (theory: of any person) 考え方 kañgaekatà, 思想 shisô

phlegm [flem] n (substance) たん tañ

phlegmatic [flegmætˈik] adj (person) の ろまな noróma na

phobia [fouˈbiːə] n (irrational fear: of insects, flying, water etc) 恐怖症 kyốfushô

phone [foun] n (system) 電話 deñwa; (apparatus) 電話器 deñwakì
♦vt ...に電話を掛ける ...ni deñwa wo kakérù
to be on the phone (BRIT: possess a phone) 電話を持っている deñwa wo mottè irù; (be calling) 電話中である deñwachū de arù

phone back vt ...に電話を掛け直す ...ni deñwa wo kakénaosù
♦vi 電話を掛け直す deñwa wo kakénaosù

phone book n (directory) 電話帳 deñwachō

phone booth n 電話ボックス deñwabokkùsu

phone box (BRIT) n 電話ボックス deñwabokkùsu

phone call n 電話 deñwa

phone-in [founˈin] (BRIT) n (RADIO, TV) 視聴者が電話で参加する番組 shichôsha ga deñwa dè sañka suru bañgumi

phonetics [fənetˈiks] n 音声学 oñseigàku

phone up vt ...に電話を掛ける ...ni deñwa wo kakérù
♦vi 電話を掛ける deñwa wo kakérù

phoney [founˈiː] adj (false: address) うそ の úsò no; (: accent) 偽の nisé no; (person) 信用できない shiñ-yō dekinài

phonograph [founˈəgræf] (US) n 蓄音機 chikúoñkì

phosphorus [fɑːsˈfərəs] n りん ríñ

photo [fouˈtou] n (photograph) 写真 shashín

photocopier [fouˈtəkɑːpiːəːr] n (machine)

写真複写機 shashínfukushakì, コピー機 kopíkì

photocopy [fouˈtəkɑːpiː] n コピー kôpì
♦vt (picture, document etc) ...のコピーを取る ...no kôpì wo tórù

photogenic [foutədʒenˈik] adj (person) 写真写りの良い shashín-utsurì no yôì

photograph [fouˈtəgræf] n 写真 shashín
♦vt (person, object, place etc) 撮影する satsúei suru

photographer [fətɑːgˈrəfəːr] n カメラマン kaméramàn

photographic [foutəgræfˈik] adj (equipment etc) 写真の shashín no

photography [fətɑːgˈrəfiː] n (art, subject) 写真撮影 shashínsatsùei

phrase [freiz] n (group of words, expression) 言方 iíkatà; (LING) 句 kú
♦vt (express) 表現する hyṓgen suru

phrase book n (foreign language aid) 表現集 hyṓgenshū

physical [fizˈikəl] adj (of the body: needs, punishment, exercise etc) 肉体的な nikútaiteki na; (geography, properties) 物理的な butsúriteki na; (world, universe, object) 自然の shizén no; (sciences) 物理学の butsúrigàku no

physical education n 体育 taíiku

physically [fizˈikliː] adv (fit, attractive) 肉体的に nikútaiteki ni

physician [fiziʃˈən] n (doctor) 医者 ishá

physicist [fizˈəsist] n 物理学者 butsúrigakushà

physics [fizˈiks] n 物理学 butsúrigàku

physiology [fiziɑːlˈədʒiː] n (science) 生理学 seírigàku; (functioning of animal, plant) 生理 seíri

physiotherapy [fiziouθeːrˈəpiː] n (MED) 物理療法 butsúriryồhô

physique [fizikˈ] n (build: of person) 体格 taíkaku

pianist [piːˈænist] n (MUS) ピアニスト piánisùto

piano [piːænˈou] n (MUS) ピアノ piáno

piccolo [pikˈəlou] n (MUS) ピッコロ pikkôro

pick [pik] n (tool: also: **pick-axe**) つるはし tsurúhàshi

♦*vt* (select) 選ぶ erábù; (gather: fruit, flowers) 摘む tsúmù; (remove, take) 取る tórù; (lock) こじ開ける kojíakerù

take your pick (choose) 選ぶ erábù

the pick of (best) ...からえり抜かれた物 ...kara erínukaretà mónð

to pick one's nose/teeth 鼻〔歯〕をほじる haná(há)wò hojírù

to pick a quarrel (with someone) (...に) けんかを売る (...ni) keñka wò urú

pick at *vt fus* (food) ちびちび食べる chíbìchibi tabérù

picket [pik'it] *n* (in strike) ピケ piké

♦*vt* (factory, workplace etc) ...にピケを張る ...ni piké wò hárù

pickle [pik'əl] *n* (*also*: **pickles**: as condiment) ピクルス píkurusu; (*fig*: mess) 苦境 kukyő

♦*vt* (CULIN: in vinegar) 酢漬にする suzúke ni surù; (: in salt water) 塩漬にする shiózuke ni surù

pick on *vt fus* (person: criticize) 非難する hinán suru; (: treat badly) いじめる ijímerù

pick out *vt* (distinguish) 識別する shikíbetsu suru; (choose from a group) 選び出す erábidasù, ピックアップする pikkúappù suru

pickpocket [pik'pɑːkit] *n* すり súrì

pick up *vi* (improve: health, economy, trade) 良くなる yókù naru

♦*vt* (object: from floor) 拾う hiróu; (POLICE: arrest) 逮捕する taího suru; (collect: person, parcel etc) 引取る hikítorù; (AUT: passenger) 乗せる noséru; (person: for sexual encounter) 引っ掛ける hikkákerù; (learn: language, skill etc) 覚える obóerù; (RADIO) 受信する jushín suru

to pick up speed 加速する kasóku suru

to pick oneself up (after falling etc) 起き上る okíagarù

pickup [pik'ʌp] *n* (small truck) ピックアップ pikkúappù

picnic [pik'nik] *n* (outdoor meal) ピクニック pikunikku

picture [pik'tʃər] *n* (painting, drawing, print) 絵 é; (photograph) 写真 shashín;

(TV) 画像 gaző; (film) 映画 éìga; (*fig*: description) 描写 byősha; (: situation) 事態 jítaì

♦*vt* (imagine) 想像する sőzō suru

picture book *n* 絵本 ehóñ

pictures [pik'tʃərz] (*BRIT*) *npl*: *the pictures* (cinema) 映画 éìga

picturesque [piktʃəresk'] *adj* (place, building) 風情のある fúzèi no árù

pie [pai] *n* (CULIN: vegetable, meat, fruit) パイ páì

piece [piːs] *n* (bit or part of larger thing) かけら kakéra; (portion: of cake, chocolate, bread etc) 一切れ hitókìre; (length: of string, ribbon) 一本 íppòn; (item): *a piece of clothing/furniture/advice* 1つ hitótsù

♦*vt*: *to piece together* (information) 総合する sőgō suru; (parts of a whole) 継ぎ合せる tsugíawaserù

to take to pieces (dismantle) 分解する buñkai suru

piecemeal [piːs'miːl] *adv* (irregularly) 少しずつ sukóshizutsù

piecework [piːs'wəːrk] *n* 出来高払いの仕事 dekídakabarài no shigóto

pie chart *n* 円形グラフ eñkeiguràfu

pier [piːr] *n* 桟橋 sañbashi

pierce [piːrs] *vt* (puncture: surface, material, skin etc) 貫通する kañtsū suru

piercing [piːrs'iŋ] *adj* (*fig*: cry) 甲高い kañdakaì; (: eyes, stare) 鋭い surúdoì; (wind) 刺す様な sásù yō na

piety [pai'əti] *n* (REL) 信心 shiñjìñ

pig [pig] *n* (ZOOL) ブタ butá; (*pej*: unkind person) 畜生 chikúshő; (: greedy person) 欲張り目 yokúbarimè

pigeon [pidʒ'ən] *n* (bird) ハト hátò

pigeonhole [pidʒ'ənhoul] *n* (for letters, messages) 小仕切り kojíkìri

piggy bank [pig'iː-] *n* (money box) 貯金箱 chokíñbako

pigheaded [pig'hedid] (*pej*) *adj* (stubborn) 頑固な gañko na

piglet [pig'lit] *n* 子ブタ kobúta

pigment [pig'mənt] *n* 色素 shikíso

pigskin [pig'skin] *n* ブタのなめし革 butá no naméshigàwa

pigsty [pig'stai] n (on farm) ブタ小屋 butágoya

pigtail [pig'teil] n (plait) お下げ o-ságe

pike [paik] n (fish) カワカマス kawákamàsu, パイク páîku

pilchard [pilt'ʃərd] n (fish) イワシ iwáshi

pile [pail] n (heap, stack) 山 yamá; (of carpet, cloth) 毛足 keáshi, パイル páîru
♦vt (also: **pile up**): objects) 積上げる tsumíagerù
♦vi (also: **pile up**): objects) 積重なる tsumíkasanarù; (problems, work) たまる tamárù

pile into vt fus (car) ...に乗込む ...ni noríkomù

piles [pailz] npl (MED) じ ji

pile-up [pail'ʌp] n (AUT) 衝突事故 shótotsujìkò

pilfering [pil'fəriŋ] n (petty thieving) くすねる事 kusúnerù kotó

pilgrim [pil'grim] n (REL) 巡礼者 juñreishà

pilgrimage [pil'grəmidʒ] n (REL) 巡礼 juñreí

pill [pil] n (MED: tablet) 錠剤 jốzai
the pill (contraceptive pill) 経口避妊薬 keíkōhinìñ-yaku, ピル pírù

pillage [pil'idʒ] vt (loot: house, town etc) 略奪する ryakúdatsu suru

pillar [pil'ə:r] n (ARCHIT) 柱 hashíra

pillar box (BRIT) n (MAIL) ポスト pósùto

pillion [pil'jən] n: **to ride pillion** (on motorcycle) 後ろに相乗りする ushíro nì aínori surù

pillory [pil'ə:ri:] vt (criticize strongly) 非難する hinán suru

pillow [pil'ou] n (cushion: for head) まくら mákùra

pillowcase [pil'oukeis] n (cover: for pillow) 枕カバー makúrakabà, ピロケース pírôkèsu

pilot [pai'lət] n (AVIAT) 操縦士 sốjūshi, パイロット páîrotto
♦cpd (scheme, study etc) 試験的な shikénteki na
♦vt (aircraft) 操縦する sốjū suru

pilot light n (on cooker, boiler, fire) 口火 kuchíbi

pimp [pimp] n ポン引き poñbiki, ひも himó

pimple [pim'pəl] n にきび níkìbi

pin [pin] n (metal: for attaching, fastening) ピン píñ
♦vt (fasten with pin) ピンで止める píñ de tomérù
pins and needles (in arms, legs etc) しびれが切れる事 shibíre gà kirérù kotó
to pin someone down (fig) ...に約束させる ...ni yakúsoku saserù, ...にくぎを刺す ...ni kugí wo sásù
to pin something on someone (fig) ...に ...のぬれぎぬを着せる ...ni ...no nuréginù wo kisérù

pinafore [pin'əfɔ:r] n (also: **pinafore dress**) エプロンドレス epúrondorèsu

pinball [pin'bɔ:l] n (game) スマートボール sumátobồru; (machine) スマートボール機 sumátobồruki

pincers [pin'sə:rz] npl (TECH) やっとこ yattôko, ペンチ péñchi; (of crab, lobster etc) はさみ hasámi

pinch [pintʃ] n (small amount: of salt etc) 一つまみ hitótsùmami
♦vt (person: with finger and thumb) つねる tsunérù; (inf: steal) くすねる kusúnerù
at a pinch 緊急の場合 kiñkyū nò baái

pincushion [pin'kuʃən] n (SEWING) 針刺し harísashì

pine [pain] n (also: **pine tree**) マツ mátsù; (wood) マツ材 matsúzài
♦vi: **to pine for** (person, place) 思い焦がれる omóikogarerù

pineapple [pain'æpəl] n (fruit) パイナップル paínappùru

pine away vi (gradually die) 衰弱して死ぬ suíjaku shite shinú

ping [piŋ] n (noise) ぴゅーんという音 pyūn to iú otó

ping-pong [piŋ'pɔːŋ] ® n (sport) 卓球 takkyū, ピンポン píñpon

pink [piŋk] adj ピンク色の piñkuiro no
♦n (color) ピンク色 piñkuiro; (BOT) ナデシコ nadéshìko

pinnacle [pin'əkəl] *n* (of building, mountain) 天辺 teppéň; (*fig*) 頂点 chốteň

pinpoint [pin'pɔint] *vt* (discover) 発見する hakkéň suru; (explain) 説明する setsúmei suru; (position of something) 正確に示す sefkaku nǐ shimésù

pint [paint] *n* (*US*: = 473 cc; *BRIT*: = 568 cc) パイント painto
a pint of beer, (BRIT: inf) a pint ビール1パイント bǐru ichípainto

pin-up [pin'ʌp] *n* (picture) ピンナップ写真〔絵〕piňnappushashiň〔e〕

pioneer [paiəni:r'] *n* (initiator: of scheme, science, method) 先駆者 seňkushà, パイオニア paíonìa; (early settler) 開拓者 kaítakushà

pious [pai'əs] *adj* (person) 信心深い shiňjiňbukai

pip [pip] *n* (seed of fruit) 種 tané; (*BRIT*: time signal on radio) 時報 jihó

pipe [paip] *n* (*gen*, also for smoking) パイプ paípu; (*also*: **water pipe**) 水道管 suídōkan; (*also*: **gas pipe**) ガス管 gasúkan
♦*vt* (water, gas, oil) パイプで運ぶ paípu de hakóbu

pipes [paipz] *npl* (*also*: **bagpipes**) バグパイプ bagúpaìpu

pipe cleaner *n* パイプクリーナー paípukurīnā

pipe down (*inf*) *vi* (be quiet) 黙る damárù

pipe dream *n* (hope, plan) 夢想 musó

pipeline [paip'lain] *n* (for oil, gas) パイプライン paípurain

piper [pai'pər] *n* (bagpipe player) バグパイプ奏者 bagúpaipu sòsha

piping [pai'piŋ] *adv*: *piping hot* (water, food, coffee) うんと熱い úňto atsúì

piquant [pi:'kənt] *adj* (food: spicy) ぴりっとした piríttò shitá; (*fig*: interesting, exciting) 興味深い kyómibùkai

pique [pi:k] *n* 立腹 rippúku

pirate [pai'rit] *n* (sailor) 海賊 kaízoku
♦*vt* (book, video tape, cassette etc) ...の海賊版を作る ...no kaízokubaň wo tsukúrù

pirate radio (*BRIT*) *n* 海賊放送 kaízokuhōsō

pirouette [piru:et'] *n* つま先旋回 tsumásakiseñkai

Pisces [pai'si:z] *n* (ASTROLOGY) 魚座 uózà

piss [pis] (*inf!*) *vi* (urinate) おしっこする oshíkkò suru

pissed [pist] (*inf!*) *adj* (*US*) 怒った okóttà; (*BRIT*: drunk) 酔っ払った yoppáratà

pistol [pis'təl] *n* けん銃 keňjū, ピストル pisútoru

piston [pis'tən] *n* ピストン písùton

pit [pit] *n* (hole in ground) 穴 aná; (in surface of something) くぼみ kubómi; (*also*: **coal pit**) 炭坑 taňkō; (quarry) 採石場 saísekijō
♦*vt*: *to pit one's wits against someone* ...と知恵比べをする ...to chiékuràbe wo suru

pitch [pitʃ] *n* (*BRIT*: SPORT: ground) グラウンド guráundo; (MUS) 調子 chōshi, ピッチ pitchi; (*fig*: level, degree) 度合 doai; (tar) ピッチ pítchǐ
♦*vt* (throw) 投げる nagérù
♦*vi* (fall forwards) つんのめる tsuňnomerù
to pitch a tent (erect) テントを張る téňto wo hárù

pitch-black [pitʃ'blæk'] *adj* (night, place) 真っ暗な makkúra na

pitched battle [pitʃt-] *n* (violent fight) 激戦 gekísen

pitchfork [pitʃ'fɔːrk] *n* ホーク hóku

piteous [pit'i:əs] *adj* (sight, sound etc) 悲惨な hisán na

pitfall [pit'fɔːl] *n* (difficulty, danger) 落し穴 otóshiàna, 危険 kikén

pith [piθ] *n* (of orange, lemon etc) わた watá

pithy [piθ'i:] *adj* (comment, saying etc) 中身の濃い nakámǐ no kóǐ

pitiful [pit'ifəl] *adj* (touching: appearance, sight) 哀れな awáre na

pitiless [pit'ilis] *adj* (person) 冷酷な refkoku na

pits [pits] *npl* (AUT) ピット pitto

pittance [pit'əns] *n* (very small income) スズメの涙 suzúme no namǐda

pity [pit'i:] n (compassion) 哀れみ awáremì
♦vt 哀れむ awáremù
what a pity! (expressing disappointment) 残念だ zańnen da

pivot [piv'ət] n (TECH) 旋回軸 señkaijìku, ピボット píbòtto; (fig) 中心 chūshin

pizza [pi:t'sə] n ピッツァ píttsà, ピザ pízà

placard [plæk'ɑ:rd] n (sign: in public place) 看板 kańban; (: in march etc) プラカード purákàdo

placate [plei'keit] vt (person, anger) なだめる nadámerù

place [pleis] n (in general: point, building, area) 所 tokóro, 場所 bashó; (position: of object) 位置 íchì; (seat) 席 sékì; (job, post etc) 職 shokú, ポスト pósùto; (home): **at/to his place** 彼の家で[へ] kárè no ié de(e); (role: in society, system etc) 役割 yakúwarì
♦vt (put: object) 置く okú; (identify: person) 思い出す omóidasù
to take place (happen) 起る okórù
out of place (not suitable) 場違いの bachígai no
in the first place (first of all) まず第一に mázù daíchi nì
to change places with someone ...と交代する ...to kõtai suru
to be placed (in race, exam) 入賞する nyúsho suru

place of birth n 出生地 shusséichì

placenta [pləsen'tə] n 胎盤 taíban

placid [plæs'id] adj (person) 穏和な ońwa na

plagiarism [plei'dʒə:rizəm] n ひょう窃 hyósetsu, 盗作 tõsaku

plague [pleig] n (MED) 伝染病 deńsenbyò; (fig: of locusts etc) 異常発生 ijõhassèi
♦vt (fig: subj: problems, difficulties) 悩ます nayámasù

plaice [pleis] n inv (fish) カレイ kárèi

plaid [plæd] n (cloth) チェックの生地 chékkù no kíjì

plain [plein] adj (unpatterned) 無地の mújì no; (simple: dress, food) 質素な shís[so na; (clear, easily understood) 明白な meíhaku na; (not beautiful) 不器量な bukíryo na
♦adv (wrong, stupid etc) 全く mattáku
♦n (area of land) 平原 heígen

plain chocolate n ブラックチョコレート burákku chokorèto

plain-clothes [plein'klouz] adj (police officer) 私服の shifúku no

plainly [plein'li:] adv (obviously) 明白に meíhaku ni; (hear, see, easily) はっきりと hakkírì to; (state: clearly) ざっくばらんに zákkùbaran ni

plaintiff [plein'tif] n (LAW) 原告 geńkoku

plaintive [plein'tiv] adj (cry, voice) 哀れっぽい awáreppoì

plait [plæt] n (of hair) お下げ o-ságe; (of rope, leather) 編みひも状の物 amíhimojõ no monó

plan [plæn] n (scheme, project) 計画 keíkaku, プラン púràn; (drawing) 図面 zúmèn; (schedule) 予定表 yotéihyo
♦vt (work out in advance: crime, holiday, future etc) 計画する keíkaku suru
♦vi (think ahead) 計画する keíkaku suru
to plan to do ...しようと計画する ...shiyõ to keíkaku suru

plane [plein] n (AVIAT) 飛行機 hikõki; (MATH) 面 mén; (fig: level) 段階 dańkai; (tool) かんな kanna; (also: **plane tree**) スズカケノキ suzúkake no ki, プラタナス purátanàsu

planet [plæn'it] n 惑星 wakúsei

plank [plæŋk] n (of wood) 板 ítà

planner [plæn'ə:r] n (gen) 計画をする人 keíkaku wo suru hitõ; (also: **town planner**) 都市計画担当者 toshíkeikaku tantõshà; (of TV program, project) 計画者 keíkakushà ●

planning [plæn'iŋ] n (of future, project, event etc) 計画 keíkaku; (also: **town planning**) 都市計画 toshíkeíkaku
family planning 家族計画 kazõkukeíkaku

planning permission n 建築許可 keńchikukyoka

plant [plænt] n (BOT) 植物 shokúbùtsu;

(machinery) 設備 sétsùbi; (factory) プラント puráñto

♦vt (seed, plant, ...) に植える ...ni uérù; (field, garden) ...に植える ...ni uérù; (secretly: microphone, bomb, incriminating evidence etc) 仕掛ける shikákerù

plantation [plæntei'ʃən] n (of tea, rubber, sugar etc) 農園 nôeñ; (area planted out with trees) 植林地 shokúriñchi

plaque [plæk] n (commemorative plaque: on building etc) 銘板 meíbaǹ; (on teeth) 歯こう shíkô

plasma [plæz'mə] n 血清 kesséi

plaster [plæs'tə:r] n (for walls) しっくい shikkúì; (also: **plaster of Paris**) 石こう sekkô; (BRIT: also: **sticking plaster**) ばんそうこう bañsôkô

♦vt (wall, ceiling) ...にしっくいを塗る ...ni shikkúì wo nurú; (cover): **to plaster with** ...に...をべったり張る ...ni ...wo bettárì hárù

plastered [plæs'tə:rd] (inf) adj 酔っ払った yopparáttà

plasterer [plæs'tərə:r] n (of walls, ceilings) 左官屋 sakáñ-ya

plastic [plæs'tik] n 合成樹脂 gôseijushì, プラスチック purásuchikkù

♦adj (made of plastic: bucket, chair, cup etc) プラスチック製の purásuchikkusei no

plastic bag n ポリ袋 poríbukuro

Plasticine [plæs'tisi:n]® n 合成粘土 gôseineñdo

plastic surgery n 整形手術 seíkeishujùtsu

plate [pleit] n (dish) 皿 sará; (plateful: of food, biscuits etc) 一皿 hitósàra; (in book: picture, photograph) 1ページ大の挿絵 ichípêjidai nò sashîè, プレート púrêto; (dental plate) 入れ歯 iréba

gold/silver plate 貴金属の食器類 kikínzoku no shokkírùi

plateau [plætou'] (pl **plateaus** or **plateaux**) n (GEO) 高原 kôgen

plate glass n (for window, door) 板ガラス itágaràsu

platform [plæt'fɔ:rm] n (at meeting, for band) 演壇 eñdan; (raised structure: for

landing, loading on etc) 台 dâi; (RAIL) ホーム hômu; (BRIT: of bus) 踏段 fumídan, ステップ sutéppù; (POL) 綱領 kôryô

platinum [plæt'ənəm] n 白金 hakkín, プラチナ puráchina

platitude [plæt'ətu:d] n 決り文句 kimárimoñku

platonic [plətɑ'nik] adj 純粋に精神的な juñsui nì seíshinteki na, プラトニックな purátoniku na

platoon [plətu:n'] n 小隊 shôtai

platter [plæt'ə:r] n 盛皿 morízara

plausible [plɔ:'zəbəl] adj (theory, excuse, statement) もっともらしい mottômorashiî; (person) 口先のうまい kuchísaki nò umaî

play [plei] n (THEATER, RADIO, TV) 劇 gékì

♦vt (subj: children: game) ...して遊ぶ ...shite asóbù; (football, tennis, chess) やる yarú; (compete against) ...と試合をする ...to shiái wò suru; (part, role: in play, film etc) 演ずる eñzurù, ...にふんする ...ni funsuru; (instrument, tune) 演奏する eñsô suru; (listen to: tape, record) 聞く kíkù

♦vi (children: on beach, swings etc) 遊ぶ asóbù; (MUS: orchestra, band) 演奏する eñsô suru; (: record, tape, radio) かかる kakárù

to play safe 大事を取る daíji wo tórù

playboy [plei'bɔi] n プレーボーイ purébôi

play down vt 軽く扱う karúku atsukaù

player [plei'ə:r] n (SPORT) 選手 séñshu, プレーヤー puréyà; (MUS) 奏者 sôsha; (THEATER) 役者 yakúsha

playful [plei'fəl] adj (person, animal) 遊び好きの asóbizuki no

playground [plei'graund] n (in park) 遊び場 asóbiba; (in school) 校庭 kôtei, 運動場 uñdôjô

playgroup [plei'gru:p] (BRIT) n 保育園 hoíkuèn

playing card [plei'iŋ-] n トランプ toráñpu

playing field n グラウンド guráundo

playmate [plei'meit] n 遊び友達 asóbitomòdachi

play-off [plei'ɔ:f] *n* (SPORT) 優勝決定戦 yūshōketteīsen, プレーオフ purēofù

playpen [plei'pen] *n* ベビーサークル bebīsākuru

plaything [plei'θiŋ] *n* おもちゃ omóchà

playtime [plei'taim] *n* (SCOL) 休み時間 yasúmijikàn

play up *vi* (cause trouble: machine) 調子が悪くなる chōshi gà wáruku naru; (: children) 行儀を悪くする gyōgi wò wáruku suru

playwright [plei'rait] *n* 劇作家 gekísakka

plc [pi:elsi:'] *abbr* (= *public limited company*) 有限株式会社 yúgen kabushikigaishā

plea [pli:] *n* (request) 懇願 kofígan; (LAW) 申立て mōshitate

plead [pli:d] *vt* (LAW) 申立てる mōshitaterù; (give as excuse: ignorance, ill health etc) ...だと言い訳する ...dá tò iíwake surù

♦*vi* (LAW) 申立てる mōshitaterù; (beg): *to plead with someone* ...に懇願する ...ni kofígan suru

pleasant [plez'ənt] *adj* (agreeable, nice: weather, chat, smile etc) 気持の良い kimóchi no yoĩ; (agreeable: person) 愛想の良い aíso no yoĩ

pleasantries [plez'əntri:z] *npl*: *to exchange pleasantries* あいさつを交わす áĩsatsu wo kawásù

please [pli:z] *excl* (polite request) どうぞ dōzo, どうか dōka; (polite acceptance): *yes, please* ええ, 有難う eé, arígatò; (to attract someone's attention) 済みません sumímaseñ

♦*vt* (give pleasure or satisfaction to) 喜ばす yorókobasù

♦*vi* (give pleasure, satisfaction) 人を喜ばす hitó wò yorókobasù; (think fit): *do as you please* お好きな様にして下さい o-súki na yṓ ni shité kudasaí

please yourself! (*inf*) ご勝手に go-káttè nĩ

pleased [pli:zd] *adj* (happy, satisfied): *pleased (with)* (...で) 満足している

(...de) mañzoku shite irù

pleased to meet you 初めまして hajímemashìte

pleasing [pli:'ziŋ] *adj* (remark etc) 愉快な yúkai na, うれしい uréshiĩ; (picture) 楽しい tanóshiĩ; (person) 愛敬のある aíkyo no arù

pleasure [pleʒ'ə:r] *n* (happiness, satisfaction) 快楽 káiraku; (activity of enjoying oneself, enjoyable experience) 楽しみ tanóshimì

it's a pleasure どういたしまして dṓ itáshimashitè

pleasure boat *n* 遊覧船 yūransen

pleat [pli:t] *n* ひだ hídà, プリーツ purītsù

pledge [pledʒ] *n* (promise) 約束 yakúsoku

♦*vt* (promise: money, support, help) 約束する yakúsoku suru

plentiful [plen'tifəl] *adj* (food, supply, amount) 豊富な hōfu na

plenty [plen'ti:] *n*: *plenty of* (much, many) 沢山の takúsan no; (sufficient) 十分な jūbun na

pleurisy [plu:r'isi:] *n* ろく膜炎 rokúmakuèn

pliable [plai'əbəl] *adj* (material) しなやかな shináyàka na; (fig: person) 素直な súnào na

pliant [plai'ənt] *adj* = **pliable**

pliers [plai'ə:rz] *npl* ペンチ péñchi

plight [plait] *n* (of person, country) 苦境 kukyṓ

plimsolls [plim'səlz] (BRIT) *npl* 運動靴 uñdṑgutsu, スニーカー suníkà

plinth [plinθ] *n* 台座 daíza

plod [plɑ:d] *vi* (walk) とぼとぼ歩く tóbòtobo arúkù; (fig) 何とかやる náñ to ka yárù

plonk [plɑ:ŋk] (*inf*) *n* (BRIT: wine) 安ワイン yasúwaìn

♦*vt*: *to plonk something down* たたきつける様に...を置く tatákitsukeru yṓ ni ...wo ókù

plot [plɑ:t] *n* (secret plan) 陰謀 iñbṓ; (of story, play, film) 筋 sújì, プロット puróttò; (of land) 区画 kukáku

♦*vt* (sb's downfall etc) たくらむ takúra-

mù; (AVIAT, NAUT: position on chart)
地図 に 書き込む chízu ni kakíkomù;
(MATH: point on graph) グラフにする
gúrafu ni suru

♦vi (conspire) 陰謀を企てる iñbō wò kuwádaterù

plotter [pla:t'ə:r] n (instrument) 製図道
具 seízudōgu

plough [plau] (US also: **plow**) n (AGR)
すき sukí

♦vt (earth) 耕す tagáyasù

to plough money into (company, project etc) ...に金をつぎ込む ...ni kané wò
tsugíkomù

ploughman's lunch [plau'mənz-] (BRIT)
n 軽食 keíshoku ◇パブのランチで、パ
ン、チーズ、ピクルスからなる pábù no
ráñchi de, pán, chízu, píkùrusu kara
nárù

plough through vt fus (crowd) ...をか
き分けて歩く ...wo kakíwakete arukù

plow [plau] (US) = **plough**

ploy [plɔi] n 策略 sakúryaku

pluck [plʌk] vt (fruit, flower, leaf) 摘む
tsúmù; (musical instrument) つま弾く
tsumábikù; (bird) ...の羽をむしる ...no
hané wò mushírù; (remove hairs from:
eyebrow) ...の毛を抜く ...no ké wo nukú

♦n (courage) 勇気 yūki

to pluck up courage 勇気を出す yūki
wo dásù

plug [plʌg] n (ELEC) 差込み sashíkomi,
プラグ púragu; (stopper: in sink, bath) 栓
séñ; (AUT: also: **spark(ing) plug**) スパー
クプラグ supákupuragu

♦vt (hole) ふさぐ fuságù; (inf: advertise)
宣伝する señden suru

plug in vt (ELEC) ...のプラグを差込む
...no púragu wo sashíkomù

plum [plʌm] n (fruit) プラム púramu

♦cpd (inf): *plum job* 甘い汁を吸える職
amái shirù wo suérù shokú

plumage [plu:'mid3] n 羽毛 hané ◇鳥の体
を覆う羽の総称 torí nò karáda wo ōù
hané no sōshō

plumb [plʌm] vt: *to plumb the depths*
(fig) (of unpleasant emotion) 辛酸をなめ
尽す shiñsan wò namétsukusù; (of un-

pleasant expression) ...を極端に表現する
...wo kyokútan nì hyōgen suru

plumber [plʌm'ə:r] n 配管工 haíkankō

plumbing [plʌm'iŋ] n (piping) 水道設備
suídōsetsubì; (trade, work) 配管業 haíkan-
gyō

plume [plu:m] n (of bird) 羽 hané; (on helmet, horse s head) 前立 maédate

plummet [plʌm'it] vi: *to plummet
(down)* (bird, aircraft) 真っ直ぐに落下
する massúgù ni rakká surù; (price,
amount, rate) 暴落する bóraku suru

plump [plʌmp] adj (person) ぽっちゃりし
た potchárì shita

♦vi: *to plump for* (inf: choose) 選ぶ
erábù

plump up vt (cushion, pillow) 膨らませ
る fukúramaserù

plunder [plʌn'də:r] n (activity) 略奪 ryakúdatsu; (stolen things) 分捕り品 buñdo-
rihiñ

♦vt (steal from: city, tomb) 略奪する
ryakúdatsu suru

plunge [plʌnd3] n (dive: of bird, person)
飛込み tobíkomi; (fig: of prices, rates
etc) 暴落 bóraku

♦vt (hand, knife) 突っ込む tsukkómù

♦vi (fall: person, thing) 落ちる ochírù;
(dive: bird, person) 飛込む tobíkomù;
(fig: prices, rates etc) 暴落する bóraku
suru

to take the plunge 冒険する bōken suru

plunger [plʌn'd3ə:r] n (for sink) プラン
ジャー puráñjā ◇長い棒の付いたゴムカ
ップ nagáì bō no tsuità gomúkappù

plunging [plʌn'd3iŋ] adj (neckline) 切込
みの深い kiríkomi no fukaì

pluperfect [plu:pə:r'fikt] n 過去完了形
kakókanryōkei

plural [plu:'rəl] adj 複数の fukúsū no

♦n 複数形 fukúsūkei

plus [plʌs] n (also: **plus sign**) 加符号 ka-
fúgō, プラス púrasu

♦prep (MATH) ...に ...を加算して ...ni
...wo kasán shite, ...に ...を足して ...ni
...wo tashíte; (in addition to) ...に加えて
...ni kuwáete

2 plus 2 is 4 2足す2は4 ní tasú ní wà yóñ

ten/twenty plus (more than) 10〔20〕以上 jū́ 〔nijū́〕ijō

plush [plʌʃ] *adj* (car, hotel etc) 豪華な gṓka na

plutonium [plu:tou'ni:əm] *n* プルトニウム purútonìumu

ply [plai] *vt* (a trade) 営む itónamù
♦*vi* (ship) 往復する ṓfuku suru
♦*n* (of wool, rope) 太さ futósa
to ply someone with drink ...に強引に酒を勧める ...ni gṓiñ nì sakê wò susúmerù

plywood [plai'wud] *n* ベニヤ板 beníyaità

P.M. [pi:'em'] *abbr* = **Prime Minister**

p.m. [pi:'em'] *adv abbr* (= *post meridiem*) 午後 gógo

pneumatic [nu:mæt'ik] *adj* (air-filled) 空気で膨らませた kū́ki dè fukúramasetà; (powered by air) 空気... kū́ki...

pneumatic drill *n* 空気ドリル kū́kidorìru

pneumonia [nu:moun'jə] *n* 肺炎 haíeñ

poach [poutʃ] *vt* (steal: fish) 密漁する mitsúryo suru; (: animals, birds) 密猟する mitsúryō suru; (cook: egg) 落し卵にする otóshitamagò ni suru, ポーチトエッグにする pṓchitoeggù ni suru; (: fish) 煮る nirú
♦*vi* (steal: fish) 密漁する mitsúryō suru; (: animals, birds) 密猟する mitsúryō suru

poached [poutʃt] *adj*: *poached egg* 落し卵 otóshitamagò, ポーチトエッグ pṓchitoeggù

poacher [pou'tʃə:r] *n* (of fish) 密漁者 mitsúryōshà; (of animals, birds) 密猟者 mitsúryōshà

P.O. Box [pi:'ou-] *n abbr* = **Post Office Box**

pocket [pɑ:k'it] *n* (on jacket, trousers, suitcase, car door etc) ポケット pokéttò; (*fig*: small area) 孤立地帯 korítsuchitài
♦*vt* (put in one's pocket) ポケットに入れる pokéttò ni irérù; (steal) くすねる kusúnerù
to be out of pocket (*BRIT*) 損する sóñ suru

pocketbook [pɑ:k'itbuk] (*US*) *n* (wallet) 財布 saífu; (handbag) ハンドバッグ hañdobaggù

pocket calculator *n* 電卓 deñtaku

pocket knife *n* ポケットナイフ pokéttonaìfu

pocket money *n* 小遣い kózùkai

pod [pɑ:d] *n* さや sáyà

podgy [pɑ:dʒ'i:] *adj* 小太りの kobútòri no

podiatrist [pədai'ətrist] (*US*) *n* 足治療医 ashíchiryòi

poem [pou'əm] *n* 詩 shi

poet [pou'it] *n* 詩人 shijín

poetic [pouet'ik] *adj* (relating to poetry) 詩の shi no; (like poetry) 詩的な shitéki na

poet laureate *n* 桂冠詩人 keikanshijin

poetry [pou'itri:] *n* (LITERATURE) 詩歌 shíika

poignant [pɔin'jənt] *adj* (emotion, look, grief etc) 痛ましい itámashiì

point [pɔint] *n* (gen) 点 teñ, ポイント poíñto; (sharp end: of needle, knife etc) せん端 señtan; (purpose) 目的 mokúteki; (significant part) 要点 yṓteñ; (detail, aspect, quality) 特徴 tokúchō; (particular place or position) 地点 chitéñ; (moment) 時点 jítèn; (stage in development) 段階 dañkai; (score: in competition, game, sport) 得点 tokúten, 点数 teñsū; (*BRIT*: ELEC: socket) コンセント kóñsento; (*also*: **decimal point**) 小数点 shṓsùten; (in numbers): *2 point 3 (2.3)* 2点3 ní teñ sañ
♦*vt* (show, mark) 指す sásù; (gun etc): *to point something at someone* ...に...を向ける ...ni ...wo mukérù
♦*vi*: *to point at* (with finger, stick etc) ...を指す ...wo sásù

to be on the point of doing something ...をする所である ..wo suru tokoró de árù

to make a point of doing 努めて...する tsutómete ...surū

to get/miss the point 相手が言わんとする事が分かる〔分からない〕aíte gà iwáñ to suru kotõ ga wakárù〔wakáranaì〕

to come to the point 要点を言う yṓteñ

wǒ iú

there's no point (in doing) (...するのは) 無意味だ (...surú no wà) muími dà

point-blank [pɔint'blæŋk'] *adv* (say, ask) ずばり zubárì; (refuse) あっさり assárì; (*also*: **at point-blank range**) 至近距離で shikínkyorì de

pointed [pɔin'tid] *adj* (stick, pencil, chin, nose etc) とがった togátta; (*fig*: remark) 辛らつな shínratsu na

pointedly [pɔin'tidli:] *adv* (reply etc) 意味深長に ímìshinchō ni

pointer [pɔin'tə:r] *n* (on chart, machine) 針 hárì; (*fig*: piece of information or advice) ヒント hínto

pointless [pɔint'lis] *adj* (useless, senseless) 無意味な muími na

point of view *n* (opinion) 観点 kańten

point out *vt* (in debate etc) ...を指摘する ...wo shitéki suru

points [pɔints] *npl* (AUT) ポイント poíñto; (RAIL) 転てつ機 teńtetsukì, ポイント poíñto

point to *vt fus* (*fig*) ...を指摘する ...wo shitéki suru

poise [pɔiz] *n* (composure) 落ち着き ochítsuki

poison [pɔi'zən] *n* (harmful substance) 毒 dokú

♦*vt* (person, animal: kill with poison) 毒殺する dokúsatsu suru; (: give poison to) ...に毒を飲ませる ...ni dokú wò nomáserù

poisonous [pɔi'zənəs] *adj* 有毒な yúdoku na, 毒... dokú...

poke [pouk] *vt* (jab with finger, stick etc) つつく tsutsúkù; (put): *to poke something in(to)* ...の中へ...を突っ込む ...no nákà e ...wo tsukkómù

poke about *vi* (search) 物色する busshóku suru

poker [pou'kə:r] *n* (metal bar) 火かき棒 hikákibō; (CARDS) ポーカー pōkà

poky [pou'ki:] *adj* (room, house) 狭苦しい semákurushiì

Poland [pou'lənd] *n* ポーランド pōrando

polar [pou'lə:r] *adj* (GEO, ELEC) 極地の kyókùchi no

polar bear *n* 北極グマ hokkyókugùma

polarize [pou'lə:raiz] *vt* 分裂させる buńretsu saserù

Pole [poul] *n* ポーランド人 pōrandojìn

pole [poul] *n* (post, stick) 棒 bǒ, さお sáò; (GEO, ELEC) 極 kyókù

flag pole 旗ざお hatázao

telegraph/telephone pole 電柱 deńchū

pole bean (*US*) *n* (runner bean) インゲン íñgen

pole vault *n* 棒高飛び bǒtakàtobi

police [pəli:s'] *n* (organization) 警察 keísatsu; (members) 警官 keíkan

♦*vt* (street, area, town) ...の治安を維持する ...no chián wò íjì suru

police car *n* パトカー patókà

policeman [pəli:s'mən] (*pl* **policemen**) *n* 警官 keíkan

police state *n* (POL) 警察国家 keísatsukokkà

police station *n* 警察署 keísatsusho

policewoman [pəli:s'wumən] (*pl* **policewomen**) *n* 婦人警官 fujínkeìkan, 婦警 fukéi

policy [pɑ:l'isi:] *n* (POL, ECON: set of ideas, plans) 政策 seísaku; (*also*: **insurance policy**) 保険証券 hokénshōken

polio [pou'li:ou] *n* 小児麻ひ shǒnimahì, ポリオ pórìo

Polish [pou'liʃ] *adj* ポーランドの pōrando no; (LING) ポーランド語の pōrandogo no

♦*n* (LING) ポーランド語 pōrandogo

polish [pɑ:l'iʃ] *n* (*also*: **shoe polish**) 靴墨 kutsúzumi; (for furniture, floors etc) 光沢剤 kǒtakuzài; (shine: on shoes, floors, furniture etc) 光沢 kǒtaku; (*fig*: refinement) 洗練 seńren

♦*vt* (put polish on, make shiny) 磨く migákù

polished [pɑ:l'iʃt] *adj* (*fig*: person, style) 洗練された seńren sareta

polish off *vt* (work) 仕上げる shiágerù; (food) 平らげる taíragerù

polite [pəlait'] *adj* (person: well-mannered) 礼儀正しい reígitadashiì; (socially superior: company, society) 上流の jǒryū no

politeness [pəlait'nis] n 礼儀正しさ reígitadashisa

political [pəlit'ikəl] adj (relating to politics) 政治の seíji no; (person) 政治に関心ある seíji nî kañshin arû

politically [pəlit'ikli:] adv 政治的に seíjiteki ni

politician [pɑ:litiʃ'ən] n 政治家 seíjika

politics [pɑ:l'itiks] n (activity) 政治 seíji; (subject) 政治学 seíjigàku
♦npl (beliefs, opinions) 政治的思想 seíjitekishisǒ

poll [poul] n (also: **opinion poll**) 世論調査 yorónchôsa; (political election) 選挙 séñkyo
♦vt (in opinion poll) ...の意見を聞く ...no îkèn wo kikû; (number of votes) 獲得する kakûtoku suru

pollen [pɑ:l'ən] n 花粉 kafún

polling day [pou'liŋ-] (BRIT) n 投票日 tôhyôbi

polling station (BRIT) n 投票所 tôhyôjo

pollute [pəlu:t'] vt (air, water, land) 汚染する osén suru

pollution [pəlu:'ʃən] n (process) 汚染 osén; (substances) 汚染物質 osénbusshîtsu

polo [pou'lou] n (sport) ポロ pôrô

polo-necked [pou'lounekt] adj (sweater) とっくりえりの tokkúrierî no

poltergeist [poul'tə:rgaist] n けん騒霊 keñsôrei, ポルターガイスト porútāgaìsuto

polyester [pɑ:li:es'tə:r] n ポリエステル porñesuteru

polyethylene [pɑ:li:eθ'əli:n] (US) n ポリエチレン porñechirèn

polystyrene [pɑ:li:stai'ri:n] n ポリスチレン porñsuchirèn

polytechnic [pɑ:li:tek'nik] n 科学技術専門学校 kagákugijutsu senmongakkǒ ◊ 英国では大学レベルの高等教育機関 eîkoku de wà daígakurebèru no kôtôkyôìku kikaǹ

polythene [pɑ:l'əθi:n] (BRIT) n = **polyethylene**

pomegranate [pɑ:m'əgrænit] n ザクロ zákùro

pomp [pɑ:mp] n 華やかさ hanáyàkasa

pompom [pɑ:m'pɑ:m] n ポンポン pôñpon

pompon [pɑ:m'pɑ:n] n = **pompom**

pompous [pɑ:m'pəs] (pej) adj (person, piece of writing) もったい振った mottáibuttà

pond [pɑ:nd] n (natural, artificial) 池 ikê

ponder [pɑ:n'də:r] vt 熟考する jukkô suru

ponderous [pɑ:n'də:rəs] adj (large and heavy) 大きくて重い ókikute omôî; (speech, writing) 重苦しい omôkurushîî

pong [pɔ:ŋ] (BRIT: inf) n 悪臭 akúshū

pontificate [pɑ:ntif'ikeit] vi (fig): **to pontificate (about)** (...について) もったい振って話す (...ni tsûíte) mottáibuttê hanásù

pontoon [pɑ:ntu:n'] n (platform) ポンツーン poñtsûn; (for seaplane etc) フロート fûrôto

pony [pou'ni:] n ポニー pônî

ponytail [pou'ni:teil] n (person's hairstyle) ポニーテール ponîtèru

pony trekking [-trek'iŋ] (BRIT) n 乗馬旅行 jôbaryokô

poodle [pu:'dəl] n プードル pùdoru

pool [pu:l] n (also: **pool of water**) 水たまり mizútamari; (pond) 池 ikê; (also: **swimming pool**) プール pûru; (fig: of light, liquid) たまり tamári; (SPORT) 玉突 tamátsuki, ビリヤード biríyàdo
♦vt (money, knowledge, resources) 出し合う dashíaù, プールする pûru suru
typing pool タイピストのプール taípisùto no pûru

pools [pu:lz] npl (football pools) トトカルチョ totókarùcho

poor [pu:r] adj (not rich: person, place, country) 貧しい mazúshiî, 貧乏な bíñbô na; (bad) 粗末な sómàtsu na
♦npl: **the poor** 貧乏人 biñbônin ◊総称 sôshō

poor in (resources etc) ...が不足している ...ga fusôku shite irû

poorly [pu:r'li:] adj (ill) 病気の byôki no
♦adv (badly: designed) 粗末に sómàtsu ni; (paid, furnished) 不十分に fujûbùn ni

pop [pɑ:p] n (MUS) ポップス pôppùsu;

(fizzy drink) 炭酸飲料 tansan-iñryō, ソー
ダ水 sōdasùi; (*inf*: father) 父ちゃん tō-
chan, パパ pápà; (sound) ぽんという音
póñ to iú otò

♦*vt* (put quickly) 突っ込む tsukkómù

♦*vi* (balloon) 破裂する harétsu suru;
(cork) 飛出す tobídasù

popcorn [pɑːpˈkɔːrn] *n* ポップコーン
poppúkòñ

pope [poup] *n* 法王 hōō

pop in *vi* 立寄る tachíyorù

poplar [pɑːpˈlər] *n* ポプラ pópùra

poplin [pɑːpˈlin] *n* ポプリン pópùrin

pop out *vi* 飛出る tobíderù

popper [pɑːpˈəːr] *n* (*BRIT*: for fastening) スナップ sunáppù

poppy [pɑːpˈiː] *n* ケシ keshí

Popsicle [pɑːpˈsikəl] ((R) *US*) *n* (ice lolly)
アイスキャンディー aísukyañdì

pop star *n* ポップスター poppúsutà

populace [pɑːpˈjələs] *n* 大衆 taíshū

popular [pɑːpˈjələːr] *adj* (well-liked: person, place, thing) 人気のある niñki no
arù; (of ordinary people: idea, belief) 一
般の ippán no, 流行の ryūkō no; (non-
academic) 一般向けの ippánmuke no;
(POL) 国民の kokúmin no

popularity [pɑːpjələːˈiti] *n* (of person,
thing, activity) 人気 niñki

popularize [pɑːpˈjələraiz] *vt* (sport,
music, fashion) 普及させる fukyū sase-
rù; (science, ideas) 分かりやすくする wa-
káriyasukù suru

population [pɑːpjəleiˈʃən] *n* (inhabitants:
of country, area) 住民 jūmin; (number of
inhabitants) 人口 jiñkō

populous [pɑːpˈjələs] *adj* (country, city,
area) 人口の多い jiñkō no ōi

pop up *vi* 現れる aráwarerù

porcelain [pɔːrˈsəlin] *n* 磁器 jíkì

porch [pɔːrtʃ] *n* (ARCHIT: entrance) 玄
関 genkan; (*US*) ベランダ beránda

porcupine [pɔːrˈkjəpain] *n* ヤマアラシ
yamáarashi

pore [pɔːr] *n* (ANAT) 毛穴 keána; (BOT)
気孔 kikō; (GEO) 小穴 koána

♦*vi*: **to pore over** (book, article etc) 熟
読する jukúdoku suru

pork [pɔːrk] *n* 豚肉 butániku

pornographic [pɔːrnəgræfˈik] *adj* (film,
book, magazine) わいせつな waísetsu
na, ポルノの poruno no

pornography [pɔːrnɑːˈgrəfiː] *n* (films,
books, magazines) ポルノ pórùno

porous [pɔːrˈəs] *adj* (soil, rock, clay etc)
小穴の多い koána nò ōi

porpoise [pɔːrˈpəs] *n* イルカ irúka

porridge [pɔːrˈidʒ] *n* オートミール ōto-
mīru

port [pɔːrt] *n* (harbor) 港 mináto;
(NAUT: left side) 左げん sagén; (wine)
ポートワイン pōtowaìn

port of call 寄港地 kikōchì

portable [pɔːrˈtəbəl] *adj* (television,
typewriter, telephone etc) 携帯用の keítai yō no, ポータブルの pōtaburu no

porter [pɔːrˈtəːr] *n* (for luggage) 赤帽 a-
kábō, ポーター pōtā; (doorkeeper) 門番
moñban

portfolio [pɔːrtfouˈliːou] *n* (case) かばん
kabán; (POL) 大臣の職 dáijin no shokú;
(FINANCE) ポートフォリオ pōtoforìo;
(of artist) 代表作品集 daíhyōsakuhiñshū

porthole [pɔːrtˈhoul] *n* げん窓 geñsō

portion [pɔːrˈʃən] *n* (part) 部分 búbùn;
(helping of food) 一人前 ichíninmaè

portly [pɔːrtˈliː] *adj* (man) 太った futóttà

portrait [pɔːrˈtrit] *n* (picture) 肖像 shō-
zō, ポートレート pōtorèto

portray [pɔːrtreiˈ] *vt* (subj: artist) 描く
egákù; (: actor) 演じる eñjiru

portrayal [pɔːrtreiˈəl] *n* (artist's: *also*
representation in book, film etc) 描写
byósha; (actor's) 演技 eñgi

Portugal [pɔːrˈtʃəgəl] *n* ポルトガル porútogàru

Portuguese [pɔːrtʃəgiːzˈ] *adj* ポルトガル
の porútogàru no; (LING) ポルトガル語
の porútogarugò no

♦*n inv* ポルトガル人 porútogarujìn;
(LING) ポルトガル語 porútogarugò

pose [pouz] *n* (posture) ポーズ pōzu

♦*vi* (pretend): **to pose as** ...を装う ...wo
yosóoù, ...の名をかたる ...no ná wð katárù

♦*vt* (question) 持出す mochídasù; (prob-

lem, danger) ...である ...de árù
   to pose for (painting etc) ...のためにポーズを取る ...no tamé nì pṓzu wo tórù

posh [pɑːʃ] (*inf*) *adj* (smart: hotel, restaurant etc) 高級な kṓkyū na; (upper class: person, behavior) 上流階級の jṓryūkaī-kyū no

position [pəziʃ'ən] *n* (place: of house, thing, person) 位置 ichì; (of person's body) 姿勢 shiséi; (social status) 地位 chíi; (job) 職務 shokù; (in race, competition) 第...位 dái ...i; (attitude) 態度 taído; (situation) 立場 tachíba
   ♦*vt* (person, thing) 置く okú

positive [pɑːz'ətiv] *adj* (certain) 確かな táshìka na; (hopeful, confident) 確信している kakúshin shite irù; (definite: decision, action, policy) 積極的な sekkyṓku-teki na

posse [pɑːs'iː] (*US*) *n* 捜索隊 sṓsakutai

possess [pəzes'] *vt* (have, own: car, watch, radio etc) 所有する shoyū suru, 保有する hoyū suru; (quality, ability) ...がある ...ga árù, ...を持っている ...wo mótte irù; (subj: feeling, belief) 支配する shíhai suru

possession [pəzeʃ'ən] *n* (state of possessing) 所有 shoyū
   to take possession of 占領する seńryō suru

possessions [pəzeʃ'ənz] *npl* (belongings) 持物 mochímòno

possessive [pəzes'iv] *adj* (of another person) ...の愛情を独占したがる ...no aíjō wò dokúsen shitagarù; (of things) 他人に使わせたがらない tanín nì tsukáwasetagaranài; (LING) 所有を表す shoyū wò aráwasù

possibility [pɑːsəbil'əti:] *n* 可能性 kanṓsei; (possible event) 可能な事 kanṓ na kotò

possible [pɑːs'əbəl] *adj* (which can be done) 可能な kanṓ na; (event, reaction) 有り得る aríurù; (candidate, successor) 成り得る naríurù
   it's possible (may be true) そうかも知れない sṓ ka mò shirénaì
   as fast as possible できるだけ早く de-

kíru dakè hayákù

possibly [pɑːs'əbli:] *adv* (perhaps) あるいは arúīwa; (expressing surprise, shock, puzzlement) ...が考えられない ...ga kańgaerarenài; (emphasizing someone's efforts) できる限り dekíru kagirí
   I cannot possibly come どう合っても私は行かれません dṓatté mo watákushi wà ikáremaseñ

post [poust] *n* (*BRIT*: service, system) 郵便 yūbin; (: letters) 郵便(物) yūbin (bùtsu); (delivery) 配達 haítatsu ◊1回分の配達郵便を指す ikkáībun no haítatsu-yūbin wo sásù; (pole) 柱 hashíra; (job, situation) 職務 shokù; (MIL) 持場 mochíba
   ♦*vt* (*BRIT*: send by post) 郵送する yū́sō suru; (: put in mailbox) 投かんする tṓkan suru; (: appoint): *to post someone to* ...を...へ配置する ...wo ...e haíchi suru

postage [pous'tidʒ] *n* (charge) 郵便料金 yūbin ryṓkin

postage stamp *n* (郵便)切手 (yūbin) kitté

postal [pous'təl] *adj* (charges, service, strike) 郵便の yūbin no

postal order *n* 郵便為替 yūbin kawàse

postbox [poust'bɑːks] (*BRIT*) *n* (郵便)ポスト (yūbin)pósùto

postcard [poust'kɑːrd] *n* (郵便)葉書 (yūbin) hagáki

postcode [poust'koud] (*BRIT*) *n* 郵便番号 yūbin bańgō

postdate [poust'deit] *vt* (check) ...に先の日付を付ける ...ni sakí nò hizúke wò tsukérù

poster [pous'tər] *n* ポスター pósùtā

poste restante [poust res'tɑːnt] (*BRIT*) *n* 局留 kyokúdome

posterity [pɑːster'iti:] *n* 後世 kṓsei

postgraduate [poustgrædʒ'uːit] *n* 大学院生 daígakuiñsei

posthumous [pɑːs'tʃəməs] *adj* (award, publication) 死後の shígo no

postman [poust'mən] (*pl* **postmen**) *n* 郵便屋 yūbin-ya

postmark [poust'mɑːrk] *n* 消印 keshíin

post-mortem [poustmɔːr'təm] *n* 司法解剖 shihṓkaibō, 検死解剖 keńshikaibō

post office n (building) 郵便局 yūbiṅkyoku; (organization): *the Post Office* 郵政省 yūseíshō

Post Office Box n 私書箱 shishóbàko

postpone [poustpoun'] vt 延期する eṅki suru

postscript [poust'skript] n 追伸 tsuíshin

posture [pɑːs'tʃəːr] n (position of body) 姿勢 shiséi; (fig) 態度 taído

postwar [poust'wɔːr'] adj (building, period, politics) 戦後の seṅgo no

posy [pou'ziː] n 花束 hanátàba ◊小さい花束を指す chíisai hanátàba wo sásù

pot [pɑt] n (for cooking) なべ nábè; (also: **teapot**) ティーポット tíipottò; (also: **coffeepot**) コーヒーポット kṓhīpottò; (tea/coffee in pot) ティー[コーヒー]ポット一杯 tí(kṓhī)pottò íppài; (bowl, container: for paint etc) つぼ tsubó; (flowerpot) 植木鉢 uékibàchi; (inf: marijuana) マリファナ marífàna

◆vt (plant) 鉢に植える hachí nì uérù

to go to pot (inf: work, performance) 駄目になる damé ni narù

potato [pətei'tou] (pl **potatoes**) n ジャガイモ jagáimo

potato peeler [-piː'ləːr] n 皮むき器 kawámukìkì

potent [pout'ənt] adj (powerful: weapon, argument, drink) 強力な kyṓryoku na; (man) 性的能力のある seítekinṓryoku no árù

potential [pəten'tʃəl] adj (candidate) 成り得る narúrù; (sales, success) 可能な kanṓ na; (danger etc) 潜在する seṅzai suru

◆n (talents, abilities) 潜在能力 seṅzainṓryoku; (promise, possibilities) 将来性 shṓraisei

potentially [pəten'tʃəliː] adv 潜在的に seṅzaiteki ni

pothole [pɑt'houl] n (in road) 穴ぼこ anábòko; (BRIT: underground) 洞くつ dṓkutsu

potholing [pɑt'houliṅ] (BRIT) n: *to go potholing* 洞くつを探検する dṓkutsu wo taṅken suru

potion [pou'ʃən] n (of medicine, poison etc) 水薬 mizúgusùri

potluck [pɑt'lʌk] n: *to take potluck* 有り合せの物で間に合せる aríawase no monð de ma ní awaserù

potted [pɑt'id] adj (food) つぼ詰めの tsubózume no; (plant) 鉢植えの hachíue no; (abbreviated: account, biography etc) 要約した yṓyaku shita

potter [pɑt'əːr] n (pottery maker) 陶芸家 tṓgeika

◆vi: *to potter around/about in the garden* (BRIT) ぶらぶらと庭いじりをする búràbura to niwáijìri wo suru

pottery [pɑt'əːriː] n (pots, dishes etc) 陶器 tṓki; (factory, workshop) 陶器製造所 tṓkiseizòjo

potty [pɑt'iː] adj (inf: mad) 狂った kurúttà

◆n (for child) おまる o-máru

pouch [pautʃ] n (for tobacco, coins etc) 小袋 kobúkuro; (ZOOL) 袋 fukúro

poultry [poul'triː] n (live chickens, ducks etc) 家きん kakín; (meat from chickens etc) 鳥肉 toríniku

pounce [pauns] vi: *to pounce on* (animal, person) …に襲い掛る …ni osóikakarù; (fig: mistake, idea etc) 攻撃する kṓgeki suru

pound [paund] n (unit of weight) ポンド póṅdo; (BRIT: unit of money) ポンド póṅdo

◆vt (beat: table, wall etc) 強くたたく tsúyòku tatákù; (crush: grain, spice etc) 砕く kudákù

◆vi (heart) どきどきする dókìdoki suru

pound sterling n ポンド póṅdo

pour [pɔːr] vt (tea, wine, cereal etc) つぐ tsugú

◆vi (water, blood, sweat etc) 流れ出る nagárederù

to pour someone a drink …に酒をついでやる …ni saké wð tsuíde yarù

pour away/off vt 流して捨てる nagáshite suterù

pour in vi (people) ぞろぞろと入って来る zórðzoro to haítte kurù; (information) 続々と入る zókùzoku to haírù

pouring [pɔːr'iṅ] adj: *pouring rain* 土砂

降りの雨 dosháburi no amě

pour out vi (people) ぞろぞろと出て来る zórōzoro to deté kurů

♦vt (tea, wine etc) つぐ tsugú; (fig: thoughts, feelings, etc) せきを切った様に吐き出す sékî wo kittá yō ni hakídasù

pout [paut] vi 膨れっ面をする fukúrettsura wò suru

poverty [pɑ:v'ə:rti:] n 貧乏 bínbō

poverty-stricken [pɑ:v'ə:rti:strikən] adj (people, town, country) 非常に貧しい hijō nì mazúshiî

powder [pau'də:r] n (tiny particles of solid substance) 粉 koná; (face powder) おしろい oshíroi, パウダー páudā

♦vt: **to powder one's face** 顔におしろいをつける kaő ni oshíroi wð tsukérù

powder compact n コンパクト kőnpakuto

powdered milk [pau'də:rd-] n 粉ミルク konámirùku

powder puff n パフ páfù

powder room n 化粧室 keshőshîtsu

power [pau'ə:r] n (control: over people, activities) 権力 kénryòku; (ability, opportunity) 能力 nőryoku; (legal right) 権利 kénri; (of explosion, engine) 威力 íryòku; (electricity) 電力 dénryoku

to be in power (POL etc) 権力を握っている kénryoku wo nigítte irů

power cut (BRIT) n 停電 teíden

powered [pau'ə:rd] adj: **powered by** ...で動く ...de ugőkù

power failure n 停電 teíden

powerful [pau'ə:rfəl] adj (person, organization) 有力な yűryoku na; (body) 力強い chikárazuyoî; (blow, kick etc) 強力な kyőryoku na; (engine) 馬力の強い baríki no tsuyoî; (speech, piece of writing) 力強い chikárazuyoî

powerless [pau'ə:rlis] adj (without control or influence) 無力な múryòku na

powerless to do ...する力がない ...súrù chikára ga naî

power point (BRIT) n コンセント kőnsento

power station n 発電所 hatsúdensho

p.p. [pi:'pi:'] abbr (= per procurationem): **p.p. J. Smith** J.Smithの代理として jē sumísù no daíri tòshité; (= pages) ページ pēji

PR [pi:ɑ:r'] abbr = **public relations**

practicable [præk'tikəbəl] adj (scheme, task, idea) 実用的な jitsúyōteki na

practical [præk'tikəl] adj (not theoretical: difficulties, experience etc) 実際の jissái no; (person: sensible) 現実的な génjitsuteki na; (: good with hands) 器用な kíyō na; (ideas, methods) 現実的な génjitsuteki na; (clothes, things: sensible) 実用的な jitsúyōteki na

practicality [præktikæl'iti:] n (no pl) 現実主義 génjitsushùgi; (of situation etc) 現実 génjitsu

practical joke n 悪ふざけ warúfuzàke

practically [præk'tikli:] adv (almost) ほとんど hotőndo

practice [præk'tis] n (habit) 習慣 shúkan; (of profession) 業務 győmu; (REL) おきてを守る事 okíte wð mamóru kotŏ; (exercise, training) 練習 reńshū; (MED, LAW: business) 開業 kaígyō

♦vt (train at: musical instrument, sport etc) 練習する reńshū suru; (carry out: custom, craft etc) 行う okónaù; (religion) ...のおきてを守る ...no okíte wo mamóru; (profession) ...に従事する ...ni jūji suru

♦vi (train) 練習する reńshū suru; (lawyer, doctor etc) ...の業務をする ...no győmu wo suru

in practice (in reality) 実際には jissái ni wà

out of practice 腕が鈍って udé gà nibúttè

practicing [præk'tisin] (BRIT **practising**) adj (Christian etc) おきてを守っている okíte wð mamótte irù; (doctor, lawyer) 業務をしている győmu wo shité irù

practise [præk'tis] vt, vi (BRIT) = **practice**

practitioner [præktiʃ'ənə:r] n (MED): **medical practitioner** 医者 ishá

pragmatic [prægmæt'ik] adj (person, reason etc) 現実的な génjitsuteki na

prairie [pre:r'i:] n 草原 sőgen

praise [preiz] n (expression of approval, admiration) 賞賛 shōsan
♦vt (express approval, admiration: of person, thing, action etc) ほめる homérù

praiseworthy [preiz'wə:rði:] adj (person, act etc) ほめるべき homérùbeki

pram [præm] (BRIT) n 乳母車 ubágurùma

prance [præns] vi (person) 威張って歩く ibátte arúkù; (horse) 躍る様に歩く odóru yŏ ni arúkù

prank [præŋk] n いたずら itázura

prawn [prɔ:n] n エビ ebí

pray [prei] vi (REL) 祈る inórù; (fig) 祈る inórù, 願う negáù

prayer [pre:r] n (REL: activity, words) 祈り inóri

preach [pri:tʃ] vi (REL) 説教する sékkyō suru; (pej: moralize) お説教する o-sékkyō suru
♦vt (peace, doctrine etc) 説く tókù
to preach a sermon 説教する sékkyō suru

preacher [pri:'tʃə:r] n (REL) 説教者 sekkyŏshà

preamble [pri:'æmbəl] n (to spoken words) 前置き maéoki; (to written words) 前書 maégaki

precarious [prike:r'i:əs] adj (dangerous: position, situation) 不安定な fuántei na; (fig) 危険な kikén na

precaution [prikɔ:'ʃən] n 用心 yŏjin

precede [prisi:d'] vt (event, period of time) ...の前に起る ...no máè ni okórù; (person) ...の前を歩く ...no máè wo arúkù; (sentence, paragraph, chapter) ...の前にある ...no máè ni árù

precedence [pres'idəns] n (priority) 優先 yūsen

precedent [pres'idənt] n (action, official decision) 判例 haírei; (something that has happened before) 先例 seírei

preceding [prisi:'diŋ] adj (chapter, programme, day) 前の máè no

precept [pri:'sept] n おきて okíte

precinct [pri:'siŋkt] n (US: part of city) 管区 kánku
pedestrian precinct (BRIT) 歩行者天

国 hokōshateñgoku
shopping precinct (BRIT) ショッピングセンター shoppíñgu séñtā ◇車が閉出される kurúma gà shimédasarerù

precincts [pri:'siŋkts] npl (of a large building) 構内 kónai

precious [preʃ'əs] adj (commodity: valuable, useful) 貴重な kichŏ na; (object, material) 高価な kŏka na

precious stone n 宝石 hŏseki

precipice [pres'əpis] n 断崖 dañgai

precipitate [prisip'iteit] vt (hasten) 早める hayámerù

precise [prisais'] adj (exact: time, nature etc) 正確な seíkaku na; (detailed: instructions, plans etc) 細かい komákaì

precisely [prisais'li:] adv (accurately) 正確に seíkaku ni; (exactly) その通り sonó tōri

precision [prisiʒ'ən] n 正確さ seíkakusa

preclude [priklu:d'] vt (action, event) 不可能にする fukánō ni suru

precocious [prikou'ʃəs] adj (child, talent) 早熟な sŏjuku na

preconceived [pri:kənsi:vd'] adj:
preconceived idea 先入観 seínyūkan

precondition [pri:kəndiʃ'ən] n 前提条件 zeñteijŏken

precursor [prikə:r'sə:r] n (person) 先駆者 señkushà; (thing) 前触れ maébure

predator [pred'ətə:r] n 捕食者 hoshókushà

predecessor [pred'isesə:r] n (person) 前任者 zeñniñsha

predestination [pri:destinei'ʃən] n 予定説 yoteísetsu

predicament [pridik'əmənt] n 苦境 kukyŏ

predict [pridikt'] vt 予言する yogén suru

predictable [pridikt'əbəl] adj (event, behavior etc) 予知できる yóchì dekírù

prediction [pridik'ʃən] n 予言 yogén

predominantly [prida:m'ənəntli:] adv 圧倒的に attŏteki ni

predominate [prida:m'əneit] vi (person, thing) ...が圧倒的に多い ...ga attŏteki ni ŏi; (feature, quality) 目立つ medátsù

pre-eminent [pri:em'ənənt] adj (person,

thing) 優れた sugúretà

pre-empt [pri:empt] vt (decision, action, statement) 先取りする sakídori suru

preen [pri:n] vt: **to preen itself** (bird) 羽繕いをする hazúkùroi wo suru
  to preen oneself 得意がる tokúìgaru

prefab [pri:'fæb] n プレハブ住宅 puréhabujũtaku

prefabricated [pri:fæb'rikeitid] adj (buildings) プレハブの puréhabu no

preface [pref'is] n (in book) 前書 maégakì

prefect [pri:'fekt] (BRIT) n (in school) 監督生 kańtokuseì

prefer [prifər'] vt (like better: person, thing, activity) ...の方を好む ...no hố wò konómù
  to prefer doing/to do ...する方が好きである ...suru hố gà sukí de arù

preferable [pref'ə:rəbəl] adj ...が望ましい ...ga nozómashiì

preferably [prifə:r'əbli:] adv できれば dekírèba

preference [pref'ə:rəns] n (liking) 好み konómi
  to give preference to ...を優先的に扱う ...wo yúsenteki nĭ atsúkaù

preferential [prefərən'tʃəl] adj: **preferential treatment** 優先的な取扱い yúsenteki nā toríatsukai

prefix [pri:'fiks] n 接頭辞 settốjì

pregnancy [preg'nənsi:] n (of woman, female animal) 妊娠 nińshin

pregnant [preg'nənt] adj (woman, female animal) 妊娠している nińshin shite irù

prehistoric [pri:histɔ:r'ik] adj (person, dwelling, monster etc) 有史以前の yúshiizèn no

prejudice [predʒ'ədis] n (unreasonable dislike) 偏見 heńken; (bias in favor) ひいき híiki

prejudiced [predʒ'ədist] adj (person: prejudiced against) ...に対して偏見のある ...ni tãíshite heńken no arù; (: prejudiced in favor) ...をひいきにした ...wo híiki ni shitá

preliminary [prilim'əne:ri:] adj (action,

discussion) 予備的な yobíteki na

prelude [prei'lu:d] n (preliminary event) 前兆 zeńchō; (MUS) 序曲 jókyòku

premarital [pri:mær'itəl] adj 婚前の końzen no

premature [pri:mətʃu:r'] adj (earlier than expected: baby) 早産の sōzan no; (death, arrival) 早過ぎた hayásugita; (too early: action, event etc) 時期尚早の jíkìshōsō no
  premature aging 早老 sốrō

premeditated [primed'əteitid] adj 計画的な keíkakuteki na

premier [primji:r'] adj (best) 最良の saíryō no
  ♦n (POL) 総理大臣 sōridaìjin, 首相 shushố

première [primji:r'] n (of film) 初公開 hatsúkōkai; (of play) 初演 shoén

premise [prem'is] n 前提 zeńtei

premises [prem'isiz] npl (of business, institution) 構内 kốnai
  on the premises 構内で kốnai de

premium [pri:'mi:əm] n (COMM: extra sum of money) 割増金 warímashikin, プレミアム purémìamu; (: sum paid for insurance) 掛金 kakékin
  to be at a premium (expensive) 高価である kốka de árù; (hard to get) 手に入りにくい té nì haírinikùi

premium bond (BRIT) n 割増金付き債券 warímashikintsukisaíken ◇抽選による賞金が付く chúsen ni yorù shốkin ga tsukù

premonition [preməniʃ'ən] n 予感 yokán

preoccupation [pri:ɑ:kjəpei'ʃən] n (obsession) 専念する事 seńnen surù kotó; (worry) 気掛りな事 kigákàri na kotó

preoccupied [pri:ɑ:k'jəpaid] adj (person) 上の空になった uwánosora ni náttà

prep [prep] n (SCOL: study) 勉強 beńkyō

prepaid [pri:peid'] adj (paid in advance) 支払い済みの shiháraizumi no

preparation [prepərei'ʃən] n (activity) 準備 júnbi; (food) 料理 ryőri; (medicine) 薬品 yakúhin; (cosmetic) 化粧品 keshőhin

preparations [prepərei'ʃənz] npl (arrangements) 準備 júnbi

preparatory [pripær'əto:ri:] adj (report) 予備の yóbì no; (training) 準備の júñbi no

preparatory school n (US) 予備校 yo-bíkō; (BRIT) 私立小学校 shírtsu shō-gakkō

prepare [pripe:r'] vt (make ready: plan, speech, room etc) 準備する júñbi suru; (CULIN) 調理する chōri suru
◆vi: to prepare for (event, action) ...の準備をする ...no júñbi wo suru
prepared to (willing) ...する用意がある ...surú yōi ga árù
prepared for (ready) ...の用意ができている ...no yōi ga dékìte irú

preponderance [pripɑ:n'də:rəns] n (of people, things) 大多数 daítasū

preposition [prepəzíʃ'ən] n 前置詞 zeñchishi

preposterous [pripɑ:s'tə:rəs] adj (suggestion, idea, situation) 途方もない tohō-monaì

prep school n = preparatory school

prerequisite [prirek'wizit] n 必要条件 hitsúyōjōken

prerogative [prərɑ:g'ətiv] n (of person, group) 特権 tokkén

Presbyterian [prezbiti:r'i:ən] adj 長老派の chōrōha no
◆n 長老派の信者 chōrōha no shíñja

preschool [pri:'sku:l'] adj (age, child, education) 就学前の shūgakumaè no

prescribe [priskraib'] vt (MED: medicine) 処方する shohō suru; (treatment) 命ずる meízurù

prescription [priskríp'ʃən] n (MED: slip of paper) 処方せん shohōsen; (: medicine) 処方薬 shohōyàku

presence [prez'əns] n (state of being somewhere) ...に居る事 ...ni irú kotò; (fig: strong personal quality) 風さい fūsai; (spirit, invisible influence) 霊 reí
in someone's presence ...の居る前で ...no irú maè de

presence of mind n 機転 kitén

present [adj, n prez'ənt vb prizent'] adj (current: person, thing) 現在の geñzai no; (in attendance) 出席している shussé-

ki shite irù
◆n (actuality): the present 現在 geñzai; (gift) 贈り物 okúrimono, プレゼント pu-rézènto
◆vt (give: prize, award etc) 贈る okúrù; (cause, provide: difficulty, threat etc) ...になる ...ni nárù; (information) 与える atáerù; (describe: person, thing) 描写する byósha suru; (RADIO, TV) 提供する teíkyō suru; (formally introduce: person) 紹介する shōkai suru
to give someone a present ...にプレゼントを上げる ...ni purézènto wo agérù
at present 今の所 imá no tokoro

presentable [prizen'təbəl] adj (person) 人前に出られる hitómae nì derárerù

presentation [prezəntei'ʃən] n (of plan, proposal, report etc) 提出 teíshutsu; (appearance) 体裁 teísai; (formal ceremony) 贈呈式 zōteishìki

present-day [prez'əntdei'] adj 現代の geñdai no

presenter [prizen'tə:r] n (RADIO, TV) 司会者 shikaísha

presently [prez'əntli:] adv (soon) 間もなく mamónàku; (now) 現在 geñzai

preservation [prezə:rvei'ʃən] n (act of preserving) 保存 hozón; (state of being preserved) 保存状態 hozóñjotai

preservative [prizə:r'vətiv] n (for food, wood, metal etc) 保存剤 hozóñzài

preserve [prizə:rv'] vt (maintain: situation, condition) 維持する íji suru; (: building, manuscript) 保存する hozón suru; (food) 保存する hozón suru
◆n (often pl: jam, marmalade) ジャム jámù

preside [prizaid'] vi: to preside (over) (meeting, event etc) (...の) 議長をする (...no) gichō wo suru

presidency [prez'idənsi:] n (POL: post) 大統領職 daítōryōshokù; (: time in office) 大統領の任期 daítōryō no níñki

president [prez'idənt] n (POL) 大統領 daítōryō; (of organization) ...長 ...chō

presidential [preziden'tʃəl] adj 大統領の daítōryō no

press [pres] n: the Press (newspapers)

報道機関 hōdōkikàn; (journalists) 報道陣 hōdōjin; (printing press) 印刷機 iñsatsukī; (of switch, button, bell) 押す事 osú kotò

◆vt (hold one thing against another) 押付ける oshítsukerù; (button, switch, bell etc) 押す osú; (iron: clothes) ...にアイロンを掛ける ...ni aíron wò kakérù; (put pressure on: person) せき立てる sekítaterù; (insist): **to press something on someone** ...に...を押付ける ...ni ...wo oshítsukerù

◆vi (squeeze) 押える osáerù; (pressurize): **to press for** (improvement, change etc) ...のために働く ...no tamé nì határakù; (forcibly) 強要する kyōyō suru

we are pressed for time/money 時間〔金〕が足りない jíkàn〔kané〕ga tarínai

press agency n 通信社 tsūshíñsha

press conference n 記者会見 kishákaìken

pressing [pres'iŋ] adj (engagement, decision etc) 緊急の kiñkyū no

press on vi (despite problems etc) ひるまずに続ける hirúmazù ni tsuzúkerù

press stud (BRIT) n スナップ sunáppù

press-up [pres'ʌp] (BRIT) n 腕立て伏せ udétatefùse

pressure [preʃ'ə:r] n (physical force: also fig) 圧力 atsúryòku; (also: **air pressure**) 気圧 kiátsu; (also: **water pressure**) 水圧 suíatsu; (also: **oil pressure**) 油圧 yuátsu; (stress) 圧迫 appáku, プレッシャー purésshā

to put pressure on someone (to do) (...する様に) ...に圧力を掛ける (...surú yō ni) ...ni atsúryòku wo kakérù

pressure cooker n 圧力ガマ atsúryokugàma

pressure gauge n 圧力計 atsúryokukei

pressure group n (POL) 圧力団体 atsúryokudañtai, プレッシャーグループ purésshāgurùpu

pressurized [preʃ'əraizd] adj (cabin, container, spacesuit) 気圧を一定に保った kiátsu wò ittéi ni tamottá

prestige [presti:ʒ'] n 名声 meísei

prestigious [prestidʒ'əs] adj 著名な cho-

méi na

presumably [prizu:'məbli:] adv たぶん tábùn, おそらく osóràku

presume [prizu:m'] vt: **to presume (that)** (suppose) (...だと) 推定する (...dá tò) suítei suru

presumption [prizʌmp'ʃən] n (supposition) 推定 suítei

presumptuous [prizʌmp'tʃu:əs] adj せん越な señ-etsu na

presuppose [pri:səpouz'] vt ...を前提とする ...wo zeñtei tò suru

pretence [pritens'] (US also: **pretense**) n (false appearance) 見せ掛け misékake

under false pretences うそを言って úsò wo itté

pretend [pritend'] vt (feign) ...の振りをする ...no furí wò suru

◆vi (feign) 見せ掛ける misékakerù

to pretend to do ...する振りをする ...suru furí wò suru

pretense [pritens'] (US) n = **pretence**

pretentious [priten'tʃəs] adj (claiming importance, significance: person, play, film etc) うぬぼれた unúboreta

pretext [pri:'tekst] n 口実 kōjitsu

pretty [prit'i:] adj (person, thing) きれいな kírèi na

◆adv (quite) かなり kánàri

prevail [priveil'] vi (be current: custom, belief) はやる hayárù; (gain acceptance, influence: proposal, principle) 勝つ kátsù

prevailing [privei'liŋ] adj (wind) 卓越風 takúetsufù; (dominant: fashion, attitude etc) 一般の ippán no

prevalent [prev'ələnt] adj (common) 一般的な ippánteki na

prevent [privent'] vt: **to prevent someone from doing something** ...が...をするのを妨げる ...ga ...wo suru no wò samátagerù

to prevent something from happening ...が起るのを防ぐ ...ga okórù no wo fuségù

preventative [priven'tətiv] adj = **preventive**

prevention [priven'tʃən] n 予防 yobō

preventive [priven'tiv] *adj* (measures, medicine) 予防の yobō no

preview [pri:'vju:] *n* (of film) 試写会 shishákài; (of exhibition etc) 招待展示内覧 shōtaitenjinairan

previous [pri:'vi:əs] *adj* (earlier: event, thing, period of time) 前の máe no

previously [pri:'vi:əsli:] *adv* 前に máe ni

pre-war [pri:'wɔ:r] *adj* 戦前の senzen no

prey [prei] *n* 獲物 emóno

♦*vi*: **to prey on** (animal: feed on) ...を捕食する ...wo hoshóku suru

it was preying on his mind 彼はそれを気にしていた kárè wa soré wò ki ní shite itá

price [prais] *n* (amount of money) 値段 nedán; (*fig*) 代償 daíshō

♦*vt* (goods) ...に値段を付ける ...ni nedán wò tsukérù

priceless [prais'lis] *adj* 非常に貴重な hijō nì kichṓ na

price list *n* 値段表 nedánhyō

prick [prik] *n* (short, sharp pain) ちくっとする痛み chikúttō suru itámi

♦*vt* (make hole in) 鋭い物で刺す surúdoi monó dè sásù; (cause pain) ちくっと刺す chikúttō sásù

to prick up one's ears (listen eagerly) 耳を澄まして聞く mimí wò sumáshite kikù

prickle [prik'əl] *n* (of plant) とげ togé; (sensation) ちくちくする痛み chíkùchiku suru itámi

prickly [prik'li:] *adj* (plant) とげだらけの togédaràke no; (fabric) ちくちくする chíkùchiku suru

prickly heat *n* 汗も asémo

pride [praid] *n* (satisfaction) 誇り hokóri; (dignity, self-respect) 自尊心 jisónshin, プライド puráido; (*pej*: feeling of superiority) 高慢 kōman

♦*vt*: **to pride oneself on** ...を誇りとする ...wo hokóri tò suru

priest [pri:st] *n* (Christian: Catholic, Anglican etc) 司祭 shisái; (non-Christian) 僧侶 sōryo

priestess [pri:s'tis] *n* (non-Christian) みこ míkò

priesthood [pri:st'hud] *n* (position) 司祭職 shisáishokù

prig [prig] *n* 気取り屋 kidóriya

prim [prim] (*pej*) *adj* (formal, correct) 堅苦しい katákurushiì; (easily shocked) 上品ぶった jōhinbutta

primarily [praimer'ili:] *adv* (above all) 主に ōmò ni

primary [prai'me:ri:] *adj* (first in importance) 主要な shuyō na

♦*n* (*US*: election) 予備選挙 yobísenkyo

primary school *n* 小学校 shōgakkō

primate [prai'meit] *n* (ZOOL) 霊長類 reíchōrui

prime [praim] *adj* (most important) 最も重要な mottómò jūyō na; (best quality) 最上の saíjō no

♦*n* (of person's life) 盛り sakári

♦*vt* (wood) ...に下塗りをする ...ni shitánuri wò suru; (*fig*: person) ...に教え込む ...ni oshíekomù

prime example (typical) 典型的な例 tenkeiteki nà reí

Prime Minister *n* 総理大臣 sōridaìjin, 首相 shushō

primeval [praimi:'vəl] *adj* (existing since long ago): *primeval forest* 原生林 genseírin; (feelings, tribe) 原始的な genshiteki na

primitive [prim'ətiv] *adj* 原始的な genshiteki na

primrose [prim'rouz] *n* ツキミソウ tsukímiso

primus (stove) [prai'məs-] (*BRIT*) *n* 石油こんろ sekíyukonro

prince [prins] *n* (son of king etc) 王子 ōji; (son of Japanese emperor) 親王 shinnō

princess [prin'sis] *n* (daughter of king etc) 王女 ōjo; (daughter of Japanese emperor) 内親王 naíshinnō

principal [prin'səpəl] *adj* (most important: reason, character, aim etc) 主要な shuyō na

♦*n* (of school) 校長 kōchō; (of college) 学長 gakúchō

principle [prin'səpəl] *n* (moral belief) 信念 shinnen; (general rule) 原則 gensoku; (scientific law) 法則 hōsoku *in principle* (theoretically) 原則として geńsoku tòshité

on principle (morally) 主義として shugí tòshité

print [print] *n* (letters and numbers on page) 印刷文字 ińsatsumojì; (ART) 版画 hañga; (PHOT) 陽画 yōga, プリント purínto; (footprint) 足跡 ashíatò; (fingerprint) 指紋 shimón

♦*vt* (produce: book, newspaper, leaflet) 印刷する ińsatsu suru; (publish: story, article etc) 記載する kisái suru; (cloth) ...になっ染する ...ni nassén suru; (write in capitals) 活字体で書く katsújitai dè kákù

out of print 絶版で zeppán de

printed matter [prin'tid-] *n* 印刷物 ińsatsubùtsu

printer [prin'tə:r] *n* (person, firm) 印刷屋 ińsatsuyà; (machine) 印刷機 ińsatsukì

printing [prin'tiŋ] *n* (act, art) 印刷 ińsatsu

printout [print'aut] *n* (COMPUT) プリントアウト puríntoaùto

prior [prai'ə:r] *adj* (previous: knowledge, warning, consent etc) 事前の jizén no; (more important: claim, duty) より重要な yorí júyō na

prior to ...の前に ...no máè ni

priority [praiɔ:r'iti:] *n* (most urgent task) 優先課題 yūsenkadài; (most important thing, task) 最重要課題 saíjūyōkadài

to have priority (over) (...に) 優先する (...ni) yūsen suru

prise [praiz] *vt*: *to prise open* こじ開ける kojíakerù

prism [priz'əm] *n* プリズム purízumu

prison [priz'ən] *n* (building) 刑務所 keímusho

♦*cpd* 刑務所の keímusho no

prisoner [priz'ənə:r] *n* (in prison) 囚人 shūjin; (captured person) 捕虜 hóryo

prisoner of war *n* 戦争捕虜 seńsohoryò

pristine [pris'ti:n] *adj* (condition: new) 真新しい maátarashiì; (: like new) 新品同様の shińpindōyō no

privacy [prai'vəsi:] *n* プライバシー puráĭbashī

private [prai'vit] *adj* (not public: property, club etc) 私有の shiyū no, プライベートの puráĭbēto no; (not state-owned: industry, service) 民間の mińkan no; (discussion, sitting etc) 非公開の hikókai no; (personal: activities, belongings) 個人の kójin no; (: thoughts, plans) 心の中の kokóro no naka no; (quiet: place) 奥まった okúmattà; (: person) 内気な uchíki na; (confidential) 内密の naímitsu no; (intimate) 部外者立入禁止の bugáisha tachfirikinshi no

♦*n* (MIL) 兵卒 heísotsu

「*private*」 (on envelope) 親展 shiñten; (on door) 部外者立入禁止 bugáisha tachíririkinshi

in private 内密に naímitsu ni

private enterprise *n* (not state owned) 民間企業 mińkan kigyō; (owned by individual) 個人企業 kójin kigyò

private eye *n* 私立探偵 shirítsutañtei

private property *n* 私有地 shiyūchi

private school *n* (fee-paying) 私立学校 shirítsugakkò

privatize [prai'vətaiz] *vt* (government-owned company etc) 民間に払い下げる mińkan nì haráì sagerù

privet [priv'it] *n* イボタノキ ibótanoki

privilege [priv'əlidʒ] *n* (advantage) 特権 tokkén; (opportunity) 光栄な機会 kōei na kikaì

privileged [priv'əlidʒd] *adj* (having advantages) 特権のある tokkén no arù; (having special opportunity) 光栄な機会を得た kōei na kikaì wo etá

privy [priv'i:] *adj*: *to be privy to* 内々に関知している naínai nì kañchi shité irù

prize [praiz] *n* (reward) 賞 shō

♦*adj* (first class) 典型的な teńkeiteki na

♦*vt* 重宝する chōhō suru

prize-giving [praiz'givīŋ] *n* 表彰式 hyō-shōshìki

prizewinner [praiz'winə:r] *n* 受賞者 ju-shōshā

pro [prou] *n* (SPORT) 職業選手 shokú-gyōseñshu, プロ púrò

♦*prep* (in favor of) ...に賛成して ...ni sańsei shite

the pros and cons 賛否両論 sáńpiryōron

probability [prɑːbəbilˈəti:] *n* (likelihood): *probability of/that* ...の〔...が起る〕公算 ...no〔...ga okórù〕kốsan

in all probability たいてい taítei

probable [prɑːbˈəbəl] *adj* (likely to happen) 起りそうな okórisồ na; (likely to be true) ありそうな arísồ na

probably [prɑːbˈəbli:] *adv* たぶん tábùn, おそらく osóràku

probation [prəbeiˈʃən] *n: on probation* (LAW) 保護観察で hogókańsatsu de; (employee) 見習いで mínárai de

probe [proub] *n* (MED) ゾンデ zóńde; (SPACE) 探査衛星 tańsaeisèi; (enquiry) 調査 chốsa

♦*vt* (investigate) 調査する chốsa suru; (poke) つついて探る tsutsúìte sagúrù

problem [prɑːbˈləm] *n* 問題 mońdai

problematic(al) [prɑːbləmætˈik(əl)] *adj* 問題になる mońdai ni narú

procedure [prəsiːˈdʒəːr] *n* (way of doing something) やり方 yaríkata; (ADMIN, LAW) 手続 tetsúzuki

proceed [prəsiːdˈ] *vi* (do afterwards): *to proceed to do something* ...をし始める ...wo shihájimerù; (continue): *to proceed (with)* (...を) 続ける (...wo) tsuzúkerù; (activity, event, process: carry on) 続ける tsuzúkerù; (person: go) 行く ikú

proceedings [prəsiːˈdiŋz] *npl* (organized events) 行事 gyốji; (LAW) 訴訟手続き soshốtetsuzùki

proceeds [prouˈsiːdz] *npl* 収益 shúeki

process [prɑːsˈes] *n* (series of actions: *also* BIOL, CHEM) 過程 katéi, プロセス purósèsu

♦*vt* (raw materials, food) 加工する kakố suru; (information) 処理する shốri suru

processing [prɑːsˈesiŋ] *n* (PHOT) 現像 geńzō

procession [prəseʃˈən] *n* 行列 gyốretsu

proclaim [prəkleimˈ] *vt* (announce) 宣言する seńgen suru

proclamation [prɑːkləmeiˈʃən] *n* 宣言 seńgen

procrastinate [prəkræsˈtəneit] *vi* 先に延ばす sakí nì nobásù

procreation [proukriːeiˈʃən] *n* 生殖 seíshoku

procure [prəkjuːrˈ] *vt* 調達する chốtatsu suru

prod [prɑːd] *vt* (push: with finger, stick, knife etc) つつく tsutsúkù

♦*n* (with finger, stick, knife etc) 一突き hitótsuki

prodigal [prɑːdˈəgəl] *adj: prodigal son/daughter* 放とう息子〔娘〕hốtōmusùko〔musùme〕

prodigious [prədidʒˈəs] *adj* 巨大な kyódai na

prodigy [prɑːdˈədʒi:] *n* 天才 teńsai

produce [*n* prouˈduːs *vb* prəduːsˈ] *n* (AGR) 農産物 nốsanbùtsu

♦*vt* (cause: effect, result etc) 起す okósù; (make, create: object) 作る tsukúrù; (BIOL: fruit, seeds) つける tsukérù, ...には...がなる ...ni wà ...ga narú; (: young) 産む umú; (CHEM) 作り出す tsukúridasù; (*fig*: evidence, argument) 示す shimésù; (: bring or take out) 取出す torídasù; (play, film, program) 製作する seísaku suru

producer [prəduːˈsəːr] *n* (of film, play, program, record) 製作者 seísakushà, プロデューサー puródyūsà; (country: of food, material) 生産国 seísankòku; (company: of food, material) 生産会社 seísangaìsha

product [prɑːdˈəkt] *n* (thing) 産物 sańbutsu; (result) 結果 kekká

production [prədʌkˈʃən] *n* (process of manufacturing, growing) 生産 seísan; (amount of goods manufactured, grown) 生産高 seísandaka; (THEATER) 上演 jồen

electricity production 発電 hatsúden

production line *n* 工程ライン kốteiraìn, ライン raín

productive [prədʌkˈtiv] *adj* (person, thing: *also fig*) 生産的な seísanteki na

productivity [prɑːdəktivˈəti:] *n* 生産能

力 seísannôryoku

profane [prəfein'] *adj* (secular, lay) 世俗的な sezôkuteki na; (language etc) 下品な gehín na

profess [prəfes'] *vt* (claim) 主張する shuchô suru; (express: feeling, opinion) 明言する meígen suru

profession [prəfeʃ'ən] *n* (job requiring special training) 知的職業 chitékishokugyô; (people) 同業者仲間 dôgyōshanakàma

professional [prəfeʃ'ənəl] *adj* (skill, organization, advice) 専門職の seímonshoku no; (not amateur: photographer, musician etc) プロの púrð no; (highly trained) 専門家の seímonka no; (of a high standard) 本職らしい honshokurashiî
♦*n* (doctor, lawyer, teacher etc) 知的職業者 chitékishokugyôshà; (SPORT) プロ púrð; (skilled person) 玄人 kúrðto

professor [prəfes'ə:r] *n* (US) 教師 kyôshi, 先生 seísei; (BRIT) 教授 kyôju

proficiency [prəfiʃ'ənsi:] *n* 熟練 jukúren

proficient [prəfiʃ'ənt] *adj* 熟練した jukúren shita

profile [prou'fail] *n* (of person's face) 横顔 yokôgað; (fig: article) 経歴 keíreki

profit [pra:f'it] *n* (COMM) 利益 rîeki
♦*vi*: to profit by/from (fig) ...がために なる ...ga tamé nì nárù

profitability [pra:fitəbil'əti:] *n* (ECON) 収益性 shúekiseī

profitable [pra:f'itəbəl] *adj* (ECON) 利益になる rîeki ni nárù

profound [prəfaund'] *adj* (great: shock, effect) 強い tsuyôî; (intellectual: idea, work) 深遠な shiñ-en na

profusely [prəfju:s'li:] *adv* (bleed) 多量に taryô ni; (thank) 重ね重ね kasánegasàne

profusion [prəfju:'ʒən] *n* 大量 tafryō

prognoses [pra:gnou'si:z] *npl of* **prognosis**

prognosis [pra:gnou'səs] (*pl* **prognoses**) *n* (forecast) 予想 yosô; (of illness) 予後 yôgð

program [prou'græm] (BRIT **programme**) *n* (of actions, events) 計画 keíkaku; (RADIO, TV) 番組 bañgumi; (leaflet) プログラム púrðguràmu; (COMPUT) プログラム púrðguràmu
♦*vt* (machine, system) ...にプログラムを入れる ...ni púrðguràmu wo irérù

programing [prou'græmiŋ] (BRIT **programming**) *n* (COMPUT) プログラム作成 púrðguramu sakùseì, プログラミング púrðguramiñgu

programmer [prou'græmə:r] *n* (COMPUT) プログラマー púrðgurámà

progress [*n* pra:g'res *vb* prəgres'] *n* (process of getting nearer to objective) 前進 zeńshin; (changes, advances in society) 進歩 shíñpo; (development) 発展 hattén
♦*vi* (become more advanced, skilled) 進歩する shíñpo suru; (become higher in rank) 昇進する shôshin suru; (continue) 続く tsuzúkù

in progress (meeting, battle, match) 進行中で shiñkôchū de

progression [prəgreʃ'ən] *n* (gradual development) 進展 shiñten; (series) 連続 reñzoku

progressive [prəgres'iv] *adj* (person) 進歩的な shíñpoteki na; (change) 段階的な dañkaiteki na

prohibit [prouhib'it] *vt* (forbid, make illegal) 禁じる kiñjirù

prohibition [prouəbiʃ'ən] *n* (law, rule) 禁則 kiñsoku; (forbidding of: strikes, alcohol etc) 禁止 kiñshi; (US): *Prohibition* 禁酒法時代 kiñshuhōjidài

prohibitive [prouhib'ətiv] *adj* (price etc) 法外な hôgai na, 手が出ない様な tê gà dénai yō na

project [*n* pra:dʒ'ekt *vb* prədʒekt'] *n* (large-scale plan, scheme) 計画 keíkaku; (SCOL) 研究テーマ keñkyūtềma
♦*vt* (plan) 計画する keíkaku suru; (estimate: figure, amount) 見積る mitsúmorù; (light) 投射する tôsha suru; (film, picture) 映写する eísha suru
♦*vi* (stick out) 突出る tsukíderù

projectile [prədʒek'təl] *n* 弾丸 dañgan

projection [prədʒek'ʃən] *n* (estimate) 見積り mitsúmori; (overhang) 突起 tokkí;

(CINEMA) 映写 eísha

projector [prədʒek'tər] n 映写機 eísha-kì

proletarian [prouliteːr'iːən] adj 無産階級の musánkaìkyū no, プロレタリアの puróretarìa no

proletariat [prouliteːr'iːət] n 無産階級 musánkaìkyū, プロレタリア puróretarìa

proliferate [prouliˈfːəːreit] vi 急増する kyúzo suru

prolific [prouliˈfˈik] adj (artist, composer, writer) 多作の tasáku no

prologue [prou'lɔːg] n (of play) 序幕 jomáku, プロローグ purórōgu; (of book) 序言 jogén

prolong [prəlɔːˈŋ'] vt (life, meeting, holiday) 引延ばす hikínobasù, 延長する eńchō suru

prom [prɑːm] n abbr = **promenade**; (US: ball) 学生舞踏会 gakúseibutòkai

promenade [prɑːməneid'] n (by sea) 海岸の遊歩道 kaígan nò yūhòdō

promenade concert (BRIT) n 立見席のある音楽会 tachímisèki no árù ońgakukài

prominence [prɑːm'ənəns] n (importance) 重要性 júyōsei

prominent [prɑːm'ənənt] adj (important) 重要な júyō na; (very noticeable) 目立つ medátsù

promiscuous [prəmisˈkjuːəs] adj (person) 相手構わずにセックスをする aíte kamawazù ni sékkusu wo suru

promise [prɑːm'is] n (vow) 約束 yakúsoku; (talent) 才能 saínō; (hope) 見込み mikómi

♦vi (vow) 約束する yakúsoku suru

♦vt: **to promise someone something, promise something to someone** ...に...を約束する ...ni ...wo yakúsoku suru

to promise (someone) to do something/that (...に) ...すると約束する (...ni) ...surú tò yakúsoku suru

promising [prɑːm'isiŋ] adj (person, thing) 有望な yūbō na

promote [prəmout'] vt (employee) 昇進させる shőshin saserù; (product, pop star) 宣伝する seńden suru; (ideas) 促進

する sokúshin suru

promoter [prəmou'tər] n (of event) 興業主 kőgyōshù, プロモーター purómōtā; (of cause, idea) 推進者 suíshinsha

promotion [prəmou'ʃən] n (at work) 昇進 shőshin; (of product, event, idea) 宣伝 seńden

prompt [prɑːmpt] adj (rapid: reaction, response etc) 迅速な jińsoku na

♦adv (exactly) 丁度 chődo

♦n (COMPUT) プロンプト puróńputo

♦vt (cause) ...の原因となる ...no geń-in tò nárù; (when talking) ...に水を向ける ...ni mizú wò mukérù

to prompt someone to do something ...が...をするきっ掛けとなる ...ga ...wo suru kikkáke to narù

promptly [prɑːmpt'liː] adv (immediately) 直ちに tádachi ni; (exactly) 丁度 chődo

prone [proun] adj (lying face down) うつ伏せの utsúbuse no

prone to (inclined to) ...しがちな ...shigáchi na

prong [prɔːŋ] n (of fork) 歯 há

pronoun [prou'naun] n 代名詞 daímeìshi

pronounce [prənauns'] vt (word) 発音する hatsúon suru; (declare) 宣言する seńgen suru; (give verdict, opinion) 言渡す ifwatasù

pronounced [prənaunst'] adj (marked) 著しい ichíjirushiì

pronunciation [prənʌnsiːei'ʃən] n 発音 hatsúon

proof [pruːf] n (evidence) 証拠 shóko; (TYP) 校正刷り kőseizuri, ゲラ gerá

♦adj: **proof against** ...に耐えられる ...ni taérarerù

prop [prɑːp] n (stick, support: also fig) 支え sasáe

♦vt (also: **prop up**) 支える sasáerù; (lean): **to prop something against** ...を...に立掛ける ...wo ...ni tatékakerù

propaganda [prɑːpəgæn'də] n 宣伝 seńden, プロパガンダ purópagaǹda

propagate [prɑːp'əgeit] vt (idea, information) 普及させる fukyű saserù

propel [prəpel'] vt (vehicle, boat,

machine) 推進する suíshin suru; (fig: person) 駆立てる karítaterù

propeller [prəpel'ə:r] n プロペラ puróperà

propensity [prəpen'siti:] n 傾向 keíkō

proper [prɑ:p'ə:r] adj (real, authentic) ちゃんとした cháñto shita; (correct) 正しい tadashiî; (suitable) 適当な tekítō na; (socially acceptable) 社会の通念にかなった shákài no tsûnen ni kanáttà; (referring to place): **the village proper** 村その もの murá sono monò

properly [prɑ:p'ə:rli:] adv (adequately: eat, study) 充分に júbun ni; (decently: behave) 正しく tadáshìku

proper noun n 固有名詞 koyúmeìshi

property [prɑ:p'ə:rti:] n (possessions) 財産 zaísan; (building and its land) 物件 bukkén; (land owned) 所有地 shoyúchì; (quality: of substance, material etc) 特性 tokúsei

property owner n 地主 jinúshi

prophecy [prɑ:f'isi:] n 予言 yogén

prophesy [prɑ:f'isai] vt (predict) 予言する yogén suru

prophet [prɑ:f'it] n (REL) 予言者 yogéñsha

prophetic [prəfet'ik] adj (statement, words) 予言的な yogéñteki na

proportion [prəpɔ:r'ʃən] n (part: of group, amount) 割合 waríai; (number: of people, things) 数 kázù; (ratio) 率 rítsù

proportional [prəpɔ:r'ʃənəl] adj: **proportional (to)** (...に) 比例する (...ni) hiréi suru

proportional representation n 比例代表制 hiréidaihyōsei

proportionate [prəpɔ:r'ʃənit] adj: **proportionate (to)** (...に) 比例する (...ni) hiréi suru

proposal [prəpou'zəl] n (plan) 提案 teían

a proposal (of marriage) 結婚の申込み kekkón nò móshikomi, プロポーズ purópòzu

propose [prəpouz'] vt (plan, idea) 提案する teían suru; (motion) 提出する teíshutsu suru; (toast) ...の音頭を取る ... no óñdo wo tórù

♦vi (offer marriage) 結婚を申込む kekkón wò móshikomù, プロポーズする purópòzu suru

to propose to do ...するつもりでいる ...suru tsumóri de irù

proposition [prɑ:pəziʃ'ən] n (statement) 主張 shuchō; (offer) 提案 teían

proprietor [prəprai'ətə:r] n (of hotel, shop, newspaper etc) 持主 mochínushi, オーナー ōnā

propriety [prəprai'əti:] n (seemliness) 礼儀正しさ reígitadashìsa

pro rata [-rɑ:'tə] adv 比例して hiréi shite

prosaic [prouzei'ik] adj (person, piece of writing) 散文的な sañbunteki na

prose [prouz] n (not poetry) 散文 sañbun

prosecute [prɑ:s'əkju:t] vt (LAW) 訴追する sotsúi suru

prosecution [prɑ:səkju:'ʃən] n (action) 訴追 sotsúi; (accusing side) 検察側 keñsatsugàwa

prosecutor [prɑ:s'əkju:tə:r] n (also: **public prosecutor**) 検察官 keñsatsukàn

prospect [prɑ:s'pekt] n (possibility) 可能性 kanōsei; (outlook) 見込み mikómi

♦vi: **to prospect (for)** (gold etc) (...を) 探鉱する (...wo) tañkō suru

prospecting [prɑ:s'pektiŋ] n (for gold, oil etc) 探鉱 tañkō

prospective [prəspek'tiv] adj (son-in-law, customer, candidate etc) ...になろうとしている ...ni narō tò shité irù

prospects [prɑ:s'pekts] npl (for work etc) 見込み mikómi

prospectus [prəspek'təs] n (of college, school, company) 要綱 yōkō

prosper [prɑ:s'pə:r] vi (person, business, city etc) 繁栄する hañ-ei suru

prosperity [prɑ:sper'iti:] n 繁栄 hañ-ei

prosperous [prɑ:s'pə:rəs] adj (person, city etc) 裕福な yúfuku na; (business etc) 繁盛している hañjō shite irù

prostitute [prɑ:s'titu:t] n (female) 売春婦 baíshuñfu; (male) 男娼 dañshō

prostrate [prɑ:s'treit] adj (face down) うつ伏せの utsúbuse no

protagonist [proutæg'ənist] n (supporter) 支援者 shiénsha; (leading participant: in event, movement) リーダー格の人 rídākaku nò hitó; (THEATER) 主役 shuyáku; (in story etc) 主人公 shujínkō

protect [prətekt'] *vt* (person, thing) 守る mamórù, 保護する hógò suru

protection [prətek'ʃən] *n* 保護 hógò

protective [prətek'tiv] *adj* (clothing, layer, etc) 防護の bōgo no; (gesture) 防衛の bōei no; (person) 保護的な hogóteki na

protégé [prou'təʒei] *n* 偉い人のひいきを受ける人 erái hitó nò hiíki wò ukérù hitó

protein [prou'ti:n] *n* たんぱく質 tañpakushítsu

protest [*n* prou'test *vb* prətest'] *n* (strong expression of disapproval, opposition) 抗議 kōgi

♦*vi*: *to protest about/against/at* ...に抗議する ...ni kōgi suru

♦*vt* (insist): *to protest (that)* (...だと) 主張する (...dá tò) shuchō suru

Protestant [prɑːt'istənt] *adj* 新教の shíñkyō no, プロテスタントの purótesutànto no

♦*n* 新教徒 shiñkyōto, プロテスタント教徒 purótesutànto kyōto

protester [prətes'tə:r] *n* 抗議者 kōgishà

protocol [prou'təkɔ:l] *n* 外交儀礼 gaíkōgirèi

prototype [prou'tətaip] *n* 原型 geñkei

protracted [proutræk'tid] *adj* (absence, meeting etc) 長引いた nagábiità

protrude [proutru:d'] *vi* (rock, ledge, teeth etc) 突出る tsukíderù

proud [praud] *adj* (pleased): *proud of* ...を誇りとする ...wo hokóri tò suru; (dignified) プライドのある puráido no arù; (arrogant) 尊大な soñdai na

prove [pru:v] *vt* (verify) 立証する risshō suru

♦*vi*: *to prove (to be) correct etc* 結局 ...が正しいと判明する kekkyóku ...ga tadáshiì to hañmei suru

to prove oneself 自分の才能を立証する jibún nò saínō wò risshō suru

proverb [prɑːv'ə:rb] *n* ことわざ kotówaza

proverbial [prəvə:r'bi:əl] *adj* ことわざの kotówaza no

provide [prəvaid'] *vt* (give) 与える atáerù; (make available) 供給する kyōkyū suru

to provide someone with something ...に...を供給する ...ni ...wo kyōkyō suru

provided (that) [prəvai'did-] *conj* ...という条件で ...tó iù jōken de

provide for *vt fus* (person) ...の面倒を見る ...no meñdō wò mírù

♦*vt* (future event) ...に備える ...ni sonáerù

Providence [prɑːv'idəns] *n* 摂理 sétsùri

providing [prəvai'diŋ] *conj*: *providing (that)* ...という条件で ...tó iù jōken de

province [prɑːv'ins] *n* (of country) 県 kéñ; (fig) 管轄 kañkatsu

provincial [prəvin'tʃəl] *adj* (town, newspaper etc) 地方の chihō no; (pej) 田舎じみた inákajimità

provision [prəviʒ'ən] *n* (supplying) 供給 kyōkyū; (of contract, agreement) 規定 kitéi

provisional [prəviʒ'ənəl] *adj* (government, agreement, arrangement etc) 暫定的な zañteiteki na

provisions [prəviʒ'ənz] *npl* (food) 食料 shokuryō

proviso [prəvai'zou] *n* 規定 kitéi

provocation [prɑːvəkei'ʃən] *n* 挑発 chōhatsu

provocative [prəvɑːk'ətiv] *adj* (remark, article, gesture) 挑発的な chōhatsuteki na; (sexually stimulating) 扇情的な señjōteki na

provoke [prəvouk'] *vt* (annoy: person) 怒らせる okóraserù; (cause: fight, argument etc) 引起こす hikíokosù

prow [prau] *n* へさき hesáki, 船首 séñshu

prowess [prau'is] *n* (outstanding ability) 手腕 shúwàn

prowl [praul] *vi* (*also*: **prowl about**, **prowl around**) うろつく urótsukù

♦*n*: *on the prowl* あさり歩いて asáriaruìte

prowler [prau'lə:r] *n* うろつく人 urótsuku hitó

proximity [prɑːksimˈitiː] n 近さ chikása

proxy [prɑːkˈsiː] n: *by proxy* 代理を通じて daíri wð tsújite

prude [pruːd] n 上品ぶる人 jôhiñburu hitð

prudence [pruːˈdəns] n (care, sense) 慎重さ shiñchôsa

prudent [pruːˈdənt] adj (careful, sensible) 慎重な shiñchô na

prune [pruːn] n 干しプラム hoshípuràmu
♦vt (bush, plant, tree) せん定する sefitei suru

pry [prai] vi: *to pry (into)* (...を) せん索する (...wo) señsaku suru

PS [piːesˈ] abbr = **postscript**

psalm [sɑːm] n 詩編 shihén

pseudo- [suːˈdou] prefix 偽... nisé...

pseudonym [suːˈdənim] n 筆名 hitsúmei, ペンネーム peñnèmu

psyche [saiˈkiː] n 精神 seíshin

psychiatric [saikiːætˈrik] adj (hospital, problem, treatment) 精神科の seíshinka no

psychiatrist [sikaiˈətrist] n 精神科医 seíshinka-ì

psychiatry [sikaiˈətriː] n 精神医学 seíshin-igàku

psychic [saiˈkik] adj (person: also: **psychical**) 霊媒の reíbai no; (of the mind) 精神の seíshin no

psychoanalysis [saikouənælˈisis] n 精神分析 seíshinbuñseki

psychoanalyst [saikouænˈəlist] n 精神分析医 seíshinbunseki-ì

psychoanalyze [saikouænˈəlaiz] vt ...の精神分析をする ...no seíshinbuñseki wo suru

psychological [saikəlɑːdʒˈikəl] adj (related to the mind: difference, problem etc) 精神的な seíshinteki na; (related to psychology: test, treatment etc) 心理的な shiñriteki na

psychologist [saikɑːlˈədʒist] n 心理学者 shiñrigakùsha

psychology [saikɑːlˈədʒiː] n (study) 心理学 shiñrigàku; (mind) 心理 shíñri

psychopath [saiˈkəpæθ] n 精神病質者 seíshinbyōshitsushà

psychosomatic [saikousoumætˈik] adj 精神身体の seíshinshiñtai no

psychotic [saikɑːtˈik] adj 精神病の seíshinbyô no

PTO [piːtiːouˈ] abbr (= please turn over) 裏面に続く rímen ni tsuzukù

pub [pʌb] n abbr (= public house) 酒場 sakába, パブ pábù

puberty [pjuːˈbəːrtiː] n 思春期 shishúñki

pubic [pjuːˈbik] adj: *pubic hair* 陰毛 iñmō

public [pʌbˈlik] adj (of people: support, opinion, interest) 国民の kokúmin no; (for people: building, service) 公共の kôkyō no; (for people to see: statement, action etc) 公の ðyake no
♦n: *the public* (all people of country, community) 公衆 kôshū; (particular set of people) ...層 ...sð; (fans, supporters) 支持者 shijísha
in public 公に ðyake ni, 人前で hitómaè de
to make public 公表する kðyō suru

public address system n 場内放送 (装置) jðnaihōsô(sòchi)

publican [pʌbˈlikən] n パブの亭主 pábù no teíshu

publication [pʌblikeiˈʃən] n (act) 出版 shuppán; (book, magazine) 出版物 shuppáñbutsu

public company n 株式会社 kabúshiki-gaìsha

public convenience (BRIT) n 公衆便所 kôshūbeñjo

public holiday n 休日 kyûjitsu

public house (BRIT) n 酒場 sakába, パブ pábù

publicity [pʌblisˈətiː] n (information) 宣伝 señden; (attention) 広く知られる事 hírðku shiráreru kotð

publicize [pʌbˈləsaiz] vt (fact, event) 報道する hðdō suru

publicly [pʌbˈlikliː] adv 公に ðyake ni, 人前で hitómaè de

public opinion n 世論 yðròn

public relations n 広報活動 kôhōkatsu-dð, ピーアール píàru

public school n (US) 公立学校 kðritsugakkō; (BRIT) 私立学校 shirítsugakkō

public-spirited [pʌb'likspir'itid] adj 公共心のある kōkyōshin nò árù

public transport n 公共輸送機関 kōkyō-yusōkikaǹ

publish [pʌb'liʃ] vt (book, magazine) 出版する shuppán suru, 発行する hakkō suru; (letter etc: in newspaper) 記載する kisái suru; (subj: person: article, story) 発表する happyō suru

publisher [pʌb'liʃə:r] n (person) 発行者 hakkṓshà; (company) 出版社 shuppán-sha

publishing [pʌb'liʃiŋ] n (profession) 出版業 shuppangyō

puce [pjuːs] adj 暗かっ色の aǹkasshoku no

pucker [pʌk'ə:r] vt (part of face) ...をしかめる ...wo shikámerù; (fabric etc) ...にしわを寄せる ...ni shiwá wò yoserù

pudding [pud'iŋ] n (cooked sweet food) プディング púdingu; (BRIT: dessert) デザート dezāto

　black pudding ブラッドソーセージ buráddosōsēji

puddle [pʌd'əl] n (also: **a puddle of water**) 水溜まり mizutamari; (of blood etc) 溜まり tamari

puff [pʌf] n (of cigarette, pipe) 一服 ippú-ku; (gasp) あえぎ aégi; (of air, smoke) 一吹き hitófuki

　♦vt: **to puff one's pipe** パイプをふかす páipu wo fukásù

　♦vi (breathe loudly) あえぐ aégù

puffed [pʌft] (inf) adj (out of breath) 息を切らせた íkì wo kirásetà

puff out vt (fill with air: one's chest, cheeks) 膨らます fukúramasù

puff pastry パイ皮 páíkawa

puffy [pʌf'iː] adj (eye) はれぼったい ha-rébottaì; (face) むくんだ mukúnda

pull [pul] n (tug): **to give something a pull** ...を引っ張る ...wo hippárù

　♦vt (gen) 引く hikú; (tug: rope, hair etc) 引っ張る hippárù

　♦vi (tug) 引く hikú, 引っ張る hippárù

　to pull to pieces 引裂く hikísakù

　to pull one's punches 手加減する teká-

gen suru

　to pull one's weight 仲間同様に働く nakámadōyo ni határakù

　to pull oneself together 落着きを取り戻す ochítsuki wò torímodosù

　to pull someone's leg (fig) ...をからかう ...wo karákaù

pull apart vt (break) ばらばらにする barábara nì suru

pull down vt (building) 取壊す toríko-wasù

pulley [pul'iː] n 滑車 kasshá

pull in vi (AUT: at the curb) ...に停車する ...ni teísha suru; (RAIL) 到着する tō-chaku suru

pull off vt (take off: clothes etc) 脱ぐ núgù; (fig: difficult thing) ...に成功する ...ni seíkō suru

pull out vi (AUT: from curb) 発進する hasshín suru; (RAIL) 出発する shuppá-tsu suru

　♦vt (extract) 取出す torídasù

pull over vi (AUT) 道路わきに寄せて停車する dōrowaki ni yosetè teísha suru

pullover [pul'ouvə:r] n セーター sētā

pull through vi (MED) 治る naórù

pull up vi (AUT, RAIL: stop) 停車する teísha suru

　♦vt (raise: object, clothing) 引上げる hi-kíagerù; (uproot) 引抜く hikínukù

pulp [pʌlp] n (of fruit) 果肉 kaníku

pulpit [pul'pit] n 説教壇 sekkyṓdaǹ

pulsate [pʌl'seit] vi 脈動する myakúdō suru

pulse [pʌls] n (ANAT) 脈拍 myakúhaku; (rhythm) 鼓動 kodō; (BOT) 豆類 mamé-rùi

pulverize [pʌl'və:raiz] vt (crush to a powder) 砕く kudákù; (fig: destroy) 破壊する hakái suru

puma [puː'mə] n ピューマ pyūma

pummel [pʌm'əl] vt 続けざまにげんこつで打つ tsuzúkezama nì geńkotsu de utsù

pump [pʌmp] n (for water, air, petrol) ポンプ póǹpu; (shoe) パンプス páǹpusu

　♦vt (force: in certain direction: liquid, gas) ポンプで送る póǹpu de okúrù; (obtain supply of: oil, **water**, **gas**) ポンプ

で汲む póǹpu de kúmù

pumpkin [pʌmp'kin] n カボチャ kabó-cha

pump up vt (inflate) ポンプで膨らます póǹpu de fukúramasù

pun [pʌn] n しゃれ sharé

punch [pʌntʃ] n (blow) げんこつで打つ事 geǹkotsu dè útsu kotó, パンチ páǹchi; (tool: for making holes) パンチ páǹchi; (drink) ポンチ póǹchi
♦vt (hit): **to punch someone/something** げんこつで...を打つ geǹkotsu de ...wo útsu

punchline [pʌntʃ'lain] n 落ち ochí

punch-up [pʌntʃ'ʌp] n (BRIT: inf) けんか keǹka

punctual [pʌŋk'tʃuəl] adj 時間を厳守する jíkàn wo geǹshu suru

punctuation [pʌŋktʃuei'ʃən] n 句読法 kutóhō

puncture [pʌŋk'tʃəːr] n パンク paǹku
♦vt ...に穴を開ける ...ni aná wò akérù

pundit [pʌn'dit] n 物知り monóshiri

pungent [pʌn'dʒənt] adj (smell, taste) 刺激的な shigékiteki na

punish [pʌn'iʃ] vt (person, crime) 罰する bassúrù

punishment [pʌn'iʃmənt] n (act) 罰する事 bassúrù kotó; (way of punishing) 罰 bátsù

punk [pʌŋk] n (also: **punk rock**) パンクロック paǹkurokkù; (also: **punk rocker**) パンクロッカー paǹkurokkằ; (US: inf: hoodlum) ちんぴら chíǹpira

punt [pʌnt] n (boat) ボート bôto ◇底が平らで さおで川底を突いて進める物を指す sokó ga taira dè sáò de kawázoko wo tsuitè susúmeru mono wò sásù

punter [pʌn'təːr] n (BRIT: gambler) ばくち打ち bakúchiùchi; (inf: client, customer) 客 kyakú

puny [pju:'ni:] adj (person, effort) ちっぽけな chippókè na

pup [pʌp] n (young dog) 子イヌ koínu

pupil [pju:'pəl] n (SCOL) 生徒 seíto; (of eye) どう孔 dókō

puppet [pʌp'it] n (doll) 操り人形 ayátsu-riníǹgyō; (fig: person) かいらい kaírai

puppy [pʌp'i:] n 子イヌ koínu

purchase [pəːr'tʃis] n (act of buying) 購入 kóǹyū; (item bought) 買い物 kaímono
♦vt (buy: house, book, car etc) 買う káù

purchaser [pəːr'tʃisəːr] n 買い手 kaíte

pure [pjuːr] adj (not mixed with anything: silk, gold etc) 純粋な juǹsui na; (clean, healthy: water, air etc) 清潔な seíketsu na; (fig: woman, girl) 純潔な juǹketsu na; (complete, total: chance, bliss) 全くの mattáku no

purée [pjurei'] n (of tomatoes, potatoes, apples etc) ピューレ pyūre

purely [pjur'li:] adv 単に táǹ ni

purgatory [pəːr'gətɔ:ri:] n (REL) れん獄 reǹgoku; (fig) 地獄 jigóku

purge [pəːrdʒ] n (POL) 粛正 shukúsei, パージ pầji
♦vt (organization) 粛正する shukúsei suru, パージする pầji suru

purify [pjuːr'əfai] vt (air, water etc) 浄化する jōka suru

purist [pjuːr'ist] n 純正主義者 juǹseishugishà

puritan [pjuːr'itən] n 禁欲主義者 kiǹyoku shugishà

purity [pjuːr'iti:] n (of silk, gold etc) 純粋さ juǹsuisa; (of water, air etc) 清潔 seíketsu; (fig: of woman, girl) 純潔 juǹketsu

purple [pəːr'pəl] adj 紫色の murásakiiro no

purport [pəːr'pɔ:rt] vi: **to purport to be/do** ...である〔...ができる〕と主張する ...de árù(...ga dekírù)to shuchō suru

purpose [pəːr'pəs] n (reason) 目的 mokúteki; (objective: of person) 目標 mokúhyō

on purpose 意図的に itóteki ni, わざと wázà to

purposeful [pəːr'pəsfəl] adj (person, look, gesture) 果敢な kakán na

purr [pəːr] vi (cat) ごろごろとのどを鳴らす górògoro to nódò wo narásù

purse [pəːrs] n (for money) 財布 saífu; (US: handbag) ハンドバッグ haǹdobaggù
♦vt (lips) すぼめる subómerù

purser [pəːr'səːr] n (NAUT) 事務長 jimúchō, パーサー pāsā

pursue [pəːrsuː'] vt (follow: person, thing) 追う ōu, 追跡する tsuíseki suru; (fig: activity, interest) 行う okonau; (: plan) 実行する jikkō suru; (: aim, result) 追い求める oímotomerù

pursuer [pəːrsuː'əːr] n 追跡者 tsuísekishà

pursuit [pəːrsuːt'] n (chase: of person, thing) 追跡 tsuíseki; (fig: of happiness, pleasure etc) 追求 tsuíkyū; (pastime) 趣味 shúmì

pus [pʌs] n うみ umí

push [puʃ] n 押す事 osú kotò
♦vt (press, shove) 押す osú; (promote) 宣伝する seńden suru
♦vi (press, shove) 押す osú; (fig: demand urgently): **to push for** 要求する yōkyū suru

push aside vt 押しのける oshínokerù

pushchair [puʃ'tʃeːr] n (BRIT) いす型ベビーカー isúgata bebíkā

pusher [puʃ'əːr] n (drug pusher) 売人 baínin

push off (inf) vi: **push off!** 消えうせろ kiéuserò

push on vi (continue) 続ける tsuzúkerù

pushover [puʃ'ouvəːr] (inf) n: **it's a pushover** 朝飯前だ asámeshimaè da

push through vi (crowd etc) ...を押し分けて進む ...wo oshíwakete susumù
♦vt (measure, scheme etc) 押し通す oshítōsu

push up vt total, prices 押し上げる oshíagerù

push-up [puʃ'ʌp] (US) n (press-up) 腕立て伏せ udétatefùse

pushy [puʃ'iː] (pej) adj 押しの強い oshí no tsuyoì

puss [pus] (inf) n ネコちゃん nékòchan

pussy(cat) [pus'iː(kæt)] (inf) n ネコちゃん nékòchan

put [put] (pt, pp **put**) vt (place: thing) 置く okú; (: person: in institution etc) 入れる irérù; (express: idea, remark etc) 表現する hyōgen suru; (present: case, view) 説明する setsúmei suru; (ask: question) する súrù; (place: person: in state, situa-

tion) 追込む oíkomù, 置く okú; (estimate) 推定する suítei suru; (write, type: word, sentence etc) 書く kákù

put about/around vt (rumor) 広める hirómerù

put across vt (ideas etc) 分からせる wakáraserù

put away vt (store) 仕舞っておく shimátte okù

put back vt (replace) 戻す modósù; (postpone) 延期する eñki suru; (delay) 遅らせる okúraserù

put by vt (money, supplies etc) 蓄えておく takúwaete okù

put down vt (on floor, table) 下ろす orósù; (in writing) 書く kákù; (riot, rebellion) 鎮圧する chiń-atsu suru; (kill: animal) 安楽死させる ańrakushi saserù; (attribute): **to put something down to** ...を...のせいにする ...wo ...no seí ni surù

put forward vt (ideas, proposal) 提案する teían suru

put in vt (application, complaint) 提出する teíshutsu suru; (time, effort) つぎ込む tsugíkomù

put off vt (delay) 延期する eñki suru; (discourage) いやにさせる iyá ni naserù

put on vt (shirt, blouse, dress etc) 着る kírù; (hat etc) かぶる kabúrù; (shoes, pants, skirt etc) はく hakú; (gloves etc) はめる hamérù; (make-up, ointment etc) つける tsukérù; (light etc) つける tsukérù; (play etc) 上演する jōen suru; (brake) かける kakérù; (record, tape, video) かける kakérù; (kettle, dinner etc) 火にかける hí nì kakérù; (assume: look, behavior etc) 装う yosóoù; (gain): **to put on weight** 太る futórù

put out vt (fire, candle, cigarette, light) 消す kesú; (take out: rubbish, cat etc) 出す dásù; (one's hand) 伸ばす nobásù; (inf: person): **to be put out** 怒っている okótte irù

putrid [pjuː'trid] adj 腐った kusáttà

putt [pʌt] n (GOLF) パット pátto

put through vt (TEL: person, call) つなぐ tsunágù; (plan, agreement) 成功させる seíkō saserù

putting green [pʌt'iŋ-] n (GOLF: smooth area around hole) グリーン gurín; (: for practice) パット練習場 páttòreñshūjō

putty [pʌt'i:] n パテ pátè

put up vt (build) 建てる tatérù; (raise: umbrella) 広げる hirógerù; (: tent) 張る hárù; (: hood) かぶる kabúrù; (poster, sign etc) 張る harú; (increase: price, cost) 上げる agérù; (accommodate) 泊める tomérù

put-up [put'ʌp]: **put-up job** (BRIT) n 八百長 yaőchō

put up with vt fus 我慢する gámàn suru

puzzle [pʌz'əl] n (question, game) なぞなぞ nazónazo; (toy) パズル pázùru; (mystery) なぞ naző
♦vt 当惑させる tőwaku saserù
♦vi: to puzzle over something ...を思案する ...wo shíàn suru

puzzling [pʌz'liŋ] adj (thing, action) 訳の分からない wákè no wakáranaī

pyjamas [pədʒɑːm'əz] (BRIT) npl = **pajamas**

pylon [pai'lɑːn] n (for electric cables) 鉄塔 tettő

pyramid [pir'əmid] n (ARCHIT) ピラミッド pirámiddð; (shape, object, pile) ピラミッド状の物 pirámiddojő no monő

Pyrenees [pir'əniːz] npl: **the Pyrenees** ピレネー山脈 pírènē sáňmyaku

python [pai'θɑːn] n ニシキヘビ nishíkihebì

Q

quack [kwæk] n (of duck) がーがー gãgã; (pej: doctor) やぶ医者 yabúisha

quad [kwɑːd] abbr = **quadrangle**; **quadruplet**

quadrangle [kwɑːd'ræŋgəl] n (courtyard) 中庭 nakániwa

quadruple [kwɑːdruː'pəl] vt (increase fourfold) 4倍にする yońbai ni suru
♦vi 4倍になる yońbai ni naru

quadruplets [kwɑːdrʌ'plits] npl 四つ子 yotsúgo

quagmire [kwæg'maiər] n (bog) 湿地 shitchí; (muddy place) ぬかるみ nukárumi

quail [kweil] n (bird) ウズラ uzúra
♦vi: to quail at/before (anger, prospect) ...の前でおじけづく ...no maè de ojíkezùku

quaint [kweint] adj (house, village) 古風で面白い kofū de omóshiroì; (ideas, customs) 奇妙な kimyō na

quake [kweik] vi (with fear) 震える furúeru
♦n abbr = **earthquake**

Quaker [kwei'kər] n クエーカー教徒 kuékākyōto

qualification [kwɑːləfəkei'ʃən] n (often pl: training, degree, diploma) 資格 shikáku; (skill, quality) 能力 nōryòku; (reservation, modification) 限定 geñtei, 条件 jōken

qualified [kwɑːl'əfaid] adj (trained) 資格のある shikáku no aru; (fit, competent): **qualified to** ...する能力がある ...suru nōryòku ga aru; (limited) 条件付きの jőkentsuki no

qualify [kwɑːl'əfai] vt (make competent) ...に資格を与える ...ni shikáku wo ataerù; (modify) 限定する gentei suru
♦vi (pass examination(s)): **to qualify (as)** ...の資格を取る ...no shikáku wo torù; (be eligible): **to qualify (for)** (...の) 資格がある (...no) shikáku ga aru; (in competition): **to qualify (for)** (...に進む) 資格を得る (...ni susúmu) shikáku wo eru

quality [kwɑːl'iti:] n (standard: of work, product) 品質 hiñshitsu; (characteristic: of person) 性質 seíshitsu; (: of wood, stone etc) 特徴 tokúchō

qualm [kwɑːm] n (doubt) 疑問 gimőn
qualms of conscience 良心のか責 ryőshin nò kasháku

quandary [kwɑːn'dri:] n: **to be in a quandary** 途方に暮れる tohő ni kuréru

quantity [kwɑːn'titi:] n (amount: of uncountable thing) 量 ryő; (: of countable things) 数 kazù

quantity surveyor n 積算士 sekĭsan-shi ◇工事などの費用を見積りで計算する人 kŏji nadŏ no hĭyŏ wo mitsŭmori dè keĭsan suru hitŏ

quarantine [kwɔːrˈəntiːn] n (isolation) 隔離 kakŭri

quarrel [kwɔːrˈəl] n (argument) けんか kenˈka
♦vi: *to quarrel (with)* (...と) けんかする (...to) keñka suru

quarrelsome [kwɔːrˈəlsəm] adj けんか早い kénkappayaĭ

quarry [kwɔːrˈiː] n (for stone) 石切り場 ishĭkiriba, 採石場 saĭsekijŏ; (animal) 獲物 emŏno

quart [kwɔːrt] n クォート kwŏto

quarter [kwɔːrˈtəːr] n (fourth part) 4分の1 yoñbun no ichi; (US: coin) 25セント玉 nijŭgosentodamà; (of year) 四半期 shihâñki; (district) 地区 chikŭ
♦vt (divide by four) 4等分する yoñtŏbun suru; (MIL: lodge) 宿泊させる shukŭhaku saseru
a quarter of an hour 15分 jūgŏfun

quarter final n 準々決勝 juñjunkesshŏ

quarterly [kwɔːrˈtəːrliː] adj (meeting, payment) 年4回の nèn-yoñkai no
♦adv (meet, pay) 年4回に nèn-yoñkai ni

quarters [kwɔːrˈtəːrz] npl (barracks) 兵舎 heĭsha; (living quarters) 宿舎 shúkusha

quartet(te) [kwɔːrtetˈ] n (group: of instrumentalists) 四重奏団 shijūsŏdan, カルテット karŭtetto; (: of singers) 四重唱団 shijŭshŏdan, カルテット karŭtetto; (piece of music) 四重奏曲 shijŭsŏkyokù

quartz [kwɔːrts] n 水晶 suĭshō

quash [kwɑːʃ] vt (verdict, judgement) 破棄する hakĭ suru

quasi- [kweiˈzai] prefix 疑似... gijĭ...

quaver [kweiˈvəːr] n (BRIT: MUS) 八分音符 hachĭbun oñpu
♦vi (voice) 震える furŭeru

quay [kiː] n (also: **quayside**) 岸壁 gañpeki

queasy [kwiːˈziː] adj (nauseous) 吐気がする hakĭke ga suru

queen [kwiːn] n (monarch) 女王 joŏ; (king's wife) 王妃 ŏhĭ; (ZOOL: also:

queen bee 女王バチ joŏbachi; (CARDS, CHESS) クイーン kuĭñ

queen mother n 皇太后 kŏtaigŏ

queer [kwiːr] adj (odd) 変な heñ na
♦n (inf: homosexual) ホモ homŏ

quell [kwel] vt (opposition) 鎮める shizŭmeru; (unease, fears) なだめる nadámeru, 静める shizŭmeru

quench [kwentʃ] vt: *to quench one's thirst* のどの乾きをいやす nodŏ no kawákĭ wo iyásù

querulous [kweˈrələs] adj (person, voice) 愚痴っぽい guchĭppòi

query [kwiəˈriː] n (question) 質問 shitsŭmon
♦vt (question) ...に聞く ...ni kikú, ...に質問する ...ni shitsŭmon suru

quest [kwest] n 探求 tañkyū

question [kwesˈtʃən] n (query) 質問 shitsŭmon; (doubt) 疑問 gimŏn; (issue) 問題 moñdai; (in test: problem) 問 toĭ
♦vt (ask) ...に聞く ...ni kikú, ...に質問する ...ni shitsŭmon suru; (interrogate) 尋問する jiñmon suru; (doubt) ...に疑問を投げ掛ける ...ni gimŏn wo nagékakeru
beyond question 疑いもなく utágai mo naku
out of the question 全く不可能で mattáku fúkanŏ de

questionable [kwesˈtʃənəbəl] adj (doubtful) 疑わしい utágawashii

question mark n 疑問符 gimŏnfu

questionnaire [kwestʃəneːrˈ] n 調査票 chŏsàhyō, アンケート añkētŏ

queue [kjuː] n (BRIT) n 列 retsŭ
♦vi (also: **queue up**) 列を作る retsù wo tsukúru

quibble [kwibˈəl] vi 詰まらない議論をする tsumáranaĭ giròn wo suru

quiche [kiːʃ] n キッシュ kisshù ◇パイの一種 paĭ no isshù

quick [kwik] adj (fast: person, movement, action etc) 早い hayáĭ; (agile) 素早い subáyai; (: mind) 理解の早い rikái no hayáĭ; (brief: look, visit) 短い mijíkài, ちょっとした chottŏ shita
♦n: *cut to the quick* (fig) ...の感情を害する ...no kañjō wo gaĭ sùru

be quick! 急いで isóide

quicken [kwik'ən] *vt* (pace, step) 早める hayámeru

♦*vi* (pace, step) 早くなる hayáku naru

quickly [kwik'li:] *adv* 早く hayáku

quicksand [kwik'sænd] *n* 流土砂 ryūdo-sha, クイックサンド kuíkkusando

quick-witted [kwik'wit'id] *adj* (alert) 機敏な kibín na

quid [kwid] (*BRIT: inf*) *n inv* ポンド poñdo

quiet [kwai't] *adj* (not loud or noisy) 静かな shizúka na; (silent) 何も言わない nanī mo iwánai; (peaceful: place) 平和な heiwa na; (calm: person) もの静かな monōshizuka na; (without fuss etc: ceremony) 簡単な kañtan na

♦*n* (peacefulness) 静けさ shizúkesa; (silence) 静かにする事 shizúka ni suru koto

♦*vi* (US: also: **quiet down**) (grow calm) 落着く ochitsuku; (grow silent) 静かになる shizúka ni naru

♦*vt* (person, animal) 落着かせる ochítsukaserù

quieten [kwai'itən] (*BRIT*) = **quiet** *vi, vt*

quietly [kwai'itli] *adv* (speak, play) 静かに shizúka ni; (silently) 黙って damáttè

quietness [kwai'itnis] *n* (peacefulness) 静けさ shizúkesa; (silence) 静かにする事 shizúka ni suru koto

quilt [kwilt] *n* (covering) ベッドカバー beddòkabā; (also: **continental quilt**) 掛布団 kakebuton, キルト kirúto

quin [kwin] *n abbr* = **quintuplet**

quinine [kwai'nain] *n* キニーネ kinínè

quintet(te) [kwintet'] *n* (group) 五重奏団 gojūsōdan, クインテット kuíntetto; (piece of music) 五重奏曲 gojūsōkyoku

quintuplets [kwintʌ'plits] *npl* 五つ子 itsútsugo

quip [kwip] *n* 警句 keíku

quirk [kwə:rk] *n* (unusual characteristic) 癖 kusé; (accident: of fate, nature) 気まぐれ kimágure

quit [kwit] (*pt, pp* **quit** *or* **quitted**) *vt* (smoking, grumbling) やめる yaméru;

(job) 辞める yaméru; (premises) ...から出ていく ...kara detè iku

♦*vi* (give up) やめる yaméru; (resign) 辞める yaméru

quite [kwait] *adv* (rather) かなり kanári; (entirely) 全く mattáku, 完全に kañzen ni; (following a negative: almost): *that's not quite big enough* それはちょっと小さい soré wa chottó chiisai

I saw quite a few of them 私はそれらをかなり沢山見ました watákushi wa soréra wo kanári takúsan mimashita

quite (so)! 全くその通り mattáku sonó tōri

quits [kwits] *adj*: **quits (with)** (...と) おあいこである (...to) o-áiko de aru

let's call it quits もうこれでおあいこにしましょう o-aíko ni shimáshō; (stop working etc) やめましょう yamémashō

quiver [kwiv'ə:r] *vi* (tremble) 震える furúerù

quiz [kwiz] *n* (game) クイズ kuízu; (US: short test) 小テスト shótesùto

♦*vt* (question) 尋問する jiñmon suru

quizzical [kwiz'ikəl] *adj* (look, smile) なぞめいた nazómeìta

quorum [kwɔ:r'əm] *n* (of members) 定足数 teísokusū

quota [kwou'tə] *n* 割当数〔量〕waríatesū〔ryō〕

quotation [kwoutei'ʃən] *n* (from book, play etc) 引用文 iñ'yōbuñ; (estimate) 見積り mitsúmori

quotation marks *npl* 引用符 iñyōfù

quote [kwout] *n* (from book, play etc) 引用文 iñyōbuñ; (estimate) 見積り mitsúmori

♦*vt* (sentence, proverb etc) 引用する iñyō suru; (figure, example) 引合いに出す hikíai ni dasù; (price) 見積る mitsúmorù

♦*vi*: *to quote from* (book, play etc) ...から引用する ...kara iñ'yō suru

quotes [kwouts] *npl* (quotation marks) 引用符 iñ-yōfù

quotient [kwou'ʃənt] *n* (factor) 指数 shisū

R

rabbi [ræb'ai] n ラビ rábi ◇ユダヤ教の聖職者 yudáyakyō nò seíshokushà

rabbit [ræb'it] n ウサギ usági

rabbit hutch n ウサギ小屋 uságigoyà

rabble [ræb'əl] (pej) n 群衆 guńshū

rabies [rei'bi:z] n 恐犬病 kyốkeǹbyō

RAC [ɑːreisiː'] (BRIT) n abbr (= Royal Automobile Club) 英国自動車連盟 eíkoku jidṓsha reńmei

raccoon [rækuːn'] n アライグマ aráigùma

race [reis] n (species) 人種 jíñshu; (competition: for speed) 競走 kyṓsō, レース rḗsù; (: for power, control) 競争 kyṓsō; (public gambling event: also: **horse race**) 競馬 keíba; (: also: **bicycle race**) 競輪 keírin; (: also: **motorboat race**) 競艇 kyṓtei
♦vt (horse) 競馬に出場させる keíba nì shutsújō saserù; (compete against: person) ...と競走する ...to kyṓsō suru
♦vi (compete: for speed) 競走する kyṓsō suru; (: for power, control) 競争する kyṓsō suru; (hurry) 急いで行く isṓide ikù; (pulse) どきどきする dókìdoki suru; (engine) 空回りする karámawarì suru

race car (US) n レーシングカー rḗshingukà

race car driver (US) n レーサー rḗsà

racecourse [reis'kɔːrs] n 競馬場 keíbajō

racehorse [reis'hɔːrs] n 競走馬 kyṓsōba

racetrack [reis'træk] n (for people) トラック toràkkù; (for cars) サーキット sàkitto

racial [rei'ʃəl] adj 人種の jíñshu no, 人種 ...jíñshu...

racing [rei'siŋ] n (horses) 競馬 keíba; (bicycles) 競輪 keírin; (motorboats) 競艇 kyṓtei; (cars) 自動車レース jidṓsharèsu; (motorcycles) オートレース ōtorḕsu

racing car (BRIT) n = **race car**

racing driver (BRIT) n = **race car driver**

racism [rei'sizəm] n 人種差別 jíñshusabètsu

racist [rei'sist] adj (statement, policy) 人種差別的な jíñshusabetsuteki na
♦n 人種差別主義者 jíñshusabetsushugi-shà

rack [ræk] n (also: **luggage rack**) 網棚 amídana; (shelf) 棚 taná; (also: **roof rack**) ルーフラック rṹfurakkù; (dish rack) 水切りかご mizúkirikago
♦vt: **racked by** (pain, anxiety) ...でもだえ苦しんで ...de modáekurushiǹde
to rack one's brains 知恵を絞る chié wò shibórù

racket [ræk'it] n (for tennis, squash etc) ラケット rakéttò; (noise) 騒音 sṓon; (swindle) 詐欺 ságì

racoon [rækuːn'] n = **raccoon**

racquet [ræk'it] n (for tennis, squash etc) ラケット rakéttò

racy [rei'siː] adj きびきびした kíbìkibi shita

radar [rei'dɑːr] n レーダー rḕdā

radial [rei'di:əl] adj (also: **radial-ply**) ラジアルの rájìaru no

radiance [rei'di:əns] n (glow) 光 hikári

radiant [rei'di:ənt] adj (happy, joyful) 輝く kagáyakù

radiate [rei'di:eit] vt (heat) 放射する hṓsha suru; (emotion) ...で輝く ...de kagáyakù
♦vi (lines) 放射状に広がる hṓshajō nì hiṟógarù

radiation [reidiːeiʃən] n (radioactive) 放射能 hṓshanō; (from sun etc) 放射 hṓsha

radiator [rei'di:eitər] n ラジエーター rajíètā

radical [ræd'ikəl] adj (change etc) 抜本的な bappóntekì na; (person) 過激な kagéki na; (organization) 過激派の kagéki-ha no, 過激派... kagékiha...

radii [rei'di:ai] npl of **radius**

radio [rei'di:ou] n (broadcasting) ラジオ放送 rajíohōsō; (device: for receiving broadcasts) ラジオ rájìo; (: for transmitting and receiving signals) 無線通信機 muséntsūshiǹki
♦vt (person) ...と無線で通信する ...to musén dè tsūshin suru
on the radio ラジオで rájìo de

radioactive [reidi:ouæk'tiv] *adj* 放射性
の hōshasei no

radiography [reidi:ɑːg'rəfi:] *n* レントゲ
ン撮影 reñtogensatsuèi

radiology [reidi:ɑːl'ədʒi:] *n* 放射線医学
hōshasen-igàku

radio station *n* ラジオ放送局 rajío hō-
sōkyòku

radiotherapy [reidi:ouθe:r'əpi:] *n* 放射
線療法 hōshasenryòhò

radish [ræd'iʃ] *n* はつかだいこん hatsuka-
kadaìkon

radius [rei'di:əs] (*pl* **radii**) *n* (of circle) 半
径 hañkei; (from point) 半径内の範囲 hañ-
keinai nò háñ-i

RAF [ɑːreief'] *n abbr* = **Royal Air
Force**

raffle [ræf'əl] *n* 宝くじ takárakùji ◇当る
と金ではなく賞品をもらえる物を指す a-
tárù to kanè de wa nakù shóhin wò
moráerù monó wò sásù

raft [ræft] *n* (craft) いかだ ikáda; (*also*:
life raft) 救命いかだ kyúmei ikàda

rafter [ræf'tə:r] *n* はり harí

rag [ræg] *n* (piece of cloth) ぞうきん zó-
kin; (torn cloth) ぼろ bőrò; (*pej*: newspaper) 三流紙 sañryúshi; (*BRIT*: UNI-
VERSITY: for charity) 慈善募金運動 ji-
zéñbokin-uñdō

rag-and-bone man [rægənboun'-]
(*BRIT*) *n* = **ragman**

rag doll *n* 縫いぐるみ人形 nuíguruminìñ-
gyō

rage [reidʒ] *n* (fury) 憤怒 fúñdo
◆*vi* (person) 怒り狂う ikárikuruù;
(storm) 荒れ狂う arékuruù; (debate) 荒れ
る arérù
it's all the rage (very fashionable) 大
流行している dafryúkō shite irù

ragged [ræg'id] *adj* (edge) ぎざぎざの gi-
zágiza no; (clothes) ぼろぼろの borőboro
no; (appearance) 不ぞろいの fuzórdi no

ragman [ræg'mæn] (*pl* **ragmen**) *n* くず
屋 kuzúyà

rags [rægz] *npl* (torn clothes) ぼろぼろの
衣服 borőboro no ifùku

raid [reid] *n* (MIL) 襲撃 shúgeki; (criminal) 不法侵入 fuhóshiñnyū; (by police) 手

入れ teíre
◆*vt* (MIL) 襲撃する shúgeki suru; (crimi-
nally) ...に不法侵入する ...ni fuhóshiñnyū
suru; (subj: police) 手入れする teíre suru

rail [reil] *n* 手すり tesúri
by rail (by train) 列車で resshá de

railing(s) [rei'liŋ(z)] *n*(*pl*) (fence) さく
sakú

railroad [reil'roud] (*US*) *n* (track) 線路
señro; (company) 鉄道 tetsúdō

railroader [reil'roudə:r] (*US*) *n* 鉄道員
tetsúdōìn

railroad line (*US*) *n* 鉄道線 tetsúdōsen

railroad station (*US*) *n* 駅 ékì

rails [reilz] *npl* (for train) レール rèru

railway [reil'wei] (*BRIT*) *n* = **railroad
etc**

railwayman [reil'weimən] (*BRIT*: *pl*
railwaymen) *n* = **railroader**

rain [rein] *n* 雨 ámè
◆*vi* 雨が降る ámè ga fúrù
in the rain 雨の中で ámè no nákà de
it's raining 雨が降っている ámè ga futté irù

rainbow [rein'bou] *n* にじ nijí

raincoat [rein'kout] *n* レーンコート réñ-
kòto

raindrop [rein'drɑːp] *n* 雨の一滴 ámè no
ittéki

rainfall [rein'fɔːl] *n* 降雨量 kőuryò

rainy [rei'ni:] *adj* 雨模様の amémoyò no

raise [reiz] *n* (payrise) 賃上げ chiñ-age
◆*vt* (lift) 持上げる mochíagerù;
(increase: salary) 上げる agérù; (: production) 増やす fuyásù; (improve:
morale) 高める takámerù; (: standards)
引上げる hikíagerù; (produce: doubts,
question) 引起こす hikíokosù; (rear: cattle) 飼育する shifku suru; (: family) 育て
る sodáterù; (cultivate: crop) 栽培する
saíbai suru; (get together: army, funds,
loan) 集める atsúmerù
to raise one's voice 声を大きくする
kőè wo őkiku suru

raisin [rei'zin] *n* 干しぶどう hoshíbudò,
レーズン rèzun

rake [reik] *n* (tool) レーキ rèki
◆*vt* (garden) レーキで...の土をならす rè-

ki de ...no tsuchí wo narásù; (leaves) か
き集める kakátsumerù; (with machine
gun) 掃射する sṓsha suru

rally [ræl'i:] n (POL etc) 集会 shū́kai;
(AUT) ラリー rarī́; (TENNIS etc) ラリ
ー rárī
◆vt (support) 集める atsúmerù
◆vi (sick person, Stock Exchange) 持直
す mochínaosù

rally round vt fus (fig: give support to)
...の支援に駆け付ける ...no shién nī kaké-
tsukerù

RAM [ræm] n abbr = **(random access
memory)** ラム rámù

ram [ræm] n (ZOOL) 雄ヒツジ osúhitsùji
◆vt (crash into) ...に激突する ...ni gekítotsu suru; (push: bolt, fist etc) 押込む oshíkomù

ramble [ræm'bəl] n (walk) ハイキング
háìkingu
◆vi (walk) ハイキングする háìkingu suru; (talk: also: **ramble on**) だらだらしゃ
べる dáràdara shabérù

rambler [ræm'blə:r] n (walker) ハイカー
háìkā; (BOT) ツルバラ tsurúbara

rambling [ræm'bliŋ] adj (speech) 取留め
のない torítome no naì; (house) だだっ広
い dadáppiroì; (BOT) つる性の tsurúsei
no

ramp [ræmp] n 傾斜路 keísharo
on/off ramp (US: AUT) 入口〔出口〕ラ
ンプ iríguchi〔degúchi〕raǹpu

rampage [ræm'peidʒ] n: **to be on the
rampage** 暴れ回っている abáremawatte
irù
◆vi: **they went rampaging through
the town** 彼らは町中暴れ回った kárèra
wa machíjū abaremawattà

rampant [ræm'pənt] adj (crime) はびこ
る habíkorù; (disease) まん延する maǹ-en
suru

rampart [ræm'pɑːrt] n (fortification) 城
壁 jōheki

ramshackle [ræm'ʃækəl] adj (house,
car, table) がたがたの gatágata no

ran [ræn] pt of **run**

ranch [ræntʃ] n 牧場 bokújō

rancher [ræn'tʃəːr] n 牧場主 bokújōshu

rancid [ræn'sid] adj (butter, bacon etc)
悪くなった wárùku natta

rancor [ræn'kəːr] (BRIT **rancour**) n 恨
み urámi

random [ræn'dəm] adj (arrangement,
selection) 手当り次第の teátarishidài no;
(COMPUT, MATH) 無作為の musákùi
no
◆n: **at random** 手当り次第に teátarishidài ni

random access n (COMPUT) ランダム
アクセス rańdamuakùsesu

randy [ræn'di:] (inf) adj セックスをした
がっている sékkùsu wo shítagatte irù

rang [ræŋ] pt of **ring**

range [reindʒ] n (also: **mountain range**)
山脈 sańmyaku; (of missile) 射程距離
shatéikyorì; (of voice) 声域 seíiki;
(series: of proposals, offers, products) 一
連の... ichíren no ...; (MIL: also: **shooting range**) 射撃場 shagékijō; (also:
kitchen range) レンジ réǹji
◆vt (place) 歩き回る arúkimawarù;
(arrange) 並べる naráberù
◆vi: **to range over** (extend) ...にわたる
...ni watárù
to range from ... to ... ...から...までに
わたる ...kárà ...mádè ni watárù

ranger [rein'dʒəːr] n 森林警備隊員 shiń-
rinkeibitaiin, レンジャー réǹjā

rank [ræŋk] n (row) 列 rétsù; (MIL) 階級
kaíkyū; (status) 地位 chíì; (BRIT: also:
taxi rank) タクシー乗場 takúshīnorìba
◆vi: **to rank among** ...のうちに数えられ
る ...no uchí nì kazóerarerù
◆adj (stinking) 臭い kusáì
the rank and file (fig: ordinary members) 一般の人 ippáǹ no hitò, 一般人 ip-
pánjin

rankle [ræŋ'kəl] vi (insult) わだかまる
wadákamarù

ransack [ræn'sæk] vt (search) 物色する
busshóku suru; (plunder) 略奪する ryakúdatsu suru

ransom [ræn'səm] n (money) 身代金 mi-
nóshirokiǹ
to hold to ransom (fig: nation, company, individual) ...に圧力を掛ける ...ni

atsúryòku wo kakérù

rant [rænt] *vi* (rave) わめく wamékù

rap [ræp] *vt* (on door, table) たたく tatákù

rape [reip] *n* (of woman) 強かん gókan; (BOT) アブラナ abúranà

♦*vt* (woman) 強かんする gókan suru

rape(seed) oil [reip'(si:d)-] *n* ナタネ油 natáneabùra

rapid [ræp'id] *adj* (growth, development, change) 急速な kyúsoku na

rapidity [rəpid'iti:] *n* (speed) 速さ háyàsa

rapidly [ræp'idli:] *adv* (grow, develop, change) 急速に kyúsoku ni

rapids [ræp'idz] *npl* (GEO) 早瀬 hayáse

rapist [rei'pist] *n* 強かん者 gókañsha

rapport [ræpɔ:r'] *n* 親和関係 shiñwakaǹkei

rapture [ræp'tʃə:r] *n* (delight) 歓喜 káǹki

rapturous [ræp'tʃə:rəs] *adj* (applause) 熱狂的な nekkyóteki na

rare [re:r] *adj* (uncommon) まれな maré na; (unusual) 珍しい mezúrashiǐ; (CULIN: steak) レアの rêâ no

rarely [reə:r'li:] *adv* (seldom) めったに...ない méttà ni ...naǐ

raring [re:r'iŋ] *adj*: **raring to go** (*inf*: keen) 意気込んでいる ikígoǹde irù

rarity [re:r'iti:] *n* (exception) 希有な物 kéù na monó; (scarcity) 希少性 kishósei

rascal [ræs'kəl] *n* (rogue) ごろつき gorótsuki; (mischievous child) いたずらっ子 itázurakkò

rash [ræʃ] *adj* (person) 向こう見ずの mukómìzu no; (promise, act) 軽率な keísotsu na

♦*n* (MED) 発しん hasshín; (spate: of events, robberies) 多発 tahátsu

rasher [ræʃ'ə:r] *n* (of bacon) 一切れ hitókìre

raspberry [ræz'be:ri:] *n* キイチゴ kiíchìgo

rasping [ræs'piŋ] *adj*: **a rasping noise** きしむ音 kishímù otó

rat [ræt] *n* ネズミ nezúmi

rate [reit] *n* (speed) 速度 sókùdo; (of change, inflation) 進行度 shiñkòdo;

(ratio: *also* of interest) 率 rítsù; (price: at hotel etc) 料金 ryókin

♦*vt* (value, estimate) 評価する hyóka suru

to rate someone/something as ...を...と評価する ...wo ...to hyóka suru

rateable value [rei'təbəl-] (*BRIT*) *n* 課税評価額 kazéi hyókagàku

ratepayer [reit'peiə:r] (*BRIT*) *n* 納税者 nózeìsha ◊固定資産税の納税者について言う kotéishisañzei no nózeìsha ni tsuíte iú

rates [reits] *npl* (*BRIT*: property tax) 固定資産税 kotéishisañzei; (fees) 料金 ryókin

rather [ræð'ə:r] *adv* (quite, somewhat) かなり kánàri; (to some extent) 少し sukóshì; (more accurately): *or rather* 正確に言えば seíkaku nì iébà

it's rather expensive (quite) かなり値段が高い kánàri nedán gà takáǐ; (too) 値段が高過ぎる nedán gà takásugirù

there's rather a lot かなり沢山ある kánàri takúsan arù

I would rather go どちらかというと行きたいと思う dóchìra ka to iú tò ikítaǐ to omóù

ratify [ræt'əfai] *vt* (agreement, treaty) 批准する hijún suru

rating [rei'tiŋ] *n* (assessment) 評価 hyóka; (score) 評点 hyóten; (NAUT: *BRIT*: sailor) 海軍兵卒 kaígunheìsotsu

ratings [rei'tiŋz] *npl* (RADIO, TV) 視聴率 shichórìtsu

ratio [rei'ʃou] *n* 率 rítsù

in the ratio of 100 to 1 100に1つといっう割合で hyakú ni hitotsù to iu waríai de

ration [ræʃ'ən] *n* (allowance: of food, petrol etc) 配給分 haíkyùbun

♦*vt* (food, petrol etc) 配給する haíkyù suru

rational [ræʃ'ənəl] *adj* (solution, reasoning) 合理的な góriteki na; (person) 訳の分かる wáke no wakáru

rationale [ræʃənæl'] *n* 根拠 kóǹkyo

rationalize [ræʃ'ənəlaiz] *vt* (justify) 正当化する seítoka suru

rationally [ræʃ'ənəliː] adv (sensibly) 合理的に gōriteki ni

rationing [ræʃ'əniŋ] n (of food, petrol etc) 配給 haikyū

rations [rei'ʃənz] npl (MIL) 兵糧 hyōrō

rat race n 競争の世界 kyōsō nò sēkai

rattle [ræt'əl] n (of door, window) がたがたという音 gátàgata to iú oto; (of train, car, engine etc) ごう音 gōon; (of coins) じゃらじゃらという音 járàjara to iú oto; (of chain) がらがらという音 gáràgara to iú oto; (object: for baby) がらがら garágarà

♦vi (small objects) がらがら鳴る gáràgara narú; (car, bus): **to rattle along** がたがた走る gatagata hashírù

♦vt (unnerve) どぎまぎさせる dógìmagi sasérù

rattlesnake [ræt'əlsneik'] n ガラガラヘビ garágarahebì

raucous [rɔː'kəs] adj しゃがれ声の shagáregoè no

ravage [ræv'idʒ] vt (damage) 荒す arásù

ravages [ræv'idʒiz] npl (of time, weather) 荒廃 kōhai

rave [reiv] vi (in anger) わめく wamékù; (with enthusiasm) ...をべたぼめする ...wo betábòme surú; (MED) うわごとを言う uwágoto wò iú

raven [rei'vən] n ワタリガラス watárigaràsu

ravenous [ræv'ənəs] adj 猛烈におなかがすいた mōretsu nì onáka ga suìta

ravine [rəvin'] n 渓谷 keíkoku

raving [rei'viŋ] adj: **raving lunatic** どき違い dokíchigai

ravishing [ræv'iʃiŋ] adj (beautiful) 悩殺する nōsatsu suru

raw [rɔː] adj (uncooked) 生の námà no; (not processed: cotton, sugar etc) 原料のままの geńryō no mamá no; (sore) 赤むけした akámuke shità; (inexperienced) 青二才の aónisài no; (weather, day) 肌寒い hadázamuì

raw deal (inf) n ひどい仕打 hidóì shiúchi

raw material n (coal, oil, gas etc) 原料 geńryō

ray [rei] n (also: **ray of light**) 光線 kōsen; (also: **ray of heat**) 熱線 nessèn

the rays of the sun 太陽の光線 táiyō no kōsen

a ray of hope 希望のひらめき kibō nò hirámeki

rayon [rei'ɑːn] n レーヨン rèyon

raze [reiz] vt 根こそぎ破壊する nekósògi hakái suru

razor [rei'zəːr] n (open razor) かみそり kamísorì; (safety razor) 安全かみそり ańzenkamisòri; (electric razor) 電気かみそり deńkikamisòri

razor blade n かみそりの刃 kamísorì no há

Rd n abbr = **road**

re [rei] prep (with regard to) ...に関して ...ni káň shite

reach [riːtʃ] n (range: of arm) 手が届く範囲 té gà todókù háň-i; (scope: of imagination) 範囲 háň-i; (stretch: of river etc) 区域 kúìku

♦vt (arrive at: place) ...に到着する ...ni tōchaku suru; (: conclusion, agreement, decision, end) ...に達する ...ni tassúrù; (be able to touch) ...に手が届く ...ni té gà todókù; (by telephone) ...に連絡する ...ni refiraku suru

♦vi (stretch out one's arm) 手を伸ばす té wò nobásù

within reach 手の届く所に té nò todókù tokórò ni

out of reach 手の届かない所に té nò todókanaì tokórò ni

within reach of the shops/station 商店街(駅)の近くに shōteńgai〔ékì〕no chikákù ni

「**keep out of the reach of children**」子供の手が届かない所に保管して下さい kodómo nò té gà todókanaì tokórò ni hokán shitè kudásaì

reach out vt (hand) 伸ばす nobásù

♦vi 手を伸ばす té wò nobásù

to reach out for something ...を取ろうとして手を伸ばす ...wo toró tò shite té wò nobásù

react [riːækt'] vi (CHEM): **to react (with)** (...と) 反応する (...to) hańnō su-

ru; (MED): *to react (to)* (...に対して)
副作用が起る (...ni táishite) fukúsayō ga
okórù; (respond): *to react (to)* (...に)
反応する (...ni) hańnō suru; (rebel): *to
react (against)* (...に) 反発する (...ni)
hańpatsu suru

reaction [ri:ǽkʹʃən] *n* (response): *reaction (to)* (...に対する) 反応 (...ni taísu-
rù) hańnō; (rebellion): *reaction
(against)* (...に対する) 反発 (...ni taí-
surù) hańpatsu; (belief in conservatism)
反動 hańdō; (CHEM) 反応 hańnō; (MED)
副作用 fukúsayō

reactionary [ri:ǽkʹʃəneri:] *adj* (forces,
attitude) 反動的な hańdōteki na

reactions [ri:ǽkʹʃənz] *npl* (reflexes) 反
応 hańnō

reactor [ri:ǽkʹtə:r] *n* (*also*: **nuclear
reactor**) 原子炉 geńshiró

read [ri:d] (*pt, pp* **read**) *vi* (person, child)
...を読む ...wo yómù; (piece of writing,
letter etc) ...と書いてある ...to káîte árù
♦*vt* (book, newspaper, music etc) 読む
yómù; (mood, thoughts) 読取る yomíto-
rù; (meter, thermometer etc) 読む yómù;
(study: at university) 学ぶ manábù

readable [ri:ʹdəbəl] *adj* (writing) 読める
yomérù; (book, author etc) 読ませる yo-
máserù

reader [ri:ʹdə:r] *n* (of book, newspaper
etc) 読者 dókùsha; (book) リーダー rīdā;
(*BRIT*: at university) 助教授 jokyóju
an avid reader 読書家 dokúshòka

readership [ri:ʹdə:rʃip] *n* (of newspaper
etc) 読者 dókùsha の総称 sōshо

readily [redʹəli:] *adv* (willingly) 快く ko-
kóroyokù; (easily) たやすく tayásukù;
(quickly) 直ぐに súgù ni

readiness [redʹi:nis] *n* (preparedness) 用
意ができている事 yōi ga dekite iru koto;
(willingness) ...する意志 ...suru ishi
in readiness (prepared) 用意ができて
yōi ga dekite

reading [ri:ʹdiŋ] *n* (of books, newspapers
etc) 読書 dokusho; (in church, as entertainment) 朗読 rōdoku; (on meter, thermometer etc) 記録 kiroku

readjust [ri:ʹədʒʌstʹ] *vt* (alter: position,

knob, mirror etc) 調節する chōsetsu suru
♦*vi* (adapt): *to readjust (to)* (...に) な
れる (...ni) nareru

ready [redʹi:] *adj* (prepared) 用意ができ
ている yōi ga dekíte iru; (willing) ...する
意志がある ...surú ishì ga árù; (available)
用意されている yōi sárete irù
♦*n*: *at the ready* (MIL) 銃を構えて jū
wo kamáetè
to get ready
♦*vi* 支度する shitáku suru
♦*vt* 準備する júnbi suru

ready-made [redʹi:meidʹ] *adj* 既製の kiséi no

ready money *n* 現金 geńkiń

ready reckoner [-rekʹənə:r] *n* 計算表
keísańhyō

ready-to-wear [redʹi:təwe:rʹ] *adj* 既製
の kiséi no

reaffirm [ri:əfə:rmʹ] *vt* 再び言明する futátabi geńmei suru

real [ri:l] *adj* (actual, true: reason, interest, result etc) 本当の hońtō no; (not artificial: leather, gold etc) 本物の hofmono
no; (not imaginary: life, feeling) 実際の
jissái no; (for emphasis): *a real idiot/
miracle* 正真正銘のばか〔奇跡〕shōshin-
shōmei no báká〔kiséki〕
in real terms 事実は jíjìtsu wa

real estate *n* 不動産 fudōsan

realism [ri:ʹəlizəm] *n* (practicality) 現実
主義 geńjitsushugī; (ART) リアリズム ri-
árizùmu

realist [ri:ʹəlist] *n* 現実的な人 geńjitsuteki nà hitó

realistic [ri:əlisʹtik] *adj* (practical) 現実
的な geńjitsuteki na; (true to life) 写実的
な shajítsuteki na

reality [ri:ǽlʹiti:] *n* (actuality, truth) 事
実 jíjìtsu
in reality 事実は jíjìtsu wa

realization [ri:ələzeiʹʃən] *n* (understanding: of situation) 実感 jikkán; (fulfilment: of dreams, hopes) 実現 jitsúgen;
(of asset) 現金化 geńkiňka

realize [ri:ʹəlaiz] *vt* (understand) 実感す

る jikkán suru; (fulfil: a dream, hope, project etc) 実現する jitsúgen suru; (COMM: asset) 現金に替える geñkiñ ni kaérù

really [ri:'əli:] *adv* (for emphasis) 実にjitsú ni, とても totémo; (actually): *what really happened* 実際に起った事は jissái nì okótta kotǒ wa

really? (indicating interest) そうですかsǒ desu ka; (expressing surprise) 本当ですか hoñtō desu ka

really! (indicating annoyance) うんもう！úñ mǒ!

realm [relm] *n* (of monarch) 王国 ǒkoku; (*fig*: area of activity or study) 分野 búñya

realtor [ri:'əltə:r] (*US*) *n* 不動産業者 fudǒsangyǒsha

reap [ri:p] *vt* (crop) ...の刈入れをする ...no karíire wò suru; (*fig*: benefits, rewards) 収穫する shǔkaku suru

reappear [ri:əpi:r'] *vi* 再び現れる futátabi arawarerù

rear [ri:r] *adj* (back) 後ろの ushíro no
♦*n* (back) 後ろ ushíro
♦*vt* (cattle) 飼育する shíiku suru; (family) 育てる sodáterù
♦*vi* (*also*: **rear up**: animal) 後足で立ち上る atóashi de tachfagarù

rearguard [ri:r'gɑ:rd] *n* (MIL) 後衛 kǒei

rearmament [ri:ɑ:rm'əmənt] *n* 再軍備 saíguñbi

rearrange [ri:əreindʒ'] *vt* 並べ直す narábenaosù

rear-view mirror [ri:r'vju:'-] *n* (AUT) バックミラー bakkúmirǎ

reason [ri:'zən] *n* (cause) 理由 riyǔ; (ability to think) 理性 riséi
♦*vi*: *to reason with someone* ...の説得に当る ...no settóku nì atárù
it stands to reason that ...という事は当然である ...to iú kotò wa tǒzen de arù

reasonable [ri:'zənəbəl] *adj* (sensible) 訳の分かる wákè no wakárù; (fair: number, amount) 程々の hodóhodo no; (: quality) まあまあの mǎmā no; (: price) 妥当な datǒ na

reasonably [ri:'zənəbli:] *adv* (sensibly)

常識的に jǒshikiteki ni; (fairly) 程々に hodóhodo ni

reasoned [ri:'zənd] *adj* (argument) 筋の通った sújì no tǒttà

reasoning [ri:'zəniŋ] *n* (process) 推理 sufri

reassurance [ri:əʃu:r'əns] *n* 安ど áñdo

reassure [ri:əʃu:r'] *vt* (comfort) 安心させる añshin saserù
to reassure someone of ...に...だと安心させる ...ni ...dá tò añshin saserù

reassuring [ri:əʃu:r'iŋ] *adj* (smile, manner) 安心させる añshin saserù

rebate [ri:'beit] *n* (on tax etc) リベート ribǔto

rebel [*n* reb'əl *vb* ribel'] *n* (against political system) 反逆者 hañgyakushà; (against society, parents etc) 反抗分子 hañkōbuñshi
♦*vi* (against political system) 反乱を起す hañran wò okósù; (against society, parents etc) 反抗する hañkō suru

rebellion [ribel'jən] *n* (against political system) 反乱 hañran; (against society, parents etc) 反抗 hañkō

rebellious [ribel'jəs] *adj* (subject) 反逆者の hañgyakushà no; (child, behavior) 反抗的な hañkōteki na

rebirth [ri:bə:rθ'] *n* 復活 fukkátsu

rebound [*vb* ri:baund' *n* ri:'baund] *vi* (ball) 跳ね返る hanékaerù
♦*n*: *on the rebound* (ball) 跳ね返った所を hanékaetta tokórò wo; (*fig*: person) ...した反動で ...shítà hañdō de

rebuff [ribʌf'] *n* 拒絶 kyozétsu

rebuild [ri:bild'] (*pt, pp* **rebuilt**) *vt* (town, building etc) 建直す taténaosù; (economy, confidence) 立直す taténaosù

rebuke [ribju:k'] *vt* しかる shikárù

rebut [ribʌt'] *vt* しりぞける shirízokerù

recalcitrant [rikæl'sitrənt] *adj* (child, behavior) 反抗的な hañkōteki na

recall [ri:kɔ:l'] *vt* (remember) 思い出す omóidasù; (parliament, ambassador etc) 呼戻す yobímodosù
♦*n* (ability to remember) 記憶 kióku; (of ambassador etc) 召還 shǒkan

recant [rikænt'] *vi* 自説を取消す jisétsu

wǒ toríkesù

recap [riːˈkæp] vt (summarize) 要約する yōyaku suru
♦vi ...を要約する ...wo yōyaku suru

recapitulate [riːkəpitʃˈuːleit] vt, vi = recap

recapture [riːˈkæptʃər] vt (town, territory etc) 奪環する dakkán suru; (atmosphere, mood etc) 取戻す torímodosù

rec'd abbr = received

recede [risiːdˈ] vi (tide) ひく hikú; (lights etc) 遠のく tōnokù; (memory) 薄らぐ usúragù; (hair) はげる hagérù

receding [risiːˈdiŋ] adj (hair) はげつつある hagétsutsu arù; (chin) 無いに等しい náī ni hitóshiī

receipt [risiːtˈ] n (document) 領収書 ryōshūsho; (from cash register) レシート reshīto; (act of receiving) 受取る事 ukétorù kotó

receipts [risiːtsˈ] npl (COMM) 収入 shūnyū

receive [risiːvˈ] vt (get: money, letter etc) 受け取る ukétorù; (criticism, acclaim) 受ける ukérù; (visitor, guest) 迎える mukáerù
to receive an injury けがする kegá surù

receiver [risiːˈvər] n (TEL) 受話器 juwákì; (RADIO, TV) 受信機 jushínkì; (of stolen goods) 故買屋 kobáìya; (COMM) 管財人 kańzainìn

recent [riːˈsənt] adj (event, times) 近ごろの chikágòro no

recently [riːˈsəntliː] adv 近ごろ chikágòro

receptacle [risepˈtəkəl] n 容器 yōkì

reception [risepˈʃən] n (in hotel, office, hospital etc) 受付 ukétsuke; (party) レセプション resépùshon; (welcome) 歓迎 kańgei; (RADIO, TV) 受信 jushín

reception desk n 受付 ukétsuke, フロント furôǹto

receptionist [risepˈʃənist] n 受付係 ukétsukegakàri

receptive [risepˈtiv] adj (person, attitude) 前向きの maémuki no

recess [riːˈses] n (in room) 壁のくぼみ

kabé nò kubómi; (secret place) 奥深い所 okúfukaì tokórò; (POL etc: holiday) 休憩時間 kyūkeijikàn

recession [riseʃˈən] n 景気後退 keíkikòtai

recharge [riːtʃɑːrdʒˈ] vt (battery) 充電する jūden suru

recipe [resˈəpiː] n (CULIN) 調理法 chōrihō; (fig: for success) 秘けつ hikétsu; (: for disaster) やり方 yaríkata

recipient [risipˈiːənt] n (of letter, payment etc) 受取人 ukétorinìn

reciprocal [risipˈrəkəl] adj (arrangement, agreement) 相互の sōgò no

recital [risaitˈəl] n (concert) リサイタル risáìtaru

recite [risaitˈ] vt (poem) 暗唱する ańshō suru

reckless [rekˈlis] adj (driving, driver) 無謀な mubô na; (spending) 無茶な múchà na

recklessly [rekˈlisliː] adv (drive) 無謀に mubô ni; (spend) むやみに múyàmi ni

reckon [rekˈən] vt (calculate) 計算する keísan suru; (think): I reckon that ... ...だと思う ...dá tò omóù

reckoning [rekˈəniŋ] n (calculation) 計算 keísan

reckon on vt fus (expect) 当てにする a-té nì suru

reclaim [rikleimˈ] vt (demand back) ...の返還を要求する ...no heńkan wò yōkyū suru; (land: by filling in) 埋め立てる umétaterù; (: by draining) 干拓する kańtaku suru; (waste materials) 再生する saísei suru

reclamation [rekləmeiˈʃən] n (of land: by filling in) 埋め立て umétate; (: by draining) 干拓 kańtaku

recline [riklainˈ] vi (sit or lie back) もたれる motárerù

reclining [riklainˈiŋ] adj: reclining seat リクライニングシート rikúrainingushìto

recluse [rekˈluːs] n 隠とん者 ińtoǹsha

recognition [rekəgniʃˈən] n (of person, place) 認識 nińshiki; (of problem, fact) 意識 íshìki; (of achievement) 認める事

mitómeru kotð

transformed beyond recognition 見分けが付かない程変化した miwáke ga tsukánai hodo hénka shita

recognizable [rekəgnai'zəbəl] *adj*: ***recognizable (by)*** (...で) 見分けが付く (...de) miwáke ga tsukú

recognize [rek'əgnaiz] *vt* (person, place, attitude, illness) ...だと分かる ...dá tð wakárù; (qualification, need) 意識する íshìki suru; (qualification, achievement) 認める mitómerù; (government) 承認する shónin suru

to recognize by/as ...で〔として〕分かる ...de 〔toshítè〕 wakárù

recoil [rikɔil'] *vi* (person): ***to recoil from doing something*** ...するのをいやがる ...surú no wð iyágarù

♦*n* (of gun) 反動 hañdō

recollect [rekəlekt'] *vt* (remember) 思い出す omóidasù

recollection [rekəlek'ʃən] *n* (memory) 思い出 omóide; (remembering) 思い出す事 omóidasu kotð

recommend [rekəmend'] *vt* (book, shop, person) 推薦する suísen suru; (course of action) 勧める susúmerù

recommendation [rekəmendei'ʃən] *n* (of book, shop, person) 推薦 suísen; (of course of action) 勧告 kañkoku

recompense [rek'əmpens] *n* (reward) 報酬 hóshū

reconcile [rek'ənsail] *vt* (two people) 仲直りさせる nakánaðri sasérù; (two facts, beliefs) 調和させる chówa saserù

to reconcile oneself to something (unpleasant situation, misery etc) ...だとあきらめる ...dá tð akíramerù

reconciliation [rekənsili:ei'ʃən] *n* (of people etc) 和解 wakái; (of facts etc) 調和 chówa

recondition [ri:kəndi'ʃən] *vt* (machine) 修理する shúri suru

reconnaissance [rikɑ:n'isəns] *n* (MIL) 偵察 teísatsu

reconnoiter [ri:kənɔi'tə:r] (*BRIT* **reconnoitre**) *vt* (MIL: enemy territory) 偵察する teísatsu suru

reconsider [ri:kənsid'ə:r] *vt* (decision, opinion etc) 考え直す kañgaenaosù

reconstruct [ri:kənstrʌkt'] *vt* (building) 建直す taténaosù; (policy, system) 練り直す nerínaosù; (event, crime) 再現する saígen suru

reconstruction [ri:kənstrʌk'ʃən] *n* (of building, country) 再建 saíken; (of crime) 再現 saígen

record [*n* rek'ə:rd *vb* rekɔ:rd'] *n* (*gen*) 記録 kiróku; (MUS: disk) レコード rekódð; (history: of person, company) 履歴 riréki; (*also*: **criminal record**) 前科 zénka

♦*vt* (write down) 記録する kiróku suru; (temperature, speed etc) 表示する hyóji suru; (MUS: song etc) 録音する rokúon suru

in record time 記録的速さで kirókuteki hayása de

off the record *adj* (remark) オフレコの ofúreko no

♦*adv* (speak) オフレコで ofúreko de

record card *n* (in file) ファイルカード faírukàdo

recorded delivery [rikɔ:r'did-] (*BRIT*) *n* (MAIL) 簡易書留 kañ-i kakítome

recorder [rikɔ:r'də:r] *n* (MUS: instrument) リコーダー rikódà

record holder *n* (SPORT) 記録保持者 kiróku hojishà

recording [rikɔ:r'diŋ] *n* 録音 rokúon

record player *n* レコードプレーヤー rekódopurèyà

recount [rikaunt'] *vt* (story, event etc) 述べる nobérù

re-count [*n* ri:'kaunt *vb* ri:kaunt'] *n* (POL: of votes) 数え直し kazóenaoshi

♦*vt* (votes etc) 数え直す kazóenaosù

recoup [riku:p'] *vt*: ***to recoup one's losses*** 損失を取戻す sońshitsu wð torímodosù

recourse [ri:'kɔ:rs] *n*: ***to have recourse to*** ...を用いる ...wo mochíirù

recover [rikʌv'ə:r] *vt* (get back: stolen goods, lost items, financial loss) 取戻す torímodosù

♦*vi*: ***to recover (from)*** (illness) (...が)

治る (...ga) naórù; (operation, shock, experience) (...から) 立直る (...kará) tachínaorù

recovery [rikʌv'ə:ri:] n (from illness, operation: in economy etc) 回復 kaífuku; (of stolen, lost items) 取戻し torímodoshi

re-create [ri:kri:eit'] vt 再現する saígen suru

recreation [rekri:ei'ʃən] n (play, leisure activities) 娯楽 goráku

recreational [rekri:ei'ʃənəl] adj 娯楽の goráku no

recrimination [rikrimənei'ʃən] n 責合い seméai

recruit [rikru:t'] n (MIL) 新兵 shíñpei; (in company, organization) 新入社〔会〕員 shíñnyūsha(kai)ìn
♦vt 募集する boshū́ suru

recruitment [rikru:t'mənt] n 募集 boshū́

rectangle [rek'tæŋgəl] n 長方形 chōhōkei

rectangular [rektæŋ'gjələ:r] adj (shape, object etc) 長方形の chōhōkei no

rectify [rek'təfai] vt (correct) 正す tadásù

rector [rek'tə:r] n (REL) 主任司祭 shunínshisài

rectory [rek'tə:ri:] n (house) 司祭館 shisáikan

recuperate [riku:'pə:reit] vi (recover: from illness etc) 回復する kaífuku suru

recur [rikə:r'] vi (error, event) 繰返される kuríkaesarerù; (illness, pain) 再発する saíhatsu suru

recurrence [rikə:r'əns] n (of error, event) 繰返し kuríkaeshi; (of illness, pain) 再発 saíhatsu

recurrent [rikə:r'ənt] adj 頻繁に起る hiñpan ni okórù

red [red] n (color) 赤 ákà; (pej: POL) 過激派 kagékiha
♦adj 赤い akáì
to be in the red (bank account, business) 赤字になっている akáji nì natté irù

red carpet treatment n 盛大な歓迎式 seídai nà kañgeishìki

Red Cross n 赤十字 sekíjūji

redcurrant [red'kʌr'ənt] n アカフサスグリ akáfusasugùri

redden [red'ən] vt (turn red) 赤くする a-kákù suru
♦vi (blush) 赤面する sekímen suru

reddish [red'iʃ] adj 赤っぽい akáppòi

redeem [ridi:m'] vt (fig: situation, reputation) 救う sukúù; (something in pawn, loan) 請出す ukédasù; (REL: rescue) 救う sukúù

redeeming [ridi:'miŋ] adj: *redeeming feature* 欠点を補う取柄 kettén wò ogínaù toríe

redeploy [ri:diplɔi'] vt (resources) 配置し直す haíchi shinaosù

red-haired [red'he:rd] adj 赤毛の akáge no

red-handed [red'hæn'did] adj: *to be caught red-handed* 現行犯で捕まる geñkòhan de tsukámarù

redhead [red'hed] n 赤毛の人 akáge no hitò

red herring n (fig) 本論から注意をそらす物 hoñron karà chūì wo sorásù monò

red-hot [red'hɑ:t'] adj (metal) 真っ赤に焼けた makká nì yakétà

redirect [ri:dərekt'] vt (mail) 転送する teñsō suru

red light n: *to go through a red light* (AUT) 信号無視をする shiñgōmùshi wo suru

red-light district [red'lait-] n 赤線地区 akásenchikù

redo [ri:du:'] (pt redid pp redone) vt やり直す yarínaosù

redolent [red'ələnt] adj: *redolent of* (smell: also fig) ...臭い ...kusáì

redouble [ri:dʌb'əl] vt: *to redouble one's efforts* 一層努力を issō doryòku suru

redress [ridres'] n (compensation) 賠償 baíshō
♦vt (error, wrong) 償う tsugúnaù

Red Sea n: *the Red Sea* 紅海 kṓkai

redskin [red'skin] n (pej) インディアン ín-dian

red tape n (fig) 形式的手続き keíshikiteki tetsuzúki

reduce [ridu:s'] *vt* (decrease: spending, numbers etc) 減らす herásù

to reduce someone to (begging, stealing) ...を余儀なくさせる ...wo yogínaku saserù

to reduce someone to tears 泣かせる nakáserù

to reduce someone to silence 黙らせる damáraserù

「*reduce speed now*」(AUT) 徐行 jokō

at a reduced price (goods) 割引で waríbiki de

reduction [ridʌk'ʃən] *n* (in price) 値下げ neságe; (in numbers etc) 減少 geńshō

redundancy [ridʌn'dənsi:] *n* (dismissal) 解雇 káiko; (unemployment) 失業 shitsúgyō

redundant [ridʌn'dənt] *adj* (worker) 失業中の shitsúgyōchū no; (detail, object) 余計な yokéi na

to be made redundant 解雇される káiko sarérù

reed [ri:d] *n* (BOT) アシ ashí; (MUS: of clarinet etc) リード rīdo

reef [ri:f] *n* (at sea) 暗礁 ańshō

reek [ri:k] *vi*: *to reek (of)* (...の) においがぷんぷんする (...no) nióì ga púnpun suru

reel [ri:l] *n* (of thread, string) 巻 makí; (of film, tape: *also* on fishing-rod) リール rīru; (dance) リール rīru
♦*vi* (sway) よろめく yorómekù

reel in *vt* (fish, line) 手繰り寄せる tagúriyoserù

ref [ref] (*inf*) *n abbr* = **referee**

refectory [rifek'tə:ri:] *n* 食堂 shokúdō

refer [rifə:r'] *vt* (person, patient): *to refer someone to* ...を...に回す ...wo ...ni mawásù; (matter, problem): *to refer something to* ...を...に委託する ...wo ...ni itáku suru
♦*vi*: *to refer to* (allude to) ...に言及する ...ni geńkyū suru; (consult) ...を参照する ...wo sańshō suru

referee [refəri:'] *n* (SPORT) 審判員 shińpaǹ-in, レフェリー réferì; (*BRIT*: for job application) 身元保証人 mimótohoshōnìn

♦*vt* (football match etc) ...のレフェリーをやる ...no réferì wo yárù

reference [ref'ə:rəns] *n* (mention) 言及 geńkyū; (in book, paper) 引用文献 iń-yō buńken; (for job application: letter) 推薦状 suíseñjō

with reference to (COMM: in letter) ...に関しては ...ni kańshite wa

reference book *n* 参考書 sańkōsho

reference number *n* 整理番号 seíribaǹgō

referenda [refəren'də] *npl of* **referendum**

referendum [refəren'dəm] (*pl* **referenda**) *n* 住民投票 jūmintōhyō

refill [*vb* ri:fil' *n* ri:'fil] *vt* (glass etc) ...にもう一杯つぐ ...ni mō ippai tsugú; (pen etc) ...に...を詰替える ...ni ...wo tsumékaerù
♦*n* (of drink etc) お代り o-káwari; (for pen etc) スペーア supéà

refine [rifain'] *vt* (sugar, oil) 精製する seísei suru; (theory, idea) 洗練する sefiren suru

refined [rifaind'] *adj* (person, taste) 洗練された sefiren saretà

refinement [rifain'mənt] *n* (of person) 優雅さ yūgasa; (of system) 精度 seído

reflect [riflekt'] *vt* (light, image) 反射する hańsha suru; (situation, attitude) 反映する hań-ei suru
♦*vi* (think) じっくり考える jikkúrì kańgaerù

it reflects badly/well on him それは彼の悪い〔いい〕所を物語っている sore wa kárè no warúî 〔ſi〕tokórò wo monógatatte irú

reflection [riflek'ʃən] *n* (of light, heat) 反射 hańsha; (image) 影 kágè; (of situation, attitude) 反映する物 hań-ei suru monò; (criticism) 非難 hínàn; (thought) 熟考 jukkō

on reflection よく考えると yókù kańgaerù to

reflector [riflek'tə:r] *n* 反射器 hańshakì

reflex [ri:'fleks] *adj* (action, gesture) 反射的な hańshateki na
♦*n* (PHYSIOLOGY, PSYCH) 反射 hań-

sha

reflexive [riflek'siv] *adj* (LING) 再帰の saíki no

reform [rifɔ:rm'] *n* (of sinner, character) 改心 kaíshin; (of law, system) 改革 kaíkaku
◆*vt* (sinner) 改心させる kaíshin saseru; (law, system) 改革する kaíkaku suru

Reformation [refər'mei'ʃən] *n: the Reformation* 宗教改革 shūkyōkaíkaku

reformatory [rifɔ:r'mətɔ:ri:] (*US*) *n* 感化院 kañkaìn

refrain [rifrein'] *vi: to refrain from doing* ...をしない様にする ...wo shinái yō ni suru
◆*n* (of song) 繰返し kuríkaeshi, リフレイン rifúreìn

refresh [rifreʃ'] *vt* (subj: sleep, drink) 元気付ける geñkizukerù
to refresh someone's memory ...に思い出させる ...ni omóidasaserù

refresher course [rifreʃ'ə:r-] (*BRIT*) *n* 研修会 keñshūkài

refreshing [rifreʃ'iŋ] *adj* (drink) 冷たくておいしい tsumétakùte oíshiì; (sleep) 気分をさわやかにする kíbùn wo sawáyàka ni suru

refreshments [rifreʃ'mənts] *npl* (food and drink) 軽食 keíshoku

refrigeration [rifridʒərei'ʃən] *n* (of food) 冷蔵 reízō

refrigerator [rifridʒ'ə:reitə:r] *n* 冷蔵庫 reízōko

refuel [ri:fju:'əl] *vi* 燃料を補給する neñryō wo hokyū suru

refuge [ref'ju:dʒ] *n* (shelter) 避難場所 hináñbasho
to take refuge in ...に避難する ...ni hínàn suru

refugee [refjudʒi:'] *n* 難民 nañmin

refund [*n* ri:'fund *vb* rifʌnd'] *n* 払い戻し haráimodoshi
◆*vt* (money) 払い戻す haráimodosù

refurbish [ri:fə:r'biʃ] *vt* (shop, theater) 改装する kaísō suru

refusal [rifju:'zəl] *n* 断り kotôwari, 拒否 kyóhì
first refusal (option) オプション権 o-

púshoñken

refuse[1] [rifju:z'] *vt* (request, offer, gift) 断る kotôwarù; (invitation) 辞退する jítài suru; (permission, consent) 拒む kobámù
◆*vi* (say no) 断る kotôwarù; (horse) 飛越を拒否する hiétsu wò kyóhì suru
to refuse to do something ...するのを拒む ...surú no wò kobámù

refuse[2] [ref'ju:s] *n* (rubbish) ごみ gomí

refuse collection *n* ごみ収集 gomíshūshū

refute [rifju:t'] *vt* (argument) 論破する roñpa suru

regain [rigein'] *vt* (power, position) 取戻す torímodosù

regal [ri:'gəl] *adj* 堂々とした dôdō to shitā

regalia [rigei'li:ə] *n* (costume) 正装 seísō

regard [rigɑ:rd'] *n* (gaze) 視線 shisen; (attention, concern) 関心 kañshin; (esteem) 尊敬 soñkei
◆*vt* (consider) 見なす minásù
to give one's regards to ...から...によろしく伝える ...kará ...nì yoróshikù tsutáerù
with kindest regards 敬具 keígu
regarding, as regards, with regard to (with reference to, concerning) ...に関して ...ni kañshitè

regardless [rigɑ:rd'lis] *adv* (carry on, continue) 構わずに kamáwazù ni
regardless of (danger, consequences) ...を顧みず ...wo kaérimizù

regatta [rigæt'ə] *n* ヨット〔ボート〕競技会 yottô 〔bôto〕 kyōgikài

regenerate [ri:dʒen'ə:reit] *vt* (inner cities, arts) よみがえらせる yomígaeraserù

regent [ri:'dʒənt] *n* 摂政 sesshô

regime [reiʒi:m'] *n* (system of government) 政治体制 seíjitaìsei

regiment [redʒ'əmənt] *n* (MIL) 連隊 reñtai

regimental [redʒəmen'təl] *adj* 連隊の reñtai no

region [ri:'dʒən] *n* (area: of land) 地区 chíkù; (: of body) ...部 ...bù; (administra-

tive division of country) 行政区 gyṓseï-
ku

in the region of (*fig*: approximately)
約 yákù

regional [riːˈdʒənəl] *adj* (organization,
wine, geography) 地元の jimóto no; (provincial) 地方の chihṓ no

register [redʒˈistɑːr] *n* (list: of births,
marriages, deaths, voters) 登録簿 tṓro-
kùbo; (SCOL: of attendance) 出席簿
shussékibò; (MUS: of voice) 声域 seíiki;
(: of instrument) 音域 oñ-iki

♦*vt* (birth, death, marriage) 届出る todǒ-
kederù; (car) 登録する tṓroku suru;
(MAIL: letter) 書留にする kakítome nì
suru; (subj: meter, gauge) 示す shimésù

♦*vi* (at hotel) チェックインする chekkúïn
suru; (for work) 名前を登録する namáe
wo tṓroku suru; (as student) 入学手続き
をする nyúgakutetsuzuki wò suru;
(make impression) ぴんと来る piñ tò kúrù

registered [redʒˈistəːrd] *adj* (MAIL: letter, parcel) 書留の kakítome no

registered trademark *n* 登録商標 tǒ-
rokushṓhyó

registrar [redʒˈistrɑːr] *n* (official) 戸籍
係 kosékigakàri; (in college, university)
教務係 kyṓmugakàri; (*BRIT*: in hospital) 医務吏員 imúriìn

registration [redʒistreiˈʃən] *n* (*gen*) 登録
tṓroku; (of birth, death) 届出 todókede;
(AUT: *also*: **registration number**) ナン
バー náñbā

registry [redʒˈistri] *n* 登記所 tṓkisho

registry office (*BRIT*) *n* 戸籍登記所
kosékitōkisho

to get married in a registry office 戸
籍登記所で結婚する kosékitōkisho dè
kekkóñ suru

regret [rigretˈ] *n* (sorrow) 悔み kuyámi

♦*vt* (decision, action) 後悔する kṓkai suru; (loss, death) 悔む kuyámù; (inability
to do something) 残念に思う zañneñ nì
omóù; (inconvenience) 済まないと思う
sumánaì to omóù

regretfully [rigretˈfəliː] *adv* (sadly) 残念
ながら zañneñ nagàra

regrettable [rigretˈəbəl] *adj* (unfortunate: mistake, incident) あいにくの aínì-
ku no

regular [regˈjələːr] *adj* (even: breathing,
pulse etc) 規則的な kisókuteki na;
(evenly-spaced: intervals, meetings etc)
定期的な teíkiteki na; (symmetrical: features, shape etc) 対称的な taíshōteki na;
(frequent: raids, exercise etc) 頻繁な hiñpan na; (usual: time, doctor, customer
etc) 通常の tsújō no; (soldier) 正規の seíki no; (LING) 規則変化の kisókuhènka
no

♦*n* (client etc) 常連 jṓren

regularity [regjəlærˈitiː] *n* (frequency)
高頻度 kṓhiñdo

regularly [regˈjələːrliː] *adv* (at evenly-
spaced intervals) 規則的に kisókuteki
ni; (symmetrically: shaped etc) 対称的に
taíshōteki ni; (often) 頻繁に hiñpan ni

regulate [regˈjəleit] *vt* (conduct, expenditure) 規制する kiséi suru; (traffic, speed)
調整する chṓsei suru; (machine, oven) 調
節する chṓsetsu suru

regulation [regjəleiˈʃən] *n* (of conduct,
expenditure) 規制 kiséi; (of traffic,
speed) 調整 chṓsei; (of machine, oven) 調
節 chṓsetsu; (rule) 規則 kisóku

rehabilitation [riːhəbiləteiˈʃən] *n* (of
criminal, addict) 社会復帰 shakáifukkì,
リハビリテーション rihábiritēshon

rehearsal [rihəːrˈsəl] *n* リハーサル rihā́-
sàru

rehearse [rihəːrsˈ] *vt* (play, dance,
speech etc) ...のリハーサルをする ...no
rihā́sàru wo suru

reign [rein] *n* (of monarch) 治世 chiséi;
(*fig*: of terror etc) 支配 shíhài

♦*vi* (monarch) 君臨する kuñrin suru;
(*fig*: violence, fear etc) はびこる habíkorù; (: peace, order etc) 行渡る ikíwatarù

reimburse [riːimbəːrsˈ] *vt* (pay back)
...に弁償する ...ni beñshō suru

rein [rein] *n* (for horse) 手綱 tazúna

reincarnation [riːinkɑːrneiˈʃən] *n*
(belief) 輪ね ríñne

reindeer [reinˈdiːr] *n inv* トナカイ tonā́-
kài

reinforce [ri:infɔːrsʼ] *vt* (strengthen: object) 補強する hokyō suru; (: situation) 強化する kyōka suru; (support: idea, statement) 裏付ける urázukerù

reinforced concrete [ri:infɔːrstʼ-] *n* 鉄筋コンクリート tekkín konkurīto

reinforcement [ri:infɔːrsʼmənt] *n* (strengthening) 補強 hokyō

reinforcements [ri:infɔːrsʼmənts] *npl* (MIL) 援軍 eńgun

reinstate [ri:insteitʼ] *vt* (worker) 復職させる fukúshoku saserù; (tax, law, text) 元通りにする motódōri ni surù

reiterate [ri:itʼəreit] *vt* (repeat) 繰返す kuríkaesù

reject [*n* ri:ʼdʒekt *vb* ridʒektʼ] *n* (COMM) 傷物 kizúmono
♦*vt* (plan, proposal etc) 退ける shi
rízokerù; (offer of help) 断る kotówarù; (belief, political system) 拒絶する kyozétsu suru; (candidate) 不採用にする fusáiyō ni suru; (coin) 受付けない ukétsuke-nài; (goods, fruit etc) 傷物として処分する kizúmono toshite shóbùn suru

rejection [ridʒekʼʃən] *n* (of plan, proposal, offer of help etc) 拒否 kyóhì; (of belief etc) 拒絶 kyozétsu; (of candidate) 不採用 fusáiyō

rejoice [ridʒɔisʼ] *vi*: **to rejoice at/over** ...を喜ぶ ...wo yorókobù

rejuvenate [ridʒuːʼvəneit] *vt* (person) 若返らせる wakágaeraserù

relapse [rilæpsʼ] *n* (MED) 再発 saíhatsu

relate [rileitʼ] *vt* (tell) 話す hanásù; (connect) 結び付ける musúbitsukerù
♦*vi*: **to relate to** (person, subject, thing) ...に関係がある ...ni kańkei ga arù

related [rileiʼtid] *adj* (person) 血縁がある ketsúen ga arù; (animal, language) 近縁の kiń-en no
related to ...に関係がある ...ni kańkei ga arù

relating [rileiʼtiŋ]: **relating to** *prep* ...に関する ...ni kań suru

relation [rileiʼʃən] *n* (member of family) 親せき shińseki; (connection) 関係 kańkei

relations [rileiʼʃənz] *npl* (dealings) 関係

kańkei; (relatives) 親せき shińseki

relationship [rileiʼʃənʃip] *n* (between two people, countries, things) 関係 kańkei; (*also*: **family relationship**) 親族関係 shińzokukańkei

relative [relʼətiv] *n* (member of family) 親類 shińrui, 親せき shińseki
♦*adj* (comparative) 相対的な sōtaiteki na; (connected): **relative to** ...に関する ...ni kań suru

relatively [relʼətivliː] *adv* (comparatively) 比較的 hikákuteki

relax [rilæksʼ] *vi* (person: unwind) くつろぐ kutsúrogù; (muscle) 緩む yurúmù
♦*vt* (one's grip) 緩める yurúmerù; (mind, person) くつろがせる kutsúrogaserù; (rule, control etc) 緩める yurúmerù

relaxation [ri:lækseiʼʃən] *n* (rest) 休みyasúmi; (of muscle, grip) 緩み yurúmi; (of rule, control etc) 緩和 kańwa; (recreation) 娯楽 goráku

relaxed [rilækstʼ] *adj* (person) 落着いたochítsuità; (discussion, atmosphere) くつろいだ kutsúroìda

relaxing [rilækʼsiŋ] *adj* (holiday, afternoon) くつろいだ kutsúroìda

relay [ri:ʼlei] *n* (race) リレー rírē
♦*vt* (message, question) 伝える tsutáerù; (programme, signal) 中継する chúkei suru

release [riliːsʼ] *n* (from prison) 釈放 shakúhō; (from obligation) 免除 mēnjo; (of gas, water etc) 放出 hōshutsu; (of film) 封切 fúkiri; (of book, record) 発売 hatsúbai
♦*vt* (prisoner: from prison) 釈放する shakúhō suru; (: from captivity) 解放する kaíhō suru; (gas etc) 放出する hōshutsu suru; (free: from wreckage etc) 救出する kyūshutsu suru; (TECH: catch, spring etc) 外す hazúsù; (book, record) 発売する hatsúbai suru; (film) 公開する kōkai suru; (report, news) 公表する kōhyō suru

relegate [relʼəgeit] *vt* (downgrade) 格下げする kakúsage suru; (*BRIT*: SPORT): **to be relegated** 格下げされる kakúsage sarerù

relent [rilentʼ] *vi* (give in) ...の態度が軟化

する ...no táido ga nañika suru

relentless [rilent'lis] *adj* (unceasing) 絶間ない taémanaì; (determined) 執念深い shúneñbukai

relevance [rel'əvəns] *n* (of remarks, information) 意義 ígì; (of question etc) 関連 kañren

relevant [rel'əvənt] *adj* (fact, information, question) 意義ある ígì árù

relevant to (situation, problem etc) ...に関連のある ...ni kañren no arù

reliability [rilaiəbil'əti:] *n* (of person, machine) 信頼性 shíñraisei; (of information) 信びょう性 shiñpyōsei

reliable [rilai'əbəl] *adj* (person, firm) 信頼できる shíñrai dekirù; (method, machine) 信頼性のある shíñraisei no arù; (news, information) 信用できる shiñyō dekirù

reliably [rilai'əbli:] *adv*: *to be reliably informed that ...* 確かな情報筋によると... táshìka na jōhōsùjì ni yorú tò ...

reliance [rilai'əns] *n*: *reliance (on)* (...への) 依存 (...é nò) ìzòn

relic [rel'ik] *n* (REL) 聖遺物 seíbùtsu; (of the past) 遺物 ibútsu

relief [rili:f'] *n* (from pain, anxiety etc) 緩和 kañwa; (help, supplies) 救援物資 kyúenbusshì; (ART) 浮彫 ukíbori, レリーフ rerífù; (GEO) 際立つ事 kiwádatsu kotò

relieve [riliːv'] *vt* (pain, fear, worry) 緩和する kañwa suru; (patient) 安心させる añshin saserù; (bring help to: victims, refugees etc) ...に救援物資を届ける ...ni kyúenbusshì wo todókerù; (take over from: colleague, guard) ...と交替する ...to kótai suru

to relieve someone of something (load) ...の ...を持って上げる ...no ...wo móttè agérù; (duties, post) ...を解任する ...wo kaínin suru

to relieve oneself 小便する shṓben suru

religion [rilidʒ'ən] *n* 宗教 shúkyō

religious [rilidʒ'əs] *adj* (activities, faith) 宗教の shúkyō no; (person) 信心深い shíñjiñbukai

relinquish [riliŋ'kwiʃ] *vt* (authority) ...から手を引く ...kara té wò hikú; (plan, habit) やめる yamérù

relish [rel'iʃ] *n* (CULIN) レリッシュ rerísshù; (enjoyment) 楽しみ tanóshimi

♦*vt* (enjoy: food, competition) 楽しむ tanóshimù

to relish the thought/idea/prospect of something/doing something ...を 〔...するのを〕心待ちに待つ ...wo 〔... surú nò wo〕 kokóromachi nì mátsù

relocate [ri:lou'keit] *vt* 移動させる idṓ saserù

♦*vi* 移動する idṓ suru

reluctance [rilʌk'təns] *n* (unwillingness) 気が進まない事 kí gà susúmanai kotò

reluctant [rilʌk'tənt] *adj* (unwilling) 気が進まない kí gà susúmanaì

reluctantly [rilʌk'təntli:] *adv* (unwillingly) いやいやながら iyáiyanagàra

rely on [rilai'-] *vt fus* (depend on) ...に頼る ...ni tayórù; (trust) ...を信用する ...wo shiñ-yō suru

remain [rimein'] *vi* (survive, be left) 残る nokórù; (continue to be) 相変らず...である aíkawarazù ...de árù; (stay) とどまる todómarù

remainder [rimein'də:r] *n* (rest) 残り nokóri

remaining [rimei'niŋ] *adj* 残りの nokóri no

remains [rimeinz'] *npl* (of meal) 食べ残り tabénokori; (of building) 廃虚 haíkyo; (corpse) 遺体 itái

remand [rimænd'] *n*: *on remand* 拘置中で kóchichū de

♦*vt*: *to be remanded in custody* 拘置される kóchi sarerù

remand home (*BRIT*) *n* 少年院 shṓnen-ìn

remark [rimɑːrk'] *n* (comment) 発言 hatsúgen

♦*vt* (comment) 言う iú

remarkable [rimɑːr'kəbəl] *adj* (outstanding) 著しい ichíjirushiî

remarry [riːmær'iː] *vi* 再婚する saíkon suru

remedial [rimiː'diəl] *adj* (tuition, clas-

ses) 補修の hoshū no; (exercise) 矯正の
kyōsei no

remedy [rem'idi:] n (cure) 治療法 chiryō-
hō

♦vt (correct) 直す naósù

remember [rimem'bəːr] vt (call back to
mind) 思い出す omóidasù; (bear in mind)
忘れない様にする wasúrenai yō ni suru;
(send greetings): *remember me to him*
彼によろしくお伝え下さい kárè ni yoró-
shikù o-tsútae kudasài

remembrance [rimem'brəns] n (memory: of dead person) 思い出 omóide;
(souvenir: of place, event) 記念品 kinénhin

remind [rimaind'] vt: *to remind someone to do something* ...するのを忘れな
い様に...に注意する ...surú no wò wasúrenai yō ni ...ni chū suru

to remind someone of something ...に
...を思い出させる ...ni ...wo omóidasasè-
ru

she reminds me of her mother 彼女を
見ると彼女の母親を思い出す kánòjo wo
mírù to kánòjo no haháoya wò omóidasa-
sù

reminder [rimaind'əːr] n (souvenir) 記念
品 kinénhin; (letter) 覚書 obóegaki

reminisce [remənis'] vi (about the past)
追憶する tsuíoku suru

reminiscent [remənis'ənt] adj: *to be
reminiscent of something* ...を思い出
させる ...wo omóidasaserù

remiss [rimis'] adj (careless) 不注意な fuchū na

it was remiss of him 彼は不注意だっ
た kárè wa fuchū dáttà

remission [rimiʃ'ən] n (of debt) 免除 mén-
jo; (of prison sentence) 減刑 geñkei; (of
illness) 緩解 kañkai; (REL: of sins) 許し
yurúshi

remit [rimit'] vt (send: money) 送金する
sōkin suru

remittance [rimit'əns] n (payment) 送金
sōkin

remnant [rem'nənt] n (small part
remaining) 残り nokóri; (of cloth) 切れ端
kiréhashi

remnants [rem'nənts] npl (COMM) 端切
れ hagíre

remorse [rimɔːrs'] n (guilt) 後悔 kōkai

remorseful [rimɔːrs'fəl] adj (guilty) 後悔
している kōkai shite irù

remorseless [rimɔːrs'lis] adj (fig: noise,
pain) 絶間ない taēmanaì

remote [rimout'] adj (distant: place,
time) 遠い tōì; (person) よそよそしい yo-
sóyososhiì; (slight: possibility, chance)
かすかな kásùka na

remote control n 遠隔操作 eñkakusō-
sa, リモートコントロール rimótokonto-
rōru

remotely [rimout'li:] adv (distantly) 遠く
に tōku ni; (slightly) かすかに kásùka ni

remould [ri:'mould] (BRIT) n (tire) 再生
タイヤ saíseitaiya

removable [rimu:'vəbəl] adj (detachable) 取外しのできる toríhazushi nò dekírù

removal [rimu:'vəl] n (taking away) 取
除く事 torínozoku kotò; (of stain) 消し
取る事 keshítoru kotò; (BRIT: from
house) 引っ越し hikkóshi; (from office:
dismissal) 免職 meñshoku; (MED) 切除
sétsùjo

removal van (BRIT) n 引っ越しトラッ
ク hikkóshi torakkù

remove [rimu:v'] vt (gen) 取除く torínozokù; (clothing) 脱ぐ núgù; (bandage etc)
外す hazúsù; (stain) 消し取る keshítorù;
(employee) 解雇する káìko suru; (MED:
lung, kidney, appendix etc) 切除する sétsùjo suru

removers [rimu:'vəːrz] (BRIT) npl
(company) 引っ越し屋 hikkóshiyà

remuneration [rimju:nəːrei'ʃən] n (payment) 報酬 hōshū

Renaissance [ren'isɑːns] n: *the Renaissance* ルネッサンス runéssànsu

render [ren'dəːr] vt (give: thanks, service) する surú; (make) させる sasérù

rendering [ren'dəːriŋ] n (MUS: instrumental) 演奏 eñsō; (: song) 歌い方 utái-
katà

rendez-vous [rɑːn'deivuː] n (meeting) 待
ち合せ machíawase; (place) 待ち合せの

場所 machíawase nò básho

renegade [ren'əgeid] *n* 裏切者 urágirimono

renew [rinu:'] *vt* (resume) 再び始める futátabi hajimerù; (loan, contract etc) 更新する kóshin suru; (negotiations) 再開する saíkai suru; (acquaintance, relationship) よみがえらせる yomígaeraserù

renewal [rinu:'əl] *n* (resumption) 再開 saíkai; (of license, contract etc) 更新 kóshin

renounce [rinauns'] *vt* (belief, course of action) 捨てる sutérù; (claim, right, peerage) 放棄する hóki suru

renovate [ren'əveit] *vt* (building, machine) 改造する kaízō suru

renovation [renəvei'ʃən] *n* 改造 kaízō

renown [rinaun'] *n* (fame) 名声 meísei

renowned [rinaund'] *adj* (famous) 有名な yūmei na

rent [rent] *n* (for house) 家賃 yáchìn
♦*vt* (take for rent: house) 賃借する chíñshaku suru; (: television, car) レンタルで借りる réñtaru de karírù; (also: **rent out**: house) 賃貸する chíñtai suru; (: television, car) 貸出す kashídasù

rental [ren'təl] *n* (for television, car) レンタル réñtaru

renunciation [rinʌnsiei'ʃən] *n* 放棄 hóki

reorganize [ri:ɔːr'gənaiz] *vt* 再編成する saíhensei suru

rep [rep] *n abbr* (COMM) = **representative**; (THEATER) = **repertory**

repair [ripe:r'] *n* (of clothes, shoes) 修繕 shúzen; (of car, road, building etc) 修理 shúri
♦*vt* (clothes, shoes) 修繕する shúzen suru; (car, engine, road, building) 修理する shúri suru
in good/bad repair 整備が行届いている〔いない〕 seíbi gà ikítodoite irù〔inái〕

repair kit *n* 修理キット shúrikittò

repatriate [ri:pei'tri:eit] *vt* (refugee, soldier) 送還する sókan suru

repay [ripei'] (*pt, pp* **repaid**) *vt* (money, debt, loan) 返済する heñsai suru; (person) ...に借金を返済する ...ni shakkíñ wo

heñsaí suru; (sb's efforts) ...に答える ...ni kotáerù; (favor) ...の恩返しをする ...no oñgaeshi wò suru

repayment [ripei'mənt] *n* (amount of money) 返済金 heñsaikiñ; (of debt, loan etc) 返済 heñsai

repeal [ripi:l'] *n* (of law) 廃止する haíshi suru
♦*vt* (law) 廃止 haíshi

repeat [ripi:t'] *n* (RADIO, TV) 再放送 saíhōso
♦*vt* (say/do again) 繰返す kuríkaesù; (RADIO, TV) 再放送する saíhōso surù
♦*vi* 繰返す kuríkaesù

repeatedly [ripi:t'idli:] *adv* (again and again) 再三 saísan

repel [ripel'] *vt* (drive away: enemy, attack) 撃退する gekítai suru; (disgust: subj: appearance, smell) ...に不快な感じを与える ...ni fukaí na kañji wò atáerù

repellent [ripel'ənt] *adj* 不快な fukaí na
♦*n: insect repellent* 虫よけ mushíyoke

repent [ripent'] *vi: to repent (of)* (sin, mistake) (...を) 後悔する (...wo) kókai suru

repentance [ripen'təns] *n* 後悔 kókai

repercussions [ri:pə:rkʌʃ'ənz] *npl* 反響 hañkyō

repertoire [rep'ə:rtwɑ:r] *n* レパートリー repátorī

repertory [rep'ə:rtɔ:ri:] *n* (also: **repertory theater**) レパートリー演劇 repátorīeñgeki

repetition [repitiʃ'ən] *n* (repeat) 繰返し kuríkaeshi

repetitive [ripet'ətiv] *adj* (movement, work) 単純反復の tañjunhañpuku no; (speech) くどい kudói; (noise) 反復される hañpuku sarerù

replace [ripleis'] *vt* (put back) 元に戻す móto ni modósù; (take the place of) ...に代る ...ni kawárù

replacement [ripleis'mənt] *n* (substitution) 置き換え okíkae; (substitute) 代りの物 kawári no monò

replay [ri:plei'] *n* (of match) 再試合 saíshiai; (of tape, film) 再生 saísei

replenish [riplen'iʃ] *vt* (glass) ...にもう一

杯つぐ ...ni mố ippài tsugú; (stock etc) 補充する hojū suru

replete [ripli:t'] *adj* (well-fed) 満腹の mañpuku no

replica [rep'ləkə] *n* (copy) 複製 fukúsei, レプリカ repúrika

reply [riplai'] *n* (answer) 答え kotáè
◆*vi* (to question, letter) 答える kotáèru

reply coupon *n* 返信券 heńshiñken ◇切手と交換できる券 kitté tò kốkan dekirù kén

report [ripɔ:rt'] *n* (account) 報告書 hốkokushò; (PRESS, TV etc) 報道 hốdò; (*BRIT: also:* **school report**) レポート repốtò; (of gun) 銃声 júsei
◆*vt* (give an account of: event, meeting) 報告する hốkoku suru; (PRESS, TV etc) 報道する hôdō suru; (theft, accident, death) 届け出る todôkederù
◆*vi* (make a report) 報告する hốkoku suru; (present oneself): *to report (to someone)* (...に) 出頭する (...ni) shuttố suru; (be responsible to): *to report to someone* ...が直属の上司である ...ga chokúzoku nò jốshi de arù

report card (*US, SCOTTISH*) *n* 通知表 tsúchihyồ

reportedly [ripɔ:r'tidli:] *adv* うわさによると uwása ni yoru tò

reporter [ripɔ:r'tə:r] *n* (PRESS, TV etc) 記者 kishá

repose [ripouz'] *n*: *in repose* (face, mouth) 平常で heîjō de

reprehensible [reprihen'səbəl] *adj* (behavior) 不届きな futôdòki na

represent [reprizent'] *vt* (person, nation) 代表する daîhyō suru; (view, belief) ...の典型的な例である ...no teñkeiteki nà reî de árù; (symbolize: idea, emotion) ...のシンボルである ...no shíñboru de árù; (constitute) ...である ...de árù; (describe): *to represent something as* ...を...として描写する ...wo ...toshite byốsha suru; (COMM) ...のセールスマンである ...no sérusumàn de árù

representation [reprizentei'ʃən] *n* (state of being represented) 代表を立てている事 daîhyō wò tátète irú kotò; (pic-ture) 絵 é; (statue) 彫像 chốzō; (petition) 陳情 chíñjō

representations [reprizentei'ʃənz] *npl* (protest) 抗議 kồgi

representative [reprizen'tətiv] *n* (of person, nation) 代表者 daîhyōsha; (of view, belief) 典型 teñkei; (COMM) セールスマン sérusumàn; (*US: POL*) 下院議員 kaîngiìn
◆*adj* (group, survey, cross-section) 代表的な daîhyōteki na

repress [ripres'] *vt* (people, revolt) 抑圧する yokúatsu suru; (feeling, impulse) 抑制する yokúsei suru

repression [ripreʃ'ən] *n* (of people, country) 抑圧 yokúatsu; (of feelings) 抑制 yokúsei

repressive [ripres'iv] *adj* (society, measures) 抑圧的な yokúatsuteki na

reprieve [ripri:v'] *n* (LAW) 執行延期 shikkốeñki ◇特に死刑について言う tókù ni shikéi ni tsuitè iú; (*fig:* delay) 延期 eñki

reprimand [rep'rəmænd] *n* (official rebuke) 懲戒 chốkai
◆*vt* 懲戒する chốkai suru

reprint [*n* ri:'print *vb* ri:print'] *n* 復刻版 fukkốkuban
◆*vt* 復刻する fukkốku suru

reprisal [riprai'zəl] *n* 報復 hốfuku

reprisals [riprai'zəlz] *npl* (acts of revenge) 報復行為 hốfukukồi

reproach [riproutʃ'] *n* (rebuke) 非難 hínàn
◆*vt*: *to reproach someone for something* ...の...を非難する ...no ...wo hínàn suru

reproachful [riproutʃ'fəl] *adj* (look, remark) 非難めいた hinánmeìta

reproduce [ri:prədu:s'] *vt* (copy: document etc) 複製する fukúsei suru; (sound) 再生する saîsei suru
◆*vi* (mankind, animal, plant) 繁殖する hañshoku suru

reproduction [ri:prədʌk'ʃən] *n* (copy: of document, report etc) 複写 fukúsha; (of sound) 再生 saîsei; (of painting, furni-ture) 複製品 fukúseìhin; (of mankind, animal etc) 繁殖 hañshoku

reproductive [ri:prəd∧k'tiv] *adj* (system, process) 繁殖の hañshoku no

reproof [ripru:f'] *n* しっ責 shissḗki

reprove [ripru:v'] *vt*: **to reprove someone for something** ...の事で...をしっ責する ...no kotṓ dè ...wo shissḗki suru

reptile [rep'tail] *n* は虫類 hachū́rùi

republic [rip∧b'lik] *n* 共和国 kyṓwakò-ku

republican [rip∧b'likən] *adj* (system, government etc) 共和国の kyṓwakòku no; (US: POL): **Republican** 共和党の kyṓwatṑ no

repudiate [ripju:'di:eit] *vt* (accusation, violence) 否定する hitḗi suru

repugnant [rip∧g'nənt] *adj* 不愉快な fuyúkài na

repulse [rip∧ls'] *vt* (enemy, attack) 撃退する gekítai suru

repulsive [rip∧l'siv] *adj* (sight, idea) 不愉快な fuyúkài na

reputable [rep'jətəbəl] *adj* 評判の良い hyṓban no yoî

reputation [repjətei'ʃən] *n* 評判 hyṓban

reputed [ripju:'tid] *adj* (supposed) ...とされる ...to sarérù

reputedly [ripju:'tidli:] *adv* (supposedly) 人の言うには hitṓ nò iú nì wà

request [rikwest'] *n* (polite demand) 願い negái; (formal demand) 要望 yṓbō; (RADIO, TV) リクエスト rikúesùto

◆*vt*: **to request something of/from someone** (politely) ...に ...をお願いする ...ni ...wo o-négai suru; (formally) ...に ...を要望する ...ni ...wo yṓbō suru; (RADIO, TV) リクエストする rikúesùto suru

request stop (*BRIT*) *n* 随時停留所 zuíjiteiryùjo ◇乗降客がいる時だけバスが留る停留所 jṓkōkyaku ga irú toki dakè básù ga tomárù teíryùjo

requiem [rek'wi:əm] *n* (REL) 死者のためのミサ shíshà no tamḗ nò mísà; (MUS) 鎮魂曲 chiñkoñkyoku, レクイエム rekúíemu

require [rikwaiə:r'] *vt* (need) ...が必要である ...ga hitsúyō de arù; (order): **to**

require someone to do something ...に ...する事を要求する ...ni ...surú kotò wo yṓkyū suru

requirement [rikwaiə:r'mənt] *n* (need) 必要条件 hitsúyōjòken; (want) 要求 yṓkyū

requisite [rek'wizit] *n* (requirement) 必要条件 hitsúyōjòken

◆*adj* (required) 必要な hitsúyō na

requisition [rekwizi'ʃən] *n*: **requisition (for)** (demand) (...の) 請求 (...no) seíkyū

◆*vt* (MIL) 徴発する chṓhatsu suru

resale [ri:'seil] *n* 転売 teñbai

rescind [risind'] *vt* (law) 廃止する haíshi suru; (contract, order etc) 破棄する hákì suru

rescue [res'kju:] *n* (help) 救援 kyūen; (from drowning, accident) 人命救助 jiñmeikyùjo

◆*vt*: **to rescue (from)** (person, animal) (...から) 救う (...kara) sukúù; (company) 救済する kyūsai suru

rescue party *n* 救援隊 kyū́entai, レスキュー隊 resúkyūtai

rescuer [res'kju:ə:r] *n* 救助者 kyū́joshà

research [risə:rtʃ'] *n* 研究 keñkyū

◆*vt* (story, subject) 研究する kefikyū suru; (person) ...について情報を集める ...ni tsúite jṓhō wò atsúmerù

researcher [risə:r'tʃə:r] *n* 研究者 keñkyūsha

resemblance [rizem'bləns] *n* (likeness) 似ている事 nitḗ iru kotò

resemble [rizem'bəl] *vt* ...に似ている ...ni nitḗ irù

resent [rizent'] *vt* ...に対して腹を立てる ...ni táìshite hará wò tatérù

resentful [rizent'fəl] *adj* 怒っている o-kótte irù

resentment [rizent'mənt] *n* 恨み urámi

reservation [rezə:rvei'ʃən] *n* (booking) 予約 yoyáku; (doubt) 疑い utágai; (for tribe) 居留地 kyoryúchì

reserve [rizə:rv'] *n* (store) 備蓄 bichíku, 蓄え takúwae; (SPORT) 補欠 hokétsu; (game reserve) 保護区 hogókù; (restraint) 遠慮 eñryo

♦*vt* (keep) 取って置く tôttè oku; (seats, table etc) 予約する yoyáku suru

in reserve 蓄えてあって takúwaete attè

reserved [rizə:rvd'] *adj* (restrained) 遠慮深い eñryobùkai

reserves [rizə:rvz'] *npl* (MIL) 予備軍 yobígùn

reservoir [rez'ə:rvwɑ:r] *n* (of water) 貯水池 chosúchì

reshuffle [ri:ʃʌf'əl] *n*: *Cabinet reshuffle* (POL) 内閣改造 naíkakukaizò

reside [rizaid'] *vi* (person: live) 住む súmù

residence [rez'idəns] *n* (formal: home) 住い sumáì; (length of stay) 滞在 taízai

residence permit (*BRIT*) *n* 在留許可 zaíryūkyokà

resident [rez'idənt] *n* (of country, town) 住民 júmin; (in hotel) 泊り客 tomárikyakù

♦*adj* (population) 現住の geñjū no; (doctor) レジデントの réjìdento no

residential [reziden'tʃəl] *adj* (area) 住宅の jútaku no; (course) 住込みの sumíkomi no; (college) 全寮制の zeñryōsei no

residue [rez'idu:] *n* (remaining part) 残留物 zañryūbutsu

resign [rizain'] *vt* (one's post) 辞任する jinín suru

♦*vi* (from post) 辞任する jinín suru

to resign oneself to (situation, fact) あきらめて…を認める akírametè …wo mitômerù

resignation [rezignei'ʃən] *n* (post) 辞任 jinín; (state of mind) あきらめ akírame

resigned [rizaind'] *adj* (to situation etc) あきらめている akíramete irù

resilience [rizil'jəns] *n* (of material) 弾力 dañryoku; (of person) 回復力 kaífukuryòku

resilient [rizil'jənt] *adj* (material) 弾力のある dañryoku no arù; (person) 立直りの速い tachínaori nò hayáî

resin [rez'in] *n* 樹脂 júshì

resist [rizist'] *vt* 抵抗する teíkō suru

resistance [rizis'təns] *n* (*gen*) 抵抗 teíkō; (to illness, infection) 抵抗力 teíkōryoku

resolute [rez'əlu:t] *adj* (person) 意志の強

い ishì no tsuyóî; (refusal) 断固とした dáñko to shitá

resolution [rezəlu:'ʃən] *n* (decision) 決心 kesshín; (determination) 決意 kétsùi; (of problem, difficulty) 解決 kaíketsu

resolve [rizɑ:lv'] *n* (determination) 決意 kétsùi

♦*vt* (problem, difficulty) 解決する kaíketsu suru

♦*vi*: *to resolve to do* …しようと決心する …shiyô tò kesshín suru

resolved [rizɑ:lvd'] *adj* (determined) 決心している kesshín shité irù

resonant [rez'ənənt] *adj* 朗朗たる rôrô taru

resort [rizɔ:rt'] *n* (town) リゾート rizôtò; (recourse) 利用 riyô

♦*vi*: *to resort to* …を利用する …wo riyô suru

in the last resort 結局 kekkyókù

resound [rizaund'] *vi*: *to resound (with)* (…の音が…中に) 鳴り響く (…no otô ga …jû ni) narîhibikù

resounding [rizaun'diŋ] *adj* (noise) 響き渡る hibíkiwatarù; (*fig*: success) 完全な kañzen na

resource [ri:'sɔ:rs] *n* (raw material) 資源 shígèn

resourceful [risɔ:rs'fəl] *adj* (quick-witted) やり手の yaríte no

resources [ri:'sɔ:rsiz] *npl* (coal, iron, oil etc) 天然資源 teñnenshigèn; (money) 財産 záísan

respect [rispekt'] *n* (consideration, esteem) 尊敬 soñkei

♦*vt* 尊敬する soñkei suru

with respect to …に関して …ni káñ shite

in this respect この点では konô ten de wà

respectability [rispektəbil'əti:] *n* 名声 meísei

respectable [rispek'təbəl] *adj* (morally correct) 道理にかなった dôri nì kanáttà; (large: amount) かなりの kánàri no; (passable) まあまあの mǎmǎ no

respectful [rispekt'fəl] *adj* (person, behavior) 礼儀正しい reígitadashíî

respective [rispek'tiv] *adj* (separate) そ
れぞれの sorézòre no

respectively [rispek'tivli:] *adv* それぞれ
sorézòre

respects [rispekts'] *npl* (greetings) あい
さつ áisatsu

respiration [respərei'ʃən] *n see* **artificial respiration**

respite [res'pit] *n* (rest) 休息 kyúsoku

resplendent [risplen'dənt] *adj* 華やかな
hanáyàka na

respond [rispɑ:nd'] *vi* (answer) 答える
kotáerù; (react: to pressure, criticism)
反応する hañnō suru

response [rispɑ:ns'] *n* (answer) 答え kotáè; (reaction) 反応 hañnō

responsibility [rispɑ:nsəbil'əti:] *n* (liability) 責任 sekínin; (duty) 義務 gímù

responsible [rispɑ:n'səbəl] *adj* (liable):
responsible (for) (...の) 責任がある
(...no) sekínin gà árù; (character, person)
責任感のある sekíninkan no aru; (job) 責
任の重い sekínin nò omóì

responsive [rispɑ:n'siv] *adj* (child, gesture) 敏感な biñkan na; (to demand,
treatment) よく応じる yókù ōjirù

rest [rest] *n* (relaxation) 休み yasúmi;
(pause) 休止 kyúshi; (remainder) 残り nokóri; (object: to support something) 台
dái; (MUS) 休止符 kyúshifù

♦*vi* (relax) 休む yasúmù; (stop) 休止する
kyúshi suru: *to rest on* (idea) ...に基づく
...ni motózukù; (weight, object) ...に置か
れている ...ni okárete irù

♦*vt* (head, eyes, muscles) 休ませる yasú-
maserù; (lean): *to rest something on/
against* ...を...に置く〔寄り掛ける〕...wo
...ni okú〔yoríkakerù〕

the rest of them (people) 残りの人たち
nokóri nò hitótachi; (objects) 残りの物
nokóri no monò

it rests with him to ... ...するのは彼の
責任だ ...surú no wà kárè no sekínin dà

restaurant [res'tə:rənt] *n* レストラン résùtoran

restaurant car (*BRIT*) *n* 食堂車 sho-
kúdōsha

restful [rest'fəl] *adj* 心を落着かせる ko-

kórò wo ochítsukaserù

rest home *n* 養老院 yóròin

restitution [restitu:'ʃən] *n*: *to make
restitution to someone for something*
(compensate) ...に対して...の弁償をする
...ni táishite ...no beñshō wo surù

restive [res'tiv] *adj* (person, crew) 反抗
的な hañkōteki na; (horse) 言う事を聞か
ない iú kotò wo kikánaî

restless [rest'lis] *adj* (person, audience)
落着かない ochítsukanaî

restoration [restərei'ʃən] *n* (of building
etc) 修復 shúfuku; (of law and order,
faith, health) 回復 kaífuku; (of something stolen) 返還 heñkan; (to power,
former state) 復旧 fukkyū

restore [ristɔ:r'] *vt* (building) 修復する
shúfuku suru; (law and order, faith,
health) 回復する kaífuku suru; (something stolen) 返す káèsu; (to power, former state) 元に戻す mótò ni modósù

restrain [ristrein'] *vt* (feeling, growth,
inflation) 抑制する yokúsei suru; (per-
son): *to restrain (from doing)* (...し
ない様に) 抑える ...shínaî yō ni) osáerù

restrained [ristreind'] *adj* (style, person)
控え目な hikáeme na

restraint [ristreint'] *n* (restriction) 抑制
yokúsei; (moderation) 程々 hodóhodo;
(of style) 控え目な調子 hikáeme nà chōshi

restrict [ristrikt'] *vt* (limit: growth,
numbers etc) 制限する seígen suru;
(: vision) 邪魔する jámà suru; (confine:
people, animals) ...の動きを制限する
...no ugóki wò seígen suru; (: activities,
membership) 制限する seígen suru

restriction [ristrik'ʃən] *n* (gen) 制限 seígen; (of vision) 妨げ samátagè; (limitation): *restriction (on)* (...の) 制限
(...no) seígen

restrictive [ristrik'tiv] *adj* (environment) 束縛的な sokúbakuteki na; (clothing) きつい kitsúî

restrictive practices *npl* (INDUS-
TRY) 制限的慣行 seígentekikañkō

rest room (*US*) *n* お手洗 o-téaraì

restructure [ri:strʌk't'ʃər] *vt* (business,

economy) 再編成する saíheńsei suru

result [rizʌlt'] n (of event, action) 結果 kekká; (of match) スコア sukóa; (of exam, competition) 成績 seíseki

♦vi: **to result in** ...に終る ...ni owáru

as a result of ...の結果 ...no kekká

resume [ri:zu:m'] vt (work, journey) 続ける tsuzúkerù

♦vi (start again) また始まる matá hàjimaru

résumé [rez'u:mei] n (summary) 要約 yóyaku; (US: curriculum vitae) 履歴書 rirékishò

resumption [rizʌmp'ʃən] n (of work, activity) 再開 saíkai

resurgence [risər'dʒəns] n 復活 fukkátsu

resurrection [rezərek'ʃən] n (of hopes, fears) よみがえらせる事 yomígaeraserù kotó; (REL): **the Resurrection** キリストの復活 kirísuto no fukkátsu

resuscitate [risʌs'əteit] vt (MED) 々 生させる soséi saserù

resuscitation [risʌsətei'ʃən] n 々 生 soséi

retail [ri:'teil] adj (trade, department, shop, goods) 小売の koúri no

♦adv 小売で koúri de

retailer [ri:'teilə:r] n (trader) 小 売 業 者 koúrigyòsha

retail price n 小売価格 koúrikakàku

retain [ritein'] vt (keep) 保つ tamótsù

retainer [ritei'nə:r] n (fee) 依 頼 料 iráiryò

retaliate [ritæl'i:eit] vi: **to retaliate (against)** (attack, ill-treatment) (...に対して) 報復する (...ni taíshite) hófuku suru

retaliation [ritæli:ei'ʃən] n 報復 hófuku

retarded [ritɑr'did] adj (child) 知恵遅れ の chiéokùre no; (development, growth) 遅れた okúretà

retch [retʃ] vi むかつく mukátsukù

retentive [riten'tiv] adj (memory) 優れた sugúretà

reticent [ret'isənt] adj 無 口 な múkùchi na

retina [ret'ənə] n (ANAT) 網膜 mómaku

retire [ritaiə:r'] vi (give up work: gen) 引退する iñtai suru; (: at a certain age) 定年退職する teínentaìshoku suru; (withdraw) 引下がる hikísagarù; (go to bed) 寝る nérù

retired [ritaiə:rd'] adj (person: gen) 引退した iñtai shita; (: at certain age) 定年退職した teínentaìshoku shita

retirement [ritaiə:r'mənt] n (giving up work: gen) 隠退 iñtai; (: at certain age) 定年退職 teínentaìshoku

retiring [ritaiə:r'iŋ] adj (leaving) 退職する taíshoku suru; (shy) 内気な uchíki na

retort [ritɔ:rt'] vi しっぺ返しをする shippégaèshi wo suru

retrace [ri:treis'] vt: **to retrace one's steps** 来た道を戻る kitá michì wo modórù

retract [ritrækt'] vt (statement, offer) 撤回する tekkái suru; (claws, aerial etc) 引っ込める hikkómerù

retrain [ri:trein'] vt 再訓練する saíkuńren suru

retraining [ri:trei'niŋ] n 再訓練 saíkuńren

retread [ri:'tred] n (tire) 再生タイヤ saíseitaìya

retreat [ritri:t'] n (place) 隠れ家 kakúregà; (withdrawal) 避難 hínan; (MIL) 退却 taíkyaku

♦vi (from danger, enemy) 避難する hínan suru; (MIL) 退却する taíkyaku suru

retribution [retrəbju:'ʃən] n 天罰 teñbatsu

retrieval [ritri:'vəl] n (of object) 回収 kaíshù; (of situation) 繕う事 tsukúrou kotò; (of honor) ばん回 bañkai; (of error) 償い tsugúnaì; (loss) 取返し toríkaeshi

retrieve [ritri:v'] vt (object) 回収する kaíshù suru; (situation) 繕う tsukúroù; (honor) ばん回する bañkai suru; (error) 償う tsugúnaù; (loss) 取返す toríkaesù

retriever [ritri:'və:r] n (dog) リトリーバ 犬 ritórībàken

retrograde [ret'rəgreid] adj 後戻りの a-tómodòri no

retrospect [ret'rəspekt] n: **in retrospect** 振返ってみると furíkaette miru tò

retrospective [retrəspek'tiv] adj (exhibition) 回顧的な kaíkoteki na; (feeling, opinion) 過去にさかのぼる kákò ni sakánoborù; (law, tax) そ及する sokyú suru

return [ritə:rn'] n (going or coming back) 帰り kaéri; (of something stolen, borrowed etc) 返還 henkan; (FINANCE: from land, shares, investment) 利回り rimáwari

◆cpd (journey) 帰りの kaéri no; (BRIT: ticket) 往復の őfuku no; (match) 雪辱の setsújoku no

◆vi (person etc: come or go back) 帰る kaérù; (feelings, symptoms etc) 戻る modórù; (regain): **to return to** (consciousness) ...を回復する ...wo kaífuku suru; (power) ...に返り咲く ...ni kaérizakù

◆vt (favor, love etc) 返す kaésù; (something borrowed, stolen etc) 返却する henkyaku suru; (LAW: verdict) ...と答申する ...to tőshin suru; (POL: candidate) 選出する senshutsu suru; (ball) 返す kaésù

in return (for) (...の) お返しに (...no) o-káeshi ni

by return of post 折返し郵便で oríkaeshiyūbin de

many happy returns (of the day)! お誕生日おめでとう o-tánjòbi omédető

returns [ritə:rnz'] npl (COMM) 利益 ríèki

reunion [ri:ju:n'jən] n (of family) 集い tsudói; (of school, class etc) 同窓会 dősőkai; (of two people) 再会 saíkai

reunite [ri:ju:nait'] vt (bring or come together again) 元のさやに収めさせる mótò no sáyà ni osámesaserù; (reconcile) 和解させる wakái saserù

rev [rev] n abbr (AUT: = revolution) 回転 kaíten

◆vt also: **rev up**: engine) ふかす fukásù

revamp [ri:væmp'] vt (organization, company, system) 改革する kaíkaku suru

reveal [rivi:l'] vt (make known) 明らかにする akírāka ni suru; (make visible) 現す aráwasù

revealing [rivi:'liŋ] adj (action, statement) 手の内を見せるよ té nò uchí wò misérù; (dress) 肌をあらわにする hádà

wo arawa ni suru

reveille [rev'əli:] n (MIL) 起床らっぱ kishő rappà

revel [rev'əl] vi: **to revel in something/ in doing something** (enjoy) ...を〔...するのを〕楽しむ ...wo [...surú no wò]tanőshimù

revelation [revəlei'ʃən] n (fact, experience) 意外な新知識 igái nà shíchishìki

revelry [rev'əlri:] n どんちゃん騒ぎ donchan sawàgi

revenge [rivendʒ'] n (for injury, insult) 復しゅう fukúshū

to take revenge on (enemy) ...に復しゅうする ...ni fukúshū suru

revenue [rev'ənu:] n (income: of individual, company, government) 収入 shűnyu

reverberate [rivə:r'bəreit] vi (sound, thunder etc: also fig) 響く hibíkù

reverberation [rivə:rbərei'ʃən] n (of sound, etc: also fig) 響き hibíki

revere [rivi:r'] vt 敬愛する keíai suru

reverence [rev'ə:rəns] n 敬愛 keíai

Reverend [rev'ə:rənd] adj (in titles) ...師 ...shī ◇聖職者の名前に付ける敬称 seíshokushà no namáè ni tsukérù keíshō

reversal [rivə:r'səl] n (of order) 反転 hanten; (of direction) 逆戻り gyakúmodòri; (of decision, policy) 逆転 gyakúten; (of roles) 入れ代わり irékawari

reverse [rivə:rs'] n (opposite) 反対 hantái; (back) 裏 urá; (AUT: also: **reverse gear**) バック bákkù; (setback, defeat) 失敗 shippái

◆adj (opposite: order, direction, process) 反対の hantai no, 逆の gyakú no; (: side) 裏の urá no

◆vt (order, position, direction) 逆にする gyakú ni surù; (process, policy, decision) 引っ繰り返す hikkúrikaèsu; (roles) 入れ替える irékaerù; (car) バックさせる bákkù saserù

◆vi (BRIT: AUT) バックする bákkù suru

reverse-charge call [rivə:rs'tʃɑ:rdʒ-] (BRIT) n 受信人払い電話 jushínninbarai denwa

reversing lights [rivə:r'siŋ-] (BRIT)

npl (AUT) バックライト bakkúraìto

revert [rivə:rt'] *vi: to revert to* (former state) ...に戻る ...ni modórù; (LAW: money, property) ...に帰属する ...ni kizóku surù

review [rivju:'] *n* (magazine) 評論雑誌 hyóronzasshì; (MIL) 閲兵 eppéi; (of book, film etc) 批評 hihyṑ; (examination: of situation, policy etc) 再検討 saíkentō

♦*vt* (MIL) 閲兵する eppéi suru; (book, film etc) ...の批評を書く ...no hihyṑ wò kákù; (situation, policy etc) 再検討する saíkentō suru

reviewer [rivju:'ə:r] *n* (of book, film etc) 批評者 hihyóshà

revile [rivail'] *vt* (insult) 侮辱する bujóku suru

revise [rivaiz'] *vt* (manuscript) 修正する shúsei suru; (opinion, price, procedure) 変える kaérù

♦*vi* (BRIT: study) 試験勉強する shikénbenkyō suru

revision [riviʒ'ən] *n* (amendment) 修正 shúsei; (for exam) 試験勉強 shikénbenkyō

revitalize [ri:vai'təlaiz] *vt* ...に新しい活力を与える ...ni atárashìi katsúryòkù wo atáerù

revival [rivai'vəl] *n* (recovery) 回復 kaífuku; (of interest, faith) 復活 fukkátsu; (THEATER) リバイバル ribáibaru

revive [rivaiv'] *vt* (person) ...の意識を回復させる ...no íshìki wo kaífuku saserù; (economy, industry) 復興させる fukkṑ saserù; (custom, hope, courage) 復活させる fukkátsu saserù; (play) 再上演する saíjōen suru

♦*vi* (person: from faint) 意識を取戻す íshìki wo torímodosù; (: from ill-health) 元気になる génki ni nárù; (activity, economy etc) 回復する kaífuku suru; (faith, interest etc) 復活する fukkátsu suru

revoke [rivouk'] *vt* 取消す toríkesù

revolt [rivoult'] *n* (rebellion) 反逆 hangyaku

♦*vi* (rebel) 反逆する hangyaku suru

♦*vt* (disgust) むかつかせる mukátsukaserù

revolting [rivoul'tiŋ] *adj* (disgusting) むかつかせる mukátsukaserù

revolution [revəlu:'ʃən] *n* (POL) 革命 kakúmei; (rotation: of wheel, earth etc: also AUT) 回転 kaíten

revolutionary [revəlu:'ʃəneːri:] *adj* (method, idea) 革命的な kakúmeiteki na; (leader, army) 革命の kakúmei no

♦*n* (POL: person) 革命家 kakúmeika

revolutionize [revəlu:'ʃənaiz] *vt* (industry, society etc) ...に大変革をもたらす ...ni daíhenkaku wo motárasù

revolve [riva:lv'] *vi* (turn: earth, wheel etc) 回転する kaíten suru; (life, discussion): *to revolve (a)round* ...を中心に展開する ...wo chūshin nì tenkai suru

revolver [riva:l'və:r] *n* けん銃 kenjū, リボルバー ribórùbā ◇回転式の物を指す kaítenshiki no monò wò sásù

revolving [riva:l'viŋ] *adj* (chair etc) 回転式の kaítenshiki no

revolving door *n* 回転ドア kaíten doà

revue [rivju:'] *n* (THEATER) レビュー rébyū

revulsion [rivʌl'ʃən] *n* (disgust) 嫌悪 kén-o

reward [riwo:rd'] *n* (for service, merit, work) 褒美 hóbi; (money for capture of criminal, information etc) 賞金 shókin

♦*vt: to reward (for)* (effort) (...のために) 褒美を与える (... no tamé nì) hóbi wò atáerù

rewarding [riwo:rd'iŋ] *adj* (fig: worthwhile) やりがいのある yarígai no arù

rewind [ri:waind'] (pt, pp **rewound**) *vt* (tape, cassette) 巻戻す makímodosù

rewire [ri:waiə:r'] *vt* (house) ...の電気配線をし直す ...no deńki haìsen wo shináosù

rewrite [ri:rait'] (pt **rewrote**, pp **rewritten**) *vt* 書き直す kakínaosù

rhapsody [ræp'sədi:] *n* (MUS) 狂想曲 kyóshikyòku, ラプソディー rápùsodī

rhetorical [rito:r'ikəl] *adj* (question, speech) 修辞的な shújiteki na

rheumatic [ru:mæt'ik] *adj* リューマチの ryúmachi no

rheumatism [ruː'mətizəm] *n* リューマチ ryūmachi

Rhine [rain] *n*: **the Rhine** ライン川 raíngawa

rhinoceros [rainɔ's'əːrəs] *n* サイ sáî

rhododendron [roudədən'drən] *n* シャクナゲ shakúnage

Rhone [roun] *n*: **the Rhone** ローヌ川 rōnùgawa

rhubarb [ruː'baːrb] *n* ルバーブ rubábù

rhyme [raim] *n* (of two words) 韻 iń; (verse) 詩 shi; (technique) 韻を踏む事 iń wò fumú kotð

rhythm [rið'əm] *n* リズム rízumu

rhythmic(al) [rið'mik(əl)] *adj* リズミカルな rizúmikàru na

rib [rib] *n* (ANAT) ろっ骨 rokkótsu
♦*vt* (tease) からかう karákaù

ribbon [rib'ən] *n* リボン ríbòn
in ribbons (torn) ずたずたになって zutázuta ni nattè

rice [rais] *n* (grain) 米 komé; (cooked) 御飯 góhàn

rice pudding *n* ライスプディング raísu pudíñgu ◇御飯にミルク、卵、砂糖などを加えたデザート góhàn ni mírùku, tamágo, satō nadð wo kuwáetà dezátð

rich [ritʃ] *adj* (person, country) 金持の kanémochi no; (clothes, jewels) 高価な kôka na; (soil) 肥えた koétà, 肥よくな hiyóku na; (food, diet) 濃厚な nôkō na; (color, voice, life) 豊かな yútàka na; (abundant): **rich in** (minerals, resources etc) …に富んだ …ni tôñda
♦*npl*: **the rich** 金持 kanémochi ◇総称 sôshō

riches [ritʃ'iz] *npl* (wealth) 富 tômî

richly [ritʃ'liː] *adv* (dressed, decorated) 豪華に gôka ni; (rewarded, deserved, earned) 十分に júbuñ ni

rickets [rik'its] *n* くる病 kurúbyō

rickety [rik'əti] *adj* (shaky) がたがたの gatágata no

rickshaw [rik'ʃɔ] *n* 人力車 jiñrikishà

ricochet [rikəʃei'] *vi* (bullet, stone) 跳ね飛ぶ hanétobù

rid [rid] (*pt, pp* **rid**) *vt*: **to rid someone of something** …の…を取除く …no …wo

to get rid of (something no longer required) 捨てる sutérù; (something unpleasant or annoying) …を取除く …wo torínozokù

ridden [rid'ən] *pp of* **ride**

riddle [rid'əl] *n* (conundrum) なぞなぞ nazónazo; (mystery) なぞ nazð
♦*vt*: **to be riddled with** …だらけである …dáràke de árù

ride [raid] *n* (in car, on bicycle, horse) 乗る事 norú kotð; (distance covered) 道のり michínori
♦*vb* (*pt* **rode**, *pp* **ridden**)
♦*vi* (as sport) 乗馬をする jôba wo suru; (go somewhere: on horse, bicycle, bus) 乗って行く notté ikù
♦*vt* (a horse, bicycle, motorcycle) …に乗る …ni nórù; (distance) 行く ikú
to take someone for a ride (*fig*: deceive) ぺてんに掛ける petéñ nî kakérù
to ride a bicycle 自転車に乗る jitéñsha ni norú
to ride at anchor (NAUT) 停泊する teíhaku suru

rider [rai'dəːr] *n* (on horse) 乗り手 noríte; (on bicycle, motorcycle) 乗る人 norú hitð, ライダー ráìdā

ridge [ridʒ] *n* (of hill) 尾根 ónè; (of roof) 天辺 teppéñ; (wrinkle) うね unê

ridicule [rid'əkjuːl] *n* あざけり azákerî
♦*vt* あざける azákerù

ridiculous [ridik'jələs] *adj* (foolish) ばかげた bakágetà

riding [rai'diŋ] *n* (sport, activity) 乗馬 jôba

riding school *n* 乗馬学校 jôbagakkô

rife [raif] *adj*: **to be rife** (bribery, corruption, superstition) はびこる habíkorù
to be rife with (rumors, fears) …がはびこっている …ga habíkotte irù

riffraff [rif'ræf] *n* (rabble) ろくでなしの連中 rokúdenashi nð reńchū

rifle [rai'fəl] *n* (gun) ライフル ráìfuru
♦*vt* (steal from: wallet, pocket etc) …の中身を盗む …no nakámi wo nusúmù

rifle range *n* (for sport) 射撃場 shageki-jō; (at fair) 射的 shatéki

rifle through *vt fus* (papers) ...を かき 回して捜す ...wo kakímawashite sagásù

rift [rift] *n* (split: in ground) 亀裂 kirétsu; (: in clouds) 切れ間 kiréma; (*fig*: disagreement) 仲たがい nakátagaì

rig [rig] *n* (*also*: **oil rig**) 油井掘削装置 yuséi kussaku sóchi
◆*vt* (election, game etc) 不正操作をする fuséisōsa suru

rigging [rig'iŋ] *n* (NAUT) 索具 sakúgù

right [rait] *adj* (correct: answer, solution, size etc) 正しい tadáshiì; (suitable: person, clothes, time) 適当な tekítō na; (: decision etc) 適切な tekísetsu na; (morally good) 正当な seítō na; (fair, just) 公正な kōsei na; (not left) 右の migí no
◆*n* (what is morally right) 正義 seígi; (entitlement) 権利 kénri; (not left) 右 migí
◆*adv* (correctly: answer etc) 正しく tadáshìku; (properly, fairly: treat etc) 公正に kōsei ni; (not on the left) 右に migí ni; (directly, exactly): **right now** 今すぐ ímà súgù
◆*vt* (put right way up: ship, car etc) 起す okósù; (correct: fault, situation, wrong) 正す tadásù
◆*excl* では dé wà

to be right (person) ...の言う事が合っている ...no iú kotò ga atté irù; (answer) 正解である seíkai de árù; (clock, reading etc) 合っている atté irù

by rights 当然 tōzen

on the right 右に migí ni

to be in the right ...の方が正しい ...no hō gà tadáshiì

right away すぐに súgù ni

right in the middle 丁度真ん中に chódo maṅnaka ni

right angle *n* (MATH) 直角 chokkáku

righteous [rai'tʃəs] *adj* (person) 有徳な yútoku na; (anger) 当然な tōzen na

rightful [rait'fəl] *adj* (heir, owner) 合法の góhō no; (place, share) 正当な seítō na

right-handed [rait'hændid] *adj* (person) 右利きの migíkiki no

right-hand man [rait'hænd'-] *n* 右腕 migíude

right-hand side *n* 右側 migígawa

rightly [rait'li:] *adv* (with reason) 当然 tōzen

right of way *n* (on path etc) 通行権 tsúkōken; (AUT) 先行権 seṅkōken

right-wing [rait'wiŋ] *adj* (POL) 右翼の úyòku no

rigid [ridʒ'id] *adj* (structure, back etc) 曲らない magáranaì; (attitude, views etc) 厳格な geñkaku na; (principle, control etc) 厳しい kibíshiì

rigmarole [rig'məroul] *n* (procedure) 手続 tetsúzùki

rigor [rig'ə:r] (*BRIT* **rigour**) *n* (strictness) 厳格さ geñkakusa; (severity): **rigors of life/winter** 生活〔冬〕の厳しさ seíkatsu(fuyú)nò kibíshisa

rigorous [rig'ə:rəs] *adj* (control, test) 厳密な geñmitsu na; (training) 厳しい kibíshiì

rig out (*BRIT*) *vt*: **to rig out as** ...の仮装をする ...no kasō wò suru

to rig out in ...を着る ...wo kírù

rig up *vt* 作り上げる tsukúriagerù

rile [rail] *vt* (annoy) ...を怒らせる ...wo okóraserù

rim [rim] *n* (of glass, dish) 縁 fuchí; (of spectacles) フレーム furémù; (of wheel) リム rímù

rind [raind] *n* (of bacon, fruit, cheese) 皮 kawá

ring [riŋ] *n* (of metal, light, smoke) 輪 wá; (for finger) 指輪 yubíwà; (of spies, drug-dealers etc) 組織 sóshìki; (for boxing, of circus) リング ríngu; (bullring) 闘牛場 tōgyūjō; (sound of bell) ベルの音 bérù no otó
◆*vb* (*pt* **rang**, *pp* **rung**)
◆*vi* (person: by telephone) 電話を掛ける deñwa wo kakérù; (telephone, bell, doorbell) 鳴る narú; (*also*: **ring out**: voice, words) 鳴り響く naríhibikù
◆*vt* (*BRIT*: TEL) ...に電話を掛ける ...ni deñwa wò kakérù; (bell etc) 鳴らす narásù

a ring of people 車座になった人々 kurúmaza ni nattá hitóbìto

a ring of stones 環状に並んだ石 kaňjō

ni naranda ishí

to give someone a ring (*BRIT*: TEL)
...に電話を掛ける ...ni deńwa wò kakérù

my ears are ringing 耳鳴りがする mimínari ga surù

ring back (*BRIT*) *vt* (TEL) ...に電話を掛け直す ...ni deńwa wò kakénaosù

♦*vi* (TEL) 電話を掛け直す deńwa wò kakénaosù

ringing [riŋ'iŋ] *n* (of telephone, bell) 鳴る音 narú otò; (in ears) 耳鳴り mimínari

ringing tone *n* (TEL) ダイヤルトーン dafyarutòn

ringleader [riŋ'li:də:r] *n* (of gang) 主犯 shuhàn

ringlets [riŋ'lits] *npl* (of hair) 巻き毛 makíge

ring off (*BRIT*) *vi* (TEL) 電話を切る deńwa wò kírù

ring road (*BRIT*) *n* 環状線 kańjōsen

ring up (*BRIT*) *vt* (TEL) ...に電話を掛ける ...ni deńwa wò kakérù

rink [riŋk] *n* (*also*: ice rink) スケートリンク sukétoriǹku

rinse [rins] *n* (of dishes, hands) すすぎ susúgi; (of hair) リンスする事 rínsu suru kotò; (dye: for hair) リンス rínsu

♦*vt* (dishes, hands etc) すすぐ susúgù; (hair etc) リンスする rínsu suru; (*also*: rinse out: clothes) すすぐ susúgù; (: mouth) ゆすぐ yusúgù

riot [rai'ət] *n* (disturbance) 騒動 sódō

♦*vi* (crowd, protestors etc) 暴動を起す bódō wò okósù

a riot of colors 色取り取り irótoridòri

to run riot (children, football fans etc) 大騒ぎをする ósawàgi wo suru

riotous [rai'ətəs] *adj* (mob, assembly etc) 暴動的な bódōteki na; (behavior, living) 遊とうざんまい yútōzaǹmai; (party) どんちゃん騒ぎの dońchan sawàgi no

rip [rip] *n* (tear) 破れ目 yabúremè

♦*vt* (paper, cloth) 破る yabúrù

♦*vi* (paper, cloth) 破れる yabúrerù

ripcord [rip'kɔ:rd] *n* (on parachute) 引き網 hikízùna

ripe [raip] *adj* (fruit, grain, cheese) 熟した jukú shità

ripen [rai'pən] *vt* (subj: sun) 熟させる jukú saserù

♦*vi* (fruit, crop) 熟する jukú suru

ripple [rip'əl] *n* (wave) さざ波 sazánami; (of laughter, applause) ざわめき zawámeki

♦*vi* (water) さざ波が立つ sazánami gà tátsù

rise [raiz] *n* (slope) 上り坂 nobórizaka; (hill) 丘 oká; (increase: in wages: *BRIT*) 賃上げ chiń-age; (: in prices, temperature) 上昇 jóshō; (*fig*: to power etc) 出世 shussé

♦*vi* (*pt* **rose**, *pp* **risen**) (prices, numbers) 上がる agárù; (waters) 水かさが増す mizúkasa gà masú; (sun, moon) 昇る nobórù; (person: from bed etc) 起きる okírù; (sound, voice) 大きくなる ókiku nárù; (*also*: rise up: tower, building) そびえる sobíerù; (: rebel) 立ち上がる tachíagarù; (in rank) 昇進する shóshin suru

to give rise to ...を起す ...wo okósù

to rise to the occasion 腕前を見せる udémaè wo misérù

risen [riz'ən] *pp* of **rise**

rising [rai'ziŋ] *adj* (increasing: number, prices) 上がる agárù; (tide) 満ちる michírù; (sun, moon) 昇る nobórù

risk [risk] *n* (danger) 危険 kikén; (INSURANCE) リスク rísuku

♦*vt* (endanger) 危険にさらす kikén nì sarásù; (chance) ...の危険を冒す ...no kinén wò okásù

to take/run the risk of doing ...する危険を冒す ...súrù kikén wò okásù

at risk 危険にさらされて kikén nì sarasáretè

at one's own risk 自分の責任で jibún nò sekínin de

risky [ris'ki:] *adj* (dangerous) 危険な kikén na

risqué [riskei'] *adj* (joke) わいせつがかった waísetsugakatta

rissole [ris'ɑ:l] *n* (of meat, fish etc) メンチカツ meńchikatsù

rite [rait] *n* 儀式 gíshìki

last rites (REL) 終油の秘蹟 shúyu nò hiséki

ritual [ritʃuəl] adj (law, dance) 儀式的な gishíkiteki na
♦n 儀式 gíshìki

rival [rai'vəl] n ライバル ráìbaru
♦adj ライバルの ráìbaru no
♦vt (match) ...に匹敵する ...ni hittéki su-ru

rivalry [rai'vəlri:] n (competition) 競争 kyōsō

river [riv'ə:r] n 川 kawá
♦cpd (port, traffic) 川の kawá no
up/down river 川上〔下〕へ kawákami 〔shimo〕 e

riverbank [riv'ə:rbæŋk] n 川岸 kawágishi

riverbed [riv'ə:rbed] n 河原 kawára

rivet [riv'it] n (bolt) リベット ribéttò
♦vt (fig): to rivet one's eyes/atten-tion on ...に注目する ...ni chūmoku suru

Riviera [rivi:er'ə] n: the (French) Riviera リビエラ ribíèra
the Italian Riviera イタリアのリビエ ラ itária nò ribíèra

road [roud] n (gen) 道 michí, 道路 dōro
♦cpd (accident, sense) 交通の kōtsu no
major/minor road 優先〔非優先〕道路 yūsen〔hiyūsen〕dōro

roadblock [roud'bla:k] n 検問所 keńmonjo

roadhog [roud'hɔːg] n マナーの悪いドラ イバー mánā no warúi doráìbā

road map n 道路地図 dōrochizu

road safety n 交通安全 kōtsūaǹzen

roadside [roud'said] n 道路脇 dōrowaki

roadsign [roud'sain] n 道路標識 dōro-hyōshiki

road user n ドライバー doráìbā

roadway [roud'wei] n 車道 shadō

roadworks [roud'wə:rks] npl 道路工事 dōrokōji

roadworthy [roud'wə:rði:] adj (car) 整備状態のいい seíbijōtai no íi

roam [roum] vi (wander) さまよう samá-yoù

roar [rɔːr] n (of animal) ほえ声 hoégoè; (of crowd) どよめき doyómeki; (of vehi-cle, storm) とどろき todóroki
♦vi (animal) ほえる hoérù; (person) どな

る donárù; (crowd) どよめく doyómekù; (engine, wind etc) とどろく todórokù
a roar of laughter 大笑い ōwarai
to roar with laughter 大笑いする ō-warài suru
to do a roaring trade ...の商売が繁盛 する ...no shōbai gà hańjō suru

roast [roust] n (of meat) ロースト rōsuto
♦vt (meat, potatoes) オーブンで焼く ō-bun de yakú; (coffee) いる írù

roast beef n ローストビーフ rōsutobīfu

rob [ra:b] vt (person, house, bank) ...から 盗む ...kara nusúmù
to rob someone of something ...から ...を盗む ...kará ...wo nusúmù; (fig: deprive) 奪う ubáù

robber [ra:b'ə:r] n 泥棒 doróbō

robbery [ra:b'ə:ri:] n (theft) 盗み nusúmi

robe [roub] n (for ceremony etc) ローブ rōbu; (also: bath robe) バスローブ basú-rōbu; (US) ひざ掛け hizákake

robin [ra:b'in] n コマドリ komádòri

robot [rou'bət] n ロボット robóttò

robust [roubʌst'] adj (person) たくましい takúmashiì; (economy) 健全な keńzen na; (appetite) おう盛な ōsei na

rock [ra:k] n (substance) 岩石 gańseki; (boulder) 岩 iwá; (US: small stone, peb-ble) 小石 koíshi; (BRIT: sweet) 氷砂糖 kōrizatō
♦vt (swing gently: cradle) 優しく揺する yasáshiku yusurù; (: child) あやす ayásù; (shake: subj: explosion, waves etc) 激し く揺すぶる hagéshiku yusuburù
♦vi (object) 揺れる yurérù; (person) 震え る furúerù
on the rocks (drink) オンザロックで oń-zarokkù de; (marriage etc) 危ぶまれて ayábumaretè

rock and roll n ロックンロール rokkún-rōru

rock-bottom [ra:k'ba:t'əm] adj (fig: lowest point) 最低の saítei no

rockery [ra:k'ə:ri:] n (in garden) 庭石 ni-wá-ishi ◇総称 sōshō

rocket [ra:k'it] n (space rocket) ロケッ ト rokéttò; (missile) ロケット弾 rokétto-daǹ; (firework) ロケット花火 rokétto hanàbi

rocking chair [rɑ:k'iŋ-] n 揺りいす yurîisu

rocking horse n 揺り木馬 yurîmokùba

rocky [rɑ:k'i:] adj (covered with rocks) 岩だらけの iwádaràke no; (unsteady: table) 不安定な fuántei na; (unstable: business, marriage) 危ぶまれている ayábumarete irù

rod [rɑ:d] n (pole) さお saó; (also: **fishing rod**) 釣ざお tsurízao

rode [roud] pt of **ride**

rodent [rou'dənt] n げっ歯類 gesshírùi

rodeo [rou'di:ou] n ロデオ ródèo

roe [rou] n (species: also: **roe deer**) ノロジカ norójìka; (of fish) 卵 tamágò
  hard roe 腹子 haráko
  soft roe 白子 shirákò

rogue [roug] n 野郎 yaró

role [roul] n 役 yakú

roll [roul] n (of paper, cloth etc) 巻きまきmakí; (of banknotes) 札束 satsútabà; (also: **bread roll**) ロールパン rôrupaǹ; (register, list) 名簿 meíbo; (sound: of drums etc) とどろき todóroki
  ◆vt (ball, stone etc) 転がす korógasù; (also: **roll up**: string) 巻く makú; (: sleeves) まくる makúrù; (cigarette) 巻く makú; (eyes) 白黒させる shíròkuro sasérù; (also: **roll out**: pastry) 延ばす nobású; (flatten: lawn, road, surface) ならす narásù
  ◆vi (ball, stone etc) 転がる korógarù; (drum) 鳴り響く naríhibikù; (vehicle: also: **roll along**) 走る hashírù; (ship) 揺れる yurérù

roll about/around vi 転がる korógarù

roll by vi (time) 過ぎる sugírù

roll call n 点呼 tênko

roller [rou'lər] n (gen) ローラー rôrā; (for hair) カーラー kârā

roller coaster [-kous'tər] n ジェットコースター jettókōsutā

roller skates npl ローラースケート rôrāsukèto

roll in vi (mail, cash) 大量に入る taíryo nì haírù

rolling [rou'liŋ] adj (landscape) うねりの

多い unéri no òi

rolling pin n めん棒 méǹbo

rolling stock n (RAIL) 車両 sharyô ◇総称 sôshò

roll over vi 寝返りを打つ negáeri wò útsù

roll up vi (inf: arrive) やって来る yatté kurù
  ◆vt (carpet, newspaper, umbrella etc) 巻く makú

ROM [rɑ:m] n abbr (COMPUT: = **read only memory**) ロム rômù

Roman [rou'mən] adj ローマの rôma no

Roman Catholic adj ローマカトリックの rômakatorikkù no
  ◆n ローマカトリック信者 rômakatorikkù shiǹja

romance [roumæns'] n (love affair) 恋愛 reñ-ai; (charm) ロマンス rômànsu; (novel) 恋愛小説 reñ-ai shôsetsu

Romania [roumei'ni:ə] n = **Rumania**

Roman numeral n ローマ数字 rômasù-ji

romantic [roumæn'tik] adj ロマンチックな románchikkù na

Rome [roum] n ローマ rôma

romp [rɑ:mp] n 騒々しい遊び sôzòshiì asóbi
  ◆vi (also: **romp about**: children, dogs etc) はしゃぎ回る hashágimawarù

rompers [rɑ:m'pə:rz] npl ロンパース roñpāsu

roof [ru:f] (pl **roofs**) n 屋根 yáne, ルーフ rûfu
  ◆vt (house, building etc) 屋根を付ける yáne wo tsukérù
  the roof of one's mouth 口がい kôgai

roofing [ru:'fiŋ] n 屋根ふき材 yanéfuki-zài

roof rack n (AUT) ルーフラック rûfurakkù

rook [ruk] n (bird) ミヤマガラス miyámagaràsu; (CHESS) ルック rúkkù

room [ru:m] n (in house, hotel etc) 部屋 heyá; (space) 空間 kûkan, 場所 bashò; (scope: for improvement, change etc) 余地 yôchì
  「**rooms for rent**」, 「**rooms to let**」貸間

あり kashíma arí

single/double room シングル〔ダブル〕部屋 shínguru〔dáburu〕beyà

rooming house [ruː'miŋ-] (US) n 下宿屋 geshúkuya

roommate [ruːm'meit] n ルームメート rúmumēto ◇寄宿舎などで同室に泊まる人 kishúkushà nádò de dōshitsu nǐ tomárù hitó

rooms [ruːmz] npl (lodging) 下宿 geshúku

room service n (in hotel) ルームサービス rūmusābisu

roomy [ruː'miː] adj (building, car) 広々とした hiróbiro to shità; (garment) ゆったりした yuttári shità

roost [ruːst] vi (birds) ねぐらにつく negúra ni tsukù

rooster [ruːs'təːr] n オンドリ oñdòri

root [ruːt] n (BOT) 根 né; (MATH) 根 kóñ; (of problem, belief) 根源 koñgen
♦vi (plant) 根を下ろす né wò orósù; (belief) 定着する teíchaku suru
the root of a hair 毛根 mōkon
the root of a tooth 歯根 shikón

root about vi (fig: search) かき回す kakímawasù

root for vt fus (support) ...を応援する ...wo ōen surù

root out vt (find) 捜し出す sagáshidasù

roots [ruːts] npl (family origins) ルーツ rūtsu

rope [roup] n (thick string) ロープ rṓpu; (NAUT) 綱 tsuná; (for climbing) ザイル zaíru
♦vt (tie) 縛る shibárù; (climbers: also: **rope together**) ザイルでつなぐ zaíru de tsunágù; (an area: also: **rope off**) 縄で仕切る nawá dè shikírù
to know the ropes (fig: know how to do something) こつが分かっている kotsú gà wakátte irù

rope in vt (fig: person) 誘い込む sasóikomù

rope ladder n 縄ばしご nawábashigo

rosary [rou'zəːriː] n ロザリオ rozárìo

rose [rouz] pt of **rise**
♦n (single flower) バラ bará; (shrub) バ

ラの木 bará nò kí; (on watering can) はす口 hasúkuchi

rosé [rouzei'] n ロゼワイン rozéwaìn

rosebud [rouz'bʌd] n バラのつぼみ bará nò tsubómi

rosebush [rouz'buʃ] n バラの木 bará no ki

rosemary [rouz'meːriː] n ローズマリー rōzumarī

rosette [rouzet'] n ロゼット rozéttò

roster [rɑːs'təːr] n: **duty roster** 勤務当番表 kiñmutōbañhyō

rostrum [rɑːs'trəm] n 演壇 eñdan

rosy [rou'ziː] adj (color) バラ色の bará-iro no; (face, cheeks) 血色のいい kesshóku no iì; (situation) 明るい akáruì
a rosy future 明るい見通し akáruì mitóshi

rot [rɑːt] n (decay) 腐敗 fuhái; (fig: pej: rubbish) でたらめ detárame
♦vt (cause to decay: teeth, wood, fruit etc) 腐らす kusárasù
♦vi (decay: teeth, wood, fruit etc) 腐る kusárù

rota [rou'tə] (BRIT) n 勤務当番表 kiñmutōbañhyō

rotary [rou'təːriː] adj (revolving) 回転式の kaíteñshiki no

rotate [rou'teit] vt (revolve) 回転させる kaíten saserù; (change round: jobs) 交替でやる kṓtai de yarù
♦vi (revolve) 回転する kaíten suru

rotating [rou'teitiŋ] adj (movement) 回転する kaíten suru

rotation [routei'ʃən] n (revolving) 回転 kaíten; (changing round: jobs) 交替 kṓtai; (of crops) 輪作 riñsaku

rote [rout] n: **by rote** 暗記で añki de

rotor [rou'təːr] n (also: **rotor blade**) 回転翼 kaíteñyoku, ローター rōta

rotten [rɑːt'ən] adj (decayed: fruit, meat, wood, eggs etc) 腐った kusátta; (fig: person, situation) いやな iyá nà; (inf: bad) ひどい hidóì
a rotten tooth 虫歯 mushíba
to feel rotten (ill) 気分が悪い kíbùn ga warúì

rotund [routʌnd'] adj (person) 丸々と太

った marúmarù to futóttá

rouble [ru:'bəl] (*BRIT*) *n* = **ruble**

rouge [ru:ʒ] *n* ほお紅 hóbeni

rough [rʌf] *adj* (skin, surface, cloth) 粗い aráì; (terrain, road) 凸凹の dekóboko no; (voice) しゃがれた shagáretà; (person, manner: violent) 荒っぽい aráppoì; (: brusque) ぶっきらぼうな bukkírabò na; (treatment) 荒い aráì; (weather, sea) 荒れた arétà; (town, area) 治安の悪い chiánnò warúì; (plan, sketch) 大まかな ōmaka na; (guess) 大よその ōyoso no

♦*n* (GOLF): **in the rough** ラフに ráfù ni

to rough it 原始的な生活をする geñshiteki nà séfkatsu wò suru

to sleep rough (*BRIT*) 野宿する nójùku suru

roughage [rʌf'idʒ] *n* 繊維 séñ-i

rough-and-ready [rʌf'ənred'i:] *adj* 原始的な geñshiteki na

roughcast [rʌf'kæst] *n* (for wall) 小石を混ぜたしっくい koíshi wò mazétà shikkúì

rough copy *n* 下書き shitágaki

rough draft *n* 素案 soán

roughly [rʌf'li:] *adv* (handle) 荒っぽく aráppokù; (make) 大まかに ōmaka ni; (speak) ぶっきらぼうに bukkírabò ni; (approximately) 大よそ ōyoso

roughness [rʌf'nis] *n* (of surface) 荒さ arása; (of manner) がさつさ gasátsusa

roulette [ru:let'] *n* ルーレット rúretto

Roumania [ru:mei'ni:ə] *n* = **Rumania**

round [raund] *adj* 丸い marúì; (figures, sum) 概数の gaísū no

♦*n* (*BRIT*: of toast) 一切 hitókire; (of policeman, milkman, doctor) 巡回 juñkai; (game: of cards) 一勝負 hitóshòbu; (: in competition) ...回戦 ...kaísen; (of ammunition) 一発 ippátsu; (BOXING) ラウンド ráùndo; (*also*: **round of golf**) ラウンド ráùndo; (of talks) 一回 ichíran

♦*vt* (corner) 回る mawárù

♦*prep* (surrounding): **round his neck/the table** 首〔家〕の回りに kubí(ié)nò mawári ni; (in a circular movement): **to move round the room** 部屋の中を一回りする heyá no nakà wo hitómawarì

suru; **to sail round the world** 世界一周の航海をする sékàìisshū nò kōkai wò suru; (in various directions): **to move round a room/house** 部屋〔家〕の中を動き回る heyá〔ie〕no nakà wo ugókimawaprù; (approximately): **round about 300** 大よそ300 ōyoso saňbyaku

♦*adv*: **all round** 回りに mawári ni

a round of golf ゴルフのワンラウンド górùfu no wañraùndo

the long way round 遠回り tōmawari

all the year round 一年中 ichínenjū

it's just round the corner (*fig*) 直ぐそこまで来ている súgù sokó madè kité irú

to go round to someone's (house) ...のうちへ行く ...no uchí è ikú

to go round the back 裏に回る urá nì mawárù

to go round a house ある家を訪ねる árù ié wò tazúnerù

enough to go round みんなに足りる程 miñna nì tarírù hodó

a round of applause 拍手 hákùshu

a round of drinks/sandwiches みんなに一通りの飲み物〔サンドウイッチ〕をおごる事 miñna nì hitótòri no nomímòno〔safidouicchì〕wo ogórù kotó

roundabout [raund'əbaut] (*BRIT*) *n* (AUT) ロータリー rōtarī; (at fair) メリーゴーラウンド meríḡoraundo

♦*adj* (route) 遠回りの tōmawàri no; (means) 遠回しの tōmawàshi no

rounders [raun'dəːrz] *npl* (game) ラウンダーズ raúndàzu ◇野球に似た英国のゲーム yakyū ni nità eŕkoku no gēmu

roundly [raund'li:] *adv* (*fig*: criticize) 厳しく kibíshikù

round off *vt* (speech etc) 終える oérù

round-shouldered [raund'ʃoulдəːrd] *adj* ねこ背の nekózè no

round trip *n* 往復旅行 ōfukuryokō

round up *vt* (cattle, people) 駆集める karfatsumerù; (price, figure) 概数にする gaísū ni suru

roundup [raund'ʌp] *n* (of news, information) まとめ matóme; (of animals) 駆集め karfatsume; (of criminals) 一斉逮捕

isséitaĭho

rouse [rauz] vt (wake up) 起す okốsù; (stir up) 引起す hikíokosù

rousing [rau'ziŋ] adj (cheer, welcome) 熱狂的な nekkyốteki na

rout [raut] n (MIL) 敗走 haĭsō
♦vt (defeat) 敗走させる haĭsō saserù

route [ru:t] n (way) ルート rǔto; (of bus, train) 路線 rosén; (of shipping) 航路 kốro; (of procession) 通り道 tốrimìchi

route map (BRIT) n (for journey) 道路地図 dốrochizù

routine [ru:ti:n'] adj (work) 日常の nichíjō no; (procedure) お決りの o-kímari no
♦n (habits) 習慣 shūkan; (drudgery) 反復作業 hañpukusagyồ; (THEATER) お決りの演技 o-kímari nò éñgi

rove [rouv] vt (area, streets) はいかいする haíkai suru

row[1] [rou] n (line of people, things) 列 rétsù; (KNITTING) 段 dáñ; (in boat) こぐ事 kogú kotồ
♦vi (in boat) こぐ kogú
♦vt (boat) こぐ kogú
in a row (fig) 一列に ichíretsu ni

row[2] [rau] n (racket) 騒ぎ sáwàgi; (noisy quarrel) 口論 kôron; (dispute) 論争 roñsō; (BRIT inf: scolding) 小言 kogóto
to give someone a row ...に大目玉を食らわす ...ni ốmedàma wo kuráwasù
♦vi (argue) 口論する kôron suru

rowboat [rou'bout] (US) n ボート bốto

rowdy [rau'di:] adj (person: noisy) 乱暴な rañbō na; (occasion) 騒々しい sốzōshiǐ

rowing [rou'iŋ] n (sport) ボートレース bốtorēsu

rowing boat (BRIT) n = **rowboat**

royal [rɔi'əl] adj 国王〔女王〕の kokúố〔jòồ〕no

Royal Air Force (BRIT) n 英国空軍 eĭkokukūgun

royalty [rɔi'əlti:] n (royal persons) 王族 ốzoku; (payment to author) 印税 iñzei

rpm [ɑ:rpi:em'] abbr (= revolutions per minute) 毎分回転数 maĭfunkaiteñsū

RSVP [ɑ:resvi:pi:'] abbr (= répondez s'il vous plaît) 御返事を請う go-héñji wò kôû

Rt Hon. (BRIT) abbr (= Right Hon-

ourable) 閣下 kákkà

rub [rʌb] vt こする kosúrù
♦n: to give something a rub こする kosúrù
to rub one's hands (together) もみ手をする momíde wò suru
to rub someone the wrong way (US) or **to rub someone up the wrong way** (BRIT) 怒らせる okóraserù

rubber [rʌb'ə:r] n (substance) ゴム gốmù; (BRIT: eraser) 消しゴム keshígomu

rubber band n 輪ゴム wagómu

rubber plant n ゴムの木 gómù no ki

rubbery [rʌb'ə:ri:] adj (material, substance) ゴムの様な gómù no yồ na; (meat, food) 固い katáĭ

rubbish [rʌb'iʃ] n (waste material) ごみ gomí; (junk) 廃品 haíhin; (fig: pej: nonsense) ナンセンス náñsensu

rubbish bin (BRIT) n ごみ箱 gomíbako

rubbish dump n ごみ捨て場 gomísuteba

rubble [rʌb'əl] n (debris) がれき garéki; (CONSTR) バラス bárasu

ruble [ru:'bəl] (BRIT **rouble**) n (currency) ルーブル rǔburu

rub off vi (paint) こすり取る kosúritorù

rub off on vt fus ...に移る ...ni utsúrù

rub out vt (erase) 消す késù

ruby [ru:'bi:] n ルビー rǔbǐ

rucksack [rʌk'sæk] n リュックサック ryukkúsakkù

rudder [rʌd'ə:r] n (of ship) かじ kajî; (of plane) 方向かじ hốkōda

ruddy [rʌd'i:] adj (face, complexion) 血色の良い kesshốku no yoĭ; (BRIT: inf: damned) くそったれの kusóttarè no

rude [ru:d] adj (impolite: person, manners, word) 無礼な buréi na; (shocking: word, behavior) 下品な gehín na

rudeness [ru:d'nis] n (impoliteness) 無礼 buréi

rudimentary [ru:dəmen'tə:ri:] adj (equipment, knowledge) 原始的な geñshiteki na

rudiments [ru:'dəmənts] npl (basics) 基本 kihón

rueful [ru:'fəl] adj 悲しい kanáshiĭ

ruffian [rʌf'i:ən] n ごろつき gorótsuki

ruffle [rʌf'əl] vt (hair) 乱す midásù; (clothes) しわくちゃにする shiwákucha ni surù; (fig: person) 怒らせる okóraserù

rug [rʌg] n (on floor) じゅうたん jútan; (BRIT: blanket) ひざ掛け hizákake

rugby [rʌg'bi:] n (also: **rugby football**) ラグビー rágùbī

rugged [rʌg'id] adj (landscape) 岩だらけの iwádarake no; (features) ごつい gotsúì; (character) 無愛想な buáiso na

rugger [rʌg'ə:r] (BRIT: inf) n ラグビー rágùbī

ruin [ru:'in] n (destruction: of building) 破壊 hakái; (: of hopes, plans) ざ折 zasétsu; (downfall) 失墜 shittsúi; (bankruptcy) 破産 hasán; (remains: of building) 廃虚 haíkyo

♦vt (destroy: building) 破壊する hakái suru; (: hopes, plans, health) 壊す kowásù; (: future) 台無しにする daínashi ni surù; (: person) 失墜させる shittsúi saserù; (: financially) 破産に追込む hasán ni oikomù

ruinous [ru:'inəs] adj (expense, interest) 破滅的な hamétsuteki na

ruins [ru:'inz] npl (of building, castle etc) 廃虚 haíkyo

rule [ru:l] n (norm, regulation) 規則 kisóku; (government) 君臨 kuñrin; (ruler) 物差し monósashi

♦vt (country, person) 支配する shíhai suru

♦vi (leader, monarch etc) 君臨する kuñrin suru; (LAW) 裁定する saítei suru

as a rule 普通は futsū wà

ruled [ru:ld] adj (paper) けい紙 keíshi

rule out vt (idea, possibility etc) 除外する jogái suru

ruler [ru:'lə:r] n (sovereign) 元首 géñshu; (for measuring) 物差し monósashi

ruling [ru:'liŋ] adj 支配する shíhai suru

♦n (LAW) 決定 kettéi

ruling party 与党 yótō

ruling class 支配階級 shihaikaíkyū

rum [rʌm] n ラム酒 ramúshu

Rumania [ru:mei'ni:ə] n ルーマニア rúmania

Rumanian [ru:mei'ni:ən] adj ルーマニアの rúmania no; (LING) ルーマニア語の rúmaniagò no

♦n (person) ルーマニア人 rúmaniajìn; (LING) ルーマニア語 rúmaniagò

rumble [rʌm'bəl] n ごう音 gốon, とどろき todóroki

♦vi (make rumbling noise: heavy truck) ごう音を響かせて走る gốon wò hibíkasète hashírù; (: stomach) 鳴る narú; (: pipes) ゴボゴボいう góbògobo iū; (: thunder) とどろく todórokù

rummage [rʌm'idʒ] vi (search) 引っかき回して捜す hikkákimawashìtè sagásù

rumor [ru:'mə:r] (BRIT **rumour**) n うわさ uwása

♦vt: **it is rumored that ....** ...だとうわさされている ...dá tò uwása sarete irù

rump [rʌmp] n (of animal) しり shirí; (of group, political party) 残党 zaňtō

rump steak n ランプステーキ raňpusutēki

rumpus [rʌm'pəs] n 騒ぎ sawági

run [rʌn] n (fast pace: move) 駆け足 kakéashi; (for exercise) ジョギング jogíngu; (in car) ドライブ dóràibu; (distance traveled) 行程 kōtei; (journey) 区間 kukáñ; (series) 継続 keízoku; (SKI) ゲレンデ geréňde; (CRICKET, BASEBALL) 得点 tokúten; (THEATER) 上演期間 jōenkikan; (in tights, stockings) ほころび hokórobi

♦vb (pt **ran**, pp **run**)

♦vt (race, distance) 走る hashírù; (operate: business, hotel) 経営する keíei suru; (: competition, course) 行う okónaù; (: house) ...の切盛りをする ...no kirímori wò suru; (COMPUT) 走らせる hashíraserù; (pass: hand) 通す tōsu; (water) 出す dásù; (bath) ...に水をはる ...ni mizú wò hárù; (PRESS: feature) 載せる nosérù

♦vi (move quickly) 走る hashírù; (flee) 逃げる nigérù; (work: machine) 作動する sadō suru; (bus, train: operate) 動く ugókù; (: travel) 走る hashírù; (continue: play) 上演される jōen sarerù; (: contract) 継続する keízoku suru; (flow: river, liquid) 流れる nagárerù; (colors) 落ちる ochírù; (washing) 色落ちする iróochi suru; (in election) 立候補する rikkṓho suru; (nose) 鼻水が出る hanámizu ga derù

there was a run on ... (meat, tickets) 人々は...を買いに殺到した hitóbìto wa ...wo kaí nì sattố shità

in the long run 行く行く（は）yukú-yuku (wà)

on the run 逃亡中で tṓbōchū de

I'll run you to the station 駅まで車で送ろう ékì made kurúma dè okúrō

to run a risk 危険を冒す kikén wò okásù

run about/around *vi* (children) はしゃぎ回る hashágimawarù

run across *vt fus* (find) 偶然に見付ける gū́zen nì mitsúkerù

run away *vi* (from home, situation) 逃げる nigérù

runaway [rʌn'əwei] *adj* (horse, truck) 暴走の bṓsō no; (person) 逃走中の tṓsōchū no

run down *vt* (production, factory) ...の規模を縮小する ...no kĩbo wo shukúshō suru; (AUT: person) ひく hikú; (criticize) けなす kenásù

to be run down (person: tired) へとへとになっている hetóheto nì natté irù

rung [rʌŋ] *pp of* **ring**

♦*n* (of ladder) 一段 ichídàn

run in (BRIT) *vt* (car) ...のならし運転をする ...no naráshiuǹten wo suru

run into *vt fus* (meet: person, trouble) ...に出会う ...ni deáù; (collide with) ...にぶつかる ...ni butsúkarù

runner [rʌn'əːr] *n* (in race: person) 競走の選手 kyṓsō nò seńshu, ランナー ráǹnā; (: horse) 競走馬 kyṓsōba; (on sledge) 滑り足 subérigi, ランナー ráǹnā; (for drawer etc) レール rḕru

runner bean (BRIT) *n* サヤインゲン sayáiǹgen

runner-up [rʌnəːrʌp'] *n* 第2位入賞者 daí ni-i nyū́shōsha

running [rʌn'iŋ] *n* (sport) ジョギング jogíngu; (of business, organization) 経営 keíei

♦*adj* (water) 水道の suídō no

to be in/out of the running for something ...の候補者である〔でなくなっている〕 ...no kṓhoshà de árù〔de nakúnatte irù〕

6 days running 連続6日間 reńzoku muikakàn

running commentary *n* 生中継 namáchūkei

running costs *npl* (of car, machine etc) 維持費 ijíhi

runny [rʌn'iː] *adj* (honey, egg) 緩い yurúì; (nose) 垂れる tarérù; (eyes) 目やにの出る meyáni nò dérù

run off *vt* (water) ...から流れ落ちる ...kara nagáreochirù; (copies) 印刷する iǹsatsu suru

♦*vi* (person, animal) 逃げる nigérù

run-of-the-mill [rʌnəvðəmil'] *adj* (ordinary) ごく普通の gókù futsū́ no

run out *vi* (person) 走って出る hashítte derù; (liquid) 流れ出る nagárederù; (lease, passport) 切れる kirérù; (money) なくなる nakúnarù

run out of *vt fus* (money, time, ideas) ...がなくなる ...ga nakúnarù

run over *vt* (AUT) ひく hikú

♦*vt fus* (revise) おさらいする o-sárai suru

run through *vt fus* (instructions) ...に目を通す ...ni mé wo tṓsu; (rehearse, practice: play) 一通り練習する hitótōri reńshū suru

run up *vt* (debt) ...がかさむ ...ga kasámù

to run up against (difficulties) ...にぶつかる ...ni butsúkarù

run-up [rʌn'ʌp] *n* (BRIT): **run-up to** (election etc) ...への準備期間 ...é nò juǹbikikàn

runway [rʌn'wei] *n* (AVIAT) 滑走路 kassṓrò

rupee [ruːpiː'] *n* (currency) ルピー rúpī̀

rupture [rʌp'tʃəːr] *n* (MED) ヘルニア herúnia

rural [ruːr'əl] *adj* (area) 田舎の ináka no; (economy) 地方の chihṓ no

ruse [ruːz] *n* 策略 sakúryaku

rush [rʌʃ] *n* (hurry) 大急ぎ ōisogi; (COMM: sudden demand) 急激な需要 kyūgeki nà juyō; (of water, current) 奔流 hońryū; (of feeling, emotion) 高まり takámari; (BOT) イグサ igúsa

♦*vt* (hurry) 急がせる isógaserù

♦*vi* (person) 急ぐ isógù; (air, water) 速く流れる háyaku nagárerù

rush hour *n* ラッシュアワー rasshúawà

rusk [rʌsk] *n* (biscuit) ラスク rásùku

Russia [rʌʃə] *n* ロシア róshìa

Russian [rʌʃ'ən] *adj* ロシアの róshìa no; (LING) ロシア語の roshíagò no

♦*n* (person) ロシア人 roshíajìn; (LING) ロシア語 roshíagò

rust [rʌst] *n* さび sabí

♦*vi* (iron, steel etc) さびる sabírù

rustic [rʌs'tik] *adj* (style, furniture) 田舎風の ináka-fū no

rustle [rʌs'əl] *vi* (leaves) かさかさいう kásàkasa iú

♦*vt* (paper) かさかさ動かす kásàkasa ugókasù; (*US*: cattle) 盗む nusúmù

rustproof [rʌst'pru:f] *adj* (car, machine) さびない sabínaì

rusty [rʌs'ti:] *adj* (car) さびた sábìta; (*fig*: skill) ...の勘が鈍くなった ...no kań gà níbuku natta

rut [rʌt] *n* (groove) わだち wadáchi; (ZOOL: season) 発情期 hatsújòki

to be in a rut 型にはまっている katá nì hamátte irù

ruthless [ru:θ'lis] *adj* (person) 血も涙もない chí mò namída mò náì; (action) 残酷な zańkoku na

rye [rai] *n* (cereal) ライ麦 raímugì

rye bread *n* ライパン raípaǹ

S

Sabbath [sæb'əθ] *n* (Jewish) 土曜日 doyōbi; (Christian) 日曜日 nichíyòbi

sabbatical [səbæt'ikəl] *n* (*also*: **sabbatical year**) 一年休暇 ichínen kyùka ◊7年置きに大学教授などに与えられる1年の長期有給休暇 nanáneǹ okí nì daígakukyòju nádò ni atáerarerù ichínen no chōkiyū-

kyūkyūka

sabotage [sæb'əta:ʒ] *n* 破壊工作 hakái-kōsaku

♦*vt* (machine, building) 破壊する hakái suru; (plan, meeting) 妨害する bōgai suru

saccharin(e) [sæk'ə:rin] *n* サッカリン sakkárìn

sachet [sæʃei'] *n* (of shampoo, sugar, etc) 小袋 kobúkùro ◊一回分ずつのシャンプー、砂糖などを入れた小さな包 ikkáìbun zutsu no sháńpū, satō nádò wo iréta chiīsana tsutsúmi

sack [sæk] *n* (bag: for flour, coal, grain, etc) 袋 fukúro

♦*vt* (dismiss) 首にする kubí ni surù; (plunder) 略奪する ryakúdatsu suru

to get the sack 首になる kubí ni narù

sacking [sæk'iŋ] *n* (dismissal) 解雇 káìko; (material) ズック zúkkù

sacrament [sæk'rəmənt] *n* (ceremony: Protestant) 聖礼典 seíreiteǹ; (: Catholic) 秘跡 hiséki

sacred [sei'krid] *adj* (of religion: music, history, writings) 宗教の shūkyō no; (holy: animal, building, memory) 神聖な shińsei na

sacrifice [sæk'rəfais] *n* (offering of someone/something) 犠牲 giséi; (thing/person offered) いけにえ ikénie

♦*vt* (animal) 殺す korósu; (*fig*: human lives, health, career) 犠牲にする giséi ni surù

sacrilege [sæk'rəlidʒ] *n* 冒とく bōtoku

sacrosanct [sæk'rousæŋkt] *adj* (*also fig*) 神聖な shińsei na

sad [sæd] *adj* (unhappy: person, day, story, news) 悲しい kanáshii; (: look) 悲しそうな kanáshisō na; (deplorable: state of affairs) 嘆かわしい nagékawashiì

saddle [sæd'əl] *n* (for horse) くら kurá; (of bicycle) サドル sadoru

♦*vt* (horse) ...にくらを付ける ...ni kurá wò tsukérù

to be saddled with (*inf*) ...の重荷を負わされる ...no omóni wò owásarerù

saddlebag [sæd'əlbæg] *n* (on bicycle) サ

ドルバッグ sadórubaggù

sadism [sei'dizəm] *n* サディズム sadízumu

sadistic [sədis'tik] *adj* サディスティックな sadísutikkù na

sadly [sæd'li:] *adv* (unhappily) 悲しそうに kanáshisō ni; (unfortunately) 残念ながら zañneñnagara; (seriously: mistaken, neglected) ひどく hídòku

sadly lacking (in) 残念ながら (…が) ない zañneñnagara (…ga) nái

sadness [sæd'nis] *n* 悲しみ kanáshimi

sae [eseii:'] *abbr* (= *stamped addressed envelope*) 返信用封筒 heñshin-yō fútō ◇ 宛先を書き，切手を張った物を指す atésaki wò kákì, kitté wò hattá mono wò sásù

safari [səfɑː'ri:] *n* サファリ sáfàri

safe [seif] *adj* (out of danger) 安全な場所にいる〔ある〕 añzen na bashò ni irú 〔árù〕; (not dangerous, sure: place) 安全な añzen na; (unharmed: return, journey) 無事な bují na; (without risk: bet, subject, appointment) 安全な añzen na, 安心できる añshin dekirù; (: seat in parliament) 落選する恐れのない rakúsen suru osore nò nái

◆*n* (for valuables, money) 金庫 kíñko

safe from (attack) …される心配のない場所にいる〔ある〕 …saréru shiñpai no nái báshò ni irú 〔árù〕

safe and sound (return, sleep, etc) 無事で bují de

(just) to be on the safe side 念のために neñ no tame nì

safe-conduct [seif'kɑːn'dʌkt] *n* (right to pass) 通行許可 tsúkōkyokà

safe-deposit [seif'dipɑːzit] *n* (vault) 貸金庫室 kashíkìñkoshitsu; (*also*: **safe deposit box**) 貸金庫 kashíkìñko

safeguard [seif'gɑːrd] *n* 保護手段 hogóshudàn

◆*vt* 保護する hógò suru

safekeeping [seifki:'piŋ] *n* 保管 hokán

safely [seif'li:] *adv* (without risk: assume, say) 安心して añshin shite; (without mishap: drive) 安全に añzen ni; (arrive) 無事に bují ni

safety [seif'ti:] *n* 安全 añzen

safety belt *n* 安全ベルト añzenberùto, シートベルト shítoberùto

safety pin *n* 安全ピン añzeñpin

safety valve *n* 安全弁 añzeñben

saffron [sæf'rən] *n* (powder) サフラン sáfùran

sag [sæg] *vi* (breasts, hem) 垂れ下がる tarésagarù; (roof) 凹む kubómu

saga [sæg'ə] *n* (long story, *also fig*) 長編物語 chóhenmonogatàri

sage [seidʒ] *n* (herb) セージ sèji; (wise man) 賢人 keñjiñ

Sagittarius [sædʒiteːr'i:əs] *n* (sign of Zodiac) 射手座 ítèzà

Sahara [səheːr'ə] *n: the Sahara (Desert)* サハラ砂漠 sahára sabàku

said [sed] *pt, pp of* **say**

sail [seil] *n* (on boat) 帆 hó; (trip): *to go for a sail* ヨットに乗る yóttò ni noru

◆*vt* (boat) 操縦する sójū suru

◆*vi* (travel: ship) 航海する kókai suru; (SPORT) ヨットに乗る yóttò ni norú; (begin voyage: ship) 出航する shukkő suru; (: passenger) 船で出発する fúnè de shuppátsu suru

they sailed into Copenhagen 彼らはコペンハーゲンに入港した kárèra wa kopénhàgen ni nyúkō shità

sailboat [seil'bout] (*US*) *n* ヨット yóttò

sailing [sei'liŋ] *n* (SPORT) ヨット遊び yottóasòbi

to go sailing ヨットに乗る yóttò ni norú, ヨット遊びをする yottóasòbi wo suru

sailing boat *n* ヨット yóttò

sailing ship *n* 帆船 hañsen

sailor [sei'ləːr] *n* (seaman) 船乗り funánòri

sail through *vt fus* (fig. exams, interview etc) …に楽々と合格する …ni rakúrakù to gókaku suru

saint [seint] *n* (*also fig*) 聖人 sèjin

saintly [seint'li:] *adj* (person, life, expression) 聖人の様な sèjin no yő nà

sake [seik] *n: for the sake of someone/something* …のために …no tamé nì

salad [sæl'əd] *n* サラダ sáràda

salad bowl *n* サラダボール sarádabòru

salad cream (*BRIT*) *n* マヨネーズ mayónèzu

salad dressing *n* サラダドレッシング sarádadoresshìngu

salami [səlɑ:'mi:] *n* サラミ sáràmi

salary [sæl'ə:ri:] *n* 給料 kyú̀ryò

sale [seil] *n* (act of selling: commercial goods etc) 販売 hañbai; (: house, land etc) 売却 baíkyaku; (at reduced prices) 安売り yasúuri, セール sèru; (auction) 競売 kyóbai

「**for sale**」売物 urímono

on sale 発売中 hatsúbaichū

on sale or return (goods) 委託販売で itákuhañbai de

saleroom [seil'ru:m] *BRIT n* = **salesroom**

sales [seilz] *npl* (total amount sold) 売上 uríage

sales clerk (*BRIT* **sales assistant**) *n* 店員 teñ-in

salesman [seilz'mən] (*pl* **salesmen**) *n* (in shop) 男子店員 dañshiteñ-in; (representative) セールスマン sérusumàn

salesroom [seilz'ru:m] (*US*) *n* 競売場 kyóbaijo

saleswoman [seilz'wumən] (*pl* **saleswomen**) *n* 女子店員 joshíteñ-in

salient [sei'li:ənt] *adj* (features, points) 重要な júyò na

saliva [səlaiv'ə] *n* だ液 daéki

sallow [sæl'ou] *adj* (complexion) 血色の悪い kesshóku nò warúi

salmon [sæm'ən] *n inv* サケ sákè

salon [səlɑn'] *n* (hairdressing salon, beauty salon) 美容院 biyóìn

saloon [səlu:n'] *n* (*US*: bar) 酒場 sakába; (*BRIT*: AUT) セダン sédàn; (ship's lounge) 広間 hírōma

salt [sɔ:lt] *n* 塩 shió
◆*vt* (preserve: fish, beef, etc) 塩漬にする shiózukè ni suru; (put salt on) ...に塩を掛ける ...ni shió wò kakérù

salt cellar *n* 塩入れ shió-ire

saltwater [sɔ:lt'wɔ:tə:r] *adj* (fish, plant) 海水の kaísui no

salty [sɔ:l'ti:] *adj* しょっぱい shoppái

salutary [sæl'jəte:ri:] *adj* (lesson, reminder) ためになる tamé ni narù

salute [səlu:t'] *n* (MIL) 敬礼 keírei; (with guns) 礼砲 reíhō; (*gen*: greeting) あいさつ áisatsu
◆*vt* (MIL) ...に敬礼する ...ni keírei suru; (*fig*) ...に敬意を表す ...ni kéì wo aráwasù

salvage [sæl'vidʒ] *n* (action: *gen*) 救助作業 kyújo sagyò; (: of shipwreck) 海難救助作業 kaínan kyújo sagyò; (things saved) サルベージ sarúbèji, 救助された物 kyújo sareta monó
◆*vt* 救助する kyújo suru; (*fig*: situation etc) 収拾する shúshu suru

salvation [sælvei'ʃən] *n* (REL) 霊魂の救い reíkon no sukúi; (economic etc) 救済 kyúsai

Salvation Army *n* 救世軍 kyúseigùn

salvo [sæl'vou] *n* (in battle) 一斉射撃 isséishagèki; (ceremonial) 一斉祝砲 isséishukùhō

same [seim] *adj* 同じ onáji
◆*pron: the same* 同じ物 onáji monò
the same book as ...と同じ本 ...to onáji hoñ
at the same time (at the same moment) 同時に dójì ni; (yet) とはいえ tó wà ie
all/just the same それにしても soré ni shite mò
to do the same (as someone) (...と) 同じ事をする (...to) onáji koto wò suru
the same to you! お前もだ omáe mo dà ◇侮辱を返す時に言う bujóku wò kaésu toki nì iú

sample [sæm'pəl] *n* (MED: blood/urine sample) 検体 keñtai, サンプル sáñpuru; (of work, merchandise) 見本 mihón, サンプル sáñpuru
◆*vt* (food) 試食する shishóku suru; (drink) 試飲する shiín suru

sanatoria [sænətɔ:r'i:ə] *npl of* **sanatorium**

sanatorium [sænətɔ:r'i:əm] (*pl* **sanatoria**) *n* = **sanitarium**

sanctify [sæŋk'təfai] *vt* 神聖にする shiñsei ni surù

sanctimonious [sæŋktəmou'ni:əs] *adj*

(person, remarks) 宗教心を装う shúkyō-shin wo yosóoú

sanction [sæŋk'ʃən] n (approval) お墨付き osúmitsùki, 認可 nínka

♦vt (give approval to) 認可する nínka suru

sanctions [sæŋk'ʃənz] npl (severe measures) 制裁処置 seísaishochì

sanctity [sæŋk'titi:] n 神聖さ shiñseisa

sanctuary [sæŋk'tʃuːeːriː] n (also: **bird sanctuary**) 鳥類保護区 chōruihogokù, サンクチュアリ sañkuchùari; (place of refuge) 避難所 hináñjo; (REL: in church) 内陣 naíjin

sand [sænd] n (material, fine grains) 砂 suná; (beach: also: **sands**) 砂浜 sunáhama

♦vt (piece of furniture: also: **sand down**) 紙やすりで磨く kamíyasùri de migáku

sandal [sæn'dəl] n (shoe) サンダル sañdaru

sandbox [sænd'baːks] US n (for children) 砂場 sunába

sandcastle [sænd'kæsəl] n 砂の城 suná no shirò

sand dune n 砂丘 sakyū́

sandpaper [sænd'peipəːr] n 紙やすり kamíyasùri, サンドペーパー sañdopèpā

sandpit [sænd'pit] (BRIT) n = **sandbox**

sandstone [sænd'stoun] n 砂岩 ságàn

sandwich [sænd'witʃ] n サンドイッチ sañdoitchì

♦vt: **sandwiched between** ...の間に挟まれて ...no aída nì hasámarète

cheese/ham sandwich チーズ〔ハム〕サンドイッチ chízù 〔hámù〕sañdoitchì

sandwich course (BRIT) n サンドイッチコース sañdoitchikòsu ◇勉強と現場実習を交互に行う課程 beñkyō tò geñbajisshū wo kōgo ni okónaù katéi

sandy [sæn'diː] adj (beach) 砂の suná no; (color) 砂色の suná-iro no

sane [sein] adj (person) 正気の shōki no; (sensible: action, system) 合理的な gōriteki na

sang [sæŋ] pt of **sing**

sanitarium [sæniterr'iːəm] (US) n 療養所 ryōyōjo, サナトリウム sanátoriùmu

sanitary [sæn'iteːriː] adj (system, arrangements, inspector) 衛生の eísei no; (clean) 衛生的な eíseiteki na

sanitary napkin (BRIT **sanitary towel**) n 生理用ナプキン seíriyō napùkin

sanitation [sænitei'ʃən] n (in house) 衛生設備 eíseisetsùbi; (in town) 下水道設備 gesúidōsetsùbi

sanitation department (US) n 清掃局 seísōkyòku

sanity [sæn'iti:] n (quality of being sane: of person) 正気 shōki; (common sense: of suggestion etc) 合理性 gōrisei

sank [sæŋk] pt of **sink**

Santa Claus [sæn'tə klɔːz] n サンタクロース sañtakurōsu

sap [sæp] n (of plants) 樹液 juéki

♦vt (strength, confidence) 失わせていく ushínawasete ikù

sapling [sæp'liŋ] n 苗木 naégi

sapphire [sæf'aiəːr] n サファイア safáìa

sarcasm [sɑːr'kæzəm] n 皮肉 hiníku

sarcastic [sɑːrkæs'tik] adj (person) いやみ好きな iyámisukì na; (remark, smile) 皮肉な hiníku na

sardine [sɑːrdiːn'] n イワシ iwáshi

Sardinia [sɑːrdin'iːə] n サルディニア島 sarúdiniatò

sardonic [sɑːrdɑːn'ik] adj (smile) あざける様な azákeru yō na

sari [sɑː'riː] n サリー sárì

sash [sæʃ] n (Western) サッシュ sásshù; (Japanese) 帯 óbì

sat [sæt] pt, pp of **sit**

Satan [sei'tən] n 大魔王 daímaò, サタン sátàn

satchel [sætʃ'əl] n (child's) かばん kabán

satellite [sæt'əlait] n (body in space) 衛星 eísei; (communications satellite) 通信衛星 tsūshin-eisèi

satellite dish n パラボラアンテナ parábora añtena

satin [sæt'ən] n サテン sátèn

♦adj サテンの sátèn no

satire [sæt'aiəːr] n (form of humor) 風刺 fūshi; (novel) 風刺小説 fūshishōsetsu; (play) 風刺劇 fūshigekì

satirical [sətir'ikəl] adj (remarks, drawings etc) 風刺の fúshi no

satisfaction [sætisfæk'ʃən] n (pleasure) 満足 mánzoku; (refund, apology etc) 謝罪 shazái

satisfactory [sætisfæk'tə:ri:] adj (patient's condition) 良い yói; (results, progress) 満足できる mánzoku dekirù

satisfy [sæt'isfai] vt (please) 満足させる mánzoku saserù; (meet: needs, demand) …に応じる …ni ójirù; (convince) 納得させる nattóku saserù

satisfying [sæt'isfaiiŋ] adj (meal, job, feeling) 満足な mánzoku na

saturate [sæt'ʃərei] vt: to saturate (with) (also fig) (…で)一杯にする (…de) ippái ni surù

saturation [sætʃərei'ʃən] n (also fig) 飽和状態 hówajòtai

Saturday [sæt'ə:rdei] n 土曜日 doyóbì

sauce [sɔ:s] n (sweet, savory) ソース sósù

saucepan [sɔ:s'pæn] n ソースパン sósupàn

saucer [sɔ:'sə:r] n 受皿 ukézàra, ソーサ sósà

saucy [sɔ:'si:] adj (cheeky) ずうずうしい zúzùshiì

Saudi [sau'di:]: **Saudi Arabia** n サウジアラビア saújiaràbia

Saudi (Arabian) adj サウジアラビアの saújiaràbia no

sauna [sɔ:'nə] n サウナ sáùna

saunter [sɔ:n'tə:r] vi のんびりと歩く noñbirì to árùku

sausage [sɔ:'sidʒ] n ソーセージ sósèji

sausage roll n ソーセージパン sósèjipàn

sauté [sɔ:tei'] adj: sauté potatoes フライポテト furáipotèto

savage [sæv'idʒ] adj (cruel, fierce: dog) どうもうな dómò na; (: attack) 残忍な zañnin na; (primitive: tribe) 未開な mikái na
♦n 野蛮人 yabáñjin

savagery [sæv'idʒri:] n 残忍さ zanninsa

save [seiv] vt (rescue: someone, someone's life, marriage) 救う sukúu; (economize on: money, time) 節約する setsúyaku suru; (put by: receipts etc) 取って置く tótte oku; (: money) 蓄える takúwaeru;

(COMPUT) 格納する kakúnô suru, セーブする sèbu suru; (avoid: work, trouble) 省く habúkù; (keep: seat) 確保する kákùho suru; (SPORT: shot, ball) セーブする sèbu suru
♦vi (also: **save up**) 貯金する chokín suru
♦n (SPORT) セーブ sébu
♦prep (except) (…を) 除いて (…wo) nozóite

saving [sei'viŋ] n (on price etc) 節約 setsúyaku
♦adj: the saving grace of something …の唯一の長所 …no yúitsu no chôshò

savings [sei'viŋz] npl (money) 貯金 chokín

savings account n 普通預金口座 futsúyokinkôza

savings bank n 普通銀行 futsúgiñkō

savior [seiv'jə:r] (BRIT **saviour**) n (gen) 救い主 sukúinùshi; (REL) 救世主 kyúseìshu

savor [sei'və:r] (BRIT **savour**) vt (food, drink, experience) 味わう ajíwaù

savory [sei'və:ri:] (BRIT **savoury**) adj (dish: not sweet: spicy) ぴりっとした piríttò shita; (: salt-flavored) 塩味の shióajì no

saw [sɔ:] n (tool) のこぎり nokógirì
♦vt (pt **sawed**, pp **sawed** or **sawn**) のこぎりで切る nokógirì de kírù
♦pt of see

sawdust [sɔ:'dʌst] n のこくず nokókuzù

sawed-off [sɔ:d'ɔ:f] n (US): **sawed-off shotgun** 短身散弾銃 tañshin sandanjû ◊ のこぎりで銃身を短くした散弾銃 nokógirì de jûshin wò mijíkaku kittà sañdanjû

sawmill [sɔ:'mil] n 製材所 seízaisho

sawn-off [sɔ:n'ɔ:f] adj (BRIT) = **sawed-off**

saxophone [sæk'səfoun] n サキソホーン sakísohôn

say [sei] n: to have one's say 意見を言う íkèn wo iú
♦vt (pt, pp **said**) 言う iú
to have a/some say in something …についてある程度の発言権がある …ni tsuíte áru teidò no hatsúgeñken ga árù

to say yes/no 承知する〔しない〕shōchi suru (shinaī)

could you say that again? もう一度言ってくれませんか mō ichidò itté kuremaseň ka

that is to say つまり tsúmari

that goes without saying それは言うまでもない soré wà iú made mo naī

saying [sei'iŋ] *n* (proverb) ことわざ kotówaza; (words of wisdom) 格言 kakúgen; (often repeated phrase) 愛用の言葉 aíyō no kotoba

scab [skæb] *n* (on wound) かさぶた kasábuta; (*pej*: strike-breaker) スト破り sutóyabùri

scaffold [skæf'əld] *n* (for execution) 死刑台 shikéidai; (for building etc) = **scaffolding**

scaffolding [skæf'əldiŋ] *n* 足場 ashíba

scald [skɔːld] *n* やけど yakédo ◇熱湯や蒸気などによるやけどを指す nettō yà jōkí nado ni yórù yakédo wò sásù

◆*vt* (burn: skin) やけどさせる yakédo saserù

scale [skeil] *n* (*gen*: set of numbers) 目盛 memóri; (of salaries, fees etc) 表 hyō; (of fish) うろこ uróko; (MUS) 音階 oňkai; (of map, model) 縮小率 shukúshōrītsu; (size, extent) 規模 kíbò

◆*vt* (mountain, tree) 登る nobórù

on a large scale 大規模で daíkibò de

scale of charges 料金表 ryōkinhyò

scale down *vt* 縮小する shukúshō suru

scales [skeilz] *npl* (for weighing) 量り hakári

scallop [skɑːl'əp] *n* (ZOOL) ホタテガイ hotátegài; (SEWING) スカラップ sukárappù

scalp [skælp] *n* 頭の皮膚 atáma no hifù, 頭皮 tōhi

◆*vt* ...の頭皮をはぐ ...no tōhî wo hágù

scalpel [skæl'pəl] *n* メス mésù

scamper [skæm'pəːr] *vi*: ***to scamper away/off*** (child, animal) ぱたぱた走って行く pátàpata hashítte ikù

scampi [skæm'pi:] *npl* エビフライ ebífuràì

scan [skæn] *vt* (examine: horizon) 見渡す miwátasu; (glance at quickly: newspaper) ...にさっと目を通す ...ni sáttò mé wò tōsù; (TV, RADAR) 走査する sōsa suru

◆*n* (MED) スキャン sukyán

scandal [skæn'dəl] *n* (shocking event) 醜聞 shūbun, スキャンダル sukyáňdaru; (defamatory: reports, rumors) 陰口 kagéguchi; (gossip) うわさ uwása; (*fig*: disgrace) 恥ずべき事 hazúbeki kotó

scandalize [skæn'dəlaiz] *vt* 憤慨させる fuňgai saserù

scandalous [skæn'dələs] *adj* (disgraceful, shocking: behavior etc) 破廉恥な harénchi na

Scandinavian [skændənei'vi:ən] *adj* スカンディナビアの sukáňdinabìa no

scant [skænt] *adj* (attention) 不十分な fujūbun na

scanty [skæn'ti:] *adj* (meal) ささやかな sasáyàka na; (underwear) 極めて小さい kiwámète chíísaì

scapegoat [skeip'gout] *n* 身代り migáwari

scar [skɑːr] *n* (on skin: *also fig*) 傷跡 kizúato

◆*vt* (*also fig*) 傷跡を残す kizúato wò nokósù

scarce [ske:rs] *adj* (rare, not plentiful) 少ない sukúnaì

to make oneself scarce (*inf*) 消えうせる kiéuserù

scarcely [ske:rs'li:] *adv* (hardly) ほとんど...ない hotóňdo ...naî; (with numbers: barely) わずかに wázùka ni

scarcity [ske:r'siti:] *n* (shortage) 不足 fusóku

scare [ske:r] *n* (fright) 恐怖 kyōfu; (public fear) 恐慌 kyōkō

◆*vt* (frighten) 怖がらす kowágarasù

bomb scare 爆弾騒ぎ bakúdan sawàgi

to scare someone stiff ...に怖い思いをさせる ...ni kowái omoì wo saserù

scarecrow [ske:r'krou] *n* かかし kakáshi

scared [ske:rd] *adj*: ***to be scared*** 怖がる kowágarù

scare off/away *vt* おどかして追払う odókashite oiharaù

scarf [skɑ:rf] (*pl* **scarfs** *or* **scarves**) *n* (long) マフラー máfūrā; (square) スカーフ sukáfù

scarlet [skɑ:r'lit] *adj* (color) ひ色 hííro

scarlet fever *n* しょう紅熱 shōkōnetsu

scarves [skɑ:rvz] *npl of* **scarf**

scary [ske:r'i:] (*inf*) *adj* 怖い kowáî

scathing [skei'ðiŋ] *adj* (comments, attack) 辛らつな shiríratsu na

scatter [skæt'ə:r] *vt* (spread: seeds, papers) まき散らす makíchirasù; (put to flight: flock of birds, crowd of people) 追散らす oíchirasù

◆*vi* (crowd) 散る chirú

scatterbrained [skæt'ə:rbreind] (*inf*) *adj* (forgetful) おつむの弱い o-tsúmù no yowáî

scavenger [skæv'indʒə:r] *n* (person) くず拾い kuzúhiroǐ

scenario [sine:r'i:ou] *n* (THEATER, CINEMA) 脚本 kyakúhon, シナリオ shinárìo; (*fig*) 筋書 sujígaki

scene [si:n] *n* (THEATER, *fig*) 場 ba, シーン shìn; (of crime, accident) 現場 geńba; (sight, view) 景色 késhìki; (fuss) 騒ぎ sáwàgi

scenery [si:'nə:ri:] *n* (THEATER) 大道具 ódōgu; (landscape) 景色 késhìki

scenic [si:'nik] *adj* (picturesque) 景色の美しい késhìki no utsúkushiî

scent [sent] *n* (pleasant smell) 香り kaóri; (track) 通った後のにおい tōtta átò no nióì; (*fig*) 手がかり tegákàri; (liquid perfume) 香水 kōsui

scepter [sep'tə:r] (*BRIT* **sceptre**) *n* しゃく shaku

sceptic [skep'tik] (*BRIT*) *n* = **skeptic** *etc*

schedule [skedʒ'u:l] *n* (of trains, buses) 時間割 jikánwari; (list of events and times) 時刻表 jikókuhyō; (list of prices, details etc) 表 hyō

◆*vt* (timetable, visit) 予定する yotéi suru

on schedule (trains, buses) 定刻通りに teíkokudòri ni; (project etc) 予定通りに yotéidòri ni

to be ahead of schedule 予定時間より

早い yotéijikàn yórì hayáî

to be behind schedule 予定時間に遅れる yotéijikàn ni okúrerù

scheduled flight [skedʒ'u:ld-] *n* 定期便 teíkibin

schematic [ski:mæt'ik] *adj* (diagram etc) 模式的な moshíkiteki na

scheme [ski:m] *n* (personal plan, idea) もくろみ mokúromi; (dishonest plan, plot) 陰謀 iñbō; (formal plan: pension plan etc) 計画 keíkaku, 案 áñ; (arrangement) 配置 haíchi

◆*vi* (intrigue) たくらむ takúramù

scheming [ski:'miŋ] *adj* 腹黒い haráguroî

◆*n* たくらむ事 takúramù kotó

schism [skiz'əm] *n* 分裂 buńretsu

schizophrenic [skitsəfren'ik] *adj* 精神分裂症の seíshinbunretsushō no

scholar [skɑ:l'ə:r] *n* (pupil) 学習者 gakúshùsha; (learned person) 学者 gakúsha

scholarly [skɑ:l'ə:rli:] *adj* (text, approach) 学問的な gakúmonteki na; (person) 博学的な hakúgakuteki na

scholarship [skɑ:l'ə:rʃip] *n* (academic knowledge) 学問 gakúmòn; (grant) 奨学金 shōgakukìn

school [sku:l] *n* (place where children learn: *gen*) 学校 gakkō; (*also:* **elementary school**) 小学校 shōgakkō; (*also:* **secondary school:** lower) 中学校 chūgakkō; (: higher) 高(等学)校 kō(tōgak)kō; (*US:* university) 大学 daígaku

◆*cpd* 学校の gakkō no

school age *n* 学齢 gakúrei

schoolbook [sku:l'buk] *n* 教科書 kyōkashò

schoolboy [sku:l'bɔi] *n* 男子生徒 dañshiseíto

schoolchildren [sku:l'tʃildrən] *npl* 生徒 seíto

schooldays [sku:l'deiz] *npl* 学校時代 gakkōjidài

schoolgirl [sku:l'gə:rl] *n* 女子生徒 joshíseíto

schooling [sku:'liŋ] *n* (education at school) 学校教育 gakkōkyōiku

schoolmaster [sku:l'mæstə:r] *n* 教師

kyōshi, 教員 kyōin, 先生 señsei ◇男子教員 dañshikyōin

schoolmistress [sku:l'mistris] *n* 教師 kyōshi, 教員 kyōin, 先生 señsei ◇女子教員 joshíkyōin

schoolteacher [sku:l'ti:tʃə:r] *n* 教師 kyōshi, 教員 kyōin, 先生 señsei ◇男女を問わず使う dáñjo wo tōwàzu tsukáù

schooner [sku:'nə:r] *n* (ship) 帆船 hañsen

sciatica [saiæt'ikə] *n* 座骨神経痛 zakótsushinkeìtsū

science [sai'əns] *n* (study of natural things) 科学 kágàku; (branch of such knowledge) ...学 ...gàku

science fiction *n* 空想科学物語 kūsōkagakumonogatàri, SF esuéfu

scientific [saiəntif'ik] *adj* (research, instruments) 科学の kágàku no

scientist [sai'əntist] *n* 科学者 kagákushà

scintillating [sin'təleitiŋ] *adj* (*fig*: conversation, wit, smile) 輝く様な kagáyakù yō na

scissors [siz'ə:rz] *npl* (*also*: **a pair of scissors**) はさみ hasámi

scoff [ska:f] *vt* (*BRIT*: *inf*: eat) がつがつ食う gátsùgatsu kúù
◆*vi*: **to scoff (at)** (mock) ...をあざける ...wo azákerù

scold [skould] *vt* しかる shikárù

scone [skoun] *n* スコーン sukóñ ◇小さなホットケーキの一種 chíisa na hottókèki no ísshù

scoop [sku:p] *n* (measuring scoop: for flour etc) スコップ sukóppù; (for ice cream) サーバー sábà; (*PRESS*) スクープ sukúpù

scoop out *vt* すくい出す sukúidasù

scoop up *vt* すくい上げる sukúiagerù

scooter [sku:'tə:r] *n* (*also*: **motor scooter**) スクーター sukútà; (toy) スクーター sukútà ◇片足を乗せて走る遊び道具 katáashi wo nosetè hashírù asóbidògu

scope [skoup] *n* (opportunity) 機会 kikái; (range: of plan, undertaking) 範囲 háñ-i; (: of person) 能力 nōryoku

scorch [skɔ:rtʃ] *vt* (clothes) 焦がす kogásù; (earth, grass) 枯らす karásù

score [skɔ:r] *n* (total number of points etc) 得点 tokúteñ, スコア sukóà; (*MUS*) 楽譜 gakúfu; (twenty) 20 nijū
◆*vt* (goal, point, mark) 取る tórù; (achieve: success) 収める osámerù
◆*vi* (in game) 得点する tokúteñ suru; (*FOOTBALL etc*) トライする torái suru; (keep score) 得点を記録する tokúteñ wo kirókù suru

scores of (very many) 多数の tasū no

on that score その点に関して sonó teñ ni kañshitè

to score 6 out of 10 10回中6回成功する jukkáichū rokkaì seíkò suru

scoreboard [skɔ:r'bɔ:rd] *n* スコアボード sukóabòdo

score out *vt* 線を引いて消す séñ wo hiíte kesú

scorn [skɔ:rn] *n* 軽べつ keíbetsu
◆*vt* 軽べつする keíbetsu suru

scornful [skɔ:rn'fəl] *adj* (laugh, disregard) 軽べつ的な keíbetsuteki na

Scorpio [skɔ:r'pi:ou] *n* (sign of Zodiac) さそり座 sasóriza

scorpion [skɔ:r'pi:ən] *n* サソリ sasóri

Scot [ska:t] *n* スコットランド人 sukóttorandojìn

Scotch [ska:tʃ] *n* (whisky) スコッチ sukótchì

scotch [ska:tʃ] *vt* (end: rumor) 消し止める keshítomerù; (plan, idea) 没にする bótsù ni suru

scot-free [ska:t'fri:'] *adv*: **to get off scot-free** (unpunished) 何の罰も受けない náñ no bátsù mo ukénaì

Scotland [ska:t'lənd] *n* スコットランド sukóttorandò

Scots [ska:ts] *adj* (accent, people) スコットランドの sukóttorandò no

Scotsman [ska:ts'mən] (*pl* **Scotsmen**) *n* スコットランドの男性 sukóttorandò no dansei

Scotswoman [ska:ts'wumən] (*pl* **Scotswomen**) *n* スコットランドの女性 sukóttorandò no joséi

Scottish [ska:t'iʃ] *adj* (history, clans, people) スコットランドの sukóttorandò no

scoundrel [skaun'drəl] n 悪党 akútō

scour [skauər] vt (search: countryside etc) くまなく捜し回る kumánaku sagáshimawarù

scourge [skərdʒ] n (cause of trouble: also fig) 悩みの種 nayámi no tanè

scout [skaut] n (MIL) 斥候 sekkō; (also: **boy scout**) ボーイスカウト bōisukaùto

girl scout (US) ガールスカウト gārusukaùto

scout around vi 捜し回る sagáshimawarù

scowl [skaul] vi 顔をしかめる káò wo shikámerù

to scowl at someone しかめっつらをして …をにらむ shikámettsura wò shité …wo nirámù

scrabble [skræb'əl] vi (claw): **to scrabble (at)** (…を)引っかく (…wo) hikkákù; (also: **scrabble around**: search) 手探りで探す teságùri de sagásù

◆n: **Scrabble** ® スクラッブル sukúrabbùru ◇単語作りゲーム tañgozukurigēmu

scraggy [skræg'i:] adj (animal, body, neck etc) やせこけた yasékoketà

scram [skræm] (inf) vi (get away fast) うせる usérù

scramble [skræm'bəl] n (difficult climb) よじ上り yojínobori; (struggle, rush) 奪い合い ubáiai

◆vi: **to scramble out/through** 慌てて出る〔通る〕 awátete derù〔tōru〕

to scramble for …の奪い合いをする …no ubáiai wo surù

scrambled eggs [skræm'bəld-] npl いり卵 iritamago, スクランブルエッグ sukúranburu eggù

scrap [skræp] n (bit: of paper, material etc) 切れ端 kiréhashi, (: of information) 少し sukóshì; (fig: of truth) 欠けら kakéra; (fight) けんか keñka; (also: **scrap iron**) くず鉄 kuzútetsu

◆vt (discard: machines etc) くず鉄にする kuzútetsu ni surù; (fig: plans etc) 捨てる sutérù

◆vi (fight) けんかする keñka suru

scrapbook [skræp'buk] n スクラップブック sukúrappubukkù

scrap dealer n くず鉄屋 kuzútetsuyà

scrape [skreip] n (fig: difficult situation) 窮地 kyūchi

◆vt (scrape off: potato skin etc) むく mukú; (scrape against: hand, car) こする kosúrù

◆vi: **to scrape through** (exam etc) …をどうにか切抜ける …wo dō ni ka kirínukerù

scrape together vt (money) かき集める kakíatsumerù

scrap heap n (fig): **on the scrap heap** 捨てられて sutérarete

scrap merchant n (BRIT) = **scrap dealer**

scrap paper n 古い紙 furúi kamí, 古紙 kóshì, ほご hógò

scrappy [skræp'i:] adj (piece of work) 雑な zatsú na

scraps [skræps] npl (leftovers: food, material etc) くず kúzù

scratch [skrætʃ] n (cut: on body, furniture: also from claw) かき傷 kakíkizu

◆cpd: **scratch team** 寄集めチーム yoséatsumechīmu

◆vt (rub: one's nose etc) かく kákù; (damage: paint, car) 傷付ける kizútsukerù; (with claw, nail) ひっかく hikkákù

◆vi (rub one's body) …をかく …wo kákù

to start from scratch 何もない所から始める naní mo naí tokóro karà hajímerù

to be up to scratch いい線をいっている íi séñ wo itté irù

scrawl [skrɔːl] n なぐり書き nagúrigaki

◆vi なぐり書きする nagúrigaki suru

scrawny [skrɔː'ni:] adj (person, neck) やせこけた yasékoketà

scream [skri:m] n 悲鳴 himéi

◆vi 悲鳴を上げる himéi wo agerù

scree [skri:] n 岩くず iwákuzu ◇崩れ落ちてたい積した岩くずを指す kuzúreochitè taíseki shità iwákuzu wo sasú

screech [skri:tʃ] vi (person) 金切り声を出す kanákirigoè wo dásù; (bird) きーきー声で鳴く kīkīgoè de nakú; (tires, brakes) きーきーと鳴る kīkī to nárù

screen [skri:n] n (CINEMA) スクリーン

sukúrìn; (TV, COMPUT) ブラウン管bu-
ráunkan; (movable barrier) ついたて
tsuítate; (fig: cover) 幕 makú

♦vt (protect, conceal) 覆い隠す ốikakusù; (from the wind etc) ...の...によけになる
...no...ni narù; (film) 映写する eísha
suru; (television program) 放映する hốei
suru; (candidates etc) 審査する shínsa
suru

screening [skri:'niŋ] n (MED) 健康診断
keńkōshiñdan

screenplay [skri:n'plei] n 映画脚本 eígakyakùhon

screw [skru:] n (for fixing something) ね
じ néjì

♦vt (fasten) ねじで留める neji de tomérù

screwdriver [skru:'draivə:r] n ねじ回し
nejímawashì

screw up vt (paper etc) くしゃくしゃに
する kushákùsha ni suru

to screw up one's eyes 目を細める mé
wò hosómerù

scribble [skrib'əl] n 走り書き hashírigaki

♦vt (write carelessly: note etc) 走り書き
する hashírigaki suru

♦vi (make meaningless marks) 落書する
rakúgaki suru

script [skript] n (CINEMA etc) 脚本
kyakúhon, スクリプト sukúripùto; (system of writing) 文字 mójì

scripture(s) [skrip'tʃə:r(z)] n(pl) (holy
writing(s) of a religion) 聖典 seíten

scroll [skroul] n (official paper) 巻物 makímono

scrounge [skraundʒ] vt (inf): *to
scrounge off/from someone* ...に...をねだる ...ni...wo nedárù

♦n: *on the scrounge* たかって takátte

scrub [skrʌb] n (land) 低木地帯 teíbokuchitài

♦vt (rub hard: floor, hands, pan, washing) ごしごし洗う góshìgoshi aráù; (inf:
reject: idea) 取り止める toríyamerù

scruff [skrʌf] n: *by the scruff of the
neck* 首筋をつかんで kubísuji wò tsukáñde

scruffy [skrʌf'i:] adj (person, object,
appearance) 薄汚い usúgitanaì

scrum(mage) [skrʌm'(idʒ)] n (RUGBY)
スクラム sukúràmu

scruple [skru:'pəl] n (gen pl) 良心のとが
め ryőshìn no togáme

scrupulous [skru:'pjələs] adj (painstaking: care, attention) 細心の saíshin
no; (fair-minded: honesty) 公正な kősei
na

scrutinize [skru:'tənaiz] vt (examine
closely) 詳しく調べる kuwáshikù shiráberù

scrutiny [skru:'təni:] n (close examination) 吟味 gíñmi

to keep someone under scrutiny ...を
監視する ...wo kañshi suru

scuff [skʌf] vt (shoes, floor) すり減らす
suríherasù

scuffle [skʌf'əl] n (fight) 乱闘 rañtō

sculptor [skʌlp'tə:r] n 彫刻家 chốkoku-ka

sculpture [skʌlp'tʃə:r] n 彫刻 chōkoku

scum [skʌm] n (on liquid) 汚い泡 kitánaì
awá; (pej: people) 人間のくず niñgen nồ
kúzù

scupper [skʌp'ə:r] (BRIT: inf) vt (plan,
idea) 邪魔して失敗させる jamá shitè
shippái saserù

scurrilous [skə:r'ələs] adj 口汚い kuchígitanaì

scurry [skə:r'i:] vi ちょこちょこ走る chókòchoko hashírù

scurry off vi ちょこちょこ走って行く
chókòchoko hashítte ikù

scuttle [skʌt'əl] n (also: **coal scuttle**) 石
炭入れ sekítan-ire

♦vt (ship) 沈没させる chiñbotsu saserù

♦vi (scamper): *to scuttle away/off* ち
ょこちょこ走っていく chókòchoko hashítte ikù

scythe [saið] n 大がま ồgama ◇柄も刃も
長いかま mố hấ mò nagáì kámà

sea [si:] n 海 úmì; (fig: very many) 多数
tasū; (: very much) 多量 taryố

♦cpd (breeze, bird, air etc) 海の úmì no

by sea (travel) 海路で kấiro de

on the sea (boat) 海上で kaíjō de;
(town) 海辺の umíbe no

out to/at sea 沖に okí ni
to be all at sea (fig) 頭が混乱している atáma gà końran shité irù
a sea of faces (fig) 顔の海 kaó nò úmì

seaboard [siːˈbɔːrd] *n* 海岸 kaígan

seafood [siːˈfuːd] *n* 魚介類 gyokáirùi, シーフード shífùdo ◇料理に使う魚介類を指す ryốri ni tsukáù gyokáirùi wo sásù

seafront [siːˈfrʌnt] *n* 海岸 kaígan ◇海辺の町などの海沿いの部分を指す umíbe no machí nadò no umízoi no bubún wo sásù

sea-going [siːˈgouiŋ] *adj* (ship) 遠洋航海用の eń-yōkōkaiyồ no

seagull [siːˈgʌl] *n* カモメ kamóme

seal [siːl] *n* (animal) アザラシ azárashi ◇セイウチを除いて全てのひれ足類を含む seíuchì wo nozóìte súbète no hiréashirùi wo fúkumù; (official stamp) 印章 ińshō; (closure) 封印 fúin
♦*vt* (close: envelope) ...の封をする ...no fú wò suru; (: opening) 封じる fújirù

sea level *n* 海抜 kaíbatsu

sea lion *n* トド tódò

seal off *vt* (place) 封鎖する fūsa suru

seam [siːm] *n* (line of stitches) 縫目 nuíme; (where edges meet) 継目 tsugíme, 合せ目 awáseme; (of coal etc) 薄層 hakúsō

seaman [siːˈmən] (*pl* **seamen**) *n* 船乗り funánòri

seamy [siːˈmiː] *adj*: *the seamy side of* ...の汚い裏面 ...no kitánaì rímèn, ...の恥部 ...no chíbù

seance [seiˈɑːns] *n* 降霊会 kốreìkai

seaplane [siːˈplein] *n* 水上飛行機 suíjōhikồki

seaport [siːˈpɔːrt] *n* 港町 minátomàchi

search [səːrtʃ] *n* (hunt: for person, thing) 捜索 sōsaku; (COMPUT) 探索 tańsaku, 検索 keńsaku; (inspection: of someone's home) 家宅捜査 katákusòsa
♦*vt* (look in: place) ...の中を捜す ...no nákà wo sagásù; (examine: memory) 捜す sagásù; (person) ...の身体検査をする ...no shińtaikeǹsa wo suru
♦*vi*: *to search for* ...を捜す ...wo sagásù
in search of ...を求めて ...wo motómetè

searching [səːrˈtʃiŋ] *adj* (question, look) 鋭い surúdoì

searchlight [səːrtʃˈlait] *n* サーチライト sáchiraìto

search party *n* 捜索隊 sōsakutai

search through *vt fus* ...の中をくまなく捜す ...no nákà wo kumánàku sagásù

search warrant *n* 捜査令状 sōsareijồ

seashore [siːˈʃɔːr] *n* 海岸 kaígan

seasick [siːˈsik] *adj* 船酔いになった funáyòi ni náttà

seaside [siːˈsaid] *n* 海辺 umíbe

seaside resort *n* 海辺の行楽地 umíbe nò kốrakuchì

season [siːˈzən] *n* (of year) 季節 kisétsu; (time of year for something: football season etc) シーズン shízun; (series: of films etc) シリーズ shírìzu
♦*vt* (food) ...に味を付ける ...ni ají wò tsukérù
in season (fruit, vegetables) しゅんで shúń de
out of season (fruit, vegetables) 季節外れで kisétsuhàzure de

seasonal [siːˈzənəl] *adj* (work) 季節的な kisétsuteki na

seasoned [siːˈzənd] *adj* (fig: traveler) 経験豊かな keíken yutàka na

seasoning [siːˈzəniŋ] *n* 調味料 chốmiryồ, 薬味 yakúmi

season ticket *n* (RAIL) 定期券 teíkikèn; (THEATER) シーズン入場券 shízun nyūjồken

seat [siːt] *n* (chair) いす isú; (in vehicle, theater: place) 席 sékì; (PARLIAMENT) 議席 giséki; (buttocks: *also* of trousers) しり shirí
♦*vt* (place: guests etc) 座らせる suwáraserù; (subj: table, theater: have room for) ...人分の席がある ...nińbun no sékì ga árù
to be seated 座る suwárù

seat belt *n* シートベルト shítoberùto

sea water *n* 海水 kaísui

seaweed [siːˈwiːd] *n* 海草 kaísō

seaworthy [siːˈwəːrðì] *adj* (ship) 航海に耐えられる kốkai nì taérarerù

sec. *abbr* = **second(s)**

secluded [sikluːˈdid] *adj* (place) 人里離れた hitózato hanaretà; (life) 隠とんの ińton no

seclusion [sıklu:'ʒən] *n* 隔離 kákùri

second [sek'ənd] *adj* (after first) 第二 (の) dái nī (no)
♦*adv* (come, be placed: in race etc) 二番 に níbàn ni; (when listing) 第二に dái nī ni
♦*n* (unit of time) 秒 byǒ; (AUT: *also*: **second gear**) セカンド sekándo; (COMM: imperfect) 二流品 niryūhìn; (BRIT: SCOL: degree) 2級優等卒業学位 níkyū yūtō sotsugyō gakùi ¶ *see also* **first**
♦*vt* (motion) ...に支持を表明する ...ni shíjì wo hyṓmei suru; (BRIT: worker) 派遣 する hakén suru

secondary [sek'ənde:ri:] *adj* (less important) 二次的な nijíteki na

secondary school *n* 中等高等学校 chútōkōtōgakkṓ

second-class [sek'əndklæs'] *adj* (hotel, novel, work) 二流の niryū no; (tickets, transport) 2等の nitṓ no
♦*adv* (travel) 2等で nitṓ de

secondhand [sek'əndhænd'] *adj* (clothing, car) 中古の chūko no

second hand *n* (on clock) 秒針 byōshìn

secondly [sek'əndli:] *adv* 2番目に nibánme ni

secondment [sek'əndmənt] (BRIT) *n* 派遣 hakén

second-rate [sek'əndreit'] *adj* (film etc) 二流の niryū no

second thoughts *npl* ためらい tamérai
on second thought (US) *or* *thoughts* (BRIT) 気が変って ki gá kawattè

secrecy [si:'krisi:] *n*: *to swear someone to secrecy* ...に秘密を誓わせる ...ni hímìtsu wò chikáwaserù

secret [si:'krit] *adj* (plan, passage, agent) 秘密の hímitsu no; (admirer, drinker) ひそかな hisókà na
♦*n* 秘密 hímìtsu
in secret 内密に naímitsu ni

secretarial [sekrite:r'i:əl] *adj* (work, course, staff, studies) 秘書の hishó no

secretariat [sekrite:r'i:ət] *n* 事務局 jimúkyòku

secretary [sek'rite:ri:] *n* (COMM) 秘書 hishó; (of club) 書記 shokí
Secretary of State (for) (BRIT: POL) (...)大臣 (...)dáìjin

secretion [sikri:'ʃən] *n* (substance) 分泌物 bunpitsubùtsu

secretive [si:'kritiv] *adj* 秘密主義の hímìtsushùgi no

secretly [si:'kritli:] *adv* (tell, marry) 内密に naímitsu ni

sect [sekt] *n* 宗派 shūha

sectarian [sekte:r'i:ən] *adj* (riots etc) 宗派間の shūhakàn no

section [sek'ʃən] *n* (part) 部分 búbùn; (department) ...部 ...bù; (of document) 章 shō; (of opinion) 一部 ichíbù; (cross-section) 断面図 dañmenzù

sector [sek'tə:r] *n* (part) 部門 búmòn; (MIL) 戦闘地区 señtōchikù

secular [sek'jələ:r] *adj* (music, society etc) 世俗の sezóku no; (priest) 教区の kyṓku no

secure [sikjur'] *adj* (safe: person) 安全な場所にいる añzen na bashò ni irú; (: money) 安全な場所にある añzen na bashò ni árù; (: building) 防犯対策完備の bṓhantaisakukañbi no; (firmly fixed, strong: rope, shelf) 固定された kotéi saretà
♦*vt* (fix: rope, shelf etc) 固定する kotéi suru; (get: job, contract etc) 確保する kakúho suru

security [sikju:r'iti:] *n* (protection) 警備 kéĩbi; (for one's future) 保証 hoshṓ; (FINANCE) 担保 tánpo

sedan [sidæn'] (US) *n* (AUT) セダン sédàn

sedate [sideit'] *adj* (person, pace) 落着いた ochítsuità
♦*vt* (MED: with injection) ...に鎮静剤を注射する ...ni chíñseizài wo chūshà suru; (: with pills etc) ...に鎮静剤を飲ませる ...ni chíñseizài wo nomáserù

sedation [sidei'ʃən] *n* (MED): *under sedation* 薬で鎮静されて kusúri dè chíñsei saretè

sedative [sed'ətiv] *n* 鎮静剤 chíñseizài

sedentary [sed'ənte:ri:] *adj* (occupation,

work) 座ってする suwátte surù

sediment [sed'əmənt] n (in bottle) おり orí; (in lake etc) 底のたい積物 sokó nò taísekibùtsu

seduce [sidu:s'] vt (entice: gen) 魅了する miryō̂ suru; (: sexually) 誘惑する yūwaku suru, たらし込む taráshikomù

seduction [sidʌk'ʃən] n (attraction) 魅惑 miwáku; (act of seducing) 誘惑 yūwaku

seductive [sidʌk'tiv] adj (look, voice, also fig offer) 誘惑的な yūwakuteki na

see [si:] (pt **saw**, pp **seen**) vt (gen) 見る mírù; (accompany): **to see someone to the door** ...を戸口まで送る ...wo tógùchi mádè okúrù; (understand) 分かる wakárù

◆vi (gen) 見える miérù; (find out) 調べる shiráberù

◆n (REL) 教区 kyṓkù

to see that someone does something ...が...する様に気を付ける ...ga...surú yō ni kí wo tsukérù

see you soon! またね matá nè

see about vt fus ...の問題を調べて片付ける ...no moñdai wò shirábete katazùkeru

seed [si:d] n (of plant, fruit) 種 tánè; (sperm) 精液 seíeki; (fig: gen pl) 種 tánè; (TENNIS) シード shīdo

to go to seed (plant) 種ができる tánè ga dekírù; (fig) 衰える otóroerù

seedling [si:d'liŋ] n 苗 náè

seedy [si:'di:] adj (shabby: person, place) 見すぼらしい misúborashiì

seeing [si:'iŋ] conj: **seeing (that)** ...だから ...dákàra

seek [si:k] (pt, pp **sought**) vt (truth, shelter, advice, post) 求める motómerù

seem [si:m] vi ...に見える ...ni miérù

there seems to be ... ...がある様です ...ga árù yṓ desù

seemingly [si:'miŋli:] adv ...らしく ...rashíkù

seen [si:n] pp of **see**

see off vt ...を見送る ...wo miókurù

seep [si:p] vi (liquid, gas) 染み透る shimítòru

seesaw [si:'sɔ:] n シーソー shísò

seethe [si:ð] vi (place: with people/things) 騒然としている sōzen shite irù

to seethe with anger 怒りで煮え繰り返る ikári dè niékurikaerù

see through vt 最後までやり通す saígo madè yarítòsu

◆vt fus 見抜く minúkù

see-through [si:'θru:] adj (blouse etc) すけすけルックの sukésukerukkù no

see to vt fus ...の世話をする ...no sewá wò suru

segment [seg'mənt] n (part: gen) 一部 ichíbù; (of orange) ふさ fusá

segregate [seg'rəgeit] vt 分ける wakérù

seismic [saiz'mik] adj (activity) 地震の jishín no

seize [si:z] vt (grasp) つかむ tsukámù; (take possession of: power, control, territory) 奪う ubáù; (: hostage) 捕まえる tsukámaerù; (opportunity) 捕える toráerù

seize up vi (TECH: engine) 焼き付く yakétsukù

seize (up)on vt fus ...に飛付く ...ni tobítsukù

seizure [si:'ʒə:r] n (MED) 発作 hossá; (LAW) 没収 bosshū; (: of power) 強奪 gōdatsu

seldom [sel'dəm] adv めったに...ない méttà ni...náì

select [silekt'] adj (school, group, area) 一流の ichíryū no

◆vt (choose) 選ぶ erábù

selection [silek'ʃən] n (being chosen) 選ばれる事 erábareru kotò; (COMM: range available) 選択 seńtaku

selective [silek'tiv] adj (careful in choosing) 選択的な seńtakuteki na; (not general: strike etc) 限られた範囲の kagíraretà háñ-i no

self [self] (pl **selves**) n: **the self** 自我 jígà

◆prefix 自分で(の)... jibúñ de (no) ...

self-assured [self'əʃu:rd'] adj 自信のある jishín no arù

self-catering [self'kei'tə:riŋ] adj (BRIT: holiday, apartment) 自炊の jisúi no

self-centered [self'sen'tə:rd] (BRIT **self-centred**) adj 自己中心の jikóchūshinno

self-colored [self'kʌl'ə:rd] (*BRIT* **self-coloured**) *adj* (of one color) 単色の tañshoku no

self-confidence [self'ka:n'fidəns] *n* 自信 jishín

self-conscious [self'ka:n'tʃəs] *adj* (nervous) 照れる teréru

self-contained [self'kənteind'] (*BRIT*) *adj* (flat) 設備完備の setsúbikañbi no

self-control [self'kəntroul'] *n* 自制 jiséi

self-defense [self'difens'] (*BRIT* **self-defence**) *n* 自己防衛 jikóbòei
 in self-defense 自己防衛で jikóbòei de

self-discipline [self'dis'əplin] *n* 気力 kíryòku

self-employed [self'implɔid'] *adj* 自営業の jiéigyò no

self-evident [self'ev'idənt] *adj* 自明の jiméi no

self-governing [self'gʌv'ə:rniŋ] *adj* 独立の dokúritsu no

self-indulgent [self'indʌl'dʒənt] *adj* 勝手気ままな kattékimama na

self-interest [self'in'trist] *n* 自己利益 jikórièki

selfish [sel'fiʃ] *adj* 身勝手な migátte na

selfishness [sel'fiʃnis] *n* 利己主義 rikóshùgi

selfless [self'lis] *adj* 献身的な keñshinteki na

self-made [self'meid'] *adj*: *self-made man* 自力でたたき上げた人 jiríki dè tatákiageta hitò

self-pity [self'pit'i:] *n* 自己れんびん jikóreñbin

self-portrait [self'pɔ:r'trit] *n* 自画像 jigázò

self-possessed [self'pəzest'] *adj* 落着いた ochítsuità

self-preservation [self'prezə:rvei'ʃən] *n* 本能的自衛 hoñnōtekijièi

self-respect [self'rispekt'] *n* 自尊心 jisóñshin

self-righteous [self'rai'tʃəs] *adj* 独善的な dokúzenteki na

self-sacrifice [self'sæk'rəfais] *n* 献身 keñshin

self-satisfied [self'sæt'isfaid] *adj* 自己満足の jikómañzoku no

self-service [self'sə:r'vis] *adj* (shop, restaurant, service station) セルフサービスの serúfusàbisu no

self-sufficient [self'səfiʃ'ənt] *adj* (farm, country) 自給自足の jikyūjisòku no; (person) 独立独歩の dokúritsudoppò no

self-taught [self'tɔ:t'] *adj* 独学の dokúgàku no

sell [sel] (*pt, pp* **sold**) *vt* (*gen*) 売る urú; (*fig*: idea) 売込む uríkomù
 ♦*vi* (goods) 売れる urérù
 to sell at/for $10 値段は10ドルである nedán wà 10 dórù de árù

sell-by date [sel'bai-] (*BRIT*) *n* 賞味期限 shōmikigèn

seller [sel'ə:r] *n* 売手 uríte

selling price [sel'iŋ-] *n* 値段 nedán

sell off *vt* 売払う uríharaù

sell out *vi* (use up stock): *to sell out (of something)* (...が)売切れる (...ga) uríkirerù
 the tickets are sold out 切符は売切れだ kippú wà uríkire da

sellotape [sel'əteip] ® (*BRIT*) *n* セロテープ serótèpu

selves [selvz] *pl of* **self**

semaphore [sem'əfɔ:r] *n* 手旗 tebáta

semblance [sem'bləns] *n* 外観 gaíkan

semen [si:'mən] *n* 精液 seíeki

semester [simes'tə:r] (*US*) *n* 学期 gakkí

semi... [sem'i:] *prefix* 半分の... hañbun no ...

semicircle [sem'i:sə:rkəl] *n* 半円形 hañeñkei

semicolon [sem'i:koulən] *n* セミコロン semíkòroñ

semiconductor [semi:kəndʌk'tə:r] *n* 半導体 hañdōtai

semidetached (house) [semi:ditætʃt'] (*BRIT*) *n* 二戸建て住宅 nikódate jùtaku

semifinal [semi:fai'nəl] *n* 準決勝 juñkesshò

seminar [sem'əna:r] *n* セミナー sémìnā

seminary [sem'əne:ri:] *n* (REL) 神学校 shiñgakkò

semiskilled [semi:skild'] *adj* (work,

worker) 半熟練の hañjukùren no

senate [sen'it] *n* 上院 jóin

senator [sen'ətər] *n* 上院議員 jóingiìn

send [send] (*pt, pp* **sent**) *vt* (dispatch) 送る okúrù; (transmit: signal) 送信する sōshin suru

send away *vt* (letter, goods) 送る okúrù; (unwelcome visitor) 追払う oíharaù

send away for *vt fus* 郵便で注文する yūbin dè chūmon suru

send back *vt* 送り返す okúrikaesù

sender [send'ər] *n* 差出人 sashídashinìn

send for *vt fus* (thing) 取寄せる toríyoseru; (person) 呼寄せる yobíyoserù

send off *vt* (goods) 送る okúrù; (*BRIT*: SPORT: player) 退場させる taíjō saserù

send-off [send'ɔːf] *n: a good send-off* 素晴らしい送別 subárashii sōbetsu

send out *vt* (invitation) 送る okúrù; (signal) 発信する hasshín suru

send up *vt* (price, blood pressure) 上昇させる jōshō saserù; (astronaut) 打上げる uchíagerù; (*BRIT*: parody) 風刺する fūshi suru

senile [si:'nail] *adj* 老いぼれた oíboretà, ぼけた bókèta; (*MED*) 老人性の rōjinsei no

senior [si:n'jə:r] *adj* (older) 年上の toshíue no; (on staff: position, officer) 幹部の kánbu no; (of higher rank: partner) 上級の jókyū no

senior citizen *n* 老人 rōjin, 高齢者 kōreishà

seniority [si:njɔːr'iti:] *n* (in service) 年功 nefíkō

sensation [sensei'ʃən] *n* (feeling) 感覚 kañkaku; (great success) 大成功 daísei-kō

sensational [sensei'ʃənəl] *adj* (wonderful) 素晴らしい subárashiî; (causing much interest: headlines) 扇情的な señjōteki na; (: result) センセーショナルな señsēshònaru na

sense [sens] *n* (physical) 感覚 kañkaku; (feeling: of guilt, shame etc) 感じ kañji; (good sense) 常識 jōshiki; (meaning: of word, phrase etc) 意味 ímì

◆*vt* (become aware of) 感じる kañjirù

it makes sense (can be understood) 意味が分かる ímì ga wakáru; (is sensible) 賢明だ kefímei dà

sense of humor ユーモアを解する心 yūmòa wo kaí surù kokórò, ユーモアのセンス yūmòa no sénsu

senseless [sens'lis] *adj* (pointless: murder) 無意味な muími na; (unconscious) 気絶した kizétsu shità

sensible [sen'səbəl] *adj* (person) 利口な, rikő na; (reasonable: price, advice) 合理的な gőriteki na; (: decision, suggestion) 賢明な kefímei na

sensitive [sen'sətiv] *adj* (understanding) 理解のある ríkai no árù; (nerve, skin) 敏感な bíñkan na; (instrument) 高感度の kőkando no; (*fig*: touchy: person) 怒りっぽい okórippòi; (: issue) 際どい kiwádoì

sensitivity [sensətiv'əti:] *n* (understanding) 理解 ríkai; (responsiveness: to touch etc) 敏感さ bíñkansa; (: of instrument) 感度 kándo; (touchiness: of person) 怒りっぽさ okórippòsa; (delicate nature: of issue etc) 際どさ kiwádosà

sensual [sen'ʃuːəl] *adj* (of the senses: rhythm etc) 官能的な kafínōteki na; (relating to sexual pleasures) 肉感的な nikkánteki na

sensuous [sen'ʃuːəs] *adj* (lips, material etc) 官能的な kafínōteki na

sent [sent] *pt, pp of* **send**

sentence [sen'təns] *n* (LING) 文 búñ; (LAW) 宣告 señkoku

◆*vt: to sentence someone to death/to 5 years in prison* ...に死刑〔懲役5年〕の判決を言渡す ...ni shikéi〔chōeki gonèn〕nò hañketsu wò iíwatasù

sentiment [sen'təmənt] *n* (tender feelings) 感情 kañjō; (opinion, *also* pl) 意見 íkèn

sentimental [sentəmen'təl] *adj* (song) 感傷的な kañshōteki na, センチメンタルな señchimeñtaru na; (person) 情にもろい jō nì morói

sentry [sen'tri:] *n* 番兵 bañpei

separate [*adj* sep'rit *vb* sep'əreit] *adj* (distinct: piles, occasions, ways, rooms) 別々の betsúbetsu no

◆*vt* (split up: people, things) 分ける wakérù; (make a distinction between: twins) 見分ける miwákerù; (: ideas etc) 区別する kubétsu suru

◆*vi* (split up, move apart) 分かれる wakárerù

separately [sep'ritli:] *adv* 別々に betsúbetsu ni

separates [sep'rits] *npl* (clothes) セパレーツ sepárētsu

separation [separei'ʃən] *n* (being apart) 分離 bunri; (time spent apart) 別れ別れになっている期間 wakárewakàre ni natté irù kikàn; (LAW) 別居 bekkyó

September [septem'bə:r] *n* 9月 kúgatsu

septic [sep'tik] *adj* (wound, finger etc) 感染した kañsen shita

septic tank *n* 浄化槽 jókasò

sequel [si:'kwəl] *n* (follow-up) 後日談 gojítsudàn; (of film, story) 続編 zokúhen

sequence [si:'kwins] *n* (ordered chain) 連続 reñzoku; (also: **dance sequence, film sequence**) 一場面 ichíbamèn, シークエンス shíkuensu

sequin [si:'kwin] *n* シークイン shíkuìn, スパンコール supánkòru

serene [səri:n'] *adj* (smile, expression etc) 穏やかな odáyàka na

serenity [səren'iti:] *n* 穏やかさ odáyàkasa

sergeant [sɑ:r'dʒənt] *n* (MIL etc) 軍曹 gúñsō; (POLICE) 巡査部長 juñsabuchō

serial [si:r'i:əl] *n* 連続物 reñzokumono

serialize [si:r'i:əlaiz] *vt* (in newspaper, magazine) 連載する reñsai suru; (on radio, TV) 連続物として放送する reñzokumono toshitè hősò suru

serial number *n* 製造番号 seízōbañgō

series [si:r'i:z] *n inv* (group) 一連 ichíren; (of books, TV programs) シリーズ shirízù

serious [si:r'i:əs] *adj* (person, manner) 真剣な shiñken na; (important: matter) 大事な daíji na; (grave: illness, condition) 重い omóì

seriously [si:r'i:əsli:] *adv* (talk, take) 真剣に shiñken ni; (hurt) ひどく hídòku

seriousness [si:r'i:əsnis] *n* (of person,

manner) 真剣さ shiñkensa; (importance) 重大さ júdaisa; (gravity) 重さ omósa

sermon [sə:r'mən] *n* (also *fig*) 説教 sekkyó

serrated [se:rei'tid] *adj* (edge, knife) のこぎり状の nokógirijō no

serum [si:r'əm] *n* 血清 kesséi

servant [sə:r'vənt] *n* (gen) 召使い meshítsukài; (*fig*) 人に仕える物 hitó nì tsukáerù monő

serve [sə:rv] *vt* (gen: company, country) 仕える tsukáerù; (in shop: goods) 売る urú; (: customer) ...の用をうかがう ...no yő wò ukágaù; (subj: train) ...の足になる ...no ashí nì naru; (apprenticeship) 務める tsutómerù

◆*vi* (at table) 給仕する kyúji suru; (TENNIS) サーブする sábu suru; (be useful):

to serve as/for ...として役に立つ ...toshîtè yakú ni tatsù

◆*n* (TENNIS) サーブ sábu

to serve to do ...をするのに役に立つ ...wo suru nò ni yakú ni tatsù

it serves him right 自業自得だ jigőjitòku da

to serve a prison term 服役する fukúeki suru

serve out/up *vt* (food) 出す dásù

service [sə:r'vis] *n* (gen: help) 役に立つ事 yakú ni tatsù koto; (in hotel) サービス sábisu; (REL) 式 shikí; (AUT) 整備 seíbi; (TENNIS) サーブ sábu; (plates, dishes etc) 一そろい hitósoroì; (also: **train service**) 鉄道の便 tetsúdō nò bén; (also: **plane service**) 空の便 sórà no bén

◆*vt* (car, washing machine) 整備する seíbi suru

military/national service 兵役 heîeki

to be of service to someone ...に役に立つ ...ni yakú ni tatsù

serviceable [sə:r'visəbəl] *adj* 役に立つ yakú ni tatsù

service area *n* (on motorway) サービスエリア sábisu erîa

service charge (*BRIT*) *n* サービス料 sábisuryő

serviceman [sə:r'vismæn] (*pl* **servicemen**) *n* (MIL) 軍人 guñjin

Services [sə:r'visiz] *npl*: *the Services* (army, navy etc) 軍隊 gúñtai

service station *n* ガソリンスタンド gasórinsutañdo; (*BRIT*: on motorway) サービスエリア sábisu erìa

serviette [sə:rvi:et'] (*BRIT*) *n* 紙ナプキン kamínapùkin

servile [sə:r'vail] *adj* (person, obedience) おもねる様な omóneru yō na

session [sej'ən] *n* (period of activity: recording/drinking session) ...するために集まる事 ...surú tame nì atsúmaru kotò

to be in session (court) 開廷中である kaíteichū de arù; (Parliament etc) 開会中である kaíkaichū de arù

set [set] *n* (collection of things) 一そろい hitósoroì, 一式 isshíki, セット séttò; (radio set) ラジオ rájìo; (TV set) テレビ térèbi; (TENNIS) セット séttò; (group of people) 連中 reñchū; (MATH) セット séttò; (CINEMA, THEATER) 舞台装置 butáisōchi, セット séttò; (HAIRDRESSING) セット séttò

♦*adj* (fixed: rules, routine) 決りの kimári no; (ready) 用意ができた yōi ga dekíta

♦*vb* (*pt, pp* set)

♦*vt* (place) 置く ókù; (fix, establish: time, price, rules etc) 決める kimérù; (: record) 作る tsukúrù; (adjust: alarm, watch) セットする séttò suru; (impose: task) 命ずる meízurù; (: exam) 作る tsukúrù

♦*vi* (sun) 沈む shizúmù; (jam, jelly, concrete) 固まる katámarù; (broken bone) 治る naórù

to set the table 食卓の用意をする shokútaku nò yōi wo suru

to be set on doing something どうしても...をすると決めている dōshite mo ...wo suru tò kiméte irù

to set to music ...に曲を付ける ...ni kyokú wo tsukérù

to set on fire ...に火を付ける ...ni hí wò tsukérù

to set free 放してやる hanáshite yarù, 自由にする jiyū ni surù

to set something going ...を始めさせる

...wo hajímesaserù

to set sail 出航する shukkō suru

set about *vt fus* (task) 始める hajímerù

set aside *vt* (money etc) 取って置く tóttè oku; (time) 空けておく akéte okù

set back *vt* (cost): *to set someone back $5* 5ドル払わなければならない go dőrù haráwànakereba naránaì; (in time): *to set someone back (by)* ...を (...) 遅らせる ...wo (...) okúraserù

setback [set'bæk] *n* (hitch) 苦難 kúnàn

set menu *n* 定食メニュー teíshokumenyū

set off *vi* 出発する shuppátsu suru

♦*vt* (bomb) 爆発させる bakúhatsu saserù; (alarm) 鳴らす narásù; (chain of events) ...の引金となる ...no hikígane to narù; (show up well: jewels) 引立たせる hikítataserù

set out *vi* (depart) 出発する shuppátsu suru

♦*vt* (arrange: goods etc) 並べて置く narábete okù; (state: arguments) 述べる nobérù

to set out to do something ...をするつもりである ...wo suru tsumori de arù

settee [seti:'] *n* ソファー sófà

setting [set'iŋ] *n* (background) 背景 haíkei; (position: of controls) セット séttò; (of jewel) はめ込み台 hamékomidài

the setting of the sun 日没 nichíbotsu

settle [set'əl] *vt* (argument, matter) ...に決着を付ける ...ni ketcháku wò tsukérù; (accounts) 清算する seísan suru; (MED: calm: person) 落着かせる ochítsukaserù

♦*vi* (*also*: **settle down**) 一カ所に落着く ikkáshò ni ochítsukù; (bird) 降りる orírù; (dust etc) つく tsukú; (calm down: children) 静まる shizúmarù

to settle for something ...で我慢する ...de gámàn suru

to settle on something ...に決める ...ni kimérù

settle in *vi* 新しい所に落着く atárashiì tokórò ni ochítsukù

settle up *vi*: *to settle up with someone* ...に借金を返す ...ni shakkíñ wo káèsu

settlement [set'əlmənt] n (payment) 清算 seísan; (agreement) 和解 wakái; (village etc) 集落 shúraku

settler [set'lə:r] n 入植者 nyúshokushà

set up vt (organization) 設立する setsúritsu suru

setup [set'ʌp] n (organization) 機構 kikó; (situation) 様子 yósu, 状況 jókyō

seven [sev'ən] num 七(の) nánà (no), 七つ(の) nanátsù (no)

seventeen [sev'ənti:n'] num 十七(の) júnanà (no)

seventh [sev'ənθ] num 第七(の) dái nanà (no)

seventy [sev'ənti:] num 七十(の) nanájù (no)

sever [sev'ə:r] vt (artery, pipe) 切断する setsúdan suru; (relations) 切る kírù, 断つ tátsù

several [sev'ə:rəl] adj (things) 幾つかの íkutsu ka no; (people) 幾人かの íkunin ka no

♦pron 幾つか íkùtsu ka

several of us 私たちの中から幾人か watákushitàchi no nákà kara íkunin ka

severance [sev'ə:rəns] n (of relations) 断交 daňkō

severance pay n 退職金 taíshokukin

severe [sivi:r'] adj (serious: pain) 激しい hagéshiì; (: damage) 大きな ōkì na; (: shortage) 深刻な shiňkoku na; (hard: winter, climate) 厳しい kibíshiì; (stern) 厳格な geňkaku na; (plain: dress) 簡素な káňso na

severity [siver'iti:] n (seriousness: of pain) 激しさ hagéshisa; (: of damage) 大きさ ōkisa; (: of shortage) 深刻さ shiňkokusa; (bitterness: of winter, climate) 厳しさ kibíshisa; (sternness) 厳格さ geňkakusa; (plainness: of dress) 簡素さ kaňsosa

sew [sou] (pt **sewed**, pp **sewn**) vt 縫う núù

sewage [su:'idʒ] n (waste) 汚水 osúì

sewer [su:'ə:r] n 下水道 gesúìdō

sewing [sou'iŋ] n (activity) 裁縫 saíhō; (items being sewn) 縫物 nuímono

sewing machine n ミシン míshìn

sewn [soun] pp of **sew**

sew up vt (item of clothing) 縫い合せる nuíawaserù

sex [seks] n (gender) 性別 seíbetsu; (lovemaking) セックス sékkùsu

to have sex with someone …とセックスをする …to sékkùsu wo suru

sexist [seks'ist] adj 性差別の seísabètsu no

sextet [sekstet'] n (group) セクステット sekúsutettò

sexual [sek'ʃu:əl] adj (of the sexes: reproduction) 有性の yúsei no; (: equality) 男女の dáňjo no; (of sex: attraction) 性的な seíteki na; (: relationship) 肉体の nikútai no

sexy [sek'si:] adj (pictures, underwear etc) セクシーな sékùshī na

shabby [ʃæb'i:] adj (person, clothes) 見すぼらしい misúborashiì; (trick, treatment) 卑劣な hirétsu na

shack [ʃæk] n バラック barákkù

shackles [ʃæk'əlz] npl (on foot) 足かせ ashíkasè; (on hands) 手かせ tékàse; (fig) 束縛 sokúbaku

shade [ʃeid] n (shelter) 日陰 hikáge; (also: **lampshade**) ランプのかさ ráňpu no kásà; (of colour) 色合 iróaì; (small quantity): **a shade too large** ちょっと大き過ぎる chottó ōkisugirù

♦vt (shelter) …の日よけになる …no hiyóke ni narù; (eyes) …に手をかざす …ni té wò kazásù

in the shade 日陰に hikáge ni

a shade more もうちょっと mó chottò

shadow [ʃæd'ou] n 影 kágè

♦vt (follow) 尾行する bikó suru

shadow cabinet (BRIT) n (POL) 影の内閣 kágè no naíkaku

shadowy [ʃæd'oui:] adj (in shadow) 影の多い kágè no ōì; (dim: figure, shape) 影の様な kágè no yó nà

shady [ʃei'di:] adj (place) 日陰のある hikáge no arù; (trees) 日よけになる hiyóke ni narù; (fig: dishonest: person, deal) いかがわしい ikágawashiì

shaft [ʃæft] n (of arrow) 矢柄 yagára; (of spear) 柄 e; (AUT, TECH) 回転軸 kaíteňjiku, シャフト sháfùto; (of mine) 縦坑 tatékō; (of elevator) 通路 tsūrò

a shaft of light 一条の光 ichíjō no hikarì

shaggy [ʃæg'iː] *adj* (appearance, beard, dog) ぼさぼさの bosábosa no

shake [ʃeik] (*pt* **shook**, *pp* **shaken**) *vt* (*gen*) 揺すぶる yusúburù; (bottle) 振る fúrù; (cocktail) シェイクする shéikù suru; (building) 揺るがす yurúgasù; (weaken: beliefs, resolve) ぐらつかせる gurátsukaserù; (upset, surprise) ...にショックを与える ...ni shókkù wo atáerù

♦*vi* (tremble) 震える furúerù

to shake one's head (in refusal, dismay) 頭を振る atáma wò fúrù

to shake hands with someone ...と握手をする ...to ákùshu wo suru

shaken [ʃei'kən] *pp* of **shake**

shake off *vt* (lit) 振り落す furíotosù; (*fig*: pursuer) まく makú

shake up *vt* (lit: ingredients) よく振る yókù furu; (*fig*: organization) 一新する isshín suru

shaky [ʃei'kiː] *adj* (hand, voice) 震える furúerù; (table, building) ぐらぐらする gúràgura suru

shall [ʃæl] *aux vb*: *I shall go* 行きます ikímasù

shall I open the door? ドアを開けましょうか dóà wo akémashō ka

I'll get some, shall I? 少し取ってきましょうか sukóshì totté kimashō ka

shallow [ʃæl'ou] *adj* (water, box, breathing) 浅い asáì; (*fig*: ideas etc) 浅薄な seńpaku na

sham [ʃæm] *n* いんちき íñchiki

♦*vt* ...の振りをする ...no furí wò suru

shambles [ʃæm'bəlz] *n* 大混乱 daíkoñran

shame [ʃeim] *n* (embarrassment) 恥 hají; (disgrace) 不面目 fuméñboku

♦*vt* 辱める hazúkashimerù

it is a shame that ... ...であるのは残念だ ...de árù no wa zañneñ da

it is a shame to do ... ...するのはもったいない ...surú no wà mottáinaì

what a shame! 残念だ zañneñ da

shamefaced [ʃeim'feist] *adj* 恥ずかしそうな hazúkashisō na

shameful [ʃeim'fəl] *adj* (disgraceful) 恥ずべき hazúbeki

shameless [ʃeim'lis] *adj* (liar, deception) 恥知らずの hajíshirazù no

shampoo [ʃæmpuː'] *n* シャンプー sháñpū

♦*vt* シャンプーする sháñpū suru

shampoo and set シャンプーとセット sháñpū to séttò

shamrock [ʃæm'rɑːk] *n* ツメクサ tsumékusa, クローバー kuróbằ

shandy [ʃæn'diː] *n* シャンディー sháñdī ◇ ビールをレモネードで割った飲物 bírù wo remónềdo de wattá nomimonò

shan't [ʃænt] = **shall not**

shanty town [ʃæn'tiː-] *n* バラック集落 barákkushūraku

shape [ʃeip] *n* (form, outline) 形 katáchi

♦*vt* (fashion, form) 形作る katáchizukurù; (someone's ideas, life) 方向付ける hốkōzukerù

to take shape (painting) 段々格好がつく dańdan kakkō ga tsukù; (plan) 具体化してくる gutáika shite kurù

-shaped [ʃeipt] *suffix*: *heart-shaped* ハート形の hátõgata no

shapeless [ʃeip'lis] *adj* 不格好な bukákkō na

shapely [ʃeip'liː] *adj* (woman, legs) 美しい utsúkushiì

shape up *vi* (events) 具体化してくる gutáika shite kurù; (person) 期待通りに進歩する kitáidðri ni shiñpo suru

share [ʃeːr] *n* (part received) 分け前 wakémaè; (part contributed) 持分 mochíbun, 負担分 futáñbun; (COMM) 株 kabú

♦*vt* (books, toys, room) 共用する kyốyō suru; (cost) 分担する buńtan suru; (one's lunch) 分けてやる wakéte yarù; (have in common: features, qualities etc) ...の点で似ている ...no téñ de nité irù

shareholder [ʃeːr'houldəːr] *n* 株主 kabúnùshi

share out *vi* 分配する buñpai suru

shark [ʃɑːrk] *n* サメ samé

sharp [ʃɑːrp] *adj* (razor, knife) よく切れる yókù kirérù; (point, teeth) 鋭い surúdoì; (nose, chin) とがった togáttà; (outline) くっきりした kukkíri shitá; (pain)

鋭い surúdoî; (cold) 身を切る様な mí wò kírù yō na; (taste) 舌を刺す様な shitá wò sásù yō na; (MUS) ピッチが高過ぎる pítchì ga takásugìrù; (contrast) 強い tsuyóî; (increase) 急な kyū na; (voice) 甲高い kańdakaî; (person: quick-witted) 抜け目のない nukéme no naî; (dishonest: practice etc) 不正な fuséi na

♦n (MUS) えい音記号 eîonkigō, シャープ shắpù

♦adv (precisely): **at 2 o'clock sharp** 2 時きっかりに nîjī kikkárì ni

sharpen [ʃɑːr'pən] vt (stick etc) とがらせる togáraserù; (pencil) 削る kezúrù; (fig: appetite) そそる sosórù

sharpener [ʃɑːr'pənə:r] n (also: **pencil sharpener**) 鉛筆削り eñpitsukezúri

sharp-eyed [ʃɑːrp'aid] adj 目の鋭い mé nò surudoî

sharply [ʃɑːrp'liː] adv (turn, stop) 急に kyū ni; (stand out) くっきりと kukkírì to; (contrast) 強く tsuyókù; (criticize, retort) 辛らつに shifiratsu ni

shatter [ʃæt'əːr] vt (break) 割る warú, 木っ端みじんにする kóppàmijin ni suru; (fig: ruin) 台無しにする daínashi ni surù; (: upset) がっくりさせる gakkúrì saserú

♦vi (break) 割れる waréru

shave [ʃeiv] vt (person, face, legs etc) そる sórù

♦vi ひげをそる higé wò sórù

♦n: **to have a shave** (at barber's) ひげをそってもらう higé wò sóttè moráù; (oneself) ひげをそる higé wò sórù

shaver [ʃei'vəːr] n (also: **electric shaver**) 電気かみそり defikikamísori

shaving [ʃei'viŋ] n (action) ひげをそる事 higé wò sórù kotó

shaving brush n シェービングブラシ shébinguburàshi

shaving cream, shaving foam n シェービングクリーム shébingukurímu

shavings [ʃei'viŋz] npl (of wood etc) かんなくず kańnakuzù

shawl [ʃɔːl] n 肩掛 katákàke, ショール shōru

she [ʃiː] pron 彼女は〔が〕kánòjo wa 〔ga〕

sheaf [ʃiːf] (npl **sheaves**) n (of corn, papers)

束 tábà

shear [ʃiː'əːr] (pt **sheared**, pp **shorn**) vt (sheep) ...の毛を刈る ...no ké wò karú

shear off vi 折れる orérù

shears [ʃiː'əːrz] npl (for hedge) はさみ hasámi

sheath [ʃiːθ] n (of knife) さや sáyà; (contraceptive) コンドーム koñdōmu, スキン sukíñ

sheaves [ʃiːvz] npl of **sheaf**

she-cat [ʃiː'kæt] n 雌ネコ mesúneko

shed [ʃed] n 小屋 koyá

♦vt (pt, pp **shed**) (leaves, fur, hair etc) 落す otósù; (skin) 脱皮する dappí suru; (tears) 流す nagásù

to shed blood 人を殺す hitó wò korósù

to shed a load (subj: truck etc) 荷崩れを起す nikúzure wò okósù

she'd [ʃiːd] = **she had; she would**

sheen [ʃiːn] n つや tsuyá

sheep [ʃiːp] n inv ヒツジ hitsúji

sheepdog [ʃiːp'dɔːg] n 牧用犬 bokúyōken

sheepish [ʃiː'piʃ] adj 恥ずかしそうな hazúkashisò na

sheepskin [ʃiːp'skin] n ヒツジの毛皮 hitsúji nò kegáwa, シープスキン shípusukiñ

sheer [ʃiːr] adj (utter) 全くの mattáku no; (steep) 垂直の suíchoku no; (almost transparent) ごく薄手の gókù usúde no

♦adv (straight up: rise) 垂直に suíchoku ni

sheet [ʃiːt] n (on bed) シーツ shítsù; (of paper, glass, metal) 一枚 ichímaî

a sheet of ice アイスバーン aísubàn

sheik(h) [ʃiːk] n 首長 shuchō

shelf [ʃelf] (pl **shelves**) n 棚 taná

shell [ʃel] n (on beach) 貝殻 kaígara; (of egg, nut etc) 殻 kará; (explosive) 弾丸 dañgan; (of building) 外壁 sotókabe

♦vt (peas) むく múkù; (MIL: fire on) 砲撃する hógeki suru

she'll [ʃiːl] = **she will; she shall**

shellfish [ʃel'fiʃ] n inv (crab) カニ kaní; (prawn, shrimp etc) エビ ebf; (lobster) ロブスター robúsùtā; (scallop, clam etc) 貝 kái ◇料理用語として殻のある海の生物を指す ryőriyōgo toshite kará no arù úmì no seíbutsu wo sásù

shelter [ʃel'tər] n (building) シェルター shérūtā; (protection: for hiding) 隠れ場所 kakúrebashò; (: from rain) 雨宿りの場所 amáyàdori no bashó
♦vt (protect) 守る mamórù; (give lodging to: homeless, refugees) ...に避難する場所を提供する ...ni hínàn no bashó wò teíkyo suru; (: wanted man) かくまう kakúmaù
♦vi (from rain etc) 雨宿りをする amáyàdori wo suru; (from danger) 避難する hínàn suru; (hide) 隠れる kakúrerù

sheltered [ʃel'tərd] adj (life) 世間の荒波から守られた sékèn no aránami karà mamóraretà; (spot) 雨風を避けられる ámèkaze wo sakérarerù
sheltered housing 老人・身障者用住宅 rójìn, shíńshōshayō jútaku

shelve [ʃelv] vt (fig: plan) 棚上げにする taná-age ni surú

shelves [ʃelvz] npl of **shelf**

shepherd [ʃep'ərd] n ヒツジ飼い hitsújikài
♦vt (guide) 案内する añnai suru

shepherd's pie (BRIT) n シェパードパイ shepádopaì ◇ひき肉にマッシュポテトを乗せて焼いた料理 hikíniku nì masshúpotetò wo noséte yaità ryórì

sheriff [ʃe:r'if] (US) n 保安官 hoáñkan

sherry [ʃe:r'i:] n シェリー酒 sheríshù

she's [ʃi:z] = **she is**; **she has**

Shetland [ʃet'lənd] n (also: **the Shetlands, the Shetland Isles**) シェットランド諸島 shettóràndo shotō

shield [ʃi:ld] n (MIL) 盾 tátè; (SPORT: trophy) 盾型トロフィー tatégata toròfī; (protection) ...よけ ...yókè
♦vt: **to shield (from)** ...の(...)よけになる ...no (...) yóke ni narù

shift [ʃift] n (change) 変更 heñkō; (workperiod) 交替 kótai; (group of workers) 交替組 kótaigumì
♦vt (move) ...の位置を変える ...no íchì wo kaérù; (remove: stain) ふく nukú
♦vi (move: wind, person) 変る kawárù

shiftless [ʃift'lis] adj (person) ろくでなしの rokúdenashi no

shift work n 交替でする作業 kótai de suru sagyō

shifty [ʃif'ti:] adj (person, eyes) うさん臭い usánkusaì

shilling [ʃil'iŋ] (BRIT) n シリング shírìngu ◇かつての英国の硬貨でポンドの1/20 kátsùte no eíkoku no kõka de póňdo no nijúbùn no ichí

shilly-shally [ʃil'i:ʃæli:] vi ぐずぐずする gúzùguzu suru

shimmer [ʃim'ər] vi ちらちら光る chírà-chira hikárù

shin [ʃin] n 向こうずね mukózune

shine [ʃain] n つや tsuyá
♦vb (pt, pp **shone**)
♦vi (sun) 照る térù; (torch, light, eyes) 光る hikárù; (fig: person) 優れる sugúrerù
♦vt (glasses) ふく fukú; (shoes) 磨く migákù
to shine a torch on something ...を懐中電燈で照す ...wo kaíchūdeñtō de terásù

shingle [ʃiŋ'gəl] n (on beach) 砂利 jarí

shingles [ʃiŋ'gəlz] n (MED) 帯状ヘルペス taíjōherupèsu

shiny [ʃai'ni:] adj (coin) ぴかぴかの pikápika no; (shoes, hair, lipstick) つやつやの tsuyátsuya no

ship [ʃip] n 船 fúnè
♦vt (transport by ship) 船で運ぶ fúnè de hakóbù; (send: goods) 輸送する yusō suru

shipbuilding [ʃip'bildiŋ] n 造船 zõsen

shipment [ʃip'mənt] n (goods) 輸送貨物 yusōkamōtsu

shipper [ʃip'ər] n 送り主 okúrinùshi

shipping [ʃip'iŋ] n (transport of cargo) 運送 uñsō; (ships collectively) 船舶 séñpaku

shipshape [ʃip'ʃeip] adj きちんとした kichín to shita

shipwreck [ʃip'rek] n (event) 難破 nañpa; (ship) 難破船 nañpasen
♦vt: **to be shipwrecked** 難破する nañpa suru

shipyard [ʃip'jɑ:rd] n 造船所 zõsenjo

shire [ʃaiə:r] (BRIT) n 郡 gúñ

shirk [ʃə:rk] vt (work, obligations) 怠る

okótarù

shirt [ʃəːrt] n (man's) ワイシャツ waíshatsu; (woman's) シャツブラウス shatsúburaùsu

in (one's) shirt sleeves 上着を脱いで uwági wò núìde

shit [ʃit] *(inf!)* excl くそっ kusót

shiver [ʃiv'əːr] n (act of shivering) 身震い mibúruì

◆vi 震える furúerù

shoal [ʃoul] n (of fish) 群れ muré; *(fig: also:* **shoals**) 大勢 ōzeì

shock [ʃɑːk] n (start, impact) 衝撃 shōgekì; (ELEC) 感電 kañden; (emotional) 打撃 dagéki, ショック shókkù; (MED) ショック shókkù

◆vt (upset, offend) ...にショックを与える ...ni shókkù wo atáerù

shock absorber n 緩衝器 kañshōkì

shocking [ʃɑk'iŋ] adj (awful: standards, accident) ひどい hidóì; (outrageous: play, book) 衝撃的な shōgekiteki na

shod [ʃɑd] pt, pp of **shoe**

shoddy [ʃɑd'iː] adj (goods, workmanship) 粗雑な sozátsu na

shoe [ʃuː] n (for person) 靴 kutsú; (for horse) てい鉄 teítetsu

◆vt (pt, pp **shod**) (horse) ...にてい鉄を付ける ...ni teítetsu wò tsukérù

shoebrush [ʃuː'brʌʃ] n 靴ブラシ kutsúburàshi

shoelace [ʃuː'leis] n 靴ひも kutsúhìmo

shoe polish n 靴磨き kutsúmigàki

shoeshop [ʃuː'ʃɑːp] n 靴屋 kutsúyà

shoestring [ʃuː'striŋ] n *(fig): on a shoestring* わずかの金で wázùka no kané de

shone [ʃoun] pt, pp of **shine**

shoo [ʃuː] excl しっ shítt ◇動物を追っ払う時に言う言葉 dóbutsu wò oíharaù toki ni iú kotoba

shook [ʃuk] pt of **shake**

shoot [ʃuːt] n (on branch, seedling) 若枝 wakáèda

◆vb (pt, pp **shot**)

◆vt (gun) 撃つ útsù; (arrow) 射る írù; (kill: bird, robber etc) 撃ち殺す uchíkorosù; (wound) 撃つ sogéki suru; (execute) 銃殺する jūsatsu suru; (film) 撮影する satsúei suru

◆vi (with gun/bow): *to shoot (at)* (...を目掛けて)撃つ〔射る〕(...wo megákete) útsù 〔írù〕; (SOCCER) シュートする shūto suru

shoot down vt (plane) 撃ち落とす uchíotosù

shoot in/out vi (rush) 飛込む〔飛出す〕 tobíkomù 〔tobídasù〕

shooting [ʃuː'tiŋ] n (shots) 発砲事件 happójikèn; (HUNTING) 狩猟 shuryō

shooting star n 流れ星 nagárebòshi

shoot up vi *(fig)* 急上昇する kyūjōshō suru

shop [ʃɑːp] n (selling goods) 店 misé; *(also:* **workshop**) 作業場 sagyōbà

◆vi *(also:* **go shopping**) 買物をする kaímono suru

shop assistant *(BRIT)* n 店員 teñ-in

shop floor *(BRIT)* n 労働側 rōdōgawa

shopkeeper [ʃɑːp'kiːpəːr] n 店主 teñshu

shoplifting [ʃɑːp'liftiŋ] n 万引 mañbiki

shopper [ʃɑːp'əːr] n (person) 買物客 kaímonokyàku

shopping [ʃɑːp'iŋ] n (goods) 買物 kaímono

shopping bag n ショッピングバッグ shoppíngubaggù

shopping center *(BRIT* **shopping centre**) n ショッピングセンター shoppíngusentà

shop-soiled [ʃɑːp'sɔild] adj (goods) 棚ざらしの tanázaràshi no

shop steward *(BRIT)* n (INDUSTRY) 職場代表 shokúbadaihyō

shop window n ショーウインドー shōuiñdō

shore [ʃɔːr] n 岸 kishí

◆vt: *to shore up* 補強する hokyō suru

on shore 陸に rikú ni

shorn [ʃɔːrn] pp of **shear**

short [ʃɔːrt] adj (not long) 短い mijíkaì; (person: not tall) 背の低い se nò hikúì; (curt) ぶっきらぼうな bukkírabò na; (insufficient) 不足している fusóku shite irù

to be short of something ...が不足している ...ga fusóku shite irù

in short 要するに yō surù ni

short of doing ... ...をしなければ ...wo shinákerėba

it is short for それは...の短縮形です soré wā ... no tañshukukei desu

to cut short (speech, visit) 予定より短くする yotéi yorī mijíkakù suru

everything short of ... ...を除いて何でも ...wo nozóite náñ de mo

to fall short of ...に達しない ...ni tasshínai

to run short of ...が足りなくなる ...ga tarínakunarù

to stop short (while walking etc) 急に立止まる kyū ni tachidomarù; (while doing something) 急にやめる kyū ni yamerù

to stop short of ...まではしない ...mádè wa shinái

shortage [ʃɔ́ːrtɪdʒ] *n*: *a shortage of* ...不足 ...busóku

shortbread [ʃɔ́ːrtˈbred] *n* ショートブレッド shōtóbureddò ◇小麦粉、バター、砂糖で作った菓子 komúgiko, bátā, satō dè tsukútta kashī

short-change [ʃɔ́ːrtˈtʃeindʒ] *vt* ...に釣銭を少なく渡す ...ni tsurísen wò sukúnakù watásù

short-circuit [ʃɔ́ːrtsər'kit] *n* (ELEC) ショート shṓto

shortcoming [ʃɔ́ːrtˈkʌmiŋ] *n* 欠点 kettéñ

short(crust) pastry [ʃɔ́ːrt('krʌst)-] (*BRIT*) *n* パイ生地 páikijì

shortcut [ʃɔ́ːrtˈkʌt] *n* 近道 chikámichi

shorten [ʃɔ́ːrtən] *vt* (clothes, visit) 短くする mijíkakù suru

shortfall [ʃɔ́ːrtˈfɔːl] *n* 不足 fusóku

shorthand [ʃɔ́ːrtˈhænd] *n* 速記 sokkí

shorthand typist (*BRIT*) *n* 速記もできるタイピスト sokkí mo dekirù taípisutò

shortlist [ʃɔ́ːrtˈlist] *n* (for job) 予備審査の合格者リスト yobíshiñsa no gṓkakusha risùto

short-lived [ʃɔ́ːrtˈlivd] *adj* つかの間の tsuká no ma no

shortly [ʃɔ́ːrtˈliː] *adv* 間もなく ma mó nàku

shorts [ʃɔ́ːrts] *npl*: *(a pair of) shorts* (short trousers) 半ズボン hañzùbon;

(men's underwear) パンツ páñtsu

short-sighted [ʃɔ́ːrtˈsai'tid] (*BRIT*) *adj* 近眼の kiñgan no; (*fig*) 先見の明のない señken no meī no nai

short-staffed [ʃɔ́ːrtˈstæft'] *adj*: *to be short-staffed* 人手不足である hitódebùsoku de aru

short story *n* 短編小説 tañpenshōsetsu

short-tempered [ʃɔ́ːrtˈtempə'rd] *adj* 短気な táñki na

short-term [ʃɔ́ːrtˈtə'rm] *adj* (effect, borrowing) 短期の táñki no

shortwave [ʃɔ́ːrtˈweiv'] *n* (RADIO) 短波 táñpa

shot [ʃɑt] *pt, pp of* **shoot**

◆*n* (of gun) 発砲 happṓ; (try, *also* SOCCER etc) シュート shūto; (injection) 注射 chūsha; (PHOT) ショット shóttò

a good/poor shot (person) 射撃のうまい〔下手な〕人 shagéki no umaī〔hetà na〕hitó

like a shot (without any delay) 鉄砲玉の様に teppṓdama no yṓ ni

shotgun [ʃɑtˈgʌn] *n* 散弾銃 sañdañjū

should [ʃud] *aux vb*: *I should go now* もうおいとましなくては mṓ o-ítoma shinakute wā

he should be there now 彼は今あそこにいるはずです kárè wa ímà asóko nī irú hazù desu

I should go if I were you 私だったら、行きますよ watákushi dattàra, ikímasù yó

I should like to ...をしたいと思いますが ...wo shitái tò omóimasù ga

shoulder [ʃoul'də'r] *n* (ANAT) 肩 kátà

◆*vt* (*fig*: responsibility, blame) 負う óu

shoulder bag *n* ショルダーバッグ shorúdābaggù

shoulder blade *n* 肩甲骨 keñkōkotsu

shoulder strap *n* ショルダーストラップ shorúdāsutorappù

shouldn't [ʃud'ənt] = **should not**

shout [ʃaut] *n* 叫び声 sakébigoè

◆*vt* 大声で言う ṓgoè de iú

◆*vi* (*also*: **shout out**) 叫ぶ sakébù

shout down *vt* (speaker) どなって黙らせる donáttè damáraserù

shouting [ʃaut'iŋ] n 叫び声 sakébigoè

shove [ʃʌv] vt 押す osú; (inf: put): *to shove something in* ...を...に押込む ...wo...ni oshíkomù

shovel [ʃʌv'əl] n (gen) スコップ sukóppù, シャベル shábèru; (mechanical) パワーシャベル pawáshabèru
♦vt (snow) かく kákù; (coal, earth) すくう sukúù

shove off vi: *shove off!* (inf) うせろ usérò

show [ʃou] n (demonstration: of emotion) 表現 hyógen; (semblance) 見せ掛け misékake; (exhibition: flower show etc) 展示会 teñjikai, ショー shō; (THEATER, TV) ショー shō
♦vb (pt showed, pp shown)
♦vt (indicate) 示す shimésù, 見せる misérù; (exhibit) 展示する teñji suru; (courage etc) 示す shimésù; (illustrate, depict) 描写する byósha suru; (film: in movie theater) 上映する jóei suru; (program, film: on television) 放送する hōsō suru
♦vi (be evident) 見える miérù; (appear) 現れる aráwarerù
for show 格好だけの kakkő dake no
on show (exhibits etc) 展示中 teñjichū

show business n 芸能界 geínōkai

showdown [ʃou'daun] n 対決 taíketsu

shower [ʃau'ər] n (of rain) にわか雨 niwákaamè; (of stones etc) ...の雨 ...no ámè; (for bathing in) シャワー sháwā
♦vi 降ってくる futté kurù
♦vt: *to shower someone with* ...の上に...を降らす ...no uế nì...wo furásù
to have a shower シャワーを浴びる sháwā wo abírù

showerproof [ʃau'ə:rpru:f] adj 防水の bốsui no ◇にわか雨程度なら耐えられるが強い雨にはぬれてしまうコートなどについて言う niwákaamè téido nara taérarerù ga tsuyói amè ni wa nuréteshimau kōto nado ni tsuíte iú

show in vt (person) 中へ案内する nákà e aññai suru

showing [ʃou'iŋ] n (of film) 上映 jóei

show jumping [-dʒʌmp'iŋ] n (of horses) 障害飛越 shōgaihiètsu

shown [ʃoun] pp of show

show off vi (pej) 気取る kidórù
♦vt (display) 見せびらかす misébirakasù

show-off [ʃou'ɔ:f] (inf) n (person) 自慢屋 jimán-yà

show out vt (person) 出口へ案内する déguchi e aññai suru

showpiece [ʃou'pi:s] n (of exhibition etc) 立派な見本 rippá nà mihón

showroom [ʃou'ru:m] n ショールーム shốrūmu

show up vi (stand out) 目立つ medátsù; (inf: turn up) 現れる aráwarerù
♦vt (uncover: imperfections etc) 暴露する bákùro suru

shrank [ʃræŋk] pt of shrink

shrapnel [ʃræp'nəl] n 弾丸の破片 dañgan nò hahén

shred [ʃred] n (gen pl) 切れ端 kiréhashi
♦vt (gen) ずたずたにする zutázuta ni surù; (CULIN) 刻む kizámù

shredder [ʃred'ə:r] n (vegetable shredder) 削り器 kezúrikì; (document shredder) シュレッダー shuréddằ

shrewd [ʃru:d] adj (businessman) 抜け目のない nukéme no naì; (assessment) 賢明な keñmei na

shriek [ʃri:k] n 金切り声 kanákirigoè
♦vi 金切り声を出す kanákirigoè wo dásù

shrill [ʃril] adj (cry, voice) 甲高い kañdakaì

shrimp [ʃrimp] n (shellfish) えび ebí

shrine [ʃrain] n (place of worship) 礼拝堂 reíhaidō; (for relics) 聖遺物容器 seíbutsutsuyōki; (fig: building) 殿堂 deñdō; (: place) 聖地 seichi

shrink [ʃriŋk] (pt shrank, pp shrunk) vi (cloth) 縮む chijímù; (be reduced: profits, audiences) 減る herú; (move: also: **shrink away**) 縮こまって逃げる chijíkomattè nigérù
♦vt (cloth) 縮める chijímerù
♦n (inf: pej: psychiatrist) 精神科医 seíshinka-ì
to shrink from (doing) something ...を(するのを)いやがる ...wo (surú no wò) iyágarù

shrinkage [ʃriŋk'idʒ] *n* 縮まる分 chijímarù bún

shrinkwrap [ʃriŋk'ræp] *vt* ラップで包む ráppù de tsutsúmù

shrivel [ʃriv'əl] (*also*: **shrivel up**) *vt* しおれさせる shíóresaserù
♦*vi* しおれる shiórerù

shroud [ʃraud] *n* 覆い ói
♦*vt*: *shrouded in mystery* なぞに包まれて nazó nì tsutsúmaretè

Shrove Tuesday [ʃrouv-] *n* 謝肉祭の火曜日 shaníkusài no kayóbi

shrub [ʃrʌb] *n* 低木 teíboku

shrubbery [ʃrʌb'əri:] *n* 植込み uékomi

shrug [ʃrʌg] *n* 肩をすくめる事 kátà wo sukúmerù kotó
♦*vt*, *vi*: *to shrug (one's shoulders)* 肩をすくめる kátà wo sukúmerù

shrug off *vt* (criticism) 受流す ukénagasù; (illness) 無視する múshì suru

shrunk [ʃrʌŋk] *pp* of **shrink**

shudder [ʃʌd'əːr] *n* 身震い mibúrùi
♦*vi* (person: with fear, revulsion) 身震いする mibúrùi suru

shuffle [ʃʌf'əl] *vt* (cards) 混ぜる mazérù
♦*vi* (walk) 足を引きずって歩く ashí wò hikízutte arukù
to shuffle (one's feet) (while standing, sitting) 足をもぞもぞ動かす ashí wò mózòmozo ugókasù

shun [ʃʌn] *vt* (publicity, neighbors etc) 避ける sakérù

shunt [ʃʌnt] *vt* (train) 分岐線に入れる buñkisen ni irerù; (object) 動かす ugókasù

shut [ʃʌt] (*pt*, *pp* **shut**) *vt* (door) 閉める shimérù; (shop) しまう shimáù; (mouth, eyes) 閉じる tojírù
♦*vi* (door, eyes, shop) 閉る shimárù

shut down *vt* (for a time) 休業させる kyúgyò saserù; (forever) 閉鎖する heísa suru
♦*vi* (for a time) 休業する kyúgyò surù; (forever) 閉鎖になる heísa ni narù

shut off *vt* (supply etc) 遮断する shadán suru

shutter [ʃʌt'əːr] *n* (on window: *also* PHOT) シャッター sháttà

shuttle [ʃʌt'əl] *n* (plane etc) シャトル

shátòru; (*also*: **space shuttle**) スペースシャトル supésushatòru; (*also*: **shuttle service**) 折り返し運転 oríkaeshi uñten

shuttlecock [ʃʌt'əlkɑːk] *n* シャットルコック shattórukokkù

shut up *vi* (*inf*: keep quiet) 黙る damárù
♦*vt* (close) しまう shimau; (silence) 黙らせる damáraserù

shy [ʃai] *adj* (timid: animal) 臆病な okúbyò na; (reserved) 内気な uchíki na

shyness [ʃai'nis] *n* (timidity: of animal) 臆病 okúbyò; (reservedness) 内気 uchíki na

Siamese [saiəmiːz'] *adj*: *Siamese cat* シャムネコ shamúneko

Siberia [saibíːriːə] *n* シベリア shibéria

sibling [sib'liŋ] *n* 兄弟 kyódai ◇男兄弟にも女兄弟 (姉妹) にも使う otókokyòdai ni mo oñnakyòdai (shímài) ni mo tsukáù

Sicily [sis'iliː] *n* シチリア shichíria

sick [sik] *adj* (ill) 病気の byóki no; (nauseated) むかついた mukátsuita; (humor) 病的な byóteki na; (vomiting): *to be sick* 吐く hákù
to feel sick むかつく mukátsukù
to be sick of (fig) ...にうんざりしている ...ni uñzari shite irù

sick bay *n* (on ship) 医務室 imúshìtsu

sicken [sik'ən] *vt* むかつかせる mukátsukaserù

sickening [sik'əniŋ] *adj* (fig) 不快な fukái na

sickle [sik'əl] *n* かま kámà

sick leave *n* 病気休暇 byókikyùka

sickly [sik'liː] *adj* (child, plant) 病気がちな byókigachi na; (causing nausea: smell) むかつかせる mukátsukaserù

sickness [sik'nis] *n* (illness) 病気 byóki; (vomiting) おう吐 ōto

sick pay *n* 病気手当 byókiteàte

side [said] *n* (of object) 横 yokó; (of body) 脇腹 wakíbara; (of lake) 岸 kishí; (aspect) 側面 sokúmen; (team) 側 gawá
♦*adj* (door, entrance) 横の yokó no
♦*vi*: *to side with someone* ...の肩を持つ ...no kátà wo mótsù
the side of the road 路肩 rokáta
the side of a hill 山腹 sañpuku
by the side of ...の横に ...no yokó ni

side by side 横に並んで yokó ni naraǹde

from side to side 左右に sáyū ni

from all sides 四方八方から shihōhappō kara

to take sides (with) (...に)味方する (...ni) mikáta suru

sideboard [said'bɔːrd] *n* 食器戸棚 shokkítodàna, サイドボード saídobòdo

sideboards [said'bɔːrdz] (*BRIT*) *npl* = **sideburns**

sideburns [said'bəːrnz] *npl* もみあげ momíage

side drum *n* (MUS) 小太鼓 kodáìko

side effect *n* (MED, *fig*) 副作用 fukúsayō

sidelight [said'lait] *n* (AUT) 車幅灯 shafúkutō

sideline [said'lain] *n* (SPORT) サイドライン saídoraìn; (*fig*: supplementary job) 副業 fukúgyō

sidelong [said'lɔːŋ] *adj*: *to give someone/something a sidelong glance* ...を横目で見る ...wo' yokóme de mirù

sidesaddle [said'sædəl] *adv*: *to ride sidesaddle* 馬に横乗りする umá nì yokónori surù

side show *n* (stall at fair, circus) 見世物屋台 misémonoyatài

sidestep [said'step] *vt* (*fig*) 避けて通る sakétetòru

side street *n* わき道 wakímichi

sidetrack [said'træk] *vt* (*fig*) ...の話を脱線させる ...no hanáshi wò dassén saserù

sidewalk [said'wɔːk] (*US*) *n* 歩道 hodō

sideways [said'weiz] *adv* (go in) 横向きに yokómuki ni; (lean) 横へ yokó e

siding [said'diŋ] *n* (RAIL) 側線 sokúsen

sidle [sai'dəl] *vi*: *to sidle up (to)* (...に)こっそり近寄る (...ni) kossórì chikáyorù

siege [siːdʒ] *n* (*gen*, MIL) 包囲 hōi

siesta [siːes'tə] *n* 昼寝 hirúne

sieve [siv] *n* ふるい furúi

♦*vt* ふるう furúu

sift [sift] *vt* (*fig*: *also*: **sift through**: information) ふるい分ける furúiwakerù; (sieve) ふるう furúu

sigh [sai] *n* ため息 taméikì

♦*vi* ため息をつく taméiki wo tsukú

sight [sait] *n* (faculty) 視覚 shikáku; (spectacle) 光景 kōkei; (on gun) 照準器 shōjunki

♦*vt* 見掛ける mikákerù

in sight 見える所に miérù tokórò ni

on sight (shoot) 見付け次第 mitsúkeshidài

out of sight 見えない所に miénaì tokórò ni

sightseeing [sait'siːiŋ] *n* 名所見物 meíshokeñbutsu

to go sightseeing 名所見物に行く meíshokeñbutsu ni ikú

sign [sain] *n* (with hand) 合図 aízu; (indication: of present condition) しるし shirúshi; (: of future condition) 兆し kizáshi; (notice) 看板 kanban; (written) 張紙 harígami

♦*vt* (document) ...に署名〔サイン〕する ...ni shoméi〔saín〕suru; (player) 雇う yatóù

to sign something over to someone ...を...に譲渡する ...wo...ni jótò suru

signal [sig'nəl] *n* (*gen*) 信号 shingō; (equipment on highway, railway) 信号機 shingōki

♦*vi* (make signs: *also* AUT) 合図をする aízu wo suru

♦*vt* (person) ...に合図をする ...ni aízu wo suru; (message) ...する様に合図をする ...suru yō ni aizu wo suru

signalman [sig'nəlmən] (*pl* **signalmen**) *n* (RAIL) 信号手 shingōshu

signature [sig'nətʃəːr] *n* 署名 shoméi, サイン saín

signature tune *n* テーマ音楽 témaoňgaku

signet ring [sig'nit-] *n* 印章指輪 iñshōyubiwà

significance [signif'əkəns] *n* (importance) 重要性 jūyōsei

significant [signif'ikənt] *adj* (full of meaning: look, smile) 意味深い imíbukài; (important: amount, discovery) 重要な jūyō na

signify [sig'nəfai] *vt* 意味する ímì suru

sign language *n* 手話 shúwa

sign on vi (MIL) 入隊する nyútai surù; (BRIT: as unemployed) 失業手当を請求する shitsúgyōteàte wo seíkyū suru; (for course) 受講手続をする jukótetsuzùki wo suru

♦vt (MIL: recruits) 入隊させる nyútai saserù; (employee) 雇う yatôù

signpost [sain'poust] n 案内標識 añnaihyōshiki

sign up vi (MIL) 入隊する nyútai suru; (for course) 受講手続をする jukótetsuzùki wo suru

silence [sai'ləns] n (of person) 沈黙 chímmoku; (of place) 静けさ shizúkesà

♦vt (person, opposition) 黙らせる damáraserù

silencer [sai'lənsə:r] n (on gun) 消音器 shóoñki, サイレンサー saíreñsā; (BRIT: AUT) 消音器 shóoñki, マフラー máfurā

silent [sai'lənt] adj (person) 黙っている damátte irù; (place) しんとした shíñtò shitá; (machine) 音のない otó no naî; (film) 無声の muséi no

to remain silent 黙っている damátte irù

silent prayer 黙とう mokútō

silent partner n (COMM) 出資者 shusshísha ◇資金の一部を出すが、業務に直接関与しない社員について言う shihóñkin no ichíbù wo dásù ga, gyômù ni chokúsetsu kañyo shináî shá-ìn ni tsuite iú

silhouette [silu:et'] n シルエット shírùetto

silicon chip [sil'ikən-] n シリコンチップ shírikonchippù

silk [silk] n 絹 kínù

♦adj (scarf, shirt) 絹の kínù no

silky [sil'ki:] adj (material, skin) 絹の様な kínù no yố nà

silly [sil'i:] adj (person, idea) ばかな bákà na

silo [sai'lou] n (on farm, for missile) サイロ saíro

silt [silt] n (in harbor, river etc) 沈泥 chíndei

silver [sil'və:r] n (metal) 銀 gíñ; (coins) 硬貨 kókà; (items made of silver) 銀製品

gíñseihin

♦adj (color) 銀色の gíñ-iro no; (made of silver) 銀の gíñ no

silver paper (BRIT) n 銀紙 gíñgami

silver-plated [sil'və:rplei'tid] adj 銀めっきの gíñmekkî no

silversmith [sil'və:rsmiθ] n 銀細工師 gíñzaikushì

silvery [sil'və:ri:] adj (like silver) 銀の様な gíñ no yố nà

similar [sim'ələr] adj: **similar (to)** (...に)似た (...ni) nitá

similarity [siməlær'iti:] n 似ている事 nité irù kotó

similarly [sim'ələ:rli:] adv 同じ様に onáji yố ni

simile [sim'əli:] n 例え tatóè

simmer [sim'ə:r] vi (CULIN) ぐつぐつ煮える gútsùgutsu niérù

simpering [sim'pə:riŋ] adj (person) ばかみたいな作り笑いをする bákàmitai na tsukúriwarài wo suru

a simpering smile ばかみたいな作り笑い bákàmitai na tsukúriwarài

simple [sim'pəl] adj (easy) 簡単な kañtan na; (plain: dress, life) 素朴な sobóku na, シンプルな shíñpuru na; (foolish) ばかな bákà na; (COMM: interest) 単純な tañjun na

simplicity [simplis'əti:] n (ease) 簡単さ kañtansa; (plainness) 素朴さ sobókusa; (foolishness) 白痴 hakuchi

simplify [sim'pləfai] vt 簡単にする kañtan ni surù

simply [sim'pli:] adv (in a simple way: live) 素朴に sobóku ni; (talk) 平易に héîi ni; (just, merely) 単に tán ni

simulate [sim'jəleit] vt (enthusiasm, innocence) 装う yosóoù

simulated [sim'jəleitid] adj (hair, fur) 偽の nisé no, 人工の jiñkō no; (nuclear explosion) 模擬の mógì no

simultaneous [saiməltei'ni:əs] adj (translation, broadcast) 同時の dôjì no

simultaneously [saiməltei'ni:əsli:] adv 同時に dôjì ni

sin [sin] n 罪 tsúmì

♦vi 罪を犯す tsúmì wo okásù

since [sins] *adv* それ以来 soré irái
♦*prep* ...以来 ...írai
♦*conj* (time) ...して以来 ...shité irái; (because) ...ので ...nóde
since then, ever since それ以来 soré irái

sincere [sinsí:r] *adj* 誠実な seíjitsu na

sincerely [sinsí:rli:] *adv*: *yours sincerely* (in letters) 敬具 keígu

sincerity [sinsér'iti:] *n* 誠実さ seíjitsusa

sinew [sín'ju:] *n* (of person, animal) けん kéñ, 筋 súji

sinful [sín'fəl] *adj* (thought, person) 罪深い tsumíbukaì

sing [siŋ] (*pt* **sang**, *pp* **sung**) *vt* 歌う utáù
♦*vi* (*gen*) 歌う utáù; (bird) 鳴く nakú

Singapore [síŋ'gəpɔ:r] *n* シンガポール shiŋgapóru

singe [sindʒ] *vt* 焦がす kogásù

singer [síŋ'ə:r] *n* 歌手 káshù

singing [síŋ'i:] *n* (noise: of people) 歌声 utágoè; (: of birds) 鳴声 nakígoè; (art) 声楽 seígaku

single [síŋ'gəl] *adj* (individual) 一つ一つの hitótsuhitótsu no; (unmarried) 独身の dokúshin no; (not double) 一つだけの hitótsu dake nò
♦*n* (*BRIT: also*: **single ticket**) 片道乗車券 katámichijōshakèn; (record) シングル盤 shíŋguruban

single-breasted [síŋ'gəlbres'tid] *adj* (jacket, suit) シングルの shíŋguru no

single file *n*: *in single file* 一列縦隊で ichíretsujūtai de

single-handed [síŋ'gəlhæn'did] *adv* (sail, build something) 一人で hitórì de

single-minded [síŋ'gəlmain'did] *adj* 一つだけの目的を追う hitótsu dake nò mokúteki wò oú

single out *vt* (choose) 選び出す erábidasù; (distinguish) 区別する kúbetsu suru

single room *n* シングル部屋 shíŋgurubeya

singles [síŋ'gəlz] *n* (TENNIS) シングルス shíŋgurusu

singly [síŋ'gli:] *adv* (alone, one by one: people) 一人ずつ hitórì zutsu; (: things) 一つずつ hitótsu zutsu

singular [síŋ'gjələr] *adj* (odd: occurrence) 変った kawátta; (outstanding: beauty) 著しい ichíjirushiĩ; (LING) 単数のtañsū no
♦*n* (LING) 単数 tañsū

sinister [sín'istə:r] *adj* 怪しげな ayáshige na

sink [siŋk] *n* 流し nagáshi
♦*vb* (*pt* **sank**, *pp* **sunk**)
♦*vt* (ship) 沈没させる chíñbotsu sasèrù; (well, foundations) 掘る hórù
♦*vi* (ship) 沈没する chíñbotsu suru; (heart, spirits) しょげる shogérù, がっかりする gakkárì suru; (ground) 沈下する chíñka suru; (*also*: **sink back**, **sink down**: into chair) 身を沈める mí wò shizúmerù; (: to one's knees etc) しゃがみ込む shágamikomù; (: head etc) うなだれる unádarerù
to sink something into (teeth, claws etc) ...に ...を食込ませる ...ni...wo kuíkomaserù

sink in *vi* (*fig*: words) 理解される ríkài sarérù, 身にしみる mí nì shimírù

sinner [sín'ə:r] *n* 罪人 tsumíbìto

sinus [sai'nəs] *n* (ANAT) 副鼻こう fukúbikō

sip [sip] *n* 一口 hitókuchi
♦*vt* ちびりちびり飲む chibírìchibiri nómù

siphon [sai'fən] *n* サイホン sáihon

siphon off *vt* (liquid) サイホンで汲み出す sáihon de kumídasù; (money etc) ほかへ回す hoká è mawásù

sir [sə:r] *n* ◇男性に対する丁寧な呼び掛け。日本語では表現しない dañsei ni tai surù teĩnei na yobíkake. nihóñgo de wa hyṓgen shinaĩ
Sir John Smith ジョン・スミス卿 jóñ sumísukyo
yes sir はい hái

siren [sai'rən] *n* サイレン sáiren

sirloin [sə:r'lɔin] *n* (*also*: **sirloin steak**) サーロインステーキ sároinsutēki

sissy [sís'i:] (*inf*) *n* 弱虫 yowámùshi

sister [sís'tə:r] *n* (relation: *gen*) 女きょうだい oñnakyōdai, 姉妹 shímài; (*also*: **older sister**) 姉 ané, 姉さん nếèsan; (*also*:

younger sister) 妹 imōto; (nun) 修道女 shūdōjo; (BRIT: nurse) 婦長 fuchō

sister-in-law [sis'tə:rinlɔ:] (pl **sisters-in-law**) n (older) 義理の姉 girí nò ané; (younger) 義理の妹 girí nò imōto

sit [sit] (pt, pp **sat**) vi (sit down) 座る suwárù, 腰掛ける koshíkakerù; (be sitting) 座っている suwátte irù, 腰掛けている koshíkakete irù; (assembly) 会期中である kaíkichū de arù; (for painter) モデルになる mòdèru ni nárù
◆vt (exam) 受ける ukérù

sitcom [sit'kɑːm] n abbr (= situation comedy) 連続放送コメディー refizoku hōsōkomèdī

sit down vi 座る suwárù, 腰掛ける koshíkakerù

site [sait] n (place) 場所 bashó; (also: **building site**) 用地 yóchì
◆vt (factory, cruise missiles) 置く ókù

sit-in [sit'in] n (demonstration) 座り込み suwárikomi

sit in on vt fus (meeting) 傍聴する bōchō suru

sitting [sit'iŋ] n (of assembly etc) 開会 kaíkai; (in canteen) 食事の時間 shokúji nò jikán

we have two sittings for lunch 昼食は2交代で出されます chūshoku wà nikōtai de dasáremasù

sitting room n 居間 imá

situated [sitʃ'u:eitid] adj ...にある ...ni árù

situation [sitʃu:ei'ʃən] n (state) 状況 jōkyō; (job) 職 shokú; (location) 立地条件 ritchíjōken

「*situations vacant*」 (BRIT) 求人 kyūjin ◇新聞などの求人欄のタイトル shínbun nadò no kyūjinrañ no táìtoru

sit up vi (after lying) 上体を起こす jōtai wò okósù; (straight) きちんと座る kichíñto suwárù; (not go to bed) 起きている ókìte irú

six [siks] num 六 (の) rokú (no), 六つ (の) múttsù (no)

sixteen [siks'ti:n'] num 十六 (の) jūroku (no)

sixth [siksθ] num 第六(の) dáì roku (no)

sixty [siks'ti:] num 六十 (の) rokújù (no)

size [saiz] n (gen) 大きさ ókisa; (extent: of project etc) 規模 kíbò; (of clothing, shoes) サイズ sáìzu; (glue) サイズ sáìzu ◇紙のにじみ止め kamí nò nijímidome

sizeable [sai'zəbəl] adj (crowd, income etc) かなり大きい kánàri ókìì

size up vt (person, situation) 判断する hañdan suru

sizzle [siz'əl] vi (sausages etc) じゅうじゅうと音を立てる jūjū to otó wò tatérù

skate [skeit] n (ice skate) スケート sukétò; (roller skate) ローラースケート rôrāsukèto; (fish) エイ eí
◆vi スケートをする sukétò wo suru

skateboard [skeit'bɔ:rd] n スケートボード sukétobòdo

skater [skei'tə:r] n スケートをする人 sukétò wo suru hito, スケーター sukétā

skating [skei'tiŋ] n (SPORT) スケート sukétò

skating rink n スケートリンク sukétoriñku

skeleton [skel'itən] n (bones) がい骨 gáìkotsu; (TECH: framework) 骨組 honégumi; (outline) 骨子 kósshì

skeleton staff n 最小限度の人員 saíshōgeñdo no jiñ-in

skeptic [skep'tik] (US) n 疑い深い人 utágaibukaì hitó

skeptical [skep'tikəl] (US) adj 疑っている utagátte irù, 信用しない shiñ-yō shinaì

skepticism [skep'tisizəm] (US) n 疑問 gímon

sketch [sketʃ] n (drawing) スケッチ sukétchì; (outline) 骨子 kósshì; (THEATER, TV) 寸劇 suñgeki, スキット sukíttò
◆vt スケッチする sukétchì suru; (also: **sketch out**: ideas) ...のあらましを言う ...no arámashi wò iú

sketchbook [sketʃ'buk] n スケッチブック sukétchibukkù

sketchy [sketʃ'i:] adj (coverage, notes etc) 大雑把な ōzappà na

skewer [skju:'ə:r] n くし kushí

ski [ski:] *n* スキー sukī
♦*vi* スキーをする sukī wo surú

ski boot *n* スキー靴 sukígùtsu

skid [skid] *n* (AUT) スリップ suríppù
♦*vi* (*gen*, AUT) スリップする suríppù suru

skier [ski:'əːr] *n* スキーヤー sukíyà

skiing [ski:'iŋ] *n* スキー sukī

ski jump *n* スキージャンプ sukíjaǹpu

skilful [skil'fəl] (*BRIT*) *adj* = **skillful**

ski lift *n* スキーリフト sukírifùto

skill [skil] *n* (ability, dexterity) 熟練 jukúren; (work requiring training: computer skill etc) 技術 gíjùtsu

skilled [skild] *adj* (able) 上手な jōzu na; (worker) 熟練の jukúren no

skillful [skil'fəl] (*BRIT*: **skilful**) *adj* 上手な jōzu na

skim [skim] *vt* (milk) ...の上澄みをすくい取る ...no uwázumi wò sukúitorù; (glide over) ...すれすれに飛ぶ ...surésure nì tobú
♦*vi*: **to skim through** (book) ...をざっと読む ...wo záttò yómù

skimmed milk [skimd-] *n* 脱脂乳 dasshínyù

skimp [skimp] *vt* (*also*: **skimp on**: work) いいかげんにする iíkagen nì suru; (: cloth etc) けちる kechírù

skimpy [skim'pi:] *adj* (meager: meal) 少な過ぎる sukúnasugirù; (too small: skirt) 短過ぎる mijíkasugirù

skin [skin] *n* (*gen*: of person, animal) 皮膚 hífù; (: of fruit) 皮 kawá; (complexion) 顔の肌 kaó nò hádà
♦*vt* (fruit etc) ...の皮をむく ...no kawá wò múkù; (animal) ...の皮を剥ぐ ...no kawá wò hágù

skin-deep [skin'di:p'] *adj* (superficial) 表面だけの hyṓmeǹ daké no

skin-diving [skin'daiviŋ] *n* スキンダイビング sukíndaìbingu

skinny [skin'i:] *adj* (person) やせた yaséta

skintight [skin'tait] *adj* (jeans etc) 体にぴったりの karáda nì pittári no

skip [skip] *n* (movement) スキップ sukíppù; (*BRIT*: container) ごみ箱 gomíbàko
♦*vi* (jump) スキップする sukíppù suru; (with rope) 縄跳びする nawátobi suru
♦*vt* (pass over: boring parts) とばす tobásù; (miss: lunch) 抜く nukú; (: lecture) すっぽかす suppókasù

ski pants *npl* スキーズボン sukízubòn

ski pole *n* スキーストック sukísutokkù

skipper [skip'əːr] *n* (NAUT) 船長 señchō; (SPORT) 主将 shushō, キャプテン kyápùten

skipping rope [skip'iŋ-] (*BRIT*) *n* 縄跳びの縄 nawátobi nò nawá

skirmish [skəːr'miʃ] *n* (*also* MIL) こぜりあい kozériai

skirt [skəːrt] *n* スカート sukátò
♦*vt* (*fig*: go round) 避けて通る sákète tṓrù

skirting board [skəːr'tiŋ-] (*BRIT*) *n* 幅木 habáki

ski slope *n* ゲレンデ geréǹde

ski suit *n* スキー服 sukífùku

skit [skit] *n* スキット sukíttò

skittle [skit'əl] *n* スキットルのピン sukíttòru no píň

skittles [skit'əlz] *n* (game) スキットル sukíttòru ◇9本のピンを木のボールで倒すボーリングに似た遊び kyúhòn no píň wo kí no bṓru de taosu bōringu ni nita asobì

skive [skaiv] (*BRIT*: *inf*) *vi* サボる sabórù

skulk [skʌlk] *vi* うろつく urótsukù

skull [skʌl] *n* (ANAT) 頭がい骨 zugáìkotsu

skunk [skʌŋk] *n* (animal) スカンク sukáňku

sky [skai] *n* 空 sórà

skylight [skai'lait] *n* 天窓 teñmado

skyscraper [skai'skreipəːr] *n* 摩天楼 matéňrō

slab [slæb] *n* (stone) 石板 sekíban; (of cake, cheese) 厚い一切れ atsúi hitokìre

slack [slæk] *adj* (loose: rope, trousers etc) たるんでいる tarúnde irù; (slow: period) 忙しくない isógashikunaì; (careless: security, discipline) いい加減な iíkagen na

slacken [slæk'ən] (*also*: **slacken off**) *vi*

slacks [slæks] *npl* ズボン zubóń, スラックス surákkùsu

slag heap [slæg-] *n* ぼた山 botáyama

slag off (*BRIT: inf*) *vt* (criticize) ...の悪口を言う ...no waróguchi wo iú

slain [slein] *pp of* **slay**

slalom [slɑː'ləm] *n* 回転競技 kaítenkyōgi, スラローム surárōmu

slam [slæm] *vt* (door) ばたんと閉める batáń to shimérù; (throw) 投げ付ける nagétsukerù; (criticize) 非難する hínán suru
◆*vi* (door) ばたんと閉まる batáń to shimárù

slander [slæn'də:r] *n* 中傷 chúshō

slang [slæŋ] *n* (informal language) 俗語 zokúgo, スラング suráňgu; (jargon: prison slang etc) 符丁 fuchō

slant [slænt] *n* (sloping: position) 傾斜 keísha; (fig: approach) 見方 mikáta

slanted [slæn'tid] *adj* (roof) 傾斜のある keísha no arù; (eyes) つり上った tsuríagattà

slanting [slæn'tiŋ] *adj* = **slanted**

slap [slæp] *n* (hit) 平手打ち hiráteuchi, びんた bíñta
◆*vt* (child, face) ぴしゃりと打つ pishárî to útsù
◆*adv* (directly) まともに matómo nì
to slap something on something (paint etc) ...を...にいい加減に塗り付ける ...wo ...ni iíkagen nì nurítsukerù

slapdash [slæp'dæʃ] *adj* (person, work) いい加減な iíkagen na

slapstick [slæp'stik] *n* (comedy) どたばた喜劇 dotábata kigèki

slap-up [slæp'ʌp] *adj: a slap-up meal* (*BRIT*) 御馳走 gochísō

slash [slæʃ] *vt* (cut: upholstery, wrists etc) 切る kírù ◊特に長くて深い切傷を付けるという意味で使う tókù ni nágakute fukáì kiríkîzu wo tsukérù to iú imì de tsukáù; (fig: prices) 下げる sagérù

slat [slæt] *n* (of wood, plastic) 板 ítà ◊百葉箱に使われる様な薄くて細い板を指す

(demand) 減る herú; (speed) 落ちる ochírù
◆*vt* (trousers) 緩める yurúmeru; (speed) 緩める yurúmerù, 落す otósù

hyakúyōbàko ni tsukáwareru yō na usúkùte hosóì ítà wo sásù

slate [sleit] *n* (material) 粘板岩 neñbangan; (piece: for roof) スレート surétò
◆*vt* (fig: criticize) けなす kenásù

slaughter [slɔː'tə:r] *n* (of animals) と殺 tosátsu; (of people) 虐殺 gyakúsatsu
◆*vt* (animals) と殺する tosátsu suru; (people) 虐殺する gyakúsatsu suru

slaughterhouse [slɔː'tə:rhaus] *n* と殺場 tosátsujō

Slav [slɑːv] *adj* スラブ民族の surábumiñzoku no

slave [sleiv] *n* 奴隷 doréi
◆*vi* (*also: slave away*) あくせく働く ákùseku határakù

slavery [slei'və:ri:] *n* (system) 奴隷制度 doréiseìdo; (condition) 奴隷の身分 doréi no mîbùn

slavish [slei'viʃ] *adj* (obedience) 卑屈な hikútsu na; (copy) 盲目的な mōmokuteki na

slay [slei] (*pt* **slew**, *pp* **slain**) *vt* 殺す korósù

sleazy [sliː'ziː] *adj* (place) 薄汚い usúgitanaì

sledge [sledʒ] *n* そり sórì

sledgehammer [sledʒ'hæmə:r] *n* 大づち ōzùchi

sleek [sliːk] *adj* (shiny, smooth: hair, fur etc) つやつやの tsuyátsuyà no; (car, boat etc) 優雅な yūga na

sleep [sliːp] *n* 睡眠 suímin
◆*vi* (*pt, pp* **slept**) (*gen*) 眠る nemúrù, 寝る nerú; (spend night) 泊る tomárù
to go to sleep (person) 眠る nemúrù, 寝る neru

sleep around *vi* 色々な人とセックスをする iróiro na hito tò sékkùsu wo suru

sleeper [sliː'pə:r] (*BRIT*) *n* (RAIL: on track) まくら木 makúragi; (: train) 寝台列車 shiñdairesshà

sleep in *vi* (oversleep) 寝坊する nebó suru

sleeping bag [sliː'piŋ-] *n* 寝袋 nebúkùro

sleeping car *n* (RAIL) 寝台車 shiñdaishà

sleeping partner (*BRIT*) *n* (COMM)

= **silent partner**

sleeping pill n 睡眠薬 suímiñ-yaku

sleepless [sli:p'lis] adj: *a sleepless night* 眠れない夜 nemúrenai yorù

sleepwalker [sli:p'wɔ:kə:r] n 夢遊病者 muyûbyôshà

sleepy [sli:'pi:] adj (person) 眠い nemúi; (fig: village etc) ひっそりとした hissôrì to shita

sleet [sli:t] n みぞれ mizóre

sleeve [sli:v] n (of jacket etc) そで sodé; (of record) ジャケット jákètto

sleeveless [sli:v'lis] adj (garment) そでなしの sodénashi no, スリーブレスの suríburešu no

sleigh [slei] n そり sórì

sleight [slait] n: *sleight of hand* 奇術 kíjùtsu

slender [slen'də:r] adj (slim: figure) ほっそりした hossôrì shita, スリムな súrìmu na; (small: means, majority) わずかな wázùka na

slept [slept] pt, pp of **sleep**

slew [slu:] vi (BRIT) = **slue**
♦pt of **slay**

slice [slais] n (of meat, bread, lemon) スライス suráisu; (utensil: fish slice) フライ返し furáigaèshi; (: cake slice) ケーキサーバー kékisàbā
♦vt (bread, meat etc) スライスする suráisu suru

slick [slik] adj (skillful: performance) 鮮やかな azáyàka na; (clever: salesman, answer) 抜け目のない nukéme no naì
♦n (also: **oil slick**) 油膜 yumáku

slid [slid] pt, pp of **slide**

slide [slaid] n (downward movement) 下落 geráku; (in playground) 滑り台 subéridài; (PHOT: also: **hair slide**) 髪留 kamídòme, ヘアクリップ heákurìppu
♦vb (pt, pp **slid**)
♦vt 滑らせる subéraserù
♦vi (slip) 滑る subérù; (glide) 滑る様に動く subéru yô ni ugókù

slide rule n 計算尺 keísanjaku

sliding [slai'diŋ] adj: *sliding door* 引戸 hikídò

sliding scale n スライド制 suráidosei

slight [slait] adj (slim: figure) やせ型の yaségata no; (frail) か弱い kayówaì; (small: increase, difference) わずかな wázùka na; (error, accent, pain etc) ちょっとした chôttò shita; (trivial) ささいな sásài na
♦n (insult) 侮辱 bujóku
not in the slightest 少しも...ない sukóshì mo ...náì

slightly [slait'li:] adv (a bit, rather) 少し sukóshì

slim [slim] adj (person, figure) ほっそりした hossôrì shita; (chance) わずかな wázùka na
♦vi (lose weight) やせる yasérù

slime [slaim] n ぬるぬるした物 núrùnuru shita monó

slimming [slim'iŋ] n (losing weight) そう身 sôshin

slimy [slai'mi:] adj (pond) ぬるぬるした物に覆われた núrùnuru shita monó nì ówaretà

sling [sliŋ] n (MED) 三角きん sañkakùkin; (for baby) 子守り帯 komóriobì; (weapon) 石投げ器 ishínagekì
♦vt (pt, pp **slung**) (throw) 投げる nagérù

slip [slip] n (while walking) 踏外し fumíhazushi; (of vehicle) スリップ suríppù; (mistake) 過ち ayámachì; (underskirt) スリップ suríppù; (also: **slip of paper**) 一枚の紙 ichímaì no kamí ◇通常メモ用紙, 伝票などの様な小さい紙を指す tsújō memoyôshi, deñpyō nadò no yô nà chiísaì kamí wò sásù
♦vt (slide) こっそり...を...にやる kossórì ...wo ...ni yarú
♦vi (slide) 滑る subérù; (lose balance) 踏外す fumíhazusù; (decline) 悪くなる wárùku nárù; (move smoothly): *to slip into/out of* (room etc) そっと入る〔出て行く〕 sôttò háìru 〔détè iku〕
to give someone the slip ...をまく ...wo mákù
a slip of the tongue うっかり言ってしまう事 ukkárì itté shimaù kotó
to slip something on/off さっと...を着る〔脱ぐ〕 sáttò ...wo kírù 〔nugu〕

slip away vi (go) そっと立ち去る sóttò tachísaru

slip in vt (put) こっそり入れる kossórī irérù

♦vi (errors) いつの間にか入ってしまう itsú no ma ni kà haítte shimaù

slip out vi (go out) そっと出て行く sóttò détè ikú

slipped disc [slipt-] n (carpet slipper) スリッパ surīppà

slipper [slip'əːr] n (carpet slipper) スリッパ surīppà

slippery [slip'əːriː] adj (road) 滑りやすい subériyasuî; (fish etc) つかみにくい tsukáminikuî

slip road (BRIT) n (on motorway: access road) 入路 nyúro; (: exit road) 出口 deguchi

slipshod [slip'ʃɑːd] adj いい加減な iîkagen na

slip up vi (make mistake) 間違いをする machígai wò suru

slip-up [slip'ʌp] n (error) 間違い machígaî

slipway [slip'wei] n 造船台 zōsendài

slit [slit] n (cut) スリット surīttò; (opening) すき間 sukíma

♦vt (pt, pp **slit**) 切り開く kiríhirakù

slither [sliŏ'əːr] vi (person) 足を取られながら歩く ashî wò torárenagara arukù; (snake etc) はう háù

sliver [sliv'əːr] n (of glass, wood) 破片 hahén; (of cheese etc) 一切れ hitókìre

slob [slɑːb] (inf) n (man) だらしない野郎 daráshinai yarō; (woman) だらしないあま daráshinaî amá

slog [slɑːg] (BRIT) vi (work hard) あくせく働く ákùseku határaku

♦n: it was a hard slog 苦労した kurō shitá

slogan [slou'gən] n スローガン surōgàn

slop [slɑːp] vi (also: slop over) こぼれる kobórerù

♦vt こぼす kobósù

slope [sloup] n (gentle hill) 坂道 sakámìchi; (side of mountain) 山腹 sańpuku; (ski slope) ゲレンデ geréndè; (slant) 傾斜 keísha

♦vi: to slope down 下り坂になる kudárizaka ni narù

slope up vi 上り坂になる nobórizaka ni narù

sloping [slou'piŋ] adj (ground, roof) 傾斜になっている keísha ni natte irù; (handwriting) 斜めの nanáme no

sloppy [slɑːp'iː] adj (work, appearance) だらしない daráshinaî

slot [slɑːt] n (in machine) 投入口 tónyūguchi, スロット suróttò

♦vt: to slot something into ... (のスロットなど) に ...を入れる ... (no suróttò nado) ni ...wo irérù

sloth [slɔːθ] n (laziness) 怠惰 táìda

slot machine n (BRIT: vending machine) 自動販売機 jidóhanbaikî; (for gambling) スロットマシーン suróttomashīn

slouch [slautʃ] vi (person) だらしない姿勢で...する daráshinaî shiséi dè ...suru

slovenly [slʌv'ənliː] adj (dirty: habits, conditions) 汚い kitánaî; (careless: piece of work) だらしない daráshinaî

slow [slou] adj (music, journey) ゆっくりした yukkúrì shita; (service) 遅い osóî, のろい noróî; (person: not clever) 物覚えの悪い monóoboe no warúî; (watch, clock): to be slow 遅れている okúrete irù

♦adv ゆっくりと yukkúrì to, 遅く osókù

♦vt (also: slow down, slow up: vehicle) ...のスピードを落す ...no supídò wo otósù; (: business etc) 低迷させる teímei saserù

♦vi (also: slow down, slow up: vehicle) スピードを落す supídò wo otósù; (: business etc) 下火になる shitábi nì narú

「slow」 (road sign) 徐行 jokō

slowly [slou'liː] adv ゆっくりと yukkúrì to, 遅く osókù

slow motion n: in slow motion スローモーションで surōmōshon de

sludge [slʌdʒ] n (mud) へどろ hedóro

slue [sluː] (US veer) vi スリップする suríppù suru

slug [slʌg] n (creature) なめくじ namékujî; (bullet) 弾丸 dańgan, 鉄砲玉 teppōdama

sluggish [slʌg'iʃ] *adj* (stream, engine, person) 緩慢な kańman na; (COMM: trading) 不活発な fukáppatsu na

sluice [slu:s] *n* (*also*: **sluicegate**) 水門 suímon; (channel) 水路 suíro

slum [slʌm] *n* (house) 汚い家 kitánaì ié; (area) 貧民街 hińmiñgai, スラム súràmu

slump [slʌmp] *n* (economic) 不景気 fukéiki; (COMM) スランプ suráñpu
♦*vi* (fall: person) 崩れ落ちる kuzúreochirù; (: prices) 暴落する bŏraku suru

slung [slʌŋ] *pt, pp of* **sling**

slur [slə:r] *n* (*fig*): **slur (on)** (...の)悪口 (...no) warúkuchi
♦*vt* (words) 口ごもって言う kuchígomottè iú

slush [slʌʃ] *n* (melted snow) 溶けかかった雪 tokékakattà yukí

slush fund *n* 裏金用資金 uráganeyōshikiñ

slut [slʌt] (*inf!*) *n* ばいた baíta

sly [slai] *adj* (smile, expression, remark) 意味ありげな ímiarige na; (person: clever, wily) ずるい zuruí

smack [smæk] *n* (slap) 平手打ち hiráteuchi; (on face) びんた bíñta
♦*vt* (hit: *gen*) 平手で打つ hiráte dè útsù; (: child) ぶつ bútsù; (: on face) ...にびんたを食らわす ...ni bíñta wo kurawásù
♦*vi*: **to smack of** (smell of) ...くさい ...kusáì; (remind one of) ...を思わせる ...wo omówaserù

small [smɔːl] *adj* (person, object) 小さいchiísaì; (child: young) 幼い osánaì; (quantity, amount) 少しの sukóshì no

small ads (*BRIT*) *npl* 分類広告 buńruikŏkoku

small change *n* 小銭 kozéni

small fry *npl* (unimportant people) 下っ端 shitáppa

smallholder [smɔːl'houldər] (*BRIT*) *n* 小自作農 shŏjisakunŏ

small hours *npl*: **in the small hours** 深夜に shíñya ni

smallpox [smɔːl'pɑːks] *n* 天然痘 teñnentŏ

small talk *n* 世間話 sekénbanàshi

smart [smɑːrt] *adj* (neat, tidy) きちんとした kichíñ to shitá; (fashionable: clothes etc) しゃれた sharéta, いきな ikí na, スマートな sumátò na; (: house, restaurant) しゃれた shareta, 高級な kŏkyū na; (clever) 頭がいい atáma ga iî; (quick) 早い hayáî

smarten up [smɑːr'tən-] *vi* 身なりを直す mínàri wo naósù
♦*vt* きれいにする kírèi ni suru

smash [smæʃ] *n* (collision: *also*: **smash-up**) 衝突 shŏtotsu; (smash hit) 大ヒット daíhittŏ
♦*vt* (break) めちゃめちゃに壊す mechámecha nì kowásù; (car etc) 衝突してめちゃめちゃにする shŏtotsu shitè mechámecha ni surù; (SPORT: record) 破る yabúrù
♦*vi* (break) めちゃめちゃに壊れる mechámecha nì kowárerù; (against wall etc) 激突する gekítotsu suru

smashing [smæʃ'iŋ] (*inf*) *adj* 素晴らしい subárashiî

smattering [smæt'əːriŋ] *n*: **a smattering of** ...をほんの少し ...wo hoñno sukoshì

smear [smiːr] *n* (trace) 染み shimí; (MED) スミア sumía
♦*vt* (spread) 塗る nurú; (make dirty) 汚す yogósù

smear campaign *n* 中傷作戦 chúshōsakuseñ

smell [smel] *n* (odor) におい nióì; (sense) 臭覚 kyúkaku
♦*vb* (*pt, pp* **smelt** *or* **smelled**)
♦*vt* (become aware of odor) ...のにおいがする ...no nioi ga suru; (sniff) かぐ kagú
♦*vi* (*pej*) におう nióù, 臭い kusáì; (food etc) ...においがする ...nióì ga suru
to smell of ...のにおいがする ...no nióì ga suru

smelly [smel'iː] *adj* (cheese, socks) 臭い kusáì

smile [smail] *n* ほほえみ hohóemi
♦*vi* ほほえむ hohóemù

smirk [smə:rk] n にやにや笑い niyániya warài

smithy [smiθ'i:] n 鍛冶屋の仕事場 kajíya no shigótoba

smock [smɑːk] n (gen) 上っ張り uwáppari; (children's) スモック sumókkù; (US: overall) 作業着 sagyōgì

smog [smɑːg] n スモッグ sumóggù

smoke [smouk] n 煙 kemúri
♦vi (person) タバコを吸う tabáko wò súù; (chimney) 煙を出す kemúri wò dásù
♦vt (cigarettes) 吸う súú

smoked [smoukt] adj (bacon etc) 薫製の kuńsei no; (glass) いぶした ibúshita

smoker [smou'kər] n (person) タバコを吸う人 tabáko wò súú hito, 喫煙者 kitsúeñsha; (RAIL) 喫煙車 kitsúeñsha

smokescreen [smouk'skri:n] n (also fig) 煙幕 éñmaku

smoking [smou'kiŋ] n (act) 喫煙 kitsúen
「no smoking」(sign) 禁煙 kiń-en

smoky [smou'ki:] adj (atmosphere, room) 煙い kemúî; (taste) 薫製の（様な）kuńsei no (yō na)

smolder [smoul'dər] (US) vi (fire: also fig: anger, hatred) くすぶる kusúburù

smooth [smuːð] adj (gen) 滑らかな naméràka na; (sauce) つぶつぶのない tsubútsubu no nai; (flat: sea) 穏やかな odáyàka na; (flavor, whisky) まろやかな maróyàka na; (movement) 滑らかな naméràka na; (pej: person) 口先のうまい kuchísaki nò umáî
♦vt (also: smooth out: skirt, piece of paper etc) ...のしわを伸ばす ...no shiwá wò nobásù; (: creases) 伸ばす nobásù; (: difficulties) 除く torínozokù

smother [smʌð'əːr] vt (fire) ...に...をかぶせて消す ...ni ...wo kabúsete kesù; (suffocate: person) 窒息させる chissóku sasérù; (repress: emotions) 抑える osáerù

smoulder [smoul'dəːr] (BRIT) vi = smolder

smudge [smʌdʒ] n 汚れ yogóre
♦vt 汚す yogósù

smug [smʌg] adj 独り善がりの hitóriyogarî no

smuggle [smʌg'əl] vt (diamonds etc) 密

smuggler [smʌg'ləːr] n 密輸者 mitsúyushã

smuggling [smʌg'liŋ] n (traffic) 密輸 mitsúyu

smutty [smʌt'i:] adj (fig: joke, book) わいせつな waísetsu na

snack [snæk] n (light meal) 軽食 keíshoku; (food) スナック sunákkù

snack bar n スナックバー sunákkubà, スナック sunákkù

snag [snæg] n 障害 shōgai

snail [sneil] n カタツムリ katátsumùri ◊一般に水生の巻貝をも指す ippán nì suísei nò makígai wo mo sásù

snake [sneik] n (gen) ヘビ hébî

snap [snæp] n (sound) ぱちっという音 pachíttò iú otò; (photograph) 写真 shashín
♦adj (decision etc) 衝動的な shōdōteki na
♦vt (break) 折る őrù; (fingers) 鳴らす narásù
♦vi (break) 折れる orérù; (fig: person: speak sharply) 辛らつな事を言う shíñratsu na kotó wo iú
to snap shut (trap, jaws etc) がちゃっと閉まる gacháttò shimárù

snap at vt fus (subj: dog) かみつこうとする kamítsukố to suru

snap off vi (break) 折れる orérù ◊折れて取れる場合に使う őrete torérù baái nì tsukáù

snappy [snæp'i:] (inf) adj (answer, slogan) 威勢のいい iséi no ĩ
make it snappy (hurry up) 早くしなさい háyàku shinásaî

snapshot [snæp'ʃɑːt] n 写真 shashín

snap up vt (bargains) すぐ買う súgù káù

snare [sneːr] n わな wánà

snarl [snɑːrl] vi (animal) うなる unárù; (person) どなる donárù

snatch [snætʃ] n (small piece: of conversation, song etc) 断片 dañpeñ
♦vt (snatch away: handbag, child etc) ひったくる hittákurù; (fig: opportunity) 利用する riyō suru; (: look, some sleep etc)

急いでやる isóide yarú

sneak [sni:k] (*pt, pp* **sneaked** *also US* **snuck**) *vi*: *to sneak in/out* こっそり入る〔出る〕kossóri háiru 〔deru〕

♦*n* (*inf*) 告げ口するひと tsugéguchi suru hitó

to sneak up on someone ...に忍び寄る ...ni shinóbiyorú

sneakers [sni:'kə:rz] *npl* 運動靴 uñdōgutsu, スニーカー suníkā

sneer [sni:r] *vi* (laugh nastily) 冷笑する reíshō suru; (mock): *to sneer at* ...をあざわらう ...wo azáwaraú

sneeze [sni:z] *n* くしゃみ kushámì

♦*vi* くしゃみをする kushámì wo suru

sniff [snif] *n* (sound) 鼻をくんくん鳴らす音 haná wò kúñkun narásù otò; (smell: by dog, person) くんくんかぐ事 kúñkun kagú kotò

♦*vi* (person: when crying etc) 鼻をくんくん鳴らす haná wò kúñkun narásù

♦*vt* (*gen*) かぐ kagú; (glue, drugs) 鼻で吸う haná dè súù

snigger [snig'ə:r] *vi* くすくす笑う kúsùkusu waráù

snip [snip] *n* (cut) はさみで切る事 hasámi dè kírù koto; (*BRIT*: *inf*: bargain) 掘出し物 horídashimonò

♦*vt* (cut) はさみで切る hasámi dè kírù

sniper [snai'pə:r] *n* 狙撃兵 sogékihèi

snippet [snip'it] *n* (of information, news) 断片 dañpen

snivelling [sniv'əliŋ] *adj* (whimpering) めそめそ泣く mésòmeso nakú

snob [sna:b] *n* 俗物 zokúbutsu

snobbery [sna:b'ə:ri:] *n* 俗物根性 zokúbutsukoñjò

snobbish [sna:b'iʃ] *adj* 俗物的な zokúbutsuteki na

snooker [snuk'ə:r] *n* ビリヤード biríyàdo

snoop [snu:p] *vi*: *to snoop about* こっそりのぞき回る kossóri nozókimawarù

snooty [snu:'ti:] *adj* (person, letter, reply) 横柄な óhèi na

snooze [snu:z] *n* 昼寝 hirúne

♦*vi* 昼寝する hirúne suru

snore [sno:r] *n* いびき ibíki

♦*vi* いびきをかく ibíki wò kákù

snorkel [sno:r'kəl] *n* (for swimming) シュノーケル shunōkèru

snort [sno:rt] *n* 鼻を鳴らす事 haná wò narásù koto

♦*vi* (animal, person) 鼻を鳴らす haná wò narásù

snout [snaut] *n* ふん fúñ

snow [snou] *n* 雪 yukí

♦*vi* 雪が降る yukí gà fúrù

snowball [snou'bɔ:l] *n* 雪のつぶて yukí nò tsubúte

♦*vi* (*fig*: problem, campaign) どんどん大きくなる dóñdon ōkiku nárù

snowbound [snou'baund] *adj* (people) 雪に閉じ込められた yukí ni tojíkomerarèta; (vehicles) 雪で立ち往生した yukí dè tachíōjō shita

snowdrift [snou'drift] *n* 雪の吹きだまり yukí nò fukídamarì

snowdrop [snou'dra:p] *n* 雪の花 yukíno-hanà

snowfall [snou'fɔ:l] *n* (amount) 降雪量 kōsetsuryò; (a fall of snow) 降雪 kōsetsu

snowflake [snou'fleik] *n* 雪のひとひら yukí nò hitóhìra

snowman [snou'mæn] (*pl* **snowmen**) *n* 雪だるま yukídaruma

snowplow [snou'plau] (*BRIT* **snowplough**) *n* 除雪車 josétsushà

snowshoe [snou'ʃu:] *n* かんじき kañjiki

snowstorm [snou'stɔ:rm] *n* 吹雪 fúbùki

snub [snʌb] *vt* (person) 鼻であしらう haná dè ashíraù

♦*n* 侮辱 bujóku

snub-nosed [snʌb'nouzd] *adj* 鼻先の反った hanásaki nò sottá

snuck [snʌk] (*US*) *pt, pp of* **sneak**

snuff [snʌf] *n* かぎタバコ kagítabàko

snug [snʌg] *adj* (sheltered: person, place) こじんまりした kojínmari shita; (person) 心地好い kokóchiyoì; (well-fitting) ぴったりした pittárì shita

snuggle [snʌg'əl] *vi*: *to snuggle up to someone* ...に体を擦付ける ...ni karáda wò surítsukerù

KEYWORD

so [sou] *adv* 1 (thus, likewise) そう só, その通り sonô tōri

so saying he walked away そう言って彼は歩き去った só itté kárě wa arúkisattà

while she was so doing, he ... 彼女がそれをやっている間彼は... kánòjo ga soré wò yatté iru aĭda kárě wa...

if so だとすれば dá tò suréba

do you enjoy soccer? if so, come to the game フットボールが好きですか、だったら試合を見に来て下さい futtóbōru ga sukí desù ká, dáttàra shiái wò mi nĭ kite kudasaĭ

I didn't do it - you did so! やったのは私じゃない -いや、お前だ yattá no wà watákushi ja naĭ -iyá, omáe dà

so do I, so am I etc 私もそうです watákushi mò só desù

I like swimming - so do I 私は水泳が好きです -私もそうです watákushi wà suíei gà sukí desù -watákushi mò só desù

I'm still at school - so am I 私はまだ学生です -私もそうです watákushi wà máda gakúsei desù -watákushi mò só desù

I've got work to do - so has Paul 私には仕事がありますから -ポールもそうですよ watákushi ni wà shigóto gà arímasu karà -pōru mo só desù yó

it's 5'o'clock - so it is! 5時です -あっ、そうですね gójì desu -át, só desù né

I hope so そう希望します só kibō shimasù

I think so そうだと思います só da tò omóimasù

so far これまで koré mdè

how do you like the book so far? これまでその本はどうでしたか koré mdè sonô hoň wa dó deshíta ka

so far I haven't had any problems ここまでは問題はありません kokó mdè wa moñdai wà arímaseñ

2 (in comparisons etc: to such a degree) そんなに soňna nĭ

so quickly (that) (...がある程) 素早く (...ga áru hodo) subáyàku, とても素早く (...した ので ...) totémo subáyàku (...shitá no dè ...)

so big (that) (...がある程) 大きな (...ga árù hodo) ōkina, とても大きい (ので...) totémo ōkii (...)

she's not so clever as her brother 彼女は兄さん程利口ではない kánòjo wa niísaň hodo ríkō de wa naĭ

we were so worried 私たちはとても心配していましたよ watákushitàchi wa totémo shiñpai shite imashíta yó

I wish you weren't so clumsy あなたの不器用さはどうにかなりませんかね anáta no bukíyòsa wa dó ni ka nárimasen ka né

I'm so glad to see you あなたを見てほっとしました anátà wo mítě hóttò shimáshità

3: *so much* *adv* そんなに沢山で soňna nĭ takúsaň de

♦*adj* そんなに沢山の soňna nĭ takúsaň de

I've got so much work 私は仕事が山程あります watákushi wà shigóto gà yamá hodo arímasù

I love you so much あなたを心から愛しています anátà wo kokórò kara áĭ shite imasu

so many そんなに沢山 (の) soňna nĭ takúsaň (no)

there are so many things to do する事が山程あります surú kotò ga yamá hodo arímasù

there are so many people to meet 私が会うべき人たちは余りにも大勢です watákushi gà áùbeki hitótàchi wa amári ni mò ōzei desù 4 (phrases): *10 or so* 10個ぐらい júkkò gurai

so long! (*inf*: goodbye) じゃね já nè, またね matá nè

♦*conj* 1 (expressing purpose): *so as to do* ...する様(ため)に ...surú yō(tame)ni

we hurried so as not to be late 遅れない様に急いで行きました okúrenai yō ni isóĭde ikímashità

so (that) ...する様(ため)に ...surú yō

〔tamè〕ni

I brought it so (that) you could see it あなたに見せるために持ってきました anátā ni misérù tame ni mottè kimashíta

2 (expressing result) ...であるから... ...de árù kara ..., ...ので... ...nó de ...

he didn't arrive so I left 彼が来なかったので私は帰りました kárè ga kónàkatta nó de watákushi wà kaérimashìta

so I was right after all 結局私の言った通りでした kekkyòkù watákushi nò ittá tòri deshita

so you see, I could have gone ですかられ, 行こうと思えば行けたんです désù kara né, ikō tò omóebà ikétan desu

soak [souk] *vt* (drench) ずぶぬれにする zubúnure nǐ suru; (steep in water) 水に漬ける mizú nǐ tsukéru

♦*vi* (dirty washing, dishes) 漬かる tsukárù

soak in *vi* (be absorbed) 染み込む shimíkomù

soak up *vt* (absorb) 吸収する kyūshū surù

soap [soup] *n* 石けん sekkén

soapflakes [soup'fleiks] *npl* フレーク石けん furékusekkèn ◇洗濯用の固形石けんをフレークにした物を指す señtakuyō no kokéisekkèn wo furékù ni shitá monð wo sásù

soap opera *n* メロドラマ meródorama ◇テレビやラジオの連続物を指す térèbi ya rájìo no reñzokumonð wo sásù

soap powder *n* 粉石けん konásekkèn

soapy [sou'pi:] *adj* (hands etc) 石けんのついた sekkén no tsuità

soapy water 石けん水 sekkéñsui

soar [sɔːr] *vi* (on wings) 舞上がる maîagarù; (rocket) 空中に上がる kūchū nǐ agárù; (price, production, temperature) 急上昇する kyūjōshō suru; (building etc) そびえたつ sobíetatsù

sob [sɑːb] *n* しゃくり泣き shakúrinaki

♦*vi* 泣きじゃくる nakíjakurù

sober [sou'bə:r] *adj* (serious) まじめな majíme na; (dull: color, style) 地味なji-

mí na; (not drunk) しらふの shírafu no

sober up *vt* ...の酔いを覚ます ...no yoí wò samásù

♦*vi* 酔いが覚める yoí gà samérù

so-called [sou'kɔːld'] *adj* (friend, expert) いわゆる iwáyurù ◇多くの場合不信や軽べつなどを表す ōkù no baái fushín yà keíbetsu nadð wo aráwasù

soccer [sɑːk'əːr] *n* サッカー sákkà

sociable [sou'ʃəbəl] *adj* 愛想の良い aísō no yoì

social [sou'ʃəl] *adj* (gen: history, structure, background) 社会の shákāi no; (leisure: event, life) 社交的な shakōteki na; (sociable: animal) 社会性のある shakáisei no arù

♦*n* (party) 懇親会 koñshiñkai

social club *n* 社交クラブ shakōkurabu

socialism [sou'ʃəlizəm] *n* 社会主義 shakáishugì

socialist [sou'ʃəlist] *adj* 社会主義の shakáishugì no

♦*n* 社会主義者 shakáishugishà

socialize [sou'ʃəlaiz] *vi*: *to socialize (with)* (...と) 交際する (...to) kōsai suru

socially [sou'ʃəli:] *adv* (visit) 社交的に shakōteki ni; (acceptable) 社会的に shakáiteki ni

social security (*BRIT*) *n* 社会保障 shakáihoshō

social work *n* ソーシャルワーク sōsharuwāku

social worker *n* ソーシャルワーカー sōsharuwākā

society [səsai'əti:] *n* (people, their lifestyle) 社会 shákāi; (club) 会 kâi; (*also*: *high society*) 上流社会 jōryūshakāi

sociologist [sousi:ɑːl'ədʒist] *n* 社会学者 shakáigakushà

sociology [sousi:ɑːl'ədʒi:] *n* 社会学 shakáigaku

sock [sɑːk] *n* 靴下 kutsúshita

socket [sɑːk'it] *n* (gen: cavity) 受け口 ukégùchi; (ANAT: of eye) 眼か gáñka; (ELEC: for light bulb) ソケット sokéttð; (*BRIT*: ELEC: wall socket) コンセント kōñsento

sod [sɑːd] n (of earth) 草の生えた土 kusá nò háèta tsuchí; (BRIT: inf!) くそ kusó

soda [sou'də] n (CHEM) ナトリウム化合物 natóriùmu kagóbutsu ◊一般にか性ソーダ, 重曹などを指す ippán nì kaséisòda, jūsō nadò wo sásù; (also: **soda water**) ソーダ水 sōdàsui; (US: also: **soda pop**) 清涼飲料 seíryoiñryo

sodden [sɑːd'ən] adj びしょぬれの bishónure no

sodium [sou'diːəm] n ナトリウム natóriùmu

sofa [sou'fə] n ソファー sófà

soft [sɔːft] adj (not hard) 柔らかい yawárakaì; (gentle, not loud: voice, music) 静かな shízùka na; (not bright: light, color) 柔らかな yawárakà na; (kind: heart, approach) 優しい yasáshii

soft drink n 清涼飲料水 seíryoiñryōsui

soften [sɔːf'ən] vt (gen: make soft) 柔らかくする yawárakàku suru; (effect, blow, expression) 和らげる yawáragerù
◆vi (gen: become soft) 柔らかくなる yawárakaku narù; (voice, expression) 優しくなる yasáshiku narù

softly [sɔːft'liː] adv (gently) 優しく yasáshiku; (quietly) 静かに shízùka ni

softness [sɔːft'nis] n (gen) 柔らかさ yawárakasa; (gentleness) 優しさ yasáshisa

soft spot n: **to have a soft spot for someone** ...が大好きである ...ga dáisuki de árù

software [sɔːft'weːr] n (COMPUT) ソフトウエア sofútouèà

soggy [sɑːg'iː] adj (ground, sandwiches etc) ぐちゃぐちゃの guchágucha no

soil [sɔil] n (earth) 土壌 dójō; (territory) 土地 tochí
◆vt 汚す yogósù

solace [sɑːl'is] n 慰め nagúsame

solar [sou'lər] adj (eclipse, power etc) 太陽の táiyò no

sold [sould] pt, pp of **sell**

solder [sɑːd'əːr] vt はんだ付けにする hañdazuke nì suru
◆n はんだ hañda

soldier [soul'dʒəːr] n (in army) 兵隊 heítai; (not a civilian) 軍人 guñjin

sold out adj (COMM: goods, tickets, concert etc) 売切れで uríkire de

sole [soul] n (of foot) 足の裏 ashí nò urá; (of shoe) 靴の底 kutsú nò sokó; (fish: pl inv) シタビラメ shitábiràme
◆adj (unique) 唯一の yuítsu no

solely [soul'liː] adv ...だけ ...dáke

solemn [sɑːl'əm] adj (person) 謹厳な kiñgen na; (music) 荘重な sōchō na; (promise) 真剣な shíñken na

sole trader n (COMM) 自営業者 jiéigyòsha

solicit [səlis'it] vt (request) 求める motómerù
◆vi (prostitute) 客引きする kyakúbiki suru

solicitor [səlis'itəːr] (BRIT) n (for wills etc, in court) 弁護士 beñgoshi

solid [sɑːl'id] adj (not hollow) 中空でない chūkū de naí; (not liquid) 固形の kokéi no; (reliable: person, foundations etc) しっかりした shikkárì shita; (entire) まる... marú...; (pure: gold etc) 純粋の juñsui no
◆n (solid object) 固体 kotái

solidarity [sɑːlidær'itiː] n 団結 dañketsu

solidify [səlid'əfai] vi (fat etc) 固まる katámarù

solids [sɑːl'idz] npl (food) 固形食 kokéishòku

solitaire [sɑːl'iteːr] n (gem) 一つはめの宝石 hitótsuhame nò hōseki; (game) 一人遊び hitóriasobì

solitary [sɑːl'iteriː] adj (person, animal, life) 単独の tañdoku no; (alone: walk) 一人だけする hitórì dake de suru; (isolated) 人気のない hitóke no naì; (single: person) 一人だけの hitórì dake no; (: animal, object) 一つだけの hotótsu dake no

solitary confinement n 独房監禁 dokúbō kañkin

solitude [sɑːl'ətuːd] n 人里を離れている事 hitózato wò hanárete iru kotò

solo [sou'lou] n (piece of music, performance) 独奏 dokúsō
◆adv (fly) 単独で tañdoku de

soloist [sou'louist] n 独奏者 dokúsōshà

soluble [sɑːl'jəbəl] adj (aspirin etc) 溶ける tokérù

solution [səluː'ʃən] n (of puzzle, problem, mystery: answer) 解決 kaíketsu; (liquid) 溶液 yōeki

solve [sɑːlv] vt (puzzle, problem, mystery) 解決する kaíketsu suru

solvent [sɑːl'vənt] adj (COMM) 支払い能力のある shiháuráinōryoku no aru
♦n (CHEM) 溶剤 yōzai

somber [sɑːm'bəːr] (BRIT **sombre**) adj (dark: color, place) 暗い kurái; (serious: person, view) 陰気な íṅki na

---

KEYWORD

---

some [sʌm] adj 1 (a certain amount or number of) 幾らかの íkuraka no, 幾つかの íkùtsuka no, 少しの sukóshì no

some tea/water/biscuits お茶〔水, ビスケット〕o-chá(mizú, bisúkettò) ◇この用法では日本語で表現しない場合が多い konó yōhō de wa nihóngo dè hyōgen shinaí baái gà ói

some children came 何人かの子供が来た nánninka no kodómo gà kíta

there's some milk in the fridge 冷蔵庫にミルクがあります reízōko ni mírùku ga arímasu

he asked me some questions 彼は色々な事を聞きました kárè wa iróiro na kotò wo kikímashìta

there were some people outside 数人の人が外に立っていた sūnin no hitó gà sótò ni tatté ità

I've got some money, but not much 金はあるにはありますが, 少しだけです kanè wà árù ni wa arímasù gá, sukóshì dake dèsu

2 (certain: in contrasts) ある árù

*some people say that ... ...*と言っている人がいます ...tò itté irú hitó ga imásu

some people hate fish, while others love it 魚の嫌いな人もいれば大好きな人もいます sakána no kirái na hitó mo irébà daísuki na hitó mo imásù

some films were excellent, but most were mediocre 中には優れた映画もあった, 大半は平凡な物だった nákà ni wa sugúreta eíga mo attá gà, taíhan wa heíbon na monò dáttà

3 (unspecified) 何かの nánìka no, だれかの dárèka no

some woman was asking for you だれか女の人があなたを訪ねていましたよ dárèka oñna no hitó ga anátà wo tazúnete imashìta yó

he was asking for some book (or other) 彼は何かの本を捜していました kárè wa nánika no hòn wo sagáshite imashìta

some day いつか ítsùka, そのうち sonó uchì

we'll meet again some day そのうちまた会うチャンスがあるでしょう sonó uchì matá áù cháñsu ga árù deshō

shall we meet some day next week? 来週のいつかに会いましょうか raíshū nò ítsùka ni aímashō kà

♦pron 1 (a certain number) 幾つか íkùtsuka

I've got some (books etc) 私は幾つか持っています watákushi wà íkùtsuka móttè imasu

some (of them) have been sold 数個は売れてしまいました sūkò wa uréte shimaimashìta

some went for a taxi and some walked 何人かはタクシーを拾いに行ったが, 残りの人は歩いた nánninka wa tákùshī wo hirói ni itta gà, nokóri nò hitó wà arúita

2 (a certain amount) 幾分か ikúbun kà

I've got some (money, milk) 私は幾分か持っています watákushi wà ikúbun kà móttè imasu

some was left 少し残っていた sukóshì nokótte ità

could I have some of that cheese? そのチーズを少しもらっていいかしら sonó chīzu wo sukóshì morátte ii kashìra

I've read some of the book その本の一部を読みました sonó hòn no ichíbù wo yomímashita

♦adv: *some 10 people* 10人ぐらい júnin gurai

somebody [sʌm'bɑːdiː] pron = **someone**
somehow [sʌm'hau] adv (in some way)

何とかして nán to ka shite; (for some reason) どういう訳か dō iu wákè ka

KEYWORD

someone [sʌm'wʌn] *pron* だれか dárèka, 人 hitó
there's someone coming 人が来ます hitó gà kimásù
I saw someone in the garden だれか庭にいました dárèka niwá nì imáshìta

someplace [sʌm'pleis] (*US*) *adv* = **somewhere**

somersault [sʌm'əːrsɔːlt] *n* とんぼ返り toñbogaèri
♦*vi* (person, vehicle) とんぼ返りする toñbogaèri suru

KEYWORD

something [sʌm'θiŋ] *pron* 何か nánìka
something nice 何かいい物 nánìka íi mono
something to do 何かする事 nánìka surú kotò
there's something wrong 何かおかしい nánìka okáshìi
would you like something to eat/drink? 何か食べません〔飲みません〕か nánìka tabémaseñ(nomímaseñ)ká

sometime [sʌm'taim] *adv* (in future) いつか ítsùka; (in past): *sometime last month* 先月のいつか señgetsu no ítsùka

sometimes [sʌm'taimz] *adv* 時々 tokídoki

somewhat [sʌm'wʌt] *adv* 少し sukóshì

KEYWORD

somewhere [sʌm'weːr] *adv* (be) どこかに〔で〕dókòka ni〔de〕; (go) どこかへ dókòka e
I must have lost it somewhere どこかに落した様です dókòka ni otóshita yō desu
it's somewhere or other in Scotland スコットランドのどこかにあります sukóttoraňdo no dókòka ni arímasù
somewhere else (be) どこか外の所に

〔で〕dókòka hoká no tokorò ni〔de〕; (go) どこか外の所へ dókòka hoká no tokorò e

son [sʌn] *n* 息子 musúko

sonar [sou'nɑːr] *n* ソナー sónā

song [sɔːŋ] *n* (MUS) 歌 utá; (of bird) さえずり saézurì

sonic [sɑːn'ik] *adj*: *sonic boom* ソニックブーム soníkkubūmu

son-in-law [sʌn'inlɔː] (*pl* **sons-in-law**) *n* 義理の息子 girí no musuko

sonnet [sɑːn'it] *n* ソネット sonéttò

sonny [sʌn'iː] (*inf*) *n* 坊や bòya

soon [suːn] *adv* (in a short time) もうすぐ mō sugù; (a short time after) 間もなく mamónàku; (early) 早く hayákù
soon afterwards それから間もなく soré karà mamónàku ¶ *see also* **as**

sooner [suː'nəːr] *adv* (time) もっと早く móttò hayákù; (preference): *I would sooner do that* 私はむしろあれをやりたい watákushi wà múshìro aré wò yarítaì
sooner or later 遅かれ早かれ osókare hayakàre

soot [sut] *n* すす súsù

soothe [suːð] *vt* (calm: person, animal) 落着かせる ochítsukaserù; (reduce: pain) 和らげる yawáragerù

sophisticated [səfis'tikeitid] *adj* (woman, lifestyle, audience) 世慣れた yonárèta; (machinery) 精巧な seíkō na; (arguments) 洗練された señren sarèta

sophomore [sɑːf'əmɔːr] (*US*) *n* 2年生 niñènsei

soporific [sɑːpərif'ik] *adj* (speech) 眠気を催させる nemúke wò moyóosaserù; (drug) 睡眠の suímin no

sopping [sɑːp'iŋ] *adj*: *sopping (wet)* (hair, clothes etc) びしょぬれの bishónure no

soppy [sɑːp'iː] (*pej*) *adj* (sentimental) センチな señchi na

soprano [səpræn'ou] *n* (singer) ソプラノ sopúrano

sorcerer [sɔːr'sərəːr] *n* 魔法使い mahṓtsukài

sordid [sɔːˈdɪd] *adj* (dirty: bed-sit etc) 汚らしい kitánarashìi; (wretched: story etc) 浅ましい asámashìi, えげつない egétsunaì

sore [sɔːr] *adj* (painful) 痛い itáì
♦*n* (shallow) ただれ tadáre; (deep) かいよう kaíyō

sorely [sɔːrˈliː] *adv*: *I am sorely tempted to* よほど...しようと思っている yohódo ...shiyō to omótte irù

sorrow [sɑːrˈou] *n* (regret) 悲しみ kanáshimi

sorrowful [sɑːrˈoufəl] *adj* (day, smile etc) 悲しい kanáshiì

sorrows [sɑːrˈouz] *npl* (causes of grief) 不幸 fúkō

sorry [sɑːrˈiː] *adj* (regretful) 残念な zańneǹ na; (condition, excuse) 情けない nasákenaì

sorry! (apology) 済みません sumímaseǹ
sorry? (pardon) はい？ haí? ◇相手の言葉を聞取れなかった時に言う aíte no kotòba wo kikítorenakatta tokí ni iú
to feel sorry for someone ...に同情する ...ni dōjō suru

sort [sɔːrt] *n* (type) 種類 shúrùi
♦*vt* (*also*: **sort out**: papers, mail, belongings) より分ける yoríwakerù; (: problems) 解決する kaíketsu suru

sorting office [sɔːrˈtiŋ-] *n* 郵便物振分け場 yūbinbutsufuriwakejō

SOS [esoues'] *n* エスオーエス esú ō esù

so-so [sou'sou'] *adv* (average) まあまあ maámaà

soufflé [suːfleiˈ] *n* スフレ súfùre

sought [sɔːt] *pt, pp of* **seek**

soul [soul] *n* (spirit etc) 魂 támashìi; (person) 人 hitó

soul-destroying [soulˈdɪstrɔiiŋ] *adj* (work) ぼけさせる様な bokésaseru yō na

soulful [soulˈfəl] *adj* (eyes, music) 表情豊かな hyōjō yutàka na

sound [saund] *adj* (healthy) 健康な keńkō na; (safe, not damaged) 無傷の múkizu no; (secure: investment) 安全な ańzen na; (reliable, thorough) 信頼できる shińrai dekirù; (sensible: advice) 堅実な keńjitsu na
♦*adv*: *sound asleep* ぐっすり眠って gussúrì nemútte
♦*n* (noise) 音 otó; (volume on TV etc) 音声 ôńsei; (GEO) 海峡 kaíkyo
♦*vt* (alarm, horn) 鳴らす narásù
♦*vi* (alarm, horn) 鳴る narú; (*fig*: seem) ...の様である ...no yō de árù
to sound like ...の様に聞える ...no yō ni kikôerù

sound barrier *n* 音速障害 ońsokushō-gai

sound effects *npl* 音響効果 ońkyōkòka

soundly [saundˈliː] *adv* (sleep) ぐっすり gussúrì; (beat) 手ひどく tehídokù

sound out *vt* (person, opinion) 打診する dashín suru

soundproof [saundˈpruːf] *adj* (room etc) 防音の bôon no

soundtrack [saundˈtræk] *n* (of film) サウンドトラック saúndotorakkù

soup [suːp] *n* スープ sūpu
in the soup (*fig*) 困って komáttè

soup plate *n* スープ皿 sūpuzarà

soupspoon [suːpˈspuːn] *n* スープスプーン sūpusupùn

sour [sauˈər] *adj* (bitter) 酸っぱい suppáì; (milk) 酸っぱくなった suppákù náttà; (*fig*: bad-tempered) 機嫌の悪い kigén no waruì
it's sour grapes (*fig*) 負け惜しみだ makéoshimi da

source [sɔːrs] *n* (*also fig*) 源 mínàmoto

south [sauθ] *n* 南 mínàmi
♦*adj* 南の mínàmi no
♦*adv* (movement) 南へ mínàmi e; (position) 南に mínàmi ni

South Africa *n* 南アフリカ mínàmi a-fūrika

South African *adj* 南アフリカの mínàmi afùrika no
♦*n* 南アフリカ人 mínàmi afurikajìn

South America *n* 南米 nańbei

South American *adj* 南米の nańbei nò
♦*n* 南米人 nańbeijìn

south-east [sauθˈist'] *n* 南東 nańtō

southerly [sʌðˈərliː] *adj* (to/towards the south: aspect) 南への mínàmi e nò; (from the south: wind) 南からの mínàmi kara nò

southern [sʌð'ə:rn] *adj* (in or from the south of region) 南 の minámi no; (to/towards the south) 南向きの minámimuki no

the southern hemisphere 南半球 mínámihañkyū

South Pole *n* 南極 nañkyoku

southward(s) [sauθ'wə:rd(z)] *adv* 南 へ minámi e

south-west [sauθwest'] *n* 南西 nañsei

souvenir [su:vəni:r'] *n* (memento) 記念品 kinéñhin

sovereign [sɑːv'rin] *n* (ruler) 君主 kúñshu

sovereignty [sɑːv'rənti:] *n* 主権 shukéñ

soviet [sou'vi:it] *adj* ソビエトの sobíetò no

the Soviet Union ソ連 sóрèn

sow[1] [sau] *n* (pig) 牝豚 mesúbùta

sow[2] [sou] (*pt* **sowed**, *pp* **sown**) *vt* (*gen*: seeds) まく mákù; (*fig*: spread: suspicion etc) 広める hirómerù

soy [sɔi] (*BRIT* **soya**) *n*: *soy bean* 大豆 dáizu

soy sauce しょう油 shóyù

spa [spɑː] *n* (*also*: **spa town**) 鉱泉町 kóseñmachi; (*US*: *also*: **health spa**) ヘルスセンター herúsuseñtā

space [speis] *n* (gap) すき間 sukíma, ギャップ gyáppù; (place) 空所 kúsho, 余白 yoháku; (room) 空間 kúkan; (beyond Earth) 宇宙空間 uchúkūkan, スペース supèsu; (interval, period) 間 ma

♦*cpd* 宇宙... úchū...

♦*vt* (*also*: **space out**: text, visits, payments) 間隔を置く kañkaku wò okú

spacecraft [speis'kræft] *n* 宇宙船 uchúsen

spaceman [speis'mæn] (*pl* **spacemen**) *n* 宇宙飛行士 uchúhikōshi

spaceship [speis'ʃip] *n* = **spacecraft**

spacewoman [speis'wumən] (*pl* **spacewomen**) *n* 女性宇宙飛行士 joséi uchūhikōshi

spacing [spei'siŋ] *n* (between words) スペース supèsu

spacious [spei'ʃəs] *adj* (car, room etc) 広い hirói

spade [speid] *n* (tool) スコップ sukóppù; (child's) おもちゃのスコップ omóchà no sukóppù

spades [speidz] *npl* (CARDS: suit) スペード supèdo

spaghetti [spəget'i:] *n* スパゲッティ supágettì

Spain [spein] *n* スペイン supéñ

span [spæn] *n* (of bird, plane) 翼長 yokúchō; (of arch) スパン supáñ; (in time) 期間 kikáñ

♦*vt* (river) ...にまたがる ...ni matágarù; (*fig*: time) ...に渡る ...ni watárù

Spaniard [spæn'jə:rd] *n* スペイン人 supéinjìn

spaniel [spæn'jəl] *n* スパニエル supánièru

Spanish [spæn'iʃ] *adj* スペインの supéñ no; (LING) スペイン語の supéiñgo no

♦*n* (LING) スペイン語 supéiñgo

♦*npl: the Spanish* スペイン人 supéinjìn ◇総称 sôshō

spank [spæŋk] *vt* (someone, someone's bottom) ...のしりをたたく ...no shirí wò tatáků

spanner [spæn'ə:r] (*BRIT*) *n* スパナ supánà

spar [spɑːr] *n* (pole) マスト másùto

♦*vi* (BOXING) スパーリングする supárìngu suru

spare [spe:r] *adj* (free) 空きの akí no; (surplus) 余った amáttà

♦*n* = **spare part**

♦*vt* (do without: trouble etc) ...なしで済ます ...nàshí de sumásù; (make available) 与える atáerù; (refrain from hurting: person, city etc) 助けてやる tasúkete yarù

to spare (surplus: time, money) 余った amáttà

spare part *n* 交換用部品 kókan-yōbuhiñ

spare time *n* 余暇 yóka

spare wheel *n* (AUT) スペアタイア supéataià

sparing [spe:r'iŋ] *adj*: *to be sparing with* ...を倹約する ...wo keñ-yaku suru

sparingly [spe:r'iŋli:] *adv* (use) 控え目に

hikáeme ni

spark [spɑːrk] *n* 火花 híbàna, スパーク supákù; (*fig*: of wit etc) ひらめき hirámekî

spark(ing) plug [spɑːrk'(iŋ)-] *n* スパークプラグ supákupuràgu

sparkle [spɑːr'kəl] *n* きらめき kirámekî
♦*vi* (shine: diamonds, water) きらめく kirámekù

sparkling [spɑːr'kliŋ] *adj* (wine) 泡立つ awádatsù; (conversation, performance) きらめく様な kirámeku yô na

sparrow [spær'ou] *n* スズメ suzúme

sparse [spɑːrs] *adj* (rainfall, hair, population) 少ない sukúnaî

spartan [spɑːr'tən] *adj* (*fig*) 簡素な kánso na

spasm [spæz'əm] *n* (MED) けいれん keíren

spasmodic [spæzmɑːd'ik] *adj* (*fig*: not continuous, irregular) 不規則な fukísoku na

spastic [spæs'tik] *n* 脳性麻ひ患者 nôseimahikanja

spat [spæt] *pt, pp of* **spit**

spate [speit] *n* (*fig*): *a spate of* (letters, protests etc) 沢山の takúsan no

spatter [spæt'əːr] *vt* (liquid, surface) ...を...にはねかす ...wo ...ni hanékasù

spatula [spætʃ'ələ] *n* (CULIN, MED) へら hérà

spawn [spɔːn] *vi* (fish etc) 産卵する sañran suru
♦*n* (frog spawn etc) 卵 tamágò

speak [spiːk] (*pt* **spoke**, *pp* **spoken**) *vt* (language) 話す hanásù; (truth) 言う iú
♦*vi* (use voice) 話す hanásù; (make a speech) 演説する eñzetsu suru
to speak to someone ...に話し掛ける ...ni hanáshikakerù
to speak to someone of/about something ...に...のことを話す ...ni ...no kotó wò hanásù
speak up! もっと大きな声で話しなさい móttò ôkìna kôè de hanáshi nasaî

speaker [spiː'kəːr] *n* (in public) 演説者 eñzetsushà; (*also*: **loudspeaker**) スピーカー supíkà; (POL): *the Speaker* (US,

BRIT) 下院議長 ka-íngichô

spear [spi'əːr] *n* (weapon) やり yarí
♦*vt* 刺す sásù

spearhead [spi:r'hed] *vt* (attack etc) ...の先頭に立つ ...no señtô nì tátsù

spec [spek] (*inf*) *n*: *on spec* 山をかけて yamá wo kakète

special [speʃ'əl] *adj* 特別な tokúbetsu na
special delivery 速達 sokútatsu
special school (*BRIT*) 特殊学校 tokúshugakkò
special adviser 特別顧問 tokúbetsukomòn
special permission 特別許可 tokúbetsukyokà

specialist [speʃ'əlist] *n* (*gen*) 専門家 señmonka; (MED) 専門医 señmoñ-i

speciality [speʃi:æl'əti:] *n* = **specialty**

specialize [speʃ'əlaiz] *vi*: *to specialize (in)* (...を) 専門的にやる (...wo) señmonteki ni yarù

specially [speʃ'əli:] *adv* (especially) 特に tôkù ni; (on purpose) 特別に tokúbetsu ni

specialty [speʃ'əlti:] *n* (dish) 名物 meíbutsu; (study) 専門 señmon

species [spiː'ʃi:z] *n inv* 種 shú

specific [spisif'ik] *adj* (fixed) 特定の tokútei no; (exact) 正確な seíkaku na

specifically [spisif'ikli:] *adv* (especially) 特に tôkù ni; (exactly) 明確に meíkaku ni

specification [spesəfəkei'ʃən] *n* (TECH) 仕様 shiyô; (requirement) 条件 jôkeñ

specifications [spesəfəkei'ʃənz] *npl* (TECH) 仕様 shiyô

specify [spes'əfai] *vt* (time, place, color etc) 指定する shitéi suru

specimen [spes'əmən] *n* (single example) 見本 mihôn; (sample for testing, *also* MED) 標本 hyôhon

speck [spek] *n* (of dirt, dust etc) 粒 tsúbù

speckled [spek'əld] *adj* (hen, eggs) 点々模様の teñteñmoyô no

specs [speks] (*inf*) *npl* 眼鏡 mégàne

spectacle [spek'təkəl] *n* (scene) 光景 kôkei; (grand event) スペクタクル supékùtakuru

spectacles [spek'təkəlz] *npl* 眼 鏡 mégàne

spectacular [spektæk'jələr] *adj* (dramatic) 劇的な gekíteki na; (success) 目覚しい mezámashiî

spectator [spek'teitər] *n* 観 客 kañkyaku

specter [spek'tər] (*US*) *n* (ghost) 幽 霊 yūrei

spectra [spek'trə] *npl of* **spectrum**

spectre [spek'tər] (*BRIT*) = **specter**

spectrum [spek'trəm] (*pl* **spectra**) *n* (color/radio wave spectrum) スペクトル supékùtoru

speculate [spek'jəleit] *vi* (FINANCE) 投機をする tôki wo suru; (try to guess): *to speculate about* ...についてあれこれと憶測する ...ni tsuîte arékòre to okúsoku suru

speculation [spekjəlei'ʃən] *n* (FINANCE) 投機 tôki; (guesswork) 憶測 okúsoku

speech [spi:tʃ] *n* (faculty) 話す能力 hanásu nõryoku; (spoken language) 話し言葉 hanáshikotòba; (formal talk) 演説 eñzetsu, スピーチ supîchi; (THEATER) せりふ serífù

speechless [spi:tʃ'lis] *adj* (be, remain etc) 声も出ない kôè mo denái

speed [spi:d] *n* (rate, fast travel) 速度 sókùdo, スピード supîdò; (haste) 急ぎ isógi; (promptness) 素早さ subáyasà

at full/top speed 全速力で zeñsokuryòku de

speed boat *n* モーターボート môtàbôto

speedily [spi:'dili] *adv* 素早く subáyakù

speeding [spi:'diŋ] *n* (AUT) スピード違反 supîdo-ihàn

speed limit *n* 速度制限 sokúdoseìgen

speedometer [spi:dɑːm'itər] *n* 速 度 計 sokúdokeì

speed up *vi* (*also fig*) 速度を増す sókùdo wo masú

♦*vt* (*also fig*) ...の速度を増す ...no sókùdo wo masú, 速める hayámerù

speedway [spi:d'wei] *n* (sport) オートレース ôtorēsu

speedy [spi:'di:] *adj* (fast: car) スピードの出る supîdò no dérù; (prompt: reply, recovery, settlement) 速い hayáî

spell [spel] *n* (*also:* **magic spell**) 魔法 mahô; (period of time) 期間 kikán

♦*vt* (*pt, pp* **spelled** *or* (*Brit*) **spelt**) (*also:* **spell out**) ...のつづりを言う ...no tsuzúri wò iú; (*fig:* advantages, difficulties) ...の兆しである ...no kizáshi de arù

to cast a spell on someone ...に魔法を掛ける ...ni mahô wò kakérù

he can't spell 彼はスペルが苦手だ kárè wa supérù ga nigáte dà

spellbound [spel'baund] *adj* (audience etc) 魅せられた miséraretà

spelling [spel'iŋ] *n* つづり tsuzúri, スペリング supériñgu

spend [spend] (*pt, pp* **spent**) *vt* (money) 使う tsukáù; (time, life) 過す sugósù

spendthrift [spend'θrift] *n* 浪費家 rôhikà

spent [spent] *pt, pp of* **spend**

sperm [spəːrm] *n* 精子 séîshi

spew [spju:] *vt* 吐き出す hakídasù

sphere [sfi:r] *n* (round object) 球 kyû; (area) 範囲 hán-i

spherical [sfe:r'ikəl] *adj* (round) 丸 い marúî

sphinx [sfiŋks] *n* スフィンクス sufíñkusu

spice [spais] *n* 香辛料 kôshiñryō, スパイス supáìsu

♦*vt* (food) ...にスパイスを入れる ...ni supáìsu wo irérù

spick-and-span [spik'ənspæn'] *adj* きちんときれいな kichíñ to kírèi na

spicy [spai'si:] *adj* (food) スパイスの利いた supáìsu no kiítà

spider [spai'dəːr] *n* クモ kúmò

spike [spaik] *n* (point) くい kuî; (BOT) 穂 hô

spill [spil] (*pt, pp* **spilt** *or* **spilled**) *vt* (liquid) こぼす kobósù

♦*vi* (liquid) こぼれる kobórerù

spill over *vi* (liquid: *also fig*) あふれる afúrerù

spin [spin] *n* (trip in car) ドライブ doráìbu; (AVIAT) きりもみ kirímomi; (on ball) スピン supíñ

♦*vb* (*pt, pp* **spun**)

♦*vt* (wool etc) 紡ぐ tsumúgù; (ball, coin) 回転させる kaíten saserù

♦*vi* (make thread) 紡ぐ tsumúgù; (person, head) 目が回る mé gà mawárù

spinach [spin'itʃ] *n* (plant, food) ホウレンソウ hôrèñsō

spinal [spai'nəl] *adj* (injury etc) 背骨の sebóne no

spinal cord *n* せき髄 sekízùi

spindly [spind'li:] *adj* (legs, trees etc) か細い kabósoì

spin-dryer [spindrai'ə:r] (*BRIT*) *n* 脱水機 dassúikî

spine [spain] *n* (ANAT) 背骨 sebóne; (thorn: of plant, hedgehog etc) とげ tógè

spineless [spain'lis] *adj* (*fig*) 意気地なしの ikújinàshi no

spinning [spin'iŋ] *n* (art) 紡績 bôseki

spinning top *n* こま kómà

spinning wheel *n* 紡ぎ車 tsumúgiguru̅ma

spin-off [spin'ɔ:f] *n* (*fig*: by-product) 副産物 fukúsañbutsu

spin out *vt* (talk, job, money, holiday) 引延ばす hikínobasù

spinster [spin'stə:r] *n* オールドミス ôrudomisù

spiral [spai'rəl] *n* ら旋形 rasêñkei

♦*vi* (*fig*: prices etc) うなぎ登りに上る unáginobòri ni nobórù

spiral staircase *n* ら旋階段 rasêñkaidàn

spire [spai'ə:r] *n* せん塔 sentō

spirit [spir'it] *n* (soul) 魂 támàshii; (ghost) 幽霊 yūrei; (energy) 元気 génki; (courage) 勇気 yūki; (frame of mind) 気分 kíbùn; (sense) 精神 seíshin

in good spirits 気分上々で kíbùn jôjō de

spirited [spir'itid] *adj* (performance, retort, defense) 精力的な seíryokuteki na

spirit level *n* 水準器 suíjuñki

spirits [spir'its] *npl* (drink) 蒸留酒 jôryūshu

spiritual [spir'itʃu:əl] *adj* (of the spirit: home, welfare, needs) 精神的な seíshinteki na; (religious: affairs) 霊的な reíteki

na

♦*n* (*also*: **Negro spiritual**) 黒人霊歌 kokújinreîka

spit [spit] *n* (for roasting) 焼きぐし yakígushi; (saliva) つばき tsubáki

♦*vi* (*pt, pp* **spat**) (throw out saliva) つばを吐く tsúbà wo hákù; (sound: fire, cooking) じゅうじゅういう júju̅ iu; (rain) ぱらつく parátsukù

spite [spait] *n* 恨み urámi

♦*vt* (person) ...に意地悪をする ...ni ijíwarù wo suru

in spite of ...にもかかわらず ...ní mò kakáwarazù

spiteful [spait'fəl] *adj* (child, words etc) 意地悪な ijíwarù na

spittle [spit'əl] *n* つばき tsubáki

splash [splæʃ] *n* (sound) ざぶんという音 zabúñ to iú otò; (of color) 派手なはん点 hadé nà hañten

♦*vt* はね掛ける hanékakerù

♦*vi* (*also*: **splash about**) ぴちゃぴちゃ水をはねる pichápìcha mizú wò hanérù

spleen [spli:n] *n* (ANAT) ひ臓 hizô

splendid [splen'did] *adj* (excellent: idea, recovery) 素晴らしい subárashiî; (impressive: architecture, affair) 立派な rippá na

splendor [splen'də:r] (*BRIT* **splendour**) *n* (impressiveness) 輝き kagáyakì

splendors [splen'də:rz] *npl* (features) 特色 tokúshoku

splint [splint] *n* 副木 fukúboku

splinter [splin'tə:r] *n* (of wood, glass) 破片 hahén; (in finger) とげ tógè

♦*vi* (bone, wood, glass etc) 砕ける kudákerù

split [split] *n* (crack) 割れ目 waréme; (tear) 裂け目 sakéme; (*fig*: division) 分裂 buñretsu; (: difference) 差異 sá-ì

♦*vb* (*pt, pp* **split**)

♦*vt* (divide) 割る wárù, 裂く sákù; (party) 分裂させる buñretsu saserù; (share equally: work) 手分けしてやる tewáke shite yarù; (: profits) 山分けする yamáwake suru

♦*vi* (divide) 割れる warérù

split up *vi* (couple) 別れる wakárerù;

(group, meeting) 解散する kaísan suru

splutter [splʌt'əːr] vi (engine etc) ぱちぱち音を立てる páchìpachi otŏ wò tatérù; (person) どもる domórù

spoil [spɔil] (pt, pp **spoilt** or **spoiled**) vt (damage, mar) 台無しにする daínashi ni surù; (child) 甘やかす amáyakasù

spoils [spɔilz] npl (loot: also fig) 分捕り品 buńdorihìn

spoilsport [spɔil'spɔːrt] n 座を白けさせる人 zá wò shirákesaserù hitŏ

spoke [spouk] pt of **speak**
◆n (of wheel) スポーク supŏkù

spoken [spou'kən] pp of **speak**

spokesman [spouks'mən] (pl **spokesmen**) n スポークスマン supŏkusumàn

spokeswoman [spouks'wumən] (pl **spokeswomen**) n 女性報道官 joséi hŏdŏkan, 女性スポークスマン joséi supŏkusumàn

sponge [spʌndʒ] n (for washing with) スポンジ supóñji; (also: **sponge cake**) スポンジケーキ supóñjikèki
◆vt (wash) スポンジで洗う supóñji de aráù
◆vi: **to sponge off/on someone** ...にたかる ...ni takárù

sponge bag (BRIT) n 洗面バッグ señmenbaggù ◇洗面道具を入れて携帯するバッグ señmendŏgu wo irête keitai surù bággù

sponsor [spɑːn'səːr] n (of player, event, club, program) スポンサー supóñsā; (of charitable event etc) 協賛者 kyŏsañsha; (for application) 保証人 hoshŏnin; (for bill in parliament etc) 提出者 teíshutsushã
◆vt (player, event, club, program etc) ...のスポンサーになる ...no supóñsā ni nárù; (charitable event etc) ...の協賛者になる ...no kyŏsañsha ni nárù; (applicant) ...の保証人になる ...no hoshŏnin ni nárù; (proposal, bill etc) 提出する teíshutsu suru

sponsorship [spɑːn'səːrʃip] n (financial support) 金銭的の援助 kińsentekieñjo

spontaneous [spɑːntei'niːəs] adj (unplanned: gesture) 自発的な jihátsuteki

na

spooky [spuː'kiː] (inf) adj (place, atmosphere) お化けが出そうな o-báke gà desŏ nà

spool [spuːl] n (for thread) 糸巻 itómàki; (for film, tape etc) リール rŕru

spoon [spuːn] n さじ sají, スプーン supűn

spoon-feed [spuːn'fiːd] vt (baby, patient) スプーンで食べさせる supŭn de tabésaserù; (fig: students etc) ...に一方的に教え込む ...ni ippŏteki nì oshíekomù

spoonful [spuːn'ful] n スプーン一杯分 supŭn ippái̇̀bun

sporadic [spɔːræd'ik] adj (glimpses, attacks etc) 散発的な sañpatsuteki na

sport [spɔːrt] n (game) スポーツ supŏtsu; (person) 気さくな人 kisáku nà hitŏ
◆vt (wear) これみよがしに身に付ける korémiyogàshi ni mi ni tsukérù

sporting [spɔːr'tiŋ] adj (event etc) スポーツの supŏtsu no; (generous) 気前がいい kimáe gà íi
to give someone a sporting chance ...にちゃんとしたチャンスを与える ...ni chañtò shita cháñsu wo atáerù

sport jacket (US) n スポーツジャケット supŏtsujakettò

sports car [spɔːrts-] n スポーツカー supŏtsukã

sports jacket (BRIT) n = **sport jacket**

sportsman [spɔːrts'mən] (pl **sportsmen**) n スポーツマン supŏtsumàn

sportsmanship [spɔːrts'mənʃip] n スポーツマンシップ supŏtsumanshippù

sportswear [spɔːrts'weəːr] n スポーツウエア supŏtsuueà

sportswoman [spɔːrts'wumən] (pl **sportswomen**) n スポーツウーマン supŏtsuũman

sporty [spɔːr'tiː] adj (good at sports) スポーツ好きの supŏtsuzuki no

spot [spɑːt] n (mark) 染み shimí; (on pattern, skin etc) はん点 hañten; (place) 場所 bashŏ; (RADIO, TV) コーナー kŏnā; (small amount): **a spot of** 少しの sukóshì no
◆vt (notice: person, mistake etc) ...に気

が付く ...ni kí gà tsúkù

on the spot (in that place) 現場に geńba ni; (immediately) その場で sonó ba de, 即座に sókùza ni; (in difficulty) 困って komáttè

spot check n 抜取り検査 nukítorikeñsa

spotless [spɑːt'lis] adj (shirt, kitchen etc) 清潔な seíketsu na

spotlight [spɑːt'lait] n スポットライト supóttoraìto

spotted [spɑːt'id] adj (pattern) はん点模様の hañtenmoyō no

spotty [spɑːt'i:] adj (face, youth: with freckles) そばかすだらけの sobákasudaràke no; (: with pimples) にきびだらけの nikíbidaràke no

spouse [spaus] n (male/female) 配偶者 haígùsha

spout [spaut] n (of jug) つぎ口 tsugígùchi; (of pipe) 出口 dégùchi
♦vi (flames, water etc) 噴出す fukídasù

sprain [sprein] n ねんざ neñza
♦vt: **to sprain one's ankle/wrist** 足首〔手首〕をねんざする ashíkùbi〔tékùbi〕wo neñza suru

sprang [spræŋ] pt of **spring**

sprawl [sprɔːl] vi (person: lie) 寝そべる nesóberù; (: sit) だらしない格好で座る daráshinai kakkō de suwárù; (place) 無秩序に広がる muchítsujo ni hirógarù

spray [sprei] n (small drops) 水煙 mizúkemùri; (sea spray) しぶき shíbùki; (container: hair spray etc) スプレー supúrè; (garden spray) 噴霧器 fuñmukì; (of flowers) 小枝 koéda
♦vt (sprinkle) 噴霧器で...に...を掛ける fuñmukì de ...ni ...wo kakérù; (crops) 消毒する shōdoku suru

spread [spred] n (range, distribution) 広がり hirógari; (CULIN: for bread) スプレッド supúreddò; (inf: food) ごちそう gochísò
♦vb (pt, pp **spread**)
♦vt (lay out) 並べる naráberù; (butter) 塗る núrù; (wings, arms, sails) 広げる hirógerù; (workload, wealth) 分配する buñpai suru; (scatter) まく mákù
♦vi (disease, news) 広がる hirógarù;

(also: **spread out**: stain) 広がる hirógarù

spread-eagled [spred'i:gəld] adj 大の字に寝た daí no jì ni netá

spread out vi (move apart) 散らばる chirábarù

spreadsheet [spred'ʃi:t] n (COMPUT) スプレッドシート supúreddoshìto

spree [spri:] n: **to go on a spree** ...にふける ...ni fukérù

sprightly [sprait'li:] adj (old person) かくしゃくとした kakúshaku to shitá

spring [spriŋ] n (leap) 跳躍 chóyaku; (coiled metal) ばね bánè; (season) 春 hárù; (of water) 泉 izúmi
♦vi (pt **sprang**, pp **sprung**) (leap) 跳ぶ tobú

in spring (season) 春に hárù ni

springboard [spriŋ'bɔːrd] n スプリングボード supúringubōdo

spring-cleaning [spriŋ'kli:'niŋ] n 大掃除 ōsōji ◇春とは関係なく言う hárù to wa kañkeinakù iú

springtime [spriŋ'taim] n 春 hárù

spring up vi (thing: appear) 現れる aráwarerù

sprinkle [spriŋ'kəl] vt (scatter: liquid) まく mákù; (: salt, sugar) 振り掛ける furíkakerù

to sprinkle water on, sprinkle with water ...に水をまく ...ni mizú wò mákù

sprinkler [spriŋ'klɔːr] n (for lawn, to put out fire) スプリンクラー supúrinkurà

sprint [sprint] n (race) 短距離競走 tañkyorikyōsō, スプリント supúriñto
♦vi (run fast) 速く走る háyàku hashírù; (SPORT) スプリントする supúriñto suru

sprinter [sprin'tɔːr] n スプリンター supúriñtà

sprout [spraut] vi (plant, vegetable) 発芽する hatsúga suru

sprouts [sprauts] npl (also: **Brussels sprouts**) 芽キャベツ mekyábètsu

spruce [spruːs] n inv (BOT) トウヒ tōhì
♦adj (neat, smart) スマートな sumátò na

sprung [sprʌŋ] pp of **spring**

spry [sprai] adj (old person) かくしゃく

とした kakúshaku to shitá

spun [spʌn] *pt, pp of* **spin**

spur [spə:r] *n* 拍車 hakúsha; (*fig*) 刺激 shigéki

♦*vt* (*also*: **spur on**) 激励する gekírei suru

on the spur of the moment とっさに tossá ni

spurious [spju:r'i:əs] *adj* (false: attraction) 見せ掛けの misékake no; (: argument) 間違った machígattá

spurn [spə:rn] *vt* (reject) はねつける hanétsukerù

spurt [spə:rt] *n* (of blood etc) 噴出 fuńshutsu; (of energy) 奮発 funpatsu

♦*vi* (blood, flame) 噴出す fukídasù

spy [spai] *n* スパイ supáî

♦*vi*: *to spy on* こっそり見張る kossóri mihárù

♦*vt* (see) 見付ける mitsúkerù

spying [spai'iŋ] *n* スパイ行為 supáikòi

sq. *abbr* = **square**

squabble [skwɑːb'əl] *vi* 口げんかする kucñgeňka suru

squad [skwɑːd] *n* (MIL, POLICE) 班 háñ; (SPORT) チーム chîmu

squadron [skwɑːd'rən] *n* (MIL) 大隊 daítai

squalid [skwɑːl'id] *adj* (dirty, unpleasant: conditions) 汚らしい kitánarashiî; (sordid: story etc) えげつない egétsunaî

squall [skwɔːl] *n* (stormy wind) スコール sukôrù

squalor [skwɑːl'ə:r] *n* 汚い環境 kitánai kańkyō

squander [skwɑːn'də:r] *vt* (money) 浪費する rôhi suru; (chances) 逃す nogásù

square [skwe:r] *n* (shape) 正方形 seîhô-kei; (in town) 広場 hírôba; (*inf*: person) 堅物 katábutsu

♦*adj* (in shape) 正方形の seîhôkei no; (*inf*: ideas, tastes) 古臭い furúkusaî

♦*vt* (arrange) ...を...に一致させる ...wo ...ni itchî saserù; (MATH) 2乗する nijô suru; (reconcile) ...を...と調和させる ...wo ...to chôwa saserù

all square 貸し借りなし kashíkàri náshì

a square meal 十分な食事 júbùn na

shokúji

2 meters square 2メーター平方 ni mêtā heíhô

2 square meters 2平方メーター ni heíhô mêtā

squarely [skwe:r'li:] *adv* (directly: fall, land etc) まともに matómo nî; (fully: confront) きっぱりと kippárî to

squash [skwɑːʃ] *n* (*US*: marrow etc) カボチャ kabócha; (*BRIT*: drink): *lemon/orange squash* レモン〔オレンジ〕スカッシュ remóñ〔oréñji〕sukasshù; (SPORT) スカッシュ sukásshù

♦*vt* つぶす tsubúsu

squat [skwɑːt] *adj* ずんぐりした zuñgurî shita

♦*vi* (*also*: **squat down**) しゃがむ shagá-mù

squatter [skwɑːt'ə:r] *n* 不法居住者 fuhô-kyojùsha

squawk [skwɔːk] *vi* (bird) ぎゃーぎゃー鳴く gyágyà nakú

squeak [skwi:k] *vi* (door etc) きしむ kishímù; (mouse) ちゅーちゅー鳴く chûchū nakú

squeal [skwi:l] *vi* (children) きゃーきゃー言う kyákyà iú; (brakes etc) キーキー言う kîkī iú

squeamish [skwi:'miʃ] *adj* やたら...に弱い yatárà ...ni yowáî

squeeze [skwi:z] *n* (*gen*: of hand) 握り締める事 nigírishimerù kotó; (ECON) 金融引締め kiñ-yúhikishime

♦*vt* (*gen*) 絞る shibórù; (hand, arm) 握り締める nigírishimerù

squeeze out *vt* (juice etc) 絞り出す shi-bóridasù

squelch [skweltʃ] *vi* ぐちゃぐちゃ音を立てる gúchàgucha otó wò tatérù

squid [skwid] *n* イカ iká

squiggle [skwig'əl] *n* のたくった線 notá-kuttà séñ

squint [skwint] *vi* (have a squint) 斜視である sháshì de árù

♦*n* (MED) 斜視 sháshì

squire [skwai'ə:r] *n* (*BRIT*) 大地主 ôjinúshi

squirm [skwə:rm] *vi* 身もだえする mimódàe suru

squirrel [skwəːr'əl] n リス rísù

squirt [skwəːrt] vi 噴出す fukídasù
♦vt 噴掛ける fukíkakerù

Sr abbr = **senior**

St abbr = **saint**; **street**

stab [stæb] n (with knife etc) ひと刺し hitósàshi; (inf: try): **to have a stab at (doing) something** ...をやってみる ...wo yatté mirù
♦vt (person, body) 刺す sásù
a stab of pain 刺す様な痛み sásù yō na itámi

stability [stəbil'əti:] n 安定 añtei

stabilize [stei'bəlaiz] vt (prices) 安定させる añtei saserù
♦vi (prices, one's weight) 安定する añtei suru

stable [stei'bəl] adj (prices, patient's condition) 安定した añtei shita; (marriage) 揺るぎない yurúgi naì
♦n (for horse) 馬小屋 umágoya

staccato [stəkɑː'tou] adv スタッカート sutákkàto

stack [stæk] n (pile) ...の山 ...no yamá
♦vt (pile) 積む tsumú

stadium [stei'di:əm] n 競技場 kyőgijō, スタジアム sutájìamu

staff [stæf] n (work force) 職員 shokúìn; (BRIT: SCOL) 教職員 kyőshokuìn
♦vt ...の職員として働く ...no shokúìn toshite határakù

stag [stæg] n 雄ジカ ójìka

stage [steidʒ] n (in theater etc) 舞台 bútài; (platform) 台 dái; (profession): **the stage** 俳優業 haíyūgyò; (point, period) 段階 dañkai
♦vt (play) 上演する jően suru; (demonstration) 行う okónaù
in stages 少しずつ sukóshi zutsù

stagecoach [steidʒ'koutʃ] n 駅馬車 ekíbashà

stage manager n 舞台監督 butáikañtoku

stagger [stæg'əːr] vi よろめく yorómekù
♦vt (amaze) 仰天させる győten saserù; (hours, holidays) ずらす zurásù

staggering [stæg'əːriŋ] adj (amazing) 仰天させる győten saserù

stagnant [stæg'nənt] adj (water) よどんだ yodóñda; (economy etc) 停滞した teítai shita

stagnate [stæg'neit] vi (economy, business, person) 停滞する teítai suru; (person) だれる darérù

stag party n スタッグパーティ sutággupàti

staid [steid] adj (person, attitudes) 古めかしい furúmekashì

stain [stein] n (mark) 染み shimí; (coloring) 着色剤 chakúshokuzài, ステイン sutéǹ
♦vt (mark) 汚す yogósù; (wood) ...にステインを塗る ...ni suténñ wo núrù

stained glass window [steind-] n ステンドグラスの窓 suténdoguràsu no mádò

stainless steel [stein'lis-] n ステンレス suténtresu

stain remover [-rimuː'vəːr] n 染み抜き shimínuki

stair [steːr] n (step) 段 dáñ, ステップ sutéppù

staircase [steːr'keis] n 階段 kaídan

stairs [steːrz] npl (flight of steps) 階段 kaídan

stairway [steːr'wei] n = **staircase**

stake [steik] n (post) くい kúì; (COMM: interest) 利害関係 rigáikañkei; (BETTING: gen pl) 賞金 shőkin
♦vt (money, life, reputation) かける kakérù
to stake a claim to ...に対する所有権を主張する ...ni taí surù shoyúken wò shuchő suru
to be at stake 危ぶまれる ayábumarerù

stalactite [stəlæk'tait] n しょう乳石 shőnyūseki

stalagmite [stəlæg'mait] n 石じゅん sekíjun

stale [steil] adj (bread) 固くなった katáku nattà; (food, air) 古くなった fúrùku natta; (air) よどんだ yodóñda; (smell) かび臭い kabíkusaì; (beer) 気の抜けた kí nò nukétà

stalemate [steil'meit] *n* (CHESS) ステールメート sutérumèto; (*fig*) 行き詰り ikízumari

stalk [stɔːk] *n* (of flower, fruit) 茎 kukí
♦*vt* (person, animal) ...に忍び寄る ...ni shinóbiyorù

stalk off *vi* 威張って行く ibátte ikù

stall [stɔːl] *n* (in market) 屋台 yátài; (in stable) 馬房 babó
♦*vt* (AUT: engine, car) エンストを起す eñsuto wo okósù; (*fig*: delay: person) 引止める hikítomerù; (: decision etc) 引延ばす hikínobasù
♦*vi* (AUT: engine, car) エンストを起す eñsuto wo okósù; (*fig*: person) 時間稼ぎをする jikánkasegi wò suru

stallion [stæl'jən] *n* 種ウマ tanéùma

stalls [stɔːlz] *npl* (BRIT: in cinema, theater) 特別席 tokúbetsusèki

stalwart [stɔːl'wəːrt] *adj* (worker, supporter, party member) 不動の fudó no

stamina [stæm'inə] *n* スタミナ sutámìna

stammer [stæm'əːr] *n* どもり dómòri
♦*vi* どもる domórù

stamp [stæmp] *n* (postage stamp) 切手 kitté; (rubber stamp) スタンプ sutáñpu; (mark, *also fig*) 特徴 tokúchō
♦*vi* (*also*: **stamp one's foot**) 足を踏み鳴らす ashí wò fumínarasù
♦*vt* (letter) ...に切手を張る ...ni kitté wò harú; (mark) 特徴付ける tokúchōzukerù; (with rubber stamp) ...にスタンプを押す ...ni sutáñpu wo osú

stamp album *n* 切手帳 kittéchō

stamp collecting [-kəlek'tiŋ] *n* 切手収集 kittéshūshū

stampede [stæmpi:d'] *n* (of animal herd) 暴走 bōsō; (*fig*: of people) 殺到 sattó

stance [stæns] *n* (way of standing) 立っている姿勢 tatté irù shiséi; (*fig*) 姿勢 shiséi

stand [stænd] *n* (position) 構え kámàe; (for taxis) 乗場 noríba; (hall, music stand) 台 dái; (SPORT) スタンド sutáñdo; (stall) 屋台 yátài
♦*vb* (*pt, pp* **stood**)
♦*vi* (be: person, unemployment etc) ...になっている ...ni natté irù; (be on foot) 立つ tátsù; (rise) 立ち上る tachíagarù; (remain: decision, offer) 有効である yū́kō de arù; (in election etc) 立候補する rikkóho suru
♦*vt* (place: object) 立てる tatérù; (tolerate, withstand: person, thing) ...に耐える ...ni taérù; (treat, invite to) おごる ogórù

to make a stand (*fig*) 立場を執る tachíba wò tórù

to stand for parliament (*BRIT*) 議員選挙に出馬する gíñsenkyo ni shutsúba suru

standard [stæn'dəːrd] *n* (level) 水準 suíjun; (norm, criterion) 基準 kijún; (flag) 旗 hatá
♦*adj* (normal: size etc) 標準的な hyójunteki na; (text) 権威のある kéñ-i no árù

standardize [stæn'dəːrdaiz] *vt* 規格化する kikákuka suru

standard lamp (*BRIT*) *n* フロアスタンド furóasutañdo

standard of living *n* 生活水準 seíkatsusuijùn

standards [stæn'dəːrdz] *npl* (morals) 道徳基準 dótoku kijùn

stand by *vi* (be ready) 待機する táìki suru
♦*vt fus* (opinion, decision) 守る mamórù; (person) ...の力になる ...no chikára ni narù

stand-by [stænd'bai] *n* (reserve) 非常用の物 hijóyō no monó

to be on stand-by 待機している táìki shité irù

stand-by ticket *n* (AVIAT) キャンセル待ちの切符 kyáñserumachi nò kippú

stand down *vi* (withdraw) 引下がる hikísagarù

stand for *vt fus* (signify) 意味する ímì suru; (represent) 代表する daíhyō suru; (tolerate) 容認する yóninn suru

stand-in [stænd'in] *n* 代行 daíkō

stand in for *vt fus* (replace) ...の代役を務める ...no daíyaku wò tsutómerù

standing [stæn'diŋ] *adj* (on feet: ovation) 立ち上ってする tachíagatte surù; (permanent: invitation) 持続の jizóku no, 継続の keízoku no

♦*n* (status) 地位 chíi

of many years' standing 数年前から続いている sǔnen maè kara tsuzúite irù

standing joke *n* お決りの冗談 o-kímari nò jódañ

standing order (*BRIT*) *n* (at bank) 自動振替 jidófuríkae ◇支払額が定額である場合に使う shiháraígaku ga teígaku de arù báaì ni tsukáù

standing room *n* 立見席 tachímisèki

stand-offish [stændɔ:f'iʃ] *adj* 無愛想な buáīsō na

stand out *vi* (be prominent) 目立つ medátsù

standpoint [stænd'point] *n* 観点 kañteñ

standstill [stænd'stil] *n: at a standstill* (*also fig*) 滞って todókòtte

to come to a standstill 止ってしまう tomátte shimaù

stand up *vi* (rise) 立ち上る tachíagarù

stand up for *vt fus* (defend) 守る mamórù

stand up to *vt fus* (withstand: *also fig*) ...に立向かう ...ni tachímukaù

stank [stæŋk] *pt of* **stink**

staple [stei'pəl] *n* (for papers) ホチキスの針 hóchìkisu no hárì

♦*adj* (food etc) 主要な shuyó no

♦*vt* (fasten) ホチキスで留める hóchìkisu de toméru

stapler [stei'plər] *n* ホチキス hóchìkisu

star [star] *n* (in sky) 星 hoshí; (celebrity) スター sutá

♦*vi: to star in* ...で主演する ...de shuén suru

♦*vt* (THEATER, CINEMA) 主役とする shuyáku to surù

starboard [star'bərd] *n* 右げん úgeñ

starch [startʃ] *n* (for shirts etc) のり norí; (CULIN) でんぷん deñpun

stardom [star'dəm] *n* スターの身分 sutá no mibúñ

stare [ster] *n* じろじろ見る事 jírðjiro mírù koto

♦*vi: to stare at* じろじろ見る jírðjiro mírù

starfish [star'fiʃ] *n* ヒトデ hitode

stark [stark] *adj* (bleak) 殺風景な sap-

púkèi na

♦*adv: stark naked* 素っ裸の suppádàka no

starling [star'liŋ] *n* ムクドリ mukúdòri

starry [star'i:] *adj* (night, sky) 星がよく見える hoshí gà yókù miérù

starry-eyed [star'i:aid] *adj* (innocent) 天真らん漫な teñshinranman na

stars [starz] *npl: the stars* (horoscope) 星占い hoshíuranaì

start [start] *n* (beginning) 初め hajíme; (departure) 出発 shuppátsu; (sudden movement) ぎくっとする事 gikúttò suru kotð; (advantage) リード rído

♦*vt* (begin) 始める hajímerù; (cause) 引起こす hikíokosù; (found: business etc) 創立する sóritsu suru; (engine) かける kakérù

♦*vi* (begin) 始まる hajímarù; (with fright) ぎくっとする gikúttò suru; (train etc) 出発する shuppátsu suru

to start doing/to do something ...をし始める ...wo shihájimerù

starter [star'tər] *n* (AUT) スターター sutátà; (SPORT: official) スターター sutátà; (*BRIT*: CULIN) 最初の料理 saísho no ryórì

starting point [star'tiŋ-] *n* 出発点 shuppátsuteñ

startle [star'təl] *vt* 驚かす odórokasù

startling [start'liŋ] *adj* (news etc) 驚く様な odóroku yð na

start off *vi* (begin) 始める hajímerù; (begin moving) 出発する shuppátsu suru

start up *vi* (business etc) 開業する kaígyō suru; (engine) かかる kakárù; (car) 走り出す hashíridasù

♦*vt* (business etc) 創立する sóritsu suru; (engine) かける kakérù; (car) 走らせる hashíraserù

starvation [starvei'ʃən] *n* 飢餓 kígà

starve [starv] *vi* (*inf*: be very hungry) おなかがぺこぺこである onáka gà pekópeko dè árù; (*also*: **starve to death**) 餓死する gáshì suru

♦*vt* (person, animal: not give food to) 飢えさせる uésaserù; (: to death) 餓死させる gáshì saserù

state [steit] *n* (condition) 状態 jốtai; (government) 国 kuní
♦*vt* (say, declare) 明言する meígen suru
to be in a state 取乱している torímidashite irú

stately [steit'li:] *adj* (home, walk etc) 優雅な yúga na

statement [steit'mənt] *n* (declaration) 陳述 chíñjutsu

States [steits] *npl*: *the States* 米国 beíkoku

statesman [steits'mən] (*pl* **statesmen**) *n* リーダー格の政治家 rídākaku nò seíjikà

static [stæt'ik] *n* (RADIO, TV) 雑音 zatsúon
♦*adj* (not moving) 静的な seíteki na

static electricity *n* 静電気 seídeñki

station [stei'ʃən] *n* (RAIL) 駅 ékì; (police station etc) 署 shó; (RADIO) 放送局 hốsōkyoku
♦*vt* (position: guards etc) 配置する haíchi suru

stationary [stei'ʃəne:ri:] *adj* (vehicle) 動いていない ugóite inaì

stationer [stei'ʃənə:r] *n* 文房具屋 buñbōguya

stationer's (shop) [stei'ʃənə:rz-] *n* 文房具店 buñbōguteñ

stationery [stei'ʃəne:ri:] *n* 文房具 buñbōgu

stationmaster [stei'ʃənmæstə:r] *n* (RAIL) 駅長 ekíchō

station wagon (*US*) *n* ワゴン車 wagóñsha

statistic [stətis'tik] *n* 統計値 tốkeichì

statistical [stətis'tikəl] *adj* (evidence, techniques) 統計学的な tốkeigakuteki na

statistics [stətis'tiks] *n* (science) 統計学 tốkeigàku

statue [stætʃ'u:] *n* 像 zố

stature [stætʃ'ə:r] *n* 身長 shíñchō

status [stei'təs] *n* (position) 身分 míbùn; (official classification) 資格 shikáku; (importance) 地位 chíì
the status quo 現状 geñjō

status symbol *n* ステータスシンボル sutếtasushiñboru

statute [stætʃ'u:t] *n* 法律 hốritsu

statutory [stætʃ'u:tɔ:ri:] *adj* (powers, rights etc) 法定の hốtei no

staunch [stɔ:ntʃ] *adj* (ally) 忠実な chújitsu na

stave off [steiv-] *vt* (attack, threat) 防ぐ fuségù

stay [stei] *n* (period of time) 滞在期間 taízaikikàn
♦*vi* (remain) 居残る inókorù; (with someone, as guest) 泊る tomárù; (in place: spend some time) とどまる todómarù
to stay put とどまる todómarù
to stay the night 泊る tomárù

stay behind *vi* 居残る inókorù

stay in *vi* (at home) 家にいる ié nì irú

staying power [stei'iŋ-] *n* 根気 koñki

stay on *vi* 残る nokórù

stay out *vi* (of house) 家に戻らない ié nì modóranaì

stay up *vi* (at night) 起きている ókìte irú

stead [sted] *n*: *in someone's stead* ...の代りに ...no kawári ni
to stand someone in good stead ...の役に立つ ...no yakú ni tatsù

steadfast [sted'fæst] *adj* 不動の fudố no

steadily [sted'ili:] *adv* (firmly) 着実に chakújitsu ni; (constantly) ずっと zuttố; (fixedly) じっと jittố; (walk) しっかりと shikkárì to

steady [sted'i:] *adj* (constant: job, boyfriend, speed) 決った kimátta, 変らない kawáranaì; (regular: rise in prices) 着実な chakújitsu na; (person, character) 堅実な keñjitsu na; (firm: hand etc) 震えない furúenaì; (calm: look, voice) 落着いた ochítsùita
♦*vt* (stabilize) 安定させる añtei saserù; (nerves) 静める shizúmerù

steak [steik] *n* (*also*: **beefsteak**) ビーフステーキ bífusutěki; (beef, fish, pork etc) ステーキ sutékì

steal [sti:l] (*pt* **stole**, *pp* **stolen**) *vt* 盗む nusúmù
♦*vi* (thieve) 盗む nusúmù; (move secretly) こっそりと行く kossórì to ikú

stealth [stelθ] *n*: **by stealth** こっそりと kossórì to

stealthy [stel'θi:] *adj* (movements, actions) ひそかな hisókà na

steam [sti:m] *n* (mist) 水蒸気 suíjòki; (on window) 曇り kumóri
◆*vt* (CULIN) 蒸す músù
◆*vi* (give off steam) 水蒸気を立てる suíjòki wo tatérù

steam engine *n* 蒸気機関 jòkikikàn

steamer [sti:'mər] *n* 汽船 kisén

steamroller [sti:m'roulər] *n* ロードローラー ròdoròrà

steamship [sti:m'ʃip] *n* = steamer

steamy [sti:'mi:] *adj* (room) 湯気でもうもうの yúgè de mómò no; (window) 湯気で曇った yúgè de kumóttà; (heat, atmosphere) 蒸暑い mushíatsuì

steel [sti:l] *n* 鋼鉄 kótetsu
◆*adj* 鋼鉄の kótetsu no

steelworks [sti:l'wərks] *n* 製鋼所 seíkòjo

steep [sti:p] *adj* (stair, slope) 険しい kewáshiì; (increase) 大幅な ōhaba na; (price) 高い takáì
◆*vt* (fig: soak) 浸す hitásù

steeple [sti:'pəl] *n* せん塔 seńtō

steeplechase [sti:'pəltʃeis] *n* 障害レース shógairèsu

steer [sti:r] *vt* (vehicle) 運転する uñten suru; (person) 導く michíbikù
◆*vi* (maneuver) 車を操る kurúma wò ayátsurù

steering [sti:r'iŋ] *n* (AUT) ステアリング sutéaringu

steering wheel *n* ハンドル hańdòru

stem [stem] *n* (of plant) 茎 kukí; (of glass) 足 ashí
◆*vt* (stop: blood, flow, advance) 止める tomérù

stem from *vt fus* (subj: condition, problem) …に由来する …ni yurái suru

stench [stentʃ] *n* 悪臭 akúshū

stencil [sten'səl] *n* (lettering) ステンシルで書いた文字 sutéñshiru de káìta mójì; (pattern used) ステンシル steńshiru
◆*vt* (letters, designs etc) ステンシルで書く sutéñshiru de kákù

stenographer [stənɑːg'rəfər] (*US*) *n* 速記者 sokkíshà

step [step] *n* (footstep, *also fig*) 一歩 íppò; (sound) 足音 ashíoto; (of stairs) 段 dáñ, ステップ sutéppù
◆*vi*: **to step forward** 前に出る máè ni dérù **to step back** 後ろに下がる ushíro nì sagárù

in/out of step (with) (…と) 歩調が合って〔ずれて〕(…to) hochó ga attè〔zurète〕

stepbrother [step'brʌðər] *n* 異父〔異母〕兄弟 ífù〔íbò〕kyódài

stepdaughter [step'dɔːtər] *n* まま娘 mamámusùme

step down *vi* (*fig*: resign) 辞任する jinín suru

stepfather [step'fɑːðər] *n* まま父 mamáchichi

stepladder [step'lædər] *n* 脚立 kyatátsu

stepmother [step'mʌðər] *n* まま母 mamáhaha

step on *vt fus* (something: walk on) 踏む fumú

stepping stone [step'iŋ-] *n* 飛石 tobíishi

steps [steps] (*BRIT*) *npl* = stepladder

stepsister [step'sistər] *n* 異父〔異母〕姉妹 ífù〔íbò〕shímài

stepson [step'sʌn] *n* まま息子 mamámusùko

step up *vt* (increase: efforts, pace etc) 増す masú

stereo [ster'i:ou] *n* (system) ステレオ sutéreo; (record player) レコードプレーヤー rekódopurèyà
◆*adj* (*also*: **stereophonic**) ステレオの sutéreo no

stereotype [ster'i:ətaip] *n* 固定概念 kotéigaìnen

sterile [ster'əl] *adj* (free from germs: bandage etc) 殺菌した sakkín shita; (barren: woman, female animal) 不妊の funín no; (: man, male animal) 子供を作れない kodómo wò tsukúrenaì; (land) 不毛の fumó no

sterilize [ster'əlaiz] *vt* (thing, place) 殺菌する sakkín suru; (woman) …に避妊手術をする …ni hinínshujùtsu wo suru

sterling [stəːr'liŋ] *adj* (silver) 純銀の juńgin no
♦*n* (ECON) 英国通貨 eíkokutsúka
one pound sterling 英貨1ポンド éíka ichí pońdo

stern [stəːrn] *adj* (father, warning etc) 厳しい kibíshíi
♦*n* (of boat) 船尾 séńbi

stethoscope [steθ'əskoup] *n* 聴診器 chóshiñki

stew [stuː] *n* シチュー shichū
♦*vt* (meat, vegetables) 煮込む nikómù; (fruit) 煮る nirú

steward [stuː'əːrd] *n* (on ship, plane, train) スチュワード suchúwàdo

stewardess [stuː'əːrdis] *n* (especially on plane) スチュワーデス suchúwàdesu

stick [stik] *n* (gen: of wood) 棒 bō; (as weapon) こん棒 końbō; (walking stick) つえ tsúè
♦*vb* (*pt*, *pp* **stuck**)
♦*vt* (with glue etc) 張る harú; (*inf*: put) 置く okú; (: tolerate) ...の最後まで我慢する ...no saígo made gámàn surù; (thrust): **to stick something into** ...の中へ...を突っ込む ...no nákà e ...wo tsukkómù
♦*vi* (become attached) くっつく kuttsúkù; (be immovable) 引っ掛る hikkákarù; (in mind etc) 焼付く yakítsukù
a stick of dynamite ダイナマイト1本 dainamaito ippon

sticker [stik'əːr] *n* ステッカー sutékkà

sticking plaster [stik'iŋ-] *n* ばんそうこう bańsōkō

stickler [stik'ləːr] *n*: **to be a stickler for** ...に関してやかましい ...ni káñ shite yakámashìi

stick out *vi* (ears etc) 突出る tsukíderù

stick up *vi* (hair etc) 立つ tátsù

stick-up [stik'ʌp] (*inf*) *n* ピストル強盗 písutoru gòtō

stick up for *vt fus* (person) ...の肩をもつ ...no kátà wo mótsù; (principle) 守る mamórù

sticky [stik'iː] *adj* (messy: hands etc) べたべたしている bétàbeta shité irù; (label) 粘着の neńchaku no; (*fig*: situation) 厄介な yákkài na

stiff [stif] *adj* (hard, firm: brush) 堅い katáì; (hard: paste, egg-white) 固まった katámattà; (moving with difficulty: arms, legs, back) こわばった kowábattà; (: door, zip etc) 堅い katáì; (formal: manner, smile) 堅苦しい katágurushìi; (difficult, severe: competition, sentence) 厳しい kibíshìi; (strong: drink, breeze) 強い tsuyóì; (high: price) 高い takáì
♦*adv* (bored, worried, scared) ひどく hídòku

stiffen [stif'ən] *vi* (body, muscles, joints) こわばる kowábarù

stiff neck *n* 首が回らない事 kubí gà mawáranaì kotó

stifle [stai'fəl] *vt* (cry, yawn) 抑える osáerù; (opposition) 抑圧する yokúatsu suru

stifling [staif'liŋ] *adj* (heat) 息苦しい ikígurushìi

stigma [stig'mə] *n* (*fig*: of divorce, failure, defeat etc) 汚名 ómèi

stile [stail] *n* 踏段 fumídan ◇牧場のさくの両側に設けられ、人間が越えられるが家畜が出られない様にした物 bokújō nò sakú no ryógawa nì mókerarè, niñgen gà koérarerù ga kachíku gà derárenai yō ni shitá monò

stiletto [stilet'ou] (*BRIT*) *n* (*also:* **stiletto heel**) ハイヒール haíhìru

still [stil] *adj* (person, water, air) 動かない ugókanaì; (place) 静寂な seíjaku na
♦*adv* (up to this time, yet) まだ mádà; (even) 更に sárà ni; (nonetheless) それにしても soré ni shite mò

stillborn [stil'bɔːrn] *adj* 死産の shízàn no

still life *n* 静物画 seíbutsugà

stilt [stilt] *n* (pile) 脚柱 kyakúchū; (for walking on) 竹馬 takéuma

stilted [stil'tid] *adj* (behavior, conversation) 堅苦しい katákurushìi

stimulant [stim'jələnt] *n* 覚せい剤 kakúseizai

stimulate [stim'jəleit] *vt* (person, demand) 刺激する shigéki suru

stimulating [stim'jəleitiŋ] *adj* (conversation, person, experience) 刺激的な shigékiteki na

stimuli [stim'jəlai] *npl of* **stimulus**

stimulus [stim'jələs] (*pl* **stimuli**) *n* (encouragement, *also* MED) 刺激 shigéki

sting [stiŋ] *n* (wound) 虫刺され mushísasarè; (pain) 刺す様な痛み sásù yō na itámi; (organ) 針 hárì
♦*vb* (*pt, pp* **stung**)
♦*vt* (insect, plant etc) 刺す sásù; (*fig*) 傷付ける kizútsukerù
♦*vi* (insect, plant etc) 刺す sásù; (eyes, ointment etc) しみる shimírù

stingy [stin'dʒi:] *adj* けちな kéchì na

stink [stiŋk] *n* (smell) 悪臭 akúshū
♦*vi* (*pt* **stank**, *pp* **stunk**) (smell) におう níòu

stinking [stiŋ'kiŋ] (*inf*) *adj* (*fig*) くそったれの kusóttàre no

stint [stint] *n* 仕事の期間 shigóto no kikaǹ
♦*vi*: **to stint on** (work, ingredients etc) ...をけちる ...wo kechírù

stipulate [stip'jəleit] *vt* ...の条件を付ける ...no jōken wò tsukérù

stir [stəːr] *n* (*fig*: agitation) 騒ぎ sáwàgi
♦*vt* (tea etc) かき混ぜる kakímazerù; (*fig*: emotions) 刺激する shigéki suru
♦*vi* (move slightly) ちょっと動く chóttò ugókù

stirrup [stəːr'əp] *n* あぶみ abúmi

stir up *vt* (trouble) 引起こす hikíokosù

stitch [stitʃ] *n* (SEWING, MED) 一針 hitóhàri; (KNITTING) ステッチ sutétchì; (pain) わき腹のけいれん wakíbara nò keíren
♦*vt* (sew: *gen*, MED) 縫う núù

stoat [stout] *n* てん téǹ

stock [staːk] *n* (supply) 資源 shígèn; (COMM) 在庫品 zaíkohìn; (AGR) 家畜 kachíku; (CULIN) 煮出し汁 nidáshijiru, ストック sutókkù; (descent) 血統 kettō; (FINANCE: government stock etc) 株式 kabúshìki
♦*adj* (*fig*: reply, excuse etc) お決りの o-kímàri no
♦*vt* (have in stock) 常備する jōbì suru
stocks and shares 債券 saíken
in/out of stock 在庫がある〔ない〕zaí-

ko gà árù〔nai〕

to take stock of (*fig*) 検討する keńtō suru

stockbroker [staːk'broukəːr] *n* 株式仲買人 kabúshikinakagainìn

stock cube (*BRIT*) *n* 固形スープの素 kokéi sūpu no moto

stock exchange *n* 株式取引所 kabúshikitorihikijò

stocking [staːk'iŋ] *n* ストッキング sutókkìngu

stockist [staːk'ist] (*BRIT*) *n* 特約店 tokúyakutèn

stock market *n* 株式市場 kabúshikishijò

stock phrase *n* 決り文句 kimárimoǹku

stockpile [staːk'pail] *n* 備蓄 bichíku
♦*vt* 貯蔵する chozō suru

stocktaking [staːk'teikiŋ] (*BRIT*) *n* (COMM) 棚卸し tanáoroshi

stock up with *vt* ...を仕入れる ...wo shiírérù

stocky [staːk'i:] *adj* (strong, short) がっしりした gasshírì shita; (short, stout) ずんぐりした zuǹgurì shita

stodgy [staːdʒ'i:] *adj* (food) こってりした kottérì shita

stoical [stou'ikəl] *adj* 平然とした heízen tò shita

stoke [stouk] *vt* (fire, furnace, boiler) ...に燃料をくべる ...ni neńryð wo kubérù

stole [stoul] *pt of* **steal**
♦*n* ストール sutórù

stolen [stou'lən] *pp of* **steal**

stolid [staːl'id] *adj* (person, behavior) 表情の乏しい hyōjò no toboshiì

stomach [stʌm'ək] *n* (ANAT) 胃 i; (belly) おなか onáka
♦*vt* (*fig*) 耐える taérù

stomachache [stʌm'əkeik] *n* 腹痛 fukútsu

stone [stoun] *n* (rock) 石 ishî; (pebble) 小石 koíshi; (gem) 宝石 hōseki; (in fruit) 種 táně; (MED) 結石 kesséki; (*BRIT*: weight) ストーン sutóǹ ◊体重の単位，約6.3 kg taíjū no taň-i, yákù 6.3 kg
♦*adj* (pottery) ストーンウエアの sutóǹ-ueà no

♦*vt* (person) ...に石を投付ける ...ni ishi wo nagetsukeru; (fruit) ...の種を取る ...no tánè wo tórù

stone-cold [stoun'kould'] *adj* 冷え切った hiékittá

stone-deaf [stoun'def'] *adj* かなつんぼの kanátsuñbo no

stonework [stoun'wə:rk] *n* (stones) 石造りの物 ishízùkùri no mono

stony [stou'ni:] *adj* (ground) 石だらけの ishídàrake no; (*fig*: glance, silence etc) 冷淡な reítan na

stood [stud] *pt, pp of* **stand**

stool [stu:l] *n* スツール sutsūrù

stoop [stu:p] *vi* (*also*: **stoop down**: bend) 腰をかがめる koshí wò kagámerù; (*also*: **have a stoop**) 腰が曲っている koshí gà magátte irú

stop [sta:p] *n* (halt) 停止 teíshi; (short stay) 立寄り tachíyori; (in punctuation: *also*: **full stop**) ピリオド pírìodo; (bus stop etc) 停留所 teíryūjo

♦*vt* (break off) 止める tomérù; (block: pay, check) ...の支払を停止させる ...no shihárài wo teíshi saserù; (prevent: *also*: **put a stop to**) やめさせる yamésaserù

♦*vi* (halt: person) 立ち止る tachídomarù; (: watch, clock) 止まる tomárù; (end: rain, noise etc) やむ yamú

to stop doing something ...するのをやめる ...surú no wò yamérù

stop dead *vi* 急に止る kyū ní tomárù

stopgap [sta:p'gæp] *n* (person/thing) 間に合せの人〔物〕ma ní awase nò hitó 〔monő〕

stop off *vi* 立寄る tachíyorù

stopover [sta:p'ouvə:r] *n* (gen) 立寄って泊る事 tachíyottè tomáru kotð; (AVIAT) 給油着陸 kyūyuchakùriku

stoppage [sta:p'idʒ] *n* (strike) ストライキ sutóraìki; (blockage) 停止 teíshi

stopper [sta:p'ə:r] *n* 栓 séñ

stop press *n* 最新ニュース saíshinnyùsu

stop up *vt* (hole) ふさぐ fuságù

stopwatch [sta:p'wɑ:tʃ] *n* ストップウオッチ sutóppuuotchì

storage [stɔ:r'idʒ] *n* 保管 hokán

storage heater *n* 蓄熱ヒーター chikú-

netsuhītā ◇深夜など電気需要の少ない時に熱を作って蓄え、昼間それを放射するヒーター shîñ-ya nádð deñkíjuyð no sukúnai tokî ni netsú wo tsukúttè takúwa-è, hirúma sorê wð hõsha suru hîtā

store [stɔ:r] *n* (stock) 蓄え takúwaè; (depot) 倉庫 sõko; (*BRIT*: large shop) デパート depắtò; (*US*) 店 misé; (reserve) 備蓄 bichíku

♦*vt* (provisions, information etc) 蓄える takúwaerù

in store 未来に待構えて mírai ni machíkamaetè

storeroom [stɔ:r'ru:m] *n* 倉庫 sõko

stores [stɔ:rz] *npl* (provisions) 物資 bússhì

store up *vt* (nuts, sugar, memories) 蓄える takúwaerù

storey [stɔ:r'i:] (*BRIT*: floor) *n* = **story**

stork [stɔ:rk] *n* コウノトリ kõnotòri

storm [stɔ:rm] *n* (bad weather) 嵐 áràshi; (*fig*: of criticism, applause etc) 爆発 bakúhatsu

♦*vi* (*fig*: speak angrily) どなる donárù

♦*vt* (attack: place) 攻撃する kõgeki suru

stormy [stɔ:r'mi:] *adj* (weather) 荒れ模様の arémoyð no; (*fig*: debate, relations) 激しい hagéshiì

story [stɔ:r'i:] *n* (gen: *also*: history) 物語 monőgàtari; (lie) うそ úsð; (*US*) 階 kaî

storybook [stɔ:r'i:buk] *n* 童話の本 dõwa no hoñ

stout [staut] *adj* (strong: branch etc) 丈夫な jõbu na; (fat) 太った futőttà; (resolute: friend, supporter) 不動の fudõ no

♦*n* (beer) スタウト sutáùto

stove [stouv] *n* (for cooking) レンジ réñji; (for heating) ストーブ sutőbù

stow [stou] *vt* (*also*: **stow away**) しまう shimáù

stowaway [stou'əwei] *n* 密航者 mikkő-shà

straddle [stræd'əl] *vt* (chair, fence etc: *also fig*) ...にまたがる ...ni matágarù

straggle [stræg'əl] *vi* (houses etc) 散在する sañzai suru; (people etc) 落ごする rakúgo suru

straggly [stræg'li:] *adj* (hair) ぼさぼさし

た bósabosa shita

straight [streit] *adj* (line, road, back, hair) 真っ直ぐの massúgù no; (honest: answer) 正直な shójiki na; (simple: choice, fight) 簡潔な kańketsu na
♦*adv* (directly) 真っ直ぐに massúgù ni; (drink) ストレートで sutórèto de
to put/get something straight (make clear) 明らかにする akíràka ni suru
straight away, straight off (at once) 直ちに tádàchi ni

straighten [strei'tən] *vt* (skirt, bed etc) 整える totónoerù

straighten out *vt* (*fig*: problem, situation) 解決する kaíketsu suru

straight-faced [streit'feist] *adj* まじめな顔をした majíme nà kaó wo shità

straightforward [streitfɔːr'wəːrd] *adj* (simple) 簡単な kañtan na; (honest) 正直な shójiki na

strain [strein] *n* (pressure) 負担 fután; (TECH) ひずみ hizúmi; (MED: tension) 緊張 kińchō; (breed) 血統 kettő
♦*vt* (back etc) 痛める itámerù; (stretch: resources) ...に負担をかける ...ni fután wò kakérù; (CULIN: food) こす kosú
back strain (MED) ぎっくり腰 gikkúrigòshi

strained [streind] *adj* (back, muscle) 痛めた itámetà; (relations) 緊迫した kińpaku shità
a strained laugh 作り笑い tsukúriwarài

strainer [strei'nəːr] *n* (CULIN) こし器 koshíkì

strains [streinz] *npl* (MUS) 旋律 seńritsu

strait [streit] *n* (GEO) 海峡 kaíkyō

strait-jacket [streit'dʒækit] *n* 拘束衣 kōsokuì

strait-laced [streit'leist] *adj* しかつめらしい shikátsumerashiì

straits [streits] *npl*: *to be in dire straits* (*fig*) 困り果てている komárihatete irù

strand [strænd] *n* (of thread, hair, rope) 一本 íppòn

stranded [stræn'did] *adj* (holiday-makers) 足留めされた ashídome saretà

strange [streindʒ] *adj* (not known) 未知の míchi no; (odd) 変な hén na

strangely [streindʒ'liː] *adv* (act, laugh) 変った風に kawátta fū ni ¶ *see also* **enough**

stranger [strein'dʒəːr] *n* (unknown person) 知らない人 shiránai hitò; (from another area) よそ者 yosómono

strangle [stræŋ'gəl] *vt* (victim) 絞殺す shimékorosù; (*fig*: economy) 圧迫する appáku suru

stranglehold [stræŋ'gəlhould] *n* (*fig*) 抑圧 yokúatsu

strap [stræp] *n* 肩ひも katáhimo, ストップ sutórappù

strapping [stræp'iŋ] *adj* たくましい takúmashiì

strata [stræt'ə] *npl of* **stratum**

stratagem [stræt'ədʒəm] *n* 策略 sakúryàku

strategic [strəti'dʒik] *adj* (positions, withdrawal, weapons etc) 戦略的な seńryakuteki na

strategy [stræt'idʒiː] *n* (plan, *also* MIL) 作戦 sakúsen

stratum [strei'təm] (*pl* **strata**) *n* (*gen*) 層 ső; (in earth's surface) 地層 chiső; (in society) 階層 kaíső

straw [strɔː] *n* (dried stalks) わら wárà; (drinking straw) ストロー sutórő
that's the last straw! もう我慢できない mő gámàn dekínaì

strawberry [strɔː'beːriː] *n* イチゴ ichígo

stray [strei] *adj* (animal) のら norá...; (bullet) 流れ... nagáre...; (scattered) 点在する teńzai suru
♦*vi* (children, animals) はぐれる hagúrerù; (thoughts) 横道にそれる yokómichi nì sorérù

streak [striːk] *n* (stripe: *gen*) 筋 sújì
♦*vt* ...に筋を付ける ...ni sújì wo tsukérù
♦*vi*: *to streak past* 猛スピードで通り過ぎる mősupìdo de tőrisugirù

stream [striːm] *n* (small river) 小川 ogáwa; (of people, vehicles, smoke) 流れ nagáre; (of questions, insults etc) 連続 reńzoku

◆*vt* (SCOL: students) 能力別に分ける nő-ryokubètsu ni wakérù

◆*vi* (water, oil, blood) 流れる nagárerù

to stream in/out (people) 流れ込む〔出る〕nagárekomù〔derù〕

streamer [stri:'mə:r] *n* 紙テープ kamítē-pu

streamlined [stri:m'laind] *adj* 流線形の ryūseñkei no

street [stri:t] *n* 道 michí

streetcar [stri:t'kɑ:r] (*US*) *n* 路面電車 roméndeñsha

street lamp *n* 街灯 gaítō

street plan *n* 市街地図 shigáichizù

streetwise [stri:t'waiz] (*inf*) *adj* 裏町の悪知恵を持っている urámachi no warújie wò motté irù

strength [streŋkθ] *n* (physical) 体力 taíryoku; (of girder, knot etc) 強さ tsúyòsa; (*fig*: power, number) 勢力 seíryoku

strengthen [streŋk'θən] *vt* (building, machine) 補強する hokyō suru; (*fig*: group, argument, relationship) 強くする tsúyòku suru

strenuous [stren'ju:əs] *adj* (energetic: exercise) 激しい hagéshiì; (determined: efforts) 精力的な seíryokuteki na

stress [stres] *n* (force, pressure, *also* TECH) 圧力 atsúryòku; (mental strain) ストレス sutórèsu; (emphasis) 強調 kyōchō

◆*vt* (point, importance etc) 強調する kyōchō suru; (syllable) ...にアクセントを置く ...ni ákùsento wo okú

stretch [stretʃ] *n* (area: of sand, water etc) 一帯 ittái

◆*vi* (person, animal) 背伸びする sénòbi suru; (extend): *to stretch to/as far as* ...まで続く ...mádè tsuzúkù

◆*vt* (pull) 伸ばす nobásù; (subj: job, task: make demands of) ...に努力を要求する ...ni dóryòku wo yōkyū suru

stretcher [stretʃ'ə:r] *n* 担架 táǹka

stretch out *vi* 体を伸ばす karáda wò nobásù

◆*vt* (arm etc) 伸ばす nobásù; (spread) 広げる hirógerù

strewn [stru:n] *adj*: *strewn with* ...が散らばっている ...ga chirábatte irù

stricken [strik'ən] *adj* (person) 打ちひしがれた uchíhishigaretà; (city, industry etc) 災いに見舞われた wazáwai nì mimáwaretà

stricken with (arthritis, disease) ...にかかっている ...ni kakátte irù

strict [strikt] *adj* (severe, firm: person, rule) 厳しい kibíshiì; (precise: meaning) 厳密な geñmitsu na

strictly [strikt'li:] *adv* (severely) 厳しく kibíshikù; (exactly) 厳密に geñmitsu ni

stridden [strid'ən] *pp of* **stride**

stride [straid] *n* (step) 大またの一歩 ốmàta no íppò

◆*vi* (*pt* **strode**, *pp* **stridden**) 大またに歩く ốmàta ni arúkù

strident [straid'ənt] *adj* (voice, sound) 甲高い kañdakaì

strife [straif] *n* 反目 hañmoku

strike [straik] *n* (of workers) ストライキ sutóraìki; (of oil etc) 発見 hakkén; (MIL: attack) 攻撃 kốgeki

◆*vb* (*pt*, *pp* **struck**)

◆*vt* (hit: person, thing) 打つ útsù; (*fig*: subj: idea, thought) ...の心に浮ぶ ...no kókòro ni ukábù; (oil etc) 発見する hakkén suru; (bargain, deal) 決める kimérù

◆*vi* (go on strike) ストライキに入る sutóraìki ni haírù; (attack: soldiers) 攻撃する kốgeki suru; (: illness) 襲う osóù; (: disaster) 見舞う mimáù; (clock) 鳴る narú

on strike (workers) ストライキ中で sutóraikichù de

to strike a match マッチを付ける mátchì wo tsukérù

strike down *vt* (kill) 殺す korósù; (harm) 襲う osóù

striker [strai'kə:r] *n* (person on strike) ストライキ参加者 sutóraikisankashà; (SPORT) 攻撃選手 kốgekiseñshu

strike up *vt* (MUS) 演奏し始める eñsō shihájimerù; (conversation) 始める hajímerù; (friendship) 結ぶ musúbù

striking [strai'kiŋ] *adj* (noticeable) 目立つ medátsù; (attractive) 魅力的な miryóku-teki na

string [striŋ] n (thin rope) ひも himó; (row: of beads etc) 数珠つなぎの物 juzútsunàgi no monó; (: of disasters etc) 一連 ichíren; (MUS) 弦 gén

♦vt (pt, pp strung): to string together つなぐ tsunágù

a string of islands 列島 rettő

to pull strings (fig) コネを利用する kónè wo riyő suru

to string out 一列に並べる ichíretsu nì naráberù

string bean n さや豆 sayámame

string(ed) instrument [striŋ(d)-] n (MUS) 弦楽器 geñgakkì

stringent [strin'dʒənt] adj (rules, measures) 厳しい kibíshiì

strings [striŋz] npl: the strings (MUS: section of orchestra) 弦楽器 geñgakkì

strip [strip] n (gen) 細長い切れ hosónagaì kiré; (of land, water) 細長い一帯 hosónagaì ittái

♦vt (undress) 裸にする hadáka ni surù; (paint) はがす hagásù; (also: strip down: machine) 分解する buñkai suru

♦vi (undress) 裸になる hadáka ni narù

strip cartoon n 四こま漫画 yoñkoma mañga

stripe [straip] n (gen) しま shima; (MIL, POLICE) 袖章 sodéshoō

striped [straipt] adj しま模様の shimámoyō no

strip lighting n 蛍光灯 keíkōtō

stripper [strip'ə:r] n ストリッパー sutórippā

striptease [strip'ti:z] n ストリップショー sutórippushō

strive [straiv] (pt strove, pp striven) vi: to strive for something/to do something ...しようと努力する ...shiyő tò dóryòku suru

striven [striv'ən] pp of strive

strode [stroud] pt of stride

stroke [strouk] n (blow) 一撃 ichígeki; (SWIMMING) ストローク sutórōku; (MED) 脳卒中 nōsotchū; (of paintbrush) 筆の運び fudé nò hakóbi

♦vt (caress) なでる nadérù

at a stroke 一気に íkkì ni

stroll [stroul] n 散歩 sañpo

♦vi 散歩する sañpo suru

stroller [strou'lə:r] (US) n (pushchair) いす型ベビーカー isúgata bebìkā

strong [strɔ:ŋ] adj (person, arms, grasp) 強い tsuyőì; (stick) 丈夫な jőbu na; (wind) 強い tsuyőì; (imagination) 想像力のある sőzōryoku no árù; (personality) 気性の激しい kishō nò hagéshiì; (influence) 強い tsuyőì; (nerves) 頑丈な gañjō na; (smell) 強烈な kyőretsu na; (coffee) 濃い kóì; (taste) 際立った kiwádattà

they are 50 strong 50人いる gojúnìn irú

stronghold [strɔ:ŋ'hould] n とりで toríde; (fig) 根城 néjìro

strongly [strɔ:ŋ'li:] adv (solidly: construct) 頑丈に gañjō ni; (with force: push, defend) 激しく hagéshikù; (deeply: feel, believe) 強く tsúyòku

strongroom [strɔ:ŋ'ru:m] n 金庫室 kiñkoshìtsu

strove [strouv] pt of strive

struck [strʌk] pt, pp of strike

structural [strʌk'tʃə:rəl] adj (damage, defect) 構造的な kőzoteki na

structure [strʌk'tʃə:r] n (organization) 組織 sőshìki; (building) 構造物 kőzōbùtsu

struggle [strʌg'əl] n 闘争 tősō

♦vi (try hard) 努力する dóryòku suru; (fight) 戦う tatákaù

strum [strʌm] vt (guitar) つま弾く tsumábikù

strung [strʌŋ] pt, pp of string

strut [strʌt] n (wood, metal) 支柱 shichū

♦vi 威張って歩く ibátte arukù

stub [stʌb] n (of check, ticket etc) 控え hikáè; (of cigarette) 吸殻 suígara

♦vt: to stub one's toe つま先をぶつける tsumásaki wò butsúkerù

stubble [stʌb'əl] n (AGR) 切株 kiríkàbu; (on chin) 不精ひげ bushőhìge

stubborn [stʌb'ə:rn] adj (child, determination) 頑固な gáñko na

stub out vt (cigarette) もみ消す momíkesù

stuck [stʌk] pt, pp of stick

◆*adj* (jammed) 引っ掛っている hikká-katte iru

stuck-up [stʌk'ʌp'] (*inf*) *adj* 天ぐになっている tengu ni natté irú

stud [stʌd] *n* (on clothing etc) 飾りボタン kazáribotàn; (earring) 丸玉 marúdamà (on sole of boot) スパイク supáiku; (*also*: **stud farm**) 馬の繁殖牧場 umá nò hañ-shokubokujò; (*also*: **stud horse**) 種馬 tanéuma

◆*vt* (*fig*): **studded with** ...をちりばめた ...wo chiríbametà

student [stu:'dənt] *n* (at university) 学生 gakúsei; (at lower schools) 生徒 seíto

◆*adj* (nurse, life, union) 学生の gakúsei no

student driver (*US*) *n* 仮免許運転者 karímenkyo unteñsha

studies [stʌd'iːz] *npl* (subjects studied) 勉強の科目 beñkyō nò kamóku

studio [stu:'diːou] *n* (TV etc) スタジオ sutájìo; (sculptor's etc) アトリエ atóriè

studio apartment (*BRIT* **studio flat**) *n* ワンルームマンション wañrūmu mâñshon

studious [stu:'diːəs] *adj* (person) 勉強家の beñkyōka no; (careful: attention) 注意深い chūibukaì

studiously [stu:'diːəsliː] *adv* (carefully) 注意深く chūibukakù

study [stʌd'iː] *n* (activity) 勉強 beñkyō; (room) 書斎 shosái

◆*vt* (learn about: subjects) 勉強する beñkyō suru; (examine: face, evidence) 調べる shiráberù

◆*vi* 勉強する beñkyō suru

stuff [stʌf] *n* (thing(s)) 物 monó, 事 kotó; (substance) 素質 soshítsu

◆*vt* (soft toy: *also* CULIN) ...に詰める ...ni tsumérù; (dead animals) はく製にする hakúsei ni surù; (*inf*: push: object) 差込む sashíkomù

stuffing [stʌf'iŋ] *n* (*gen*, CULIN) 詰物 tsumémòno

stuffy [stʌf'iː] *adj* (room) 空気の悪い kúki nò waruî; (person, ideas) 古臭い furúkusaì

stumble [stʌm'bəl] *vi* つまづく tsumázu-kù

to stumble across/on (*fig*) ...に出くわす ...ni dekúwasù

stumbling block [stʌm'bliŋ-] *n* 障害 shōgai

stump [stʌmp] *n* (of tree) 切株 kiríkàbu; (of limb) 断端 dañtan

◆*vt*: **to be stumped** まごつく magótsu-kù

stun [stʌn] *vt* (subj: news) あ然とさせる azen to sasérù; (: blow on head) 気絶させる kizetsu sasérù

stung [stʌŋ] *pt, pp of* **sting**

stunk [stʌŋk] *pp of* **stink**

stunning [stʌn'iŋ] *adj* (*fig*: news, event) 仰天させる gyōten saserù; (: girl, dress) 美しい utsúkushiî

stunt [stʌnt] *n* (in film) スタント sutáñto; (*also*: **publicity stunt**) 宣伝用のトリック señden-yō no toríkkù

stunted [stʌn'tid] *adj* (trees, growth etc) 成長を阻害された seíchō wò sogái sare-tà

stuntman [stʌnt'mən] (*pl* **stuntmen**) *n* スタントマン sutáñtoman

stupefy [stu:'pəfai] *vt* ぼう然とさせる bōzen to saserù

stupendous [stu:pen'dəs] *adj* 途方もない tohōmonaî

stupid [stu:'pid] *adj* (person, question etc) ばかな bákà na

stupidity [stu:pid'itiː] *n* 愚かさ orókasà

stupor [stu:'pəːr] *n* 前後不覚 zéñgofukáku

sturdy [stəːr'diː] *adj* (person, thing) がっちりした gatchírî shita

stutter [stʌt'əːr] *n* どもり dómòri

◆*vi* どもる domórù

sty [stai] *n* (*also*: **pigsty**) 豚小屋 butágo-ya

stye [stai] *n* (MED) ものもらい monómo-raì

style [stail] *n* (way, attitude) やり方 yaríkata; (elegance) 優雅さ yūgàsa; (design) スタイル sutáîru

stylish [stai'liʃ] *adj* 優雅な yūgà na

stylus [stai'ləs] *n* (of record player) 針 harí

suave [swɑːv] *adj* 物腰の丁寧な monógòshi no teínei na

subconscious [sʌbkɑːn'tʃəs] *adj* (desire etc) 潜在意識の seńzaiishìki no

subcontract [sʌbkəntrækt'] *vt* 下請に出す shitáuke nì dásù

subdivide [sʌbdivaid'] *vt* 小分けする kowáke suru

subdue [səbduː'] *vt* (rebels etc) 征服する seífuku suru; (passions) 抑制する yokúsei suru

subdued [səbduːd'] *adj* (light) 柔らかな yawárakà na; (person) 落込んだ ochíkoñda

subject [*n* sʌb'dʒikt *vb* səbjekt'] *n* (matter) 話題 wadái; (SCOL) 学科 gakká; (of kingdom) 臣民 shiñmiñ; (GRAMMAR) 主語 shúgò

♦*vt*: **to subject someone to something** ...を...にさらす ...wo ...ni sarásù

to be subject to (law) ...に服従しなければならない ...ni fukújū shinakerèba naránaì; (heart attacks) ...が起りやすい ...ga okóriyasuì

to be subject to tax 課税される kazéi sarerù

subjective [səbdʒek'tiv] *adj* 主観的な shukánteki na

subject matter *n* (content) 内容 naíyō

subjugate [sʌb'dʒəgeit] *vt* (people) 征服する seífuku suru

subjunctive [səbdʒʌŋk'tiv] *n* 仮定法 katéihò

sublet [sʌb'let] *vt* また貸しする matágashi suru

sublime [səblaim'] *adj* 素晴らしい subárashiì

submachine gun [sʌbməʃiːn'-] *n* 軽機関銃 keíkikañjū

submarine [sʌb'məriːn] *n* 潜水艦 seńsuikan

submerge [səbmərdʒ'] *vt* 水中に沈める suíchū nì shizúmerù

♦*vi* (submarine, sea creature) 潜る mogúrù

submission [səbmiʃ'ən] *n* (state) 服従 fukújū; (claim) 申請書 shińseishò; (of plan) 提出 teíshutsu

submissive [səbmis'iv] *adj* 従順な jújun na

submit [səbmit'] *vt* (proposal, application etc) 提出する teíshutsu suru

♦*vi*: **to submit to something** ...に従う ...ni shitágaù

subnormal [sʌbnɔːr'məl] *adj* (below average: temperatures) 通常以下の tsújōìkà no

subordinate [səbɔːr'dənit] *adj* 二次的な nijíteki na

♦*n* 部下 búkà

subpoena [səpiː'nə] *n* (LAW) 召喚状 shókañjò

subscribe [səbskraib'] *vi*: **to subscribe to** (opinion) ...に同意する ...ni dóì suru; (fund) ...に寄付する ...ni kifú suru; (magazine etc) ...を購読する ...wo kódoku suru

subscriber [səbskraib'əːr] *n* (to periodical, telephone) 購読者 kódokushà; (to telephone) 加入者 kanyúsha

subscription [səbskrip'ʃən] *n* (to magazine etc) 購読契約 kódokukeiyàku

subsequent [sʌb'səkwənt] *adj* (following) その後の sonó atò no; (resulting) その結果として起る sonó kekkà toshite okórù

subsequently [sʌb'səkwəntliː] *adv* その後 sonó atò

subside [səbsaid'] *vi* (feeling) 収る osámarù; (flood) ひく hikú; (wind) やむ yamú

subsidence [səbsaid'əns] *n* (in road etc) 陥没 kañbotsu

subsidiary [səbsid'iːeːriː] *adj* (question, details) 二次的な nijíteki na

♦*n* (*also*: **subsidiary company**) 子会社 kogáìsha

subsidize [sʌb'sidaiz] *vt* (education, industry etc) ...に補助金を与える ...ni hojókìn wo atáerù

subsidy [sʌb'sidiː] *n* 補助金 hojókìn

subsistence [səbsis'təns] *n* (ability to live) 最低限度の生活水準 saíteigeñdo no seíkatsusuijùn

subsistence allowance (*BRIT*) *n* (advance payment) 支度金 shitákukìn;

(for expenses etc) 特別手当 tokúbetsu teáte

substance [sʌb'stəns] n (product, material) 物質 busshítsu

substantial [səbstæn'tʃəl] adj (solid) 頑丈な gañjō na; (fig: reward, meal) 多い ối

substantially [səbstæn'tʃəli:] adv (by a large amount) 大いに ối ni; (in essence) 本質的に hoñshitsuteki ni

substantiate [səbstæn'tʃi:eit] vt 裏付ける urázukerù

substitute [sʌb'stitu:t] n (person) 代人 daínin; (thing) 代用品 daíyōhìn

♦vt: to substitute A for B Bの代りにA を置く B nò kawári nì A wò okú

substitution [sʌbstitu:'ʃən] n (act of substituting) 置換え okíkae; (SOCCER) 選手交代 señshukốtai

subterfuge [sʌb'tə:rfju:dʒ] n 策略 sakúryàku

subterranean [sʌbtərei'ni:ən] adj 地下の chiká no

subtitle [sʌb'taitəl] n 字幕スーパー jimákusūpā

subtle [sʌt'əl] adj (slight: change) 微妙な bimyố na; (indirect: person) 腹芸のうまい harágei no umái

subtlety [sʌt'əlti:] n (small detail) 微妙な所 bimyố nà tokórò; (art of being subtle) 腹芸 harágei

subtotal [sʌbtou'təl] n 小計 shốkei

subtract [səbtrækt'] vt ...から...を引く ...kárà ...wò hikú

subtraction [səbtræk'ʃən] n 引算 hikízan

suburb [sʌb'ə:rb] n 都市周辺の自治体 toshíshūhen no jichítai

suburban [səbə:r'bən] adj (train, lifestyle etc) 郊外の kốgai no

suburbia [səbə:r'bi:ə] n 郊外 kốgai

suburbs [sʌb'ə:rbz] npl: the suburbs (area) 郊外 kốgai

subversive [səbvə:r'siv] adj (activities, literature) 破壊的な hakáiteki na

subway [sʌb'wei] n (US: underground railway) 地下鉄 chikátetsu; (BRIT: underpass) 地下道 chikádồ

succeed [səksi:d'] vi (plan etc) 成功する

seíkō suru; (person: in career etc) 出生する shusshố suru

♦vt (in job) ...の後任になる ...no kốnin ni narú; (in order) ...の後に続く ...no átò ni tsuzúkù

to succeed in doing ...する事に成功する ...surú kotò ni seíkō suru

succeeding [səksi:'diŋ] adj (following) その後の sonó átò no

success [səkses'] n (achievement) 成功 seíkō; (hit, also person) 大ヒット daíhittò

successful [səkses'fəl] adj (venture) 成功した seíkō shita; (writer) 出生した shusshố shita

to be successful 成功する seíkō suru

to be successful in doing ...する事に成功する ...surú kotò ni seíkō suru

successfully [səkses'fəli:] adv (complete, do) うまく úmaku

succession [səkseʃ'ən] n (series) 連続 reñzoku; (to throne etc) 継承 keíshō

in succession 立続けに tatétsuzuke ni

successive [səkses'iv] adj 連続の reñzoku no

successor [səkses'ə:r] n 後任 kốnin

succinct [səksiŋkt'] adj 簡潔な kañketsu na

succulent [sʌk'jələnt] adj 汁が多くておいしい shírù ga ốkute oíshiì

succumb [səkʌm'] vi (to temptation) 負ける makérù; (to illness: become very ill) ...で倒れる ...de taórerù; (: die) ...で死ぬ ...de shinú

such [sʌtʃ] adj (emphasizing similarity) この〔その, あの〕様な konó〔sonó, anố〕yỗ na; (of that kind): such a book そんな本 soñna hoñ; (so much): such courage そんな勇気 soñna yūki

♦adv こんな〔そんな, あんな〕に koñna〔soñna, añna〕nì

such books そんな本 soñna hoñ

such a long trip あんなに長い旅行 añna nì nagái ryokō

such a lot of そんなに沢山の soñna nì takúsan no

such as (like) ...の様な ...no yỗ na

as such その物 sonố monố

such-and-such [sʌtʃ'ənsʌtʃ] *adj* しかじ かの shikájìka no

suck [sʌk] *vt* (*gen*: ice-lolly etc) なめ る namérù; (bottle, breast) 吸う súù

sucker [sʌk'ə:r] *n* (ZOOL) 吸盤 kyúban; (*inf*: easily cheated person) かも kámò

suction [sʌk'ʃən] *n* 吸引 kyúin

Sudan [su:dæn'] *n* スーダン súdan

sudden [sʌd'ən] *adj* (unexpected, rapid: increase, shower, change) 突然の totsúzen no

all of a sudden (unexpectedly) 突然 totsúzen

suddenly [sʌd'ənli:] *adv* (unexpectedly) 突然 totsúzen

suds [sʌdz] *npl* 石けんの泡 sekkén no a-wà

sue [su:] *vt* ...を相手取って訴訟を起す ...wo aítedottè soshṑ wò okósù

suede [sweid] *n* スエード suédò

suet [su:'it] *n* 脂肪 shibṑ ◇料理に使うウ シやヒツジの堅い脂肪を指す ryōrì ni tsukáù ushí yà hitsúji nò katáì shibṑ wò sásù

Suez [su:'ez] *n*: **the Suez Canal** スエズ 運河 suézu uñga

suffer [sʌf'ə:r] *vt* (undergo: hardship etc) 経験する keíken suru; (bear: pain, rudeness) 我慢する gámàn suru
♦*vi* (be harmed: person, results etc) 苦し む kurúshimù; (results etc) 悪くなる wá-rùku nárù

to suffer from (illness etc) ...の病気にか かっている ...no byōkì ni kakátte irù

sufferer [sʌf'ə:rə:r] *n* (MED) 患者 kañja

suffering [sʌf'ə:riŋ] *n* (hardship) 苦しみ kurúshimi

suffice [səfais'] *vi* 足りる tarírù

sufficient [səfiʃ'ənt] *adj* 十分な júbùn na

sufficiently [səfiʃ'əntli:] *adv* 十分に jú-bùn ni

suffix [sʌf'iks] *n* 接尾辞 setsúbijì

suffocate [sʌf'əkeit] *vi* 窒息する chissó-ku suru

suffocation [sʌfəkei'ʃən] *n* 窒息 chissó-ku

suffrage [sʌf'ridʒ] *n* (right to vote) 参政 権 sañseikèn

suffused [səfju:zd'] *adj*: **suffused with** (light, color, tears) ...で満たされた ...de mitásaretà

sugar [ʃug'ə:r] *n* 砂糖 satṑ
♦*vt* (tea etc) ...に砂糖を入れる ...ni satṑ wò irérù

sugar beet *n* サトウダイコン satṑdaìkon

sugar cane *n* サトウキビ satṑkìbi

suggest [səgdʒest'] *vt* (propose) 提案する teían suru; (indicate) 示唆する shísà suru

suggestion [səgdʒes't'ʃən] *n* (proposal) 提案 teían; (indication) 示唆 shísà

suggestive [səgdʒes'tiv] (*pej*) *adj* (re-marks, looks) 卑わいな hiwái na

suicide [su:'isaid] *n* (death, *also fig*) 自殺 jisátsu; (person) 自殺者 jisátsushà ¶ *see also* **commit**

suit [su:t] *n* (man's) 背広 sebíro; (woman's) スーツ sútsu; (LAW) 訴訟 soshṑ; (CARDS) 組札 kumífùda
♦*vt* (*gen*: be convenient, appropriate) ...に都合がいい ...ni tsugṑ ga íì; (color, clothes) ...に似合う ...ni niáù; (adapt): **to suit something to** ...を...に合せる ...wo ...ni awáserù

well suited (well matched: couple) お似 合いの o-níaì no

suitable [su:'təbəl] *adj* (convenient: time, moment) 都合のいい tsugṑ no íì; (appro-priate: person, clothes etc) 適当な tekítṑ na

suitably [su:'təbli:] *adv* (dressed) 適当に tekítṑ ni; (impressed) 期待通りに kitái-dòri ni

suitcase [su:t'keis] *n* スーツケース sútsu-kèsu

suite [swi:t] *n* (of rooms) スイートルーム suítorùmu; (MUS) 組曲 kumíkyòku; (furniture): **bedroom / dining room suite** 寝室〔食堂〕用家具の一そろい shiñ-shitsu〔shokúdō〕yṑ kágù no hitósòroi

suitor [su:'tə:r] *n* 求婚者 kyúkoǹsha

sulfur [sʌl'fə:r] (*US*) *n* 硫黄 iṑ

sulk [sʌlk] *vi* すねる sunérù

sulky [sʌl'ki:] *adj* (child, silence) すねた sunétà

sullen [sʌl'ən] *adj* (person, silence) すね た sunétà

sulphur [sʌl'fəːr] n = **sulfur**

sultan [sʌl'tən] n サルタン sárùtan ◇ イスラム教国の君主 isúramukyṓkoku no kúñshu

sultana [sʌltæn'ə] n (fruit) 白いレーズン shirōī rḗsùn

sultry [sʌl'triː] adj (weather) 蒸暑い mushíatsuì

sum [sʌm] n (calculation) 計算 keísan; (amount) 金額 kiñgaku; (total) 合計 gṓkei

summarize [sʌm'əːraiz] vt 要約する yṓyaku suru

summary [sʌm'əːriː] n 要約 yṓyaku

summer [sʌm'əːr] n 夏 natsú
◆adj (dress, school) 夏の natsú no
in summer 夏に natsú ni

summer holidays npl 夏休み natsúyasùmi

summerhouse [sʌm'əːrhaus] n (in garden) 東屋 azúmayà

summertime [sʌm'əːrtaim] n (season) 夏 natsú

summer time n (by clock) サマータイム samátaìmu

summer vacation (US) n 夏休み natsúyasùmi

summit [sʌm'it] n (of mountain) 頂上 chōjō; (also: **summit conference/meeting**) 首脳会議 shunṓkaìgi, サミット samíttò

summon [sʌm'ən] vt (person, police, help) 呼ぶ yobú; (to a meeting) 召集する shōshū suru; (LAW: witness) 召喚する shōkan suru

summons [sʌm'ənz] n (LAW) 召喚書 shṓkañsho; (fig) 呼出し yobídashi
◆vt (JUR) 召喚する shōkan suru

summon up vt (strength, energy, courage) 奮い起す furúiokosù

sump [sʌmp] (BRIT) n (AUT) オイルパン oírupañ

sumptuous [sʌmp'tʃuːəs] adj 豪華な gṓkà na

sum up vt (describe) 要約する yṓyaku suru
◆vi (summarize) 要約する yṓyaku suru

sun [sʌn] n (star) 太陽 táìyō; (sunshine)

日光 níkkò

sunbathe [sʌn'beið] vi 日光浴する nikkṓyòku suru

sunburn [sʌn'bəːrn] n (painful) 日焼け hiyáke

sunburnt [sʌn'bəːrnt] adj (tanned) 日に焼けた hi ní yaketà; (painfully) ひどく日焼けした hídòku hiyáke shita

Sunday [sʌn'dei] n 日曜日 nichíyòbi

Sunday school n 日曜学校 nichíyōgakkò

sundial [sʌn'dail] n 日時計 hidókèi

sundown [sʌn'daun] n 日没 nichíbotsu

sundries [sʌn'driːz] npl (miscellaneous items) その他 sonó tà

sundry [sʌn'driː] adj (various) 色々な iróiro na
all and sundry だれもかも dárè mo kámò

sunflower [sʌn'flauəːr] n ヒマワリ himáwàri

sung [sʌŋ] pp of **sing**

sunglasses [sʌn'glæsiz] npl サングラス sañguràsu

sunk [sʌŋk] pp of **sink**

sunlight [sʌn'lait] n 日光 níkkò

sunlit [sʌn'lit] adj 日に照らされた hi ní terasaretà

sunny [sʌn'iː] adj (weather, day) 晴れた háreta; (place) 日当りの良い hiátari no yoì

sunrise [sʌn'raiz] n 日の出 hi nó de

sun roof n (AUT) サンルーフ sañrūfu

sunset [sʌn'set] n 日没 nichíbotsu

sunshade [sʌn'ʃeid] n (over table) パラソル párasòru

sunshine [sʌn'ʃain] n 日光 níkkò

sunstroke [sʌn'strouk] n 日射病 nisshábyō

suntan [sʌn'tæn] n 日焼け hiyáke

suntan lotion n 日焼け止めローション hiyákedome rōshon

suntan oil n サンタンオイル sañtan oirù

super [suː'pəːr] (inf) adj 最高の saíkō no

superannuation [suːpəːrænjuːei'ʃən] n 年金の掛金 neñkin nò kakékìn

superb [suːpəːrb'] adj 素晴らしい subárashiĩ

supercilious [su:pər'sil'i:əs] *adj* (disdainful, haughty) 横柄な ōhei na

superficial [su:pər'fiʃ'əl] *adj* (wound) 浅い asáì; (knowledge) 表面的な hyōmenteki na; (shallow: person) 浅はかな asáhàka na

superfluous [su:pər'flu:əs] *adj* 余計な yokéi na

superhuman [su:pər'hju:'mən] *adj* 超人的な chōjinteki na

superimpose [su:pər'rimpouz'] *vt* 重ね合せる kasáneawaserù

superintendent [su:pər'rinten'dənt] *n* (of place, activity) ...長 ...chō; (POLICE) 警視 keíshi

superior [səpi:r'i:ə:r] *adj* (better) (より) すぐれた (yorí) sugúretà; (more senior) 上位の jōī no; (smug) 偉ぶった erábuttà
♦*n* 上司 jōshì

superiority [səpi:ri:ɔ:r'iti:] *n* 優位性 yūìsei

superlative [səpə:r'lətiv] *n* (LING) 最上級 saíjōkyū

superman [su:'pə:rmæn] (*pl* **supermen**) *n* 超人 chōjin

supermarket [su:'pə:rma:rkit] *n* スーパー sūpā

supernatural [su:pər'nætʃ'ə:rəl] *adj* (creature, force etc) 超自然の chōshizen no
♦*n*: *the supernatural* 超自然の現象 chōshizen no genshō

superpower [su:pər'pau'ə:r] *n* (POL) 超大国 chōtaikòku

supersede [su:pə:rsi:d'] *vt* ...に取って代る ...ni tōttè kawárù

supersonic [su:pər'sa:n'ik] *adj* (flight, aircraft) 超音速の chōonsoku no

superstar [su:'pə:rsta:r] *n* (CINEMA, SPORT etc) スーパースター sūpāsutà

superstition [su:pər'stiʃ'ən] *n* 迷信 meíshin

superstitious [su:pər'stiʃ'əs] *adj* (person) 迷信深い meíshinbùkai; (practices) 迷信的な meíshinteki na

supertanker [su:'pə:rtæŋkə:r] *n* スーパータンカー sūpātañkà

supervise [su:'pə:rvaiz] *vt* (person, activity) 監督する kañtoku suru

supervision [su:pə:rviʒ'ən] *n* 監督 kañtoku

supervisor [su:'pə:rvaizə:r] *n* (of workers, students) 監督 kañtoku

supine [su:'pain] *adj* 仰向きの aómuki no

supper [sʌp'ə:r] *n* (early evening) 夕食 yūshoku; (late evening) 夜食 yashōku

supplant [səplænt'] *vt* (person, thing) ...に取って代る ...ni tōttè kawárù

supple [sʌp'əl] *adj* (person, body, leather etc) しなやかな shináyàka na

supplement [*n* sʌp'ləmənt *vb* sʌp'ləment] *n* (additional amount, e.g. vitamin supplement) 補給品 hokyūhin; (of book) 補遺 hōì; (of newspaper, magazine) 付録 furóku
♦*vt* 補足する hosóku suru

supplementary [sʌpləmen'tə:ri:] *adj* (question) 補足的な hosókuteki na

supplementary benefit (*BRIT*) *n* 生活保護費 seíkatsuhogò

supplier [səplai'ə:r] *n* (COMM: person, firm) 供給業者 kyōkyūgyòsha

supplies [səplai'z] *npl* (food) 食料 shokúryō; (MIL) 軍需品 guñjuhìn

supply [səplai'] *vt* (provide) 供給する kyōkyū suru; (equip): *to supply (with)* (...を) 支給する (...wo) shikyū suru
♦*n* (stock) 在庫品 zaíkohìn; (supplying) 供給 kyōkyū

supply teacher (*BRIT*) *n* 代行教師 daíkōkyòshi

support [səpɔ:rt'] *n* (moral, financial etc) 支援 shién; (TECH) 支柱 shichū
♦*vt* (morally: football team etc) 支援する shién suru; (financially: family etc) 養う yashínaù; (TECH: hold up) 支える saáerù; (sustain: theory etc) 裏付ける urázukerù

supporter [səpɔ:r'tə:r] *n* (POL etc) 支援者 shiénshà; (SPORT) ファン fáñ

suppose [səpouz'] *vt* (think likely) ...だと思う ...dá tò omóù; (imagine) 想像する sōzō suru; (duty): *to be supposed to do something* ...する事になっている ...surú kotò ni nattè irù

supposedly [səpou'zidli:] *adv* ...だとされ

て ...dá tò saretè

supposing [səpou'ziŋ] *conj* も し ... mô-shî...

suppress [səpres'] *vt* (revolt) 鎮圧する chíñ-atsu suru; (information) 隠す kakúsù; (feelings, yawn) 抑える osáerù

suppression [səpreʃ'ən] *n* (of revolt) 鎮圧 chíñ-atsu; (of information) 隠ぺい íñpei; (of feelings etc) 抑制 yokúsei

supremacy [səprem'əsi:] *n* 優越 yűetsu

supreme [səpri:m'] *adj* (in titles: court etc) 最高の saíkō no; (effort, achievement) 最上の saíjō no

surcharge [sər'tʃɑːrdʒ] *n* (extra cost) 追加料金 tsuíkaryōkin

sure [ʃuːr] *adj* (definite, convinced) 確信 している kakúshin shite irù; (aim, remedy) 確実な kakújitsu na; (friend) 頼りになる táyòri ni nárù

to make sure of something ...を確かめる ...wo tashíkamerù

to make sure that ...だと確かめる ...dá tò tashíkamerù

sure! (of course) いいとも íi to mo

sure enough 案の定 añ no jō

sure-footed [ʃuːr'fut'id] *adj* 足のしっか りした ashí nò shikkárì shita

surely [ʃuːr'li:] *adv* (certainly: *US: also:* **sure**) 確かに táshìka ni

surety [ʃuːr'əti:] *n* (money) 担保 táñpo

surf [səːrf] *n* 打寄せる波 uchíyoseru namì

surface [səːr'fis] *n* (of object) 表面 hyṓmen; (of lake, pond) 水面 suímen

♦*vt* (road) 舗装する hosṓ suru

♦*vi* (fish, person in water: *also fig*) 浮上 する fujṓ suru

surface mail *n* 普通郵便 futsúyùbin

surfboard [səːrf'bɔːrd] *n* サーフボード sáfubòdo

surfeit [səːr'fit] *n*: *a surfeit of* ...の過剰 ...no kajṓ

surfing [səːr'fiŋ] *n* サーフィン sáfìn

surge [səːrdʒ] *n* (increase: *also fig*) 高ま り takámarì

♦*vi* (water) 波打つ namíutsù; (people, vehicles) 突進する tosshín suru; (emotion) 高まる takámarù

surgeon [səːr'dʒən] *n* 外科医 geká-ì

surgery [səːr'dʒəri:] *n* (treatment) 手術 shújùtsu; (*BRIT:* room) 診察室 shíñsatsushìtsu; (: *also:* **surgery hours**) 診療時 間 shíñryō jikan

surgical [səːr'dʒikəl] *adj* (instrument, mask etc) 外科用の gekáyō no; (treatment) 外科の geká no

surgical spirit (*BRIT*) *n* 消毒用アルコ ール shṓdokuyō arúkòru

surly [səːr'li:] *adj* 無愛想な buáìso na

surmount [səːrmaunt'] *vt* (*fig*: problem, difficulty) 乗越える noríkoerù

surname [səːr'neim] *n* 名字 myṓji

surpass [səːrpæs'] *vt* (person, thing) しの ぐ shinógù

surplus [səːr'pləs] *n* (extra, *also* COMM, ECON) 余剰分 yojṓbùn

♦*adj* (stock, grain etc) 余剰の yojṓ no

surprise [səːrpraiz'] *n* (unexpected) 思い 掛け無い物 omóigakenaì monó; (astonishment) 驚き odóroki

♦*vt* (astonish) 驚かす odórokasù; (catch unawares: army, thief) ...の不意を突く ...no fuí wò tsukú

surprising [səːrprai'ziŋ] *adj* 驚くべき o-dórokubèki

surprisingly [səːrprai'ziŋli:] *adv* (easy, helpful) 驚く程 odóroku hodò

surrealist [səːri:'əlist] *adj* (paintings etc) 超現実主義の chṓgenjitsushùgi no

surrender [səren'dəːr] *n* 降伏 kṓfuku

♦*vi* (army, hijackers etc) 降伏する kṓfuku suru

surreptitious [səːrəptiʃ'əs] *adj* ひそかな hisókà na

surrogate [səːr'əgit] *n* 代理の daírī no

surrogate mother *n* 代理母 daírihahà

surround [səraund'] *vt* (subj: walls, hedge etc) 囲む kakómù; (MIL, POLICE etc) 包囲する hṓi suru

surrounding [səraun'diŋ] *adj* (country-side) 周囲の shũi no

surroundings [səraun'diŋz] *npl* 周辺 shúhen

surveillance [səːrvei'ləns] *n* 監視 kañshi

survey [*n* səːr'vei *vb* səːrvei'] *n* (examination: of land, house) 測量 sokúryō;

(investigation: of habits etc) 調査 chṓsa
♦vt (land, house etc) 測量する sokúryō
suru; (look at: scene, work etc) 見渡す
miwátasù

surveyor [sə:rvei'ə:r] n (of land, house)
測量技師 sokúryōgishi

survival [sə:rvai'vəl] n (continuation of
life) 生存 seízon; (relic) 遺物 ibútsu

survive [sə:rvaiv'] vi (person, thing) 助か
る tasúkarù; (custom etc) 残る nokórù
♦vt (outlive: person) ...より長生きする
...yórì nagáikì suru

survivor [sə:rvai'və:r] n (of illness, accident) 生存者 seízonsha

susceptible [səsep'təbəl] adj: **susceptible (to)** (affected by: heat, injury)
(...に) 弱い ...ni yowáì; (influenced by:
flattery, pressure) (...に) 影響されやす
い (...ni) eíkyō sareyasuì

suspect [adj, n sʌs'pekt vb səspekt']
adj 怪しい ayáshiì
♦n 容疑者 yōgìsha
♦vt (person) ...が怪しいと思う ...ga ayáshiì to omóù; (think) ...ではないかと思う
...dé wa naí ka to omóù

suspend [səspend'] vt (hang) つるす tsu-
rúsù; (delay, stop) 中止する chū́shi suru;
(from employment) 停職処分にする teí-
shokushobùn ni suru

suspended sentence [səspen'did-] n
(LAW) 執行猶予付きの判決 shikkṓyūyo-
tsuki no hañketsu

suspender belt [səspen'də:r-] n ガーター
ーベルト gátāberùto

suspenders [səspen'də:rz] npl (US) ズボ
ンつり zubóñtsuri; (BRIT) ガーターベル
トのストッキング留め gátāberùto no su-
tókkingudòme

suspense [səspens'] n (uncertainty) 気掛
り kigakárì; (in film etc) サスペンス sá-
sùpensu
to keep someone in suspense はらはら
させる hárahara sasérù

suspension [səspen'tʃən] n (from job,
team) 停職 teíshoku; (AUT) サスペンシ
ョン sasúpeñshon; (of driver's license,
payment) 停止 teíshi

suspension bridge n つり橋 tsuríbàshi

suspicion [səspiʃ'ən] n (distrust) 疑い u-
tágai; ((bad) feeling) 漠然とした感じ bakúzen to shità kañji

suspicious [səspiʃ'əs] adj (suspecting:
look) 疑い深い utágaibukaì; (causing
suspicion: circumstances) 怪しげな ayá-
shigè na

sustain [səstein'] vt (continue: interest
etc) 維持する íjī suru; (subj: food, drink)
...に力を付ける ...ni chikára wò tsukérù;
(suffer: injury) 受ける ukérù

sustained [səsteind'] adj (effort, attack)
絶間ない taémanaì

sustenance [sʌs'tənəns] n 食物 shokúmòtsu

swab [swɑ:b] n (MED) 綿球 meñkyū

swagger [swæg'ə:r] vi 威張って歩く i-
bátte arukù

swallow [swɑ:l'ou] n (bird) ツバメ tsubá-
me
♦vt (food, pills etc) 飲込む nomíkomù;
(fig: story) 信じ込む shiñjikomù;
(: insult) ...に黙って耐える ...ni damáttè
taérù; (one's pride, one's words) 抑える
osáerù

swallow up vt (savings etc) 飲込む nomíkomù

swam [swæm] pt of **swim**

swamp [swɑ:mp] n 沼地 numáchi
♦vt (with water etc) 水没させる suíbotsu
saserù; (fig: person) 圧倒する attṓ suru

swan [swɑ:n] n ハクチョウ hakúchō

swap [swɑ:p] n 交換 kṓkan
♦vt: **to swap (for)** (exchange (for))
(...) と交換する (...to) kṓkan suru;
(replace (with)) (...と) 取替える (...to)
toríkaerù

swarm [swɔ:rm] n (of bees) 群れ muré;
(of people) 群衆 guñshū
♦vi (bees) 群れで巣別れする muré dè su-
wákarè suru; (people) 群がる murágarù;
(place): **to be swarming with** ...に...が
うじゃうじゃいる ...ni ...ga újàuja irú

swarthy [swɔ:r'ði:] adj 浅黒い aságuroì

swastika [swɑ:s'tikə] n かぎ十字 kagíjū-
ji

swat [swɑ:t] vt (insect) たたく tatákù

sway [swei] vi (person, tree) 揺れる yurérù

♦vt (influence) 揺さぶる yusáburù

swear [swe'ə:r] (pt **swore**, pp **sworn**) vi (curse) 悪態をつく akútai wò tsukú

♦vt (promise) 誓う chikáu

swearword [swe:r'wə:rd] n 悪態 akútai

sweat [swet] n 汗 ásè

♦vi 汗をかく ásè wo kákù

sweater [swet'ə:r] n セーター sếtā

sweatshirt [swet'ʃə:rt] n トレーナー torếnā

sweaty [swet'i:] adj (clothes, hands) 汗ばんだ asébànda

Swede [swi:d] n スウェーデン人 suéēdenjìn

swede [swi:d] (BRIT) n スウェーデンカブ suéēdeñkabu

Sweden [swi:d'ən] n スウェーデン suéēden

Swedish [swi:'diʃ] adj スウェーデンの suéēden no; (LING) スウェーデン語の suéēdeñgo no

♦n (LING) スウェーデン語 suéēdeñgo

sweep [swi:p] n (act of sweeping) 掃く事 hákù kotố; (also: **chimney sweep**) 煙突掃除夫 eñtotsusōjifù

♦vb (pt, pp **swept**)

♦vt (brush) 掃く hákù; (with arm) 払う haráù; (subj: current) 流す nagásù

♦vi (hand, arm) 振る furù; (wind) 吹きまくる fukímakurù

sweep away vt 取除く torínozokù

sweeping [swi:'piŋ] adj (gesture) 大振りな ốburi na; (generalized: statement) 十把一からげの jíppàhitôkàrage no

sweep past vi (at great speed) 猛スピードで通り過ぎる mōsupído de tốrisugirù; (majestically) 堂々と通り過ぎる dốdō tò tốrisugiru

sweep up vi 掃き取る hakítorù

sweet [swi:t] n (candy) あめ amé; (BRIT: pudding) デザート dezâto

♦adj (not savory: taste) 甘い amáì; (fig: air, water, smell, sound) 快い kokóroyoî; (: kind) 親切な shíñsetsu na; (attractive: baby, kitten) かわいい kawáîî

sweetcorn [swi:t'kɔ:rn] n トウモロコシ tốmorðkoshi

sweeten [swi:t'ən] vt (add sugar to) 甘くする amáku surù; (soften: temper) なだめる nadámerù

sweetheart [swi:t'hɑ:rt] n (boyfriend/girlfriend) 恋人 koîbito

sweetness [swi:t'nis] n (amount of sugar) 甘さ amása; (fig: of air, water, smell, sound) 快さ kokóroyosà; (kindness) 親切 shiñsetsu; (attractiveness: of baby, kitten) かわいさ kawáisà

sweetpea [swi:t'pi:] n スイートピー suítopì

swell [swel] n (of sea) うねり unéri

♦adj (US: inf: excellent) 素晴らしい subárashiì

♦vi (pt **swelled**, pp **swollen** or **swelled**) (increase: numbers) 増える fuérù; (get stronger: sound, feeling) 増す masú; (also: **swell up**: face, ankle etc) はれる harérù

swelling [swel'iŋ] n (MED) はれ haré

sweltering [swel'tə:riŋ] adj (heat, weather, day) うだる様な udáru yō na

swept [swept] pt, pp of **sweep**

swerve [swə:rv] vi (person, animal, vehicle) それる sorérù

swift [swift] n (bird) アマツバメ amátsubàme

♦adj (happening quickly: recovery) じん速な jiñsoku na; (moving quickly: stream, glance) 早い hayáì

swiftly [swift'li:] adv (move, react, reply) 早く háyàku

swig [swig] (inf) n (drink) がぶ飲み gabúnomi

swill [swil] vt (also: **swill out**, **swill down**) がぶがぶ飲む gábùgabu nómù

swim [swim] n: **to go for a swim** 泳ぎに行く oyógi ni ikú

♦vb (pt **swam**, pp **swum**)

♦vi (person, animal) 泳ぐ oyốgù; (head, room) 回る mawárù

♦vt (the Channel, a length) 泳いで渡る oyőĩde watárù

swimmer [swim'ə:r] n 泳ぐ人 oyốgù hitố

swimming [swim'iŋ] n 水泳 suíei

swimming cap n 水泳用の帽子 suíeiyō no bốshi

swimming costume (*BRIT*) *n* 水着 mizúgi

swimming pool *n* 水泳プール suíeipūru

swimming trunks *npl* 水泳パンツ suíeipañtsu

swimsuit [swim'su:t] *n* 水着 mizúgi

swindle [swin'dəl] *n* 詐欺 ságì
♦*vt* ぺてんにかける petén nì kakérù

swine [swain] (*inf!*) *n* 畜生 chikúshōme

swing [swiŋ] *n* (in playground) ぶらんこ búranko; (movement) 揺れ yuré; (change: in opinions etc) 変動 heñdō; (MUS: *also* rhythm) スイング suíñgu
♦*vb* (*pt, pp* **swung**)
♦*vt* (arms, legs) 振る furú; (*also*: **swing round**: vehicle etc) 回す mawásù
♦*vi* (pendulum) 揺れる yurérù; (on a swing) ぶらんこに乗る búranko ni norú; (*also*: **swing round**: person, animal) 振向く furímukù; (: vehicle) 向きを変える múkì wo kaérù

to be in full swing (party etc) たけなわである takénawa de arù

swing bridge *n* 旋回橋 señkaikyō

swingeing [swin'dʒiŋ] (*BRIT*) *adj* (blow, attack) 激しい hagéshiì; (cuts) 法外な hṓgai na

swinging door [swiŋ'iŋ-] (*BRIT* **swing door**) *n* 自在ドア jizáidòa

swipe [swaip] *vt* (hit) たたく tatákù; (*inf*: steal) かっ払う kappáraù

swirl [swə:rl] *vi* (water, smoke, leaves) 渦巻く uzúmakù

swish [swiʃ] *vt* (tail etc) 音を立てて振る otó wò tátète furú
♦*vi* (clothes) 衣ずれの音を立てる kinúzure nò otó wò tatérù

Swiss [swis] *adj* スイスの suísu no
♦*n inv* スイス人 suísujìn

switch [switʃ] *n* (for light, radio etc) スイッチ suítchì; (change) 取替え toríkae
♦*vt* (change) 取替える toríkaerù

switchboard [switʃ'bɔ:rd] *n* (TEL) 交換台 kōkandai

switch off *vt* (light, radio) 消す kesú; (engine, machine) 止める tomérù

switch on *vt* (light, radio, machine) つ

ける tsukérù; (engine) かける kakérù

Switzerland [swit'sə:rlənd] *n* スイス suísu

swivel [swiv'əl] *vi* (*also*: **swivel round**) 回る mawárù

swollen [swou'lən] *pp of* **swell**

swoon [swu:n] *vi* 気絶する kizétsu suru

swoop [swu:p] *n* (by police etc) 手入れ te-íre
♦*vi* (*also*: **swoop down**: bird, plane) 舞降りる maíorirù

swop [swɑ:p] = **swap**

sword [sɔ:rd] *n* 刀 katána

swordfish [sɔ:rd'fiʃ] *n* メカジキ mekájìki

swore [swɔ:r] *pt of* **swear**

sworn [swɔ:rn] *pp of* **swear**
♦*adj* (statement, evidence) 宣誓付きの señseitsuki no; (enemy) 年来の néñrai no

swot [swɑ:t] *vi* がり勉する garíben suru

swum [swʌm] *pp of* **swim**

swung [swʌŋ] *pt, pp of* **swing**

sycamore [sik'əmɔ:r] *n* カエデ kaéde

syllable [sil'əbəl] *n* 音節 oñsetsu

syllabus [sil'əbəs] *n* 講義概要 kōgigaiyō

symbol [sim'bəl] *n* (sign, *also* MATH) 記号 kigō; (representation) 象徴 shóchō

symbolic(al) [simbɑ:l'ik(əl)] *adj* 象徴的な shóchōteki na

symbolism [sim'bəlizəm] *n* 象徴的意味 shóchōteki imì

symbolize [sim'bəlaiz] *vt* 象徴する shóchō suru

symmetrical [simet'rikəl] *adj* 対称的な taíshōteki na

symmetry [sim'itri:] *n* 対称 taíshō

sympathetic [simpəθet'ik] *adj* (showing understanding) 同情的な dṓjōteki na; (likeable: character) 人好きのする hitózuki no surù; (showing support): *sympathetic to(wards)* ...に好意的である ...ni kṓiteki de arù

sympathies [sim'pəθi:z] *npl* (support, tendencies) 支援 shién

sympathize [sim'pəθaiz] *vi*: *to sympathize with* (person) ...に同情する ...ni dṓjō suru; (feelings, cause) ...に共感する ...ni kyṓkan suru

sympathizer [sim'pǝθaizǝːr] *n* (POL) 支援者 shiéñsha

sympathy [sim'pǝθi:] *n* (pity) 同情 dốjō
with our deepest sympathy 心からお悔みを申上げます kokórò kara o-kúyami wò mōshiagemasù
in sympathy (workers: come out) 同情して dốjō shite

symphony [sim'fǝni:] *n* 交響曲 kốkyồkyoku

symposia [simpou'zi:ǝ] *npl of* **symposium**

symposium [simpou'zi:ǝm] (*pl* **symposiums** *or* **symposia**) *n* シンポジウム shiñpojiùmu

symptom [simp'tǝm] *n* (indicator: MED) 症状 shốjồ; (: *gen*) しるし shirúshi

synagogue [sin'ǝgɑːg] *n* ユダヤ教会堂 yudáyakyōkaidō

synchronize [siŋ'krǝnaiz] *vt* (watches, sound) 合せる awáserù

syncopated [siŋ'kǝpeitid] *adj* (rhythm, beat) シンコペートした shiñkopèto shita

syndicate [sin'dǝkit] *n* (of people, businesses, newspapers) シンジケート shiñjikèto

syndrome [sin'droum] *n* (*also* MED) 症侯群 shốkồgun

synonym [sin'ǝnim] *n* 同意語 dốigò

synopses [sinɑːp'si:z] *npl of* **synopsis**

synopsis [sinɑːp'sis] (*pl* **synopses**) *n* 概要 gaíyồ

syntax [sin'tæks] *n* (LING) 統語法 tốgohồ, シンタックス shiñtakkùsu

syntheses [sin'θǝsi:z] *npl of* **synthesis**

synthesis [sin'θǝsis] (*pl* **syntheses**) *n* (of ideas, styles) 総合する sốgồ suru

synthetic [sinθet'ik] *adj* (man-made: materials) 合成の gōseí no

syphilis [sif'ǝlis] *n* 梅毒 baídoku

syphon [sai'fǝn] = **siphon**

Syria [siːr'iːǝ] *n* シリア shírìa

Syrian [siːr'iːǝn] *adj* シリアの shírìa no
♦*n* シリア人 shírìajin

syringe [sǝrindʒ'] *n* 注射器 chúshakì

syrup [sir'ǝp] *n* シロップ shiróppù

system [sis'tǝm] *n* (organization) 組織 sồshìki; (POL): *the system* 体制 taísei; (method) やり方 yaríkata; (the body) 身体 shíntai
the digestive system (MED) 消化器系 shốkakikềi
the nervous system (MED) 神経系 shiñkeikềi

systematic [sistǝmæt'ik] *adj* (methodical) 組織的な soshíkiteki na

system disk *n* (COMPUT) システムディスク shisútemu disùku

systems analyst [sis'tǝmz-] *n* システムアナリスト shisútemu anarisùto

T

ta [tɑː] (*BRIT: inf*) *excl* (thanks) どうも dốmo

tab [tæb] *n* (on file etc) 耳 mimí; (on drinks can etc) プルタブ purútàbu, プルトップ purútoppù; (label: name tab) 名札 nafúda
to keep tabs on (*fig*) 監視する kañshi suru

tabby [tæb'i:] *n* (*also*: **tabby cat**) とら毛のネコ toráge nò nékò

table [tei'bǝl] *n* (piece of furniture) テーブル tēburu; (MATH, CHEM etc) 表 hyố
♦*vt* (*BRIT*: motion etc) 上程する jốtei suru; (*US*: put off: proposal etc) 棚上げにする taná-age ni surù
to lay/set the table 食卓に皿を並べる shokútaku nì sará wò naráberù

tablecloth [tei'bǝlklɔːθ] *n* テーブルクロス tếburukurosù

table d'hôte [tæb'ǝl dout'] *adj* (menu, meal) 定食の teíshoku no

table lamp *n* 電気スタンド deñki sutàndo

tablemat [tei'bǝlmæt] *n* (for plate) テーブルマット tềburumattð; (for hot dish) なべ敷 nabéshìki

table of contents *n* 目次 mokúji

tablespoon [tei'bǝlspuːn] *n* (type of spoon) テーブルスプーン tếburusupùn; (*also*: **tablespoonful**: as measurement) 大さじ一杯 ốsaji ippài

tablet [tæb'lit] *n* (MED) 錠剤 jốzai

a stone tablet 石板 sekíban

table tennis *n* 卓球 takkyū

table wine *n* テーブルワイン téburuwaiñ

tabloid [tæb'lɔid] *n* (newspaper) タブロイド新聞 tabúroido shiñbun

taboo [təbu:'] *n* (religious, social) タブー tabū

♦*adj* (subject, place, name etc) タブーの tabū no

tabulate [tæb'jəleit] *vt* (data, figures) 表にする hyō ni surū

tacit [tæs'it] *adj* (agreement, approval etc) 暗黙の afimoku no

taciturn [tæs'itəːrn] *adj* (person) 無口な múkuchi na

tack [tæk] *n* (nail) びょう byō; (*fig*) やり方 yaríkata

♦*vt* (nail) びょうで留める byō de toméru; (stitch) 仮縫いする karínui suru

♦*vi* (NAUT) 間切る magíru

tackle [tæk'əl] *n* (gear: fishing tackle etc) 道具 dṓgu; (for lifting) ろくろ rókùro, 滑車 kásshà; (FOOTBALL, RUGBY) タックル tákkùru

♦*vt* (deal with: difficulty) ...と取組む ...to toríkumù; (challenge: person) ...に掛合う ...ni kakéaù; (grapple with: person, animal) ...と取組む ...to toríkumù; (FOOTBALL, RUGBY) タックルする tákkùru suru

tacky [tæk'iː] *adj* (sticky) べたべたする bétàbeta suru; (*pej*: of poor quality) 安っぽい yasúppoì

tact [tækt] *n* 如才なさ josáinasà

tactful [tækt'fəl] *adj* 如才ない josáinaì

tactical [tæk'tikəl] *adj* (move, withdrawal, voting) 戦術的な señjutsuteki na

tactics [tæk'tiks] *n* 用兵学 yṓheigàku

♦*npl* 駆引き kakéhìki

tactless [tækt'lis] *adj* 気転の利かない kitéñ no kikanaì

tadpole [tæd'poul] *n* オタマジャクシ otámajakùshi

taffy [tæf'iː] (*US*) *n* (toffee) タフィー táfìi ◇あめの一種 amé nò ísshu

tag [tæg] *n* (label) 札 fudá

tag along *vi* ついて行く tsúìte ikú

tail [teil] *n* (of animal) しっ尾 shíppò; (of plane) 尾部 bíbù; (of shirt, coat) すそ susō

♦*vt* (follow: person, vehicle) 尾行する bikṓ suru

tail away/off *vi* (in size, quality etc) 次第に減る shidái ni herù

tailback [teil'bæk] (*BRIT*) *n* (AUT) 交通渋滞 kṓtsūjūtai

tail end *n* 末端 mattáñ

tailgate [teil'geit] *n* (AUT: of hatchback) 後尾ドア kōbidòa

tailor [tei'ləːr] *n* 仕立屋 shitáteya

tailoring [tei'ləːriŋ] *n* (cut) 仕立て方 shitátekata; (craft) 仕立職 shitáteshòku

tailor-made [tei'ləːrmeid] *adj* (suit) あつらえの atsúraè no; (*fig*: part in play, person for job) おあつらえ向きの o-átsuraemuki no

tails [teilz] *npl* (formal suit) えん尾服 eñbifúku

tailwind [teil'wind] *n* 追風 oíkàze

tainted [teint'id] *adj* (food, water, air) 汚染された osén saretà; (*fig*: profits, reputation etc) 汚れた yogóretà

Taiwan [tai'wɑːn] *n* 台湾 taíwàñ

take [teik] (*pt* **took**, *pp* **taken**) *vt* (photo, notes, holiday etc) とる tórù; (shower, walk, decision etc) する surú; (grab: someone's arm etc) 取る tórù; (gain: prize) 得る érù; (require: effort, courage, time) ...が必要である ...ga hitsúyō de arù; (tolerate: pain etc) 耐える taérù; (hold: passengers etc) 収容する shūyō suru; (accompany, bring, carry: person) 連れて行く tsuréte ikù; (: thing) 持って行く motté ikù; (exam, test) 受ける ukérù

to take something from (drawer etc) ...を...から取出す ...wo ...kárà torídasù; (steal from: person) ...を...から盗む ...wo ...kárà nusúmù

I take it that ... ...だと思っていいですね ...dá tò omótte iî desu né

take after *vt fus* (resemble) ...に似ている ...ni nité ù

take apart *vt* 分解する buñkai suru

take away *vt* (remove) 下げる sagérù; (carry off) 持って行く motté ikù; (MATH) 引く hikú

takeaway [teiˈkəwei] *(BRIT)* n = **take-out**

take back vt (return) 返す kaésù; (one's words) 取消す toríkesù

take down vt (dismantle: building) 解体する kaítai suru; (write down: letter etc) 書き取る kakítorù

take in vt (deceive) だます damásù; (understand) 理解する rikái suru; (include) 含む fukúmù; (lodger) 泊める tomérù

take off vi (AVIAT) 離陸する riríku suru; (go away) 行ってしまう itté shimaù
♦vt (remove) 外す hazúsù

takeoff [teikˈɔːf] n (AVIAT) 離陸 riríku

take on vt (work) 引受ける hikíukerù; (employee) 雇う yatóù; (opponent) ...と戦う ...to tatákaù

take out vt (invite) 外食に連れて行く gaíshoku nì tsuréte ikù; (remove) 取出す torídasù

takeout [teikˈaut] *(US)* n (shop, restaurant) 持帰り料理店 mochíkaeriryōritèn; (food) 持帰り料理 mochíkaeriryòri

take over vt (business, country) 乗っ取る nottórù
♦vi: **to take over from someone** ...と交替する ...to kótai suru

takeover [teikˈouvəːr] n (COMM) 乗っ取り nottóri

take to vt fus (person, thing, activity) 気に入る ki ní irù, 好きになる sukí ni narù; (engage in: hobby etc) やり出す yarídasù

take up vt (a dress) 短くする mijíkakù suru; (occupy: time, space) ...に付く ...ni tsukú; (: time) ...がかかる ...ga kakárù; (engage in: hobby etc) やり出す yarídasù
to take someone up on something (offer, suggestion) ...に応じる ...ni ójirù

takings [teiˈkiŋz] npl 売上金 uríage

talc [tælk] n (also: **talcum powder**) タルカムパウダー tarúkamupaùda

tale [teil] n (story, account) 物語 monógatàri
to tell tales (fig: to teacher, parents etc) 告げ口する tsugéguchi suru

talent [tælˈənt] n 才能 saínō

talented [tælˈəntid] adj 才能ある saínō arù

talk [tɔːk] n (a (prepared) speech) 演説 eñzetsu; (conversation) 話 hanáshi; (gossip) うわさ uwása
♦vi (speak) 話す hanásù; (give information) しゃべる shabérù
to talk about ...について話す ...ni tsuíte hanásù
to talk someone into doing something ...する様に...を説得する ...surú yō ni ...wo settóku suru
to talk someone out of doing something ...しない様に...を説得する ...shinái yō ni ...wo settóku suru
to talk shop 仕事の話をする shigóto nò hanáshi wo surù

talkative [tɔːˈkətiv] adj おしゃべりな o-shábèri na

talk over vt (problem etc) 話し合う hanáshiaù

talks [tɔːks] npl (POL etc) 会談 kaídan

talk show n おしゃべり番組 o-sháberi baňgumi

tall [tɔːl] adj (person) 背が高い sé gà takáî; (object) 高い takáî
to be 6 feet tall (person) 身長が6フィートである shiñchō gà 6 fíto de árù

tall story n ほら話 horábanàshi

tally [tælˈiː] n (of marks, amounts of money etc) 記録 kiróku
♦vi: **to tally (with)** (subj: figures, stories etc) (...と) 合う (...to) áù

talon [tælˈən] n かぎづめ kagízume

tambourine [tæmˈbəriːn] n タンバリン táňbarin

tame [teim] adj (animal, bird) なれた nárèta; (fig: story, style) 平凡な heíbon na

tamper [tæmˈpəːr] vi: **to tamper with something** ...をいじる ...wo ijírù

tampon [tæmˈpɑːn] n タンポン táňpon

tan [tæn] n (also: **suntan**) 日焼け hiyáke
♦vi (person, skin) 日に焼ける hi ní yakerù
♦adj (color) 黄かっ色の ókasshòku no

tandem [tænˈdəm] n: **in tandem** (together) 2人で futári dè

tang [tæŋ] n (smell) 鼻をつくにおい haná wò tsukú nióì; (taste) ぴりっとした味 píríttò shita ají

tangent [tæn'dʒənt] n (MATH) 接線 sessén

to go off at a tangent (fig) わき道へそ れる wakímìchi e sorérù

tangerine [tændʒəri:n'] n ミカン míkàn

tangible [tæn'dʒəbəl] adj (proof, bene- fits) 具体的な gutáiteki na

tangle [tæŋ'gəl] n もつれる motsúre

to get in(to) a tangle (also fig) もつれ る motsúrerù

tank [tæŋk] n (also: **water tank**) 貯水タ ンク chosúitàñku; (for fish) 水槽 suísò; (MIL) 戦車 séñsha

tanker [tæŋk'ə:r] n (ship) タンカー táñ- kā; (truck) タンクローリー tañkurōrī

tanned [tænd] adj (skin) 日に焼けた hi ní yaketà

tantalizing [tæn'təlaiziŋ] adj (smell, possibility) 興味をそそる kyṓmi wò so- sórù

tantamount [tæn'təmaunt] adj: *tanta- mount to* ...も同然である ...mo dṓzen de arù

tantrum [tæn'trəm] n かんしゃく kañ- shaku

tap [tæp] n (on sink etc) 蛇口 jagúchi; (also: **gas tap**) ガスの元栓 gásù no motó- sen; (gentle blow) 軽くたたく事 karúku tatakù kotó

◆vt (hit gently) 軽くたたく karúku tata- kù; (resources) 利用する riyṓ suru; (tele- phone) 盗聴する tṓchō suru

on tap (fig: resources) いつでも利用でき る ítsùdemo riyṓ dekirù

tap-dancing [tæp'dænsiŋ] n タップダン ス tappúdàñsu

tape [teip] n (also: **magnetic tape**) 磁気 テープ jikítèpu; (cassette) カセットテー プ kaséttotèpu; (sticky tape) 粘着テープ neñchakutèpu; (ひも) himó

◆vt (record: sound) 録音する rokúon su- ru; (: image) 録画する rokúga suru; (stick with tape) テープで張る tèpu de harú

tape deck n テープデッキ tēpudekkì

tape measure n メジャー méjā

taper [tei'pə:r] n (candle) 細いろうそく hosóì rōsokù

◆vi (narrow) 細くなる hósòku nárù

tape recorder n テープレコーダー té- purekōdā

tapestry [tæp'istri:] n (object) タペスト リー tapésutòrī; (art) ししゅう shishū

tar [ta:r] n コールタール kṓrutàru

tarantula [təræn'tʃələ] n タランチュラ taráñchura

target [ta:r'git] n (thing aimed at, also fig) 的 matō

tariff [tær'if] n (tax on goods) 関税 kañ- zei; (BRIT: in hotels, restaurants) 料金 表 ryōkiñhyō

tarmac [ta:r'mæk] n (BRIT: on road) ア スファルト asúfarùto; (AVIAT) エプロ ン épùron

tarnish [ta:r'niʃ] vt (metal) さびさせる sabísaserù; (fig: reputation etc) 汚す yo- gósù

tarpaulin [ta:rpɔ:'lin] n シート shīto

tarragon [tær'əgən] n タラゴン táràgon ◇香辛料の一種 kōshíñryō no ísshu

tart [ta:rt] n (CULIN) タルト tarúto ◇菓 子の一種 káshì no ísshù; (BRIT: inf: prostitute) ばいた bâìta

◆adj (flavor) 酸っぱい suppáì

tartan [ta:r'tən] n タータンチェック tá- tanchekkù

◆adj (rug, scarf etc) タータンチェックの tátanchekkù no

tartar [ta:r'tə:r] n (on teeth) 歯石 shiséki

tartar(e) sauce [ta:r'ta:r-] n タルタルソ ース tarútarusòsu

tart up (BRIT) vt (inf: object) 派手にす る hadé nì suru

to tart oneself up おめかしをする o-mékashi wò suru

task [tæsk] n 仕事 shigóto

to take to task ...の責任を問う ...no sekínin wò tōu

task force n (MIL, POLICE) 機動部隊 kidṓbùtai

Tasmania [tæzmei'ni:ə] n タスマニア ta- súmanìa

tassel [tæs'əl] n 房 fusá

taste [teist] *n* (*also*: **sense of taste**) 味覚 mikáku; (flavor: *also*: **aftertaste**) 味 ajî; (sample) 一 口 hitókùchi; (*fig*: glimpse, idea) 味わい ajíwaì
♦*vt* (get flavor of) 味わう ajíwaû; (test) 試食する shishóku suru
♦*vi*: **to taste of**/**like** (fish etc) ...の味がする ...no ajî ga suru
   you can taste the garlic (in it) (含まれている) ニンニクの味がする (fukúmarete irû) nînìniku nô ajî ga surù
   in good/**bad taste** 趣味がいい〔悪い〕 shúmì ga íi〔warúì〕

tasteful [teist'fəl] *adj* (furnishings) 趣味の良い shúmì no yóì

tasteless [teist'lis] *adj* (food) 味がない ajî ga naî; (remark, joke, furnishings) 趣味の悪い shúmì no warúì

tasty [teis'ti:] *adj* (food) おいしい oíshiî

tatters [tæt'əːrz] *npl*: **in tatters** (clothes, papers etc) ずたずたになって zutázuta ni natté

tattoo [tætu:'] *n* (on skin) 入れ墨 irézumi; (spectacle) パレード parédò
♦*vt* (name, design) ...の入れ墨をする ...no irézumi wo suru

tatty [tæt'i:] (*BRIT*: *inf*) *adj* (*inf*) 薄汚い usúgitanaì

taught [tɔ:t] *pt*, *pp* of **teach**

taunt [tɔ:nt] *n* あざけり azákerì
♦*vt* あざける azákerù

Taurus [tɔ:r'əs] *n* 牡牛座 oúshizà

taut [tɔ:t] *adj* ぴんと張った píñ tò hattá

tavern [tæv'əːrn] *n* (old) 酒場 sakába

tax [tæks] *n* 税金 zeîkin
♦*vt* (earnings, goods etc) ...に税金をかける ...ni zeîkin wo kakérù; (*fig*: test: memory) 最大限に使う saídaìgen ni tsukaû; (patience) 試練にかける shírèn ni kakérù

taxable [tæk'səbəl] *adj* (income) 課税される kazéi sarerù

taxation [tæksei'ʃən] *n* (system) 課税 kazéi; (money paid) 税金 zeîkin

tax avoidance [-əvɔi'dəns] *n* 節税 setsúzei

tax disc (*BRIT*) *n* (AUT) 納税ステッカー nôzeisutekkằ

tax evasion *n* 脱税 datsúzei

tax-free [tæks'fri:'] *adj* (goods, services) 免税の meñzei no

taxi [tæk'si:] *n* タクシー tákùshī
♦*vi* (AVIAT: plane) 滑走する kassô suru

taxi driver *n* タクシーの運転手 tákùshī no uñteñshu

taxi rank (*BRIT*) *n* = **taxi stand**

taxi stand *n* タクシー乗場 takúshīnorìba

tax payer [-pei'əːr] *n* 納税者 nôzeishà

tax relief *n* 減税 geñzei

tax return *n* 確定申告書 kakúteishiñkokushò

TB [ti:bi:'] *n* *abbr* = **tuberculosis**

tea [ti:] *n* (drink: Japanese) お茶 o-chá; (: English) 紅茶 kôcha; (*BRIT*: meal) おやつ o-yátsù
   high tea (*BRIT*) 夕食 yúshoku ◇夕方早目に食べる食事 yúgata hayáme nì tabérù shokúji

tea bag *n* ティーバッグ tîbaggù

tea break (*BRIT*) *n* 休憩 kyúkei

teach [ti:tʃ] (*pt*, *pp* **taught**) *vt* (*gen*) 教える oshíerù; (be a teacher of) ...(の)教師をする ...(no)kyôshi wo suru
♦*vi* (be a teacher: in school etc) 教師をする kyôshi wô suru

teacher [ti:'tʃəːr] *n* 教師 kyôshi, 先生 señseî

teaching [ti:'tʃiŋ] *n* (work of teacher) 教職 kyôshoku

tea cosy *n* お茶帽子 o-chábòshi

tea cup *n* (Western) ティーカップ tîkappù; (Japanese) 湯飲み茶碗 yunómijawàn, 湯飲み yunómi

teak [ti:k] *n* チーク chîku

tea leaves *npl* 茶殻 chagára

team [ti:m] *n* (of people: *gen*, SPORT) チーム chîmu; (of animals) 一組 hitókumi

teamwork [ti:m'wəːrk] *n* チームワーク chîmuwàku

teapot [ti:'pɑ:t] *n* きゅうす kyûsu

tear¹ [te:r] *n* (hole) 裂け目 sakéme
♦*vb* (*pt* **tore**, *pp* **torn**)
♦*vt* (rip) 破る yabúrù
♦*vi* (become torn) 破れる yabúrerù

tear² [ti:r] *n* (in eye) 涙 námìda
   in tears 泣いている naîte irù

tear along vi (rush) 猛スピードで走って行く mốsupīdò de hashítte ikù

tearful [tir'fəl] adj (family, face) 涙ぐんだ namídaguǹda

tear gas n 催涙ガス saíruigasù

tearoom [ti:'ru:m] n 喫茶店 kissáteǹ

tear up vt (sheet of paper etc) ずたずたに破る zutázuta nì yabúrù

tease [ti:z] vt からかう karákaù

tea set n 茶器セット chakísettò

teaspoon [ti:'spu:n] n (type of spoon) ティースプーン tīsupūǹ; (also: **teaspoonful**: as measurement) 小さじ一杯 kosáji ippài

teat [ti:t] n (ANAT) 乳首 chikúbì; (also: **bottle teat**) ほ乳瓶の乳首 honyū́bìn no chikúbì

teatime [ti:'taim] n おやつの時間 o-yátsu no jikáǹ

tea towel (BRIT) n ふきん fukíǹ

technical [tek'nikəl] adj (terms, advances) 技術の gíjutsu no

technical college (BRIT) n 高等専門学校 kốtōsenmongakkồ

technicality [teknikæl'iti:] n (point of law) 法律の専門的細目 hốritsu nò seńmonteki saimòku; (detail) 細かい事 komákaì kotó

technically [tek'nikli:] adv (strictly speaking) 正確に言えば seíkaku nì iébà; (regarding technique) 技術的に gíjutsuteki ni

technician [tekniʃ'ən] n 技術者 gijútsushà

technique [tekni:k'] n 技術 gíjutsu

technological [teknəla:dʒ'ikəl] adj 技術的な gíjutsuteki na

technology [teknɑ:l'ədʒi:] n 科学技術 kagákugijùtsu

teddy (bear) [ted'i:-] n クマのぬいぐるみ kumá nò nuígurumi

tedious [ti:'di:əs] adj (work, discussions etc) 退屈な taíkutsu na

tee [ti:] n (GOLF) ティー tī

teem [ti:m] vi: **to teem with** (visitors, tourists etc) ...がぞろぞろ来ている ...ga zõrozoro kité irù

it is teeming (with rain) 雨が激しく降っている ámè ga hagéshikù futté irù

teenage [ti:n'eidʒ] adj (children, fashions etc) ティーンエージャーの tín-ējā no

teenager [ti:n'eidʒə:r] n ティーンエージャー tín-ējā

teens [ti:nz] npl: **to be in one's teens** 年齢は10代である neńrei wà jūdai de árù

tee-shirt [ti:'ʃə:rt] n = **T-shirt**

teeter [ti:'tə:r] vi (also fig) ぐらつく gurátsukù

teeth [ti:θ] npl of **tooth**

teethe [ti:ð] vi (baby) 歯が生える há gà haérù

teething ring [ti:'ðiŋ-] n おしゃぶり o-shábùri ◇リング状の物を指す ríngujò no monó wò sásù

teething troubles npl (fig) 初期の困難 shókì no kốnnan

teetotal [ti:tout'əl] adj (person) 酒を飲まない saké wò nománaì

telecommunications [teləkəmju:nikei'ʃənz] n 電気通信 deńkitsùshin

telegram [tel'əgræm] n 電報 deńpō

telegraph [tel'əgræf] n (system) 電信 deńshin

telegraph pole n 電柱 deńchū

telepathic [teləpæθ'ik] adj テレパシーの terápashī no

telepathy [təlep'əθi:] n テレパシー terápashī

telephone [tel'əfoun] n 電話 deńwa

◆vt (person) ...に電話をかける ...ni deńwa wò kakérù; (message) 電話で伝える deńwa dè tsutáerù

on the telephone (talking) 電話中で deńwachū de; (possessing phone) 電話を持っている deńwa wò mótte irù

telephone booth n 電話ボックス deńwabokkùsu

telephone box (BRIT) n = **telephone booth**

telephone call n 電話 deńwa

telephone directory n 電話帳 deńwachō

telephone number n 電話番号 deńwabañgō

telephonist [telə'founist] (BRIT) n 電話交換手 deńwakōkañshu

telescope [tel'əskoup] *n* 望遠鏡 bóenkyō

telescopic [teliskɑːp'ik] *adj* (lens) 望遠の bóen no; (collapsible: tripod, aerial) 入れ子式の irékoshìki no

television [tel'əviʒən] *n* (all senses) テレビ térèbi

on television テレビで térèbi de

television set *n* テレビ受像機 terébijuzŏki

telex [tel'eks] *n* テレックス terékkùsu

♦*vt* (company) ...にテレックスを送る ...ni terékkùsu wo okúrù; (message) テレックスで送る terékkùsu de okúrù

tell [tel] (*pt, pp* **told**) *vt* (say) ...に言う ...ni iú; (relate: story) 述べる nobérù; (distinguish): *to tell something from* ...から ...を区別する ...kará ...wò kúbètsu suru

♦*vi* (talk): *to tell (of)* ...について話す ...ni tsúìte hanásù; (have an effect) 効果的である kốkateki de arù

to tell someone to do something ...に ...する様に言う ...ni ...surú yồ ni iú

teller [tel'ə:r] *n* (in bank) 出納係 suítōgakàri

telling [tel'iŋ] *adj* (remark, detail) 意味深い imíbukài

tell off *vt*: *to tell someone off* しかる shikaru

telltale [tel'teil] *adj* (sign) 証拠の shốko no

telly [tel'i:] (*BRIT: inf*) *n abbr* = **television**

temerity [təmer'iti:] *n* ずうずうしさ zúzūshisà

temp [temp] *n abbr* (= *temporary*) 臨時職員 rińjishokuìn

temper [tem'pə:r] *n* (nature) 性質 seíshitsu; (mood) 機嫌 kigén; (fit of anger) かんしゃく kańshaku

♦*vt* (moderate) 和らげる yawáragerù

to be in a temper 怒っている okótte irù

to lose one's temper 怒る okórù

temperament [tem'pə:rəmənt] *n* (nature) 性質 seíshitsu

temperamental [tempə:rəmen'təl] *adj* (person, *fig*: car) 気まぐれな kimágùre na

temperate [tem'pə:rit] *adj* (climate, country) 温暖な ońdan na

temperate zone *n* 温帯 ońtai

temperature [tem'pə:rətʃə:r] *n* (of person, place) 温度 óñdo

to have/run a temperature 熱がある netsú ga arù

tempest [tem'pist] *n* 嵐 árashi

tempi [tem'pi:] *npl of* **tempo**

temple [tem'pəl] *n* (building) 神殿 shińden; (ANAT) こめかみ komékami

tempo [tem'pou] (*pl* **tempos** *or* **tempi**) *n* (MUS) テンポ teńpo; (*fig*: of life etc) ペース pếsu

temporarily [tempə:re:r'ili:] *adv* 一時的に ichíjiteki ni

temporary [tem'pə:re:ri:] *adj* (passing) 一時的な ichíjiteki na; (worker, job) 臨時の rińji no

tempt [tempt] *vt* 誘惑する yúwaku suru

to tempt someone into doing something ...する様に...を誘惑する ...surú yồ ni ...wo yúwaku suru

temptation [temptei'ʃən] *n* 誘惑 yúwaku

tempting [temp'tiŋ] *adj* (offer) 魅惑的な miwákuteki na; (food) おいしそうな ofshisồ na

ten [ten] *num* 十（の）jú (no)

tenacity [tənæs'iti:] *n* (of person, animal) 根気強さ końkizùyosa

tenancy [ten'ənsi:] *n* (possession of room, land etc) 賃借 chińshaku; (period of possession) 賃借期間 chińshakukikàn

tenant [ten'ənt] *n* (rent-payer) 店子 tanáko, テナント tenáñto

tend [tend] *vt* (crops, sick person) ...の世話をする ...no sewá wð suru

♦*vi*: *to tend to do something* ...しがちである ...shigáchi de arù

tendency [ten'dənsi:] *n* (of person, thing) 傾向 keíkō

tender [ten'də:r] *adj* (person, heart, care) 優しい yasáshiĩ; (sore) 触ると痛い sawáru tò itáĩ; (meat) 柔らかい yawárakaĩ; (age) 幼い osánaĩ

♦*n* (COMM: offer) 見積り mitsúmori; (money): *legal tender* 通貨 tsúkà

◆*vt* (offer, resignation) 提出する teíshutsu suru

to tender an apology 陳謝する chínsha suru

tenderness [ten'dərnis] *n* (affection) 優しさ yasáshisà; (of meat) 柔らかさ yawárakasà

tendon [ten'dən] *n* けん kéñ

tenement [ten'əmənt] *n* 安アパート yasúapàto

tenet [ten'it] *n* 信条 shiñjō

tennis [ten'is] *n* テニス téñisu

tennis ball *n* テニスボール teñisubòru

tennis court *n* テニスコート teñisukòto

tennis player *n* テニス選手 teníseñshu

tennis racket *n* テニスラケット teníturakettò

tennis shoes *npl* テニスシューズ teníshūzu

tenor [ten'ə:r] *n* (MUS) テノール tenőrù

tenpin bowling [ten'pin-] *n* ボウリング bőriñgu

tense [tens] *adj* (person, smile, muscle) 緊張した kiñchō shita; (period) 緊迫した kiñpaku shita

◆*n* (LING) 時制 jiséi

tension [ten'ʃən] *n* (nervousness) 緊張 kiñchō; (between ropes etc) 張力 chōryoku

tent [tent] *n* テント téñto

tentacle [ten'təkəl] *n* (of octopus etc) あし ashí

tentative [ten'tətiv] *adj* (person, step, smile) 自信のない jishín no naì; (conclusion, plans) 差し当っての sashíatattè no

tenterhooks [ten'tə:rhuks] *npl*: *on tenterhooks* はらはらして háràhara shite

tenth [tenθ] *num* 第十（の）dáijū (no)

tent peg *n* テントのくい téñto no kuí

tent pole *n* テントの支柱 téñto no shichū

tenuous [ten'ju:əs] *adj* (hold, links, connection etc) 弱い yowáì

tenure [ten'jə:r] *n* (of land, buildings etc) 保有権 hoyúken; (of office) 在職期間 zaíshokukikàn

tepid [tep'id] *adj* (tea, pool etc) ぬるい nurúì

term [tə:rm] *n* (word, expression) 用語 yőgo; (period in power etc) 期間 kikáñ; (SCOL) 学期 gakkí

◆*vt* (call) ...と言う ...to iú

in the short/long term 短〔長〕期間で tañ(chő)kikàn de

terminal [tə:r'mənəl] *adj* (disease, cancer, patient) 末期の mákkì no

◆*n* (ELEC) 端子 táñshi; (COMPUT) 端末機 tañmatsukì; (*also*: **air terminal**) ターミナルビル tắminarubirù; (*BRIT*: *also*: **coach terminal**) バスターミナル basútàminaru

terminate [tə:r'məneit] *vt* (discussion, contract, pregnancy) 終らせる owáraserù, 終える oérù; (contract) 破棄する hákì suru; (pregnancy) 中絶する chűzetsu suru

termini [tə:r'məni:] *npl of* **terminus**

terminology [tə:rmənɑ:l'ədʒi:] *n* 用語 yőgo ◇総称 sőshō

terminus [tə:r'mənəs] (*pl* **-mini**) *n* (for buses, trains) ターミナル táminaru

terms [tə:rmz] *npl* (conditions: *also* COMM) 条件 jőken

to be on good terms with someone ...と仲がいい ...to nákà ga íì

to come to terms with (problem) ...と折合いがつく ...to oríaì ga tsukú

terrace [ter'əs] *n* (*BRIT*: row of houses) 長屋 nagáyà; (patio) テラス téràsu; (AGR) 段々畑 dañdanbatàke

terraced [ter'əst] *adj* (house) 長屋の nagáyà no; (garden) ひな壇式の hinádañshiki no

terraces [ter'əsiz] (*BRIT*) *npl* (SPORT): *the terraces* 立見席 tachímisèki

terracotta [terəkɑ:t'ə] *n* テラコッタ terácottà

terrain [tərein'] *n* 地面 jímèn

terrible [te:r'əbəl] *adj* ひどい hidóì

terribly [te:r'əbli:] *adv* (very) とても totémo; (very badly) ひどく hídòku

terrier [te:r'i:ə:r] *n* テリア térìa

terrific [tərif'ik] *adj* (very great: thunderstorm, speed) 大変な taíhen na; (wonderful: time, party) 素晴らしい subárashiî

terrify [te:r'əfai] vt おびえさせる obíesaserù

territorial [te:ritɔ:r'i:əl] adj (waters, boundaries, dispute) 領土の ryṓdò no

territory [te:r'itɔ:ri:] n (gen) 領土 ryṓdò; (fig) 縄張 nawábarî

terror [te:r'ə:r] n (great fear) 恐怖 kyṓfu

terrorism [te:r'ə:rizəm] n テロ térò

terrorist [te:r'ə:rist] n テロリスト teró-risùto

terrorize [te:r'ə:raiz] vt おびえさせる o-bíesaserù

terse [tə:rs] adj (style) 簡潔な kańketsu na; (reply) そっけない sokkénaî ◇言葉数が少なく無愛想な返事などについて言う kotóbakazù ga sukúnakù buáîso na heñji nadò ni tsúîte iú

Terylene [te:r'əli:n] ® n テリレン térìren ◇人工繊維の一種 jiñkōseñ-i no ísshù

test [test] n (trial, check: also MED, CHEM) テスト tésùto; (of courage etc) 試練 shíren; (SCOL) テスト tésùto; (also: **driving test**) 運転免許の試験 uñtenmeñkyo no shíken
♦vt (gen) テストする tésùto suru

testament [tes'təmənt] n 証拠 shṓko
the Old/New Testament 旧〔新〕約聖書 kyū́ (shiñ)yaku seisho

testicle [tes'tikəl] n こう丸 kṓgan

testify [tes'təfai] vi (LAW) 証言する shṓgen suru
to testify to something ...が...だと証言する ...ga ...dà tò shṓgen suru

testimony [tes'təmouni:] n (LAW: statement) 証言 shṓgen; (clear proof) 証拠 shṓko

test match n (CRICKET, RUGBY) 国際戦 kokúsaisen, 国際試合 kokúsaijiài

test pilot n テストパイロット tesútopairottò

test tube n 試験管 shikéñkan

tetanus [tet'ənəs] n 破傷風 hashṓfū

tether [teð'ə:r] vt (animal) つなぐ tsunágù
♦n: *at the end of one's tether* 行き詰って ikízumattè

text [tekst] n 文書 búñsho

textbook [tekst'buk] n 教科書 kyṓkasho

textiles [teks'tailz] npl (fabrics) 織物 o-rímòno; (textile industry) 織物業界 orímonogyōkai

texture [teks'tʃə:r] n (of cloth, skin, soil, silk) 手触り tezáwari

Thailand [tai'lənd] n タイ tái

Thames [temz] n: *the Thames* テムズ川 témùzugawa

than [ðæn] conj (in comparisons) ...より (も) ...yórì(mo)
you have more than 10 あなたは10個以上持っています anátà wa júkkò íjò móttè imasu
I have more than you/Paul 私はあなた〔ポール〕より沢山持っています watákushi wà anátà (pṓrù)yori takúsaň móttè imasu
I have more pens than pencils 私は鉛筆よりペンを沢山持っています watákushi wà eñpitsu yorì péñ wo takúsaň móttè imasu
she is older than you think 彼女はあなたが思っているより年ですよ kánojo wa anátà ga omóttè irù yórì toshí desù yó
more than once 数回 súkài

thank [θæŋk] vt (person) ...に感謝する ...ni káñsha suru
thank you (very much) (大変) 有難うございました (taíhen) arígàtō gozáimashità
thank God! ああ良かった ầ yókàtta

thankful [θæŋk'fəl] adj: *thankful (for)* (...を) 有難く思っている (...wo) arígatakù omótte irù

thankless [θæŋk'lis] adj (task) 割の悪い warî no waruî

thanks [θæŋks] npl 感謝 kánsha
♦excl (also: *many thanks*, *thanks a lot*) 有難う arígàtō

Thanksgiving (Day) [θæŋksgiv'iŋ-] n 感謝祭 kañshasaî

thanks to prep ...のおかげで ...no o-káge dè

KEYWORD

that [ðæt] (*demonstrative adj, pron: pl* **those**) *adj* (demonstrative) その sonó, あの anó

that man/woman/book その〔あの〕男性〔女性, 本〕 sonó〔anó〕dañsei〔jòsei, hoñ〕

leave those books on the table その本をテーブルの上に置いていって下さい sonó hoñ wo tḕburu no ué nì oíte ittè kudásaì

that one それ soré, あれ aré

that one over there あそこにある物 asóko nì árù monó

I want this one, not that one 欲しいのはこれです, あれは要りません hoshíi no wà koré desù, aré wà irímaseñ

◆*pron* **1** (demonstrative) それ soré, あれ aré

who's/what's that? あれはだれですか〔何ですか〕aré wà dárè desu ká〔náñ desu ká〕

is that you? あなたですか anátá desu ká

I prefer this to that あれよりこちらの方が好きです aré yorì kochíra no hǒ ga sukí desù

will you eat all that? あれを全部食べるつもりですか aré wò zéñbu tabérù tsumóri desù ká

that's my house 私の家はあれです watákushi nò ié wà aré desù

that's what he said 彼はそう言いましたよ kárè wa sǒ iimashìta yó

what happened after that? それからどうなりましたか soré karà dǒ narimashìta ká

that is (to say) つまり tsúmàri, すなわち sunáwàchi

2 (relative): *the book (that) I read* 私の読んだ本 watákushi nò yóñda hóñ

the books that are in the library 図書館にある本 toshókàn ni árù hóñ

the man (that) I saw 私の見た男 watákushi nò mítà otóko

all (that) I have 私が持っているだけ watákushi gà móttè irú dàke

the box (that) I put it in それを入れた箱 soré wò iréta hakó

the people (that) I spoke to 私が声を掛けた人々 watákushi gà kóè wo kákèta hitóbìto

3 (relative: of time): *the day (that) he came* 彼が来た日 kárè ga kitá hì

the evening/winter (that) he came to see us 彼が私たちの家に来た夜〔冬〕kárè ga watákushitàchi no ié ni kitá yorù〔fuyù〕

◆*conj* ...だと ...dá tò

he thought that I was ill 私が病気だと彼は思っていました watákushi gà byǒkì dá tò kárè wa omótte imashìta

she suggested that I phone you あなたに電話する様にと彼女は私に勧めました anátá ni deñwa suru yǒ ni to kánòjo wa watákushi nì susúmemashìta

◆*adv* (demonstrative) それ程 soré hodò, あれ程 aré hodò, そんなに soñna nì, あんなに añna nì

I can't work that much あんなに働けません añna nì határakemaseñ

I didn't realize it was that bad 事態があれ程悪くなっているとは思っていませんでした jítai ga aré hodò wárùku natté irù to wa omótte imaseñ deshìta

that high あんなに高い añna nì takái

the wall's about that high and that thick 塀はこれぐらい高くてこれぐらい厚い heí wà koré gurài tákàkute koré gurài atsúi

thatched [θætʃt] *adj* (roof, cottage) わらぶきの warábuki no

thaw [θɔː] *n* 雪解けの陽気 yukídokè no yǒkì

◆*vi* (ice) 溶ける tokérù; (food) 解凍される kaítō sarerù

◆*vt* (food: *also*: **thaw out**) 解凍する kaítō suru

KEYWORD

the [ðə] *def art* **1** (gen) その sonó ◇ 通常日本語では表現しない tsǔjō nihóngo de wà hyǒgen shinaì

the history of France フランスの歴史

furánsu nò rekíshi

the books/children are in the library 本〔子供たち〕は図書館にあります〔います〕hón〔kodómotàchi〕wa toshókàn ni arímasù〔imásù〕

she put it on the table/gave it to the postman 彼女はテーブルに置きました〔郵便屋さんにあげました〕kánòjo wa tèburu ni okímashìta〔yúbin-yasan nì agémashìta〕

he took it from the drawer 彼は引出しから取り出しました kárè wa hikídashi karà torídashimashìta

I haven't the time/money 私にはそれだけの時間〔金〕がありません watákushi ni wà soré dakè no jikán〔kané〕gà arímasèñ

to play the piano/violin ピアノ〔バイオリン〕をひく piáno〔baíorin〕wo hikú

the age of the computer コンピュータの時代 kóñpyùta no jídái

I'm going to the butcher's/the cinema 肉屋に〔映画を見に〕行って来ます nikúyà ni 〔eíga wò mí nì〕ittè kimasù

2 (+ adjective to form noun)

the rich and the poor 金持と貧乏人 kanémochì to bíñbònin

the wounded were taken to the hospital 負傷者は病院に運ばれた fushóshà wa byóìn ni hakóbaretà

to attempt the impossible 不可能な事をやろうとする fukánó na kotò wo yaró to surù

3 (in titles): *Elizabeth the First* エリザベス1世 erízabèsu íssèi

Peter the Great ビョートル大帝 pyótòru taítei

4 (in comparisons): *the more he works the more he earns* 彼は働けば働く程もうかる kárè wa határakèba határaku hodò mókarù

the more I look at it the less I like it 見れば見る程いやになります mírèba míru hodò iyá ni narimasù

theater [θiː'ətər] (*BRIT* **theatre**) *n* (building with stage) 劇場 gekíjō; (art form) 演劇 eñgeki; (*also*: **lecture thea-**

ter) 講義室 kőgishìtsu; (MED: *also*: **operating theater**) 手術室 shujútsushìtsu

theater-goer [θiː'ətə:rgouə:r] *n* 芝居好き shibáizùki

theatrical [θiːæt'rikəl] *adj* (event, production) 演劇の eñgeki no; (gestures) 芝居染みた shibáijimìta

theft [θeft] *n* 窃盗 settó

their [ðeːr] *adj* 彼らの kárèra no ¶ *see also* **my**

theirs [ðeːrz] *pron* 彼らの物 kárèra no monó ¶ *see also* **mine**

them [ðem] *pron* (direct) 彼らを kárèra wo; (indirect) 彼らに kárèra ni; (stressed, after prep) 彼ら kárèra ¶ *see also* **me**

theme [θiːm] *n* (main subject) 主題 shudái, テーマ tèma; (MUS) テーマ tèma

theme park *n* テーマ遊園地 témayūeñchi

theme song *n* 主題歌 shidáīka

themselves [ðəmselvz'] *pl pron* (reflexive) 彼ら自身を karéra jishìn wo; (after prep) 彼ら自身 karéra jishìn ¶ *see also* **oneself**

then [ðen] *adv* (at that time) その時(に) sonó tokì (ni); (next, later, and also) それから soré karà

♦*conj* (therefore) だから dá kàra

♦*adj*: *the then president* 当時の大統領 tőjì no daítōryố

by then (past) その時 sonó tokì; (future) その時になったら sonó tokì ni nattárà

from then on その時から sonó tokì kara

theology [θiːɑːl'ədʒi] *n* 神学 shiñgaku

theorem [θiːr'əm] *n* 定理 teíri

theoretical [θiːəret'ikəl] *adj* (biology, possibility) 理論的な rirónteki na

theorize [θiː'ə:raiz] *vi* 学説を立てる gakúsetsu wò tatérù

theory [θiː'ri] *n* (all senses) 理論 rírön

in theory 理論的には rirónteki ni wà

therapeutic(al) [θeːrəpju:'tik(əl)] *adj* 治療の chiryō no

therapist [θeːr'əpist] *n* セラピスト serápisùto

therapy [θe:r'əpi:] n 治療 chiryō

KEYWORD

there [ðe:r] adv 1: *there is, there are
...*があ[いる] ...ga árù(irú)

there are 3 of them (things) 3つありま
す míttsu arímasù; (people) 3人 い ます
saññiñ imásù

there is no one here だれもいません
dáre mo imáseñ

there is no bread left パンがなくなり
ました páñ ga nakúnarimashìta

there has been an accident 事故があ
りました jíkò ga arímashìta

there will be a meeting tomorrow 明
日会議があります asú káigi ga arímasù

2 (referring to place) そこに〔で, へ〕so-
kó nì〔dè, e〕, あそこに〔で, へ〕asokó nì
〔dè, e〕

where is the book? - it's there 本はど
こにありますか-あそこにあります hóñ
wa dókò ni arímasù ká - asóko nì arímasù

put it down there そこに置いて下さい
sokó nì oíte kudasaì

he went there on Friday 彼は金曜日
に行きました kárè wa kiñ-yōbi ni ikímashìta

I want that book there そこの本が欲
しい sokó nò hóñ ga hoshíi

there he is! いました imáshìta

3: *there, there* (especially to child) よし
よし yóshì yóshì

*there, there, it's not your fault/
don't cry* よしよし, お前のせいじゃな
いから〔泣かないで〕 yóshì yóshì, omáe
nò seí ja naì kara(nakánaìde)

---

thereabouts [ðe:r'əbauts] adv (place) そ
こら辺 sokórahen; (amount) それぐらい
soré gurai

thereafter [ðe:r'æf'tə:r] adv それ以来 soré irài

thereby [ðe:r'bai'] adv それによって soré
ni yottè

therefore [ðe:r'fɔ:r] adv だから dá kàra

there's [ðe:rz] = there is; there has

thermal [θə:r'məl] adj (underwear) 防寒

用の bốkan-yō no; (paper) 感熱の kañne-
tsu no; (printer) 熱式の netsúshìki no

thermal spring n 温泉 oñsen

thermometer [θə:rmɑ:m'itə:r] n (for
room/body temperature) 温度計 ofido-
kèi

Thermos [θə:r'məs]® n (also: **Thermos
flask**) 魔法瓶 mahốbìn

thermostat [θə:r'məstæt] n サーモスタ
ット sámosutattò

thesaurus [θisɔ:r'əs] n シソーラス shisố-
rāsu

these [ði:z] pl adj これらの korérà no
♦pl pron これらは〔を〕 korérà wa(wo)

theses [θi:'si:z] npl of **thesis**

thesis [θi:'sis] (pl **theses**) n (for doctor-
ate etc) 論文 roñbun

they [ðei] pl pron 彼らは〔が〕 kárèra wa
〔ga〕

they say that ... (it is said that) ...と言
われている ...to iwárete irù

they'd [ðeid] = they had; they would

they'll [ðeil] = they shall, they will

they're [ðe:r] = they are

they've [ðeiv] = they have

thick [θik] adj (in shape: slice, jersey etc)
厚い atsúì; (line) 太い futóì; (in consistency: sauce, mud, fog etc) 濃い kóì;
(: forest) 深い fukáì; (stupid) 鈍い nibúì
♦n: *in the thick of the battle* 戦いの
さなかに tatákai nò sánàka ni

it's 20 cm thick 厚さは20センチだ a-
tsúsa wà nijússeñchi da

thicken [θik'ən] vi (fog etc) 濃くなる kốkù naru; (plot) 込入ってくる komítte
kurù
♦vt (sauce etc) 濃くする kốkù suru

thickness [θik'nis] n 厚み atsúmi

thickset [θik'set'] adj (person, body) が
っちりした gatchírì shita

thickskinned [θik'skind] adj (fig: person) 無神経な mushíñkei na

thief [θi:f] (pl **thieves**) n 泥棒 doróbō

thieves [θi:vz] npl of **thief**

thigh [θai] n 太もも futómomo

thimble [θim'bəl] n 指抜き yubínuki

thin [θin] adj (gen) 薄い usúì; (line) 細い
hosóì; (person, animal) やせた yasétà;

(crowd) まばらな mabára na

♦vt: **to thin (down)** (sauce, paint) 薄める usúmerù

thing [θiŋ] n (gen) 物事 monógòto; (physical object) 物 monó; (matter) 事 kotó:
to have a thing about someone/something (mania) ...が大嫌いである ...ga dáikirai de árù; (fascination) ...が大好きである ...ga dáisuki de árù
poor thing かわいそうに kawáisò ni
the best thing would be to ... ...するのが一番いいだろう ...surú no gà ichíban iî darò
how are things? どうですか dô desu ká

things [θiŋz] npl (belongings) 持物 mochímòno

think [θiŋk] (pt, pp thought) vi (reflect) 考える kañgaerù; (believe) 思う omóù
♦vt (imagine) ...だと思う ...dá tò omóù
what did you think of them? 彼らの事をどう思いましたか kárèra no kotó wo dô omóimashìta ka
to think about something/someone ...について考える ...ni tsúite kañgaerù
I'll think about it 考えておくね kañgaete okù né
to think of doing something ...しようと思う ...shiyô tò omóù
I think so/not そうだ〔違う〕と思う sô dà〔chigáù〕to omóù
to think well of someone ...に対して好感を持つ ...ni táishite kôkan wò mótsù

think over vt (offer, suggestion) よく考える yókù kañgaerù

think tank n シンクタンク shiñkutañku

think up vt (plan, scheme, excuse) 考え出す kañgaedasù

thinly [θin'li:] adv (cut, spread) 薄く usúkù

third [θə:rd] num 第三（の）dái san (no)
♦n (fraction) 3分の1 sañbun no ichí; (AUT: also: third gear) サードギヤ sâdogiyà; (BRIT: SCOL: degree) 3級優等卒業学位 sañkyū yūtō sotsugyō gakùi
¶ see also **first**

thirdly [θə:rd'li:] adv 第三に dái san ni

third party insurance (BRIT) n 損害倍償保険 sofgaibaishōhoken

third-rate [θə:rd'reit'] adj 三流の sañryū no

Third World n: **the Third World** 第三世界 dái san sékài

thirst [θə:rst] n 渇き kawáki

thirsty [θə:rs'ti:] adj (person, animal) のどが渇いた nódò ga kawáita; (work) のどが渇く nódò ga kawákù
to be thirsty (person, animal) のどが渇いている nódò ga kawáite irù

thirteen [θə:r'ti:n'] num 十三（の）jûsan (no)

thirty [θə:r'ti:] num 三十（の）sáñjū (no)

KEYWORD

this [ðis] (pl **these**) adj (demonstrative) この konó
this man/woman/book この男性〔女性, 本〕konó dansei〔josei, hon〕
these people/children/records この人たち〔子供たち, レコード〕konó hitotàchi〔kodomotàchi, rekôdo〕
this one これ koré
it's not that picture but this one that I like 私が好きなのはあの絵ではなくて、この絵です watákushi gà sukí na no wà anó e de wa nakùte, konó e desù
♦pron (demonstrative) これ koré
what is this? これは何ですか koré wà nán desu ká
who is this? この方はどなたですか konó katà wa dónàta desu ká
I prefer this to that 私はあれよりこの方が好きです watákushi wà aré yorì konó hô ga sukí desù
this is where I live 私の住いはここです watákushi no sumài wa kokó desù
this is what he said 彼はこう言いました kárè wa kô iimashìta
this is Mr Brown (in introductions/photo) こちらはブラウンさんです kochíra wà buráûnsan desu; (on telephone) こちらはブラウンですが kochíra wà burá-

ùn desu ga

♦*adv* (demonstrative): *this high/long*
高さ〔長さ〕はこれぐらいで tákàsa〔nágàsa〕wa koré gùrài de
it was about this big 大きさはこれぐらいでした ốkìsa wa korégùrài deshita
the car is this long 車の長さはこれぐらいです kurúma no nagàsa wa koré gùrài desu
we can't stop now we've gone this far ここまで来たらやめられません kokó madè kitára yaméraremaseǹ

thistle [θis'əl] *n* アザミ azámi

thong [θɔ:ŋ] *n* バンド bándo

thorn [θɔ:rn] *n* とげ togé

thorny [θɔːr'niː] *adj* (plant, tree) とげの多い togé no ōi; (problem) 厄介な yákkài na

thorough [θəːr'ou] *adj* (search, wash) 徹底的な tettéiteki na; (knowledge, research) 深い fukáĩ; (person: methodical) きちょうめんな kichốmen na

thoroughbred [θəːr'oubred] *adj* (horse) サラブレッド sarábureddò

thoroughfare [θəːr'oufeːr] *n* 目抜き通り menúkidòri
「*no thoroughfare*」通行禁止 tsúkōkiǹshi

thoroughly [θəːr'ouliː] *adv* (examine, study, wash, search) 徹底的に tettéiteki ni; (very) とても totémo

those [ðouz] *pl adj* それらの sorérà no, あれらの arérà no
♦*pl pron* それらを sorérà wo, あれらを arérà wo

though [ðou] *conj* ...にもかかわらず ...ní mò kakáwarazù
♦*adv* しかし shikáshì

thought [θɔ:t] *pt, pp of* think
♦*n* (idea, reflection) 考え kañgaè; (opinion) 意見 íkeñ

thoughtful [θɔ:t'fəl] *adj* (person: deep in thought) 考え込んでいる kañgaekonde irù; (: serious) 真剣な shiñken na; (considerate: person) 思いやりのある omóiyari no arù

thoughtless [θɔ:t'lis] *adj* (inconsiderate:

behavior, words, person) 心ない kokóronaĩ

thousand [θau'zənd] *num* 千 (の) séñ (no)
two thousand 二千 (の) niséñ (no)
thousands of 何千もの... nañzeñ mo no ...

thousandth [θau'zəndθ] *num* 第千 (の) dái sen (no)

thrash [θræʃ] *vt* (beat) たたく tatákù; (defeat) ...に快勝する ...ni kaíshō suru
thrash about/around *vi* のたうつ notáutsù
thrash out *vt* (problem) 討議する tốgi suru

thread [θred] *n* (yarn) 糸 ítò; (of screw) ねじ山 nejíyama
♦*vt* (needle) ...に糸を通す ...ni ítò wo tốsù

threadbare [θred'beːr] *adj* (clothes, carpet) 擦切れた suríkiretà

threat [θret] *n* (*also fig*) 脅し odóshi; (*fig*) 危険 kikéñ

threaten [θret'ən] *vi* (storm, danger) 迫る semárù
♦*vt: to threaten someone with/to do* ...で〔...すると言って〕...を脅す ...de 〔...surú to itté〕...wŏ odósù

three [θri:] *num* 三 (の) sañ (no)

three-dimensional [θri:'dimen'tʃənəl] *adj* 立体の rittái no

three-piece suit [θri:'pi:s-] *n* 三つぞろい mitsúzoròi

three-piece suite *n* 応接三点セット ốsetsu santensettò

three-ply [θri:'plai] *adj* (wool) 三重織りの sañjūori no

thresh [θreʃ] *vt* (AGR) 脱穀する dakkóku suru

threshold [θreʃ'ould] *n* 敷居 shikíi

threw [θru:] *pt of* throw

thrift [θrift] *n* 節約 setsúyaku

thrifty [θrif'ti:] *adj* 節約家の setsúyakukà no

thrill [θril] *n* (excitement) スリル súrìru; (shudder) ぞっとする事 zottó suru kotò
♦*vt* (person, audience) わくわくさせる wákùwaku sasérù

to be thrilled (with gift etc) 大喜びである ốyorðkobi de árù

thriller [θril'əːr] n (novel, play, film) スリラー surírā

thrilling [θril'iŋ] adj (ride, performance, news etc) わくわくさせる wákùwaku sasérù

thrive [θraiv] (pt **throve**, pp **thrived** or **thriven**) vi (grow: plant) 生茂る oíshigerù; (: person, animal) よく育つ yốkù sodátsù; (: business) 盛んになる sakán ni narù; (do well): **to thrive on something** ...で栄える ...de sakáerù

thriven [θraivən] pp of **thrive**

thriving [θraiv'iŋ] adj (business, community) 繁盛している háňjō shité irù

throat [θrout] n のど nódò

to have a sore throat のどが痛い nódò ga itáī

throb [θrɑːb] n (of heart) 鼓動 kodố; (of wound) うずき uzúki; (of engine) 振動 shiñdố

♦vi (heart) どきどきする dốkìdoki suru; (head, arm: with pain) ずきずきする zúkìzuki suru; (machine: vibrate) 振動する shiñdố suru

throes [θrouz] npl: **in the throes of** (war, moving house etc) ...と取組んでいるさなかに ...to toríkunde irù sánàka ni

thrombosis [θrɑːmbou'sis] n 血栓症 kessếňshō

throne [θroun] n 王座 ốza

throng [θrɔːŋ] n 群衆 guñshū

♦vt (streets etc) ...に殺到する ...ni sattố suru

throttle [θrɑːt'əl] n (AUT) スロットル surốttòru

♦vt (strangle) ...ののどを絞める ...no nódò wo shimérù

through [θruː] prep (space) ...を通って ...wo tốttè; (time) ...の間中 ...no aídà jū; (by means of) ...を使って ...wo tsukáttè; (owing to) ...が原因で ...ga geñ-in dè

♦adj (ticket, train) 直通の chokútsū no

♦adv 通して tốshìte

to put someone through to someone (TEL) ...を...につなぐ ...wo ...ni tsunágù

to be through (TEL) つながれる tsuná-

garerù; (relationship: finished) 終る owárù

「**no through road**」(BRIT) 行き止りikídomarì

throughout [θruːaut'] prep (place) ...の至る所に ...no itárù tokoro ni; (time) ...の間中 ...no aídà jū

♦adv 至る所に itárù tokoro ni

throve [θrouv] pt of **thrive**

throw [θrou] n (gen) 投げる事 nagérù kotð

♦vt (pt **threw**, pp **thrown**) (object) 投げる nagérù; (rider) 振り落す furíotosù; (fig: person: confuse) 迷わせる mayốwaserù

to throw a party パーティをやる pấtī wo yárù

throw away vt (rubbish) 捨てる sutérù; (money) 浪費する rốhi suru

throwaway [θrou'əwei] adj (toothbrush) 使い捨ての tsukáisùte no; (line, remark) 捨てぜりふ染みた sutézerifujimìta

throw-in [θrou'in] n (SPORT) スローイン surốīn

throw off vt (get rid of: burden, habit) かなぐり捨てる kanágurisuterù; (cold) ...が治る ...ga naốrù

throw out vt (rubbish, idea) 捨てる sutérù; (person) ほうり出す hốridasù

throw up vi (vomit) 吐く hákù

thru [θruː] (US) = **through**

thrush [θrʌʃ] n (bird) つぐみ tsugúmi

thrust [θrʌst] n (TECH) 推進力 suíshiñryoku

♦vt (pt, pp **thrust**) (person, object) 強く押す tsúyðku osú

thud [θʌd] n ばたんという音 batán to iú otð

thug [θʌg] n (pej) ちんぴら chiñpira; (criminal) 犯罪者 hañzaìsha

thumb [θʌm] n (ANAT) 親指 oyáyubi

♦vt: **to thumb a lift** ヒッチハイクする hitchíhaìku suru

thumbtack [θʌm'tæk] (US) n 画びょう gabyố

thumb through vt fus (book) 拾い読みする hirðiyomi suru

thump [θʌmp] n (blow) 一撃 ichígeki; (sound) どしんという音 doshíñ to iú otò
♦vt (person, object) たたく tatákù
♦vi (heart etc) どきどきする dókìdoki suru

thunder [θʌn'də:r] n 雷 kamínari
♦vi 雷が鳴る kamínari ga narù; (fig: train etc): **to thunder past** ごう音を立てて通り過ぎる góon wò tátète tōrisugirù

thunderbolt [θʌn'də:rboult] n 落雷 rakúrai

thunderclap [θʌn'də:rklæp] n 雷鳴 raímei

thunderstorm [θʌn'də:rstɔ:rm] n 雷雨 ráìu

thundery [θʌn'də:ri:] adj (weather) 雷が鳴る kamínarì ga narú

Thursday [θə:rz'dei] n 木曜日 mokúyòbi

thus [ðʌs] adv (in this way) こうして kōshìte; (consequently) 従って shitágattè

thwart [θwɔ:rt] vt (person, plans) 邪魔する jamá suru

thyme [taim] n タイム táìmu

thyroid [θai'rɔid] n (also: **thyroid gland**) 甲状腺 kōjōsen

tiara [ti:e:r'ə] n ティアラ tíàra

Tibet [tibet'] n チベット chibéttò

tic [tik] n チック chíkkù

tick [tik] n (sound: of clock) かちかち káchìkachi; (mark) 印 shirúshi; (ZOOL) だに danî; (BRIT: inf): **in a tick** もうすぐ mố sugù
♦vi (clock, watch) かちかちいう káchìkachi iú
♦vt (item on list) …に印を付ける …ni shirúshi wò tsukérù

ticket [tik'it] n (for public transport, theater etc) 切符 kippú; (in shop: on goods) 値札 nefúda; (for raffle, library etc) チケット chikéttò; (also: **parking ticket**) 駐車違反のチケット chūsha-ihàn no chikéttò

ticket collector n 改札係 kaísatsugakàri

ticket office n (RAIL, theater etc) 切符売場 kippú urìba

tickle [tik'əl] vt (person, dog) くすぐる kusúguru
♦vi (feather etc) くすぐったい kusúguttai

ticklish [tik'liʃ] adj (person) くすぐったがる kusúguttagàru; (problem) 厄介な yákkài na

tick off vt (item on list) …に印を付ける …ni shirúshi wò tsukérù; (person) しかる shikárù

tick over vi (engine) アイドリングする aídoriñgu suru; (fig: business) 低迷する teímei suru

tidal [taid'əl] adj (force) 潮の shió no; (estuary) 干満のある kañman no arù

tidal wave n 津波 tsunámi

tidbit [tid'bit] (US) n (food) うまいもの一口 umái monò hitókùchi; (news) 好奇心をあおり立てるうわさ話 kôkishìn wo aôritaterù uwásabanàshi

tiddlywinks [tid'li:wiŋks] n おはじき ohájìki

tide [taid] n (in sea) 潮 shió; (fig: of events, fashion, opinion) 動向 dôkô
high/low tide 満〔干〕潮 mañ〔kañ〕chō

tide over vt (help out) …の一時的な助けになる …no ichíjiteki na tasúke ni narù

tidy [tai'di:] adj (room, dress, desk, work) きちんとした kichíñ to shita; (person) きれい好きな kiréîzuki na
♦vt (also: **tidy up**: room, house etc) 片付ける katázukerù

tie [tai] n (string etc) ひも himó; (BRIT: also: **necktie**) ネクタイ nékùtai; (fig: link) 縁 éñ; (SPORT: even score) 同点 dóten
♦vt (fasten: parcel) 縛る shibárù; (: shoelaces, ribbon) 結ぶ musúbù
♦vi (SPORT etc) 同点になる dóten nì narù
to tie in a bow ちょう結びにする chômusùbi ni suru
to tie a knot in something …に結び目を作る …ni musúbime wo tsukúrù

tie down vt (fig: person: restrict) 束縛する sokúbaku suru; (: to date, price etc) 縛り付ける shibáritsukerù

tier [ti:r] n (of stadium etc) 列 rétsù; (of cake) 層 số

tie up vt (parcel) ...にひもを掛ける ...ni himó wò kakérù; (dog, boat) つなぐ tsunagu; (prisoner) 縛る shibárù; (arrangements) 整える totónoerù
to be tied up (busy) 忙しい isógashiî

tiger [tai'gə:r] n トラ torá

tight [tait] adj (firm: rope) ぴんと張った piń tò hattá; (scarce: money) 少ない sukúnaî; (narrow: shoes, clothes) きつい kitsúî; (bend) 急な kyū na; (strict: security, budget, schedule) 厳しい kibíshiî; (inf: drunk) 酔っ払った yopparattá
♦adv (hold, squeeze, shut) 堅く katákù

tighten [tait'ən] vt (rope, screw) 締める shimérù; (grip) 固くする katáku suru; (security) 厳しくする kibíshikù suru
♦vi (grip) 固くなる katáku narù; (rope) 締る shimárù

tightfisted [tait'fis'tid] adj けちな kéchi na

tightly [tait'li:] adv (grasp) 固く katáku

tightrope [tait'roup] n 綱渡りの綱 tsunáwatàri no tsuná

tights [taits] npl タイツ táîtsu

tile [tail] n (on roof) かわら kawára; (on floor, wall) タイル táîru

tiled [taild] adj (roof) かわらぶきの kawárabuki no; (floor, wall) タイル張りの taírubari no

till [til] n (in shop etc) レジの引出し réjì no hikídashi
♦vt (land: cultivate) 耕す tagáyasù
♦prep, conj = until

tiller [til'ə:r] n (NAUT) だ柄 dahéi, チラー chírā

tilt [tilt] vt 傾ける katámukerù
♦vi 傾く katámukù

timber [tim'bə:r] n (material) 材木 zaímoku; (trees) 材木用の木 zaímokuyò no kí

time [taim] n (gen) 時間 jíkàn; (epoch: often pl) 時代 jidái; (by clock) 時刻 jíkòku; (moment) 瞬間 shuńkan; (occasion) 回 káî; (MUS) テンポ téñpo
♦vt (measure time of: race, boiling an egg etc) ...の時間を計る ...no jíkàn wo hakárù; (fix moment for: visit etc) ...の時期を選ぶ ...no jíkì wo erábù; (remark

etc) ...のタイミングを合せる ...no taímiñgu wo awáserù
a long time 長い間 nagái aidà
for the time being 取りあえず toríaezù
4 at a time 4つずつ yottsú zùtsu
from time to time 時々 tokídoki
at times 時には tokí ni wà
in time (soon enough) 間に合って ma ní attè; (after some time) やがて yagáte; (MUS) ...のリズムに合せて ...no rízùmu ni awásetè
in a week's time 1週間で isshūkàn de
in no time 直ぐに súgù ni
any time now いつでも ítsù de mo
on time 間に合って ma ní attè
5 times 5 5かける5 gó kakerù gó
what time is it? 何時ですか náñji desu ká
to have a good time 楽しむ tanóshimù

time bomb n 時限爆弾 jigénbakùdan

time lag n 遅れ okúre

timeless [taim'lis] adj 普遍的な fuhénteki na

time limit n 期限 kígèn

timely [taim'li:] adj (arrival, reminder) 時宜を得た jígì wo étà, 丁度いい時の chódo ii tokí no, タイムリーな taímurī na

time off n 休暇 kyūka

timer [tai'mə:r] n (time switch) タイムスイッチ taímusuitchì; (in cooking) タイマー taímā

time scale (BRIT) n 期間 kíkàn

time-share [taim'ʃe:r] n リゾート施設の共同使用権 rizótoshisètsu no kyódòshiyōken

time switch n タイムスイッチ taímusuitchì, タイマー taímā

timetable [taim'teibəl] n (RAIL etc) 時刻表 jikókuhyō; (SCOL etc) 時間割 jikánwari

time zone n 時間帯 jikántai

timid [tim'id] adj (shy) 気が小さい ki gá chíìsai; (easily frightened) 臆病な okúbyò na

timing [tai'miŋ] n (SPORT) タイミング taímingu
the timing of his resignation 彼の辞

退のタイミング kárè no jítai no taímingu

timpani [tim'pəni:] *npl* ティンパニー tínpanī

tin [tin] *n* (material) すず súzù; (*also*: **tin plate**) ブリキ buríki; (container: biscuit tin etc) 箱 hakó; (: *BRIT*: can) 缶 kán

tinfoil [tin'fɔil] *n* ホイル hóîru

tinge [tindʒ] *n* (of color) 薄い色合 usúî iróaî; (of feeling) 気味 kimí
◆*vt*: **tinged with** (color) ...の色合を帯びた ...no iróaî wo óbìta; (feeling) ...の気味を帯びた ...no kimí wò óbìta

tingle [tiŋ'gəl] *vi* (person, arms etc) ぴりぴりする bírìbiri suru

tinker [tiŋk'ə:r]: **to tinker with** *vt fus* いじくる ijíkurù

tinned [tind] (*BRIT*) *adj* (food, salmon, peas) 缶詰の kañzumè no

tin opener [-ou'pənə:r] (*BRIT*) *n* 缶切り kañkirì

tinsel [tin'səl] *n* ティンセル tínseru

tint [tint] *n* (color) 色合い iróaî; (for hair) 染毛剤 senmōzai

tinted [tin'tid] *adj* (hair) 染めた sométa; (spectacles, glass) 色付きの irótsuki no

tiny [tai'ni:] *adj* 小さな chíisa na

tip [tip] *n* (end: of paintbrush etc) 先端 señtan; (gratuity) チップ chíppù; (*BRIT*: for rubbish) ごみ捨て場 gomí suteba; (advice) 助言 jogén
◆*vt* (waiter) ...にチップをあげる ...ni chíppù wo agérù; (tilt) 傾ける katámukerù; (overturn: *also*: **tip over**) 引っ繰り返す hikkúrikaesù; (empty: *also*: **tip out**) 空ける akérù

tip-off [tip'ɔ:f] *n* (hint) 内報 naíhō

tipped [tipt] (*BRIT*) *adj* (cigarette) フィルター付きの firútatsuki no

Tipp-Ex [tip'eks] (®) *BRIT*) *n* 修正ペン shūseipeñ ◊白い修正液の出るフェルトペン shiróî shūseieki no derù ferútopeñ

tipsy [tip'si:] (*inf*) *adj* 酔っ払った yoppárattà

tiptoe [tip'tou] *n*: **on tiptoe** つま先立って tsumásakidattè

tiptop [tip'tɑ:p] *adj*: **in tiptop condition** 状態が最高で jōtai gà saíkō dè

tire [taiə'r] *n* (*BRIT* **tyre**) タイヤ táîya
◆*vt* (make tired) 疲れさせる tsukáresaserù
◆*vi* (become tired) 疲れる tsukárerù; (become wearied) うんざりする uñzarì suru

tired [taiə:rd'] *adj* (person, voice) 疲れた tsukáreta
to be tired of something ...にうんざりしている ...ni uñzarì shité irù

tireless [taiə:r'lis] *adj* (worker) 疲れを知らない tsukáre wò shiránaî; (efforts) たゆまない tayúmanaî

tire pressure *n* タイヤの空気圧 táîya no kúkiatsù

tiresome [taiə:r'səm] *adj* (person, thing) うんざりさせる uñzarì saserù

tiring [taiə:r'iŋ] *adj* 疲れさせる tsukáresaserù

tissue [tiʃ'u:] *n* (ANAT, BIO) 組織 sóshìki; (paper handkerchief) ティッシュ tísshù

tissue paper *n* ティッシュペーパー tisshúpēpā

tit [tit] *n* (bird) シジュウカラ shijúkàra
to give tit for tat しっぺ返しする shippégaèshi suru

titbit [tit'bit] = **tidbit**

titillate [tit'əleit] *vt* 刺激する shigéki suru ◊特に性的描写などについて言う tókù ni seíteki byōsha nádò ni tsúîte iú

title [tait'əl] *n* (of book, play etc) 題 dáî; (personal rank etc) 肩書 katágaki; (BOXING etc) タイトル táîtoru

title deed *n* (LAW) 権利証書 keñrishòsho

title role *n* 主役 shuyáku

titter [tit'ə:r] *vi* くすくす笑う kusúkusu waraù

TM [ti:em'] *abbr* = **trademark**

KEYWORD

to [tu:] *prep* **1** (direction) ...へ ...é
to go to France/London/school/the station フランス〔ロンドン, 学校, 駅〕へ行く furánsu〔róñdon, gakkō, ékì〕e ikù
to go to Claude's/the doctor's クロー

528 **to**

ドの家〔医者〕へ行く kuródò no ié〔ishá〕e ikù

the road to Edinburgh エジンバラへの道 ejínbara é nò michí

to the left/right 左〔右〕へ hidári〔migí〕e

2 (as far as) ...まで ...mádè

from here to London ここからロンドンまで kokó karà róndon madè

to count to 10 10まで数える jú madè kazőerù

from 40 to 50 people 40ないし50人の人 yőnjū náishi gojűnin no hitó

3 (with expressions of time): *a quarter to 5* 5時15分前 gójí júgofùn máè

it's twenty to 3 3時20分前です sánji nijúppùn máè desu

4 (for, of) ...の...no

the key to the front door 玄関のかぎ génkan no kagí

she is secretary to the director 彼女は所長の秘書です kánòjo wa shochő nò hishő desù

a letter to his wife 妻への手紙 tsúmà e no tegámi

5 (expressing indirect object) ...に ...ni

to give something to someone ...に...を与える ...ni ...wò atáerù

to talk to someone ...に話す ...ni hanásù

I sold it to a friend 友達にそれを売りました tomódachi nì soré wò urímashìta

to cause damage to something ...に損害を与える ...ni sofigai wò atáerù

to be a danger to someone/something ...を危険にさらす ...wò kikén nì sarásù

to carry out repairs to something ...を修理する ...wò shűrí suru

you've done something to your hair あなたは髪型を変えましたね anátà wa kamígata wò kaémashìta né

6 (in relation to) ...に対して ...ni táìshite

A is to B as C is to D A対Bの関係はC対Dの関係に等しい A táì B no kañkei wà C táì D no kañkei nì hitóshìì

3 goals to 2 スコアは3対2 sukőà wa sañ táì ní

30 miles to the gallon ガソリン1ガロンで30マイル走れる gasórin ichígaròn de sañjūmaìru hashírerù

7 (purpose, result): *to come to someone's aid* ...を助けに来る ...wò tasúke nì kúrù

to sentence someone to death ...に死刑の宣告を下す ...ni shikéi nò señkoku wò kudásù

to my surprise 驚いた事に odőroita kotð ni

◆*with vb* **1** (simple infinitive): *to go/eat* 行く〔食べる〕事 ikú〔tabérù〕kotð

2 (following another verb): *to want to do* ...したい ...shitái

to try to do ...をしようとする ...wò shiyő tð suru

to start to do ...をし始める ...wò shihájimerù

3 (with vb omitted): *I don't want to* それをしたくない soré wò shitákùnai

you ought to あなたはそうすべきです anátà wa ső sùbeki desu

4 (purpose, result) ...するために ...surú tamè ni, ...する様に ...surú yő ni, ...しに ...shí nì

I did it to help you あなたを助け様と思ってそれをしました anátà wo tasúke-yő to omőttè soré wò shimáshìta

he came to see you 彼はあなたに会いに来ました kárè wa anátà ni áì ni kimáshìta

I went there to meet him 彼に会おうとしてあそこへ行きました kárè ni aő tð shite asóko e ikimáshìta

5 (equivalent to relative clause): *I have things to do* 色々とする事があります irőiro tð suru kotð ga arímasù

he has a lot to lose if ... ...が起れば、彼は大損をするだろう ...gà okőrèba, kárè wa őzòn wo suru darő

the main thing is to try 一番大切なのは努力です ichíban taìsetsu ná nò wà dőryòku desu

6 (after adjective etc): *ready to go* 行く準備ができた ikú juñbi ga dékìta

too old/young to ... ...するのに年を取り過ぎている〔若過ぎる〕...surú no nì to-

shí wŏ torísugite irú (wakásugirù)
it's too heavy to lift 重くて持上げられ
ません omókùte mochíageraremaseñ
◆*adv: push/pull the door to* ドアを閉
める dóàwo shimérù ◇ぴったり閉めない
場合に使う pittárì shiménài baái nì tsukáù

toad [toud] *n* ヒキガエル hikígàeru
toadstool [toud'stu:l] *n* キノコ kínòko
toast [toust] *n* (CULIN) トースト tōsuto;
(drink, speech) 乾杯 kañpai
◆*vt* (CULIN: bread etc) 焼く yákù;
(drink to) ...のために乾杯する ...no tamé
nì kañpai suru
toaster [tous'tə:r] *n* トースター tōsutā
tobacco [təbæk'ou] *n* タバコ tabáko
tobacconist [təbæk'ənist] *n* タバコ売り
tabákòuri
tobacconist's (shop) [təbæk'ənists-] *n*
タバコ屋 tabákòya
toboggan [təba:g'ən] *n* (*also* child's) ト
ボガン tobógañ
today [tədei'] *adv* (*also* fig) 今日(は) kyố
(wà)
◆*n* 今日 kyố; (fig) 現在 geñzai
toddler [ta:d'lə:r] *n* 幼児 yōjì
to-do [tədu:'] *n* (fuss) 騒ぎ sáwàgi
toe [tou] *n* (of foot) 足 ashíyùbi; (of
shoe, sock) つま先 tsumásàki
◆*vt: to toe the line* (fig) 服従する fukújū suru
toenail [tou'neil] *n* 足のつめ ashí no tsu-
mè
toffee [tɔ:f'i:] *n* = taffy
toffee apple [tɔ:f'i:-] *n* (BRIT) タフィー衣のり
んご tafígoromo no riñgo
toga [tou'gə] *n* トーガ tōga
together [tu:geð'ə:r] *adv* (with each
other) 一緒に ísshò ni; (at same time) 同
時に dōji ni
together with ...と一緒に ...to ísshò ni
toil [tɔil] *n* 労苦 rōkù
◆*vi* あくせく働く ákùseku határakù
toilet [tɔi'lit] *n* (apparatus) 便器 béñki,
トイレ tōïre; (room with this apparatus)
便所 beñjo, お手洗い o-téarài, トイレ tōïre

toilet bag (for woman) 化粧バッグ ke-
shōbaggù; (for man) 洗面バッグ señmenbaggù
toilet paper *n* トイレットペーパー toírettopēpā
toiletries [tɔi'litri:z] *npl* 化粧品 keshōhìn
toilet roll *n* トイレットペーパーのロー
ル toírettopēpā no rōru
toilet soap *n* 化粧石けん keshōsekkèn
toilet water *n* 化粧水 keshōsùi
token [tou'kən] *n* (sign, souvenir) 印 shi-
rúshì; (substitute coin) コイン kóìn
◆*adj* (strike, payment etc) 名目の meí-
moku no
book/record/gift token (BRIT) 商品
券 shōhiñken
Tokyo [tou'ki:jou] *n* 東京 tōkyō
told [tould] *pt, pp of* tell
tolerable [ta:l'ə:rəbəl] *adj* (bearable) 我
慢できる gámàn dekírù; (fairly good) ま
あまあの mãmā no
tolerance [ta:l'ə:rəns] *n* (patience) 寛容
kañ-yō; (TECH) 耐久力 taíkyūryòku
tolerant [ta:l'ə:rənt] *adj: tolerant (of)*
(...に) 耐えられる (...ni) taérarerù
tolerate [ta:l'ə:reit] *vt* (pain, noise, injustice) 我慢する gámàn suru
toll [toul] *n* (of casualties, deaths) 数 kázù; (tax, charge) 料金 ryōkin
◆*vi* (bell) 鳴る narú
tomato [təmei'tou] (*pl* tomatoes) *n* トマ
ト tómàto
tomb [tu:m] *n* 墓 haká
tomboy [ta:m'bɔi] *n* お転婆 o-téñba
tombstone [tu:m'stoun] *n* 墓石 haká-ishi
tomcat [ta:m'kæt] *n* 雄ネコ osúneko
tomorrow [təmɔ:r'ou] *adv* (*also* fig) 明
日 asú, あした ashíta
◆*n* (*also* fig) 明日 asu, あした ashíta
the day after tomorrow あさって a-
sáttè
tomorrow morning あしたの朝 ashíta
nò ása
ton [tʌn] *n* トン tóñ ◇BRIT = 1016 kg;
US = 907 kg
tons of (*inf*) ものすごく沢山の monósu-
gòku takúsan no
tone [toun] *n* (of voice) 調子 chōshi; (of

instrument) 音色 ne-íro; (of color) 色調 shikíchō

♦*vi* (colors: *also:* **tone in**) 合う áù

tone-deaf [toun'def] *adj* 音痴の ónchi no

tone down *vt* (color, criticism, demands) 和らげる yawáragerù; (sound) 小さくする chíisakù suru

tone up *vt* (muscles) 強くする tsúyòku suru

tongs [tɔːŋz] *npl* (*also:* **coal tongs**) 炭ば さみ sumíbasàmi; (curling tongs) 髪ごて kamígòte

tongue [tʌŋ] *n* (ANAT) 舌 shitá; (CULIN) タン táñ; (language) 言語 géñgo

tongue in cheek (speak, say) からかっ て karákattè

tongue-tied [tʌŋ'taid] *adj* (*fig*) ものも言 えない monó mò iénaì

tongue-twister [tʌŋ'twistə:r] *n* 早口言 葉 hayákuchi kotobà

tonic [tɑːn'ik] *n* (MED, *also fig*) 強壮剤 kyōsōzai; (*also:* **tonic water**) トニックウ オーター toníkkuuōtà

tonight [tənait'] *adv* (this evening) 今日 の夕方 kyō no yūgata; (this night) 今夜 kóñ-ya

♦*n* (this evening) 今日の夕方 kyō no yūgata; (this night) 今夜 kóñ-ya

tonnage [tʌn'idʒ] *n* (NAUT) トン数 toñsū

tonsil [tɑːn'səl] *n* へんとうせん heñtōsen

tonsillitis [tɑːnsəlai'tis] *n* へんとうせん 炎 heñtōsen-èn

too [tuː] *adv* (excessively) あまりに...過ぎ る amári nì ...sugírù; (*also*) ...も (また) ...mo (matá)

too much adv あまり沢山で amári takusañ de

♦*adj* あまり沢山の amári takusañ no

too many adv あまり沢山の amári takusañ no

♦*pron* あまり沢山 amári takusañ

took [tuk] *pt of* **take**

tool [tuːl] *n* 道具 dṓgù

tool box *n* 道具箱 dṓgubàko

toot [tuːt] *n* (of horn) ぶーぶー pūpū; (of whistle) ぴーぴー pīpī

♦*vi* (with car-horn) クラクションを鳴ら す kurákùshon wo narásù

tooth [tuːθ] (*pl* **teeth**) *n* (ANAT, TECH) 歯 há

toothache [tuːθ'eik] *n* 歯の痛み há nò itámi, 歯痛 shitsū

toothbrush [tuːθ'brʌʃ] *n* 歯ブラシ habúrashi

toothpaste [tuːθ'peist] *n* 歯磨き hamigaki

toothpick [tuːθ'pik] *n* つまようじ tsumáyòji

top [tɑːp] *n* (of mountain, tree, head, ladder) 天辺 teppéñ; (page) 頭 atáma; (of cupboard, table, box) ...の上 ...no ué; (of list etc) 筆頭 hittṓ; (lid: of box, jar, bottle) ふた futá; (blouse etc) トップ tóppù; (toy) こま kóma

♦*adj* (highest: shelf, step) 一番上の ichíban ue no; (: marks) 最高の saíkō no; (in rank: salesman etc) ぴか一の piká-ichì no

♦*vt* (be first in: poll, vote, list) ...の首位 に立つ ...no shúì ni tátsù; (exceed: estimate etc) 越える koérù

on top of (above) ...の上に ...no ué nì; (in addition to) ...に加えて ...ni kuwáetè

from top to bottom 上から下まで ué karà shitá madè

top floor *n* 最上階 saíjōkai

top hat *n* シルクハット shirúkuhattò

top-heavy [tɑːp'hevi:] *adj* (object) 不安 定な fuáñtei na; (administration) 幹部の 多過ぎる káñbu no ōsugìrù

topic [tɑːp'ik] *n* 話題 wadái

topical [tɑːp'ikəl] *adj* 時事問題の jijímoñdai no

topless [tɑːp'lis] *adj* (bather, waitress, swimsuit) トップレスの tóppùresu no

top-level [tɑːp'lev'əl] *adj* (talks, decision) 首脳の shunṓ no

topmost [tɑːp'moust] *adj* (branch etc) 一番上の ichíban ue no

top off (*US*) *vt* = **top up**

topple [tɑːp'əl] *vt* (government, leader) 倒す taósù

♦*vi* (person, object) 倒れる taórerù

top-secret [tɑːp'siː'krit] *adj* 極秘の gokúhi no

topsy-turvy [tɑ:p'si:tər'vi:] adj (world) はちゃめちゃの háchàmecha no

♦adv (fall, land etc) 逆様に sakásama ni

top up vt (bottle etc) 一杯にする ippái ni suru

torch [tɔ:rtʃ] n (with flame) たいまつ táimatsu; (BRIT: electric) 懐中電とう kaíchūdeñtō

tore [tɔ:r] pt of tear

torment [n tɔ:r'ment vb tɔ:rment'] n 苦しみ kurúshimì

♦vt (subj: feelings, guilt etc) 苦しませる kurúshimaserù, 悩ませる nayámaserù; (fig: annoy: subj: person) いじめる ijímerù

torn [tɔ:rn] pp of tear

tornado [tɔ:rnei'dou] (pl tornadoes) n 竜巻 tatsúmaki

torpedo [tɔ:rpi:'dou] (pl torpedoes) n 魚雷 gyorái

torrent [tɔ:r'ənt] n (flood) 急流 kyúryū; (fig) 奔流 hoñryū

torrential [tɔ:ren'tʃəl] adj (rain) 土砂降りの dosháburi no

torrid [tɔ:r'id] adj (sun) しゃく熱の shakúnetsu no; (love affair) 情熱的な jónetsuteki na

torso [tɔ:r'sou] n 胴 dō

tortoise [tɔ:r'təs] n カメ kámè

tortoiseshell [tɔ:r'təsʃel] adj べっ甲の bekkō no

tortuous [tɔ:r'tʃu:əs] adj (path) 曲りくねった magárikunettà; (argument) 回りくどい mawárikudoì; (mind) 邪悪な jaáku na

torture [tɔ:r'tʃər] n (also fig) 拷問 gómon

♦vt (also fig) 拷問にかける gómon nì kakérù

Tory [tɔ:r'i:] (BRIT) adj 保守党の hoshútō no

♦n 保守党員 hoshútòin

toss [tɔ:s] vt (throw) 投げる nagérù; (one's head) 振る furú

to toss a coin コインをトスする kóìn wo tósù suru

to toss up for something コインをトスして...を決める kóìn wo tósù shité ...wò

to toss and turn (in bed) ころげ回る korógemawarù

tot [tɑ:t] n (BRIT: drink) おちょこ一杯 ochókò íppài; (child) 小さい子供 chiísaì kodómo

total [tout'əl] adj (complete: number, workforce etc) 全体の zeñtai no; (: failure, wreck etc) 完全な kañzen na

♦n 合計 gókei

♦vt (add up: numbers, objects) 合計する gókei suru; (add up to: X dollars/ pounds) 合計は...になる gókei wà ...ni nárù

totalitarian [toutæelite:r'i:ən] adj 全体主義の zeñtaishùgi no

totally [tou'təli:] adv (agree, write off, unprepared) 全く mattáku

totter [tɑ:t'ə:r] vi (person) よろめく yorómekù

touch [tʌtʃ] n (sense of touch) 触覚 shokkáku; (contact) 触る事 sawárù kotó

♦vt (with hand, foot) ...に触る ...ni sawárù; (tamper with) いじる ijíru; (make contact with) ...に接触する ...ni sesshóku suru; (emotionally) 感動させる kañdō saserù

a touch of (fig: frost etc) 少しばかり sukóshi bakàri

to get in touch with someone ...に連絡する ...ni reñraku suru

to lose touch (friends) ...との連絡が途絶える ...tó nò reñraku ga todáerù

touch-and-go [tʌtʃ'əngou'] adj 危ない abúnai

touchdown [tʌtʃ'daun] n (of rocket, plane: on land) 着陸 chakúriku; (: on water) 着水 chakúsui; (US FOOTBALL) タッチダウン tatchídaùn

touched [tʌtʃt] adj (moved) 感動した kañdō shita

touching [tʌtʃ'iŋ] adj 感動的な kañdōteki na

touchline [tʌtʃ'lain] n (SPORT) サイドライン saídoraìn

touch on vt fus (topic) ...に触れる ...ni furérù

touch up vt (paint) 修正する shūsei suru

touchy [tʌtʃi:] adj (person) 気難しい ki-múzukashii

tough [tʌf] adj (strong, hard-wearing: material) 丈夫な jõbu na; (meat) 固い ka-tái; (person: physically) 頑丈な gañjõ na; (: mentally) 神経が太い shiñkei gà futõí; (difficult: task, problem, way of life) 難しい muzúkashiì; (firm: stance, negotiations, policies) 譲らない yuzúranaì

toughen [tʌf'ən] vt (someone's character) 強くする tsúyòku suru; (glass etc) 強化する kyõka suru

toupée [tu:pei'] n かつら katsúra ◇男性のはげを隠す小さな物を指す dañsei no hagè wo kakúsù chiīsa na monò wo sásù

tour [tu:r] n (journey) 旅行 ryokõ; (also: **package tour**) ツアー tsúâ; (of town, factory, museum) 見学 keñgaku; (by pop group etc) 巡業 juñgyõ

◆vt (country, city, factory etc) 観光旅行する kañkõryokõ suru; (city) 見物する keñbutsu suru; (factory etc) 見学する keñgaku suru

tourism [tu:r'izəm] n (business) 観光 kañkõ

tourist [tu:r'ist] n 観光客 kañkõkyaku

◆cpd (attractions etc) 観光の kañkõ no

tourist class (on ship, plane) ツーリストクラス tsúrisutokuràsu

tourist office n 観光案内所 kañkõan-naisho

tournament [tu:r'nəmənt] n トーナメント tõnàmento

tousled [tau'zəld] adj (hair) 乱れた midáretà

tout [taut] vi: **to tout for business** (business) 御用聞きする goyõkìki suru

◆n (also: **ticket tout**) だふ屋 dafúyà

tow [tou] vt (vehicle, caravan, trailer) 引く hikú, けん引する keñ in suru

「**in** (US) or (BRIT) **on tow**」 (AUT) けん引中 keñ-iñchū

toward(s) [tɔ:rd(z)] prep (direction) ...の方へ ...no hõ è; (attitude) ...に対して ...ni táīshite; (purpose) ...に向かって ...ni mukátte; (in time) ...のちょっと前に ...no chõttò máè ni

towel [tau'əl] n (hand/bath towel) タオル táòru

towelling [tau'əliŋ] n (fabric) タオル地 taõrujī

towel rack (BRIT: **towel rail**) n タオル掛け taõrukàke

tower [tau'ə:r] n 塔 tõ

tower block (BRIT) n 高層ビル kõsõbirù

towering [tau'ə:riŋ] adj (buildings, trees, cliffs) 高くそびえる tákàku sobíerù; (figure) 体の大きな karáda nò õkì na

town [taun] n 町 machí

to go to town 町に出掛ける machí nì dekákerù; (fig: on something) 思い切りやる omóikiri yarù, 派手にやる hadé nì yárù

town center n 町の中心部 machí nò chūshiñbu

town council n 町議会 chõgikài

town hall n 町役場 machíyakùba

town plan n 町の道路地図 machí nò dõrochizù

town planning n 開発計画 kaíhatsuke-ikàku

towrope [tou'roup] n けん引用ロープ keñ-in-yõ rõpù

tow truck (US) n (breakdown lorry) レッカー車 rekkáshà

toxic [tɑ:k'sik] adj (fumes, waste etc) 有毒の yúdoku no

toy [tɔi] n おもちゃ omóchà

toyshop [tɔi'ʃɑːp] n おもちゃ屋 omóchayà

toy with vt fus (object, food) いじくり回す ijíkurimawasù; (idea) ...しようかなと考えてみる ...shiyõ kà na to kañgaete mirù

trace [treis] n (sign) 跡 átò; (small amount) 微量 biryõ

◆vt (draw) トレースする torésù suru; (follow) 追跡する tsuíseki suru; (locate) 見付ける mitsúkerù

tracing paper [trei'siŋ-] n トレーシングペーパー torḗshingupḕpā

track [træk] n (mark) 跡 átò; (path: gen) 道 michí; (: of bullet etc) 弾道 dáñdõ; (: of suspect, animal) 足跡 ashíatò; (RAIL) 線路 señro; (on tape, record: also SPORT)

トラック torákkù

◆vt (follow: animal, person) 追跡する tsuíseki suru

to keep track of ...を監視する ...wo kañshi suru

track down vt (prey) 追詰める oítsumerù; (something lost) 見付ける mitsúkerù

tracksuit [træk'su:t] n トレーニングウエア toréningu ueà

tract [trækt] n (GEO) 地帯 chitái; (pamphlet) 論文 rońbun

traction [træk'ʃən] n (power) けん引力 keń-iñryoku; (MED): *in traction* けん引療法中 keń-inryōhōchū

tractor [træk'tɚr] n トラクター toráku-tā

trade [treid] n (activity) 貿易 bóeki; (skill) 技術 gíjutsu; (job) 職業 shokúgyō

◆vi (do business) 商売する shóbai suru

◆vt (exchange): *to trade something (for something)* (...と) ...を交換する (...to) ...wò kókan suru

trade fair n トレードフェアー torédofeà

trade in vt (old car etc) 下取に出す shitádori nì dásù

trademark [treid'mɑ:rk] n 商標 shóhyō

trade name n 商品名 shóhiñmei

trader [trei'dɚr] n 貿易業者 bóekigyōsha

tradesman [treidz'mən] (pl **tradesmen**) n 商人 shóniñ

trade union n 労働組合 ródōkumìai

trade unionist [-ju:n'jənist] n 労働組合員 ródōkumiaìin

tradition [trədiʃ'ən] n 伝統 deñtō

traditional [trədiʃ'ənəl] adj (dress, costume, meal) 伝統的な deñtōteki na

traffic [træf'ik] n (movement: of people, vehicles) 往来 órai; (: of drugs etc) 売買 báibai; (air traffic, road traffic etc) 交通 kótsū

◆vi: *to traffic in* (liquor, drugs) 売買する báibai suru

traffic circle (US) n ロータリー rótarī

traffic jam n 交通渋滞 kótsūjūtai

traffic lights npl 信号(機) shiñgō(kì)

traffic warden n 違反駐車取締官 ihán-

chūsha toríshimarikàn

tragedy [trædʒ'idi:] n 悲劇 higéki

tragic [trædʒ'ik] adj (death, consequences) 悲劇的な higékiteki na; (play, novel etc) 悲劇の higéki no

trail [treil] n (path) 小道 kómìchi; (track) 足跡 ashíatò; (of smoke, dust) 尾 ó

◆vt (drag) 後に引く átò ni hikú; (follow: person, animal) 追跡する tsuíseki suru

◆vi (hang loosely) 後ろに垂れる ushíro nì tarérù; (in game, contest) 負けている makéte irù

trail behind vi (lag) 遅れる okúrerù

trailer [trei'lɚr] n (AUT) トレーラー torérà; (US: caravan) キャンピングカー kyañpingukà; (CINEMA) 予告編 yokókuheñ

trailer truck (US) n トレーラートラック torératorakkù

train [trein] n (RAIL) 列車 resshá; (underground train) 地下鉄 chikátetsu; (of dress) トレイン toréiñ

◆vt (educate: mind) 教育する kyóiku suru; (teach skills to: apprentice, doctor, dog etc) 訓練する kuñren suru; (athlete) 鍛える kitáerù; (point: camera, hose, gun etc): *to train on* 向ける mukérù

◆vi (learn a skill) 訓練を受ける kuñren wò ukérù; (SPORT) トレーニングする toréniñgu suru

one's train of thought 考えの流れ kañgaè no nagáre

trained [treind] adj (worker, teacher) 技術が確かな gíjutsu ga táshika na; (animal) 訓練された kuñren saretá

trainee [treini:'] n (apprentice: hairdresser etc) 見習 mináru; (teacher etc) 実習生 jisshúsei

trainer [trei'nɚr] n (SPORT: coach) コーチ kóchi; (: shoe) スニーカー suníkà; (of animals) 訓練師 kuñreñshi

training [trei'niŋ] n (for occupation) 訓練 kúñren; (SPORT) トレーニング toréniñgu

in training トレーニング中 toréningu-chū

training college n (gen) 職業大学 shokúgyōdaigàku; (for teachers) 教育大学

kyōikudaigaku

training shoes *npl* スニーカー suníkà

traipse [treips] *vi* 足を棒にして歩き回る ashí wò bō ni shitè arúkimawarù

trait [treit] *n* 特徴 tokúchō

traitor [trei'tə:r] *n* 裏切者 urágirimòno

tram [træm] *n* (*also*: **tramcar**) 路面電車 roméndeǹsha

tramp [træmp] *n* (person) ルンペン rúǹpen; (*inf: pej*: woman) 浮気女 uwákioǹna

◆*vi* どしんどしん歩く doshíǹdoshin arúkù

trample [træm'pəl] *vt*: **to trample (underfoot)** 踏み付ける fumítsukerù

trampoline [træmpəli:n'] *n* トランポリン toráǹporin

trance [træns] *n* (*gen*) こん睡状態 koǹsuijōtai; (*fig*) ぼう然とした状態 bōzen to shitá jōtai

tranquil [træŋ'kwil] *adj* (place, old age) 平穏な heíon na; (sleep) 静かな shízùka na

tranquillity [træŋkwil'iti:] *n* 平静さ heíseisà

tranquillizer [træŋ'kwəlaizə:r] *n* (MED) 鎮静剤 chiǹseizai

transact [trænsækt'] *vt*: **to transact business** 取引する toríhìki suru

transaction [trænsæk'ʃən] *n* (piece of business) 取引 toríhìki

transatlantic [trænsətlæn'tik] *adj* (trade, phone-call etc) 英米間の eíbeikàn no

transcend [trænsend'] *vt* 越える koérù

transcript [træn'skript] *n* (of tape recording etc) 記録文書 kiróku buǹsho

transfer [træns'fə:r] *n* (moving: of employees etc) 異動 idō; (: of money) 振替 furíkaè; (POL: of power) 引継ぎ hikítsugi; (SPORT) トレード torédò; (picture, design) 写し絵 utsúshiè

◆*vt* (move: employees) 転任させる teǹnin saserù; (: money) 振替える furíkaerù; (: power) 譲る yuzúrù

to transfer the charges (*BRIT*: TEL) コレクトコールにする korékutokòru ni suru

transform [trænsfɔ:rm'] *vt* 変化させる

héǹka saserù

transformation [trænsfə:rmei'ʃən] *n* 変化 héǹka

transfusion [trænsfju:'ʒən] *n* (*also*: **blood transfusion**) 輸血 yukétsu

transient [træn'ʃənt] *adj* 一時的な ichíjiteki na

transistor [trænzis'tə:r] *n* (ELEC) トランジスタ toráǹjisùta; (*also*: **transistor radio**) トランジスタラジオ toráǹjisuta rajìo

transit [træn'sit] *n*: **in transit** (people, things) 通過中の tsūkachū no

transition [trænziʃ'ən] *n* 移行 ikō

transitional [trænziʃ'ənəl] *adj* (period, stage) 移行の ikō no

transitive [træn'sətiv] *adj* (LING): **transitive verb** 他動詞 tadōshì

transit lounge *n* (at airport etc) トランジットラウンジ toráǹjitto raùnji

transitory [træn'sitɔ:ri:] *adj* つかの間の tsuká no ma nò

translate [trænz'leit] *vt* (word, book etc) 翻訳する hoń-yaku suru

translation [trænzlei'ʃən] *n* (act/result of translating) 訳 yákù

translator [trænslei'tə:r] *n* 訳者 yákùsha

transmission [trænsmiʃ'ən] *n* (of information, disease) 伝達 deńtatsu; (TV: broadcasting, program broadcast) 放送 hōsō; (AUT) トランスミッション toráǹsumisshòn

transmit [trænsmit'] *vt* (message, signal, disease) 伝達する deńtatsu suru

transmitter [trænsmit'ə:r] *n* (piece of equipment) トランスミッタ toráǹsumittà

transparency [trænsper'ənsi:] *n* (of glass etc) 透明度 tōmeìdo; (PHOT: slide) スライド suráìdo

transparent [trænsper'ənt] *adj* (seethrough) 透明の tōmei no

transpire [trænspaiə:r'] *vi* (turn out) 明らかになる akíràka ni nárù; (happen) 起る okórù

transplant [*vb* trænzplænt' *n* trænz'plænt] *vt* (seedlings: *also*: MED: organ)

移植する ishóku suru
◆*n* (MED) 移植 ishóku

transport [*n* trǽns'pɔːrt *vb* trænspɔːrt'] *n* (moving people, goods) 輸送 yusō; (*also*: **road/rail transport** *etc*) 輸送機関 yusōkikàn; (car) 車 kurúma
◆*vt* (carry) 輸送する yusō suru

transportation [trænspəːrtei'ʃən] *n* (transport) 輸送 yusō; (means of transport) 輸送機関 yusōkikàn

transport café (*BRIT*) *n* トラック運転手向きのレストラン torákkuunteǹshu mukí nò resútoraǹ

transvestite [trænsves'tait] *n* 女装趣味の男性 josōshùmi no daǹsei

trap [træp] *n* (snare, trick) わな wánà; (carriage) 軽馬車 keíbashà
◆*vt* (animal) わなで捕える wánà de toraérù; (person: trick) わなにかける wánà ni kakérù; (: confine: in bad marriage, burning building): **to be trapped** 逃げられなくなっている nigérarenakù natté irù

trap door *n* 落し戸 otóshidò

trapeze [træpi:z'] *n* 空中ぶらんこ kūchūburaǹko

trappings [træp'iŋz] *npl* 飾り kazári

trash [træʃ] *n* (rubbish: *also pej*) ごみ gomí; (: nonsense) でたらめ detáramè

trash can (*US*) *n* ごみ入れ gomíirè

trauma [trɔː'mə] *n* 衝撃 shōgeki, ショック shókkù

traumatic [trɔːmæt'ik] *adj* 衝撃的な shōgekiteki na

travel [træv'əl] *n* (traveling) 旅行 ryokō
◆*vi* (person) 旅行する ryokō suru; (news, sound) 伝わる tsutáwarù; (wine etc): **to travel well/badly** 運搬に耐えられる〔耐えられない〕uǹpan nì taérarerù (taérarenaì)
◆*vt* (distance) 旅行する ryokō suru

travel agency *n* 旅行代理店 ryokódairitèn

travel agent *n* 旅行業者 ryokōgyòsha

traveler [træv'ələːr] (*BRIT* **traveller**) *n* 旅行者 ryokōshà

traveler's check [træv'ələːrz-] (*BRIT* **traveller's cheque**) *n* トラベラーズチェ

ック toráberāzuchekkù

traveling [træv'əliŋ] (*BRIT* **travelling**) *n* 旅行 ryokō

travels [træv'əlz] *npl* (journeys) 旅行 ryokō

travel sickness *n* 乗物酔い norímonoyoì

travesty [træv'isti] *n* パロディー páròdī

trawler [trɔː'ləːr] *n* トロール漁船 torōrugyòsen

tray [trei] *n* (for carrying) お盆 o-bóǹ; (on desk) デスクトレー desúkutorè

treacherous [tretʃ'əːrəs] *adj* (person, look) 裏切りの urágirimòno no; (ground, tide) 危険な kikén na

treachery [tretʃ'əːri] *n* 裏切り urágirì

treacle [tri:'kəl] *n* 糖みつ tōmitsu

tread [tred] *n* (step) 歩調 hochō; (sound) 足音 ashíotò; (of stair) 踏面 fumízùra; (of tire) トレッド toréddò
◆*vi* (*pt* **trod**, *pp* **trodden**) 歩く arúkù

tread on *vt fus* 踏む fumú

treason [tri:'zən] *n* 反逆罪 haǹgyakuzài

treasure [treʒ'əːr] *n* (gold, jewels etc) 宝物 takáramono; (person) 重宝な人 chōhō nà hitó
◆*vt* (value: object) 重宝する chōhō suru; (: friendship) 大事にしている daíji nì shité irù; (: memory, thought) 心に銘記する kokórò ni méìki suru

treasurer [treʒ'əːrəːr] *n* 会計 kaíkei

treasures [treʒ'əːrz] *npl* (art treasures etc) 貴重品 kichōhìn

treasury [treʒ'əːri] *n*: (*US*) **the Treasury Department**, (*BRIT*) **the Treasury** 大蔵省 ōkurashō

treat [tri:t] *n* (present) 贈物 okúrimono
◆*vt* (handle, regard: person, object) 扱う atsúkaù; (MED: patient, illness) 治療する chiryō suru; (TECH: coat) 処理する shōrì suru

to treat someone to something ...に...をおごる ...ni ...wo ogórù

treatment [tri:t'mənt] *n* (attention, handling) 扱い方 atsúkaikata; (MED) 治療 chiryō

treaty [tri:'ti:] *n* 協定 kyōtei

treble [treb'əl] *adj* 3倍の saǹbai no;

(MUS) 高音部の kŏonbu no
♦vt 3倍にする sañbai nǐ suru
♦vi 3倍になる sañbai ni narù

treble clef n (MUS) 高音部記号 kŏonbu-kigŏ

tree [tri:] n 木 kí

tree trunk n 木の幹 kí nò míkì

trek [trek] n (long difficult journey: on foot) 徒歩旅行 tohóryokŏ; (: by car) 自動車旅行 jidŏsharyokŏ; (tiring walk) 苦しい道のり kurúshiì michínori

trellis [trel'is] n (for climbing plants) 棚 taná

tremble [trem'bəl] vi (voice, body, trees: with fear, cold etc) 震える furúerù; (ground) 揺れる yurérù

tremendous [trimen'dəs] adj (enormous: amount etc) ばく大な bakúdai na; (excellent: success, holiday, view etc) 素晴らしい subárashiì

tremor [trem'əːr] n (trembling: of excitement, fear: in voice) 震え furúè; (also: **earth tremor**) 地震 jishín

trench [trentʃ] n (channel) 溝 mizó; (for defense) ざんごう zañgō

trend [trend] n (tendency) 傾向 keíkō; (of events) 動向 dŏkō; (fashion) トレンド toréñdo

trendy [tren'di:] adj (idea, person, clothes) トレンディな toréñdi na

trepidation [trepidei'ʃən] n (apprehension) 不安 fuáñ

trespass [tres'pæs] vi: **to trespass on** (private property) ...に不法侵入する ...ni fuhŏshiñnyū suru
「**no trespassing**」立入禁止 tachíirikiñshi

trestle [tres'əl] n (support for table etc) うま umá

trial [trail] n (LAW) 裁判 saíban; (test: of machine etc) テスト tésùto
on trial (LAW) 裁判に掛けられて saíban ni kakéraretè
by trial and error 試行錯誤で shikŏsakùgo de

trial period n テスト期間 tesúto kikàn

trials [trailz] npl (unpleasant experiences) 試練 shírèn

triangle [trai'æŋgəl] n (MATH) 三角 sáñkaku; (MUS) トライアングル toráiañguru

triangular [traiæŋ'gjələːr] adj 三角形の sañkakkèi no

tribal [trai'bəl] adj (warrior, warfare, dance) 種族の shúzòku no

tribe [traib] n 種族 shúzòku

tribesman [traibz'mən] (pl **tribesmen**) n 種族の男性 shúzòku no dañsei

tribulations [tribjəlei'ʃənz] npl 苦労 kúrò, 苦難 kúnàn

tribunal [traibju:'nəl] n 審判委員会 shiñpan iiñkai

tributary [trib'jəte:ri:] n 支流 shiryū

tribute [trib'ju:t] n (compliment) ほめの言葉 homé no kotobà
to pay tribute to ...をほめる ...wò homérù

trice [trais] n: **in a trice** あっという間に áttò iú ma nǐ

trick [trik] n (magic trick) 手品 téjìna; (prank, joke) いたずら itázura; (skill, knack) こつ kotsú; (CARDS) トリック toríkkù
♦vt (deceive) だます damásù
to play a trick on someone ...にいたずらをする ...ni itázura wò suru
that should do the trick これでいいはずだ koré de iì hazú dà

trickery [trik'əːri:] n 計略 keíryaku

trickle [trik'əl] n (of water etc) 滴り shitátari
♦vi (water, rain etc) 滴る shitátarù

tricky [trik'i:] adj (job, problem, business) 厄介な yákkài na

tricycle [trai'sikəl] n 三輪車 sañriñsha

trifle [trai'fəl] n (small detail) ささいな事 sásài na kotŏ; (CULIN) トライフル toráìfuru◇カステラにゼリー, フルーツ, プリンなどをのせたデザート kasútera nǐ zérì, furútsù, púrìn nádò wo nosétà dezátò
♦adv: **a trifle long** ちょっと長い chóttò nagáì

trifling [traif'liŋ] adj (detail, matter) ささいな sásài na

trigger [trig'əːr] n (of gun) 引金 hikígane

trigger off vt (reaction, riot) ...の引金となる ...no hikígane tò nárù

trigonometry [trigənə:m'ətri:] n 三角法 sañkakuhõ

trill [tril] vi (birds) さえずる saézurù

trim [trim] adj (house, garden) 手入れの行届いた teíre nò ikítodoità; (figure) すらっとした suráttò shitá

♦n (haircut etc) 刈る事 karú kotò; (on car) 飾り kazári

♦vt (cut: hair, beard) 刈る karú; (decorate): **to trim (with)** (...で) 飾る (...de) kazárù; (NAUT: a sail) 調節する chõsetsu surú

trimmings [trim'iŋz] npl (CULIN) お飾りの付け合せ o-kímàri no tsukéawase

trinket [triŋ'kit] n (ornament) 安い置物 yasúì okímono; (piece of jewellery) 安い装身具 yasúì sōshiñgu

trio [tri:'ou] n (gen) 三つ組 mitsúgumi; (MUS) 三重奏 tórìo

trip [trip] n (journey) 旅行 ryokõ; (outing) 遠足 eñsoku; (stumble) つまずき tsumázuki

♦vi (stumble) つまずく tsumázukù; (go lightly) 軽快に歩く keíkai nì arúkù
on a trip 旅行中で ryokõchū de

tripe [traip] n (CULIN) トライプ toráìpu◇ウシ、ブタなどの胃の料理 ushí, butá nadò no i no ryõri; (pej: rubbish) 下らない物 kudaranai mono◇特に人の発言や文書について言う tókù ni hitó nò hatsúgen yà búñsho ni tsúìte iú

triple [trip'əl] adj (ice cream, somersault etc) トリプルの torípùru no

triplets [trip'lits] npl 三つ子 mitsúgo

triplicate [trip'ləkit] n: **in triplicate** 三通で sañtsū de

tripod [trai'pa:d] n 三脚 sañkyaku

trip up vi (stumble) つまずく tsumázukù

♦vt (person) つまずかせる tsumázukaserù

trite [trait] adj 陳腐な chíñpu na

triumph [trai'əmf] n (satisfaction) 大満足 daímañzoku; (great achievement) 輝かしい勝利 kagáyakashiî shõrì

♦vi: **to triumph (over)** (...に) 打勝つ (...ni) uchíkatsù

triumphant [traiʌm'fənt] adj (team, wave, return) 意気揚々とした íkìyõyõ to shitá

trivia [triv'i:ə] npl 詰まらない事 tsumáranai kotõ

trivial [triv'i:əl] adj (unimportant) 詰まらない tsumáranaî; (commonplace) 平凡な heíbon na

trod [tra:d] pt of tread

trodden [tra:d'ən] pp of tread

trolley [tra:l'i:] n (for luggage, shopping, also in supermarkets) 手車 tegúruma; (table on wheels) ワゴン wágòn; (also: **trolley bus**) トロリーバス toróríbasu

trombone [tra:mboun'] n トロンボーン toróñbōn

troop [tru:p] n (of people, monkeys etc) 群れ muré

troop in/out vi ぞろぞろと入って来る〔出て行く〕zóròzoro to haítte kurù〔détè iku〕

trooping the color [tru:p'iŋ-] (BRIT) n (ceremony) 軍旗敬礼の分列行進 kuñkikeírei no buñretsu kõshin

troops [tru:ps] npl (MIL) 兵隊 heítai

trophy [trou'fi:] n トロフィー tóròfī

tropic [tra:p'ik] n 回帰線 kaíkisèn
the tropics 熱帯地方 nettái chihõ

tropical [tra:p'ikəl] adj (rain forest etc) 熱帯 (地方) の nettái(chihõ) no

trot [tra:t] n (fast pace) 小走り kobáshìri; (of horse) 速足 hayáàshi, トロット toróttò

♦vi (horse) トロットで駆ける toróttò de kakérù; (person) 小走りで行く kobáshìri de ikú

on the trot (BRIT: fig) 立続けに tatétsuzuke ni

trouble [trʌb'əl] n (difficulty) 困難 koñnan; (worry) 心配 shíñpai; (bother, effort) 苦労 kúrõ; (unrest) トラブル torábùru; (MED): **heart etc trouble** ...病 ...byõ

♦vt (worry) ...に心配を掛ける ...ni shiñpai wò kakérù; (person: disturb) 面倒をかける meñdõ wo kakérù

♦*vi*: *to trouble to do something* わざわざ...する wázawaza ...suru

to be in trouble (*gen*) 困っている komátte irù; (ship, climber etc) 危険にあっている kikén ni atte irù

it's no trouble! 迷惑ではありませんから mêiwaku de wa arímasen kará

what's the trouble? (with broken television etc) どうなっていますか dô natté imasù ká; (doctor to patient) いかがですか ikága desù ká

troubled [trʌb'əld] *adj* (person, country, life, era) 不安な fuáñ na

troublemaker [trʌb'əlmeikər] *n* トラブルを起す常習犯 toráburu wo okósù jôshūhan; (child) 問題児 mofídaìji

troubles [trʌb'əlz] *npl* (personal, POL etc) 問題 mofídai

troubleshooter [trʌb'əlʃuːtər] *n* (in conflict) 調停人 chôteinìn

troublesome [trʌb'əlsəm] *adj* (child, cough etc) 厄介な yákkai na

trough [trɔːf] *n* (*also*: **drinking trough**) 水入れ mizúirè; (feeding trough) えさ入れ esá-irè; (depression) 谷間 taníma

troupe [truːp] *n* (of actors, singers, dancers) 団 dáñ

trousers [trau'zəːrz] *npl* ズボン zubóñ

short trousers 半ズボン hañzubòn

trousseau [truː'sou] (*pl* **trousseaux** *or* **trousseaus**) *n* 嫁入り道具 yomé-iri dògu

trout [traut] *n inv* マス masu

trowel [trau'əl] *n* (garden tool) 移植ごて ishókugòte; (builder's tool) こて kotê

truant [truː'ənt] (*BRIT*) *n*: *to play truant* 学校をサボる gakkô wo sabórù

truce [truːs] *n* 休戦 kyûsen

truck [trʌk] *n* (*US*) トラック torákkù; (RAIL) 台車 daíshà

truck driver *n* トラック運転手 torákku unteñshu

truck farm (*US*) *n* 野菜農園 yasáinòen

trudge [trʌdʒ] *vi* (*also*: **trudge along**) とぼとぼ歩く tóbotobo arúkù

true [truː] *adj* (real: motive) 本当の hoñtô no; (accurate: likeness) 正確な seíkaku na; (genuine: love) 本物の hoñmono no; (faithful: friend) 忠実な chûjitsu na

to come true (dreams, predictions) 実現される jitsúgen sarerù

truffle [trʌf'əl] *n* (fungus) トリュフ tóryùfu; (sweet) トラッフル toráffùru ◇菓子の一種 káshì no ísshù

truly [truː'liː] *adv* (really) 本当に hoñtô ni; (truthfully) 真実に shíñjitsu ni; (faithfully): *yours truly* (in letter) 敬具 keígu

trump [trʌmp] *n* (*also*: **trump card**: *also fig*) 切札 kirífùda

trumped-up [trʌmpt'ʌp'] *adj* (charge, pretext) でっち上げた detchíagetà

trumpet [trʌm'pit] *n* トランペット toráñpetto

truncheon [trʌn'tʃən] *n* 警棒 keíbō

trundle [trʌn'dəl] *vt* (push chair etc) ごろごろ動かす górògoro ugókasù

♦*vi*: *to trundle along* (vehicle) 重そうに動く omósò ni ugókù; (person) ゆっくり行く yukkúrì ikú

trunk [trʌŋk] *n* (of tree, person) 幹 mfkì; (of person) 胴 dô; (of elephant) 鼻 haná; (case) トランク toráñku; (*US*: AUT) トランク toráñku

trunks [trʌŋks] *npl* (*also*: **swimming trunks**) 水泳パンツ suíei pañtsu

truss [trʌs] *n* (MED) ヘルニアバンド herúnia bañdo

truss (up) *vt* (CULIN) 縛る shibárù

trust [trʌst] *n* (faith) 信用 shiñ-yō; (responsibility) 責任 sekínin; (LAW) 信託 shíntaku

♦*vt* (rely on, have faith in) 信用する shiñyō suru; (hope) きっと ...だろうね kittó ...dárò né; (entrust): *to trust something to someone* ...を...に任せる ...wo ...ni makáserù

to take something on trust (advice, information) 証拠なしで...を信じる shôko nashì de ...wo shiñjirù

trusted [trʌs'tid] *adj* (friend, servant) 信用された shiñ-yō saretà

trustee [trʌstiː'] *n* (LAW) 受託者 jutákushà; (of school etc) 理事 ríjì

trustful/trusting [trʌst'fəl/trʌs'tiŋ] *adj* (person, nature, smile) 信用する shiñyō suru

trustworthy [trʌst'wəːrðiː] *adj* (person,

report) 信用できる shiń-yō dekirù
truth [tru:θ] *n* (true fact) 真実 shíńjitsu; (universal principle) 真理 shíńri
truthful [tru:θ'fəl] *adj* (person, answer) 正直な shójiki na
try [trai] *n* (attempt) 努力 dóryoku; (RUGBY) トライ toráī
◆*vt* (attempt) やってみる yatté mirù; (test: something new: *also*: **try out**) 試す tamésù; (LAW: person) 裁判にかける sáiban ni kakérù; (strain: patience) ぎりぎりまで追込む girígiri madè oíkomù
◆*vi* (make effort, attempt) 努力する dóryoku suru
to have a try やってみる yatté mirù
to try to do something (seek) ...をしようとする ...wo shíyō to suru
trying [trai'iŋ] *adj* (person) 気難しい kimúzukashiĩ; (experience) 苦しい kurúshiĩ
try on *vt* (dress, hat, shoes) 試着する shicháku suru
tsar [zɑ:r] *n* ロシア皇帝 roshía kótei
T-shirt [ti:'ʃə:rt] *n* Tシャツ tíshatsu
T-square [ti:'skwe:r] *n* T定規 tíjōgi
tub [tʌb] *n* (container: shallow) たらい taráī; (: deeper) おけ ókè; (bath) 湯舟 yúbùne
tuba [tu:'bə] *n* チューバ chúba
tubby [tʌb'i:] *adj* 太った futóttà
tube [tu:b] *n* (pipe) 管 kúdà; (container, in tire) チューブ chúbu; (BRIT: underground) 地下鉄 chikátetsu
tuberculosis [tu:bə:rkjəlou'sis] *n* 結核 kekkáku
tube station (BRIT) *n* 地下鉄の駅 chikátetsu nò ékì
tubular [tu:'bjələr] *adj* (furniture, metal) 管状の kańjō no; (furniture) パイプ型の paípusei no
TUC [ti:ju:si:'] *n abbr* (BRIT: = Trades Union Congress) 英国労働組合会議 eíkoku ródōkumiai kaígi
tuck [tʌk] *vt* (put) 押込む oshíkomù
tuck away *vt* (money) 仕舞い込む shimáikomù; (building): *to be tucked away* 隠れている kakúrete irù
tuck in *vt* (clothing) 押込む oshíkomù;

(child) 毛布にくるんで寝かせる mófù ni kurúnde nekáserù
◆*vi* (eat) かぶりつく kabúritsukù
tuck shop (BRIT) *n* 売店 baíten ◇学校内でお菓子などを売る売店を指す gakkónaī de o-káshi nadò wo urú baíten wò sásù
tuck up *vt* (invalid, child) 毛布にくるんで寝かせる mófù ni kurúnde nekáserù
Tuesday [tu:z'dei] *n* 火曜日 kayóbì
tuft [tʌft] *n* (of hair, grass etc) 一房 hitófùsa
tug [tʌg] *n* (ship) タグボート tagúbòto
◆*vt* 引っ張る hippárù
tug-of-war [tʌg'əvwɔ:r'] *n* (SPORT) 綱引き tsunáhiki; (fig) 競り合い seríaī ◇二者間の競り合いを指す nishákàn no seríaī wo sásù
tuition [tu:iʃ'ən] *n* (BRIT) 教授 kyójù; (: private tuition) 個人教授 kojínkyòju; (US: school fees) 授業料 jugyóryð
tulip [tu:'lip] *n* チューリップ chúrippu
tumble [tʌm'bəl] *n* (fall) 転ぶ事 koróbu kotð
◆*vi* (fall: person) 転ぶ koróbù; (water) 落ちる ochírù
to tumble to something (inf) ...に気が付く ...ni ki gá tsukù
tumbledown [tʌm'bəldaun] *adj* (building) 荒れ果てた aréhatetà
tumble dryer (BRIT) *n* 乾燥機 kańsōki
tumbler [tʌm'blə:r] *n* (glass) コップ koppú
tummy [tʌm'i:] (inf) *n* (belly, stomach) おなか onáka
tumor [tu:'mə:r] (BRIT **tumour**) *n* しゅよう shuyó
tumult [tu:'mʌlt] *n* 大騒ぎ ósawàgi
tumultuous [tu:mʌl'tʃuːəs] *adj* (welcome, applause etc) にぎやかな nigíyàka na
tuna [tu:'nə] *n inv* (also: **tuna fish**) マグロ maguro; (in can, sandwich) ツナ tsúnà
tune [tu:n] *n* (melody) 旋律 seńritsu
◆*vt* (MUS) 調律する chóritsu suru; (RADIO, TV) 合せる awáserù; (AUT) チューンアップする chún-appù suru
to be in/out of tune (instrument, singer)

調子が合って〔外れて〕いる chōshi gà atte 〔hazúrete〕irù

to be in/out of tune with (fig) ...と気が合っている〔いない〕...to ki gá atte irù 〔inái〕

tuneful [tuːnˈfəl] *adj* (music) 旋律のきれいな senritsu no kírèi na

tuner [tuːˈnəːr] *n*: *piano tuner* 調律師 chōritsushì

tune in *vi* (RADIO, TV): *to tune in (to)* (...を) 聞く (...wo) kikú

tune up *vi* (musician, orchestra) 調子を合せる chōshi wò awáserù

tunic [tuːˈnik] *n* (passage) チュニック chuníkkù

Tunisia [tuːniːˈʒə] *n* チュニジア chuníjìa

tunnel [tʌnˈəl] *n* (passage) トンネル toníneru; (in mine) 坑道 kōdo

♦*vi* トンネルを掘る toníneru wo hórù

turban [təːrˈbən] *n* ターバン tában

turbine [təːrˈbain] *n* タービン tábìn

turbulence [təːrˈbjələns] *n* (AVIAT) 乱気流 rankiryū

turbulent [təːrˈbjələnt] *adj* (water) 荒れ狂う arékuruù; (fig: career) 起伏の多い kífùku no ōi

tureen [təriːnˈ] *n* スープ鉢 sūpubàchi, チューリン chūrìn

turf [təːrf] *n* (grass) 芝生 shibáfu; (clod) 芝土 shibátsuchi

♦*vt* (area) 芝生を敷く shibáfu wò shikú

turf out (inf) *vt* (person) 追出す oídasù

turgid [təːrˈdʒid] *adj* (speech) 仰々しい gyōgyōshíì

Turk [təːrk] *n* トルコ人 torúkojìn

Turkey [təːrˈkiː] *n* トルコ tórùko

turkey [təːrˈkiː] *n* (bird, meat) 七面鳥 shichímenchò, ターキー tákì

Turkish [təːrˈkiʃ] *adj* トルコの tórùko no; (LING) トルコ語の torúkogò no

♦*n* (LING) トルコ語 torúkogò

Turkish bath *n* トルコ風呂 torúkobùro

turmoil [təːrˈmoil] *n* 混乱 koñran

in turmoil 混乱して koñran shitè

turn [təːrn] *n* (change) 変化 héñka; (in road) カーブ kābu; (tendency: of mind, events) 傾向 keíkō; (performance) 出し物 dashímòno; (chance) 番 báñ; (MED) 発作 hossá

♦*vt* (handle, key) 回す mawásù; (collar, page) めくる mekúrù; (steak) 裏返す urágaesù; (change): *to turn something into* ...を...に変える ...wo ...ni kaérù

♦*vi* (object) 回る mawárù; (person: look back) 振向く furímukù; (reverse direction: in car) Uターンする yūtàn suru; (: wind) 向きが変る múkì ga kawárù; (milk) 悪くなる wáruku nárù; (become) なる nárù

a good turn 親切 shíñsetsu

it gave me quite a turn ああ、怖かった ā, kowákattà

「no left turn」 (AUT) 左折禁止 sasétsukinshi

it's your turn あなたの番です anáta nò báñ desu

in turn 次々と tsugítsugi tò

to take turns (at) 交替で (...を) する kōtai dè (...wo) suru

turn away *vi* 顔をそむける kaó wò somúkerù

♦*vt* (applicants) 門前払いする moñzenbarài suru

turn back *vi* 引返す hikíkaesù

♦*vt* (person, vehicle) 引返させる hikíkaesaserù; (clock) 遅らせる okúraserù

turn down *vt* (refuse: request) 断る kotówarù; (reduce: heating) 弱くする yówàku suru; (fold: bedclothes) 折返す oríkaesù

turn in *vi* (inf: go to bed) 寝る nerú

♦*vt* (fold) 折込む oríkomù

turning [təːrˈniŋ] *n* (in road) 曲り角 magárikadò

turning point *n* (fig) 変り目 kawárimè

turnip [təːrˈnip] *n* カブ kábù

turn off *vi* (from road) 横道に入る yokómichi nì háìru

♦*vt* (light, radio etc) 消す kesú; (tap) ...の水を止める ...no mizú wò tomérù; (engine) 止める tomérù

turn on *vi* (light, radio etc) つける tsukérù; (tap) ...の水を出す ...no mizú wò dásù; (engine) かける kakérù

turn out *vt* (light, gas) 消す kesú; (produce) 作る tsukúrù

♦*vi* (voters) 出る dérù

to turn out to be (prove to be) 結局...で あると分かる kekkyókú ...de árù to wa-karu

turnout [təːrnˈaut] *n* (of voters etc) 人出 hitóde

turn over *vi* (person) 寝返りを打つ ne-gáeri wò utsù
♦*vt* (object) 引っ繰り返す hikkúrikaesu; (page) めくる mekúrù

turnover [təːrnˈouvəːr] *n* (COMM: amount of money) 売上高 uríagedàka; (: of goods) 回転率 kaíteńritsu; (: of staff) 異動率 idóritsu

turnpike [təːrnˈpaik] (*US*) *n* 有料道路 yūryódòro

turn round *vi* (person) 振り向く furímu-kù; (vehicle) Uターンする yútàn suru; (rotate) 回転する kaíten suru

turnstile [təːrnˈstail] *n* ターンスタイル táǹsutaìru

turntable [təːrnˈteibəl] *n* (on record player) ターンテーブル táǹtèburu

turn up *vi* (person) 現れる aráwarerù; (lost object) 見付かる mitsúkarù
♦*vt* (collar) 立てる tatérù; (radio, stereo etc) ...のボリュームを上げる ...no boryú-mu wò agérù; (heater) 強くする tsúyòku suru

turn-up [təːrnˈʌp] (*BRIT*) *n* (on trousers) 折返し oríkaeshi

turpentine [təːrˈpəntain] *n* (*also*: **turps**) テレビン油 teríbiǹ-yu

turquoise [təːrˈkɔiz] *n* (stone) トルコ石 torúkoìshi
♦*adj* (color) 青みどりの aómidòri no

turret [təːrˈit] *n* (on building) 小塔 shótò; (on tank) 旋回砲塔 seńkaihōtō

turtle [təːrˈtəl] *n* カメ kámè

turtleneck (sweater) [təːrˈtəlnek-] *n* タートルネック tátorunekkù

tusk [tʌsk] *n* きば kíbà

tussle [tʌsˈəl] *n* (fight, scuffle) 取っ組み合い tokkúmiaì

tutor [tuːˈtəːr] *n* (SCOL) チューター chū-tā; (private tutor) 家庭教師 katéikyòshi

tutorial [tuːtɔːrˈiːəl] *n* (SCOL) 討論授業 tóroñjugyō

tuxedo [tʌksiːˈdou] (*US*) *n* タキシード ta-kíshìdo

TV [tiːviː] *n abbr* = **television**

twang [twæŋ] *n* (of instrument) びゅんという音 byún to iú otò; (of voice) 鼻声 hanágoè

tweed [twiːd] *n* ツイード tsuídò

tweezers [twiːˈzəːrz] *npl* ピンセット píǹ-setto

twelfth [twelfθ] *num* 第十二の dáí jūni no

twelve [twelv] *num* 十二 (の) júnì (no)
at twelve (o'clock) (midday) 正午に shógò ni; (midnight) 零時に reiji ni

twentieth [twenˈtiːiθ] *num* 第二十の dáí níjù no

twenty [twenˈtiː] *num* 二十 (の) níjù (no)

twice [twais] *adv* 2回 nikáí
twice as much ...の二倍 ...no nibái

twiddle [twidˈəl] *vt* いじくる ijíkurù
♦*vi: to twiddle (with) something* ...をいじくる ...wo ijíkurù
to twiddle one's thumbs (*fig*) 手をこまねく té wò kománekù

twig [twig] *n* 小枝 kóeda
♦*vi* (*inf*: realize) 気が付く ki gá tsukù

twilight [twaiˈlait] *n* 夕暮 yūgure

twin [twin] *adj* (sister, brother) 双子の futágo no; (towers, beds etc) 対の tsuí no, ツインの tsuíñ no
♦*n* 双子の一人 futágo nò hitórì
♦*vt* (towns etc) 姉妹都市にする shimáitoshì ni suru

twin-bedded room [twinˈbedid-] *n* ツインルーム tsuíǹrùmu

twine [twain] *n* ひも himó
♦*vi* (plant) 巻付く makítsukù

twinge [twindʒ] *n* (of pain) うずき uzúki; (of conscience) かしゃく kasháku; (of regret) 苦しみ kurúshimi

twinkle [twiŋˈkəl] *vi* (star, light, eyes) きらめく kirámekù

twirl [twəːrl] *vt* くるくる回す kúrùkuru mawásù
♦*vi* くるくる回る kúrùkuru mawárù

twist [twist] *n* (action) ひねり hinéri; (in road, coil, flex) 曲りmagári; (in story) ひねり hinéri

♦*vt* (turn) ひ ねる hinérù; (injure: ankle etc) ねんざする neñza suru; (weave) より合さる yoríawasarù; (roll around) 巻付ける makítsukerù; (fig: meaning, words) 曲げる magérù

♦*vi* (road, river) 曲りくねる magárikunerù

twit [twit] (*inf*) *n* ばか bákà

twitch [twitʃ] *n* (pull) ぐいと引く事 guítò hikú kotò; (nervous) 引きつり hikítsuri

♦*vi* (muscle, body) 引きつる hikítsurù

two [tu:] *num* 二（の）ní (no), 二つ（の）futátsū (no)

to put two and two together (*fig*) あれこれを総合してなぞを解く arékòre wo sōgō shitè nazó wò tókù

two-door [tu:'dɔ:r] *adj* (AUT) ツードアの tsúdoà no

two-faced [tu:'feist] (*pej*) *adj* (person) 二枚舌の nimáijita no

twofold [tu:'fould] *adv*: *to increase twofold* 倍になる bai ni narù

two-piece (suit) [tu:'pi:s-] *n* ツーピースの服 tsúpìsu no fukú

two-piece (swimsuit) *n* ツーピースの水着 tsúpìsu no mizúgi

twosome [tu:'səm] *n* (people) 二人組 futárigùmi

two-way [tu:'wei'] *adj*: *two-way traffic* 両方向交通 ryṓhōkōkōtsū

tycoon [taiku:n'] *n*: *(business) tycoon* 大物実業家 ōmonojitsugyōka

type [taip] *n* (category, model, example) 種類 shúrùi; (TYP) 活字 katsúji

♦*vt* (letter etc) タイプする táìpu suru

type-cast [taip'kæst] *adj* (actor) はまり役の hamáriyaku no

typeface [taip'feis] *n* 書体 shotái

typescript [taip'skript] *n* タイプライターで打った原稿 taípuraìtā de úttà geñkō

typewriter [taip'raitə:r] *n* タイプライター taípuraìtā

typewritten [taip'ritən] *adj* タイプライターで打った taípuraìtā de úttà

typhoid [tai'fɔid] *n* 腸チフス chốchifùsu

typhoon [taifu:n'] *n* 台風 taffū

typical [tip'ikəl] *adj* 典型的な teñikeiteki na

typify [tip'əfai] *vt* ...の典型的な例である ...no teñikeiteki na reí de arù

typing [tai'piŋ] *n* タイプライターを打つ事 taípuraìtā wo útsù kotó

typist [tai'pist] *n* タイピスト taípisùto

tyranny [ti:r'əni:] *n* 暴政 bōsei

tyrant [tai'rənt] *n* 暴君 bốkun

tyre [taiə:r] (*BRIT*) *n* = **tire**

tzar [zɑ:r] *n* = **tsar**

U

U-bend [ju:'bend] *n* (in pipe) トラップ toráppù

ubiquitous [ju:bik'witəs] *adj* いたる所にある itáru tokoro nì aru

udder [ʌd'ə:r] *n* 乳房 chibúsa ◇ ウシ, ヤギなどについて言う ushí, yagí nado ni tsuite iú

UFO [ju:efou'] *n abbr* (= *unidentified flying object*) 未確認飛行物体 mikákunin hikōbuttài, ユーフォー yūfố

Uganda [ju:gæn'də] *n* ウガンダ ugáñda

ugh [ʌ] *excl* おえっ oét

ugliness [ʌg'li:nis] *n* 醜さ miníkusà

ugly [ʌg'li:] *adj* (person, dress etc) 醜い miníkuì; (dangerous: situation) 物騒な bussố nà

UK [ju:'kei'] *n abbr* = **United Kingdom**

ulcer [ʌl'sə:r] *n* かいよう kaíyō

Ulster [ʌl'stə:r] *n* アルスター arùsutā

ulterior [ʌlti:r'i:ə:r] *adj*: *ulterior motive* 下心 shitágokòro

ultimate [ʌl'təmit] *adj* (final: aim, destination, result) 最後の saígo no; (greatest: insult, deterrent, authority) 最大の saídai no

ultimately [ʌl'təmitli:] *adv* (in the end) やがて yagáte; (basically) 根本的に koñponteki ni

ultimatum [ʌltimei'təm] *n* 最後通ちょう saígotsùchō

ultrasound [ʌl'trəsaund] *n* (MED) 超音波 chốōñpa

ultraviolet [ʌltrəvai'əlit] *adj* (rays, light) 紫外線の shigáisen no

umbilical cord [ʌmbil'ikəl-] *n* へその緒 hesó no o

umbrella [ʌmbrel'ə] *n* (for rain) 傘 kasà, 雨傘 amágasà; (for sun) 日傘 higása, パラソル parásoru

umpire [ʌm'paiə:r] *n* (TENNIS, CRICKET) 審判 shinpan, アンパイア añpaīa

◆*vt* (game) ...のアンパイアをする ...no añpaīa wo suru

umpteen [ʌmp'ti:n'] *adj* うんと沢山の uñto takusan no

umpteenth [ʌmp'ti:nθ'] *adj*: **for the umpteenth time** 何回目か分からないが nañkaime kà wakáranaì ga

UN [ju:'en'] *n abbr* = **United Nations**

unable [ʌnei'bəl] *adj*: **to be unable to do something** ...する事ができない ...surú koto gà dekínai

unaccompanied [ʌnəkʌm'pəni:d] *adj* (child, woman) 同伴者のいない dōhañsha no inai; (luggage) 別送の bessō no; (song) 無伴奏の mubáñsō no

unaccountably [ʌnəkaunt'əbli:] *adv* 妙に myō nì

unaccustomed [ʌnəkʌs'təmd] *adj*: **to be unaccustomed to** (public speaking, Western customs etc) ...になれていない ...ni narète inai

unanimous [ju:næn'əməs] *adj* (vote) 満場一致の mañjōitchi no; (people) 全員同意の zeñ-indōi su

unanimously [ju:næn'əməsli:] *adv* (vote) 満場一致で mañjōitchi de

unarmed [ʌna:rmd'] *adj* (person) 武器を持たない búkì wo motánaì, 丸腰の marúgoshi no

unarmed combat 武器を使わない武術 búkì wo tsukáwanaì bújutsu

unashamed [ʌnəʃeimd'] *adj* (greed) 恥知らずの hajíshirāzu no; (pleasure) 人目をはばからない hitóme wo habákaranaì

unassuming [ʌnəsu:'miŋ] *adj* (person, manner) 気取らない kidóranai

unattached [ʌnətætʃt'] *adj* (person) 独身の dokúshin no; (part etc) 遊んでいる a-sōnde iru

unattended [ʌnəten'did] *adj* (car, luggage, child) ほったらかしの hottáraka-shi no

unattractive [ʌnətræk'tiv] *adj* (person, character) いやな iyá na; (building, appearance, idea) 魅力のない miryóku no nai

unauthorized [ʌnɔ:'θə:raizd] *adj* (visit, use, version) 無許可の mukyóka no

unavoidable [ʌnəvɔi'dəbəl] *adj* (delay) 避けられない sakérarenài

unaware [ʌnəwe:r'] *adj*: **to be unaware of** ...に気が付いていない ...ni ki gá tsuìte inai

unawares [ʌnəwe:rz'] *adv* (catch, take) 不意に fuí ni

unbalanced [ʌnbæl'ənst] *adj* (report) 偏った katáyottà; (mentally) 狂った kurútta

unbearable [ʌnbe:r'əbəl] *adj* (heat, pain) 耐えられない taérarenài; (person) 我慢できない程いやな gamàn dekínaì hodo iyá na

unbeatable [ʌnbi:'təbəl] *adj* (team) 無敵の mutéki no; (quality) 最高の saíkō no; (price) 最高に安い saíkō ni yasuì

unbeknown(st) [ʌnbinoun(st)'] *adv*: **unbeknown(st) to me/Peter** 私(ピーター)に気付かれずに watákushi(pìtā)ni kizúkarezù ni

unbelievable [ʌnbili:'vəbəl] *adj* 信じられない shiñjirarenài

unbend [ʌnbend'] (*pt, pp* **bent**) *vi* (relax) くつろぐ kutsúrogù

◆*vt* (wire) 真っ直ぐにする massúgù ni suru

unbiased [ʌnbai'əst] *adj* (person, report) 公正な kōsei na

unborn [ʌnbɔ:rn'] *adj* (child, young) おなかの中の onáka no nakà no

unbreakable [ʌnbrei'kəbəl] *adj* (glassware, crockery etc) 割れない warénai; (other objects) 壊れない kowárenai

unbroken [ʌnbrou'kən] *adj* (seal) 開けてない akéte naì; (silence, series) 続く tsuzúku; (record) 破られていない yabúrarète inai; (spirit) くじけない kujíkenài

unbutton [ʌnbʌt'ən] *vt* ...のボタンを外す ...no botán wo hazúsu

uncalled-for [ʌnkɔ:ld'fɔ:r] *adj* (remark)

余計な yokéi na; (rudeness etc) いわれの ない iwáre no nai

uncanny [ʌnkǽn'i:] adj (silence, resemblance, knack) 不気味な bukími na

unceasing [ʌnsi:'siŋ] adj 引っ切り無しの hikkírinashī no

unceremonious [ʌnse:rəmou'ni:əs] adj (abrupt, rude) ぶしつけな bushítsuke na

uncertain [ʌnsə:r'tən] adj (hesitant: voice, steps) 自信のない jishín no nai; (unsure) 不確実な fukákùjitsu na

uncertainty [ʌnsə:r'tənti:] n (not knowing) 不確実さ fukákùjitsusa; (also pl: doubts) 疑問 gimón

unchanged [ʌntʃeind3d'] adj (condition) 変っていない kawátte inai

unchecked [ʌntʃekt'] adv (grow, continue) 無制限に muséīgen ni

uncivilized [ʌnsiv'ilaizd] adj (gen: country, people) 未開の mikái no; (fig: behavior, hour etc) 野蛮な yabán na

uncle [ʌŋ'kəl] n おじ ojí

uncomfortable [ʌnkʌmf'tərbəl] adj (physically, also furniture) 使い心地の悪い tsukáigokochi nò warūī; (uneasy) 不安な fuán na; (unpleasant: situation, fact) 厄介な yakkái na

uncommon [ʌnkɑ:m'ən] adj (rare, unusual) 珍しい mezúrashii

uncompromising [ʌnkɑ:m'prəmaiziŋ] adj (person, belief) 融通の利かない yūzū no kikánai

unconcerned [ʌnkənsə:rnd'] adj (indifferent) 関心がない kańshin ga naī; (not worried) 平気な heíki na

unconditional [ʌnkəndiʃ'ənəl] adj 無条件の mujōkèn no

unconscious [ʌnkɑ:n'tʃəs] adj (in faint, also MED) 意識不明の ishíkifumei no; (unaware): *unconscious of* ...に気が付かない ...ni kí ga tsukanaī
♦n: *the unconscious* 潜在意識 seńzaiishīki

unconsciously [ʌnkɑ:n'tʃəsli:] adv (unawares) 無意識に muíshiki ni

uncontrollable [ʌnkəntrou'ləbəl] adj (child, animal) 手に負えない te nǐ oénai; (temper) 抑制のきかない yokúsei no ki-

kánai; (laughter) やめられない yaméra-renài

unconventional [ʌnkənven'tʃənəl] adj 型破りの katáyabùri no

uncouth [ʌnku:θ'] adj 無様な buzáma na

uncover [ʌnkʌv'ə:r] vt (take lid, veil etc off) ...の覆いを取る ...no ōī wo torū; (plot, secret) 発見する hakkén suru

undecided [ʌndisai'did] adj (person) 決定していない kettéi shite inai; (question) 未決定の mikettéi no

undeniable [ʌndinai'əbəl] adj (fact, evidence) 否定できない hitéi dekínaī

under [ʌn'də:r] prep (beneath) ...の下に ...no shitá ni; (in age, price: less than) ...以下に ...ikà ni; (according to: law, agreement etc) ...によって ...ni yottè; (someone's leadership) ...のもとに ...no motò ni
♦adv (go, fly etc) ...の下に〔で〕 ...no shitá ni(de)
under there あそこの下に〔で〕 asóko no shitá ni(de)
under repair 修理中 shūrìchū

under... prefix の下... shitá no...

under-age [ʌndə:reid3'] adj (person, drinking) 未成年の miséīnen no

undercarriage [ʌndə:rkær'id3] (BRIT) n (AVIAT) 着陸装置 chakúrikusōchi

undercharge [ʌndə:rtʃɑ:rd3] vt ...から正当な料金を取らない ...kara séitō na ryōkìn wo toránaī

underclothes [ʌn'də:rklouz] npl 下着 shitági

undercoat [ʌn'də:rkout] n (paint) 下塗り shitánuri

undercover [ʌndə:rkʌv'ə:r] adj (work, agent) 秘密の himítsu no

undercurrent [ʌn'də:rkə:rənt] n (fig: of feeling) 底流 teíryu

undercut [ʌn'də:rkʌt] (pt, pp undercut) vt (person, prices) ...より低い値段で物を売る ...yorī hikúi nedàn de monő wo urú

underdog [ʌn'də:rdɔ:g] n 弱者 jakúsha

underdone [ʌn'də:rdʌn'] adj (CULIN) 生焼けの namáyake no

underestimate [ʌndə:res'təmeit] vt (person, thing) 見くびる mikúbiru

underexposed [ʌndə:rikspouzd'] *adj*
(PHOT) 露出不足の roshútsubusòku no

underfed [ʌndə:rfed'] *adj* (person, animal) 栄養不足の eíyōbusòku no

underfoot [ʌndə:rfut'] *adv* (crush, trample) 足の下に〔で〕 ashí no shitá ni(de)

undergo [ʌndə:rgou'] (*pt* **underwent** *pp* **undergone**) *vt* (test, operation, treatment) 受ける ukérù

to undergo change 変る kawáru

undergraduate [ʌndə:rgrædʒ'u:it] *n* 学部の学生 gakùbu no gakúsei

underground [ʌn'də:rgraund] *n* (BRIT: railway) 地下鉄 chikátetsu; (POL) 地下組織 chikásoshiki
♦*adj* (car park) 地下の chiká no; (newspaper, activities) 潜りの mogúrì no
♦*adv* (work) 潜りで mogúrì de; (fig): *to go underground* 地下に潜る chiká ni mogúrù

undergrowth [ʌn'də:rgrouθ] *n* 下生え shitábae

underhand [ʌn'də:rhænd] *adj* (fig) ずるい zurúi

underhanded [ʌn'də:rhæn'did] *adj* = **underhand**

underlie [ʌndə:rlai'] (*pt* **underlay** *pp* **underlain**) *vt* (fig: be basis of) ...の根底になっている ...no koñtei ni nattè iru

underline [ʌn'də:rlain] *vt* 下線する kasén suru, ...にアンダーラインを引く ...ni añdārain wo hikú; (fig) 強調する kyốchō suru

underling [ʌn'də:rliŋ] (*pej*) *n* 手下 teshíta

undermine [ʌn'də:rmain] *vt* (confidence) 失わせる ushínawaseru; (authority) 弱める yowámerù

underneath [ʌndə:rni:θ'] *adv* 下に〔で〕 shitá ni(de)
♦*prep* ...の下に〔で〕 ...no shitá ni(de)

underpaid [ʌndə:rpeid'] *adj* 安給料の yasúkyūryò no

underpants [ʌn'də:rpænts] *npl* パンツ pañtsu

underpass [ʌn'də:rpæs] (BRIT) *n* 地下道 chikádō

underprivileged [ʌndə:rpriv'əlidʒd] *adj*
(country, race, family) 恵まれない megúmarenai

underrate [ʌndə:reit'] *vt* (person, power etc) 見くびる mikúbirù; (size) 見誤る miáyamarù

undershirt [ʌn'də:rʃə:rt] (US) *n* アンダーシャツ añdāshatsù

undershorts [ʌn'də:rʃɔːrts] (US) *npl* パンツ pañtsu

underside [ʌn'də:rsaid] *n* (of object) 下側 shitágawa; (of animal) おなか onáka

underskirt [ʌn'də:rskə:rt] (BRIT) *n* アンダースカート añdāsukàto

understand [ʌndə:rstænd'] (*pt, pp* **understood**) *vt* 分かる wakárù, 理解する rikái suru
♦*vi* (believe): *I understand that* ...だそうですね ...da sốdesù ne, ...だと聞いていますが ...da tò kíìte imasu gà

understandable [ʌndə:rstæn'dəbəl] *adj*
(behavior, reaction, mistake) 理解できる rikái dekírù

understanding [ʌndə:rstæn'diŋ] *adj*
(kind) 思いやりのある omóiyari no aru
♦*n* (gen) 理解 rikái; (agreement) 合意 gōī

understatement [ʌndə:rsteit'mənt] *n*
(of quality) 控え目な表現 hikáeme na hyốgen

that's an understatement! それは控え目過ぎるよ sore wa hikáemesugírù yo

understood [ʌndə:rstud'] *pt, pp of* **understand**
♦*adj* (agreed) 合意された gōī sareta; (implied) 暗黙の añmoku no

understudy [ʌn'də:rstʌdi:] *n* (actor, actress) 代役 daíyaku

undertake [ʌndə:rteik'] (*pt* **undertook** *pp* **undertaken**) *vt* (task) 引受ける hikíukerù

to undertake to do something ...する事を約束する ...surú koto wo yakúsoku suru

undertaker [ʌn'də:rteikə:r] *n* 葬儀屋 sốgiyà

undertaking [ʌn'də:rteikiŋ] *n* (job) 事業 jigyồ; (promise) 約束 yakúsoku

undertone [ʌn'də:rtoun] *n*: *in an undertone* 小声 kogóe

underwater [ʌn'də:rwɔ:t'ə:r] adv (use) 水中に〔で〕suíchū ni(de); (swim) 水中に潜って suíchū ni mogútte
♦adj (exploration) 水中の suíchū no; (camera etc) 潜水用の sénsuiyō no

underwear [ʌn'də:rwe:r] n 下着 shítagi

underworld [ʌn'də:rwə:rld] n (of crime) 暗黒街 añkokugai

underwriter [ʌn'də:raitə:r] n (INSURANCE) 保険業者 hokéngyōshà

undesirable [ʌndizaiə:r'əbəl] adj (person, thing) 好ましくない konómashiku-nai

undies [ʌn'di:z] (inf) npl 下着 shítagi ◊ 女性用を指す joséiyō wo sasù

undisputed [ʌndispju:'tid] adj (fact) 否定できない hitéi dekinaì; (champion etc) 断トツの dañtotsu no

undo [ʌndu:'] (pt **undid** pp **undone**) vt (unfasten) 外す hazúsu; (spoil) 台無しにする daínashi ni suru

undoing [ʌndu:'iŋ] n 破滅 hamétsu

undoubted [ʌndau'tid] adj 疑う余地のない utágau yochì no naì

undoubtedly [ʌndau'tidli:] adv 疑う余地なく utágau yochì naku

undress [ʌndres'] vi 服を脱ぐ fukú wo nugù

undue [ʌndu:'] adj (excessive) 余分な yobún na

undulating [ʌn'dʒəleitiŋ] adj (countryside, hills) 起伏の多い kifúku no ōì

unduly [ʌndu:'li:] adv (excessively) 余分に yobún ni

unearth [ʌnə:rθ'] vt (skeleton etc) 発掘する hakkútsu suru; (fig: secrets etc) 発見する hakkén suru

unearthly [ʌnə:rθ'li:] adj (hour) とんでもない toñde mo naì

uneasy [ʌni:'zi:] adj (person: not comfortable) 窮屈な kyúkutsu na; (: worried: also feeling) 不安な fuán na; (peace, truce) 不安定な fuáñtei na

uneconomic(al) [ʌni:kənɑ:m'ik(əl)] adj 不経済な fukéizai na

uneducated [ʌnedʒ'u:keitid] adj (person) 教育のない kyóiku no nai

unemployed [ʌnemplɔid'] adj (worker)

失業中の shitsúgyōchū no
♦npl: **the unemployed** 失業者 shitsú-gyōshà ◊総称 sōshō

unemployment [ʌnemplɔi'mənt] n 失業 shitsúgyō

unending [ʌnen'diŋ] adj 果てし無い ha-téshí naì

unerring [ʌnə:r'iŋ] adj (instinct etc) 確実な kakújitsu na

uneven [ʌni:'vən] adj (not regular: teeth) 不ぞろいの fuzórōi no; (performance) むらのある murá no aru; (road etc) 凸凹の dekóboko no

unexpected [ʌnikspek'tid] adj (arrival) 不意の fuí no; (success etc) 思い掛けない omóigakenaì, 意外な igái na

unexpectedly [ʌnikspek'tidli:] adv (arrive) 不意に fuí ni; (succeed) 意外に igái ni

unfailing [ʌnfei'liŋ] adj (support, energy) 尽きる事のない tsukíru koto no naì

unfair [ʌnfe:r'] adj: **unfair (to)** (…に対して) 不当な (…ni taishite) futó na

unfaithful [ʌnfeiθ'fəl] adj (lover, spouse) 浮気な uwáki na

unfamiliar [ʌnfəmil'jə:r] adj (place, person, subject) 知らない shiránai
to be unfamiliar with …を知らない …wo shiránai

unfashionable [ʌnfæʃ'ənəbəl] adj (clothes, ideas, place) はやらない hayá-ranaì

unfasten [ʌnfæs'ən] vt (undo) 外す hazú-su; (open) 開ける akéru

unfavorable [ʌnfei'və:rəbəl] (BRIT **unfavourable**) adj (circumstances, weather) 良くない yokúnai; (opinion, report) 批判的の hihánteki na

unfeeling [ʌnfi:'liŋ] adj 冷たい tsumétai, 冷酷な reíkoku na

unfinished [ʌnfin'iʃt] adj (incomplete) 未完成の mikáñsei no

unfit [ʌnfit'] adj (physically) 運動不足の uñdōbusoku no; (incompetent): **unfit (for)** (…に) 不向きな (…ni) fumúki na
to be unfit for work 仕事に不向きである shigóto ni fumúki de aru

unfold [ʌnfould'] vt (sheets, map) 広げる hirógeru

♦vi (situation) 展開する teñkai suru

unforeseen [ʌnfɔːrsiːn'] adj (circumstances etc) 予期しなかった yokī shinákatta, 思い掛けない omóigakenaī

unforgettable [ʌnfərget'əbəl] adj 忘れられない wasúrerarenaī

unforgivable [ʌnfərgiv'əbəl] adj 許せない yurúsenaī

unfortunate [ʌnfɔːr'tʃənit] adj (poor) 哀れな awáre na; (event) 不幸な fukō na; (remark) まずい mazúi

unfortunately [ʌnfɔːr'tʃənitliː] adv 残念ながら zañneñnagara

unfounded [ʌnfaun'did] adj (criticism, fears) 根拠のない koñkyo no nái

unfriendly [ʌnfrend'liː] adj (person, behavior, remark) 不親切な fushíñsetsu na

ungainly [ʌngein'liː] adj ぎこちない gikóchinaī

ungodly [ʌngɑːd'liː] adj (hour) とんでもない tofídemonaī

ungrateful [ʌngreit'fəl] adj (person) 恩知らずの oñshirázu no

unhappiness [ʌnhæp'iːnis] n 不幸せ fushíawàse, 不幸 fukō

unhappy [ʌnhæp'iː] adj (sad) 悲しい kanáshii; (unfortunate) 不幸な fukō na; (childhood) 恵まれない megúmarenaī; (dissatisfied): *unhappy about/with* (arrangements etc) ...に不満がある ...ni fumán ga aru

unharmed [ʌnhɑːrmd'] adj 無事な bují na

unhealthy [ʌnhel'θiː] adj (person) 病弱な byōjaku na; (place) 健康に悪い keñkōni warúi; (fig: interest) 不健全な fukéñzen na

unheard-of [ʌnhərd'əv] adj (shocking) 前代未聞の zeñdaimimon no; (unknown) 知られていない shirárete inaī

unhurt [ʌnhərt'] adj 無事な bují na

unidentified [ʌnaiden'təfaid] adj 未確定の mikákútei no ¶ see also UFO

uniform [juː'nəfɔːrm] n 制服 seífuku, ユニフォーム yunífōmù

♦adj (length, width etc) 一定の ittéi no

uniformity [juːnəfɔːr'mitiː] n 均一性 kiñítsusei

unify [juː'nəfai] vt 統一する tōitsu suru

unilateral [juːnəlæt'əːrəl] adj (disarmament etc) 一方的な ippóteki na

uninhabited [ʌninhæb'itid] adj (island etc) 無人の mujín no; (house) 空き家になっている akíya ni nattē iru

unintentional [ʌninten'tʃənəl] adj 意図的でない itōteki de naī

union [juː'njən] n (joining) 合併 gappéi; (grouping) 連合 reñgō; (also: **trade union**) 組合 kumíai

♦cpd (activities, leader etc) 組合の kumíai no

Union Jack n 英国国旗 eíkokukòkki, ユニオンジャック yunîonjakkù

unique [juːniːk'] adj 独特な dokútoku na, ユニークな yunīkù na

unisex [juː'niseks] adj (clothes, hairdresser etc) ユニセックスの yunísekkusu no

unison [juː'nisən] n: *in unison* (say) 一同に ichídō ni; (sing) 同音で dōon de, ユニゾンで yunízon de

unit [juː'nit] n (single whole, *also* measurement) 単位 tañ-i; (section: of furniture etc) ユニット yunītto; (team, squad) 班 hán

kitchen unit 台所用ユニット daídokoroyō yunītto

unite [juːnait'] vt (join: *gen*) 一緒にする isshō ni suru, 一つにする hitótsu ni suru; (: country, party) 結束させる kessokusaseru

♦vi 一緒になる isshò ni naru, 一つになる hitótsù ni naru

united [juːnai'tid] adj (gen) 一緒になった isshò ni natta, 一つになった hitótsù ni natta; (effort) 団結した dañketsu shita

United Kingdom n 英国 eíkoku

United Nations (Organization) n 国連 kokúren

United States (of America) n (アメリカ) 合衆国 (américa)gasshúkoku

unit trust (BRIT) n ユニット型投資信託 yunīttogata tōshishiñtaku

unity [ju:'niti:] *n* 一致 itchí

universal [ju:nə'vər:'səl] *adj* 普遍的な fuhénteki na

universe [ju:'nə'vər:rs] *n* 宇宙 uchū

university [ju:nə'vər:'siti:] *n* 大学 daígaku

unjust [ʌndʒʌst'] *adj* 不当な futō na

unkempt [ʌnkempt'] *adj* (appearance) だらしのない daráshi no naí; (hair, beard) もじゃもじゃの mojàmoja no

unkind [ʌnkaind'] *adj* (person, behavior, comment etc) 不親切な fushínsetsu na

unknown [ʌnnoun'] *adj* 知られていない shiráretè inaì

unlawful [ʌnlɔː'fəl] *adj* (act, activity) 非合法な higōhō na

unleash [ʌnliːʃ'] *vt* (*fig*: feeling, forces etc) 爆発させる bakúhatsu saseru

unless [ʌnles'] *conj* ...しなければ〔でなければ〕...shinákereba〔denákereba〕

unless he comes 彼が来なければ karè ga konákereba

unlike [ʌnlaik'] *adj* (not alike) 似ていない nitê inaî; (not like) 違った chigátta

◆*prep* (different from) ...と違って ...to chigátte

unlikely [ʌnlaik'li:] *adj* (not likely) ありそうもない arísō mo naî; (unexpected: combination etc) 驚くべき odórokubeki

unlimited [ʌnlim'itid] *adj* (travel, wine etc) 無制限の muséīgen no

unlisted [ʌnlis'tid] (*BRIT* **ex-directory**) *adj* (ex-directory) 電話帳に載っていない deńwachō ni nottè inaî

unload [ʌnloud'] *vt* (box, car etc) ...の積み荷を降ろす ...no tsumíni wo orósù

unlock [ʌnlɑːk'] *vt* ...のかぎを開ける ...no kagí wo akéru

unlucky [ʌnlʌk'i:] *adj* (person) 運の悪い uñ no warúî; (object, number) 縁起の悪い eñgi no warúî

to be unlucky (person) 運が悪い uñ ga warúî

unmarried [ʌnmær'i:d] *adj* (person) 独身の dokúshin no; (mother) 未婚の mikón no

unmask [ʌnmæsk'] *vt* (reveal: thief etc) ...の正体を暴く ...no shōtaî wo abákù

unmistakable [ʌnmistei'kəbəl] *adj* (voice, sound, person) 間違え様のない machígaeyō no naî

unmitigated [ʌnmit'əgeitid] *adj* (disaster etc) 紛れもない magíre mò naî

unnatural [ʌnnætʃ'ə:rəl] *adj* 不自然な fushízèn na

unnecessary [ʌnnes'ise:ri:] *adj* 不必要な fuhítsuyō na

unnoticed [ʌnnou'tist] *adj*: (*to go/pass*) *unnoticed* 気付かれない kizúkarenai

UNO [u:'nou] *n abbr* = **United Nations Organization**

unobtainable [ʌnəbtei'nəbəl] *adj* (item) 手に入らない te nî haíranaì; (*TEL*): *this number is unobtainable* この電話番号は現在使用されていません konó deñwa-bangō wa geñzai shiyō sarete imásèn

unobtrusive [ʌnəbtru:'siv] *adj* (person) 遠慮がちな eñryogachi na; (thing) 目立たない medátanaî

unofficial [ʌnəfiʃ'əl] *adj* (news) 公表されていない kōhyō sarete inaî; (strike) 公認されていない kōnin sarete inaî

unorthodox [ʌnɔːr'θədɑːks] *adj* (treatment) 通常でない tsūjō de nai; (*REL*) 正統でない seítō de nai

unpack [ʌnpæk'] *vi* 荷物の中身を出して片付ける nimòtsu no nakámi wo dashíte katázukerù

◆*vt* (suitcase etc) ...の中身を出して片付ける ...no nakamì wo dashíte katázukerù

unpalatable [ʌnpæl'ətəbəl] *adj* (meal) まずい mazúî; (truth) 不愉快な fuyúkài na

unparalleled [ʌnpær'əleld] *adj* (unequalled) 前代未聞の zeñdaimimon no

unpleasant [ʌnplez'ənt] *adj* (disagreeable: thing) いやな iyà na; (: person, manner) 不愉快な fuyúkài na

unplug [ʌnplʌg'] *vt* (iron, TV etc) ...のプラグを抜く ...no puràgu wo nukú

unpopular [ʌnpɑːp'jələ:r] *adj* (person, decision etc) 不評の fuhyō no

unprecedented [ʌnpres'identid] *adj* 前代未聞の zeñdaimimon no

unpredictable [ʌnpridik'təbəl] *adj*

(weather, reaction) 予測できない yosóku dekínaì; (person): *he is unpredictable* 彼のする事は予測できない karè no suru koto wa yosóku dekínai

unprofessional [ʌnprəfe'ʃənəl] *adj* (attitude, conduct) 職業倫理に反する shokúgyōrìnri ni haǹ suru

unqualified [ʌnkwɑ:l'əfaid] *adj* (teacher, nurse etc) 資格のない shikáku no nai; (complete: disaster) 全くの mattáku no, 大...daî...; (: success) 完全な kaǹzen na, 大...daî...

unquestionably [ʌnkwes'tʃənəbli:] *adv* 疑いもなく utágai mò naku

unravel [ʌnræv'əl] *vt* (ball of string) ほぐす hogúsù; (mystery) 解明する kaímei suru

unreal [ʌnri:l'] *adj* (not real) 偽の nisé no; (extraordinary) うその様な usò no yō na

unrealistic [ʌnri:əlis'tik] *adj* (person, project) 非現実的な higénjitsuteki na

unreasonable [ʌnri:'zənəbəl] *adj* (person, attitude) 不合理な fugôri na; (demand) 不当な futô na; (length of time) 非常識な hijôshìki na

unrelated [ʌnrilei'tid] *adj* (incident) 関係のない kaǹkei no naî, 無関係な mukáǹkei na; (family) 親族でない shiǹzoku de naî

unrelenting [ʌnrilen'tiǹ] *adj* 執念深い shûnenbukai

unreliable [ʌnrilai'əbəl] *adj* (person, firm) 信頼できない shiǹrai dekinaî; (machine, watch, method) 当てにならない atê ni naranaî

unremitting [ʌnrimit'iǹ] *adj* (efforts, attempts) 絶間ない taêma naî

unreservedly [ʌnrizə:r'vidli:] *adv* 心から kokórò kara

unrest [ʌnrest'] *n* (social, political, industrial etc) 不安 fuán

unroll [ʌnroul'] *vt* 広げる hirôgeru

unruly [ʌnru:'li:] *adj* (child, behavior) 素直でない sunáo de nai, 手に負えない te oénaì; (hair) もじゃもじゃの mojámoja no

unsafe [ʌnseif'] *adj* (in danger) 危険にさ

らされた kiṅkén ni sarásareta; (journey, machine, bridge etc) 危険な kikén na, 危ない abúnai

unsaid [ʌnsed'] *adj*: *to leave something unsaid* ...を言わないでおく ...wo iwánaide okù

unsatisfactory [ʌnsætisfæk'tə:ri:] *adj* (progress, work, results) 不満足な fumáǹzoku na

unsavory [ʌnsei'və:ri:] (*BRIT* **unsavoury**) *adj* (*fig*: person, place) いかがわしい ikágawashiì

unscathed [ʌnskeiðd'] *adj* 無傷の mukîzu no

unscrew [ʌnskru:'] *vt* (bottletop etc) ねじって開ける nejítte akéru; (sign, mirror etc) ...のねじを抜く ...no nejî wo nukú

unscrupulous [ʌnskru:p'jələs] *adj* (person, behavior) 悪徳... akútoku...

unsettled [ʌnset'əld] *adj* (person) 落付かない ochítsukanài; (weather) 変りやすい kawáriyasuî

unshaven [ʌnʃei'vən] *adj* 不精ひげの bushôhìge no

unsightly [ʌnsait'li:] *adj* (mark, building etc) 醜い minîkuì, 目障りな mezáwàri na

unskilled [ʌnskild'] *adj* (work, worker) 未熟練の mijúkuren no

unspeakable [ʌnspi:'kəbəl] *adj* (indescribable) 言語に絶する geṅgo ni zéssuru, 想像を絶する sôzō wo zéssurù; (awful) ひどい hidôî

unstable [ʌnstei'bəl] *adj* (piece of furniture) ぐらぐらする gurágura suru; (government) 不安定な fuántei na; (mentally) 情緒不安定な jôchofuántei na

unsteady [ʌnsted'i:] *adj* (step, legs) ふらふらする furáfura suru; (hands, voice) 震える furúeru; (ladder) ぐらぐらする gurágura suru

unstuck [ʌnstʌk'] *adj*: *to come unstuck* (label etc) 取れてしまう toréte shimaù; (*fig*: plan, scheme etc) 失敗する shippái suru

unsuccessful [ʌnsəkses'fəl] *adj* (attempt) 失敗した shippái shita; (writer) 成功しない seíkō shinaî; (proposal) 採用されなかった saíyō sarènakatta *to be unsuccessful* (in attempting something) 失敗する shippai suru; (application) 採用されない saíyō sarénai

unsuccessfully [ʌnsəkses'fəli:] *adv* (try) 成功せずに seíkō sezu ni

unsuitable [ʌnsu:'təbəl] *adj* (inconvenient: time, moment) 不適当な futékìtō na; (inappropriate: clothes) 場違いの bachígaì no; (: person) 不適当な futékìtō na

unsure [ʌnʃu:r'] *adj* (uncertain) 不確実な fukákùjitsu na

unsure about ...について確信できない ...ni tsuíte kakúshin dekinaì

to be unsure of oneself 自信がない jishín ga nai

unsuspecting [ʌnsəspek'tiŋ] *adj* 気付いていない kizúite inai

unsympathetic [ʌnsimpəθet'ik] *adj* (showing little understanding) 同情しない dōjō shinai; (unlikeable) いやな iyá na

untapped [ʌntæpt'] *adj* (resources) 未開発の mikáìhatsu no

unthinkable [ʌnθiŋk'əbəl] *adj* 考えられない kaṅgaerarenaì

untidy [ʌntai'di:] *adj* (room) 散らかった chírakatta; (person, appearance) だらしない daráshi nai

untie [ʌntai'] *vt* (knot, parcel, ribbon) ほどく hodókù; (prisoner) ...の縄をほどく ...no nawá wo hodókù; (parcel, dog) ...のひもをほどく ...no himó wo hodókù

until [ʌntil'] *prep* ...まで madè
♦*conj* ...するまで ...suru madè
until he comes 彼が来るまで karè ga kurù made
until now 今まで imámadè
until then その時まで sonó toki madè

untimely [ʌntaim'li:] *adj* (inopportune: moment, arrival) 時機の悪い jikì no warúì
an untimely death 早死に hayájini, 若死に wakájini

untold [ʌntould'] *adj* (story) 明かされていない akásarete inai; (joy, suffering, wealth) 想像を絶する sōzō wo zessúru

untoward [ʌntɔ:rd'] *adj* 困った komáttà

unused [ʌnju:zd'] *adj* (not used: clothes, portion etc) 未使用の mishíyō no

unusual [ʌnju:'ʒu:əl] *adj* (strange) 変った kawátta; (rare) 珍しい mezúrashiì; (exceptional, distinctive) 並外れた namíhazureta

unveil [ʌnveil'] *vt* (statue) ...の除幕式を行う ...no jomákushìki wo okónau

unwanted [ʌnwɔ:n'tid] *adj* (clothing etc) 不要の fuyō no; (child, pregnancy) 望まれなかった nozómarenakatta

unwavering [ʌnwei'və:riŋ] *adj* (faith) 揺るぎ無い yurúginaì; (gaze) じっとした jittō shita

unwelcome [ʌnwel'kəm] *adj* (guest) 歓迎されない kaṅgeisarenaì; (news) 悪い warúì

unwell [ʌnwel'] *adj*: *to feel unwell* 気分が悪い kibùn ga warúì
to be unwell 病気である byōki de aru

unwieldy [ʌnwi:l'di:] *adj* (object, system) 大きくて扱いにくい ōkìkute atsúkainikuì

unwilling [ʌnwil'iŋ] *adj*: *to be unwilling to do something* ...するのをいやがっている ...surú no wo iyagatte iru

unwillingly [ʌnwil'iŋli:] *adv* いやがって iyágatte

unwind [ʌnwaind'] (*pt*, *pp* **unwound**) *vt* (undo) ほどく hodókù
♦*vi* (relax) くつろぐ kutsúrogù

unwise [ʌnwaiz'] *adj* (person) 思慮の足りない shiryò no tarínai; (decision) 浅はかな asáhàka na

unwitting [ʌnwit'iŋ] *adj* (victim, accomplice) 気付かない kizúkànai

unworkable [ʌnwə:r'kəbəl] *adj* (plan) 実行不可能な jikkófukanō na

unworthy [ʌnwə:r'ði:] *adj* ...の値打がない ...no neúchi ga naì

unwrap [ʌnræp'] *vt* 開ける akéru

unwritten [ʌnrit'ən] *adj* (law) 慣習の kaṅshū no; (agreement) 口頭での kőtō de no

---

KEYWORD

---

up [ʌp] *prep*: *to go up something* ...を登る ...wo nobóru
to be up something ...の上に（登って）いる ...no ué ni nobotte iru

he went up the stairs/the hill 彼は階段〔坂〕を登った karè wa kaídan〔sakà〕 wo nobótta

the cat was up a tree ネコは木の上にいた nekò wa ki nò uè ni ita

we walked/climbed up the hill 私たちは丘を登った watákushitachi wa oká wo nobótta

they live further up the street 彼らはこの道をもう少し行った所に住んでいます karèra wa konó michi wo mó sukoshi ittá tokoro ni suǹde imasu

go up that road and turn left この道を交差点まで行って左に曲って下さい konó michi wo kôsaten màde itte hidári ni magátte kudásaì

♦*adv* 1 (upwards, higher) 上に〔で, へ〕 ué ni〔de, e〕

up in the sky/the mountains 空〔山の上〕に sorà〔yamá no ué〕ni

put it a bit higher up もう少し高い所に置いて下さい mó sukoshì takáì tokoro ni oíte kudásaì

up there あの上に anó ue ni

what's the cat doing up there? ネコは何であの上にいるのかしら nekò wa naǹde anó ue nì irú no kashira

up above 上の方に〔で〕 ué no hô nì〔de〕

there's a village and up above, on the hill, a monastery 村があって, その上の丘に修道院がある murá ga atte, sonó ue no oká ni shûdōìn ga aru

2: *to be up* (out of bed) 起きている okíte iru; (prices, level) 上がっている agátte iru; (building) 建ててある tatéte aru, 立っている tattè iru; (tent) 張ってある hattê aru

3: *up to* (as far as) ...まで ...made

I've read up to p.60 私は60ページまで読みました watákushi wa rokújupēji madè yomímashita

the water came up to his knees 水深は彼のひざまでだった suíshin wa karè no hizá madè datta

up to now 今〔これ〕まで imà〔korè〕madè

I can spend up to \$10 10ドルまで使えます jûdòru made tsukáemasu

4: *to be up to* (depending on) ...の責任である ...no sekínin de aru, ...次第である ...shidái de aru

it's up to you あなた次第です anàta shidái desu

it's not up to me to decide 決めるのは私の責任ではない kiméru no wa watá-kushi no sekínin de wa naì

5: *to be up to* (equal to) ...に合う ...ni aù

he's not up to it (job, task etc) 彼にはその仕事は無理です karè ni wa sonó shigoto wa murì desu

his work is not up to the required standard 彼の仕事は基準に合いません karè no shigóto wa kijún ni aìmasen

6: *to be up to* (inf: be doing) やっている yattè iru

what is he up to? (showing disapproval, suspicion) あいつは何をやらかしているんだろうね aìtsu wa nanì wo yarákashite irún darô nè

♦*n*: *ups and downs* (in life, career) 浮き沈み ukíshizumi

we all have our ups and downs だれだっていい時と悪い時がありますよ darè datte iì toki to warúì toki ga arimasu yo

his life had its ups and downs, but he died happy 彼の人生には浮き沈みが多かったが, 死ぬ時は幸せだった karè no jiǹsei ni wa ukíshizumi ga ōkattà ga, shinú toki wa shiáwase datta

upbringing [ʌp'briŋiŋ] *n* 養育 yóiku

update [ʌpdeit'] *vt* (records, information) 更新する kôshin suru

upgrade [ʌp'greid'] *vt* (improve: house) 改築する kaíchiku suru; (job) 格上げする kakúage suru; (employee) 昇格させる shôkaku saseru

upheaval [ʌphi:'vəl] *n* 変動 héndō

uphill [*adj* ʌp'hil *adv* ʌp'hil'] *adj* (climb) 上りの nobóri no; (fig: task) 困難な koǹnan na

♦*adv*: *to go uphill* 坂を上る sakà wo nobóru

uphold [ʌphould'] (*pt, pp* upheld) *vt* (law, principle, decision) 守る mamórù

upholstery [ʌphoul'stəːri:] *n* いすに張っ

た生地 isú ni hattá kijí

upkeep [ʌp'ki:p] *n* (maintenance) 維持 ijí

upon [əpɑ:n'] *prep* ...の上に〔で〕...no ué ni 〔de〕

upper [ʌp'əːr] *adj* 上の方の ué no hō nò
♦*n* (of shoe) 甲皮 kóhi

upper-class [ʌp'əːrklæs'] *adj* (families, accent) 上流の jốryū no

upper hand *n*: *to have the upper hand* 優勢である yūsei de aru

uppermost [ʌp'əːrmoust] *adj* 一番上の i-chíban ué no
what was uppermost in my mind 私が真っ先に考えたのは watákushi ga massákì ni kañgaèta no wa

upright [ʌp'rait] *adj* (straight) 直立の chokúritsu no; (vertical) 垂直の suíchoku no; (fig: honest) 正直な shốjiki na

uprising [ʌp'raiziŋ] *n* 反乱 hañran

uproar [ʌp'rɔːr] *n* (protests, shouts) 大騒ぎ ōsáwagi

uproot [ʌpruːt'] *vt* (tree) 根こそぎにする nekósogi ni suru; (fig: family) 故郷から追出す kokyố kara oídasu

upset [*n* ʌp'set *vb* ʌpset'] (*pt*, *pp* **upset**) *n* (to plan etc) 失敗 shippái
♦*vt* (knock over: glass etc) 倒す taósù; (routine, plan) 台無しにする daínashi ni suru; (person: offend, make unhappy) 動転させる dốten saseru
♦*adj* (unhappy) 動転した dốten shita
to have an upset stomach 胃の具合が悪い i nò gúai ga warúī

upshot [ʌp'ʃɑːt] *n* 結果 kekká

upside down [ʌp'said-] *adv* (hang, hold) 逆様に〔で〕 sakásama ni〔de〕
to turn a place upside down (fig) 家中を引っかき回す iéjū wo híkkakìmawasu

upstairs [ʌp'steːrz] *adv* (be) 2階に〔で〕 nikái ni〔de〕; (go) 2階へ nikái e
♦*adj* (window, room) 2階の nikái no
♦*n* 2階 nikái

upstart [ʌp'stɑːrt] *n* 横柄な奴 ōhèi na yatsú

upstream [ʌp'striːm] *adv* 川上に〔で、へ〕kawákami ni〔de, e〕, 上流に〔で、へ〕jốryū ni〔de, e〕

uptake [ʌp'teik] *n*: *to be quick/slow on the uptake* 物分かりがいい〔悪い〕 mo-nốwakàri ga iì〔warui〕

uptight [ʌp'tait] *adj* ぴりぴりした pirī-piri shita

up-to-date [ʌp'tədeit'] *adj* (most recent: information) 最新の saíshin no; (person) 最新の情報に通じている saíshin no jốhō ni tsūjíte irù

upturn [ʌp'təːrn] *n* (in luck) 好転 kốten; (COMM: in market) 上向き uwámuki

upward [ʌp'wəːrd] *adj* (movement, glance) 上への ué e no

upwards [ʌp'wəːrdz] *adv* (move, glance) 上の方へ ué no hō è; (more than): *upward(s) of* ...以上の ...ijō no

uranium [jurei'ni:əm] *n* ウラン urān, ウラニウム urániumù

urban [əːr'bən] *adj* 都会の tokái no

urbane [əːrbein'] *adj* 上品な jốhin na

urchin [əːr'tʃin] *n* (child) がき gakí; (waif) 浮浪児 furốjī

urge [əːrdʒ] *n* (need, desire) 衝動 shốdō
♦*vt*: *to urge someone to do something* ...する様に...を説得する ...surú yō ni ...wo settóku suru

urgency [əːr'dʒənsi:] *n* (importance) 緊急性 kiñkyūseì; (of tone) 緊迫した調子 kiñpaku shita chốshi

urgent [əːr'dʒənt] *adj* (need, message) 緊急な kiñkyū na; (voice) 切迫した seppáku shita

urinal [juːr'ənəl] *n* 小便器 shốbeñki

urinate [juːr'əneit] *vi* 小便をする shốbeñ wo suru

urine [juːr'in] *n* 尿 nyố, 小便 shốbeñ

urn [əːrn] *n* (container) 骨つぼ kotsútsubo; (*also*: **coffee/tea urn**) 大型コーヒー〔紅茶〕メーカー ōgátakōhī〔kốcha〕mèkā

Uruguay [juː'rəgwei] *n* ウルグアイ urū-guai

us [ʌs] *pron* 私たちを〔に〕watákushitachi wo〔ni〕 ¶ *see also* **me**

US(A) [juː'es'(ei')] *n abbr* = **United States (of America)**

usage [juː'sidʒ] *n* (LING) 慣用 kañyō

use [*n* juːs *vb* juːz] *n* (using) 使用 shíyố; (usefulness, purpose) 役に立つ事 yakú ni tatsu koto 利益 rîeki

♦vt (object, tool, phrase etc) 使う tsuká-u, 用いる mochíìru, 使用する shíyō suru
in use 使用中 shíyōchū
out of use 廃れて sutáretè
to be of use 役に立つ yakú ni tatsu
it's no use (not useful) 使えません tsukáemasen; (pointless) 役に立ちません yakú ni tachimasen, 無意味です muímí desu
she used to do it 前は彼女はそれをする習慣でした maè wa kanòjo wa soré wo suru shūkan deshita
to be used to ...に慣れている ...ni narète iru

used [juːzd] adj (object) 使われた tsuká-wareta; (car) 中古の chūkò no

useful [juːsˈfəl] adj 役に立つ yakú ni tatsu, 有益な yūeki na, 便利な benri na

usefulness [juːsˈfəlnıs] n 実用性 jitsúyō-sei

useless [juːsˈlıs] adj (unusable) 使えない tsukáenai, 役に立たない yakú ni tatanai; (pointless) 無意味な múimí na, 無駄な mudá na; (person: hopeless) 能無しの nō-nashi no, 役に立たない yakú ni tatanai

user [juːˈzəːr] n 使用者 shiyōsha

user-friendly [juːˈzəːrfrend'liː] adj (computer) 使いやすい tsukáiyasuî, ユーザーフレンドリーな yūzāfuréndorî na

use up vt 全部使ってしまう zeñbu tsukátte shimaù, 使い尽す tsukáitsukusù

usher [ʌʃˈəːr] n (at wedding) 案内係 añnaigakàri

usherette [ʌʃəˈret'] n (in cinema) 女性案内係 joséi añnaigakàri

USSR [juːesesaːr'] n: *the USSR* ソ連 soreñ

usual [juːˈʒuːəl] adj (time, place etc) いつもの itsùmo no
as usual いつもの様に itsúmo no yō ni

usually [juːˈʒuːaliː] adv 普通は futsū wa

usurp [juːsəːrpˈ] vt (title, position) 強奪する gōdatsu suru

utensil [juːten'səl] n 用具 yōgu
kitchen utensils 台所用具 daídokoro yōgu

uterus [juːˈtəːrəs] n 子宮 shikyū

utility [juːtilˈitiː] n (usefulness) 有用性 yūyōsei, 実用性 jitsúyosei; (also: **public utility**) 公益事業 kōekijigyō

utility room n 洗濯部屋 señtakubeya

utilize [juːˈtəlaiz] vt (object) 利用する riyō suru, 使う tsukáu

utmost [ʌtˈmoust] adj 最大の saídai no
♦n: *to do one's utmost* 全力を尽す zeñryoku wo tsukusù

utter [ʌtˈəːr] adj (total: amazement, fool, waste, rubbish) 全くの mattáku no
♦vt (sounds) 出す dasù, 発する hassúru; (words) 口に出す kuchí ni dasù, 言う iû

utterance [ʌtˈəːrəns] n 発言 hatsúgen, 言葉 kotóba

utterly [ʌtˈəːrliː] adv 全く mattáku

U-turn [juːˈtəːrn] n Uターン yūtāñ

V

v. abbr = **verse**; **versus**; **volt**; (= **vide**) ...を見よ ...wo mîyo

vacancy [vei'kənsiː] n (BRIT: job) 欠員 ketsúin; (room) 空き部屋 akíbeya

vacant [vei'kənt] adj (room, seat, toilet) 空いている aíte iru; (look, expression) うつろの utsúro no

vacant lot (US) n 空き地 akíchi

vacate [vei'keit] vt (house, one's seat) 空ける akéru; (job) 辞める yaméru

vacation [veikei'ʃən] n (esp US: holiday) 休暇 kyūka; (SCOL) 夏休み natsúyasùmi

vaccinate [væk'səneit] vt: *to vaccinate someone (against something)* ...に (...の) 予防注射をする ...ni (...no) yobō-chūsha wo suru

vaccine [væksiːn'] n ワクチン wakùchin

vacuum [væk'juːm] n (empty space) 真空 shiñkū

vacuum cleaner n (真空) 掃除機 (shiñ-kū)sōjikî

vacuum-packed [væk'juːmpækt'] adj 真空パックの shiñkūpakkū no

vagabond [væg'əbaːnd] n 浮浪者 furō-shà, ルンペン ruñpen

vagina [vədʒai'nə] n ちつ chitsú

vagrant [vei'grənt] n 浮浪者 furōshà, ルンペン ruñpen

vague [veig] *adj* (blurred: memory, outline) ぼんやりとした boń-yarĭ to shita; (uncertain: look, idea, instructions) 漠然とした bakúzen to shita; (person: not precise) 不正確な fuseǐkaku na; (: evasive) 煮え切らない niékirànài

vaguely [veig'li:] *adv* (not clearly) ぼんやりとして boń-yarĭ to shite; (without certainty) 漠然と bakúzen to, 不正確に fuseǐkaku ni; (evasively) あいまいに aímai ni

vain [vein] *adj* (conceited) うぬぼれた unúboreta; (useless: attempt, action) 無駄な mudá na

in vain 何のかいもなく nań no kaí mo nakù

valentine [væl'əntain] *n* (*also:* **valentine card**) バレンタインカード baréntaiñkādo; (person) バレンタインデーの恋人 baréntaiñdē no koǐbito

valet [vælei'] *n* 召使い meshítsukài

valiant [væl'jənt] *adj* (attempt, effort) 勇敢な yūkan na

valid [væl'id] *adj* (ticket, document) 有効な yūkō na; (argument, reason) 妥当な datō na

validity [vəlid'iti:] *n* (of ticket, document) 有効性 yūkōseǐ; (of argument, reason) 妥当性 datōseǐ

valley [væl'i:] *n* 谷(間) tanǐ(ma)

valor [væl'ə:r] (*BRIT* **valour**) *n* 勇ましさ isámashisà

valuable [væl'ju:əbəl] *adj* (jewel etc) 高価な kōka na; (time, help, advice) 貴重な kichō na

valuables [væl'ju:əbəlz] *npl* (jewellery etc) 貴重品 kichōhin

valuation [vælju:ei'ʃən] *n* (worth: of house etc) 価値 kachǐ; (judgment of quality) 評価 hyōka

value [væl'ju:] *n* (financial worth) 価値 kachǐ, 価格 kakáku; (importance, usefulness) 価値 kachǐ

◆*vt* (fix price or worth of) ...に値を付ける ...ni ne wǒ tsukérù; (appreciate) 大切にする taǐsetsu ni suru, 重宝する chōhō suru

values [væl'ju:z] *npl* (principles, beliefs)

価値観 kachǐkaň

value added tax [-æd'id-] (*BRIT*) *n* 付加価値税 fukákachizèi

valued [væl'ju:d] *adj* (appreciated: customer, advice) 大切な taǐsetsu na

valve [vælv] *n* 弁 beň, バルブ barúbu

vampire [væm'paiə:r] *n* 吸血鬼 kyūketsùki

van [væn] *n* (AUT) バン bań

vandal [væn'dəl] *n* 心無い破壊者 kokóronaǐ hakáisha

vandalism [væn'dəlizəm] *n* 破壊行動 hakáikōdō

vandalize [væn'dəlaiz] *vt* 破壊する hakái suru

vanguard [væn'ga:rd] *n* (*fig*): *in the vanguard of* ...の先端に立って ...no seńtan ni tattè

vanilla [vənil'ə] *n* バニラ banǐra

vanilla ice cream *n* バニラアイスクリーム banǐra aísukurīmu

vanish [væn'iʃ] *vi* (disappear suddenly) 見えなくなる miénàku narù, 消える kiéru

vanity [væn'iti:] *n* (of person: unreasonable pride) 虚栄心 kyoéishiň

vantage point [væn'tidʒ-] *n* (lookout place) 観察点 kańsatsuten; (viewpoint) 有利な立場 yūri na tachǐba

vapor [vei'pə:r] (*BRIT* **vapour**) *n* (gas) 気体 kitái; (mist, steam) 蒸気 jōki

variable [ve:r'i:əbəl] *adj* (likely to change: mood, quality, weather) 変りやすい kawáriyasuǐ; (able to be changed: temperature, height, speed) 調節できる chōsetsu dekírù

variance [ve:r'i:əns] *n*: *to be at variance (with)* (people) (...と) 仲たがいしている (...to) nakátagai shité iru; (facts) (...と) 矛盾している (...to) mujúnshité iru

variation [ve:ri:ei'ʃən] *n* (change in level, amount, quantity) 変化 heńka, 変動 heńdō; (different form: of plot, musical theme etc) 変形 heńkei

varicose [vær'əkous] *adj*: *varicose veins* 拡張蛇行静脈 kakúchōdakōjōmyàku

varied [ve:r'i:d] *adj* (diverse: opinions, reasons) 様々な sámazama na; (full of changes: career) 多彩な tasái na

variety [vərai'əti:] *n* (degree of choice, diversity) 変化 heñka, バラエティー baráetī; (varied collection, quantity) 様々な物 sámazama na mono; (type) 種類 shurúi

variety show *n* バラエティーショー baráetīshō

various [ve:r'i:əs] *adj* 色々な iróiro na

varnish [vɑ:r'niʃ] *n* (product applied to surface) ニス nísù

♦*vt* (apply varnish to: wood, piece of furniture etc) ...にニスを塗る ...ni nísù wo nuru; (: nails) ...にマニキュアをする ...ni maníkyua wo suru

nail varnish マニキュア maníkyua

vary [ve:r'i:] *vt* (make changes to: routine, diet) 変える kaéru

♦*vi* (be different: sizes, colors) ...が色々ある ...ga iróiro aru; (become different): *to vary with* (weather, season etc) ...によって変る ...ni yótte kawáru

vase [veis] *n* 花瓶 kabín

Vaseline [væs'əli:n] ® *n* ワセリン wasérin

vast [væst] *adj* (wide: area, knowledge) 広い hiróì; (enormous: expense etc) ばく大な bakúdai na

VAT [væt] *n abbr* = **value added tax**

vat [væt] *n* 大おけ ōokè

Vatican [væt'ikən] *n*: *the Vatican* (palace) バチカン宮殿 bachíkan kyūdeñ; (authority) ローマ法王庁 rōma hōōchō

vault [vɔ:lt] *n* (of roof) 丸天井 marúteñjō; (tomb) 地下納骨堂 chikánōkotsudō; (in bank) 金庫室 kiñkoshitsú

♦*vt* (*also*: **vault over**) 飛越える tobíkoerù

vaunted [vɔ:n'tid] *adj*: *much-vaunted* ご自慢の go-jíman no

VCR [vi:si:ɑ:r'] *n abbr* = **video cassette recorder**

VD [vi:di:'] *n abbr* = **venereal disease**

VDU [vi:di:ju:'] *n abbr* = **visual display unit**

veal [vi:l] *n* 子ウシ肉 koúshiniku

veer [vi:r] *vi* (vehicle, wind) 急に向きを変える kyū ni mukí wo kaéru

vegetable [vedʒ'təbəl] *n* (BOT) 植物 shokúbutsu; (edible plant) 野菜 yasái

♦*adj* (oil etc) 植物性の shokúbutsusei no

vegetarian [vedʒite:r'i:ən] *n* 菜食主義者 saíshokushugishà

♦*adj* (diet etc) 菜食主義の saíshokushugi no

vegetate [vedʒ'iteit] *vi* 無為に暮す muí ni kurásu

vegetation [vedʒitei'ʃən] *n* (plants) 植物 shokúbutsu ◊総称 sōshō

vehement [vi:'əmənt] *adj* (strong: attack, passions, denial) 猛烈な mōretsu na

vehicle [vi:'ikəl] *n* (machine) 車 kurúma; (*fig*: means of expressing) 手段 shudán

veil [veil] *n* ベール bēru

veiled [veild] *adj* (*fig*: threat) 隠された kakúsareta

vein [vein] *n* (ANAT) 静脈 jōmyaku; (of ore etc) 脈 myakú

vein of a leaf 葉脈 yōmyaku

velocity [vəlɑs'iti:] *n* 速度 sokúdo

velvet [vel'vit] *n* ビロード biródo, ベルベット berúbetto

♦*adj* ビロードの biródo no, ベルベットの berúbettò no

vendetta [vendet'ə] *n* 復しゅう fukúshū

vending machine [ven'diŋ-] *n* 自動販売機 jidóhanbaiki

vendor [ven'də:r] *n* (of house, land) 売手 uríte; (of cigarettes, beer etc) 売子 uríko

veneer [vəni:r'] *n* (on furniture) 化粧張り keshōbari; (*fig*: of person, place) 虚飾 kyoshóku

venereal [vəni:r'i:əl] *adj*: *venereal disease* 性病 seíbyō

Venetian blind [vəni:'ʃən-] *n* ベネシャンブラインド beñéshanburaindò

Venezuela [venizwei'lə] *n* ベネズエラ benézuera

vengeance [ven'dʒəns] *n* (revenge) 復しゅう fukúshū

with a vengeance (*fig*: to a greater extent) 驚く程 odórokù hodo

venison [ven'isən] *n* シカ肉 shikániku

venom [ven'əm] n (of snake, insect) 毒 dokú; (bitterness, anger) 悪意 ákui

venomous [ven'əməs] adj (poisonous: snake, insect) 毒... dokú...; (full of bitterness: look, stare) 敵意に満ちた tekíi ni michíta

vent [vent] n (also: **air vent**) 通気孔 tsúkikō; (in jacket) ベンツ beñtsu
◆vt (fig: feelings, anger) ぶちまける buchímakeru

ventilate [ven'təleit] vt (room, building) 換気する kañki suru

ventilation [ventəlei'ʃən] n 換気 kañki

ventilator [ven'təleitə:r] n (TECH) 換気装置 kañkisōchi, ベンチレーター beñchirētā; (MED) 人工呼吸器 jiñkōkokyūkì, レスピレタ resúpireta

ventriloquist [ventril'əkwist] n 腹話術師 fukúwajùtsushi

venture [ven'tʃə:r] n (risky undertaking) 冒険 bōken
◆vt (opinion) おずおず言う ozúozu iú
◆vi (dare to go) おずおず行く ozúozu ikú
business venture 投機 tōki

venue [ven'ju:] n (place fixed for something) 開催地 kaísaichi

veranda(h) [vəræn'də] n ベランダ beránda

verb [və:rb] n 動詞 dōshi

verbal [və:r'bəl] adj (spoken: skills etc) 言葉の kotóba no; (: translation etc) 口頭の kótō no; (of a verb) 動詞の dōshi no

verbatim [və:rbei'tim] adj 言葉通りの kotóbadōri no
◆adv 言葉通りに kotóbadōri ni

verbose [və:rbous'] adj (person) 口数の多い kuchíkazu no ōì; (speech, report etc) 冗長な jōchō na

verdict [və:r'dikt] n (LAW) 判決 hañketsu; (fig: opinion) 判断 hañdan

verge [və:rdʒ] n (BRIT: of road) 路肩 rokáta
「*soft verges*」(BRIT: AUT) 路肩軟弱 rokáta nanjaku
to be on the verge of doing something ...する所である ...surú tokoro dè arù

verge on vt fus ...同然である ...dōzen de arù

verify [ve:r'əfai] vt (confirm, check) 確認する kakúnin suru

veritable [ve:r'itəbəl] adj (reinforcer: = real) 全くの mattáku no

vermin [və:r'min] npl (animals) 害獣 gaíjū; (fleas, lice etc) 害虫 gaíchū

vermouth [və:rmu:θ'] n ベルモット berúmottò

vernacular [və:rnæk'jələ:r] n (language) その土地の言葉 sonó tochi no kotóba

versatile [və:r'sətəl] adj (person) 多才の tasái no; (substance, machine, tool etc) 使い道の多い tsukáimichi no ōì

verse [və:rs] n (poetry) 詩 shi; (one part of a poem: also in bible) 節 setsú

versed [və:rst] adj: *(well-)versed in* ...に詳しい ...ni kuwáshii

version [və:r'ʒən] n (form: of design, production) 型 katá; (: of book, play etc) ...版 ...bañ; (account: of events, accident etc) 説明 setsúmei

versus [və:r'səs] prep ...対... ...tai ...

vertebra [və:r'təbrə] (pl vertebrae) n せきつい sekítsùi

vertebrae [və:r'təbrei] npl of vertebra

vertebrate [və:r'təbreit] n せきつい動物 sekítsuidōbutsu

vertical [və:r'tikəl] adj 垂直の suíchoku no

vertigo [və:r'təgou] n めまい memáì

verve [və:rv] n (vivacity) 気迫 kiháku

very [ve:r'i:] adv (+ adjective, adverb) とても totémo, 大変 taíhen, 非常に hijō ni
◆adj: *it's the very book he'd told me about* 彼が話していたのは正にその本だ karè ga hanáshite ita no wà masá ni sonó hon dà
the very last 正に最後の masá ni saígo no
at the very least 少なくとも sukunàkutomo
very much 大変 taíhen

vessel [ves'əl] n (NAUT) 船 funè; (container) 容器 yóki see **blood**

vest [vest] n (US: waistcoat) チョッキ chókki; (BRIT) アンダーシャツ añdāshatsù

vested interests [ves'tid-] *npl* 自分の利益 jibún no rièki, 私利 shirì

vestige [ves'tidʒ] *n* 残り nokóri

vet [vet] (*BRIT*) *n abbr* = **veterinary surgeon**
♦*vt* (examine: candidate) 調べる shirábe-rù

veteran [vet'ərən] *n* (of war) …戦争で戦った人 …seńsō de tatákatta hito; (former soldier) 退役軍人 taíekigunjin; (old hand) ベテラン betéran

veterinarian [vetə:rənə:r'i:ən] (*US*) *n* 獣医 jūi

veterinary [vet'ə:rəne:ri:] *adj* (practice, care etc) 獣医の jūi no

veterinary surgeon (*BRIT*) *n* = **veterinarian**

veto [vi:'tou] (*pl* **vetoes**) *n* (right to forbid) 拒否権 kyohìken; (act of forbidding) 拒否権の行使 kyohìken no kōshì
♦*vt* …に拒否権を行使する …ni kyohìken wo kōshì suru

vex [veks] *vt* (irritate, upset) 怒らせる o-kóraserù

vexed [vekst] *adj* (question) 厄介な yak-kãi na

via [vai'ə] *prep* (through, by way of) …を経て …wo hetè, …経由 …keíyu

viable [vai'əbəl] *adj* (project) 実行可能な jikkṓkanō na; (company) 存立できる sofíritsu dekirù

viaduct [vai'ədʌkt] *n* 陸橋 rikkyṓ

vibrant [vai'brənt] *adj* (lively) 力強い chikárazuyoì; (bright) 生き生きした ikíi-kì shita; (full of emotion: voice) 感情のこもった kańjō no komótta

vibrate [vai'breit] *vi* (house, machine etc) 振動する shíndō suru

vibration [vaibrei'ʃən] *n* 振動 shíndō

vicar [vik'ə:r] *n* 主任司祭 shunínshisaì

vicarage [vik'ə:ridʒ] *n* 司祭館 shisáikaň

vicarious [vaike:r'i:əs] *adj* (pleasure) 他人の身になって感じる tańín no mi nì nattè kańjirù

vice [vais] *n* (moral fault) 悪徳 akútoku; (TECH) 万力 mańriki

vice- [vais] *prefix* 副… fukú…

vice-president [vais'prez'idənt] *n* (*US* POL) 副大統領 fukúdaitōryō

vice squad *n* 風俗犯罪取締班 fūzokuhań-zai toríshimarihaň

vice versa [vais'və:r'sə] *adv* 逆の場合も同じ gyakú no baái mo onáji

vicinity [visin'əti:] *n* (area): *in the vicinity (of)* (…の) 近所に (…no) kiń-jo ni

vicious [viʃ'əs] *adj* (violent: attack, blow) 猛烈な mōretsu na; (cruel: words, look) 残酷な zańkoku na; (horse, dog) どう猛な dṓmō na

vicious circle *n* 悪循環 akújuňkan

victim [vik'tim] *n* (person, animal, business) 犠牲者 giséisha

victimize [vik'təmaiz] *vt* (strikers etc) 食い物にする kuímono nì suru

victor [vik'tə:r] *n* 勝利者 shōrísha

Victorian [viktour'i:ən] *adj* ヴィクトリア朝の bikútoriachō no

victorious [viktɔ:r'i:əs] *adj* (triumphant: team, shout) 勝ち誇る kachíhokoru

victory [vik'tə:ri:] *n* 勝利 shōrī

video [vid'i:ou] *cpd* ビデオの bideo no
♦*n* (video film) ビデオ bídeo, ビデオ映画 bídeo eíga; (*also*: **video cassette**) ビデオカセット bídeokasettò; (*also*: **video cassette recorder**) ビデオテープレコーダー bídeo tēpùrekōdằ, VTR buitíāru

video tape *n* ビデオテープ bídeotēpù

vie [vai] *vi*: *to vie (with someone)(for something)* (…のために) (…と) 競り合う (…no tamè ni) (…to) seríaù

Vienna [vi:en'ə] *n* ウィーン uíň

Vietnam [vi:etna:m'] *n* ベトナム betónamu

Vietnamese [vi:etna:mi:z'] *adj* ベトナムの betónamu no; (LING) ベトナム語の betónamugð no
♦*n inv* (person) ベトナム人 betónamujìn; (LING) ベトナム語 betónamugð

view [vju:] *n* (sight) 景色 keshìki; (outlook) 見方 mikáta; (/: opinion) 意見 ikèn
♦*vt* (look at: *also fig*) 見る mirù
on view (in museum etc) 展示中 teńjichū
in full view (of) (…の) 見ている前で (…no) mitè iru maè de

in view of the weather こういう天気
だから kō fu teñki da karà
in view of the fact that ...だという事
を考えて ...da tō iu koto wo kañgaetè
in my view 私の考えでは watákushi no
kañgae de wà

viewer [vju:'ə:r] *n* (person) 見る人 mirù
hito

viewfinder [vju:'faində:r] *n* ファインダ
ー faíndā

viewpoint [vju:'point] *n* (attitude) 考え
方 kañgaekata, 見地 keñchi; (place) 観察
する地点 kañsatsu suru chitén

vigil [vidʒ'əl] *n* 不寝番 fushíñban

vigilance [vidʒ'ələns] *n* 用心 yōjin

vigilant [vidʒ'ələnt] *adj* 用心する yōjin
surù

vigor [vig'ə:r] (*BRIT* **vigour**) *n* (energy:
of person, campaign) 力強さ chikárazu-
yosà

vigorous [vig'ə:rəs] *adj* (full of energy:
person) 元気のいい geñki no iì; (: action,
campaign) 強力な kyōryoku na; (: plant)
よく茂った yokù shigétta

vile [vail] *adj* (evil: action) 下劣な gerétsu na; (: language) 下品な gehíñ na; (unpleasant: smell, weather, food, temper)
ひどい hidoì

villa [vil'ə] *n* (country house) 別荘 bessō;
(suburban house) 郊外の屋敷 kōgài no
yashikí

village [vil'idʒ] *n* 村 murá

villager [vil'idʒə:r] *n* 村民 soñmiñ

villain [vil'in] *n* (scoundrel) 悪党 akútò;
(in novel) 悪役 akúyaku; (*BRIT*: criminal) 犯人 hañniñ

vindicate [vin'dikeit] *vt* (person: free
from blame) ...の正しさを立証する ...no
tadashīsa wo risshō suru; (action: justify)
...が正当である事を立証する ...ga seítō
de arù koto wo risshō suru

vindictive [vindik'tiv] *adj* (person) 執念
深い shúnenbukaì; (action etc) 復しゅう
心による fukúshūshiñ ni yoru

vine [vain] *n* (climbing plant) ツル tsurù;
(grapevine) ブドウの木 budō no ki

vinegar [vin'əgə:r] *n* 酢 su

vineyard [vin'jə:rd] *n* ブドウ園 budōen

vintage [vin'tidʒ] *n* (year) ブドウ収穫年
budō shūkakuneñ
♦*cpd* (classic: comedy, performance etc)
典型的な teñkeiteki na

vintage car *n* クラシックカー kura-
shīkku kā

vintage wine *n* 当り年のワイン atári-
doshi no waiñ

vinyl [vai'nil] *n* ビニール biníru

viola [viːou'lə] *n* (MUS) ビオラ biòra

violate [vai'əleit] *vt* (agreement, peace)
破る yaburù; (graveyard) 汚す kegasù

violation [vaiəlei'ʃən] *n* (of agreement
etc) 違反 ihán

violence [vai'ələns] *n* (brutality) 暴力 bōryòku; (strength) 乱暴 rañbō

violent [vai'ələnt] *adj* (brutal: behavior)
暴力の bōryòku no, 乱暴な rañbō na;
(intense: debate, criticism) 猛烈な mōré-
tsu na
a violent death 変死 heñshi

violet [vai'əlit] *adj* 紫色の murásakiiro
no
♦*n* (color) 紫 murásàki; (plant) スミレ
sumíre

violin [vaiəlin'] *n* バイオリン baíorin

violinist [vaiəlin'ist] *n* バイオリン奏者
baíorinsōsha, バイオリニスト baíorinisu-
to

VIP [viːaipiː'] *n abbr* (= *very important
person*) 要人 yōjin, 貴賓 kihín, ブイアイ
ピー buíaipī, ビップ bippù

viper [vai'pə:r] *n* クサリヘビ kusárihebì

virgin [və:r'dʒin] *n* (person) 処女 shojò,
バージン bājin
♦*adj* (snow, forest etc) 処女... shojò...

virginity [və:rdʒin'əti:] *n* (of person) 処
女 shojò

Virgo [və:r'gou] *n* (sign) 乙女座 otómeza

virile [vir'əl] *adj* 男らしい otókorashiì

virility [vəril'əti:] *n* (sexual power) 性的
能力 seítekinōryoku; (*fig*: masculine
qualities) 男らしさ otókorashisà

virtually [və:r'tʃuːəliː] *adv* (almost) 事実
上 jijítsujō

virtue [və:r'tʃu:] *n* (moral correctness) 徳
tokú, 徳行 tokkō; (good quality) 美徳 bitóku; (advantage) 利点 ritén, 長所 chō-

shō

by virtue of ...である事で ... de arù kotō de

virtuosi [vəːrtʃuːou'zi:] *npl of* **virtuoso**

virtuoso [vəːrtʃuːou'zou] (*pl* **virtuosos** *or* **virtuosi**) *n* 名人 meíjin

virtuous [vəːr'tʃuːəs] *adj* (displaying virtue) 良心的な ryōshínteki na, 高潔な kōkétsu na, 敬けんな keíken na

virulent [vir'jələnt] *adj* (disease) 悪性の akúsei no 危険な kiken na; (actions, feelings) 憎悪に満ちた zōo ni michíta

virus [vai'rəs] *n* ウイルス uírusu

visa [viː'zə] *n* 査証 sashō, ビザ bizá

vis-à-vis [viːzaːviː'] *prep* (compared to) ...と比べて ...to kurábete; (in regard to) ...に関して ...ni kaň shite

viscose [vis'jkouz] *n* ビスコース人絹 bisúkōsùjíňkeň, ビスコースレーヨン bisúkōsùrēyòn

viscous [vis'kəs] *adj* ねばねばした nebàneba shita

visibility [vizəbil'əti:] *n* 視界 shikái

visible [viz'əbəl] *adj* (able to be seen or recognized: *also fig*) 目に見える me ní mierù

vision [viʒ'ən] *n* (sight: ability) 視力 shiryōku; (: sense) 視覚 shikáku; (foresight) ビジョン bijòn; (in dream) 幻影 geň-ei

visit [viz'it] *n* (to person, place) 訪問 hōmon

◆*vt* (person: *US also:* visit with) 訪問する hōmon suru, 訪ねる tazúnerù, ...の所へ遊びに行く ...no tokóro e asóbi ni ikú; (place) 訪問する hōmon suru, 訪ねる tazúneru

visiting hours [viz'itiŋ-] *npl* (in hospital etc) 面会時間 meňkaijikan

visitor [viz'itər] *n* (person visiting, invited) 客 kyakú; (tourist) 観光客 kaňkōkyàku

visor [vai'zər] *n* (of helmet etc) 面 meň; (of cap etc) ひさし hisáshi; (AUT: *also:* **sun visor**) 日よけ hiyóke

vista [vis'tə] *n* (view) 景色 keshíki

visual [viʒ'uːəl] *adj* (arts etc) 視覚の shikáku no

visual aid *n* 視覚教材 shikákukyōzai

visual display unit *n* モニター monítā, ディスプレー dísupurē

visualize [viʒ'uːəlaiz] *vt* (picture, imagine) 想像する sōzō suru

vital [vait'əl] *adj* (essential, important, crucial) 重要な jūyō na; (full of life: person) 活発な kappátsu na; (necessary for life: organ) 生命に必要な seímei ni hitsúyō na

vitality [vaitæl'iti:] *n* (liveliness) 元気 geňki

vitally [vai'təli:] *adv*: *vitally important* 極めて重要な kiwámete jūyō na

vital statistics *npl* (of population) 人口動態統計 jíňkōdōtaitōkei; (*inf*: woman's measurements) スリーサイズ surísaizù

vitamin [vai'təmin] *n* ビタミン bitámin

vivacious [vivei'ʃəs] *adj* にぎやかな nigìyàka na

vivid [viv'id] *adj* (clear: description, memory) 鮮明な seímei na; (bright: color, light) 鮮やかな azáyàka na; (imagination) はつらつとした hatsúratsu to shitá

vividly [viv'idli:] *adv* (describe) 目に見える様に me ní mierù yō ni; (remember) はっきりと hakkírì to

vivisection [vivisek'ʃən] *n* 生体解剖 seítaikaibō

V-neck [viː'nek] *n* (*also:* **V-neck jumper/pullover**) V ネックセーター buínekkusētā

vocabulary [voukæb'jələːri:] *n* (words known) 語い goì

vocal [vou'kəl] *adj* (of the voice) 声の koè no; (articulate) はっきり物を言う hakkírì monó wo iú

vocal c(h)ords *npl* 声帯 seítai

vocation [voukei'ʃən] *n* (calling) 使命感 shiméìkan; (chosen career) 職業 shokugyō

vocational [voukei'ʃənəl] *adj* (training etc) 職業の shokugyō no

vociferous [vousif'əːrəs] *adj* (protesters, demands) やかましい yakámashii, しつこい shitsúkoì

vodka [vad'kə] *n* ウォッカ uókkā

vogue [voug] *n* 流行 ryūkō

in vogue 流行して ryūkṓ shite

voice [vɔis] *n* (of person) 声 koè
♦*vt* (opinion) 表明する hyṓmei suru

void [vɔid] *n* (emptiness) 空虚 kūkyò; (hole) 穴 aná, 空間 kūkan
♦*adj* (invalid) 無効の mukṓ no; (empty): *void of* ...が全くない ...ga mattáku naì

volatile [vɑː'lətəl] *adj* (liable to change: situation) 不安定な fuañtei na; (: person) 気まぐれな kimágure na; (: liquid) 揮発性の kihátsusei no

volcanic [vɑːlkæn'ik] *adj* (eruption) 火山の kazàn no; (rock etc) 火山性の kazánsei no

volcano [vɑːlkei'nou] (*pl* **volcanoes**) *n* 火山 kazàn

volition [vouliʃ'ən] *n*: *of one's own volition* 自発的に jihátsuteki ni, 自由意志で jiyūishì de

volley [vɑːl'iː] *n* (of stones etc) 一斉に投げられる ... isséi ni nagérareru ...; (of questions etc) 連発 reñpatsu; (TENNIS etc) ボレー borè
a volley of gunfire 一斉射撃 isséishagèki

volleyball [vɑːl'iːbɔːl] *n* バレーボール barḗbōru

volt [voult] *n* ボルト borúto

voltage [voul'tidʒ] *n* 電圧 deñ-atsu

voluble [vɑːl'jəbəl] *adj* (person) 口達者な kuchídasshà na; (speech etc) 流ちょうな ryūchṓ na

volume [vɑːl'juːm] *n* (space) 容積 yōsèki; (amount) 容量 yōryṓ; (book) 本 hoñ; (sound level) 音量 oñryō, ボリューム boryū́mu
Volume 2 第2巻 daínikan

voluminous [vəlu:'minəs] *adj* (clothes) だぶだぶの dabúdabu no; (correspondence, notes) 大量の taíryō no, 多数の tasù no

voluntarily [vɑːləntɛːr'iliː] *adv* (willingly) 自発的に jihátsuteki ni, 自由意志で jiyūishì de

voluntary [vɑːl'əntɛːri:] *adj* (willing, done willingly: exile, redundancy) 自発的な jihátsuteki na, 自由意志による jiyū́ishi ni yoru; (unpaid: work, worker) 奉仕

の hōshí no

volunteer [vɑːləntiːr'] *n* (unpaid helper) 奉仕者 hōshísha, ボランティア boráñtia; (to army etc) 志願者 shigáñsha
♦*vt* (information) 自発的に言う jihátsuteki ni iú, 提供する teíkyō suru
♦*vi* (for army etc) ...への入隊を志願する ...e no nyū́tai wo shigàn suru
to volunteer to do ...しようと申し出る ...shiyṓto mōshíderu

voluptuous [vəlʌp'tʃuːəs] *adj* (movement, body, feeling) 官能的な kañnōteki na, 色っぽい iróppoi

vomit [vɑːm'it] *n* 吐いた物 haíta monó, 反吐 hedò
♦*vt* 吐く hakù
♦*vi* 吐く haku

vote [vout] *n* (method of choosing) 票決 hyōketsu; (indication of choice, opinion) 投票 tōhyō; (votes cast) 投票数 tōhyōsū; (also: *right to vote*) 投票権 tōhyōkèn
♦*vt* (elect): *to be voted chairman etc* 座長に選出される zachō ni señshutsu saréru; (propose): *to vote that* ...という事を提案する ...to iú koto wo teían suru
♦*vi* (in election etc) 投票する tōhyō suru
vote of thanks 感謝決議 kañshaketsugì

voter [vou'təːr] *n* (person voting) 投票者 tōhyōshà; (person with right to vote) 有権者 yūkeñsha

voting [vou'tiŋ] *n* 投票 tōhyō

vouch for [vautʃ-] *vt fus* (person, quality etc) 保証する hoshṓ suru

voucher [vau'tʃəːr] *n* (for meal: *also*: **luncheon voucher**) 食券 shokkèn; (with petrol, cigarettes etc) クーポン kū́pon; (*also*: **gift voucher**) ギフト券 gifútokeñ

vow [vau] *n* 誓い chikái
♦*vt*: *to vow to do/that* ...する事[...だという事]を誓う ...surú koto[...da to iú koto]wo chikáu

vowel [vau'əl] *n* 母音 boín

voyage [vɔi'idʒ] *n* (journey: by ship, spacecraft) 旅 tabí, 旅行 ryokṓ

V-sign [viː'sain] (*BRIT*) *n* V サイン buísain ◇手の甲を相手に向けると軽べつのサイン；手のひらを向けると勝利のサイ

ン té no kō wo aíte ni mukéru to keíbetsu no saín; te nō hirā wo mukéru to shōrī no saín

vulgar [vʌl'gə:r] *adj* (rude: remarks, gestures, graffiti) 下品な gehín na; (in bad taste: decor, ostentation) 野暮な yabò na

vulgarity [vʌlgær'iti:] *n* (rudeness) 下品な言葉 gehín na kotóba; (ostentation) 野暮ったい事 yabóttaī kotó

vulnerable [vʌl'nə:rəbəl] *adj* (person, position) やられやすい yaráreyasuī, 無防備な mubóbī na

vulture [vʌl'tʃə:r] *n* ハゲタカ hagétaka

W

wad [wɑːd] *n* (of cotton wool, paper) 塊 katámari; (of banknotes etc) 束 tabà

waddle [wɑːd'əl] *vi* (duck, baby) よちよち歩く yochìyochi arúkù; (fat person) よたよた歩く yotàyota arúkù

wade [weid] *vi*: **to wade through** (water) ...の中を歩いて通る ...no nakà wo arúite tōrù; (*fig*: a book) 苦労して読む kurō shité yomù

wafer [wei'fə:r] *n* (biscuit) ウエハース uéhāsu

waffle [wɑː'fəl] *n* (CULIN) ワッフル waffùru; (empty talk) 下らない話 kudáranai hanáshi
♦*vi* (in speech, writing) 下らない話をする kudáranai hanáshi wo suru

waft [wæft] *vt* (sound, scent) 漂わせる tadàyowaseru
♦*vi* (sound, scent) 漂う tadáyou

wag [wæg] *vt* (tail, finger) 振る furù
♦*vi*: **the dog's tail was wagging** イヌはしっぽを振っていた inú wà shippò wo futté itá

wage [weidʒ] *n* (*also*: **wages**) 賃金 chíngin, 給料 kyūryō
♦*vt*: **to wage war** 戦争をする señsō wo suru

wage earner [-ə:r'nə:r] *n* 賃金労働者 chínginródōshà

wage packet *n* 給料袋 kyúryōbukùro

wager [wei'dʒə:r] *n* かけ kakè

waggle [wæg'əl] *vt* (hips) 振る furu; (eyebrows etc) ぴくぴくさせる pikùpiku saséru

wag(g)on [wæg'ən] *n* (*also*: **horse-drawn wag(g)on**) 荷馬車 nibáshà; (*BRIT*: RAIL) 貨車 kashá

wail [weil] *n* (of person) 泣き声 nakígoè; (of siren etc) うなり unári
♦*vi* (person) 泣き声をあげる nakígoè wo agéru; (siren) うなる unarù

waist [weist] *n* (ANAT, *also* of clothing) ウエスト uésuto

waistcoat [weist'kout] (*BRIT*) *n* チョッキ chốkki, ベスト besùto

waistline [weist'lain] *n* (of body) 胴回り dốmawàri, ウエスト uésùto; (of garment) ウエストライン uésùtorain

wait [weit] *n* (interval) 待ち時間 machí jikan
♦*vi* 待つ matsù
to lie in wait for ...を待伏せする ...wo machíbuse suru
I can't wait to (*fig*) 早く...したい hayáku ...shitái
to wait for someone/something ...を待つ ...wo matsu

wait behind *vi* 居残って待つ inokotte matsù

waiter [wei'tə:r] *n* (in restaurant etc) 給仕 kyūjì, ウエーター uétā, ボーイ bối

waiting [wei'tiŋ] *n*: 「*no waiting*」(*BRIT*: AUT) 停車禁止 teísha kínshi

waiting list *n* 順番待ちの名簿 juñbanmachi no meībo

waiting room *n* (in surgery, railway station) 待合室 machíaīshitsu

wait on *vt fus* (people in restaurant) ...に給仕する ...ni kyūjì suru

waitress [wei'tris] *n* ウエートレス uétòresu

waive [weiv] *vt* (rule) 適用するのをやめる tekíyō suru no wò yaméru; (rights etc) 放棄する hōkī suru

wake [weik] (*pt* **woke** *or* **waked**, *pp* **woken** *or* **waked**) *vt* (*also*: **wake up**) 起す okósù
♦*vi* (*also*: **wake up**) 目が覚める me gá samérù

♦*n* (for dead person) 通夜 tsuyà, tsūya; (NAUT) 航跡 kōseki

waken [wei'kən] *vt, vi* = **wake**

Wales [weilz] *n* ウェールズ uērùzu

the Prince of Wales プリンスオブウェールズ purínsu obu uērùzu

walk [wɔːk] *n* (hike) ハイキング haīkingu; (shorter) 散歩 sanpo; (gait) 歩調 hochō; (in park, along coast etc) 散歩道 sanpomichi, 遊歩道 yūhodō

♦*vi* (go on foot) 歩く arúkù; (for pleasure, exercise) 散歩する sanpo suru

♦*vt* (distance) 歩く arúkù; (dog) 散歩に連れて行く sanpo ni tsuréte ikú

10 minutes' walk from here ここから徒歩で10分の所に kokó karà tohò do juppùn no tokóro ni

people from all walks of life あらゆる身分の人々 aráyurù mibún no hitóbìto

walker [wɔːk'əːr] *n* (person) ハイカー haīkā

walkie-talkie [wɔːˈkiːtɔːˈkiː] *n* トランシーバー toránshībā

walking [wɔːˈkiŋ] *n* ハイキング haīkingu

walking shoes *npl* 散歩靴 sanpogutsu

walking stick *n* ステッキ sutékkì

walk out *vi* (audience) 出て行く detè ikú; (workers) ストライキをする sutóraìki wo suru

walkout [wɔːˈkaut] *n* (of workers) ストライキ sutóraìki

walk out on (*inf*) *vt fus* (family etc) 見捨てる misúteru

walkover [wɔːˈkouvəːr] (*inf*) *n* (competition, exam etc) 朝飯前 asámeshimaè

walkway [wɔːˈkwei] *n* 連絡通路 renrakutsūrō

wall [wɔːl] *n* (gen) 壁 kabé; (city wall etc) 城壁 jōheki

walled [wɔːld] *adj* (city) 城壁に囲まれた jōheki ni kakómareta; (garden) 塀をめぐらした heí wo megúrashita

wallet [wɑːˈlit] *n* 札入れ satsúire, 財布 saífu

wallflower [wɔːlˈflauəːr] *n* ニオイアラセイトウ nióiaraseitō

to be a wallflower (*fig*) だれもダンスの相手になってくれない darè mo dánsu no aíte ni nattè kurénai, 壁の花である kabé no hana de arù

wallop [wɑːˈləp] (*inf*) *vt* ぶん殴る bufínaguru

wallow [wɑːˈlou] *vi* (animal: in mud, water) ころげ回る korógemawarù; (person: in sentiment, guilt) ふける fukérù

wallpaper [wɔːˈlpeipəːr] *n* 壁紙 kabégami

♦*vt* (room) ...に壁紙を張る ...ni kabégami wo harú

wally [weiˈliː] (*BRIT*: *inf*) *n* ばか bakà

walnut [wɔːlˈnʌt] *n* (nut) クルミ kurúmi; (*also*: **walnut tree**) クルミの木 kurúmi no ki; (wood) クルミ材 kurúmizaì

walrus [wɔːˈlrəs] (*pl* **walrus** *or* **walruses**) *n* セイウチ seíuchì

waltz [wɔːlts] *n* (dance, MUS) 円舞曲 enbukyòku, ワルツ warùtsu

♦*vi* (dancers) ワルツを踊る warùtsu wo odóru

wan [wɑːn] *adj* (person, complexion) 青白い aójiroi; (smile) 悲しげな kanáshige nà

wand [wɑːnd] *n* (*also*: **magic wand**) 魔法の棒 mahō no bō

wander [wɑːnˈdəːr] *vi* (person) ぶらぶら歩く burábura arúkù; (attention) 散漫になる safíman ni narù; (mind, thoughts: here and there) さまよう samáyoù; (: to specific topic) 漂う tadáyoù

♦*vt* (the streets, the hills etc) ...をぶらぶら歩く ...wo burúbura arúkù

wane [wein] *vi* (moon) 欠ける kakérù; (enthusiasm, influence etc) 減る herú

wangle [wæŋˈgəl] (*inf*) *vt* うまい具合に獲得する umái guái ni kakútoku suru

want [wɑːnt] *vt* (wish for) 望む nozómu, ...が欲しい ...ga hoshíì; (need, require) ...が必要である ...ga hitsúyō de arù

♦*n: for want of* ...がないので ...ga naì no de

to want to do ...したい ...shitái

to want someone to do something ...に...してもらいたい ...ni ...shité moraitaì

wanted [wɑːntˈid] *adj* (criminal etc) 指名手配中の shiméitehàichū no 「*wanted*」(in advertisements) 求む motómù

wanting [wɑːn'tiŋ] *adj*: *to be found wanting* 期待を裏切る kitái wo urágirù

wanton [wɑːn'tən] *adj* (gratuitous) 理由のない riyú no naì; (promiscuous) 浮気な uwáki na

wants [wɑːnts] *npl* (needs) 必要とする物 hitsuyó to suru monò, ニーズ nīzù

war [wɔːr] *n* 戦争 seńsō
to make war (on) (*also fig*) ...と戦う ...to tatákau

ward [wɔːrd] *n* (in hospital) 病棟 byótō; (POL) 区 ku; (LAW: child: *also*: **ward of court**) 被後見人 hikókennin

warden [wɔːr'dən] *n* (of park, game reserve, youth hostel) 管理人 kańriniñ; (of prison etc) 所長 shochó; (*BRIT*: *also*: **traffic warden**) 交通監視官 kōtsūkanshikañ

warder [wɔːr'dəːr] *n* (*BRIT*) 看守 kańshu

ward off *vt* (attack, enemy) 食止める kuítomeru; (danger, illness) 防ぐ fuségù

wardrobe [wɔːr'droub] *n* (for clothes) 洋服だんす yófukudañsu; (collection of clothes) 衣装 ishó; (CINEMA, THEATER) 衣装部屋 ishóbeya

warehouse [we:r'haus] *n* 倉庫 sōkò

wares [we:rz] *npl* 商品 shóhin, 売物 urímono

warfare [wɔːr'fe:r] *n* 戦争 seńsō

warhead [wɔːr'hed] *n* 弾頭 dańtō

warily [we:r'ili:] *adv* 用心深く yōjínbukakù

warlike [wɔːr'laik] *adj* (nation) 好戦的な kósenteki na; (appearance) 武装した busóshita

warm [wɔːrm] *adj* (meal, soup, day, clothes etc) 暖かい atátakaì; (thanks) 心からの kokóro kara no; (applause, welcome) 熱烈な netsúretsu na; (person, heart) 優しい yasáshii, 温情のある onjó no arù
it's warm (just right) 暖かい atátakaì; (too warm) 暑い atsúì
I'm warm 暑い atsúì
warm water ぬるま湯 murúmayù

warm-hearted [wɔːrm'hɑːr'tid] *adj* 心の優しい kokóro no yasáshii

warmly [wɔːrm'li:] *adv* (applaud, welcome) 熱烈に netsúretsu ni
to dress warmly 厚着する atsúgi suru

warmth [wɔːrmθ] *n* (heat) 暖かさ atátakasa; (friendliness) 温かみ atátakami

warm up *vi* (person, room, soup, etc) 暖まる atátamarù; (weather) 暖かくなる atátakaku narù; (athlete) 準備運動をする juńbiundō wo suru, ウォーミングアップする uōminguappù suru
♦*vt* (hands etc) 暖める atátamerù; (engine) 暖気運転する dańkiuñten suru

warn [wɔːrn] *vt* (advise): *to warn someone of/that* ...に...があると/...だと)警告する ...ni ...ga arù to (...da to)keíkoku suru
to warn someone not to do ...に...しないよう警告する ...ni ...shinái yō keíkoku suru

warning [wɔːr'niŋ] *n* 警告 keíkoku

warning light *n* 警告灯 keíkokutō

warning triangle *n* (AUT) 停止表示板 teíshihyōjibañ

warp [wɔːrp] *vi* (wood etc) ゆがむ yugámu
♦*vt* (*fig*: character) ゆがめる yugámeru

warrant [wɔːr'ənt] *n* (voucher) 証明書 shómeíshò; (LAW: for arrest) 逮捕状 taíhojò; (: search warrant) 捜索令状 sōsakureíjò

warranty [wɔːr'ənti:] *n* (guarantee) 保証 hoshó

warren [wɔːr'ən] *n* (*also*: **rabbit warren**) ウサギ小屋 uságigoya; (*fig*: of passages, streets) 迷路 meíro

warrior [wɔːr'i:əːr] *n* 戦士 seńshi

Warsaw [wɔːr'sɔː] *n* ワルシャワ warúshawa

warship [wɔːr'ʃip] *n* 軍艦 guńkan

wart [wɔːrt] *n* いぼ ibó

wartime [wɔːr'taim] *n*: *in wartime* 戦時中 seńjichū

wary [we:r'i:] *adj* 用心深い yōjinbukaì

was [wʌz] *pt of* **be**

wash [wɔːʃ] *vt* (gen) 洗う aráu; (clothes etc) 洗濯する seńtaku suru

♦*vi* (person) 手を洗う te wò aráu; (sea etc): *to wash over/against something* ...に打寄せる ...ni uchíyoseru, ...を洗う ...wo aráu

♦*n* (clothes etc) 洗濯物 señtakumono; (washing program) 洗い arái; (of ship) 航跡の波 kóseki no namî

to have a wash 手を洗う te wò aráu

to give something a wash ...を洗う ...wo aráu

washable [wɔːʃʼəbəl] *adj* 洗濯できる señtaku dekirû

wash away *vt* (stain) 洗い落す araiotosu; (subj: flood, river etc) 流す nagasu

washbasin [wɔːʃʼbeisin] (*US also:* **washbowl**) *n* 洗面器 señmeñki

washcloth [wɔːʃʼklɔːθ] (*US*) *n* (face cloth) フェースタオル fêsutaorù

washer [wɔːʃʼəʳ] *n* (TECH: metal) 座金 zagáne, ワッシャー wasshá; (machine) 洗濯機 señtakuki

washing [wɔːʃʼiŋ] *n* (dirty, clean) 洗濯物 señtakumono

washing machine *n* 洗濯機 señtakuki

washing powder (*BRIT*) *n* 洗剤 señzai

washing-up [wɔːʃʼiŋʌpʼ] (*BRIT*) *n* (action) 皿洗い saráaraì; (dirty dishes) 汚れた皿 yogóretà sará

washing-up liquid (*BRIT*) *n* 台所用洗剤 daídokoroyô senzai

wash off *vi* 洗い落される aráiotosàreru

wash-out [wɔːʃʼaut] (*inf*) *n* (failed event) 失敗 shippaí

washroom [wɔːʃʼruːm] (*US*) *n* お手洗い o-téaraì

wash up *vi* (*US*) 手を洗う te wò aráu; (*BRIT*) 皿洗いをする saráaraì wo suru

wasn't [wʌzʼənt] = **was not**

wasp [wɑːsp] *n* アシナガバチ ashínagabàchi ◇スズメバチなど肉食性のハチの総称 suzúmebàchi nado nikúshokuseî no hachi no sôshō

wastage [weisʼtidʒ] *n* (amount wasted, loss) 浪費 rôhi

natural wastage 自然消耗 shizénshōmō

waste [weist] *n* (act of wasting: life, money, energy, time) 浪費 rôhi; (rubbish)

廃棄物 haíkibutsu; (*also:* **household waste**) ごみ gomí

♦*adj* (material) 廃棄の haíki no; (left over) 残り物の nokórimono no; (land) 荒れた aréta

♦*vt* (time, life, money, energy) 浪費する rôhi suru; (opportunity) 失う ushínau, 逃す nogásù

to lay waste (destroy: area, town) 破壊する hakái suru

waste away *vi* 衰弱する suíjaku suru

waste disposal unit (*BRIT*) *n* ディスポーザー disúpōzà

wasteful [weistʼfəl] *adj* (person) 無駄使いの多い mudázùkai no ôî; (process) 不経済な fukeízai na

waste ground (*BRIT*) *n* 空き地 akíchi

wastepaper basket [weistʼpeipəːr-] *n* くずかご kuzúkàgo

waste pipe *n* 排水管 haísuîkan

wastes [weists] *npl* (area of land) 荒れ野 aréno

watch [wɑːtʃ] *n* (*also:* **wristwatch**) 腕時計 udédokeì; (act of watching) 見張り mihári; (vigilance) 警戒 keíkai; (group of guards: MIL, NAUT) 番兵 bañpei; (NAUT: spell of duty) 当直 tôchoku, ワッチ watchî

♦*vt* (look at: people, objects, TV etc) 見る mírù; (spy on, guard) 見張る miháru; (be careful of) ...に気を付ける ...ni ki wó tsukerú

♦*vi* (look) 見る mírù; (keep guard) 見張る miháru

watchdog [wɑːtʃʼdɔːg] *n* (dog) 番犬 bañken; (*fig*) 監視者 kañshisha, お目付け役 o-métsukeyaku

watchful [wɑːtʃʼfəl] *adj* 注意深い chúibukaì

watchmaker [wɑːtʃʼmeikəːr] *n* 時計屋 tokéiya

watchman [wɑːtʃʼmən] (*pl* **watchmen**) *n* *see* night

watch out *vi* 気を付ける ki wó tsukerù, 注意する chúi suru

watch out! 危ない！ abúnai!

watch strap *n* 腕時計のバンド udédokeì no bañdo

water [wɔː'təːr] n (cold) 水 mizú; (hot) (お) 湯 (o)yú

♦vt (plant) ...に水をやる ...ni mizú wo yarú

♦vi (eyes) 涙が出る namída ga derú; (mouth) よだれが出る yodáre ga derú

in British waters 英国領海に〔で〕eíkokuryōkái ni(de)

water cannon n 放水砲 hōsuihō

water closet (BRIT) n トイレ toìre

watercolor [wɔː'təːrkʌləːr] n (picture) 水彩画 suísaiga

watercress [wɔː'təːrkres] n クレソン kuréson

water down vt (milk etc) 水で薄める mizú de usúmeru; (fig: story) 和らげる yawáragerù

waterfall [wɔː'təːrfɔːl] n 滝 takí

water heater n 湯沸器 yuwákashikì

watering can [wɔː'təːriŋ-] n じょうろ jōrō

water level n 水位 suíi

water lily n スイレン suíren

waterline [wɔː'təːrlaìn] n (NAUT) 喫水線 kíssúisen

waterlogged [wɔː'təːrlɔːgd] adj (ground) 水浸しの mizúbitashi no

water main n 水道本管 suídōhonkań

watermelon [wɔː'təːrmeləņ] n スイカ suíka

waterproof [wɔː'təːrpruːf] adj (trousers, jacket etc) 防水の bōsui no

watershed [wɔː'təːrʃed] n (GEO: natural boundary) 分水界 buńsuikaì; (: high ridge) 分水嶺 buńsuìrei; (fig) 分岐点 buńkitèn

water-skiing [wɔː'təːrskiːiŋ] n 水上スキー suíjōsukī

watertight [wɔː'təːrtait] adj (seal) 水密の suímitsu no

waterway [wɔː'təːrwei] n 水路 suíro

waterworks [wɔː'təːrwəːrks] n (building) 浄水場 jōsuijō

watery [wɔː'təːriː] adj (coffee) 水っぽい mizúppoì; (eyes) 涙ぐんだ namídagundà

watt [wɑːt] n ワット wattō

wave [weiv] n (of hand) 一振り hitófuri; (on water) 波 namí; (RADIO) 電波 deńpà; (in hair) ウェーブ uébù; (fig: surge) 高まり takámarì, 急増 kyūzō

♦vi (signal) 手を振る te wò furù; (branches, grass) 揺れる yuréru; (flag) なびく nabíkù

♦vt (hand, flag, handkerchief) 振る furù; (gun, stick) 振回す furímawasù

wavelength [weiv'leŋkθ] n (RADIO) 波長 hachō

on the same wavelength (fig) 気が合って ki gà attè

waver [wei'vəːr] vi (voice) 震える furúeru; (love) 揺らぐ yurágu; (person) 動揺する dōyō suru

his gaze did not waver 彼は目を反らさなかった kárè wa mé wò sorásanakattà

wavy [wei'viː] adj (line) くねくねした kunékune shita; (hair) ウェーブのある uébù no aru

wax [wæks] n (polish, for skis) ワックス wakkùsu; (also: **earwax**) 耳あか mimíakà

♦vt (floor, car, skis) ...にワックスを掛ける ...ni wakkùsu wo kakérù

♦vi (moon) 満ちる michíru

waxworks [wæks'wəːrks] npl (models) ろう人形 rōniǹgyō

♦n (place) ろう人形館 rōniǹgyōkan

way [wei] n (route) ...へ行く道 ...e ikú michí; (path) 道 michí; (access) 出入口 deíriguchi; (distance) 距離 kyórì; (direction) 方向 hōkō; (manner, method) 方法 hōhō; (habit) 習慣 shūkan

which way? - this way どちらへ？-こちらへ dochìra é ? -kochíra e

on the way (en route) 途中で tochū de

to be on one's way 今向かっている imá mukátte irù, 途途中である imá tochū de arù

to be in the way (also fig) 邪魔である jamá de arù

to go out of one's way to do something わざわざ...する wazàwaza ...suru

under way (project etc) 進行中で shiñkōchū de

to lose one's way 道に迷う michí ni mayóù

in a way ある意味では arù imì de wa

in some ways ある面では arù men de wa

no way! (*inf*) 絶対に駄目だ zettái ni damé dà

by the way ... ところで tokóro dè

「*way in*」(BRIT) 入口 iríguchi

「*way out*」(BRIT) 出口 degùchi

the way back 帰路 kirò

「*way*」(BRIT: AUT) 進路譲れ shìnro yuzúre

waylay [weilei'] (*pt*, *pp* **waylaid**) *vt* 待伏せする machíbuse suru

wayward [wei'wərd] *adj* (behavior, child) わがままな wagamáma na

W.C. [dʌb'əlju:si:'] (BRIT) *n* トイレ toírè

we [wi:] *pl pron* 私たちは〔が〕watákushi-tàchi wa〔ga〕

weak [wi:k] *adj* (*gen*) 弱い yowáì; (dollar, pound) 安い yasúi; (excuse) 下手な hetá nà; (argument) 説得力のない settókuryoku no naì; (tea) 薄い usúi

weaken [wi:'kən] *vi* (person, resolve) 弱る yowárù; (health) 衰える otóroerù; (influence, power) 劣る otóru

◆*vt* (person, government) 弱くする yowákù suru

weakling [wi:k'liŋ] *n* (physically) 虚弱児 kyojákuji; (morally) 骨無し honénashi

weakness [wi:k'nis] *n* (frailty) 弱さ yowása; (fault) 弱点 jakúten

to have a weakness for ...に目がない ...ni me gà naì

wealth [welθ] *n* (money, resources) 富 tomí, 財産 zaísan; (of details, knowledge etc) 豊富さ hófu na

wealthy [wel'θi:] *adj* (person, family, country) 裕福な yúfùku na

wean [wi:n] *vt* (baby) 離乳させる rinyǘ saséru

weapon [wep'ən] *n* 武器 bukì

wear [we:r] *n* (use) 使用 shiyǒ; (damage through use) 消耗 shǒmō; (clothing): *sportswear* スポーツウェア supótsùuea

◆*vb* (*pt* **wore**, *pp* **worn**)

◆*vt* (shirt, blouse, dress etc) 着る kirú; (hat etc) かぶる kabúrù; (shoes, pants, skirt etc) はく hakú; (gloves etc) はめる

haméru; (make-up) つける tsukérù; (damage: through use) 使い古す tsukáifurusù

◆*vi* (last) 使用に耐える shiyǒ ni taérù; (rub through etc: carpet, shoes, jeans) すり減る suríherù

babywear 幼児ウェア yōjíuea

evening wear イブニングウェア ibúningu ueà

wear and tear *n* 消耗 shǒmō

wear away *vt* すり減らす suríherasu

◆*vi* (inscription etc) すり減って消える suríhette kíeru

wear down *vt* (heels) すり減らす suríherasu; (person, strength) 弱くする yowákù suru, 弱らせる yowáraserù

wear off *vi* (pain etc) なくなる nakúnaru

wear out *vt* (shoes, clothing) 使い古す tsukáifurusù; (person) すっかり疲れさせる sukkárì tsukáresaséru; (strength) なくす nakúsu

weary [wi:r'i:] *adj* (tired) 疲れ果てた tsukárehatetà; (dispirited) がっかりした gakkárì shita

◆*vi*: *to weary of* ...に飽きる ...ni akírù

weasel [wi:'zəl] *n* イタチ itáchi

weather [weð'ər] *n* 天気 teñki, 天候 teñkō

◆*vt* (storm, crisis) 乗切る noríkirù

under the weather (*fig*: ill) 気分が悪い kibûn ga warúì

weather-beaten [weð'ə:rbi:tən] *adj* (face, skin, building, stone) 風雪に鍛えられた fǔsetsu ni kitáeraretà

weathercock [weð'ə:rkɑ:k] *n* 風見鶏 kazámidòri

weather forecast *n* 天気予報 teñkiyohǒ

weatherman [weð'ə:rmæn] (*pl* **weathermen**) *n* 天気予報係 teñkiyohǒgakarì

weather vane [-vein] *n* = **weathercock**

weave [wi:v] (*pt* **wove**, *pp* **woven**) *vt* (cloth) 織る orù; (basket) 編む amù

weaver [wi:'və:r] *n* 機織職人 hatáorishokunin

weaving [wi:'viŋ] *n* (craft) 機織 hatáori

web [web] n (also: **spiderweb**) クモ の巣 kumó no su; (on duck's foot) 水かき mizúkaki; (network, also fig) 網 amí

we'd [wi:d] = **we had; we would**

wed [wed] (pt, pp **wedded**) vt (marry) ...と結婚する ...to kekkón suru
◆vi ...の重さは...である ...no omósa wa ...de arú

wedding [wed'iŋ] n 結婚式 kekkónshiki
silver/golden wedding (anniversary) 銀〔金〕婚式 giń〔kiń〕kónshiki

wedding day n (day of the wedding) 結婚の日 kekkón no hi; (US: anniversary) 結婚記念日 kekkón kinenbi

wedding dress n 花嫁衣装 hanáyome ishō, ウエディングドレス uédingudorèsu

wedding present n 結婚祝い kekkón iwaî

wedding ring n 結婚指輪 kekkón yubíwa

wedge [wedʒ] n (of wood etc) くさび kusábi; (of cake) 一切れ hitókirè
◆vt (jam with a wedge) くさびで留める kusábi dè toméru; (pack tightly: of people, animals) 押込む oshíkomù

Wednesday [wenz'dei] n 水曜日 suíyòbi

wee [wi:] (SCOTTISH) adj (little) 小さい chíísaì

weed [wi:d] n 雑草 zassó
◆vt (garden) ...の草むしりをする ...no kusámushìri wo suru

weedkiller [wi:d'kilə:r] n 除草剤 josôzai

weedy [wi:'di:] adj (man) 柔そうな yawásō na

week [wi:k] n 週間 shúkan
a week today/on Friday 来週の今日〔金曜日〕raíshū no kyō〔kiń-yòbi〕

weekday [wi:k'dei] n (gen, COMM) 平日 heíjitsu, ウイークデー uíkùdē

weekend [wi:k'end] n 週末 shūmátsu, ウイークエンド uíkueñdo

weekly [wi:k'li:] adv (deliver etc) 毎週 maíshū
◆adj (newspaper) 週刊の shúkan no; (payment) 週払いの shúbarai no; (visit etc) 毎週の maishū no
◆n (magazine) 週刊誌 shúkanshi; (newspaper) 週刊新聞 shúkanshínbun

weep [wi:p] (pt, pp **wept**) vi (person) 泣く naku

weeping willow [wi:'piŋ-] n シダレヤナギ shidáreyanàgi

weigh [wei] vt ...の重さを計る ...no omósa wo hakáru
◆vi ...の重さは...である ...no omósa wa ...de arú
to weigh anchor いかりを揚げる ikári wo agéru

weigh down vt (person, pack animal etc) ...の重さで動きが遅くなる ...no omósa de ugóki ga osóku narù; (fig: with worry): *to be weighed down* ...で沈み込む ...de shizúmikomù

weight [weit] n (metal object) 重り omóri; (heaviness) 重さ omósa
to lose/put on weight 体重が減る〔増える〕taíjū ga herú〔fueru〕

weighting [wei'tiŋ] (BRIT) n (allowance) 地域手当 chiíkiteatè

weightlifter [weit'liftə:r] n 重量挙げ選手 jūryóage señshu

weighty [wei'ti:] adj (heavy) 重い omói; (important: matters) 重大な júdai na

weigh up vt (person, offer, risk) 評価する hyōka suru

weir [wi:r] n せき sekì

weird [wi:rd] adj 奇妙な kimyō na

welcome [wel'kəm] n (visitor, suggestion, change) 歓迎すべき kangeisubeki; (news) うれしい ureshii
◆n 歓迎 kañgei
◆vt (visitor, delegation, suggestion, change) 歓迎する kañgei suru; (be glad of: news) うれしく思う uréshiku omóù
thank you - you're welcome! どうも有難う-どういたしまして dōmò arígàtō - dō.itáshimashìtè

weld [weld] n 溶接 yósetsu
◆vt 溶接する yósetsu suru

welfare [wel'fe:r] n (well-being) 幸福 kófuku, 福祉 fukúshî; (social aid) 生活保護 seíkatsuhogò

welfare state n 福祉国家 fukúshikokkà

welfare work n 福祉事業 fukúshijigyò

well [wel] n (for water) 井戸 idô; (also: **oil well**) 油井 yuséi

♦*adv* (to a high standard, thoroughly: *also* for emphasis with adv, adj or prep phrase) よく yokù

♦*adj: to be well* (person: in good health) 元気である geńkì de árù

♦*excl* そう，ねえ sò, nē

as well (in addition) も mo

as well as (in addition to) ...の外に ...no hoká ni

well done! よくやった yokù yattá

get well soon! 早く治ります様に hayàku naôrimasu yō nì, お大事に o-dáiji ni

to do well (person) 順調である juńchō de arù; (business) 繁盛する hańjō suru

we'll [wiːl] = we will; we shall

well-behaved [welbiheivd'] *adj* (child, dog) 行儀の良い gyôgi no yoí

well-being [wel'biː'iŋ] *n* 幸福 kôfuku, 福祉 fukúshi

well-built [wel'bilt'] *adj* (person) 体格の良い taíkaku no yoí

well-deserved [wel'dizə:rvd'] *adj* (success, prize) 努力相応の doryòkusôô no

well-dressed [wel'drest'] *adj* 身なりの良い minári no yoí

well-heeled [wel'hiːld'] (*inf*) *adj* (wealthy) 金持の kanémochì no

wellingtons [wel'iŋtənz] *npl* (*also:* **wellington boots**) ゴム長靴 gomúnagagutsu

well-known [wel'noun'] *adj* (famous: person, place) 有名な yûmei na

well-mannered [wel'mæn'ə:rd] *adj* 礼儀正しい reígitádashiì

well-meaning [wel'miː'niŋ] *adj* (person) 善意の zeń-i no; (offer etc) 善意に基づく zeń-i ni motózuku

well-off [wel'ɔ:f'] *adj* (rich) 金持の kanémochì no

well-read [wel'red'] *adj* 博学の hakúgaku no

well-to-do [wel'tədu:'] *adj* 金持の kanémochì no

well up *vi* (tears) こみ上げる komíageru

well-wisher [wel'wiʃə:r] *n* (friends, admirers) 支持者 shijìsha, ファン fañ

Welsh [welʃ] *adj* ウェールズの uèruzu no; (LING) ウェールズ語の uèruzugo no

♦*n* (LING) ウェールズ語 uèruzugo

Welsh *npl: the Welsh* ウェールズ人 uèruzujin

Welshman/woman [welʃ'mən/wumən] (*pl* **Welshmen/women**) *n* ウェールズ人の男性〔女性〕 uèruzujin no dańsei〔joséi〕

Welsh rarebit [-reːr'bit] *n* チーズトースト chīzùtôsùto

went [went] *pt of* go

wept [wept] *pt, pp of* weep

we're [wiːr] = we are

were [wəːr] *pt of* be

weren't [wəːr'ənt] = were not

west [west] *n* (direction) 西 nishí; (part of country) 西部 seíbu

♦*adj* (wing, coast, side) 西の nishí no, 西側の nishígawa no

♦*adv* (to/towards the west) 西へ nishí e

west wind 西風 nishíkaze

West *n: the West* (POL: US plus western Europe) 西洋 seíyō

West Country: *the West Country* (*BRIT*) *n* 西部地方 seíbuchihō

westerly [wes'tə:rli] *adj* (point) 西寄りの nishíyori no; (wind) 西からの nishí kara no

western [wes'tə:rn] *adj* (of the west) 西の nishí no; (POL: of the West) 西洋の seíyō no

♦*n* (CINEMA) 西部劇 seíbugeki

West Germany *n* 西ドイツ nishídoitsu

West Indian *adj* 西インド諸島の nishíindoshotò nð

♦*n* 西インド諸島の人 nishíindoshotō no hitð

West Indies [-in'di:z] *npl* 西インド諸島 nishíindoshotō

westward(s) [west'wə:rd(z)] *adv* 西へ nishí e

wet [wet] *adj* (damp) 湿った shimétta; (wet through) ぬれた nuréta; (rainy: weather, day) 雨模様の amémòyō no

♦*n* (*BRIT*: POL) 穏健派の人 onkénha no hitð

to get wet (person, hair, clothes) ぬれる nuréru

「*wet paint*」ペンキ塗立て peńki nurítate

to be a wet blanket (*fig*) 座を白けさせ

る za wò shirákesaseru

wet suit n ウェットスーツ uéttòsūtsu

we've [wi:v] = **we have**

whack [wæk] vt たたく tatákù

whale [weil] n (ZOOL) クジラ kujíra

wharf [wɔ:rf] (pl **wharves**) n 岸壁 gañpeki

wharves [wɔ:rvz] npl of **wharf**

KEYWORD

what [wʌt] adj 1 (in direct/indirect questions) 何の náñ no, 何... nánì...

what size is it? サイズは幾つですか sáìzu wa íkùtsu desu ká

what color is it? 何色ですか nánì iro desu ká

what shape is it? 形はどうなっていますか katáchi wà dô nattè imásù ká

what books do you need? どんな本がいりますか dóñna hóñ ga irímasù ká

he asked me what books I needed 私にはどんな本がいるかと彼は聞いていました watákushi ni wà dóñna hóñ ga irú kà to kárè wa kiíte imáshìta

2 (in exclamations) 何て...náñte...

what a mess! 何て有様だ náñte arísama dà

what a fool I am! 私は何てばかだ watákushi wà náñte bákà da

◆pron 1 (interrogative) 何 nánì, 何 náñ

what are you doing? 何をしていますか nánì wo shité imasù ká

what is happening? どうなっていますか dô nattè imásù ká

what's in there? その中に何が入っていますか sonó nakà ni nánì ga háìtte imasu ká

what is it? - it's a tool 何ですか-道具です náñ desu ká - dôgu desu

what are you talking about? 何の話ですか náñ no hanáshì desu ká

what is it called? これは何と言いますか kórè wa náñ to iímasù ká

what about me? 私はどうすればいいんですか watákushi wà dô surèba iíñ desu ká

what about doing ...? ...しませんか ...shimáseñ ká

2 (relative): **is that what happened?** 事件は今話した通りですか jíkèn wa ímà hanáshita tôri desu ká

I saw what you did/was on the table あなたのした事〔テーブルにあった物〕を見ました anátà no shitá kotò〔tēburu ni attá monò〕wo mimáshìta

he asked me what she had said 彼は彼女の言った事を私に尋ねた kárè wa kánòjo no ittá kotò wo watákushi nì tazúnetà

tell me what you're thinking about 今何を考えているか教えて下さい ímà nánì wo kañgaete irù ká oshíete kudasai

what you say is wrong あなたの言っている事は間違っています anátà no itté iru kotò wà machígattè imásù

◆excl (disbelieving) 何 nánì

what, no coffee! 何, コーヒーがないんだって? nánì, kôhī gà naíñ dattè?

I've crashed the car - what! 車をぶつけてしまった-何? kurúma wò butsúkete shimattà - nánì?

---

whatever [wʌtev'ə:r] adj: **whatever book** どんな本でも doñna hoñ de mo

◆pron: **do whatever is necessary/you want** 何でも必要〔好き〕な事をしなさい nañ de mo hitsúyō〔sukí〕na koto wò shinásai

whatever happens 何が起っても naní ga okôtte mo

no reason whatever/whatsoever 全く理由がない mattáku riyû ga nai

nothing whatever 全く何もない mattáku nanî mo nai

whatsoever [wʌtsouev'ə:r] adj = **whatever**

wheat [wi:t] n 小麦 komúgi

wheedle [wi:d'əl] vt: **to wheedle someone into doing something** ...を口車に乗せて...させる ...wo kuchíguruma ni noséte ...sasèru

to wheedle something out of someone 口車に乗せて...を...からだまし取る kuchíguruma ni noséte ...wo ...karà damáshitorù

wheel [wi:l] n (of vehicle etc) 車 kurúma,

車輪 sharín, ホイール hoíru; (*also*: **steering wheel**) ハンドル handoru; (NAUT) だ輪 darín
♦*vt* (pram etc) 押す osú
♦*vi* (birds) 旋回する senkai suru; (*also*: **wheel round**: person) 急に向き直る kyū ni mukínaorù

wheelbarrow [wi:l'bærou] *n* 一輪車 ichírīnsha, ネコ車 nekóguruma

wheelchair [wi:l'tʃe:r] *n* 車いす kurúmaisù

wheel clamp *n* (AUT) ◇違反駐車の自動車車輪に付けて走れなくする金具 ihánchūsha ni jidōshàsharin ni tsukéte hashírenaku surù kanágu

wheeze [wi:z] *vi* (person) ぜいぜいいう zeízei iú

KEYWORD

when [wen] *adv* いつ ítsù
when did it happen? いつ起ったんですか ítsù okóttan desu ká
I know when it happened いつ起ったかはちゃんと分かっています ítsù okótta kà wa chanto wakátte imasù
when are you going to Italy? イタリアにはいつ行きますか itárìa ni wa ítsù ikímasù ká
when will you be back? いつ帰って来ますか ítsù kaétte kimasù ká
♦*conj* 1 (at, during, after the time that) ...する時 ...surú tokì, ...すると ...surú tò, ...したら ...shitárà, ...してから ...shité karà
she was reading when I came in 私が部屋に入った時彼女は本を読んでいました watákushi gà heyá nì háitta toki kánòjo wa hôn wo yónde imáshìta
when you've read it, tell me what you think これを読んだらご意見を聞かせて下さい kóre wo yóndara go-íkèn wo kikásete kudasaì
be careful when you cross the road 道路を横断する時には気を付けてね dōro wo ôdàn suru tokì ni wa kí wò tsukéte nè
that was when I needed you あなたにいて欲しかったのはその時ですよ aná-

tà ni íté hoshikàtta no wa sonó tokì desu yô
2: (on, at which): *on the day when I met him* 彼に会った日は kárè ni áttà hí wà
one day when it was raining 雨が降っていたある日 ámè ga futté ità árù hí
3 (whereas): *you said I was wrong when in fact I was right* あなたは私が間違っていると言いましたが、事実は間違っていませんでした anátà wa watákushi gà machígatte irù to iímashita gà, jíjìtsu wa machígattè imásen deshìta
why did you buy it when you can't afford it? 金の余裕がないのになぜあれを買ったんですか kané nò yoyú gà náì no ni názè aré wò kattán desu ká

whenever [wenev'ə:r] *adv* いつか ítsù ka
♦*conj* (any time) ...するといつも ...surù to itsùmo...; (every time that) ...する度に ...surù tabí ni

where [we:r] *adv* (place, direction) どこ(に, で) dókò (ni, de)
♦*conj* ...の所に(で) ...no tokóro ni(de)
this is where ... これは...する所です koré wa ... surù tokoro desu

whereabouts [we:r'əbauts] *adv* どの辺に donò hen ni
♦*n*: *nobody knows his whereabouts* 彼の居場所は不明だ karè no ibásho wa fuméi da

whereas [we:ræz'] *conj* ...であるのに対して ...de arù no ni taìshite

whereby [we:rbai'] *pron* それによって soré ni yottè

whereupon [we:rəpa:n'] *conj* すると surú to

wherever [we:rev'ə:r] *conj* (no matter where) どこに(で)...しても dokò ni(de) ...shite mo; (not knowing where) どこに...か知らないが dokò ni ...ká shiranai ga
♦*adv* (interrogative: surprise) 一体全体どこに(で) ittái zentai dokò ni(de)

wherewithal [we:r'wiθɔ:l] *n* 金 kané

whet [wet] *vt* (appetite) そそる sosóru

whether [weð'ə:r] *conj* ...かどうか ...ka dô kà

I don't know whether to accept or not 引受けるべきかどうかは分からない hikĩukerubeki kà dõ kà wa wakãranai
whether you go or not 行くにしても行かないにしても ikũ nĩ shité mò ikãnai nĩ shité mò
it's doubtful whether he will come 彼はたぶん来ないだろう karè wa tabùn kõnai darō

KEYWORD

which [witʃ] *adj* 1 (interrogative: direct, indirect) どの dõnò, どちらの dõchīra no
which picture do you want? どちらの絵がいいんですか dõchīra no é gà iĩ desu ká
which books are yours? あなたの本はどれとどれですか anãta no hõn wa dõre to dõre desu ká
tell me which picture/books you want どの絵〔本〕が欲しいか言って下さい dõnò é〔hõn〕gà hoshíi kà itté kudasai
which one? どれ dõrè
which one do you want? どれが欲しいんですか dõre ga hoshíin desu ká
which one of you did it? あなたたちのだれがやったんですか anãta tachi no dárè ga yattãn desu ká
2: *in which case* その場合 sonõ baài
the train may be late, in which case don't wait up 列車が遅れるかもしれないが, その場合先に寝て下さい rèsshá ga okũreru ka mò shirênai ga, sonõ baài sakí ni netè kudasai
by which time その時 sonõ tokì
we got there at 8 pm, by which time the cinema was full 映画館に着いたのは夜の8時でしたが, もう満席になっていました eigãkan ni tsuíta no wa yõrubu no hachíjī deshita ga, mõ mañseki ni nattè imashíta

◆*pron* 1 (interrogative) どれ dõrè
which (of these) are yours? どれとどれがあなたの物ですか dõre to dõre ga anãta no monõ desù ká
which of you are coming? あなたたちのだれとだれが一緒に来てくれますか a-nãtatachi no dárè to dárè ga ísshò ni

kité kuremasù ká
here are the books/files - tell me which you want 本〔ファイル〕はこれだけありますが, どれとどれが欲しいですか hõn〔fáiru〕wa korè dakè arĩmasù ga, dõre to dõre ga hoshíin desu ká
I don't mind which どれでもいいんですよ dõre de mo iĩ desu yó
2 (relative): *the apple which is on the table* あなたの食べた〔テーブルにある〕りんご anãta no tãbèta〔tèburu ni árù〕riñgo
the meeting (which) we attended 私たちが出席した会議 watãkushitãchi ga shusséki shitã kãigi
the chair on which you are sitting あなたが座っているいす anãta ga suwãt-te irù ísu
the book of which you spoke あなたが話していた本 anãta ga hanãshite itã hõn
he said he knew, which is true/I feared 彼は知っていると言ったが, その通りでした〔私の心配していた通りでした〕 kárè wa shitté irù to ittã ga, sonõ tòri deshita〔watãkushi nõ shiñpai shite ita tòri deshita〕
after which その後 sonõ atò

whichever [witʃ'ev'ə:r] *adj:* *take whichever book you prefer* どれでもいいから好きな本を取って下さい doré de mo iĩ kara sukí nà hon wo tottè kudasai
whichever book you take あなたがどの本を取っても anãta ga donõ hon wo tottè mo

whiff [wif] *n* (of perfume, gasoline, smoke) ちょっと...のにおいがすること chottõ ...no nióī ga suru koto

while [wail] *n* (period of time) 間 aĩda
◆*conj* (at the same time as) ...する間 ...surú aida; (as long as) ...する限りは ...surú kagìri wa; (although) ...するにもかかわらず ...surú nĩ mo kakãwarazu
for a while しばらくの間 shibãraku no aĩda

while away *vt* (time) つぶす tsubúsu

whim [wim] *n* 気まぐれ kimãgure

whimper [wim'pər] n (cry, moan) 哀れ
っぽい泣き声 awáreppoî nakígoè
♦vi (child, animal) 哀れっぽいなき声を
出す awáreppoî nakígoè wo dasù

whimsical [wim'zikəl] adj (person) 気ま
ぐれな kimágure na; (poem) 奇抜な kibátsu na; (look, smile) 変な heñ na

whine [wain] n (of pain) 哀れっぽいなき
声 awáreppoî nakígoè; (of engine, siren)
うなり unári
♦vi (person, animal) 哀れっぽいなき声を
出す awáreppoî nakígoè wo dasù;
(engine, siren) うなる unárù; (fig: complain) 愚痴をこぼす guchî wo kobósù

whip [wip] n (lash, riding whip) むち mu-
chî; (POL) 院内幹事 ínnaikañji
♦vt (person, animal) むち打つ muchíutsù; (cream, eggs) 泡立てる awádaterù,
ホイップする hoíppù suru; (move quickly): **to whip something out/off** さっと
取出す〔はずす, 脱ぐ〕sattò torídasu
(hazúsu, nugù)

whipped cream [wipt-] n ホイップクリ
ーム hoíppukurīmù

whip-round [wip'raund] (BRIT) n 募金
bokín

whirl [wə:rl] vt (arms, sword etc) 振回す
furímawasù
♦vi (dancers) ぐるぐる回る gurùguru
mawáru; (leaves, water etc) 渦巻く uzúmakù

whirlpool [wə:rl'pu:l] n 渦巻 uzúmàki

whirlwind [wə:rl'wind] n 竜巻 tatsúmaki

whir(r) [wə:r] vi (motor etc) うなり unári

whisk [wisk] n (CULIN) 泡立て器 awá-
datekì
♦vt (cream, eggs) 泡立てる awádaterù
to whisk someone away/off ...を素早
く連去る ...wo subáyakù tsurésarù

whiskers [wis'kə:rz] npl (of animal,
man) ひげ higé

whiskey [wis'ki:] (BRIT **whisky**) n ウイ
スキー uísukì

whisper [wis'pə:r] n (low voice) ささや
き sasáyaki
♦vi ささやく sasáyakù

♦vt ささやく sasáyakù

whist [wist] (BRIT) n ホイスト hoísuto

whistle [wis'əl] n (sound) 口笛 kuchíbue;
(object) 笛 fuě
♦vi (person) 口笛を吹く kuchíbue wo fukù; (bird) ぴーぴーさえずる pîpî saézurù;
(bullet) ひゅーとうなる hyû to unárù;
(kettle) ぴゅーと鳴る pyû to narú

white [wait] adj (color) 白い shiróî; (pale:
person, face) 青白い aójiroî; (with fear)
青ざめた aózamèta
♦n (color) 白 shiró; (person) 白人 hakújin;
(of egg) 白身 shirómì

white coffee (BRIT) n ミルク入りコー
ヒー mirúkuirikōhī

white-collar worker [wait'ka:'lə:r-] n
サラリーマン sarárīmàn, ホワイトカラー
howáitokarā

white elephant n (fig) 無用の長物 mu-
yố no chōbutsu

white lie n 方便のうそ hōbèn no usò

white paper n (POL) 白書 hakùsho

whitewash [wait'wa:ʃ] n (paint) のろ norò ◇石灰, 白亜, のりを水に混ぜた塗料
sekkài, hakùa, norí wo mizú ni mazèta
toryò
♦vt (building) ...にのろを塗る ...ni norò
wo nurù; (fig: happening, career, reputation) ...の表面を繕う ...no hyốmeñ wo
tsukúroù

whiting [wai'tiŋ] n inv (fish) タラ tarà

Whitsun [wit'sən] n 聖霊降臨節 seírei-
kōriñsetsu

whittle [wit'əl] vt: **to whittle away,
whittle down** (costs: reduce) 減らす herásu

whiz(z) [wiz] vi: **to whizz past/by** (person, vehicle etc) ぴゅーんと通り過ぎる
byûn to tõrisugirù

whiz(z) kid (inf) n 天才 teñsai

who [hu:] pron 1 (interrogative) だれ dárè, どなた dónata
who is it?, who's there? だれですか
dárè desu ká
who are you looking for? だれを捜し
ているんですか dárè wo sagáshite irùn

desu ká

I told her who I was 彼女に名乗りました kánòjo ni nanórimashìta

I told her who was coming to the party パーティの出席予定者を彼女に知らせました páti no shussékiyoteìsha wo kánòjo ni shirásemashìta

who did you see? だれを見ましたか dárè wo mimáshìta ká

2 (relative): *my cousin who lives in New York* ニューヨークに住んでいるいとこ nyúyòku ni súnde iru itókò

the man/woman who spoke to me 私に話しかけた男性〔女性〕watákushi nì hanáshikaketà dañséi〔joséi〕

those who can swim 泳げる人たち oyógerù hitótàchi

whodunit [hu:dʌn'it] (*inf*) *n* 探偵小説 tañteishōsetsu

whole [houl] *adj* (entire) 全体の zeñtai no; (not broken) 無傷の mukîzu no

♦*n* (entire unit) 全体 zeñtai; (all): *the whole of* 全体の zeñtai no

the whole of the town 町全体 machízeñtai

on the whole, as a whole 全体として zeñtai toshite

whole food(s) [houl'fu:d(z)] *n(pl)* 無加工の食べ物 mukákō no tabémonò

wholehearted [houl'hɑ:r'tid] *adj* (agreement etc) 心からの kokóro kàra no

wholemeal [houl'mi:l] *adj* (bread, flour) 全粒の zeñryū no, 全麦の zeñbaku no

wholesale [houl'seil] *n* (business) 卸 oróshi, 卸売 oróshiuri

♦*adj* (price) 卸の oróshi nò; (destruction) 大規模の daíkibò no

♦*adv* (buy, sell) 卸で oróshi dè

wholesaler [houl'seilə:r] *n* 問屋 toñ-ya

wholesome [houl'səm] *adj* (food, climate) 健康に良い keñkō ni yoì; (person) 健全な keñzen na

wholewheat [houl'wi:t] *adj* = **wholemeal**

wholly [hou'li:] *adv* (completely) 完全に kañzen ni

whom [hu:m] *pron* **1** (interrogative) だれを dáre wo, どなたを dónàta wo

whom did you see? だれを見ましたか dárè wo mimáshìta ká

to whom did you give it? だれに渡しましたか dárè ni watáshimashìta ká

tell me from whom you received it だれに〔から〕それをもらったかを教えて下さい dárè ni〔kárà〕soré wò morátta kà wo oshíete kudasaì

2 (relative): *the man whom I saw/to whom I spoke* 私が見た〔話し掛けた〕男性 watákushi gà mítà(hanáshikaketà) dañséi

the lady with whom I was talking 私と話していた女性 watákushi tò hanáshite ità joséi

whooping cough [wu:'piŋ-] *n* 百日ぜき hyakúnichizèki

whore [hɔːr] (*inf: pej*) *n* 売女 baíta

whose [hu:z] *adj* **1** (possessive: interrogative) だれの dáre no, どなたの dónàta no

whose book is this?, whose is this book? これはだれの本ですか koré wà dáre no hón desu ká

whose pencil have you taken? だれの鉛筆を持って来たんですか dárè no efñpitsu wò mottê kitañ desu ká

whose daughter are you? あなたはどなたの娘さんですか anátà wa dónàta no musúme-sañ desu ká

I don't know whose it is だれの物か私には分かりません dárè no monó kà watákushi ni wà wakárimaseñ

2 (possessive: relative): *the man whose son you rescued* あなたが助けた子供の父親 anátà ga tasúketa kodomò no chichíoya

the girl whose sister you were speaking to あなたと話していた女性の妹 anátà to hanáshite ità joséi no imótò

the woman whose car was stolen 車を盗まれた女性 kurúma wò nusúmaretà josếi

◆*pron* だれの物 dárè no monố, どなたの物 dốnàta no monố

whose is this? これはだれのですか kő-rè wa dárè no desu ká

I know whose it is だれの物か知っています dárè no monố kà shitté imasù

whose are these? これらはだれの物ですか korếra wa dárè no monố desù ká

whose do you come too? あなたも来ませんか anátà mo kimásèn ká

KEYWORD

why [wai] *adv* なぜ názè, どうして dőshìte

why is he always late? どうして彼はいつも遅刻するのですか dőshìte kárè wa ítsùmo chikőku suru nò desu ká

why don't you come too? あなたも来ませんか anátà mo kimásèn ká

I'm not coming - why not? 私は行きません-どうしてですか watákushi wà i-kímasèn - dőshìte desu ká

fancy a drink? - why not? 一杯やろうか-いいね íppài yárố ká - fí nế

why not do it now? 今すぐやりませんか ímà súgù yarímasèn ká

◆*conj* なぜ názè, どうして dőshìte

I wonder why he said that どうしてそんな事を言ったのかしら dőshìte sofina kotố wo ittá nò kashira

the reason why 理由 riyú

that's not (the reason) why I'm here 私が来たのはそのためじゃありません watákushi gà kitá no wà sonố tamè ja arímasèn

◆*excl* (expressing surprise, shock, annoyance etc) ◇日本語では表現しない場合が多い nihóngo de wà hyőgen shinaî baái gà ối

why, it's you! おや、あなたでしたか oyà, anátà deshita ká

why, that's impossible/quite unacceptable! そんな事はできません（認められません） sofina kotố wà dekímasèn 〔mitőmeraremasèn〕

I don't understand - why, it's obvious! 訳が分かりません-ばかでも分かる事だよ wákè ga wakárimasèn - bákà de

mo wakárù kotő dà yố

---

whyever [waiev'ə:r] *adv* 一体なぜ ittai názè

wicked [wik'id] *adj* (crime, man, witch) 極悪の gokúaku no; (smile) 意地悪そうな ijíwarusố na

wickerwork [wik'ə:rwə:rk] *adj* (basket, chair etc) 籐編みの tốami no, 枝編みの edáami no

◆*n* (objects) 籐編み細工品 tốamizaikuhin, 枝編み細工品 edáamizaikuhin

wicket [wik'it] *n* (CRICKET: stumps) 三柱門 sańchūmòn, ウイケット uíkètto; (: grass area) ピッチ pitchì

◇2つのウイケット間のグランド futátsu nò uíkettokàn no gurándo

wide [waid] *adj* (gen) 広い hiróî; (grin) 楽しげな tanőshigè na

◆*adv*: *to open wide* (window etc) 広く開ける hiróku akéru

to shoot wide ねらいを外す nerái wo hazúsu

wide-angle lens [waid'æŋ'gəl-] *n* 広角レンズ kőkaku reñzu

wide-awake [waid'əweik'] *adj* すっかり目が覚めた sukkárì me gà samèta

widely [waid'li:] *adv* (gen) 広く hiróku; (differing) 甚だしく hanáhadashikù

widen [wai'dən] *vt* (road, river, experience) 広くする hiróku suru, 広げる hirőgeru

◆*vi* (road, river, gap) 広くなる hiróku narù, 広がる hirőgaru

wide open *adj* (window, eyes, mouth) 大きく開けた ốkìku akéta

widespread [waidspred'] *adj* (belief etc) はびこった habíkottà

widow [wid'ou] *n* 未亡人 mibốjìn, 後家 gokế

widowed [wid'oud] *adj* (mother, father) やもめになった yamốme ni nattầ

widower [wid'ouə:r] *n* 男やもめ otőko-yamőme

width [widθ] *n* (distance) 広さ hirósa; (of cloth) 幅 habá

wield [wi:ld] *vt* (sword, power) 振るう fu-rúu

wife [waif] (*pl* **wives**) *n* (*gen*) 妻 tsumá; (one's own) 家内 kánai; (someone else's) 奥さん okúsan

wig [wig] *n* かつら katsúra

wiggle [wig'əl] *vt* (hips) くねらす kunérasù; (ears etc) ぴくぴく動かす pikùpiku ugókasù

wild [waild] *adj* (animal, plant) 野生の yaséi no; (rough: land) 荒れ果てた aréhatèta; (: weather, sea) 荒れ狂う arékuruù; (person, behavior, applause) 興奮した kófun shita; (idea) 突飛な toppí na; (guess) 当てずっぽうの atézuppō no

wilderness [wil'də:rnis] *n* 荒野 kōyà, 原野 geñ-ya, 未開地 mikáichì

wild-goose chase [waild'gu:s'-] *n* (*fig*) 無駄な捜索 mudá na sōsaku

wildlife [waild'laif] *n* (animals) 野生動物 yaséidōbùtsu

wildly [waild'li:] *adv* (behave) 狂った様に kurúttà yō ni; (applaud) 熱狂的に nekkyóteki ni; (hit) めくら滅法に mekúrameppō ni; (guess) 当てずっぽうに atézuppō ni; (happy) 最高に saíkō ni

wilds [waildz] *npl* 荒野 kōyà, 未開地 mikáichì

wilful [wil'fəl] (*US also*: **willful**) *adj* (obstinate: child, character) わがままな wagámamà na; (deliberate: action, disregard etc) 故意の koí no

---

KEYWORD

will [wil] (*vt*: *pt*, *pp* **willed**) *aux vb* **1** (forming future tense): *I will finish it tomorrow* 明日終ります ashíta owárimasù

I will have finished it by tomorrow 明日にでもなれば終るでしょう asú ni dè mo náreba owárù deshō

will you do it? - yes I will/no I won't やりますか-はい、やります〔いいえ、やりません〕yarímasù ká - hái, yarímasù(iíè, yarímasèn)

when will you finish it? いつ終りますか ítsu owárimasù ká

2 (in conjectures, predictions): *he will/he'll be there by now* 彼はもう着いているでしょう kárè wa mō tsúite irú de-

shō

that will be the postman 郵便屋さんでしょう yúbinya-san deshō

this medicine will help you この薬なら効くでしょう konó kusuri narà kikú deshō

this medicine won't help you この薬は何の役にも立ちません konó kusuri wà nań no yakú ni mò tachímaseñ

3 (in commands, requests, offers): *will you be quiet!* 黙りなさい damárinasaì

will you come? 来てくれますか kité kuremasù ká

will you help me? 手伝ってくれますか tetsúdattè kurémasù ká

will you have a cup of tea? お茶をいかがですか o-chá wò ikága desù ká

I won't put up with it! 我慢できません gámàn dekímaseñ

♦*vt: to will someone to do something* 意志の力で...に...をさせようとする íshì no chikára dè ...ni ...wò saséyō tò suru

he willed himself to go on 彼は精神力だけで続けようとした kárè wa seíshinryòku daké dè tsuzúkeyō tò shita

♦*n* (volition) 意志 íshì; (testament) 遺言 yuígon

---

willful [wil'fəl] (*US*) *adj* = **wilful**

willing [wil'iŋ] *adj* (with goodwill) 進んで...する susúnde ...surù; (enthusiastic) 熱心な nesshín na

he's willing to do it 彼はそれを引き受けてくれるそうです kárè wa soré wo hikíukète kureru sō dèsu

willingly [wil'iŋli:] *adv* 進んで susúnde

willingness [wil'iŋnis] *n* 好意 kōì

willow [wil'ou] *n* ヤナギ yanági

willpower [wil'pauə:r] *n* 精神力 seíshiñ-ryoku

willy-nilly [wil'i:nil'i:] *adv* 否応なしに i-yáō nashì ni

wilt [wilt] *vi* (flower, plant) 枯れる karéru

wily [wai'li:] *adj* (fox, move, person) ずる賢い zurúgashikoì

win [win] *n* (in sports etc) 勝利 shōrì, 勝ち kachí

♦vb (pt, pp **won**)

♦vt (game, competition) ...で勝つ ...de katsù; (election) ...で当選する ...de tōsen suru; (obtain: prize, medal) もらう moráu, 受ける ukérù; (money) 当てる atérù; (support, popularity) 獲得する kakútoku suru

♦vi 勝つ katsù

wince [wins] vi 顔がこわばる kaó ga kowábaru

winch [wintʃ] n ウインチ uínchi

wind¹ [wind] n (air) 風 kazé; (MED) 呼吸 kokyū́; (breath) 息 ikí

♦vt (take breath away from) ...の息を切らせる ...no ikí wo kiráserù

wind² [waind] (pt, pp **wound**) vt (roll: thread, rope) 巻く makú; (wrap: bandage) 巻付ける makítsukerù; (clock, toy) ...のぜんまいを巻く ...no zeńmai wo makú

♦vi (road, river) 曲りくねる magárikunerù

windfall [wind'fɔ:l] n (money) 棚ぼた tanábota

winding [wain'diŋ] adj (road) 曲りくねった magárikunettà; (staircase) らせん状の rasénjō no

wind instrument n (MUS) 管楽器 kaňgakki

windmill [wind'mil] n 風車 kazágurùma

window [win'dou] n 窓 madò

window box n ウインドーボックス uíndōbokkùsu

window cleaner n (person) 窓ふき職人 madófukishokùnin

window envelope n 窓付き封筒 madótsukifūtò

window ledge n 窓下枠 madóshitawàku

window pane n 窓ガラス madógaràsu

window-shopping [win'douʃɑ:piŋ] n ウインドーショッピング uíndōshoppìngu

windowsill [win'dousil] n 窓下枠 madóshitawàku

windpipe [wind'paip] n 気管 kikán

windscreen [wind'skri:n] (BRIT) n = **windshield**

windshield [wind'ʃi:ld] (US) n フロント

ガラス furóntogaràsu, ウインドシールド uíndoshīrùdo

windshield washer n ウインドシールドワシャー uíndoshīrudowashã̀

windshield wiper [-waip'əːr] n ワイパー waípā

windswept [wind'swept] adj (place) 吹きさらしの fukísarashi no; (person) 風で髪が乱れた kazé de kamí gà midárèta

wind up vt (clock, toy) ...のぜんまいを巻く ...no zeńmai wo makú; (debate) 終りにする owári ni suru

windy [win'di:] adj (weather, day) 風の強い kazé no tsuyoì

  it's windy 風が強い kazé ga tsuyoì

wine [wain] n ブドウ酒 budóshu, ワイン waìn

wine bar n ワインバー waínbā

wine cellar n ワインの地下貯蔵庫 waìn no chikáchozòkò

wine glass n ワイングラス waínguràsu

wine list n ワインリスト waínrisùto

wine merchant n ワイン商 waínshõ

wine waiter n ソムリエ somúrie

wing [wiŋ] n (of bird, insect, plane) 羽根 hanè, 翼 tsubàsa; (of building) 翼 yokú; (BRIT: AUT) フェンダー feńdā

winger [wiŋ'əːr] n (SPORT) ウイング uíngu

wings [wiŋz] npl (THEATER) そで sodé

wink [wiŋk] n (of eye) ウインク uíňku

♦vi (with eye) ウインクする uíňku suru; (light etc) 瞬く matátakù

winner [win'əːr] n (of prize, race, competition) 勝者 shōshà

winning [win'iŋ] adj (team, competitor, entry) 勝った kattà; (shot, goal) 決勝の kesshṓ no; (smile) 愛敬たっぷりの aíkyō tappùrí no

winnings [win'iŋz] npl 賞金 shōkin

win over vt (person: persuade) 味方にする mikáta ni suru

win round (BRIT) vt = **win over**

winter [win'təːr] n (season) 冬 fuyú

  in winter 冬には fuyú nì wa

winter sports npl ウインタースポーツ uíntāsupōtsù

wintry [win'tri:] adj (weather, day) 冬ら

しい fuyúrashiî

wipe [waip] *n*: *to give something a wipe* ...をふく ...wo fukú

◆*vt* (rub) ふく fukú; (erase: tape) 消す kesú

wipe off *vt* (remove) ふき取る fukítorù

wipe out *vt* (debt) 完済する kańsai suru; (memory) 忘れる wasúreru; (destroy: city, population) 滅ぼす horóbosù

wipe up *vt* (mess) ふき取る fukítorù

wire [wai'ə:r] *n* (metal etc) 針金 harígane; (ELEC) 電線 deñsen; (telegram) 電報 deñpō

◆*vt* (house) ...の配線工事をする ...no haísenkōji wo suru; (*also*: **wire up**: electrical fitting) 取り付ける torítsukerù; (person: telegram) ...に電報を打つ ...ni deñpō wo utsù

wireless [wai'ə:rlis] (*BRIT*) *n* ラジオ rajío

wiring [waiə:r'iŋ] *n* (ELEC) 配線 haísen

wiry [waiə:r'i:] *adj* (person) やせて強じんな yasé de kyōjin na; (hair) こわい kowáî

wisdom [wiz'dəm] *n* (of person) 知恵 chié; (of action, remark) 賢明さ tekísetsusa

wisdom tooth *n* 親知らず oyáshirazu

wise [waiz] *adj* (person, action, remark) 賢い kashíkoî, 賢明な keñmei na

...wise *suffix*: *timewise/moneywise etc* 時間〔金銭〕的に jikán〔kiñsen〕teki ni

wisecrack [waiz'kræk] *n* 皮肉な冗談 híniku na jōdañ

wish [wiʃ] *n* (desire) 望み nozómi, 希望 kibō; (specific) 望みの物 nozómi no mono

◆*vt* (want) 望む nozómù, 希望する kibō suru

best wishes (for birthday, etc) おめでとう omédetō

with best wishes (in letter) お体をお大事に o-káràda wo o-dáiji ni

to wish someone goodbye ...に別れのあいさつを言う ...ni wakáre no aísatsu wo iu, ...にさよならを言う ...ni sayōnarà wo iu

he wished me well 彼は「成功を祈る」と言いました karè wa 「seíkō wo inórù」to iímashìta

to wish to do ...したいと思う ...shitáî to omóù

to wish someone to do something ...に...してもらいたいと思う ...ni ...shité moraitaî to omóù

to wish for ...が欲しいと思う ...ga hoshíî to omóù

wishful [wiʃ'fəl] *adj*: *it's wishful thinking* その考えは甘い sonó kangaè wa amáî, それは有り得ない事だ soré wa aríenài kotó dà

wishy-washy [wiʃ'i:wɑ:ʃi:] (*inf*) *adj* (color) 薄い usúi; (ideas, person) 迫力のない hakúryoku no naî

wisp [wisp] *n* (of grass, hair) 小さな束 chíisana tabà; (of smoke) 一筋 hitósùji

wistful [wist'fəl] *adj* (look, smile) 残念そうな zañnensō na

wit [wit] *n* (wittiness) ユーモア yūmða, ウイット uíttò; (intelligence: *also*: **wits**) 知恵 chié; (person) ウイットのある人 uíttò no aru hito

witch [witʃ] *n* 魔女 majò

witchcraft [witʃ'kræft] *n* 魔術 majútsu

witch-hunt [witʃ'hʌnt] *n* (*fig*) 魔女狩り majógari

KEYWORD

with [wið] *prep* **1** (accompanying, in the company of) ...と ...to, ...と一緒に ...to ísshò ni

I was with him 私は彼と一緒にいました watákushi wà kárè to ísshò ni imáshìta

we stayed with friends 私たちは友達の家に泊りました watákushitàchi wa tomódachi nò ié nì tomárimashìta

we'll take the children with us 子供たちを一緒に連れて行きます kodómotàchi wo ísshò ni tsuréte ikimasù

mix the sugar with the eggs 砂糖を卵に混ぜて下さい satő wð tamágo nì mázète kudásaì

I'll be with you in a minute 直ぐ行きますからお待ち下さい súgù ikímasu karà o-máchi kudásaì

I'm with you (I understand) 分かります wakárimasù

to be with it (*inf*: up-to-date) 現代的である geńdaiteki de arù; (: alert) 抜け目がない nukéme gà náì

2 (descriptive): **a room with a view** 見晴らしのいい部屋 miharashi nò íi heyá

the man with the grey hat/blue eyes 灰色の帽子をかぶった[青い目の]男 haíiro nò bôshi wò kabútta[aóī mé nò]otóko

3 (indicating manner, means, cause): **with tears in her eyes** 目に涙を浮かべながら mè nì námìda wo ukábènagara

to walk with a stick つえをついて歩く tsúê wo tsuíte arúku

red with anger 怒りで顔を真っ赤にして ikári dè kaó wò makká ni shité

to shake with fear 恐怖で震える kyófu dè furúerù

to fill something with water ...を水で一杯にする ...wò mizú dè ippái nì suru

you can open the door with this key このかぎでドアを開けられます konó kagí dè dóà wo akéraremasù

---

withdraw [wiðdrɔ:'] (*pt* **withdrew** *pp* **withdrawn**) *vt* (object) 取出す torídasu; (offer, remark) 取消す toríkesu, 撤回する tekkái suru

♦*vi* (troops) 撤退する tettái suru; (person) 下がる sagárù

to withdraw money (from the bank) 金を引出す kané wo hikídasu

withdrawal [wiðdrɔ:'əl] *n* (of offer, remark) 撤回 tekkái; (of troops) 撤退 tettái; (of services) 停止 teíshi; (of participation) 取りやめる事 toríyameru koto; (of money) 引出し hikídashi

withdrawal symptoms *n* (MED) 禁断症状 kińdanshōjō

withdrawn [wiðdrɔ:n'] *adj* (person) 引っ込みがちな hikkómigachi na

wither [wið'ə:r] *vi* (plant) 枯れる karéru

withhold [wiðhould'] (*pt*, *pp* **withheld**) *vt* (tax etc) 源泉徴収する geńsenchōshū suru; (permission) 拒む kobámù; (information) 隠す kakúsù

within [wiðin'] *prep* (inside: referring to place, time, distance) ...以内に[で] ...inài ni[de]

♦*adv* (inside) 中の nakā no

within reach (of) (...に) 手が届く所に[で] (...ni) té gà todókù tokoro ni[de]

within sight (of) (...が) 見える所に[で] (...ga) miérù tokoro ni[de]

within the week 今週中に kofishūchū ni

within a mile of ...の1マイル以内に ...no ichímairu inài ni

without [wiðaut'] *prep* ...なしで ...nashì de

without a coat コートなしで kōtò nashì de

without speaking 何も言わないで naní mo iwanàìde

to go without something ...なしで済ます ...nashì de sumásù

withstand [wiðstænd'] (*pt*, *pp* **withstood**) *vt* (winds, attack, pressure) ...に耐える ...ni taérù

witness [wit'nis] *n* (person who sees) 目撃者 mokúgekishà; (person who countersigns document: *also* LAW) 証人 shōnin

♦*vt* (event) 見る mirù, 目撃する mokúgeki suru; (document) 保証人として...にサインする hoshónin toshite ...ni saín suru

to bear witness to (*fig*: offer proof of) ...を証明する ...wo shōmei suru

witness stand (*BRIT* **witness box**) *n* 証人席 shōninseki

witticism [wit'əsizəm] *n* (remark) 冗談 jōdan

witty [wit'i:] *adj* (person) ウイットのある uíttò no arù; (remark etc) おどけた odóketa

wives [waivz] *npl of* **wife**

wizard [wiz'ə:rd] *n* 魔法使い mahótsukài

wk *abbr* = **week**

wobble [wa:b'əl] *vi* (legs) よろめく yorómekù; (chair) ぐらぐらする gùragura suru; (jelly) ぷるぷるする purùpuru suru

woe [wou] *n* 悲しみ kanáshimi

woke [wouk] *pt of* **wake**

woken [wou'kən] *pp of* **wake**

wolf [wulf] (*pl* **wolves**) *n* オオカミ ōkami

wolves [wulvz] *npl of* **wolf**

woman [wum'ən] (*pl* **women**) *n* 女 oñna, 女性 joséi

woman doctor *n* 女医 joí

womanly [wum'ənli:] *adj* (virtues etc) 女性らしい joséirashii

womb [wu:m] *n* (ANAT) 子宮 shikyū

women [wim'ən] *pl of* **woman**

women's lib [wim'ənzlib'] (*inf*) *n* ウーマンリブ ūmanribù

won [wʌn] *pt, pp of* **win**

wonder [wʌn'də:r] *n* (miracle) 不思議 fushígi; (feeling) 驚異 kyōi
♦*vi*: **to wonder whether/why** ...かしら〔なぜ...かと〕と思う ...ka shira 〔nazè ...ka shira〕to omóù

to wonder at (marvel at) ...に驚く ...ni odórokù

to wonder about ...の事を考える ...no kotó wò kangaèru

it's no wonder (that) ... (という事)は不思議ではない ... (to iú koto) wà fushígi de wà naì

wonderful [wʌn'də:rfəl] *adj* (excellent) 素晴らしい subárashiì; (miraculous) 不思議な fushígi na

wonderfully [wʌn'də:rfəli:] *adv* (excellently) 素晴らしく subárashiku; (miraculously) 不思議に fushígi ni

won't [wount] = **will not**

woo [wu:] *vt* (woman) ...に言い寄る ...ni iíyorù; (audience etc) ...にこびる ...ni kobírù

wood [wud] *n* (timber) 木材 mokúzài, 木 ki; (forest) 森 morí, 林 hayáshi, 木立 kodáchi

wood carving *n* (act, object) 木彫 kibóri

wooded [wud'id] *adj* (slopes, area) 木の茂った kí nò shigéttà

wooden [wud'ən] *adj* (object) 木でできた kí dè dekita, 木製の mokúsei no; (house) 木造の mokúzō no; (*fig*: performance, actor) でくの坊の様な dekúnobò no yō nà

woodpecker [wud'pekə:r] *n* キツツキ kitsútsukì

woodwind [wud'wind] *npl* (MUS) 木管楽器 mokkángakkì

woodwork [wud'wə:rk] *n* (skill) 木材工芸 mokúzaikōgèi

woodworm [wud'wə:rm] *n* キクイムシ kikúimùshi

wool [wul] *n* (material, yarn) 毛糸 keíto, ウール ūrù

to pull the wool over someone's eyes (*fig*) ...をだます ...wo damásù

woolen [wul'ən] (*BRIT* **woollen**) *adj* (socks, hat etc) 毛糸の keíto no, ウールの ūrù no

the woolen industry 羊毛加工業界 yōmōkakōgyōkài

woolens [wul'ənz] *npl* 毛糸衣類 keítoirùi

wooly [wul'i:] (*BRIT* **woolly**) *adj* (socks, hat etc) 毛糸の keíto no, ウールの ūrù no; (*fig*: ideas) 取留めのない torítome no naì; (person) 考え方のはっきりしない kañgaekatà no hakkírì shinái

word [wə:rd] *n* (unit of language: written, spoken) 語 go, 単語 tañgo, 言葉 kotóba; (promise) 約束 yakúsoku; (news) 知らせ shiráse, ニュース nyūsu
♦*vt* (letter, message) ...の言回しを選ぶ ...no iímawashi wo erábù

in other words 言替えると iíkaerù to

to break/keep one's word 約束を破る〔守る〕yakúsoku wo yabúrù 〔mamórù〕

to have words with someone ...と口げんかをする ...to kuchígeñka wo suru

wording [wə:r'diŋ] *n* (of message, contract etc) 言回し iímawashi

word processing *n* ワードプロセシング wādopuroseshìngu

word processor [-prɑ'sesə:r] *n* ワープロ wápuro

wore [wɔ:r] *pt of* **wear**

work [wə:rk] *n* (*gen*) 仕事 shigóto; (job) 職 shokú; (ART, LITERATURE) 作品 sakúhin
♦*vi* (person: labor) 働く határaku; (mechanism) 動く ugókù; (be successful: medicine etc) 効く kikú
♦*vt* (clay, wood etc) 加工する kakó suru; (land) 耕す tagáyasù; (mine) 採掘する saíkutsu suru; (machine) 動かす ugókasù; (cause: effect) もたらす motárasù; (: miracle) 行う okónau

to be out of work 失業中である shitsúgyōchū de arù

to work loose (part) 緩む yurúmù; (knot) 解ける tokérù

workable [wəːrˈkəbəl] *adj* (solution) 実行可能な jikkókanō na

workaholic [wəːrkəhɑːˈlik] *n* 仕事中毒の人 shigótochūdoku no hito, ワーカホリック wākahorìkku

worker [wəːrˈkəːr] *n* 労働者 rōdōshà

workforce [wəːkˈfɔːrs] *n* 労働人口 rōdōjinkō

working class [wəːrˈkiŋ-] *n* 労働者階級 rōdōshakaìkyū

working-class [wəːrˈkiŋklæs] *adj* 労働者階級の rōdōshakaìkyū no

working order *n*: *in working order* ちゃんと動く状態で chańto ugokù jōtai de

workman [wəːrkˈmən] (*pl* **workmen**) *n* 作業員 sagyóìn

workmanship [wəːrkˈmənʃip] *n* (skill) 腕前 udémae

work on vt fus (task) ...に取組む ...ni toríkumu; (person: influence) 説得する settóku suru; (principle) ...に基づく ...ni motózukù

work out vi (plans etc) うまくいく umáku iku

♦*vt* (problem) 解決する kaíketsu suru; (plan) 作る tsukúrù

it works out at $100 100ドルになる hyakúdòru ni narù

works [wəːrks] *n* (*BRIT*: factory) 工場 kōjō

♦*npl* (of clock, machine) 機構 kikō

worksheet [wəːrkˈʃiːt] *n* ワークシート wākushītò

workshop [wəːrkˈʃɑːp] *n* (at home, in factory) 作業場 sagyōjò; (practical session) ワークショップ wākushoppù

work station *n* ワークステーション wākusutēshòn

work-to-rule [wəːrkˈtəruːl] (*BRIT*) *n* 順法闘争 juńpōtōsō

work up vt: *to get worked up* 怒る okórù

world [wəːrld] *n* 世界 sekái

♦*cpd* (champion) 世界... sekài...; (power, war) 国際的... kokúsaiteki..., 国際... kokúsai...

to think the world of someone (*fig*: admire) ...を高く評価する ...wo takáku hyōkā suru; (: love) ...が大好きである ...ga daìsuki de arù

worldly [wəːrldˈliː] *adj* (not spiritual) 世俗的な sezókuteki na; (knowledgeable) 世才にたけた sesái ni takèta

worldwide [wəːrldˈwaid'] *adj* 世界的な sekáiteki na

worm [wəːrm] *n* (*also*: **earthworm**) ミミズ mimízu

worn [wɔːrn] *pp of* **wear**

♦*adj* (carpet) 使い古した tsukáifurushità; (shoe) 履き古した hakífurushità

worn-out [wɔːrnˈaut'] *adj* (object) 使い古した tsukáifurushità; (person) へとへとに疲れた hetóheto ni tsukáreta

worried [wəːrˈiːd] *adj* (anxious) 心配している shiñpai shite irù

worry [wəːrˈiː] *n* (anxiety) 心配 shiñpai

♦*vt* (person) 心配させる shiñpai saserù

♦*vi* (person) 心配する shiñpai surù

worrying [wəːrˈiːiŋ] *adj* 心配な shiñpai na

worse [wəːrs] *adj* 更に悪い sarà ni waruî

♦*adv* 更に悪く sarà ni warùku

♦*n* 更に悪い事 sarà ni waruî koto

a change for the worse 悪化 akká

worsen [wəːrˈsən] *vt* 悪くする warùku suru

♦*vi* 悪くなる warùku naru

worse off *adj* (financially) 収入が減った shúñyū ga hettá; (*fig*): *you'll be worse off this way* そんな事は得策ではない sofína koto wa tokúsaku de wa naì

worship [wəːrˈʃip] *n* (act) 礼拝 reíhai

♦*vt* (god) 礼拝する reíhai suru; (person, thing) 崇拝する sūhái suru

Your Worship (*BRIT*: to mayor, judge) 閣下 kakkà

worst [wəːrst] *adj* 最悪の saíaku no

♦*adv* 最もひどく mottómo hidóku

♦*n* 最悪 saíaku

at worst 最悪の場合 saíaku no baái

worth [wəːrθ] *n* (value) 価値 kachî

◆*adj*: *to be worth $100* 価格は100ドルである kakáku wa hyakúdoru de arú

it's worth it やる価値がある yarú kachĩ ga aru

to be worth one's while (to do) (...する事は) ...のためになる (...surú koto wa) ...no tamé ni naru

worthless [wəːrθ'lis] *adj* (person, thing) 価値のない kachĩ no nai

worthwhile [wəːrθ'wail'] *adj* (activity, cause) ためになる tamé ni naru

worthy [wəːr'ðiː] *adj* (person) 尊敬すべき soñkeisubeki; (motive) 良い yoĩ

worthy of ...にふさわしい ...ni fusáwashiĩ

KEYWORD

would [wud] *aux vb* **1** (conditional tense): *if you asked him he would do it* 彼にお願いすればやってくれるでしょう kárè ni o-négai surèba yatté kureru deshō

if you had asked him he would have done it 彼に頼めばやってくれた事でしょう kárè ni tanómebà yatté kuretà kotó deshō

2 (in offers, invitations, requests): *would you like a biscuit?* ビスケットはいかがですか bisúkettò wa ikágà desu ká

would you ask him to come in? 彼に入ってもらって下さい kárè ni háitte morátte kudasaĩ

would you open the window please? 窓を開けてくれますか mádò wo akéte kuremasù ká

3 (in indirect speech): *I said I would do it* 私はやってあげると約束しました watákushi wà yatté agerù to yakúsoku shimashĩta

he asked me if I would go with him 一緒に行ってくれと彼に頼まれました isshó nĩ itté kurè to kárè ni tanómaremashĩta

4 (emphatic): *it WOULD have to snow today!* 今日に限って雪が降るなんてなあ kyō nĩ kagĩttè yukí gà fúrù náñte nã

you WOULD say that, wouldn't you! あんたの言いそうな事だ áñta no iísō na kotó dà

5 (insistence): *she wouldn't behave* あの子はどうしても言う事を聞いてくれない anó kò wa dō shite mò iú kotó wo kiĩte kurenaĩ

6 (conjecture): *it would have been midnight* だとすれば夜中の12時という事になります dà tò surèba yonáka nò júnjĩ to iú kotó ni narímasù

it would seem so そうらしいね sō rashiĩ né

7 (indicating habit): *he would go there on Mondays* 彼は毎週月曜日にそこへ行く事にしていました kárè wa maíshū getsúyòbi ni sokó è ikú kotó ni shité imashĩta

he would spend every day on the beach 彼は毎日浜でごろごろしていました kárè wa maĩnichi hamá dè górògoro shite imáshĩta

would-be [wud'biː'] *(pej) adj* ...志望の ...shibō no

wouldn't [wud'ənt] = **would not**

wound¹ [waund] *pt, pp of* **wind**

wound² [wuːnd] *n* 傷 kizú

◆*vt* ...に傷を負わせる ...ni kizú wo owáseru, 負傷させる fushō saséru

wove [wouv] *pt of* **weave**

woven [wou'vən] *pp of* **weave**

wrangle [ræŋ'gəl] *n* 口論 kŏron

wrap [ræp] *n* (stole) 肩掛 katakake, ストール sutórù; (cape) マント mañto, ケープ kēpu

◆*vt* (cover) 包む tsutsúmù; (pack: *also*: **wrap up**) こん包する koñpō suru; (wind: tape etc) 巻付ける makĩtsukerù

wrapper [ræp'əːr] *n* (on chocolate) 包み tsutsúmi; (*BRIT*: of book) カバー kabā

wrapping paper [ræp'iŋ-] *n* (brown) クラフト紙 kurấfùtoshi; (fancy) 包み紙 tsutsúmigami

wrath [ræθ] *n* 怒り ikári

wreak [riːk] *vt* (havoc) もたらす motárasù

to wreak vengeance on ...に復しゅうす

る ...ni fukúshū suru

wreath [ri:θ] n (funeral wreath) 花輪 ha-náwa

wreck [rek] n (vehicle) 残がい zaigai; (ship) 難破船 naápasen; (pej: person) 変り果てた人 kawárihatetá hitó
♦vt (car etc) めちゃめちゃに壊す mecha-mecha ni kowású; (fig: chances) 台無しにする daínashi ni surù

wreckage [rek'idʒ] n (of car, plane, ship, building) 残がい zaígai

wren [ren] n (ZOOL) ミソサザイ misósazài

wrench [rentʃ] n (TECH: adjustable) スパナ supánà; (: fixed size) レンチ reńchi; (tug) ひねり hinéri; (fig) 心痛 shíntsū
♦vt (twist) ひねる hinérù
to wrench something from someone ...から...をねじり取る ...kara ...wo nejíritorù

wrestle [res'əl] vi: *to wrestle (with someone)* (fight) (...と)格闘する (...to) kakútō suru; (for sport) (...と) レスリングする (...to) resúringu suru
to wrestle with (fig) ...と取組む ...to toríkumu, ...と戦う ...to tatákau

wrestler [res'lə:r] n レスラー resúrā

wrestling [res'liŋ] n レスリング resúringu

wretched [retʃ'id] adj (poor, unhappy) 不幸な fukō na; (inf: very bad) どうしようもない dō shiyō mo nai

wriggle [rig'əl] vi (also: **wriggle about**: person, fish, snake etc) うねうねする unéune suru

wring [riŋ] (pt, pp **wrung**) vt (wet clothes) 絞る shibórù; (hands) もむ momú; (bird's neck) ひねる hinérù; (fig): *to wring something out of someone* ...に...を吐かせる ...ni ...wo hákaserù

wrinkle [riŋ'kəl] n (on skin, paper etc) しわ shiwá
♦vt (nose, forehead etc) ...にしわを寄せる ...ni shiwá wo yoséru
♦vi (skin, paint etc) しわになる shiwá ni naru

wrist [rist] n 手首 tekúbi

wristwatch [rist'wɑːtʃ] n 腕時計 udédo-

kèi

writ [rit] n 令状 reíjō

write [rait] (pt **wrote**, pp **written**) vt 書く kakù
♦vi 書く kakù
to write to someone ...に手紙を書く ...ni tegámi wo kakù

write down vt 書く kakù, 書留める ka-kítomeru

write off vt (debt) 帳消しにする chōke-shi ni suru; (plan, project) 取りやめる to-ríyameru

write-off [rait'ɔːf] n 修理不可能な物 shūrìfukánō na mono

writer [rai'tə:r] n (author) 著者 chosha; (professional) 作家 sakká; (person who writes) 書手 kakíte

write up vt (report, minutes etc) 詳しく書く kuwáshikù kakù

writhe [raið] vi 身もだえする mimódàe suru

writing [rai'tiŋ] n (words written) 文字 mojì, 文章 buńshō; (handwriting) 筆跡 hisséki; (of author) 作品 sakúhin, 作風 sakúfū; (activity) 書物 kakímono
in writing 書面で shomén de

writing paper n 便せん bińsen

written [rit'ən] pp of **write**

wrong [rɔːŋ] adj (bad) 良くない yokúnai; (incorrect: number, address etc) 間違った machígatta; (not suitable) 不適当な futékìtō na; (reverse: side of material) 裏側の urágawa no; (unfair) 不正な fuséi na
♦adv 間違って machígatte, 誤って ayá-mattè
♦n (injustice) 不正 fuséi
♦vt (treat unfairly) ...に悪い事をする ...ni warúi koto wo surù
you are wrong to do it それは不正な事です sore wa fuséi na koto desù
you are wrong about that, you've got it wrong それは違います soré wa chigáimasù
to be in the wrong 間違っている machígatte iru
what's wrong? どうしましたか dō shi-máshita ká

to go wrong (person) 間違う machígaù; (plan) 失敗する shippái suru; (machine) 狂う kurúù

wrongful [rɔːŋ'fəl] *adj* (imprisonment, dismissal) 不当な futō na

wrongly [rɔːŋ'liː] *adv* 間違って machígattè

wrote [rout] *pt of* **write**

wrought [rɔːt] *adj*: **wrought iron** 錬鉄 reñtetsu

wrung [rʌŋ] *pt, pp of* **wring**

wry [rai] *adj* (smile, humor, expression) 皮肉っぽい hiníkuppoì

wt. *abbr* = **weight**

X

Xmas [eks'mis] *n abbr* = **Christmas**

X-ray [eks'rei] *n* (ray) エックス線 ekkúsusen; (photo) レントゲン写真 reñtogeñshashin
♦*vt* ...のレントゲンを撮る ...no reñtogeñ wo torù

xylophone [zai'ləfoun] *n* 木琴 mokkín

Y

yacht [jɑːt] *n* ヨット yottò

yachting [jɑːt'iŋ] *n* ヨット遊び yottóasobi

yachtsman [jɑːts'mən] (*pl* **yachtsmen**) *n* ヨット乗り yottónori

Yank [jæŋk] (*pej*) *n* ヤンキー yañkī

Yankee [jæŋk'iː] (*pej*) *n* = **Yank**

yap [jæp] *vi* (dog) きゃんきゃんほえる kyañkyan hoérù

yard [jɑːrd] *n* (of house etc) 庭 niwà; (measure) ヤード yādò

yardstick [jɑːrd'stik] *n* (*fig*) 尺度 shakúdò

yarn [jɑːrn] *n* (thread) 毛糸 keíto; (tale) ほら話 horábanashi

yawn [jɔːn] *n* あくび akúbi
♦*vi* あくびをする akúbi suru

yawning [jɔːn'iŋ] *adj* (gap) 大きな ōkína

yd. *abbr* = **yard(s)**

yeah [je] (*inf*) *adv* はい haì

year [jiːr] *n* 年 neñ, toshí, 1年 ichínen
to be 8 years old 8才である hassái de aru
an eight-year-old child 8才の子供 hassái no kodómo

yearly [jiːr'liː] *adj* 毎年の maínen no, maítoshi no
♦*adv* 毎年 maínen, maítoshi

yearn [jəːrn] *vi*: *to yearn for something* ...を切に望む ...wo setsù ni nozómu
to yearn to do ...をしたいと切に望む ...wo shitái to setsù ni nozómu

yeast [jiːst] *n* 酵母 kōbò, イースト īsùto

yell [jel] *n* 叫び sakébi
♦*vi* 叫ぶ sakébù

yellow [jel'ou] *adj* 黄色い kiíroi

yelp [jelp] *n* (of animal) キャンと鳴く事 kyañ to nakú koto; (of person) 悲鳴 himéi
♦*vi* (animal) きゃんと鳴く kyañ to nakú; (person) 悲鳴を上げる himéi wò agérù

yeoman [jou'mən] (*pl* **yeomen**) *n*: *yeoman of the guard* 国王の親衛隊員 kokúō no shiñ-eitaiiñ

yes [jes] *adv* はい haì
♦*n* はいという返事 haì to iú heñji
to say/answer yes 承諾する shōdaku suru

yesterday [jes'təːrdei] *adv* 昨日 kinô, sakújìtsu
♦*n* 昨日 kinô, sakújìtsu
yesterday morning/evening 昨日の朝〔夕方〕kinô no asà〔yūgata〕
all day yesterday 昨日一日 kinô ichínichi

yet [jet] *adv* まだ madà; (already) もう mō
♦*conj* がしかし ga shikáshì
it is not finished yet まだできていない madà dekíte inái
the best yet これまでの物で最も良い物 koré madè no mono dè mottōmo yoī mono
as yet まだ madà

yew [juː] *n* (tree) イチイ ichíi

Yiddish [jid'iʃ] *n* イディッシュ語 idísshugo

yield [ji:ld] *n* (AGR) 収穫 shúkaku; (COMM) 収益 shūéki

♦*vt* (surrender: control, responsibility) 譲る yuzúru; (produce: results, profit) もたらす motárasu

♦*vi* (surrender) 譲る yuzúru; (*US:* AUT) 道を譲る michí wo yuzúru

YMCA [waiemsi:ei'] *n abbr* (= *Young Men's Christian Association*) キリスト教青年会 kirísutokyōseínenkai, ワイエムシーエー waíemushīē

yog(h)ourt [jou'gə:rt] *n* ヨーグルト yōgurúto

yog(h)urt [jou'gə:rt] *n* = **yog(h)ourt**

yoke [jouk] *n* (of oxen) くびき kubíki; (*fig*) 重荷 omóni

yolk [jouk] *n* 卵黄 rañ-ō, 黄身 kimí

───── **KEYWORD** ─────

you [ju:] *pron* 1 (subj: *sing*) あなたは〔が〕 anáta wa〔ga〕; (: *pl*) あなたたちは〔が〕 anátatáchi wa〔ga〕

you are very kind あなたはとても親切ですね anáta wa totémo shíñsetsu desu ne, ご親切に有難うございます go-shíñsetsu ni arígàtō gozáimasù

you Japanese enjoy your food あなたたち日本人は食べるのが好きですね anátatáchi nihóñjìn wa tabéru no ga sukí desù né

you and I will go あなたと私が行く事になっています anáta to watákushi gà ikú kotò ni natté imasù

2 (obj: direct, indirect: *sing*) あなたを〔に〕 anáta wo〔ni〕; (: *pl*) あなたたちを〔に〕 anátatáchi wo〔ni〕

I know you 私はあなたを知っています watákushi wa anáta wo shitté imasù

I gave it to you 私はそれをあなたに渡しました watákushi wà soré wò anáta ni watáshimashìta

3 (stressed): *I told YOU to do it* やれというのはあなたに言ったんですよ yaré tò iú no wà anáta ni ittáñ desu yó

4 (after prep, in comparisons)

it's for you あなたのためです anáta no tamé desù

can I come with you? 一緒に行っていいですか isshó nì itté íi desu ká

she's younger than you 彼女はあなたより若いです kánòjo wa anáta yori wakái desu

5 (impersonal: one)

fresh air does you good 新鮮な空気は健康にいい shiñsen nà kúkì wa keñkō ni íi

you never know どうなるか分かりませんね dó narù ka wakárimaseñ né

you can't do that! それはいけません soré wà ikémaseñ

───────────────

you'd [ju:d] = **you had; you would**

you'll [ju:l] = **you will; you shall**

young [jʌŋ] *adj* (person, animal, plant) 若い wakái

♦*npl* (of animal) 子 ko; (people): *the young* 若者 wakámono

younger [jʌŋ'gə:r] *adj* (brother etc) 年下の toshíshita no

youngster [jʌŋ'stə:r] *n* 子供 kodómo

your [ju:r] *adj* (singular) あなたの anáta no; (plural) あなたたちの anátatáchi no ¶ *see also* **my**

you're [ju:r] = **you are**

yours [ju:rz] *pron* (singular) あなたの物 anáta no mono; (plural) あなたたちの物 anátatáchi no mono ¶ *see also* **mine; faithfully; sincerely**

yourself [ju:rself'] *pron* あなた自身 anáta jishìn ¶ *see also* **oneself**

yourselves [ju:rselvz'] *pl pron* あなたたち自身 anátatáchi jishìn ¶ *see also* **oneself**

youth [ju:θ] *n* (young days) 若い時分 wakái jibun; (young man: *pl* **youths**) 少年 shóneñ

youth club *n* 青少年クラブ seíshōnèn kurábu

youthful [ju:θ'fəl] *adj* (person) 若い wakái; (looks) 若々しい wakáwakashiì; (air, enthusiasm) 若者独特の wakámonodokútoku no

youth hostel *n* ユースホステル yūsúhosùteru

Youth Training (*BRIT*) 職業訓練 sho-

kúgyōkunreǹ ◇失業青少年のためのもの
shitsúgyōseishōnen no tamé no monò

you've [ju:v] = **you have**

Yugoslav [ju:'gouslɑ:v] *adj* ユーゴスラ
ビアの yūgosurabìa no
♦*n* ユーゴスラビア人 yūgosurabiajin

Yugoslavia [ju:'gouslɑ:'vi:ə] *n* ユーゴス
ラビア yūgosurabīa

yuppie [jʌp'i:] (*inf*) *n* ヤッピー yappì
♦*adj* ヤッピーの yappì no

YWCA [waidʌbəlju:siei'] *n abbr* (=
Young Women's Christian Association)
キリスト教女子青年会 kirísutokyōjoshì-
seínenkai, ワイダブリューシーエー waí-
daburyūshīē

Z

Zambia [zæm'bi:ə] *n* ザンビア zańbia

zany [zei'ni:] *adj* (ideas, sense of humor)
ばかげた bakágeta

zap [zæp] *vt* (COMPUT: delete) 削除する
sakújo suru

zeal [zi:l] *n* (enthusiasm) 熱情 netsújō;
(*also*: **religious zeal**) 狂信 kyōshín

zealous [zel'əs] *adj* 熱狂的な nekkyōteki
na

zebra [zi:'brə] *n* シマウマ shimáuma

zebra crossing (*BRIT*) *n* 横断歩道 ōdán-
hodō

zenith [zi:'niθ] *n* 頂点 chōtèn

zero [zi:'rou] *n* 零点 reítén, ゼロ zerð

zest [zest] *n* (for life) 熱意 netsùi; (of
orange) 皮 kawá

zigzag [zig'zæg] *n* ジグザグ jigùzagu
♦*vi* ジグザグに動く jigùzagu ni ugókù

Zimbabwe [zimbɑ:'bwei] *n* ジンバブウエ
jiñbabùue

zinc [ziŋk] *n* 亜鉛 aèn

zip [zip] *n* (*also*: **zip fastener**) = **zipper**
♦*vt* (*also*: **zip up**) = **zipper**

zip code (*US*) *n* 郵便番号 yūbinbañgō

zipper [zip'ə:r] (*US*) *n* チャック chakkù,
ジッパー jippā, ファスナー fasùnā
♦*vt* (*also*: **zipper up**) ...のチャックを締め
る ...no chakkù wo shimérù

zodiac [zou'di:æk] *n* 十二宮図 jūníkyùzu

zombie [zɑ:m'bi:] *n* (*fig*): **like a zombie**
ロボットの様に〔な〕robóttð no yð ni
〔na〕

zone [zoun] *n* (area, *also* MIL) 地帯 chitái

zoo [zu:] *n* 動物園 dðbutsùen

zoologist [zouɑ:l'ədʒist] *n* 動物学者 dð-
butsugakùsha

zoology [zouɑ:l'ədʒi:] *n* 動物学 dðbutsu-
gàku

zoom [zu:m] *vi*: **to zoom past** 猛スピー
ドで通り過ぎる mósupīdo de tōrísuguru

zoom lens *n* ズームレンズ zūmureñzu

zucchini [zu:ki:'ni:] (*US*) *n inv* ズッキー
ニ zukkīnī

SUPPLEMENT

NUMBERS

Cardinal numbers:

1	一	ichi	11	十一	jūichi	21	二十一	nijūichi
2	二	ni	12	十二	jūni	22	二十二	nijūni
3	三	san	13	十三	jūsan	etc		
4	四	yon/shi	14	十四	jūyon/jūshi	30	三十	sanjū
5	五	go	15	十五	jūgo	40	四十	yonjū
6	六	roku	16	十六	jūroku	50	五十	gojū
7	七	nana/shichi	17	十七	jūnana/jūshichi	60	六十	rokujū
8	八	hachi	18	十八	jūhachi	70	七十	nanajū/shichijū
9	九	ku/kyū	19	十九	jūku/jūkyū	80	八十	hachijū
10	十	jū	20	二十	nijū	90	九十	kyūjū

Note: the alternative forms given for 4, 7, 9 etc are not necessarily interchangeable. The choice is determined by usage.

100	百	hyaku	1,000	千 sen, 一千 issen		10,000	一万	ichiman
200	二百	nihyaku	2,000	二千	nisen	20,000	二万	niman
300	三百	sanbyaku	3,000	三千	sanzen	etc		
400	四百	yonhyaku	4,000	四千	yonsen			
500	五百	gohyaku	5,000	五千	gosen			
600	六百	roppyaku	6,000	六千	rokusen			
700	七百	nanahyaku	7,000	七千	nanasen			
800	八百	happyaku	8,000	八千	hassen			
900	九百	kyūhyaku	9,000	九千	kyūsen			

Alternate set of numbers:

These are used often for counting, particularly for counting things without "counters" (see below), and for expressing the age of children.

1	一つ	hitotsu	6	六つ	muttsu
2	二つ	futatsu	7	七つ	nanatsu
3	三つ	mittsu	8	八つ	yattsu
4	四つ	yottsu	9	九つ	kokonotsu
5	五つ	itsutsu	10	十	tō

Ordinal numbers:

"The first," "the second" etc are expressed by the formula 第 x 番目 *dai x banme*, where x is the cardinal number and *dai*, *banme* or *me* can be variously omitted. Thus "the third" can be expressed by any of the following:

> 第三番目　daisanbanme
>
> 三番目　sanbanme
>
> 三番　sanban
>
> 第三　daisan

The alternate cardinal numbers from 1 to 9 can also be made into ordinal numbers by the addition of 目 *me* alone: "the third" = 三つ目 *mittsume*.

Days of the month:

The days of the month are written straightforwardly by a cardinal number plus the character for day 日. But the reading is not straightforward and needs to be learned.

一日	tsuitachi	七日	nanoka
二日	futsuka	八日	yōka
三日	mikka	九日	kokonoka
四日	yokka	十日	tōka
五日	itsuka	二十日	hatsuka
六日	muika		

Days 11 to 19 and 21 to 31 are expressed straightforwardly by a cardinal number + *nichi*. Thus the 18th day of the month is *jūhachinichi*.

Fractions:

In Japanese you express fractions by the formula y分のx *y bun no x*, where *y* is the DENOMINATOR, not the numerator. In other words, in Japanese you say the denominator first, then the numerator, thus:

> 1/2　二分の一　nibun no ichi
>
> 2/3　三分の二　sanbun no ni
>
> 3/4　四分の三　yonbun no san

Counters:

As in English we often say "2 *head* of cattle", "a *bunch* of grapes", "a *flock* of geese", Japanese uses counters for almost all everyday things, including people. There are many counters, some common, some exotic (like using the same counter for "rabbit" as you would for "bird"). Here is a list of counters you will need for your daily life.

counter:		used for:
人	nin	people
名	mei	people (interchangeable with *nin* except in set phrases)
匹	hiki	animals in general, except birds
頭	tō	relatively large animals
羽	wa	birds
個	ko	3-dimensional, relatively rounded objects: balls, stones, apples, cups
枚	mai	thin, flat things: pieces of paper, computer disks, handkerchiefs, blankets, dishes
本	hon	long things: pencils, ropes, sticks
冊	satsu	books and things bound like books: notebooks, diaries
台	dai	cars, trucks, bicycles, large machines
足	soku	shoes, socks etc that come in matched pairs
歳	sai	age of living things in years
杯	hai	containers full of something: cupful, glassful, spoonful

Like the use in English of "an" instead of "a" before words that begin with a vowel, Japanese makes pronunciation changes depending on the last syllable of the cardinal number and the first letter of a counter. Here are the most important.

1. Counters beginning with "h"

   一本，一匹 ippon, ippiki
   二本，二匹 nihon, nihiki
   三本，三匹 sanbon, sanbiki
   四本，四匹 yonhon, yonhiki
   五本，五匹 gohon, gohiki
   六本，六匹 roppon, roppiki
   七本，七匹 nanahon, nanahiki
   八本，八匹 happon, happiki
   九本，九匹 kyūhon, kyūhiki
   十本，十匹 juppon, juppiki

2. Counters beginning with unvoiced consonants (k, s, t, ch) double the consonant after the numbers 1 and 10.

   一個，一歳 ikko, issai
   十個，十歳 jukko, jussai

3. "k" also doubles after 6.

   六個 rokko

4. The voiced consonants g, z, d, m, n, r, w generally do not change.

5. The counter 人 *nin* for persons has an atypical pronunciation for 1 and 2.

一人 hitori

二人 futari

6. The counter 歳 *sai* for age has an atypical pronunciation for 20 years of age.

二十歳 hatachi

DEMONSTRATIVES

Japanese demonstratives begin with 4 prefixes: *ko-*, *so-*, *a-*, and *do-*. *Ko-* expresses nearness to the speaker; *so-* expresses distance from the speaker but nearness to the listener; *a-* expresses distance from both speaker and listener; and *do-* forms interrogatives.

kō	like this	sō	like that	aa	like that	dō	how ?
kono	this	sono	that	ano	that	dono	which ?
kore	this (one)	sore	that (one)	are	that (one)	dore	which (one) ?
koko		soko		asoko		doko	
kotchi	here	sotchi	there	atchi	there	dotchi	where ?
kochira		sochira		achira		dochira	
konna	such a	sonna	such a	anna	such a	donna	what kind of ?

UNDERSTANDING JAPANESE

Japanese has certain characteristics not always found in the European family of languages. This shows up in particular in the way the subject of the sentence is expressed (or unexpressed, as we shall see), and in the numerous particles which take the place of declensions, prepositions, auxiliaries etc in Western languages. Although it may take years to learn to use these characteristics like a native, being aware of their existance can serve as a shortcut to a fuller understanding of Japanese.

1. The hidden subject

Consider the following sentence. It is the opening line to Yasunari Kawabata's Nobel Prize-winning "Snow Country".

国境の長いトンネルを抜けると雪国であった. kokkyō no nagai tonneru wo nukeru to yukiguni de atta.

My translation would be:

"When your train emerged from the long tunnel beneath the border, you suddenly found yourself in the snow-bound countryside."

Notice that there is no "train" or "your" or "you" expressed in the original.

Japanese prefers not to express words that are apparent from the context or the choice of expression. This happens most frequently with the grammatical subject of the sentence, not only in literature, but especially in daily conversation.

A：どちらへお出かけですか dochira e o-dekake desu ka

B：郵便局へ手紙を出しに行きます yūbinkyoku e tegami wo dashi ni ikimasu

Here there is no need for an *anata wa* in A or a *watashi wa* in B. The choice of words (the polite *dochira* with *o-...*) contains the "you" in A, and makes an "I" in B's answer superfluous.

In Japanese the verbal part of the sentence is the most important, and normally comes at the end. In a long sentence the listener has to wait till the end of the sentence in order to grasp the meaning. In English, the grammatical subject is the most important part, and is expressed at the beginning of the sentence, and auxiliary information about the subject is imparted gradually. This makes for great clarity of meaning, whereas Japanese sentences can often produce ambiguities. But this is a product of the Japanese culture, where reticence is considered virtue and outspokenness vice.

2. Particles

Japanese uses particles to make clear the relationship among words in a sentence. English frequently relies on position of words in the sentence for this. In a simple example, the meaning of A below is reversed if you reverse the position of the words, as in B.

A. John hit Sue.

B. Sue hit John.

On the other hand, consider the following example and its literal Japanese translation.

She gave me a book.

彼女は私に1冊の本をくれました.

kanojo *wa* watashi *ni* issatsu *no* hon *wo* kuremashita.

This is a standard translation. But the following are also possible, in context, without changing the meaning.

watashi *ni* kanojo *wa* issatsu *no* hon *wo* kuremashita.

issatsu *no* hon *wo* kanojo *wa* watashi *ni* kuremashita.

kuremashita, kanojo *wa* watashi *ni* issatsu *no* hon *wo*.

In other words, the particles make the meaning clear without regard to the position of the various sentence elements, even when the position is somewhat unnatural. On the other hand, if you confuse the particles, your speech becomes unintelligible. To say that someone's train of thought is illogical or contradictory, the Japanese have an old metaphor.

てにをはが合わない. te-ni-wo-ha ga awanai.

Literally, "his particles are all mixed up." This underscores the correct use of particles, even for a native speaker of Japanese.

The Japanese classify their particles as follows.

Case particles: Added to nouns and pronouns, they indicate relation to other words in the sentence: no, ga, wo, ni, e, to, yori, kara, de.

Adverbial particles: They are added to nouns, pronouns, and adverbs and restrict the meaning of the verbal parts of the sentence: sae, made, bakari, dake, hodo, kurai, nado, nanka, nante, yara, zo, ka, zutsu.

Modifying particles: They add their own meaning to the word they follow and also modify the verbal parts of the sentence: wa, mo, koso, demo (also written "de mo"), shika, datte.

Sentence particles: They conclude a sentence and indicate interrogation, exclamation, emotion, prohibition etc: ka, kai, kashira, na, zo, ze, tomo (to mo), tte, no, ne, sa, ya, yo.

Parenthetical particles: They are placed at the end of phrases and clauses and are used to adjust sentence rhythm or to express emotion, emphasis etc: na, ne, sa.

Connecting particles: They are appended to various verbal phrases and clauses to indicate their connection with what follows: ba, to, te mo (de mo), keredo (keredomo), ga, no ni, no de, kara, shi, te (de), nagara.

The following illustrate typical Japanese usage of the more important particles. The translations given show one way, but not necessarily the only way, of expressing the concept in English.

a. Case particles

§ の **no:** indicates possession, location etc

父の本　chichi no hon "my father's book" —possession

海の風　umi no kaze "a sea breeze" —location

大学の教授　daigaku no kyōju "a university professor" —affiliation

紫の花　murasaki no hana "a purple flower" —attribute

小説家の川端氏　shōsetsuka no kawabatashi "Mr. Kawabata the novelist" —apposition

§ が **ga:** follows nouns or pronouns

私が行きます　watashi ga ikimasu "I will go." —indicates subject

メロンが好きだ　meron ga suki da "I like melons." —indicates object of desire, ability, likes and dislikes etc

それがね，本当なんだよ　sore ga ne, hontō nan da yo "The thing is, the story is true." —attached to a demonstrative like a connecting particle

§ **を wo:** follows nouns or pronouns

本を読む hon wo yomu "to read a book" —indicates object of an action verb

歩道を歩く hodō wo aruku "to walk on the sidewalk" —indicates location with a verb of movement

この半年を堪え忍んだ kono hantoshi wo taeshinonda "I have suffered in silence for the past 6 months." —indicates duration of an action

朝9時に家を出る asa kuji ni ie wo deru "to leave the house at 9 o'clock" —indicates the place where an action commences

§ **に ni:** indicates the person or thing to which an action extends

朝5時に起床する asa goji ni kishō suru "to get up at 5 a.m." —indicates time

空に虹が出る sora ni niji ga deru "A rainbow appears in the sky." —indicates place

仕事に熱中する shigoto ni netchū suru "to concentrate on one's work" —indicates the object of an action

会社にたどりつく kaisha ni tadoritsuku "to reach one's office" —indicates destination or direction

悪夢にうなされる akumu ni unasareru "to be tormented by a nightmare" —indicates cause

1週間に2日はお休み isshūkan ni futsuka wa o-yasumi "We have 2 days a week off." —indicates ratio, proportion etc

犬に吠えられる inu ni hoerareru "to be barked at by a dog" —indicates the agent of an action

大人になる otona ni naru "to become an adult" —indicates the result of change

ぴかぴかに光る pikapika ni hikaru "to shine brightly" —indicates manner

§ **へ e:**

西へ進む nishi e susumu "to advance toward the west" —indicates the direction of an action

君への思い kimi e no omoi "my longing for you" —indicates the object of an action

学校へ着く gakkō e tsuku "to arrive at school" —indicates destination

兄がすぐそこへ来ています ani ga sugu soko e kite imasu "My brother is right near here." —indicates location of an action

§ **と to:**

友人と話す yūjin to hanasu "to talk with friends" —expresses the idea of "with"

以前と同じやり方 izen to onaji yarikata "the same manner as before" —indicates a term of comparison

政治家となる　seijika to naru "to become a politician" —indicates the result of change

開催地は山梨と決定した　kaisaichi wa Yamanashi to kettei shita "We decided to hold the meeting in Yamanashi." —indicates the content of an action or state

延々と続く　en-en to tsuzuku "to go on endlessly" —indicates the manner of an action or state

§ **より yori:**

父より背が高い　chichi yori se ga takai "I am taller than my father." —indicates a term of comparison

5時より前に帰る　goji yori mae ni kaeru "to be back before 5" —indicates a limit

§ **から kara:** used after nouns and pronouns, and indicates point of departure, or cause

明日から夏休み　myōnichi kara natsuyasumi "Summer vacation starts tomorrow." —indicates a spatial or temporal point of departure

窓から西日が差す　mado kara nishibi ga sasu "The western sun shines in through the window." —expresses the idea of "passing through"

何から何までお世話になりました　nani kara nani made o-sewa ni narimashita "You took wonderful care of me." —indicates extent

母から聞いた話　haha kara kiita hanashi "something I heard from my mother" —indicates a source

ビールは麦から作る　bīru wa mugi kara tsukuru "Beer is made from grain." —indicates constituent materials etc

§ **で de:**

プールで泳ぐ　pūru de oyogu "to swim in the pool" —indicates the location of an action.

ペンで書く　pen de kaku "to write with a pen" —indicates instrument, means, material etc

病気で死ぬ　byōki de shinu "to die from a sickness" —indicates cause, reason, motive

b. Adverbial particles

§ **まで made:** used after nouns and pronouns, and connects them with verbal parts or other particles

東京から北海道まで旅する　tōkyō kara hokkaidō made tabi suru "to travel from Tōkyō to Hokkaidō" —indicates the outer limits of an action in space or time

あくまで計画を実行する　aku made keikaku wo jikkō suru "to push a plan through to the finish" —expresses final extent of an action

§ だけ dake: expresses the limits of something

２人だけで話したい　futari dake de hanashitai "I want to talk to you alone." —indicates a limit

あれだけ食べたら満腹です　are dake tabetara manpuku desu "I'm full after eating all that." —expresses the idea of "that much"

§ ほど hodo: used after various noun and verb forms

後５枚ほど必要です　ato gomai hodo hitsuyō desu "I need about 5 more sheets of paper." —expresses an approximation of number or quantity

かわいそうなほどしょんぼりしている　kawaisō na hodo shonbori shite iru "He's looking so depressed I can't help feeling sorry for him." —expresses an action or state resulting from some characteristic

悪い奴ほど手が白い　warui yatsu hodo te ga shiroi "The evilest men have the whitest hands." —indicates 2 items, the second of which changes in direct proportion to change in the first

c. Modifying particles

§ は wa: used after many kinds of words. The original use was to single out one item of a group.

勉強はもう済んだ　benkyō wa mō sunda "I have finished my homework." —here singles out one item from a group of things to do

象は鼻が長い　zō wa hana ga nagai "The elephant has a long trunk." —singles out an item of subject matter about which some information is given

行きはよいよい、帰りは恐い　iki wa yoi yoi, kaeri wa kowai "Going is easy, but getting back is the problem." —expresses 2 or more contrasting judgments

君とは絶交だ　kimi to wa zekkō da "I want nothing more to do with you." —indicates emphasis

◇Note: in modern Japanese, wa is frequently used to express a word that corresponds to the grammatical subject of a sentence in English.

§ も mo: used after many kinds of words

花も実もある男　hana mo mi mo aru otoko "a man in both looks and deeds" —coordinates 2 or more concepts

料理もろくにできない　ryōri mo roku ni dekinai "She can't even cook properly." —singles out one among many other implied concepts

兄も病気になった　ani mo byōki ni natta "My older brother got sick too." —expresses the concept of "also"

そして誰もいなくなった　soshite dare mo inakunatta "And then there was no one." —used with a negative to express the idea of "nothing, no one"

§ しか **shika:**

生き残ったのは1人しかいない　ikinokotta no wa hitori shika inai "Only one person was left alive." —used with a negative to express the idea of "only"

d. Sentence particles

§ か **ka:** expresses a variety of questions

君はだれですか　kimi wa dare desu ka "Who are you?"

本当に行くのか　hontō ni iku no ka "Are you really going?"

散歩に行きませんか　sanpo ni ikimasen ka "How about going for a walk?"

こんなことができないのか　konna koto ga dekinai no ka "Can't you even do something as simple as this?"

そうか, 失敗だったのか　sō ka, shippai datta no ka "Oh, so it ended in failure, eh?"

§ ね **ne:** used at the end of a sentence

まあ, きれいな花ね　maa, kirei na hana ne "Oh, look at the pretty flower!"
　—expresses an exclamation

この本は君のですね　kono hon wa kimi no desu ne "This is your book, right?"
　—expresses a tag question

遅れてごめんなさいね　okurete gomen nasai ne "Do forgive me for being late."
　—expresses a request for the listener's understanding, sympathy, agreement etc

e. Parenthetical particles

§ ね **ne:** appended to words or phrases as a transition word, or to adjust sentence rhythm etc

そうですね, 考えておきましょう　sō desu ne, kangaete okimashō "Well, let me think about it."

私ね, その秘密知っているの　watashi ne, sono himitsu shitte iru no "Listen, I know the secret behind that."

f. Connecting particles

§ ば **ba**

雨が降れば, 旅行は中止　ame ga fureba, ryokō wa chūshi "If it rains, the trip is off." —expresses a possible condition

消息筋によれば, また株価が下がるらしい　shōsokusuji ni yoreba, mata kabuka ga sagaru rashii "According to a knowledgeable source, stock prices are going to fall again." —indicates the basis for a statement

日が沈めば夜になる　hi ga shizumeba yoru ni naru "Night comes when the sun sets." —expresses an invariable cause and effect relationship

5年前を思えば，随分楽になった　gonen mae wo omoeba, zuibun raku ni natta "Compared with 5 years ago, I am quite well off now." —indicates a past time for comparison with the present

§ **と to:** used after the present tense form of verbs

庭へ出ると，桜が咲いていた　niwa e deru to, sakura ga saite ita "When you went into the garden, you could see the cherry trees in bloom." —joins two contemporaneous actions

本を置くと，すぐ出て行った　hon wo oku to, sugu dete itta "He put down the book and left the room." —joins two successive actions

話が始まると，静かになった　hanashi ga hajimaru to, shizuka ni natta "When the lecture began, the audience became silent and listened." —expresses the beginning or cause etc of an action

はっきり言うと，それは失敗です　hakkiri iu to, sore wa shippai desu "Frankly, it's a failure." —expresses a preamble to what follows

§ **ても te mo** (with certain verbal forms it becomes でも *de mo*): used to express permission etc

果物なら食べてもいいですよ　kudamono nara tabete mo ii desu yo "Fruit is all right for you to eat."

§ **けれども keredomo:** used after verbs and -ii adjectives

貧しいけれども，心は豊かだった　mazushii keredomo, kokoro wa yutaka datta "He was poor materially, but rich in spirit." —expresses some sort of contrast

勝手な言い分ですけれども，帰らせて下さい　katte na iibun desu keredomo, kaerasete kudasai "I'm sorry to do so at this point, but I really must leave." —joins a preamble to the main point of the sentence

レコード持ってきたけれども，聞いてみる　rekōdo motte kita keredomo, kiite miru? "I brought a record along. Do you want to hear it?" —simply joins two clauses

§ **が ga:** used after verbs and -ii adjectives

ご存知のことと思いますが，一応説明します　go-zonji no koto to omoimasu ga, ichiō setsumei shimasu "I'm sure you are already familiar with the problem, but I'll run through it briefly for you anyway." —joins a preamble to the main part of the sentence

驚いて振り向いたが，もはやだれの姿もなかった　odoroite furimuita ga, mohaya dare no sugata mo nakatta "In surprise I wheeled around to look back, but whoever it was had already disappeared." —expresses a temporal relationship between two clauses

見かけは悪いが，たいへん親切な男　mikake wa warui ga, taihen shinsetsu na otoko "He doesn't look it, but he's really a very kind man." —expresses contrast

§ のに **no ni**: expresses dissatisfaction, unexpectedness etc

待っていたのに，来なかった　matte ita no ni, konakatta "I waited and waited, but he didn't come."

§ ので **no de**: expresses cause, reason, basis etc

分からないので，質問しましたwakaranai no de, shitsumon shimashita "I didn't understand, so I asked."

§ から **kara**

暑いから，のどが渇いた　atsui kara, nodo ga kawaita "It was hot, and I became very thirsty." —expresses cause, reason, basis etc

決心したからには，やり通そう　kesshin shita kara ni wa, yaritōsō "We have made the decision, so let's see it through to the end." —expresses the notion of "having done such and such, it follows that..."

DAILY JAPANESE

Here we present a selection of very typical and idiomatic Japanese words and phrases. These examples occur with a high frequency in daily life in Japan. The English translations given in boldface provide an idea of the meaning, but are not absolute. A number of translations are possible, depending on the context, tone of voice, person speaking or spoken to, etc.

Some words occur in the examples which have no English equivalent, or are unintelligible to a person unfamiliar with Japan. Foreigners living in Japan often prefer to use these as loan words in conversation, rather than resorting to some clumsy translation. Such words are marked with an asterisk (∗) in the translation, and are explained in a short glossary at the end of the section.

1. Indispensable words

私　watashi **I**

(Note: slightly formal: 私 watakushi; familiar: male: 僕 boku; female: あたし atashi; very familiar/rough/vulgar, usually male: おれ ore)

あなた anata **you**

(Note: familiar/affectionate: 君 kimi; very familiar/rough/vulgar: お前 omae; rough/vulgar: てめえ temē; insulting: きさま kisama)

彼　kare **he**

彼女　kanojo **she**

はい　hai **yes**

いいえ　iie **no**

どうぞ　dōzo **please**

ありがとう（ございます）arigatō (gozaimasu) **Thank you.**

どういたしまして　dō itashimashite **You're welcome./Don't mention it.**

いいえ、結構です　iie, kekkō desu **No, thank you.**

すみません　sumimasen **excuse me/pardon me/I'm sorry**

2. Greetings

General

お早うございます　o-hayō gozaimasu **Good morning.**

今日は　konnichi wa **Good morning./Good afternoon./Hello.** (said from about 10 a.m. to early evening)

今晩は　konban wa **Good evening.**

お休みなさい　o-yasumi nasai **Good night.**

ご機嫌いかがですか　go-kigen ikaga desu ka **How are you ?** (very formal)

お元気ですか　o-genki desu ka **How are you ?** (less formal)

ありがとう。とても元気です　arigatō. totemo genki desu **I'm fine, thank you.**

よいお天気ですね　yoi o-tenki desu ne **Nice weather, isn't it ?**

今日は寒いですね　kyō wa samui desu ne **It's cold today, isn't it ?**

さようなら　sayōnara **Goodbye.**

行って参ります　itte mairimasu (no English equivalent; said when leaving for a destination with the intention of returning)

行っていらっしゃい　itte irasshai (no English equivalent; said in response to the above)

ただ今　tadaima **I'm home./I'm back.**

お帰りなさい　o-kaeri nasai **Welcome home./Welcome back.** (said in response to the above, but the order may also be reversed)

Visiting

ごめん下さい　gomen kudasai **Hello./Anybody home ?**

いらっしゃいませ　irasshaimase **Welcome.**

おじゃまします　o-jama shimasu (no English equivalent ; said when entering a place)

どうぞこちらへ　dōzo kochira e **This way, please.**

ちょっとお待ち下さい　chotto o-machi kudasai **One moment, please.**

お掛け下さい　o-kake kudasai **Have a seat.**

お目にかかれてうれしいです　o-me ni kakarete ureshii desu **Pleased to meet you.**

長いことおじゃまいたしました　nagai koto o-jama itashimashita **Thank you for your time.**

この辺で失礼いたします　kono hen de shitsurei itashimasu **I'll be going now.**

明日またお会いしましょう　myōnichi mata o-ai shimashō **See you again tomorrow.**

Meals

お上がり下さい　o-agari kudasai **Help yourself** (literally, "please eat")

いただきます　itadakimasu (no English equivalent; said when beginning to eat or drink)

ごちそうさまでした　gochisōsama deshita **I enjoyed the meal./Thanks for the meal.**

3. Introducing oneself

私は日本人（オーストラリア人）です　watashi wa nihonjin (ōsutorariajin) desu **I am Japanese/Australian.**

名前は鈴木花子です　namae wa suzuki hanako desu **My name is Hanako Suzuki.**

私は学生です　watashi wa gakusei desu **I am a university student.**

京都からきました　kyōto kara kimashita **I come from Kyoto.**

22才です　nijūnissai desu **I am 22 years old.**

兄が2人妹が1人います　ani ga futari imōto ga hitori imasu **I have 2 older brothers and a younger sister.**

父は建築家です　chichi wa kenchikuka desu **My father is an architect.**

私は外国に行ったことがありません　watashi wa gaikoku ni itta koto ga arimasen **I have never been to a foreign country.**

私は少ししか英語を話せません　watashi wa sukoshi shika eigo wo hanasemasen **I can only speak a little English.**

趣味は音楽鑑賞です　shumi wa ongaku kanshō desu **My favorite pastime is listening to music.**

．．．が好きではありません　...ga suki de wa arimasen **I don't like ....**

私は水泳が得意です　watashi wa suiei ga tokui desu **I am a good swimmer.**

．．．が苦手です　...ga nigate desu **I am not very good at....**

4. Questions and requests

これは何ですか　kore wa nan desu ka **What is this ?**

あの人はだれですか　ano hito wa dare desu ka **Who is that?**

いつですか　itsu desu ka **When (is it etc)?**

どこから来ましたか　doko kara kimashita ka **Where did you come from/where are you from?**

どうなりましたか　dō narimashita ka **What happened/what is the matter?**

どのぐらい遠いですか　donogurai tōi desu ka **How far (away) is it?**

いくらですか　ikura desu ka **How much is it?**

何をしているのですか　nani wo shite iru no desu ka **What are you doing?**

何がほしいのですか　nani ga hoshii no desu ka **What do you want?**

… がありますか　...ga arimasu ka **Is there a .../do you have ...?**

… を持っていますか　...wo motte imasu ka **Do you have a ...?**

これをいただいてもよろしいですか　kore wo itadaite mo yoroshii desu ka **May I have this?**

… がほしい　...ga hoshii **I want a ....**

… がほしくない　...ga hoshikunai **I don't want ....**

… を取って下さい　...wo totte kudasai **Take ....**

5. Manners

ごめんなさい　gomen nasai **I'm sorry./Pardon me./Forgive me.**

失礼します　shitsurei shimasu **Excuse me./pardon me.**

すみません　sumimasen **Excuse me.** (used to get attention when seeking information, calling a waiter etc)

お手数掛けてすみません　o-tesū kakete sumimasen **I'm sorry to trouble you like this.**

よろしくお願いします　yoroshiku o-negai shimasu (no English equivalent; rather like a very formal "please")

ご迷惑でしょうか　go-meiwaku deshō ka **Is it too much trouble?**

心配いりません　shinpai irimasen **Don't worry.**

かまいません　kamaimasen **It doesn't matter.**

よろしいんですよ　yoroshiin desu yo **That's all right.**

何とおっしゃいましたか　nan to osshaimashita ka **What did you say?**

もう一度言って下さい　mō ichido itte kudasai **Please say that again.**

ゆっくり話して下さい　yukkuri hanashite kudasai **Please speak slowly.**

急いでいます　isoide imasu **I'm in a hurry.**

用意ができています　yōi ga dekite imasu **I'm ready.**

ちょっとお待ち下さい　chotto o-machi kudasai **Just a moment, please.**

6. Conveying information

私はあの少年を知っています　watashi wa ano shōnen wo shitte imasu **I know that boy.**

その人を知りません　sono hito wo shirimasen **I never heard of him/her.**

はっきりとは分かりません　hakkiri to wa wakarimasen **I really don't know for certain.**

覚えています　oboete imasu **(Yes,) I remember.**

忘れました　wasuremashita **I forgot.**

私はとても怒っています　watashi wa totemo okotte imasu **I am very angry.**

私はたいへん不愉快です　watashi wa taihen fuyukai desu **I am very upset.**

気分は最高です　kibun wa saikō desu **I feel great.**

とても幸せです　totemo shiawase desu **I feel very happy.**

残念です　zannen desu **That's too bad.**

家族と／が離ればなれで寂しい　kazoku to／ga hanarebanare de sabishii **I miss my family.**

それは正しいと思います　sore wa tadashii to omoimasu **That's correct.**

あなたは間違っています　anata wa machigatte imasu **You're mistaken.**

あなたの言う通りです　anata no iu tōri desu **It's as you say.**

一生懸命に働きます　isshōkenmei ni hatarakimasu **I'm going to work hard.**

7. Eating out

a. getting seats

私はとても空腹です　watashi wa totemo kūfuku desu **I'm very hungry.**

私はのどが渇きました　watashi wa nodo ga kawakimashita **I'm thirsty.**

食事に行きましょう　shokuji ni ikimashō **Let's go someplace to eat.**

安い店を紹介してくれませんか　yasui mise wo shōkai shite kuremasen ka **Do you know some inexpensive place?**

角のてんぷら屋がおいしいと評判です　kado no tenpuraya ga oishii to hyōban desu **They say the tempura* place on the corner is pretty good.**

1時にテーブルを予約して下さい　ichiji ni tēburu wo yoyaku shite kudasai **Reserve a table for one o'clock, will you please?**

3人連れですが、空いているテーブルありますか　sanninzure desu ga, aite iru tēburu arimasu ka **Do you have a table for 3?**

満席です　manseki desu **Sorry, we're all filled up.**

昼時はどこも混んでいます　hirudoki wa doko mo konde imasu **At noontime everywhere you go it's crowded.**

禁煙席にお願いします　kin-enseki ni o-negai shimasu **We want a non-smoking** table, please.

b. ordering

メニューを見せていただけますか　menyū wo misete itadakemasu ka **Can we see a menu, please ?**

定食はありますか　teishoku wa arimasu ka **Do you have set meals ?**

本日のおすすめ料理は何ですか　honjitsu no o-susume ryōri wa nan desu ka **What's today's specialty ?**

この地方の名物は何ですか　kono chihō no meibutsu wa nan desu ka **What's the local specialty ?**

何を食べたいですか　nani wo tabetai desu ka **What do you feel like eating ?**

これは何の料理ですか　kore wa nan no ryōri desu ka **What is this ?**

... を食べて見ませんか　...wo tabete mimasen ka **How about trying the ... ?**

私は... にしたい　watashi wa ...ni shitai **I want the ....**

私は魚が大好きです　watashi wa sakana ga daisuki desu **I just love fish.**

私は肉は嫌いです　watashi wa niku wa kirai desu **I hate meat.**

私はピーマンは食べられません　watashi wa pīman wa taberaremasen **I can't eat green peppers.**

おいしいです　oishii desu **It's delicious.**

これはまずい　kore wa mazui **It tastes awful.**

もう少しパンを下さい　mō sukoshi pan wo kudasai **Can we have some more bread, please?**

ご飯のおかわりを下さい　gohan no o-kawari wo kudasai **Another bowl of rice, please.**

塩を取って下さい　shio wo totte kudasai **Please pass the salt.**

スープがまだきていません　sūpu ga mada kite imasen **We didn't get our soup yet.**

味が薄い　aji ga usui **This needs more seasoning.**

辛すぎます　karasugimasu **It's too salty.**

おなかがいっぱいになりました　onaka ga ippai ni narimashita **I'm full.**

c. drinks

飲物は何になさいますか　nomimono wa nani ni nasaimasu ka **What will you have to drink ?**

生ビールを下さい　namabīru wo kudasai **We'll have draft beer.**

ブランディーはありますか　burandī wa arimasu ka **Do you have any brandy ?**

ミルクティーを2つ下さい　mirukutī wo futatsu kudasai **Two teas with milk,** please.

ダイエットをしているので砂糖はいりません　daietto wo shite iru no de satō wa irimasen **I'm on a diet, so no sugar, please.**

コーヒーのおかわりを下さい　kōhī no o-kawari wo kudasai **More coffee, please.**

水をもういっぱい下さい　mizu wo mō ippai kudasai **More water, please.**

このお茶は少し熱い　kono o-cha wa sukoshi atsui **This tea is too hot.**

d. paying

勘定をお願いします　kanjō wo o-negai shimasu **Can I have the bill, please?**

伝票を調べて下さい．間違っていると思います　denpyō wo shirabete kudasai. machigatte iru to omoimasu **Check this bill, will you? I think there's a mistake on it.**

サラダは取っていません　sarada wa totte imasen **I didn't order any salad.**

伝票を別々にしてくれませんか　denpyō wo betsubetsu ni shite kuremasen ka **Will you give us separate bills, please?**

e. restaurant words

レストラン　resutoran **restaurant**

軽食　keishoku **light lunches**

メニュー　menyū **menu**

勘定(書)　kanjō(gaki) **bill/check**

化粧室　keshōshitsu **restroom(s)**

ウエイトレス　ueitoresu **waitress**

ウエイター　ueitā **waiter**

板前　itamae **cook**

茶碗(㋕)　chawan **rice bowl/teacup (for Japanese tea)**

湯呑み　yunomi **teacup (for Japanese tea)**

カップ　kappu **cup/teacup/coffee cup (with handle)**

箸(㋕)　hashi **chopsticks**

つまようじ　tsumayōji **toothpick**

灰皿　haizara **ashtray**

たばこ　tabako **cigarette**

日本酒　nihonshu **sake***

銚子(㋕)／とっくり　chōshi*/tokkuri* (no English equivalent; see glossary)

熱燗(㋕)　atsukan **hot sake**

水　mizu **water**

ミルク　miruku **milk**

砂糖　satō **sugar**

紅茶　kōcha **tea**

日本茶　nihoncha **Japanese tea**

塩　shio **salt**

こしょう　koshō **pepper**

芥子(ﾟﾟ)　karashi **mustard**

油　abura **oil**

酢　su **vinegar**

正油(ﾟﾟ)　shōyu **soy sauce**

どんぶり　donburi **bowl**

味噌(ﾟ)　miso **miso***

わさび　wasabi **wasabi***

f. some Japanese dishes

すき焼き　sukiyaki　　beef cooked at table with green onions, tofu, and leafy vegetables

寿司(ﾟ)　sushi　　cooked rice seasoned with vinegar and served in various forms with a topping of fish, shellfish, and vegetables

てんぷら　tenpura　　fish, shellfish, and vegetables coated with batter and fried in deep fat

天丼(ﾟ)　tendon　　a bowl of rice topped with tempura* dipped in broth

豆腐　tōfu　　white soya-bean curd with a soft, cheeselike consistency

梅干　umeboshi　　ume* pickled with salt and a pungent seasoning

刺身　sashimi　　fish and shellfish sliced and eaten raw with soy sauce and wasabi*

納豆　nattō　　fermented soy beans

うどん　udon　　wheat-flour noodles

そば – soba　　buckwheat noodles

味噌(ﾟ)汁　misoshiru　　soup flavored with miso

お握(ﾟ)り　o-nigiri　　rice compacted into a ball or other shape for carrying on outings, to work etc

餅(ﾟ)　mochi　　glutinous rice steamed, pounded into a paste, shaped into patties, and allowed to harden

赤飯　sekihan　　glutinous rice steamed with red beans

たくあん　takuan　　radish pickled in salt and rice bran

お好み焼き　okonomiyaki　　a sort of hotcake made from wheat flour batter to which have been added various vegetables and other ingredients and fried on a hot plate

ところてん　tokoroten　　a jelly made from a species of seaweed and eaten as a refreshing dish in summer

おでん　oden　　various fish and vegetable preparations stewed in a light broth

ようかん　yōkan　　a jellied confection made from highly sweetened beans

雑煮　zōni　　a soup with vegetables, fish, and meat to which mochi are added: a traditional New Year's dish

おせち　o-sechi　　an assortment of New Year's dishes prepared several days beforehand from ingredients that will not spoil; the idea is to give the womenfolk a degree of respite from the drudgery of kitchen work on the greatest feast of the year

煎餅(ﾎ.ｶ)　senbei　　fried crackers made from rice flour

Shopping

a. going out

私は帽子が買いたい　watashi wa bōshi ga kaitai **I need a new hat.**

どのお店が一番よいですか　dono o-mise ga ichiban yoi desu ka **Do you know a good store?**

駅のそばの果物屋は安いので有名です　eki no soba no kudamonoya wa yasui no de yūmei desu **The fruit store near the station is known for its low prices.**

デパートで今セールをやっています　depāto de ima sēru wo yatte imasu **They're having a sale at the department store today.**

一緒に買い物に行きましょう　issho ni kaimono ni ikimashō **How about coming shopping with me?**

... はどこで買えますか　...wa doko de kaemasu ka **Where can you buy a ...?**

一番近い本屋はどこですか　ichiban chikai hon-ya wa doko desu ka **Where's the closest bookstore?**

靴売場はどこですか　kutsu uriba wa doko desu ka **Where is the shoe department?**

b. picking things out

店員さん，これを見せて下さい　ten-insan, kore wo misete kudasai **Excuse me, Miss, could you let me examine this item?**

... を売っていますか　...wo utte imasu ka **Do you sell ... here?**

... を買いたいのです　...wo kaitai no desu **I'm looking for ....**

こちらはいかがでしょう　kochira wa ikaga deshou **How about this one?**

何色がよろしいのですか　nani-iro ga yoroshii no desu ka **What color would you like?**

きれいな色ですね　kirei na iro desu ne **That's a pretty color, isn't it ?**

これが気に入りました　kore ga ki ni irimashita **I like this one.**

あちらの方が好きです　achira no hō ga suki desu **I like that one.**

この色はあまり好きではありません　kono iro wa amari suki de wa arimasen **I don't like this color.**

別な色のものがありますか　betsu na iro no mono ga arimasu ka **Do you have this in a different color ?**

別の品物を見せて下さい　betsu no shinamono wo misete kudasai **Show me something else.**

もっと安いものはありませんか　motto yasui mono wa arimasen ka **Do you have something cheaper ?**

予算は1万円です　yosan wa ichiman en desu **My spending limit is 10,000 yen.**

予算の枠内で買いたいのです　yosan no wakunai de kaitai no desu **I don't want to go over my limit.**

サイズはいくらですか　saizu wa ikura desu ka **What size do you take ?**

これはどのサイズですか　kore wa dono saizu desu ka **What size is this ?**

サイズ... を下さい　saizu... wo kudasai **Give me a size ....**

もっと大きいものがありますか　motto ōkii mono ga arimasu ka **Do you have something bigger ?**

大きすぎる　ōkisugiru **It's too big.**

高すぎる　takasugiru **It's too expensive.**

c. in various stores
clothing and shoes

セーターを見せて下さい　sētā wo misete kudasai **Show me some sweaters.**

ウインドーにあるのが好きです　uindō ni aru no ga suki desu **I like the one in the window.**

その着物は実に豪華ですね　sono kimono wa jitsu ni gōka desu ne **That kimono is really gorgeous.**

残念ながら着物は1人で着られません　zannennagara kimono wa hitori de kiraremasen **It's unfortunate, but a kimono is hard to put on by oneself.**

黒い絹の手袋がほしい　kuroi kinu no tebukuro ga hoshii **I want a pair of black silk gloves.**

試着していいですか　shichaku shite ii desu ka **Can I try it on ?**

胸まわりは... です　munemawari wa ...desu **My bust/chest measures ....**

ウエストは... です　uesuto wa ...desu **My waist measures ....**

襟(衿)のサイズは... です　eri no saizu wa ...desu **My collar size is....**

この色は今年の流行です　kono iro wa kotoshi no ryūkō desu **This color is in fashion this year.**

このスタイルは好きではありません　kono sutairu wa suki de wa arimasen **I don't like this style.**

コート売り場はどこですか　kōto uriba wa doko desu ka **Where do you sell coats?**

このネクタイは実におしゃれです　kono nekutai wa jitsu ni o-share desu **This necktie is really stylish.**

靴下を２足ほしい　kutsushita wo nisoku hoshii **I want 2 pairs of socks.**

ビーチサンダルがほしい　bīchisandaru ga hoshii **I want a pair of beach sandals.**

このかかとは高すぎる　kono kakato wa takasugiru **The heels are too high.**

food and drink

パンを１個下さい　pan wo ikko kudasai **One loaf of bread, please.**

冷凍食品コーナーはどこですか　reitōshokuhin kōnā wa doko desu ka **Where are the frozen foods?**

… を１キロ下さい　…wo ichikiro kudasai **Give me one kilo of ….**

牛乳を１瓶下さい　gyūnyū wo hitobin kudasai **Give me a bottle of milk.**

それは新鮮ですか　sore wa shinsen desu ka **Is that fresh?**

これは古くなっている　kore wa furuku natte iru **This isn't fresh any more.**

賞味期間を過ぎている　shōmikikan wo sugite iru **The date on this has expired.**

これは悪くなっている　kore wa waruku natte iru **This has gone bad.**

medicines

ばんそうこうを下さい　bansōkō wo kudasai **I'd like a roll of adhesive tape.**

バンドエイドを下さい　bandoeido wo kudasai **Give me a box of Band-Aids®.**

日焼け止めの薬ありますか　hiyakedome no kusuri arimasu ka **Have you got something to prevent sunburn?**

消化不良にきく薬を下さい　shōkafuryō ni kiku kusuri wo kudasai **Give me something for indigestion, please.**

のどが痛みます。トローチを下さい　nodo ga itamimasu. torōchi wo kudasai **I have a sore throat; give me a box of cough drops.**

虫刺されにきく薬をくれませんか　mushisasare ni kiku kusuri wo kuremasen ka **Can you give me something for insect bites?**

総合ビタミン剤を下さい　sōgōbitaminzai wo kudasai **I want a bottle of vitamin tablets.**

この処方箋 (⅔) を調合していただけますか　kono shohōsen wo chōgō shite itadakemasu ka **Can I have this prescription filled, please ?**

小さな救急箱はありますか　chiisana kyūkyūbako wa arimasu ka **Do you have a small first-aid kit ?**

アスピリンを1瓶下さい　asupirin wo hitobin kudasai **Give me a bottle of aspirin, please.**

newspapers, books, stationery

英字新聞は売っていますか　eijishinbun wa utte imasu ka **Do you carry English-language newspapers ?**

市街地図はありますか　shigaichizu wa arimasu ka **Do you have a city map ?**

... 著の本がありますか　...cho no hon ga arimasu ka **Do you have any books by ... ?**

ノートを2冊とボールペンを1本下さい　nōto wo nisatsu to bōrupen wo ippon kudasai **Two notebooks and a ballpoint, please.**

横書きの便せんはありますか　yokogaki no binsen wa arimasu ka **Have you got letter paper for writing left to right ?**

d. paying for things

これはいくらですか　kore wa ikura desu ka **How much is this ?**

全部でいくらになりますか　zenbu de ikura ni narimasu ka **How much all together ?**

勘定をお願いします　kanjō wo o-negai shimasu **Can I have the bill, please ?**

アメリカの通貨で売ってくれますか　amerika no tsūka de utte kuremasu ka **Can I pay in American money ?**

トラベラーズチェックで受けてくれますか　toraberāzuchekku de ukete kuremasu ka **Will you take traveler's checks ?**

少し高いですね　sukoshi takai desu ne **That's rather expensive, isn't it ?**

割引きしてくれますか　waribiki shite kuremasu ka **Can you give me a discount ?**

ここのレジは混んでいます　koko no reji wa konde imasu **The line at this checkout counter is too long.**

レシートをいただけますか　reshīto wo itadakemasu ka **Can I have a receipt ?**

おつりが間違っています　o-tsuri ga machigatte imasu **You gave me the wrong change.**

e. complaints

責任者に会いたい　sekininsha ni aitai **I want to speak to your superior.**

昨日これを買いました　sakujitsu kore wo kaimashita **I bought this yesterday.**

これは汚れている（破れている，壊れている，ひびが入っている，不良品だ）　kore wa yogorete iru (yaburete iru, kowarete iru, hibi ga haitte iru, furyōhin da) **This is stained (torn, broken, cracked, defective).**

この本には落丁があります　kono hon ni wa rakuchō ga arimasu **This book has pages missing.**

この薬は全く効果がありません　kono kusuri wa mattaku kōka ga arimasen **This medicine doesn't have any effect at all.**

店員の態度が悪い　ten-in no taido ga warui **I don't like your clerk's manners.**

これを取り替えて下さいませんか　kore wo torikaete kudasaimasen ka **Can I exchange this, please?**

お金を払い戻して下さいませんか　o-kane wo haraimodoshite kudasaimasen ka **Can I have my money back, please?**

f. repairing and mending

時計が壊れてしまいました　tokei ga kowarete shimaimashita **My watch is broken.**

修理できますか　shūri dekimasu ka **Can it be fixed?**

これを直して下さい　kore wo naoshite kudasai **Can you fix this?**

残念ながらそれはもはや修理できません　zannennagara sore wa mohaya shūri dekimasen **I'm sorry, but it's beyond repair.**

靴のかかとを新しいのとつけ替えていただけますか　kutsu no kakato wo atarashii no to tsukekaete itadakemasu ka **Can you put new heels on these shoes?**

待っている間にやってくれますか　matte iru aida ni yatte kuremasu ka **Can you do it while I wait?**

いつできますか　itsu dekimasu ka **How soon can you have it done?**

どのぐらい時間がかかりますか　dono gurai jikan ga kakarimasu ka **How long will it take?**

このジャケットのシミは抜けないでしょうか　kono jaketto no shimi wa nukenai deshō ka **Can you remove the stain on this jacket?**

このズボンのすそがほつれているので繕っていただけますか　kono zubon no suso ga hotsurete iru no de tsukurotte itadakemasu ka **The cuffs on these pants are worn. Can you mend them?**

... の具合が悪いのでみていただけますか　...no guai ga warui no de mite itadakemasu ka **The ... is out of order. Could you have a look at it, please?**

できるだけ早く直していただきたい　dekiru dake hayaku naoshite itadakitai **I want** this fixed as soon as possible.

費用はいくらですか　hiyō wa ikura desu ka **How much will it cost ?**

9. Postal and Telephone Service

a. the post office

一番近い郵便局はどこですか　ichiban chikai yūbinkyoku wa doko desu ka **Where is the nearest post office ?**

郵便局は何時まで開いていますか　yūbinkyoku wa nanji made aite imasu ka **What time does the post office close ?**

ポストはどこにありますか　posuto wa doko ni arimasu ka **Do you know where there's a mailbox ?**

ちょうど記念切手を売り出しているところです　chōdo kinenkitte wo uridashite iru tokoro desu **They have just issued a new commemorative stamp.**

カナダまで葉書はいくらですか　kanada made hagaki wa ikura desu ka **How much is a postcard to Canada ?**

アメリカまで航空便はいくらですか　amerika made kōkūbin wa ikura desu ka **How much is an air mail letter to America ?**

イギリスまで船便ではいくらですか　igirisu made funabin de wa ikura desu ka **How much is surface mail to Britain ?**

この小包をお願いします　kono kozutsumi wo o-negai shimasu **I want to mail this package.**

この手紙を速達で送りたい　kono tegami wo sokutatsu de okuritai **I want to send this letter by express mail.**

この手紙を書留にしたい　kono tegami wo kakitome ni shitai **I want to send this letter by registered mail.**

官製葉書を10枚下さい　kanseihagaki wo jūmai kudasai **Ten government postcards*, please.**

大体何日頃届きますか　daitai nannichi goro todokimasu ka **Do you know how many days it will take to get there ?**

b. telephones and telegrams

一番近い電話ボックスはどこですか　ichiban chikai denwabokkusu wa doko desu ka **Where is the nearest telephone booth ?**

電話を掛けたい　denwa wo kaketai **I want to make a phone call.**

オーストラリアに電話したい　ōsutoraria ni denwa shitai **I want to make a phone call to Australia.**

小銭が不足しています．テレフォンカードをお持ちですか　kozeni ga fusoku shite

imasu. terefonkādo wo o-mochi desu ka **I don't have enough small change. Do you have a telephone card ?**

コレクトコールにしたい　korekutokōru ni shitai **I want to make a collect call.**

もしもし... さんですか　moshimoshi ...san desu ka **Hello. Is this Mr. ... ?**

どちら様ですか　dochirasama desu ka **Who is this calling, please ?**

内線... 番をお願いします　naisen ...ban wo o-negai shimasu **Give me extension ..., please.**

そのままお待ち下さい　sono mama o-machi kudasai **Please hold the line a moment.**

... はただ今外出中です　...wa tadaima gaishutsuchū desu **... is out at the moment.**

... はいつお戻りですか　...wa itsu o-modori desu ka **When will ... be back ?**

伝言をお願いできますか　dengon wo o-negai dekimasu ka **Will you take a message, please ?**

... より電話があったと彼に伝えて下さい　...yori denwa ga atta to kare ni tsutaete kudasai **Please tell him that ... called.**

後ほどお電話します　nochihodo o-denwa shimasu **I'll call again later.**

私に電話するように伝えて下さい　watashi ni denwa suru yō ni tsutaete kudasai **Please tell him to call me.**

話し中です　hanashichū desu **The line is busy.**

電話番号が間違っています　denwabangō ga machigatte imasu **You have the wrong number.**

留守番電話にメッセージが入っています　rusubandenwa ni messēji ga haitte imasu **There's a message on the answering machine.**

電報を打ちたい　denpō wo uchitai **I want to send a telegram.**

1語あたりいくらですか　ichigo atari ikura desu ka **How much is it for each word ?**

祝電(弔電)を打ちたい　shukuden (chōden) wo uchitai **I want to send a telegram of congratulation [condolence].**

10. Transport

a. trains

駅はどこにありますか　eki wa doko ni arimasu ka **Where is the train station ?**

新幹線のホームはどこですか　shinkansen no hōmu wa doko desu ka **Where are the shinkansen* tracks ?**

切符は自動発券機で買えます　kippu wa jidōhakkenki de kaemasu **You can buy your ticket at the automatic ticket machine.**

新幹線の座席指定はこの用紙に必要事項を記入します shinkansen no zaseki shitei wa kono yōshi ni hitsuyōjikō wo kinyū shimasu **You have to fill out this form to get a reserved seat on the shinkansen*.**

9：30分発京都行きの特急に乗りたいのですが kujisanjippunhatsu kyōtoyuki no tokkyū ni noritai no desu ga **I want a ticket on the 9:30 special express to Kyōto, please.**

禁煙席を希望します kin-enseki wo kibō shimasu **If possible I want a non-smoking seat.**

往復の切符を買いたい ōfuku no kippu wo kaitai **I want a round-trip ticket.**

寝台車を予約したい shindaisha wo yoyaku shitai **I want to reserve a berth on a sleeping car.**

寝台車はいくらですか shindaisha wa ikura desu ka **How much does a sleeping car ticket cost ?**

急行列車ですか，それとも普通列車ですか kyūkōressha desu ka, soretomo futsūressha desu ka **Do you want the express train or the local train ?**

この電車は... へ行きますか kono densha wa ..e ikimasu ka **Does this train go to ... ?**

もっと早くでる列車はありますか motto hayaku deru ressha wa arimasu ka **Isn't there an earlier train ?**

この列車には食堂車がありますか kono ressha ni wa shokudōsha ga arimasu ka **Is there a dining car on this train ?**

... まで片道３枚下さい ...made katamichi sanmai kudasai **Three one-way tickets to ..., please.**

この切符は何日間有効ですか kono kippu wa nannichikan yūkō desu ka **How long is this ticket valid ?**

この列車は何時に発車しますか kono ressha wa nanji ni hassha shimasu ka **What time does this train leave ?**

... 行きの列車は何番ホームから発車しますか ...yuki no ressha wa nanban hōmu kara hassha shimasu ka **Where do I get the train for ... ?**

... には何時に到着しますか ...ni wa nanji ni tōchaku shimasu ka **What time does the train get to ... ?**

... からの列車は何時に到着しますか ...kara no ressha wa nanji ni tōchaku shimasu ka **What time does the train from ... get in ?**

この列車は... に停まりますか kono ressha wa .. ni tomarimasu ka **Does this train stop at ... ?**

この列車は遅れていますか kono ressha wa okurete imasu ka **Is this train running late ?**

指定券を持っています　shiteiken wo motte imasu **I have a reservation.**

車掌が検札に来ました　shashō ga kensatsu ni kimashita **The conductor is here to check the tickets.**

この席は空いていますか　kono seki wa aite imasu ka **Is this seat taken？** (literally, "Is this seat open？")

どこで乗換えですか　doko de norikae desu ka **Where do I transfer？**

時刻表はどこにありますか　jikokuhyō wa doko ni arimasu ka **Where is the time-table？**

近ごろは自動改札が増えました　chikagoro wa jidōkaisatsu ga fuemashita **Nowadays you see more and more automatic wickets.**

b. buses

バス停はどこですか　basutei wa doko desu ka **Where is the bus stop？**

... 行きのバスの発着所はどこですか　...yuki no basu no hatchakujo wa doko desu ka **Where do I get the bus for ...？**

このバスは... に停まりますか　kono basu wa ...ni tomarimasu ka **Does this bus stop at ...？**

... までどのぐらい時間がかかりますか　...made dono gurai jikan ga kakarimasu ka **How long does it take to get to ...？**

定期観光バスに乗りたい　teiki kankōbasu ni noritai **I want to ride a scheduled sightseeing bus.**

そのバスは何時に... に着きますか　sono basu wa nanji ni ...ni tsukimasu ka **What time does the bus reach ...？**

そのバスは何時に発車しますか　sono basu wa nanji ni hassha shimasu ka **What time does the bus leave？**

このバスはどのぐらいの間隔で出ていますか　kono basu wa donogurai no kankaku de dete imasu ka **How often does this bus leave？**

次のバスは何時ですか　tsugi no basu wa nanji desu ka **What time is the next bus？**

... の近くを通りますか　...no chikaku wo tōrimasu ka **Does the bus pass near ...？**

... 行きのバスはどれですか　...yuki no basu wa dore desu ka **Which is the bus for ...？**

... まで行きたい　...made ikitai **I want to go to ....**

どこで降りたらいいでしょうか　doko de oritara ii deshō ka **Where should I get off？**

最終バスは出てしまいましたか　saishūbasu wa dete shimaimashita ka **Has the last** bus already left ?

c. taxis

タクシー乗り場はどこですか　takushīnoriba wa doko desu ka **Where is the taxi stand ?**

空車が来ました　kūsha ga kimashita **Here comes an empty taxi.**

... ホテルまで行って下さい　...hoteru made itte kudasai **Take me to the ... Hotel.**

遅れているので少し急いでくれませんか　okurete iru no de sukoshi isoide kuremasen ka **I'm late, so could you go a little faster ?**

ここで止って下さい　koko de tomatte kudasai **Stop here, please.**

待っていて下さい　matte ite kudasai **Wait for me, please.**

名所旧跡がみたい　meishokyūseki ga mitai **I want to go sightseeing.**

そこは遠いですか　soko wa tōi desu ka **Is it very far from here ?**

... までどのぐらいの時間ですか　...made dono gurai no jikan desu ka **How long does it take to get there ?**

いくらですか　ikura desu ka **How much is it ?**

d. airplanes

航空会社の営業所はどこにありますか　kōkūgaisha no eigyōsho wa doko ni arimasu ka **Where is the airline office ?**

日曜日の午後の便で... まで3席予約したい　nichiyōbi no gogo no bin de ...made sanseki yoyaku shitai **I want 3 tickets to ... on the Sunday afternoon flight.**

金曜日に... までの便がありますか　kinyōbi ni ...made no bin ga arimasu ka **Is there a flight to ... on Friday ?**

その便は何時に発ますか　sono bin wa nanji ni tachimasu ka **What time does that flight leave ?**

その便は何時に到着しますか　sono bin wa nanji ni tōchaku shimasu ka **What time does that flight arrive ?**

... の予約をキャンセルして下さい　...no yoyaku wo kyanseru shite kudasai **Please cancel my reservation for ...**

予約を変更したい　yoyaku wo henkō shitai **I want to change my reservation.**

次の便は何時ですか　tsugi no bin wa nanji desu ka **When is the next flight ?**

市内から空港までのバスがありますか　shinai kara kūkō made no basu ga arimasu ka **Is there a bus from the city center to the airport ?**

e. boats

その船は何時に出航ですか　sono fune wa nanji ni shukkō desu ka **What time does the boat leave ?**

次の出航は何時ですか　tsugi no shukkō wa nanji desu ka **When does the next boat leave ?**

その船はどこに入港ですか　sono fune wa doko ni nyūkō desu ka **What stops does the boat make ?**

その船は... に寄港しますか　sono fune wa ...ni kikō shimasu ka **Does the boat stop at ... ?**

... まで船便がありますか　...made funabin ga arimasu ka **Is there a boat to ... ?**

この船でどのぐらい時間がかかりますか　kono fune de dono gurai jikan ga kakarimasu ka **How much time does this boat take to get there ?**

一人用船室を予約できますか　hitoriyō senshitsu wo yoyaku dekimasu ka **Can I reserve a single stateroom ?**

部屋にはいくつ寝台がありますか　heya ni wa ikutsu shindai ga arimasu ka **How many beds are there in the stateroom ?**

いつ入港しますか　itsu nyūkō shimasu ka **When will we reach port ?**

何時に乗船しなければなりませんか　nanji ni jōsen shinakereba narimasen ka **By what time do we have to be on board ?**

港にどのぐらい停泊しますか　minato ni dono gurai teihaku shimasu ka **How long will the boat stay in port ?**

f. cars

運転免許証を持っています　unten menkyoshō wo motte imasu **I have a driver's license.**

友人とドライブに出かけましょう　yūjin to doraibu ni dekakemashō **Let's go for a drive with some friends.**

いい車ですね. 自家用車ですか　ii kuruma desu ne. jikayōsha desu ka **Nice car. Is it yours ?**

いいえ. レンタカーです　iie. rentakā desu **No, it's rented.**

どこで車を借りられますか　doko de kuruma wo kariraremasu ka **Where can I rent a car ?**

レンタカーは1時間いくらですか　rentakā wa ichijikan ikura desu ka **What's the fee per hour to rent this car ?**

一番近いガソリンスタンドはどこですか　ichiban chikai gasorinsutando wa doko desu ka **Where is the nearest gas station ?**

満タンにして下さい　mantan ni shite kudasai **Fill it up, please.**

ガソリン，リッターあたりいくらですか　gasorin, rittā atari ikura desu ka **How much is gasoline per liter ?**

洗車して下さい　sensha shite kudasai **Wash the car, please.**

道路地図はありますか　dōrochizu wa arimasu ka **Do you have a road map ?**

駐車場はどこですか　chūshajō wa doko desu ka **Where is the parking lot ?**

ここは駐車禁止ですか　koko wa chūsha kinshi desu ka **Is this a no parking zone ?**

今どこでしょうか　ima doko deshō ka **Where are we now ?**

地図で示して下さい　chizu de shimeshite kudasai **Show me on the map.**

次のドライブインで昼食にしましょう　tsugi no doraibuin de chūshoku ni shimashō **Let's have lunch at the next drive-in.**

... にはどう行けばいいですか　...ni wa dō ikeba ii desu ka **How do you get to ... ?**

... はどこにありますか　...wa doko ni arimasu ka **Where is ... ?**

... への自動車道にはどう行けばいいですか　...e no jidōshadō ni wa dō ikeba ii desu ka **How do you get to the expressway for ... ?**

... へはどの道を行けば一番いいですか　...e wa dono michi wo ikeba ichiban ii desu ka **What's the best road to ... ?**

... までどのぐらいの距離がありますか　...made dono gurai no kyori ga arimasu ka **How far is it to ... ?**

... に夕刻までには着くのでしょうか　...ni yūkoku made ni wa tsuku no deshō ka **Will we reach ... by evening ?**

高速道路は混んでいます　kōsokudōro wa konde imasu **The expressway is clogged with heavy traffic.**

渋滞に巻き込まれました　jūtai ni makikomaremashita **I got caught in heavy traffic.**

抜け道がありますか　nukemichi ga arimasu ka **Is there a back road to get around the traffic ?**

このまま5キロほどまっすぐ行って下さい　kono mama 5 kiro hodo massugu itte kudasai **Go straight along this road for 5 kilometers.**

次の信号を右に曲がって下さい　tsugi no shingō wo migi ni magatte kudasai **Turn right at the next signal.**

車の鍵（š）をなくさないように　kuruma no kagi wo nakusanai yō ni **Don't lose your car keys.**

　　some road signs

右側通行　migigawa tsūkō **keep right**

一方通行道路　ippōtsūkōdōrò **one way**

迂回　ukai **detour**

駐車禁止　chūsha kinshi **no parking**

追い越し禁止　oikoshi kinshi **no passing**

進入禁止　shinnyū kinshi **no entry**

前方道路工事中　zenpō dōro kōjichū **construction ahead**

11. Hotels

安くてよいホテルを紹介して下さい　yasukute yoi hoteru wo shōkai shite kudasai **Can you tell me the name of a hotel that is good and also cheap ?**

今夜部屋はありますか　kon-ya heya wa arimasu ka **Do you have a vacancy for tonight ?**

2人で泊まれる部屋がありますか　futari de tomareru heya ga arimasu ka **Do you have a room for two ?**

シングルの部屋を3室予約します　shinguru no heya wo sanshitsu yoyaku shimasu **I would like to reserve 3 single rooms.**

その部屋は何階にありますか　sono heya wa nangai ni arimasu ka **What floor is that room on ?**

2階の部屋は空いていますか　nikai no heya wa aite imasu ka **Do you have a room on the second floor ?**

この部屋にします　kono heya ni shimasu **I'll take this room.**

別の部屋がありませんか　betsu no heya ga arimasen ka **Don't you have some other room ?**

ツインしかありません　tsuin shika arimasen **We only have a twin room.**

空き室はこれだけです　akishitsu wa kore dake desu **This is the only vacancy we have.**

和室の部屋はありますか　washitsu no heya wa arimasu ka **Do you have a Japanese-style room ?**

この部屋は1泊いくらですか　kono heya wa ippaku ikura desu ka **What's the rate for this room ?**

もっと安い部屋はありませんか　motto yasui heya wa arimasen ka **Don't you have something cheaper ?**

明朝7：30分に起して下さい　myōchō shichiji sanjuppun ni okoshite kudasai **Please wake me up at 7:30 tomorrow morning.**

私の部屋にはタオルがありません　watashi no heya ni wa taoru ga arimasen **There are no towels in my room.**

シーツが汚れています　shītsu ga yogorete imasu **The sheets are dirty.**

トイレの水が流れません　toire no mizu ga nagaremasen **The toilet won't flush.**

シャワーの出がよくありません　shawā no de ga yoku arimasen **There's no pressure in the shower.**

窓が空きません．開けて下さい　mado ga akimasen. akete kudasai **I can't get the window open. Please open it.**

暑すぎます　atsusugimasu **It's too hot in here.**

暖房を強くできますか　danbō wo tsuyoku dekimasu ka **Can you turn up the heat?**

冷房がきいていません　reibō ga kiite imasen **The air conditioning isn't working.**

鍵(ぎ)を下さい　kagi wo kudasai **Give me my key, please.**

私宛のメッセージがありますか　watashi ate no messēji ga arimasu ka **Are there any messages for me?**

この洋服を洗濯してほしい　kono yōfuku wo sentaku shite hoshii **I want to get this dress cleaned.**

このスーツにアイロンを掛けてほしい　kono sūtsu ni airon wo kakete hoshii **I want to get this suit pressed.**

明日の午前中までにできますか　myōnichi no gozenchū made ni dekimasu ka **Can you have it done by tomorrow morning?**

食堂はどこですか　shokudō wa doko desu ka **Where is the dining room?**

明後日の朝立ちます　asatte no asa tachimasu **I'll be leaving the day after tomorrow in the morning.**

勘定書きを用意してくれますか　kanjōgaki wo yōi shite kuremasu ka **Will you get my bill ready, please?**

荷物を下におろしていただけますか　nimotsu wo shita ni oroshite itadakemasu ka **Can you have my luggage taken downstairs, please?**

10時にタクシーを1台呼んでいただけますか　jūji ni takushī wo ichidai yonde itadakemasu ka **Will you call me a taxi for 10 o'clock, please?**

お世話になりました　o-sewa ni narimashita **I enjoyed my stay.**

12. Leisure time

a. sightseeing

名所旧跡を見物しましょう　meishokyūseki wo kenbutsu shimashō **Let's go sightseeing.**

ガイドブックを持ってきましたか　gaidobukku wo motte kimashita ka **Did you bring the guidebook?**

当地の見所は何ですか　tōchi no midokoro wa nan desu ka **What is there to see** around here ?

この建物は何ですか　kono tatemono wa nan desu ka **What is this building ?**

いつ建てられましたか　itsu tateraremashita ka **When was it built ?**

誰(⑤)が建てましたか　dare ga tatemashita ka **Who built it ?**

このお寺は何と言いますか　kono o-tera wa nan to iimasu ka **What's the name of this temple ?**

これは美術館ですか　kore wa bijutsukan desu ka **Is this an art museum ?**

… は何時に開きますか　...wa nanji ni akimasu ka **What time does ... open ?**

何曜日が休館ですか　nanyōbi ga kyūkan desu ka **What days is it closed on ?**

入場料はいくらですか　nyūjōryō wa ikura desu ka **How much is the entrance fee ?**

切符はどこで買えますか　kippu wa doko de kaemasu ka **Where do they sell the tickets ?**

カメラを持ってきましたか　kamera wo motte kimashita ka **Did you bring your camera ?**

写真をとって下さい　shashin wo totte kudasai **Take a picture of that.**

写真をとってもいいですか　shashin wo totte mo ii desu ka **Is it all right to take pictures ?**

撮影は禁止です　satsuei wa kinshi desu **Picture-taking is forbidden.**

ガイドさんについて行って下さい　gaidosan ni tsuite itte kudasai **Follow the guide.**

ガイドは英語を話せますか　gaido wa eigo wo hanasemasu ka **Can the guide speak English ?**

ガイドはいりません　gaido wa irimasen **I don't need a guide.**

少し足をのばしてみましょう　sukoshi ashi wo nobashite mimashō **Let's walk on a little further.**

城に行くのはどのバスですか　shiro ni iku no wa dono basu desu ka **Which is the bus that goes to the castle ?**

… に行く道はこれですか　...ni iku michi wa kore desu ka **Is this the road that goes to ... ?**

… に行くにはどう行ったらよいですか　...ni iku ni wa dō ittara yoi desu ka **How can I get to ... ?**

歩いて行けますか　aruite ikemasu ka **Is it close enough to walk ?**

当地の名物料理は何ですか　tōchi no meibutsuryōri wa nan desu ka **What kind of cooking is this place known for ?**

有名なお店を教えて下さい　yūmei na o-mise wo oshiete kudasai **Can you tell me the names of important stores in this area ?**

土産には何を買ったらいいですか　miyage ni wa nani wo kattara ii desu ka **What kind of souvenirs should I buy to take home with me ?**

民芸品のお店を紹介して下さい　mingeihin no o-mise wo shōkai shite kudasai **Can you direct me to a place that sells folk art ?**

b. sports

プロ野球の観戦に行きたい　puroyakyū no kansen ni ikitai **I want to go to a professional baseball game.**

一番安い席はいくらですか　ichiban yasui seki wa ikura desu ka **How much is the cheapest ticket ?**

何時に始まりますか　nanji ni hajimarimasu ka **What time does the game start ?**

テニスをやりたい　tenisu wo yaritai **I want to play tennis.**

この海岸で泳げますか　kono kaigan de oyogemasu ka **Can you swim at this beach ?**

水泳禁止です　suiei kinshi desu **It's a no swimming zone.**

私は美容のためにヨガとエアロビクスをやっています　watashi wa biyō no tame ni yoga to earobikusu wo yatte imasu **I do yoga and aerobics for beauty care.**

相撲は日本の国技です　sumō wa nippon no kokugi desu **Sumo is the Japanese national sport.**

兄は柔道5段剣道2段です　ani wa jūdō godan kendō nidan desu **My older brother holds a fifth dan in judo and a second dan in kendo.**

釣りに行きませんか　tsuri ni ikimasen ka **Would you like to go fishing with me ?**

ボートを借りられますか　bōto wo kariraremasu ka **Can we rent a boat ?**

なかなかゴルフの腕前が上がりません　nakanaka gorufu no udemae ga agarimasen **I don't seem to make any progress at golf.**

私はマリンスポーツが得意です　watashi wa marin supōtsu ga tokui desu **I specialize in marine sports.**

運動し過ぎて体じゅうの筋肉が痛い　undō shisugite karadajū no kinniku ga itai **I exercised too hard, and all my muscles are sore.**

子供とキャッチボールをします　kodomo to kyatchibōru wo shimasu **I play catch with my son.**

家族と一緒にアウトドアスポーツを楽しみました　kazoku to issho ni autodoa supōtsu wo tanoshimimashita **I had fun playing outdoors with my family.**

c. events

映画館で何かおもしろいものをやっていますか　eigakan de nanika omoshiroi mono

wo yatte imasu ka **Is there some good movie playing at the theater now ?**

コンサートがありますか　konsāto ga arimasu ka **Are there any concerts scheduled ?**

... デパートで生け花展があります　...depāto de ikebanaten ga arimasu **There is an ikebana* exhibition at the ... Department Store.**

... ホールで明晩オペラがあります　...hōru de myōban opera ga arimasu **There is an opera tomorrow night at the ... Hall.**

S席のチケットを2枚ほしい　esu-seki no chiketto wo nimai hoshii **I want 2 S tickets*, please.**

来週の火曜日の席を予約したい　raishū no kayōbi no seki wo yoyaku shitai **I want a reserved seat for next Tuesday.**

前売り券は明日から売り出します　maeuriken wa myōnichi kara uridashimasu **Advance tickets go on sale tomorrow.**

開演は何時ですか　kaien wa nanji desu ka **What time does the play start ?**

演目は何ですか　enmoku wa nan desu ka **What's the title of the play ?**

指揮者は誰ですか　shikisha wa dare desu ka **Who is the conductor ?**

配役を教えて下さい　haiyaku wo oshiete kudasai **Tell me the names of the actors.**

プログラムを2部下さい　puroguramu wo nibu kudasai **Two programs, please.**

日本の古典芸能に関心がありますか　nippon no kotengeinō ni kanshin ga arimasu ka **Do you have any interest in classical Japanese theater ?**

歌舞伎は見たことがありますか　kabuki wa mita koto ga arimasu ka **Have you ever been to see Kabuki* ?**

能はまだ一度も見たことがありません　nō wa mada ichido mo mita koto ga arimasen **I have never seen a Noh* play.**

13. Sickness and Accidents

a. sickness

病院へ行きたいのですが，どこがいいでしょうか　byōin e ikitai no desu ga, doko ga ii deshō ka **I want to get medical attention. Can you recommend a good hospital ?**

お医者さんを呼んで下さい　o-ishasan wo yonde kudasai **Please call a doctor.**

救急車を呼んで下さい　kyūkyūsha wo yonde kudasai **Please call an ambulance.**

私は病気です　watashi wa byōki desu **I am sick.**

とても気分が悪い　totemo kibun ga warui **I feel terrible.**

吐き気がする　hakike ga suru **I feel nauseated.**

頭ががんがん痛い　atama ga gangan itai **I have a splitting headache.**

視力が急に落ちた　shiryoku ga kyū ni ochita **My eyesight has gotten bad all of a sudden.**

耳なりがひどいのです　miminari ga hidoi no desu **I have a terrible ringing in my ears.**

虫歯が痛くてたまりません　mushiba ga itakute tamarimasen **I have a terrible toothache.**

歯医者さんへ行かなければなりませんか　haishasan e ikanakereba narimasen ka **Do you need to see a dentist?**

食あたりをしたようです　shokuatari wo shita yō desu **I must've eaten something that didn't agree with me.**

胃をこわしました　i wo kowashimashita **I've got an upset stomach.**

消化不良を起こしました　shōkafuryō wo okoshimashita **I've got indigestion.**

風邪をひきました　kaze wo hikimashita **I have a cold.**

息苦しい　ikigurushii **I have trouble breathing.**

目まいがする　memai ga suru **I feel dizzy.**

私はずっと糖尿病を煩っています　watashi wa zutto tōnyōbyō wo wazuratte imasu **I have had diabetes for a long time.**

全く食欲がありません　mattaku shokuyoku ga arimasen **I have no appetite.**

熟睡できません　jukusui dekimasen **I have trouble sleeping.**

寒気がします　samuke ga shimasu **I'm getting chills.**

咳が止まりません　seki ga tomarimasen **I can't stop coughing.**

持病の...が悪化したようです　jibyō no ...ga akka shita yō desu **His chronic ... has gotten worse.**

足首を捻挫した　ashikubi wo nenza shita **I sprained my ankle.**

右腕を骨折した　migiude wo kossetsu shita **I broke my right arm.**

やけどをした　yakedo wo shita **I burnt myself.**

切り傷をした　kirikizu wo shita **I cut myself.**

いつからそんな状態ですか　itsu kara sonna jōtai desu ka **How long have you been like this?**

昨日からこんな状態です　sakujitsu kara konna jōtai desu **I've been like this since yesterday.**

どこが痛いですか　doko ga itai desu ka **Where do you hurt?**

寝ていないといけませんか　nete inai to ikemasen ka **Do I absolutely have to stay in bed?**

絶対安静が必要です　zettai ansei ga hitsuyō desu **You need absolute rest.**

口を開けなさい　kuchi wo akenasai **Open your mouth.**

舌を出しなさい　shita wo dashinasai **Stick out your tongue.**

横になりなさい　yoko ni narinasai **Lie down.**

息を吸いなさい〔吐きなさい〕　iki wo suinasai 〔hakinasai〕 **Breathe in 〔out〕.**

薬局にこの処方箋（ま）を持って行きなさい　yakkyoku ni kono shohōsen wo motte ikinasai **Take this prescription to a pharmacy.**

1日に3回これを飲んで下さい　ichinichi ni sankai kore wo nonde kudasai **Take this 3 times a day.**

注射しましょう　chūsha shimashō **I'll give you an injection.**

袖（そ）をまくりなさい　sode wo makuri nasai **Roll up your sleeve.**

少し気分がよくなりました　sukoshi kibun ga yoku narimashita **I feel a little better now.**

おかげさまですっかり元気になりました　o-kagesama de sukkari genki ni narimashita **Thanks to you, I am completely cured.**

b. accidents and disasters

交番はどこですか　kōban wa doko desu ka **Is there a police box* around here ?**

警察を呼んで下さい　keisatsu wo yonde kudasai **Call the police.**

大至急110番して下さい　daishikyū hyakutōban shite kudasai **Quick, dial 110.**

領事館に知らせて下さい　ryōjikan ni shirasete kudasai **Please inform my consulate.**

私のカバンが盗まれました　watashi no kaban ga nusumaremashita **My briefcase has been stolen.**

財布をすられました　saifu wo suraremashita **A pickpocket stole my wallet.**

パスポートがなくなりました　pasupōto ga nakunarimashita **My passport is missing.**

交通事故にあいました　kōtsūjiko ni aimashita **I have had a traffic accident.**

… に車をぶつけました　...ni kuruma wo butsukemashita **I crashed my car into a ....**

駅の階段から落ちました　eki no kaidan kara ochimashita **I fell down the stairs in the station.**

雪道で滑りました　yukimichi de suberimashita **I slipped on the snowy street.**

大けがをしました．救急車を呼んで下さい　ōkega wo shimashita. kyūkyūsha wo yonde kudasai **I am badly hurt. Please call an ambulance.**

重傷です．そっと担架に乗せて下さい　jūshō desu. sotto tanka ni nosete kudasai **He is badly hurt. Go easy when you put him on the stretcher.**

意識を失っています．大丈夫でしょうか　ishiki wo ushinatte imasu. daijōbu deshō ka **She's unconscious. Will she be okay ?**

火事だ！火事だ！　kaji da! kaji da! **Fire! Fire!**

消火器はどこですか　shōkaki wa doko desu ka **Where's the fire extinguisher?**

今朝の地震にはびっくりしました　kesa no jishin ni wa bikkuri shimashita **The earthquake this morning was frightening.**

台風の大雨で床下浸水になりました　taifū no ōame de yukashita shinsui ni narimashita **The heavy rains of the typhoon flooded my house almost up to floor level.**

家の前の川が反乱しました　ie no mae no kawa ga hanran shimashita **The river in front of my house overflowed its banks.**

... が行方不明です　...ga yukuefumei desu **...is missing.**

山で遭難しました。救助隊を呼んで下さい　yama de sōnan shimashita. kyūjotai wo yonde kudasai **We've had a bad accident on the mountain. Please call out the rescue squad.**

仕事の現場で事故にあいました　shigoto no genba de jiko ni aimashita **He had an accident at the construction site.**

補償はどうなるのでしょうか　hoshō wa dō naru no deshō ka **What does he have to do to get compensation?**

14. At the office

新入社員の... です。よろしく　shinnyūshain no ...desu. yoroshiku **I have just joined the company and my name is .... I am happy to meet you.**

今日からアルバイトをする事になった... です　kyō kara arubaito wo suru koto ni natta ...desu **My name is ... and I have started today as a part-timer here.**

会社の中を案内しましょうか　kaisha no naka wo annai shimashō ka **Shall I show you around the place?**

名刺をいただけませんか　meishi wo itadakemasen ka **Could I have your card, please?**

私のデスクはどこですか　watashi no desuku wa doko desu ka **Which is my desk?**

初めに何をしたらいいですか　hajime ni nani wo shitara ii desu ka **What's the first thing I need to do?**

この小包を出してきて下さい　kono kozutsumi wo dashite kite kudasai **Go mail this package, will you?**

会議室はどこですか　kaigishitsu wa doko desu ka **Where is the conference room?**

会議を始めます　kaigi wo hajimemasu **The meeting will now come to order.**

食事に行きます　shokuji ni ikimasu **I'm going out to lunch.**

毎日忙しい　mainichi isogashii **Every day is a busy one for me.**

残業をしなければなりません　zangyō wo shinakereba narimasen **I have to work overtime today.**

お先に失礼します　o-saki ni shitsurei shimasu (no English equivalent; said when going home ahead of one's colleagues)

お疲れさまでした　o-tsukaresama deshita (no English equivalent; said as a polite goodbye in response to the above)

忙しくていやになります　isogashikute iya ni narimasu **I'm so busy it isn't funny.**

昨日も終電で帰ったのです　kinō mo shūden de kaetta no desu **Yesterday also I worked till it was time for the last train.**

ストレスがたまっています　sutoresu ga tamatte imasu **I'm all stressed out.**

ファックスは今使っています　fakkusu wa ima tsukatte imasu **The fax machine is busy now.**

コンピュータ通信ができる人はだれですか　konpyūtatsūshin ga dekiru hito wa dare desu ka **Is there someone here who knows how to send electronic mail ?**

コピーをして下さい　kopī wo shite kudasai **Make me a copy of this, please.**

ワープロを打って下さい　wāpuro wo utte kudasai **Type this out on the word processor, will you ?**

ファックスを送って下さい　fakkusu wo okutte kudasai **Fax this out, will you please ?**

これ、すぐお願いできますか　kore, sugu o-negai dekimasu ka **Can you handle this right away, please ?**

今、ちょっと忙しいんだけど　ima, chotto isogashiin da kedo **Sorry, I'm terribly busy right now.**

この件、すぐに調べて下さい　kono ken, sugu ni shirabete kudasai **Will you look into this right away, please ?**

これから課長と打ち合わせです　kore kara kachō to uchiawase desu **I've got a meeting with the manager now.**

出張で大阪へ行ってきました　shutchō de ōsaka e itte kimashita **I just got back from Osaka on a business trip.**

もうじき人事異動があります　mō jiki jinjiidō ga arimasu **There's going to be some personnel changes soon.**

根回しがうまくいっていません　nemawashi ga umaku itte imasen **The prearrangements* aren't going well.**

忘年会はだれが幹事ですか　bōnenkai wa dare ga kanji desu ka **Who's in charge of the bonenkai* ?**

二次会はどこに決まりましたか　nijikai wa doko ni kimarimashita ka **Where are** you going for the nijikai* ?

彼は企画部のベテランです　kare wa kikakubu no beteran desu **He's a veteran employee of the planning department.**

この資料に目を通して下さい　kono shiryō ni me wo tōshite kudasai **I want you to read through this material, would you ?**

このパソコンの操作を教えて下さい　kono pasokon no sōsa wo oshiete kudasai **Can you show me how to run this computer ?**

… さんを応接室へお通し下さい　...san wo ōsetsushitsu e o-tōshi kudasai **Show ... to the reception room, please.**

帰りにいっぱい飲みませんか　kaeri ni ippai nomimasen ka **How about a drink on the way home ?**

もういっぱいいかがですか　mō ippai ikaga desu ka **Have another drink ?**

ちょっと酔ったからタクシーで帰ります　chotto yotta kara takushī de kaerimasu **I'm drunk, so I'll take a taxi home.**

仕事にやっと慣れました　shigoto ni yatto naremashita **I've finally gotten used to my work.**

昇進おめでとうございます　shōshin omedetō gozaimasu **Congratulations on your promotion.**

… についてご意見を聞かせて下さい　...ni tsuite go-iken wo kikasete kudasai **We'd like to hear your opinion on this matter.**

会社を辞めることにしました　kaisha wo yameru koto ni shimashita **I have decided to leave the company.**

転職することに決めました　tenshoku suru koto ni kimemashita **I have decided to look for a new job.**

15. Calendar events

a. January

日本のお正月は初めてです　nihon no o-shōgatsu wa hajimete desu **This is my first experience of the New Year's celebration in Japan.**

明けましておめでとうございます　akemashite omdetō gozaimasu **Happy New Year !**

初詣(½)では人がいっぱいでした　hatsumōde wa hito ga ippai deshita **The temples and shrines were crowded with people out for the first prayers of the year.**

みんなで百人一首をやりませんか　minna de hyakuninisshu wo yarimasen ka **How about all of us playing hyakunin-isshu* ?**

雑煮とお節料理を召し上がれ　zōni to o-sechiryōri wo meshiagare **Help yourself to** the zoni* and New Year's dishes.

年賀状がたくさん来ました　nengajō ga takusan kimashita **I received a whole lot of New Year's cards.**

b. February

2月3日は節分です　nigatsu mikka wa setsubun desu **February 3 is the setsubun* festivity.**

冬が終わって新春を迎える日です　fuyu ga owatte shinshun wo mukaeru hi desu **It is the day for celebrating the end of winter and the advent of spring.**

豆まきをして家の中に福を呼び込みます　mamemaki wo shite ie no naka ni fuku wo yobikomimasu **People throw beans and invoke happiness on their households.**

バレンタインデーは憂鬱(ウ)です　barentaindē wa yūutsu desu **I hate Valentine's Day.**

どうしてチョコレート売り場に女性が殺到するのか不思議です　dōshite chokorēto uriba ni josei ga sattō suru no ka fushigi desu **I never cease to wonder at all those women and girls crowding the chocolate candy counters.**

c. March

3月3日は桃の節句です　sangatsu mikka wa momo no sekku desu **March 3 is the peach blossom festival.**

女の子のいる家ではお雛(ビ)様を飾ります　onna no ko no iru ie de wa o-hinasama wo kazarimasu **In households with female children they set up a display of dolls.**

そろそろお花見のシーズンですね　sorosoro o-hanami no shīzun desu ne **It's about time for the cherry blossom season.**

桜の花が満開になりました　sakura no hana ga mankai ni narimashita **The cherry trees are in full blossom.**

卒業式帰りの女子大生をよく見かけます　sotsugyōshikigaeri no joshigakusei wo yoku mikakemasu **A conspicuous sight is women university students returning from their graduation ceremony.**

d. April

エープリルフールで以前ひどいいたずらをされました　ēpurirufūru de izen hidoi itazura wo saremashita **I once had a terrible prank played on me on April Fools' Day.**

新入生がお母さんの手に引かれて学校へ行きます　shinnyūsei ga o-kaasan no te ni

hikarete gakkō e ikimasu **Little children walk hand in hand with their mothers to their first day of school.**

会社も新しい社員が入って活気に満ちています　kaisha mo atarashii shain ga haitte kakki ni michite imasu **Companies are busy welcoming their new employees.**

e. May

5月5日は端午の節句です　gogatsu itsuka wa tango no sekku desu **May 5 is the Boys' Festival.**

男の子のいる家では鯉(こ)のぼりを飾ります　otoko no ko no iru ie de wa koinobori wo kazarimasu **Households with male children fly big cloth carps on a pole.**

まちにまったゴールデンウイークの到来　machi ni matta gōruden-uīku no tōrai **Now comes the long-awaited Golden Week*.**

今年は何連休ですか　kotoshi wa nanrenkyū desu ka **How many days off will we have this year ?**

どこへ行っても混んでいるから家でゴロゴロします　doko e itte mo konde iru kara ie de gorogoro shimasu **Everywhere you go it will be crowded, so I'm just going to lie around at home.**

f. June

梅雨に入りました　tsuyu ni hairimashita **The rainy season has started.**

毎日雨ばかりでうっとうしいですね　mainichi ame bakari de uttōshii desu ne **Isn't it dreary, all this rain day in and day out ?**

g. July

7月7日は七夕です　shichigatsu nanoka wa tanabata desu **July 7 is the Star Festival.**

何か星に願いをかけましょうか　nanika hoshi ni negai wo kakemashō ka **Shall we pray to the stars for something ?**

ようやく梅雨が上がり暑さがきびしくなりました・yōyaku tsuyu ga agari atsusa ga kibishikunarimashita **The rainy season has ended and the heat has become oppressive.**

土用の丑(?)の日には夏ばて防止にウナギを食べる習慣です　doyō no ushi no hi ni wa natsubate bōshi ni unagi wo taberu shūkan desu **On the day of the Ox in the dog days of summer, people customarily eat eel so as not to succumb to the heat.**

夏休みの計画は立てましたか　natsuyasumi no keikaku wa tatemashita ka **Have you made your plans for the summer vacation ?**

h. August

海水浴に行きませんか　kaisuiyoku ni ikimasen ka **Do you care to go to the beach with me ?**

お盆の帰省ラッシュのピークはいつですか　o-bon no kisei rasshu no pīku wa itsu desu ka **When is the back-to-the-country rush going to reach its peak during this o-bon* ?**

盆踊りを見に行きましょう　bon-odori wo mi ni ikimashō **Let's go watch the bon-odori*.**

花火大会があります　hanabi taikai ga arimasu **There is going to be a fireworks display.**

金魚すくいはなかなか難かしい　kingyōsukui wa nakanaka muzukashii **It's hard to catch goldfish with these paper nets.**

i. September

新学期が始まります　shingakki ga hajimarimasu **The new school term starts.**

今夜は仲秋の名月です　kon-ya wa chūshū no meigetsu desu **This is the night of the harvest moon.**

今年は台風が多いです　kotoshi wa taifū ga ōi desu **There are a lot of typhoons this year.**

j. October

あちこちで運動会があります　achikochi de undōkai ga arimasu **Many schools are having Field Day.**

芸術の秋です．美術館を散策します　geijutsu no aki desu. bijutsukan wo sansaku shimasu **Autumn is the season for art. I like to visit art museums at this time.**

食欲の秋です．また焼き芋(⅛)を買ってしまった　shokuyoku no aki desu. mata yaki-imo wo katte shimatta **The autumn air stimulates the appetite. I bought some roasted sweet potatoes again.**

公園の樹々が見事に紅葉しています　kōen no kigi ga migoto ni kōyō shite imasu **The trees in the park are beautiful in their autumn colors.**

k. November

だんだん寒くなってきました　dandan samuku natte kimashita **It is gradually**

getting colder.
あちこちの大学で学園祭が催されます　achikochi no daigaku de gakuensai ga moyōsaremasu **Many universities are holding their school festival.**

l. December

師走は何となく気ぜわしい月です　shiwasu wa nan to naku kizewashii tsuki desu **Somehow December always makes me feel restless.**
クリスマスのプレゼントはもう買いましたか　kurisumasu no purezento wa mō kaimashita ka **Have you finished your Christmas shopping?**
クリスマスイブは誰(誰)と過ごしますか　kurisumasuibu wa dare to sugoshimasu ka **Who are you going to spend Christmas Eve with?**
年賀状はもう書きましたか　nengajō wa mō kakimashita ka **Have you written your New Year's cards yet?**
忘年会が続いて少し胃がもたれました　bōnenkai ga tsuzuite sukoshi i ga motaremashita **I have been to so many year-end parties that my stomach feels queasy.**

m. Japanese public holidays

Jan. 1 元旦 gantan **New Year's Day**
Jan. 15 成人の日 seijin no hi **Coming-of-Age Day**
Feb. 11 建国記念日 kenkoku kinenbi **National Foundation Day**
March 20 春分の日 shunbun no hi **Spring Equinox**
April 29 緑の日 midori no hi **Nature Day**
May 3 憲法記念日 kenpō kinenbi **Constitution Day**
May 4 国民の休日 kokumin to kyūjitsu **Citizens' Day**
May 5 子供の日 kodomo no hi **Children's Day**
Sept. 15 敬老の日 keirō no hi **Senior Citizens' Day**
Sept 23 秋分の日 shunbun no hi **Autumn Equinox**
Oct. 10 体育の日 taiiku no hi **Sports Day**
Nov. 3 文化の日 bunka no hi **Culture Day**
Nov. 23 勤労感謝の日 kinrō kansha no hi **Labor Day**
Dec. 23 天皇誕生日 tennō tanjōbi **The Emperor's Birthday**
振替休日 furikae kyūjitsu **substitute holiday***

16. Dates and Times
日 hi/nichi **day**
朝 asa **morning**

昼 hiru **noon/daytime**
夕方 yūgata **evening**
夜 yoru **night**
午前 gozen **morning** (from daybreak to noon)
正午 shōgo **12 noon**
午後 gogo **afternoon**
真夜中 mayonaka **midnight**
今朝 kesa **this morning**
午前中 gozenchū **during the morning**
深夜 shin-ya **late at night**
今日 kyō **today**
昨日 kinō/sakujitsu **yesterday**
明日 ashita/asu/myōnichi **tomorrow**
明後日 asatte/myōgonichi **the day after tomorrow**
一昨日 ototoi/issakujitsu **the day before yesterday**
週 shū **week**
今週 konshū **this week**
先週 senshū **last week**
来週 raishū **next week**
日曜日 nichiyōbi **Sunday**
月曜日 getsuyōbi **Monday**
火曜日 kayōbi **Tuesday**
水曜日 suiyōbi **Wednesday**
木曜日 mokuyōbi **Thursday**
金曜日 kin-yōbi **Friday**
土曜日 doyōbi **Saturday**
月 tsuki/getsu **month**
今月 kongetsu **this month**
先月 sengetsu **last month**
来月 raigetsu **next month**
1 月 ichigatsu **January**
2 月 nigatsu **February**
3 月 sangatsu **March**
4 月 shigatsu **April**
5 月 gogatsu **May**
6 月 rokugatsu **June**
7 月 shichigatsu **July**

8月 hachigatsu **August**

9月 kugatsu **September**

10月 jūgatsu **October**

11月 jūichigatsu **November**

12月 jūnigatsu **December**

年 nen/toshi **year**

今年 kotoshi/konnen **this year**

去年 kyonen **last year**

昨年 sakunen **last year**

来年 rainen **next year**

西暦 seireki **Western calendar year**

1993年 senkyūhyakukyūjūsannen **nineteen ninety-three**

年号 nengō **Japanese calendar year name**

平成5年 heisei gonen **the fifth year of Heisei (= 1993)**

季節 kisetsu **season**

四季 shiki **the four seasons**

春 haru **spring**

夏 natsu **summer**

秋 aki **autumn/fall**

冬 fuyu **winter**

閏年 uruudoshi **leap year**

今日は何日ですか kyō wa nannichi desu ka **What's today's date?**

3月3日です sangatsu mikka desu **It's March (the) third.**

今日は何曜日ですか kyō wa nan-yōbi desu ka **What day of the week is it today?**

水曜日です suiyōbi desu **It's Wednesday.**

今年は何年ですか kotoshi wa nannen desu ka **What year is it?**

1993年です senkyūhyakukyūjūsannen desu **It's nineteen ninety-three.**

今何時ですか ima nanji desu ka **What time is it?**

8時15分です hachiji jūgofun desu **It's eight fifteen.**

10時15分前です jūji jūgofun mae desu **It's fifteen to ten.**

いつ来ましたか itsu kimashita ka **When did you get here?**

お昼過ぎです o-hirusugi desu **A little after noon.**

GLOSSARY

bon-odori: A community dance held on certain evenings around the time of the o-bon festival.

bonenkai: A traditional party held at the end of the year by various work and social groups to bring the year to a happy end.

choshi: A tokkuri (see below) full of sake (see below).

Golden Week: Seven or more days, usually beginning April 29, during which 4 national holidays and 1 or 2 weekends occur.

government postcards: Postcards issued by the government on which the postage has been prepaid, so that no further postage is necessary; said in contrast to picture postcards etc which require a postage stamp.

hyakunin-isshu: A card game played at New Year's.

ikebana: The Japanese art of flower arranging.

Kabuki: A form of classical Japanese drama based on popular legends, with male actors in both male and female roles.

miso: Fermented bean paste.

nijikai: An informal drinking party taking place after a more formal party or banquet.

Noh: A form of classical Japanese drama based on religious or mythical themes and featuring very stylized dancing.

o-bon: The festival of the dead, held to commemorate one's ancestors. It is marked in modern times by a great exodus from the cities as people return to their ancestral homes in the country for the celebration. In most regions it is held on August 13, 14, and 15.

police box: A small local police station manned by 2 or more policemen 24 hours a day. It usually consists of a small office with toilet and sleeping facilities. In the cities there may be one every several hundred meters, depending on the population density.

prearrangements: Also called by their Japanese name, *nemawashi*, such arrangements usually consist of informal, often secret meetings with individual members of some decision-making committee etc to argue one's case before the full committee meets.

S tickets: Tickets to the S seats, i.e., the best reserved seats in the house in a theater or concert hall.

sake: A kind of wine made from fermented rice and often drunk hot.

setsubun: A festivity where people throw beans toward the outside of their houses to ward off devils.

shinkansen: The Japanese name for the so-called "bullet trains" that run at great speeds on wide, elevated tracks.

substitute holiday: The name given to a Monday observed as a holiday following a national holiday that fell on a Sunday.

tempura: Fish, shellfish, and vegetables dipped in batter and fried in deep fat. Spelled with an *n* in romaji, but with an *m* as an English loan word.

tokkuri: A small bottle for heating sake (see above).

ume: A green, very sour relative of the plum, used for various kinds of pickles and flavorings. Its tree, also called ume, is also cultivated for its beautiful white, pink, or red blossoms, which open in very early spring.

wasabi: A kind of horseradish, cultivated in cold mountain streams, and used as a pungent spice.

zoni: A broth containing vegetables and mochi (see page 605) and eaten at New Year's.